2009
THE**YELLOW**BOOK

Published by The National Gardens Scheme

A company limited by guarantee • Registered in England & Wales
Charity No. 1112664 • Company No. 5631421
Registered & Head Office: Hatchlands Park, East Clandon,
Guildford, Surrey, GU4 7RT
T 01483 211535 F 01483 211537 W www.ngs.org.uk
© The National Gardens Scheme 2009

Front cover: Jacksons Wold, Yorkshire. Photograph: Val Corbett.
This page, above: Woottens, Suffolk. Photograph: Viv Kemp.
Top right: Sixpenny Moon, Devon. Photograph: Heather Edwards.
Bottom right: The Old Vicarage, Yorkshire. Photograph: Jerry Harpur.

A GUIDE
TO VISITING
THOUSANDS
OF GARDENS
IN ENGLAND
AND WALES

ngs gardens open for charity

CONTENTS

The Yellow Book 2009

Left: South Newington House, Oxfordshire
Photograph: Andrew Lawson

| Production Team: Elna Broe, Valerie Caldwell, Julia Grant, Tracey Layzell, Kali Masure, Elizabeth Milner, Chris Morley, Wendy Morton, Janet Oldham, Valerie Piggott, Sue Reeve, Jane Sennett. With thanks to our NGS County Volunteers | Unless otherwise stated, photographs are kindly supplied by permission of the garden owner | Copyright of the photographs belongs to the individual photographers | Design by James Pembroke Publishing | Maps designed and produced by Global Mapping | Map Data © The People's Map | Data manipulation and image setting by Chat Noir Design, France | Printing and binding by William Clowes Limited |

HRH The Prince of Wales

has been patron of the NGS since 2002. On page 21 he shares his enthusiasm for kitchen gardens…

A nation of gardens

TV gardener Toby Buckland introduces *The Yellow Book* 2009

Toby Buckland, Photograph: Panmedia UK Ltd

For me, the wonderful thing about joining *BBC Gardeners' World* is that I get to spend time pursuing my favourite activity – gardening! I can experiment and share ideas, try out new plants and potter around in a gorgeous garden. And that's really what the gardeners who generously open their gardens for the NGS are doing. They are sharing what they love, the highs as well as the lows – and inviting us in to see their borders at their triumphant best.

I always think of *The Yellow Book* as an adventure guide for gardeners, taking you to places, towns and villages you wouldn't ordinarily visit and opening up your horticultural horizons to new plant combinations and design ideas.

Past visits to friends' open gardens have always been a real celebration – not just of the plot and the plants growing in it but the best the season has to offer, as well as the owner's hard work and imagination. So don't miss your chance. Plan another great year of gardening and garden visiting, and don't forget to put your feet up in front of *Gardeners' World* on Friday evenings!

Toby Buckland
Presenter, *BBC Gardeners' World*

Photograph: Nicola Stocken Tomkins

Chairman's message

Thank you for buying this book, which will lead you to wonderful gardens – many privately owned, opened by owners who are happy to share their gardens and welcome you through their garden gate.

Once again this year we are supported by Rensburg Sheppards, who continue to sponsor us. To them, to our garden owners and you, the visiting public, our warmest thanks for helping us to raise the magnificent sums we are able to pass on to our benefiting charities.

I would also like to thank our voluntary County Teams who work tirelessly to support our owners and promote their openings, together with our dedicated staff, all of whom contribute to the wonderful total this unique charity raises.

I am honoured to have been appointed Chairman of The National Gardens Scheme, following Nicholas Payne who has taken the NGS forward in the last six years with such energy and enthusiasm. Nicholas will remain as County Organiser in Cheshire, so we're not losing him altogether and, of course, he still opens his own garden for the NGS. Enjoy your visits and thank you for your support.

Penny Snell, Chairman

Pastures new for the
NGS Chairman

2008 marked the end of an era for The National Gardens Scheme, as Nicholas Payne was succeeded as Chairman of the NGS by Penny Snell

Nicholas took up the Chairmanship in November 2002. He and his wife, Mona, first opened their garden for The National Gardens Scheme in 1991, although Nicholas's first involvement was as a boy in the 1950s, when he helped his great aunt by taking the gate money at her garden openings. Before becoming Chairman, Nicholas had already served for seven years on the NGS's Council.

In 1992, Nicholas took on the role of County Organiser (CO) for Cheshire and Wirral, with the aim of increasing visitor numbers and adding to the number of gardens opening in the county. There are now over 20,000 visitors being welcomed to 94 Cheshire and Wirral gardens, compared with 8,641 visitors to 31 gardens in 1991. Nicholas will continue as CO for Cheshire and Wirral.

In paying tribute to Nicholas's years of service, Ann Trevor-Jones, Vice-President, thanked him for his work, praising his good humour, sense of fairness, dedication and aplomb.

Commenting on her appointment, Penny Snell, who has been the County Organiser for London for 28 years, said how delighted she was to become Chairman of the NGS.

"Consolidating on Nicholas Payne's excellent work, I look forward to a progressive future with all our garden owners, supported by the volunteer county teams and staff," she says.

Since she became London County Organiser in 1980, the number of gardens opening in Greater London has increased from 31 to 230, raising more than £1.5 million for charity. Penny opens her own garden for the NGS and last year raised over £2,000. Her experience as County Organiser, and the 10 years she has served on the NGS Council of Trustees, means Penny is well placed to take on the role of Chairman – providing guidance, support and encouragement as the NGS continues to grow.

Pudding Poke Barn, Cumbria
Photograph: Linda Greening

Come and enjoy the world's greatest gardens

garden journeys 2009

ENGLAND
Finest Gardens & Chelsea
Flower Show on Members' Day

FRANCE
Paris, the Loire Valley,
Dordogne & the Lot

ITALY
Classic Gardens of Rome, Tuscany,
Venice & the Italian Lakes

JAPAN
Cherry Blossoms, Bonsai &
Exquisite Gardens

CHINA
The Complete Heritage,
Gardens & Cultural Tour

NEW ZEALAND
An Exclusive Selection of
Gardens in the Wine Country

OUTBACK AUSTRALIA
The True Australian Experience
in Comfort & Style

WESTERN AUSTRALIA
Wildflowers, Ancient Landscapes
& Aboriginal Rock Art

TASMANIA, AUSTRALIA
Glorious cool climate gardens at
their peak of spring flowering.

Graham Ross founded Ross Garden Tours in 1980. He is descendant from a long line of well known British gardeners, back to Thomas Hay V.C.O., V.M.H. (1874 - 1952), Superintendent of Hyde & St. James Parks & the gardens at Buckingham & Kensington Palaces during the reign of King George V & Queen Mary. Thomas' son Roy Hay M.B.E. (1910 - 1989) was one of Britain's first media gardeners presenting gardening radio shows, editing Gardener's Chronicle, & publishing many gardening titles. Roy founded the Dig for Victory campaign & Britain in Bloom campaign that continues today. Graham continues this legacy presenting gardening for radio and television. His first garden tour was to Japan in 1980 and has enjoyed sharing his love of gardens on over 400 tours ever since. Now in its 29th year Ross Garden Tours offers an unrivalled programme of luxury garden tours all over the world.

Call now for a free brochure
UK 08451 222 650
USA/Canada 1800 661 7176
www.rosstours.co.uk

ross
garden tours
Established 1980

in association with World of Experience Tours (UK) & Travel Concepts (Canada)

60 Mill Lane, Essex
Photograph: Sara Lee

Protect our gardens

NGS President Zac Goldsmith raises his concerns
about the de-greening of South East England

All around Britain, our green spaces are under threat. Flood plains are being built upon, the green belt is being developed, playing fields are still being sold off, and we are losing our beautiful gardens. Campaigners believe London alone is losing up to 30,000 gardens a year to developers – the equivalent of twice the area of Hyde Park.

Why? Instead of being cherished as havens for wildlife, not to mention the sheer pleasure they bring communities, gardens are now officially regarded as 'brownfield' sites with the same status as neglected industrial wasteland.

Whatever protection the planning laws once provided has been seriously eroded, and that, combined with an unwillingness by local authorities to put up a fight, means residents are increasingly powerless to prevent their loss, and neighbourhoods are being transformed.

Of course there is immense housing pressure on South East England. Investment in affordable high-speed rail would help relieve that, as it would make it easier for businesses to locate North of London and reoccupy areas of the UK that are being abandoned.

But more immediately, garden lovers are calling for urgent change. Our gardens are not 'brownfield' sites. They must be re-classified as 'greenfield' sites. They are havens and they need our protection.

Zac Goldsmith, President

New from **Thames & Hudson**

The Garden Visitor's Companion
Louisa Jones

A beautifully illustrated and inspirational guide for all garden visitors,
owners and designers, created by the doyenne of garden writing.

ISBN 978 0500 514634   **£16.95** hb
Available March 2009

Thames & Hudson
Sixty years of making a splash

For further details of our list, news of events
and special offers, visit us online at
www.thamesandhudson.com

The Pump House, Hertfordshire
Photograph: Mike Howes

Become a Friend of the NGS Free!

Opportunities to talk with existing and potential Friends over the last year have given us valuable feedback to steer the way the NGS runs this project in future. It seems that the primary motivation for joining Friends is to get a *Yellow Book* and a newsletter. This quote from one garden lover in London is very typical:

"I really just want a way of joining so that I can receive a **Yellow Book** *each year without having to remember to send for one. I hope that becoming a Friend will allow me to do this. I am happy to support the Scheme as a Friend in a small financial way. I live in Central London and have no garden, so am only able to join as a 'spectator' rather than a gardening member, but I still love to visit gardens whenever I can."*

The new programme in 2009 will focus on *The Yellow Book* and a twice-yearly newsletter as the main benefits. All you have to do is fill in your name and contact details on the tear-off flap on the back cover and send it to our Freepost address and we will send you a copy of *Roots* newsletter in the Spring and Autumn. You will also be able to take advantage of discounts and promotional offers for NGS events, and two-for-one entry at selected attractions.

And next year, you can buy *The Yellow Book 2010* direct from the NGS for the same low price – and have all these benefits. Who said there's no such thing as a free lunch?

25 Years
with Ambrose Place

How Marie Pringle coped with extraordinary publicity surrounding
the 25th opening of Ambrose Place back gardens

There was never any doubt that the 25th year of opening Ambrose Place back gardens in Worthing, West Sussex, was going to be a momentous event. Once it became clear, in the summer of 2007, that the editor of *The Times Magazine* was seriously interested in featuring the gardens and their owners in the 2008 Chelsea Flower Show edition, we knew that this was going to be special. But had we bitten off more than we could chew? After all, our 14 back gardens, behind a classic Regency terrace, are very restricted in size and access, and there is a limit to how many can physically pass through in six hours.

The 14 gardens are all different, with amazing variety ranging from country cottage style with a colourful profusion of seasonal flowers, to more formal landscaping, to exotic, Mediterranean-style plantings.

However, 'the story' for the media is the community – an entire street of people opening their gardens. The gardeners – all amateurs – range from busy young professionals with families and jobs to

juggle, to retirees with more time on their hands. The young newcomers to the street have embraced the NGS concept and devoted precious leisure time to develop their gardens. A major factor in recent success has been all the gardens opening.

So, come the 25th anniversary opening, and having had a front cover and seven pages in *The Times Magazine,* live broadcasts by *GMTV* from the gardens, (with all residents up at 5.30am), local radio and media coverage, plus an official opening by the Mayor of Worthing, the day was as hectic as expected. We more than doubled attendees to 2,200, and income to over £12,000. We were stretched – people queued to get out of the gardens, never mind getting in – and we regretted that some visitors gave up because of the crowds. But what a huge success! We were so pleased and relieved as we relaxed at our celebratory barbecue afterwards.

2008 was always going to be exceptional, but we shall be happy next year, with less pressure and a more comfortable experience for our visitors.

BARTLETT

BECAUSE EVERY TREE IS A FAMILY TREE.

Today, more than ever, property value is as much about your landscape as it is your home. The trees and shrubs that grow along with you and your family are valuable assets that deserve care and protection. For over 100 years, Bartlett Tree Experts has led both the science and services that make your landscape thrive. No matter the size or scope of your needs, our tree surgeons bring a rare mix of groundbreaking research, global resources and a local service approach to every task at hand. Trees add so much value to our lives. And Bartlett adds even more value to your trees.

BARTLETT TREE EXPERTS

SCIENTIFIC TREE CARE SINCE 1907

For the life of your trees.

Exclusive Emma Bridgewater mugs

Emma Bridgewater introduces the gorgeous mugs that she has designed for the NGS

"Tea in the garden is one of my favourite ways to spend an afternoon, and now we are working with the NGS, an organisation which allows you to visit over 3,600 gardens around the country which are open to us all. We've collaborated with the NGS and designed a range of six half-pint flower mugs; and for each mug sold, we will make a donation to the NGS. When you've finished your cup of tea, turn the mug over to find a backstamp with details about each of the flowers on it. As pretty as a bunch of blooms, these mugs look gorgeous on a winter table, and make me think of sunny springtime days all-year round." Each mug costs £15.95.

Prizewinning pub garden
The Wych Elm pub, Kingston upon Thames

Thanks to the superb efforts of Janet Turnes, this prize-winning floriferous pub garden, famed for its brilliant colour displays from eaves to pavement, is opening for the first time in 2009. There is a Mediterranean atmosphere in the back garden, which features pampered exotic plants, a cool, shady corner and hot colours on the terrace. All you need is a warm summer evening sitting out under the pergola festooned with exotic climbers, which protect banana and other tender plants… and you'll be transported to an island in the sun!

150-year milestone

2009 marks the 150th anniversary of the founding of district nursing in England and Wales

The Queen's
Nursing Institute

William Rathbone, a Liverpool-based merchant and philanthropist, employed a nurse, Mary Robinson, to care for his dying wife. After his wife's death in 1859, Mary was employed by William to provide health care in the city's poorest district. William spent the rest of his life working to develop the service and soon district nursing, based on the Liverpool model, began to appear across the country.

In 1887 Queen Victoria's Jubilee Institute for Nurses was founded, centralising training for district nurses, or Queen's Nurses as they became known. The charity, which later became The Queen's Nursing Institute (QNI), continues to support community nurses. Today district nurses continue to provide a vital, if sometimes low-profile, healthcare service to people in their own homes. This year more than 2.6 million people

will receive healthcare from a district nurse. The NGS was originally established in 1927 to raise funds for the QNI, and since then has been its most generous supporter.

Help the Hospices

Help the Hospices is the national charity for hospice care. We support local hospices to provide the best possible care to people facing the end of life, and to those who love them. There is a local hospice close to many NGS gardens, and for 11 years the NGS has helped us to help train the doctors, nurses and other hospice staff delivering this essential care.

See History
in Full Bloom

Follow in the footsteps of royalty, discover the source of Shakespeare's inspiration and admire glorious blooms from Beatrix Potter's point of view. The National Trust has over 200 gardens to choose from, including celebrated landscapes, national flower collections and working kitchen gardens. Come and enjoy history growing on you.

Visit **www.nationaltrust.org.uk** for more information on historic houses and gardens throughout England, Wales and Northern Ireland.
For National Trust membership enquiries, please call 0844 800 1895.

The Walled Garden, Houghton, Norfolk
Photograph: Val Corbett

NGS charitable donations top £30 million

Rensburg Sheppards

Investment managers Rensburg Sheppards tot up the total raised by the NGS during their 15 year sponsorship

Having sponsored the NGS since 1994, and as investment managers having more than a passing interest in matters of finance, we thought we should blow a trumpet on behalf of the NGS by highlighting the amount of money it has raised for charitable purposes during the past 15 years. In 2008 the cumulative total rose above £30 million – a remarkable and very worthwhile figure, made possible by the huge amount of voluntary work by the garden owners, which makes these figures a reality.

We are proud to have played our part in enabling this successful fund-raising effort, by supporting this well-respected and revered reference book which both informs and guides

its readers to the places of beauty, tranquillity and inspiration that are the NGS Gardens.

It is a source of great satisfaction that this huge total has been achieved during the period of our support. We understand the value of long-term relationships, and this is one such example which has demonstrably been a success, and which we are delighted to continue.

Steve Elliott

Steve Elliott
Chief Executive, Rensburg Sheppards
www.rensburgsheppards.co.uk

The NGS welcomes Warner Leisure Hotels

The NGS is delighted to welcome Warner Leisure Hotels and four of its historic hotel gardens into the Scheme. The hotel group won the Hotel Chain of the Year Award 2008/2009, and this is an opportunity to raise money and also encourage hotel guests to visit other NGS gardens.

Thoresby Hall Hotel & Spa (pictured) is a Grade 1-listed mansion on the edge of Sherwood Forest, set in 50 acres designed by Sir Humphry Repton.

Littlecote House Hotel in Berkshire is a Tudor mansion with 40 acres, including a topiary avenue and rose garden and Roman ruins in its grounds.

Holme Lacy House is a Grade 1-listed Georgian home nestled in the Wye Valley, with 20 acres of landscaped parkland in a lakeside setting.

Cricket St Thomas Hotel in Somerset has 160 acres of gardens and parkland, including its famous Wildlife Park and Manor House, which was the setting for the BBC series *To The Manor Born*.

For further information visit
www.warnerleisurehotels.co.uk

Private garden tours at Hampton Court

Gossip, scandal, murder, healing – you'll find it all within the formal gardens at Hampton Court Palace. This year, NGS visitors have the chance to visit these famous gardens in the company of one of the Palace's specialist tour guides. Tours will be available from April to September, starting at 6:30pm and costing only £6 per person, booking is essential. Each tour will have its own unique feature, whether it's the story of the Great Vine, the magic and mystery of the Hampton Court Maze, a chance to visit the nurseries or a behind-the-scenes look in the glasshouses.

All tours will include the new Tudor Heraldic Courtyard garden built to mark the 500th Anniversary of Henry VIII's accession to the English throne in 1509. **For more information visit** www.ngs.org.uk

NGS gardens feature in Kew photographic competition

Garden photography is quite a solitary profession but we have always enjoyed getting together at annual events like the Chelsea Flower Show. At Chelsea one year, a group of us resolved to meet up again in the quiet winter months. Thus the Garden Photographers' Association (GPA) was born, 10 years ago this October. The first meetings of the group were mainly social occasions. It was good to put faces to bylines, and to share experiences.

Since then, the GPA has expanded to over 100 members, and we have joined forces with the garden writers in the Garden Media Guild (GMG). Although our photographers are competitors, we are also friends, and the GPA is a very supportive self-help organisation. As a group we are especially concerned to nourish good relationships with garden owners.

At the end of our first year we organised an exhibition of garden photography – a modest affair with just 61 framed prints, one from each of our members at the time. This project has grown over the years and has transmuted into the International Garden Photographer of the Year competition (www.igpoty.com). Out of many thousands of entries worldwide, the winners are exhibited at an outdoor show at Kew all summer. **For further information visit** www.gpauk.org

Photograph: www.philip-hartley.co.uk/Amateur Gardening

NGS gardens on TV

Laurence Llewelyn-Bowen was on location last summer at Haddon Lake House filming Channel 5's 'I own Britain's Best Home and Garden'. The following gardens from the programme have all opened for the NGS: Dipley Mill, Hampshire; The Manor House, Upton Grey, Hampshire; Rustling End, Hertfordshire; High Glanau Manor, Gwent; The Manor House, Bedfordshire; Wollerton Old Hall, Shropshire; Cwm-Weeg, Powys; Greystone, Oxfordshire; The Coach House, Hampshire; The Exotic Garden, Norfolk; Haddon Lake House, IOW.

"Most of the money that you donate at the garden gate goes straight to our beneficiary charities"

Green Island, Essex,
Photograph: Marianne Majerus

Gardens doing good

Visit an NGS garden and help raise millions for charity. This is how you help...

Most of the 3,600 gardens which open for the NGS are privately owned, and more than half a million people visited these gardens last year. In doing so they helped raise more than £2 million for nursing, gardening and other charitable causes.

Since 1927, we've raised almost £42 million to support these charities; £25 million in the last ten years alone. We keep our overheads low, so most of your donation goes straight to our charities.

The NGS is **Macmillan Cancer Support**'s biggest single donor, donating over £11.6 million since 1985 and funding 130 Macmillan services, such as nursing posts, financial advice and counselling, supporting hundreds of thousands of people affected by cancer.

Support to **Marie Curie Cancer Care** has helped fund the Marie Curie Nursing Service. The charity provides free nursing care to give people with terminal illnesses the choice of dying at home, supported by their families.

Over two million UK carers of working age (66 per cent) combine work and caring. Our donation allows **Crossroads** to support working carers.

In 2008 the NGS assisted **Help the Hospices** with funding towards training for nurses and hospice staff, so they can give the best possible care.

The NGS keeps up its tradition of funding nursing care through **The Queen's Nursing Institute** which celebrates its 150th anniversary this year. Our donation to **The Royal Fund for Gardeners' Children** supports orphaned and needy horticulturist's children. With our support, **Perennial – Gardeners' Royal Benevolent Society**, helps people from the gardening trades who are in need. Our donations to **The National Trust** help fund the Trust's 'gardening careership' programme, to train and educate the heritage gardeners of the future.

All of which is only made possible by you visiting an NGS garden – **Thank you!**

HRH The Prince of Wales...

...has been Patron of The National Gardens Scheme (NGS) since 2002. His Royal Highness is also patron of Macmillan Cancer Support and Marie Curie Cancer Care. These charities welcomed donations of £1 million from the NGS in 2008. Here he shares his enthusiasm for kitchen gardens, and on the following pages we pick some of the best NGS examples of this great gardening tradition.

"There could not be a better time to encourage people to grow their own food wherever possible. And it doesn't need an acre of garden, because a window-box is a very good start"

A speech by HRH The Prince of Wales during a visit to the Garden Organic's Golden Jubilee Garden Festival, Ryton, 25th July 2008

Growing Inspiration

NGS gardens are a wonderful source of ideas for a productive garden, either for fruit and veg for the table, or flowers for the house. An added bonus is that there is often produce for sale at garden openings.

1 **96 East Sheen Avenue** London

A productive area within the main garden creates vibrancy, texture and added interest. This small plantaholic's garden also boasts a shed with a green roof. At the end of the garden are hidden allotments, also open.

Photograph: Jacqui Hurst

2 **Old Rectory, Sudborough** Northamptonshire

A runner-bean arch, step-over apple trees and formal rose circle (by Rosemary Verey) make you want to explore this lovely garden. Herbaceous borders, a woodland walk and a pond guarantee a successful visit.

Photograph: Brian & Nina Chapple

3 **Guanock House** Lincolnshire

The topiary and mixture of vegetables and plants in this walled kitchen garden are magnificent. Five acres in the Lincolnshire fens offers knot garden, rose garden and lime walk; orchard, Italian garden and more.

Photograph: Rosalind Simon

4 **Greenacre** Lancashire

Small, raised beds are a popular design for a productive garden and are used to good effect at Greenacre. This large garden on the edge of Ribble Valley is colour phased throughout the year, with a late-summer wow factor. Original sculpture in a woodland setting adds another dimension. A continually evolving garden.

Photograph: Fiona Lea

5 **Kemble Mill** Gloucestershire

This lovely mill garden on the banks of the infant Thames is for adults and children to enjoy, with a formal, walled garden, cottage garden, raised vegetable beds, pond, an island garden bordered by mill race, apple orchard and woodland walk. There's an 8-acre field full of donkeys and chickens, and a playground.

Photograph: Mandy Bradshaw

4

5

NOTHING ELSE IS A HARTLEY

A Hartley Glasshouse is the natural choice of horticultural professionals and enthusiasts alike. Our name has remained synonymous with enduring style and excellence for over 70 years, and is uniquely recognised by one of the most respected and prestigious worldwide authorities, The Royal Botanic Gardens Kew.

FOR A BROCHURE AND OUR LATEST OFFERS CALL

0800 783 8083

tyb@hartleybotanic.co.uk

hartleybotanic.co.uk

HARTLEY BOTANIC

Hartley Botanic Limited, Wellington Road, Greenfield. OL3 7AG

6 **Bonython Manor** Cornwall

Willow looks wonderful as an edging medium or container in both the productive and flower garden. This magnificent 20-acre colourful garden has a sweeping hydrangea drive, herbaceous walled garden, potager with vegetables and picking flowers; three lakes in a valley planted with ornamental grasses, perennials and South African flowers. A 'must see' for all-seasons colour.

Photograph: Brian & Nina Chapple

7 **Horsell Allotments** Surrey

These magnificent allotments are such an inspiration to get digging. There are over 100 individual plots growing a variety of flowers, fruit and vegetables. A mixture of modern, well-known, heritage and unusual vegetables, many not seen in supermarkets!

8 **Langton Farm** Yorkshire

What healthy cabbages – they obviously enjoy growing in the border! This riverside garden comprises formal and informal gravel areas, a nuttery, romantic flower garden with mixed borders and pebble pool. All run on organic principles.

Photograph: Jerry Harpur

9 **Wild Rose Cottage, Lode Gardens** Cambridgeshire

An overflowing cottage garden, with a rose tunnel, wildlife pond and circular vegetable garden edged with lavender and sage. A wild flower spiral entered through arches of roses and clematis adds to this pretty garden. An added bonus is the opportunity to visit the other lovely gardens in this group.

Photograph: Howard Rice

3 issues for £1

WHEN YOU SUBSCRIBE TO GARDENS ILLUSTRATED

Feed your imagination with gorgeous gardens and irresistible plants by subscribing to GARDENS ILLUSTRATED. Revel all year round in the unique mix of stunning images, expert insights and useful advice that makes GARDENS ILLUSTRATED the perfect read for any passionate gardener.

SPECIAL INTRODUCTORY SUBSCRIPTION OFFER

- Your first three issues for **just £1**
- After your trial period **save 25%** on the magazine's shop price
- Spread the cost at **just £8.60** every 3 issues by Direct Debit
- FREE UK delivery
- Never miss an issue

SUBSCRIBE ONLINE AT
www.subscribeonline.co.uk/gardensillustrated

or call our hotline **0844 844 0253*** quoting NGSYB09

*Calls to this number from a BT landline will cost no more than 5p per minute. Calls from mobiles and other providers may vary

Close to home

Save money and the planet by visiting a garden local to you

Emerald House, London
Photograph: Jacqui Hurst

You don't have to drive long distances to find a garden opening as part of the National Gardens Scheme. With the recent focus on reducing the distances driven, either to offset the impact on the environment or as a consequence of rising fuel prices, it's good to know that there will be an NGS garden close by for you to visit.

Just consider the following: within a three-mile radius of central London, more than 80 gardens opened on behalf of the NGS in 2008. Extend that boundary to include all the postcodes in inner and outer London and the number jumps to an incredible 150.

A similar picture emerges from other major urban areas in England and Wales. 56 gardens located in Birmingham postcodes opened for the NGS in 2008, and more than 30 gardens in the county of Lancashire, whose postcodes include Manchester, Liverpool and Preston. Add to this the gardens from Cheshire and the Wirral, and the number rises to well over 100. Over the border, there are 62 gardens located close to Cardiff and Swansea, while the postcodes of Leeds, Sheffield, Bradford and York account for a further 72 gardens.

So in total, nearly 500 gardens which opened to support the NGS in 2008, are all within a relatively short driving distance of major centres of population in both England and Wales.

"You can have a great afternoon out with tea and cake for under £10"

Finding the gardens

By buying this copy of *The Yellow Book* you've taken the first step in finding out the opening dates and times of the gardens you may want to visit in 2009. You can also find this information online; visit the NGS website at www.ngs.org.uk – using the 'Garden Finder' section you'll be able to find gardens that will be opening near to you. The website has a search option, so you just need to type in your postcode, select the distance you wish to travel and the dates of possible visits. Hit 'search' and within seconds the list of gardens will open within the area and dates you have specified. In addition the 'Local to You' section provides information about the NGS in your part of the country.

45A Combe Park, Somerset
Photograph: Julia Phillips

Stones and Roses Garden, Lancashire
Photograph: Fiona Lea

Great value for money

Besides the cost savings that visiting local gardens can give you, a visit to an
NGS garden really does give you excellent value for money. During 2008
the average admittance charge to NGS gardens was less than £3. So, if there
are two of you, you can have a great afternoon out looking at some truly
wonderful gardens, order a cup of tea and a slice of cake each or maybe
buy a plant (if the garden owner is having a plant sale), all for under £10.
What's more, you spend that money in the knowledge that you will also be
donating it to some very good causes. That's the real beauty and joy of the
NGS – the garden owners get to display their many hours of hard work and
dedication, and you get to see some 'real' gardens knowing that the donation
you have made, by way of an entrance fee or purchase, is going to charity.
Additionally, children are welcome and over 2,000 of the gardens admit
children aged 16 and under for free.

If you want to keep a wary eye on the distances that you are driving,
whether for financial or environmental reasons, use *The Yellow Book* or the
website to plan your visits to local gardens. With the wide choice of gardens
that open for the NGS, we are sure you will locate a garden close to wherever
you are, that you will want to visit.

Waltham Place Organic Farm & Gardens

"An inspirational naturalistic garden"

Open May-September 2009

NGS Day Wednesday

Tuesday & Thursday by appointment

Education tours and courses available

Organic Farm Shop & Tea Room

Open Tuesday-Friday: 10am-4pm

For further information contact:

Estate Office, Waltham Place,

Church Hill, White Waltham,

Berkshire, SL6 3JH

Tel: 01628 825517

www.walthamplace.com

Cool for kids

Many of our gardens are a wonderland of adventure and exploration for children. Here's our pick of places to inspire them

Showing children that gardening is fun is essential to grab their interest and produce our future gardeners. Combining garden visiting with children is easy when you choose an NGS garden. Over 2,000 NGS gardens welcome youngsters aged 16 and under to visit without charge. Many also offer activities to keep children amused, such as quizzes and treasure hunts, while other gardens are created with the involvement of children themselves. Included amongst these are several schools who welcome visitors to their grounds, plus gardens with animals for the children to admire. There's plenty to inspire budding young gardeners, and of course, the promise of a delicious cake to round off the visit!

Two, large, closely located schools in Sussex, are award-winning gardens created by teachers, volunteers and children with special needs.

Pond dipping on an NGS open day at Palatine

1 **The Palatine School Garden** Sussex

This garden is the work in progress of children, teachers and volunteers at a special school. Over the years the grounds have been transformed into a series of themed gardens. Centred around three ponds, the gardens have a calm and spiritual quality. The inspirational motto of 'Green Fingers and Growing Minds' reflects the recreational and educational goals of the school.

2 **Oak Grove College** Sussex

Oak Grove opened for the first time for the NGS in 2008, and is a garden in the making, showing how much can be achieved in less than three years. The areas within the garden include water-wise gardens, a large courtyard with seating area, water features, sculptures and extensive planting, memorial gardens, spiral herb garden, large food growing area, poly tunnels, living willow features and some reclaimed woodland.

1

2

3 **The Old Vicarage** Nottinghamshire

This lovely and very welcoming garden is a children's haven. The two acres are surrounded by woodland and fields and is a plantsman's delight. Begun 12 years ago from nothing, this undulating landscape has plenty of texture, colour, and unusual plants and trees. Peaceful rooms, with plenty of nooks and crannies to discover. Delicious cakes to add to the enjoyment.

4 **Treffos School** Gwynedd

The children's involvement can be seen and enjoyed as they all join in growing fruit, flowers and vegetables in a number of classroom-linked projects. There are 7 acres of woodland, herbaceous borders and productive gardens in this rural, child-friendly garden, surrounding a C17 house which is now run as a school.

3

4

5 **Watendlath** Worcestershire

A diverse garden with lots of interesting corners and a fine view has something for everyone, particularly children. A secret garden, pond, chickens and with an emphasis on being friendly to wildlife, the garden has been created by people who love flowering plants, colour and scent. Inspiration can be gained from densely packed herbaceous borders, island beds, vegetables and many containers.

6 **Potash** Berkshire

Children and dogs are very welcome in this 5-acre garden which is open by appointment throughout the year. There is a wide range of plants with many unusual specimens and interest for every season; from snowdrops and daffodils to autumn colour. Enjoy plenty of space to explore, or just to sit and contemplate the view.

5

6

From plant pots to teapots

Sitting down to tea in a beautiful garden is one of life's great pleasures. And to do your teatime justice, you need the great taste of Yorkshire Tea. Not forgetting our classic cakes and buttery biscuits, of course.

To find out more, please visit **yorkshiretea.co.uk**

Yorkshire Tea. Try it. You'll see.

7 **9 Bourne Street** Cheshire

Roughly 60x120ft, this mature garden has evolved over three generations in one family, having been started in 1924 on the site of an existing orchard. It has Victorian and Japanese influences, including rhododendrons, azaleas and a magnificent wisteria. A peaceful secret garden with a surprise around every corner, and a delight for children of all ages.

8 **33 Peerley Road** Sussex

Combine a garden visit with a trip to the seaside! This small garden is packed full of ideas and unusual plants using every inch of space to create unusual rooms and places for adults and children to play. The owner specialises in unusual plants that grow well in seaside conditions. A must for any suburban gardener. Great winter interest.

Photograph: Nicola Stocken Tomkins

7

8

New additions

Here's our pick of the most recent gardens to open for the NGS. Their owners describe what they've accomplished – welcome them to the Scheme by paying them a visit to see for yourself!

High View, Worcestershire
Owners: Carole and Mike Dunnett
Open: 9 August 2009 and by appointment for groups

Work on our garden began in 1972. We inherited magnificent south-easterly views over the Teme Valley but the 2 ½ acre plot was all nettles, thistles and half-dead fruit trees. Investment in clearing, ground improvement and tree planting means we now have large trees, giving the garden splendid maturity.

In the early 80s we started to develop the garden that we have today. We planned a garden that had to be explored, so you could only see a small part at a time. We wanted to create a surprise around every corner, to be informal with variety of atmospheres. Above all, we decided to carry out all the work ourselves whenever possible. Apart from building the pond and some tree surgery, we've managed this.

The largest part of the garden is some distance from the house and is planted for summer. Although, as we enjoy the garden all year round, we've included spring and autumn-interest plants. The areas nearest the house are crammed with plants that are attractive in winter.

Adjacent to the house is a patio, seating areas and two formal ponds.

Steps lead to a small vegetable garden, greenhouse and propagation area. The patio is decorated with containers of bulbs in the spring, bedding during summer and interesting shrubs in winter.

The lower garden is reached via steps descending through a wildflower area. As far as we're aware this south-east facing, alkaline bank had never been cultivated. Now we encourage local flora and have many Worcestershire wildflowers, including three species of orchid. Here we have a fascinating mixture of trees, conifers, shrubs, herbaceous plants and grasses. There are many specimen trees, including *Picea breweriana*, Colorado white fir and ghost tree. *Helleborus* and specimen *Hamamelis* give splashes of winter colour and the large wildlife pond is backed by a small native wood. Several *Lonicera nitida* varieties are clipped to produce intriguing topiary, and sculptures and structures add interest. Summer and autumn colour comes from *Dahlia*, *Penstemons gladioli* and *lilies*. A paddock is planted with *Narcissus* to give long-lasting spring colour.

It has been a great joy to us to share the garden with our visitors – not to mention a surprise and delight when we won *Worcestershire Life* magazine's Best Private Garden 2008.

24 Brunswick Street, London E17
Owner: Martyn Cox
Open: 28 June 2009

When I moved into my mid-terrace house five years ago, I inherited an ugly, uninspiring back garden. The 30x15ft south-facing space was an expanse of concrete slabs and a 'lawn' – a few scraggy tufts of grass sitting glumly on a sea of mud. There were a couple of lilacs, a rosemary, some lanky roses and a near-derelict old shed.

I adopted a scorched-earth policy; ripping everything from the ground, reducing the shed to kindling with a sledgehammer. There were a few hiccups… like the day when the house was taped off by the police, for the bomb squad to investigate an unusual metallic object found by my digging. A few hours later they emerged with an old zinc bucket.

Left with a blank canvas, I had to think carefully about how to make the most of the space. A shed was out of the question, so I tucked a small, fence-mounted tool store into a corner. There's further storage with a raised brick storage seat. Step down from the slate patio onto a path of slate shingle between beds crammed with unusual plants along with a few prosaic but hard-working specimens. In the bottom corner a small deck covered with a shade sail is ideal for our young children to play. The tiniest cracks have been filled with plants and every vertical surface has been utilised. Pots cling to drainpipes, baskets to walls and evergreen climbers to fences, along with a grape vine, kiwifruit and an apricot (there are 12 types of fruit in the garden, from berries to figs).

After creating the garden from scratch I applied to open it for the NGS, so that other small garden owners might be inspired. I expected a crushing phone call to say it was too small or not interesting enough, but was overjoyed to learn I'd been given the go ahead. I'm seriously excited about welcoming other garden lovers into my private plot.
Martyn Cox writes gardening columns for The Mail on Sunday and Saga Magazine. His books include 101 Ideas for Small Gardens (BBC Books, March 2009) and RHS Wildlife Garden (Dorling Kindersley, April 2009).

Quality Garden Tours in Britain and Ireland 2009

Royal Horticultural Society

Brightwater Holidays have produced a unique collection of Garden Holidays throughout the United Kingdom and Ireland. Some gardens are large and famous, some are small and rarely open to visitors; all our tours include a balanced selection of gardens, complement each other and offer variety, colour and interest - rather like a good herbaceous border.

Among our tours in England are the Private Gardens of Cornwall, Gardens of Kent and Sussex, Somerset and Devon, the Cream of the Cotswolds and Gardens of Northumberland. In Scotland we visit Gardens of the Far North, including the Castle of Mey and Highland and Island Gardens that features some magical gardens in Argyll. We cross the Irish Sea to discover the verdant gardens in the Emerald Isle and we also have a tour of the Welsh Principality along with tours that visit RHS events such as the Tatton, Chelsea and Hampton Court Flower Shows.

In addition Brightwater Holidays organise quality garden tours throughout the world.

To obtain a copy of our comprehensive brochures for 2009, please call Brightwater Holidays on:

01334 657155

brightwater
holidays

Brightwater Holidays Ltd
Eden Park House, Cupar, Fife KY15 4HS
rhs@brightwaterholidays.com
www.brightwaterholidays.com

Photographs: Fiona McLeod

Maryfield, Buckinghamshire
Owners: Jacqueline and
Roger Andrews
Open: 23 & 24 May, 4 July
and 19 September 2009

We'd always intended to share our garden, but never found a vehicle to do it formally. Meeting with the NGS team and opening Maryfield last year was a wonderful experience. We had little idea what to expect, and were amazed by the volume of interest and feedback we got. The involvement and support from the NGS has been superb.

Setting the dates in *The Yellow Book* galvanised us into action. Having just dug up a tennis court and replaced it with a vegetable garden, we had a lot to get done!

Other than the garden itself, getting organised for the opening was relatively straightforward. We recruited neighbours to help with the plant sale and serving teas and then, basically, we opened the gates!

The two days that we opened exceeded our expectations. We hadn't anticipated the level of appreciation for the garden and were delighted that visitors seemed to take great enjoyment in pottering around, and were inspired by what they saw. They saw things in it that we'd lost sight of. It reminded us that we should literally stop and smell the flowers a little more.

We held a romantic vision of the quintessential English garden; an afternoon in late spring, with people wandering around enjoying tea.

In turn, this has inspired us to work harder on developing Maryfield. We've started work on a bronze goblet-shaped pool and a large lily-pool on the main lawn.

Our garden is a work in progress, which we hope to share over the years. We are looking forward to our second year in *The Yellow Book* and will be opening four days this year. We look forward to other gardeners sharing developments at Maryfield.

J's Pots & Potted Gardens

Garden Antiques, Pots & Ornaments

Based in Hertfordshire with all current stock displayed on the website:

www.jsgardens.co.uk

Tel: 01992 443055 or 07930 576881
Email: julia@jsgardens.co.uk

Gardens

122nd

SHREWSBURY Flower Show

14th & 15th August 2009

Tel. No. 01743 239183
Book online at:
www.shrewsburyflowershow.org.uk

Credit Card Hotline **01743 239181**
No dogs on showground

SPECIAL ATTRACTIONS

Superb Floral Attractions
over 3 million blooms
Chris Beardshaw
TV Gardening personality
Flying Gunners
Motorcycle Display Team
3 Top Military Bands
Dog Display team
Grade A Showjumping
Huge Trade Shopping Area

TICKETS

Advance Price until the 8th August
Adult £16.00 **Over 60s** £14.00
Children 16 & under free when accompanied by an Adult

Pots with Panache

Having created the gardens at East Ruston Old Vicarage in Norfolk from nothing, its owner Alan Gray reveals the secrets behind his glorious container planting

Pots play a very important part in the furnishing and structure of my garden. They adorn steps, they stand impressively like ranks of soldiers on the terrace, they bring intimacy to doorways and gateways and they are even elevated to such importance that they form the centrepiece of parts of my garden. However, to get the maximum amount of impact – even length of flowering period – from them, there are a few rules to follow.

Let us start with the container first. This should always be as large as possible, I see so many good attempts at pot planting ruined because the pot is too small, which means that the display fizzles out by midsummer. For summer pots, let me begin with the large specimen plants that I use in my garden. Years ago, I fell head over heels in love with the scent of Brugmansias while on a continental holiday, and soon after I acquired some plants of my own. I still have them, but they are larger than ever; I like to be able to look up into their trumpets and in the evenings I enjoy the swooningly sweet scent. To get the best from these I allow each a very large pot.

The preparation for all my pots starts with crocks over the drainage hole, then a layer of very good compost, I use equal parts of John Innes No.3 and a ready-prepared, peat-based mix. Then a layer of well-rotted manure nine to twelve inches deep; this is important because summer plants are greedy feeders. The pots are then topped up with the compost mix. With plants like Brugmansias, I start a twice-weekly liquid feeding regime after four weeks which ensures that my plants keep on producing wave after wave of blossom getting ever better as the season progresses, their finale can result in them carrying as many as 200 flowers on each plant.

I think it important that due consideration be given to the centrepiece of each pot. Years ago I used standard Fuchsias, but these became somewhat ubiquitous, so I made standards of Solanum *rantonnetii* and Tibouchina

urvilleana, both with rich, papal-purple flowers. I then work out my colour palette for the whole pot, which is kept quite simple; it may be purple and pink, or purple and yellow, or purple and white… the important point is to keep the tonal quality of your planting similar. For instance, keep the pinks pure and on the red side, omitting any hint of orange. Similarly, with yellow, either keep it to a sharp, acid tone or to a warmer, more orange tint.

The flowering plants that I choose are quite ordinary: Verbenas, Petunias, Pelargoniums… in fact, I use any ingredient that suits my purpose, but I always include some good, architectural foliage. This will come to the fore later in the season when some of the flowering plants start to dissolve into an amorphorous mass. Plants like Melianthus *major,* with its gorgeous glaucous leaves, or Sparrmannia *africana* with huge, bright-green paddles, then take over the scene and grab everyone's attention.

If you are in any doubt, why not plant a white-themed pot? Nothing could be simpler or look smarter. One of my best pots last summer was composed of a tall, growing, small-flowered Fuchsia 'Hawkshead', Gaura *lindheimeri,* Verbenas, the silver foliage of Dichondra 'Silver Falls' and Melianthus *major* for late interest. White and silver: so simple, so good! *Alan Gray is a gardener, author, radio and television personality. As an NGS Ambassador he also opens his own garden to NGS visitors*

White and silver: Fuschia 'Hawkshead' and Dichondra

Alan Gray, owner

The Romantic garden

Celebrity pottery designer Emma Bridgewater waxes lyrical about the gardens she loves…

Photograph: Ian Gowland

Sometimes it's the gardens that *might be* wonderful that affect me most. A perfect lawn is a treat, but so is the old grass court grown meadow-high, the fine fescues and lawn grasses interspersed with cinquefoil and daisies brushing against the sagging net.

The love affair with the Picturesque, the Romantic and the Gothic is particularly English, starting in the 17th and 18th century. I am not immune, and felt excited returning to a house we left empty. Wading through the prairie lawns and seeing the borders drift deep in Scots thistle and other volunteers, I loved the abandon and feeling of chaos taking over.

My childhood holidays were split between Norfolk and Cornwall, my father's spiritual home. He rented various cliff-side pleasure-domes along the north coast, mainly in Treyarnon where his grandmother, who lived nearby in Bodmin, built a holiday house. Walking along the coast path I was drawn into a gateway. Looking over a rusted but elegant gate revealed a further entrance; Alice-like, I was led from outdoor room to room, walled in feathery tamarisk or sea buckthorn, glaucous leaves contrasting with their iron red stalks. Abandoned lawns and grassed-over paths led to a well with sinuous over-structure, and on through a tunnel formed by banks of Cornish slate laid in characteristic herringbone pattern, the gaps between the slate crammed with clusters of elegant lemon yellow-and-cream banded snails. The ruins of a kitchen garden came next, enclosed by rolling banks of tamarisk. Ancient gooseberry bushes, chalky grey with hanging lichens like Spanish moss, great antlered currant bushes and the ghosts of fruit cages, their rusting posts melting into the Cornish soil. Last of all, a hanging wrought-iron gate guarded a long-deserted swimming pool.

The autumnal leaf-covered pool at the end of *The Great Gatsby*

"In the ruins of a kitchen garden…
the ghosts of fruit cages, their rusting
posts melting into the Cornish soil"

*Main image: Hanham Court,
Somerset and Bristol.
Insert: Lower Severalls,
Somerset and Bristol.
Photograph: Rachel Warne*

reveals Gatsby's fate. Pools, as any owner knows, are all maintenance – and if you relax that regime for a moment the gin-clear water can turn, in weeks, to a murky pond complete with miraculous draught of frogs or newts. But if the neglect becomes long-term, an atmosphere of utter Triste can establish. This Cornish ruined pool, lined in aquamarine and turquoise tiles that Fired Earth would kill for, summoned up long-gone Joan Hunter-Dunnes diving forcefully in after tennis, or midnight bathing with holidaying neighbours… secluded and silent, it's a memorial to Edwardian summer loveliness.

Despite the most cursory maintenance and the almost complete absence of flowers, just a few hardy blooms surviving the neglect, this is one of my favourite gardens. An indication that it's framework and ground plan that really lasts, and that manicured tidiness is not everything.

Not all romantic gardens are in

*Take inspiration from Cilgwyn Lodge, Carmarthenshire
Photograph: Rowan Isaac*

walls, Elizabethan staircase, a fairytale medieval tower, a15th-century tithe barn. The house morphs imperceptibly into the medieval church. But all this is just a picturesque backdrop to a many-levelled and roomed garden that winds along the contours of this little valley. A spotless lawn with pea-shingle paths is edged by two grand borders, of the sort long abandoned by more feeble-minded gardeners. This leads to a baroque gateway, all volutes and pediment but made of muscular green oak, and on to a belvedere looking along the valley towards the Rowntrees chocolate factory.

On the right is a wooded gorge with ponds and streams under planted with giant tree ferns bought from Homebase, and drifts of the more esoteric snowdrops. Further round, a walled enclosure – sitting 10 feet above a meadow in which sheep gaze under lime-green walnut trees – contains the swimming pool. It's black, small and hot, and around it grottos of ecclesiastical ruins are heaped up in ways never intended by their original sculptors. Old roses and pots of giant *Agapanthus* crowd around the walls and the whole effect is entrancing.

And on it goes, lots of loving, stylish and inspiring gardening such as we could never contemplate doing ourselves. This year it is open from April under the NGS' auspices, so while to recommend the Cornish garden would be to suggest trespass, Hanham Court is available for all to see. Just the king of surprising private gardens that the NGS helps you to find.

states of disrepair. Try Hanham Court on the fringes of Bristol. The approach is uninspiring, as high street turns to tatty housing estates. Then, suddenly, lyrical meadows and scattered stone buildings herald the gates. The inviting curved drive leads to one of England's most extraordinary gardens – the home of Julian and Isabelle Bannerman, two of the country's leading garden designers (they've worked at Highgrove, Waddesden and Houghton, designed the English 9/11 memorial gardens in New York and, recently, the dazzling Collector Earls garden at Arundel Castle, based on an unrealised scheme of Inigo Jones).

Hanham Court is a house of almost every period: 17th-century

Gardens through the ages

Take a tour through time, from Middle Ages water-gardens to the 21st-century, via Jane Austen rose arbours, and be inspired by gardening through the centuries

1 **14th Century Dunsborough Park** Surrey

The landscaped grounds date from the 14th Century, but set within these splendid surroundings you will find extensive formal and walled gardens of six acres redesigned by Penelope Hobhouse and Rupert Golby. Truly a garden across time.

Photograph: Nicola Stocken Tomkins

2 **15th Century Hodges Barn** Gloucestershire

Featuring an unusual 15th Century dovecote (now a family home), this is a wonderful English summer garden. Local Cotswold stone walls host many climbing plants and hedges create formality around the house. Explore the water and woodland gardens.

Photograph: Mandy Bradshaw

3 **16th Century Littlecote House Hotel** Berkshire (New for 2009)

A stunning 16th Century mansion set in exquisite manicured lawns. Here, in 1535, Henry VIII wooed Jane Seymour. As well as the Tudor avenue, there's a walled rose garden and the north topiaried avenue with the very essence of times past.

Photograph: Warner Leisure Hotels

2

3

Gardd Fotaneg Genedlaethol Cymru

Mae'r Ardd ar agor gydol y flwyddyn ac yn cynnig diwrnod allan arbennig i'r teulu i gyd. Dewch i weld y Tŷ Gwydr un haen mwyaf yn y byd, a nifer o atyniadau eraill gan gynnwys:

- Tŷ Gwydr Mawr
- Tŷ Gwydr Trofannol Newydd
- Yr Ardd Japaneaidd
- Gardd Wenyn
- Oriel y Stablau
- Canolfan Ymwelwyr a Siop Rhoddion
- Theatr Botanica
- Planhigion i Iachau Exhibition
- Lle Chwarae i Blant
- Gwarchodfa Natur Genedlaethol Waun Las

Rydym ar agor bob dydd ac eithrio Dydd Nadolig
Haf : 10am - 6pm | Gaeaf : 10am - 4.30pm

- Oedolion £8 • Gostyngiadau £6.50 • Plant (5-16) £4
- Dan 5 AM DDIM • Tocyn Teulu (2 Oedolyn a 4 o blant) £19.50

Gallai'r prisiau newid yn y gaeaf

Mae cyfleusterau cynadleddo ac arlwyo ar gael ar gyfer hyd at 400 o bobl. Addas iawn ar gyfer ymweliadau ysgol.

I gael prisiau a rhagor o wybodaeth cysylltwch â :
Gardd Fotaneg Genedlaethol Cymru, Llanarthne, Sir Gaerfyrddin SA32 8HG

National Botanic Garden of Wales

Open all year, the Garden offers a great day out for all the family. See the world's largest single span glass house and the many varied attractions including:

- Great Glasshouse
- Tropical House
- Japanese Garden
- Bee Garden
- Stables Gallery
- Gift Shop & Visitor Centre
- Theatr Botanica
- Plants for Health Exhibition
- Children's Play Area
- Waun Las National Nature Reserve

Open every day except Christmas Day
Summer : 10am - 6pm | Winter : 10am - 4.30pm

- Adults £8 • Concessions £6.50 • Children (5-16) £4
- Under 5's FREE • Family (2 Adults, 4 children) £19.50

Prices may vary in winter

Conference and catering facilities for up to 400 people available. School visits highly recommended.

For prices and further information contact :
The National Botanic Garden of Wales, Llanarthne, Carmarthenshire SA32 8HG

National Botanic Garden of Wales
Gardd Fotaneg Genedlaethol Cymru

01558 668768
www.gardenofwales.org.uk

Visit Wales National Tourism Awards 2007 - UK's favourite Lottery-funded Environment Project

LOTTERY FUNDED

Wales Cymru

4 17th Century **Newtimber Place** Sussex

This Sussex moated house, built of flint and brick with a roof of Horsham stone, was probably built by Richard Bellingham's son, who was Sheriff of Sussex in 1567. What could be more wonderful than exploring these delightful gardens? Bulbs and wildflowers in the spring, and roses and herbaceous borders in high summer.

Photograph: David Gadsby

5 18th Century **Mere House** Kent

The wonderful lake was created in 1780 by canalising a stream feeding the Mereworth Castle lakes. The existing garden is almost entirely the work of the mid 20th Century, by the present owners' parents, with an emphasis on foliage contrast and the lake.

Photograph: Leigh Clapp

6 Georgian **Old Rectory, Haselbech** Northamptonshire

One-acre garden set in 9 acres of parkland surrounding a Georgian rectory. It's not hard to imagine Jane Austen's characters in such a setting, with its old walled garden, rose garden, small potager vegetable gardens – and not forgetting the ha-ha and magnificent trees.

Photograph: Clive Nichols

7 19th Century **Thornbridge Hall** Derbyshire (New for 2009)

A stunning 100-acre garden overlooking rolling Derbyshire countryside. Established in the late 19th Century, this rarely opened, privately owned garden has many distinct areas including Italian, knot and water gardens, 110ft herbaceous border, working potager, koi lake, summer house and glass houses.

Photograph: Lu Jeffery

6

7

Your gateway to the international auction market

8 Early 20th Century **Whalton Manor Gardens**
Durham & Northumberland

The historic manor here was altered by Lutyens in 1908. He also designed the three acres of walled gardens with the help of Gertrude Jekyll. The Manor is owned by the Norland family, who have been developing the gardens since the 1920s. The 30-yard peony border is well worth a visit.

9 Mid 20th Century **Melplash Court** Dorset

Originally designed in the late 1950s, the gardens have evolved over the last 25 years under the enthusiastic ownership of the late Timothy Lewis with the assistance of Terry Baker of the Botanic Gardens, Atworth in Wiltshire. Together they have designed and planted new borders and a number of special areas of interest. Don't miss the formal kitchen and herb garden.

Photograph: Carole Drake

8

9

10 21st Century **Temple Guiting Manor** Gloucestershire

Set in approximately 14.5 acres with wonderful views across the Windrush valley. This beautiful Tudor house is set in a series of contemporary walled gardens designed by Jinny Blom, which make the most of the views and local landscape. New gardens are currently being developed and will be completed in 2009.

Photograph: Andrew Lawson

11 21st Century **Linden Barn** Hampshire

This 1/3-acre garden was created from a farmyard in 2001. The owners have placed a garden with emphasis on structure and colour combinations. The planting scheme creates drifts of colour using classic cottage garden plants alongside contemporary species. With a backdrop of the village church, the past really does meet the present.

Photograph: Nicola Stocken Tomkins

10

11

Naturetrek

Escorted botanical holidays you can't afford to miss!

SOUTH AFRICA'S DRAKENSBURG
7 – 20 Jan £2,995

NEW ZEALAND
15 Jan – 3 Feb £4,395

CYPRUS
21 – 29 Mar,
29 Mar – 5 Apr £1,045

SRI LANKA
29 Mar – 9 Apr £1,995

SPAIN – WESTERN ANDALUCIA
11 – 18 Mar, 18 – 25 Mar £995

CRETE
7 – 14 Apr, 14 – 21 Apr,
21 – 28 Apr £1,095
13 – 20 Oct £995

KAZAKHSTAN & TIEN SHAN
11 – 26 Apr £2,790

ITALY – SORRENTO
15 – 22 Apr £1,095

CROATIA
18 – 25 Apr, 5 – 12 Sep £1,295

THE ISLAND OF SAMOS
18 – 26 Apr £1,095

ITALY – THE GARGANO
19 – 26 Apr, 26 Apr – 3 May £995

BHUTAN
23 Apr – 10 May £4,395

SARDINIA
26 Apr – 3 May £1,095

FRANCE – PROVENCE
28 Apr – 5 May £1,095

SICILY
29 Apr – 6 May £1,095

MENORCA
1 – 8 May £1,095

ITALY – TUSCANY
3 – 10 May £1,295

SPAIN – CATALONIA
9 – 16 May £1,095

CORSICA
10 – 17 May, 20 – 27 Sep £1,195

FRANCE – THE CEVENNES
13 – 20 May £995

FRANCE – LA BRENNE
16 – 23 May £1,095

FRANCE – THE LOT VALLEY
16 – 23 May £995

FRANCE – THE VERCORS
17 – 24 May, 24 – 31 May £1,095

MOROCCO
17 – 31 May £1,295

THE SPANISH PYRENEES
17 – 24 May, 24 – 31 May £995

FRANCE – THE DORDOGNE
24 – 31 May £995

IRELAND – THE BURREN
26 – 29 May £395

ITALY – THE APENNINES
27 May – 3 Jun £1,085

SWEDEN – OLAND
28 May – 3 Jun £1,295

CHINA – YUNNAN
2 – 20 Jun £3,795

MADEIRA
3 – 10 Jun £985

FRANCE – THE LOIRE VALLEY
6 – 10 Jun £675

SLOVAKIA
6 – 13 Jun £1,295

ITALY – SIBILLINI MOUNTAINS
7 – 14 Jun £1,085

ESTONIA
9 – 14 Jun £1,995

FRANCE – THE AUVERGNE
14 – 21 Jun, 12 – 19 Sep £995

THE HAMPSHIRE DOWNS
19 – 21 Jun £265

ALPINES IN THE TIEN SHAN
20 Jun – 2 Jul £2,690

BULGARIA
20 – 27 Jun £1,050

CHINA – SICHUAN
21 Jun – 12 Jul £3,795

ROMANIA
23 – 30 Jun £1,195

THE ITALIAN DOLOMITES
24 Jun – 1 Jul £995

WENGEN, THE SWISS ALPS
28 Jun – 5 Jul £1,095

ITALIAN & FRENCH ALPS
1 – 8 Jul £1,195

SWITZERLAND – ENGADINE
5 – 12 Jul £1,095

NORWAY – GOL PLATEAU
11 – 18 Jul £1,285

LADAKH'S MARKHA VALLEY
24 Jul – 9 Aug £1,995

SOUTH AFRICA
17 Aug – 2 Sep £3,995

CAPE & NAMAQUALAND (SOUTH AFRICA)
20 Aug – 2 Sep,
2 Sep – 15 Sep £TBC

WESTERN AUSTRALIA
4 – 20 Sep £3,995

FRENCH PYRENEES
6 – 13 Sep £995

SOUTH AFRICA'S GARDEN ROUTE
16 – 29 Sep £TBC

MADAGASCAR'S FLORA
20 Sep – 3 Oct £3,495

ECUADOR – ANDEAN FLORA
26 Sep – 11 Oct £2,995

Call **01962 733051**
or visit **www.naturetrek.co.uk**

Gardd Bodnant | Bodnant Garden

Caleidosgop o liwau a ffurfiau newidiol | A kaleidoscope of changing colour and form

Touch the Senses
2009 DIAMOND JUBILEE YEAR

28 February to **1 November**, open daily **10-5pm**
2 November to **15 November**, open daily **10-4pm**
(last entry 30 minutes prior to closing)

8 mls south of Llandudno, off A470; exit A55 Jct 19

Tal-y-Cafn, near Colwyn Bay, Conwy.   Tel: 01492 650460
www.bodnant-garden.co.uk

How to use
The Yellow Book

Main image:
Devils End, Norfolk
Photograph: Jerry
Harpur

The following pages list gardens all over the country you can visit. Joe Swift reveals the different ways to find a garden…

Like the first tender shoots of spring, the publication of *The Yellow Book* heralds a new season of garden opening for you to enjoy. When I have a spare moment, or between filming assignments, I take the opportunity to leaf through *The Yellow Book* to find gardens that I want to visit, and to plan my garden visiting.

I always keep a copy of *The Yellow Book* to hand when I'm travelling, so I can see if there are any gardens nearby to visit. Using *The Yellow Book* is easy – either look at the listings for the county you're in, then check the description and opening dates. Alternatively, if you know the name of a particular garden but not where it is, the garden names are listed in an index at the back of the book.

There are so many great *Yellow Book* gardens to see, so why not stop off at some on your holidays and travels? Many welcome visitors by appointment, which gives you extra flexibility when planning your trip.

One area of *The Yellow Book* that I see continuing to grow are gardens in one village or street that open on the same day. This is a great way to see a group of gardens in one location and to appreciate how each owner imposes their own style on their garden, under similar growing conditions to their neighbour. The group openings also represent great value for money, as the admission fee will cover a number of gardens and generally works out cheaper than if you were to visit each garden separately. Everyone pitches in together, and there's a really good community feel to the opening.

The helpful editorial team at the NGS have made these popular group openings easier to find this year – look out for the new green headings in the listings section.

The garden information listed in *The Yellow Book* is also available via the website, www.ngs.org.uk (listed at the bottom of each page). Images of some of the gardens accompany their description, giving you a sneak preview of what they look like. The website also provides up-to-date gardening news stories, articles, and updates about forthcoming special NGS events. There's loads on there, so take a look.

There's bound to be a garden opening close to your home, so read on to see which gardens are opening this year!

113 Corringham Road, London. Photograph: Susie Gibbons

And now for the gardens . . .

'There's bound to be a garden opening close to your home, so read on to see which gardens are opening this year!'
Joe Swift

Visit a garden near you

The Yellow Book 2009 lists over 3600 gardens all over England & Wales. With hundreds of new entries to be discovered this year, there's sure to be a garden near you!

The map at the start of each county section shows the location of the gardens – green ovals for gardens within that county, and grey ovals for those in adjacent counties.

NGS counties do not necessarily follow exact government boundaries, nor do they always acknowledge the unitary authorities or the large cities which lie within them.

So if you can't find a garden in England or Wales, try looking here...

Where to find the gardens

Place/area	Section listing
Anglesey	Gwynedd & Anglesey
Avon	Somerset, Bristol Area & South Gloucestershire
Bath	Somerset, Bristol Area & South Gloucestershire
Birmingham	Warwickshire
Bristol	Somerset, Bristol Area & South Gloucestershire
Cambrian Coast	See individual Welsh counties
Cardiff	Glamorgan
Colwyn	Denbigh & Colwyn
Conwy	Gwynedd & Anglesey
Coventry	Warwickshire
County Durham	Durham & Northumberland
South Gloucestershire	Somerset, Bristol Area & South Gloucestershire
Hull	Yorkshire
Leeds	Yorkshire
Liverpool	Lancashire
Manchester	Lancashire
Merseyside	Lancashire
Monmouthshire	Gwent
Newcastle	Durham & Northumberland
Northumberland	Durham & Northumberland
Sheffield	Yorkshire
Swansea	Glamorgan
Teeside	Durham & Northumberland
Tyne and Wear	Durham & Northumberland
West Midlands, county of	Staffordshire and Warwickshire
Wirral	Cheshire & Wirral
Wrexham	Flintshire & Wrexham

Remember, with GardenFinder ® at www.ngs.org.uk, you can search for gardens by name, county, postcode, distance from home or by special features.

While every effort is made to ensure that entries are accurate, with so many gardens there will inevitably be last-minute changes. Where possible these will be publicised locally, but please visit www.ngs.org.uk for up-to-date opening information, as well as garden news and information on special events all over the country.

For further information, contact details of local volunteer teams are at the end of each section. Alternatively email ngs@ngs.org.uk or phone 01483 211535.

Geographical Area Guide

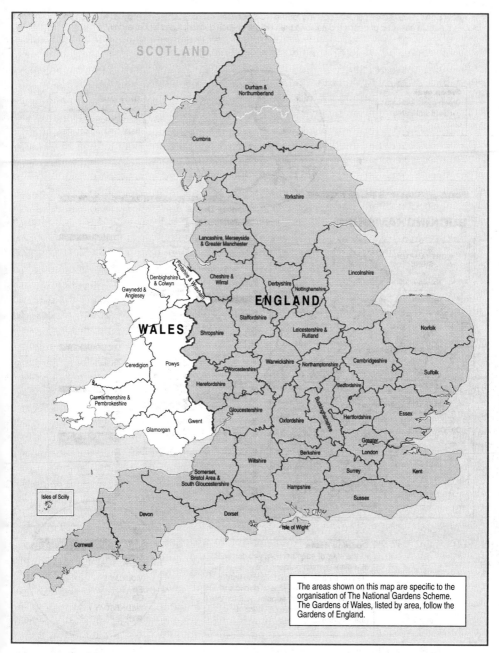

The areas shown on this map are specific to the organisation of The National Gardens Scheme. The Gardens of Wales, listed by area, follow the Gardens of England.

Understanding this book

A simple guide to getting the most out of the listings section

Overview

The Yellow Book 2009 lists all gardens opening for the NGS between January 2009 and early 2010. Each county section includes a map, a calendar of opening dates and then details of each garden, listed alphabetically.

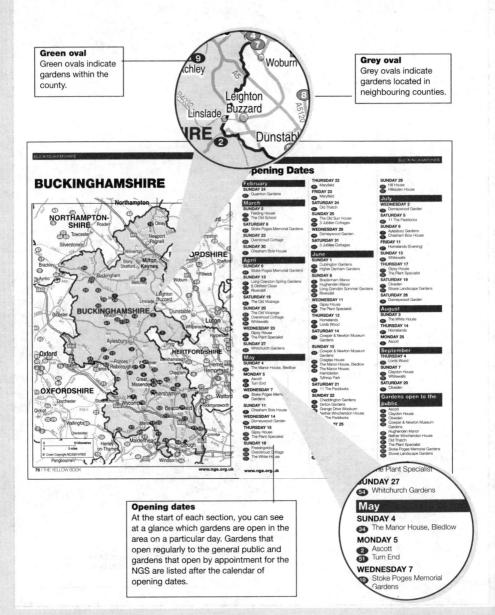

Green oval
Green ovals indicate gardens within the county.

Grey oval
Grey ovals indicate gardens located in neighbouring counties.

Opening dates
At the start of each section, you can see at a glance which gardens are open in the area on a particular day. Gardens that open regularly to the general public and gardens that open by appointment for the NGS are listed after the calendar of opening dates.

County name
Gardens in England are listed first, followed by gardens in Wales.

Directions
A simple set of directons to each garden. Most gardens also list postcodes for use with computer or satellite navigation systems.

Description
A short description of each garden covers the main features. This is written by garden owners and reviewed each year.

Admission price
The admission price applies to all visitors unless exceptions are noted e.g. child free.

---

40 THE OLD SUN HOUSE
Pednor HP5 2SZ. Mr & Mrs M Sharpley. 3m E of Gt Missenden, 2m W of Chesham. From Gt Missenden take B485 to Chesham, 1st L & follow signs approx 2m. From Chesham Church St (B485) follow signs approx 1½ m. Home-made teas. **Adm £3, chd free. Sun 25 May (2-6).**
5-acre garden, abundant with wildlife, set on a Chiltern ridge giving superb views. The garden is surrounded by mature trees with inner plantings of unusual trees and shrubs. Features incl large ornamental pond with walkway, vegetable and herb garden, interesting woodland walk, white peafowl, guinea fowl, pheasantry and chickens.

BUCKINGHAMSHIRE

36 NEW MARYFIELD
SL6 0EX. Jacqueline & Roger Andrews. 1m S Cliveden, ½m E Maidenhead. From M4 J7 or M40 J4 follow signs for Taplow. House on bend of High St. Light refreshments & teas. **Adm £3.50, chd free (share to Thames Valley Adventure Playground).** Thur 22, Fri 23 May (2-6).
2-acres wrapped around our Victorian home in the heart of Taplow Village. New walled vegetable and herb garden bordered by fruit trees, over-looked by a mature lime walk, extends into herbaceous planting, mature yew hedging, pond area, orchard and Japanese inspired garden. Cake sale.

37 THE OLD SCHOOL
Church Lane, Oving HP22 4HL. Mr & Mrs M Ryan. Off A413, 1m W of Whitchurch, between pub & church. Light refreshments & teas. **Combined with Fielding House, Whitchurch Adm £2.50, chd free.** Sun 2 Mar (12-4).
Playground now a walled lawn backed by herbaceous borders. Fine views from old orchard planted with roses and spring bulbs, enclosed patio with collection of scented-leaf geraniums, hellebore collection.

40 THE OLD SUN HOUSE
Pednor HP5 2SZ. Mr & Mrs M Sharpley. 3m E of Gt Missenden, 2m W of Chesham. From Gt Missenden take B485 to Chesham, 1st L & follow signs approx 2m. From Chesham Church St (B485) follow signs approx 1½ m. Home-made teas. **Adm £3, chd free.** Sun 25 May (2-6).
5-acre garden, abundant with wildlife, set on a Chiltern ridge giving superb views. The garden is surrounded by mature trees with inner plantings of unusual trees and shrubs. Features incl large ornamental pond with walkway, vegetable and herb garden, interesting woodland walk, white peafowl, guinea fowl, pheasantry and chickens.

41 OLD THATCH
Coldmoorholme Lane, Well End SL8 5PS. Jacky & David Hawthorne, 01628 527518, www.jackyshawthorne.co.uk. 3m E Marlow, 1m W Bourne End. Off A4155. Thatched house on L just before the Spade Oak PH. Public car park 100yds

UpCorner, on to Silver Hill. At top of hill fork R into Dodds Lane. N Down is 6th opening on L. Limited parking in Dodds Lane. **Adm £3, chd free.** Visitors welcome by appt, May to Oct, groups welcome, no coaches.
¾ -acre sloping N-facing compartmentalised site with mature trees. Difficult stony soil. Designed with scenic effect in mind and interest throughout the yr. Large grassed areas with island beds of mixed perennials, shrubs and some unusual plants. Variety of rhododendrons, azaleas, acers, 70+ clematis and other climbers. Displays of sempervivum varieties, alpines, grasses and ferns. Small patio/water feature. Greenhouse. Italianate front patio to owner's design.

43 THE OLD VICARAGE
Thornborough Road, Padbury MK18 2AH. Mr & Mrs H Morley-Fletcher, 01280 813045, belindamfli@freenet.co.uk. 2m S of Buckingham, 4m NW of Winslow. On A413, signed in village. Home-made teas. **Adm £3, chd free.** Sat 19, Sun 20 Apr (2-6). Visitors also welcome by appt.
2½ acres on 3 levels, flowering shrubs and trees. Vegetable garden, pond and sunken garden, parterre and millennium arch. Magnolias and trilliums. Sunken garden can be viewed from above by wheelchair users.

45 6 OLDFIELD CLOSE
Little Chalfont HP6 6SU. Jolyon & Phyllis Lea, 01494 762384. 3m E of Amersham. Take A404 E through Little Chalfont, 1st R after railway bridge, R again into Oakington Ave. Teas. **Adm £2, chd free.** Sun 13 Apr (2-5). Visitors also welcome by appt. Mature ½ -acre garden of shrub borders, peat beds, rock plants, troughs and alpine house. Over 2,000 species and varieties of rare and interesting plants, incl spring bulbs, cyclamen and dwarf rhododendrons. Wide range of plants for sale.

46 OVERSTROUD COTTAGE
The Dell, Frith Hill, Gt Missenden HP16 9QE. Mr & Mrs Jonathan Brooke, 01494 862701, susie@jandsbrooke.co.uk. ½ m E Gt Missenden. Turn E off A413 at Gt Missenden onto B485 Frith Hill to Chesham rd. White Gothic cottage set back in lay-by 100yds up hill on L. Parking on R at church. Cream teas at Parish Church. **Adm £2.50, chd 50p.**

39 NETHER WINCHENDON HOUSE
Nether Winchendon HP18 0DY. Mr Robert Spencer Bernard, 01844 290101, www.netherwinchendonhouse.com, 6m SW of Aylesbury, 6m from Thame. **Adm £3, chd free.** For NGS: Sun 22 June (2-5.30).
5 acres of fine and rare trees and shrubs, a variety of hedges, herbaceous borders and naturalised spring bulbs. Founder garden (1927) Medieval and Tudor manor house (not open) in picturesque village with beautiful church. Unfenced river bank.

38 NORTH DOWN
Dodds Lane, Chalfont St Giles HP8 4EL. Merida Saunders, 01494 872928. 4m SE of Amersham, 4m NE of Beaconsfield. Opp the green in centre of village. At Crown Inn turn into

84 | THE YELLOW BOOK

www.ngs.org.uk

Symbols explained

4 The garden's position on the county or area map.

NEW Garden opening this year for the first time or reopening after a long break or under new ownership.

♦ Denotes a garden that is open to the public on a regular basis. Gardens which carry this symbol contribute to the NGS either by opening on a specific day or days and/or by giving a guaranteed contribution to the Scheme.

♿ Wheelchair access to at least the main features of the garden. Often disabled parking is available close by, or in the owner's driveway.

🐕 No dogs except guide dogs. Where dogs are allowed they must be on short leads.

✿ Plants usually for sale, often propagated by the garden owners. If proceeds go elsewhere, this is shown at the garden opening.

NCCPG Garden that holds a NCCPG National Plant Collection.

🛏 Gardens that offer accommodation. For a detailed listing see the Accommodation index beginning on page 685.

☕ Refreshments are available, normally at a charge. Detailed information is given in the garden's entry. Wine is often available at Evening Openings. If proceeds go elsewhere, this is shown at the garden opening.

☎ Gardens showing this symbol welcome visitors by prior arrangement. They are listed at the start of each county or area section. Some can accommodate clubs, some only small parties and some have limited parking. Please telephone, email or write to make an appointment.

Coach parties
Please contact the garden direct to make arrangements.

Children must be accompanied by an adult.

Toilets are not usually available at private gardens.

Photographs
Where taken at a garden opening, photographs must not be used for sale or reproduction without prior permission of the owner.

Share To
If 'share to' is shown in a garden text, it indicates that a proportion of the money collected will be given to the nominated charity.

Group Opening

A group of gardens opening together on the same day or days – a great afternoon out!

BEDFORDSHIRE

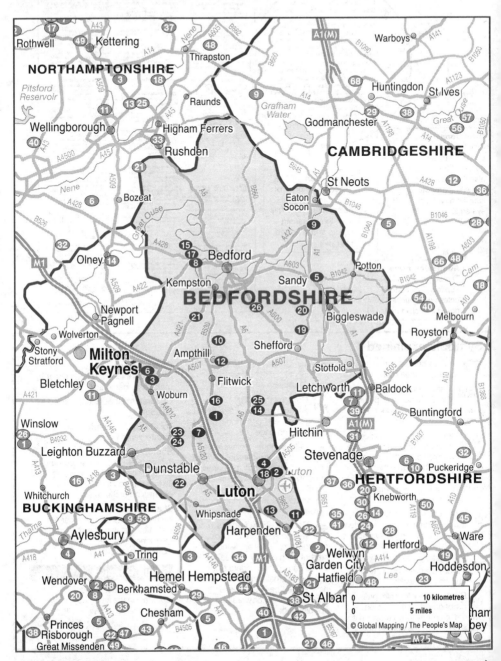

www.ngs.org.uk

Opening Dates

January

SUNDAY 25
⑫ King's Arms Garden

March

SUNDAY 29
⑩ How End Cottage
⑯ The Old Vicarage

April

SATURDAY 18
⑧ 59 Grange Lane

SUNDAY 19
⑧ 59 Grange Lane
⑳ Swiss Garden

May

SATURDAY 9
⑪ The Hyde Walled Garden

SUNDAY 10
⑦ The Folly

SUNDAY 17
㉒ Valley Forge

SUNDAY 24
① Briarwood (Day & Evening)

SUNDAY 31
⑤ The Firs

June

SUNDAY 7
⑥ Flaxbourne Farm
⑰ Park End Thatch
⑲ Southill Park

SUNDAY 14
⑬ Luton Hoo
⑮ Manor House, Stevington

SUNDAY 21
⑩ How End Cottage
⑯ The Old Vicarage

SUNDAY 28
⑪ The Hyde Walled Garden
㉓ Watergate Farm
㉔ Watergate Lodge
㉖ 16 Wood Lane

July

SUNDAY 5
⑥ Flaxbourne Farm

SATURDAY 11
⑨ 8 Great North Road

SUNDAY 12
⑨ 8 Great North Road
㉑ Treize

SUNDAY 19
② Conifers

⑱ Seal Point

August

SUNDAY 9
⑥ Flaxbourne Farm

SUNDAY 23
⑭ The Manor House, Barton-Le-Clay
㉕ Wayside Cottage

September

SUNDAY 6
㉒ Valley Forge

October

SUNDAY 25
⑫ King's Arms Garden

January 2010

SUNDAY 31
⑫ King's Arms Garden

Gardens open to the public

⑫ King's Arms Garden
⑮ Manor House, Stevington

By appointment only

③ Dawnedge Lodge
④ 14 Fairford Avenue

Also open by appointment ☎

③ Dawnedge Lodge
④ 14 Fairford Avenue
⑤ The Firs
⑥ Flaxbourne Farm
⑧ 59 Grange Lane
⑨ 8 Great North Road
⑭ The Manor House, Barton-Le-Clay
⑰ Park End Thatch
⑱ Seal Point
㉕ Wayside Cottage

Japanese-style garden, pergola walk with climbers, rockery surrounding ornamental fish-pond with waterfall . . .

The Gardens

ASCOTT
See Buckinghamshire.

① BRIARWOOD
Toddington Road, Harlington
LU5 6LA. Jenny & Andrew Asbury.
From M1 J12 take A5120 heading towards Flitwick, bear R at 1st mini r'about signed for Harlington Stn. Double gates 500yds on L. Ample parking available. Disabled parking in drive. Adm £3.50, chd free (share to BDSSG). **Afternoon & Evening Opening** light refreshments & teas, wine, Sun 24 May (3-9).
In years gone by this 7 acre plot would have been a hive of activity being the remains of old brickworks. The 2 lakes are now a haven for wildlife. Features incl stunning boardwalks, walled garden with Victorian greenhouse, bridges, summerhouse and thatched willow. Children will love this place, with plenty to do for all ages incl an outdoor playground and climbing frames. Disabled access to boardwalk.
♿ ⊕ ☕

100 CHURCH GREEN ROAD
See Buckinghamshire.

② CONIFERS
40 Sowerby Avenue, Luton LU2 8AF.
June & Richard Giles, 01582 415846.
3½ m NE of Luton town centre. Take A505 towards Hitchin. R at Jansell House r'about (Stopsley) into Ashcroft Rd. After 200yds L into Wigmore Lane, Sowerby Ave 3rd on L. Adm £3, chd free. Combined with **Seal Point** adm £6. Sun 19 July (2-5).
Interesting mature garden created over 10yrs and set within ¼ acre plot featuring large colourful borders with trees, shrubs and herbaceous planting. Japanese-style garden, pergola walk with climbers, rockery surrounding ornamental fish-pond with waterfall. Rose arch and rose beds, greenhouse and vegetable garden.
✈ ⊕ ☕

COWPER & NEWTON MUSEUM GARDENS
See Buckinghamshire.

CUBLINGTON GARDENS
See Buckinghamshire.

Rare, exotic and unusual plants abound ... year round interest where plants provide structure and form . . .

3 DAWNEDGE LODGE

Woburn Lane, Aspley Guise MK17 8JH. Phil & Lynne Wallace, 01908 582233, lynnewallace@hotmail.co.uk. 5m W of Ampthill. 3m from J13 M1. In Aspley Guise, turn L in centre of village at Moore Place Hotel. Home-made teas. **Adm £3, chd free. Visitors welcome by appt May, June & July, also groups.**
1-acre garden on top of a hill with great views to Woburn. Victorian walled garden, rescued 10yrs ago, with colour themed island beds, pergolas, terracotta pots on stone patio. Cutting garden, Alitex greenhouse. Alliums and agapanthus good. If groups wish, I will exhibit my patchwork quilts, some of which are for sale in aid of NGS.

4 14 FAIRFORD AVENUE

Luton LU2 7ER. Brian & Ann Biddle, 01582 735669, biddle.ba@sky.com. 2m N of Luton town centre. Fairford Ave leads directly from Bradgers Hill Rd, past Luton VI college situated off the Old Bedford Rd parallel to A6. **Adm £3, chd free. Visitors welcome by appt and small groups.**
1/4 -acre hillside garden, with many changes of level, twists and turns, disguising the long, narrow plot and giving some surprise views. Variety of shrubs, trees and herbaceous plants which will tolerate poor, chalky soil give yr-round interest from snowdrops and hellebores to autumn flowering perennials.

5 THE FIRS

33 Bedford Road, Sandy SG19 1EP. Mr & Mrs D Sutton, 01767 691992, d.sutton7@ntworld.com. 7m E of Bedford. On B1042 towards town centre. On rd parking. Home-made teas. **Adm £2.50, chd free. Sun 31 May (2-5). Visitors also welcome by appt.**
1/4 -acre town garden with many different features. This garden has been designed and created from scratch since 2000 and is productive in fruit, flowers, vegetables and wildlife. Run organically, this garden has everything from shrubs, trees, perennials, to water features. Featured in 'Womens Weekly' & 'Daily Telegraph'. Gravel drive at front of house.

6 FLAXBOURNE FARM

Salford Road, Aspley Guise MK17 8HZ. Geoff & Davina Barrett, 01908 585329, carole@boa.uk.com. 5m W of Ampthill. 1m S of J13 of M1.Turn R in village centre, 1m over railway line. Home-made teas. **Adm £5, concession £4 (June), adm £4, concessions £3.50 (July, Aug) chd free (share to St Botolph Church). Special opening Sun 7 June (10-5); Suns 5 July; 9 Aug (2-6). Visitors also welcome by appt groups or 10+, coaches permitted.**
A beautiful and entertaining fun garden of 2 acres, lovingly developed with numerous water features, windmill, modern arches and bridges, small moated castle, lily pond, herbaceous borders. Shrubs and trees recently established, newly constructed Greek temple ruin, fernery and crow's nest. Bring the whole family and discover many more inspirational features, incl huge roman stone arched gateway as recently featured in ITV's 'This Morning' programme. Plant Fair and Party Day adm £5, Sun 7 June. Woburn Sands Band play - June & Aug.

7 THE FOLLY

69 Leighton Road, Toddington LU5 6AL. Gillian & Edward Ladd. 5m N of Dunstable. J12 M1 follow B5120 to village. Turn R at Bell PH. Garden 0.2m on L. Light refreshments & teas. **Adm £3, chd free. Sun 10 May (11-5).**
Wheelchair friendly 1/4 acre created over 14yrs. Many mature shrubs and trees with various foliage. Small woodland walk, orchard and vegetable garden. Greenhouse and potting shed with cacti garden. Many interesting features incl numerous old farmimg implements.

8 59 GRANGE LANE

Bromham MK43 8PA. Mrs Mary Morris, 01234 822215, mary.morris59@ntlworld.com. 3m W of Bedford. A428 to Bromham, sign Oakley, into Village Rd. 3rd turning on L (Grange Lane), 59 is opp Springfield Drive on L. Home-made teas. **Adm £3, chd free. Sat 18, Sun 19 Apr (2-5). Visitors also welcome by appt April & May.**
An informal 150ft organic garden developed over 25yrs. Herbaceous border with colour groupings; mixed border; small woodland garden with camellias and many spring flowers and bulbs. Gravel areas. Some unusual plants; hardy geraniums; pulmonarias. Formal pond and white border. Vegetable garden using raised beds and companion planting. Visitors always welcome. Paintings for sale - 20% to NGS.

9 8 GREAT NORTH ROAD

Chawston MK44 3BD. D G Parker, 01480 213284. 2m S of St Neots. Between Wyboston & Blackcat r'about on S-bound lane of A1. Turn off at McDonalds, at end of filling station forecourt turn L. Light refreshments & teas. **Adm £3, chd free. Sat 11, Sun 12 July (2-6). Visitors also welcome by appt Apr to Sept, no coaches.**
1 acre garden, 1/2 acre young trees and shrubs. Cottage garden of 1/2 acre crammed with bulbs, herbaceous, water and bog plants, ferns, grasses, shrubs and trees. Rare, exotic and unusual plants abound, large pond, level grass paths. Yr round interest where plants provide structure and form, 2500sq metre glasshouse mainly growing Chinese vegetables.

10 HOW END COTTAGE

Houghton Conquest MK45 3JT. Jeremy & Gill Smith. 1m N of Ampthill. Turn R 1m from Ampthill off B530 towards Houghton Conquest. How End Rd 300yds on RH-side. Garden at end of rd, approx 1/2 m. Home-made teas. **Adm £3, chd free. Suns 29 Mar; 21 June (2.30-5.30).**
Approx 1 acre garden with 2 ponds, large vegetable garden, greenhouse and orchard. Large lawn gives an

uninterrupted view of Houghton House. The garden contains mature trees and beds with many types of slow growing fir trees. Flower beds contain home grown bedding plants and roses. 3 acres of paddocks, wood and further pond. Many spring bulbs.

 ♾ 🚦 ☕

⑪ THE HYDE WALLED GARDEN
East Hyde, Luton LU2 9PS. D J J Hambro Will Trust. *2m S of Luton. M1 exit J10/10a. A1081 S take 2nd L. At E Hyde turn R then immed L. Junction entrance on R. From A1 exit J4. Follow A3057 N to r'about, 1st L to B653 Wheathamstead/Luton to E Hyde.* Home-made teas. **Adm £3, chd free.** **Sat 9 May; Sun 28 June** (2-5). Walled garden adjoins the grounds of The Hyde (house NOT open). Extends to approx 1 acre and features rose garden, seasonal beds and herbaceous borders, imaginatively interspersed with hidden areas of formal lawn. An interesting group of Victorian greenhouses, coldframes and cucumber house are serviced from the potting shed in the adjoining vegetable garden. Bluebell walk in season. Gravel paths.

♾ 🚦 ❊ ☕

⑫ ♦ KING'S ARMS GARDEN
Ampthill MK45 2PP. Ampthill Town Council, 01525 755648, bryden.k@ntlworld.com. *8m S of Bedford. Free parking in town centre. Entrance opp old Market Place, down King's Arms Yard.* **Adm £2, chd free.** **Last Sun of month 2.30-5, except 12 Apr & 3 May.** For NGS: **Suns 25 Jan** (2-4); **25 Oct** (2-4.30); **31 Jan 2010.** Small woodland garden of about 1½ acres created by plantsman the late William Nourish. Trees, shrubs, bulbs and many collections giving interest thoughout the yr. The winter garden, with swathes of snowdrops, early daffodils and hellebores, magnificent mahonias and hemmamelis, is of particular interest. Maintained since 1987 by 'The Friends of the Garden' on behalf of Ampthill Town Council.

♾ 🚦 ❊ ☕

⑬ NEW LUTON HOO
Luton Hoo Hotel Golf & Spa, The Mansion House, Luton Hoo, Luton LU1 3TQ. *Approx 1m from J10 M1, take London Rd A1081 signed Harpenden for approx ½ m - entrance on L for Luton Hoo.* **Adm £5, chd free.** **Sun 14 June** (11-4). The gardens and parkland designed by Capability Brown are of national historic significance and lie in a conservation area. Main features - lakes, woodland and pleasure grounds, Victorian grass tennis court and late C19 sunken rockery. Italianate garden with herbaceous borders and topiary garden. Gravel paths, gentle slopes down to garden.

♾ 🚦 🛌 ❊ ☕

⑮ ♦ MANOR HOUSE, STEVINGTON
Church Road, nr Bedford MK43 7QB. Kathy Brown, 01234 822064, www.kathybrownsgarden.homestead.com. *Off A428 through Bromham.* **Adm £4.50, chd free.** **3, 4, 24, 25 May, 2, 30, 31 Aug, 20 Sept, Tues June & July.** For NGS: **Sun 14 June** (12-5). Great swathes of roses and then late flowering clematis abound in this modern country garden designed and cared for by owners Simon and Kathy Brown. The French Garden with its jury scene, cottage garden, wild flower meadow, and several major container displays (most are longterm), offer contrasting areas of interest with wonderful ornamental grass borders echoing works of art by Hepworth, Hokusai and Monet. Topiary Rothko rooms and Mondrian 'Boogie Woogie' dance floor add to the 'Art Garden' theme. Featured in 'English Garden', 'Gardeners World'; Chanel 5/NGS Gold Medal Award Garden.

♾ 🚦 ❊ ☕

⑭ NEW THE MANOR HOUSE, BARTON-LE-CLAY
87 Manor Road. MK45 4NR. Mrs Veronica Pilcher. *Off A6 between Bedford & Luton. Take old A6 (Bedford Rd) through Barton-le-Clay Village (not the by-pass) and, Manor Rd is off Bedford Rd. Parking in paddock.* Home-made teas. **Combined with Wayside Cottage adm £4, chd free.** **Sun 23 Aug** (2-6). Visitors also welcome by appt please apply in writing. The garden was beautifully landscaped during the 1930s and much interest is created by picturesque stream which incorporates a series of waterfalls, colourful streamside planting incl an abundance of arum lilies. Sunken garden with lily pond and a magnificent wisteria thrives at the rear of the house. Partial wheelchair access.

♾ ❊ ☕ ☏

THE MENAGERIE
See Northamptonshire.

⑯ THE OLD VICARAGE
Church Road, Westoning MK45 5JW. Ann & Colin Davies. *4m S of Ampthill. Off A5120, 2m N of M1 J12. ¼ m up Church Rd, next to church.* Cream teas at church. **Adm £3.50, chd free.** **Suns 29 Mar; 21 June** (2-5.30). Traditional 2 acre Victorian vicarage garden on sandy soil with box and laurel hedges, formal lawn, large magnolia grandiflora and other mature shrubs and trees. Colour co-ordinated herbaceous beds, rose garden, pond, rockery, meadow, copse and small vegetable gardens. Spring interest with hellebores and daffodils. Featured in 'Garden News'.

♾ 🚦 ❊ ☕

⑰ PARK END THATCH
58 Park Road, Stevington MK43 7QG. Susan Young, 01234 826430. *5m NW of Bedford. Off A428 through Bromham.* Tea & cakes. **Adm £3, chd free.** **Sun 7 June** (1-5). Visitors also welcome by appt, July, Aug, groups 6-10, no coaches. ½ -acre cottage garden set within old orchard. View of Stevington windmill. Sunny borders of flowering shrubs with herbaceous planting. Fragrant roses and climber covered pergola. Winding paths shaded by trees. Trellice border

Picturesque stream which incorporates a series of waterfalls, colourful streamside planting incl an abundance of arum lilies . . .

featuring colour and texture groupings. Fruit production and herbs. Garden cultivated to be drought tolerant. Wildlife friendly. Gravel path on slight slope, some uneven surfaces.

RAGGED HALL
See Hertfordshire.

ROSE COTTAGE
See Buckinghamshire.

18 SEAL POINT
7 Wendover Way, Luton LU2 7LS. Mrs Danae Johnston, 01582 611567. *2m from Luton town centre. In NE Luton, turning N off Stockingstone Rd A505 into Felstead Way then 2nd L Wendover Way.* Adm £3, chd free. Combined with Conifers adm £6. Sun 19 July (2-5). Visitors also welcome by appt for small groups & coaches.
A garden of delight, incls wildlife spinney, lovely grasses, unusual trees and shrubs; 3 water features and tree-top balcony on which to enjoy refreshments. Danae won Gardener of the year E and SE 1999. We both love visitors to see our clipped topiary cats, dogs and King Kong! In 2007 the garden had an upgrade and is looking super with new vistas and waterfall. Wheelchair access only in dry weather - grassy hill slippery.

19 SOUTHILL PARK
nr Biggleswade SG18 9LL. Mr & Mrs Charles Whitbread. *3m W of Biggleswade. In the village of Southill. 3m from A1 junction at Biggleswade.* Cream teas. Adm £3.50, chd free. Sun 7 June (2-5).
Large garden, with mature trees and flowering shrubs, herbaceous borders, rose garden and wild garden. Large conservatory with tropical plants. The parkland was designed by Lancelot 'Capability' Brown in 1777.

20 SWISS GARDEN
Old Warden Park SG18 9EP. Shuttleworth Trust in Partnership with Bedfordshire County Council, 01767 627924, karen.wilsher@shuttleworth.org, www.shuttleworth.org. *2m W of Biggleswade. Signed from A1 & A600.* Light refreshments & teas. Adm £5, chd free (share to Friends of the Swiss Garden). Sun 19 Apr (10-5). Designed in 1820s. 9-acre miniature

landscape garden with winding paths, intertwining ponds, wrought iron bridges, fernery grotto and tiny buildings. Peacocks wander around splendid trees and shrubs, with daffodils, rhododendrons and roses in season. Adjacent further acres of native woodland. Gravel paths, some steep slope, bridges.

21 TREIZE
Cranfield Road, Wootton Green, Bedford MK43 9EA. Roger & Anna Skipper. *5m SW of Bedford. 10m NE of Milton Keynes. C70 Kempston to Cranfield rd, 1/2 m SW of Wootton. Private Lane on R opp Wootton Green Hamlet sign. Bungalow 100yds along lane on R. Car parking on open day in adjacent meadow (depending on weather).* Home-made teas. Adm £3.50, chd free. Sun 12 July (2-6).
1-acre plantsman's garden set out for yr-round interest on heavy clay. Hidden gardens and established herbaceous borders; formal pond; rockery, gravel beds. Many varieties of established and younger trees, shrubs and vast collection of perennials, incl over 150 varieties and species of penstemon. Wood Turning Demonstration.

22 VALLEY FORGE
213 Castle Hill Road, Totternhoe LU6 2DA. Pat & Mike Sutcliffe. *2m W of Dunstable. Turn R off B489 Aston Clinton rd, 1/2 m from Dunstable centre, signed Totternhoe. Fronting main rd, corner of Chapel Lane, 1m through village. On rd parking.* Home-made teas. Adm £3.50, chd free. Suns 17 May; 6 Sept (2-5).
A true cottage garden to rear of C17 grade 2 listed thatched cottage (not open). 1/2 -acre sloping site planted from scratch by owners 16yrs ago. Imaginatively landscaped, terraced on 4 levels, long pergola, archways and steps connecting to meandering pathways that lead intriguingly through the foliage. Small gravel garden, 'sun trap' garden planted with an orange /yellow theme. Ponds on 2 levels connected by small cascade. Large range of shrubs, perennials and trees compatible with chalk, including the indigenous Aylesbury Prune. The site also houses The Mike Sutcliffe Collection of early Leyland buses (1908-1934).

23 NEW WATERGATE FARM
Woburn Road, Hockliffe LU7 9LN. Henry & Phyllis Hunt. *From A5 Hockliffe T-lights take A4012 towards Woburn Farm approx 3/4 m on R, approx 200yds past sign for Battlesden, gated rd. From Woburn take A4012 towards Hockliffe. Farm on L approx 4m down drive with trees.* Home-made teas. Combined with Watergate Lodge adm £4, chd free. Sun 28 June (2-5).
Approach by long drive with trees. Small orchard on L with roses on wall. 2 borders in yard with small vegetable plot behind wall. Garden in tranquil setting overlooking fields and grazing sheep. Mostly shrub and perennials, small water feature and summerhouse with large sycamore being dominant.

> Garden in tranquil setting overlooking fields and grazing sheep . . .

24 NEW WATERGATE LODGE
Woburn Road, Hockliffe, Leighton Buzzard LU7 9LN. Chris & Mary Hunt. *1/2 m E of Hockliffe. From A5 take A4012 towards Woburn 1/2 m on R. From Woburn continue on A4012 approx 1/4 m after 2nd Battlesden turn on L.* Home-made teas. Combined with Watergate Farm adm £4, chd free. Sun 28 June (2-5).
Approx 1 acre country garden in an elevated position with far reaching views approached by tree lined drive. Lawn divided by shrub and herbaceous borders, small orchard and vegetable garden. A pleasant 10 min stroll through fields between farm and lodge.

25 NEW WAYSIDE COTTAGE
Manor Road, Barton-Le-Clay
MK45 4NR. Mr Denis Hibburd,
01582 881419. *1m off A6. Take
old A6 (Bedford Rd) through
Barton-Le-Clay Village (not the bypass), Manor Rd is off Bedford Rd.
Parking in paddock at the Manor
House.* Home-made teas.
**Combined with The Manor
House, Barton Le Clay** adm £4,
chd free. Sun 23 Aug (2-6).
Visitors also welcome by appt
all-yr round.
The garden is sited on a $1/2$ -acre
plot. Developed over 50yrs it has
mature trees, shrubs and flower
borders. A well-stocked pond with
fountain and waterfalls. A variety of
attractive outbuildings nestle within
the old walled garden for a tranquil
scene with plenty of hidden
corners.

26 16 WOOD LANE
Cotton End MK45 3AJ. Lesley
Bunker-Nixon & Eddie Wilkins. *2m S
of Bedford. A600 signed Shefford from
Bedford, 2nd L at The Bell PH, into
Wood Lane, past Hall Way on RH-side.*
Light refreshments & teas. **Adm £2.50,
chd free. Sun 28 June (12-5).**
150ft garden consisting of cottage
style garden, containers and bygones.
Formal garden with large koi pond with
beautiful fish, borders and lawns.
Japanese garden with bonsai trees,
wooded area with stream. Vegetable
garden based on an allotment. Wildlife
area with folly and chickens, also
facade of an old water mill.

Japanese
garden with
bonsai trees . . .

Bedfordshire County Volunteers

County Organisers
Mike & Pat Sutcliffe, Valley Forge, 213 Castle Hill Road, Totternhoe, Dunstable LU6 2DA, 01525 221676,
    sutcliffes@leylandman.co.uk

County Treasurer
David Johnston, Seal Point, 7 Wendover Way, Luton LU2 7LS, 01582 611567

Publicity
Geoff & Davina Barrett, Flaxbourne Farm, Aspley Guise, Milton Keynes MK17 8HZ, 01908 585329, carole@boa.com

BERKSHIRE

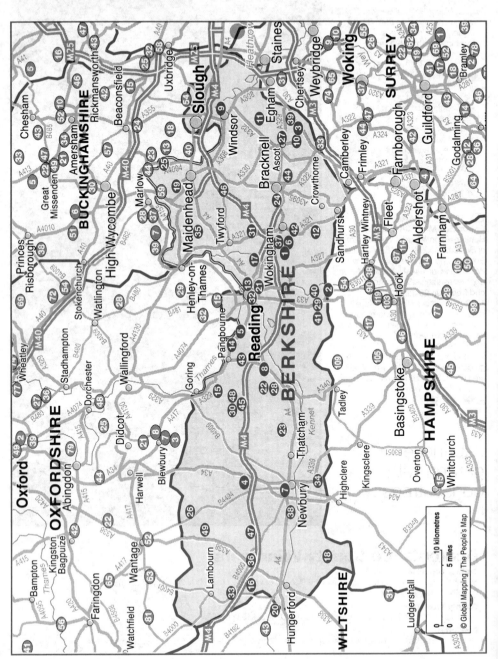

Opening Dates

April

WEDNESDAY 1
16 Inholmes

SUNDAY 19
13 The Harris Garden
26 The Old Rectory Farnborough

MONDAY 20
19 Little Harwood

WEDNESDAY 22
38 Stockcross House

SUNDAY 26
25 Odney Club

WEDNESDAY 29
33 Rooksnest

May

SUNDAY 3
24 Moor Close Gardens

MONDAY 4
24 Moor Close Gardens

WEDNESDAY 6
24 Moor Close Gardens
46 Waltham Place Gardens

SATURDAY 9
32 The RISC Roof Garden, Reading

SUNDAY 10
26 The Old Rectory Farnborough
32 The RISC Roof Garden, Reading

WEDNESDAY 13
46 Waltham Place Gardens

SUNDAY 17
1 Bearwood College

WEDNESDAY 20
46 Waltham Place Gardens
47 Welford Park

SUNDAY 24
10 Fairacre

MONDAY 25
39 Sunningdale Park

TUESDAY 25
11 Frogmore House

WEDNESDAY 27
46 Waltham Place Gardens

SUNDAY 31
14 Highveldt
37 21 Simons Lane
38 Stockcross House

June

WEDNESDAY 3
46 Waltham Place Gardens

SUNDAY 7
15 Hook End Farm

18 Kirby House
49 Woolley Park

MONDAY 8
19 Little Harwood

WEDNESDAY 10
15 Hook End Farm
20 Littlecote House Hotel
46 Waltham Place Gardens

SATURDAY 13
9 Eton College Gardens

SUNDAY 14
15 Hook End Farm
22 Mariners
34 Sandleford Place
36 Shefford Woodlands House
43 The Tithe Barn

WEDNESDAY 17
20 Littlecote House Hotel
46 Waltham Place Gardens

SUNDAY 21
2 Border Cottage
26 The Old Rectory Farnborough
29 The Priory
41 Thrive's Trunkwell Garden Project

WEDNESDAY 24
16 Inholmes
33 Rooksnest
46 Waltham Place Gardens

SUNDAY 28
30 Pyt House
48 Willow Tree Cottage

July

WEDNESDAY 1
46 Waltham Place Gardens

SUNDAY 5
4 Chieveley Manor

WEDNESDAY 8
20 Littlecote House Hotel
46 Waltham Place Gardens

FRIDAY 10
7 Donnington Castle House

SATURDAY 11
21 The M.E.R.L. Garden
32 The RISC Roof Garden, Reading

SUNDAY 12
21 The M.E.R.L. Garden
32 The RISC Roof Garden, Reading
40 Swallowfield Horticultural Society

WEDNESDAY 15
46 Waltham Place Gardens

SUNDAY 19
3 Boxwood House

WEDNESDAY 22
46 Waltham Place Gardens

SUNDAY 26
10 Fairacre

WEDNESDAY 29
46 Waltham Place Gardens

August

WEDNESDAY 5
46 Waltham Place Gardens

SATURDAY 8
32 The RISC Roof Garden, Reading

SUNDAY 9
32 The RISC Roof Garden, Reading
44 Two Bracknell Gardens

WEDNESDAY 12
46 Waltham Place Gardens

WEDNESDAY 19
46 Waltham Place Gardens

WEDNESDAY 26
46 Waltham Place Gardens

SUNDAY 30
27 Old Waterfield

September

WEDNESDAY 2
46 Waltham Place Gardens

WEDNESDAY 9
46 Waltham Place Gardens

SATURDAY 12
32 The RISC Roof Garden, Reading

SUNDAY 13
32 The RISC Roof Garden, Reading

MONDAY 14
19 Little Harwood

WEDNESDAY 16
46 Waltham Place Gardens

WEDNESDAY 23
46 Waltham Place Gardens

Gardens open to the public

8 Englefield House
21 The M.E.R.L. Garden
46 Waltham Place Gardens
47 Welford Park

By appointment only

5 17 Clevedon Road
6 6 Crecy Close
12 Glenmere
17 Ivydene
23 Miles's Green House
28 Potash
31 Reynolds Farm
35 Scotlands
42 Timberlea

45 Two Gardens at Ashampstead Common

Also open by appointment

- **1** Bearwood College
- **10** Fairacre
- **15** Hook End Farm
- **16** Inholmes
- **20** Littlecote House Hotel
- **22** Mariners
- **24** Moor Close Gardens
- **26** The Old Rectory Farnborough
- **29** The Priory
- **30** Pyt House
- **33** Rooksnest
- **34** Sandleford Place
- **36** Shefford Woodlands House
- **37** 21 Simons Lane
- **44** Devonia, Two Bracknell Gardens
- **44** 10 Shaftesbury Close, Two Bracknell Gardens
- **45** Baggage Chute, Two Gardens at Ashampstead Common
- **45** Farriers Cottage, Two Gardens at Ashampstead Common
- **48** Willow Tree Cottage

The Gardens

1 BEARWOOD COLLEGE
Winnersh RG41 5BG, 0118 974 8300, secondmaster@ bearwoodcollege.co.uk. *5m SE of Reading. Off B3030, 1m S of A329/ B3030 intersection at Winnersh, midway between Reading and Wokingham. Look for Bearwood Rd & College sign.* Cream teas. **Adm £3, chd free. Sun 17 May (2-5). Visitors also welcome by appt for groups 8+.**
Late C19 mansion and parkland now an independent school. Walks through mature woodland, pinetum, rhododendrons and grassland. Lake and natural margins. Pulham water garden under restoration. Some mansion rooms open. New family nature trail and environmental stalls.

2 NEW BORDER COTTAGE
Benham Lane, Riseley RG7 1RY. David & Caroline Cotton. *8m S Reading. From B3349 in Riseley take Part Lane opp Bull PH and then 1st R.* **Adm £2.50, chd free (share to Thrive). Sun 21 June (11-4).**
Small secluded country cottage garden in a lovely rural setting. Traditional and unusual shrubs are topped up with perennial borders and pots. A working well and unusual water feature. Kitchen garden with fruit, vegetables and herbs and where colour and design are just as important as the produce. Gravel paths.

3 BOXWOOD HOUSE
Heathfield Avenue, Sunninghill SL5 0AL. Mr J P H Morrow & Mr R E G Beard. *6m S of Windsor. From A30 at Sunningdale, take Broomhall Lane, after 1/2 m follow signs to car park. From A329 turn into Silwood Rd and R to Larch Ave.* Home-made teas. **Adm £3, chd free (share to Battersea Dogs & Cats Home). Sun 19 July (2-6).**
3/4 -acre designer's, plantsman's and flower arrangers garden in woodland setting with emphasis to plant and colour association. Large range of herbaceous perennials, large leaved hostas, acers, grasses, topiary, climbers, interesting foliage plants with pergola, woodland garden, natural style pond and many tender plant combinations in pots.

4 CHIEVELEY MANOR
RG20 8UT. Mr & Mrs C J Spence. *5m N of Newbury. Take A34 N, pass under M4, then L to Chieveley. After 1/2 m L up Manor Lane.* Home-made teas. **Adm £3, chd free (share to St Mary's Church). Sun 5 July (2-5).**
Large garden with fine views over stud farm. Walled garden containing borders, shrubs and rose garden. Listed house (not open). Newly planted bed.

5 17 CLEVEDON ROAD
Tilehurst RG31 6RL. G Emmerick & G Preston, 0118 427 317, jpgae@aol.com. *3m W Reading centre. A329 to Tilehurst stn, L into Carlisle rd, R into Clevedon rd.* **Adm £2.50, chd free. Visitors welcome by appt from 18 July to 16 Aug.**
1/4 -acre yr-round town garden on 3 levels featuring a circular lawn and octagonal vegetable plot, planted with a mix of English and Mediterranean horticultural delights, incl grasses, climbers, shrubs, fruit and trees. A tranquil oasis with views to Arthur Newbery Park.

6 6 CRECY CLOSE
Wokingham RG41 3UZ. John & Anne Massey, 0118 9019099, anne.massey@ntlworld.com, www.acorngardenservices.co.uk. *Take A329 towards Reading. 1m after town centre, L at Woosehill roundabout, end of dual carriageway turn R, take 1st L and 5th on L.* **Adm £2.50, chd free. Visitors welcome by appt from May to Sept, evening only, groups 10+.**
Lovely award winning garden designed by the owners, now professional garden designers, and offering many ideas for the small garden together with interesting and unusual plants.

DIPLEY MILL
See Hampshire.

7 DONNINGTON CASTLE HOUSE
Castle Lane. RG14 2LE. Mr & Mrs B Stewart-Brown. *1m N of Newbury. Follow signs to Donnington Castle. Entrance on R towards top of main castle entrance. Car park through wooden gates.* Home-made teas. **Adm £4, chd free. Fri 10 July (10-5).**
Large mature garden with additional planting during last 5yrs. Attractive herbaceous borders, roses, mixed borders, fine mature trees, lawns, woodland and garden walks.

8 ◆ ENGLEFIELD HOUSE
RG7 5EN. Mr & Mrs Richard Benyon, 01189 302221, www.englefield.co.uk. *6m W of Reading. 1½ m from J12 M4. 1m from Theale. Entrance on A340 3m S of Pangbourne.* **Adm £3, chd free. Mon all yr, Mon to Thurs incl from 1 Apr to 1 Nov (10-6).**

Kitchen garden where colour and design are just as important as the produce . . .

9-acre woodland garden with interesting variety of trees and shrubs, stream, water garden descending to formal terraces with stone balustrades making background for deep borders. Small enclosed gardens of differing character incl children's garden with joke fountains. All enclosed by deer park with lake. Majority of garden can be viewed by wheelchair users, access difficult.

9 ETON COLLEGE GARDENS
SL4 6DB. Eton College. *½ m N of Windsor. Parking off B3022 Slough to Eton rd, signed to R, S of junction with Datchet Rd (Pocock's Lane), walk across playing fields to entry. Cars with disabled badges will be directed further.* Cream teas. **Museum, Private Gardens and Garden Adm £5, Garden only Adm £3, chd free. Sat 13 June (2-5).**
A group of 4 central college gardens surrounded by ancient school buildings incl Luxmoore's garden on an island in the Thames reached across an attractive bridge. Some private gardens and Eton's Natural History Museum also open. Gravel paths, mown grass to Luxmoore's. No wheelchair access to private gardens or museum.

10 FAIRACRE
Ravensdale Road, South Ascot SL5 9HJ. David & Mary Nichols, 01344 624535, mary@nichols624.wanadoo.co.uk. *6m E of Bracknell. On A330 ½ m S of Ascot Racecourse, turn R into Coronation Rd, 2nd R to Woodlands Ride, Ravensdale Rd 150yds on R. No cars except disabled in unmade Ravensdale Rd.* Home-made teas. **Adm £3, chd free. Suns 24 May; 26 July (2-5). Visitors also welcome by appt.**
1½ acres. Banks of large rhododendrons and azaleas, sunken garden with mix of annuals and perennials, beds of flowering shrubs, herbaceous borders, collection of conifers, kitchen garden. Some re-planting and new additions each year.

11 FROGMORE HOUSE GARDEN
Windsor SL4 2HT. Her Majesty The Queen, www.royal.gov.uk. *1m SE of Windsor. Entrance via Park St gate into Long Walk (follow AA signs). Visitors*

are requested kindly to keep on the route to the garden & not stray into the Home Park. Stn & bus stop in Windsor (20 mins walk from gardens), Green Line bus no 701, from London. Limited parking for cars only (free). Coaches by appointment only. Light refreshments & teas. **Garden only adm £4.50, chd free. House adm £5, child £3, concessions £4. Tue 26 May (10-5.30 last adm 4pm).**
30 acres of landscaped gardens rich in history and beauty. Large lake, fine trees, lawns, flowers and flowering shrubs. Gravel paths. For advance tickets apply to NGS, Hatchlands Park, East Clandon, Guildford, Surrey GU4 7RT, Tel 01483 211535, www.ngs.org.uk. Tickets also available on the day.

12 GLENMERE
246 Nine Mile Ride, Finchampstead RG40 3PA. Heather Bradly & John Kenney, 01189 733274, heather@gino-graphics.com. *7m J10 M4. 3m Crowthorne or Wokingham. On B3430 E of California Crossroads r'about.* Home-made teas. **Adm £3, chd free (share to Salt of the Earth). Visitors welcome by appt anytime, max 15.**
Japanese style garden with waiting arbour, raked gravel area, tea house, Torii gate, dry stream bed with bridge and pond. Vegetable garden, greenhouse and soft fruit area.

GRANGE DRIVE WOOBURN
See Buckinghamshire.

13 THE HARRIS GARDEN
Whiteknights. RG6 6AS. The University of Reading, School of Biological Sciences, www. friendsoftheharrisgarden.org.uk. *1½ m S of Reading town centre. Off A327, Shinfield Rd. Turn R just inside Pepper Lane entrance to campus.* Home-made teas. **Adm £3, chd free. Sun 19 Apr (2-6).**
12-acre research and teaching garden. Rose gardens, herbaceous borders, winter garden, herb garden, jungle garden. Extensive glasshouses. Many plants labelled. Some uneven (but manageable) paths.

HEARNS HOUSE
See Oxfordshire.

HECKFIELD PLACE
See Hampshire.

HIGHER DENHAM GARDENS
See Buckinghamshire.

14 NEW HIGHVELDT
Beech Road, Purley-on-Thames RG8 8DS. Ben & Dorothy Viljoen. *4m NW Reading, off A329. Coming from Pangbourne Beech Rd is 1st R as you enter Purley. From Reading, cross T-lights at Long Lane, cross r'about, take 1st L.* Teas. **Adm £2.50, chd free. Sun 31 May (2-6).**
Attractive ⅓ -acre terraced garden retaining much of original 1930s layout. Down steps through trellis arch to circular lawn with box balls and lavender. Pass through a new secret garden that shows a very small space used to maximum effect, then into main terracing incl herbaceous borders, lawns and Chiltern views.

HILLCREST
See Buckinghamshire.

. . . through trellis arch to circular lawn with box balls and lavender . . .

15 HOOK END FARM
Upper Basildon RG8 8SD. David & Fiona Ambler, 01491 671255, fiona@hookendfarm.com. *3m W of Pangbourne. From A329 L into Hook End Lane, 1m on R.* Home-made teas. **Adm £3.50, chd free. Sun 7, Wed 10, Sun 14 June (2-5). Visitors also welcome by appt in June, groups 10+.**
2-acre hillside walled garden and orchard in a tranquil rural valley with outstanding views. Atmospheric garden with a wild natural look. Over 250 varieties of roses, other interesting plants and shrubs filling box parterres, secret corners and arbours. Collection of stationary engines.

16 INHOLMES

Woodlands St Mary RG17 7SY. Lady Williams, 07811 381 211 (Head Gardener), paddy.hoare@down-to-earth.org.uk. *3m SE Lambourn. From A338 take B4000 towards Lambourn, Inholmes signed.* Home-made teas. Adm £4, chd free or £6 combined with **Rooksnest** on 24 June. **Weds 1 Apr; 24 June** (11-4). Visitors also welcome by appt from April-July on written application.

Newly re-established, incl spring bulbs, colour co-ordinated walled garden, formal gardens, parkland walk with specimen trees leading to bluebell wood. Gravel paths.

17 IVYDENE

283 Loddon Bridge Road, Woodley RG5 4BE. Janet & Bill Bonney, 0118 969 7591, janetbonney2003@aol.com. *3½ m E of Reading. A4 from Reading towards Maidenhead. Woodley lies midway between. Loddon Bridge Rd is the main rd through the small town. Garden about 100yds S of 'Just Tiles' roundabout. Parking in adjacent rd.* Adm £2.50, chd free. **Visitors welcome by appt.**

Small urban gardener's garden approx 120ft x 30ft, specialising in ornamental grasses with over 50 varieties integrated into both front and back gardens. Autumn viewing shows grasses to best advantage. Cottage garden and stained glass features.

KAYALAMI
See Buckinghamshire.

18 KIRBY HOUSE

Inkpen RG17 9ED. Mr & Mrs R Astor. *3½ m SE of Hungerford. A4 to Kintbury. L at Xrds in Kintbury (by Corner Stores) towards Coombe. 2m out of Kintbury turn L immed beyond Crown & Garter PH, turn L at junction, house at bottom of hill on R.* Adm £3.50. **Sun 7 June** (2-5).

6 acres in beautiful setting with views of S Berkshire Downs across lawn and parkland. C18 Queen Anne House (not open). Formal rose borders, double herbaceous border in kitchen garden, colour themed border between yew buttress hedges. Lily pond garden, reflecting pond with fountain, lake. Recently designed walled garden.

19 LITTLE HARWOOD

Choke Lane, Pinkneys Green SL6 6PL. Mr & Mrs David Harrold. *2½ m NW of Maidenhead. A308 towards Marlow from Maidenhead. At Pinkneys Green turn R into Winter Hill Rd signed to Winter Hill & Cookham Dean. Where rd forks continue on main rd towards Cookham Dean, now Choke Lane. 500yds along Choke Lane you reach a Z bend & SLOW sign. Little Harwood is on the L.* Light refreshments & teas. Adm £3.50, chd free. **Mons 20 Apr; 8 June; 14 Sept** (10.30-4).

2-acre mature, formal and informal, terraced gardens, incl water garden, rock garden, herbaceous border completely redesigned spring 2007, herb bed and contemporary garden buildings. Large specimen trees and clipped yew and hawthorn hedges. 16-acre bluebell woodland walk and wild flower meadow. Good autumn colour, stunning views. A plantsman's garden, well labelled.

Good autumn colour, stunning views . . .

20 NEW LITTLECOTE HOUSE HOTEL

RG17 0SU. Warner Leisure Hotels, 01488 682509, functions.littlecote@bourne-leisure.co.uk. *2m W of Hungerford. From A4 turn R onto B4192 signed Swindon. 1½ m exit L & follow signs.* Light refreshments. Adm £4, sorry no children. **Weds 10, 17 June; 8 July** (10-4). Visitors also welcome by appt.

Beautiful setting with views of the Kennet Valley over lawns and parkland. Herbaceous borders, rose and herb garden, clipped yew and box hedging. Carp pond and large selection of hanging baskets and planters. Some rooms of G1 Tudor Manor House open. Roman Villa and Orpheus Mosaic. Ice house in woods. Sorry, no children. Gravel paths.

21 NEW ◆ THE M.E.R.L. GARDEN

Redlands Road. RG1 5EX. Museum of English Rural Life, University of Reading. *Central Reading. From M4 J11 take A329(M). Take 2nd exit (A4) to central Reading. Turn L after Royal Berks Hosp.* Light refreshments & teas. Adm £2.50, chd free, £4 combined with **RISC Roof Garden.** For NGS: **Sat 11, Sun 12 July** (2-4.30).

Approx 1 acre, herb physic garden with fruit trees, lavender walk, Victorian border and naturalistic perennial planting. Collection of ash trees, wildflower meadow, allotments and lawn. Museum, 'Grow Your Own' Exhibition, talks by Head Gardener, family activities. Some gravel & uneven paths.

THE MANOR HOUSE, HAMBLEDEN
See Buckinghamshire.

22 MARINERS

Mariners Lane, Bradfield RG7 6HU. Anthony & Fenja Anderson, 0118 974 5226, fenjaanderson@aol.com, www.mariners-garden.com. *10m W of Reading. M4 J12 take A4 direction Newbury 1m. At roundabout exit A340 direction Pangbourne. 400yds turn L direction Bradfield. After 1m, turn L direction Southend Bradfield. After 1m opp signpost direction Tutts Clump turn R into Mariners Lane.* Adm £4, chd free. **Sun 14 June** (2-6). Visitors also welcome by appt from 15 June-24 July.

1½ -acre sloping site with creative feature made of slopes. Rich mixture of herbaceous planting incl unusual plants and grasses arranged in colour themes with emphasis on plant form and texture. Garden of old varieties of shrub roses, species and climbing roses. Streamside walk, orchard, sundial garden and 1-acre wild flower meadow. Featured in 'GGG*', 'The English Garden' & 'Berkshire Life'. Gravel paths, steep grass slope.

23 MILES'S GREEN HOUSE

Briff Lane, Bucklebury RG7 6SH. Mr & Mrs Eric Lloyd, lloydmgh@googlemail.com. *6m NE of Newbury, off A4. From Thatcham take Harts Hill Rd N to Bucklebury.* Adm £3.50, chd free. **Visitors** welcome by appt from 18 May to 19 Jun, no coach access.

3-acre tranquil valley garden in a woodland setting with small lake, bog garden and adjacent pool. Specimen trees and shrubs feature on well-maintained sloping lawns with island beds of choice and unusual plants. Herbaceous beds combine shrubs, roses and perennials with a subtle blend of colours. Meadow with grass paths.

✗ ⏺ ☎

24 MOOR CLOSE GARDENS
Popeswood Road, Binfield RG42 4AN. Newbold College, 01344 452427/407583, autm96@dsl.pipex.com/pdyckhoff@newbold.ac.uk. *2m W of Bracknell. Off B3408. From Bracknell turn R at Binfield T-lights, from A329(M) take B3408, turn L at Binfield T-lights. Follow signs.* Home-made teas. **Adm £2.50, chd free. Sun 3, Mon 4, Wed 6 May (2-5). Visitors also welcome by appt except Sats.**
A small GII listed garden designed 1911-13 by Oliver Hill and a rare example of his early work. Lavender garden, water parterre, remains of Italianate garden. Undergoing long-term restoration, it currently offers most interest in its historical architecture rather than planting. Garden history tours by appointment.

✗ ⏺ ☎

25 ODNEY CLUB
Odney Lane, Cookham SL6 9SR. John Lewis Partnership. *3m N of Maidenhead. Off A4094 S of Cookham Bridge. Car park in grounds.* Cream teas, 3-4.30. **Adm £4, chd free (share to Thames Valley Adventure Playground). Sun 26 Apr (2-6).**
This 120-acre site beside the Thames is continuously developing and, with lovely riverside walks, can take a full afternoon to visit. A favourite with Stanley Spencer who featured our magnolia in his work. Magnificent wisteria, specimen trees, herbaceous borders, side gardens, spring bedding and ornamental lake. Some gravel paths.

♿ ⏺

26 THE OLD RECTORY FARNBOROUGH
Wantage OX12 8NX. Mr & Mrs Michael Todhunter. *4m SE of Wantage. Take B4494 Wantage-Newbury Rd, after 4m turn E at sign for Farnborough.* Home-made teas. **Adm £3.50, chd free (share to**

Farnborough PCC). **Suns 19 Apr; 10 May; 21 June (2-5.30). Visitors also welcome by appt on written application.**
In a series of immaculately tended garden rooms, incl herbaceous borders, arboretum, boules, rose, pool and vegetable gardens, there is an explosion of rare and interesting plants, beautifully combined for colour and texture. With stunning views across the countryside, it is the perfect setting for the 1749 rectory (not open), once home of John Betjeman, in memory of whom John Piper created a window in the local church. Featured in 'Country Life' and on Radio Berks.

✗ ✿ ⏺ ☎

A favourite with Stanley Spencer who featured our magnolia in his work . . .

OLD THATCH
See Buckinghamshire.

27 OLD WATERFIELD
Winkfield Road, Ascot SL5 7LJ. Hugh & Catherine Stevenson. *6m SW of Windsor. On A330 (Winkfield Rd) midway between A329 and A332 to E of Ascot Racecourse. Parking on Practice Ground (by kind permission of Royal Ascot Golf Club) adjacent to house.* Home-made teas. **Adm £3, chd free (share to Ascot Day Centre). Sun 30 Aug (2.30-5.30).**
Nestling in 4 acres adjacent to Ascot Race Course the original cottage garden has attractive herbaceous borders and lovely views. Large productive kitchen garden full of fruit and vegetables, natural pond, specimen trees, a young orchard and mixed hedging.

♿ ✗ ✿ ⏺

28 POTASH
Mariners Lane, Southend Bradfield RG7 6HU. Mr & Mrs J W C Mooney, 0118 9744264, john@potash.plus.com. *10m W of Reading. From M4 J12 take A4 W 1m. At roundabout exit A340 direction Pangbourne, turn L after 400yds direction Bradfield. After 1m turn L direction Southend Bradfield. 1m opp sign to Tutts Clump turn R. Potash is*

400yds on L by beech hedge. **Adm £4, chd free. Visitors welcome by appt all year incl groups. Teas on request.**
5-acre garden. Wide range of plants, many unusual specimens and interest throughout the yr from snowdrops to autumn colour. Daffodils a feature, shrubs, tea roses, herbaceous borders, bog garden feeding a clay-lined pond, young woodland and space to sit and contemplate the view. Children and dogs very welcome.

♿ ⏺ ☎

THE PRIORS FARM
See Hampshire.

29 THE PRIORY
Beech Hill RG7 2BJ. Mr & Mrs C Carter, 01189 883146. *5m S of Reading. M4 J11. Follow signs to A33, then L at roundabout signed Swallowfield. After 1¼ m, R by Murco garage to Beech Hill. When in village turn opp church into Wood Lane, then R down Priory Drive - house at end.* Home-made teas. **Adm £3.50, chd free. Sun 21 June (2-6). Visitors also welcome by appt anytime for groups 10+.**
Extensive gardens in grounds of former C12 Benedictine Priory (not open), rebuilt 1648. Beside the R Loddon, the mature gardens are being restored and re-developed. Large formal walled garden with espalier fruit trees, lawns, extensive mixed and recently replanted herbaceous borders, vegetables and roses. Woodland, lake and new Italian style water garden in progress. Fine trees. A lot of gravel paths.

♿ ✗ ✿ ⏺ ☎

30 NEW PYT HOUSE
Ashampstead RG8 8RA. Hans & Virginia von Celsing, virginiacelsing@gmail.com. *4m W of Pangbourne. From Yattendon head towards Reading. Rd forks L into a beech wood towards Ashampstead. Keep L and join lower rd. ½ m turn L just before houses.* **Adm £3.50, chd free, £5 combined with Willow Tree Cottage. Sun 28 June (2-5). Visitors also welcome by appt for groups 10+.**
4-acres planted over the last 5yrs. Mature trees, yew, hornbeam and beech hedges, pleached limes, modern perennial borders, orchard and vegetable garden.

♿ ✗ ⏺ ☎

31 REYNOLDS FARM

Broad Common Lane, Hurst RG10 0RE. Mr & Mrs Christopher Wells, 01189 345296/0207 5894475. *1m S of Twyford. From Twyford turn L off A321 at Hurst into Broad Common Road. After 2/3 m L into Broad Common Lane.* **Adm £3, chd free. Visitors welcome by appt for groups 10+ incl coaches. Best April - June.**
And now for something quite different - wild woodland garden planted from scratch by present owners over past 40yrs, objective being to maximise pleasure and minimise maintenance. Planting policy has been driven by greed, followed by indigestion - can't resist it, but oh! where to put it? Densely planted woodland walks leave little space for weeds whilst providing fun for ourselves, the dog and we hope you as well especially in April, May and June. Best if wheelchairs have thick tyres.

32 THE RISC ROOF GARDEN, READING

35-39 London Street. RG1 4PS. Reading International Solidarity Centre. *5 mins walk from Oracle shopping centre.* **Adm £2.50, chd free (share to WEB/RISC), £4 combined with The M.E.R.L. Garden on 11 & 12 July only. Sats & Suns 9, 10 May; 11, 12 July; 8, 9 Aug; 12, 13 Sept (12-4).**
Small town centre roof forest garden developed to demonstrate sustainability and our dependance on plants. All plants in the garden have an economic use for food, clothing, medicine etc, and come from all over the world. Water harvesting and irrigation systems powered by renewable energy. Garden accessed by external staircase. Featured in 'The Sunday Times' and at The World Green Roof Congress.

33 ROOKSNEST

Ermine Street, Lambourn Woodlands RG17 7SB. Dr & Mrs M D Sackler, 07766 130398, lisa.rooksnest@hotmail.co.uk. *2m S of Lambourn. From A338 Wantage rd, along B4000. Rooksnest signed.* Light refreshments & teas. **Adm £4, chd free or £6 combined with Inholmes on 24 June. Weds 29 Apr; 24 June (11-4). Visitors also welcome by appt.**
Approx 10-acre exceptionally fine traditional English garden. Rose and herbaceous garden, pond, herb

garden, organic vegetables and glasshouses. Many specimen trees and fine shrubs, orchard and terraces renovated and replanted for 2009. Garden mostly designed by Arabella Lennox-Boyd from 1980 to today. Some gravel paths. We are happy to assist.

34 SANDLEFORD PLACE

Newtown RG20 9AY. Mr & Mrs Alan Gatward, 01635 40726, melgatward@bigfoot.com. *1½ m S of Newbury on A399. House is at W side of Swan r'about.* Home-made teas. **Adm £4, chd free. Sun 14 June (2-6). Visitors also welcome by appt.**
4-acre grounds, more exuberant than manicured, around a former old mill and granary. Many varied shrub and herbaceous borders crammed with plants for romantic, naturalistic effect. Walled garden with a wide range of plants arranged for yr-round interest, flowers, foliage and scent. Kitchen garden and herb bed. Long herbaceous border flanks wild flowers in meadow and along R Enborne. Unusual plants for sale, some seen in the garden.

> Planting policy has been driven by greed, followed by indigestion . . .

35 SCOTLANDS

Cockpole Green, Wargrave RG10 8QP. The Payne Family, 01628 822648. *6m W of Maidenhead, 4m E of Henley. In centre of triangle formed by A4130, A321 to Wargrave & A4 at Knowl Hill - midway between Warren Row Village & Cockpole Green.* **Adm £3.50, chd free. Visitors welcome by appt.**
4-acre garden surrounding C17 farmhouse (not open). Clipped yews surrounding oval swimming pool, shrub borders, grass paths through trees to woodland and pond gardens, within brick and flint partly walled garden. Rocks with waterfall and gazebo of C18 design. Featured in 'GGG'.

36 SHEFFORD WOODLANDS HOUSE

RG17 7AG. Mrs Verina Black, 01488 648220. *3m N of Hungerford. M4 J14 take A338 N. 1/2 m turn R onto B4000, R again for Shefford Woodlands & L in front of church.* **Adm £3, chd free. Sun 14 June (2-6). Visitors also welcome by appt in June & July, groups 10 max on written request.**
4-acre garden. Formal entrance with pond and topiary. Herbaceous borders, incl many old-fashioned roses, delphiniums, clematis, white garden and clipped yews all designed by Arabella Lennox-Boyd. Informal gardens with trees, woodland area, shrubs,vegetable and cutting garden. Parterre garden with fountain, Gold and Silver border. Raffle for garden tools/plants. Part of garden can be seen from wheelchair. Gravel driveway and steps.

37 21 SIMONS LANE

Wokingham RG41 3HG. Jill Wheatley, 0118 9780500, jill.wheatley@btinternet.com, www.jillsgarden.co.uk. *1m W of Wokingham. Off A329 between Woosehill roundabout and Sainsburys, on L.* Home-made teas. **Adm £3, chd free. Sun 31 May (2-5). Visitors also welcome by appt in May & June.**
Organically-run small garden, developed since 1996, intensively planted with wide variety of shrubs, herbaceous perennials, climbers and fruit. Rear garden is designed around pond with water lilies. In courtyard garden there is a large hosta collection. HDRA information available on organic methods. Front has apple, pear, cherry and plum trees, raspberries, blackcurrants and gooseberries together with a pond. Display of quilts and ceramics. Some gravel paths.

38 STOCKCROSS HOUSE

Stockcross RG20 8LP. Susan & Edward Vandyk. *3m W of Newbury. From M4, J13, take A34 S to A4 junction. Exit direction Hungerford, take B4000 to Stockcross.* Home-made teas 31 May only. **Adm £3, chd free (share to Helen & Douglas House Hospice). Wed 22 Apr (11-4); Sun 31 May (2-5.30).**
1½ -acre garden developed over past 15yrs with an emphasis on plant partnerships and colour combinations. Winter bulbs and hellebores, herbaceous borders, shrubs, roses,

pergola and pond, vegetable and cutting gardens, all maintained to a high standard. Music in the garden, members of Newbury Symphony Orchestra on 31 May. Gravel courtyard to cross, slope to lower garden.

STOKE POGES MEMORIAL GARDENS
See Buckinghamshire.

39 SUNNINGDALE PARK
Larch Avenue, Ascot SL5 0QE. National School of Government/Verve Venues. *6m S of Windsor. On A30 at Sunningdale take Broomhall Lane. After ½ m turn R into Larch Ave. From A329 turn into Silwood Rd towards Sunningdale.* Home-made teas. **Adm £4, chd free. Mon 25 May (2-5).**
Over 20 acres of beautifully landscaped gardens reputedly designed after Capability Brown. Terrace garden and Victorian rockery designed by Pulham incl cave and water features. Lake area with paved walks, extensive lawns with specimen trees and flower beds, impressive massed rhododendrons. Beautiful 1m woodland walk. Grade II listed building (not open). Free garden history tour at 3.30.

40 SWALLOWFIELD HORTICULTURAL SOCIETY
RG7 1QX. *5m S of Reading. M4 J11 & A33/B3349, signed Swallowfield. Tickets and maps at village hall in centre.* Light refreshments & teas. **Combined adm £4, chd free. Sun 12 July (11-5).**
Swallowfield has survived as a real village beside the Blackwater meadows and offers a minimum of 8 gardens to visit, ranging from tiny and perfect to large and shaggy (some immaculate ones too). Some are full of special plants, others developed in a variety of styles. Model trains, donkeys and you may see rare breed fowl. There are always views to love.

41 THRIVE'S TRUNKWELL GARDEN PROJECT
Beech Hill, Reading RG7 2AT. Thrive, www.thrive.org.uk. *7m S of Reading. M4 J11, follow signs to A33, L at roundabout signed Swallowfield. After 1¼ m, R by Murco garage to Beech Hill. From S keep through Swallowfield on B3349, after Mill House restaurant turn L, bear R, then L*

at Xrds to Beech Hill. Signs in village. Teas. **Adm £3.50, chd £1 (share to THRIVE). Sun 21 June (2-4.30).**
3-acre site with Victorian walled garden run by Thrive, a national charity which uses gardening to support and inspire disabled people. Formal and informal interest, nature trail, pond, butterfly garden, trained fruit and cut flower areas, potager, glasshouse, sensory and cottage gardens.

42 TIMBERLEA
17 Oaklands Drive, Wokingham RG41 2SA. Mr & Mrs F Preston, 0118 978 4629. *1m SW of Wokingham. M4 J10 or M3 J3. From Wokingham take A321 under 2 railway bridges, Tesco store is between. Immed turn R at mini roundabout, Molly Millars Lane. 3rd rd on L is Oaklands Drive. After 100yds, R into cul-de-sac.* Light refreshments & teas. **Adm £2.50, chd free. Visitors welcome by appt from June to Sept, groups max 30, incl coaches.**
Something of interest at every turn! Triangular plot lends itself to hidden corners with different levels and vistas. Arches, pergolas and walls give height to replanted borders, water feature with shade loving plants. Kitchen garden has raised beds, fruit cage and greenhouses. Front garden incl small waterfall, stream, pond and private decking. Wheelchairs limited by woodchip & 3 shallow steps.

43 NEW THE TITHE BARN
Tidmarsh RG8 8ER. Fran Wakefield. *1m S of Pangbourne, off A340. From J12 M4 take A340 to Pangbourne. Turn R at Greyhound PH in Tidmarsh, over bridge, R into Mill Corner field.* Home-made teas. **Adm £2.50, chd free. Sun 14 June (2-5).**
Newly designed small walled ¼-acre garden formally laid out with gravel paths and box hedging and planted with roses, herbaceous and shrubs. Working beehives. Visit Norman Church next door. Willow craft demonstration.

44 TWO BRACKNELL GARDENS
RG12 9BH. *1m S of Bracknell town centre. From M4 take A329(M), from M3 take A322, towards Bracknell and follow each garden directions.* Teas at Shaftesbury Close. **Combined adm £3.50, chd free. £3 per garden by appointment, £5 incl refreshments. Sun 9 Aug (2-5).**

DEVONIA
Broad Lane. Andrew Radgick, 01344 450914, aradgick@aol.com. *From A329M take 3rd roundabout, 2nd exit into Broad Lane and over 2 r'abouts. 3rd house on L after railway bridge. From A322, Horse & Groom r'about, take 4th exit into Broad Lane.* **Visitors also welcome by appt.**
⅓ -acre plantaholic's garden designed for all seasons and planted to require minimal watering. Divided into several areas to provide appropriate conditions for over 1200 different shrubs, climbers, perennials, bulbs and alpines, incl many rare and unusual. Hot and dry front garden, shady and sheltered corners to the rear.

10 SHAFTESBURY CLOSE
Harmanswater. Gill Cheetham, 01344 423440, gillcheetham @btopenworld.com. *At sports centre roundabout exit to Harmanswater. L on 2 mini r'abouts into Nightingale Crescent. Shaftesbury Close is 2nd on R.* **Visitors also welcome by appt.**
Woodland garden, with many different ericaceous shrubs and plants. Walled garden. Beds planted to reflect climatic changes incl Mediterranean and scree. Colour themed herbaceous borders.

Something of interest at every turn! . . . hidden corners with different levels and vistas . . .

Group opening

45 TWO GARDENS AT ASHAMPSTEAD COMMON

RG8 8QT. *7m J12 M4. 2m E of Yattendon along Yattendon Lane. L into Sucks Lane, 1/2 m, R opp common.* Home-made teas. **Combined adm £5, chd free. Visitors welcome by appt from April to Sept, incl groups.**

2 gardens linked by pretty walk through medieval woodland. Stunning bluebells in May. No wheelchair access.

BAGGAGE CHUTE

Colin & Caroline Butler, 01635 210399, baggchute@aol.com
Lower terraced garden with colourful mix of shrubs and perennials leading to large informal pond. Vegetable and cutting garden. Hillside slopes feature prairie style mix of flowers and grasses with long views over surrounding countryside.

FARRIERS COTTAGE

Jackie Lomas, 01635 202993, jacqaranda@btinternet.com
Small immaculate cottage garden designed and planted by owner. Formal front garden in woodland setting leading to colourful mix of shrubs and herbaceous planting at the back.

TYLNEY HALL HOTEL
See Hampshire.

THE VYNE
See Hampshire.

46 ◆ WALTHAM PLACE GARDENS

Church Hill, White Waltham SL6 3JH. Mr & Mrs N Oppenheimer, 01628 825517, www.walthamplace.com. *31/2 m S of Maidenhead. From M4 J8/9 take A404. Follow signs for White Waltham. Pass airfield on RH-side. Take L turn signed Windsor/Paley St. Pass the church, turn R before car parking. From Bracknell/Wokingham A3095 to A330 direction Maidenhead. Turn L at Paley St B3024 to White Waltham. Follow parking signs.* **Adm £4, chd £1. Tues & Thurs, 5 May-25 Sept by appointment. Fris, 11am & 2pm walks with the gardener. For NGS: Weds, 6 May to 23 Sept (10-4).**
Designed by Henk Gerritsen the gardens embrace a naturalistic philosophy and seek to combine forces with nature to produce a haven for an abundance of insect and animal life, fungi and indigenous flora. They feature walled gardens, long borders, woodlands and an organic and bio-dynamic kitchen garden and farm. Featured in 'House & Garden'.

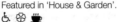

47 ◆ WELFORD PARK

Newbury RG20 8HU. Mrs J H Puxley, 01488 608203, www.welfordpark.co.uk. *6m NW of Newbury. On Lambourn Valley Rd. Entrance on Newbury-Lambourn rd. Please use clearly marked car park.* **Adm £4, chd free. See website for details. For NGS: Wed 20 May (11-6).**
Formal garden with attractive herbaceous borders and rose pergolas. Spacious parkland and wonderful trees. Gravel and uneven paths.

WHITE GABLES
See Hampshire.

48 NEW WILLOW TREE COTTAGE

Ashampstead RG8 8RA. Katy & David Weston, westonkaty@hotmail.com. *4m W of Pangbourne. From Yattendon head towards Reading. L fork in beechwood to Ashampstead, keep L, join lower rd, 1/2 m turn L before houses.* Teas at Pyt House. **Adm £5 combined with Pyt House. Sun 28 June (2-5). Visitors also welcome by appt with Pyt House.**
Small pretty garden of the cottage that was originally build for gardener at Pyt House. Substantially redesigned and replanted over last 5 yrs. Perennial borders, vegetable garden, pond with ducks and chickens.

1 WOGSBARNE COTTAGES
See Hampshire.

49 WOOLLEY PARK

Wantage OX12 8NJ. Lady Wroughton. *5m S of Wantage. A338. Turn L at sign to Woolley.* Light refreshments & teas. **Adm £2.50, chd free. Sun 7 June (2-5).**
Large park, fine trees and views. Two linked walled gardens sensitively planted with a wide variety of interesting plants. Gravel paths.

For Bristol see Somerset

A haven for an abundance of insect and animal life, fungi and indigenous flora . . .

Berkshire County Volunteers

County Organiser
Heather Skinner, 5 Liddell Close, Finchampstead, Wokingham RG40 4NS, 01189 737197, heatheraskinner@aol.com

County Treasurer
Hugh Priestley, Jennets Hill House, Stanford Dingley, Reading RG7 6JP, 01189 744349, hughpriestley1@aol.com

Press Officer
Fenja Anderson, Mariners, Mariners Lane, Southend, Reading RG7 6HU, 01189 745226, fenjaanderson@aol.com

Assistant County Organisers
Nigel Evans, 21 Cottrell Close, Hungerford RG17 0HF, 01488 681405, n.evans669@btinternet.com
Elspeth Ewen, Blossoms, Clay Lane, Beenham RG7 5PA, 01189 712856, ken.ewen@btinternet.com
Nina Preston, Timberlea, 17 Oaklands Drive, Wokingham RG41 2SA, 01189 784629, fred.nina@tiscali.co.uk
Jill Wheatley, 21 Simons Lane, Wokingham RG41 3HG, 01189 780500, jill.wheatley@btinternet.com

Mark your diary with these special events in 2009

EXPLORE SECRET GARDENS DURING CHELSEA & HAMPTON COURT FLOWER SHOW WEEKS

Tue 19 May, Wed 20 May, Thur 21 May, Fri 22 May, Wed 8 July, Thur 9 July
Full day tours from £82 per person, 10% discount for groups
Advance booking required, telephone +44 (0)20 8693 1015 or email j.wookey@btinternet.com
Specially selected gardens in London, Essex, Kent, Hampshire and South Oxfordshire. The tour price includes transport and lunch with wine at a popular restaurant or pub.

HAMPTON COURT PALACE

Thur 2 Apr, Tue 23 June, Thur 25 June, Wed 15 July, Tue 4 Aug, Thur 10 Sept
Evening tours in the company of one of the Palace's specialist tour guides from 6.30 – 8pm
Tickets £6 per person. Advance booking required, telephone +44 (0)1483 211535 or visit www.ngs.org.uk for more information
Gossip, scandal, murder, healing – you'll find it all within the Formal Gardens at Hampton Court Palace. Each tour will have its own unique feature whether it's the story of the Great Vine or the magic and mystery of the Maze.

FROGMORE – A ROYAL GARDEN (BERKSHIRE)

Tue 26 May 10am – 5.30pm (last admission 4pm)
Garden adm £4.50, chd free. Tickets available in advance or on the day.
Advance booking for groups and coaches, telephone
+44 (0) 1483 211535 or email orders@ngs.org.uk
A rare opportunity to explore 30 acres of landscaped garden, rich in history and beauty.

FLAXBOURNE FARM – FUN & SURPRISES (BEDFORDSHIRE)

Sun 7 June 10am – 5pm. Adm £5, chd free
No booking required, come along on the day!
Bring the whole family and have fun in this surprising and entertaining garden of 2 acres. Enjoy the large plant fair, live music, pets corner, birds of prey, dog agility show and much more.

WISLEY RHS GARDEN – MUSIC IN THE GARDEN (SURREY)

Fri 11 Sept 6 – 9pm
Adm (incl RHS members) £7, chd under 15 free
Save money on advance bookings for groups of 4 or more, telephone +44 (0)1483 211535 or visit www.ngs.org.uk for more information
A special evening opening of this famous garden, exclusively for the NGS. Enjoy music and entertainment as you explore the gardens and the floral marquee on the first day of the Wisley Flower Show.

For further information visit www.ngs.org.uk or telephone 01483 211535

BUCKINGHAMSHIRE

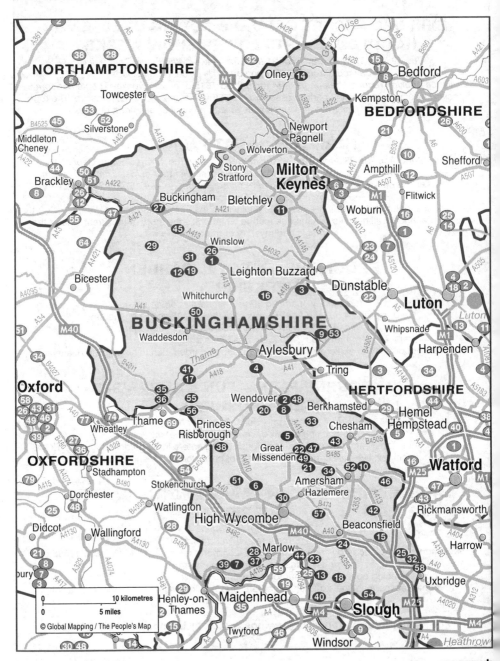

Opening Dates

February

SUNDAY 22
- 23 Grange Drive Wooburn
- 50 Quainton Gardens

March

SATURDAY 14
- 54 Stoke Poges Memorial Gardens

SUNDAY 29
- 10 Chesham Bois House

April

SUNDAY 12
- 47 Overstroud Cottage

MONDAY 13
- 52 Rivendell

SUNDAY 19
- 35 Long Crendon Spring Gardens
- 46 6 Oldfield Close
- 54 Stoke Poges Memorial Gardens
- 59 Whitewalls

THURSDAY 23
- 22 Gipsy House & One Church Street
- 49 The Plant Specialist

SATURDAY 25
- 45 The Old Vicarage

SUNDAY 26
- 45 The Old Vicarage

May

SUNDAY 3
- 38 The Manor House, Bledlow

MONDAY 4
- 3 Ascott
- 55 Turn End

SUNDAY 10
- 21 Fressingwood
- 47 Overstroud Cottage

WEDNESDAY 13
- 18 Dorneywood Garden
- 22 Gipsy House & One Church Street
- 49 The Plant Specialist
- 54 Stoke Poges Memorial Gardens

SUNDAY 17
- 10 Chesham Bois House
- 33 The Lee Gardens at Swan Bottom

SATURDAY 23
- 40 Maryfield

SUNDAY 24
- 40 Maryfield
- 43 The Old Sun House
- 58 The White House

WEDNESDAY 27
- 18 Dorneywood Garden

SATURDAY 30
- 31 3 Jubilee Cottages

SUNDAY 31
- 15 Craiglea House
- 19 East Claydon and Verney Junction Gardens
- 25 Higher Denham Gardens
- 41 Nether Winchendon House
- 50 Quainton Gardens

June

SATURDAY 6
- 44 Old Thatch

SUNDAY 7
- 15 Craiglea House
- 16 Cublington Gardens
- 34 Little Missenden Gardens
- 36 Long Crendon Summer Gardens
- 52 Rivendell

THURSDAY 11
- 20 Ellesborough Village Gardens
- 22 Gipsy House & One Church Street
- 49 The Plant Specialist

SATURDAY 13
- 14 Cowper & Newton Museum Gardens

SUNDAY 14
- 14 Cowper & Newton Museum Gardens
- 38 The Manor House, Bledlow
- 39 The Manor House, Hambleden
- 47 Overstroud Cottage

THURSDAY 18
- 37 Lords Wood

SATURDAY 20
- 2 Acer Corner
- 48 11 The Paddocks

SUNDAY 21
- 2 Acer Corner
- 4 Aylesbury Gardens
- 6 Bradenham Manor
- 7 Burrow Farm
- 9 Cheddington Gardens
- 17 Cuddington Gardens
- 30 Hughenden Manor
- 48 11 The Paddocks

TUESDAY 23
- 28 Hillcrest

FRIDAY 26
- 31 3 Jubilee Cottages (Evening)
- 48 11 The Paddocks (Evening)
- 53 Rose Cottage (Evening)

SUNDAY 28
- 23 Grange Drive Wooburn

- 29 Hillesden House

July

WEDNESDAY 1
- 18 Dorneywood Garden

SATURDAY 4
- 40 Maryfield
- 48 11 The Paddocks

SUNDAY 5
- 47 Overstroud Cottage

TUESDAY 7
- 28 Hillcrest

FRIDAY 10
- 20 Ellesborough Village Gardens (Evening)

SUNDAY 12
- 10 Chesham Bois House
- 12 Claydon House
- 32 Kayalami
- 56 Tythrop Park
- 59 Whitewalls

WEDNESDAY 15
- 22 Gipsy House & One Church Street
- 49 The Plant Specialist

SATURDAY 18
- 13 Cliveden

SATURDAY 25
- 2 Acer Corner
- 18 Dorneywood Garden

SUNDAY 26
- 2 Acer Corner

August

THURSDAY 13
- 20 Ellesborough Village Gardens

MONDAY 31
- 3 Ascott

September

SUNDAY 6
- 59 Whitewalls

THURSDAY 10
- 37 Lords Wood

SATURDAY 19
- 13 Cliveden
- 40 Maryfield

February 2010

SUNDAY 21
- 23 Magnolia House, Grange Drive Wooburn

SUNDAY 28
- 50 Quainton Gardens

Gardens open to the public

- **3** Ascott
- **6** Bradenham Manor
- **12** Claydon House
- **13** Cliveden
- **14** Cowper & Newton Museum Gardens
- **30** Hughenden Manor
- **41** Nether Winchendon House
- **44** Old Thatch
- **49** The Plant Specialist
- **54** Stoke Poges Memorial Gardens

By appointment only

- **1** Abbotts House
- **5** Blossoms
- **8** Cedar House
- **11** 100 Church Green Road
- **24** Hall Barn
- **26** 19 Highfield Road
- **27** Hill House
- **42** North Down
- **51** Red Kites
- **57** Watercroft

Also open by appointment ☎

- **2** Acer Corner
- **4** Aylesbury Gardens
- **7** Burrow Farm
- **10** Chesham Bois House
- **15** Craiglea House
- **20** Ellesborough Village Gardens
- **23** Grange Drive Wooburn
- **28** Hillcrest
- **29** Hillesden House
- **32** Kayalami
- **33** The Lee Gardens at Swan Bottom
- **36** Long Crendon Summer Gardens
- **38** The Manor House, Bledlow
- **40** Maryfield
- **45** The Old Vicarage
- **46** 6 Oldfield Close
- **47** Overstroud Cottage
- **50** Quainton Gardens
- **59** Whitewalls

Various specimen exotics . . .

The Gardens

① ABBOTTS HOUSE
10 Church Street, Winslow MK18 3AN. Mrs Jane Rennie, 01296 712326. *9m N of Aylesbury. On A413 into Winslow. From town centre take Horn St & R into Church St.* **Adm £2.50, chd free. Visitors welcome by appt.**
Garden on different levels divided into 4. Courtyard near house with arbour and pots, woodland garden (planted 4yrs ago) with rose arbour, swimming pool garden with grasses. Walled Victorian kitchen garden with glass houses, potager, fruit pergola, wall trained fruit and many mediterranean plants.

✗ ☎

② NEW ACER CORNER
10 Manor Rd, Wendover HP22 6HQ. Jo Naiman, 07872 059867, jo@acercorner.com. *3m S of Aylesbury. Follow A413 into Wendover. L at clock tower r'about into Aylesbury Rd. R at next r'about into Wharf Rd, continue past schools on L, garden on R.* **Adm £2.50, chd free. Sats, Suns 20, 21 June; 25, 26 July (2-6). Visitors also welcome by appt May to Oct, check website for best autumn colour.**
Medium-sized garden with Japanese influence and a large collection of Japanese maples. The enclosed front garden is oriental in style, whilst back garden is divided into 3 distinct areas; patio area surrounded by shrubs, densely-planted area with many acers and roses and an area recently developed with greenhouse, waste area and deck.

❀ ☎

③ ◆ ASCOTT
Wing LU7 0PS. Sir Evelyn de Rothschild, The National Trust, 01296 688242, info@ascottestate.co.uk. *2m SW of Leighton Buzzard, 8m NE of Aylesbury.* **House and Garden £8.40, chd £4.20, Garden only £4.20, chd £2.10. Phone or see website for other openings. For NGS: Mons 4 May; 31 Aug (2-6).**
Combining Victorian formality with early C20 natural style and recent plantings to lead it into the C21, with a recently completed garden designed by

Jacques and Peter Wirtz who designed the gardens at Alnwick Castle, and also a Richard Long Sculpture. Terraced lawns with specimen and ornamental trees, panoramic views to the Chilterns. Naturalised bulbs, mirror-image herbaceous borders, impressive topiary incl box and yew sundial.

&. ✗ ❀

Group opening

④ AYLESBURY GARDENS
HP21 7LR. *¾ m SE of Aylesbury Centre. 5 town gardens S of town centre, 3 off A413, 2 on A41.* Home-made teas at 2 Spenser Road. **Combined adm £4, chd free. Sun 21 June (2-6).**
A group of mainly mature town gardens showing a range of ideas and specialities. Each garden displays the individuality of its owner and their passions.

☕

16 MILTON ROAD
Roger & Frances King
Mature suburban garden featuring Mediterranean and oriental patios and pergolas with woodland fernery and wildlife pond.

✗

2 SPENSER ROAD
Mr & Mrs G A Brown
Tranquil cottage style garden with many ornamental trees raised from seed. Victorian greenhouse with original features containing a collection of pelargoniums and tender plants.

✗ ❀

NEW TOLVERNE
185 Tring Rd. Bill Nuttycombe
1930's 140ft cottage-style garden completely redesigned in 2007. Large fish pond and small wildlife pond, various beds, shrubs, rose beds, pergolas and patios and various specimen exotics.

NEW 110 TRING ROAD
Mr & Mrs K Keasley
Established town garden with mature trees, variety of perennial plants, rose bed and gazebo, pond, alpine raised bed and troughs and vegetable parterre.

&. ✗

NEW 13 WALTON DENE
Joe & Marian Benham
Town garden with a mixture of planting incl alpines and alpine house, perennials, shrubs, a selection of ferns and grasses, vegetables and some exotics.

Small fountain at base of ancient elder tree . . .

---

5 BLOSSOMS
Cobblers Hill HP16 9PW. Dr & Mrs F Hytten, 01494 863140. *2¹/₂ m NW of Great Missenden. By Rignall Rd, signed Butler's Cross, to Kings Lane 1¹/₂ m on R, then to top of Cobblers Hill. Turn R at yellow stone marker & after 50yds turn R again at stone, marked Blossoms.* Home-made teas. **Adm £3, chd free. Visitors welcome by appt, no coach access.**
4 acres began as hill-top fields, plus 1-acre beechwood. Lawns, old apple orchard, small lake, water, troughs, scree and patio gardens. Large areas of bluebells, wild daffodils and other spring bulbs. Large climbing roses, flowering cherries and many other interesting trees incl acers, eucalyptus and willows. Foliage effects throughout yr. Dogs on short leads only.

6 ◆ BRADENHAM MANOR
HP14 4HF. The National Trust. *2¹/₂ m NW of High Wycombe, 5m S of Princes Risborough. On A4010, turn by Red Lion Pub, car park signed on village green.* Light refreshments & teas. **Adm £3.50, chd free. Sun 21 June (1-4.30).**
Unique opportunity to see the on-going restoration of the C17 gardens, with views of the village and countryside. Reinstated victorian summer border, yew hedges, parterre and wilderness at various stages of restoration. Guided tour at 2pm, £1 donation. Refreshments on village green at cricket pavilion. Limited wheelchair access, gravel paths, steep grass slopes.

---

7 NEW BURROW FARM
Hambleden RG9 6LT. David Palmer, 01491 571256/571267. *1m SE of Hambleden. On A4155 between Henley and Marlow, turn N at Mill End. After 300yds, R onto Rotten Row. After ¹/₂ m, Burrow Farm entrance on R.* Home-made teas. **Adm £5, chd free (share to Buckinghamshire Foundation). Sun 21 June (11-5). Visitors also welcome by appt June/July. Groups 40 max.**
Burrow Farm and the adj Cottages (not open) are part Tudor and part Elizabethan, set in the Chilterns above Hambleden Valley where it meets the Thames. Views of pasture and woodlands across the ha-ha greatly enhance the setting. Special features are the parterre, arboretum and C15 barn, where teas are served.

8 CEDAR HOUSE
Bacombe Lane, Wendover HP22 6EQ. Sarah Nicholson, 01296 622131, jeremynicholson@btinternet.com. *5m SE Aylesbury. From Gt Missenden take A413 into Wendover. Take 1st L before row of cottages, house at top.* **Adm £3.50, chd free. Visitors welcome by appt from May-Sept for groups 10+, no coaches, parking for 10 cars only.**
Chalk garden with beautiful views. Lawn leads to swimming pond with aquatic plants. Shaped borders contain a great variety of perennial plants and shrubs. In summer, colour co-ordinated half hardy plants in pots, well stocked lodge greenhouse. Steep slope.

CHARLTON GARDENS
See Northamptonshire.

Group opening

9 CHEDDINGTON GARDENS
LU7 0RQ. *11m E of Aylesbury, 7m S of Leighton Buzzard. Turn off B489 at Pitstone. Turn off B488 at Cheddington stn, turn off Cheddington/Long Marston rd.* Home-made teas at Methodist Church on green. **Combined adm £4.50, chd free (share to Cheddington Methodist Church & Cheddington Church St Giles). Sun 21 June (2-6).**

Long village with green. Maps for visitors. Runner-up best kept village in Bucks.

THE OLD POST OFFICE
27 High St. Alan & Wendy Tipple
Cottage-style garden, softly planted with lavender, roses, clematis, herbaceous borders, shaded area and a small pond. Interesting low maintenance gravel garden to front.

ROSE COTTAGE
68 High Street. Mrs Margery Jones
(See separate entry).

21 STATION ROAD
Mr & Mrs P Jay
¹/₂ -acre informal garden with wild flower and wildlife conservation area, herbaceous and shrub borders, trees, herbs and kitchen garden.

WOODSTOCK COTTAGE
42 High St. Mr & Mrs D Bradford
Front garden laid to gravel with assorted shrubs. Back courtyard and patio with small fountain at base of ancient elder tree.

---

10 CHESHAM BOIS HOUSE
85 Bois Lane, Chesham Bois HP6 6DF. Julia Plaistowe, 01494 726476, julia.plaistowe@yahoo.co.uk, www.cheshamboishouse.co.uk. *1m N of Amersham-on-the-Hill. From Amersham-on-the-Hill follow Sycamore Rd, over double mini r'about, which turns into Bois Lane. Past village shops, house is ¹/₂ m on L. Parking in road or on R at school & at scout hut.* Home-made teas. **Adm £3.50, chd free. Suns 29 Mar; 17 May; 12 July (2-5.30). Visitors also welcome by appt.**
Up a drive of mostly old lime trees, a late Georgian house (not open) surrounded by 3-acre garden of yr-round interest. Walled garden, small ornamental canal and rill with gazebo, lovely herbaceous borders with some tender and unusual plants, topiaried trees and wide lawns. Winding walks through old orchard and over ancient bowling green. In spring, fine display of primroses, daffodils and hellebores. Gravel area to front.

⑪ 100 CHURCH GREEN ROAD

Bletchley, Milton Keynes MK3 6BY. Rosemary & Gordon Farr, 01908 379289, gordonandrosie@tiscali.co.uk. *13m E of Buckingham, 11m N of Leighton Buzzard. Off A421. Turn into Church Green Rd, take L fork. House is half way down.* Home-made teas. **Adm £2.50, chd free (share to Willen Hospice). Visitors welcome by appt in June & July.**
Divided into rooms, this very long and narrow garden offers lots of interest and ideas for the visitor. The garden is informally planted incl beautiful fern collection, herbaceous and shrub borders. A meandering path takes you past several water features and seating areas. Winner Milton Keynes News Garden of the Year Competition.

✖ ❀ ☕ ☎

⑫ ◆ CLAYDON HOUSE

Middle Claydon MK18 2EX. Sir Edmund & Lady Verney, 01296 730252, www.claydonestate.co.uk. *4m S of Buckingham. Signed, nr village, adjacent to church.* **Adm £3.50, chd free. Sat to Wed, Mar-Oct (1-5). For NGS: Sun 12 July (2-5).**
Large country house garden under gradual redevelopment and redesign. Herbaceous borders, mixed plantings, shrubs, annuals and tender perennials. 2-acre Victorian kitchen garden planted with vegetables and flowers and adjacent walled flower garden with large pond, borders, and a restored Victorian glasshouse.

♿ ✖ ❀ ☕

⑬ ◆ CLIVEDEN

Taplow SL6 0JA. The National Trust, 01628 605069, cliveden@nationaltrust.org.uk. *2m N of Taplow. Leave M4 at J7 or M40 at J4 & follow brown tourism signs.* **Adm £8, chd £4. For NGS: Sats 18 July (11-6); 19 Sept (2-6).**
Separate gardens within extensive grounds first laid out in C18. Water garden, secret garden, topiary, herbaceous borders, woodland walks and views of R Thames. Timber steps lead down yew tree walk to river.

♿ ✖ ❀

⑭ ◆ COWPER & NEWTON MUSEUM GARDENS

Market Place, Olney MK46 4AJ. Mrs E Knight, 01234 711516, www.cowperandnewtonmuseum. org.uk. *5m N of Newport Pagnell. 12m S of Wellingborough. On A509. Please*

park on Market Place, Cattle Market Car Park or in High Street. **Adm £2, chd free. Tues to Sat, 1 Mar to 23 Dec (10.30-4.30). For NGS: Sat 13, Sun 14 June (10.30-4.30).**
Restored walled flower garden with plants pre 1800, many mentioned by C18 poet, William Cowper, who said of himself 'Gardening was, of all employments, that in which I succeeded best'. Summerhouse garden in Victorian kitchen style with organic, new and old vegetables. Herb and medicinal plant borders in memory of the garden's original use by an apothecary.

♿ ✖ ❀ ☕

⑮ CRAIGLEA HOUSE

Austenwood Lane, Chalfont St Peter, Gerrards Cross SL9 9DA. Jeff & Sue Medlock, 01753 884852, jeffmedlock@hotmail.com. *6m SE Amersham. From Gerrards Cross take B416 towards Amersham. Take L fork after 1/2 m into Austenwood Lane, garden 1/3 m. Park at St Joseph's Church or Priory Road.* Home-made teas. **Adm £4, chd free. Suns 31 May; 7 June (2-5). Visitors also welcome by appt.**
1 acre landscaped to reflect the Edwardian house. Formal white garden bordered by pleached hornbeam and trellis with central fountain. Lawns edged by herbaceous and mixed borders, separated from rose garden by a pergola underplanted with lavender. Less formal area with wildlife pond, vegetables and beds of mixed planting.

♿ ✖ ❀ ☕ ☎

Group opening

⑯ CUBLINGTON GARDENS

LU7 0LQ. *5m SE Winslow, 5m NE Aylesbury. From Aylesbury take A413 Buckingham Rd. After 4m, at Whitchurch, turn R to Cublington.* Home-made teas at The Old Rectory. **Combined adm £4, chd free. Sun 7 June (2-6).**

♿ ❀ ☕

LARKSPUR HOUSE

Wing Road. Mr & Mrs S I Jenkins
S-facing family garden planted in 1996 to create a mix of moods and style, eclectic planting suggests a Mediterranean patio, moving to a tropical shade garden then to a cottage garden. Small kitchen garden.

✖

THE OLD RECTORY

High Street. Mr & Mrs J Naylor
2-acre country garden with herbaceous border, rose beds, shrubs and mature trees, vegetables, ponds and climbing plants.

❀

THE OLD STABLES

Reads Lane. Mr & Mrs George
Large family garden with separate walled garden. Features incl maze, large ponds, kitchen garden, variety of shrubs and herbaceous plants. Revolving summerhouse and arbour. Some gravel paths.

❀

NEW 1 STEWKLEY ROAD

Tom & Helen Gadsby
Part-walled rear garden, organic kitchen garden, small orchard and courtyard. Strong focus on home-grown food. Established 2002.

✖

Herb and medicinal plant borders . . .

Group opening

⑰ CUDDINGTON GARDENS

Thame HP18 0AP. *3 1/2 m NE Thame, 5m SW Aylesbury. Off A418. Parking signed in village. Wheelchair visitor parking phone 01844 291526 or 01844 299455.* Home-made teas at Tyringham Hall/The Bernard Hall. **Combined adm £5, chd free. Sun 21 June (2-6).**
Picturesque Midsomer Murders village. Cottage garden plantings provide colour throughout and complement the pretty village greens. C13 church with attractive churchyard and wild flower reserve. Romantic dell with waterfall in Tibbys Lane adjoining Tyringham Hall. Plants at The Bernard Hall. Film location for Midsomer Murders. Buckinghamshire Winners of Calor Village of the Year and nominated to represent the county in 2008/2009. Runner-up in regional Best Kept Village competition.

♿ ❀

NEW 33 BERNARD CLOSE
Mr & Mrs Tony Orchard
The accent is on colour with an amazing kaleidoscope of annuals set in borders, beds, troughs, pots and hanging baskets. Established shrubs and, would you believe it, the gardener's double!

NEW BOX COTTAGE
Lower Church St. Mr & Mrs Tony Picot
Sensual cottage garden perfectly complementing its 'chocolate-box' timber-framed, thatched cottage. Enticing roses and babbling pools draw you through to reveal the 'secrets' of the back garden.

NEW THE OLD PLACE
Dr & Mrs Michael Straiton
Partially-walled 1½ -acre garden surrounding ancient cottage (not open). Mixed beds and lawns with glass and willow sculptures. Stunning valley view.

NEW THE OLD SCHOOL HOUSE
Mrs Margaret Spurrell
Charming flower-arranger's garden. Well-stocked borders and island beds with established shrubs and perennials and some new planting. Rustic pergola supporting varied climbers. 2 resident peacocks.

TYRINGHAM HALL
Mrs Sherry Scott
Medieval house that will be partly open. Flower filled patios, large lawns, herbaceous borders. Mature trees, bog area featuring water garden with tufted ducks. Raised beds with organic vegetables. Filming location for Midsomer Murders.

18 DORNEYWOOD GARDEN
Burnham SL1 8PY. The National Trust, 01628 665361, secretary.dorneywood@btopenworld.com. *1m E of Taplow, 5m S of Beaconsfield. From Burnham village take Dropmore Rd, at end of 30mph limit take R fork into Dorneywood Rd. Entrance is 1m on R. From M40 J2, take A355 to Slough then 1st R to Burnham, 2m then 2nd L after Jolly Woodman, signed Dorneywood Rd. Dorneywood is about 1m on L.* **Adm £4.50, chd under 5 free, NT**

members £3.50. **Admission only by written application, or e-mail (to the Secretary) 2 weeks in advance for all dates Weds 13, 27 May; 1 July, Sat 25 July (2-5).** 8-acre country house garden on several levels with herbaceous borders, greenhouses, rose, cottage and kitchen gardens, lily pond and conservatory.

. . . would you believe it, the gardener's double! . . .

Group opening

19 EAST CLAYDON AND VERNEY JUNCTION GARDENS
MK18 2ND. *1½ m SW Winslow. In Winslow turn R off High St, follow NT signs to Claydon House (E Claydon) or carry straight out of Winslow on Vicarage Rd (Verney Junction).* Home-made teas at The Old Vicarage. **Combined adm £3.50, chd free. Sun 31 May (2-6).**
2 small villages, originally part of the Claydon Estate (Claydon House, NT is 1½ m). Typical N Bucks cottages and railway history.

INGLENOOKS
St Mary's Road. Mr & Mrs David Polhill
Informal cottage garden with different areas of interest, many roses, surrounding C17 timber-framed thatched cottage (not open).
♿

3 JUBILEE COTTAGES
Verney Junction, Robert & Jane O'Connell
(See seperate entry)

THE OLD VICARAGE
Church Way. Nigel & Esther Turnbull
Large garden on clay started from scratch in 1991. Mixed borders, scented garden, dell, shrub roses, vegetables and natural clay pond. Small meadow area and planting to encourage wildlife. Access via gravel drive.

Group opening

20 NEW ELLESBOROUGH VILLAGE GARDENS
HP17 0XD. *6m SE of Aylesbury, 4m NE of Princes Risborough. On B4010, 1½ m W of Wendover. Spring Lane is between the village hall at Butlers Cross & St Peter & St Pauls Church. Narrow Lane, uneven surface.* Home-made teas at Homelands. **Combined adm £4.50, chd free. Thurs 11 June; 13 Aug (2-5). Evening Opening £4.50, wine, Fri 10 July (6-9).**
Ellesborough is on the escarpment of the Chilterns in AONB. Coombe Hill is the highest point. The picturesque church is surrounded by cottages and former almshouse. Close by is Chequers, the country home of British Prime Ministers. Plant and feature-oriented treasure hunt for children Aug. Homelands featured in 'Chiltern Life & Berkshire'.

HOMELANDS
Springs Lane, Ellesborough. Jean & Tony Young, 01296 622306. Visitors also welcome by appt.
¾ -acre garden on chalk, evolving design; wide range of features incl secluded seating areas, wildlife pond, mature wild flower meadow, deep borders and new gravel beds with exotic late summer and autumn planting.
☎

NEW WOODLAND HOUSE
Springs Close. Kim & Barry White
New garden developed over 3 yrs on ⅓ -acre site. Shaded woodland garden and various other borders reclaimed from solid chalk. Emphasis on interesting colour and foliage combinations.
❀

EVENLEY WOOD GARDEN
See Northamptonshire.

21 FRESSINGWOOD
Hare Lane, Little Kingshill HP16 0EF. John & Maggie Bateson. *1m S of Gt Missenden, 4m W of Amersham. From A413 Amersham to Aylesbury rd, turn L at Chiltern Hospital, signed Gt & Little Kingshill. Take 1st L into Nags Head Lane. Turn R under railway bridge & 1st L into New Rd. At top, turn into Hare Lane, 1st house on R.* Home-

made teas. **Adm £3, chd free.** Sun 10 May (2-6).

Thoughtfully designed garden with yr-round colour. Shrubbery with ferns, grasses and hellebores, small formal garden, herb garden, pergolas with wisteria, roses and clematis, topiary and landscaped terrace. Formal pond, herbaceous borders and bonsai collection. Many interesting features.

Water garden with reed beds and koi carp . . .

Group opening

22 GIPSY HOUSE & ONE CHURCH STREET
Great Missenden HP16 0AL. *5m NW Amersham. A413 to Gt Missenden. One Church St can be found at the Missenden Abbey end of High St, on corner of Church St. For Gipsy House, take Whitefield Lane, opp Missenden Abbey entrance, under railway bridge. Small Georgian house on R, park in field opp.* Home-made teas. **Combined adm £5, chd free.** Thur 23 Apr; Wed 13 May; Thur 11 June; Wed 15 July (2-5). Also open **The Plant Specialist.**
In village of Great Missenden, home of Roald Dahl, an opportunity to visit 2 very different gardens and exceptional plant nursery with a wide range of unusual plants.

GIPSY HOUSE
Mrs Felicity Dahl
Garden of late Roald Dahl. York stone terrace, pleached lime walk with hosta and allium. Sunken garden, maze, topiary oaks, herbaceous borders with perennials and assorted roses. Walled vegetable garden with espalier fruits, vine, peaches and nectarines.

NEW ONE CHURCH STREET
Lyndsey Keeling
Walled courtyard and water garden designed by Andy Sturgeon. Mixture of grasses, alliums and olive trees. Water garden with reed beds and koi carp.

Group opening

23 GRANGE DRIVE WOOBURN
Wooburn Green HP10 0QD. *On A4094, 2m SW of A40, between Bourne End & Wooburn. From the church, heading to Maidenhead, Grange Drive is on the L.* Light refreshments & teas Feb/home-made teas June at Magnolia House. **Combined adm £3.50, chd free, £2.50 Feb.** Sun 22 Feb for snowdrops (11-3); Sun 28 June (2-5). Sun 21 Feb 2010 (Magnolia House only).
Private tree-lined drive which formed the entrance to a country house. Display of local paintings/crafts.

MAGNOLIA HOUSE
Alan & Elaine Ford, 01628 525818, sales@lanford.co.uk.
Sun 21 Feb 2010. Visitors also welcome by appt.
½ acre containing 24 mature trees incl magnificent copper beech and magnolia reaching the rooftop. Small cactus bed, ferns, stream leading to pond, small vegetable garden, greenhouses. Small aviary. 10,000 snowdrops in spring and many hellebores.

THE SHADES
Pauline & Maurice Kirkpatrick.
Not open 22 Feb.
Drive approached through mature trees, area of shade-loving plants, beds of shrubs, 60 various roses and herbaceous plants. Rear garden with natural well surrounded by shrubs, conifers and acers. Original green slate water features and scree garden with alpine plants.

24 HALL BARN
Windsor End, Beaconsfield HP9 2SD. The Hon Mrs Farncombe, jenefer@farncombe01.demon.co.uk. *½ m S of Beaconsfield. Lodge gate 300yds S of St Mary and All Saints' Church in Old Town centre.* **Adm £3, chd free.** Visitors welcome by appt by written application, ample parking, no min number.
Historical landscaped garden laid out between 1680-1730 for the poet Edmund Waller and his descendants. Features 300-yr-old 'cloud formation' yew hedges, formal lake and vistas ending with classical buildings and statues. Wooded walks around the

grove offer respite from the heat on sunny days. One of the original gardens opening in 1927 for the NGS. Open-air Shakespeare festival in mid-June (covered seating). Gravel paths.

Group opening

25 HIGHER DENHAM GARDENS
Higher Denham UB9 5EN. *6m E of Beaconsfield. From A40 take A412. ¼ m from the junction turn L at part-time traffic lights into Old Rectory Lane. 1m on turn into Lower Rd signed Higher Denham.* **Combined adm £4, chd free** (share to Higher Denham Community Association, Trees Fund). Sun 31 May (1-5).
Small semi-rural village nestling in the delightful Misbourne Valley with its idyllic chalk stream. A map will guide you firstly to our star 3-acre garden then onto the 2 smaller gardens.

19 LOWER ROAD
Helene White
Flower arranger's garden backing onto stream. Shrubs, perennials and bulbs planted to create a garden with all-yr interest and plenty of cutting material for arrangements.

19 MIDDLE ROAD
Sonia Harris. *From Lower Rd turn into Middle Cresent, becomes Middle Rd*
A garden crowded with as many plants as possible, many cuttings from friends or small plants from holidays. Some fruit bushes, a few vegetables. Terrace overlooking the garden, full of pots and ornamental pond. Gravel gardens at front of house.

WIND IN THE WILLOWS
Moorhouse Farm Lane off Lower Rd. Ron James, 07740 177038, r.james@company-doc.co.uk. Visitors also welcome by appt with at least 3 weeks notice please.
3-acre wildlife-friendly yr-round garden comprising informal, woodland and wild gardens separated by streams lined by iris and primulas. Over 300 shrubs and trees, many variegated or uncommon, marginal and bog plantings incl a collection of 80 hostas. 'Stunning' was the word

most often used by visitors last year. Level gravel paths in woodland garden.

 ♿ ✈ ☎

26 19 HIGHFIELD ROAD

Winslow MK18 3DU. Mrs Gwladys Tonge, 18002 01296 713489 (type talk relay service), mail@gwladystonge.co.uk. *5m SE of Buckingham, 9m N of Aylesbury. On A413 Winslow to Buckingham, take last turning L, 200yds after garage, 50yds before turning to Great Horwood.* **Adm £4 incl tea & home-made cake, chd free, £3 garden only. Visitors welcome by appt,** Feb (snowdrops) to Sept, max 10.
Very small garden with extensive range of attractive hardy plants providing beauty and excitement for each season. Trees, shrubs, rose pergola, clematis and other climbers, bulbs, incl interesting snowdrop collection, ferns, grasses, evergreen and herbaceous perennials demonstrate ingenious use of space and grow happily together. Experimenting with growing fruit and vegetables in containers.

✈ ❀ ☕ ☎

27 HILL HOUSE

Castle Street, Buckingham MK18 1BS. Mr & Mrs P Thorogood, 07860 714758, leonie@pjtassociates.com. *Town centre. On L of vehicle entrance to Parish Church (spire very visible). Castle St clearly marked as you face Old Town Hall at central town r'about.* **Adm £2.50, chd free. Visitors welcome by appt** from June to end Sept.
1/3 -acre town garden on old castle walls, aiming at ease of maintenance, yr-round interest and colour. Slope.

 ♿ ✈ ☎

28 HILLCREST

6 Frieth Road, Marlow SL7 2QT. Mr & Mrs Ivan Pierce, 01628 483063, marianpierce@talktalk.net. *2m W of Marlow. At Marlow turn off A4155 into Oxford rd (by Platts of Marlow). Continue and rd becomes Chalkpit Lane. Approx 2m up past Valley View Stables, Hillcrest is 3rd house on R.* Home-made teas. **Adm £3, chd free. Tues 23 June; 7 July (11-5). Visitors also welcome by appt from 22 June to 17 July, groups 15+.**
Sloping 1/3 acre developed over the last few yrs. Topiary garden with water feature, gravel beds with variety of

grasses. Several well stocked island beds with perennials and shrubs. Many pots of hostas, ferns and summer annuals. Large vegetable garden and fruit cage, small wildlife pond. Pleasant countryside view. Wheelchair access to patio to view garden and countryside beyond. Garden has slope.

 ♿ ✈ ❀ ☕ ☎

29 HILLESDEN HOUSE

Church End, Hillesden MK18 4DB. Mr & Mrs R M Faccenda, 01296 730451, suefaccenda@aol.com. *3m S of Buckingham. Next to church in Hillesden.* Home-made teas. **Adm £4, chd free. Sun 28 June (2-5).** Visitors also welcome by appt in March/April, June/July, groups 10+.
By superb church 'Cathedral in the Fields'. Carp lakes, fountains and waterfalls. Mature trees and large conservatory. Rose, alpine, foliage and herbaceous gardens. 5 acre formal area surrounded by about 100 acres of deer park, wild flower areas and extensive lakes developed by owner. Lovely walks, lots of wildlife and many birds.

 ♿ ❀ ☕ ☎

30 ◆ HUGHENDEN MANOR

High Wycombe HP14 4LA. The National Trust, 01494 755573, www.nationaltrust.org.uk. *1½ m N of High Wycombe. On W side of Gt Missenden Rd A4128, past church, into NT woodland car-park.* **House and Garden £7.40, chd £3.70, Garden only £2.90, chd £2.20. 1 Apr to 31 Oct, Wed to Sun. For NGS: Sun 21 June (11-5).**
Mary Anne Disraeli's colour schemes inspire spring and summer bedding in formal parterre. Unusual conifers, planted from photographs taken at time of Disraeli's death. Old English apple orchard with picnic area. Beech woodland walks. Mediterranean border. The walled garden Learning Zone will be open too, with guides available. Meet the NT Head Gardener at the 'Gardeners Question Corner' (NT Marquee) ready to help with your garden questions. Access to main features but slopes require help.

 ♿ ✈ ❀ ☕

31 3 JUBILEE COTTAGES

Verney Junction MK18 2JZ. Robert & Jane O'Connell. *2½ m SW of Winslow. Turn in High St by Windmill vets and follow road out of Winslow.* Home-made teas. **Adm £2.50, chd free. Sat 30 May (2-6). Evening**

Opening wine, Fri 26 June (6-9). Established but continually evolving mid-terrace garden. Ornamental garden divided into rooms linked by a boardwalk. Vegetable garden, greenhouses, small orchard with summerhouse and further borders. Also open with East Clayden and Verney Junction Gardens.

🐕 ❀ ☕

32 NEW KAYALAMI

The Pyghtle, off Village Rd, Denham Village UB9 5BD. Hazel de Quervain, 07747 856468, hazel@connexions4africa.com. *3m NW of Uxbridge, 7m E of Beaconsfield. Village Rd is next to village green, opp Falcon PH. 3rd house down The Pyghtle.* Home-made teas. **Adm £4, chd free. Sun 12 July (2-5). Visitors also welcome by appt.**
In 1993 the owner started creating this charming 1-acre garden. Beautifully manicured lawns lead to large herbaceous borders packed with a wide variety of plants providing a riot of colour and foliage. Other highlights of this peaceful garden incl rockery, pond, vegetable patch, compost area and greenhouse. Gravel drive, plenty of seats.

 ♿ ☎

Evolving mix of plantings for sun and shade, moist and dry . . .

Group opening

33 THE LEE GARDENS AT SWAN BOTTOM

Gt Missenden HP16 9NU. *3m N of Great Missenden, 3m SE of Wendover. Follow A413 Gt Missenden to Wendover. Turn 3rd R up Rocky Lane. After 2m turn L at 1st Xrds. 200yds turn R down drive.* Cream teas at Kingswood House. **Combined adm £5, chd free (share to The Lee PCC). Sun 17 May (2-6).**
Swan Bottom is a hamlet less that 1m N of the secluded and picturesque village of The Lee, at the centre of which is the green created by Arthur Liberty who founded Libertys of Regent Street. C13 church with fine wall paintings.

2 KINGSWOOD COTTAGES

Swan Lane, The Lee. Jon & Trish Swain, 01494 837752, swaino@talk21.com. *3m SE Wendover, 3m N Gt Missenden. From A413, Gt Missenden to Wendover, take 3rd R up Rocky Lane. After 2m turn L at 1st X-rds. 200yds turn L down unmade road, 1st drive on R.* **Visitors also welcome by appt in May & June, groups 20+.**
2-acre informal garden in the peaceful Chiltern Hills. Children (and adults) love following winding paths, discovering sculptures and artefacts en route. Slate herb garden, sundial table, wildlife pond, beehives, chickens, specimen trees. Gravel paths, some narrow.

KINGSWOOD HOUSE

Mr & Mrs T Hart, 01494 837328, judy.hart@virgin.net. **Visitors also welcome by appt in May & June, groups 20+.**
4-acre mature garden in an AONB. Mixed borders with many unusual plants. White garden surrounding a formal pond, sundial garden, fruit and vegetable areas. Some gravel paths.

A riot of colour and foliage . . .

Group opening

34 LITTLE MISSENDEN GARDENS

HP7 0RD. *2½ m NW of Old Amersham.* On A413. Home-made teas at Church. **Combined adm £4, chd free. Sun 7 June (2-6).**
Attractive Chiltern village in an area of outstanding natural beauty. (Anglo-saxon church built 975). Village used several times as a 'set' for film and TV.

HOLLYDYKE HOUSE

Bob and Sandra Wetherall
3-acre garden, herbaceous borders, shrubs and trees. Old fashioned roses, koi and lily ponds, collection of conifers.

NEW KINGS BARN

Penfold Lane. Mr & Mrs A Playle
A new garden in an old setting. We have tried to reflect the rectangular form of the barn and its plot by picking this theme in its design. It relies on indigenous species and traditional forms. Sculpture studio open. Gravel drive.

THE MANOR HOUSE

Mr & Mrs T A Cuff
9-acres, in a glorious setting. Gravel paths.

NEW MILL HOUSE

Mr & Mrs J B White
The gardens surround the C17 Mill House with the R Misbourne running through. A variety of shrubs, roses, clematis and many mature trees. To the front are brick paths with assorted shrubs and lavender. At the rear there are lawns and shrub beds together with a patio and pergola.

MISSENDEN HOUSE

Wilf Stevenson
A mixture of traditional and modern. Herbaceous and lawns together with a Zen garden by Christopher Bradley Hole and bamboo playground. Lawn and gravel paths.

Group opening

35 LONG CRENDON SPRING GARDENS

HP18 9AN. *2m N of Thame. On B4011 Thame-Bicester rd.* Home-made teas at Church House. **Combined adm £4, chd free (share to (10%) Long Crendon Day Centre). Sun 19 Apr (2-6).**
Attractive large village with many old and listed buildings and a large variety of gardens. Partial wheelchair access.

BARRY'S CLOSE

Mr & Mrs Richard Salmon
2-acre sloping garden with interesting collection of trees and shrubs. Herbaceous border, spring-fed pools and water garden.

NEW 48 CHILTON ROAD

Mr & Mrs M Charnock
Pretty ¼-acre garden, mostly shrub and herbaceous perennial borders with summerhouse and small vegetable plot.

MANOR HOUSE

114 High St. Mr & Mrs West
4-acre garden. Lawns sweep down to 2 ornamental lakes each with small island, fine views towards Chilterns. Evolving mix of plantings for sun and shade, moist and dry. New courtyard borders. Partial wheelchair access, steep slopes down to lakes.

NEW 2 NAPPINS CLOSE

Nicky Donnelly
Maximising a small space, a modern courtyard with patio area and a communal garden.

THE OLD CROWN

97 Bicester Rd. Mr & Mrs R H Bradbury
1¼ -acre on SW slope. More than 250 assorted roses, colourful annual and perennial plants in numerous beds, incl 50-60 clematis, flowering shrubs, assorted colourful pots and containers, statues, 2 sizeable vegetable plots. Great variety and very many spring bulbs.

Group opening

36 LONG CRENDON SUMMER GARDENS

HP18 9AN. *2m N of Thame. On Thame/Bicester rd B4011.* Home-made teas at Church House & Croft House, refreshments at Nappins Close. **Combined adm £5, chd free (share to (10%) Long Crendon Day Centre). Sun 7 June (2-6).** A great variety of gardens in attractive large village with many old/listed buildings. Maps available for all visitors.

CROFT HOUSE

Cdr & Mrs Peter Everett, 01844 208451, peverett@nildram.co.uk. Visitors also welcome by appt. 1/2 -acre walled garden with a variety of plants and shrubs, some unusual and of interest to flower arrangers. Water feature, greenhouse and conservatory.

NEW 25 ELM TREES

Carol Price A small cottage-style garden, friendly to wildlife, with trees, shrubs, climbers and herbaceous perennials. Different areas incl a fruit and vegetable plot, wildlife pond, rockery, sunken patio, and main lawn with deep borders.

KETCHMORE HOUSE

9 Chearsley Road. Mr & Mrs C Plumb Very attractive wildlife friendly cottage garden laid out in 3 sections; courtyard with raised pond, entertaining area with bog garden and lawn and vegetable area. Great variety of plants and shrubs.

MANOR HOUSE

114 High Street. Mr & Mrs N West 4-acre garden, lawns sweep down to 2 ornamental lakes each with small island. Fine views towards Chilterns, evolving mix of plantings for sun and shade, moist and dry, new courtyard borders. Partial wheelchair access.

MULBERRY HOUSE

Mr & Mrs C Weston 1-acre, old vicarage garden, recently restored. Set amongst mature trees, now incl formal knot garden, woodland walk, pond, vegetable garden, numerous beds and lawns, a notable monkey puzzle tree and a mulberry tree.

NEW NAPPINS CLOSE

Nicky Donnelly Maximising a small space, a modern courtyard with patio area and a communal garden.

THE OLD CROWN

97 Bicester Road. Mr & Mrs R H Bradbury 1 1/4 acre on SW slope. More than 250 assorted roses, colourful annual and perennial plants in numerous beds, incl 50-60 clematis, flowering shrubs, assorted colourful pots and containers, statues, 2 sizeable vegetable plots. Great variety and very many spring bulbs.

TOMPSONS FARM

Mr D Tye Large woodland garden with mature trees and lawns sweeping down to an ornamental lake.

37 LORDS WOOD

Frieth Road, Marlow Common SL7 2QS. Mr & Mrs Messum. *1 1/2 m NW Marlow. Off A4155, turn at Platts Garage into Oxford Rd, towards Frieth, 1 1/2 m. Garden is 100yds past Marlow Common turn, on L.* Home-made teas. **Adm £4, chd free (share to NSPCC). Thurs 18 June; 10 Sept (11-5).** Family home to the Messums since 1976, Lords Wood boasts fantastic views over the Chilterns. 5-acre garden, large orchard, woodland and meadow. Varied planting styles throughout, extensive borders, large water garden and rockery. This garden never stands still, with something new to enjoy on each visit. Gravel, steep slopes.

38 THE MANOR HOUSE, BLEDLOW

HP27 9PB. **The Lord & Lady Carrington.** *9m NW of High Wycombe, 3m SW of Princes Risborough. 1/2 m off B4009 in middle of Bledlow village.* Teas (May), Home made teas (Jun). **Adm £5, chd free. Suns 3 May; 14 June (2-6). Visitors also welcome by appt for groups** 10+ incl coaches. By written application only to 32a Ovington Street, London SW3 1LR. Paved garden, parterres, shrub borders, old roses and walled kitchen garden. Water garden with paths, bridges and walkways, fed by 14 chalk springs. Also 2 acres with sculptures and landscaped planting.

A notable monkey puzzle tree and a mulberry tree . . .

---

39 THE MANOR HOUSE, HAMBLEDEN

RG9 6SG. Maria Carmela, Viscountess Hambleden. *3 1/2 m NE Henley-on-Thames, 8m SW High Wycombe. 1m N of A4155.* **Adm £3.50, chd free. Sun 14 June (2-6).** Informal garden, sweeping lawns, mature trees and an exceptional rose garden designed by Peter Beales with a profusion of old fashioned scented roses. Large terrace on the S side of the house takes you to a magnificent conservatory with stunning plants climbing 30ft.

40 MARYFIELD

High Street. SL6 0EX. Jacqueline & Roger Andrews, 01628 667246, japrivate@btinternet.com. *1m S Cliveden, 1/2 m E Maidenhead. From M4 J7 or M40 J4 follow signs for Taplow. House on bend of High St.* Light refreshments & teas. **Adm £4, chd free. Sat 23, Sun 24 May; Sats 4 July; 19 Sept (2-6). Visitors also welcome by appt.** 2-acres wrapped around our Victorian home in the heart of Taplow Village. Walled vegetable and herb garden bordered by fruit trees, over-looked by a mature lime walk, newly laid out lily pond, extends into herbaceous planting, mature yew hedging, pond area, orchard and Japanese inspired garden.

41 ◆ NETHER WINCHENDON HOUSE
Nether Winchendon HP18 0DY. Mr Robert Spencer Bernard, 01844 290101, www.netherwinchendonhouse.com. *6m SW of Aylesbury, 6m from Thame.* Adm £3, chd free. For NGS: Sun 31 May (2-5.30). House open NGS day only, adm £8, guided tours 2.45, 3.45, 4.45.
5 acres of fine and rare trees and shrubs, a variety of hedges, herbaceous borders and naturalised spring bulbs. Founder garden (1927) Medieval and Tudor manor house in picturesque village with beautiful church.

42 NORTH DOWN
Dodds Lane, Chalfont St Giles HP8 4EL. Merida Saunders, 01494 872928. *4m SE of Amersham, 4m NE of Beaconsfield. Opp the green in centre of village. At Crown Inn turn into UpCorner, on to Silver Hill. At top of hill fork R into Dodds Lane. N Down is 6th opening on L. Limited parking in Dodds Lane.* Adm £3, chd free. Visitors welcome by appt from May to Sept, incl groups, no coaches.
3/4 -acre sloping N-facing compartmentalised site with mature trees. Difficult stony soil. Designed with scenic effect in mind and interest throughout the yr. Large grassed areas with island beds of mixed perennials, shrubs and some unusual plants. Variety of rhododendrons, azaleas, acers, 70+ clematis and other climbers. Displays of sempervivum varieties, alpines, grasses and ferns. Small patio/water feature. Greenhouse. Italianate front patio to owner's design.

ODNEY CLUB
See Berkshire.

43 THE OLD SUN HOUSE
Pednor HP5 2SZ. Mr & Mrs M Sharpley. *3m E of Gt Missenden, 2m W of Chesham. From Gt Missenden take B485 to Chesham, 1st L & follow signs approx 2m. From Chesham Church St (B485) follow signs approx 1 1/2 m.* Home-made teas. Adm £3.50, chd free. Sun 24 May (2-6).
5-acre garden, abundant with wildlife, set on a Chiltern ridge giving superb views. The garden is surrounded by mature trees with inner plantings of unusual trees and shrubs. Features incl large ornamental pond with walkway, vegetable and herb garden, interesting woodland walk, white peafowl, guinea fowl, pheasantry and chickens. Gravel drive, some slopes.

Over 2,000 species and varieties of rare and interesting plants . . .

44 ◆ OLD THATCH
Coldmoorholme Lane, Bourne End SL8 5PS. Jacky & David Hawthorne, 01628 527518, www.jackyhawthorne.co.uk. *1m W Bourne End, 3m E Marlow. Off A4155. Thatched house on L just before the Spade Oak PH. Public car park 100yds on, towards the R Thames.* Adm £4, chd £1. 23 May-31 Aug, Sat, Suns, Weds & BH Mons. For NGS: Sat 6 June (2-5.30).
Listed thatched cottage (not open), famous home of Enid Blyton and source of many of her stories. 2 acres, re-designed by Jacky Hawthorne in 2000, now contain beautiful palettes of colour, stunning ornamental grasses and wonderful design features. Cottage garden, lavender terrace, rose and clematis walk, formal garden, water circle. Teas in room claimed by EB to be Dick Turpin's stable, containing secret treasures. Featured in various press & publications.

45 THE OLD VICARAGE
Thornborough Road, Padbury MK18 2AH. Mr & Mrs H Morley-Fletcher, 01280 813045, belindamf@freenet.co.uk. *2m S of Buckingham, 4m NW of Winslow. On A413, signed in village.* Home-made teas. Adm £3, chd free. Sat 25, Sun 26 Apr (2-6). Visitors also welcome by appt.
2 1/2 acres on 3 levels, flowering shrubs and trees. Vegetable garden, pond and sunken garden, parterre and millennium arch. Magnolias and trilliums.

46 6 OLDFIELD CLOSE
Little Chalfont HP6 6SU. Jolyon & Phyllis Lea, 01494 762384. *3m E of Amersham. Take A404 E through Little Chalfont, 1st R after railway bridge, R again into Oakington Ave.* Home-made teas. Adm £2, chd free. Sun 19 Apr (2-5). Visitors also welcome by appt.
Mature 1/6 -acre garden of shrub borders, peat beds, rock plants, troughs and alpine house. Over 2,000 species and varieties of rare and interesting plants, incl spring bulbs, cyclamen and dwarf rhododendrons. Wide range of plants for sale.

47 OVERSTROUD COTTAGE
The Dell, Frith Hill, Gt Missenden HP16 9QE. Mr & Mrs Jonathan Brooke, 01494 862701, susie@jandsbrooke.co.uk. *1/2 m E Gt Missenden. Turn E off A413 at Gt Missenden onto B485 Frith Hill to Chesham rd. White Gothic cottage set back in lay-by 100yds up hill on L. Parking on R at church.* Cream teas at Parish Church. Adm £3, chd 50p. Suns 12 Apr; 10 May; 14 June; 5 July (2-6). Visitors also welcome by appt March to July, groups 15+, incl coaches.
Artistic chalk garden on 2 levels. Collection of C17/C18 plants. Potager/herb garden, spring bulbs, hellebores, succulents, primulas, pulmonarias, geraniums, species/old fashioned roses and lily pond. Garden studio with painting exhibition. Cottage was once C17 fever house for Missenden Abbey. Featured in 'Creative Vegetable Gardening' by Joy Larkcom.

48 11 THE PADDOCKS
Wendover HP22 6HE. Mr & Mrs E Rye. *5m from Aylesbury, on A413. At Wendover after approx 1/2 m, turn L at mini-r'about into Wharf Rd. Entrance is 2nd on L. From Gt Missenden, turn L at Clock Tower, then R at next mini-r'about.* Adm £2, chd free. Sat 20, Sun 21 June; Sat 4 July (2-6). Evening Opening £2, wine, Fri 26 June (5-8).
Small peaceful garden with mixed borders of colourful herbaceous perennials and a special show of David Austin roses and delphiniums. Cool hosta walk and tremendous variety of plants in a small area. White garden with peaceful arbour 'The Magic of Moonlight'. Many unusual plants. Entry to BBC 'Gardener of the Decade' at Eden Project.

49 ◆ **THE PLANT SPECIALIST**
Whitefield Lane, Gt Missenden
HP16 0BH. Sean Walter, 01494
866650,
www.theplantspecialist.co.uk. *5m
NW Amersham. A413 to Gt
Missenden. Whitefield Lane opp
Missenden Abbey. Under railway
bridge on the L.* **Nursery open
Apr to end Oct, Wed to Sat (10-5)
Sun (10-4).** 10% for NGS on Thurs
23 Apr; Weds 13 May; 11 June;
15 July (2-5). Also open **Gipsy
House & One Church Street.**
Plant nursery with herbaceous
perennials and grasses, container
grown bulbs and half hardy perennials
in attractive garden setting and display
garden.

Secluded
water garden
and many
attractive
walks . . .

Group opening

50 **QUAINTON GARDENS**
HP22 4BW. *7m NW of Aylesbury, 7m
SW of Winslow. Nr Waddesdon turn
off A41.* Tea & soup at parish church,
mulled wine at Capricorner (Feb),
Home-made teas at parish church
(May). **Combined adm £2.50 (Feb),
£3.50 (May) chd free. Suns 22 Feb
(12-4); 31 May (2-6); 28 Feb 2010.**
Village lies at the foot of the Quainton
Hills. Fine views over the vale of
Aylesbury & the Chiltern Hills. C14
parish church & C19 working windmill
(open to visitors). Heavy clay but well-
watered by spring from Quainton Hills.

CAPRICORNER
Mrs Davis
Small garden planted for yr-round
interest with many scented plants,
winter flowering shrubs and bulbs,
small woodland glade with
interesting trees.

NEW 135A STATION ROAD
Mr & Mrs Carter. Not open 22
Feb 2009.
Mature and secluded heavily
planted garden with shrubs giving
all-yr shape and form. Established
herbaceous areas incl roses and
climbers. Vegetable patch with
small fruit trees.

THE VINE
Upper Street. Mr & Mrs D A
Campbell, 01296 655243,
david@dacampbell.com. **Visitors
also welcome by appt anytime.**
Lying at the foot of the Quainton
Hills, a stream runs through the
bog garden into a pond, many
exotic plants particularly from the
Himalayas and China. Winter
flowering shrubs and spring bulbs.

RAGGED HALL
See Hertfordshire.

---

51 **NEW RED KITES**
46 Haw Lane, Bledlow Ridge
HP14 4JJ. Mag & LesTerry,
01494 481474,
les.terry@lineone.net. *4m S of
Princes Risborough. Off A4010
halfway between Princes
Risborough and West Wycombe.
At Hearing Dogs sign in
Saunderton turn to Haw Lane,
then 3/4 m on L.* Home-made teas.
**Adm £3, chd free. Visitors
welcome by appt for groups of
15+.**
Chiltern hillside garden with
terracing and superb views.
Planted for yr-round interest, the
1 1/4 acres encompasses various
mixed and herbaceous borders,
wild flower orchard, established
pond, vegetable garden, managed
woodland area and hidden garden.
Wide use of climbers and clematis
throughout.

52 **RIVENDELL**
13 The Leys, Amersham HP6 5NP.
Janice & Mike Cross. *Off A416. Take
A416 N towards Chesham. The Leys is
on L 1/2 m after Boot & Slipper PH.
Park at Beacon School, 100yds N.*
**Adm £3, chd free. Mons 13 Apr;
7 June (2-5).**
S-facing garden featuring a series of

---

different areas with wide variety of
perennials, especially hellebores. Alpine
bed, box-edged herbaceous beds,
sedum and thyme path leading to rose
and clematis arbour. Raised woodland
bed under mature trees, bog garden,
gravel area with grasses and pond,
vegetable plot, developing topiary.

53 **ROSE COTTAGE**
68 High St, Cheddington LU7 0RQ.
Margery R Jones. *11m S of
Aylesbury, 7m S of Leighton Buzzard.
Turn off B489 at Pitstone, turn off B488
at Cheddington Stn, turn off
Cheddington, Long Marston rd.* Wine.
**Adm £2, chd free. Evening
Opening** wine, Fri 26 June (6-8.30).
1/2 -acre cottage garden filled with small
rooms with maximum use of space. A
balance of evergreens and deciduous
resulting in a garden for all seasons,
incl a late border with herbs, vegetable
parterre and wildlife pond. Also open
with Cheddington Gardens. Gravel
paths.

54 ◆ **STOKE POGES MEMORIAL
GARDENS**
Church Lane. SL2 4NZ. South
Bucks District Council, 01753
537619, graham.pattison@
southbucks.gov.uk. *1m N of Slough,
1m S of Stoke Poges. From Stoke
Poges, B416 towards Slough, R at
Church Lane. From Slough, Stoke
Poges Lane, leads into Church Lane.
By St Giles Church.* **Adm £3.50, chd
free.** For NGS: Sat 14 Mar; Sun
19 Apr; Wed 13 May (2-5).
Unique 20-acre Grade II registered
garden constructed 1934-9. Rock and
water gardens, sunken colonnade,
rose garden incl 500 individual gated
gardens. Spring garden, bulbs,
wisteria, rhododendrons. Recently
completed £1m renovation. Guided
tours, 2,3,4pm. Winner of Green Flag
Heritage Site Award and Green Flag
Award.

55 **TURN END**
Townside, Haddenham HP17 8BG.
Peter Aldington. *3m NE of Thame,
5m SW of Aylesbury. Turn off A418 to
Haddenham. Turn at Rising Sun to
Townside. Please park at a distance
with consideration for neighbours.*
Home-made teas. **Adm £3, chd £1.
Mon 4 May (2-5.30).**
Architect's own post-war listed house
(not open). Garden less than 1 acre,

space used to create illusion of size. Series of enclosed gardens, sunken or raised, sunny or shady, each different yet harmonious, contrast with lawns, borders and glades. Spring bulbs, irises, old roses and climbers. Courtyard with fish pool. Heather Hunter - artist in residence - will be demonstrating print making in the studio. Some gravel paths and steps.

&♿ ❀ ☕

TURWESTON MILL
See Northamptonshire.

TURWESTON HOUSE
See Northamptonshire.

Spectacular view of weir . . .

56 TYTHROP PARK
Kingsey HP17 8LT. Nick & Chrissie Wheeler. *2m E of Thame, 4m NW of Princes Risborough. Via A4129, lodge gates just outside Kingsey.* Light refreshments & home-made teas. **Adm £4.50, chd free (share to St Nicholas' Church). Sun 12 July (2-6).** Anyone who has visited Tythrop in the past will agree there is huge potential for an outstanding garden. The new owners are developing a fresh plan and hope to realise that potential. The 7 acres of formal gardens already have many features incl fine specimen trees and shrubs, an intricate box parterre, large walled garden, secluded water garden and many attractive walks with old roses.

✈ ☕

VERSIONS FARM
See Northamptonshire.

57 WATERCROFT
Church Road, Penn HP10 8NX. Mr & Mrs Paul Hunnings, 01494 816535. *3m NW of Beaconsfield, 3m W of Amersham. On B474 from Beaconsfeld, 600yds on L past Holy Trinity Church, Penn.* Home-made teas. **Visitors welcome by appt June & July only, groups 20+.** Mature 3-acre chalk and clay garden. Unusual spring bulbs and hellebores. Large weeping ash. Rose walk with 350 roses. Courtyard with summer pots and box topiary. Large natural old pond with diving ducks, newly extended and replanted perennial border. Italianate garden with 15yr-old yew hedges and fine view. Wild flower meadow with wild roses. Formal herb garden with culinary herbs, small vegetable garden with hebe hedge. Glasshouse with unusual pelargoniums.

🐕 ☕ ☎

58 THE WHITE HOUSE
Village Road, Denham Village UB9 5BE. Mr & Mrs P G Courtenay-Luck. *3m NW of Uxbridge, 7m E of Beaconsfield. Signed from A40 or A412. Parking in village rd. The White House is in centre of village.* Home-made teas. **Adm £4, chd free. Sun 24 May (2-5).** Well established 6-acre formal garden in picturesque setting. Mature trees and hedges, with R Misbourne meandering through lawns. Shrubberies, flower beds, rockery, rose garden and orchard. Large walled garden with Italian garden and developing laburnum walk. Herb garden, vegetable plot and Victorian greenhouses. Gravel entrance drive.

♿ ❀ ☕

59 WHITEWALLS
Quarry Wood Road, Marlow SL7 1RE. Mr W H Williams, 01628 482573. *½ m S Marlow. From Marlow cross over bridge. 1st L, 3rd house on L, white garden wall.* **Adm £2.50, chd free. Suns 19 Apr; 12 July; 6 Sept (2-5). Visitors also welcome by appt.** Thames-side garden approx ½ acre with . Large lily pond, interesting planting of trees, shrubs, herbaceous perennials and bedding, large conservatory.

♿ ☎

Mark your diary with these special events in 2009

EXPLORE SECRET GARDENS DURING CHELSEA & HAMPTON COURT FLOWER SHOW WEEKS

Tue 19 May, Wed 20 May, Thur 21 May, Fri 22 May, Wed 8 July, Thur 9 July
Full day tours from £82 per person, 10% discount for groups
Advance booking required, telephone +44 (0)20 8693 1015 or email j.wookey@btinternet.com
Specially selected gardens in London, Essex, Kent, Hampshire and South Oxfordshire. The tour price includes transport and lunch with wine at a popular restaurant or pub.

HAMPTON COURT PALACE

Thur 2 Apr, Tue 23 June, Thur 25 June, Wed 15 July, Tue 4 Aug, Thur 10 Sept
Evening tours in the company of one of the Palace's specialist tour guides from 6.30 – 8pm.
Tickets £6 per person. Advance booking required, telephone +44 (0)1483 211535 or visit www.ngs.org.uk for more information
Gossip, scandal, murder, healing – you'll find it all within the Formal Gardens at Hampton Court Palace. Each tour will have its own unique feature whether it's the story of the Great Vine or the magic and mystery of the Maze.

FROGMORE – A ROYAL GARDEN (BERKSHIRE)

Tue 26 May 10am – 5.30pm (last admission 4pm)
Garden adm £4.50, chd free. Tickets available in advance or on the day.
Advance booking for groups and coaches, telephone
+44 (0) 1483 211535 or email orders@ngs.org.uk
A rare opportunity to explore 30 acres of landscaped garden, rich in history and beauty.

FLAXBOURNE FARM – FUN & SURPRISES (BEDFORDSHIRE)

Sun 7 June 10am – 5pm. Adm £5, chd free
No booking required, come along on the day!
Bring the whole family and have fun in this surprising and entertaining garden of 2 acres. Enjoy the large plant fair, live music, pets corner, birds of prey, dog agility show and much more.

WISLEY RHS GARDEN – MUSIC IN THE GARDEN (SURREY)

Fri 11 Sept 6 – 9pm
Adm (incl RHS members) £7, chd under 15 free
Save money on advance bookings for groups of 4 or more, telephone +44 (0)1483 211535 or visit www.ngs.org.uk for more information
A special evening opening of this famous garden, exclusively for the NGS. Enjoy music and entertainment as you explore the gardens and the floral marquee on the first day of the Wisley Flower Show.

For further information visit www.ngs.org.uk or telephone 01483 211535

CAMBRIDGESHIRE

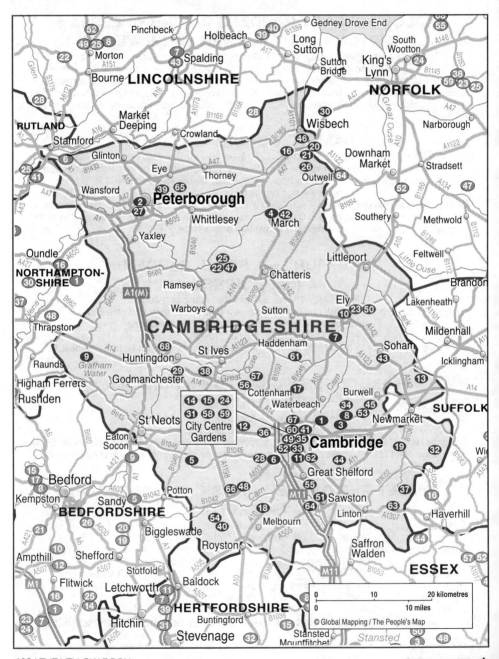

Opening Dates

March

SUNDAY 22
⑬ Chippenham Park

SUNDAY 29
㉜ Kirtling Tower
㊸ Netherhall Manor
(65) Willow Holt

April

SUNDAY 5
⑥ Barton Gardens
㉜ Kirtling Tower
㉝ Leckhampton
(60) Trinity Hall - Wychfield

SUNDAY 12
(58) Trinity College, Fellows' Garden

SUNDAY 19
⑭ Churchill College

SUNDAY 26
(65) Willow Holt
(68) Wytchwood

May

SUNDAY 3
⑪ 16 Chaucer Road
㊸ Netherhall Manor
(62) Upwater Lodge
(67) The Windmill

MONDAY 4
⑪ 16 Chaucer Road
(62) Upwater Lodge

SUNDAY 10
② Almora
㉞ Lode Gardens

SATURDAY 16
(53) Shadworth House
(61) Ty Gwyn

SUNDAY 17
⑥ Barton Gardens
⑱ Docwra's Manor
(61) Ty Gwyn

SUNDAY 24
㉖ Florence House
㉙ Island Hall
㉚ Kenilworth Smallholding (Day & Evening)

SUNDAY 31
㉓ Ely Gardens
㊲ Manna Ash House
(65) Willow Holt

June

SATURDAY 6
㊽ Rectory Farm House
(52) 4 Selwyn Gardens

SUNDAY 7
② Almora
㉞ Lode Gardens
㊹ The Old House
㊽ Rectory Farm House
(52) 4 Selwyn Gardens
(55) Stapleford Gardens

SATURDAY 13
⑳ Elm & Walsoken
(61) Ty Gwyn

SUNDAY 14
⑨ Catworth, Molesworth & Brington Gardens
⑬ Chippenham Park
⑰ Cottenham Gardens
⑳ Elm & Walsoken
㊱ Madingley Hall
(61) Ty Gwyn

WEDNESDAY 17
(65) Willow Holt

SATURDAY 20
⑤ 2 Baldwins Manor
㊺ The Paddock
(53) Shadworth House

SUNDAY 21
① 15 Abbots Way
② Almora
⑤ 2 Baldwins Manor
㉚ Kenilworth Smallholding (Day & Evening)
(56) Swavesey & Over Gardens
(64) Whittlesford Gardens

SATURDAY 27
⑤ 2 Baldwins Manor
㉑ Elm House

SUNDAY 28
⑤ 2 Baldwins Manor
㉔ Emmanuel College Garden & Fellows' Garden
㊼ Ramsey Forty Foot
(68) Wytchwood

July

SUNDAY 5
⑮ Clare College Fellows' Garden
㉛ King's College Fellows' Garden
㉞ Lode Gardens
(51) Sawston Gardens
(60) Trinity Hall - Wychfield

WEDNESDAY 8
㉟ Lucy Cavendish College

SATURDAY 11
(61) Ty Gwyn

SUNDAY 12
㉞ Lode Gardens
㊹ The Old House
(61) Ty Gwyn

SATURDAY 18
③ Anglesey Abbey, Gardens & Lode Mill
㊶ Murray Edwards College (formally New Hall)
㊻ Peckover House

SUNDAY 19
⑭ Churchill College
(66) Wimpole Hall

SUNDAY 26
(65) Willow Holt

August

SUNDAY 2
㊸ Netherhall Manor

SATURDAY 8
④ Appledene
㊷ 88 Nene Parade

SUNDAY 9
④ Appledene
㊷ 88 Nene Parade
㊸ Netherhall Manor

SATURDAY 15
(61) Ty Gwyn

SUNDAY 16
㉖ Florence House
(59) Trinity Hall
(61) Ty Gwyn

SUNDAY 23
⑦ Breakaway

SUNDAY 30
㊲ Manna Ash House
(65) Willow Holt

September

SATURDAY 5
(61) Ty Gwyn

SUNDAY 6
(61) Ty Gwyn

SUNDAY 27
(65) Willow Holt

October

SUNDAY 11
⑬ Chippenham Park

SUNDAY 25
(65) Willow Holt

Gardens open to the public

③ Anglesey Abbey, Gardens & Lode Mill
⑱ Docwra's Manor
㊳ The Manor
㊻ Peckover House
㊾ Robinson College
(66) Wimpole Hall

By appointment only

- ⑫ Childerley Hall
- ⑯ Clearview
- ⑲ Dullingham House
- ㉗ 39 Foster Road
- ㉘ Greystones
- ㊴ 38 Martinsbridge
- ㊵ Mill House
- �54 South Farm & Brook Cottage
- ㊅③ Weaver's Cottage

Also open by appointment ☎

- ⑦ Breakaway
- ⑭ Churchill College
- ㉒ The Elms
- ㉕ First Cottage
- ㉖ Florence House
- �34 Carpenters End
- �34 12 Chapel Street
- �34 21 Lode Road
- �34 Wild Rose Cottage
- �37 Manna Ash House
- ㊴ 38 Martinsbridge
- ㊵ Mill House
- ㊷ 88 Nene Parade
- ㊸ Netherhall Manor
- ㊹ The Old House
- ㊿ Rosewell House
- �53 Shadworth House
- �57 Sycamore Farm
- �61 Ty Gwyn
- �62 Upwater Lodge
- �65 Willow Holt
- ㊻ The Windmill
- ㊽ Wytchwood

The Gardens

① 15 ABBOTS WAY
Horningsea CB25 9JN. Sally & Don Edwards. *4m NE of Cambridge. ¹/₂ m off A14. No access from Abbots Way. Follow signs in Horningsea to garden & car park.* Home-made teas. **Adm £3, chd free (share to Friends of St Peter's Church Horningsea).** Sun 21 June (2-5.30).
1¹/₄ -acre sloping garden with views over R Cam and water meadows. Interesting plants, trees and use of colour. 116ft pergola with large collection of roses, clematis, and other climbers (currently being extended) and natural pond with fish and bridge.
☕

② ALMORA
91 Thorpe Road, Peterborough PE3 6JQ. Dr Robert Stebbings & Sheila Stebbings. *¹/₂ m W of railway stn. W of Thorpe Lodge Hotel. 2nd house (red brick).* **Adm £2.50, chd free.** Suns 10 May; 7, 21 June (10-4).
Small town garden 11m x 23m with pond, rockery and mix of native and exotic species. Created in 2004/5 with 120yr old Bramley and first project to replace a Leylandii hedge with native evergreens by inter-planting. Over 30 species of ferns in shade, all planned to attract native wildlife. Art exhibit will show how the garden was created. Featured in local press and on local radio.
🐾

③ ♦ ANGLESEY ABBEY, GARDENS & LODE MILL
Cambridge CB25 9EJ. The National Trust, 01223 810080, www.nationaltrust.org.uk. *6m NE of Cambridge. From A14 turn N on to B1102 through Stow-cum-Quy.* **House and Garden Adm £9.75, chd £4.90, Garden only Adm £5.80, chd £2.90. For opening dates & times, please tel or see website.** For NGS: Sat 18 July (10.30-5.30).
Set against a Jacobean-style country house these 114 acre magnificent formal and informal gardens are truly for all seasons. The breathtaking gardens and arboretum contain more than 100 pieces of sculpture. In July, the beautiful herbaceous borders and wildflower meadows are not to be missed.
♿ 🐾 ❀ ❀ ☕

④ NEW APPLEDENE
35a Westwood Avenue, March PE15 8AX. Eric Stromberg. *5mins from March town centre. Take B1099 Wisbech Rd off A141 r'about signed March. N for 8m. Continue straight on into Wisbech Rd & Dartford Rd. Westwood Ave on L, garden 200yds along on the outside of the LH-bend. Parking for 5 cars.* Home-made teas. **Combined with 88 Nene Parade adm £2.50, chd free.** Sat 8, Sun 9 Aug (10-5).
A relaxing and secluded garden of ¹/₂ - acre with trees, lawns 'tucked away' seating, and colour. Highly Commended - March Gardens in Bloom. A few wide, low steps, some narrow paths.
♿ 🐾 ☕

⑤ NEW 2 BALDWINS MANOR
SG19 3RH. Jon & Catherine Smith. *6m E of St Neots. On edge of village at junction of B1046 from Abbotsley and Waresely Rd, house 2nd on R.* **Adm £2.50, chd free.** Sats, Suns 20, 21, 27, 28 June (12-6).
Artistically designed, lovingly tended traditional cottage style garden. With glorious countryside views, something of interest at every turn. Colourful, informal, well established beds that are continuously evolving. Many quirky plants. Large natural pond surrounded by a wild meadow. Secluded vegetable patch that's always changing.
♿ ❀ ☕

Artistically designed, lovingly tended traditional cottage style garden . . .

Group opening

⑥ BARTON GARDENS
Cambridge CB23 7AY. *3¹/₂ m SW of Cambridge. M11 J12. Take A603 towards Sandy, in village turn R for Comberton Rd.* Home-made teas at village hall (Apr) & school (May). **Combined adm £5, chd free.** Suns 5 Apr; 17 May (2-5).

DORMERS
4 Comberton Road. Nigel & Jean Hobday. *Adjacent to village pond.* **Not open 5 Apr.**

FARM COTTAGE
18 High Street. Dr R M Belbin.

NEW THE GABLES
11 Comberton Road. Nigel & Sarah Pitchford. **Not open 17 May.**

GLEBE HOUSE
1 High Street. David & Sue Rapley. *Top of High St*

114 HIGH STREET
Meta & Hugh Greenfield

NEW KING'S TITHE
13a Comberton Road. Mr & Mrs Cornelius Thorne. Not open 17 May.

31 NEW ROAD
Dr & Mrs D Macdonald

THE SIX HOUSES
33-45 Comberton Road. Perennial (GRBS).

247 WIMPOLE ROAD
Ray & Nikki Scrivens

WINDY CORNER
245 Wimpole Road. Mike & Jules Webber

Delightful group of large and small gardens reflecting different approaches to gardenening. Each garden is unique in character an style, offering everything from a formal, Italian style courtyard to an established country garden with room for animals and birds. Features to look out for include the secret garden with gazebo, a hatta, loggia with climbing plants, woodland walk, walled garden, duck pond, kitchen garden and a formal fruit and herb garden. Planting includes herbaceous borders, spring flowers and bulbs, an adventurous array of shrubs and perennials and mature trees. Wheelchair access to 5 gardens, some gravel areas. Burwash Spring Fair (May). Featured in 'Garden News'.

7 BREAKAWAY
Old Stretham Station Road. CB6 3QD. Mr & Mrs Grey, 01353 649615. *3m S of Ely. From Ely follow A10 S 3m. Turn R (signed NGS). Garden 1m from A10 on L. From Cambridge 1½ m N at Stretham r'about turn L (signed NGS).* Home-made teas. **Adm £2, chd free. Sun 23 Aug (2-6). Visitors also welcome by appt from 23 Aug to 20 Sept only.** Medium sized garden containing wide range of interesting plants, shrubs, trees, and knot gardens, gravelled, grass and palm areas. Water features, summerhouse, exotic jungle area featuring bananas, gingers, tree ferns, bamboos and colocasia to name a few.

BURGHLEY HOUSE PRIVATE SOUTH GARDENS
See Lincolnshire.

Group opening

9 CATWORTH, MOLESWORTH & BRINGTON GARDENS
nr Huntingdon PE28 0PF. *10m W of Huntingdon. For Catworth & Brington turn off A14 onto B660 (Catworth S bound) approx 7m W of A14 junction with A1. Village is on the N side of A14 flyover. Molesworth is on the A14, 8m W of the A1.* Home-made teas at Molesworth House, The Poplars & Yew Tree Cottage. **Combined adm £3, chd free. Sun 14 June (2-6).**

32 HIGH STREET
Catworth. Colin Small

MOLESWORTH HOUSE
Molesworth. John Prentis.

THE POPLARS
Molesworth. Nick Frost.

YEW TREE COTTAGE
Brington. Mr & Mrs D G Eggleston.

Four varied gardens showing showing the best of planting, design and creativity representing classic traditions but with a modern twist. **32 HIGH STREET** is a long narrow garden with many rare plants including salvias and ferns. An informal patio, with containers of unusual foliage plants leads to a lawn with herbaceous borders and a native woodland area. **MOLESWORTH HOUSE** is a Victorian rectory garden with a bit of everything; old-fashioned and proud of it but with a groovy tropical house. **THE POPLARS** has been created over the last 3 yrs and uses a hillside setting to create terraces, wonderful ponds and a waterfall surrounded by excellent planting. Long low steps to pond areas. **YEW TREE COTTAGE** comprises flower beds, lawns, vegetable patch, boggy area, copses and orchard. Plants in pots and hanging baskets. Some steps around pond areas and gravel drives. Featured in 'Garden News'.

10 12 CHAPEL STREET
Ely CB6 1AD. Ken & Linda Ellis, 01353 664219, ken.ellis1@ntlworld.com. Open with **Ely Gardens** Sun 31 May (2-6) Visitors also welcome by appt May to Sept.
Small town garden with lots of interesting corners. The plants reflect the eclectic outlook of the gardeners towards plants. Themes from alpine to herbaceous border. All linked by a railway! At least, that's the excuse....

11 NEW 16 CHAUCER ROAD
Cambridge CB2 7EB. Mrs V Albutt. *1m S of Cambridge. Off Trumpngton Rd (A1309) nr Brooklands Ave junction.* **Combined with Upwater Lodge adm £5, chd free. Sun 3, Mon 4 May (2-5).**
½ -acre garden, divided by arches and hedges into separate areas, each with its own character. Spring flowering shrubs and trees, bulbs in borders and wildlife area. Greeting cards for sale.

12 CHILDERLEY HALL
Dry Drayton CB23 8BB. Mrs Jenkins, 01954 210271. *6m W of Cambridge. Between Caldecote r'about and Cambourne on old A428.* **Adm £3.50, chd free. Visitors welcome by appt May to July.**
Romantic 4-acre garden (grade II historic garden) surrounds part Tudor house (not open). Winding paths lead through herbaceous borders to secret areas. Large collection shrub roses and good variety of plants and trees.

Themes from alpine to herbaceous border . . . all linked by a railway! At least, that's the excuse . . .

⑬ CHIPPENHAM PARK
Chippenham, nr Newmarket
CB7 5PT. Mr & Mrs Eustace
Crawley. *5m NE of Newmarket. 1m off
A11.* Light refreshments. **Adm £4, chd
free. Suns 22 Mar; 14 June; 11 Oct
(11-4).**
The house (not open), gardens, lake,
canals and 350-acre park enclosed by
wall 3½ m long, built after Admiral Lord
Russell petitioned William III in 1696 for
permission to make a park. Gardens
have been extended and restocked by
Anne Crawley, descendant of John
Tharp who bought the estate in 1791.
Superb display of narcissus and early
flowering shrubs followed by extensive
summer borders and dramatic autumn
colours. Many plants stalls.
&. ⊛ ☕

Beautiful grouping of 20 Prunus Tai Haku (the great white cherry) trees . . .

**⑭ NEW CHURCHILL
COLLEGE**
CB3 0DS. University of
Cambridge, 01223 740926,
john.moore@chu.cam.ac.uk,
www.chu.cam.ac.uk. *1m from
M11 J13. 1m NW of Cambridge
city centre. Turn into Storeys Way
from Madingley Rd (A1303), or
from Huntingdon Rd (A1307).* Light
refreshments & teas in College
Buttery. **Adm £3.50, chd free.
Suns 19 Apr; 19 July (2-5).
Visitors also welcome by appt
out of university term 20 Apr to
20 June.**
42 acre site designed in 1960's for
foliage and form, providing a
peaceful and relaxing visit with
courtyards and large open spaces.
Recent additions incl 75m long
parterre incorporating 1400 box
pants and herbaceous plantings.
Beautiful grouping of 20 Prunus Tai
Haku (the great white cherry) trees
forming striking canopy in spring
and naturalised bulbs in grass
elsewhere. The planting provides a
setting for the impressive collection
of modern sculpture. Sculpture trail
and leaflets of college's trees.
&. ✕ ⊨ ☕ ☎

**⑮ CLARE COLLEGE FELLOWS'
GARDEN**
Trinity Lane, Cambridge CB2 1TL.
The Master & Fellows,
www.clare.cam.ac.uk. *Central to city.
From Queens Rd or city centre via
Senate House Passage, Old Court &
Clare Bridge.* **Adm £3.50, chd free.
Sun 5 July (2-6).**
2 acres. One of the most famous
gardens on the Cambridge Backs.
Herbaceous borders; sunken pond
garden, fine specimen trees and
tropical garden.
&. ✕

⑯ CLEARVIEW
Cross Lane, Wisbech St Mary
PE13 4TX. Margaret & Graham
Rickard, 01945 410724,
magsrick@hotmail.com. *3m SW of
Wisbech, off Barton Rd. Leave
Wisbech on Barton Rd towards
Wisbech St Mary. L at Cox Garage
Xrds into Bevis Lane. 1st L into Cross
Lane. Garden 4th on R with iron gates.*
Home-made teas. **Adm £3, chd free.
Visitors welcome by appt Apr to
July, no large coaches please.**
Approx 1-acre with lake incorporating
large wildlife area - incl beehives.
Secluded cottage garden with many
old fashioned plants, herbaceous
border, gravel garden with raised bed
and pond. Large rose bed, allotments
and small orchard. Plenty of secluded
seating. Jazz Band playing in June -
please phone for date. Wildlife Garden
of the Year Wisbech in Bloom. Access
in areas except cottage garden can be
viewed from edges.
&. ✕ ⊛ ☕ ☎

Group opening

**⑰ NEW COTTENHAM
GARDENS**
CB24 8TJ. *6m N of Cambridge.
Take B1049 from A14 through
Histon to Cottenham Green.*
Home-made teas. **Combined
adm £4, chd free (share to
James Whale Kidney Cancer
Fund). Sun 14 June (11-5).**

**NEW 3 CURRINGTONS
CLOSE**
Mr & Mrs K Marr.

NEW 103 RAMPTON ROAD
Rosemary Pawlak.

NEW 105 RAMPTON ROAD
Jean & Rob Knott.

Large village N of the University
City of Cambridge. One of largest
in Cambridgeshire since the C11.
All Saints Church is a prominent
landmark with its 'onion shaped'
pinnacles on the church tower. The
High St is one of the longest in the
country, with All Saints Church and
the village green a mile apart. **3
CURRINGTONS CLOSE** a
cottage garden with herbaceous
shrub borders, climbing roses and
clematis over structures. Gravel
garden and formal box hedge
borders.**103 RAMPTON ROAD** a
small courtyard garden with raised
beds, water feature, rockery,
hanging baskets and mixed
planting.**105 RAMPTON ROAD** is
a medium sized garden mainly
perennials, relaxed cottage garden
style. Mixed planting with roses
and shrubs. Small wildlife pond
and seating areas.
&. ✕ ⊛ ☕

⑱ ◆ DOCWRA'S MANOR
Meldreth Road, Shepreth SG8 6PS.
Mrs Faith Raven, 01763 260677,
www.docwrasmanorgarden.co.uk.
*8m S of Cambridge. ½ m W of A10.
Garden is opp the War Memorial in
Shepreth. King's Cross-Cambridge
train stop 5 min walk.* **Adm £4, chd
free. All yr Weds, Fris (10-4.30), 1st
Sun in month (11-4). For NGS: Sun
17 May (2-5.30).**
2½ acres of choice plants in series of
enclosed gardens. Tulips and Judas
trees. Opened for NGS for more than
40yrs. Quality Assured Visitor
Attraction.
&. ✕ ⊛ ☕

⑲ DULLINGHAM HOUSE
nr Newmarket CB8 9UP. Sir Martin &
Lady Nourse, 01638 508186,
lavinia.nourse@btinternet.com. *4m S
of Newmarket. Off A1304 & B1061.*
**Adm £3, chd free. Visitors welcome
by appt Jun-Jul only.**
The grounds were landscaped by
Humphrey Repton in 1799 and the
view remains virtually intact today. To
the rear there is a substantial walled
garden with magnificent long
shrub/herbaceous borders. The
garden encompasses a fine claire voie
and historic bowling green.
&. ✕ ☎

Group opening

20 ELM & WALSOKEN

PE14 0DL. *Elmfield Drive is Off A47 towards Downham Market, 1st turning L on bend opp Blacksmith's Arms PH. Walnut Lodge off A47 towards Walsoken, nr Walsoken Aquatics.* Home-made teas at Walnut Lodge. **Combined adm £3.50, chd free.** Sat 13, Sun 14 June (10-4).

22 ELMFIELD DRIVE
Elm. Vivien & Andrew Steed.

24 ELMFIELD DRIVE
Elm. Kathleen & Tony Price.

WALNUT LODGE
Shirley Lakey.

Three gardens combining water and varied and interesting planting. **24 ELMFIELD DRIVE** a variety of herbaceous plants, spring, summer and autumn bulbs together with flowering shrubs, incl over 100 clematis. Small arid garden and fish pond. **22 ELMFIELD DRIVE** Rear garden with a range of foliage plants inc. ferns, acers, bamboos and over 100 hostas. Wildlife pond. Front garden with grasses and clematis. **WALNUT LODGE** one acre of reclaimed orchard includes raised herbaceous beds, a rockery overlooking ornamental fish ponds, a rose garden and a new area designed for clematis and fuchsia. Adjacent to 4-acre wildlife orchard. 2 gardens are mostly accessible by wheelchair.

✖ ☕

21 ELM HOUSE

Main Road, Elm PE14 0AB. Mrs Diana Bullard. *2½ m SW of Wisbech. From A47 take A1101 towards Downham Market, take B1101 towards March, garden approx ¼ m on L.* Home-made teas. **Adm £3.00, chd free.** Sat 27 June (2-5).
Walled garden with arboretum, many rare trees and shrubs, mixed perennials C17 house (not open). New 3 acre meadow.

♿ ✖ ☕

22 THE ELMS

Hollow Road, Ramsey Forty Foot PE26 2YA. Mr R Shotbolt, 01487 812601, richard@shotbolt.freeserve.co.uk. *3m N of Ramsey. From Ramsey (B1096) travel through Ramsey Forty Foot, just before bridge over drain, turn R, First Cottage 300yds on R, next door to The Elmsv.* **Open wih Ramsey Forty Foot Gardens** Sun 28 (2-6). **Visitors also welcome by appt.**

1½ -acre water garden around C19 clay pit backed by massive elms. Large collection of shrubs, perennials, bog and aquatic plants. New woodland and arid plantings for 2009.

☎

Group opening

23 ELY GARDENS

CB7 4TX. *14m N of Cambridge. Approaching Ely from A10 follow signs to the cathedral, or yellow signs in Prickwillow Rd. Maps given at first garden visited.* Home-made teas at Rosewell House, teas & drinks at Bishop Woodford House. **Combined adm £4, chd free.** Sun 31 May (2-6).

BISHOP WOODFORD HOUSE
Barton Road. Ms Michelle Collins

THE BISHOP'S HOUSE
The Rt Reverend the Bishop of Ely & Mrs Russell

12 CHAPEL STREET
Ken & Linda Ellis. Visitors also welcome by appt.
(See separate entry).

HAZELDENE
36 Barton Road. Mike & Juliette Tuplin

50A PRICKWILLOW ROAD
Mr & Mrs J Hunter

ROSEWELL HOUSE
Mr & Mrs A Bullivant. Visitors also welcome by appt.
(See separate entry).

Delightful group of gardens within a historic city with famous cathedral and river frontage. Two walled gardens, one small and one large, arranged around the cloisters of a former monastery. Treats for the visitor include a rose garden, box hedging and mixed herbaceous borders created for scent colour and interest. A fusion of old favourites and modern must-haves. The gardens reflect an interest in organic methods and wildlife gardening. Gravel paths, but wheelchair access to all but Hazeldene.

♿ ✖ ❀ ☕

24 EMMANUEL COLLEGE GARDEN & FELLOWS' GARDEN

St Andrews Street, Cambridge CB2 3AP. *Car parks at Parker's Piece & Lion Yard, within 5 mins walk.* **Adm £3.50, chd free.** Sun 28 June (2-5).
One of the most beautiful gardens in Cambridge. Buildings of C17 to C20 surrounding 3 large gardens with pools, herb garden, herbaceous borders, fine trees incl dawn redwood. Access allowed to Fellows' Garden (NGS day only) with magnificent oriental plane and more herbaceous borders. Gravel paths.

♿ ✖ ❀

Bold and exotic building to a climax in the late summer . . .

25 FIRST COTTAGE

Hollow Road, Ramsey Forty Foot PE26 2YA. Mr & Mrs R Fort, 01487 813973. *3m N of Ramsey. From Ramsey (B1096) travel through Ramsey Forty Foot, just before bridge over drain, turn R, First Cottage 300yds on R, next door to The Elms.* **Open wih Ramsey Forty Foot Gardens** Sun 28 (2-6). **Visitors also welcome by appt** June & July only, coached permitted.
150ft x 40ft garden with herbaceous borders, shrub beds; natural pond. Miniature steam railway.

♿ ☎

26 FLORENCE HOUSE

Back Road, Fridaybridge, Wisbech PE14 0HU. Mr & Mrs A Stevenson, 01945 860268. *3½ m S of Wisbech. On B1101. In Fridaybridge centre turn R in front of Chequers PH on to Back Rd.* Home-made teas. **Adm £2.50, chd free.** Suns 24 May; 16 Aug (12-4). **Visitors also welcome by appt.**
Large sweeping borders in this 30yr-old 1-acre garden, growing a modern mix of trees, shrubs, perennials and grasses in C21 style. The ½ acre paddock borders planted in 2000, start bold and exotic building to a climax in the late summer. Shrubs and trees with spring bulbs and plants, winter flowering perennials shrubs and climbers. Vegetable and fruit garden. Over 30 different verities of roses. ½ m walk through grass fields surrounded by native hedging and areas that incl mulberry, medlar, walnut and greengages, also ponies and chickens. Some gravel areas.

♿ ✖ ❀ ☕ ☎ ✖

27 39 FOSTER ROAD
Campaign Avenue, Sugar Way, Woodston PE2 9RS. Robert Marshall & Richard Handscombe, 01733 555978, robfmarshall@btinternet.com. *1m SW of Peterborough City Centre. From Oundle Rd turn N into Sugar Way at T-lights, L at 2nd r'about onto Campaign Ave, R at next r'about still on Campaign Ave, 2nd R at Foster Rd. Continue to very end of rd. Entrance via rear gate in green fence.* **Adm £3 incl tea & biscuits. Visitors welcome by appt Feb to Nov.**
Plant enthusiasts' garden within typical, small, new estate plot. Informal and formal areas incl: mixed herbaceous border, woodland and shade, vestibule garden, exotic and ferns, kitchen garden, espaliered fruit trees, pergola, patio, pond, containers and octagonal greenhouse. Unusual snowdrops, over 100 hostas plus daphnes, acers and other choice plants. Featured in 'Secret Gardens'. Limited wheelchair access.

GREAT THURLOW HALL
Haverhill. See Suffolk.

28 GREYSTONES
Swaynes Lane, Comberton CB23 7EF. Alison & Lyndon Davies, 01223 262686, lyndon.alison@tiscali.co.uk. *5m SW of Cambridge. 2m from M11 J12, via Barton on B1046.* **Adm £3, chd free. Visitors welcome by appt and groups.**
Artistically designed plantswoman's garden of $\frac{1}{2}$ acre. Borders developed according to microclimate providing colour and interest throughout the yr. Peonies and salvias are particular interest. Productive summer potager beyond rose trellis.

29 ISLAND HALL
Godmanchester PE29 2BA. Mr Christopher & Lady Linda Vane Percy. *1m S of Huntingdon (A1). 15m NW of Cambridge (A14). In centre of Godmanchester next to free car park.* Home-made teas. **Adm £3, chd free. Sun 24 May (11-5).**
3-acre grounds. Mid C18 mansion (not open). Tranquil riverside setting with mature trees. Chinese bridge over Saxon mill race to an embowered island with wild flowers. Garden restored in 1983 to mid C18 formal design, with box hedging, clipped

hornbeams, parterres, topiary and good vistas over borrowed landscape, punctuated with C18 wrought iron and stone urns. Gravel paths.

30 NEW KENILWORTH SMALLHOLDING
West Drove North, Walton Highway PE14 7DP. John & Marilyn Clarke, 01945 428029, john.clarke@mcp-law.co.uk. *6m E of Wisbech. Off A47 through Walton Highway, at E end of village turn N towards Walpole St Peter, on 2nd sharp bend turn R into Farm Lane.* **Adm £3, chd free, concessions £1.50. Day & Evening Openings Suns 24 May; 21 June (11-8).**
Varied country garden set around 100yr-old Bramleys. Beds, large ponds, herb container gardens working smallholding with goats and sheep. Trees lined path past paddocks to secluded mixed desert apple orchard and copse. Teas served in outbuilding housing an exhibition of the development of the smallholding and archaeology. Trail walk to desert apple orchard. Display of 40yrs history.

31 KING'S COLLEGE FELLOWS' GARDEN
Queens Road, Cambridge CB2 1ST. Provost & Scholars of King's College. *In Cambridge, the Backs. Entry by gate at junction of Queens Rd & West Rd. Parking at Lion Yard 10mins walk, or some pay & display places in West Rd.* Cream teas. **Adm £3, chd free. Sun 5 July (2-6).**
Fine example of a Victorian garden with rare specimen trees.

32 KIRTLING TOWER
Newmarket Road, Kirtling, nr Newmarket CB8 9PA. The Lord & Lady Fairhaven. *6m SE of Newmarket. From Newmarket head towards Saxon Street village, through village to Kirtling, turn L at war memorial, entrance is signed on L.* Light refreshments & cream teas. **Adm £4, chd free (share to All Saints Church, Kirtling). Suns 29 Mar; 5 Apr (11-4).**
Kirtling Tower is surrounded on 3 sides by a moat. The garden of 5 acres was started by the present owners 7yrs

ago. Main features are the spring garden, secret, walled and cutting gardens. Original Tudor walk. The spring garden is planted with 70,000 bulbs - daffodils, narcissus and camassias in memory of The Hon Rupert Broughton (1970-2000). Recently 30,000 bulbs of muscari and chionodoxa planted along the 150m church walk. Photographic cards for sale. Enjoy organ music in the church. Featured in 'The English Garden', also on local tv and radio.

33 LECKHAMPTON
37 Grange Road, Cambridge CB2 1RH. Corpus Christi College. *Runs N to S between Madingley Rd (A1303) & A603. Drive entrance opp Selwyn College. No parking available on site.* Home-made teas. **Adm £4, chd free. Sun 5 Apr (2-6).**
10 acres comprising formal lawns and extensive wild gardens, featuring walkways and tree-lined avenues, fine specimen trees under-planted with spring bulbs, cowslips, anemones, fritillaries and a large area of lupins. Gravel and grass paths.

Trail walk to desert apple orchard . . .

Group opening

34 LODE GARDENS
CB25 9ER. *10m NE of Cambridge. Take B1102 from Stow-cum-Quy r'about, NE of Cambridge at junction with A14, Lode is 2m from r'about.* Teas at 21 Lode Road. **Combined adm £4, chd free. Suns 10 May; 7 June; 5, 12 July (11-5).**

CARPENTERS END
Mr & Mrs Paul Webb, 01223 812812646. Visitors also welcome by appt.

21 LODE ROAD
CB25 9ER. Mr Richard P Ayres, 01223 811873. Visitors also welcome by appt.

THE OLD VICARAGE
Mr & Mrs Hunter

WILD ROSE COTTAGE
Church Walk. Joy Martin. Not open Suns 7 June; 7, 14 July.

Four varied gardens set in a picturesque village to the E of Anglesey Abbey Garden. Two cottage gardens, **WILD ROSE COTTAGE** is overflowing with roses and clematis, set against a vegetable garden edged with lavender and sage and a wild flower spiral. **21 LODE ROAD** is planted with bold groups of herbaceous plants creating an element of mystery and delight. These contrast with two recently developed gardens. **CARPENTERS END** ¾ -acre recently developed garden. Shrubs, trees with fine lawn, next to church yard. **THE OLD VICARAGE** is a formal garden with an intricate design formed from box, yew and pleached lime.

35 NEW LUCY CAVENDISH COLLEGE
Lady Margaret Road, Cambridge CB3 0BU. *1m NW of Gt St Mary. College situated on corner of Lady Margaret Rd & Madingley Rd (A1303). Entrance off Lady Margaret Rd.* **Adm £3, chd free (share to Red Cross). Wed 8 July (2-5).**
The gardens of 4 late Victorian houses have been combined and developed over past 25yrs into an informal 3 acre garden. Fine mature trees shade densely planted borders. An Anglo Saxon herb garden is situated in one corner. The garden is maintained using organic methods and provides a rich wildlife habitat.

36 MADINGLEY HALL
nr Cambridge CB23 8AQ. University of Cambridge, www.cont-ed.cam.ac.uk. *4m W of Cambridge. 1m from M11 J13.* Cream teas. **Adm £3, chd free (share to Madingley Church Restoration Fund). Sun 14 June (2.30-5.30).**
C16 Hall (not open) set in 8 acres of attractive grounds. Features incl landscaped walled garden with hazel walk, alpine bed, medicinal border and rose pergola. Meadow, topiary, mature trees and wide variety of hardy plants. St Mary Magdalene Church open.

37 NEW MANNA ASH HOUSE
Common Road, Weston Coalville CB21 5NR. Will & EugĒnie Woodouse, 01223 290029, will @naturalswimmingpools.com, www.naturalswimmingpools. com. *12m E of Cambridge. 1m E of Weston Colville Village. Between Carlton & West Wickham.* Light refreshments & home-made teas. **Adm £2.50, chd free. Suns 31 May; 30 Aug (10-6). Visitors also welcome by appt.**
1¼ acre long garden with fine views over natural swimming pool and aquatic garden with exotic lilies and irises. Lush planting incl very tall grasses, wild flowers and willow varieties. Hot, dry, flint wall garden and walk with fragrant plants and open raised terrace with wild flower banks and open views over undulating Cambridgeshire countryside. Display of other gardens with natural swimming pools.

Open raised terrace with wild flower banks and open views over undulating Cambridgeshire countryside . . .

38 ◆ THE MANOR
Hemingford Grey PE28 9BN. Mrs D S Boston, 01480 463134, www.greenknowe.co.uk. *4m E of Huntingdon. Off A14. Entrance to garden by small gate off river towpath. No parking at house except for disabled by arrangement with owner. Park in village.* **Adm £3, chd free. Open daily throughout the yr 11-5 (dusk in winter).**
Garden designed and planted by author Lucy Boston, surrounds C12 manor house on which Green Knowe books were based (house open only by appt). 4 acres with topiary; over 200 old roses, bearded iris collection and large herbaceous borders with mainly scented plants. Enclosed by river, moat and wilderness. Gravel paths, but wheelchairs permitted on lawns.

39 NEW 38 MARTINSBRIDGE
Parnwell, Peterborough PE1 4YB. Maurice & Lynne Holmes, 01733 766721, maurice53@hotmail.co.uk. *Parnwell Estate, exit Frank Perkins Parkway at Oxney Rd. From Parnwell Way take 1st exit into Saltersgate then into Martinsbridge.* **Adm £2, chd free. Visitors welcome by appt May & June.**
Plant enthusiasts small town garden, planted on 3 sides for all-yr round interest. Trees, shrubs, wisteria, acers, climbing roses, clematis, bamboos and perennials. Incl water features, walled shady area, gravel and slate beds, mirrors, summerhouse, stepping stones, orfe and gold fish pond with statue. Gold Winner Award - Parnwell in Bloom. Gate threshold, owner will assist.

40 MILL HOUSE
22 Fen Road, North End, Bassingbourn SG8 5PQ. Mr & Mrs A Jackson, 01763 243491, millhouseval@btinternet.com. *2m N of Royston. On the NW outskirts of Bassingbourn. 1m from Church, on the rd to Shingay. Take North End at the war memorial in the centre of Bassingbourn which is just W of the A1198 (do not take Mill Lane).* **Adm £3.50, chd free. Visitors welcome by appt May to Sept, groups welcome.**
Garden created over many years by retired garden designer owners and divided up into interesting enclosures, providing unusual formal and informal settings for many rare trees, shrubs, herbaceous plants, clematis and topiary whiich provide yr round interest. Wonderful elevated view over countryside and garden. New winter garden with snowdrop collection. Featured in FT.

41 NEW **MURRAY EDWARDS COLLEGE (FORMALLY NEW HALL)**
Storey's Way, Cambridge CB3 0DF,
www.newhall.cam.ac.uk/grounds/gardens. *Storey's Way, off Madingley Rd & Huntingdon Rd.* Adm £4, chd free (share to Perennial). Sat 18 July (2-5).
The 1965 Grade 11 listed college buildings provide a dramatic setting for our colourful planting of perennials and annuals. Features incl student potager and orchard. Art Collection (adm free). New Hall Art Collection.

 ♿ 🐾 ✿ ☕

42 **88 NENE PARADE**
March PE15 8TA. Doreen & Neville Patrick, 01354 657796. *8m S of Wisbech. From town centre take Creek Rd, past Sainsburys, after ½ m turn R into Wigstoner Rd, then L at end into Nene Parade.* Adm £2.50, chd free. Sat 8, Sun 9 Aug (10-5). Combined with **35a Westwood Ave.** Visitors also welcome by appt during Aug, groups 10 or less.
Large garden approx 20yds x 40yds, mainly with hardy fuchsia over 100 planted around the beds and borders, with a mixture of lawn, flowers and shrubs. Featured in 'Garden News'. Winner - March Gardens in Bloom.

🐾 ☕ ☎

Round a corner there is a playhouse, golf practice net and 'flowery mead' . . .

43 **NETHERHALL MANOR**
Tanners Lane, Soham CB7 5AB. Timothy Clark Esq, 01353 720269. *6m Ely, 6m Newmarket. Enter Soham from Newmarket, Tanners Lane is 2nd R 100yds after cemetery. Enter Soham from Ely, Tanners Lane is 2nd L after War Memorial.* Home-made teas. Adm £2, chd free. Suns 29 Mar; 3 May; 2, 9 Aug (2-5). Visitors also welcome by appt.
'An elegant garden touched with antiquity' Good Gardens Guide. This is an unusual garden which will appeal to those with an historical interest in the individual collections of genera and plant groups: March - Old primroses, daffodils and Victorian double flowered hyacinths. May - Old English tulips. Aug - Victorian pelargonium, heliotrope, calceolaria and dahlias.

 ♿ 🐾 ☕ ☎

44 **THE OLD HOUSE**
2 Home End, Fulbourn CB21 5BS. Mr & Mrs Charles Comins, 01223 882907, comins@ntufton.co.uk. *4m SE of Cambridge. Opp Townley Village Hall, next to recreation ground, Home End.* Home-made teas. Adm £3.50, chd free (share to Magpas). Suns 7 June; 12 July (12-5). Visitors also welcome by appt for groups.
²/₃ -acre garden surrounded by high flint walls, mature trees, large formal pond with many fish, plants and centre fountain. Well stocked borders with bulbs, herbaceous plants, roses and shrubs with central lawn. Rockery with dwarf conifers. Close to centre of village and Fulbourn Nature Reserve.

 ♿ 🐾 ✿ ☕ ☎

45 NEW **THE PADDOCK**
43 Lower End, Swaffham Prior CB25 0HT. Mike & Judi Churcher. *10m E of Cambridge. Off B1102, 1m on L opp turning to Roger Rd.* Adm £3, chd free. Sat 20 June (2-6). Also open **Shadworth House.**
½ acre garden designed for yr round interest and an outdoor life style. Gravel paths lead though trees, shrubs and perennials linking seating areas, a reflecting pool and putting green. Round a corner there is a playhouse, golf practice net and 'flowery mead', where paths meander through grasses and perennials.

🐾

46 ◆ **PECKOVER HOUSE**
North Brink, Wisbech PE13 1JR. National Trust, 01945 583463, www.nationaltrust.org.uk. *Centre of Wisbech on N banks of R Nene. Within easy walking distance of town bus stn. Nearest car park in Chapel Rd - no parking on property. Disabled blue badge parking outside property.* House and Garden £5.80, chd £2.90, garden only £3.70, chd £1.85. Sats to Weds 14 Mar to 1 Nov. For NGS: Sat 18 July (12-5).
Said to be one of the best examples of a Victorian town house garden, Peckover is a 2-acre site offering many areas of interest. These incl herbaceous borders, bedding, roses, trees, ponds, lawns cut flower border, ferns, summerhouses and orangery with 3 very old fruiting orange trees and colourful display of pot plants throughout the season. Display and information about the NGS Careership scheme, and on-hand advice about the training scheme from our current careership student. Gravel paths.

 ♿ 🐾 ✿ ☕

Group opening

47 **RAMSEY FORTY FOOT**
nr Ramsey PE26 2YA. *3m N of Ramsey. From Ramsey (B1096) travel through Ramsey Forty Foot, just before bridge over drain, turn R, First Cottage 300yds on R, next door to The Elms.* Home-made teas at First Cottage & The Willows. Combined adm £3, chd free. Sun 28 June (2-6).

> **THE ELMS**
> Mr R Shotbolt. Visitors also welcome by appt.
> (See separate entry).

> **FIRST COTTAGE**
> Mr & Mrs Fort. Visitors also welcome by appt.
> (See separate entry).

> **THE WILLOWS**
> Jane & Andrew Sills. *Turn L down private rd opp George PH. Park in Hollow Rd*

Three interesting and contrasting gardens in the village of Ramsey Forty Foot. **THE WILLOWS** is a cottage garden with riverside location filled with old roses, herbaceous beds; shrubs, ferns; pond and a vegetable garden. See separate entries for **THE ELMS** and **FIRST COTTAGE**.

 ♿ ✿ ☕

48 **RECTORY FARM HOUSE**
Orwell SG8 5RB. Mr & Mrs Pinnington. *8m W of Cambridge. On & N of A603, towards Wimpole from Cambridge.* Home-made teas. Adm £3, chd free. Sat 6, Sun 7 June (2-5).
2-acre garden on exposed site developed from a field in 1998. Enclosed spaces filled with roses, lavender and herbaceous plants, surrounded by box and hornbeam hedges. Garden designed and planted by Peter Reynolds. Some gravel paths.

 ♿ 🐾 ☕

49 ◆ **ROBINSON COLLEGE**
Grange Road, Cambridge CB3 9AN,
01223 339100,
www.robinson.cam.ac.uk. *Grange
Rd runs N to S between Madingley Rd
(A1303) & Barton Rd (A603). Turn S on
Madingley Rd down Grange Rd, on R.
N from Barton Rd on L, opp University
Library. Park on st, (parking may be
limited). Please report to the Porters
Lodge on arrival.* **Adm £2.50, chd
free. Open June to late April for
NGS, please tel or see website for
details.**
10 original Edwardian gardens are
linked to central wild woodland water
garden focusing on Bin Brook with
small lake at heart of site. This gives a
feeling of park and informal woodland,
while at the same time keeping the
sense of older more formal gardens
beyond. Central area has a wide lawn
running down to the pond, framed by
many mature stately trees with much
of the original planting intact. More
recent planting incl herbaceous
borders and commemorative trees. No
picnics. Children must be
accompanied at all times. Wheelchair
access to most areas.
&. ✗

Model engines
on show . . .

50 **ROSEWELL HOUSE**
60 Prickwillow Road, Ely CB7 4TX.
Mr & Mrs A Bullivant, 01353 667355,
pam.bullivant@talk21.com. *From
A10 south, follow signs for Ely centre.
Turn L at traffic lights at Lamb Hotel,
then R at next traffic lights. Continue
straight on for 1m to mini r'about.
Straight across for 100m. Turn R into
'Environment Agency' road before
bends. Garden on R after 20m.*
**Open with Ely Gardens Sun 31 May
(2-6). Visitors also welcome by appt
in June. Ample parking, coaches
permitted.**
Herbaceous borders with old roses
and shrubs. Pond and kitchen garden.
Secluded 'sitting areas'. Splendid
views of Ely cathedral and surrounding
fenland. Meadow being developed to
encourage wildlife and wild flowers,
with area of cornfield planting.
Wheelchair access through sidegate.
&. ✗ ⊗ ☎

Group opening

51 **SAWSTON GARDENS**
CB22 3LA. *5m SE of Cambridge. 3m
from M11 J10. A505 follow signs to
Sawston.* Cream teas at 54 High St.
**Combined adm £4, chd free. Sun 5
July (1-6).**

1A CHURCH LANE
Mr & Mrs M Carpenter

30 CHURCHFIELD AVENUE
Mr & Mrs I Butler

DRIFT HOUSE
19a Babraham Road. Mr & Mrs
A Osborne

54 HIGH STREET
Richard & Marilyn Maunder

35 MILL LANE
Doreen Butler.

NEW THE ORCHARDS
11 Mill Lane. Tim & Rosie
Phillips.

30 QUEENSWAY
John & Tessa Capes

VINE COTTAGE
Hammonds Road. Dr & Mrs T
Wreghitt

Eight gardens set within a village with
ancient and listed building and
modern, architect designed house.
Imaginative use of features including
water, lawns and decking covered by a
grapevined pergola. Ponds, waterfalls
and mirrors are used to great effect.
Seating spaces next to a kitchen
garden, vegetable cages, herb beds
and chickens contrast with a
contemporary Japanese courtyard.
Planting includes roses and 50
varieties of hardy geranium, mixed with
hardy fuchsias and shrubs. One
garden has adopted a no watering
policy for the last 3yrs. Wheelchair
access to 5 gardens.
☕

---

52 **4 SELWYN GARDENS**
Cambridge CB3 9AX. Mr & Mrs A
Swarbrick, 01223 360797,
louiseswarbrick@yahoo.co.uk.
*Grange Rd runs N to S between
Madingley Rd (A1303) & Barton Rd
(A603).* Light refreshments & teas.
**Adm £3.50, chd free. Sat 6, Sun
7 June (2-5).**
Family garden. Walled so no vista.
Attempted to create space and interest
through dense planting and areas
within the garden itself. Lots of
traditional cottage plants with a splash
of exotic colour to catch the eye.
✗ ☕

53 **NEW** SHADWORTH
HOUSE
45 High Street, Swaffham Prior
CB25 0LD. Mr John Norris,
01638 741465,
john.norris@onetel.com. *10m E
of Cambridge. off B1102. Park at
village hall.* **Adm £3, chd free.
Sats 16 May; 20 June (10-6).
Also open The Paddock
20 June. Visitors also welcome
by appt.**
Hillside chalk garden 0.8 acre,
several terraces, access by steps
(39), fish pond and natural
waterfall. Garden mostly trees,
shrubs and bulbs in season. Site
adjacent to 2 medieval churches in
centre of the village. (Model
engines on show).
☎

54 **SOUTH FARM & BROOK
COTTAGE**
Shingay-cum-Wendy, Royston
SG8 0HR. Philip Paxman, 01223
207581, philip@south-farm.co.uk,
www.south-farm.co.uk. *12m W of
Cambridge. Off A603. 5m N of
Royston off A1198, L turn.* **Combined
adm £3, chd free. Visitors welcome
by appt Apr to Sept incl Tues/Weds
day or evening, groups of 10+.
Refreshments or 2 course meal
available.**
Garden established over 30yrs on
farmland site. 8 acres ring fenced by
hardwood planting. Eco-garden with
reed bed, wild flowers, ponds.
Extensive vegetable garden. Restored
listed barnyard (open). Also Private
Nature Reserve with lake, otters,
beautiful dragon flies and native
crayfish, wild flowers. Neighbouring
Brook Cottage (Mr & Mrs Charvile)
Countryman's cottage garden.
Abundant yr-long mixed colour, spilling
over boundary stream, intermixed with
traditional vegetables and poultry.
&. ✗ ⊨ ☎

Group opening

55 **STAPLEFORD GARDENS**
CB22 5DG. Light refreshments &
home-made teas at 59-61 London
Road. **Combined adm £4, chd free
(share to East Anglia Childrens
Hospice). Sun 7 June (2-6).**

59 - 61 LONDON ROAD
Dr & Mrs S Jones.

57 LONDON ROAD
Mrs M Spriggs.

5 PRIAMS WAY
Mr Anthony Smith.

THE STONE HOUSE
40 Mingle Lane. Sir James &
Lady Mirrlees.

NEW WILLOW END
Bar Close. Mr & Mrs Peter
Tilbury-Davis.

Contrasting gardens showing a range
of size, planting and atmosphere in this
village just S of Cambridge. The
LONDON ROAD gardens and
PRIAMS WAY form an interlocking
series of garden rooms including
herbaceous beds, kitchen garden,
alpine, pit and summer houses with
sculptures set around. **THE STONE
HOUSE** and **WILLOW END** show
trees, lawns and shrubs and a variety
of shade loving plants.

Free range chickens and ducks including rare breeds . . .

Group opening

**56 NEW SWAVESEY & OVER
GARDENS**
CB24 4TR. *Off A14, W of
Cambridge. 2m beyond Barthill.*
Home-made teas at Scyamore
Farm, Over. **Combined adm £4,
chd free.** Sun 21 June (12-5).

5 MOAT WAY
Swavesey. Mr & Mrs N Kybird.

NEW SYCAMORE FARM
Dr & Mrs R Hook. Visitors also
welcome by appt.
(See separate entry).

Two contrasting gardens showing
great flair in design and planting,
one with patio area, and one with
old fashioned rose garden.
5 MOAT WAY Colourful garden
filled with collection of trees, shrubs
and perennials. Large patio area
displaying many specimen foliage
plants in planters, incl pines,
hostas and acers. **SYCAMORE
FARM** for wildlife pond with rill, and
short woodland walk.

57 SYCAMORE FARM
New Road, Over CB24 5PJ. Dr &
Mrs R Hook, 01954 231371,
rob@sycamorefarm.org. *4m E of
A14. Disabled parking on-site, park on
New Rd.* Visitors also welcome by
appt **for groups of 10+.**
2-acre garden incl dry garden, lily
pond, herbaceous border, old
fashioned rose garden, white border,
wildlife pond with rill, and short
woodland walk.

**58 TRINITY COLLEGE,
FELLOWS' GARDEN**
Queen's Road, Cambridge
CB2 1TQ. Trinity College. *City centre.*
Adm £3.50, chd free. Sun 12 Apr
(2-5).
Garden of 8 acres, originally laid out in
the 1870s by W B Thomas. Lawns
with mixed borders, shrubs and
specimen trees. Drifts of spring bulbs.
Recent extension of landscaped area
among new college buildings to W of
main garden. Gravel paths.

59 NEW TRINITY HALL
Trinity Lane. CB2 1TJ. The
Masters & Fellows. *City Centre.
From Trinity St in city centre, Trinity
Hall is located beween Senate
House Passage & Garret Hostel
Lane.* Home-made teas. **Adm
£3.50, chd free (share to Breast
Cancer Care).** Sun 16 Aug
(11.30-3.30).
First ever opening for the historic
heart of Trinity Hill. A beautiful
series of courts and gardens incl
herbaceous, mixed borders and
recently developed fellows garden
set amongst fine buildings dating
back to the C14. Some gravel
paths.

60 TRINITY HALL - WYCHFIELD
Storeys Way, Cambridge CB3 0DZ.
The Master & Fellows,
www.trinhall.cam.ac.uk. *1m NW of
city centre. Turn into Storeys Way from
Madingley Rd (A1303).* Home-made
teas. **Adm £3.50, chd free (share to
Alzheimers Society).** Suns 5 Apr;
5 July (11.30-3.30).
A contrasting mixture and range of
garden areas within the grounds of the
Edwardian Wychfield House, now also
containing sports facilities and newly
built accommodation. The gardens
contain established lawns, majestic

trees, beautiful beds and newly planted
borders all filled with a wide range of
plants. Some gravel paths.

61 NEW TY GWYN
6 The Borough, Aldreth
CB6 3PJ. Si,n & Mark Hugo,
01353 740586, mark@artes-
mundi.co.uk, www.artes-
mundi.co.uk/garden. *7m SW of
Ely. 2m S of Haddenham. The
Borough is 2nd on L after Aldreth
Village.* Home-made teas. **Adm £3,
chd free.** Sats, Suns 16, 17 May;
13, 14 June; 11, 12 July; 15, 16
Aug; 5, 6 Sept (10-5). **Visitors
also welcome by appt.**
1 acre country garden in small
fenland hamlet. Grass path walks
around mature trees, shrubs,
perennials and climbers. Wild
flower garden, cactus greenhouse.
Vegetable patch, orchard,
fishpond. Free range chickens and
ducks incl rare breeds. Fair Trade
gift shop onsite. Perhaps a walk in
the fens to the river afterwards.
Small gravel section at entrance
which can be covered.

62 UPWATER LODGE
23 Chaucer Road, Cambridge
CB2 7EB. Mr & Mrs G Pearson,
01223 361378, jmp@pearson.co.uk.
*1m S of Cambridge. Off Trumpington
Rd (A1309), nr Brooklands Ave
junction. Parking available at MRC
Psychology Dept on Chaucer Rd.*
Home-made teas. **Adm £5, chd free.**
Sun 3, Mon 4 May (2-5). **Combined
with 16 Chaucer Rd. Visitors also
welcome by appt.**
2 gardens - 1st, 6 acres with mature
trees, fine lawns, old wisterias, and
colourful borders. A new addition for
2009 is a potager. A network of paths
through bluebell wood leading down to
water meadows by the R Cam and
small flock of rare breed sheep. 2nd,
adjoining (from same family) has rose
and wisteria covered pergolas,
colourful borders and plentiful bulbs.
Waterproof footwear advised. Some
stalls, possibly lambs. Some gravel
paths, small incline.

63 WEAVER'S COTTAGE
35 Streetly End, West Wickham,
Cambridge CB21 4RP. Miss Sylvia
Norton, 01223 892399. *8m NW of
Haverhill. On A1307 between Linton &
Haverhill turn N at Horseheath towards
W Wickham. Weaver's Cottage is 10th*

on R after 40 sign. **Adm £2.50, chd free.** Visitors welcome by appt anytime, any numbers - incl coaches. $^1/_2$ -acre garden exuberantly planted for fragrance with spring bulbs; shrubs; herbaceous; climbers; old roses. Scree garden. NCCPG National Collection of *Lathyrus.*

✕ NCCPG ☎

Group opening

64 WHITTLESFORD GARDENS
CB22 4NR. *7m S of Cambridge. 1m NE of J10 M11 & A505. Parking nr church, additional parking will be signed.* Home-made teas in Parish Church. **Combined adm £3.50, chd free. Sun 21 June (2-6).**

43 THE LAWN
Mr & Mrs R Redman

NEW 19 CHURCH CLOSE
Mr & Mrs V Massey

THE GUILDHALL
Professors P & M Spufford

NEW MARKINGS FARM
32 West End. Mr & Mrs A Jennings.

4 MIDDLEMOOR ROAD
Mr & Mrs A Osborne

23 NEWTON ROAD
Mr F Winter

14 NORTH ROAD
Mr & Mrs R Adderley

5 PARSONAGE COURT
Mrs L Button.

RAYNERS FARM
North Road. Mr & Mrs C Morton

RYECROFT
1 Middlemoor Road. Mr & Mrs P A Goodman

11 SCOTTS GARDENS
Mr & Mrs M Walker

There is a sense of going back to older, gentler times with this collection of formal and country gardens. Features

include a not garden, streams ponds and waterfalls and even an allotment consisting of vegetables, fruit, flowers and bird aviary. Informal mixed planting of herbaceous plants and vegetables contrasts with medieval-style herb beds in a C15 walled garden. Planting covers everything from trees and shrubs to herbaceous borders and shade loving plants. WCs available in church and Social Club in High St.

✖ ❀ ☕

65 ◆ WILLOW HOLT
Willow Hall Lane, Thorney PE6 0QN. Angie & Jonathan Jones, 01733 222367, janda.salix@virgin.net. *4m E of Peterborough. From A47, between Eye & Thorney turn S into Willow Hall Lane. 2m on R. NOT in Thorney Village.* Teas. **Adm £3, chd free. Suns 29 Mar; 26 Apr; 31 May (11-5); Wed 17 June (2-dusk); Suns 26 July; 30 Aug; 27 Sept (11-5); Sun 25 Oct (10-4). Visitors also welcome by appt.** Barren field and rubbish strewn hollow have been transformed over sixteen years into 2 acres of plants and wildlife. Dragonflies share ponds with newt and water vole. Bees and butterflies bask in the flower meadow and scrap steel structures dance or lurk beside meandering woodland pathways. A place of peaceful contemplation. In June watch the bats come out at dusk.

✕ ❀ ☕ ☎

66 ◆ WIMPOLE HALL
Arrington SG8 0BW. The National Trust, 01223 206000, www.wimpole.org. *7m N of Royston (A1198). 8m SW of Cambridge (A603). J12 off M11, 30 mins from A1(M).* **House & garden £8.80, chd £4.95, garden only £3.70, chd £1.95. For NGS: Sun 19 July (10.30-4.30).** Part of 350-acre park. Restored Dutch garden and Victorian parterres on N lawns. Fine trees, marked walks in park. National Collection of walnuts. New herbaceous borders over 100m

long, with mixed plantings of perennials, roses and choice shrubs. Walled vegetable garden. The recreated Sir John Soane glasshouse financed with the help of the National Gardens Scheme. No wheelchair access to House (12 steps).

♿ ✕ ❀ NCCPG ☕

67 NEW THE WINDMILL
Cambridge Road, Impington CB24 9NU. Pippa & Steve Temple, 01223 232284, mill.impington@ntlworld.com. *2$^1/_2$ m N of Cambridge. Off B1049, turn L into Cambridge Rd.* Home-made teas & wine after 6. **Sun 3 May (2-7). Visitors also welcome by appt Apr to Sept.** New owners took over this romantic wilderness of 1$^1/_2$ acres surrounding windmill. Stocked with thousands of bulbs, seasonal beds, pergolas, bog gardens, grass bed and herb bank. Secret paths and wild areas maintain the romance but still much to be done. Tour of Windmill. No wheelchair access on secret paths.

♿ ☕ ☎

68 WYTCHWOOD
7 Owl End, Great Stukeley PE28 4AQ. Mr David Cox, 01480 454835. *2m N of Huntingdon. On B1043. Parking at village hall, Owl End.* Home-made teas. **Adm £3.50, chd free. Suns 26 Apr; 28 June (1.30-5.30). Visitors also welcome by appt, May and June only.** 2-acre garden. Brightly planted borders of perennials, annuals and shrubs, lawns and ponds. 1 acre of wild plants, grasses set among rowan, maple and birch trees leading to spinney. Planted with native trees, ferns, hostas and foxgloves. Plenty of seats and shade. Haven for wildlife. Gravel drive. Featured in 'GGG'.

♿ ✕ ❀ ☕ ☎

Cambridgeshire County Volunteers

County Organiser
George Stevenson, 1a The Village, Orton Longueville, Peterborough, Cambridgeshire PE2 7DN, 01733 391506, ChrisGeorge1a@aol.com

County Treasurer
Dr Lyndon Davies, 19 Swaynes Lane, Comberton, Cambridge CB23 7EF, 01223 262686, lyndon.alison@tiscali.co.uk

Assistant County Organisers
Pam Bullivant, Rosewell House, 60 Prickwillow Road, Ely, Cambridgeshire CB7 4TX, 01353 667355, pam.bullivant@talk21.com
Alison Davies, 19 Swaynes Lane, Comberton, Cambridge CB23 7EF, 01223 262686, lyndon.alison@tiscali.co.uk
Angie Jones Willow Holt, Willow Hall Lane, Thorney, Peterborough PE6 0QN, 01733 222367 janda.salix@virgin.net
Patsy Glazebrook, 15 Bentley Road, Cambridge CB2 8AW, 01223 301302, glazebrc@doctors.net.uk

CHESHIRE & WIRRAL

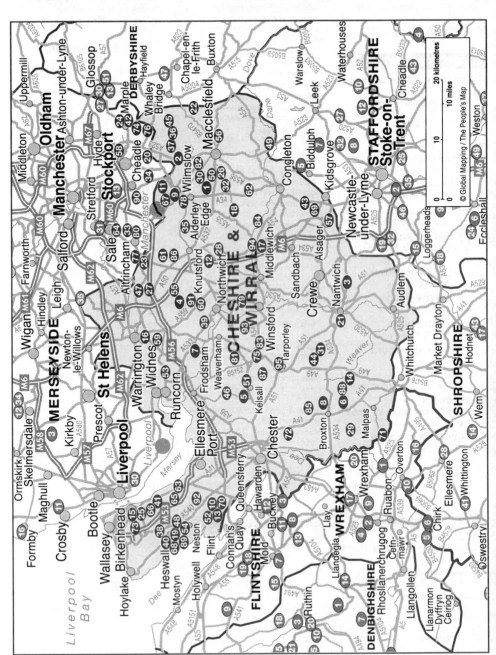

Opening Dates

January

SATURDAY 17
52 Ness Botanic Gardens

April

SUNDAY 5
60 Parm Place

WEDNESDAY 15
14 Cholmondeley Castle Garden

SUNDAY 19
23 Dunham Massey
45 Lyme Park
65 Poulton Hall

SATURDAY 25
6 Bank House
62 Pikelow Farm

SUNDAY 26
6 Bank House
7 Bluebell Cottage Gardens
10 Briarfield
44 Long Acre
84 Swettenham Village
87 Tirley Garth

WEDNESDAY 29
57 Orchard Villa
86 Tatton Park

May

SUNDAY 3
48 Maylands
72 Saighton Grange
89 69 Well Lane

MONDAY 4
48 Maylands
89 69 Well Lane

SUNDAY 10
30 Hare Hill Gardens
47 Mayfield
56 One House Nursery
87 Tirley Garth

SATURDAY 16
9 9 Bourne Street
61 Peover Hall Gardens
64 17 Poplar Grove
74 Sandsend

SUNDAY 17
3 Alma Villa
9 9 Bourne Street
21 Dorfold Hall
32 Henbury Hall
46 Manley Knoll
61 Peover Hall Gardens
64 17 Poplar Grove
68 Riverside Lodge
74 Sandsend
92 Willaston Village Gardens

SATURDAY 23
26 Far Hills
42 Leawood
50 The Mount

SUNDAY 24
26 Far Hills
42 Leawood
50 The Mount
51 Mount Pleasant

MONDAY 25
51 Mount Pleasant

WEDNESDAY 27
22 Dunge Valley Hidden Gardens

SATURDAY 30
35 Hillside

SUNDAY 31
28 Free Green Farm
31 Haughton Hall
35 Hillside

June

FRIDAY 5
77 The School House (Evening)

SATURDAY 6
5 Ashton House
6 Bank House
25 Fairview Cottage (Evening)
53 Norton Priory Museum & Gardens
55 The Old Parsonage
78 68 South Oak Lane
95 Yew Tree House

SUNDAY 7
2 Adlington Hall
5 Ashton House
6 Bank House
34 73 Hill Top Avenue
55 The Old Parsonage
78 68 South Oak Lane
81 Stonyford Cottage
95 Yew Tree House

WEDNESDAY 10
33 35 Heyes Lane
57 Orchard Villa
86 Tatton Park

FRIDAY 12
91 Westage Farm

SATURDAY 13
88 The Valve House
91 Westage Farm

SUNDAY 14
12 Bucklow Farm
15 28 Christchurch Road
29 Grafton Lodge
33 35 Heyes Lane
80 199 Stockport Road
88 The Valve House
90 West Drive Gardens

91 Westage Farm

FRIDAY 19
29 Grafton Lodge (Evening)

SATURDAY 20
1 Acton House
49 Millpool
95 Yew Tree House

SUNDAY 21
1 Acton House
19 29 Dee Park Road
44 Long Acre
49 Millpool
85 Tattenhall Hall
95 Yew Tree House

SUNDAY 28
3 Alma Villa
13 Burton Village Gardens
18 Deans Rough Farm
36 Hillside Cottage
75 Sandymere

July

THURSDAY 2
93 Wood End Cottage (Evening)

SATURDAY 4
38 18 Holmwood Drive
95 Yew Tree House

SUNDAY 5
37 Holmcroft
38 18 Holmwood Drive
95 Yew Tree House

THURSDAY 9
34 73 Hill Top Avenue (Evening)

SATURDAY 11
16 68 Cranborne Avenue
37 Holmcroft

SUNDAY 12
16 68 Cranborne Avenue
24 Edith Terrace Gardens
37 Holmcroft
47 Mayfield
60 Parm Place

FRIDAY 17
85 Tattenhall Hall (Evening)

SATURDAY 18
23 Dunham Massey
43 Little Moreton Hall
67 Quarry Bank House Garden
71 The Rowans
78 68 South Oak Lane

SUNDAY 19
11 Brooke Cottage
40 Inglewood
62 Pikelow Farm
71 The Rowans
78 68 South Oak Lane
93 Wood End Cottage

SATURDAY 25
- 59 Park House

SUNDAY 26
- 20 19 Dorchester Road
- 41 King's Lane Dawson Allotments
- 59 Park House
- 66 59 Princes Boulevard

August

SATURDAY 1
- 4 Arley Hall & Gardens
- 27 Field House
- 76 21 Scafell Close
- 79 Springbank

SUNDAY 2
- 76 21 Scafell Close
- 77 The School House
- 79 Springbank
- 80 199 Stockport Road

THURSDAY 6
- 36 Hillside Cottage (Evening)

FRIDAY 7
- 36 Hillside Cottage (Evening)

SATURDAY 8
- 95 Yew Tree House

SUNDAY 9
- 7 Bluebell Cottage Gardens
- 34 73 Hill Top Avenue
- 54 The Old Farm
- 81 Stonyford Cottage
- 84 Swettenham Village
- 95 Yew Tree House

SUNDAY 16
- 45 Lyme Park
- 63 Plymyard Hall Allotments

WEDNESDAY 19
- 57 Orchard Villa

SATURDAY 22
- 39 2 Hough Cottage
- 83 Sunnyside Farm
- 95 Yew Tree House

SUNDAY 23
- 39 2 Hough Cottage
- 83 Sunnyside Farm
- 95 Yew Tree House

September

SATURDAY 5
- 51 Mount Pleasant
- 58 39 Osborne Street
- 78 68 South Oak Lane

SUNDAY 6
- 51 Mount Pleasant
- 58 39 Osborne Street
- 78 68 South Oak Lane

SATURDAY 19
- 95 Yew Tree House

SUNDAY 20
- 95 Yew Tree House

October

SUNDAY 4
- 23 Dunham Massey

December

SUNDAY 6
- 23 Dunham Massey

January 2010

SATURDAY 16
- 52 Ness Botanic Gardens

February

SUNDAY 7
- 23 Dunham Massey

Gardens open to the public

- 2 Adlington Hall
- 4 Arley Hall & Gardens
- 7 Bluebell Cottage Gardens
- 14 Cholmondeley Castle Garden
- 22 Dunge Valley Hidden Gardens
- 23 Dunham Massey
- 30 Hare Hill Gardens
- 43 Little Moreton Hall
- 45 Lyme Park
- 51 Mount Pleasant
- 52 Ness Botanic Gardens
- 53 Norton Priory Museum & Gardens
- 61 Peover Hall Gardens
- 67 Quarry Bank House Garden
- 69 Rode Hall
- 81 Stonyford Cottage
- 84 The Quinta Arboretum
- 86 Tatton Park

By appointment only

- 8 Bolesworth Castle
- 17 Croco Brook Farm
- 70 Rosewood
- 73 St Davids House
- 82 Summerdown
- 94 Woodcroft

Also open by appointment ☎

- 3 Alma Villa
- 5 Ashton House
- 10 Briarfield
- 11 Brooke Cottage
- 20 19 Dorchester Road
- 26 Far Hills
- 29 Grafton Lodge
- 34 73 Hill Top Avenue
- 37 Holmcroft
- 40 Inglewood
- 44 Long Acre
- 47 Mayfield
- 48 Maylands
- 49 Millpool

- 50 The Mount
- 55 The Old Parsonage
- 57 Orchard Villa
- 59 Park House
- 60 Parm Place
- 64 17 Poplar Grove
- 65 Poulton Hall
- 66 59 Princes Boulevard
- 71 The Rowans
- 72 Saighton Grange
- 78 68 South Oak Lane
- 88 The Valve House
- 89 69 Well Lane
- 91 Westage Farm
- 93 Wood End Cottage

The Gardens

1 NEW ACTON HOUSE
Hocker Lane, Over Alderley
SK10 4SD. Mr & Mrs W Hunter.
*2m SE of Alderley Edge on B5087.
Turn R onto S Slade Lane, at end of lane turn R on to Hocker Lane, garden 150m on R.* Home-made teas. **Adm £3.50, chd free. Sat 20, Sun 21 June (2-5).**
Maturing country garden in 2-acre plot. Series of 'rooms' set around gravel paths, comprising walled garden, lawned areas edged by herbaceous borders, vegetable and cutting garden, orchard, courtyard, pergola, clipped hedges and topiary.
✖ 🐕 ☕

2 ◆ ADLINGTON HALL
Macclesfield SK10 4LF. Mrs Camilla Legh, 01625 829206,
www.adlingtonhall.com. *4m N of Macclesfield. Well signed off A523 at Adlington.* **Adm £5, chd free. Sun & Wed, July & Aug 2-5. For NGS: Sun 7 June (2-5).**
6 acres of formal gardens with herbaceous borders, rose garden, rockeries, yew maze, water garden. Lawns with open views across ha-ha. 32-acre wilderness with mature plantings, various follies incl a 'Temple to Diana'; woodland walk. Yew and ancient lime walks. Flower parterre. Limited wheelchair access.
✖ ❀ 🐕 ☕

Temple to
Diana . . .

❸ ALMA VILLA

73 Main Road, Shavington, Crewe CW2 5DU. Rosemary & Roger Murphy, 01270 567710. *2m E of Nantwich. From J16 M6 take A500 towards Nantwich, at 3rd r'about turn L signed Shavington, L at T-lights into village approx ½ m take 2nd R into Main Rd, garden approx 300yds on R. From Nantwich follow Shavington signs to Elephant PH turn 1st L into Main Rd, garden approx 400yds on L.* Home-made teas. **Adm £3, chd free. Suns 17 May; 28 June (1-5). Visitors also welcome by appt in June, July & Aug.**
Well stocked garden created by plantswoman for yr-round interest. Many varieties of shrubs, perennials and mature fruit trees. Pergolas and arches covered with climbing roses and clematis. An abundance of pots, containers and hanging baskets. Bog garden, water features, lavender hedge and much more. Featured in Amateur Gardening.

 ♿ 🐕 ❀ ☕ ☎

❹ ♦ ARLEY HALL & GARDENS

Northwich CW9 6NA. The Viscount Ashbrook, 01565 777353, www.arleyhallandgardens.com. *4m W of Knutsford. Well signed from M6 J19 & 20, & M56 J9 & 10.* **Adm £5.50, chd £2, concessions £5. Tues to Suns 22 March - 27 Sept; weekends in Oct. For NGS: Sat 1 Aug (11-5).**
One of Britain's finest gardens, Arley has been lovingly created by the same family over 250yrs and is famous for its yew buttressed herbaceous border, avenue of ilex columns, walled garden, pleached lime avenue and Victorian Rootree. A garden of great atmosphere, interest and vitality throughout the seasons. Specialist nursery adjacent.

 ♿ ❀ ☕

❺ ASHTON HOUSE

Church Road, Ashton Hayes CH3 8AB. Mrs M Sheppard, 01829 752761. *7m E of Chester. Off A54, take B5393 to Ashton. 200yds past Golden Lion, R into Nursery car park.* Home-made teas. **Adm £3, chd free. Sat 6, Sun 7 June (2-5). Visitors also welcome by appt evenings in June only for groups of 10+, coaches permitted.**
Country garden with stream, natural pond and interesting trees, incl old monkey puzzle and many other interesting and unusual species of trees and shrubs. Children's garden

with vegetables, herbs, living willow maze and tunnels, woodland area.

 ♿ 🐕 ☕ ☎

❻ BANK HOUSE

Goldford Lane, Bickerton SY14 8LL. Dr & Mrs M A Voisey. *4m NE of Malpas. 11m S of Chester on A41 turn L at Broxton r'about to Nantwich on A534. Take 5th R (1¾ m) to Bickerton. Take 2nd R into Goldford Lane. Bank House is nearly 1m on L. Field parking.* Home-made teas. **Adm £3.50, chd free. Sats, Suns 25, 26 Apr; 6, 7 June (2-5.30).**
1¾ -acre garden at the foot of Bickerton Hill, in area of outstanding beauty, with extensive views to Derbyshire and the Marches. Sheltered, terraced borders stocked with a wide range of shrubs, trees and herbaceous plants; established wild garden, Millennium garden with water features and productive vegetable garden. Unfenced swimming pool and ponds. Gravel paths, and some steep slopes.

 ♿ ❀ ☕

BIDDULPH GRANGE GARDEN

See Staffordshire & part of West Midlands.

❼ ♦ BLUEBELL COTTAGE GARDENS

Lodge Lane, Dutton WA4 4HP. Sue & Dave Beesley, 01928 713718, www.lodgelane.co.uk. *5m W of Northwich. From M56 (J10) take A49 (Whitchurch) turn R at T-lights towards Runcorn. Then 1st turning L.* Home-made teas. **Adm £4, chd free. Wed to Sun Apr to Sept 10-5. For NGS: Suns 26 Apr; 9 Aug (12-5).**
The 1½ -acre garden is on a quiet rural lane in the heart of Cheshire and is packed with thousands of rare and familiar hardy herbaceous perennials, shrubs and trees. Our spring opening coincides with the peak flowering in the bluebell woods, incl in the visit. Unusual plants available at adjacent nursery. Featured on Gardeners World.

 ♿ 🐕 ❀ ☕

❽ BOLESWORTH CASTLE

Tattenhall CH3 9HQ. Mrs Anthony Barbour, 01829 782210, dcb@bolesworth.co.uk. *8m S of Chester on A41. Enter by Lodge.* **Adm £5, chd free. Visitors welcome by appt during May & October, in groups.**
One of the finest collections of rhododendrons, camellias and acers in any private garden in the NW. Set on a

steep hillside accessed by a gently rising woodland walk and overlooking spectacular view of the Cheshire plain. Formal lawn beside castle with well stocked herbaceous borders. Terraces with lawn, rose gardens and many other plants.

 ☎

❾ 9 BOURNE STREET

Wilmslow SK9 5HD. Lucille Sumner & Melanie & Keith Harris, www.wilmslowgarden.co.uk. *¼ m W of central Wilmslow. Take A538 from Wilmslow towards Manchester Airport. Bourne St 2nd on L after fire stn. Or from M56 (J6), take A538 to Wilmslow. Bourne St on R.* Home-made teas. **Adm £3, chd free. Sat 16, Sun 17 May (11-5).**
Roughly 60' x 120'. Started in 1924 on the site of an existing orchard, this mature garden has evolved over 3 generations of one family. It has Victorian and Japanese influences, incl rhododendrons, azaleas and magnificent wisteria. Peaceful secret garden with a surprise around every corner. A delight for children of all ages.

 🐕 ❀ ☕

> # Bog garden, water features, lavender hedge and much more . . .

❿ BRIARFIELD

The Rake, Burton, Neston CH64 5TL. Liz Carter, 0151 336 2304, carter.burton@virgin.net. *9m NW of Chester. Turn off A540 at Willaston-Burton Xrds T-lights & follow rd for 1m to Burton village centre.* Home-made teas on Rake Cottage terrace next door to main garden. **Adm £3.50, chd free (share to Claire House Childrens Hospice). Sun 26 Apr (2-5). Also open with Burton Village Gardens Sun 28 June. Visitors also welcome by appt all year.**
Sheltered S facing sandy slope, home to many specialist plants, some available in plant sale. Colourful shrubs, bulbs, alpines and several water features compete for your attention as you wander through the four distinctly different gardens. Many beds redesigned for this season. Can you find all 7 water features?.

 🐕 ❀ ☕ ☎

⑪ BROOKE COTTAGE
Church Road, Handforth SK9 3LT.
Barry & Melanie Davy, 01625
536511. *1m N of Wilmslow. In the
centre of Handforth Village, behind the
Health Centre and Library. Turn off
Wilmslow Rd next to St Chads Parish
Church and follow Church Rd round to
R. Garden last on L. Ample parking in
Health Centre car park.* Home-made
teas. **Adm £2.50, chd free. Sun 19
July (12-5). Visitors also welcome by
appt May to Aug.**
Small secluded garden separated into
3 areas. Woodland garden redesigned
in 2008. New circular patio and original
water feature amongst tree ferns,
hellebores, astrantias, hydrangeas,
foxgloves and other shade-loving
plants, incl 16 varieties of fern. Main
patio features lush, large leaved plants
- banana, cannas, ligularias, bamboo,
dahlias, hermerocallis and small pond.
Long mixed border and island beds
planted in naturalistic style with
grasses and late flowering perennials.

Water features, herbaceous beds and lawns connected by tunnels, pathways and steps . . .

⑫ BUCKLOW FARM
Pinfold Lane, Plumley WA16 9RP.
Dawn & Peter Freeman. *2m S of
Knutsford. M6 J19, head to Chester
A556. L at 2nd set of T-lights by
Smoker PH. In 1¼ m L at concealed
Xrds, 1st R. From Knutsford A5033, L
at Sudlow Lane. Follow rd, becomes
Pinfold Lane.* Cream teas. **Adm £3.50,
chd free (share to Knutsford
Methodist Church). Sun 14 June
(2-5).**
Country garden with shrubs, perennial
borders, rambling roses, herb garden,
vegetable patch, wildlife pond/water
feature and alpines. Landscaped and
planted over the last 20yrs with
recorded changes. Free range hens.
Wheelchair access, cobbles in the yard
and entrance but reasonably flat in the
garden area.

Group opening

⑬ BURTON VILLAGE GARDENS
Neston CH64 5SJ. *9m NW of
Chester. Turn off A540 at Willaston-
Burton Xrds T-lights & follow rd for 1m
to Burton.* Home-made teas at Burton
Manor. **Combined adm £4, chd free
(share to Claire House Children's
Hospice). Sun 28 June (2-6).**
Gardens in village, signed car parks,
maps given to all visitors. Teas on
Burton Manor terrace, glorious view
across gardens to Cheshire countryside.
Each garden has a unique character.
5min walk through Burton Wood (NT)
between Briarfield and Lynwood.

BRIARFIELD
The Rake, Burton. Liz Carter.
Also open Sun 26 April (2-5).
(See separate entry).

BURTON MANOR
Burton. College Principal, Keith
Chandler
Three geometric gardens on E, S
and N sides of house, essentially
as designed by Thomas Mawson
in 1906, with mature trees, sunken
parterre, yew hedges, formal flower
beds and deep lily ponds.
Delightful setting for afternoon tea
on the terrace.

LYNWOOD
Neston Road. Pauline Wright,
0151 336 2311. Visitors also
welcome by appt from May-Sept.
Plantswoman Pauline Wright has
spent 35yrs designing this
spectacular 2 acre garden
overlooking the Dee estuary. From
the sunken sandstone pond to the
woodland area separated by
clematis-clad trellis, this garden of
differing herbaceous borders will
delight with its colour and variety of
planting.

---

⑭ ◆ CHOLMONDELEY CASTLE GARDEN
Malpas SY14 8AH. The Marchioness
of Cholmondeley, 01829 720383. *4m
NE of Malpas. Off A41 Chester-
Whitchurch rd & A49 Whitchurch-
Tarporley rd.* **Adm £5, chd £2. Weds,
Thurs, Suns & Bank Hols 5 April to
27 Sept; Suns 11, 25 Oct for Autumn
Tints. For NGS: Wed 15 Apr (11-5).**
Romantically landscaped gardens.
Azaleas, rhododendrons, flowering
shrubs, rare trees, herbaceous borders
and water gardens. Lakeside picnic
area, rare breeds of farm animals and
aviary breeds, incl llamas. Private
chapel in the park. Partial wheelchair
access.

⑮ **NEW** 28 CHRISTCHURCH ROAD
Oxton. CH43 5SF. Tom & Ruth
Foster. *1m SW of Birkenhead.
From M53 J3 take A552 to
Birkenhead. Follow rd passing
Sainsbury's cross junction at T-
lights (Halfway House PH). Bar L at
nest T-lights into Woodchurch Rd.
Continue on rd passing school on
R, then take 2nd L into
Bessborough Rd. Christchurch R is
1st L after church. Parking
available courtesy of Christchurch
Church & the Williamson Art
Gallery & Museum in Slatey Rd ñ
3mins walk.* Home-made teas.
**Adm £3.50, chd free. Sun 14
June (2-5.30).**
Grade II listed Victorian Folly with
crenellated towers forms a unique
feature in this ¼ -acre plot. The
garden is on different levels with
gravel areas, 2 water features,
herbaceous beds and lawns
connected by tunnels, pathways
and steps. Planting consists of
trees (many acers) shrubs and
perennials.

CLOUD COTTAGE
See Derbyshire.

⑯ 68 CRANBORNE AVENUE
Warrington WA4 6DE. Mr & Mrs J
Carter. *1m S of Warrington Centre.
From Stockton Heath N on A49 over
swing bridge. L at 2nd set of T-lights
into Gainsborough Rd, 4th L into
Cranborne Ave.* **Adm £2.50, chd free.
Sat 11, Sun 12 July (11-6).**
Hidden away from the passer-by -
A secret place to please the eye. -
Planting so lush, growth so high -
An oasis of calm where time will fly. -
Water and glass for attention vie -
With unusual objects over which to
sigh.

⑰ CROCO BROOK FARM
Selkirk Drive, Holmes Chapel
CW4 7DR. John & Linda Clowes,
01477 532266,
gardens@johnclowes.co.uk. *½ m W
of Holmes Chapel centre. From M6*

J18 take A54 towards Holme Chapel. After Texaco garage turn R A54 Congleton (Chester Rd). After 200yds R into Selkirk Drive, garden entrance 20yds on L. From T-lights in Holmes Chapel village take A54 towards Middlewich, Selkirk Drive 500yds on L. Park along Selkirk Dr. **Visitors welcome by appt.**
2/3 -acre garden developed since 1980 by the garden designer owner. Containing a wide range of trees, shrubs and herbaceous plants arranged to create interest all yr round. The garden encircles the old farm house (not open) providing the opportunity to create areas with different characteristics.

 ♿ ✗ ✿ ☎

⑱ DEANS ROUGH FARM
Lower Withington SK11 9DF. Mr & Mrs Brian Chesworth. *3m S of Chelford. 5m N of Holmes Chapel. A535 nr Jodrell Bank turn into Catchpenny Lane. 1¹/₂ m turn R into no through rd (opp bungalow), 400yds turn L into Deans Rough Farm.* Home-made teas. **Adm £3.50, chd free.** **Sun 28 June (2-6).**
Area of 1¹/₂ acres; informal cottage garden around house. Herbaceous and mixed borders and old roses. Potager; large natural pond with wild flowers. Woodland area with bog garden.

 ♿ ✗ ✿ ☕

⑲ 29 DEE PARK ROAD
Gayton CH60 3RG. E Lewis. *7m S of Birkenhead. From Devon Doorway/ Glegg Arms r'about at Heswall, travel SE in Chester direction on A540 for approx ¹/₄ m. Turn R into Gayton Lane, 5th L into Dee Park Rd. Garden on L after ¹/₄ m.* Home-made teas. **Adm £2.50, chd free.** **Sun 21 June (1-5.30).**
Mature trees and shrubs, climbing roses, clematis, mixed shrub, herbaceous borders and island beds provide yr-round interest. Set around gravel areas with thymes and alpines. A mirror in the secret garden reflects many shade-loving plants. A new attraction is the gated entrance by an arbour leading to a garden room with more climbing roses and clematis. 2 pergolas support climbing roses solanum and clematis. Visitor comment 'I only popped in for 5 mins - I have been here 2 hours'.

 ✗ ✿ ☕

⑳ 19 DORCHESTER ROAD
Hazel Grove SK7 5JR. John & Sandra Shatwell, 0161 440 8574, john.shatwell@firenet.ws. *4m S of Stockport. On A5143 at junction of Dorchester Rd and Jacksons Lane. From Stockport take A6 S for approx 1m, R on A5102 for 2m, L at r'about on A5143. Garden on L after mini-r'about. Parking at shops or school (further up Jacksons Lane).* Home-made teas. **Adm £3, chd free.** **Sun 26 July (1-5).** **Visitors also welcome by appt, groups of 10-20. June (roses) or week preceeding garden opening.**
Suburban garden redesigned and planted in 2003. 150sq yd front garden with David Austin and hybrid tea roses around a central gazebo. 400sq yd back garden with pond and waterfall, pergola, lawn. Colour-themed borders with perennials, annuals and small trees set against a background of beech trees. Featured in the 'Manchester Evening News'.

 ♿ ✗ ✿ ☕ ☎

㉑ DORFOLD HALL
Nantwich CW5 8LD. Mr & Mrs Richard Roundell. *1m W of Nantwich. On A534 between Nantwich & Acton.* Home-made teas. **Adm £5, chd £2.50.** **Sun 17 May (2-5.30).**
18-acre garden surrounding C17 house (not open) with formal approach; lawns and herbaceous borders; spectacular spring woodland garden with rhododendrons, azaleas, magnolias and bulbs.

 ✗ ✿ ☕

Set in rolling Pennine Hills with the sound of curlews in the air, the scent of bluebells in a wooded valley . . .

㉒ NEW ♦ DUNGE VALLEY HIDDEN GARDENS
Dunge Road, Windgather Rocks, Kettleshulme, High Peak SK23 7RF. David & Elizabeth Ketley, 01663 733787, www.dungevalley.co.uk. *6m NW of Macclesfield. 2m SE of the Macclesfield to Whaley Bridge rd. Follow white on brown signs on Macclesfield to Whaley Bridge rd, B570 towards Windgather Rocks. At Xrds take No Through Rd S to signed gateway and over cattle grid.* **Adm £3.50, chd £1.50. For opening details, please tel or see website. For NGS: Wed 27 May (10.30-5).**
Rhododendrons, azaleas and magnolias create a kaleidoscope of colour in a garden changing every yr. Set in rolling Pennine Hills with the sound of curlews in the air, the scent of bluebells in a wooded valley, with streams and waterfalls, the garden is a delight to all who visit.

 ✗ ✿ ☕

㉓ ♦ DUNHAM MASSEY
Altrincham WA14 4SJ. The National Trust, 0161 941 1025, www.nationaltrust.org.uk. *3m SW of Altrincham. Off A56. Well signed.* **House & garden £9, chd £4.50, garden only £6.50, chd £3.25. Daily 28 Feb to 1 Nov 11-5.30, 2 Nov to 26 Feb 11-4 2010. For NGS: Sun 19 Apr; Sat 18 July; Suns 4 Oct (11-5.30); 6 Dec (11-4); 7 Feb 2010.**
Great plantsman's garden. Magnificent trees reflected in moat; richly planted borders vibrant with colour and subtle textures. The Orangery, Mount and Bark House give a sense of the garden's long history. Sweeping lawns, lush borders, shady woodland, a formal parterre set the stage while collections of shade-, moisture- and acid-loving plants such as blue poppies, Chinese lilies and hydrangeas contribute to an ever-changing scene.

 ♿ ✗ ✿ ☕

Group opening

㉔ EDITH TERRACE GARDENS
Compstall, nr Marple SK6 5JF. The Edith Terrace Group. *6m E of Stockport. Take Bredbury junction off M60. Follow Romiley-Marple Bridge sign on B6104. Turn into Compstall at Etherow Country Park sign. Take 1st R, situated at end of Montagu St. Parking*

in village public car parks - short walk to Edith Terrace. Home-made teas. **Adm £4.50, chd free (share to Find a cure for Martha - Kidney Research UK). Sun 12 July (1-5).**
Series of gardens in mixed style from cottage to formal, situated to front and rear of Victorian terrace; described by BBC 'Gardeners' World' magazine as 'a colourful and beautiful living space'. Mixed herbaceous perennials, ornamental backyards and back alleyway. In lakeside setting in the conserved mill village of Compstall, adjacent to Etherow Country Park.

25 FAIRVIEW COTTAGE
15 Fairview Road, Oxton, Wirral CH43 5SD. Ian & Christine Wray. *1m SW of Birkenhead. From M53 J3, east on A552, L onto B5151 & immed 1st R into Fairview Rd.* Home-made teas. **Adm £3, chd free. Evening Opening,** Sat 6 June (5.30-8).
Architects walled garden in conservation area. Small but with creative use of space - subdivision, terraces, steps, views. Pond, woodland, shade loving plants and interesting herbaceous border. Frames 1830s sandstone cottage. Watering can collection and replica Somerset and Dorset Railway signal box.

Stable block with sedum roof . . .

26 FAR HILLS
Andertons Lane, Henbury SK11 9PB. Mr & Mrs Ian Warburton, 01625 431800. *2m W of Macclesfield. Along A537 opp Blacksmiths Arms. At Henbury go up Pepper St. Turn L into Church Lane then Andertons Lane in 100yds.* Home-made teas at The Mount. **Combined with The Mount adm £5, chd free.** Sat 23, Sun 24 May (2-5.30). Visitors also welcome by appt.
Mixed ½ -acre garden planted for yr-round interest with regard for wildlife. Trees, shrubs, herbaceous perennials, small pond, fruit and vegetable area, native copse.

10 FERN DENE
See Staffordshire & part of West Midlands.

27 NEW FIELD HOUSE
Crouchley Lane, Lymm WA13 0TQ. Emma Aspinall. *1m S/SE of Lymm Village. From Lymm Dam Head E along Church Rd (A56) past St Mary's church & The Church Green PH. Take next R into Crouchley Lane for approx 1m garden on R.* Home-made teas & wine. **Adm £3, chd free. Sat 1 Aug (1-5.30).**
New and evolving garden set in peaceful countryside on an exposed plot extending to approx 0.4 acres together with a 1 acre paddock. Stable block with sedum roof. Well stocked herbaceous borders, vegetable garden, fruit trees, orangery, water features and small rose/scented garden. Some gravel paths.

28 FREE GREEN FARM
Free Green Lane, Lower Peover WA16 9QX. Sir Philip & Lady Haworth. *3m S of Knutsford. Free Green Lane connects A50 with B5081. From Holmes Chapel on A50 turn L after Drovers Arms. From Knutsford on B5081 turn L into Broom Lane, then L into Free Green Lane.* Home-made teas. **Adm £4, chd free. Sun 31 May (2-6).**
2-acre garden with pleached limes, herbaceous borders, ponds, parterre; collection of hebes, garden of the senses and British woodland. Collection of ferns. Topiary.

GAMESLEY FOLD COTTAGE
See Derbyshire.

29 GRAFTON LODGE
Tilston, Malpas SY14 7JE. Simon Carter & Derren Gilhooley, 01829 250670, simoncar@aol.com. *12m S of Chester. A41 S from Chester turning towards Wrexham on A534 at Broxton r'about. Past Carden Park Hotel & turn at Cock-a-Barton PH towards Stretton & Tilston. Through Stretton, garden on R before reaching Tilston.* Home-made teas. **Adm £4, chd free. Sun 14 June (1.30-6). Evening Opening** wine, Fri 19 June (5-8.30). Visitors also welcome by appt.
Colourful garden of 2 acres with lawns, natural and formal ponds, specimen trees, many mature shrubs and several garden rooms incl herb garden, standard rose circle, large pergola with varied climbers, herbaceous beds,

perfumed gazebo, orchard, roof terrace with far reaching views over garden and countryside. Gravel drive.

30 ◆ HARE HILL GARDENS
Over Alderley SK10 4QB. The National Trust. *2m E of Alderley Edge. Between Alderley Edge & Prestbury. Turn off N at B5087 at Greyhound Rd.* **Adm £3.40, chd £1.70. For NGS: Sun 10 May (10-5).**
Attractive spring garden featuring a fine display of rhododendrons and azaleas; good collection of hollies and other specimen trees and shrubs. 10-acre garden incl a walled garden which hosts many wall shrubs incl clematis and vines; borders are planted with agapanthus and geraniums. Partially suitable for wheelchairs.

31 HAUGHTON HALL
Hall Lane, Haughton, Bunbury, Tarporley CW6 9RH. Mr & Mrs Phillip Posnett. *5m NW of Nantwich. Off A534 Nantwich to Wrexham rd, 6m SE of Tarporley via A49 to Whitchurch.* Home-made teas. **Adm £5, chd £2.50. Sun 31 May (2-5).**
Large garden currently being restored. Interesting collection of trees, recently planted borders leading down to lake. Fantastic display of azaleas and rhododendrons.

32 HENBURY HALL
Macclesfield SK11 9PJ. Sebastian de Ferranti Esq. *2m W of Macclesfield. On A537. Turn down School Lane Henbury at Blacksmiths Arms. East Lodge on R.* Home-made teas. **Adm £6, chd free. Sun 17 May (2-5).**
Large garden with lake, beautifully landscaped and full of variety. Azaleas, rhododendrons, flowering shrubs, rare trees and herbaceous borders.

33 35 HEYES LANE
Timperley, Altrincham WA15 6EF. Mr & Mrs David Eastwood. *1½ m NE of Altrincham. Heyes Lane, a turning off Park Rd (B5165) 1m from junction with A56 Altrincham-Manchester rd. Or from A560 turn W in Timperley Village for ¼ m. Newsagents shop on corner.* **Adm £3 incl tea, chd free. Wed 10, Sun 14 June (2-5).**
Small mature suburban garden 30' x 90' on sandy soil, maintained by a keen plantswoman member of the

Organic Movement. Improved accessibility with several changes to this yr-round garden; trees; small pond; greenhouses; many kinds of fruit with a good collection of interesting and unusual plants. A true plantspersons garden with many environmentally friendly features incl wildlife havens, media interest. Featured in 'Amateur Gardening'. Partial wheelchair access.

HIGH ROOST
See Derbyshire.

34 73 HILL TOP AVENUE
Cheadle Hulme SK8 7HZ. Mr & Mrs Martin Land, 0161 486 0055. *4m S of Stockport. Turn off A34 (new bypass) at r'about signed Cheadle Hulme (B5094). Take 2nd turn L into Gillbent Rd, signed Cheadle Hulme Sports Centre. Go to end, small r'about, turn R into Church Rd. 2nd rd on L is Hill Top Ave. From Stockport or Bramhall turn R or L into Church Rd by The Church Inn. Hill Top Ave is 1st rd on R.* Home-made teas. **Adm £3, chd free** (share to Arthritis Research Campaign). **Suns 7 June; 9 Aug (2-6). Evening Opening** wine, Thur 9 July (6-8.30). Visitors also welcome by appt, for groups of 4+. ¹⁄₆ -acre plantswoman's garden. Well stocked with a wide range of sun-loving herbaceous plants, shrub and climbing roses, many clematis varieties, pond and damp area, shade-loving woodland plants and small unusual trees, in an originally designed, long narrow garden.

35 NEW HILLSIDE
Mill Lane, Mobberley WA16 7HY. Paul Hales & Mark Rubery. *2m E of Knutsford. Entrance off Mill Lane, next door to Roebuck Inn. Roebuck is signed off Mobberley Rd.* Light refreshments & teas. **Adm £5, chd free** (share to Blackpool Zoological Park). **Sat 30, Sun 31 May (12-5).**
A magnificent garden, this 6 acre site is home to a huge collection of rare birds incl 80 flamingos. Beautiful rare plants and mature trees surround the various ponds and waterfalls. This delightful garden is also home to a rare collection of bonsai trees. Some gravel paths, narrow bridges and steps.

36 HILLSIDE COTTAGE
Shrigley Road, Pott Shrigley SK10 5SG. Anne & Phil Geoghegan. *6m N of Macclesfield. On A523. At Legh Arms T-lights turn into Brookledge Lane signed Pott Shrigley. After 1¹⁄₂ m signed Shrigley Hall turn L signed Higher Poynton. After 1m turn R at Methodist Chapel. Field parking with short walk to garden. Park & ride service 01625 572214.* Home-made teas (Sun). **Adm £3.50, chd free** (share to Great Dane Adoption Society). **Sun 28 June (2-6). Evening Openings** wine, Thur 6, Fri 7 Aug (5.30-8.30).
Set on a hillside, ¹⁄₄ -acre garden with panoramic vistas, over the treetops, of the Cheshire Plain and beyond. Filled with colour, texture and the scent of roses. Landscaped on several levels with a wide variety of shrubs, small trees and 'cottage garden' perennials. Water features and walled patio garden with container planting. Access available to main areas only.

Full of diverse planting, bordering on the chaotic . . .

37 HOLMCROFT
Wood Lane North, Adlington SK10 4PF. Iain & Karen Reddy, 01625 877317, karenreddy@mac.com. *6m N of Macclesfield. From Poynton head towards Macclesfield, turn L opp The Little Chef. Stay on Street Lane until T-junction. Turn L until Minors Arms PH, Holmcroft is opp pub car park.* Cream teas. **Adm £3.50, chd free. Sun 5, Sat 11, Sun 12 July (12-5). Visitors also welcome by appt in May, June, July.**
The garden is cottage style with mature shrubs, trees and perennial borders. 4 sections incl pond garden, small courtyard, vegetable garden and front garden, approx ¹⁄₂ acre. The gardens are on multiple levels. Limited access for wheelchairs.

38 NEW 18 HOLMWOOD DRIVE
Barnston CH61 1AU. J Rennie. *4m SW Birkenhead. From M53 J3 turn W to Arrowe Park Hospital. At 2nd T-lights L onto A551, straight over r'about, pass Basset Hound PH, turn L into Holmwood Dr, signed Murryfield Hospital, garden on R.* Teas (Sun only). **Adm £3, chd free. Sat 4, Sun 5 July (2-5).**
Full of diverse planting, bordering on the chaotic a spectacular rear terraced garden, that descends to the edge of Barnston Dales.

39 2 HOUGH COTTAGE
Hough Lane, Comberbach CW9 6AN. Carole Hough & Jeff Elms. *1m W of Anderton Lift. From Lift - towards Comberbach - 1st L Cogshall Lane 1m. From A49 take A533 Northwich, after 2m turn L Stone Heyes Lane, twice, after 1m turn R Hough Lane for ¹⁄₂ m.* Home-made teas. **Adm £3, chd free** (share to St Luke's Hospice, Winsford). **Sat 22, Sun 23 Aug (11-5).**
Countryside cottage garden with secluded secret areas, scented garden and many tranquil places to sit. Well stocked with late flowering, unusual perennials and grasses within herbaceous borders. Pond with some unusual plants, cyperus eragrostis. Featured in 'Cheshire Life, Northwich Guardian' & 'Northwich Chronicle'. Smooth Radio.

40 NEW INGLEWOOD
4 Birchmere, Heswall CH60 6TN. Colin & Sandra Fairclough, 0151 342 4645, sandra.fairclough@tiscali.co.uk. *6m S Birkenhead. From A540 Devon Doorway/Clegg Arms r'about go through Heswall. ¹⁄₄ m after Tesco's, R into Quarry Rd East, 2nd L into Tower Rd North & L into Birchmere.* Cream teas. **Adm £3.50, chd free. Sun 19 July (1-5). Visitors also welcome by appt in May to July, groups max 20.**
¹⁄₂ -acre maturing garden in secluded setting. Extensive water gardens incl planted stream, large koi pond, lily pond and bog area with mature arum lilies. Secret herbaceous garden, curving lawns and woodland area. Acers, conifers, rhododendrons, shrubs and ferns. Many tranquil places to enjoy cream teas.

Wildlife areas of bluebells and unusual shade loving plants . . . owl boxes with cameras . . .

Allotments

41 KING'S LANE DAWSON ALLOTMENTS
Bebington, Wirral CH63 8NZ. *2¹/₂ m S of Birkenhead Centre. From J4 M53 exit B5151 (Mount Rd) for Birkenhenhead. In approx 1.7m turn R into Broadway, at r'about, exit straight ahead into King's Lane. Entrance on R, opp Conville Boulevard. Parking on adjacent rds. Disabled access will be available to main path, but not necessarily to the individual allotments.* Home-made teas. **Combined with Princes Boulevard adm £3.50, chd free. Sun 26 July (2-5).**
Dawson Allotments consist of 68 plots Rented from from Wirral MBC and run as a society; they vary from novice to expert plots. Many plot-holders will be on hand to answer questions on their different approaches and crops. The opening is at the peak of the picking and showing season. Produce stall, and 'Pick Your Own' on some plots.
♿ ✻ ✦ ☕

42 NEW LEAWOOD
off Longhurst Lane, Marple Bridge SK6 5AE. **John & Mary Hartley.** *4m E Stockport. A626 to Marple - Marple Bridge, through village, signed Mellor. 100yds on L from car park.* Cream teas. **Adm £3, chd free. Sat 23, Sun 24 May (11-4).**
³/₄ -acre hidden woodland garden facing E-W surrounded by trout stream. Large lawns and flower beds of mixed planting giving rise to panoramic view of hillside with rhododendrons, azaleas and camellias. Terraced paths pass small spring fed ponds and wildlife areas of bluebells and unusual shade loving plants. Bird boxes and owl boxes with cameras. Limited wheelchair access, steep driveway.
♿ ✻ ☕

43 ♦ LITTLE MORETON HALL
Congleton CW12 4SD. **The National Trust, 01260 272018, www.national trust.org.uk.** *4m S of Congleton. On A34.* House & garden adm £6.70, chd £3.30. Weds to Suns 18 Mar to 1 Nov, 11-5. Sat & Sun 21 Feb to 15 Mar & 7 Nov to 20 Dec 11-4Sat & Sun. For NGS: Sat 18 July (11-5).
1¹/₂ -acre garden surrounded by a moat, next to finest example of timber-framed architecture in England. Herb and historic vegetable garden, orchard and borders. Knot garden. Adm includes entry to the Hall with optional free guided tours. Wheelchairs available. Picnic lawn at front of hall.
♿ ✻ ✦

44 LONG ACRE
Wyche Lane, Bunbury CW6 9PS. **Margaret & Michael Bourne, 01829 260944, mike@thebournes249. wanadoo.co.uk.** *3¹/₂ m SE of Tarporley. On A49. Turn 2nd L after Wild Boar Hotel to Bunbury. At 1st rd junction then 1st R by Nags Head PH 400yds on L. From A51 turn to Bunbury until Nags Head. Turn into Wyche Lane before PH car park. 400yds to garden. Disabled parking in lane adjacent to garden.* Home-made teas. **Adm £3.50, chd free (share to Horses & Ponies Protection Assoc & St Boniface Church Flower Fund). Suns 26 Apr; 21 June (2-5). Visitors also welcome by appt for groups of 10+.**
Plantswoman's garden of approx 1 acre with unusual plants and trees. Roses, pool gardens, small vineyard. Exotic conservatory, herbaceous, specialise in proteas, S African bulbs, clivia and streptocarpus. Spring garden with camellias, magnolias, bulbs. Newly planted area with rare trees. Featured in 'The Independent on Sunday' & 'Chester Chronical'. Gravel drive.
♿ ✻ ✦ ☕ ☎

45 ♦ LYME PARK
Disley SK12 2NX. **The National Trust, 01663 762023, lymepark@nationaltrust.org.uk.** *6m SE of Stockport. Just W of Disley on A6.* House & garden £7.20, chd £3.60, garden only £4.95, chd £2.25. Daily end March to end Oct. For NGS: Suns 19 Apr; 16 Aug (11-5).
17-acre garden retaining many original features from Tudor and Jacobean times. High Victorian style bedding, Dutch garden, Gertrude Jekyll style herbaceous border, Edwardian rose garden, Wyatt orangery and many other features. Also rare trees, lake, ravine garden, lawns, mixed borders and rare Wyatt garden. Steps, steep gravel paths - wheelchairs available please tel.
♿ ☕

46 MANLEY KNOLL
Manley Road, Manley WA6 9DX. **Mr & Mrs R Fildes.** *3m N of Tarvin. On B5393, via Ashton & Mouldsworth. 3m S of Frodsham, via Alvanley.* Home-made teas. **Adm £3.50, chd free. Sun 17 May (2-5).**
Terraced garden with rhododendrons, azaleas etc. Quarry garden with waterfalls and an air of mystery. Far reaching views over Cheshire Plain.
✻ ☕

47 MAYFIELD
The Peppers, Lymm WA13 0JA. **Janet Bashforth & Barrie Renshaw, 01925 756107, janetbashforth@talktalk.net.** *4m from J7 M56 or 2m J21 M6. In Lymm village turn by Lloyds TSB Bank into Pepper St. Follow NGS signs, take 2nd R leading into The Peppers.* Home-made teas. **Adm £3, chd free. Suns 10 May; 12 July (12-5). Visitors also welcome by appt.**
Constantly evolving plantswoman's garden, approx ¹/₃ acre. Dry shade area set under mature trees. Colourful mixed borders containing herbaceous perennials and shrubs with a wonderful display of tulips in Apr/May. Front garden has large number of grasses, and vibrant perennial border. Interesting structures and features throughout. Featured on BBC Northwest Tonight.
♿ ✻ ✦ ☕ ☎

48 MAYLANDS
Latchford Road, Gayton CH60 3RN. **John & Ann Hinde, 0151 342 8557, www.maylands.com.** *7m S of Birkenhead. From Devon Doorway/Glegg Arms r'about at Heswall travel SE in Chester direction on A540 approx ¹/₄ m. Turn R into Gayton Lane, take 3rd L into Latchford Rd. Garden on L. Park on rd or at 69 Well Lane.* Teas at 69 Well Lane. **Combined with 69 Well Lane adm £4, chd free. Sun 3, Mon 4 May (2-5). Visitors also welcome by appt in May to July.**
A plantsman's ¹/₂ acre garden, set around curving lawns, which in May is full of rhododendrons, camellias, magnolias and a large wisteria

smothering the house. In June herbaceous plants inc paeonies and roses take centre stage with hardy geraniums supporting. By July the herbaceous planting is joined increasingly by grasses. Plant list available.

✕ ☕ 🎥

49 MILLPOOL
Smithy Lane, Bosley SK11 0NZ. Joe & Barbara Fray, 01260 226581. *5m S of Macclesfield. Just off A523 at Bosley. Turn L 1m S of A54 T-lights. From Leek, turn R, 2¹/₂ m N of The Royal Oak PH at Rushton. Please follow direction to parking areas. No parking at garden.* Teas. **Adm £3, chd free. Sat 20, Sun 21 June (1-5). Visitors also welcome by appt in May, July, Aug, Sept, groups 10+.** Garden designed to extend the seasons with colour, texture and scent. Lush herbaceous borders and areas of deep shade. Small stream, pond and bog garden. Gravel plantings, containers and a fine collection of bonsai trees. An ever increasing collection of modern ceramics and a most productive vegetable garden in tubs and baskets. Popular children's discovery trail and budding artists are encouraged to draw their favourite plants.

❀ ☕ ☎

50 THE MOUNT
Andertons Lane, Whirley, Henbury, nr Macclesfield SK11 9PB. Nicholas Payne, 01625 422920, ngs@themount1.freeserve.co.uk. *2m due W of Macclesfield. Along A537 opp Blacksmiths Arms. At Henbury go up Pepper St. Turn L into Church Lane then Andertons Lane in 100yds.* Home-made teas. **Combined with Far Hills adm £5, chd free. Sat 23, Sun 24 May (2-5.30). Visitors also welcome by appt.** Approx 2 acres with interesting trees incl *Eucryphia x nymansensis,* fern leaved beech and *Sciadopitys.* Shrubberies, herbaceous border and short vista of Irish yews. Water features and landscaped swimming pool. Far views to Wales.

♿ ✕ ❀ ☕ ☎

51 ◆ MOUNT PLEASANT
Yeld Lane, Kelsall CW6 0TB. Dave Darlington & Louise Worthington, 01829 751592, www.mountpleasantgardens.co.uk. *8m E of Chester. Off A54 at T-lights into Kelsall. Turn into Yeld Lane opp*

Farmers Arms PH, 200yds on L. Do not follow Sat Nav directions. **Adm £3.50, chd free. Weds, Sats, Suns Apr to Aug; Weds, Thurs, Fris, Sats, Suns Sept. For NGS: Sun 24, Mon 25 May; Sat 5, Sun 6 Sept (12-5).** 10 acres of landscaped garden and woodland started in 1994 with impressive views over the Cheshire countryside. Steeply terraced in places. Specimen trees, rhododendrons, azaleas, conifers, mixed and herbaceous borders; 4 ponds, formal and wildlife. Vegetable garden, stumpery with tree ferns, sculptures, wild flower meadow and Japanese garden. Bog garden, tropical garden. September Sculpture Exhibition. Wheelchair access, please call prior to visit.

✕ ❀ ☕

52 ◆ NESS BOTANIC GARDENS
Ness, Neston CH64 4AY. The University of Liverpool, 0151 3530123, www.nessgardens.org.uk. *10 NW of Chester. Off A540. M53 J4, follow signs M56 & A5117 (signed N Wales). Turn onto A540 follow signs for Hoy Lake.* **Adm £5.75, chd £2.75, concession £5.25. Open all yr Feb - end Oct 10-5; Nov - end Jan 10-4. For NGS: Sat 17 Jan (10-4.30); 2010 Sat 16 Jan (10-4.30).** Gardens cover some 64 acres, and have a distinctly maritime feel and houses The National Collection of (Sorbus) Mountain Ash. Among some of the significant specimens that still flourish in the gardens are Pieris Forrestii which was collected for Bulley by George Forrest in Yunnan. Winner of numerous awrds incl Gold Medal at Tatton RHS show.

♿ ✕ ❀ NCCPG ☕

53 ◆ NORTON PRIORY MUSEUM & GARDENS
Tudor Road, Runcorn WA7 1SX. Norton Priory Museum Trust, 01928 569895, www.nortonpriory.org. *2m SW of Runcorn. From M56 J11 turn for Warrington & follow signs. From Warrington take A56 for Runcorn & follow signs.* **Normal adm prices apply. Walled Garden open. Daily Apr to Oct. For NGS: Sat 6 June (1.30-4.30).** 16 acres of gardens. Georgian summerhouses, rock garden and stream glade, 3-acre walled garden of similar date (1760s) recently restored. Rosewalk, colour borders, herb and cottage gardens. National Collection of Tree Quince, (*Cydonia oblonga*).

♿ ✕ ❀ NCCPG

Popular children's discovery trail and budding artists are encouraged to draw their favourite plants . . .

54 THE OLD FARM
Gayton Farm Road, Gayton CH60 8NN. A Gamon. *7m S of Birkenhead. SE of Heswall. From Devon Doorway r'about on A540, take the exit directly opp the Devon Doorway into Well Lane. Parking on Well Lane in approx ¹/₂ m. Garden entrance is up cobbled rd which is L as the main rd takes a R.* Home-made teas. **Adm £3, chd free. Sun 9 Aug (2-5.30).** ¹/₃ -acre, in 3rd generation ownership, set on slopes of Dee estuary, against mid C18 farm building (not open). Main garden has 3 tiers, created from old sloping, cobbled farmyard with pond, roses, vegetables, soft fruit and bedding. Rose parterre completes the garden.

☕

55 THE OLD PARSONAGE
Arley Green, via Arley Hall & Gardens CW9 6LZ. The Viscount & Viscountess Ashbrook, 01565 777277. *5m NNE of Northwich. 3m Great Budworth. M6 J19 & 20 & M56 J10. Follow signs to Arley Hall & Gardens. From Arley Hall notices to Old Parsonage which lies across park at Arley Green.* Home-made teas. **Adm £4, chd free (share to Save The Children Fund). Sat 6, Sun 7 June (2-5.30). Visitors also welcome by appt, June & July, groups of 10+.** 2-acre garden in attractive and secretive rural setting in secluded part of Arley Estate, with ancient yew hedges, herbaceous and mixed borders, shrub roses, climbers, leading to woodland garden and unfenced pond with gunnera and water plants. Rhododendrons, azaleas, meconopsis, cardiocrinums, some interesting and unusual trees. Wheelchair access over mown grass.

♿ ❀ ☕ ☎

56 ONE HOUSE NURSERY

Rainow SK11 0AD. Louise Baylis, www.onehousenursery.co.uk. *2½ m NE of Macclesfield. On A537 Macclesfield to Buxton rd. 2½ m from Macclesfield stn.* Home-made teas. **Adm £3, chd free. Sun 10 May (10-5).**

½ -acre plantswoman's garden featuring hostas, rare and unusual woodland and sun-loving perennials, rockery, gravel garden, sculptures and hornbeam arbour. Stunning views over Cheshire Plain. A short walk away is an atmospheric ⅓ -acre historic early C18 walled kitchen garden, hidden for 60yrs and recently restored. Heritage vegetables, gardening and farming bygones, orchard with rare-breed pigs. Sculpture trail and bluebell walk.

57 ORCHARD VILLA

72 Audley Road, Alsager ST7 2QN. Mr & Mrs J Trinder, 01270 874833. *6m S of Congleton. 3m W of Kidsgrove. At T-lights in Alsager town centre turn L towards Audley, house is 300yds on R beyond level Xing. Or M6 J16 to North Stoke on A500, 1st L to Alsager, 2m, just beyond Manor House Hotel on L.* Home-made teas. **Adm £2.50, chd free. Weds 29 Apr; 10 June; 19 Aug (12-5). Visitors also welcome by appt.**

Fascinated by plants from an early age, we have an unusual collection of diverse plants. Our long narrow garden is organised to accomodate shrubs, herbaceous plants, alpines, grasses, ferns and specialising in bulbs and irises.

58 NEW 39 OSBORNE STREET

Bredbury SK6 2DA. Geoff & Heather Hoyle. *1½ m E of Stockport. Osborne St is off Stockport Rd West (B6104), approx 1m from M60. Leave M60 at J27 (from S & W) or J25 (from N & E). Follow signs for Lower Bredbury and/or Bredbury Hall. Osborne St is adjacent to pelican Xing on B6104, no 39 is across from local shops.* Home-made teas. **Adm £3, chd free. Sat 5, Sun 6 Sept (1-5.30).**

This dahliaholic's garden contains over 250 dahlias in 150+ varieties, mostly of exhibition standard. Shapely lawns are surrounded by deep flower beds that are crammed with dahlias of all shapes, sizes and colours, and complemented by climbers, soft perennials and bedding plants. An absolute riot of early autumn colour.

OTTERBROOK

See Derbyshire.

59 NEW PARK HOUSE

Park Lane, Higher Walton WA4 5LH. Robert & Elaine Bilton, 07885 703926, janebilton@ntlworld.cm. *3m S of Warrington. From M56 J11 head for Warrington. After 1½ m turn R in to Park Lane.* Home-made teas. **Adm £4, chd free. Sat 25, Sun 26 July (10-5). Visitors also welcome by appt May - Aug.**

Evolving garden extending to 3 acres incl rich herbaceous planting in cottage and more formal style, sunken herb garden, woods, superb rill/fountain feature based on chelsea design, large pond, circular pergola enclosing rose garden, littered with beautifully crafted vistas. Garden set in larger grounds, some may be open for walking. Dogs on leads.

An absolute riot of early autumn colour . . .

60 PARM PLACE

High Street, Great Budworth CW9 6HF. Peter & Jane Fairclough, 01606 891131. *3m N of Northwich. Great Budworth on E side of A559 between Northwich & Warrington, 4m from J10 M56, also 4m from J19 M6. Parm Place is W of village on S side of High Street.* Home-made teas. **Adm £3.50, chd free (share to Great Ormond Street Hospital). Suns 5 Apr; 12 July (1-5). Visitors also welcome by appt.**

Well-stocked ½ -acre plantswoman's garden with stunning views towards S Cheshire. Immaculate curving lawns, shrubs, colour co-ordinated herbaceous borders, roses, water features, rockery, gravel bed with grasses. Fruit and vegetable plots. In spring large collection of bulbs and flowers, camellias, hellebores and blossom. A treat in store. Featured in 'Cheshire Life'.

61 ◆ PEOVER HALL GARDENS

Knutsford WA16 6SW. Randle Brooks Esq, 01565 830395. *4m S of Knutsford. Turn off A50 at Whipping Stocks Inn, down Stocks Lane. Follow signs to Peover Hall & Church. Entrance off Goostrey Lane clearly signed.* **Adm £4, chd free. Mons, Thurs except Bank Hols May - Aug. For NGS: Sat 16, Sun 17 May (2-5).**

15 acres. 5 walled gardens; C19 dell, rhododendrons, pleached limes, topiary. Grade II Carolean Stables and C18 park.

62 PIKELOW FARM

School Lane, Marton SK11 9HD. David & Ann Taylor. *3m N of Congleton. In Marton Village take rd signed Marton Heath Trout Pools, ¾ m down School Lane on R.* Home-made teas. **Adm £3, chd free. Sat 25 Apr; Sun 19 July (2-5).**

Peace and tranquillity of a private Nature Reserve with 3 beautifully landscaped lakes bordered by wild flowers, native trees and plants. Typical farm garden with traditional spring flowers, herbaceous borders and ponds. Echiums in the spring with amazing displays of non-stop begonias throughout the summer. A Nature Lovers Paradise. Teas, cakes, gifts, bird food etc by Macclesfield RSPB.

Allotments

63 NEW PLYMYARD HALL ALLOTMENTS

Bridle Road, Eastham CH62 8BN. *6m SE of Birkenhead. From A41 turn into Allport Rd towards Bromborough Station. ¼ m turn L at T-lights into Bridle Rd. L next to Treetops Surgery.* Home-made teas. **Adm £3, chd free. Sun 16 Aug (2-5.30).**

Allotments are sited on an area previously used as the gardens of a very large house known as Plymyard. Some features are still to be seen; ha-ha and specimen trees. The allotments are well tended and a huge variety of vegetables, fruit and flowers are on show. Some produce on sale for charity. Enjoy a plethora of plants set against the backdrop of towering trees and pleasant surroundings. History of the site information available. Wear stout footwear if wet. Wheelchair access over grassy paths.

64 17 POPLAR GROVE
Sale M33 3AX. Mr Gordon Cooke,
gordoncooke.ceramics@virgin.net.
*3m N of Altrincham. From the A6144
at Brooklands stn turn into Hope Rd.
Poplar Grove 3rd on R.* Home-made
teas. **Adm £3.50, chd free** (share to
The Stroke Assoc). **Sat 16, Sun 17
May (2-5).** Visitors also welcome by
appt May & June only.
This garden is 'deceptively spacious',
being two gardens joined together. The
owner is a ceramic artist/landscape
designer. Features incl sculpture
garden; pebble mosaic 'cave', scented
area and living roof. Many tender and
borderline plants thrive in this city
microclimate such as *Acacia dealbata;
lochroma australis* and Rhododendron
'Fragrantissima'. Garden Ceramics
Exhibition. Featured in 'Dream
Gardens' by Andrew Lawson.

65 POULTON HALL
Poulton Lancelyn, Bebington
CH63 9LN. The Lancelyn Green
Family, 0151 334 2057,
www.poultonhall.co.uk. *2m S of
Bebington. From M53, J4 towards
Bebington; at T-lights R along Poulton
Rd; house 1m on R.* Home-made teas.
**Adm £4, chd free. Sun 19 Apr (2-
5.30).** Visitors also welcome by appt
May to July.
3 acres; front lawns with view of the
house, wild flower meadow and
shrubbery. Child-friendly features incl a
surprising new approach to the walled
garden, redesigned Nursery Rhyme
area, wood sculptures of Robin Hood
and Jabberwocky by Jim Heath and
other reminders of Roger Lancelyn
Green's retellings. Sundial garden for
the visually impaired is sponsored by
Bebington Rotary club. As a powerful
memorial to Richard Lancelyn Green,
new monumental, stainless steel
sculpture of enigmatic contemporary
form has been created by Sue
Sharples, who designed the bronze
Viking head. Music: organ recital 4pm.

**66 NEW 59 PRINCES
BOULEVARD**
Higher Bebington CH63 5LJ.
Gary & Sue Bethel, 0151 644
7903, gary.bethel@sky.com. *2½
m S of Birkenhead Centre. From
J4 M53, exit B5151 (Mount Rd) for
Birkenhead. In approx 1.7m turn R
into Broadway. At r'about exit
straight ahead into Kings Lane.
Parking on Kings Lane or L into
Conville Boulevard. Entrance on
corner of Conville & Princes
Boulevards.* Teas at Kings Lane
Dawson Allotments. **Combined
adm with Kings Lane Dawson
Allotments adm £3.50, chd free.
Sun 26 July (2-5).** Visitors also
welcome by appt July onwards.
Amazing garden very tropical
looking, many unusual rare and
tender plant collections, palms and
tree ferns, butia jubaea, squarossa,
cyathea etc. Pseudopanax,
scheffera tibouchima and unusual
perennials all set amongst beautiful
lawn and pond. Landscaped
colourful small walled garden.

**67 NEW ◆ QUARRY BANK
HOUSE GARDEN**
Quarry Bank Road, Styal
SK9 4LA. The National Trust,
alan.knapper@nationaltrust.org.
uk. *Follow NT signs.* **House &
garden £9.50, chd £4.80, garden
only £5, chd £2.50. 1 March to
31 Oct.** For NGS: **Sat 18 July
(11-5).**
A 'picturesque' valley garden
created in the 1790's by cotton mill
owner Samuel Greg. The garden is
mainly a spring garden, with many
fine azaleas and rhododendrons.
Some rhododendrons are unique
to the garden having been
commisioned and introduced by
the Greg family during C19.
Featured on BBC's Country File &
Northwest News.

QUARRYSIDE
See Derbyshire.

68 NEW RIVERSIDE LODGE
19 Oldfield Road, Heswall
CH60 6SN. Tim & Margaret
Ransome. *7m S Birkenhead. From
Devon Doorway/Glegg Arms
r'about go N on Telegraph Rd for
1½ m. Turn L at Quarry Rd West.
Garden in Oldfield Rd facing
junction with Quarry Rd West.*
Home-made teas. **Adm £3.50,
chd free. Sun 17 May (1-5).**
³/₄ -acre garden set in mature trees
and shrubs, which has been
designed by the owners and
developed over the last 3 yrs.
Spectacular stonework terracing
with views to Welsh Hills, reflecting
pool, gazebo, herbaceous and
mixed planting, gravel area and
rose arches. Short slope but help
available.

69 ◆ RODE HALL
Church Lane, Scholar Green
ST7 3QP. Sir Richard & Lady Baker
Wilbraham, 01270 873237,
www.rodehall.co.uk. *5m SW of
Congleton. Between Scholar Green
(A34) & Rode Heath (A50).* **Adm £3,
Concessions £2.50. Snowdrops;
24 Jan - 1 Mar daily except Mons &
Tues (12-4). Gardens; Tues, Weds,
Thurs & Bank Hols 1 April to 30 Sept
(2-5). 1st Sat each month (9.30-
1.30).**
Nesfield's terrace and rose garden with
view over Humphry Repton's
landscape is a feature of Rode
gardens, as is the woodland garden
with terraced rock garden and grotto.
Other attractions incl the walk to the
lake, restored ice house, working
walled kitchen garden and new Italian
garden. Fine display of snowdrops in
February.

70 ROSEWOOD
Puddington CH64 5SS. Mr & Mrs C
E J Brabin, 0151 353 1193,
angela.brabin@tesco.net. *6m N of
Chester. Turn L (W) off Chester to
Hoylake A540 to Puddington. Park by
village green. Walk to Old Hall Lane,
30yds away then through archway on
L to garden. Owner will meet you at
green by appt.* **Adm £3, chd free.**
Visitors welcome by appt **all yr.**
Individuals and coaches.
All yr garden; thousands of snowdrops
in Feb, camellias in autumn, winter and
spring. Rhododendrons in April/May
and unusual flowering trees from

Spectacular stonework terracing
with views to Welsh Hills . . .

March to June. Autumn cyclamen in quantity from Aug to Nov. Perhaps the greatest delight to owner are two large Cornus capitata, flowering in June.

&. ⊛ ☎

71 THE ROWANS
Oldcastle Lane, Threapwood SY14 7AY. Paul Philpotts & Alan Bourne, 01948 770522. *3m SW of Malpas. Leave Malpas by B5069 for Wrexham, pass church on R, continue for 3m, take 1st L after Threapwood PO into Chapel Lane. L into Oldcastle Lane, garden 1st bungalow on R.* Home-made teas. **Adm £3.50, chd free. Sat 18, Sun 19 July (2-5.30). Visitors also welcome by appt, groups 10+.**
An Italian themed garden for all seasons. Restored after a period of neglect, divided into numerous areas in which to sit and enjoy the views and statuary. Features incl several ponds, woodland dell, mixed and herbaceous borders, rhododendrons, magnolias, feature trees, vegetable plots, greenhouse and secret garden. 1st place - Cheshire Year of the Garden, 2nd place Chester in Bloom - Large Garden awards.

🐾 ⊛ ☕ ☎

72 SAIGHTON GRANGE
Saighton CH3 6EN. The Governors of Abbey Gate College, 01244 332077, alan.kift@abbeygatecollege.co.uk, www.abbeygatecollege.co.uk. *4m SE of Chester. Take A41 towards Whitchurch. At far end of Waverton turn R to Saighton. Grange is at the end of village.* Cream teas. **Adm £3, chd free (share to Deeside House Educational Trust Ltd). Sun 3 May (12-4). Visitors also welcome by appt.**
The gardens at Abbey Gate College are a little masterpiece of garden design. From the symmetrical vista through the clipped yews hedges, which are undergoing restoration, to the Japanese garden, which is beginning to blossom, all provide a tantalising glimpse of what has been and what is yet to come. This garden is still in the process of restoration.

🐾 ☕ ☎

73 ST DAVIDS HOUSE
St Davids Lane, Noctorum CH43 9UD. Ian Mitchell, 0151 652 5236. *3½ m SW of Birkenhead Town Hall. Take A553 then A502 through Claughton Village. After 2 sets of T-*lights, 1st L (Noctorum Lane). After Xrds, St Davids Lane is 1st on R. **Adm £3.50, chd free. Visitors welcome by appt any time of year.**
Victorian garden of 1½ acres recently restored to original 1864 probable planting. Azaleas, camellias, rhododendrons, herbaceous and mixed borders, rockeries, pond, pine and silver birch copse with winding steep paths. Excellent views of Clwyd Hills, Snowdonia and Irish Sea.

🍴 ⊛ ☎

74 NEW SANDSEND
126 Hibbert Lane, Marple SK6 7NU. Davd & Audrey Bomford. *5m SE of Stockport. Leave M60 at J27. A626 to Marple R at Texaco garage, R at mini r'about into Hibbert Lane ½ m on R or A6 from Stockport via Hazel Grove to High Lane, L at Horseshoe PH into Windlehurst Rd 1¾ m towards Marple. Hibbert Lane starts at canal bridge on L 200yds past bridge.* Home-made teas. **Adm £3, chd free. Sat 16, Sun 17 May (1-5).**
Long narrow front and back gardens, in sun and shade, lawns and paths journey through planting for yr round colour and design with azaleas, acers, hostas, shrubs, flowering trees. Backing onto woodland, birdsong abundant. Secluded resting places, area for propagation. Sale of African craft and jewellery.

🐾 ⊛ ☕

75 SANDYMERE
Cotebrook CW6 9EH. John & Alex Timpson. *5m N of Tarporley. On A54 about 300yds W of T-lights at Xrds of A49/A54.* Home-made teas. **Adm £4.50, chd free. Sun 28 June (2-5).**
16 landscaped acres of beautiful Cheshire countryside with terraces, walled garden and amazing hosta garden. Long views, native wildlife and tranquillity of 3 lakes. Elegant planting schemes, shady seats and sun-splashed borders, mature pine woods and rolling lawns accented by graceful wooden structures. Different every year: witness the evolution of the garden that is now in its 20th yr. New for 2009, lily pond and herbaceous garden. Limited access for wheelchairs.

&. 🐾 ☕

76 NEW 21 SCAFELL CLOSE
High Lane, Stockport SK6 8JA. Lesley & Dean Stafford. *On A6 SE of Stockport. 2m past Rising Sun PH. At High Lane turn into Russell Ave opp Dog & Partridge PH, 2nd L to Kirkfell Drive & immed R onto Scafell Close, 21 on the R. Parking on L or to the end in turning circle.* Teas. **Adm £3, chd free. Sat 1, Sun 2 Aug (2-5).**
⅓ acre landscaped suburban garden. Colour themed annuals border featuring Kinder Ram and passing into vegetables, soft fruits and orchard. Returning perennial pathway leads to the fishpond and secret terraced garden with water feature and patio planting. Finally visit the blue front garden.

☕

Woodland, birdsong abundant . . . secluded resting places . . .

77 THE SCHOOL HOUSE
School Lane, Dunham Massey WA14 4SE. Andrew Bushell & Peter White. *1½ m SW of Altrincham. From M56 J7 follow signs for Dunham Massey Hall (NT). Turn into Woodhouse Lane becoming School Lane 100yds after Axe Cleaver PH. Car park available from 1pm.* Home-made teas at village hall. **Adm £3, chd free. Evening Opening wine, Fri 5 June (7-10). Sun 2 Aug (1-5).**
Cottage garden divided into rooms. In picturesque setting attached to village hall and beside the Bridgewater canal. Incl herbaceous borders, rose and bog garden. History of Dunham display in village hall. Some gravel paths.

&. 🐾 ⊛ ☕

78 68 SOUTH OAK LANE
Wilmslow SK9 6AT. Caroline & David Melliar-Smith, 01625 528147, davcaro.melliarsmith@btinternet.com. *¾ m SW of Central Wilmslow. From M56 (J6) take A528 towards Wilmslow, R into Buckingham Rd. From center Wilmslow turn R onto B5086 (Knutsford), 1st R into Gravel Lane, 4th R into South Oak Lane. Park by recreation ground.* **Adm £2.50, chd free. Sats & Suns 6, 7 June; 18, 19**

July; 5, 6 Sept (11-5). **Visitors also welcome by appt in July, Aug, mid Sept, max group 30.**
With yr round colour, scent and interest, this attractive, small, hedged cottage garden has evolved over the years into 5 natural 'rooms'. As keen members of the Hardy Plants Society, the owners passion for plant is reflected in shrubs, trees, flower borders and pond, creating havens for birds, bees and wildlife. Enjoy tranquillity and peace on this plant-packed garden 'journey'. Featured in 'Cheshire Life' & 'Amateur Gardening'.

SOUTHLANDS
See Lancashire Merseyside & Greater Manchester.

79 NEW SPRINGBANK
670 London Road, Davenham CW9 8LG. Doug & Ann Welch.
2¹/₂ m S of Northwich. From Peckmill r'about at S end of Davenham Village on A533 Davenham By-pass take rd signed Davenham & Moulton. Garden on L approx 150yds. Light refreshments & teas. **Adm £3.50, chd free. Sat 1, Sun 2 Aug (2-5).**
Lovely interesting garden in ¹/₂ acre sheltered hollow with backdrop of mature trees and shrubs. Large colourful herbaceous border, other mixed borders, rose and lavender bed, pond, bog garden, grasses, hostas and much more. Long pergola with roses, clematis and honeysuckle. High level paths giving views of garden.

80 199 STOCKPORT ROAD
Timperley WA15 7SF. Eric & Shirley Robinson. *1¹/₂ m NE of Altrincham. Take A560 out of Altrincham, in 1m take B5165 towards Timperley. B5165 is Stockport rd.* Home-made teas. **Adm £2.50, chd free. Suns 14 June; 2 Aug (1-5).**
Overstuffed cottage-style garden owned by 2 plantaholics, one an enthusiastic gardener, the other a very keen flower arranger. The garden is full of colourful herbaceous perennials, shrubs and hostas, and has a small brick-built pond complete with small koi and goldfish. You will not believe how many plants there are in such a small garden. Newly designed front garden with water feature.

81 ◆ STONYFORD COTTAGE
Stonyford Lane, Oakmere CW8 2TF. Janet & Tony Overland, 01606 888128, www.stoneyfordcottage gardens.co.uk. *5m SW of Northwich. Fom Northwich take A556 towards Chester. ³/₄ m past A49 junction turn R into Stoneyford Lane. Entrance ¹/₂ m on L.* **Adm £3.50, chd free. Tues - Suns & Bank Hol Mons April - Sept 11-5.** Guided tours for groups. For NGS: **Suns 7 June; 9 Aug (1.30-5.30).**
Set around a tranquil pool this Monet style landscape has a wealth of moisture loving plants, incl iris and candelabra primulas. Drier areas feature unusual perennials and rarer trees and shrubs. Woodland paths meander through shade and bog plantings with views across the pool to the cottage gardens. Unusual plants available at the adjacent nursery.

82 SUMMERDOWN
27 Castle Hill, Prestbury SK10 4AS. Kate & Paul Boutinot, 01625 265350, kateboutinot@ntlworld.com. *3m NW of Macclesfield. From Prestbury take A538 towards Wilmslow. Garden 3 drives on L after 2nd turning to Castlegate. Please park considerately in Castlegate or car parks in village (12min walk). No parking on property except for disabled by prior tel arrangement.* **Adm £4.50, chd free. Visitors welcome by appt June & July only, light refreshments & wine by arrangement.**
Landscaped in 2004 this 1¹/₄ acre garden has established boundaries with mature trees and distant views. Stream, pond, fountain, temple and parterre garden are compliemented by already well established plantings of David Austin roses, grasses, hostas, catalpas, tree ferns, gunneras and much more! Glasshouse and raised vegetable area. Gravel paths and slopes.

83 SUNNYSIDE FARM
Shop Lane, Little Budworth CW6 9HA. Mike & Joan Smeethe. *3m NE of Tarporley. Signed field parking is reached directly off A54 approx 1m E of T-lights at A54/A49 Xrds, take track opp Longstone Lane 250yds W of Shrewsbury Arms (limited parking for disabled at house, please tel).* Home-made teas. **Adm £4, chd free. Sat 22, Sun 23 Aug (1-5).**
Country garden of differing moods.

Cottage garden with traditional and contemporary plantings, tranquil pool garden, long border with late flowering bold perennials and dramatic grasses,¹/₈ acre decorative potager and fruit garden, orchard with beehives. 3 acre oak woodland with recently planted acer glade and wild flower meadow with mown paths. A wealth of unusual plants and interesting colour schemes. Access from car park slightly uneven.

Lovely interesting garden in ¹/₂ acre sheltered hollow . . .

Group opening

84 SWETTENHAM VILLAGE
CW12 2LD. *5m NW of Congleton. Turn off A54 N 2m W of Congleton or turn E off A535 at Twemlow Green, NE of Holmes Chapel. Follow signs to Swettenham. Parking at Swettenham Arms PH. Entrance at side of PH.* Home-made teas at Dane Edge £2.50. **Combined adm £5, chd free. Suns 26 Apr; 9 Aug (12-4).**

DANE EDGE
Mr & Mrs J Cunningham.
Garden approx 5 mins walk from car park
Steep riverside garden of 10¹/₂ acres leading down to a beautiful and partially wooded wildlife haven with pleasant walks by R Dane. Peacocks roaming the garden. Spring opening for bluebell, wild garlic, summer opening for lavender meadow at Swettenham Arms.

◆ THE QUINTA ARBORETUM
Swettenham. Tatton Garden Society, www.tattongardensociety.co.uk. **Open daily (not Christmas Day) 9-dusk.**
Arboretum on a 28-acre site established since 1948 with over 2,000 species of trees incl collections of birch, pine, oak and flowering shrubs. Bluebell bank and snowdrops. 40 camellias and 64 rhododendrons planted 2004. Collection of 120 hebes. Lake.

85 TATTENHALL HALL

High Street, Tattenhall CH3 9PX. Jen & Nick Benefield, Chris Evered & Jannie Hollins. *8m S of Chester on A41. Turn L to Tattenhall, through village, turn R at Letters PH, past war memorial on L through Sandstone pillared gates. Park on rd or in village car park.* Home-made teas (Sun). **Adm £4, chd free. Sun 21 June (2-5). Evening Opening** wine & light refreshments, Fri 17 July (5.30-8.30). Shared garden developed over 14yrs, around Jacobean house (not open). 4$1/2$ acres, incl wild flower meadows, with interesting trees, large pond, stream, walled garden with well stocked herbaceous borders, planted for succession, yew terrace overlooking meadow with views to hills. Glasshouse, vegetable garden. A relaxed garden style. Limited wheelchair access, gravel and cobbled paths, slope to field.

86 ◆ TATTON PARK

Knutsford WA16 6QN. The National Trust, leased to Cheshire County Council, 01625 374400, www.tattonpark.org.uk. *2$1/2$ m N of Knutsford. Well signed on M56 J7 & from M6 J19.* **House & garden £7, chd £3.50, park entry £4.50 per car, garden only £4.50, chd £2.50. For opening details please tel or see website. For NGS: Weds 29 Apr; 10 June (10-6).** Features include orangery by Wyatt, fernery by Paxton, restored Japanese garden, Italian and rose gardens. Greek monument and African hut. Hybrid azaleas and rhododendrons; swamp cypresses, tree ferns, tall redwoods, bamboos and pines. Fully restored productive walled gardens.

87 TIRLEY GARTH

Utkinton CW6 0LZ. *2m N of Tarporley. 2m S of Kelsall. Entrance 500yds from village of Utkinton. At N of Tarporley take Utkinton rd.* Home-made teas. **Adm £4, chd free. Suns 26 Apr; 10 May (1-5).** 40-acre garden, terraced and landscaped. Designed by Thomas Mawson, it is the only Grade II* Arts & Crafts garden in Cheshire that remains complete and in excellent condition. The garden is considered an exceptionally important example of an early C20 garden laid out in both formal and informal styles. Late April brings a profusion of blossom, magnolias,

camellias and early rhododendrons. By early May most of the gardens' 3000 azalea and rhododendron have burst into flower. Partial wheelchair access (staff pleased to help).

The garden is totally child friendly and Jean will meet and greet each time . . .

88 THE VALVE HOUSE

Egerton Green SY14 8AW. Nicola Reynolds, 01829 720057, dr.nicola@btinternet.com. *4m NE of Malpas. From Chester take A41 S, at Broxton r'about turn L onto A534, 1st R after Coppermine PH (to Bickerton). Fork L at Bickerton School. Garden 1st house L. On A49 turn opp Cholmondeley Arms to Cholmondeley Castle. Garden 3m on L.* Home-made teas. **Adm £3, chd free. Sat 13, Sun 14 June (2-5). Visitors also welcome by appt.**
$1/2$ -acre plantswoman's garden with many interesting features, well stocked herbaceous borders with, apart from many old favourites, an abundance of unusual plants, many of which we will be selling. Lavishly planted wildlife pond with Monet style bridge, productive vegetable and fruit gardens and a well stocked Victorian style conservatory. Gravel paths.

89 69 WELL LANE

Gayton CH60 8NH. Angus & Sally Clark, 0151 342 3321. *7m S of Birkenhead. From Devon Doorway/Glegg Arms r'about travel SE towards Chester for approx $1/4$ m. Turn R into Gayton Lane for about $1/2$ m then L into Well Lane. Garden on L. Park on rd or at Maylands.* Teas. **Combined with Maylands adm £4, chd free. Sun 3, Mon 4 May (2-5). Visitors also welcome by appt.** This undulating established 1-acre garden has a stunning rear setting and is surrounded by a natural woodland backdrop. Many spring flowering shrubs (rhododendron, azalea, magnolia, cornus) with surprises at every corner. Restored old farm buildings with roofless area containing

climbers and fronted by cobblestones. Large slate water feature. Limited wheelchair access.

90 WEST DRIVE GARDENS

4, 6, 9 West Drive, Gatley SK8 4JJ. Mr & Mrs D J Gane, Mr & Mrs K L Marsden & Mrs T Bishop & Mr J Needham. *4m N of Wilmslow on B5166. From J5 (M56) drive past airport to B5166 (Styal Rd). L towards Gatley. Pass over T-lights at Heald Green. West Drive is last turn on R before Gatley Village. Cul-de-sac, please do not park beyond the notice.* Home-made teas. **Combined adm £5, chd free (share to Francis House Children's Hospice). Sun 14 June (10.30-4.30).** Here are three hidden gems in a suburban setting, each with its individual character. Surrounded by mature trees and incl woodland walk, wildlife pond, unusual containers and ceramics, these gardens are a plantperson's delight. Fantastic plant stall as usual. New developments in all gardens.

91 WESTAGE FARM

Westage Lane, Great Budworth CW9 6HJ. Jean & Peter Davies, 01606 892383, pj@budworth94. fsnet.co.uk. *3m N of Northwich. 4m W of Knutsford. Gt Budworth is on E side of A559 between Northwich & Warrington, 4m from J10 M 56, and 4m from J19 M6. Garden is 400yds to E of village. Follow Gt Budworth signs.* Home-made teas. **Adm £3.50, chd free. Evening Opening** wine, Fri 12 June (7-9); Sat 13, Sun 14 June (11-5). **Visitors also welcome by appt,** May, June & July only, coaches welcome. 2 acre cottage garden with herbaceous and mixed borders with architectural planting, a new interest around every corner. Large vegetable and soft fruit area, orchard and wild flower woodland garden with interesting trees. You can walk in the field to the well and see donkeys, hens, ducks and other rare breed poultry. There are many amusing light hearted features and raised colour themed plots. We have a small vine yard and Peter will talk about his wine making. The garden is totally child friendly and Jean will meet and greet each time. Quiz for children, marquee shelter. Wheelchair access to most of garden.

Group opening

92 WILLASTON VILLAGE GARDENS

Willaston CH64 1TE. *8m N of Chester. Take A540 Chester to West Kirby rd; turn R on B5151 to Willaston; at village centre turn R into Hooton Rd. Change Lane is 3/4 m on R opp garage. All 3 gardens are entered from Change Hey garden. Parking available in field at bottom of Change Lane on RH-side. 15 mins walk from Hooton Stn along B5133 in direction of Willaston. Change Lane on LH-side opp garage. Leave M53 J5. Join A41, travel in direction of Queensferry, N Wales. 1/4 m at T- lights turn R B5133. Along Hooton Rd, after 3/4 m Hooton Stn on L. Then as from Hooton Stn.* Home-made teas at Change Hey. **Combined adm £4.50, chd free. Sun 17 May (2-5).** Bridge linking Silverburn and Change Hey not designed for wheelchairs. Alternative (separate) access possible.

CHANGE HEY

Change Lane. Keith & Joan Butcher
2-acre garden with mature trees, developing woodland area underplanted with rhododendrons and azaleas.

THE DUTCH HOUSE

Joan & Michael Ring
1/3 -acre cottage-style garden with some formality. The rear garden vista, terminating with a 1920 Boulton & Paul revolving summerhouse, is surrounded on 2 sides by mature beech, oak and pine trees. Some gravel paths.

SILVERBURN

Prof M P & Dr A M Escudier
Just under 1/2 -acre garden designed by garden owners. A plantsman's garden with interesting herbaceous beds and mixed borders, species and old-fashioned roses, rhododendrons, azaleas, attractive trees, vegetable garden and small orchard.

Stunning herbaceous borders with a long season of interest, beautiful countryside views . . .

93 WOOD END COTTAGE

Grange Lane, Whitegate CW8 2BQ. Mr & Mrs M R Everett, 01606 888236, woodendct@supanet.com. *4m SW of Northwich. Turn S off A556 (Northwich bypass) at Sandiway PO T-lights; after 1 3/4 m, turn L to Whitegate village; opp school follow Grange Lane for 300yds.* Home-made teas (Sun). **Adm £3.50, chd free (share to The Macular Disease Society). Evening Opening** wine, Thur 2 July (5.30-8); Sun 19 July (2-5). Visitors also welcome by appt, May, June & July only.
Plantsman's 1/2 acre country garden in attractive setting, gently sloping to a fast-flowing natural stream bordered by shade and moisture-loving plants. Background of mature trees. Impressive, well stocked herbaceous border backed by trellis supporting many climbing roses and clematis, featuring delphiniums (2 July), over 30 varieties of phlox (19 July) and many choice perennials. Red border, shrubs and vegetable garden.

94 WOODCROFT

1 Oakfield Rise, Holmes Chapel CW4 7DY. Mr & Mrs R Spencer, 01477 533482. *4m E of Middlewich. At Holmes Chapel at r'about take A54 to Middlewich, after 1/2 m turn L into Brookfield Dr, next R to Oakfield Rise.* Home-made teas. **Adm £2.50, chd free. Visitors welcome by appt in spring or late summer.**
This medium-sized garden continues to develop to create colour throughout the yr. Spring flowering shrubs, heathers and bulbs, followed by climbing honeysuckles and clematis, then roses, annuals and herbaceous planting. Conifers, fruit trees and bushes, small vegetable patch and greenhouse. Featured in Cheshire Life.

95 NEW YEW TREE HOUSE

Hall Lane, Hankelow CW6 0JB. Janet & Martin Blow, www.specialperennials.com. *Just off A529, 5m S of Nantwich. Park at village green, follow Hall Lane L along rear of green. Last house on R before junction wth A529.* **Adm £2.50, chd free. Sats, Suns 6, 7, 20, 21 June; 4, 5 July; 8, 9, 22, 23 Aug; 19, 20 Sept (11-5).**
1/3 acre plantsman's garden. Stunning herbaceous borders with a long season of interest, beautiful countryside views. Colourful nursery stock beds, many rare and unusual plants incl large collection of day lily, centaurea and geum. National Collection of Heleniums. Indian Runner ducks. Attached nursery selling plants grown in the garden. Some gravel paths.

Cheshire & Wirral County Volunteers

County Organiser
Nicholas Payne, The Mount, Whirley, Macclesfield SK11 9PB, 01625 422920, ngs@themount1.freeserve.co.uk

Deputy County Organiser (& Advertising)
John Hinde, Maylands, Latchford Road, Gayton, Wirral CH60 3RN, 0151 342 8557, john.hinde@maylands.com

Publicity
Peter Johnson, Church Cottage, Birtles Lane, Over Alderley, Macclesfield SK10 4RX, 01625 860206, peterandjane@talktalk.net

Assistant County Organisers
Sue Bryant, 40b Church Street, Davenham, Cheshire CW9 8NF, 01606 49175
Juliet Hill, Salterswell House, Tarporley CW6 0ED, 01829 732804
Romy Holmes, Bowmere Cottage, Bowmere Road, Tarporley CW6 0BS, 01829 732053, romy.holmes@tiscali.co.uk
Ros Mahon, Rectory Cottage, Eaton, Congleton CW12 2ND, 01260 274777
Sally Sutcliffe, Little Somerley, Woodlan Court, Utkinton, Tarporley CW6 0LJ, 01829 730149
Alex Willcocks, Crowley Lodge, Arley, Northwich CW9 6NR, 01565 777381

CORNWALL

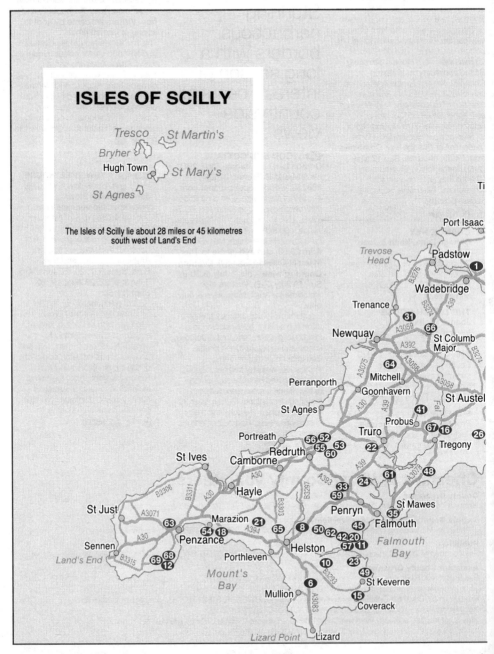

ISLES OF SCILLY

Tresco
St Martin's
Bryher
Hugh Town
St Mary's
St Agnes

The Isles of Scilly lie about 28 miles or 45 kilometres
south west of Land's End

Port Isaac
Trevose Head
Padstow
Wadebridge
Trenance
Newquay
St Columb Major
Mitchell
Perranporth
Goonhavern
St Austell
St Agnes
Probus
Truro
Tregony
Portreath
Redruth
Camborne
St Ives
Hayle
St Just
Penryn
St Mawes
Marazion
Falmouth
Sennen
Penzance
Falmouth Bay
Land's End
Porthleven
Helston
Mount's Bay
St Keverne
Mullion
Coverack
Lizard Point
Lizard

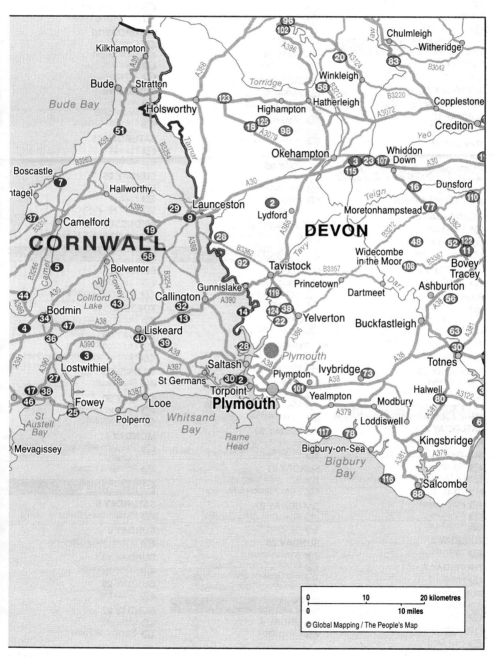

Opening Dates

February
SATURDAY 7
13 Coombegate Cottage
SUNDAY 15
13 Coombegate Cottage

March
SUNDAY 1
13 Coombegate Cottage
SATURDAY 14
61 Trelissick
SUNDAY 15
30 Ince Castle
SUNDAY 29
55 Scorrier House

April
SUNDAY 5
51 Poundstock Gardens
WEDNESDAY 8
44 Pencarrow
SUNDAY 12
63 Trengwainton
SATURDAY 18
20 Glendurgan
SUNDAY 19
30 Ince Castle
45 Penjerrick Garden
64 Trerice
SUNDAY 26
41 Nansawsan House
THURSDAY 30
25 Headland
54 St Michael's Mount

May
SATURDAY 2
35 Lamorran House
SUNDAY 3
3 Boconnoc
29 Higher Truscott
MONDAY 4
23 Hallowarren
40 Moyclare
60 Tregullow
TUESDAY 5
36 Lanhydrock
THURSDAY 7
25 Headland
SUNDAY 10
5 Bolts Quarry Farm
66 Trewan Hall
THURSDAY 14
25 Headland

SATURDAY 16
47 Pinsla Garden & Nursery
SUNDAY 17
30 Ince Castle
37 Long Hay
47 Pinsla Garden & Nursery
48 Poppy Cottage Garden
TUESDAY 19
21 Godolphin
THURSDAY 21
25 Headland
SUNDAY 24
12 Chygurno
42 Navas Hill House
43 Northwood Farm Water Gardens
MONDAY 25
12 Chygurno
23 Hallowarren
31 The Japanese Garden & Bonsai Nursery
WEDNESDAY 27
51 Poundstock Gardens

June
SUNDAY 7
16 Creed House
29 Higher Truscott
34 Kingberry
FRIDAY 12
27 Hidden Valley Gardens
SATURDAY 13
27 Hidden Valley Gardens
39 Menheniot Garden Safari
SUNDAY 14
37 Long Hay
39 Menheniot Garden Safari
68 Trewoofe House
SATURDAY 20
7 Boscastle Gardens
47 Pinsla Garden & Nursery
SUNDAY 21
7 Boscastle Gardens
47 Pinsla Garden & Nursery
SATURDAY 27
49 Porthallow Cove Gardens
52 Primrose Farm
SUNDAY 28
1 Amble Gardens
8 Bowling Green Cottage
19 Ellis Gardens and Nurseries
49 Porthallow Cove Gardens

July
SATURDAY 4
12 Chygurno

SUNDAY 5
12 Chygurno
SUNDAY 12
15 Coverack Open Gardens
59 Tregonning Lodge
SATURDAY 18
14 Cotehele
20 Glendurgan
61 Trelissick
64 Trerice
SUNDAY 19
2 Antony
30 Ince Castle
62 Trenarth
SATURDAY 25
24 Halwyn
36 Lanhydrock
SUNDAY 26
9 Byeways
24 Halwyn
50 Potager Garden
WEDNESDAY 29
51 Poundstock Gardens

August
SUNDAY 2
22 Grey Stones
28 Highcroft Gardens
TUESDAY 11
6 Bonython Manor
SUNDAY 16
28 Highcroft Gardens
43 Northwood Farm Water Gardens
WEDNESDAY 26
10 Caervallack
SUNDAY 30
53 Roseland House
63 Trengwainton
MONDAY 31
31 The Japanese Garden & Bonsai Nursery
53 Roseland House

September
SATURDAY 5
27 Hidden Valley Gardens
SUNDAY 6
27 Hidden Valley Gardens
SUNDAY 13
18 Ednovean Farm
SUNDAY 20
58 Trebartha
SUNDAY 27
14 Cotehele
56 Stencoose Farmhouse

February 2010

SATURDAY 6
⑬ Coombegate Cottage

SUNDAY 14
⑬ Coombegate Cottage

Gardens open to the public

② Antony
③ Boconnoc
⑥ Bonython Manor
⑪ Carwinion
⑫ Chygurno
⑭ Cotehele
⑰ Eden Project
⑲ Ellis Gardens and Nurseries
⑳ Glendurgan
㉑ Godolphin
㉕ Headland
㉖ The Lost Gardens of Heligan
㉗ Hidden Valley Gardens
㉛ The Japanese Garden & Bonsai Nursery
㉜ Ken Caro
㉟ Lamorran House
㊱ Lanhydrock
㊳ Marsh Villa Gardens
㊵ Moyclare
㊸ Northwood Farm Water Gardens
㊹ Pencarrow
㊺ Penjerrick Garden
㊻ Pine Lodge Gardens & Nursery
㊼ Pinsla Garden & Nursery
㊽ Poppy Cottage Garden
㊿ Potager Garden
㊽ Roseland House
㊹ St Michael's Mount
㊼ Trebah
㊅ Trelissick
㊃ Trengwainton
㊄ Trerice
㊅ Trevarno Gardens & The National Museum of Gardening
㊇ Trewithen
㊈ Trewoofe House

By appointment only

④ Bodwannick
㉝ Kennall House
㊈ Trewoofe Orchard

Garden overlooks flood plain, visited by a host of birds . . .

Also open by appointment ☎

⑤ Bolts Quarry Farm
⑩ Caervallack
⑮ Treleaver Cottage, Coverack Open Gardens
⑯ Creed House
⑱ Ednovean Farm
㉒ Grey Stones
㉓ Hallowarren
㉘ Highcroft Gardens
㊶ Nansawsan House
㊿ Southfield, Poundstock Gardens
㊼ Primrose Farm
㊾ Tregonning Lodge
㊽ Trenarth

The Gardens

Group opening

① **NEW AMBLE GARDENS**
Chapel Amble PL27 6EW. *2m N of Wadebridge. Turn off A39 signed Chapel Amble. In village pass PH and PO on R, L towards Lower Middle Amble, 4th and 6th gardens on L. Park in adj field.* Cream teas. **Combined adm £3, chd free. Sun 28 June (2-6).**
Two neighbouring gardens within unspoilt village of Chapel Amble on N Cornish coast. Bordering an area of designated scientific interest, they have a tranquil position, S-facing across the Amble Valley with far-reaching views to Breock Downs. Walmsley Bird Sanctuary nearby.
&. ⊛ ☕

NEW CALAIS
Chris & Bernice Saitch
Exposed ³/₄ -acre garden divided into rooms. Incl cottage-style sweeping herbaceous borders, raised colour-themed border, newly-planted woodland area, lawns, pond, less formal area designated to fruit, vegetables, mature trees. C19 slate piggery.
&. ⊛

NEW TREVANDOL
Frank & Carol Beck
¹/₂ -acre garden of shrubs, perennials, annuals and vegetables. Cultivation and planting of 90% of garden started 4yrs ago. Ongoing. Garden overlooks flood plain, visited by a host of birds. Granite chipping path and gradual slope.
&. ⊛

② ◆ ANTONY

Torpoint PL11 2QA. The National Trust, 01752 812191, www.nationaltrust.org.uk. *6m W of Plymouth. 2m from Torpoint town centre. Take main rd (Antony Rd) out of Torpoint and follow signs to Antony House and Gardens.* **House and garden adm £6.30, chd £3.15, garden only adm £3.25, chd £1.60. Mons, Tues, Weds Apr to Oct, shop & tearoom 12-5.30, house & garden 1-5.30. For NGS: Sun 19 July (12-5.30).**
Beautiful garden set in 35 acres of Cornish countryside. Home to the Carew-Pole family, primarily a spring and summer garden but a visit any time between April and end Oct will delight as you walk around the National Collection of hemerocallis, summer and knot garden, specimen shrubs and trees. Humphrey Repton-designed views down to R Lyner. Gravel paths, slopes.
&. ✗ ⊛ ☕

③ ◆ BOCONNOC

Lostwithiel PL22 0RG. Mr Anthony Fortescue, 01208 872507, www.boconnocenterprises.co.uk. *4m E of Lostwithiel. 2m E of A390. Turn off A390 at Middle Taphouse.* **Garden only adm £4.50, house £4, under 12 free. House and garden open Suns Apr, May (2-5) and for Cornwall Garden Society Spring Flower Show 4/5 Apr. For NGS: Sun 3 May (2-5).**
Gardens covering some 20 acres, surrounded by parkland and woods. Magnificent trees, flowering shrubs and views. Set in C18 picturesque landscape which surrounds the church and Boconnoc House (both open). Teas in the stable yard designed by Sir John Soane. Newly-planted magnolias. Hydrangeas for sale and 2 local stands.
&. ⊛ ☕

④ BODWANNICK

Nanstallon PL30 5LN. Mr P M Appleton, 01208 831427. *2¹/₂ m W of Bodmin. A389 turn at Pottery signed Nanstallon, L at Xrds signed Hoopers Bridge then sharp R.* **Visitors welcome by appt (share to FLEET).**
Approx 1-acre compact garden incl water garden, herbaceous, granite Cornish cross, roses, shade garden and shrubs. Over 50 varieties of daffodils and narcissi. Large stone circle. Plantsman's garden.
&. ☎

5 BOLTS QUARRY FARM
Penvorder Lane, St Breward
PL30 4NY. George & Jackie
Greengrass, 01208 851592,
boltsfarm@tiscali.co.uk. *8m NE of Bodmin. From village shop, downhill through village to grass triangle & bus shelter. 1st L into Penvorder Lane & drive up hill. Garden last property on L.* Light refreshments. **Adm £3, chd free. Sun 10 May (2-6). Visitors also welcome by appt May & June only.**
'Mowhay' granite garden with rhododendron walk. Many different plants and shrubs. Bluebell trail to 2-acre young broadleaf plantation and quarry garden covered in bluebells in May. Wonderful views. Natural pond garden. Recital by St Breward Silver Band. Bluebell Trail.

6 ◆ BONYTHON MANOR
Cury Cross Lanes TR12 7BA. Mr & Mrs Richard Nathan, 01326 240234, sue@bonythonmanor.co.uk. *5m S of Helston. On main A3083 Helston to Lizard Rd. Turn L at Cury Cross Lanes (Wheel Inn). Entrance 300yds on R.* **Adm £6, chd £2. Mon to Fri incl, 1 Apr to 30 Sept (closed Public Holidays) (10-4.30). For NGS: Tue 11 Aug (2-4.30).**
Magnificent 20-acre colour garden incl sweeping hydrangea drive to Georgian manor (not open). Herbaceous walled garden, potager with vegetables and picking flowers; 3 lakes in valley planted with ornamental grasses, perennials and South African flowers. A 'must see' for all seasons colour. Featured in House & Garden magazine.

Group opening

7 BOSCASTLE GARDENS
PL35 0BJ. *5m N of Camelford. Park in doctor's surgery car park at top of village (clearly signed). Limited parking for disabled at both gardens. Maps provided.* Home-made teas.
Combined adm £3, chd free. Sat 20, Sun 21 June (1.30-5.30).
Boscastle Harbour is well-known to visitors. Both gardens are in older part of village, overlooking cliff, land and sea. Garden paintings exhibition.

HALF ACRE
Carole Vincent
Sculpture in an acre of 3 gardens: cottage; small wood; the Blue Circle garden, constructed in colour concrete with coastal planting. Studio open, painting exhibition.

WILDWOOD
Alex & Ian Stewart
Garden of magic deception. Front traditional, rear - lawns leading to wood with pond, tree ferns and shade-loving shrubs.

8 BOWLING GREEN COTTAGE
Wendron TR13 0NB. Stephen & Carol Lay. *2m from Helston. Signed from Helston - Redruth rd (B3297) and Helston - Falmouth rd (A394).* Cream teas. **Adm £3, chd free. Sun 28 June (2-5.30).**
Creating the 2½ acres of gardens and woodlands has been a battle against the elements. On top of a hill, 2 windswept fields have been transformed, incl wetland areas. Evidence of mining heritage has been retained around the property. Children's nature trail. 1st prize District Garden Competition for Large Garden/Woodlands. Featured in local press, magazines and on Radio Cornwall. Some gravel. Access in woodland limited if very wet.

9 NEW BYEWAYS
Dunheved Road, Launceston
PL15 9JE. Tony & Margaret Reddicliffe. *Launceston town centre. 100yds from multistorey car park past offices of Cornish & Devon Post into Dunheved Rd, 3rd bungalow on R.* Cream teas. **Adm £2.50, chd free. Sun 26 July (1-5).**
Small town garden developed over 3yrs by 2 enthusiastic amateur gardeners, many interesting design features, herbaceous borders, pond, stream and vegetable plot. Areas of interest incl Japanese garden with many young bonsai, shingle grass area, small desert garden with mature cactus, giant rockery. Tropicals incl bananas, gingers and senecia.

Plenty of benches so you can take a rest . . .

10 CAERVALLACK
St Martin, Helston TR12 6DF. Matt Robinson & Louise McClary, 01326 221339, www.build-art.co.uk. *5m SE of Helston. Go through Mawgan village, over 2 bridges, past Gear Farm shop; garden next farmhouse on L.* Home-made teas. **Adm £3.50, chd free. Wed 26 Aug (3-5.30). Visitors also welcome by appt, please tel after 3pm only.**
An 'English' garden arranged into rooms, the collaborations between an artist and an architect. Colour and form of plants against contemporary cob walls and grade II listed farmhouse. 54ft timber and wire bridge. Mature orchard. Featured in 'Country Living', 'Cornwall Today' and various books.

11 ◆ CARWINION
Mawnan Smith TR11 5JA. Anthony & Jane Rogers, 01326 250258, www.carwinion.co.uk. *3m W of Falmouth. 500yds from centre of Mawnan Smith.* **Adm £4, chd free. Daily (10-5.30).**
Luxuriant, traditional, 14-acre Cornish valley garden with delightful walk running down to R Helford. Home of UK's premier collection of bamboos. Hardy fern nursery. Ferns and wild flowers abound. A garden of yesterday and tomorrow. Upper garden accessible, lower paths steeper, possible for electric chairs. Main path gravel, others grass.

12 ◆ CHYGURNO
Lamorna TR19 6XH. Dr & Mrs Robert Moule, 01736 732153. *4m S of Penzance. Off B3315. Follow signs for The Cove Restaurant. Garden is at top of hill, past Hotel on LH side.* **Adm £4, chd free. Weds, Thurs only Apr to Sept (2-5); other days/times by arrangement. For NGS: Sun 24, Mon 25 May; Sat 4, Sun 5 July (2-5).**
Beautiful, unique, 3-acre cliffside garden overlooking Lamorna Cove. Planting started in 1998, mainly S-hemisphere shrubs and exotics with hydrangeas, camellias and rhododendrons. Woodland area with tree ferns set against large granite outcrops. Garden terraced with steep steps and paths. Plenty of benches so you can take a rest and enjoy the wonderful views. Well worth the effort.

THE CIDER HOUSE
See Devon.

COOMBE SCULPTURE GARDEN
See Devon.

⑬ COOMBEGATE COTTAGE

St Ive PL14 3LZ. Michael Stephens.
4m E of Liskeard. From A390 at St Ive take turning signed Blunts. Use village car park immed on L, then take 2nd L for 400metres. Limited parking at house for less mobile. Home-made teas in Parish Hall. **Adm £2.50, chd free. Sat 7 Feb (11-4), Suns 15 Feb; 1 Mar (1-4); Sat 6 Feb 2010 (11-4), Sun 14 Feb 2010 (1-4).**
1-acre garden full of winter colour and scent. Witch hazels, daphnes, hellebores, early rhododendrons and interesting collection of more unusual seasonal plants. Drifts of snowdrops. Sloping site with steps. Open weather permitting - check if in doubt. Art Exhibition in Village Hall 7 Feb 2009 and 6 Feb 2010.

✗ ✿ ☕

⑭ ◆ COTEHELE

Saltash PL12 6TA. The National Trust, 01579 351346,
www.nationaltrust.org.uk. *2m E of St Dominick. 4m from Gunnislake. (Turn at St Ann's Chapel); 8m SW of Tavistock; 14m from Plymouth via Tamar Bridge.* **House and garden adm £9.20, chd £4.60, garden only adm £5.50, chd £2.75. Garden open all yr (10-dusk). For NGS: Sat 18 July; Sun 27 Sept (11-4).**
Formal garden, orchard and meadow. Terrace garden falling to sheltered valley with ponds, stream and unusual shrubs. Fine medieval house (one of the least altered in the country); armour, tapestries, furniture. Gravel paths throughout garden, some steep slopes. Map available at reception for wheelchair users.

☕ ✗ ✿ ☕

Group opening

⑮ NEW COVERACK OPEN GARDENS

TR12 6TG. *10m from Helston. From Helston take B3293 then follow directions to individual gardens.* Home-made teas/light refreshments at Waters Edge. **Combined adm £4, chd free. Sun 12 July (1-6).**
Situated on the unique Lizard Peninsular, Coverack is a traditional historic village with harbour, beach and shallow bathing. Conservation area and of geological importance (SSI). 3 very different gardens and all facilities in village will be open.

☕

NEW BODLOWEN

David & Gillian Richardson.
1m after Zoar Garage on B3293 Helston to St Keverne, R to Coverack. Garden 50m on L after village sign
Bodlowen's 1/2 -acre site, sheltered by adjacent woodland, shows how an organic, self-sustaining and productive garden has been achieved, by a series of garden rooms, terraces, ponds, greenhouses, pergolas and dedicated fruit and vegetable area. Some gravel paths and a few steps.

☕ ✿

NEW TRELEAVER COTTAGE

Pete & Glynis Merrifield, 01326 281296. *From B3293 R just before Zoar Garage. Continue for approx 1 1/2 m past T sign then 1st R. 1st bungalow on L.* **Visitors also welcome by appt Aug/Sept.**
1 1/2 -acre exposed coastal garden created from 2 fields. Lawns, several ponds, bog gardens, gravel beds, wildflower meadow and organic vegetable garden designed to work with nature and encourage butterflies, birds and other wildlife. Children's nature trail. 1st prize Kerrier District Council Garden Competitiion for Organic Vegetable Garden.

✗ ☎

NEW WATERS EDGE

North Corner. Lizzie Cartwright.
From Coverack car park walk to sea then L, garden next to Porthgwarra Nursing Home
Small, steep, narrow terraced garden leading to cliff top. Meditation garden with hidden seating, sculpture, stream, pond and artist's studio. Organic refreshments on verandah with stunning views of harbour and sea.

⑯ CREED HOUSE

Creed TR2 4SL. The Croggon family, 01872 530372. *6m SW of St Austell. From the centre of Grampound on A390, take rd signed to Creed. After 1m turn L opp Creed Church & garden is on L.* Cream teas. **Adm £3.50, chd free. Sun 7 June (2-5). Visitors also welcome by appt for groups.**
5-acre landscaped Georgian rectory garden; tranquil rural setting; spacious lawns. Tree collection; rhododendrons; sunken cobbled yard and formal

walled herbaceous garden. Trickle stream to ponds and bog. Natural woodland walk. Restoration began 1974 - continues and incl recent planting.

✿ ⇤ ☕ ☎

⑰ ◆ EDEN PROJECT

Bodelva PL24 2SG. The Eden Trust, 01726 811911,
www.edenproject.com. *4m E of St Austell. Brown signs from A30 & A390.* **Adm £15, chd £5, concessions £10, family £36. Daily except Christmas Eve/Christmas Day. Apr to Oct (10-6, last adm 4.30); Nov to Mar (10-4.30, last adm 3).**
The world's largest greenhouses nestle in a giant 50-metre deep crater the size of 30 football pitches, the centrepiece of a spectacular global garden. Eden is a gateway into the fascinating world of plants and people and a vibrant reminder of how we need each other for our mutual survival.

☕ ✗ ✿ ☕

⑱ EDNOVEAN FARM

Perranuthnoe TR20 9LZ. Christine & Charles Taylor, 01736 711883,
www.ednoveanfarm.co.uk/gardens. *3m E of Penzance. From A394 1/2 m E of Marazion, turn seawards at Perran Xrds beside Dynasty Restaurant. Continue towards Perranuthnoe, parking in field beside Perranuthnoe sign. Drive up hill to garden.* Teas. **Adm £4, chd free. Sun 13 Sept (1-5). Visitors also welcome by appt July/Aug/Sept for groups of 2+, £5pp.**
Above Mounts Bay with sweeping sea views incl St Michael's Mount. A garden of contrasts. Formal parterres and courtyards around a converted barn, opening to flowing lawns, finishing with Italian and gravel gardens. Box, date palms, olive trees and figs in the courtyards, grasses, phormiums, cordalines beyond. Sculpture exhibition.

✿ ⇤ ☕ ☎

⑲ ◆ ELLIS GARDENS AND NURSERIES

Polyphant PL15 7PS. Tim & Sue Ellis, 01566 86641,
www.ellisnurseries.co.uk. *6m W of Launceston. From A30 take turning to Blackhill Quarry. Proceed up hill to village green. L at bottom of green and keep to L round bend. Garden 4th on R.* **Adm £3, chd free. Wed to Sat, Easter to Sept (9-5). For NGS: Sun 28 June (12-5.30).**

Recently-created and developing 3/4 acre perennial flower garden with deep herbaceous borders, willow tunnel, wildlife pond and white garden. Large collection of euphorbias planted through the gardens, many for sale in the nursery. Full of colour from May to Sept. A delight to behold. Featured on BBC2 Open Gardens. If wet, wheelchair access is difficult. Deep, unfenced pond.

   ⌖ ❁ ☕

THE GARDEN HOUSE
See Devon.

⓴ ◆ GLENDURGAN
Mawnan Smith TR11 5JD. The National Trust, 01326 250906, glendurgan@nationaltrust.org.uk. *5m SW of Falmouth. Take rd to Helford Passage. Follow NT signs.* **Adm £6.40, chd £3.20. Tues to Sat, 14 Feb to 31 Oct (10.30-5.30, last entry 4.30). Closed Good Fri, open BH Mons and Mons in Aug. For NGS: Sats 18 Apr; 18 July (10.30-5.30).**
Valley garden running down to Durgan village on R Helford. In spring large displays of rhododendrons, camellias and magnolias with drifts of primroses, bluebells and aquilegia below. Many specimen trees, laurel maze dating from 1833 and giant's stride.

   🐕 ❁ ☕

㉑ ◆ GODOLPHIN
Godolphin Cross. TR13 9RD. The National Trust, 01736 763194, www.nationaltrust.org.uk. *5m NW of Helston. From Helston follow A394 towards Penzance, then B3302 to Hayle, turning L signed Godolphin Cross.* **Adm £2.70, chd £1.35. Sats to Weds, 29 Mar to 1 Nov (10-4). For NGS: Tues 19 May (10-4).**
A near-miraculous survival from C14 and C16, unchanged by fashions through the centuries. The garden is not about flowers and plants but about the surviving remains of a medieval pattern. Acquired by the National Trust in 2007. Gravel paths, steep slopes, some rough surfaces.

   ⌖ 🐕

㉒ GREY STONES
15 Trethowan Heights, off Penwethers Lane, Truro TR1 3QQ. Roddy & Rachel Macpherson-Rait, 01872 261140, r.macpherson-rait@sky.com. *1/4 m W of County Hall Truro. On A390 Truro to Redruth rd. 1st L after County Arms PH, down Penwethers Lane.* Cream teas. **Adm £3, chd free. Sun 2 Aug (1-5).**

Visitors also welcome by appt June to Sept incl garden societies. 1/2 -acre plant-lovers' garden created over last 9yrs. Winding paths lead to 2 ponds and adjoining rill. Herbaceous borders, rockery, box beds, green and white tranquil garden; bamboo/restio area complements large number of grasses, lilies and exotics. Well-stocked, colourful summer garden. Partial wheelchair access, gravel paths.

   ⌖ 🐕 ❁ ☕ ☎

Full of colour from May to September . . .

㉓ HALLOWARREN
Carne, Manaccan TR12 6HD. Mrs Amanda Osman, 01326 231224. *10m E of Helston. 1m out of the centre of Manaccan village. Downhill past inn on R, follow sign to Carne. House on R.* Cream teas. **Adm £3, chd free. Mons 4, 25 May (1-5).** Visitors also welcome by appt.
2-acre garden and orchard leading to 6-acre beautiful wooded valley and bordering stream. Mixture of the natural and cultivated, bog and cottage garden with primulas, lilies and kitchen herbs, unusual shrubs and trees. Walk along valley through old woodland full of native bluebells. The ethos of this garden is harmony with nature and it is run on organic lines. Ducks, geese and chickens.

   🐕 ❁ 🛏 ☕ ☎

㉔ NEW HALWYN
Truro TR3 6PW. Sue & Roy Sutherland-Clark. *Playing Place - Kea School, R to Porth Kea, follow rd to Higher Trelease Farm, park where signed, walk down hill to Halwyn.* Cream teas. **Adm £3, chd free. Sat 25, Sun 26 July (10-4).** Halwyn has grown from farmland. The garden is still growing because of a love for colour. No set plan, plants go where they look good and if they grow they have a home. Roses are a favourite. The newest addition is the dell, a steep garden running down to the river with a breeze house at the bottom. River and surrounding area are a conservation site with beautiful scenery and birds.

   🐕 ☕

HARTLAND ABBEY
See Devon.

㉕ ◆ HEADLAND
Battery Lane, Polruan-by-Fowey PL23 1PW. Jean Hill, 01726 870243, www.headlandgarden.co.uk. *1/2 m SE of Fowey across estuary. Passenger ferry from Fowey, 10 min walk along West St & up Battery Lane. Or follow signs to Polruan (on E of Fowey Estuary). Ignore first car park, turn L for second car park (overlooking harbour), turn L (on foot) down St Saviour's Hill.* **Adm £2.50, chd £1. Thurs only May to 3 Sept (2-6). For NGS: Thurs 30 Apr; 7, 14, 21 May (2-6).**
1 1/4 -acre cliff garden with magnificent sea, coastal and estuary views on 3 sides. Planted to withstand salty gales yet incls subtropical plants with intimate places to sit and savour the views. Paths wind through the garden past rocky outcrops down to a secluded swimming cove. Some paths steep, rocky and narrow.

   ❁ ☕

㉖ ◆ THE LOST GARDENS OF HELIGAN
Pentewan PL26 6EN. Heligan Gardens Ltd, 01726 845100, www.heligan.com. *5m S of St Austell. From St Austell take B3273 signed Mevagissey, follow signs.* **Adm £8.50, chd £5, senior citizens £7.50. Daily all year except 24, 25 Dec (10-6; 10-5 in winter; last adm 1 1/2 hrs before close).**
'The Nation's Favourite Garden' offers 200 acres for exploration with a breadth of interest around the yr. Incl Victorian productive gardens, pleasure grounds, subtropical jungle, ancient woodland and farmland where sustainable management practices promote diverse habitats and a pioneering wildlife project. National Collection of pre-1920 camellias and rhododendrons. Access guide available from website/reception. Some manual wheelchairs at reception.

   ⌖ 🐕 ❁ NCCPG ☕

㉗ ◆ HIDDEN VALLEY GARDENS
Treesmill, Par PL24 2TU. Tricia Howard, 01208 873225, www.hiddenvalleygardens.co.uk. *2m SW of Lostwithiel. From St Austell take A390 towards Lostwithiel. After 6m turn R on to B3269 signed Fowey, after 200yds turn R signed Treesmill. After 1m turn L, signed to the gardens*

(¹/₂ m). At end of lane after Colwith Farm. Cream teas on NGS days only. **Adm £2.50, chd free. Daily 20 Mar to 31 Oct (10-6). For NGS: Fri 12, Sat 13 June; Sat 5, Sun 6 Sept (10-6).**
4-acre colourful garden in secluded valley with nursery. Cottage-style planting with herbaceous borders, grasses, ferns and fruit. Gazebo with country views. Iris fairy well. Fishpond and courtyard area. New Japanese garden and vegetable potager. Irises flowering at June opening, dahlia display in Sept. Children's garden quiz. Specialist plant nursery.

⊛ ⌷ ☕

Prairie planting containing 2,500 plants . . .

28 HIGHCROFT GARDENS
Cargreen PL12 6PA. Mr & Mrs B J Richards, 01752 848048, highcroftnursery@btconnect.com. *5m NW of Saltash. 5m from Callington on A388 take Landulph Cargreen turning. 2m on, turn L at Landulph Xrds. Parking by Methodist Church.* Cream teas in Methodist Church. **Adm £3, chd free. Suns 2, 16 Aug (1.30-5.30). Visitors also welcome by appt late June to early Sept for groups of 10+, incl coaches.**
3-acre garden in beautiful Tamar Valley. Japanese-style garden, hot border, pastel border, grasses, arboretum with hemerocallis and new blue borders. Prairie planting containing 2,500 plants of herbaceous and grasses. Buddleia and shrub rose bank. Pond. All at their best in July, Aug and Sept.

⋇ ⊛ ☕ ☎

29 HIGHER TRUSCOTT
St Stephens, Launceston PL15 8LA. Mr & Mrs J C Mann. *3m NW of Launceston. From Launceston B3254 turn W at St Stephens toward Egloskerry. Signed.* Cream teas. **Adm £3, chd free (share to RNLI 3 May, St Stephens Church 7 June). Suns 3 May; 7 June (2-5.30).**
1-acre plantsman's garden. Elevated position with fine views. Trees and shrubs with interesting underplanting. Yr-round interest with climbers, herbaceous, alpines and troughs.

⋇ ⊛ ☕

30 INCE CASTLE
Saltash PL12 4RA. Lord and Lady Boyd. *3m SW of Saltash. From A38 at Stoketon Cross take turn signed Trematon, then Elmgate. No large coaches.* Home-made teas. **Adm £3.50, chd free (share to Bishop Cornish Education Centre). Suns 15 Mar; 19 Apr; 17 May; 19 July (2-5).**
5-acre garden with camellias and magnolias, woodlands, borders, orchard, bulbs, shell house and lovely views of R Lynher.

♿ ⊛ ☕

31 ◆ THE JAPANESE GARDEN & BONSAI NURSERY
St Mawgan TR8 4ET. Mr & Mrs Hore, 01637 860116, www.thebonsainursery.com. *6m E of Newquay. 1¹/₂ m from N coast. Signs from A3059 & B3276.* **Adm £3.50, chd £1.50, groups 10+ £3pp. Open daily (closed Xmas day to New Year's day) (10-6/earlier in winter). For NGS: Mons 25 May; 31 Aug (10-6).**
East meets West in unique Garden for All Seasons. Spectacular Japanese maples and azaleas, symbolic teahouse, koi pond, bamboo grove, stroll, woodland, zen and moss gardens. An oasis of tranquillity. Entrance free to adjacent specialist Bonsai and Japanese garden nurseries. Hard gravel paths.

♿ ⋇ ⊛

32 ◆ KEN CARO
Bicton, nr Liskeard PL14 5RF. Mr K R Willcock & Mrs Willcock, 01579 362446. *5m NE of Liskeard. From A390 to Callington turn off N at St Ive. Take Pensilva Rd, follow brown tourist signs, approx 1m off main rd. Plenty of parking.* **Adm £4.50, chd £2. Gps of 12+ £4. Daily 22 Feb to 30 Sept (10-5.30).**
5-acre connoisseur's garden full of interest all yr round, with lily ponds and panoramic views. Dogs welcome in meadow and woodland walk, plenty of seats in all 13 acres, picnic area. Partial wheelchair access, none to meadow/woodland.

♿ ⊛ ☕

33 ◆ KENNALL HOUSE
Ponsanooth TR3 7HJ. Mr & Mrs N Wilson-Holt, 01872 870557. *4m NW of Falmouth. A393 Falmouth to Redruth, L at Ponsanooth PO for 0.3m. Garden at end of drive marked Kennall Vale House.* **Visitors welcome by appt throughout yr.**

6-acre garden in extended grounds in valley setting. Incl mixture of typical British species and exotics. Wide variety of trees, shrubs and herbaceous plants. Bisected by fast-flowing stream with ponds and walled garden.

☎

34 KINGBERRY
Rhind Street, Bodmin PL31 2EL. Dr & Mrs M S Stead. *N side of town, 100yds uphill from Westberry Hotel. Limited parking on hill, otherwise car parks in town centre.* Cream teas. **Adm £3, chd free. Sun 7 June (2-6).**
Surprising haven in centre of this county town. ²/₃ -acre formal town garden with abundantly planted herbaceous borders, original stone walls covered in climbers, ornamental pond, gravel terrace, orchard and wild flower garden. Sculptures and unusual plants, many for sale.

⋇ ⊛ ☕

35 ◆ LAMORRAN HOUSE
Upper Castle Road, St Mawes, Truro TR2 5BZ. Robert Dudley-Cooke, 01326 270800, info@lamorrangarden.co.uk. *A3078, R past garage at entrance to St Mawes. ³/₄ m on L. ¹/₄ m from castle if using passenger ferry service.* **Adm £6.50, chd free. Weds, Fris, Apr to end Sept (10-5). For NGS: Sat 2 May (10-5).**
4-acre subtropical garden overlooking Falmouth bay. Designed by the owner in an Italianate/Cote d'Azur style. Extensive collection of Mediterranean and subtropical plants incl large collection of palms and tree ferns. Reflects both design and remarkable micro-climate. Beautiful collection of Japanese azaleas and tender rhododendrons. Large collection of S-hemisphere plants. Featured in 'Sunday Telegraph', 'Sunday Times' and 'Devon Life'.

⋇ ☕

36 ◆ LANHYDROCK
Bodmin PL30 5AD. The National Trust, 01208 265950, www.nationaltrust.org.uk. *2¹/₂ m SE of Bodmin. 2¹/₂ m on B3268. Stn: Bodmin Parkway 1³/₄ m.* **House and garden adm £10.40, chd £5.20, garden only adm £5.90, chd £2.95. Gardens open all yr (10 - 6). Please visit website or tel for house opening details. For NGS: Tues 5 May; Sat 25 July (10-5.30).**
Large formal garden laid out 1857. Good summer colour with herbaceous

borders, shrub garden with fine specimens of rhododendrons and magnolias and lovely views. Wheelchair access route around formal garden. Gravel paths and slopes to higher woodland garden.

37 LONG HAY
Treligga, Delabole PL33 9EE. Bett & Mick Hartley. *10m N of Wadebridge. Take B3314 Pendoggett to Delabole Rd. Turn L at Westdowns from Pendoggett, R fom Delabole. Signed Treligga (N). Turn L after entering hamlet. Long Hay on L, after 30yds white gate. Parking past gate, turn L into farmyard.* Cream teas. **Adm £3, chd free.** Suns 17 May; 14 June (2-5).
2/3 -acre abundant cottage garden with beautiful vistas of the N coast and sea. Herbaceous beds, shrubs, pond, greenhouse and lawns. Meadow overlooking sea with paths leading to copse, vegetable plots, orchard and greenhouse. Cornish coastal garden in beautiful but harsh environment.

... you are sure to find inspiration

38 ◆ MARSH VILLA GARDENS
St Andrew's Road, Par PL24 2LU. Judith Stephens, 01726 815920, marshvillagardens@talktalk.net, www.marshvillagardens.com. *5m E of St Austell. Leave A390 at St Blazey T-lights, by church, into Station Rd, then 1st L, garden 600yds on L.* **Adm £4, chd under 12 free.** Sun to Wed Apr to Sept (10-6).
Approx 3-acre garden featuring large pond, streams, bog garden. Extensive herbaceous beds, mixed borders, woodland and marshland walks in former estuary. New features incl alpine bed and substantial rose and clematis pergola. Large fernery/bog garden under development. Featured in 'Cornwall Life'. A few steps.

Group opening

39 NEW MENHENIOT GARDEN SAFARI
Menheniot Village PL14 3RZ. *4m SE of Liskeard. Take A38 from Liskeard to Plymouth. L at Menheniot turning. 1m to centre of village. Maps and entrance stickers from The Old School opp Parish Church, also taxi service to outlying gardens.* Light lunches (12-2) at The Old School; Cream teas (2-5.30) at Bodway Farm. **Adm £4.50 for 2 days, chd free.** Sat 13, Sun 14 June (12-5.30).
Attractive Cornish village with 10+ varied and interesting gardens incl competitively-tended allotments. Large/small/formal/cottage/sloping /nearly flat, incl natural wood. Many are new to the NGS and amongst them you are sure to find inspiration. Lovely views of the beautiful surrounding countryside. WC at The Old School. In a quiet, rural location, on both days visitors can see a Textile Art studio, where courses are offered. Display of students work.

40 ◆ MOYCLARE
Lodge Hill, Liskeard PL14 4EH. Elizabeth & Philip Henslowe, 01579 343114, www.moyclare.co.uk. *1/2 m S of Liskeard centre. Approx 300yds S of Liskeard railway stn on St Keyne-Duloe rd (B3254).* **Adm £3, chd free.** Weekend & BH Mons, Apr, May, June (2-5), also open by appointment. For NGS: Mon 4 May (2-5).
Gardened by one family for over 80 yrs; mature trees, shrubs and plants (many unusual, many variegated). Once most televised Cornish garden. Now revived and rejuvenated and still a plantsman's delight, still full of character. Camellia, Brachyglottis and Astrantia (all 'Moira Reid') and Cytisus 'Moyclare Pink' originated here. Featured in 'Cornwall Today' and local press.

41 ◆ NANSAWSAN HOUSE
Ladock TR2 4PW. Michael & Maureen Cole, 01726 882392, nansawsan@googlemail.com. *7m NE of Truro. On B3275, follow yellow signs. Use Falmouth Arms and Community Hall car parks.* Cream teas. **Adm £3, chd free.** Sun 26 Apr (2-5). Visitors also welcome by appt

April, May only for groups of 10+. 1 1/2 -acre garden, once part of Victorian estate garden. From house, paths meander through rhododendrons, camellias, azaleas and perennial borders taking in secret corners, fishpond, greenhouse, summerhouse and gazebo with wider vistas. Unusual trees, shrubs and climbers. Family vegetable garden, soft fruits and ample seating around the garden. Gravel paths.

42 NEW NAVAS HILL HOUSE
Bosanath Valley, Mawnan Smith, Falmouth TR11 5LL. Aline & Richard Turner. *1 1/2 m from Trebah and Glendurgan Gdns. Follow signs to Trebah. Pass Trebah on L, follow rd, past Budock Vean Hotel, continue for just under 1m. L just before sharp L turn at end of creek, rd to R, gdn 30yds on R.* Cream teas. **Adm £3, chd free.** Sun 24 May (1.30-5).
8 1/2 -acre garden divided into various zones; kitchen garden with greenhouses, potting shed, fruit cages, orchard; 2 plantsman areas with specialist trees and shrubs; walled rose garden; ornamental garden with water features and rockery. Seating areas with views across wooded valley, not a car in sight! Limited wheelchair access, gravel paths and slopes.

43 ◆ NORTHWOOD FARM WATER GARDENS
Northwood, St Neot PL14 6QN. Mackenzie Bell, 01579 320030, www.northwoodgardens.com. *2m NE of St Neot. From St Neot Church proceed up steep hill signed Bolventor & Northwood Water Gardens then follow signs.* Cream teas. **Adm £3, chd free.** Gardens open Suns, Mons June to mid-Sept (11-5) (closed 26/27 July). For NGS: Suns 24 May; 16 Aug (11-5).
Overlooking lovely river valley on S slopes of Bodmin Moor. AONB. 4-acre water garden. Bridges and pathways guide you through 8 delightfully landscaped ponds featuring wildlife, streams, waterfalls and fountains. Idyllic lake and romantic island, giant gunnera, vibrant hydrangeas, tree ferns, phormiums, acers, water lilies, rhododendrons, pieris, secret walled herbaceous borders. Art gallery. Live guitar and flute - weather permitting.

44 ◆ PENCARROW
Washaway, Bodmin PL30 3AG.
Molesworth-St Aubyn family, 01208
841369, www.pencarrow.co.uk. *4m
NW of Bodmin. Signed off A389 &
B3266.* House and garden adm
£8.50, chd £4, garden only adm £4,
chd £1, under 5 free. Daily 1 Mar to
31 Oct; house Sun to Thur incl 5 Apr
to 24 Sept. For NGS: Wed 8 Apr
(10-5.30).
A surprise around every corner. Family-
owned grade 2* listed garden. Find an
Iron Age fort, Victorian rockery, Italian
gardens, ice house, lakeside and
woodland walks for dogs off leads! You
can also visit the fine Georgian house
with its superb collection of paintings,
furniture, porcelain and some antique
dolls.

45 ◆ PENJERRICK GARDEN
Budock, nr Falmouth TR11 5ED.
Mrs Rachel Morin, 01872 870105,
racheltmorin@tiscali.co.uk. *3m SW
of Falmouth. Between Budock-
Mawnan Smith, opp. Penmorvah
Manor Hotel. Coach parking by
arrangement.* Adm £2.50, chd £1.50.
Mar to Sept, Sun, Wed, Fri (1.30-
4.30). For NGS: Sun 19 Apr (1.30-
4.30).
15-acre subtropical garden, home to
important rhododendron hybrids and
the C19 Quaker Fox family. The upper
garden contains rhododendrons,
camellias, magnolias, bamboos, tree
ferns and magnificent trees. Across a
bridge a luxuriant valley features pools
in a wild primeval setting. Suitable for
adventurous fit people wearing
gumboots.

**46 ◆ PINE LODGE GARDENS &
NURSERY**
Holmbush, St Austell PL25 3RQ.
Shirley & Ray Clemo, 01726 73500,
www.pinelodgegardens.co.uk. *1m E
of St Austell. On A390 between
Holmbush & St Blazey at junction of
A391.* Adm £6.50, chd £3,
concessions £6. Open daily (10-6,
last entrance 5).
30-acre estate comprises gardens
within a garden. Some 6,000 plants, all
labelled, have been thoughtfully laid out
using original designs and colour
combinations to provide maximum
interest. Rhododendrons, magnolias,
camellias, herbaceous borders with
many rare and tender plants, marsh
gardens, tranquil fish ponds, lake with
black swans within the park, pinetum.
Japanese garden and arboretum.
Holder of National Collection of

Grevilleas. 3-acre winter garden. Many
seats. Featured on French TV.
2 wheelchairs available on loan.

♿ ✕ ⊛ NCCPG ☕

**47 ◆ PINSLA GARDEN &
NURSERY**
Cardinham PL30 4AY. Mark & Claire
Woodbine, 01208 821339,
www.pinslagarden.net. *3¹/₂ m E of
Bodmin. From A30 roundabout take
A38 towards Plymouth, 1st L to
Cardinham & Fletchers Bridge, 2m on
R.* Adm £2.50, chd free. Daily 23 Feb
to 31 Oct (9-6). For NGS: Sats, Suns
16, 17 May; 20, 21 June (9-6).
Romantic 1¹/₂ acres of inspirational
planting and design surrounded by
woodland. Herbaceous and shrub
borders, jungle, ponds, cottage
garden, orchard, alpines on scree;
stone circle in meadow; tree tunnel.
Paths lined with granite boulders and
set with slate, stone and incised
abstract patterns. Featured in 'The
Guardian'. Gravel paths.

♿ ⊛ ☕

48 ◆ POPPY COTTAGE GARDEN
Ruan High Lanes TR2 5JR. Tina
Pritchard & David Primmer, 01872
501411, www.poppycottagegarden.
co.uk. *1m NW of Veryan. On the
Roseland Peninsula, 4m from Tregony
on A3078 rd to St Mawes.* Adm £3,
chd free. Tues, Weds, Thurs, Suns (2-
5.30). For NGS: Sun 17 May (2-5.30).
Inspirational plantsman's garden
combining colour, form and texture,
approx 1 acre, divided into many
rooms. From established cottage
garden, extra land acquired in 2003
enabled the creation of different
gardens filled with many beautiful and
unusual shrubs, trees, bulbs,
herbaceous and exotics, all colour-
themed. Wildlife pond with stream and
bridge. Featured in 'GGG'. Gravel area
at entrance. Wheelchair access to
most of garden.

♿ ⊛ ☕

Group opening

**49 NEW PORTHALLOW
COVE GARDENS**
TR12 6PP. *2m W of St Keverne.
14m on B3293 from Helston to St
Keverne then 2m beyond to
Porthallow. Parking on beach.
Steps to gardens, maps provided.*
Cream teas. **Combined adm £3,
chd free (share to Porthallow
Village Association).** Sat 27, Sun
28 June (12-5).

Porthallow Cove is half-way point
on SW coast path with magnificent
views across Falmouth Bay.
3 gardens, all making the most of
slopes and exposure to the winds
but all differ in their interpretations.

⊛ ☕

NEW CHY AN DOUR
Pat & Ian Gutridge. *From beach,
take path to Headland Cottage.
Follow signs to rd, R up hill,
garden on L*
¹/₃ -acre, S-facing garden with
trees, shrubs, exotics and
herbaceous plants in mixed
borders. Plenty of seating to sit
and appreciate views and vistas.
Terraced vegetable and fruit
garden.

NEW HEADLAND COTTAGE
Nikki Whiley. *From beach, up
coast path steps on L of beach
(facing seaward). Garden
alongside path*
Coastal garden with pocket-sized
lawn but crammed with interesting
plants. Border beside coast path
is particularly worth notice.
Although beach is NE-facing, the
planting has stood up to gale
force winds.

NEW TARANAKI
Dorothy Pelling. *1st house on L
coming into village by car. From
beach (parking), 100yds up St
Keverne Rd*
Small subtropical garden packed
with unusual plants, a garden to
be savoured slowly. Incl Pinus
montezumae, sciadopity and
Idesia salvias and euphorbias a
speciality. Sunny terrace for
refreshments.

⊛

PORTINGTON
See Devon.

Small subtropical garden . . . to be savoured slowly . . .

50 ◆ POTAGER GARDEN
High Cross, Constantine TR11 5RF.
Peter Skerrett, Dan Thomas & Mark
Harris, 01326 341258,
www.potagergarden.org. *7m SW of*

Falmouth. Towards Constantine. In High Cross turn L at grass triangle with white signpost to Port Navas. Garden 100yds on R. **Adm £2.50, chd free, concessions £2. Open Suns only, Apr to Sept (11-5). For NGS: Sun 26 July (11-5).**

New organic garden emerging from old nursery near Helford Estuary. Garden provides relaxed environment with informal mix of herbaceous planting accentuated with vegetables and fruit. Home-made cooking in the Glasshouse Café, hammocks, games and sculpture make Potager a friendly and peaceful retreat. Art Exhibition. Featured in 'Cornwall Country Garden', 'Cornwall Today' and 'Grow It'.

Group opening

51 POUNDSTOCK GARDENS
Poundstock EX23 0AU. *5m S of Bude, off A39.* Lunches/refreshments (Southfield) and cream teas (The Barn House). **Combined adm £4, chd free. Sun 5 Apr (The Barn House only, adm £3); Weds 27 May; 29 July (11-5).**
Direction maps given to visitors. Local C12 church and C16 guild house recently fully restored.

THE BARN HOUSE
Penhalt. Tim & Sandy Dingle.
From A39 take Widemouth, Bude (coastal route). L at Widemouth Manor Hotel towards Millook for 1/2 m
Colourful plantsman's garden within 200m of dramatic cliffs of N Cornish coast. Divided by sheltering hedges, there are herbaceous borders, prairie bed, pond, kitchen garden, all designed for yr-round colour. Setting gives extensive views over surrounding countryside. Wildlife walk through flower-rich fields to wooded valley, often full of butterflies. Partial wheelchair access.

SOUTHFIELD
Vicarage Lane. Mr P R & Mrs J A Marfleet, 01288 361233. *Off A39 at Bangor Xrds (chapel on corner). Turn into Vicarage Lane, signed Poundstock Church. Approx 200yds on L. Use church car park.* **Visitors also welcome by appt.**
3 acres of wildlife woodland and garden. Woodland walks with

daffodils, rhododendrons and hydrangeas. Mainly broadleaf trees planted 1994. Garden with borders of mixed shrubs, trees and perennial plants giving yr-round interest. Kitchen garden. Beautiful views. Many wild birds. Partial wheelchair access. Some steep slopes, difficult if wet.

---

52 PRIMROSE FARM
Skinners Bottom, Redruth TR16 5EA. Barbara & Peter Simmons, 01209 890350, babs.simmons@btinternet.com. *6m N of Truro. At Chiverton Cross roundabout on A30 take Blackwater turn. Down hill, R by Red Lion PH up North Hill, 1st L (mini Xrd), garden approx 1/2 m on L.* Home-made teas. **Adm £3, chd free. Sat 27 June (1-5). Visitors also welcome by appt.**
Rambling informal cottage-style garden with woodland glade. Mature trees and shrubs, herbaceous and mixed borders. Pond with cascades and trickling fountain. Patio area with exotic plants. Gravel path to pergola with scented climbers and summerhouse. A plantsman's garden. Featured on BBC2 Open Gardens.

&⚘🐾☕☎

53 ◆ ROSELAND HOUSE
Chacewater TR4 8QB. Mr & Mrs Pridham, 01872 560451, www.roselandhouse.co.uk. *4m W of Truro. At Truro end of main st. Parking in village car park (100yds) or surrounding rds.* **Adm £3, chd free. Tues, Weds (1-6), Apr to Sept. For NGS: Sun 30, Mon 31 Aug (2-5).**
1-acre garden subdivided by walls and trellises hosting a wide range of climbers. Mixed borders of unusual plants, Victorian conservatory and greenhouse extend the gardening yr. Holders of National Collection of Clematis *viticella cvs* and Lapageria Rosea cultivars. Some slopes.

& ⚘ **NCCPG** ☕

54 ◆ ST MICHAEL'S MOUNT
Marazion TR17 0HT. James & Mary St Aubyn, 01736 710507, www.stmichaelsmount.co.uk. *2½ m E of Penzance. 1/2 m from shore at Marazion by Causeway; otherwise by motor boat.* **Castle & garden £6.60, chd £3.30, garden only adm £3, chd £1. Gardens Mon-Fri, 1 May to 30 Jun; Thurs, Fris 1 Jul to 1 Nov. Castle Sun-Fri, 29 Mar to 1 Nov. For NGS: Thur 30 Apr (10.30-5.30).**

Flowering shrubs; rock plants, spectacular castle; fine sea views. Steep climb to castle, uneven cobbled surfaces, sensible shoes advised.

The planting reflects a relaxed style . . . many succulents inhabit stone walls . . .

55 SCORRIER HOUSE
Redruth TR16 5AU. Richard & Caroline Williams. *2½ m E of Redruth. From Truro A390, at 4th roundabout slip road A30 to Redruth for 2½ m, A3047 under railway bridge, L at mini roundabout to B3287 for 1/2 m, R on B3207 for 200yds, R by Lodge House. From Falmouth take A393 to Redruth for 7m then B3258, turn at 2nd lodge.* **Adm £3, chd free. Sun 29 Mar (2-5).**
Formal garden round old family house with herbaceous border, knot garden and conservatory. Walled garden filled with camellias, rhododendrons and magnolias. All set in parkland with ha ha. Unfenced swimming pool.

56 NEW STENCOOSE FARMHOUSE
Wheal Rose, Redruth TR16 5DQ. Mr & Mrs N J Reed. *2m E of Redruth. Leave A30 westbound at Scorrier, over flyover, 1st L to Wheal Rose/Porthtowan. R through Wheal Rose past Ethrington Meat Packing on L. Next L (public bridleway), 1/2 m along track to white farmhouse.* Cream teas. **Adm £3.50, chd free. Sun 27 Sept (11-5).**
Garden completely redesigned since 2002. The planting reflects a relaxed style with unusual trees, shrubs, perennials and grasses. Many succulents inhabit stone walls. Fruit and vegetable garden now being developed with a collection of old varieties of Cornish apples.

57 ◆ TREBAH
Mawnan Smith TR11 5JZ. Trebah
Garden Trust, 01326 252200,
www.trebah-garden.co.uk. *4m SW of
Falmouth. Follow tourist signs from
Hillhead roundabout on A39 approach
to Falmouth or Treliever Cross
roundabout on junction of A39-A394.
Parking for coaches.* **Adm £7.50 Mar-
Oct (£3 Nov-Feb), chd £2.50/£1,
concessions £6.50/£2.50. Daily all yr
(10.30-5/dusk if earlier).**
26-acre S-facing ravine garden,
planted in 1830s. Extensive collection
rare/mature trees/shrubs incl glades;
huge tree ferns 100yrs old, subtropical
exotics. Hydrangea collection covers
2¹/₂ acres. Water garden, waterfalls,
rock pool stocked with mature koi
carp. Enchanted garden for
plantsman/artist/family. Play area/trails
for children. Use of private beach.
Steep paths in places. 2 motorised
vehicles available, please book in
advance.
&♿ ❀ ☕

58 TREBARTHA
nr Launceston PL15 7PE. The
Latham Family. *6m SW of
Launceston. North Hill, SW of
Launceston nr junction of B3254 &
B3257.* Cream teas. **Adm £3, chd
free. Sun 20 Sept (2-5).**
Wooded area with lake surrounded by
walks of flowering shrubs; woodland
trail through fine woods with cascades
and waterfalls; American glade with
fine trees. No coaches.
❀ ☕

59 TREGONNING LODGE
Tregonning Road, Stithians
TR3 7DA. Pat & Jeremy Thomas,
01209 861179. *4m NW of Falmouth.
Stithians turning off A393 at Five Lanes
Xrds ³/₄ m N of Ponsanooth. In village L
at Xrds signed Trevales, garden 25yds.
On-site parking.* Cream teas. **Adm £3,
chd free. Sun 12 July (1-5). Visitors
also welcome by appt.**
New garden set on S-facing slope in 4
acres of woodland, shrubberies, beds
and 2 natural ponds. 10yrs of planting
have yielded a garden full of interest.
Herbaceous borders and waterlilies are
at their best in July and Aug. Partial
wheelchair access, gravel paths, steps.
&♿ ❀ ☕ ☎

60 TREGULLOW
Scorrier TR16 5AY. Mr & Mrs James
Williams. *2m E of Redruth. Leave A30
at Scorrier. Follow signs to St Day &
Carharrack on B3298. 1m out of*

Scorrier turn R at Tolgullow Village sign.
Go through white gates by lodge.
Cream teas. **Adm £3.50, chd £1. Mon
4 May (1.30-5.30).**
An idyllic Cornish spring garden a mere
3m from the Atlantic. Tregullow is
blessed with unfolding vistas of intense
colour as you explore your way around
its 15 acres. First planted by the
Williams family in C19, the gardens
have been carefully restored and
replanted since the 1970s. Partly
accessible to wheelchairs but 2 flights
of granite steps need to be bypassed.
&♿ ❀ ☕

A hint of quirkiness - not all is what it seems! . . .

61 ◆ TRELISSICK
Feock TR3 6QL. The National Trust,
01872 862090,
www.nationaltrust.org.uk. *4m S of
Truro. Nr King Harry Ferry. On B3289.*
**Adm £7, chd £3.50. Daily except
Christmas (10.30-5.30 14 Feb to 31
Oct; 11-4 1 Nov to 13 Feb). For
NGS: Sats 14 Mar; 18 July (10.30-
5.30).**
Planted with tender shrubs; magnolias,
camellias and rhododendrons with
many named species characteristic of
Cornish gardens. National Collection of
Photinias and Azaras. Fine woodlands
encircle the gardens through which a
varied circular walk can be enjoyed.
Superb view over Falmouth harbour.
Georgian house, not open. Now
accessible by foot ferry from Truro,
Falmouth and St Mawes, Apr-Sept.
Gravel paths, some steps, suggested
route.
&♿ 🐕 ❀ NCCPG ☕

62 TRENARTH
High Cross, Constantine TR11 5JN.
Mrs L M Nottingham, 01326 340444,
lmnottingham@tiscali.co.uk. *6m SW
of Falmouth. Nearest main rds A39-
A394 Truro to Helston-Falmouth: follow
signs for Constantine. At High Cross
garage, 1¹/₂ m before Constantine, turn
L signed Mawnan, then R after 30yds*

down dead end lane. Garden at end of
lane. Home-made teas. **Adm £3, chd
free. Sun 19 July (2-5). Visitors also
welcome by appt.**
4-acre garden surrounding C17
farmhouse in lovely pastoral setting -
not a road in sight or sound. Yr-round
interest. Emphasis on unusual plants,
structure and form, with a hint of
quirkiness - not all is what it seems!
Courtyard, C18 garden walls, yew
rooms, prize-winning vegetable
garden, traditional potting shed,
'puddled' pond, orchard, green lane
walk down to R Helford. New for 2009:
collection of dieramas and water
feature. Prizewinner Kerrier Gardens.
❀ ☕ ☎

63 ◆ TRENGWAINTON
Madron TR20 8RZ. The National
Trust, 01736 363148,
trengwainton@nationaltrust.org.uk.
*2m NW of Penzance. ¹/₂ m W of
Heamoor. On Penzance-Morvah rd
(B3312), ¹/₂ m off St Just rd (A3071).*
**Adm £5.40, chd £2.70. Suns to
Thurs, 8 Feb to 1 Nov (10.30-5). For
NGS: Sun 12 Apr; Sun 30 Aug
(10.30-5).**
Sheltered garden with an abundance
of exotic trees and shrubs. Picturesque
stream running through valley and
stunning views of Mounts Bay from
terrace. Ongoing restoration of walled
kitchen garden showcasing
contemporary varieties of fruit and
vegetables. Large collection of
camellias and rhododendrons. Free
guided tour 2pm on NGS days. Gravel
paths off main tarmac drive.
&♿ ❀ ☕

64 ◆ TRERICE
nr Newquay TR8 4PG. The National
Trust, 01637 875404,
trerice@nationaltrust.org.uk. *3m SE
of Newquay. From Newquay via A392
& A3058; turn R at Kestle Mill (NT
signs) or signed from A30 at
Summercourt via A3058.* **House and
garden adm £7, chd £3.50, garden
only adm £2.40, chd £1.20. 23 Feb-
1Nov daily except Fri. Gardens
10.30-5, house 11-4.30. For NGS:
Sun 19 Apr; Sat 18 July (11-5).**
Summer/autumn-flowering garden
unusual in content and layout and for
neutral alkaline soil varieties. Orchard
planted with old varieties of fruit trees.
Experimental Tudor garden developed
in partnership with local primary
school. Grass paths. For wheelchair
access to house please phone.
&♿ 🐕 ❀ ☕

Stunning waterfall . . .

65 ◆ **TREVARNO GARDENS AND THE NATIONAL MUSEUM OF GARDENING**
Crowntown, Helston TR13 0RU. Messrs M Sagin & N Helsby, 01326 574274, www.trevarno.co.uk. *3m NW of Helston. Signed from Crowntown on B3303. Disabled parking.* **Adm £6.50, chd £2.10, concessions £5.75. Open daily except Xmas Day & Boxing Day (10.30-5).**
Unforgettable gardening experience combining Victorian garden with fountain garden café, unique range of craft workshops and the National Museum of Gardening, Britain's largest and most comprehensive collection of antique tools, implements, memorabilia and ephemera. Vintage soap and nostalgic toy museum (small additional charge). Woodland adventure play area and estate walk. Featured on Westcountry TV Gorgeous Gardens and in Telegraph and Sunday Times. 'Access for All' pathways. Limited number of wheelchairs for loan.

66 ◆ **TREWAN HALL**
St Columb TR9 6DB. Mrs P M Hill. *6m E of Newquay. N of St Columb Major, off A39 to Wadebridge. 1st turning on L signed to St Eval & Talskiddy. Entrance ¾ m on L in woodland.* Cream teas. **Adm £3, chd free.** Sun 10 May (2-5.30).

Set in 36 acres of fields and bluebell woodland, with gardens round the house. Mixed beds, roses and specimen trees. Driveway bordered by rhododendrons and hydrangeas. Lovely views over the Lanherne Valley. Trewan Hall (not open) built in 1633 is a fine centrepiece for garden. Children welcome. Small playground, large grass area for games. Gold David Bellamy Conservation Award (6yrs).

67 ◆ **TREWITHEN**
Truro TR2 4DD. Mr & Mrs Michael Galsworthy, 01726 883647, www.trewithengardens.co.uk. *½ m E of Probus. Entrance on A390 Truro-St Austell rd. Signed.* **Adm £5. Mon to Sat, 1 Mar to 30 Sept; Suns Mar to May (10-4.30).**
Internationally renowned and historic garden of 30 acres laid out between 1912 and 1960 with much of original seed and plant material collected by Ward Forrest. Towering magnolias and rhododendrons and very large collection of camellias. Flattish ground amidst original woodland park and magnificent landscaped lawn vistas. Rose garden currently in development. Many new plantings throughout the garden which is now responding to the challenge of climate change with many new introductions.

68 ◆ **TREWOOFE HOUSE**
Lamorna TR19 6PA. Mrs H M Pigott, tel and fax 01736 810269. *4m SW of Penzance. Take B3315 from Penzance via Newlyn towards Lamorna. At top of hill take sharp turn signed Trewoofe.* **Adm £3, chd free. Suns & Weds June only (2-5). Group visits**

welcome by prior arrangement. For NGS: Sun 14 June (11-5).
2-acre garden at top of Lamorna Valley with ancient mill leat. Bog garden planted with a variety of primulas, many kinds of iris, astilbes and arums. Shrub and perennial beds planted for all-yr interest. Small fruit garden with espalier and cordon-trained apple and pear trees. Conservatory with semi-tender climbers and vine. Featured in 'Inside Cornwall'. Partial wheelchair access, grass and gravel paths.

69 **TREWOOFE ORCHARD**
Lamorna TR19 6BW. Dick & Barbara Waterson, 01736 810214. *4m SW of Penzance. on B3315, Signed from Lamorna Cove turning.* **Adm £3, chd free (share to RNLI).** Visitors welcome by appt most days, Feb to Oct (10-dusk). **Please tel to confirm before travelling any distance.**
4-acre valley garden, secluded and tranquil. bluebell woodland; more formal planting around the house. Stunning waterfall, stream, still pond and rills. Spring bulbs, camellias, arums, hostas and new tree ferns. Plenty of seats and well-defined paths. Peace and quiet in a magical setting. Water everywhere to delight the senses. Full of butterflies, bird song and busy bees. Featured in 'Cornwall Today' and 'Cornish World'. Partial wheelchair access to lower levels near stream, not to steps/steep slopes.

WICK FARM GARDENS
See Devon.

WILDSIDE
See Devon.

Cornwall County Volunteers

County Organiser
William Croggon, Creed House , Creed, Grampound, Truro TR2 4SL, 01872 530372

County Treasurer
Nigel Rimmer, 11 Melvill Road, Falmouth TR11 4AS, 01326 313429

Leaflet Coordinator
Peter Stanley, Mazey Cottage, Tangies, Gunwalloe, Helston TR12 7PU, 01326 565868, stanley.m2@sky.com

Publicity
Hugh Tapper, Trethewey Barns, Ruan Lanihorne, Tregony, Truro TR2 5TH, 01872 530567, hugh@truro.tv

Assistant County Organisers
Barry Champion, Lillys Cottage, Dicky Lane, Trelissick, Feock, Truro TR3 6QL, 01872 870750, wbchampion2003@yahoo.co.uk
Ginnie Clotworthy, Trethew, Lanlivery, Bodmin PL30 5BZ, 01208 872612 giles.clotworthy@btopenworld.com
Lally Croggon, Creed House, Creed, Grampound, Truro TR2 4SL, 01872 530372
Caroline Latham, Stonaford Manor, North Hill, Launceston PL15 7PE, 01566 782970
Alison O'Connor, Tregoose, Grampound, Truro TR2 4DB, 01726 882460
Marion Stanley, Mazey Cottage, Tangies, Gunwalloe, Helston TR12 7PU, 01326 565868
Virginia Vyvyan-Robinson, Mellingey Mill House, St Issey, Wadebridge PL27 7QU, 01841 540511

Mark your diary with these special events in 2009

EXPLORE SECRET GARDENS DURING CHELSEA & HAMPTON COURT FLOWER SHOW WEEKS

Tue 19 May, Wed 20 May, Thur 21 May, Fri 22 May, Wed 8 July, Thur 9 July
Full day tours from £82 per person, 10% discount for groups
Advance booking required, telephone +44 (0)20 8693 1015 or email j.wookey@btinternet.com
Specially selected gardens in London, Essex, Kent, Hampshire and South Oxfordshire. The tour price includes transport and lunch with wine at a popular restaurant or pub.

HAMPTON COURT PALACE

Thur 2 Apr, Tue 23 June, Thur 25 June, Wed 15 July, Tue 4 Aug, Thur 10 Sept
Evening tours in the company of one of the Palace's specialist tour guides from 6.30 – 8pm
Tickets £6 per person. Advance booking required, telephone +44 (0)1483 211535 or visit www.ngs.org.uk for more information
Gossip, scandal, murder, healing – you'll find it all within the Formal Gardens at Hampton Court Palace. Each tour will have its own unique feature whether it's the story of the Great Vine or the magic and mystery of the Maze.

FROGMORE – A ROYAL GARDEN (BERKSHIRE)

Tue 26 May 10am – 5.30pm (last admission 4pm)
Garden adm £4.50, chd free. Tickets available in advance or on the day.
Advance booking for groups and coaches, telephone
+44 (0) 1483 211535 or email orders@ngs.org.uk
A rare opportunity to explore 30 acres of landscaped garden, rich in history and beauty.

FLAXBOURNE FARM – FUN & SURPRISES (BEDFORDSHIRE)

Sun 7 June 10am – 5pm. Adm £5, chd free
No booking required, come along on the day!
Bring the whole family and have fun in this surprising and entertaining garden of 2 acres. Enjoy the large plant fair, live music, pets corner, birds of prey, dog agility show and much more.

WISLEY RHS GARDEN – MUSIC IN THE GARDEN (SURREY)

Fri 11 Sept 6 – 9pm
Adm (incl RHS members) £7, chd under 15 free
Save money on advance bookings for groups of 4 or more, telephone +44 (0)1483 211535 or visit www.ngs.org.uk for more information
A special evening opening of this famous garden, exclusively for the NGS. Enjoy music and entertainment as you explore the gardens and the floral marquee on the first day of the Wisley Flower Show.

For further information visit www.ngs.org.uk or telephone 01483 211535

CUMBRIA

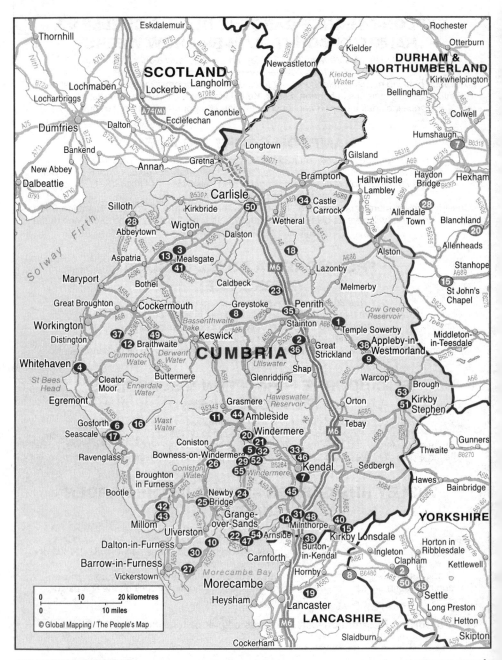

Scale:
0 — 10 — 20 kilometres
0 — 10 miles

© Global Mapping / The People's Map

Opening Dates

March

SUNDAY 1
48 Summerdale House

WEDNESDAY 25
11 Copt Howe

FRIDAY 27
11 Copt Howe

April

WEDNESDAY 1
11 Copt Howe

FRIDAY 10
11 Copt Howe

SATURDAY 11
11 Copt Howe

SUNDAY 12
11 Copt Howe
48 Summerdale House

MONDAY 13
48 Summerdale House

WEDNESDAY 15
11 Copt Howe

THURSDAY 16
44 Rydal Hall

WEDNESDAY 22
11 Copt Howe

FRIDAY 24
11 Copt Howe

SATURDAY 25
10 Conishead Priory & Buddhist
Temple
11 Copt Howe

SUNDAY 26
10 Conishead Priory & Buddhist
Temple
28 Lilac Cottage Garden

WEDNESDAY 29
11 Copt Howe

May

FRIDAY 1
8 Chapelside

SATURDAY 2
8 Chapelside

SUNDAY 3
5 Brackenrigg Lodge
48 Summerdale House
52 Windy Hall

WEDNESDAY 6
11 Copt Howe

SATURDAY 9
1 Acorn Bank
11 Copt Howe

SUNDAY 10
14 Dallam Tower

WEDNESDAY 13
11 Copt Howe
24 Lakeside Hotel

FRIDAY 15
8 Chapelside
11 Copt Howe

SATURDAY 16
8 Chapelside
29 Lindeth Fell Country House Hotel
31 Lower Rowell Farm

SUNDAY 17
15 Fell Yeat
27 Leece Village Gardens
31 Lower Rowell Farm
32 Matson Ground

FRIDAY 22
11 Copt Howe

SATURDAY 23
11 Copt Howe
18 Hazel Cottage

SUNDAY 24
6 Buckbarrow House
11 Copt Howe
16 Galesyke
36 The Nook
42 The Ridding
43 Ridding Barn

MONDAY 25
6 Buckbarrow House
7 Castle Green Hotel
16 Galesyke
36 The Nook
42 The Ridding
43 Ridding Barn

FRIDAY 29
8 Chapelside
11 Copt Howe

SATURDAY 30
8 Chapelside
40 Pudding Poke Barn (Evening)

SUNDAY 31
19 Heywood House

June

WEDNESDAY 3
11 Copt Howe

FRIDAY 5
11 Copt Howe

SATURDAY 6
1 Acorn Bank
11 Copt Howe

SUNDAY 7
2 Askham Hall
5 Brackenrigg Lodge

23 Hutton-in-the-Forest
48 Summerdale House
52 Windy Hall
54 Yewbarrow House

WEDNESDAY 10
11 Copt Howe

FRIDAY 12
8 Chapelside
11 Copt Howe

SATURDAY 13
8 Chapelside
50 Tullie House

SUNDAY 14
3 Beech House
50 Tullie House

WEDNESDAY 17
11 Copt Howe

THURSDAY 18
44 Rydal Hall

FRIDAY 19
11 Copt Howe

SUNDAY 21
9 Church View
13 Crookdake Farm
19 Heywood House
46 Sprint Mill
55 Yews

WEDNESDAY 24
11 Copt Howe
35 Newton Rigg Campus Gardens
(Day & Evening)
39 Pear Tree Cottage (Evening)

FRIDAY 26
8 Chapelside

SATURDAY 27
8 Chapelside

SUNDAY 28
28 Lilac Cottage Garden
30 Little Urswick Village
Gardens

MONDAY 29
7 Castle Green Hotel (Evening)

July

THURSDAY 2
31 Lower Rowell Farm (Evening)

SATURDAY 4
20 High Cross Lodge

SUNDAY 5
20 High Cross Lodge
48 Summerdale House
54 Yewbarrow House

WEDNESDAY 8
22 Holker Hall Gardens

FRIDAY 10
(8) Chapelside

SATURDAY 11
(8) Chapelside

SUNDAY 12
(23) Hutton-in-the-Forest
(34) Netherton
(39) Pear Tree Cottage
(41) Quarry Hill House
(49) Swinside End Farm

FRIDAY 17
(8) Chapelside

SATURDAY 18
(1) Acorn Bank
(8) Chapelside
(42) The Ridding
(43) Ridding Barn
(45) Sizergh Castle

SUNDAY 19
(42) The Ridding
(43) Ridding Barn

THURSDAY 23
(21) Holehird Gardens
(44) Rydal Hall

SATURDAY 25
(40) Pudding Poke Barn

SUNDAY 26
(26) Lawson Park
(33) Meadow House
(40) Pudding Poke Barn
(46) Sprint Mill
(51) Westview
(53) Winton Park

August

SUNDAY 2
(17) Hall Senna
(48) Summerdale House
(54) Yewbarrow House

SATURDAY 8
(12) Croftside

TUESDAY 11
(47) Stone Edge (Day & Evening)

SUNDAY 16
(38) Olde Oaks

THURSDAY 20
(44) Rydal Hall

SUNDAY 23
(4) Berridale

September

WEDNESDAY 2
(24) Lakeside Hotel

SUNDAY 6
(48) Summerdale House
(54) Yewbarrow House

SUNDAY 13
(9) Church View

SUNDAY 27
(7) Castle Green Hotel

February 2010

SUNDAY 28
(48) Summerdale House

Gardens open to the public

(1) Acorn Bank
(10) Conishead Priory & Buddhist Temple
(11) Copt Howe
(21) Holehird Gardens
(22) Holker Hall Gardens
(23) Hutton-in-the-Forest
(44) Rydal Hall
(45) Sizergh Castle
(50) Tullie House

By appointment only

(25) Langholme Mill
(37) The Old Rectory

Also open by appointment ☎

(6) Buckbarrow House
(7) Castle Green Hotel
(8) Chapelside
(9) Church View
(16) Galesyke
(17) Hall Senna
(20) High Cross Lodge
(24) Lakeside Hotel
(26) Lawson Park
(28) Lilac Cottage Garden
(29) Lindeth Fell Country House Hotel
(31) Lower Rowell Farm
(32) Matson Ground
(36) The Nook
(38) Olde Oaks
(39) Pear Tree Cottage
(41) Quarry Hill House
(46) Sprint Mill
(47) Stone Edge
(48) Summerdale House
(49) Swinside End Farm
(52) Windy Hall
(54) Yewbarrow House

The Gardens

(1) ◆ ACORN BANK
Temple Sowerby CA10 1SP. The National Trust, 017683 61893, www.nationaltrust.org.uk. *6m E of Penrith. Off A66; 1/2 m N of Temple Sowerby. Bus: Penrith-Appleby or Carlisle-Darlington; alight Culgaith Rd end.* **Adm £4, chd £2. Wed to Sun Mar to Oct. For NGS: Sats 9 May; 6 June; 18 July (10-5).**
Medium-sized walled garden; fine herb garden; orchard and mixed borders; wild garden with woodland/riverside walk leading to a partly restored watermill open to the public. Dogs on leads only in woodland walk.
&. ✕ 🐕 ❀ ☕

(2) ASKHAM HALL
Penrith CA10 2PF. Countess of Lonsdale. *5m S of Penrith. Turn off A6 for Lowther & Askham.* Home-made teas. **Adm £3, chd free (share to Askham & Lowther Churches). Sun 7 June (2-5).**
Askham Hall is a pele tower (not open), incorporating C14, C16 and early C18 elements in courtyard plan. Splendid formal outlines of garden with terraces of herbaceous borders and original topiary, probably from late C17. Herb garden and recently created meadow area with trees and pond. Increasing kitchen garden, basically organic.
✕ ❀ ☕

(3) BEECH HOUSE
Woodrow CA7 0AT. Mr & Mrs L B J McDonnell. *3m W of Wigton. On A595 take turning signed Waverton. At first xrds take turning signed Wigton. First house 250yds on L.* Home-made teas. **Adm £3, chd free. Sun 14 June (1-5).**
Approx 3/4 acre of informal garden with lawns, mixed shrub/herbaceous borders, stream and ponds.
&. ✕ ❀ ☕

Large vegetable garden with fruit trees, show class vegetables and flowers . . .

④ NEW BERRIDALE

15 Loop Road South, Whitehaven CA28 7TN. John Stanborough. *From S, A595 through T-lights onto Loop Rd approx 150yds on R. From N, A595 onto Loop Rd at Pelican Garage, garden approx 1½ m on L.* Home-made teas. Adm £3, chd free. Sun 23 Aug (2-5).

Large cottage style garden divided into several areas including Japanese style, wildlife, patio, large vegetable garden with fruit trees, show class vegetables and flowers. Large front garden, 2 lawns surrounded by flower borders and small pond. Large pond with seating area leading to greenhouse of fuchsias and plants for sale. Oil paintings; show fuchsias in baskets and pots. Featured in local press.

✕ ✿ ☕

⑤ BRACKENRIGG LODGE

Windy Hall Road, Bowness-on-Windermere LA23 3HY. Lynne Bush, www.brackenriggs.co.uk. *1m S of Bowness. Just off B5284 on Windy Hall Rd, opp Linthwaite House Hotel entrance.* Home-made teas at Windy Hall. Adm £3, chd free. Combined with Windy Hall adm £5. Suns 3 May; 7 June (10-5).

3 acres of wildlife garden run on organic lines with a combination of native and cultivated plants, shrubs and trees. Water features created from a diverted culvert giving streams, waterfall and pond. Woodland area, bog garden, wild flower meadows. Haphazard pruning and netted plants due to regular deer visitations. Stout footwear.

✕ ⊨ ☕

⑥ BUCKBARROW HOUSE

Denton Park Court, Gosforth CA20 1BN. John Maddison, 01946 725431, johnmaddgosf@aol.com. *13m S of Whitehaven. Turn off A595. Through centre of Gosforth Village. At 'Y' junction take L fork towards Wasdale. After 150yds turn L (before church) into Denton Park. Keep bearing R. House is last on R in Denton Park Court.* Adm £3, chd free. Sun 24, Mon 25 May (11-5). Also open Galesyke. Visitors also welcome by appt all year, groups max 10.

Small densely-planted garden approx 23yds x 49yds. Numerous compartments incl wildlife pond, Japanese gravel garden, shrub area, cottage garden borders and natural stream. Decking area. Decorative stone front garden. Over 30 acers, mostly Japanese palmatum. A friend (I hope) described it as 'Delightfully wild'. Included in Gardens of the Lake District by Tim Longville.

✕ ✿ ☕ ☎

⑦ NEW CASTLE GREEN HOTEL

Castle Green Lane, Kendal LA9 6RG. Castle Green Hotel, 01539 734000, www.castlegreen.co.uk. *M6, J37, 5m on R on A684.* Adm £3, chd free. Mon 25 May (1-4); Evening Opening; Mon 29 June (5-7); Sun 27 Sept (1-4). Visitors also welcome by appt.

The grounds cover approx 14 acres, spread over a mix of woodlands, wildlife areas, herbaceous perennials and rolling lawns. Mature trees incl oaks, pines, Cercidiphyllum japonica, beeches as well as ornamentals such as Catalpa bignonioides and Cystisus battandieri. Mature yews and topiary are common themes throughout. Winner Best Commercial Premises with Grounds, Kendal in Bloom. Some steep slopes.

♿ ✕ ⊨ ☕ ☎

⑧ CHAPELSIDE

Mungrisdale, Penrith CA11 0XR. Tricia & Robin Acland, 017687 79672. *12m W of Penrith. On A66 take unclassified rd N, signed Mungrisdale Village. House is far end of scattered village on L immed after tiny church on R. Use parish church room parking at foot of our short drive.* Adm £2.50, chd free (share to Mungrisdale Parish Church). Fri, Sats 1, 2, 15, 16, 29, 30 May; 12, 13, 26, 27 June; 10, 11, 17, 18 July (11-5). Visitors also welcome by appt, teas for groups by arrangement.

1 acre organic garden below fell, tiny stream, large pond. Extensive range of plants, many unusual, providing green texture and colour effects carefully or accidentally structured in closely planted relaxed style. Art constructions in and out, local stone used creatively. Fine views, so unkind winds. Wildlife friendly. Featured in 'Gardens of the Lake District'.

✕ ✿ ☎

⑨ NEW CHURCH VIEW

Bonegate, Appleby-in-Westmorland CA16 6UN. Mrs H Holmes, 017683 51397. *Northbound on A66 take B6542 to Appleby. After 2m St Michael's Church on L garden opp. Southbound on A66 take Appleby slip rd, B6542 under railway bridge, pass R Eden on R and continue up hill to Royal Oak Inn. Garden next door opp church.* Adm £3, chd free. Suns 21 June; 13 Sept (2-5). Visitors also welcome by appt.

Developed (2007 – 2008) on a sloping site. Roses and some shrubs for structure, but relying heavily on grasses and herbaceous plants to create textures, colour combinations and contrasts in a modern way. Mixed beds at front with 'woodland corner'. A small self-contained cottage garden to get lost in. Sloping gravel paths in main garden, flat surface to front and side.

♿ ✕ ⊨ ☕ ☎

Small self-contained cottage garden to get lost in . . .

⑩ ◆ CONISHEAD PRIORY & BUDDHIST TEMPLE

Ulverston, A5087 Coast Rd LA12 9QQ. Manjushri Kadampa Meditation Centre, 01229 584029, www.manjushri.org. *2m S of Ulverston on A5087 coast rd. 30 mins from M6 J36, follow A590 to Ulverston then L onto coastal rd. Car parking free.* Adm £3, chd free. Open daily except Sat 16 May to Sun 31 May and Sat 18 July to Sun 16 August incl. For NGS: Sat 25, Sun 26 Apr (2-5).

40 acres of gardens and woodland surrounding historic mansion. Temple garden an oasis of peace, lake and wildlife garden, arboretum, cottage gardens. Woodland walks to Morecambe Bay. Free guided house tours from 2pm onwards with garden ticket. Temple, cafe and gift shop.

♿ ☕

11 ◆ COPT HOWE
Chapel Stile, Great Langdale
LA22 9JR. Professor R N
Haszeldine, Please tel 015394 37685
for weekly recorded message. *5m W
of Ambleside. On B5343, 1/4 m past
Chapel Stile.* For
NGS: Weds 25, Fri 27 Mar; Wed 1
Apr; Fri 10 to Sun 12 Apr; Weds 15
Apr to 13 May; Wed 1, Fri 24, Sat 25
Apr; Sat 9 May; Fris 15 to 29 May;
Sats 9, 23, Sun 24 May; Weds, 3
June to 24 June; Fris 5 to 19 June;
Sat 6 June (12-5).
2-acre plantsman's mountain paradise
garden. Superb views Langdale Pikes.
Extensive collections of acers,
camellias, azaleas, rhododendrons,
oaks, beeches, rare shrubs, trees,
unusual perennials; herbaceous and
bulbous species; alpines, trough
gardens; rare conifers; expedition
plants from worldwide mountainous
regions. Outstanding spring and
autumn colour. Wildlife sanctuary, red
squirrels, badgers, slow-worms, hotel
for wild birds. Major new garden
extensions. Featured in many papers,
magazines, radio and TV programmes.

12 NEW CROFTSIDE
Mockerkin, Cockermouth
CA13 0ST. Anne & Ian Frazer. *5m
S of Cockermouth. From
Cockermouth A5086 towards
Egremont for 5m, turn L at sign to
Mockerkin 1/2 m on R of main rd
through village.* Light refreshments
& teas. **Adm £2.50, chd free. Sat
8 May (10-4).**
1/2 acre plot developed for year
round interest. Wide variety of
plants, fruit garden, ponds and
raised beds.

13 NEW CROOKDAKE FARM
Aspatria CA7 3SH. Kirk &
Alannah Rylands. *3m NE of
Aspatria. Between A595 & A596.
From A595 take B5299 at
Mealsgate signed Aspatria. After
2m turn sharp R in Watch Hill
signed Crookdake. House 1m on
L.* Home-made teas. **Adm £3, chd
free. Sun 21 June (1-5).**
Exposed farmhouse (not open)
garden incl densely planted
herbaceous borders, vegetables,
meadow and pond areas.

We have tried to incorporate new features . . . sympathetic to the existing buildings and landscape . . .

14 DALLAM TOWER
Milnthorpe LA7 7AG. Mr & Mrs R T
Villiers-Smith. *7m S of Kendal. 7m N
of Carnforth. Nr junction of A6 &
B5282. Stn: Arnside, 4m; Lancaster,
15m.* Cream teas. **Adm £3, chd free.
Sun 10 May (2-5).**
Large garden; natural rock garden,
water garden; wood walks, lawns,
shrubs. C19 cast iron orangery.

15 FELL YEAT
Casterton, nr Kirkby Lonsdale
LA6 2JW. Mr & Mrs O S Benson. *1m
E of Casterton Village. On the rd to Bull
Pot. Leave A65 at Devils Bridge, follow
A683 for 1m, take the R fork to High
Casterton at golf course, straight
across at two sets of Xrds, house on L,
1/4 m from no-through-rd sign.* Cream
teas. **Adm £3.50, chd free. Sun 17
May (1-5).**
1-acre country garden with mixed
planting, incl unusual trees, shrubs and
some topiary. Small woodland garden,
and woodland glades. Paved white
garden, 2 ponds which encourage
dragonflies. National Collection of
Ligularia. Several arbours. A garden to
be explored. Featured in 'Amateur
Gardening'. Some gravel paths, gentle
slopes.

16 GALESYKE
Wasdale CA20 1ET. Christine & Mike
McKinley, 019467 26267,
mckinley2112@sky.com. *From N
follow signs to Nether Wasdale,
through village take rd to The Lake &
Wasdale Head. After approx 3/4 m
Galesyke on R on sharp R-hand bend
with wooden fence. From S turn R at
Santon Bridge, follow signs to Wasdale
Head, Galesyke 21/2 m on R.* Cream
teas. **Adm £3, chd free. Sun 24, Mon
25 May (11-5).** Also open
**Buckbarrow House. Visitors also
welcome by appt May/June only.**

Partially landscaped garden of several
acres on banks of R Irt with views of
Wasdale Fells, noted for its display of
rhododendrons and azaleas.

17 NEW HALL SENNA
Hallsenna, Holmrook, Gosforth
CA19 1YB. Chris & Helen Steele,
019467 25436,
helen.steele5@btinternet.com.
*2m SW of Gosforth. Follow main
A595 either N or S. 1m S of
Gosforth turn down lane opp
Seven Acres Caravan Park,
proceed for approx 1m.* Home-
made teas. **Adm £3, chd £2
(share to Alzheimer's Society).
Sun 2 Aug (10-5). Visitors also
welcome by appt May to Sept,
individuals or small groups, no
coaches.**
Over the last 7yrs we have
developed a garden from a 1-acre
site above the house. We have
tried to incorporate new features
whilst being sympathetic to the
existing buildings and landscape.
Features incl vegetable and sunken
gardens, arbour border and folly
garden. Large lawned areas and
summerhouse. Flower arranging
display.

18 HAZEL COTTAGE
Armathwaite CA4 9PG. Mr D Ryland
& Mr J Thexton. *8m SE of Carlisle.
Turn off A6 just S of High Hesket
signed Armathwaite, after 2m house
facing you at T-junction.* Home-made
teas. **Adm £3.50, chd free. Sat 23
May (12-5).**
Developing flower arrangers and
plantsmans garden. Extending to
approx 5 acres. Incls herbaceous
borders, pergola, ponds and planting
of disused railway siding providing
home to wildlife. Many variegated and
unusual plants. Varied areas, planted
for all seasons, S-facing, some gentle
slopes. Featured in 'Flora International
Magazine'.

19 HEYWOOD HOUSE
Brookhouse LA2 9PW. Mike &
Lorraine Cave. *4m E of Lancaster.
From J34 M6, follow A683 to
Caton/Kirkby Lonsdale. At mini island
turn R to Brookhouse. At Black Bull PH
turn R, garden 3/4 m on LH-side.*
Home-made teas. **Adm £3, chd free.**

Suns 31 May; 21 June (11-5).
Secluded 2-acre garden with many unusual trees and shrubs, sweeping lawns with beautiful herbaceous borders leading to large natural wildlife pond, gravel garden, pergolas with an abundance of roses and climbers, rockery, folly, woodland garden with natural stream, under development. Garden railway train rides for adults and children.

🐾 ❀ ☕

⑳ HIGH CROSS LODGE
Bridge Lane, Troutbeck LA23 1LA. Linda Orchant, 01539 488521, lindaorchant@talktalk.net. *2¹/₂ m N of Windermere. From Windermere, after Lakes School turn R into Bridge Lane off A591, next to YHA.* Adm £3.50, chd free. Sat 4, Sun 5 July (11-4). Visitors also welcome by appt May, June & July for groups of 15+, small coaches permitted.
Tropical-style garden designed by owner for all-yr interest. 1-acre gently sloping garden in a woodland setting with local slate terracing and cascading serpentine stream. Spectacular display of over 30 tree ferns, trachycarpus, cordylines and phormiums, many other non-hardy exotics. Collection of acers, ferns and pristine slug free hostas. Perfumed white garden surrounds a delightful summerhouse. Featured in 'GGG'.

🐾 ❀ ☎

㉑ ◆ HOLEHIRD GARDENS
Windermere LA23 1NP. Lakeland Horticultural Society, 015394 46008, www.holehirdgardens.org.uk. *2m N of Windermere. Off A592 Patterdale Rd. Garden signed on R.* Adm £3, by donation, chd free. Open daily all yr. For NGS: Thur 23 July (10-5).
The garden is run by volunteers with the aim of promoting knowledge of the cultivation of alpine and herbaceous plants, shrubs and trees, especially those suited to Lakeland conditions. One of the best labelled gardens in the UK. National Collections of *Astilbe*, *Hydrangea* and *Polystichum* (ferns). Set on the fellside with stunning views over Windermere the walled garden gives protection to mixed borders whilst alpine houses protect an always colourful array of tiny gems. Consistently voted among the top gardens in Britain and Europe. Visit our website. Featured in national press, TV & radio.

♿ 🐾 ❀ NCCPG

㉒ ◆ HOLKER HALL GARDENS
Cark-in-Cartmel LA11 7PL. Lord & Lady Cavendish, 015395 58328, www.holkerhall.co.uk. *4m W of Grange-over-Sands. 12m W of M6 (J36) Follow brown 'tourist signs'.* House & garden £9.25, chd £5, concessions £8.50, garden only £5.95, chd £3, concessions £5.25. Gardens 22 March to 1 November closed Sats. For NGS: Wed 8 July (10.30-5.30).
A garden for all seasons within the Gulf Stream, benefiting plants from throughout the world incl exotic planting. Woodland garden with extensive collection of rhododendrons flowering Jan to late summer. National Collection of *Styracaceae*. Ancient oaks, magnolias, camellias and largest common lime in UK. Hourly guided tours 11-2 starting from Kiosk. Donations to NGS.

♿ 🐾 ❀ NCCPG ☕

㉓ ◆ HUTTON-IN-THE-FOREST
Penrith CA11 9TH. Lord Inglewood, 017684 84449, www.hutton-in-the-forest.co.uk. *6m NW of Penrith. On B5305, 3m from exit 41 of M6 towards Wigton.* House & garden £7, chd £3, garden only £4, chd £1.50. Garden daily except Sats 11-5. House Weds, Thurs, Suns, Bank Hol Mons 12.30-4. For NGS: Suns 7 June; 12 July (11-5).
Hutton-in-the-Forest is surrounded on two sides by distinctive yew topiary and grass terraces -, which to the S lead to C18 lake and cascade. 1730s walled garden is full of old fruit trees, tulips in spring, roses and an extensive collection of herbaceous plants in summer. Cumbria in Bloom - Top Visitor Attraction.

♿ ☕

㉔ LAKESIDE HOTEL
Lake Windermere, Newby Bridge LA12 8AT. Mr N R Talbot, 015395 30001, sales@lakesidehotel.co.uk. *1m N of Newby Bridge. On S shore of Lake Windermere. From A590 at Newby Bridge, cross the bridge which leads onto the Hawkshead rd. Follow this rd for 1m, hotel on the R. Complimentary parking available.* Light refreshments & teas. Adm £3, chd free (share to Boalbank Nursing Home). Weds 13 May; 2 Sept (11-5). Visitors also welcome by appt.
Created for year round interest, packed with choice plants, including some unusual varieties. Great lake views from terrace and roof gardens. Main garden areas with shrub roses,

herbaceous, foliage shrubs, scented and winter interest plants and seasonal bedding. Roof garden with lawn, herb filled box parterres and espaliered, local, heritage apple varieties.

🐾 ❀ ☕ ☎

㉕ LANGHOLME MILL
Woodgate, Lowick Green LA12 8ES. Judith & Graham Sanderson, 01229 885215, info@langholmemill.co.uk. *7m NW of Ulverston. Take A5092 at Greenodd towards Broughton for 3³/₄ m on L ¹/₂ m after school.* Adm £3, chd free (share to Air Ambulance). Visitors welcome by appt May to Sept.
Approx 1 acre of woodland garden surrounding mill race stream with bridges, hosting well established rhododendrons, hostas and acers. Featured in 'Cumbria Life'.

🛏 ☎

Local slate terracing and cascading serpentine stream . . .

㉖ LAWSON PARK
East of Lake Coniston. LA21 8AD. Grizedale Arts, www.lawsonpark.org. *5m E of Coniston. From Coniston Village follow signs East of Lake/Brantwood, car park signed 1m after Brantwood car park. Please use free minibus (runs every 10 mins) from Machell's Coppice Forestry Commission car park On foot 15 mins walk up footpath from car park. Route not suitable for those with limited mobility. Rough in places.* Home-made teas. Adm £3.50, chd free. Sun 26 July (12-6). Visitors also welcome by appt July to Sept only, groups of between 10 - 20 (on site parking by prior arrangement).
Approx 5 acres of reclaimed fellside in spectacular setting overlooking Old Man of Coniston. Restored over the last 8yrs to a working smallholding, now an artist's base. Informal and naturalistic herbaceous, woodland and wild gardens, incl large wild flower meadow and large organic kitchen garden of raised beds, apiary, poultry area. Extensive experimental plantings of unusual perennials and shrubs. Contemporary Art Project on site. Featured in 'Herald magazine'.

🐾 ❀ ☕

Group opening

27 LEECE VILLAGE GARDENS
LA12 0QU. *2m E of Barrow-in-Furness. 6m SW of Ulverston. J36 M6 onto A590 to Ulverston. A5087 coast rd to Barrow. Approx 8m turn R for Leece Village (signed, look for concrete sea wall on L). Village parking for gardens.* Light refreshments. **Combined adm £3.50, chd free. Sun 17 May (11-5).**
Small village on the Furness Peninsula 1½ m from Morecambe Bay, rural but not remote, with working farms centred around a tarn. Gardens of varying size and individual styles. Maps supplied to visitors.

BRIAR HOUSE
Jeff Lowden
Large informal garden with steps and steep slopes. Features incl willow yurt, green roof, white garden, haymeadow with maze. Panoramic views over Morecambe Bay. Lots of seats.

4 DALE GARTH
Steve & Gail Shaw
Mid-terrace property. Front garden with intensively planted mixed borders, lawn, small pond and paved seating area with pots. Enclosed rear garden with wild hedge, plant covered walls and fences, grass, greenhouse, and layered borders.

DOWNFIELD HOUSE
Mr & Mrs A Bolt
Approx ½ acre of mature garden containing interesting collections of hardy geraniums and ferns. Trees, shrubs, wildlife pond and vegetables. Limited parking available.

LANE END HOUSE
Mr & Mrs A Sharp
Front garden (opposite tarn) with raised beds and borders incl roses and clematis. Traditional SW facing back garden with access steps. Terraces incl cottage garden plants, herbaceous perennials. Small alpine border. Seating areas, with view over village.

RAISING HOUSE
Vivien & Neil Hudson
Plant lovers garden on SW slope. Garden planted to give interest in every season. Early summer alpine screes and garden troughs.

Clematis, shrubs and early perennials of particular interest. Access by steps and slopes. Featured in 'Garden News'.

WINANDER
Mrs Enid Cockshott
1-acre, eco-friendly garden amid mature trees on an E-facing slope. Patio area with wildlife pond; large organic vegetable and fruit area. Alpines, mixed borders, quiet seating areas with views across Leece Tarn and out to Morecambe Bay.

28 LILAC COTTAGE GARDEN
Blitterlees. CA7 4JJ. Lynn & Jeff Downham, 01697 332171, lilaccottage@tiscali.co.uk. *1m S of Silloth. On B5300 the Maryport to Silloth rd.* Home-made teas. **Adm £3, chd free. Suns 26 Apr; 28 June (11-4). Visitors also welcome by appt.**
Approx 1-acre garden set in compartments in a coastal setting. Featuring raised and woodland gardens, herbaceous borders, large lawned areas and sandstone gazebo. Each garden has an individual theme, well stocked with plants and shrubs. In the springtime the magnolias, azaleas, rhododendrons and tulip beds give a fine display of colour, which continues throughout summer and into autumn. Featured in 'Amateur Gardening'.

29 LINDETH FELL COUNTRY HOUSE HOTEL
Lyth Valley Road, Bowness-on-Windermere LA23 3JP. Air Cdr & Mrs P A Kennedy, 015394 43286, www.lindethfell.co.uk. *1m S of Bowness. On A5074. From centre of Bowness opp St Martins church turn L, signed Kendal A5074. 200yds on L after Xrds at Ferry View.* Home-made teas. **Adm £3, chd free. Sat 16 May (2-5). Visitors also welcome by appt May to Oct, short wheel base coaches only.**
6 acres of lawns and landscaped grounds on the hills above Lake Windermere, designed by Mawson around 1909; conifers and specimen trees best in spring and early summer with a colourful display of rhododendrons, azaleas and Japanese maples; grounds offer splendid views to Coniston mountains. Partial wheelchair access: To terrace in front of house looking over garden and view.

Quiet village setting with houses set around small village green . . .

Group opening

30 NEW LITTLE URSWICK VILLAGE GARDENS
LA12 0PL. *4m W of Ulverston. A590 from Ulverston approx 2m to Little Urswick.* Home-made teas. **Combined adm £3.50, chd free. Sun 28 June (11-5).**
Quiet village setting with houses set around small village green. Maps given to visitors. Featured in 'Cumbria Life', 'Lancashire Life' & 'Amateur Gardening'.

NEW BECKSIDE FARM
Ann Thomason
Interesting cottage garden with organic vegetable plot. Some areas still evolving.

NEW BURNSMEAD FARM
Anne Kenyon
Old farm courtyard with Victorian conservatory, family friendly garden, productive orchard and vegetable section.

NEW CORNAA
Mike & Bev Williams. *Behind the green, up short drive*
Small domestic garden in 2 parts. Still developing - 4yr old property.

NEW EAST VIEW
Simon & Sally Barton
Small, traditional cottage style garden, on 2 levels, with modern decking and pond. Complemented with vegetable gardens. Still being developed by owners.

NEW 21 GREENBANK GARDENS
Mr & Mrs P Rixom
Well-established garden on corner plot with lovely views towards Birkrigg. Eclectic mix of shrubs, tree conifers, herbaceous borders and perennials in an interesting setting with clearly defined pond.

NEW HILL COTTAGE
Mrs Christine Winder
Traditional cottage garden meets Mediterranean Al Fresco living. Organic lawn mowers, equestrian area and kitchen garden growing vegetables from organic compost.

REDMAYNE HALL
Jennie Werry
A very private private garden. Mature shrubs, mixed beds, former farmyard still evolving. Divided into several areas. Peaceful country setting.

31 LOWER ROWELL FARM
Milnthorpe LA7 7LU. John & Mavis Robinson, 015395 62270. *2m NE of Milnthorpe. Signed to Rowell off B6385. Garden 1/2 m up lane on L.* Home-made teas. **Adm £3, chd free. Sat 16, Sun 17 May (1-5). Evening Opening** £4.50, wine, Thur 2 July (6-9). **Visitors also welcome by appt.**
Approx 3/4 -acre garden. Borders and beds with shrubs and interesting herbaceous perennials. Retro greenhouse and vegetable plots. Very peaceful with open views to Farleton Knott, Pennines and Lakeland hills. Featured in 'Garden News'. Voted Best garden in local show.

32 MATSON GROUND
Windermere LA23 2NH. Matson Ground Estate Co Ltd, 015394 47892, info@matsonground.co.uk. *2/3 m E of Bowness. From Kendal turn R off B5284 signed Heathwaite, 100yds after Windermere Golf Club. Garden on L after 1/3 m. From Bowness turn L onto B5284 from A5074. After 1/2 m turn L at Xrds. Garden on L 1/2 m along lane.* Home-made teas. **Adm £3, chd free. Sun 17 May (2-5). Visitors also welcome by appt.**
Stream flows through ornamental garden to large pond in the wild garden of spring bulbs, later wild flowers. Azaleas, rhododendrons, large mixed shrub/herbaceous borders, topiary work, white garden, spring/summer colour. 1/2 -acre walled kitchen garden and greenhouses. 2-acre woodland.

33 MEADOW HOUSE
Garnett Bridge Road, Burneside, Kendal LA8 9AY. Paul Burrill. *4m N of Kendal. Leave A591 2m N of Kendal*

signed R towards Burneside. Continue to village centre past Premier Store. After 1/2 m turn L towards Longsleddale (opp Burneside Hall). After 3/4 m turn L signed Meadow House. Go immed R over cattle grid. Park as directed, majority of parking in field. Home-made teas. **Adm £3, chd free (share to St Mary's Hospice, Ulverston). Sun 26 July (1-5).**
11/2 -acre rural garden with superb S-facing countryside views. Of special interest are water features with ponds and streams; large vegetable and fruit garden with glasshouses and polytunnel. The garden blends ornamental beauty with food production, home to ducks, chickens and honey bees/beehives. All this and donkeys too. Featured in & on 'Cumbria Life', BBC Open Gardens.

The garden blends ornamental beauty with food production, home to ducks, chickens and honey bees/ beehives . . .

34 NEW NETHERTON
Talkin, Carlisle CA8 1LR. Dawn MacKenzie. *21/2 m S of Brampton. From Brampton take B6413 (signed Castle Carrock), 21/2 m on R.* **Adm £3.50, chd free. Sun 12 July (12-5).**
Newly created 2 acre garden, incl walled garden with young trained fruit trees and small orchard. Lawned terraces, perennials, rose pergola and hosta bed. 6 acres of mature broadleaf woodland with walk (some very steep steps).

35 NEWTON RIGG CAMPUS GARDENS
Newton Rigg, Penrith CA11 0AH. University of Cumbria, www.cumbria.ac.uk. *1m W of Penrith. 3m W from J40 & J41 off M6. 1/2 m off the B5288 W of Penrith.* **Adm £4, chd free. Afternoon & Evening**

Opening tea, wine, Wed 24 June (3-8.30).
The gardens and campus grounds have much of horticultural interest incl herbaceous borders, ponds, organic garden with fruit cage and display of composting techniques, woodland walk, summer scented garden, 2 arboretums, tropical display house, annual meadows, pleached hornbeam walkway and extensive range of ornamental trees and shrubs. Guided tour of gardens by expert gardeners from Newton Rigg, choose from 1/2 hr or 1hr tours on a range of subjects e.g. trees, organic and seasonal gardens etc. Featured in 'Cumbria Life'. Gold medal awarded at The Borders Spring Show.

36 THE NOOK
Helton CA10 2QA. Brenda & Philip Freedman, pfreedman@helton.demon.co.uk. *6m S of Penrith. A6 S from Penrith. After Eamont Bridge turn R to Pooley Bridge. Fork L to Askham. Through Askham 1m to Helton. Follow signs.* Home-made teas. **Adm £3, chd free. Sun 24, Mon 25 May (11-5). Visitors also welcome by appt June & July - max visitors 30.**
Plantsman's hillside garden with long views down Lowther Valley. Mainly alpine plants many rare and unusual. Front, cottage garden, side garden has cordon, espalier and fan trained fruit trees, soft fruit and vegetables. Main garden with species rhododendrons, scree garden, troughs, conifers, herb garden and water feature. Steps into main garden, but can provide ramp.

37 THE OLD RECTORY
Dean, Workington CA14 4TH. Mr F H & Mrs J S Wheeler, 01946 861840. *5m SW of Cockermouth. Last house in Dean on rd to Workington, on L beyond church.* **Adm £3, chd free. Visitors welcome by appt throughout the year, individuals & groups welcome.**
Over 1 acre. with interest throughout the year from aconites and spring bulbs to autumn colours. Informal rooms with wide range of trees, shrubs and herbaceous perennials, many relatively rare and tender, various shrub and climbing roses. Mixed shrubberies, woodland and damp areas, scree garden and rockeries. Featured in 'Gardens of the Lake District'.

A multi-coloured leafy mosaic punctuated by bright flower colour . . .

38 OLDE OAKS
Croft Ends, Appleby CA16 6JW.
Chantal Knight, 017683 51304,
chantalknight@midwife.plus.com.
1½ m N of Appleby. Heading N out of
Appleby take rd to Long Marton for
1m. 1st R, continue on ½ m, garden
last on R. Home-made teas. **Adm £3,
chd free. Sun 16 Aug (1-5). Visitors
also welcome by appt June to Sept.**
Beautiful views of the Pennines create
a stunning backdrop for this medium
sized cottage-style garden. Large
herbaceous borders are filled with
interesting mixed perennials and
wildlife pond. A wealth of summer
bedding adorns front of the property
with stream and pond containing koi
carp. Across the road is delightful 3-
acre mixed woodland walk. Featured in
'Amateur Gardening' & Best Village
Garden - Dufton Show.
 ♿ 🐾 ❀ ☕ ☎

39 PEAR TREE COTTAGE
Dalton, Burton-in-Kendal LA6 1NN.
Linda & Alec Greening, 01524
781624, linda@
peartreecottagecumbria. co.uk,
www.peartreecottagecumbria.co.uk.
4m W of Kirkby Lonsdale. 10m S of
Kendal. From village of Burton-in-
Kendal (A6070), follow Vicarage Lane
for 1m. Parking at farm, 50yds before
garden (signed). Home-made teas at
Bell House Barn (approx 200yds).
**Adm £3, chd free. Evening
Opening £4.50, wine & coffee, Wed
24 June (6-9). Sun 12 July (11-5).
Visitors also welcome by appt May
to July for groups of 10+.**
⅓ -acre cottage garden. A peaceful
and relaxing garden, harmonising with
its rural setting. Diverse planting areas,
including packed herbaceous borders,
rambling roses, wildlife pond and bog
garden, fernery and gravel garden.
Intensively planted, incl much to
interest the plantsman and general
garden visitor alike. Increasing
collections of ferns and hardy
geraniums. Featured in 'Amateur
Gardening' & 'Garden News'.
🐾 ❀ ☕ ☎

**40 NEW PUDDING POKE
BARN**
Moorthwaite Lane, Barbon, nr
Kirkby Lonsdale LA6 2LW. Gilly
Newbery, 015242 76284,
gandn.newb@tiscali.co.uk. 2½ m
N of Kirkby Lonsdale. Take Kirkby
Lonsdale rd to Sedbergh A683. At
small bridge with green rails turn
up to village of Barbon. At war
memorial turn R. Park at village
hall, walk back to garden turning L
ad L again (3mins). Light
refreshments & teas. **Adm £3.50,
chd free. Evening Opening
£4.50, wine, Sat 30 May (6-9).
Sat 25, Sun 26 July (11-5).**
1 acre of informal plant lover's
garden created over 13yrs from a
field mostly with a pickaxe. Organic
wildlife friendly with wild flowers in
long grass, alongside raised beds,
trees and shrubs, herbaceous,
vegetables and fruit. Gravel
garden, bog and pond. Gothic
potting shed and gypsy caravan for
children.
❀ ☕

41 QUARRY HILL HOUSE
Mealsgate CA7 1AE. Mr & Mrs
Charles Woodhouse, 016973 71225,
cfwoodhouse@btinternet.com.
1m E of Mealsgate. Between
Boltongate & Mealsgate on B5299.
½ m W of Boltongate(8m SSW of
Wigton). At Mealsgate, on A595
Cockermouth to Carlisle rd, turn E onto
B5299 for Boltongate, Ireby &
Caldbeck. Approx 1m along rd,
entrance gates to Quarry Hill House on
L. Home-made teas. **Adm £4, chd
free (share to Hospice at Home
Carlisle & N Lakeland). Sun 12 July
(1.30-5.30). Visitors also welcome by
appt.**
3 acre parkland setting country house
(not open) woodland garden with good
views. Herbaceous borders, trees,
shrubs, vegetable garden. 25 acre
park incls wild flower areas and
extensively planted arboreta with many
specimen trees, especially varieties of
sorbus with lovely woodland walks.
Much tree planting and many
regeneration projects since 2000 incl
recreation for wildlife of former
shooting ponds. Featured in
'Cumberland News' & Gardens of the
Lake District.
🐾 ❀ ☕ ☎

42 NEW THE RIDDING
The Hill, Millom LA18 5HE. Mr &
Mrs K Sawyer. 2m NE of Millom,
5m SW of Broughton in Furness.
From the A5093 at The Hill take
road signed Underhill. After ¼ m
turn R at 30mph signs. Garden is
100yds on R. Home-made teas.
**Combined with Ridding Barn
adm £3, chd free. Sun 24, Mon
25 May; Sat 18, Sun 19 July
(11-4).**
¾ -acre sloping site with some
steep steps and estuary views.
Pond, waterfall, rockery and
herbaceous beds. In May daffodils,
bluebells and rhododendrons
feature and in July shrubs and
herbaceous perennials. The
gardens is contiguous with Ridding
Barn and admission covers both
gardens. Partial wheelchair access.
♿ ☕

43 NEW RIDDING BARN
The Hill, Millom LA18 5HE. Joan
& Robin Gray. 2m NE of Millom,
5m SW of Broughton-in-Furness.
From the A5093 at The Hill take
road signed Underhill. After ¼ m
turn R at 30mph signs. Garden is
100yds on R. Home-made teas.
**Combined with The Ridding,
adm £3, chd free. Sun 24, Mon
25 May; Sat 18, Sun 19 July
(11-4).**
¾ -acre plot incl century-old
terraced flower garden, 10yr old
garden-from-a-field with sloping
lawns, mixed shrubs and trees,
bulbs, wild flowers, wildlife pond,
rocky cascade and bog garden.
The summer effect is a multi-
coloured leafy mosaic punctuated
by bright flower colour. Steps,
grassy slopes, gravel courtyard.
♿ ❀ ☕

44 NEW ◆ RYDAL HALL
Ambleside LA22 9LX. Diocese of
Carlisle, 01539 432050,
www.rydalhall.org. 2m N of
Ambleside. E from A591 at Rydal
signed Rydal Hall. **Adm £3 by
donation. Open daily, all yr. For
NGS: Thurs 16 Apr; 18 June; 23
July; 20 Aug (10-4).**
Formal Italianate gardens designed
by Thomas Mawson in 1911 set in
34 acres. The gardens have
recently been restored over a 2yr
period returning to their former
glory. Informal woodland garden,
leading to C17 viewing

station/summerhouse, fine herbaceous planting, community vegetable garden, orchard and apiary. Partial wheelchair access.

 ♿ ⊨ ☕

45 ◆ SIZERGH CASTLE
nr Kendal LA8 8AE. The National Trust, 015395 69813, www.nationaltrust.org.uk. *3m S of Kendal. Approach rd leaves A590 close to & S of A590/A591 interchange.* **Adm £4.45, chd £2.25. For opening details please see website or tel. For NGS: Sat 18 July (11-5).**
²/₃ -acre limestone rock garden, largest owned by National Trust; collection of Japanese maples, dwarf conifers, hardy ferns, primulas, gentians, perennials and bulbs; water garden, aquatic plants; hot wall border with fruiting trees; south garden with specimen roses, lilies, shrubs and ground cover. Wild flower areas, herbaceous borders, orchard with spring bulbs, 'Dutch' garden. Terraced garden and lake; kitchen garden, vegetables, herbs, flowers; fruit orchard with spring bulbs. National Collection of Asplenium, Cystopteris, Dryopteris, Osmunda. Garden tours 12pm, 1pm, 2pm, 3pm adm £3, chd £1.50.

♿ ✗ ☕

46 SPRINT MILL
Burneside LA8 9AQ. Edward & Romola Acland, 01539 725168. *2m N of Kendal. From Burneside follow signs to Skelsmergh for ¹/₂ m then L to Sprint Mill.* Home-made teas. **Adm £2.50, chd free. Suns 21 June; 26 July (11-5). Visitors also welcome by appt.**
Unorthodox organic garden (atypical NGS) combining the wild and natural alongside provision of owners' wood, fruit and vegetables. 5-acres to explore, riverside setting, hand-crafted seats, old water mill building. Large vegetable and soft fruit area, following no-dig and permaculture principles. Hand-tools prevail. Unconventional art and crafts display, green woodworking workshop, slide show of garden development.

✗ ☕ ☎

47 STONE EDGE
Jack Hill, Allithwaite LA11 7QB. Ian & Julie Chambers, 015395 33895. *2m W of Grange-over-Sands. On B5277. Jack Hill is on L just before*

Allithwaite Village. Parking available 10-4.30 in The Pheasant Inn car park at bottom of Jack Hill approx 100m. Limited parking for the not so fit nr house. Home-made teas. **Adm £3.50, chd free. Day & Evening Opening wine, Tue 11 Aug (10-8.30). Visitors also welcome by appt all year.**
Gardening on the edge, in harmony with nature; incl formal box, new agave garden, pergola with border, climbers, shrubs and perennials, herbs grown for use in the kitchen. Spectacular specimens form a Mediterranean garden; tree top balcony; woodland garden meanders down to fern garden and pond. Steep slope in woodland garden. Pots abound. Fantastic views over Morecambe Bay. New garden room with cloister conservatory, garden room, potting garden room. Featured in 'Cumbria Life' & 'The Lake District Life'.

✗ ☕ ☎

48 SUMMERDALE HOUSE
Nook, nr Lupton LA6 1PE. David & Gail Sheals, 015395 67210, sheals@btinternet.com. *7m S of Kendal, 5m W of Kirkby Lonsdale. From J36 M6 take A65 to Kirkby Lonsdale, at Nook take R turn Farleton.* Home-made soup & teas Mar/Apr, home-made teas May to Sept. **Adm £3.50, chd free. Suns 1 Mar; 12 Apr, Mon 13 Apr; Suns 3 May; 7 June; 5 July; 2 Aug; 6 Sept (11-5); 2010 28 Feb. Visitors also welcome by appt, groups of 10+.**
1¹/₂ -acre part-walled country garden restored and developed over last 10yrs by owners. Beautiful setting with fine views across to Farleton Fell. Herbaceous borders, formal and informal ponds, woodland planting, old orchard and new meadow planting. Interesting range of herbaceous perennials, many of which are propagated by owners. Adjoining nursery features in RHS 'Britains Favourite Plants'. Featured in 'Country Homes & Interiors'.

⊛ ☕ ☎

49 SWINSIDE END FARM
Scales, High Lorton CA13 9UA. Mrs Karen Nicholson, 01900 85134. *4m S of Cockermouth. From A66 take B5292 (Braithwaite) which climbs Whinlatter Forest Park, passing the Visitor Centre on your R, continue on B5292 for 1¹/₂ m, take the fork L signed Hopebeck, bearing R at next fork for Lorton, take next L & the farm is immed on L.* **Adm £3, chd free. Sun 12 July (1-4.30). Visitors also**

welcome by appt June, July, Aug only.
Lovely evolving garden surrounding farmhouse with superb views of Lorton Vale. Well-stocked herbaceous borders together with informal borders of perennials, shrubs and grasses in colour-themed area incl black border in rear garden. Planted old agricultural equipment and pergolas. Traditional planted stone walls, wishing well and summerhouse.

✗ ⊨ ☎

> Tucked away behind the town centre, this secret walled cottage garden is a little haven . . .

50 ◆ TULLIE HOUSE
Castle Street, Carlisle CA3 8TP. Carlisle City Council, 01228 618737, www.tulliehouse.co.uk. *City Centre. Signed as Museum on brown signs, see website for map.* **Adm by donation. All year, except Christmas & New Year. For NGS: Sat 13 (10-5), Sun 14 June (11-5).**
Beds in front of Jacobean house are planted to reflect C17. Mature *Arbutus unedo* and *Cornus kousa* grow alongside other recent planting incl *Fatsia japonica variegata: Eucryphia glutinosa.* Roman style planting incl fig, vines, myrtle, acanthus and variety of herbs. Music, plant stall, childrens activities. Green Flag Award.

♿ ⊛

51 WESTVIEW
Fletcher Hill, Kirkby Stephen CA17 4QQ. Reg & Irene Metcalfe. *Kirkby Stephen town centre, T-lights opp Pine Design.* **Combined with Winton Park adm £4.50, chd free. Sun 26 July (11-5).**
Tucked away behind the town centre, this secret walled cottage garden is a little haven. The main garden is filled with perennials, shrubs and large collection of hostas, with small wildlife pond. The adjacent prairie-style nursery beds are at their best in July.

✗ ⊛

4¹/₂ -acre Mediterranean style garden with magnificent views over Morecambe Bay . . .

52 WINDY HALL
Crook Road, Windermere LA23 3JA.
Diane & David Kinsman, 015394
46238,
dhewitt.kinsman@googlemail.com.
*1m S of Bowness-on-Windermere. On
B5284 up Linthwaite House Hotel
driveway.* Home-made teas. **Adm £3,
chd free. Combined with
Brackenrigg Lodge** adm **£5. Suns
3 May; 7 June (10-5).** Visitors also
welcome by appt.
4-acre owner designed and maintained
garden. Woodland underplanted with
species rhododendrons, camellias,
magnolias and hydrangeas; Japanese
influenced quarry garden; alpine area
with gunnera; wild flower meadow;
kitchen, 'privy' and 'Best' gardens.
Waterfowl garden with gunnera, many
stewartias. Redesigned pond garden
with plants raised from seed collected
by David in China. NCCPG Collections
of *Aruncus* and *Filipendula*; Naturalised
moss gardens and paths in woodland,
bluebells and foxgloves in abundance,
wide variety of native birds, many nest
in gardens. Black, multi-horned
Hebridean sheep and lambs. Rare
breeds of pheasants from China and
Nepal, exotic ducks and geese.
Waterfowl, rare pheasants and
primitive sheep. Article in Gardens in
the Lake District by T Longville.
🐾 ❀ NCCPG ☕ ☎

53 WINTON PARK
Appleby Road. CA17 4PG. Mr
Anthony Kilvington. *2m N of Kirkby
Stephen. Just N of Kirkby Stephen on
A685 turn L signed Gt
Musgrove/Warcop (B6259). After
approx 1m turn L as signed.* Home-
made teas. **Combined with
Westview** adm **£4.50, chd free.** Sun
26 July (11-5).
2 acre country garden with many fine
conifers, acers and rhododendrons,
herbaceous borders, hostas, ferns,
grasses and over 700 roses. Three
formal ponds, plus secret wildlife pond.
Stunning views.
♿ 🐾 ☕

54 YEWBARROW HOUSE
Hampsfell Road, Grange-over-
Sands LA11 6BE. Jonathan &
Margaret Denby, 015395 32469,
www.yewbarrowhouse.co.uk. *¹/₄ m
from town centre. Follow signs in
centre of Grange. Turn R at HSBC
Bank into Pig Lane, 1st L into
Hampsfell Rd. Garden 200yds on L.*
Cream teas. **Adm £3.50, chd free.**
Suns 7 June; 5 July; 2 Aug; 6 Sept

(11-4). **Visitors also welcome by
appt coaches permitted.**
New Mediterranean style garden on
4¹/₂ -acre elevated site with magnificent
views over Morecambe Bay. The
garden features a restored walled
Victorian kitchen garden; Italianate
terrace garden; exotic gravel garden;
fern garden, Japanese Hot Spring
pool. Dahlia trial beds, orangery,
sculpture and sensory gardens.
Featured in various publications.
❀ ☕ ☎

55 YEWS
Bowness-on-Windermere LA23 3JR.
Sir Oliver & Lady Scott. *1m S of
Bowness-on-Windermere. A5074.
Middle Entrance Drive, 50yds.* Home-
made teas. **Adm £3, chd free.** Sun 21
June (2-5.30).
Medium-sized formal Edwardian
garden; fine trees, ha-ha, herbaceous
borders; greenhouse. Bog area being
developed, bamboo, primula, hosta.
Young yew maze and vegetable
garden.
🐾 ❀ ☕

Cumbria County Volunteers

County Organisers
Alec & Linda Greening, Pear Tree Cottage, Dalton, Burton-in-Kendal, Carnforth LA6 1NN, 01524 781624,
    linda@peartreecottagecumbria.co.uk

County Treasurer
Derek Farman, Mill House, Winster, Windermere, Cumbria LA23 3NW, 015394 44893, farman@f2s.com

Publicity
Tony Connor, 15 Morewood Drive, Burton-in-Kendal, Carnforth LA6 1NE, 01524 781119, tonconnor@aol.com

Assistant County Organisers
Diane Hewitt, Windy Hall, Crook Road, Windermere LA23 3JA, 015394 46238, dhewitt.kinsman@googlemail.com
South West John Maddison, Buckbarrow House, Denton Park Court, Gosforth, Seascale CA20 1BN, 019467 25431,
    JohnMaddGosf@aol.com
North Alannah Rylands, Crookdake Farm, Aspatria, Wigton CA7 3SH, 016973 20413, rylands@crookdake.com

Mark your diary with these special events in 2009

EXPLORE SECRET GARDENS DURING CHELSEA & HAMPTON COURT FLOWER SHOW WEEKS

Tue 19 May, Wed 20 May, Thur 21 May, Fri 22 May, Wed 8 July, Thur 9 July
Full day tours from £82 per person, 10% discount for groups
Advance booking required, telephone +44 (0)20 8693 1015 or email j.wookey@btinternet.com
Specially selected gardens in London, Essex, Kent, Hampshire and South Oxfordshire. The tour price includes transport and lunch with wine at a popular restaurant or pub.

HAMPTON COURT PALACE

Thur 2 Apr, Tue 23 June, Thur 25 June, Wed 15 July, Tue 4 Aug, Thur 10 Sept
Evening tours in the company of one of the Palace's specialist tour guides from 6.30 – 8pm.
Tickets £6 per person. Advance booking required, telephone +44 (0)1483 211535 or
visit www.ngs.org.uk for more information
Gossip, scandal, murder, healing – you'll find it all within the Formal Gardens at Hampton Court Palace. Each tour will have its own unique feature whether it's the story of the Great Vine or the magic and mystery of the Maze.

FROGMORE – A ROYAL GARDEN (BERKSHIRE)

Tue 26 May 10am – 5.30pm (last admission 4pm)
Garden adm £4.50, chd free. Tickets available in advance or on the day.
Advance booking for groups and coaches, telephone
+44 (0) 1483 211535 or email orders@ngs.org.uk
A rare opportunity to explore 30 acres of landscaped garden, rich in history and beauty.

FLAXBOURNE FARM – FUN & SURPRISES (BEDFORDSHIRE)

Sun 7 June 10am – 5pm. Adm £5, chd free
No booking required, come along on the day!
Bring the whole family and have fun in this surprising and entertaining garden of 2 acres. Enjoy the large plant fair, live music, pets corner, birds of prey, dog agility show and much more.

WISLEY RHS GARDEN – MUSIC IN THE GARDEN (SURREY)

Fri 11 Sept 6 – 9pm
Adm (incl RHS members) £7, chd under 15 free
Save money on advance bookings for groups of 4 or more, telephone +44 (0)1483 211535 or
visit www.ngs.org.uk for more information
A special evening opening of this famous garden, exclusively for the NGS. Enjoy music and entertainment as you explore the gardens and the floral marquee on the first day of the Wisley Flower Show.

For further information visit www.ngs.org.uk or telephone 01483 211535

DERBYSHIRE

Opening Dates

March

SUNDAY 29
64 Windward

April

TUESDAY 14
52 Renishaw Hall Gardens

WEDNESDAY 15
4 Bluebell Arboretum
9 Cascades Gardens

SATURDAY 18
50 19 Portland Street

SUNDAY 19
11 10 Chestnut Way
31 37 High Street
42 Meynell Langley Trials Garden
50 19 Portland Street

SUNDAY 26
4 Bluebell Arboretum

May

MONDAY 4
7 The Burrows Gardens

SUNDAY 10
6 Broomfield Hall
13 Cloud Cottage
42 Meynell Langley Trials Garden

WEDNESDAY 13
4 Bluebell Arboretum

SUNDAY 17
13 Cloud Cottage
26 Fir Croft
38 Locko Park
55 Southfield
64 Windward

WEDNESDAY 20
9 Cascades Gardens

SATURDAY 23
22 Dove Cottage

SUNDAY 24
5 Brick Kiln Farm
13 Cloud Cottage
22 Dove Cottage
27 Gamesley Fold Cottage
32 Highfield House
36 The Leylands

MONDAY 25
5 Brick Kiln Farm
7 The Burrows Gardens
36 The Leylands

SUNDAY 31
4 Bluebell Arboretum
10 Cashel
12 13 Chiltern Drive
26 Fir Croft

June

SATURDAY 6
23 The Dower House

SUNDAY 7
23 The Dower House
31 37 High Street
37 Littleover Lane Allotments
42 Meynell Langley Trials Garden
44 Monksway
54 Shatton Hall Farm
65 Woodend Cottage

SATURDAY 13
2 334 Belper Road

SUNDAY 14
2 334 Belper Road
21 Dolly Barn
26 Fir Croft
27 Gamesley Fold Cottage
44 Monksway
47 Otterbrook
61 24 Wheeldon Avenue
62 26 Wheeldon Avenue

WEDNESDAY 17
4 Bluebell Arboretum
9 Cascades Gardens

SUNDAY 21
24 Fanshawe Gate Hall
32 Highfield House
44 Monksway
63 26 Windmill Rise

SUNDAY 28
4 Bluebell Arboretum
22 Dove Cottage
24 Fanshawe Gate Hall
48 Park Hall
60 Wharfedale

MONDAY 29
7 The Burrows Gardens

July

SUNDAY 5
1 42 Arkendale Walk
14 Clovermead
17 8 Curzon Lane
24 Fanshawe Gate Hall
30 High Roost

SUNDAY 12
1 42 Arkendale Walk
9 Cascades Gardens
17 8 Curzon Lane
24 Fanshawe Gate Hall
42 Meynell Langley Trials Garden
58 Tilford House
65 Woodend Cottage

MONDAY 13
7 The Burrows Gardens

WEDNESDAY 15
4 Bluebell Arboretum
8 Calke Abbey

SATURDAY 18
29 Hardwick Hall
33 11 Highgrove Drive
53 Rosebank
56 Sudbury Hall

SUNDAY 19
33 11 Highgrove Drive
40 2 Manvers Street
41 Markham Villa

SATURDAY 25
15 The Cottage

SUNDAY 26
4 Bluebell Arboretum
15 The Cottage
21 Dolly Barn
45 Moorfields
54 Shatton Hall Farm
55 Southfield
60 Wharfedale
64 Windward

August

SATURDAY 1
5 Brick Kiln Farm
50 19 Portland Street

SUNDAY 2
5 Brick Kiln Farm
20 62A Denby Lane
22 Dove Cottage
39 9 Main Street
41 Markham Villa
50 19 Portland Street
63 26 Windmill Rise

TUESDAY 4
52 Renishaw Hall Gardens

WEDNESDAY 5
9 Cascades Gardens

SATURDAY 8
53 Rosebank

SUNDAY 9
11 10 Chestnut Way
14 Clovermead
43 23 Mill Lane
49 22 Pinfold Close
65 Woodend Cottage

WEDNESDAY 12
4 Bluebell Arboretum

THURSDAY 13
8 Calke Abbey

SUNDAY 16
42 Meynell Langley Trials Garden

SUNDAY 23
57 Thornbridge Hall

MONDAY 24
7 The Burrows Gardens

FRIDAY 28
60 Wharfedale (Evening)

SUNDAY 30
4 Bluebell Arboretum
60 Wharfedale

MONDAY 31
59 Tissington Hall

September

TUESDAY 1
50 19 Portland Street

SUNDAY 6
37 Littleover Lane Allotments

MONDAY 7
7 The Burrows Gardens

WEDNESDAY 9
4 Bluebell Arboretum
50 19 Portland Street

SATURDAY 12
56 Sudbury Hall

SUNDAY 13
42 Meynell Langley Trials Garden

SUNDAY 27
4 Bluebell Arboretum
25 Field Farm

October

WEDNESDAY 7
4 Bluebell Arboretum

SUNDAY 11
42 Meynell Langley Trials Garden

SUNDAY 25
4 Bluebell Arboretum

Gardens open to the public

4 Bluebell Arboretum
7 The Burrows Gardens
8 Calke Abbey
9 Cascades Gardens
18 Dam Farm House
29 Hardwick Hall
35 Lea Gardens
42 Meynell Langley Trials Garden
52 Renishaw Hall Gardens
56 Sudbury Hall
59 Tissington Hall

By appointment only

3 Birchfield
16 Cuckoostone Cottage
19 Dam Stead
28 The Gardens at Dobholme Fishery
34 Hillside
51 Quarryside
66 35 Wyver Lane

Also open by appointment ☎

2 334 Belper Road
5 Brick Kiln Farm
7 The Burrows Gardens
10 Cashel
11 10 Chestnut Way
12 13 Chiltern Drive
13 Cloud Cottage
14 Clovermead
15 The Cottage
17 8 Curzon Lane
19 Dam Stead
21 Dolly Barn
22 Dove Cottage
23 The Dower House
24 Fanshawe Gate Hall
25 Field Farm
27 Gamesley Fold Cottage
30 High Roost
32 Highfield House
36 The Leylands
37 Littleover Lane Allotments
39 9 Main Street
40 2 Manvers Street
41 Markham Villa
44 Monksway
47 Otterbrook
48 Park Hall
50 19 Portland Street
54 Shatton Hall Farm
60 Wharfedale
61 24 Wheeldon Avenue
62 26 Wheeldon Avenue
64 Windward
65 Woodend Cottage

A stunning, tiny, colour themed garden in red, black, green and silver . . .

The Gardens

1 **42 ARKENDALE WALK**
Arkendale Walk, Alavaston DE24 0RJ. Mrs V Knight. *4m E of Derby. Elvaston Lane, off A6 at Alvaston. R at island, L opposite James Wyatt. L into Codbeck Close. Parking nr shops, PH and surrounding streets*. Home-made teas. **Adm £2, chd free (share to MIND). Suns 5, 12 July (2-6). Also open 8 Curzon Lane.**
A stunning, tiny, colour themed garden in red, black, green and silver, which continues through the house. Acers in containers. Lid of waterbutt planted with sempervivum. Enter through the red back gate on Codbeck Close. Garden too small for pushchairs/wheelchairs.
☕

THE BEECHES
See Staffordshire & part of West Midlands.

2 **334 BELPER ROAD**
Stanley Common DE7 6FY. Gill & Colin Hancock, 0115 930 1061. *7m N of Derby. 3m W of Ilkeston. On A609, ³/₄ m from Rose & Crown Xrds (A608). Please park in field up farm drive or Working Men's Club rear car park if wet*. Home-made teas. **Adm £2.50, chd free. Sat 13 (2-5), Sun 14 June (12-5). Visitors also welcome by appt.**
Predominantly shrubs and perennials in a ³/₄ -acre maturing garden with many seating areas. Large kitchen garden and greenhouses. Replanted pond area with bog plants, ferns and a renovated DCC workmans hut, now a summerhouse. ¹/₂ m walk around a 8yr old wood and ¹/₂ -acre lake. New grass and wildflower borders. Highly recommended home-made cakes. Featured in 'Country Life Magazine, Where to Take Tea in the Garden'.
♿ 🐕 ❀ ☕ ☎

3 **BIRCHFIELD**
Dukes Drive, Ashford in the Water, Bakewell DE45 1QQ. Brian Parker, 01629 813800, www.birchfieldgarden.com. *2m NW of Bakewell. On A6 to Buxton between New Bridge and Sheepwash Bridge.* **Adm £3, chd free (share to Thornhill Memorial Trust). Visitors welcome by appt all yr, groups or individuals.**
Beautifully situated terraced garden of approx ³/₄ acre. Designed for yr-round colour, it contains wide variety of shrubs and perennials, bulbs and water gardens. Dry garden with grasses and bamboos recently constructed. Arboretum with wild flowers has been developed on a further 1¹/₄ acres. Featured in 'Reflections' magazine.
🐕 ☕ ☎

4 ♦ **BLUEBELL ARBORETUM**
Annwell Lane, Smisby LE65 2TA.
Robert & Suzette Vernon, 01530
413700, www.bluebellnursery.com.
1m N of Ashby-de-la-Zouch.
Arboretum is clearly signed in Annwell
Lane, 1/4 m S, through village of Smisby
which is off B5006, between Ticknall &
Ashby-de-la-Zouch. **Adm £3, chd**
free. For regular opening dates and
times please see website for details.
For NGS: Weds, Suns 15, 26 Apr;
13, 31 May; 17, 28 June; 15, 26 July;
12, 30 Aug; 9, 27 Sept; 7, 25 Oct,
Weds (9-5) Suns (10.30-4).
Beautiful 9-acre arboretum planted in
last 17yrs incl many specimens of rare
trees and shrubs. Bring wellingtons in
wet weather. Please be aware this is
not a wood full of bluebells, despite the
name. Adjacent specialist nursery.
Ground difficult in wet weather.
&. ✕ ⊕

5 **NEW** **BRICK KILN FARM**
Hulland Ward, Ashbourne
DE6 3EJ. Mrs Jan Hutchinson,
01335 370440. *4m E of*
Ashbourne (A517). 1m S of
Carsington Water. From Hulland
Ward, 2nd L, Dog Lane, past
church, 100yds on R. From
Ashbourne A517, Bradley Corner,
turn L, follow sign for Carsington
Water. Approx 1m up on L. Home-
made teas. **Adm £2.50, chd free**
(share to Great Dane Adoption
Society). Sun 24, Mon 25 May;
Sat 1, Sun 2 Aug (11-5). Visitors
also welcome by appt.
Garden created 17yrs ago from
part of a field. Small courtyard area
with pond. Original well
complements the reclaimed
architectural stone work, leading to
lawned area. Well filled herbaceous
and shrub borders. Garden
featured in the book 'Spirit of
Hulland'. Owner has one friendly
Great Dane. Gravel drive, path.
Some uneven flagstones.
Unfenced pond areas.
&. ✕ ⊨ ☕ ☎

6 **BROOMFIELD HALL**
Morley DE7 6DN. Derby College. *4m*
N of Derby. 6m S of Heanor On A608.
Light refreshments & teas available at
College. **Adm £2.50, chd free. Sun 10**
May (11-4).
Landscaped garden of 25 acres.
Shrubs, trees, rose collection,
herbaceous borders; glasshouses;
walled garden; garden tour guides.

Themed gardens, plant centre.
National Collection of old roses. Partial
wheelchair access.
&. ✕ ⊕ **NCCPG** ☕

7 ♦ **THE BURROWS GARDENS**
Burrows Lane, Brailsford,
Ashbourne DE6 3BU. Mr B C
Dalton, 01335 360745,
www.burrowsgardens.com. *5m SE*
of Ashbourne; 5m NW of Derby. Follow
yellow AA signs from both Ashbourne
& Derby direction. From Ashbourne:
A52 towards Derby 5m to Brailsford.
Turn R after Rose & Crown PH, then
1st L. Continue 1/2 m, garden on R.
From Derby: leave Derby on A52
towards Ashbourne, after Kirk Langley
stay on A52 for 11/2 m. Turn L signed
Dalbury. 1/2 m R at grass triangle,
garden in front of you. **Adm £4, chd**
free. Open every Sun 3 May to 13
Sept incl. Other times by appt,
please telephone. Coaches & mini
buses can be accommodated.
Group guided tours by Mr Dalton.
For NGS: Mons 4, 25 May; 29 June;
13 July; 24 Aug; 7 Sept (10.30-4.30).
Visitors also welcome by appt.
Five acres of stunning garden set in
beautiful countryside where the
immaculate lawns show off the exotic
rare plants and trees which mix with
the old favourites in this fabulous
garden. A vast variety of styles from the
temple garden to a Cornish, Italian and
English garden plus many more are
gloriously designed and displayed.
Featured on 'BBC1 East Midlands
Today' & in '1000 Best Gardens in
Britain & Ireland', magazines, local
press and Radio Derby.
&. ✕ ⊕ ☕ ☎

8 ♦ **CALKE ABBEY**
Ticknall DE73 7LE. The National
Trust, 01332 863822. *10m S of Derby.*
On A514 at Ticknall between
Swadlincote & Melbourne. House and
garden £9.50, child £4.60, garden
only £5.90, chd £2.90. Sat to Weds
(11-5). **For NGS: Wed 15 July; Thur**
13 Aug (11-5).
Extensive late C18 walled gardens.
Flower garden with summer bedding
and famous auricula theatre.
Impressive collection of glasshouses
and garden buildings. Vegetable
garden growing heirloom varieties of
fruit and vegetables, on sale to visitors.
Guided tours available. Lift to garden
entrance from car park or mansion on
electric buggy. Wheelchair available.
Gravel paths. Some steps.
&. ✕ ⊕

Original well complements the reclaimed architectural stone work . . .

9 ♦ **CASCADES GARDENS**
Clatterway, Bonsall DE4 2AH. Alan &
Elizabeth Clements, 01629 822813,
www.derbyshiregarden.com. *5m SW*
of Matlock. From Cromford A6 T-lights
turn towards Wirksworth. Turn R along
Via Gellia, signed Buxton & Bonsall.
After 1m turn R up hill towards Bonsall
village. Cascades on R at top of hill.
Tea & coffee NGS days only. Cream
teas 12 July. **Adm £3.50, chd free.**
Weds & Suns & B Hols 1 April to 13
Sept (10-5). For NGS: Weds 15 Apr;
20 May; 17 June; 5 Aug. Sun 12
July; (10-5).
Fascinating 4-acre garden in
spectacular natural surroundings with
woodland, high cliffs, stream, ponds, a
ruined corn mill and old lead mine.
Secluded areas provide peaceful views
of the extensive collection of plants,
shrubs and trees. The nursery has a
wide range of unusual herbaceous
perennial plants. Featured on East
Midlands Today & BBC TV.
&. ⊕ ⊨ ☕

10 **CASHEL**
Kirk Ireton DE6 3JX. Anita & Jeremy
Butt, 01335 370495. *2m S of*
Wirksworth. Turn off B5023 (Duffield-
Wirksworth rd). Follow rd to Kirk Ireton,
take sharp R turn at church corner.
Follow lane for 200yds. Garden on RH-
side. Parking on LH-side 80yds
beyond house. **Adm £3, chd free.**
Sun 31 May (2-5). Visitors also
welcome by appt.
3-acre garden situated on sloping site,
featuring terraced ravine and several
wood sculptures by local artists. Open
views of surrounding countryside.
Many interesting trees, shrubs and
plants. New stone circle.
⊕ ☕ ☎

11 10 CHESTNUT WAY

Repton DE65 6FQ. Robert & Pauline Little, 01283 702267, rlittleq@googlemail.com, www.littlegarden.org.uk. *6m S of Derby. From A38, S of Derby, follow signs to Willington, then Repton. In Repton turn R at roundabout. Chestnut Way is 1/4 m up hill, on L.* Home-made teas. **Adm £2.50, chd free. Suns 19 Apr (1-5); 9 Aug (1-6). Combined with Woodend Cottage & 22 Pinfold Close adm £5, Sun 9 Aug. Visitors also welcome by appt for groups of 10+, coaches permitted.**
Meander through an acre of natural borders, spring bulbs, mature trees to a stunning butterfly bed and flower meadow. A pair of passionate, practical, organic gardeners gently manages this plantsman's garden. First August opening so expect a colourful display Plenty of seats, conservatory if wet.

&♿ ⊛ ☕ ☎

Honeysuckle, roses, jasmine and sweet peas scent the air . . .

12 13 CHILTERN DRIVE

West Hallam, Ilkeston DE7 6PA. Jacqueline & Keith Holness, 01159 305670, jacqueline.holness@yahoo.com. *Approx 6m NE of Derby. 2m W of Ilkeston on A609. Take St Wilfred's Rd to West Hallam, 1st R Derbyshire Ave, 3rd L is Chiltern Drive.* Home-made teas. **Adm £2.50, chd free. Sun 31 May (11-5). Visitors also welcome by appt, wine.**
Small, secret walled suburban garden packed with a myriad of plants, some rare and unusual. Summerhouse, two small ponds and fernery, together with 75 acers and some well-hidden lizards! Garden on two levels separated by steps. Also enjoy delicious homemade cakes.

🐾 ⊛ ☕ ☎

54 CHURCH LANE
See Nottinghamshire.

59 CHURCH LANE
See Nottinghamshire.

13 CLOUD COTTAGE

Simmondley SK13 6JN. Mr R G Lomas, 01457 862033. *1m SW of Glossop. On High Lane between Simmondley & Charlesworth. From M67 take A57, turn R at Mottram (1st T-lights) through Broadbottom & Charlesworth. In Charlesworth up Town Lane by the side of Grey Mare. Cloud Cottage is 1/2 m on R. From Glossop, A57 towards Manchester, turn L at 2nd of two mini roundabouts up Simmondley Lane, Cloud Cottage is on L after passing Hare & Hounds.* **Adm £3, chd free. Suns 10, 17, 24 May (2-5). Visitors also welcome by appt.**
1 1/4 -acre arboretum/rhododendron garden. Altitude 750ft on side of hill in Peak District National Park. Collections of conifers, most over 40yrs old. Species and hybrid rhododendron; with a wide variety of shrubs. We have extended the Japanese inspired garden by diverting a stream to make 5 ponds. Featured in 'The Review'.

&♿ ☎

14 CLOVERMEAD

Commonpiece Lane, Findern, Derby DE65 6AF. David & Rosemary Noblet, 01283 702237. *4m S of Derby. From Findern village green, turn R at church into Lower Green, R turn into Commonpiece Lane, approx 500yds on R.* Home-made teas. **Adm £2.50, chd free. Suns 5 July; 9 Aug (2-5.30). Visitors also welcome by appt.**
Cottage garden set in approx 3/4 acre. Garden rooms full of perennial flowers. Honeysuckle, roses, jasmine and sweet peas scent the air. Pergolas and archways with clematis, fishponds and bandstand with seating. Greenhouses, vegetable plot and wildlife orchard. Featured in 'Derbyshire Life'.

🐾 ⊛ ☕ ☎

7 COLLYGATE
See Nottinghamshire.

15 THE COTTAGE

25 Plant Lane, Old Sawley, Long Eaton NG10 3BJ. Ernie & Averil Carver, 0115 849 1960. *2m SW of Long Eaton. From Long Eaton green take sign for town centre. Onto B6540 through to Old Sawley, take R at Nags Head PH into Wiln Rd. 400yds take R turn into Plant Lane at the Railway Inn. Garden 200yds on R.* Light refreshments & teas. **Adm £2.50, chd free. Sat 25, Sun 26 July (2-5.30). Visitors also welcome by appt for**
groups 10+ in July.
Cottage garden full of colour, steeped in herbaceous borders. Annual plants raised from the greenhouse. Number of surprising features. Summerhouse in a walled sheltered garden, providing a charming environment. Featured in 'Amateur Gardener', 'Breeze', 'Daily Mail'.

&♿ ⊛ ☕ ☎

16 CUCKOOSTONE COTTAGE

Chesterfield Road, Matlock Moor, Matlock DE4 5LZ. Barrie & Pauline Wild, 07960 708415, pauline.wild@sky.com. *2 1/2 m N of Matlock on A632. Past Matlock Golf Course look for Cuckoostone Lane on L. Turn here & follow for 1/4 m. 1st cottage on bend.* **Adm £3, chd free. Visitors welcome by appt.**
Situated on a SW-facing, sloping, rural hillside at 850ft, this 1/2 -acre is a plantsman's garden. Developed in under 6yrs it incorporates colour-themed borders, pond, bog garden and conservatory. Large collection of unusual trees, shrubs and perennials make this a yr-round garden but best in late spring and late summer. Featured in 'Reflections'.

🐾 ☎

17 8 CURZON LANE

Alvaston, Derby DE24 8QS. Mrs Marian Gray, 01332 601596, maz@cvnation.com. *2m SE of Derby city centre. From city centre take A6 (London Rd) towards Alvaston. Curzon Lane is on L, approx 1/2 m before Alvaston shops.* **Adm £2.50, chd free. Suns 5, 12 July (1-5). Visitors also welcome by appt for groups 10+, no coaches.**
Mature garden with lawns, borders packed full of perennials, shrubs and small trees, tropical planting. Ornamental and wildlife ponds, greenhouse, gravel area, large patio with container planting.

🐾 ⊛ ☕ ☎

THE DAIRY
See Leicestershire & Rutland.

18 ◆ DAM FARM HOUSE

Yeldersley Lane, Ednaston DE6 3BA. Mrs J M Player, 01335 360291. *5m SE of Ashbourne. On A52, opp Ednaston village turn, gate on R 500yds.* **Adm £4, chd free. April to Oct. Mons, Tues & Fris, or by appointment (9-4). Not open Bank Holidays.**
3 acres incl a stunning young

arboretum, beautifully situated. Contains mixed borders, scree. Unusual plants have been collected. From spring to autumn it is full of colour with interesting rare trees and plants, many of which are propagated for sale in the nursery.

🚶 ✕ ⊗ ☕

⑲ DAM STEAD

3 Crowhole, Barlow, Dronfield S18 7TJ. Derek & Barbara Saveall, 0114 2890802. *3¹/₂ m NW of Chesterfield. From A61 Sheffield/Derby take B6051 Barlow at Chesterfield North. Through Barlow, pass Tickled Trout PH on L. Pass Springfield Road on L then R (unamed road). Last house on R.* Home-made teas. **Adm £2.50, chd free (share to The Jennifer Trust for Spinal Muscular Atrophy). Visitors welcome by appt for groups 6+.**
³/₄ acre with stream, weir and dam with an island. Long woodland path, orchard, alpine troughs/rockeries and mixed planting. A natural wildlife garden with large summerhouse with seating inside and out. Display & sale of mounted wildlife and flower photographs. Featured in local publications, 'Amateur Gardening' & 'Reflections'.

✕ ☕ ☎

⑳ 62A DENBY LANE

Loscoe DE75 7RX. Mrs J Charlesworth. *12m NW of Nottingham. Between Codnor & Heanor, on A6007. Follow Denby sign.* Light refreshments. **Adm £2, chd free. Sun 2 Aug (2-5).**
All-year round garden with hostas, ferns, grasses, perennials, dahlias, shrubs, conifers and vegetable plot. Small pond with waterfall and stream. Japanese features, pergola with seating area and summerhouse.

✕ ⊗ ☕

㉑ DOLLY BARN

Ash Lane, nr Etwall, Derby DE65 6HT. Glynis & Michael Smith, 01283 734002, dollybarn@ic24.net. *6m W of Derby. From A516 Etwall bypass turn into Ash Lane signed Sutton-on-the-Hill. After 1m take R turn at postbox. Dolly Barn 200yds on R.* Home-made teas. **Adm £3, chd free. Suns 14 June; 26 July (1-5). Visitors also welcome by appt.**
Eclectic mix of contemporary, cottage and prairie styles in 2¹/₂ acre rural setting created from a cattle field. Walled garden (formerly cow yard) with 17m rill, 2 stainless steel water features

and different planting styles from tropical to formal box hedging, with walkways. Large pond well stocked with fish and plants. Prairie and grass gardens. Large vegetable garden and greenhouse. Gravel drive.

🚶 ⊗ ☕ ☎

㉒ DOVE COTTAGE

Clifton, Ashbourne DE6 2JQ. Stephen & Anne Liverman, 01335 343545, astrantiamajor@hotmail.co.uk. *1¹/₂ m SW of Ashbourne. Enter Clifton village. Turn R at Xrds by church. Travel 100yds turn L, Dove Cottage 1st house on L. Always well signed on open days.* Home-made teas. **Adm £3, chd free (share to Ashbourne British Heart Foundation). Sat 23, Sun 24 May; Suns 28 June; 2 Aug (1-5). Visitors also welcome by appt.**
³/₄ -acre garden by River Dove, extensively replanted. Emphasis on establishing collections of hardy plants and shrubs incl alchemillas, alliums, berberis, geraniums, euphorbias, hostas, lilies, variegated and silver foliage plants inc astrantias. Plantsman's garden. Area growing new heucheras and other purple flowering plants and foliage. Woodland area planted with daffodils and shade loving plants. Worth visiting end of Mar.

✕ ⊗ ☕ ☎

㉓ THE DOWER HOUSE

Church Square, Melbourne DE73 8JH. Griselda Kerr, 01332 864756, griseldakerr@btinternet.com. *6m S of Derby. 5m W of exit 21A M1. 4m N of exit 13 M42. Church Sq is at bottom of Church St in centre of Melbourne. Enter the square & turn R before church immed after war memorial. The Dower House is at west end of Norman church. Park in & around the town & Church Square.* Home-made teas. **Adm £3, chd free. Sat 6, Sun 7 June (10-5.30). Visitors also welcome by appt.**
Beautiful view of Melbourne Pool from balustraded terrace running length of 1821 house. Garden drops steeply by way of paths, steps and shrubbery to lawn with 70' herbaceous border. Rose tunnel, peaceful glade, young orchard, small area of woodland, hellebore bed, herb garden, small cottage garden with vegetables. New planting continues. Featured in 'Derbyshire Magazine' & 'Derbyshire Life'. Limited access for wheelchairs to 75% of garden. Gravel paths & very steep paths.

🚶 🐕 ☕ ☎

> Lower courtyard with knot garden and herb border. Restored terraced orchard representing a medieval tilt yard . . .

EDITH TERRACE GARDENS
See Cheshire & Wirral.

EYNORD
See Nottinghamshire.

㉔ FANSHAWE GATE HALL

Holmesfield S18 7WA. Mr & Mrs John Ramsden, 01142 890391, www.fanshawegate.com. *2m W of Dronfield. Situated on the edge of the Peak National Park. Follow B6054 towards Owler Bar. 1st R turn after church signed Fanshawe Gate Lane.* Light refreshments. **Adm £2.50, chd free (share to Oesophageal Patients Assoc). Suns 21, 28 June; 5, 12 July (11-5). Visitors also welcome by appt June & July only, small coaches/mini buses.**
C13 seat of the Fanshawe family. Old-fashioned cottage-style garden. Many stone features, fine C16 dovecote. Upper walled garden with herbaceous, variegated and fern plantings, water features, topiary, terracing and lawns. Lower courtyard with knot garden and herb border. Restored terraced orchard representing a medieval tilt yard. Newly planted pleached hornbeam hedge. Wildlife pond. Featured in 'The Derbyshire Magazine' and GGG.

🚶 ✕ ⊗ ☕ ☎

FELLEY PRIORY
See Nottinghamshire.

25 FIELD FARM

Kirk Ireton, Ashbourne DE6 3JU.
Graham & Irene Dougan, 01335
370958, dougan@lineone.net,
www.fieldfarmgarden.info. *2m S of
Wirksworth. At top of Main St, Kirk
Ireton turn L signed Blackwall, on
sharp RH-bend find Field Lane
(unmade rd), Field Farm 400yds.
Parking in adjacent field.* Home-made
teas. **Adm £3, chd free. Sun 27 Sept
(1-5). Visitors also welcome by appt
July to end Sept, groups 10+. Coach
parties must park in village.**
A glorious 2-acre garden for all
seasons, set in superb countryside.
Gravelled courtyard with specimen
plants. Herbaceous borders, roses and
many rare trees and shrubs. Summer
fragrance and autumn colour. The
home-made cake is good too.
Featured in 'The Derbyshire' & on BBC
TV Open Gardens. Some gravel paths
& undulating lawns.

♿ ❀ ☕ ☎

26 FIR CROFT

Froggatt Road, Calver S32 3ZD.
Dr S B Furness,
www.alpineplantcentre.co.uk. *4m N
of Bakewell. At junction of B6001 with
A625 (formerly B6054), adjacent to
Power Garage.* **Adm by donation.
Sun 17, 31 May; Sun 14 June (2-5).**
Massive scree with many rarities.
Plantsman's garden; rockeries; water
garden and nursery; extensive
collection (over 3000 varieties) of
alpines; conifers; over 800
sempervivums, 500 saxifrages and
350 primulas. Tufa and scree beds.

✈ ❀

27 GAMESLEY FOLD COTTAGE

Glossop SK13 6JJ. Mrs G Carr,
01457 867856,
www.gamesleyfold.co.uk. *2m W of
Glossop. Off A626 Glossop to Marple
rd, nr Charlesworth. Turn down lane
directly opp St Margaret's School.
White cottage at bottom. Car parking
in adjacent field.* Home-made teas.
**Adm £2, chd free. Suns 24 May;
14 June (1-4). Visitors also welcome
by appt for groups during May &
June only. Coaches permitted.**
Old-fashioned cottage garden. Spring
garden with herbaceous borders,
shrubs and rhododendrons, wild
flowers and herbs in profusion to
attract butterflies and wildlife. Good
selection of herbs and cottage garden
plants for sale. Many breeds of poultry
and fan-tailed doves kept.

✈ ❀ ☕ ☎

GARDENERS COTTAGE
See Nottinghamshire.

28 THE GARDENS AT DOBHOLME FISHERY

Main Road, Troway, nr Coal Aston
S21 5RR. Paul & Pauline Calvert,
07875 839680,
calvertpj@yahoo.co.uk. *3m NE of
Dronfield. Halfway along B6056,
Dronfield to Eckington rd, 2½ m from
each. Coming from Dronfield turn L at
Blackamoor Head Inn for Troway.
Follow signs in village.* **Adm £3, chd
free. Visitors welcome by appt
June/July for groups of 15+.**
Situated in beautiful conservation area
of Moss Valley. Developed on sloping
site of approx 3 acres around fishing
ponds. Designed to encourage wildlife;
planted in a wild, natural look. Heavy
clay with many springs; stone quarried
from the site is widely used to pave the
pond sides. Sloping uneven terrain.
Potager vegetable garden and herb
garden. ☎

GORENE
See Nottinghamshire.

> A garden which has to be explored to discover its secrets . . .

GRAFTON COTTAGE
See Staffordshire & part of West
Midlands.

29 ◆ HARDWICK HALL

Doe Lea, Chesterfield S44 5QJ. The
National Trust, 01246 858400,
www.nationaltrust.org.uk. *8m SE of
Chesterfield. S of A617. Signed from
J29 M1.* **House and Garden Adm
£10.00, chd £5, Garden only Adm
£5, chd £2.50. Wed to Sun 14 Mar to
1 Nov (11-5). For NGS: Sat 18 July
(11-5).**
Grass walks between yew and
hornbeam hedges; cedar trees; herb
garden; herbaceous and rose borders.
Finest example of Elizabethan house in
the country.

♿ ✈ ☕

HARDWICK HALL
See Derbyshire.

30 HIGH ROOST

27 Storthmeadow Road,
Simmondley, Glossop SK13 6UZ.
Peter & Christina Harris, 01457
863888, peter@pharris54.fsnet.
co.uk. *¾ m SW of Glossop. From
M67 take A57, turn R at Mottram (1st
T-lights), through Broadbottom and
Charlesworth. In Charlesworth turn R
up Town Lane by side of Grey Mare
PH, continue up High Lane, past Hare
& Hounds PH, Storthmeadow Rd is
2nd turn on L. From Glossop, A57
towards Manchester, L at 2nd mini
roundabout, up Simmondley Lane,
turn R into Storthmeadow Rd, nr top,
no 27 last house on L. On road parking
nearby, please take care not to block
drives.* Light refreshments & teas. **Adm
£2, chd free (share to Manchester
Dogs Home). Sun 5 July (1-5).
Visitors also welcome by appt June
- Aug.**
Youngish suburban garden with
interesting layout on terraced slopes
with views over fields and hills. Winding
paths, archways and steps explore
different garden 'rooms' packed with
plants for yr-round interest and colour,
much of the planting designed to
attract wildlife. Herbaceous borders
give a blaze of colour in summer.
Tiered alpine bed, vegetable garden,
several small water features. Statuary,
pots, troughs and planters. A garden
which has to be explored to discover
its secrets tucked away in hidden
corners. New for 2009, 'dry' garden for
spikey, drought tolerant plants. Craft
stalls incl children's lucky dip. Featured
in 'Peak District Life'.

❀ ☕ ☎

31 37 HIGH STREET

Repton DE65 6GD. David & Jan
Roberts. *6m S of Derby. From A38,
A50 junction S of Derby follow signs to
Willington, then Repton. In Repton
continue past island and shops.
Garden on L.* Home-made teas. **Adm
£2.50, chd free. Suns 19 Apr; 7 June
(2-5.30).**
Over 1 acre of gardens with bridge
over Repton Brook which meanders
through. Formal and wildlife ponds,
mixed borders of herbaceous, shrubs
and trees. Rhododendrons and
woodland, grasses, ferns and
bamboos. Vegetable garden and
greenhouses, container planting for
spring and summer colour and alpines
troughs. A surprising garden for all
seasons with interest for everyone.

♿ ✈ ❀ ☕ ☎

32 HIGHFIELD HOUSE
Wingfield Road, Oakerthorpe, Alfreton DE55 7AP. Paul & Ruth Peat & Janet Costall, 01773 521342, peatruth@aol.com. *Approx 1m from Alfreton town centre on A615 Alfreton-Matlock Rd. From Matlock: A615 to Alfreton. Turn R into Alfreton Golf Club. From Derby: A38 to Alfreton. A615 to Matlock. After houses on L of Wingfield Rd, turn L into Alfreton Golf Club.* Light refreshments & home-made teas. **Adm £2.50, chd free. Suns 24 May; 21 June (11-5). Visitors also welcome by appt late May to July for groups 10+.**
Delightful family garden of 3/4 acre. Individual areas include a shady garden, small area of woodland, tree house, laburnum arch, orchard, lawns, herbaceous borders and newly developed productive vegetable garden. Pleasant level walk to Derbyshire Wildlife Trust Nature reserve, where there is a pond and boardwalk and beautiful spotted orchids. Some gravel paths and slopes.

33 11 HIGHGROVE DRIVE
Chellaston, Derby DE73 5XA. Ms Sarah Bacon. *2m SE of city centre. Off the A514 Derby Melbourne Rd, halfway between the ring road (A5111) and the A50.* Home-made teas. **Adm £2.50, chd free. Sat 18 (2-6), Sun 19 July (11-5).**
Small suburban garden. Lawn, paved areas, pond with waterfall, water feature, Japanese corner, Mediterranean yard, small patio with topiary. Grape, kiwi, greenhouse and garden shed in enclosed area. Pots, hanging baskets, automatic watering, lights and pond fountain. A big garden in a small space. Display of honey bee hive.

HILL PARK FARM
See Leicestershire & Rutland.

34 HILLSIDE
286 Handley Road, New Whittington, Chesterfield S43 2ET. E J Lee, 01246 454960. *3m N of Chesterfield. From A6135, take B6052 through Eckington & Marsh Lane 3m. Turn L at Xrds signed Whittington, then 1m. From Coal Aston (Sheffield), take B6056 towards Chesterfield to give way sign, then 1m. From Chesterfield, take B6052.* **Adm £2, chd free. Visitors welcome by appt all yr.**

1/3 -acre sloping site. Herbaceous borders, rock garden, alpines, streams, pools, bog gardens, asiatic primula bed, and alpine house. Acers, bamboos, collection of approx 150 varieties of ferns, eucalypts, euphorbias, grasses, conifers, Himalayan bed. 1500 plants permanently labelled. Yr-round interest.

35 ◆ LEA GARDENS
Lea, Nr Matlock DE4 5GH. Mr & Mrs J Tye, 01629 534380, www.leagarden.co.uk. *5m SE of Matlock. Off A6. Also off A615.* **Adm £4, chd 50p. Daily 20 Mar to 30 June (10-5).**
Rare collection of rhododendrons, azaleas, kalmias, alpines and conifers in delightful woodland setting. Gardens are sited on remains of medieval quarry and cover about 4 acres. Specialised plant nursery of rhododendrons and azaleas on site. Teashop offering light lunches and home-made cakes open daily. Music Day Sun 14 June.

36 NEW THE LEYLANDS
Moorwood Lane, Owler Bar (Holmesfield) S17 3BS. Richard & Chris Hibberd, 0114 289 0833, richard@rhibberd.demon.co.uk. *2m W of Dronfield. Situated on the edge of the Peak District National Park, adjacent to the B6054. Moorwood Lane is 1m from the Owler Bar junction with the A621 (Sheffield-Bakewell) or 2nd turn on R after leaving Holmesfield village if travelling W towards Owler Bar.* **Adm £2.50, chd free (share to Water Aid). Sun 24, Mon 25 May (1-5). Visitors also welcome by appt.**
2-acre country garden in which the owners, over the last 30 yrs, have indulged their individual passions for water and for plants. The result is a garden with a variety of water systems, breeding koi and plant combinations with yr-round interest. Part of the garden was a working nursery in the 1950s and has been re-developed for plant propagation. Sloping site. Some steps & uneven paths.

Allotments

37 LITTLEOVER LANE ALLOTMENTS
19 Littleover Lane, Derby DE23 6JH. Littleover Lane Allotments Assoc, 01332 770096, davidkenyon@tinyworld.co.uk. *3m SW of Derby. Off Derby ring rd A5111 into Stenson Rd. R into Littleover Lane. Garden on L. On street parking opp Foremark Ave.* Light refreshments & teas. **Adm £3, chd free. Suns 7 June; 6 Sept (11-5). Visitors also welcome by appt.**
Allotment site with plots cultivated in a variety of styles. A Schools' Centre incl greenhouses and walled garden and museum collection of heritage gardening equipment. A range of heritage and unusual vegetable varieties grown. Some slopes. Disabled WC.

38 LOCKO PARK
Spondon DE21 7BW. Mrs Lucy Palmer. *6m NE of Derby. From A52 Borrowash bypass, 2m N via B6001, turn to Spondon.* Light refreshments & teas. **Adm £3, chd free. Sun 17 May (2-5).**
Large garden; pleasure gardens; rose gardens. House (not open) by Smith of Warwick with Victorian additions. Chapel (open) Charles II, with original ceiling.

39 9 MAIN STREET
Horsley Woodhouse DE7 6AU. Ms Alison Napier, 01332 881629, ibhillib@btinternet.com. *3m SW of Heanor. 6m N of Derby. Turn off A608 Derby to Heanor rd at Smalley, towards Belper, (A609). Garden on A609, 1m from Smalley turning.* Cream teas. **Adm £2.50, accom chd free. Sun 2 Aug (2-5). Visitors also welcome by appt.**
1/3 -acre hilltop garden overlooking lovely farmland view. Terracing, borders, lawns and pergola create space for an informal layout with planting for colour effect. Features incl large wildlife pond with water lilies, bog garden and small formal pool. Emphasis on carefully selected herbaceous perennials mixed with shrubs and old-fashioned roses. Wheelchair-adapted WC.

Mediterranean yard, small patio with topiary . . .

40 2 MANVERS STREET
Ripley DE5 3EQ. Mrs D Wood & Mr D Hawkins, 01773 743962. *Ripley Town centre to Derby rd turn L opp Leisure Centre onto Heath Rd. 1st turn R onto Meadow Rd, 1st L onto Manvers St.* Home-made teas. **Adm £2, chd free. Sun 19 July (2-6). Visitors also welcome by appt, July to Aug only.**
Summer garden with backdrop of neighbouring trees, 10 borders bursting with colour surrounded by immaculate shaped lawn. Perennials incl 26 clematis, annuals, baskets, tubs and pots. Ornamental fish pond. Water features, arbour and summerhouse. Plenty of seating areas to take in this awe-inspiring oasis. First Prize and Cup Winner Ripley Town Council.

🏖 ❀ ☕ ☎ 🐕

41 MARKHAM VILLA
60 Alfreton Road, Newton DE55 5TQ. Ann & Kevin Briggs, 01773 778982, markhamvilla1@hotmail.com. *2m NE of Alfreton. A38 N from Derby. Take Alfreton/Matlock junction along A61. Turn R following Blackwell signs. 1½ m to Newton.* Home-made teas. **Adm £3, chd free. Suns 19 July; 2 Aug (11-5). Visitors also welcome by appt for groups of 15+ in Aug. Artists & photography groups welcome.**
Continually developing 2/3 acre plot with a series of gardens, walkways and seating to create areas for different purposes and moods. Extensively planted for all yr-round interest of flower, foliage, colour and texture. Fragrant parterre with camomile lawn, summerhouse, orchard, pond, wild flower mound, greenhouses and well-maintained productive vegetable plot. A delightful surprise around every corner.

🏖 ❀ ☕ ☎

42 ◆ MEYNELL LANGLEY TRIALS GARDEN
Lodge Lane (off Flagshaw Lane), Derby DE6 4NT. Robert & Karen Walker, 01332 824358, www.meynell-langley-gardens.co.uk. *4m W of Derby, nr Kedleston Hall. Head W out of Derby on A52. At Kirk Langley turn R onto Flagshaw Lane (signed to Kedleston Hall) then R onto Lodge Lane. Follow Meynell Langley Gdns sign for 1½ m. From A38 follow signs for Kedleston Hall (past first entrance).* **Adm £2.50, chd free. Open daily 19 April to**

11 Oct. For NGS: **Suns 19 Apr; 10 May; 7 June; 12 July; 16 Aug; 13 Sept; 11 Oct (10-5).**
Formal 3/4 -acre Victorian-style garden established 17 yrs, displaying and trialling new and existing varieties of bedding plants, herbaceous perennials and vegetable plants grown at the adjacent nursery. Over 180 hanging baskets and floral displays. 85 varieties of apple, pear and other fruit. Summer fruit tree pruning demonstrations 16 Aug. Apple tasting 13 Sept & 11 Oct.

♿ 🏖 ❀ ☕

Developed from a field over the last 5 years . . .

43 23 MILL LANE
Codnor, Ripley DE5 9QF. Mrs S Jackson. *12m NW of Nottingham. 10m N of Derby. Mill Lane is opp Codnor Market Place (Clock Tower) on A610. 2 car parks nearby.* Cream teas. **Adm £1.50, chd free. Sun 9 Aug (1-6).**
Lawn, herbaceous borders, pond, waterfall; clematis and Mediterranean garden. 2nd Prize 'Best Kept Garden' Codnor & Wainsgrove Parish Council.

🏖 ❀ ☕

MILLPOOL
See Cheshire & Wirral.

44 MONKSWAY
Summer Cross, Tideswell, nr Buxton SK17 8HU. Mr & Mrs R Porter, 01298 871687, www.monkswaygarden.co.uk. *9m NE of Buxton. On the B6049. Turn up Parke Rd, opp Nat West Bank, off Queen St. Take L turn at top & then 1st R onto Summer Cross. Monksway is 4th semi-detached house on L. Limited parking.* **Adm £2, chd free. Suns 7, 14, 21 June (11-5). Visitors also welcome by appt for groups of 6+.**
Gently sloping garden 1000ft above sea level. Gravel/paved paths and archways meander through well-stocked beds and borders of perennials, shrubs and climbers. Garden planted for all-yr interest. An aviary and water features complete the scene.

☎

45 NEW MOORFIELDS
257/261 Chesterfield Road, Temple Normanton, Chesterfield S42 5DE. Peter, Janet & Stephen Wright. *4m SE of Chesterfield. From Chesterfield take A617 for 2m, turn off on to B6039 through Temple Normanton, taking R fork signed Tibshelf. Garden 1/4 m on R.* Home-made teas. **Adm £2.50, chd free. Sun 26 July (1-5).**
Of these two adjacent gardens, the larger has been developed from a field over the last 5yrs and has a gravel garden, herbaceous beds, a small wild flower area, pond, fruit trees and bushes and vegetable patch. (Some uneven ground). The smaller more traditional back and front gardens of No 257 feature herbaceous borders. Limited parking on site, otherwise on-road parking. Short walk down field to pet cemetery.

🏖 ❀ ☕

THE OLD RECTORY, CLIFTON CAMPVILLE
See Staffordshire & part of West Midlands.

ONE HOUSE NURSERY
See Cheshire & Wirral.

47 OTTERBROOK
Alders Lane, Chinley, High Peak SK23 6DP. Mary & Dennis Sharp, 01663 750335. *3m W of Whaley Bridge. Otterbrook is reached by 300yd walk up Alders Lane on outskirts of village off Buxton Rd (B6062) between Chinley & Chapel-en-le-Frith. Parking is very limited at house. Please park at Buxton Road.* Home-made teas. **Adm £2.50, chd free. Sun 14 June (1-5). Visitors also welcome by appt for groups & individuals, please telephone first.**
Wander in this 1-acre garden between colour-themed beds and borders, along paths to focal points and views of the surrounding hills. Trees, shrubs and plants, many moisture-loving, provide contrasting form and texture and complement the ponds and bog garden. Pergolas and structures give cohesion. A small potager is included.

🏖 ❀ ☕ ☎

20 THE PADDOCKS
See Nottinghamshire.

48 PARK HALL
Walton Back Lane, Walton,
Chesterfield S42 7LT. Kim &
Margaret Staniforth, 01246 567412,
kim.staniforth@virgin.net. *2m SW of
Chesterfield. From Chesterfield take
A632 for Matlock. After start of 40mph
section take 1st R into Acorn Ridge
and then L into Walton Back Lane.
300yds on R, at end of high stone wall.
Park on field side of Walton Back Lane
only.* Cream teas & ploughman's
lunches. **Adm £3, chd 50p (share to
Bluebell Wood Children's Hospice).**
Sun 28 June (12-5.30). Visitors also
welcome by appt Apr to Aug for
groups of 10+.
2-acre plantsman's garden in a
beautiful setting surrounding C17
house, not open. Four main 'rooms' -
terraced garden, park area with forest
trees, croquet lawn and new
millennium garden now fully mature.
Within these are a woodland walk,
fernery, yew hedges and topiary, water
features, pergolas, arbours,
herbaceous borders, rhododendrons,
camellias, azaleas, hydrangeas, 150
roses, a circular pleached hedge, and
a small auricula theatre.
🌠 ⊛ ☕ ☎

49 NEW 22 PINFOLD CLOSE
Repton. DE65 6FR. Mr O Jowett.
*6m S of Derby. From A38, A50 J,
S of Derby follow signs to
Willington then Repton. Off Repton
High Street find Pinfold Lane,
Pinfold Close 1st L.* **Combined
adm £5, chd free. Sun 9 Aug (1-
6).** **Combined with Woodend
Cottage & 10 Chestnut Way.**
Small garden with an interest in
tropical plants. Palms, gingers, tree
ferns, canna's, bananas. Mainly
foliage plants.

50 19 PORTLAND STREET
Etwall DE65 6JF. Paul & Fran
Harvey, 01283 734360. *6m W of
Derby. In centre of Etwall Village, at
Spread Eagle PH turn into Willington
Rd then immed R into Portland St
(behind PH car park).* Home-made
teas. **Adm £2.50, chd free. Sat 18,
Sun 19 Apr; Sat 1, Sun 2 Aug; (11-5);
Tue 1, Wed 9 Sept (2-7).** Visitors also
welcome by appt.
Our tranquil garden is packed with
plants for yr-round interest. This 1/3 acre
has been developed since 1992 with
significant changes every year. Many
rare and unusual shrubs and
perennials, fabulous colour and

tremendous scent; pond, small stream;
oriental garden; pergola; exhibition
dahlias; collections incl picea,
agapanthus and crocosmia, but no
lawn. New planting in front garden -
collection of plants from New Zealand.
2009 will be the last opportunity to visit
our garden.
♿ 🌠 ☕ ☎

Small garden
with an interest
in tropical
plants . . .

51 QUARRYSIDE
1 King Charles Court, Glossop
SK13 8NJ. Sue & Ron Astles, 01457
857015, sue.astles@ctaweb.co.uk.
*1m S of Glossop town centre. From
Glossop centre take A624 towards
Hayfield & Chapel-en-le-Frith. About
3/4 m along turn L into Whitfield Ave.
At top turn R into Hague St & 1st L
into King Charles Court. Please park
on Whitfield Ave, limited parking in
Close.* **Adm £2, chd free.** Visitors
welcome by appt May, June & July,
16 max.
Small peaceful garden in quarry setting
with exposed rock strata and
interesting nooks and crannies on two
terraces, with an emphasis on texture
and colour. All yr-round natural planting
with two water features to attract
wildlife. Front garden is being redesigned for spring 2009. Featured on
UKTV Gardens.
🌠 ⊛ ☕ ☎

**52 ◆ RENISHAW HALL
GARDENS**
Renishaw, nr Sheffield S21 3WB. Sir
Reresby & Lady Sitwell, 01246
432310, www.renishaw-hall.co.uk.
*4m W of Sheffield. From J30 M1 take
A6135 towards Sheffield. Renishaw
Hall is 3m from motorway.* **Gardens,
galleries & museums adm £5, conc
£4.20. Garden only adm £3, chd
free. Thurs to Suns, BH Mons 26
Mar to 27 Sept (10.30-4.30).** For
NGS: Tues 14 Apr; 4 Aug (10.30-
3.30).
Home of Sir Reresby and Lady Sitwell.
Romantic, formal 2 Italianate gardens
divided into rooms by yew hedges.
Bluebell woods, magnolias and

rhododendrons in spring woodland
gardens. Over a thousand roses in
June with peonies and clematis. Deep
herbaceous borders with collections of
unusual plants. National Collection of
Yuccas. Separate childrens garden
with willow tunnel, maze and trails.
Pastoral music to be played in garden
(weather permitting). 10 min talk on the
Sitwell Family (11.30 & 2.30). Featured
in 'The Mail on Sunday'. Gravel & bark
pathways.
♿ ⊛ NCCPG ☕

53 ROSEBANK
303 Duffield Road, Allestree, Derby
DE22 2DF. Patrick & Carol Smith. *2m
N of Derby. Follow A6 from Derby
towards Matlock. On crossing A38
island continue for 150 metres turning
L into Gisborne Crescent then R into
service rd.* Cream teas. **Adm £2, chd
free (share to St Peter's City Centre
Church, Derby & Cruse
Bereavement Care).** Sats 18 July;
8 Aug (2-6).
Interesting garden of variety on a
gentle, upward sloping site. Access by
steps and paths. Includes colourful
borders with imaginative planting and a
water feature in a natural setting. Small
orchard and soft fruit garden, lawns,
rockery, shrubs and trees. Wildlife
friendly. Children welcomed.
⊛ ☕

SANDSEND
See Cheshire & Wirral.

54 SHATTON HALL FARM
Bamford S33 0BG. Mr & Mrs J
Kellie, 01433 620635,
jk@shatton.co.uk,
www.peakfarmholidays.co.uk. *3m W
of Hathersage. Take A6187 from
Hathersage, turn L to Shatton, after
2m (opp High Peak Garden Centre).
After 1/2 m turn R through ford, drive
1/2 m & house is on L over cattle grids.*
Home-made teas. **Adm £3, chd free.**
**Suns 7 June; 26 July (1.30-5).
Visitors also welcome by appt.**
Original walled garden of C16.
Farmhouse now spills out to water
gardens and sheltered slopes, planted
informally and merging into the
picturesque landscape. Among the
great variety of unusual plants and
shrubs, sculpture and willow features
add interest to this maturing and still
expanding garden. New planting in the
house and under the old yew tree has
now matured into a substantial feature.
Featured in 'Guardian Weekend'.
⊛ 🏠 ☕ ☎

55 SOUTHFIELD
Bullbridge Hill, Fritchley, Belper DE56 2FL. Pete & Lot Clark. *4m N of Belper. Turn off A610 between Ripley & Ambergate under railway bridge & signed Bullbridge, Frichley, Crich. Proceed up hill towards Crich. In 1/2 m garden is on junction of Allen Lane (signed Fritchley) and Bullbridge Hill. Turn R into Allen Lane & park in village.* Home-made teas. **Adm £2.50, chd free. Suns 17 May; Crich Brass band** 26 July (1-5).
1 1/2 acre all-yr round garden surrounded by mature trees. Beds and borders of rhododendrons, flowering and foliage shrubs, mixed herbaceous plants and a rockery with pond ensure interest throughout the seasons. Raised nursery beds, terrace with bedding plants and Mediterranean garden complete the picture. New for 2009, summerhouse with associated colour themed beds. Featured on BBC East Midlands Today.

Stunning 100-acre garden overlooking rolling countryside . . .

STONEHILL QUARRY GARDEN
See Staffordshire & part of West Midlands.

56 ◆ SUDBURY HALL
Ashbourne DE6 5HT. The National Trust, 01283 585337, www.nationaltrust.org.uk/sudbury. *6m E of Uttoxeter. At junction of A50 Derby-Stoke & A515 Ashbourne.* House & Museum Adm £13.20, chd £7. 14 Feb to 1 Nov. Please phone for opening times. **For NGS: Sats 18 July; 12 Sept** (10-5).
Original garden design dates from 1700s. Landscaped in 1800s in a naturalistic style popularised by Capability Brown. Wander through the meadow and small woodland, walk by the lake and stroll through our unusual quincunx. Admire the hall from the garden terraces. Some gravel paths and cobbles.

57 NEW THORNBRIDGE HALL
Ashford in the Water DE45 1NZ. Jim & Emma Harrison. *2m NW of Bakewell. From Bakewell take A6, signed Buxton. After 2m, R onto A6020. 1/2 m turn L, signed Thornbridge Hall.* Light refreshments & teas. **Adm £4.50, chd free. Sun 23 Aug** (10-4).
A stunning 100-acre garden overlooking rolling Derbyshire countryside. Established late C19 this rarely opened, privately owned garden has many distinct areas incl Italian garden with statuary, knot garden, water garden, 100ft herbaceous border, working potager, koi lake, thatched summer house and new glass houses. Also on site award winning Thornbridge Brewery. Gravel paths, some steep slopes, steps.

58 NEW TILFORD HOUSE
Hognaston, Ashbourne DE6 1PW. Mr & Mrs P R Gardner. *5m NE of Ashbourne. A517 Belper to Ashbourne. At Hulland Ward follow signs to Hognaston. Down hill (2m) to bridge. Roadside parking 100 meters.* **Adm £3, chd free. Sun 12 July** (2-5).
A 1 1/2 -acre damp, streamside country garden. Mixed borders and woodland planting alongside untamed wild areas. Raised vegetable beds and fruit. Wander through a plant lovers' garden with large collections of hostas, iris and primulas, unusual trees and shrubs, or sit, enjoy and relax. Waterproof footwear essential when wet.

59 ◆ TISSINGTON HALL
nr Ashbourne DE6 1RA. Sir Richard FitzHerbert, 01335 352200, www.tissington-hall.com. *4m N of Ashbourne. E of A515 on Ashbourne to Buxton rd.* Refreshments in village. **Adm £3.50, chd free. Tissington Hall is open to visitors throughout the year, please ring. For NGS: Mon 31 Aug** (1.30-4).
Large garden celebrating over 70 years in the NGS, with roses, herbaceous borders and 5 acres of grounds. Hall also open to visitors.

60 WHARFEDALE
34 Broadway, Duffield, Belper DE56 4BU. Roger & Sue Roberts, 01332 841905, roberts34@btinternet.com, www.garden34.co.uk. *4m N of Derby. Turn onto B5023 Wirksworth rd (Broadway) off A6 midway between Belper & Derby.* Home-made teas. **Adm £3, chd free. Suns 28 June; 26 July; 30 Aug** (11-5). **Evening Opening £5,** wine & light refreshments, **Fri 28 Aug** (6.30-10). Visitors also welcome by appt, for groups of 15+, June, July & Aug.
Plant enthusiasts' garden with over 800 varieties of choice and unusual shrubs, trees, perennials and bulbs. Themed borders incl Mediterranean, late summer tropical and single colour schemes. Cottage garden to front. 14yrs old with Italianate walled scented garden and woodland pond with raised walkway. Eclectic and unusual garden providing lots of ideas. Japanese tea garden with stream and pavilion. Fully illuminated and several sitting areas. Featured in 'Derbyshire' magazine.

61 24 WHEELDON AVENUE
Derby DE22 1HN. Laura Burnett, 01332 384893. *1m N Derby city centre. Approached directly from Kedleston Rd or from A6, Duffield Rd via West Bank Ave. Limited on street parking. Good bus services on Kedleston Rd or Duffield Rd.* Home-made teas. **Adm £2, chd free. Combined with 26 Wheeldon Ave,** adm £3.50. **Sun 14 June** (2-5). Visitors also welcome by appt for groups 6+.
Small Victorian garden, with original walling supporting many shrubs and climbers with contrasting colour and texture. Circular lawn surrounded by herbaceous border with main colour scheme of blue, purple, black, yellow and orange tones. This leads to a small area at rear of garden given to more natural planting to suit shade and natural habitat. This is a garden produced on a low income budget, with varied tones and textures throughout the planting. Sale of hand-made cards and mohair teddy bears. Featured on BBC, radio, press and in 'Derbyshire Magazine'.

62 26 WHEELDON AVENUE
Derby DE22 1HN. Ian Griffiths, 01332 342204. *1m N of Derby. 1m from city centre & approached directly off the Kedleston Rd or from A6*

Duffield Rd via West Bank Ave. Limited on-street parking. Teas & Wine. **Adm £2, chd free. Combined with 24 Wheeldon Avenue, adm £3.50. Sun 14 June** (2-5). **Visitors also welcome by appt** May to Jul, groups of 4+.
Tiny Victorian walled garden near to city centre. Lawn and herbaceous borders with old roses, lupins, delphiniums and foxgloves. Small terrace with topiary, herb garden and new lion fountain. Old rose collection restored and replanted for 2009. Featured on BBC TV, radio, press and in 'Period Living' & 'Amateur Gardening'.

63 NEW 26 WINDMILL RISE
Belper DE56 1GQ. Kathy Fairweather. *1/2 m from Belper market place. Take Chesterfield Road towards Heage. Top of hill 1st R, Marsh Lane. 1st R Windmill Lane, 1st R Windmill Rise. Please do not park on Windmill Rise.* Light refreshments & teas. **Adm £2, chd free. Suns 21 June, 2 Aug** (12.30-4.30).
Plantsman's organic garden. All yr interest with some unusual plants. Garden divided into sections; woodland spring, Japanese, 'secret garden', cottage. Edible and patio gardens. Fish and wildlife ponds, small stream. Unusual specimen Fir tree.

64 WINDWARD
62 Summer Lane, Wirksworth DE4 4EB. Audrey & Andrew Winkler, 01629 822681, audrey.winkler@w3z.co.uk, www.grandmafrogsgarden.co.uk. *5m S of Matlock. 1/2 m from Wirksworth town centre off B5023 Wirksworth to Duffield rd. After approx 300yds, turn R at mini island onto Summer Lane. Windward is approx 500yds on R, rockery at roadside.* Home-made teas. **Adm £3, chd free (share to Ruddington Framework Knitters Museum). Suns 29 Mar; 17 May; 26 July (11-5). Visitors also welcome by appt for groups of 10+.**
Lush, green garden,1-acre, with mature trees and shrubs. Woodland clearings with wild flowers. Spring bulbs, fernery, grasses, gravel garden, wildlife pond, hostas, roses, rhododendrons and poppies and an impressive Leylandii crinkle-crankle hedge. Small vegetable area. Explore the hidden paths. Find a sheltered seat. Relax and enjoy. Paintings on view in upstairs gallery.

65 WOODEND COTTAGE
134 Main Street, Repton DE65 6FB. Wendy & Stephen Longden, 01283 703259. *6m S of Derby. From A38, S of Derby, follow signs to Willington, then Repton. In Repton, straight on at roundabout through village. Woodend Cottage is 1m on R before Woodend Children's Nursery.* Home-made teas. **Adm £2.50, chd free. Suns 7 June;**

12 July (1.30-5); 9 Aug (1-6). **Combined with 10 Chestnut Way & 22 Pinfold Close adm £5, chd free, Sun 9 Aug. Visitors also welcome by appt.**
Plant lover's garden with glorious views on sloping 2 1/2 -acre site developed organically for yr-round interest. On lower levels herbaceous borders are arranged informally and connected via lawns, thyme bed, pond and pergolas. Mixed woodland and grassed labyrinth lead naturally into fruit, vegetable and herb potager with meadows beyond. Especially colourful in July and Aug. Some steps and steep slopes.

66 35 WYVER LANE
Belper DE56 2UB. Jim & Brenda Stannering, 01773 824280. *8m N of Derby. Take A6 from Derby through Belper to T-lights at triangle. Turn L for A517 to Ashbourne, over river bridge, 1st R onto Wyver Lane. Parking in River Gardens, entrance on A6.* **Entrance by donation. Visitors welcome by appt April to July, please phone.**
Cottage garden of approx 500sq yds on side of R Derwent opp Belper River Gardens. Full of hardy perennial plants with pergola, troughs, greenhouse, small pond.

Fish and wildlife ponds, small stream . . .

Derbyshire County Volunteers

County Organiser
Irene Dougan, Field Farm, Field Lane, Kirk Ireton, Ashbourne DE6 3JU, 01335 370958, dougan@lineone.net

County Treasurer
Graham Dougan, Field Farm, Field Lane, Kirk Ireton, Ashbourne DE6 3JU, 01335 370958, dougan@lineone.net

Publicity
Christine Morris, 9 Langdale Avenue, Ravenshead NG15 9EA, 01623 793827, christine@ravenshead.demon.co.uk

Leaflet Coordinator
Sarah Bacon, 11 Highgrove Drive, Chellaston, Derby DE73 5XA, 01332 690702, sarah@sarbac.wanadoo.co.uk

Assistant County Organisers
Ron & Sue Astles, Quarryside, 1 King Charles Court, Glossop SK13 8NJ, 01457 857015, sue.astles@ctaweb.co.uk
Gill & Colin Hancock, 334 Belper Road, Stanley Common, nr Ilkeston DE7 6FY, 01159 301061
Kate & Peter Spencer, The Riddings Farm, Kirk Ireton, Ashbourne DE6 3LB, 01335 370331

DEVON

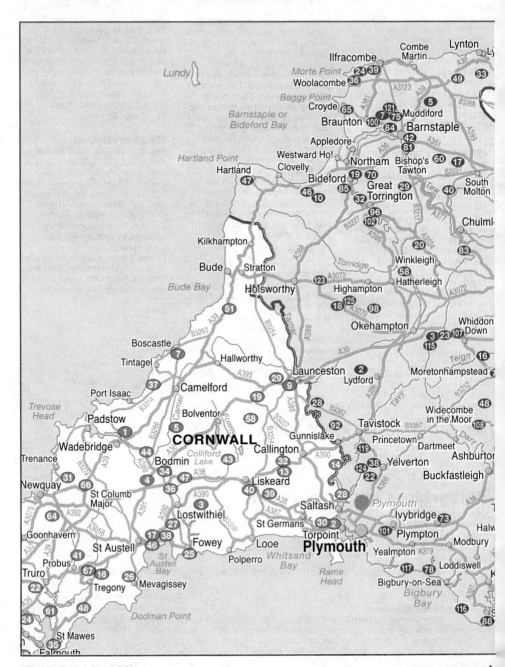

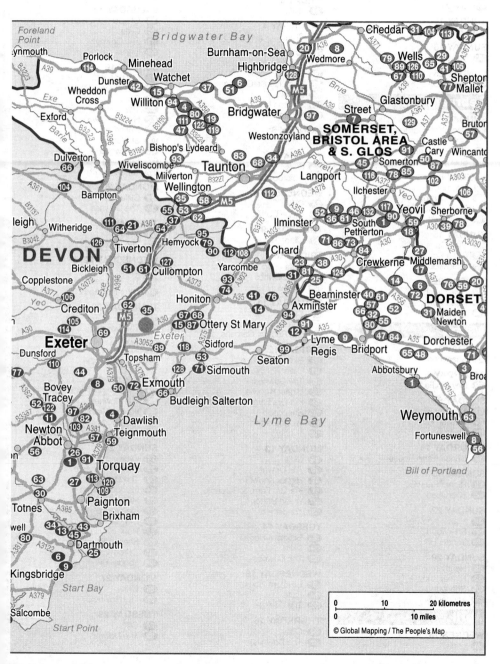

Opening Dates

January

SUNDAY 4
105 Sherwood

SUNDAY 11
105 Sherwood

SUNDAY 18
105 Sherwood

SUNDAY 25
105 Sherwood

February

SUNDAY 1
20 Cherubeer Gardens
69 Little Cumbre
90 Pikes Cottage
105 Sherwood

SUNDAY 8
20 Cherubeer Gardens
69 Little Cumbre
90 Pikes Cottage
105 Sherwood

SUNDAY 15
69 Little Cumbre
90 Pikes Cottage
105 Sherwood

SUNDAY 22
69 Little Cumbre
90 Pikes Cottage
105 Sherwood

March

SUNDAY 1
105 Sherwood

SATURDAY 7
79 Newton Farm

SUNDAY 8
63 Kingston House
79 Newton Farm
105 Sherwood

SATURDAY 14
18 Chapel Farm House

SUNDAY 15
52 Higher Knowle
105 Sherwood

SUNDAY 22
52 Higher Knowle
105 Sherwood
128 Yonder Hill

SUNDAY 29
48 Heathercombe
52 Higher Knowle
105 Sherwood
128 Yonder Hill

April

WEDNESDAY 1
24 Cliffe

THURSDAY 2
24 Cliffe

FRIDAY 3
24 Cliffe

SATURDAY 4
24 Cliffe

SUNDAY 5
24 Cliffe
52 Higher Knowle
97 Rock House Garden
105 Sherwood
110 Sowton Mill
128 Yonder Hill

MONDAY 6
24 Cliffe

TUESDAY 7
24 Cliffe
54 Holbrook Garden

WEDNESDAY 8
24 Cliffe
40 Glebe Cottage

THURSDAY 9
24 Cliffe

FRIDAY 10
24 Cliffe
32 The Downes
128 Yonder Hill

SATURDAY 11
24 Cliffe
32 The Downes
85 Old Rectory Gardens

SUNDAY 12
8 Bickham House
24 Cliffe
32 The Downes
52 Higher Knowle
61 Kia-Ora Farm & Gardens
105 Sherwood
127 Wood Barton
128 Yonder Hill

MONDAY 13
24 Cliffe
32 The Downes
52 Higher Knowle
61 Kia-Ora Farm & Gardens
127 Wood Barton
128 Yonder Hill

TUESDAY 14
8 Bickham House
24 Cliffe
32 The Downes

WEDNESDAY 15
8 Bickham House
24 Cliffe
32 The Downes

THURSDAY 16
24 Cliffe
32 The Downes

FRIDAY 17
24 Cliffe
32 The Downes

SATURDAY 18
18 Chapel Farm House
24 Cliffe
32 The Downes
53 Hillrise

SUNDAY 19
17 Castle Hill
21 Chevithorne Barton
24 Cliffe
32 The Downes
52 Higher Knowle
53 Hillrise
100 St Merryn
105 Sherwood
114 Summers Place
128 Yonder Hill

MONDAY 20
24 Cliffe
32 The Downes

TUESDAY 21
24 Cliffe
32 The Downes

WEDNESDAY 22
24 Cliffe
32 The Downes
87 Otter Nurseries

THURSDAY 23
24 Cliffe
32 The Downes

FRIDAY 24
24 Cliffe
32 The Downes

SATURDAY 25
24 Cliffe
32 The Downes
44 Haldon Grange
75 Marwood Hill
106 Shobrooke Park Gardens

SUNDAY 26
24 Cliffe
25 Coleton Fishacre
32 The Downes
44 Haldon Grange
52 Higher Knowle
61 Kia-Ora Farm & Gardens
85 Old Rectory Gardens
97 Rock House Garden
105 Sherwood
115 Taikoo
128 Yonder Hill

MONDAY 27
24 Cliffe
32 The Downes

TUESDAY 28
24 Cliffe
32 The Downes

WEDNESDAY 29
- (24) Cliffe
- (32) The Downes

THURSDAY 30
- (24) Cliffe
- (32) The Downes

May

FRIDAY 1
- (24) Cliffe
- (32) The Downes

SATURDAY 2
- (24) Cliffe
- (32) The Downes
- (44) Haldon Grange
- (78) Mothecombe House
- (90) Pikes Cottage
- (93) Pound Cottage

SUNDAY 3
- (3) Andrew's Corner
- (24) Cliffe
- (31) Dicot
- (32) The Downes
- (44) Haldon Grange
- (52) Higher Knowle
- (59) Jason's Garden
- (61) Kia-Ora Farm & Gardens
- (64) Knightshayes Court Garden
- (78) Mothecombe House
- (90) Pikes Cottage
- (103) Sedgewell Coach House Gardens
- (105) Sherwood
- (128) Yonder Hill

MONDAY 4
- (24) Cliffe
- (31) Dicot
- (32) The Downes
- (44) Haldon Grange
- (52) Higher Knowle
- (59) Jason's Garden
- (61) Kia-Ora Farm & Gardens
- (80) North Boreston Farm
- (90) Pikes Cottage
- (127) Wood Barton
- (128) Yonder Hill

TUESDAY 5
- (24) Cliffe
- (32) The Downes
- (54) Holbrook Garden
- (127) Wood Barton

WEDNESDAY 6
- (24) Cliffe
- (32) The Downes
- (44) Haldon Grange
- (87) Otter Nurseries

THURSDAY 7
- (24) Cliffe
- (32) The Downes
- (101) Saltram House

FRIDAY 8
- (24) Cliffe

- (32) The Downes
- (86) The Old Vicarage

SATURDAY 9
- (24) Cliffe
- (32) The Downes
- (44) Haldon Grange
- (83) The Old Glebe
- (86) The Old Vicarage
- (93) Pound Cottage
- (124) Wildside
- (126) Withleigh Farm

SUNDAY 10
- (3) Andrew's Corner
- (8) Bickham House
- (24) Cliffe
- (32) The Downes
- (44) Haldon Grange
- (52) Higher Knowle
- (65) Langtrees
- (80) North Boreston Farm
- (83) The Old Glebe
- (84) The Old Rectory
- (86) The Old Vicarage
- (99) Rousdon Cottage Gardens
- (103) Sedgewell Coach House Gardens
- (105) Sherwood
- (108) Southcombe Gardens
- (122) Whitstone Farm
- (126) Withleigh Farm
- (128) Yonder Hill

MONDAY 11
- (24) Cliffe
- (32) The Downes

TUESDAY 12
- (8) Bickham House
- (24) Cliffe
- (32) The Downes

WEDNESDAY 13
- (8) Bickham House
- (24) Cliffe
- (32) The Downes
- (44) Haldon Grange

THURSDAY 14
- (3) Andrew's Corner (Evening)
- (24) Cliffe
- (32) The Downes
- (36) Foamlea

FRIDAY 15
- (24) Cliffe
- (32) The Downes

SATURDAY 16
- (7) Beara Charter Barton and Little Beara
- (18) Chapel Farm House
- (24) Cliffe
- (32) The Downes
- (44) Haldon Grange
- (53) Hillrise
- (70) Little Webbery
- (83) The Old Glebe
- (106) Shobrooke Park Gardens
- (112) Springdale

SUNDAY 17
- (16) Castle Drogo
- (17) Castle Hill
- (24) Cliffe
- (32) The Downes
- (42) Gorwell House
- (44) Haldon Grange
- (48) Heathercombe
- (52) Higher Knowle
- (53) Hillrise
- (61) Kia-Ora Farm & Gardens
- (62) Killerton Garden
- (63) Kingston House
- (70) Little Webbery
- (83) The Old Glebe
- (105) Sherwood
- (112) Springdale
- (114) Summers Place
- (123) Wick Farm Gardens
- (128) Yonder Hill

MONDAY 18
- (24) Cliffe
- (32) The Downes
- (112) Springdale

TUESDAY 19
- (24) Cliffe
- (32) The Downes

WEDNESDAY 20
- (24) Cliffe
- (32) The Downes
- (44) Haldon Grange

THURSDAY 21
- (24) Cliffe
- (32) The Downes

FRIDAY 22
- (24) Cliffe
- (32) The Downes

SATURDAY 23
- (24) Cliffe
- (32) The Downes
- (44) Haldon Grange
- (48) Heathercombe
- (77) Moretonhampstead Gardens
- (90) Pikes Cottage
- (123) Wick Farm Gardens

SUNDAY 24
- (2) Alder
- (3) Andrew's Corner
- (21) Chevithorne Barton
- (24) Cliffe
- (32) The Downes
- (44) Haldon Grange
- (48) Heathercombe
- (49) Heddon Hall
- (52) Higher Knowle
- (61) Kia-Ora Farm & Gardens
- (71) Littlecourt Gardens
- (77) Moretonhampstead Gardens
- (90) Pikes Cottage
- (97) Rock House Garden
- (100) St Merryn
- (105) Sherwood
- (108) Southcombe Gardens
- (115) Taikoo

121 Westcott Barton
123 Wick Farm Gardens
128 Yonder Hill

MONDAY 25
15 Cadhay
19 Cherry Trees Wildlife Garden
24 Cliffe
32 The Downes
52 Higher Knowle
61 Kia-Ora Farm & Gardens
77 Moretonhampstead Gardens
90 Pikes Cottage
108 Southcombe Gardens
121 Westcott Barton
123 Wick Farm Gardens
128 Yonder Hill

TUESDAY 26
24 Cliffe
32 The Downes

WEDNESDAY 27
24 Cliffe
32 The Downes

THURSDAY 28
24 Cliffe
32 The Downes

FRIDAY 29
24 Cliffe
32 The Downes

SATURDAY 30
1 Abbotskerswell Gardens
24 Cliffe
32 The Downes
44 Haldon Grange
74 Luppitt Gardens
76 Membury Gardens
79 Newton Farm

SUNDAY 31
1 Abbotskerswell Gardens
3 Andrew's Corner
20 Cherubeer Gardens
24 Cliffe
32 The Downes
44 Haldon Grange
52 Higher Knowle
74 Luppitt Gardens
76 Membury Gardens
79 Newton Farm
105 Sherwood
108 Southcombe Gardens
123 Wick Farm Gardens
128 Yonder Hill

June

MONDAY 1
24 Cliffe

TUESDAY 2
24 Cliffe
54 Holbrook Garden

WEDNESDAY 3
24 Cliffe

THURSDAY 4
24 Cliffe

FRIDAY 5
24 Cliffe

SATURDAY 6
11 Bovey Tracey Gardens
24 Cliffe
41 Goren Farm
67 Little Ash Bungalow

SUNDAY 7
3 Andrew's Corner
11 Bovey Tracey Gardens
13 Bramble Torre
20 Cherubeer Gardens
24 Cliffe
30 Dartington Hall Gardens
41 Goren Farm
61 Kia-Ora Farm & Gardens
97 Rock House Garden
105 Sherwood
107 South Tawton Gardens
108 Southcombe Gardens
128 Yonder Hill

MONDAY 8
13 Bramble Torre
24 Cliffe

TUESDAY 9
24 Cliffe

WEDNESDAY 10
24 Cliffe

THURSDAY 11
24 Cliffe
36 Foamlea

FRIDAY 12
12 Bramble Hayes (Day & Evening)
15 Cadhay
24 Cliffe

SATURDAY 13
12 Bramble Hayes
24 Cliffe
53 Hillrise
89 Owls Barn
106 Shobrooke Park Gardens

SUNDAY 14
6 Ash House Farm
8 Bickham House
12 Bramble Hayes
24 Cliffe
28 Coombe Sculpture Garden
42 Gorwell House
51 Higher Burnhaies
53 Hillrise
57 Hollycombe House
82 Olchard Gardens
89 Owls Barn
92 Portington
98 Rose Cottage
99 Rousdon Cottage Gardens
102 School House
105 Sherwood
108 Southcombe Gardens
109 Southern Comfort
114 Summers Place
117 Tanglewood
128 Yonder Hill

MONDAY 15
24 Cliffe

TUESDAY 16
8 Bickham House
24 Cliffe

WEDNESDAY 17
8 Bickham House
24 Cliffe
79 Newton Farm

THURSDAY 18
24 Cliffe

FRIDAY 19
24 Cliffe
72 The Lookout

SATURDAY 20
18 Chapel Farm House
23 Cleave House
24 Cliffe
26 Collepardo
41 Goren Farm
50 High Garden
59 Jason's Garden
79 Newton Farm
90 Pikes Cottage

SUNDAY 21
6 Ash House Farm
23 Cleave House
24 Cliffe
26 Collepardo
28 Coombe Sculpture Garden
29 The Croft
31 Dicot
41 Goren Farm
50 High Garden
59 Jason's Garden
61 Kia-Ora Farm & Gardens
68 Little Ash Farm
72 The Lookout
79 Newton Farm
82 Olchard Gardens
90 Pikes Cottage
92 Portington
95 Regency House
97 Rock House Garden
98 Rose Cottage
100 St Merryn
105 Sherwood
125 Winsford Walled Garden
128 Yonder Hill

MONDAY 22
24 Cliffe
26 Collepardo
31 Dicot

TUESDAY 23
24 Cliffe
26 Collepardo

WEDNESDAY 24
24 Cliffe
26 Collepardo
79 Newton Farm

THURSDAY 25
24 Cliffe

26 Collepardo
27 Compton Castle

FRIDAY 26
24 Cliffe
26 Collepardo

SATURDAY 27
19 Cherry Trees Wildlife Garden
22 The Cider House
23 Cleave House
24 Cliffe
26 Collepardo
48 Heathercombe
55 Holcombe Court
76 Membury Gardens
79 Newton Farm
118 1 Tipton Lodge
124 Wildside

SUNDAY 28
2 Alder
3 Andrew's Corner
23 Cleave House
24 Cliffe
26 Collepardo
35 Feebers Gardens
48 Heathercombe
49 Heddon Hall
51 Higher Burnhaies
55 Holcombe Court
60 Kerscott House
71 Littlecourt Cottages
76 Membury Gardens
79 Newton Farm
105 Sherwood
107 South Tawton Gardens
118 1 Tipton Lodge
119 Walreddon Manor Gardens
128 Yonder Hill

MONDAY 29
24 Cliffe
119 Walreddon Manor Gardens

TUESDAY 30
24 Cliffe

July

WEDNESDAY 1
24 Cliffe
40 Glebe Cottage

THURSDAY 2
24 Cliffe

FRIDAY 3
24 Cliffe

SATURDAY 4
4 Appletree Cottage
24 Cliffe
41 Goren Farm
46 Harbour Lights
94 Prospect House

SUNDAY 5
4 Appletree Cottage
24 Cliffe
41 Goren Farm
46 Harbour Lights (Day & Evening)
61 Kia-Ora Farm & Gardens

63 Kingston House
94 Prospect House
105 Sherwood
110 Sowton Mill
128 Yonder Hill

MONDAY 6
4 Appletree Cottage
24 Cliffe

TUESDAY 7
4 Appletree Cottage
24 Cliffe
54 Holbrook Garden

WEDNESDAY 8
4 Appletree Cottage
24 Cliffe
104 Shapcott Barton Estate

THURSDAY 9
4 Appletree Cottage
24 Cliffe

FRIDAY 10
4 Appletree Cottage
24 Cliffe
86 The Old Vicarage

SATURDAY 11
4 Appletree Cottage
24 Cliffe
50 High Garden
81 North Devon Hospice
86 The Old Vicarage
112 Springdale

SUNDAY 12
4 Appletree Cottage
8 Bickham House
24 Cliffe
42 Gorwell House
50 High Garden
57 Hollycombe House
65 Langtrees
81 North Devon Hospice
86 The Old Vicarage
99 Rousdon Cottage Gardens
100 St Merryn
105 Sherwood
112 Springdale
128 Yonder Hill

MONDAY 13
24 Cliffe
104 Shapcott Barton Estate
112 Springdale

TUESDAY 14
8 Bickham House
24 Cliffe

WEDNESDAY 15
8 Bickham House
24 Cliffe
79 Newton Farm

THURSDAY 16
24 Cliffe
116 Tamarisks

FRIDAY 17
15 Cadhay

24 Cliffe
116 Tamarisks

SATURDAY 18
5 Arlington Court
16 Castle Drogo
18 Chapel Farm House
24 Cliffe
25 Coleton Fishacre
34 East Cornworthy Gardens
41 Goren Farm
53 Hillrise
58 Iddesleigh Gardens
64 Knightshayes Court Garden
79 Newton Farm
88 Overbeck's
101 Saltram House
104 Shapcott Barton Estate

SUNDAY 19
5 Arlington Court
24 Cliffe
29 The Croft
34 East Cornworthy Gardens
35 Feebers Gardens
41 Goren Farm
53 Hillrise
58 Iddesleigh Gardens
61 Kia-Ora Farm & Gardens
63 Kingston House (Evening)
68 Little Ash Farm
79 Newton Farm
104 Shapcott Barton Estate
105 Sherwood
125 Winsford Walled Garden
128 Yonder Hill

MONDAY 20
24 Cliffe

TUESDAY 21
24 Cliffe

WEDNESDAY 22
24 Cliffe

THURSDAY 23
24 Cliffe

FRIDAY 24
12 Bramble Hayes (Day & Evening)
24 Cliffe

SATURDAY 25
12 Bramble Hayes
24 Cliffe
37 Fossleigh
90 Pikes Cottage

SUNDAY 26
3 Andrew's Corner
12 Bramble Hayes
24 Cliffe
31 Dicot
37 Fossleigh
71 Littlecourt Cottages
90 Pikes Cottage
97 Rock House Garden
102 School House
105 Sherwood
117 Tanglewood

120 4 Wellswood Heights
128 Yonder Hill

MONDAY 27
24 Cliffe
31 Dicot
104 Shapcott Barton Estate

TUESDAY 28
24 Cliffe
104 Shapcott Barton Estate

WEDNESDAY 29
24 Cliffe
79 Newton Farm

THURSDAY 30
24 Cliffe

FRIDAY 31
24 Cliffe

August

SATURDAY 1
19 Cherry Trees Wildlife Garden
24 Cliffe
77 Moretonhampstead Gardens
104 Shapcott Barton Estate
113 Squirrels

SUNDAY 2
19 Cherry Trees Wildlife Garden
24 Cliffe
61 Kia-Ora Farm & Gardens
77 Moretonhampstead Gardens
104 Shapcott Barton Estate
105 Sherwood
113 Squirrels
128 Yonder Hill

MONDAY 3
24 Cliffe

TUESDAY 4
24 Cliffe
54 Holbrook Garden

WEDNESDAY 5
24 Cliffe

THURSDAY 6
3 Andrew's Corner (Evening)
24 Cliffe

FRIDAY 7
24 Cliffe

SATURDAY 8
24 Cliffe
79 Newton Farm
113 Squirrels

SUNDAY 9
8 Bickham House
24 Cliffe
79 Newton Farm
99 Rousdon Cottage Gardens
105 Sherwood
128 Yonder Hill

MONDAY 10
24 Cliffe

TUESDAY 11
8 Bickham House
24 Cliffe

WEDNESDAY 12
8 Bickham House
24 Cliffe

THURSDAY 13
24 Cliffe

FRIDAY 14
24 Cliffe

SATURDAY 15
18 Chapel Farm House
24 Cliffe
53 Hillrise
68 Little Ash Farm
79 Newton Farm

SUNDAY 16
24 Cliffe
29 The Croft
53 Hillrise
56 Hole Farm
61 Kia-Ora Farm & Gardens
68 Little Ash Farm
79 Newton Farm
104 Shapcott Barton Estate
105 Sherwood
122 Whitstone Farm
125 Winsford Walled Garden
128 Yonder Hill

MONDAY 17
24 Cliffe
104 Shapcott Barton Estate

TUESDAY 18
24 Cliffe

WEDNESDAY 19
24 Cliffe

THURSDAY 20
24 Cliffe

FRIDAY 21
24 Cliffe

SATURDAY 22
24 Cliffe
37 Fossleigh
79 Newton Farm
94 Prospect House
103 Sedgewell Coach House Gardens

SUNDAY 23
24 Cliffe
35 Feebers Gardens
37 Fossleigh
62 Killerton Garden
67 Little Ash Bungalow
79 Newton Farm
94 Prospect House
103 Sedgewell Coach House Gardens
105 Sherwood
128 Yonder Hill

MONDAY 24
24 Cliffe

TUESDAY 25
24 Cliffe

WEDNESDAY 26
24 Cliffe

THURSDAY 27
24 Cliffe

FRIDAY 28
24 Cliffe

SATURDAY 29
24 Cliffe
79 Newton Farm
90 Pikes Cottage
103 Sedgewell Coach House Gardens

SUNDAY 30
24 Cliffe
33 Durcombe Water
59 Jason's Garden
61 Kia-Ora Farm & Gardens
79 Newton Farm
90 Pikes Cottage
97 Rock House Garden
103 Sedgewell Coach House Gardens
105 Sherwood
121 Westcott Barton
128 Yonder Hill

MONDAY 31
24 Cliffe
33 Durcombe Water
59 Jason's Garden
61 Kia-Ora Farm & Gardens
79 Newton Farm
90 Pikes Cottage
121 Westcott Barton
128 Yonder Hill

September

TUESDAY 1
24 Cliffe
54 Holbrook Garden

WEDNESDAY 2
24 Cliffe

THURSDAY 3
24 Cliffe

FRIDAY 4
24 Cliffe

SATURDAY 5
24 Cliffe
43 Greenway Garden
81 North Devon Hospice

SUNDAY 6
8 Bickham House
24 Cliffe
81 North Devon Hospice
84 The Old Rectory
105 Sherwood
128 Yonder Hill

MONDAY 7
- 24 Cliffe

TUESDAY 8
- 8 Bickham House
- 24 Cliffe

WEDNESDAY 9
- 8 Bickham House
- 24 Cliffe

THURSDAY 10
- 24 Cliffe
- 36 Foamlea

FRIDAY 11
- 24 Cliffe

SATURDAY 12
- 24 Cliffe
- 53 Hillrise

SUNDAY 13
- 24 Cliffe
- 42 Gorwell House
- 53 Hillrise
- 57 Hollycombe House
- 61 Kia-Ora Farm & Gardens
- 65 Langtrees
- 97 Rock House Garden
- 105 Sherwood
- 125 Winsford Walled Garden
- 128 Yonder Hill

MONDAY 14
- 24 Cliffe

TUESDAY 15
- 24 Cliffe

WEDNESDAY 16
- 24 Cliffe

THURSDAY 17
- 24 Cliffe

FRIDAY 18
- 24 Cliffe

SATURDAY 19
- 18 Chapel Farm House
- 24 Cliffe
- 75 Marwood Hill
- 79 Newton Farm
- 124 Wildside

SUNDAY 20
- 24 Cliffe
- 79 Newton Farm
- 105 Sherwood
- 109 Southern Comfort
- 128 Yonder Hill

MONDAY 21
- 24 Cliffe

TUESDAY 22
- 24 Cliffe

WEDNESDAY 23
- 24 Cliffe

THURSDAY 24
- 24 Cliffe

FRIDAY 25
- 24 Cliffe

SATURDAY 26
- 24 Cliffe
- 88 Overbeck's
- 90 Pikes Cottage

SUNDAY 27
- 24 Cliffe
- 90 Pikes Cottage
- 95 Regency House
- 97 Rock House Garden
- 105 Sherwood
- 128 Yonder Hill

MONDAY 28
- 24 Cliffe

TUESDAY 29
- 24 Cliffe

WEDNESDAY 30
- 24 Cliffe
- 40 Glebe Cottage

October

SUNDAY 4
- 97 Rock House Garden
- 105 Sherwood
- 114 Summers Place
- 128 Yonder Hill

TUESDAY 6
- 54 Holbrook Garden

SUNDAY 11
- 105 Sherwood
- 128 Yonder Hill

WEDNESDAY 14
- 87 Otter Nurseries

SUNDAY 18
- 105 Sherwood
- 128 Yonder Hill

SUNDAY 25
- 97 Rock House Garden
- 105 Sherwood
- 128 Yonder Hill

November

SUNDAY 1
- 105 Sherwood

SUNDAY 8
- 105 Sherwood

SUNDAY 15
- 105 Sherwood

SUNDAY 22
- 105 Sherwood

SUNDAY 29
- 105 Sherwood

December

SUNDAY 6
- 105 Sherwood

SUNDAY 13
- 105 Sherwood

SUNDAY 20
- 105 Sherwood

SUNDAY 27
- 105 Sherwood

January 2010

SUNDAY 3
- 105 Sherwood

SUNDAY 10
- 105 Sherwood

SUNDAY 17
- 105 Sherwood

SUNDAY 24
- 105 Sherwood

SUNDAY 31
- 20 Cherubeer Gardens
- 69 Little Cumbre
- 105 Sherwood

February

SUNDAY 7
- 20 Cherubeer Gardens
- 69 Little Cumbre
- 90 Pikes Cottage
- 105 Sherwood

SUNDAY 14
- 69 Little Cumbre
- 90 Pikes Cottage
- 105 Sherwood

SUNDAY 21
- 69 Little Cumbre
- 90 Pikes Cottage
- 105 Sherwood

SUNDAY 28
- 90 Pikes Cottage
- 105 Sherwood

Gardens open to the public

- 5 Arlington Court
- 9 Blackpool Gardens
- 14 Burrow Farm Gardens
- 15 Cadhay
- 16 Castle Drogo
- 17 Castle Hill
- 25 Coleton Fishacre
- 27 Compton Castle
- 28 Coombe Sculpture Garden
- 30 Dartington Hall Gardens
- 38 The Garden House
- 40 Glebe Cottage
- 43 Greenway Garden
- 47 Hartland Abbey
- 49 Heddon Hall
- 54 Holbrook Garden
- 62 Killerton Garden
- 64 Knightshayes Court Garden
- 73 Lukesland

75 Marwood Hill
87 Otter Nurseries
88 Overbeck's
91 Plant World
96 RHS Garden Rosemoor
97 Rock House Garden
99 Green Lane Cottage, Rousdon Cottage Gardens
101 Saltram House
104 Shapcott Barton Estate
124 Wildside
125 Winsford Walled Garden

By appointment only

10 Bocombe Mill Cottage
39 The Gate House
45 Hamblyn's Coombe
66 Lee Ford
111 Spillifords Wildlife Garden

Also open by Appointment ☎

2 Alder
3 Andrew's Corner
4 Appletree Cottage
8 Bickham House
12 Bramble Hayes
13 Bramble Torre
18 Chapel Farm House
20 Higher Cherubeer, Cherubeer Gardens
22 The Cider House
23 Cleave House
29 The Croft
31 Dicot
32 The Downes
33 Durcombe Water
36 Foamlea
41 Goren Farm
42 Gorwell House
44 Haldon Grange
48 Heathercombe
51 Higher Burnhaies
52 Higher Knowle
53 Hillrise
56 Hole Farm
57 Hollycombe House
59 Jason's Garden
61 Kia-Ora Farm & Gardens
63 Kingston House
65 Langtrees
67 Little Ash Bungalow
68 Little Ash Farm
69 Little Cumbre
70 Little Webbery
76 Cleave Hill, Membury Gardens
76 Sixpenny Moon, Membury Gardens
77 Sutton Mead, Moretonhampstead Gardens
78 Mothecombe House
79 Newton Farm
80 North Boreston Farm
82 Olchard Farm, Olchard Gardens
82 Well Cottage, Olchard Gardens

84 The Old Rectory
90 Pikes Cottage
92 Portington
93 Pound Cottage
94 Prospect House
95 Regency House
98 Rose Cottage
99 Green Lane Cottage, Rousdon Cottage Gardens
100 St Merryn
102 School House
105 Sherwood
106 Shobrooke Park Gardens
108 Southcombe House, Southcombe Gardens
109 Southern Comfort
110 Sowton Mill
113 Squirrels
114 Summers Place
115 Taikoo
116 Tamarisks
118 1 Tipton Lodge
120 4 Wellswood Heights
121 Westcott Barton
122 Whitstone Farm
123 Wick Farm Gardens
126 Withleigh Farm
127 Wood Barton
128 Yonder Hill

Secret jungle garden . . .

The Gardens

ABBOTSBURY GARDENS
See Dorset.

Group opening

1 ABBOTSKERSWELL GARDENS
TQ12 5PN. *2m SW of Newton Abbot town centre. Take A381 to Totnes, sharp L turn to village. Car parking at Fairfield or in village. Route maps available.* Cream teas at Church House, village centre. **Combined adm £4, chd free (share to Friends of St Mary's). Sat 30, Sun 31 May (1-5).** Abbotskerswell is an attractive and vibrant village of 800 homes clustered around C15 church, 2 PHs, village shop and PO. Centre of village has wealth of charming thatched cottages and other houses. Have fun finding your way around the maze of hidden pathways in village to gardens, map available.

✿ ❀ ☕

1, 2 & 8 COURT FARM BARNS
Wilton Way. Pat & Tony Parsons, Mike & Beryl Veale, Pat Mackness
3 tiny courtyard gardens in barn conversion next to church, showing a variety of creative ways to make the most of a small site.

♿ ✿

BRIAR COTTAGE
1 Monk's Orchard. Peggy & David Munden
Informal, rambling cottage-style garden. Area around house set to vegetables, herbaceous, shrubs and rockery. Beyond is steep terraced slope with small coppice below. Many unusual and interesting plants abound - a plantsman's delight.

✿

COURT COTTAGE
Mr & Mrs A R W Rooth. *50yds from PO, opp Vicarage Rd*
Delightful hidden walled garden. Pretty summerhouse for outdoor living, herbaceous borders with range of interesting plants incl asphodeline, agapanthus, clematis. Small pond, pergola and vegetable patch. When choosing new plants drought conditions are uppermost as most of garden is composed of shillet.

✿

FAIRFIELD
Vicarage Rd. Christine & Brian Mackness
$3/4$-acre walled garden, herbaceous cottage-style borders. Vegetable patch, pond with stepped rill. 1-acre arboretum and wildlife copse with winding pathways. New for 2009 - wild bog garden and orchard development, friendly Shetland ponies. Wheelchair access over 4 step ramp - at users risk.

♿ ✿ ✾

NEW KARIBU
35 Wilton Way. Jenny & Dave Brook
30 yd slope to secret jungle garden with stunning views. Owner-designed, constructed from scrubland. Wander through banana, bamboos and tree ferns, cottage and Mediterranean sections with lemons, acers and a container climbing garden.

✿

1 LAKELAND
Mary & Alan Wheeler
Small cottage garden currently undergoing a makeover to incl mixed borders, raised vegetable beds and soft fruit area, greenhouse, container plants, small raised fish pond and wildlife pond under construction.

31 ODLEHILL GROVE
Christine Lewis
Small garden with good variety of shrubs, trees and flowers, incl roses and clematis.

PLUMTREE COTTAGE
Slade Lane. Derek & Jenny Bellotti
2-acre cottage garden. Established wisteria, quince, nectarine and many shrubs. Pergola, seating areas, arched walkways, greenhouse, pond and terrace. Stream with wildlife pond. A garden to be followed as it develops. Large vegetable plot in raised beds.

NEW 18 WILTON WAY
Ced & Viv Bell
From a boggy clay builder's yard, this garden has been owner-designed and constructed as an artist's canvas, using colour, texture and line to create interesting effects as the seasons change. Planters and pots give flexibility, fragrance and low maintenance.

2 ALDER
Lewdown EX20 4PJ. Bob & Anne Westlake, 01566 783909. *8m W of Okehampton, 8m E of Launceston. On old A30 (W Devon Drive).* Cream teas. **Adm £2.50, chd free. Suns 24 May; 28 June (2-6). Visitors also welcome by appt.**
Large garden created over last 22yrs with shrubs and herbaceous areas and views over landscaped valley. Woodland walks with 4-acre lake in former quarry. Bluebell wood in spring. Rill and water feature. New 170metre lime avenue leading to new pond. Gravel paths.

AMBLE GARDENS
See Cornwall.

3 ANDREW'S CORNER
Belstone EX20 1RD. Robin & Edwina Hill, 01837 840332, edwinarobinhill@btinternet.com. *3m E of Okehampton. Signed to Belstone. In village signed Skaigh. Parking restricted but cars may be left on nearby common.* Cream teas. **Adm £2.50, chd free. Suns 3, 10, 24, 31 May; 7, 28 June; 26 July (2.30-5.30). Candlelit Evening Openings £4, chd free, wine, Thurs 14 May; 6 Aug (7-10). Visitors also welcome by appt.**
Well-established, wildlife-friendly, well-labelled plantsman's garden in stunning high moorland setting. Variety of garden habitats incl woodland areas, bog garden, pond; wide range of unusual trees, shrubs, herbaceous plants for yr-round effect incl alpines, rhododendrons, bulbs and maples; spectacular autumn colour. New organic kitchen garden, greenhouse and chickens. Featured on ITV Wild Gardens and in 'Devon Life'. Wheelchair access difficult when wet.

ANTONY
See Cornwall.

4 APPLETREE COTTAGE
Higher Dawlish Water, Ashcombe Rd, Dawlish EX7 0QW. David & Sue Stephenson, 01626 895024, david@stephend.f9.co.uk. *2m NW of Dawlish. From Dawlish, follow Weech Rd to T-junction. R into Ashcombe Rd, garden on L after 1½ m. Limited parking.* **Adm £3, chd free. Daily Sat 4 July to Sun 12 July (10-5). Visitors also welcome by appt June/July only.**
SW-facing sloping site, abundantly planted. Herbaceous and mixed borders, ponds, bog garden, gazebo with board walk to larger pond. Decorative vegetable and fruit garden, greenhouse. Bordering Dawlish Water, exploiting the microclimate of Ashcombe Valley, encouraging and supporting wildlife. Unfenced stream and ponds.

5 ◆ ARLINGTON COURT
Arlington, Barnstaple EX31 4LP. The National Trust, 01271 850296, www.nationaltrust.org.uk. *7m NE of Barnstaple. On A39. From E use A399.* House and Garden Adm £8.20, chd £4.10, family £20.50. Garden only Adm £5.90, chd £2.95. House, carriage museum, gardens, tea room, shop open daily 14 Mar to

1 Nov (11-5, last adm 4.30). For NGS: Sat 18, Sun 19 July (11-5). Rolling parkland and woods with lake. Rhododendrons and azaleas; fine specimen trees; small terraced Victorian garden with herbaceous borders and conservatory. Walled garden nearly restored, produce for sale. Regency house containing fascinating collections. Carriage collection in the stables, carriage rides. Garden archaeology walk and talk plus other archaeology events (11-3), see website for details. Gravel paths, some steep slopes.

2 adjacent gardens . . .

6 ASH HOUSE FARM
Ash TQ6 0LR. Jane & Roger Davenport. *3m W of Dartmouth. From A3122 Halwell to Dartmouth rd R just before Sportsmans Arms. Follow yellow NGS signs for approx 2m. Parking on L, 300metres beyond Ash Tree Farm.* Cream teas at Ash Tree Farm Nursery. **Adm £4, chd free. Suns 14, 21 June (2-5).**
An interesting series of small gardens set within 10 acres of farmland. Formal garden areas around house mix with wild flower orchard centred about a stone circle. Walks lead to newly-planted arboretum and wetland bog area; reservoir, secluded decking area and copse.

7 NEW BEARA CHARTER BARTON AND LITTLE BEARA
Marwood EX31 4EH. Mr & Dr McCaie, Dr & Mrs Gibson. *5m NW of Barnstaple. After leaving Barnstaple via Bradiford (heading towards Marwood Hill Gardens), take 3rd L turning signed Whitehall, Middle Marwood. Drive through Whitehall and continue for approx 1m.* Home-made teas. **Adm £4, chd free. Sat 16 May (10-5).**
2 adjacent gardens created in last 15 yrs around C16 farmhouse and converted barns. They sit in a beautiful valley with several large ponds (unfenced) fed by a stream running through both properties. Several distinct areas, both formal and informal, containing many interesting trees and shrubs.

8 BICKHAM HOUSE

Kenn EX6 7XL. John & Julia Tremlett, 01392 832671, jandjtremlett@hotmail.com. *6m S of Exeter. 1m off A38. Leave A38 at Kennford Services, follow signs to Kenn. 1st R in village, follow lane for ³/₄m to end of no-through rd.* Cream teas. **Adm £3.50, chd free. Suns, Tues, Weds (2-5) 12, 14, 15 Apr; 10, 12, 13 May; 14, 16, 17 June; 12, 14, 15 July; 9, 11, 12 Aug; 6, 8, 9 Sept.** Visitors also welcome by appt for individuals and groups, coaches welcome.
7 acres in secluded wooded valley; lawns, mature trees and shrubs, naturalised bulbs, mixed borders with unusual perennials, wild flower banks for butterflies. Fern garden, small formal parterre with lily pond; 1-acre walled kitchen garden with profusion of vegetables, fruit and flowers, palm tree avenue leading to Millennium summerhouse. Lakeside walk. Featured in 'GGG', 'Devon Country Gardener' and local press.

9 ♦ BLACKPOOL GARDENS

Dartmouth TQ6 0RG. Sir Geoffrey Newman, 01803 770606, www.blackpoolsands.co.uk. *3m SW of Dartmouth. From Dartmouth follow brown signs to Blackpool Sands on A379. Entrance to gardens via Blackpool Sands car park.* **Adm £2.50, chd free. Daily Apr to Sept (10-4).**
Tenderly restored C19 subtropical plantsman's garden with collection of mature and newly-planted tender and unusual trees, shrubs and carpet of spring flowers. Paths and steps lead gradually uphill to the Captain's seat and spectacular coastal views. Recent plantings follow the S hemisphere theme with callistemons, pittosporums, acacias and buddlejas.

10 BOCOMBE MILL COTTAGE

Bocombe EX39 5PH. Mr Chris Butler & Mr David Burrows, 01237 451293, www.bocombe.co.uk. *6m E of Clovelly, 9m SW of Bideford. From A39 just outside Horns Cross village, turn to Foxdown. At Xrds take lane signed Bocombe. At T-junction turn R. 100yds on R.* **Adm £3, chd £1.** Visitors welcome by appt **Mar to Sept, groups of 10+.**

---

5 acres of gardens and wild meadow in small wooded valley, a wildlife haven. Many flower gardens. Streams, bog gardens and pools. Kitchen garden, orchard, soft fruit garden, shrubbery. All grown organically. New statue, barrel and Japanese gardens. Goats on hillside. Plan and tree guide. Circular walk (boots or wellies needed) of just under 1m. New statue, barrel and Japanese gardens. Featured in 'Pink Paper'. Many steps, some steep slopes.

BOSCASTLE GARDENS
See Cornwall.

Small town garden bursting with flowers . . .

Group opening

11 BOVEY TRACEY GARDENS

TQ13 9NA. *6m N of Newton Abbot. Gateway to Dartmoor. Take A382 to Bovey Tracey. Car parking available at Mary St, Station Rd, library car parks and at Whitstone. Limited parking at Southbrook.* Cream teas. **Combined adm £4, chd free. Sat 6, Sun 7 June (2-6).**

ASHWELL
East Street. Bill & Diane Riddell
1-acre Victorian walled garden presently undergoing restoration. On a steep slope with glorious views. Vineyard, orchard and mature trees incl impressive arbutus.

CRANBROOK
Moretonhampstead Rd. Nigel & Ann Gillingham. *Within 30yds of hospital*
S-facing garden with views of Dartmoor. Traditional vegetable garden and soft fruit. Lawned area with established herbaceous border, rockery garden and pond.

DOWN PARK
Shewte Cross. Susan Macready. *1m from Fire Station roundabout on Manaton Rd. Parking available*
Well-maintained, colourful, mature garden. Great variety of rhododendrons, azaleas, camellias and unusual shrubs. Formal pond and alpine garden.

NEW 38 PRIORY

Emma & Matthew Scott. *Park in library car park, walk down Cromwell's Way, R up hill at end*
Small town garden bursting with flowers of all kinds, especially clematis and roses. Pond and several Dartmoor finds. Seats.

NEW SOUTHBROOK COURT

Southbrook Lane. Mr & Mrs G V Horne. *1st L on A382 to Moretonhamstead from Bovey Tracey, between Hole Bridge and golf course. 1st garden on R after crossing bridge in Southbrook Lane. Parking restricted, use A382 verge*
Approx 1¹/₂ acres with mini park feel. Large pond with marginals, stream, borders with perennials and shrubs, small apple orchard, lawn featuring birch trees.

15 STORRS CLOSE

Bob & Pauline Arnold. *From Crokers Meadow follow signs to Storrs Close or park in library car park, walk down Cromwell's Way to end, down steps to Bullen's Meadow, follow hedge to bottom garden entrance*
Small garden designed and built by present owners in past 4yrs. Very easily maintained with paving and chippings. Tiny but productive vegetable plot, raspberry canes, fruit trees, herb bed, colourful flower beds and containers. Planted fish pond with water feature, attracting abundance of wildlife. Stage decking overlooks garden.

WHITSTONE HOUSE
Laura Barclay. *Park in Whitstone Quarry at top of Whitstone Lane*
Mature garden with heathers, rhododendrons and azaleas. Panoramic views of Dartmoor and Bovey valley from many levels. Woodland walk. Wheelchair access limited to upper terrace.

YONDER
Whitstone Lane,
Moretonhampstead Rd. Mr &
Mrs John Awcock
Mature cottage garden.
Restoration in progress. Many
varieties of acer and clematis.
Interesting new plantings.

🐕 ✿

---

12 BRAMBLE HAYES
Yawl Hill Lane, Uplyme DT7 3RP.
Martin & Celia Young, 01297
443084,
martin@sittingspiritually.co.uk. *3m E
of Axminster. From E A35, 100metres
E of Devon sign, L into Red Lane, over
2 Xrds into Yawl Hill Lane, garden 0.8m
on R. From W A35 through Raymonds
Hill, R into Red Lane then as above.
From Lyme Regis, B3165 through
Uplyme/Yawl to Yawl Hill Lane.* Home-
made teas. **Adm £3.50, chd free.
Sats, Suns 13, 14 June; 25, 26 July
(11-5). Day & Evening Openings**
wine, Fris 12 June; 24 July (11-
dusk). **Visitors also welcome by
appt.**
Bramble Hayes is the product of 10yrs
eco management. Very naturalistic and
free with 70% of herbaceous
perennials self setting to produce some
truly unique planting combinations.
Eclectic mix of flowers, fruit and
vegetables. Garden swing seats, made
by owner, take full advantage of views,
the perfect spot to end your visit with a
delicious tea. Garden swing seats and
art for sale.

✿ ☕ ☎

---

13 NEW BRAMBLE TORRE
Dittisham, nr Dartmouth
TQ6 0HZ. Paul & Sally Vincent,
01803 722227. *³/₄ m from
Dittisham. Leave A3122 Halwell to
Dartmouth rd at Sportsmans Arms
and head towards Dittisham. In
village turn hard L towards
Cornworthy. Garden ³/₄ m straight
ahead - L turn by gates to park.*
Home-made teas. **Adm £3, chd
free. Sun 7, Mon 8 June (2-5).
Visitors also welcome by appt
for groups, no large coaches.**
3 acres of garden follows rambling
stream through steep valley. Lily
pond, herbaceous borders,
camellias, shrubs and roses
dominated by huge Embothrium,
scarlet against a sometimes blue
sky! Further up the valley, a formal
herb and vegetable garden runs
along one side of the stream, while

chickens scratch in an orchard of
Ditsum plums and cider apples on
the other side. Donkeys and
Whiteface Dartmoor sheep quietly
graze on the hills above. Dogs on
leads welcome.

☕ ☎

---

14 ◆ BURROW FARM GARDENS
Dalwood EX13 7ET. Mary & John
Benger, 01404 831285,
www.burrowfarmgardens.co.uk.
*3¹/₂ m W of Axminster. From A35 turn
N at Taunton Xrds then follow brown
signs.* **Adm £5, chd £1. Daily 1 Apr to
31 Oct (10-7).**
Secluded 10-acre garden of informal
design with many unusual shrubs and
herbaceous plants. Pergola walk with
shrub roses. Woodland with
rhododendrons and azaleas, ponds
and large bog garden. Terraced
courtyard featuring later flowering
plants. Rill garden with water feature;
traditional stone summerhouse and
informal planting all with wonderful
views. Grass paths on gentle slopes.

♿ ✿ ☕

---

15 ◆ CADHAY
Ottery St Mary EX11 1QT. Rupert
Thistlethwayte, www.cadhay.org.uk.
1m NW of Ottery St Mary. On B3176.
**Gardens only adm £2, chd free. Fris
May to Sept (2-5.30, last adm 4.30).
Guided tours £6, chd £2. For NGS:
Mon 25 May; Fris 12 June; 17 July
(2-4.30).**
Tranquil 2-acre garden in lovely setting
between the Elizabethan Manor house
(open) and ancient stew ponds.
Carefully planned double herbaceous
borders particularly colourful in
summer. Small part-walled water
garden, roses, lilies and clematis.
Featured on ITV's Country Ways.
Limited wheelchair access in house.

♿ 🐕 ✿

---

16 ◆ CASTLE DROGO
Drewsteignton EX6 6PB. The
National Trust, 01647 434111. *12m
W of Exeter. 5m S of A30. Follow
brown signs. Limited parking until Aug.
Please phone or visit website for
adm prices and opening times.* **For
NGS: Sun 17 May; Sat 18 July
(10.30-5).**
Medium-sized Grade II* listed garden
with formal structures designed by
George Dillistone during the late
1920s. These consist of formal rose
beds, herbaceous borders and circular
croquet lawn surrounded by mature

yew hedges. Rhododendron garden
overlooks spectacular views of Teign
valley gorge and Dartmoor. Guided
tours with garden stewards.

♿ 🐕 ✿

---

17 ◆ CASTLE HILL
Filleigh EX32 0RQ. The Earl &
Countess of Arran, 01598 760336
ext 1, www.castlehilldevon.co.uk.
*4m W of South Molton. From A361
Tiverton to Barnstaple leave at
roundabout on B3226 signed Filleigh.*
Teas Suns/Bank Hols May to Aug.
**Adm £4, chd free, senior citizens
£3.50. Daily except Sats 10 Apr to
30 Sept (11-5). For NGS: Suns 19
Apr; 17 May (11-5).**
Palladian house in extensive C18
Grade I landscape park and garden.
Arboretum and woodlands with
camellias, rhododendrons, magnolias,
azaleas and other shrubs and rare
trees in abundance. Summer
millennium garden designed by Xa
Tollemache with topiary water
sculpture by Giles Rayner. Many C18
follies and a 1730 castle on the hill with
magnificent views to Exmoor,
Dartmoor and Lundy Island.

☕

Chickens
scratch in
an orchard
of Ditsum
plums . . .

---

18 ◆ CHAPEL FARM HOUSE
Halwill Junction, Beaworthy
EX21 5UF. Robin & Toshie Hull,
01409 221594. *12m NW of
Okehampton. On A3079. At W end of
village.* **Adm £3, chd free. Sats 14
Mar; 18 Apr; 16 May; 20 June; 18
July; 15 Aug; 19 Sept (11-5). Visitors
also welcome by appt all yr.**
Approx ¹/₂ -acre garden started in 1992
by present owners, landscaped with
shrub borders, heathers,
rhododendrons and azaleas. Alpine
bed. Kitchen garden. 2 small
greenhouses for mixed use. Small
bonsai collection. 3 acres of mixed
young woodland added in 1995 with
wildlife and flowers. Gravel
paths/parking area, large lawns.

♿ 🐕 ✿ ☎

---

19 CHERRY TREES WILDLIFE GARDEN

5 Sentry Corner, East The Water EX39 4BW. Henry and Evelyn Butterfield. *From Bideford Old Bridge, follow up hill past The Royal Hotel. Follow signs to Sentry Corner (approx ¾ m), parking at Pollyfield Centre.* Light refreshments & teas. **Adm £2.50, chd free. Mon 25 May; Sat 27 June; Sat 1, Sun 2 Aug (2-5).**
Small demonstration garden showing what can be done to bring wildlife into the town. Incl courtyard garden, summer cornfield, summer wildflower meadow, cottage garden border, woodland edge and ponds. Owners available for advice on wildlife gardening. Featured on BBC2 Open Gardens.

National Collection of Hostas with 1000 varieties . . .

Group opening

20 CHERUBEER GARDENS

Dolton EX19 8PP. *8m SE of Great Torrington. 2m E of Dolton. From A3124 turn S towards Stafford Moor Fisheries, take 1st R, gardens 500m on L.* Home-made/cream teas at Higher Cherubeer, home-made soup available at snowdrop openings. **Combined adm £3.50, chd free. Suns 1, 8 Feb (1-5); 31 May; Sun 7 June (2-6); 31 Jan 2010; 7 Feb 2010 (1-4).**
A family affair, the 3 Cherubeers in this ancient hamlet are gardened by Jo and Tom and their respective mothers, Jan and Heather.

CHERUBEER
Janet Brown
Cottage garden set around a C15 thatched house (not open). Garden divided into compartments with ponds, paths, and steps filled with colourful perennials and herbs set off by mature shrubs and trees.

HIGHER CHERUBEER
Jo & Tom Hynes, 01805 804265, hynesjo@gmail.com. Visitors also welcome by appt for groups.
1-acre country garden with gravelled courtyard, raised beds and alpine house, lawns, large herbaceous border, shady woodland beds, large kitchen garden, greenhouse, colourful collection of basketry willows. Winter opening for National Collection of hardy cyclamen, snowdrop varieties and hellebores. Featured on BBC2 Open Gardens. Gravel paths.

 NCCPG

MIDDLE CHERUBEER
Heather Hynes
Colourful small garden. Three separate areas with bog garden, pond and massed herbaceous perennials interlinked with paths. Many cyclamen and snowdrop bank.

21 CHEVITHORNE BARTON

Tiverton EX16 7QB. Michael & Arabella Heathcoat Amory. *3m NE of Tiverton. M5, J27, leave A361 by first exit after 300 yards, through Sampford Peverell and Halberton towards Tiverton. Immed past golf course, R then R at next T-junction. Over bridge, L through Craze Lowman, carry on through lanes to T-junction, R then 1st L.* Cream teas. **Adm £3.50, chd free. Suns 19 Apr; 24 May (2-5.30).**
Terraced walled garden, summer borders and romantic woodland of rare trees and shrubs. In spring, garden features large collection of magnolias, camellias, rhododendrons and azaleas. Also incl one of only two NCCPG oak collections situated in 12 hectares of parkland and comprising over 200 different species.

NCCPG

CHIDEOCK MANOR
See Dorset.

22 THE CIDER HOUSE

Buckland Abbey, Yelverton PL20 6EZ. Mr & Mrs M J Stone, 01822 853285, michael.stone@cider-house.co.uk. *8m N of Plymouth. From A386 Plymouth to Tavistock rd, follow NT signs to Buckland Abbey. At Xrds before Abbey entrance turn N signed Buckland Monachorum. Drive 200yds*

on L, or short walk for visitors to Abbey. Lunches & cream teas. **Adm £3, chd free. Sat 27 June (11-5).**
Also open **Wildside**. Visitors also welcome by appt.
3 acres in peaceful surroundings looking down to Tavy valley. Terrace gardens complement the medieval house (not open), herb garden, woodland and herbaceous borders, wild garden with rhododendrons, camellias and other shrubs. Former walled kitchen garden productively maintained to give abundance of fruit, vegetables and flowers.

23 CLEAVE HOUSE

Sticklepath EX20 2NL. Ann & Roger Bowden, 01837 840481, bowdens2@eclipse.co.uk, www.hostas-uk.com. *3½ m E of Okehampton. On old A30 towards Exeter. Cleave House on L in village, on main rd just past R turn for Skaigh.* **Adm £2.50, chd free. Sats, Suns 20, 21, 27, 28 June (10.30-5).** Visitors also welcome by appt.
½ -acre garden with mixed planting for all season interest. National Collection of Hostas with 1000 varieties. Some soft grass areas.

NCCPG

24 CLIFFE

Lee, Ilfracombe EX34 8LR. Dr & Mrs Humphreys. *3m W of Ilfracombe. Garden is past sea front at Lee, 150yds up steep hill on coast rd. Entrance through wrought iron gates on L. Lee Bay car park at bottom of hill (200yds) (no parking on approach rd).* **Adm £3, chd free. Daily 1 Apr to 30 Sept (9-5).**
Cliffside terraced garden with spectacular coastal views. A diverse range of habitats from Mediterranean to woodland. Always something to see. In spring, camellias and azaleas, colourful herbaceous borders throughout summer and exotic hedychiums, canna and salvias flowering into autumn. National collection of Heuchera and Schizostylis.

NCCPG

25 ◆ COLETON FISHACRE

nr Kingswear TQ6 0EQ. The National Trust, 01803 752466, www.nationaltrust.org.uk. *3m E of Dartmouth. Lower Ferry Rd. Follow brown signs. Lane leading to Coleton Fishacre is narrow and can be busy on fine days. Use of passing places and*

reversing may be necessary. Coach parties must book. **Please phone or visit website for adm prices. Weds to Suns & Bank Hol Mons 14 Mar to 1 Nov; Sats, Suns 28 Feb to 13 Mar (10.30-5). For NGS: Sun 26 Apr; Sat 18 July (10.30-5).**
30-acre garden created by Rupert and Lady Dorothy D'Oyly Carte between 1925 and 1948. Re-established and developed by NT since 1983. Wide range of tender and uncommon trees and shrubs in spectacular coastal setting.

26 COLLEPARDO
3 Keyberry Park, Newton Abbot TQ12 1BZ. Betty & Don Frampton. *Take A380 for Newton Abbot. From Penn Inn roundabout follow sign for town centre. Take 1st L, 1st R, 2nd L.* **Home-made teas. Adm £2.50, chd free. Daily Sat 20 June to Sun 28 June; (11-5).**
1/3 -acre lawn-free garden laid out in series of interlinked colour-themed smaller areas. Incl 400 metres of meandering gravel pathways, circular rockery of 20 metres, herbaceous borders, pond, walkway, gazebo and over 1,500 different varieties of plants, shrubs and trees.

27 ◆ COMPTON CASTLE
Marldon, Paignton TQ3 1TA. The National Trust, 01803 842382, www.nationaltrust.org.uk. *3m W of Torquay. 1 1/2 m N of Marldon. From Newton Abbot - Totnes rd A381 turn L at Ipplepen Xrds & W off Torbay Ring Rd via Marldon.* **Please phone or visit website for adm prices. Mons, Weds, Thurs, 30 Mar to 29 Oct (11-5). For NGS: Thur 25 June (11-5).**
Small formal courtyard gardens, rose garden, herb garden. Access to the usually private fruit and vegetable garden. Incl access to fortified Manor House with restored medieval great hall.

28 ◆ COOMBE SCULPTURE GARDEN
Bradstone Coombe, Tavistock PL19 0QS. Gary & Kay Vanstone. *9m W of Tavistock. On B3362 Tavistock to Launceston rd, garden signed.* **Home-made light lunches and cream teas on NGS days. Adm £4, chd free. Gallery and garden open Weds to Suns, 3 to 28 June (11-4). For NGS: Suns 14, 21 June (11-5).**
2-acre S-sloping garden around C17

---

farmhouse in secluded wooded valley. Variety of garden habitats preserving ancient features with an emphasis on providing for wildlife. Planted with hellebores and bulbs. Unusual trees incl magnolia campbellii, shrubs and herbaceous plants for all-yr colour. Tamar valley fruit orchard, organic vegetable garden. Spring-fed streams, pools and mill pond. Sculptures of Paul Vanstone on display and for sale. Featured in 'Tavistock Times' and 'Devon Life'. Wheelchair access to main features.

COOMBEGATE COTTAGE
See Cornwall.

COTEHELE
See Cornwall.

COTHAY MANOR GARDENS
See Somerset & Bristol.

Variety of garden habitats preserving ancient features . . .

29 THE CROFT
Yarnscombe EX31 3LW. Sam & Margaret Jewell, 01769 560535. *4m NE of Torrington, 8m S of Barnstaple. From A377, turn W opp Chapelton railway stn. After 3m drive on L at village sign. From B3232, 1/4 m N of Hunshaw TV mast Xrds, turn E for 2m. Parking in village hall car park nearby.* **Adm £3, chd free (share to N Devon Animal Ambulance). Suns 21 June; 19 July; 16 Aug (2-6). Visitors also welcome by appt.**
1-acre plantswoman's garden featuring exotic Japanese garden with tea house, koi carp pond and cascading stream, tropical garden with exotic shrubs and perennials. Herbaceous borders with unusual plants and shrubs. Bog garden with collection of irises, astilbes and moisture-loving plants, duck pond. New exotic border for 2009 and extension to Japanese garden.

---

30 ◆ DARTINGTON HALL GARDENS
Dartington TQ9 6EL. Dartington Hall Trust, 01803 862367, gardens@dartingtonhall.org. *1 1/2 m NW of Totnes. From Totnes take A384, turn R at Dartington Parish Church. Proceed up hill for 1m. Hall & gardens on R. Car parking on L.* **Adm £3, chd free. For NGS: Sun 7 June (10-6).**
28-acre modern garden, created since 1925 around C14 medieval hall (not open). Courtyard and tournament ground. Dry landscape Japanese garden. Extensive wild flower meadows and mixed shrub and herbaceous border. Peter Randall-Page sculpture. Guided tour at 2.30pm, £6 adults, chd free, proceeds to NGS. Partial wheelchair access, difficult slopes, gravel paths, steps, please contact prior to visit for advice or assistance.

31 DICOT
Chardstock EX13 7DF. Mr & Mrs F Clarkson, 01460 220364, www.dicot.co.uk. *5m N of Axminster. Axminster to Chard A358 at Tytherleigh to Chardstock. R at George Inn, L fork to Hook, R to Burridge, 2nd house on L.* **Home-made teas. Adm £3, chd £1. Suns, Mons 3, 4 May; 21, 22 June; 26, 27 July (2-5.30). Visitors also welcome by appt.**
Secret garden hidden in East Devon valley. 3 acres of unusual and exotic plants - some rare. Rhododendrons, azaleas and camellias in profusion. Meandering stream, fish pool, Japanese-style garden and interesting vegetable garden with fruit cage, tunnel and greenhouses.

32 THE DOWNES
Bideford EX39 5LB. Mrs R C Stanley-Baker, 01805 622244. *3m NW of Great Torrington. On A386 between Bideford & Torrington. Drive leads off A386 4 1/2 m from Bideford, 2 1/2 m from Torrington. Do not go to Monkleigh.* **Adm £3, chd free. Daily Fri 10 Apr to Sun 31 May (12-5). Visitors also welcome by appt.**
15 acres with landscaped lawns; fine views overlooking fields and woodlands in Torridge Valley; many unusual trees and shrubs; small arboretum; woodland walks; bluebells.

DEVON

33 DURCOMBE WATER
Furzehill, Barbrook, Lynton
EX35 6LN. Pam & David Sydenham,
01598 753658. *3m S of Lynton. From
Barnstaple take A39 towards Lynton.
On entering Barbrook go past Total
garage (do not turn to Lynton) take the
next turn R (about 100yds). Follow this
single track rd for 2m, gates on L.*
Home-made teas. **Adm £3, chd free.
Sun 30, Mon 31 Aug (11-5).** Visitors
also welcome by appt.
Set in Exmoor National Park beside
open moorland with superb views,
delightfully secluded steeply-terraced
garden providing profusion of yr-round
colour. Includes conifers, heathers and
many old-fashioned annuals and
perennials. The garden offers peace
and tranquillity enhanced by spring-fed
streams and ponds, and waterfalls
dropping 40ft via 8 tiered ponds. Fruit
and vegetable garden. Many unusual
features. Large extension in progress
(2½ acres total garden) with ponds,
waterfalls, landscaping and small
woodland.

Group opening

34 EAST CORNWORTHY GARDENS
TQ9 7HQ. *1m W of Dittisham. B3122
from Dartmouth, turn at Sportsmans
Arms for Dittisham. Keep L in village for
E Cornworthy.* Cream teas. **Combined
adm £3.50, chd free. Sat 18, Sun 19
July (2-5).**
East Cornworthy is a pretty hamlet set
in glorious countryside, 1m from R Dart
and Dittisham. Brook featured on BBC
Spotlight.

BLACK NESS HOUSE
Tim & Lesley Taylor. *From
Dittisham, last house on R before
rd turns L and up hill*
Approx ½ acre with wonderful
views. Steps down to different
levels and areas. Walled gardens,
one Mediterranean themed with
agaves, olive trees, cypresses,
lavender and myrtle. Colour-
themed beds and borders, gravel
paths.

BROOK
Peter & Bee Smyth. *From
Dittisham, 1st house on L on
bridge. From Cornworthy, last
house on R*
Particularly interesting mature trees
and shrubs. All yr flowering such as

embothrium, eucryphia, drimys
and large hoheria. Front garden
has splendid colourful herbaceous
beds each side of path to front
door. Large pond at end of garden.

5 year-old garden with full maritime exposure . . .

Group opening

35 FEEBERS GARDENS
nr Broadclyst EX5 3DQ. *8m NE of
Exeter. From B3181 Exeter to Taunton
bear E at Dog Village to Whimple. After
1½ m fork L for Westwood.* Cream
teas. **Combined adm £3, chd free.
Suns 28 June; 19 July; 23 Aug (2-6).**
3 cottage gardens in a Devon hamlet.

1 FEEBERS COTTAGE
Mr & Mrs M J Squires
Evolving cottage garden of 1 acre -
a maze of pathways, herbaceous,
shrubs and trees. In spring, 60
different snowdrops; in autumn,
colchicums and cyclamen.

2 FEEBERS COTTAGE
Bob & Ena Williams
Colourful, formal garden, set
between 2 cottage gardens.
Delightful flower beds, small alpine
house and gravel area with variety
of potted shrubs and plants. Not a
weed to be seen.

3 FEEBERS COTTAGE
Richard & Karen Burrell
Contemporary cottage garden with
formal vegetable area, established
fruit trees, flower beds and rose
arbour. Some quirky features incl
BBQ house and a mini petanque
area within 'a secret garden'.
Numerous places to sit and enjoy a
cream tea.

FERNHILL
See Somerset & Bristol.

36 NEW FOAMLEA
Chapel Hill, Mortehoe EX34 7DZ.
Beth Smith, 01271 871182,
bethmortepoint@fmail.co.uk.
*¼ m S of Mortehoe village. A361 N
from Barnstaple. L at Mullacott
Cross onto B3343 to Mortehoe.
Use village car park, L past church,
down steep hill, garden further
200yds. Also on bus route.* Home-
made teas. **Adm £3, chd free
(share to Shelterbox). Thurs 14
May; 11 June; 10 Sept (10-5).**
Visitors also welcome by appt
Easter to end Oct.
¾ -acre plantswoman's 5 yr-old
garden with full maritime exposure.
Steep steps and uneven slate
paths lead through many colourful
areas. Incl exotics and succulents
amongst a wide range of hedges,
shrubs and perennials. Adjoins SW
coastal footpath with stunning view
of Morte Point, Baggy, Hartland
and Lundy Island.

FORDE ABBEY GARDENS
See Dorset.

37 NEW FOSSLEIGH
Burlescombe EX16 7JH. David &
Glenis Beard. *3m from M5, J27.
From J27 take A38 to Wellington,
over M5, 1st L to Burlescombe.
1m L just before canal bridge.
Limited parking, public car park
150m from garden, over bridge
then immed L.* Home-made teas.
**Adm £2.50, chd free. Sats, Suns
25, 26 July; 22, 23 Aug (2-5.30).**
¼ -acre garden bordering Grand
Western Canal. Imaginative use of
space, many surprises: Water
garden, bog garden, herbaceous
borders, miniature bowling green,
sundial vegetable plot, fruit cage,
sunken walkways surrounded by
flowers and foliage. Enjoy a stroll
on canal towpath after your visit.

38 ◆ THE GARDEN HOUSE
Buckland Monachorum, Yelverton
PL20 7LQ. The Fortescue Garden
Trust, 01822 854769,
www.thegardenhouse.org.uk. *10m
N of Plymouth. Signed off A386 at
Yelverton.* Adm £5.90, chd £2.50
(5-16), concessions £5.40. Open
daily 28 Feb to 1 Nov (10.30-5).
W/E only Feb & Nov (10.30-3.30).

8 acres, incl romantic walled garden surrounding ruins of medieval vicarage. Other areas pioneering 'new naturalism' style, inspired by great natural landscapes. South African garden, quarry garden, cottage garden, acer glade. Stunning views and more than 6000 plant varieties. Famous for spring bulb meadow, rhododendrons, camellias, innovative planting and yr-round colour and interest. Limited wheelchair access, some steep slopes.

39 THE GATE HOUSE

Lee EX34 8LR. Mr & Mrs D Booker, 01271 862409, booker@loveleebay.co.uk. *3m W of Ilfracombe. Park in village car park. Take lane alongside The Grampus public house. Garden is approx 30 metres past inn buildings.* **Adm by donation. Open most days throughout the yr but wise to check by email/phone. Visitors welcome by appt.**
2¼ acres, where no chemicals are used, only few minutes walk from the sea and dramatic coastal scenery. Peaceful streamside garden with range of habitats; bog garden, National Collection of Rodgersia, at their best June/July, woodland, herbaceous borders, patio gardens with semi-hardy 'exotics' and large vegetable garden. Art & Craft Exhibition in Village Hall during Aug. Gravel paths.

Thousands of orchids! . . .

40 ◆ GLEBE COTTAGE

Warkleigh EX37 9DH. Carol Klein, 01769 540554, www.glebecottageplants.co.uk. *5m SW of South Molton. On the road between Chittlehamholt and Chittlehampton - 1m from Chittlehamholt.* **Adm £3, chd free. Garden & nursery open Weds, Thurs, Fris (10-1, 2-5). For NGS: Weds 8 Apr; 1 July; 30 Sept (2-5).**
Cottage S-facing garden with variety of situations. In spring small woodland garden with stumpery, hellebores and pulmonarias is interesting. Terraced

beds and 'brick' garden with many newly-planted areas, including hot summer and autumn flowers and foliage. Home of BBC Gardeners' World and Open Gardens presenter.

41 NEW GOREN FARM

Stockland, Honiton EX14 9EN. Julian Pady, 07770 694646, gorenfarm@hotmail.com. *6m E of Honiton. Turn off A35 N at Taunton Cross. 3m to the Stockland TV mast, next R, follow signs.* Home-made teas & light refreshments. **Adm £4, chd free 6/7 June & 4/5 July; £2, chd free other days. Sats, Suns 6, 7, 20, 21 June; 4, 5, 18, 19 July (10.30-5). Visitors also welcome by appt June/July/Aug.**
Wild flower meadow walk through 50 acres of fields not ploughed in living memory. Hedgerows managed as wildlife habitats. No chemicals. Dozens of varieties of wild flowers and grasses. Thousands of orchids! Stunning views of Blackdown Hills. Picnic areas. Dogs on leads. Seeds for sale. 2½ hr guided tours at 10.30 with cold lunches and cider June 6/7 and July 4/5. Barn camping.

42 GORWELL HOUSE

Goodleigh Rd, Barnstaple EX32 7JP. Dr J A Marston, 01271 323202, artavianjohn@gmail.com. *1m E of Barnstaple centre on Bratton Fleming rd. Drive entrance between two lodges on L.* Cream teas. **Adm £3.50, chd free. Suns 17 May; 14 June; 12 July; 13 Sept (2-6). Visitors also welcome by appt.**
Created mostly since 1979, this 4-acre garden overlooking the Taw estuary has a benign microclimate which allows many rare and tender plants to grow and thrive, both in the open and in the walled garden. Several strategically-placed follies complementing the enclosures and vistas within the garden. Featured in 'Devon Life'. Some steep slopes.

43 ◆ GREENWAY GARDEN

Galmpton nr Brixham TQ5 0ES. The National Trust, 01803 842382, www.nationaltrust.org.uk. *1½ m SE of Galmpton. A3022 towards Brixham. R turn signed Galmpton, follow brown signs for Greenway Quay. Entrance 1½ m on L. For ferry service from*

Dartmouth or Dittisham ring 01803 844010. **Please phone or visit website for adm prices. Wed to Sun incl, 28 Feb to 25 Oct (10.30-5), also Tues 21 July to 30 Aug. For NGS: Sat 5 Sept (10.30-5).**
Renowned for rare half-hardy plants underplanted with native wild flowers. Greenway has an atmosphere of wildness and timelessness, a true secret garden of peace and tranquillity with wonderful views of R Dart, associated with many fascinating characters.

44 HALDON GRANGE

Dunchideock EX6 7YE. Ted Phythian, 01392 832349. *5m SW of Exeter. From A30 at Exeter pass through Ide village to Dunchideock 5m. In centre of village turn L to Lord Haldon Hotel, Haldon Grange just past hotel drive. From A38 (S) turn L on top of Haldon Hill follow Dunchideock signs, R at village centre (at thatched house) to Lord Haldon Hotel.* Light refreshments & teas. **Adm £3, chd free (share to Devon Air Ambulance). Sat 25, Sun 26 Apr; Sats, Suns, 2 May to 31 May; Mon 4, Weds 6, 13, 20 May (1-5). Visitors also welcome by appt May to July only.**
12-acre well-established garden with camellias, magnolias, azaleas and rhododendrons; rare and mature trees; small lake and ponds with river and water cascades as a feature.

45 HAMBLYN'S COOMBE

Dittisham TQ6 0HE. Bridget McCrum, 01803 722228, www.bridgetmccrum.com. *3m N of Dartmouth. From Red Lion Inn follow The Level until it forks & go straight up steep private rd and through 'River Farm' gate. Continue straight on to end of farm track as signed.* **Adm £4, chd free. Visitors welcome by appt all yr except July & Aug. No coaches.**
7-acre garden with stunning views across the river to Greenway House and sloping steeply to R Dart at bottom of garden. Extensive planting of trees and shrubs with unusual design features accompanying Bridget McCrum's stone carvings and bronzes. Wild flower meadow and woods. Good rhododendrons and camellias, ferns and bamboos, acers and hydrangeas. Exceptional autumn colour. Featured in 'Homes and Gardens' and 'GGG'.

HANGERIDGE FARMHOUSE
See Somerset & Bristol.

46 NEW HARBOUR LIGHTS
Horns Cross, Bideford
EX39 5DW. Brian & Faith Butler.
7m W of Bideford, 3m E of Clovelly. On the main A39 between Bideford and Clovelly, half way between Hoops Inn and Bucks Cross. Cream teas, wine. **Adm £2.50, chd free.** Sat 4 July (11-6). **Day and Evening Opening** Sun 5 July (11-8).
½ -acre colourful garden with views of Lundy and countryside. A garden full of humour, wit, unusual ideas and surprises. Water features and polytunnel. Hoops Inn & Clovelly nearby.

47 ◆ HARTLAND ABBEY
Hartland, nr Bideford EX39 6DT. Sir Hugh & Lady Stucley, 01237 441234/264, www.hartlandabbey.com. *15m W of Bideford, 15m N of Bude. Turn off A39 W of Clovelly Cross to Hartland. Abbey between Hartland & Hartland Quay.* Light lunches & cream teas in aid of church. **House and Garden Adm £9, chd £2.50, Garden only Adm £5, chd £1.50.** Snowdrop Suns 8, 15 Feb (11-4); daily except Sats 1 Apr to 4 Oct (12-5).
Enchanting family home, beautiful woodland walks, C18 walled gardens and wild flower walk to the sea. Bog garden and fernery designed by Jekyll. Glasshouses. Bulbs, camellias, rhododendrons, azaleas, hydrangeas, herbaceous, tender and rare plants. Sense and Sensibility filmed here. Peacocks, donkeys and black sheep. Featured on Devon Radio and in 'Daily Telegraph' & 'Devon Life'. Limited wheelchair access, steep slopes and steps.

48 HEATHERCOMBE
Manaton TQ13 9XE. Claude & Margaret Pike Woodlands Trust, 01647 221350, gardens@heathercombe.com, www.heathercombe.com. *7m NW of Bovey Tracey. From Bovey Tracey take rd to Becky Falls and Manaton. Continue on same rd for 2m beyond village. At Heatree Cross follow sign straight ahead to Heathercombe. At top of hill continue straight ahead to Heathercombe. (From Widecombe take rd past Natsworthy).* Cream teas.

Adm £3.50, chd free. Sun 29 Mar (2-5.30); Sun 17, Sat 23, Sun 24 May (11-5.30); Sat 27 June (2-5.30), Sun 28 June (11-5.30). **Visitors also welcome by appt.**
Tranquil wooded valley 1,000 feet up on Dartmoor provides setting for variety of developing garden areas extending over 30 acres, providing yr-round interest; woodland walks beside streams, ponds and lake amongst snowdrops, daffodils and bluebells; well-labelled 'parkland' plantings incl over 100 varieties of rhododendrons and 400 specimen trees, many providing autumn colour; 2 medieval longhouse summer gardens with varied rooms of herbaceous plantings; wild flower meadow in orchard of West Country fruit trees; sandy paths.

A garden full of humour . . .

49 ◆ HEDDON HALL
Parracombe EX31 4QL. Mr & Mrs de Falbe, 01598 763541, www.heddonhallgardens.co.uk. *10m NE of Barnstaple. Follow A39 towards Lynton around Parracombe (avoiding village centre), then turn L down towards the village; entrance 200 yds on L.* **Adm £4, chd free.** Weds, Thurs, Fris May to July (12-5). For NGS: Suns 24 May; 28 June (2-5).
Stunning walled garden laid out by Penelope Hobhouse with clipped box and cordoned apple trees, herbaceous secret garden and natural rockery leading to a bog garden and 3 stew ponds. Very much a gardeners' garden, beautifully maintained, with many rare species, ferns, mature shrubs and trees all thriving in 4 acres of this sheltered Exmoor valley. Wheelchair users please phone in advance.

HIDDEN VALLEY GARDENS
See Cornwall.

50 HIGH GARDEN
Chiverstone Lane, Kenton EX6 8NJ. Chris & Sharon Britton. *5m S of Exeter on A379 Dawlish Rd. Leaving Kenton towards Exeter, L into Chiverstone Lane, 50yds along lane. Entrance clearly marked.* Home-made

teas. **Adm £2.50, chd free.** Sats, Suns 20, 21 June; 11, 12 July (2-5.30).
Recently-developed garden overlooking Exe Estuary. 70m double traditional herbaceous border for high summer colour. Unusual and choice shrubs and perennial beds. Large fruit/vegetable garden. Adjoining plantsman's nursery open on NGS days and Tues to Fri all yr.

HIGHCROFT GARDENS
See Cornwall.

51 HIGHER BURNHAIES
Butterleigh, Cullompton EX15 1PG. Richard & Virginia Holmes, 01884 855748. *3m W of Cullompton, 3m S of Tiverton. From Butterleigh, take rd to Silverton at T-junction. After ¼ m, take unmarked L fork, continue to hamlet. Very narrow lanes.* Cream teas. **Adm £3, chd free.** Suns 14, 28 June (2-6). **Visitors also welcome by appt.**
2½ -acre site started in 1997. Garden situated in the beautiful Burn Valley, surrounded by farmland. Plantsman's garden of herbaceous plantings with trees, shrubs and ponds. Informal, country feel with wild edges. Devon lane and wilderness walk. Vegetable garden. Uneven ground and steps, sometimes slippery.

52 HIGHER KNOWLE
Lustleigh TQ13 9SP. Mr & Mrs D R A Quicke, 01647 277275, quicke@connectfree.co.uk. *3m NW of Bovey Tracey. Take A382 towards Moretonhampstead. In 2½ m turn L for Lustleigh; in ¼ m L then R; in ¼ m steep drive L.* **Adm £3, chd free (share to Lustleigh Parish Church).** Every Sun & Bank Hol Mons 15 Mar to 31 May incl (11-6). **Visitors also welcome by appt March to May incl.**
3-acre woodland garden surrounds romantic 1914 Lutyens-style house (not open) with spectacular views towards R Bovey and Dartmoor. Sheltered site provides excellent conditions for tender plants. Numerous well-rounded granite boulders add natural sculpture to old oak woodland, carpeted with primroses, bluebells and other wild flowers. Collections of camellias, magnolias, rhododendrons and other acid-loving shrubs thrive here and all are labelled. Wildlife pond with fountain adds interest to this lovely garden. Featured in 'Devon Life'. Slippery steep paths.

HIGHER TRUSCOTT
See Cornwall.

53 NEW HILLRISE
24 Windsor Mead, Sidford
EX10 9SJ. Mr & Mrs D
Robertshaw, 01395 514991. *1m
N of Sidmouth. Off A3052 approx
¹/₄ m W of Sidford T-lights (towards
Exeter) signed R to Windsor Mead.
R at top of hill, last on R.* Home-
made teas. **Adm £3, chd £1.50.
Sats, Suns 18, 19 Apr; 16, 17
May; 13, 14 June; 18, 19 July;
15, 16 Aug; 12, 13 Sept (1.30-
5.30). Visitors also welcome by
appt Apr to Sept inc for groups
of 10+, month's notice if
applying in writing. Minibuses,
no large coaches.**
Plant enthusiasts' garden on S-
facing slope. Fine countryside and
sea views. Yr-round colour and
interest from wide variety of plants.
Borders for New Zealand plants,
penstemons, cannas, dahlias,
grasses with kniphofias and
hemerocalis, kaleidoscope border.
Fern garden, shaded area for
woodland plants. Greenhouse with
pelargoniums, streptocarpus, cacti
and succulents. Troughs. 1st prize
large garden category Sidmouth in
Bloom.
🐾 ✷ ☕ ☎

54 ◆ HOLBROOK GARDEN
Sampford Shrubs, Sampford
Peverell EX16 7EN. Martin Hughes-
Jones & Susan Proud, 01884
821164, www.holbrookgarden.com.
*1m NW from M5 J27. From J27 follow
brown signs to 'Minnows' camping site
then continue 300 metres up Holbrook
Hill (on Holcombe Rogus Rd).* **Adm £3,
chd free. Tues to Sats, Apr to Oct (9-
5). For NGS: Tues 7 Apr; 5 May; 2
June; 7 July; 4 Aug; 1 Sept; 6 Oct
(9-5).**
2-acre S-facing garden with innovative
plantings inspired by natural plant
populations; vibrant Mediterranean
colours; the garden continually evolves
- many experimental plantings - wet
garden, stone garden. Perfumes,
songbirds and nests everywhere in
spring and early summer. Fritillaries,
pulmonarias April; crocosmia,
National Collection of heleniums, late
perennials Aug/Sept. Organic
vegetable garden.
🐾 ✷ **NCCPG**

55 NEW HOLCOMBE COURT
Holcombe Rogus TA21 0PA. Mr
Nigel Wiggins. *5m W of
Wellington. From J26 or J27 on
M5, Holcombe Rogus is signed
from A38.* **Adm £4, chd free
(share to All Saints Church
Holcombe Rogus). Sat 27, Sun
28 June (10-5).**
7 acres of very varied gardens
around Grade I Tudor manor house
(not open). Herbaceous borders,
trout ponds and Victorian rockery.
Recently-restored and recreated
woodland garden and newly-
created vegetable parterre within
C18 walled garden. Espaliers and
apple orchard. 50% wheelchair
access.
♿ 🐾 ☕

56 HOLE FARM
nr Bickington TQ12 6PE. Rev Ian
Graham-Orlebar, 01626 821298,
ianorlebar@aol.com. *5m NE of
Ashburton. From A383 Ashburton to
Newton Abbot rd, 3m NE of Ashburton
signed Gale, Burne. Follow signs to
Farlacombe, after 2m, at top of hill,
lane on R to Hole Farm.* Light
refreshments & teas. **Adm £3, chd £1.
Sun 16 Aug (3-8). Visitors also
welcome by appt, no access for
coaches.**
2¹/₂ -acre valley garden with woodland,
wild garden, 2 ponds, 3 herbaceous
borders, bog areas and wildlife
plantation. Old farm and buildings, not
open.
♿ ☕ ☎

**57 NEW HOLLYCOMBE
HOUSE**
Manor Rd, Bishopsteignton
TQ14 9SU. Jenny & Graham
Jeley, 01626 870838,
jsc2007@hotmail.co.uk. *Newton
Abbot A381 to Teignmouth, L at
Wyevale Garden Centre, Church
Rd, R at PH, Radway Hill, L Manor
Rd, R at Rock, drive to top.* Cream
teas. **Adm £3.50, chd free. Suns
14 June; 12 July; 13 Sept (2-5).
Visitors also welcome by appt.**
Nearly 5 acres of stunning garden
with panoramic view of the Teign
Estuary. Stylish borders, shrubs for
every day of the yr. Organic
vegetables in raised beds.
Attractive large pond, full of water
lilies and fish. Alpacas, goats,
chickens and ducks. All create an
area of individuality.
☕ ☎

Borders for
New Zealand
plants . . .
kaleidoscope
border . . .

HOOPER'S HOLDING
See Somerset & Bristol.

Group opening

**58 NEW IDDESLEIGH
GARDENS**
Iddesleigh, mid-Devon
EX19 8SN. *2m S Iddesleigh
village, 7m NE of Okehampton, 3m
N of Hatherleigh, 5m S of
Winkleigh. From Hatherleigh take
route to Monkokehampton 2m, L
at Xrds 1.5m, L at Weekmoor Xrds,
2nd track on L. Group parking at
Nethercott House.* Cream teas at
Nethercott House. **Combined
adm £4, chd free (share to
Farms for City Children). Sat 18
July (2-5), Sun 19 July (2-6).**
2 very different gardens 300yds
apart. Set in the heartland of rural
Devon, both overlooking Dartmoor.
Working walled vegetable garden
in manorial setting and cottage
flower garden. Exhibition of James
Ravillious's photographs of bygone
era at Nethercott, weaving
demonstration in studio at
Sanctuary Gate.
♿ ✷ ☕

NETHERCOTT HOUSE
Iddesleigh, nr Winkleigh. Farms
for City Children. *3m NE of
Hatherleigh*
South-facing Victorian walled
working kitchen and vegetable
gardens (unregistered organic) with
herbaceous borders. Home of
Farms for City Children, the charity
that provides farm work experience
for urban city children. Superb
aspect overlooking Dartmoor.
Gravel paths.
♿ ✷

NEW SANCTUARY GATE
Debbie & Steve Phelps
Cottage garden originally serving
farm labourers' cottages opposite.
Extensive rural views incl Yes Tor,
Dartmoor. Mature garden trees and
well-planted herbaceous borders.
Original stone-lined and domed
well. Fleece insulated artist's
studio; weaving demonstration.
Gravel paths.
&. ⊛

59 JASON'S GARDEN
Eastcliff Walk, Teignmouth
TQ14 8SZ. Jason's family, 01626
776070, nev@mamma.org.uk. *Park
at East Cliff car park, follow signs, walk
up cliff rd with sea on R.* Catering at
Ian's cafe, Eastcliff Walk. **Adm £2.50,
chd free (share to Teignmouth Folk
Festival 20/21 June). Sun 3, Mon 4
May (10-4); Sat 20, Sun 21 June
(2-5); Sun 30, Mon 31 Aug (10-4).
Visitors also welcome by appt
coach parties welcome.**
Stunning clifftop garden with 180°
panoramic view of sea and S Devon
coastline. Modern, stylish design with
high quality landscaping and bold
planting, creating areas of individuality
within a harmonious whole. This
tactile garden is accessible and of
interest to all and its underlying ethos
leaves a lasting impression. Seeing is
believing. Growing collection of
sculptures with environmental ethos.
Teignmouth Folk Festival 20/21 June,
music in garden. Catering at Ian's Cafe,
Eastcliff Walk. Part of TRAIL (trail of
recycled art in the environment). Walk
to garden up steep narrow lane, no
steps.
&. ☕ ☎

KEN CARO
See Cornwall.

60 KERSCOTT HOUSE
Swimbridge EX32 0QA. Jessica &
Peter Duncan. *6m E of Barnstaple.
On Barnstaple-Swimbridge-South
Molton rd (not A361), 1m E of
Swimbridge turn R at top of hill, immed
fork L, 100yds on L, 1st gate past
house.* Cream teas. **Adm £2.50, chd
free. Sun 28 June (2-6).**
6 acres surrounding C16 farmhouse
(not open) in peaceful rural setting.
Garden evolved from scratch since
1985, owner designed/maintained.
Naturalistic site-generated planting
flowing through vistas combining dry
gravel, shady and boggy areas.
Atmospheric and harmonious, with

living willow constructions, woodland,
ponds, wildlife meadow. Unusual
plants, Mediterranean garden within
roofless barn.
&. ⊛ ☕

61 KIA-ORA FARM & GARDENS
Knowle Lane, Cullompton
EX15 1PZ. Mrs M B Disney, 01884
32347. *6m SE of Tiverton. J28 of M5.
Straight through Cullompton town
centre to roundabout, take 3rd exit into
Swallow Way, follow rd through houses
up to sharp R-hand bend. On bend
turn L into Knowle Lane, garden
beside Rugby Club.* Cream teas. **Adm
£2.50, chd free. Suns, Bank Hol
Mons 12, 13, 26 Apr; 3, 4, 17, 24, 25
May; 7, 21 June; 5, 19 July; 2, 16,
30, 31 Aug; 13 Sept (2-5.30). Visitors
also welcome by appt.**
10 acres of extensively planted
gardens and lakes. Charming, peaceful
garden with lawns, large lakes, ponds,
bog garden and various water features
incl ducks and wildlife. Many areas with
individual character, mature trees and
shrubs, rhododendrons, azaleas,
heathers, roses, herbaceous borders
and rockeries. Several different features
incl nursery avenue, wisteria walk,
novelty crazy golf and many more!
Surprises everywhere! Come and see
what's new for 2009.
&. ✕ ⊛ ☕ ☎

. . . weaving
demonstration . . .

62 ◆ KILLERTON GARDEN
Broadclyst EX5 3LE. The National
Trust, 01392 881345,
www.nationaltrust.org.uk. *8m N of
Exeter. Take B3181 Exeter to
Cullompton rd, after 7m fork left &
follow NT signs.* **House and garden
adm £8, chd £4, garden only adm
£5.90, chd £2.95. Open all yr (10.30-
earlier of 7 or dusk). For NGS: Suns
17 May; 23 Aug (11-4.30).**
20 acres of spectacular hillside
gardens with naturalised bulbs,
sweeping down to large open lawns.
Delightful walks through fine collection
of rare trees, shrubs and herbaceous
borders. Plant sales 17 May.
&. ✕ ⊛ ☕ ☕

63 KINGSTON HOUSE
Staverton TQ9 6AR. Mr & Mrs M R
Corfield, 01803 762235,
info@kingston-estate.co.uk. *4m NE
of Totnes. A384 Totnes to
Buckfastleigh, from Staverton, 1m due
N of Sea Trout Inn, follow signs to
Kingston.* Cream teas. **Adm £4, chd
50p (share to Animals in Distress).
Suns 8 Mar; 17 May; 5 July (2-6).
Evening Opening £6, wine &
nibbles, Sun 19 July (5-8). Visitors
also welcome by appt, no coaches.**
George II 1735 house Grade II (not
open). Gardens restored in keeping
with the period. Walled garden, rose
garden, pleached limes and
hornbeams, vegetable garden.
Unusual formal garden with santolinas,
lavender and camomile. Large formal
parterre. 6000 tulips in bloom mid-May,
maybe! Many gravel paths.
&. ⊨ ☕ ☎

**64 ◆ KNIGHTSHAYES COURT
GARDEN**
Tiverton EX16 7RQ. The National
Trust, 01884 254665,
www.nationaltrust.org.uk. *2m N of
Tiverton. Via A396 Tiverton to
Bampton rd; turn E in Bolham, signed
Knightshayes; entrance ½ m on L.*
**House and garden adm £8.20, chd
£4.10, garden only adm £6.50, chd
£3.25. Daily 14 Mar to 1 Nov (11-5).
House closed Fris. For NGS: Sun
3 May; Sat 18 July (11-5).**
Large 'Garden in the Wood', 50 acres
of landscaped gardens with pleasant
walks and views over Exe valley.
Choice collections of unusual plants,
incl acers, birches, rhododendrons,
azaleas, camellias, magnolias, roses,
spring bulbs, alpines and herbaceous
borders; formal gardens; walled
kitchen garden.
&. ✕ ⊛

KNOWLE FARM
See Dorset.

65 LANGTREES
10 Cott Lane, Croyde, Braunton
EX33 1ND. Paul & Helena Petrides,
01271 890202,
angelrest@lineone.net,
www.langtrees.info. *10m W of
Barnstaple. From Barnstaple A361 to
Braunton, L on B3231 to Croyde, past
Croyde Bay Holidays on L. Cott Lane
on R as rd narrows towards village
centre. No parking in lane, park in
village car park 200yds L by village hall.*
Home-made teas. **Adm £3.50, chd
free. Suns 10 May; 12 July; 13 Sept**

(2-6). Visitors also welcome by appt all yr.

1-acre plantsman's garden with eclectic selection of plants. Many S hemisphere shrubs and other tender species. Yr-round interest with landscaping and design features. Flowers all seasons from rhododendrons and magnolias in spring to salvias, cannas and ginger lilies in autumn. Interesting selection of trees.

✘ ✿ ☕ ☎

1½ acres, designed for year-round interest . . .

66 LEE FORD
Knowle, Budleigh Salterton EX9 7AJ. Mr & Mrs N Lindsay-Fynn, 01395 445894, crescent@leeford.co.uk. *3½ m E of Exmouth.* Home-made teas by arrangement. **Adm £5. Visitors welcome by appt Mon to Thur (10-4) and other times by special arrangement.**
Extensive, formal and woodland garden, largely developed in the 1950s, but recently much extended with mass displays of camellias, rhododendrons and azaleas, incl many rare varieties. Traditional walled garden filled with fruit and vegetables, herb garden, bog garden, rose garden, hydrangea collection, greenhouses. Ornamental conservatory and Adam pavilion. 45 min group tour of garden and woodlands by prior booking £20.

& ☕ ☎

LIFT THE LATCH
See Somerset & Bristol.

67 NEW LITTLE ASH BUNGALOW
Fenny Bridges, Honiton EX14 3BL. Helen & Brian Brown, 01404 850941, helenlittleash@hotmail.com. *3m W of Honiton. Leave A30 at Iron Bridge from Honiton 1m, Patteson's Cross from Exeter ½ m and follow NGS signs.* Light refreshments & teas. **Adm £3, chd**

free. Sat 6 June; Sun 23 Aug (1.30-5.30). **Visitors also welcome by appt for groups of 10+.**
1½ acres, designed for yr-round interest. Many different and unusual perennials, shrubs, bamboos and trees. Colour-coordinated mixed borders, providing much late summer colour. A natural-looking stream flows into a pebble bordered lily pond and 3 granite rollers lead the eye to glorious view towards R Otter and East Hill. Grass paths.

& ✿ ☕ ☎

68 LITTLE ASH FARM
Fenny Bridges, Honiton EX14 3BL. Sadie & Robert Reid, 01404 850271. *3m W of Honiton. Leave A30 at Iron Bridge from Honiton 1m, Patteson's Cross from Exeter ½ m, & follow NGS signs.* Home-made teas. **Adm £3, chd free. Suns 21 June; 19 July; Sat 15, Sun 16 Aug (2-6). Visitors also welcome by appt.**
Peaceful garden within 1 acre with adjoining farmland and extensive views. Immaculate lawns, new and established trees and shrubs. Three linked ponds and delightful rill through the garden. Fruit and new vegetable plot. Golf putting course. Handmade furniture workshop and showroom.

& ✘ ⊨ ☕ ☎

69 LITTLE CUMBRE
145 Pennsylvania Road, Exeter EX4 6DZ. Dr Margaret Lloyd, 01392 258315. *1m due N of city centre. From town centre take Longbrook St, continue N up hill approx 1m. Near top of hill.* **Adm £3, chd free. Suns 1, 8, 15, 22 Feb 2009; 31 Jan; 7, 14, 21 Feb 2010; (12-3.30). Visitors also welcome by appt Feb to May.**
1-acre garden and woodland on S-facing slope with extensive views. Interesting areas of garden on different levels linked by grassy paths. Wonderful display of snowdrops, many varieties, and colourful hellebores. Scented winter shrubs and camellias, spring bulbs. Top garden managed to encourage wildlife. Limited wheelchair access.

& ✘ ✿ ☎

70 LITTLE WEBBERY
EX39 4PS. Mr & Mrs J A Yewdall, 01271 858206, jayewdall@surfree.co.uk. Home-made teas. **Adm £3.50, chd free. Sat**

16, Sun 17 May (2-6). **Visitors also welcome by appt.**
Approx 3 acres in valley setting with pond, lake, mature trees and 2 ha-has. Walled kitchen garden with yew and box hedging; greenhouse; rose garden; trellises; shrubs and climbing plants. 3 mature borders. Some gravel paths.

& ✘ ✿ ☕ ☎

71 LITTLECOURT COTTAGES
Seafield Road, Sidmouth EX10 8HF. Geoffrey Ward & Selwyn Kussman. *500yds N of Sidmouth seafront. From N take B3176 to Sidmouth seafront/Bedford Car Park. Take Station Rd, past Manor Rd and immed up Seafield Rd. Garden 100yds on R. Regret no parking at garden, car parks nearby.* **Adm £3, chd free. Suns 24 May; 28 June; 26 July (2-5.30).**
Oasis of calm in middle of Sidmouth. A series of rooms for the plantaholic. Courtyard gardens behind house; in front, main lawn and water feature. Rare and tender plants everywhere. Exceptional basket colour. Featured on BBC2 Open Gardens. Winner Sidmouth in Bloom.

✘

72 THE LOOKOUT
Sowden Lane, Lympstone EX8 5HE. Will & Jackie Michelmore. *9m SE of Exeter, 2m N of Exmouth. A376 to Exmouth. 1st R after Marine Camp signed Lower Lympstone, 1st R in village into The Strand, past Londis shop, village car park next L. Follow NGS signs, 8min walk. No on-site parking or much on-road parking nearby, parking in adj field if dry. New cycle path nearby.* Home-made teas. **Adm £3, chd free. Fri 19 June (2-5), Sun 21 June (2-6).**
2 wildlife-friendly acres on edge of Exe Estuary. Lovingly created from derelict site over last 6yrs by garden designer/owner to harmonise with coast and countryside location and maximise on views. Flotsam and jetsam finds amongst naturalistic seaside planting. Circular walk through wild flower meadow to pond (unfenced), through copse and along riverbank. Walled mediterranean courtyard, small jungley area. Featured on BBC2 Open Gardens. Gravel paths, slopes and some steps so unsuitable for disabled and toddlers.

✘ ✿ ☕

73 ◆ **LUKESLAND**
Harford, Ivybridge PL21 0JF. Mrs R
Howell & Mr & Mrs J Howell, 01752
691749/893390,
www.lukesland.co.uk. *10m E of
Plymouth. Turn off A38 at Ivybridge.
1½ m N on Harford rd, E side of Erme
valley.* Adm £4.50, chd free, groups
of 20+ £4, wheelchairs free. Suns,
Weds & Bank Hols, 29 Mar to 7
June (2-6); Suns, Weds 18 Oct to
15 Nov (11-4).
24 acres of flowering shrubs, wild
flowers and rare trees with pinetum in
Dartmoor National Park. Beautiful
setting of small valley around
Addicombe Brook with lakes,
numerous waterfalls and pools.
Extensive and unusual collection of
rhododendrons, a champion
Magnolia campbellii and a huge
Davidia involucrata. Superb spring
and autumn colour. Children's Trail for
spring and autumn each yr, other
events advertised on website.
Featured in 'Country Living'. 1st prize
Rhododendron Loderi class at RHS
National Rhododendron, Camellia &
Magnolia show. Some steep slopes
and grass paths.

Group opening

74 NEW **LUPPITT GARDENS**
EX14 4TP. *2m NE of Honiton.*
Home-made teas. Adm £3.50,
chd free. Sat 30, Sun 31 May
(1-5).
Both gardens have Dumpdon
Hillfort (NT) as backdrop and are
2m apart.

POUND COTTAGE
John & Naomi Lott
(See separate entry).

NEW WOODHAYES
Mr & Mrs N Page-Turner. *Take
Dunkeswell Rd out of Honiton.
Cross R Otter, 150yds R, 1st drive
on R*
1½ acres of formal garden.
Trees, shrubs, herbaceous
borders and tree paeonies. 3 levels
divided by small stone walls and
clipped beech hedges. Rose
garden and rockery surrounded by
clipped box. Stunning views of
R Otter.

75 ◆ **MARWOOD HILL**
Marwood EX31 4EB. Dr J A
Snowdon, 01271 342528,
www.marwoodhillgarden.co.uk. *4m
N of Barnstaple. Signed from A361 &
B3230. Outside Guineaford village,
opp Marwood church. See website for
map.* Adm £4.50, chd free. Gardens
open daily except Christmas Day
(10-5.30); Plant sales/tearoom open
Mar to Oct (11-5). For NGS: Sats 25
Apr; 19 Sept (10-5.30).
20 acres with 3 small lakes. Extensive
collection of camellias under glass and
in open; daffodils, rhododendrons, rare
flowering shrubs, rock and alpine
scree; waterside planting; bog garden;
many clematis; Australian native plants
and many eucalyptus. National
Collections of Astilbe, *Iris ensata*,
Tulbaghia. Featured in 'Gardeners
World', 'The English Garden' and
'Devon Life'. Steep slopes, gravel
paths, information leaflet given to
visitors.

MELPLASH COURT
See Dorset.

Group opening

76 **MEMBURY GARDENS**
Membury EX13 7AJ. *4m NW of
Axminster.* Home-made teas.
Combined adm £3.50, chd free. Sat
30, Sun 31 May; Sat 27, Sun 28 June
(11-5).
Two artistic gardens in pretty village,
situated on edge of Blackdown Hills.

CLEAVE HILL
Andy & Penny Pritchard, 01404
881437. *From Membury Village,
follow rd down valley. 1st R after
Lea Hill B&B, last house on drive,
approx 1m.* Visitors also
welcome by appt.
Cottage-style garden, artistically
planted to provide all-season
structure, texture and colour.
Designed around pretty thatched
house and old stone barn.
Wonderful views, attractive
vegetable garden and orchard, wild
flower meadow.

SIXPENNY MOON
Lindsay & Ian Withycombe,
01404 881625, sixpenny-
moon@tiscali.co.uk. *In centre of
village nr church. Park opp Village
Hall. 2nd gate on R.* Visitors also
welcome by appt.
Small walled garden, big on plants

and naturally dividing into different
areas. This quirky garden has been
planted for yr-round interest with
emphasis on foliage, colour and
form, structural planting and
sculpture.

Cottage-style garden, artistically planted to provide all-season structure, texture and colour. . . .

Group opening

77 **MORETONHAMPSTEAD
GARDENS**
TQ13 8PW. *12m W of Exeter & N of
Newton Abbot. On E slopes of
Dartmoor National Park. Parking at
both gardens.* Combined adm £4, chd free. Sat 23,
Sun 24, Mon 25 May; Sat 1, Sun 2
Aug (2-6).
Two complementary gardens of
differing character in the geographical
centre of Devon, close to the edge of
Dartmoor. Superb walking country.
Dogs on leads welcome.

MARDON
Graham & Mary Wilson. *From
centre of village, head towards
church, turn L into Lime St. Bottom
of hill on R*
Spacious and well-maintained
4-acre garden surrounding
Edwardian house (not open) in
small Dartmoor coombe. Formal
terraces leading from rose garden
to large lawn with long herbaceous
border and wild flowers. Extensive
rhododendron planting. Woodland
walk along stream leading to
fernery and pond with thatched
boathouse. Productive vegetable
garden. New this year - wild
meadow orchard. Featured in
'Country Gardener'.

SUTTON MEAD
Edward & Miranda Allhusen, 01647 440296, miranda@allhusen.co.uk. ½ m N of village on A382. R at de-restriction sign. **Visitors also welcome by appt.**
3½ -acre garden of contrasts on gently-sloping hillside. Woodland of mature and recent plantings and rill fed round pond. Potager vegetable garden with unusual concrete greenhouse. Granite walls mingling with imaginative planting of trees and shrubs. Croquet lawn, rhododendrons, azaleas and many hydrangeas. Spring-fed ponds with granite seat at water's edge. Bog garden and new orchard. Fine views of Dartmoor from all corners of garden. Current project - restyling long borders. Featured on ITV Glorious Gardens & in 'Country Gardener' magazine.

78 MOTHECOMBE HOUSE
Holbeton, nr Plymouth PL8 1LB. Mr & Mrs A Mildmay-White, 01752 830444, annemildmaywhite@hotmail.com. *From A379 between Yealmpton & Modbury turn S for Holbeton. Continue 2m to Mothecombe.* Cream teas. **Adm £4, chd free. Sat 2, Sun 3 May (2-5). Visitors also welcome by appt.**
Queen Anne house (not open) with Lutyens additions and terraces set in private estate hamlet. Walled pleasure gardens, borders and Lutyens courtyard. Orchard with spring bulbs, unusual shrubs and trees, camellia walk. Autumn garden, streams, bog garden and pond. Bluebell woods leading to private beach. Yr-round interest. Featured in 'Country Homes & Interiors'. Gravel paths, some slopes.

MOYCLARE
See Cornwall.

79 NEWTON FARM
Hemyock EX15 3QS. Mr & Mrs J F J M Ward, 01823 680410. ½ m S of Hemyock. On Old Dunkeswell Abbey Rd, from Wellington take Monument Hemyock Rd in centre of Hemyock, turn L by pump. From Honiton take Taunton to top of hill L to Dunkeswell Cross aerodrome, turn R at first major Xrds, follow signs. Home-made teas. **Adm £2.50, chd free (share to Blackdown Support). Sats, Suns 7, 8 Mar; 30, 31 May; Weds, Sats,**

Suns 17, 20, 21, 24, 27, 28 June; 15, 18, 19, 29 July; Sats, Suns, 8 Aug to 30 Aug; Mon 31 Aug; Sat 19, Sun 20 Sept (10-5). **Visitors also welcome by appt.**
5 acres in Blackdown Hills with views over Culm Valley. S-facing garden: 8 large herbaceous borders, young maze, hornbeam walk, iris and hemerocallis garden. N garden: dwarf rhododendrons, dwarf conifers and pines. National Collections *Gentianas* and *Rhodohypoxis* and *x Rhodoxis*, bog. Woodland garden, many rare and unusual trees. Planting and development continue. New 1½ acres open grown *Iris ensata* and hemerocallis for the visitor to walk through. Wild flower meadow approx 3 acres. March opening for hellebores, Sept for gentianas. Nursery.

Waterfall and exotic planting . . .

80 NORTH BORESTON FARM
nr Moreleigh TQ9 7LD. Rob & Jan Wagstaff, 01548 821320, borestongarden@btinternet.com. *5m S of Totnes. From A381 Totnes to Kingsbridge rd, at Halwell take rd to Moreleigh. From edge of Moreleigh village, follow yellow NGS signs.* Home-made teas. **Adm £3.50, chd free. Mon 4, Sun 10 May (2-5). Visitors also welcome by appt Apr to Sept, groups welcome.**
Sloping 3-acre garden of very different areas, plus 2-acre bluebell wood. Quarry garden ablaze with alpines. Over 100 varieties each of rhododendrons and camellias. Acers with spring borders beneath; herbaceous borders nr house. Large spring-fed ponds, stream and bog garden. Bridge to exotic garden with palms, bamboos, bananas and many rare and unusual plants. Featured on ITV's Glorious Gardens and in 'Devon Life'.

81 NEW NORTH DEVON HOSPICE
Deer Park, Newport EX32 0HU. *A39 to Barnstaple, follow signs to Newport and NGS signs to Hospice. (1½ m from A39).* Cream teas. **Adm £3, chd free. Sats, Suns 11, 12 July; 5, 6 Sept (12-4.30).**

5-acre garden with lawns, trees, shrubs and ornamental planting. 2 ponds with waterfall and exotic planting. Newly-planted cherry orchard, ornamental kitchen garden and retreat garden for quiet contemplation. Extensively redesigned and rebuilt over last 2 yrs in contemporary style. No wheelchair access to orchard.

Group opening

82 OLCHARD GARDENS
Nr Ideford TQ12 3GX. *4m NNE of Newton Abbot. 1m from Ideford, 2m N of Kingsteignton, off A380 (Newton Abbot to Exeter rd).* Home-made teas at Well Cottage. **Combined adm £3.50, chd free (share to Ideford Millennium Green Trust). Suns 14, 21 June (2-6).**
Both gardens are in small hamlet consisting of only a handful of houses.

NEW OLCHARD FARM
Mr & Mrs S Allen. *S on A380, sharp L signed Olchard. Down hill, R opp postbox on pole, garden on R. N from Newton Abbot on A380, exit at Wapperwell. R under dual carriageway to T-junction. L, then almost immed R into lane signed Olchard. ½ m, L opp post box, garden on R.* **Visitors also welcome by appt.**
1½ -acre garden with walled deep herbaceous and mixed shrub borders. Water garden fed by natural spring with gunnera, tree fern and bamboo. Ancient orchard, stream and separate wildlife area (boots recommended).

WELL COTTAGE
Olchard. Joe & Wendy Taylor, 01626 852415, olchard@hotmail.com. *S on A380, sharp L exit signed Olchard. Downhill, R opp postbox on pole, garden on L. N from Newton Abbot on A380, exit at Wapperwell. R under dual carriageway to T-junction. L then almost immed R into lane signed Olchard. ½ m, L opp post box, garden on L.* **Visitors also welcome by appt.**
½ -acre of lawn/mixed borders on different levels. Beautifully planted with emphasis on creating a cottage garden.

83 THE OLD GLEBE

Eggesford EX18 7QU. Mr & Mrs Nigel Wright. *20m NW of Exeter. Turn S off A377 at Eggesford stn (halfway between Exeter & Barnstaple), cross railway & R Taw, drive straight uphill (signed Brushford) for ³/₄ m; turn R into bridleway.* Home-made teas. **Adm £3, chd £1 (share to Friends of Eggesford All Saints Trust). Sats, Suns 9, 10, 16, 17 May (2-5).**
7-acre garden of former Georgian rectory (not open) with mature trees and several lawns, courtyard, walled herbaceous borders, bog garden and small lake; emphasis on species and hybrid rhododendrons and azaleas, 750 varieties. Adjacent rhododendron nursery open by appt.

♿ ✗ ❀ ☕

Imaginatively-designed with surprises round every corner . . .

84 THE OLD RECTORY

Ashford, Barnstaple EX31 4BY. Mrs Ann Burnham, 01271 377408, annburnham@btinternet.com. *3m W of Barnstaple. A361 to Braunton. At end of dual carriageway, R to Ashford. Approx 1m, follow rd round to L, 1st house on L.* Light refreshments & cream teas. **Adm £3, chd free. Suns 10 May; 6 Sept (11-5). Visitors also welcome by appt.**
Recently-created garden of approx 1¹/₂ acres. Open, S-facing with superb views of Taw Estuary. Top garden has been redesigned with new and interesting planting. Lower garden, previously a paddock, now included in flower garden. Jazz duo. Lower garden is sloping.

♿ ❀ ⛰ ☕ ☎

85 NEW OLD RECTORY GARDENS

Littleham EX39 5HW. Mr & Mrs J J Smith. *3m S of Bideford. Turn off A39 'Atlantic Highway' at Abbotsham Cross r'about. In Littleham, follow signs to church for designated parking areas in gardens.* Cream teas. **Adm £3.50, chd free (share to St Swithun's Church). Sat 11, Sun 26 Apr (12-5).**
This former rectory with its neighbouring cottage and fine church stand together at the head of a secluded valley. 5 acres of garden and grounds with landscaped lawns and a variety of contrasting areas incl pretty cottage garden, large collection of unusual trees and shrubs, specimen conifers, ponds and wild flowers. Gravel paths and sloping wild flower areas.

♿ ⛰ ☕

THE OLD RECTORY, LITTON CHENEY

See Dorset.

THE OLD RECTORY, NETHERBURY

See Dorset.

86 THE OLD VICARAGE

West Anstey EX36 3PE. Tuck & Juliet Moss, 01398 341604. *9m E of South Molton. From South Molton 9m E on B3227 to Jubilee Inn. Sign to West Anstey. Turn L for ¹/₄ m then dog-leg L then R following signs. Through Yeomill to T-junction. R following sign. Garden 1st house on L.* Cream teas. **Adm £2.50, chd free. Fri, Sat, Sun 8, 9, 10 May; 10, 11, 12 July (2-5). Visitors also welcome by appt.**
Croquet lawn leads to multi-level garden overlooking three large ponds with winding paths, climbing roses and overviews. Brook with waterfall flows through garden past fascinating summerhouse built by owner. Benched deck overhangs first pond. Features rhododendrons, azaleas and primulas in spring and large collection of Japanese iris in summer.

 ☕

87 ◆ OTTER NURSERIES

Gosford Road, Ottery St Mary EX11 1LZ. Malcolm & Marilyn White, 01404 815815 ext 241. *Follow brown tourist signs on A30 Honiton to Exeter rd.* **Adm £1, chd free. Mon - Sat (9-5.30); Wed (Mar - Dec) until 8pm;**
Suns (10-4,.30). For NGS: Wed 22 Apr; Wed 6 May; Wed 14 Oct (10-5.30).
Not a garden but a fascinating 'behind the scenes' tour of one of Devon's favourite garden centres. Guided walks around nursery growing areas. Spring tours look at young plants raised to bring gardens to glorious summer colour. Autumn tour reveals the secrets of growing poinsettias, colourful cyclamen, autumn and winter plants. Featured in press. Regret not suitable for wheelchairs.

✗ ❀

88 ◆ OVERBECK'S

Sharpitor, Salcombe TQ8 8LW. The National Trust, 01548 842893, www.nationaltrust.org.uk. *1¹/₂ m SW of Salcombe. Follow NT signs.* **Adm £6.40, chd £3.20. For NGS: Sats 18 July; 26 Sept (11-5).**
7-acre exotic coastal garden, Grade II* listed, with rare plants and shrubs; spectacular views over Salcombe estuary. Garden tour at 2.30.

✗

89 OWLS BARN

The Chestnuts, Aylesbeare EX5 2BY. Pauline & Ray Mulligan. *3m E of Exeter airport. A3052 Exeter to Sidmouth, fork L after Halfway Inn. 50yds, park in Village Way. Garden on R past school. From Ottery St Mary, go through West Hill, L onto B3180, R at Tipton X. At Aylesbeare, L through village, garden signed on L. Disabled parking only at The Chestnuts.* Home-made teas. **Adm £3, chd free. Sat 13, Sun 14 June (2-5.30).**
Peaceful ³/₄ -acre village garden, a haven for wildlife. Small woodland, natural bog with pond and gravel areas. All on N-facing slope of heavy clay. Contrasting foliage with plenty of unusual perennials, grasses, billowing roses, clematis, fruit and vegetables. Imaginatively-designed with surprises round every corner. Gravel drive, wheelchair access to most areas.

♿ ✗ ❀ ☕

90 PIKES COTTAGE

Madford, Hemyock EX15 3QZ. Christine Carver, 01823 680345, bridget.carver@btinternet.com. *7m N of Honiton. Off A30 to Wolford Chapel & through Dunkeswell towards Hemyock, then follow signs from Gypsy Cross. Or 7m S of Wellington off M5 J26 to Hemyock, then follow signs. Turn in at gates signed Pikes Cottage downhill from Madford Farm & up rough farm track.* Cream teas. **Adm**

£2.50, chd free. Suns, 1 Feb to 22 Feb (1-5); Sats, Suns, Mons 2, 3, 4, 23, 24, 25 May; Sats, Suns 20, 21 June; 25, 26 July; Sat 29, Sun 30, Mon 31 Aug; Sat 26, Sun 27 Sept; (2-6); Suns, 7 Feb to 28 Feb 2010 (1-5). Visitors also welcome by appt May to Sept, minibuses but no coaches.
Set in 19 acres of bluebell woods (hilly access). 6 acres of cultivated garden incl herb garden, scree, prarie planting, sensory garden, rhododendrons and other shrubs. 1¹/₂ -acre lawn slopes to large pond and bog garden. Wisteria tunnel, steps to snowdrops (Feb) and arboretum. Children's quiz, playground, model village. Ample seating. Limited wheelchair access.

A gem, not to be missed . . .

91 ◆ PLANT WORLD
St Marychurch Road, Newton Abbot TQ12 4SE. Ray Brown, 01803 872939, www.plant-world-seeds.com. *2m SE of Newton Abbot. 1¹/₂ m from Penn Inn roundabout. Follow brown tourist signs at the end of the A380 dual carriageway from Exeter.* Adm £3, chd free. Daily 10 Apr to 31 Oct (9.30-5).
The 4 acres of landscape gardens with fabulous views have been called Devon's 'Little Outdoor Eden'. Representing each of the five continents, they offer an extensive collection of rare and exotic plants from around the world. Superb mature cottage garden and Mediterranean garden will delight the visitor. Featured in 'Sunday Telegraph', 'Gardeners World' and on regional TV.

92 PORTINGTON
nr Lamerton PL19 8QY. Mr & Mrs I A Dingle, 01822 870364. *3m NW of Tavistock. From Tavistock B3362 to Launceston. ¹/₄ m beyond Blacksmiths Arms, Lamerton, fork L (signed Chipshop). Over Xrds (signed Horsebridge) first L then L again (signed Portington). From Launceston*

turn R at Carrs Garage and R again (signed Horsebridge), then as above. Home-made teas. Adm £2.50, chd free (share to Plymouth Samaritans). Suns 14, 21 June (2-5.30). Visitors also welcome by appt June/July only.
Garden in peaceful rural setting with fine views over surrounding countryside. Mixed planting with shrubs and borders. Walk to small lake through woodland and fields, which have recently been designated a county wildlife site.

93 POUND COTTAGE
Beacon, Honiton EX14 4TT. John & Naomi Lott, 07790 961310, naomilott@yahoo.co.uk. *4m E of Honiton. A30 from Honiton, pass Little Chef, 1st L signed Luppitt. Over bridge, 1.8m up hill, 1st R. Straight on at Pound Farm (no through rd), garden on L. Parking in field on R (limited parking if wet).* Home-made teas. Adm £3, chd free. Sats 2, 9 May. Also open with **Luptitt Gardens** 30, 31 May. Visitors also welcome by appt.
1-acre hillside garden with magnificent views, designed and developed by owners over 25yrs. Collection of over 150 species rhododendrons plus camellias, azaleas, pieris and many unusual shrubs and trees, most of which labelled. Bluebells, vegetable garden and 1 acre across lane still under development with orchard and pond. Featured on ITV Georgeous Gardens.

POUNDSTOCK GARDENS
See Cornwall.

94 PROSPECT HOUSE
Lyme Road, Axminster EX13 5BH. Peter Wadeley, 01297 631210, wadeley@btinternet.com. *From Axminster town centre (Trinity Square) proceed uphill past George Hotel into Lyme St & Lyme Rd. Garden approx ¹/₂ m up rd on R, just before petrol stn.* Home-made teas. Adm £3, chd free. Sats, Suns 4, 5 July; 22, 23 Aug (1.30-5.30). Visitors also welcome by appt.
1-acre plantsman's garden hidden behind high stone walls and with Axe valley views. Well-stocked borders with rare shrubs, many reckoned to be borderline tender. 200 varieties of salvia and late summer perennials. A gem, not to be missed.

95 REGENCY HOUSE
Hemyock EX15 3RQ. Mrs Jenny Parsons, jenny.parsons@ btinternet.com. *8m N of Honiton. M5 J26. From Hemyock take Dunkeswell-Honiton rd. Entrance ¹/₂ m on R from Catherine Wheel PH & church. Disabled parking (only) at house.* Cream teas. Adm £3.50, chd free. Suns 21 June; 27 Sept (11-6). Visitors also welcome by appt no coaches.
5-acre plantsman's garden approached across a private ford. Many interesting and unusual trees and shrubs. Visitors can try their hand at identifying plants with the plant list. Home-made teas or plenty of space to eat your own picnic. Walled vegetable and fruit garden, lake, ponds, bog plantings and sweeping lawns. Horses, Dexter cattle and Jacob sheep. Gravel paths and slopes.

96 ◆ RHS GARDEN ROSEMOOR
Great Torrington EX38 8PH. The Royal Horticultural Society, 01805 624067, www.rhs.org.uk/rosemoor. *1m SE of Great Torrington. On A3124 to Exeter.* Adm £6, chd £2. Oct to Mar (10-5), Apr to Sept (10-6).
65-acre plantsman's garden plus woodlands; rhododendrons (species and hybrids), ornamental trees and shrubs, woodland garden, species and old-fashioned roses, scree and raised beds with alpine plants, arboretum. 2000 roses in 200 varieties, two colour-theme gardens, herb garden, potager, 220yds of herbaceous border, large stream and bog garden, cottage garden, foliage and fruit and vegetable garden.

97 ◆ ROCK HOUSE GARDEN
Station Hill, Chudleigh TQ13 0EE. Mrs D B & B Boulton, 01626 852134, www.therockgardens.co.uk. *8m SW of Exeter. A38 Exeter to Plymouth signed Chudleigh. S edge of town. Entrance at Rock Nursery.* Adm £3, chd free. Daily except Christmas week. For NGS: Suns 5, 26 Apr; 24 May; 7, 21 June; 26 July; 30 Aug; 13, 27 Sept; 4, 25 Oct (9-5).
Garden in ancient bishop's palace quarry with massive limestone rock. Delights for all seasons. Rare and unusual trees and shrubs. Massed bulbs in spring. Autumn brings one of the finest displays of cyclamen. Cave and ponds with koi and orfe. Walk with spectacular views of Dartmoor and

access to Chudleigh rock, glen and waterfall. Wheelchair access to part of garden only, tea shop and nursery.

♿ ☕

98 ROSE COTTAGE
Crowden Road, Northlew
EX20 3ND. Irene & Ron Oldale,
01409 221106. *6m NW of Okehampton. Off A386 at Hilltown Cross to Northlew (6m). In Northlew Square, NW corner, take rd signed Highampton. Follow signs. L after 400yds, garden 1/2 m. Limited parking if wet.* Home-made teas. **Adm £2.50, chd free. Suns 14, 21 June (2-5.30). Visitors also welcome by appt.**
2-acre naturalistic informal stroller's garden of winding grass paths and hidden views. Exuberantly-planted mixed herbaceous borders; attractive and productive kitchen garden with vegetables, fruit, herbs and flowers; mixed orchard with crab apple walk; bog and water garden; wild flower meadows; young woodland copse, all developed over last 10yrs.

🐕 ✿ ☕ ☎ 📞

Group opening

99 ROUSDON COTTAGE GARDENS
Rousdon DT7 3XW. *3m E of Seaton. On A3052 midway between Seaton and Lyme Regis. Look for roadside signs.* Home-made teas at both gardens. **Combined adm £3.50, chd free (share to Himalayan Learning). Suns 10 May; 14 June; 12 July; 9 Aug (11-5).**
Two delightful cottage gardens buried in the Devon countryside, each gardening organically and encouraging over 50 species of wild birds and animals from the tiny goldcrest to badgers, hedgehogs and the occasional deer. Sit and chat a while on sunny terraces or secluded benches whilst enjoying wonderful homemade cakes and scones. Photographic display 'Green Lane Cottage Garden in All Seasons'.

🐕 ✿ ☕

NEW CHARTON TREE COTTAGE
Jane & Sid Gibson. *Just off A3052 at Charton Cross, 1 1/2 m W of Lyme Regis*
S-facing garden at 500ft, just under 1 acre with 7 rooms, 2 herbaceous borders and water feature. Spring area planted with erythroniums, snowdrops,

---

bluebells, hellebores, pulmonaria plus unusual plants. Kitchen garden with raised beds. New hot border, summerhouse, greenhouse and numerous seating areas.

🐕 ✿

GREEN LANE COTTAGE
Green Lane. Toni & Helena Williams-Pugh, 01297 443712, helena@himalayanlearning.org. *On the edge of Rousdon Village just off A3052, 2m from Lyme Regis.* **Visitors also welcome by appt March to Sept, groups of 10+.**
Triple pond water feature, curving lawns and flowerbeds crammed with a succession of colour-themed flowers. Small church window set in tiny folly and sunken walled patio. Wooden staircase to pergola of antique carved pillars from Turkistan and dovecots for over 100 aviaried doves. Featured in 'The English Garden', 'Amateur Gardening' and 'Devon Country Life'.

🐕 ✿ ☎

---

100 ST MERRYN
Higher Park Road, Braunton
EX33 2LG. Dr W & Mrs Ros Bradford, 01271 813805, ros@st-merryn.co.uk. *5m W of Barnstaple. In centre of Braunton turn R at T-lights round Nat West Bank. At top of Heanton St turn L and immed R into Lower Park Rd. Continue until you see Tyspane Nursing Home on L then turn L into unmarked lane & R at top. Pink house 200yds on R. Parking where available.* Home-made teas. **Adm £3, chd free. Suns 19 Apr; 24 May; 21 June; 12 July (2-6). Visitors also welcome by appt.**
Very sheltered 3/4 -acre, S-facing, cottage garden with emphasis on scent, colour and all-yr interest. Thatched summerhouse leading down to herbaceous borders; many seating areas; winding paths through lawns, shrubs and mature trees. Fish ponds. New: Studio/gallery, grassy knoll, gravel garden and discreet resiting of greenhouse.

♿ 🐕 ✿ 🛏 ☕ ☎

101 ◆ SALTRAM HOUSE
Plympton PL7 1UH. The National Trust, 01752 333503, www.nationaltrust.org.uk. *3m E of Plymouth. S of A38, 2m W of Plympton.* **House and garden adm**

£9.20, chd £4.60, garden only adm £4.60, chd £2.30. **Garden open all yr, house Mar to Nov, please phone for details. For NGS: Thur 7 May; Sat 18 July (11-4.30).**
20 acres with fine specimen trees; spring garden; rhododendrons and azaleas. C18 orangery and octagonal garden house. (George II mansion with magnificent plasterwork and decorations, incl 2 rooms designed by Robert Adam). Good variety of evergreens, incl many tender and unusual shrubs, esp from the S hemisphere. Long grass areas with bulbs and wild flowers.

♿ 🐕 ✿ ☕

Garden at 500ft with 7 rooms . . .

---

102 SCHOOL HOUSE
Little Torrington, Torrington
EX38 8PS. Mr & Mrs M Sampson, 01805 623445. *2m S Torrington on A386. Village of Little Torrington signed, follow signs to village green, park here, walk 50yds along bridle path to School House.* Cream teas at Village Hall. **Adm £2.50, chd free. Suns 14 June; 26 July (2-5.30). Visitors also welcome by appt, no coaches.**
2/3 -acre informally planted cottage garden. Wildlife pond with adjacent 'natural' planting under old apple tree. 2 ornamental pools. Arbour and pergola with a variety of climbers. Trees, shrubs, herbaceous and annual planting with some colour-themed areas. Small raised bed for alpines. Village gardens open also, not for NGS.

🐕 ✿ ☕ 📞

103 SEDGEWELL COACH HOUSE GARDENS
Olchard TQ12 3GU. Heather Jansch, www.heatherjansch.com. *4m N of Newton Abbot. 12m S of Exeter on A380, L for Olchard, straight ahead on private drive.* **Adm £3, chd free. Suns 3, 10 May; Sats, Suns 22, 23, 29, 30 Aug (10-5).**

Heather Jansch, world-famous sculptor, brings innovative use of recycled materials to gardening. 14 acres incl stunning driftwood sculpture, fabulous views from thrilling woodland bluebell trail down to timeless stream-bordered water meadow walk, pools, herbaceous border, medicinal herb garden. Plentiful seating, come and picnic. Limited level wheelchair access.

104 ◆ SHAPCOTT BARTON ESTATE

(East Knowstone Manor), East Knowstone, South Molton EX36 4EE. Anita Allen, 01398 341664. *13m NW of Tiverton. J27 M5 take Tiverton exit. 6½ m to roundabout, take exit South Molton 10m, on A361. Turn R signed Knowstone (picnic area). Leave A361 at this point, travel 1¼ m to Roachhill, through hamlet, turn L at Wiston Cross, entrance on L ¼ m.* **Adm £3, chd free. Open Apr to Oct (10-4.30) for NCCPG collections. For NGS: Wed 8, Mon 13, Sat 18, Sun 19, Mon 27, Tue 28 July; Sat 1, Suns 2, 16, Mon 17 Aug (11-4.30).**
Large garden of 200-acre estate around ancient historic manor house. Wildlife garden. Rare swallowtail butterflies seen in 2006. Restored old fish ponds, stream and woodland rich in birdlife. Many exotic breeds of poultry can be seen here, showing how a garden can cope with wildlife on a working farm. Unusual fruit orchard. Narcissi in May. June is even more floriferous before the flowering burst in July/Aug of National Plant Collections *Leucanthemum superbum* (shasta daisies) and Buddleja davidii. No photography without permission. Featured in 'Gardens Illustrated', 'RHS The Garden' and 'Devon Country Garden'.

105 SHERWOOD

Newton St Cyres, Exeter EX5 5BT. John & Prue Quicke, 01392 851216. *2m SE of Crediton. Off A377 Exeter to Barnstaple rd, ¾ m Crediton side of Newton St Cyres, signed Sherwood, entrance to drive in 1¾ m.* **Adm £4, chd free (share to Newton St Cyres Parochial Church). Every Sun, 4 Jan 2009 to 28 Feb 2010 (2-5). Visitors also welcome by appt, large coaches must stop at bottom of drive, smaller coaches can turn at house.**
15 acres, 2 steep wooded valleys. Wild flowers, especially daffodils; extensive

collections of magnolias, camellias, rhododendrons, azaleas, berberis, heathers, maples, cotoneasters, buddleias, hydrangeas and late summer flowering perennials. Woodland garden with shade-loving perennials and epimediums. National Collections of Magnolias, Knaphill azaleas and berberis. Limited wheelchair access, steep in places.

106 SHOBROOKE PARK GARDENS

Crediton EX17 1DG. Dr & Mrs J R Shelley, 01363 775153, jack@shobrookepark.com, www.shobrookepark.com. *1m NE of Crediton. On A3072. Cream teas.* **Adm £3, chd free. Sats 25 Apr; 16 May; 13 June (2-5). Visitors also welcome by appt April/May/June only for groups of 15+.**
15-acre woodland garden laid out in mid-C19 incl extensive Portland Stone terraces with views over 200-acre park with ponds. In process of being restored with extensive new planting amongst old rhododendrons incl reconstructed Victorian rose garden.

Clearings blaze with wild flowers . . .

Group opening

107 SOUTH TAWTON GARDENS

EX20 2LP. *6m E of Okehampton. Park in village square, walk through churchyard. Home-made teas at Glebe House.* **Combined adm £4, chd free. Suns 7, 28 June (2-5.30).**
Small village built around Parish Church. Historic church rooms recently restored open to public. Display of paintings and photographs at Blackhall Manor.

BLACKHALL MANOR

Roger & Jacqueline Yeates
Small cottage garden around C16 thatched listed house (not open) on

N edge of Dartmoor. Planted with trees, shrubs and herbaceous perennials to give interest throughout the year. Cobbled paths and pond.

GLEBE HOUSE

John & Welmoed Perrin. *Turning next to Seven Stars. Glebe House facing at end of rd*
Space with backdrop of hills, moor and meadow. A ha-ha conceals a young vineyard; mature trees frame two ponds and living arches. Rockeries support well stocked borders; an original courtyard creates a small orangerie.

Group opening

108 SOUTHCOMBE GARDENS

Dartmoor, Widecombe-in-the-Moor TQ13 7TU. *6m W of Bovey Tracey. Take B3387 from Bovey Tracey. After village church take rd SW for 400yds then sharp R, signed Southcombe, up steep hill. After 200yds, pass C17 farmhouse & park on L. Alternatively park in public car park in village and walk. Home-made teas.* **Combined adm £3.50, chd free. Suns 10, 24, Mon 25, Sun 31 May; Suns 7, 14 June (2-5).**
Village famous for its Fair, Uncle Tom Cobley and its C14 church - the 'Cathedral of the Moor'. Featured in RHS 'The Garden'.

SOUTHCOMBE BARN

Amanda Sabin & Stephen Hobson
3-acre woodland garden with exotic and native trees between long lawn and rocky stream. Clearings blaze with wild flowers and survivor garden flowers. Meadow in recently-cleared area.

SOUTHCOMBE HOUSE

Widecombe-in-the-Moor. Dr & Mrs J R Seale, 01364 621365. **Visitors also welcome by appt May/June only.**
5 acres, SE-facing garden, arboretum and wild flower meadow with bulbs in spring and four orchid species (early purple, southern marsh, common spotted and greater butterfly). On steep slope at 900ft above sea level with fine views to nearby tors.

109 **NEW** **SOUTHERN COMFORT**
Meadfoot Sea Road, Torquay TQ1 2LQ. Dr Maciej Pomian-Srzednicki & Mrs Ewa Pomian-Srzednicka, 01803 201813, maciej@pomian.co.uk. $1/2$ m from Torquay Harbour. From harbourside clock tower take rd uphill towards Babbacombe. 1st R at T-lights, follow main rd up hill. Garden 200yds on L (opp Clevedon Hotel) after brow of hill. Light refreshments & teas. **Adm £2.50, chd free. Suns 14 June; 20 Sept (2-5). Visitors also welcome by appt March-June/Sept/Oct, min 5, max 15.**
$1/4$ -acre town plot, part-naturalistic planting; exotic/tender species rarely tried outside. Palms, ferns, agaves, aloes, bromeliads, aroids and numerous individualistic plants grow in the exceptional microclimate of Meadfoot Valley. Variety of microhabitats, spring-fed pond and rill. Emphasis on foliage. Specimens. Recommended for exotica enthusiasts. Children over 12 only, please. Featured in local press.

110 **SOWTON MILL**
Dunsford EX6 7JN. A Cooke & S Newton, 01647 252347/252263, sonianewton@sowtonmill.eclipse.co.uk. 7m W of Exeter. From Dunsford take B3193 S for $1/2$ m. Entrance straight ahead off sharp R bend by bridge. From A38 N along Teign valley for 8m. Sharp R after humpback bridge. Home-made teas. **Adm £3, chd free (share to Cygnet Training Theatre). Suns 5 Apr; 5 July (2-6). Visitors also welcome by appt.**
4 acres laid out around former mill (not open), leat and river. Part woodland with multitudes of wild flowers in spring, ornamental trees and shrubs, mixed borders and scree. Yr-round interest.

111 **SPILLIFORDS WILDLIFE GARDEN**
Lower Washfield, Tiverton EX16 9PE. Dr Gavin Haig, 01884 252422, gavinhaig@googlemail.com. 3m N of Tiverton. Take A396 Tiverton to Bampton rd, turn L over iron bridge signed Stoodleigh. Turn L again after crossing bridge marked Washfield, & L again on hill following Washfield sign.

Bridge is approx 2m from link rd roundabout. Spillifords is 1st house on L after Hatswell - some 400 metres onwards. Parking in top field. Home-made teas £2. **Adm £3, chd free. Visitors welcome by appt, no coaches please.**
Specialist wildlife garden leading down to R Exe. Banks and islands of mixed wild flowers and herbs. Many nesting birds, including flycatchers and warblers; breeding butterflies; reptiles. Ponds and marsh areas. About 50 nestboxes. Annually 30 different butterflies - including rare Marsh Fritillary. Picnic areas. About 4 acres. Kingfisher, dipper and otter frequent visitors. Featured in many television programmes illustrating Spillifords Wildlife Garden.

112 **SPRINGDALE**
Smeatharpe, Honiton EX14 9RF. Graham & Ann Salmon, 01823 601182. 8m N of Honiton. Park in field behind Village Hall, N end of Smeatharpe. Garden is through gate in hedge and down bridleway. Cream teas. **Adm £3.50, chd free (share to Blackdown Support Group). Sats, Suns, Mons 16, 17, 18 May; 11, 12, 13 July (2-6).**
Astride Devon/Somerset border, set high in the magnificent Blackdown Hills, is a developing 2-acre plantsman's garden with adjoining 16 acres of SSSI. Hundreds of wild orchids in flower early summer. Extensive planting of choice trees, shrubs and perennials, waterside and alpine beds complemented by cacti and auricula collections. Damp, acid garden designed for plants, wildlife and people to enjoy. Featured in 'Devon Country Gardener' and 'NCCPG Devon'.

Exotic/tender species rarely tried outside . . .

113 **SQUIRRELS**
98 Barton Road, Torquay TQ2 7NS. Graham & Carol Starkie, 01803 329241, calgra@calgra.freeserve.co.uk. From Newton Abbot take A380 to Torquay. After Focus DIY on L, turn L at T-lights up Old Woods Hill. 1st L into Barton Rd, bungalow 200yds on L. **Adm £3, chd free. Sat 1, Sun 2, Sat 8 Aug (2-5). Visitors also welcome by appt for groups 1st 2 weeks Aug only.**
Plantsman's small town garden landscaped with small ponds and 7ft waterfall. Interlinked areas incl Japanese, Italianate, Tropical. Specialising in fruit incl peaches, figs, kiwi. Tender plants incl bananas, tree fern, brugmansia, lantanas, oleanders, abutilons, bougainvilleas. Colourful pergolas and lawn area. Environmentally-friendly garden with rain water storage, large disguised compost heaps, home-made solar hot-water panel, many nesting boxes and ducks on slug patrol. Featured in 'Devon Life'. Winner Torbay in Bloom Environmentally Friendly & Wildlife Garden.

STOWLEYS
See Somerset & Bristol.

114 **SUMMERS PLACE**
Little Bowlish, Whitestone EX4 2HS. Mr & Mrs Stafford Charles, 01647 61786. 6m NW of Exeter. From Exeter/M5, A30 towards Okehampton, 10m turn to Tedburn St Mary, L at end of village, $3/4$ m to Heath Cross, L (Crediton), garden $3/4$ m on L, car park further on R. Heath Cross is 1m beyond Whitstone from Exeter. From Crediton, follow Whitestone rd (through Fordton) 3m, well-signed. Home-made teas. **Adm £3, chd free. Suns 19 Apr; 17 May; 14 June; 4 Oct (2-5). Visitors also welcome by appt, at least one day's notice please.**
Sizeable sylvan haven; sympathetic plantings on steep North slope, now with wooded valley and ponds plus new projects. Nature nurtured and enlivened with garden cultivars, many unusual. Single flowers and large leaves typify this relationship. Rustic (renewable) paths, steps and walkways lead to arbours, seats and follies. Climber-clad divisions create intimate areas around house with more quirky features. Arab mares and foals on view. Featured in National and local press.

115 TAIKOO

Belstone EX20 1QZ. Richard & Rosamund Bernays, 01837 840217, richard@bernays.net. *3m SE of Okehampton. Fork L at stocks in middle of village. 300yds on R. Park in field.* Cream teas. **Adm £3.50, chd free. Suns 26 Apr; 24 May (2-5). Visitors also welcome by appt.**
3-acre hillside moorland garden, restored over past 12yrs, recently extended to incl heathers and moorland plants. Interesting collections of rhododendrons, fuchsias, hydrangeas, magnolias, camellias, roses and other shrubs and trees. Herb garden and water features. Magnificent views over Dartmoor from terraces of Taipan's house (not open).

116 TAMARISKS

Inner Hope Cove, Kingsbridge TQ7 3HH. Barbara Anderson, 01548 561745, bba@talktalk.net. *6m SW of Kingsbridge. Turn off A381 at Malborough between Kingsbridge & Salcombe. 2m further, on entering Hope Cove, turn L at sign to Inner Hope. After 1/4 m, turn R into lane beneath Sun Bay Hotel. Tamarisks is next house. Park opp hotel or in lane (larger car park in Outer Hope, follow path leading to Inner Hope into lane).* Home-made teas. **Adm £2.50, chd free (share to Butterfly Conservation & BTO Birdwatch). Thur 16, Fri 17 July (11-6). Visitors also welcome by appt.**
Sloping 1/3 acre directly above sea with magnificent view. Garden is exciting with rustic steps, extensive stonework, ponds, rockeries, feature corners, patios, 'wild' terrace overlooking sea. Very colourful. Demonstrates what can flourish at seaside - notably hydrangeas, mallows, crocosmia, achillea, sea holly, convolvulus, lavender, sedum, roses, grasses, ferns, fruit trees. Bird and butterfly haven. Butterfly Conservation and BTO Birdwatch tables with representatives, pamphlets etc. Craft demonstration - glass blowing, enamel work. Featured in 'Devon Life'.

117 TANGLEWOOD

8 Perches Close, Membland, Newton Ferrers PL8 1HZ. Paul & Shirley Fleming. *12m E of Plymouth. From A379 between Yealmpton and Brixton at Kitley follow signs towards Newton Ferrers and Noss Mayo, L signed Bridgend. From Bridgend take rd inland signed Membland. At top of hill (1/2 m), Perches Close on R, garden at far end of cul-de-sac.* Home-made teas. **Adm £2.50, chd free. Suns 14 June; 26 July (2-6).**
Maturing plantsman's 3/4 -acre garden now 10 yrs old. Situated on SW-facing valley site and backing onto woods. Many unusual trees, shrubs and herbaceous plants providing yr-round interest and colour. Secluded seating areas give varied aspects of the garden, incl ponds with small stream and owners' ceramic sculptures.

> Fully working organic estate gardens . . . beautiful views . . .

118 1 TIPTON LODGE

Tipton St John. EX10 0AW. Angela Avis & Robin Pickering, 01404 813371. *3m N of Sidmouth. From Exeter take A3052 towards Sidmouth. L on B3176 at Bowd Inn toward Ottery St Mary. After 1 1/2 m turn into Tipton St John. After village sign, 1 Tipton Lodge is the second driveway on R about 100yds before Golden Lion PH. Parking for disabled only, other parking in village.* Home-made teas. **Adm £2.50, chd free. Sat 27, Sun 28 June (11-5). Visitors also welcome by appt.**
3/4 acre designed to reflect mid-Victorian house. Formal grass walks between double herbaceous borders and avenue of white weeping roses. Old shrub roses, small woodland area incl tree ferns, potager-style vegetable garden. All organic. Exuberant romantic planting.

TREBARTHA
See Cornwall.

119 NEW WALREDDON MANOR GARDENS

Whitchurch, Tavistock PL19 9EQ. Walreddon Manor Farm. *1 1/2 m from Tavistock. From Tavistock take A386 Plymouth rd, at cemetery R on mini r'about towards Walreddon onto Brook Lane. Continue for 1 1/2 m to manor on R.* Home-made teas. **Adm £4, chd free (share to Dartmoor Heritage Trust). Sun 28, Mon 29 June (12-5).**
Fully working organic estate gardens surrounding C15 manor house (not open). Productive and extensive terraced vegetable garden with cut flower bed. Wildflower meadow with roses. Brand new rose garden full of climbers, floribundas, T and shrub with old scented varieties. Orchard with wild flowers, apple store. At front, herbaceous borders, shrubs, climbers, mature magnolias, lawns, ha-ha, with beautiful views over parkland, Tavy Valley and beyond. Wildlife area with deep, dangerous ponds, wildflowers, fruit trees, mown paths and gentle woodland walk. Pond area not suitable for wheelchairs.

WAYFORD MANOR
See Somerset & Bristol.

120 4 WELLSWOOD HEIGHTS

Higher Erith Rd, Wellswood TQ1 2NH. Mr & Mrs S W Tiller, 01803 296387. *1m from Torquay town centre. From Torquay harbourside towards Babbacombe, Burlington Hotel on R. R after red post box on R into Lincombe Hill Rd then R at top, garden immed on L.* Home-made teas. **Adm £2.50, chd free. Sun 26 July (2-5). Visitors also welcome by appt June to Sept, max 20.**
Small exotic garden. Large variety of exotics incl palms, tree ferns, aloes and other unusual trees, shrubs and succulents mainly from S hemisphere. Featured in local press and on West Country ITV.

121 WESTCOTT BARTON

Marwood, Barnstaple EX31 4EF. Howard Frank, 01271 812842, westcott_barton@yahoo.co.uk, www.westcottbarton.co.uk. *4m N of Barnstaple. From Barnstaple 4m N to Guineaford, continue N for 1m. Turn L,*

signed *Middle Marwood and Patsford, 2nd L at Westcott Barton sign.* Cream teas. **Adm £3, chd free. Sun 24, Mon 25 May; Sun 30, Mon 31 Aug (2-6). Visitors also welcome by appt (no large coaches).**
2-acre developing valley garden with stream, bridge and several ponds. Wide variety of planting: rhododendrons, camellias, clematis, hydrangeas, gunnera, rose garden. Masses of interest. Garden surrounds C12 farmhouse (not open) with cobbled courtyard, range of outbuildings and water wheel.

  ✗ ⌷ ☕ ❀ ☎

⑫ WHITSTONE FARM
Whitstone Lane, Bovey Tracey TQ13 9NA. Katie & Alan Bunn, 01626 832258,
katie@whitstonefarm.co.uk. *¹/₂ m N of Bovey Tracey. From A382 turn toward hospital (signed opp golf range) after ¹/₃ m turn L at swinging sign 'Private road leading to Whitstone'. Follow lane uphill & bend to L. Whitstone Farm on R at end of long barn. Limited parking.* Home-made teas. **Adm £3, chd free.** Suns 10 May; 16 Aug (2-5). **Visitors also welcome by appt May to end Sept, groups welcome.**
Over 3 acres of steep hillside garden with stunning views of Haytor and Dartmoor. An aboretum planted 38yrs ago of over 200 trees from all over the world, incl magnolias, camellias, acers, alders, betula and sorbus. Water feature. Major plantings of rhododendron and cornus. New Aug opening date for flowering eucryphias.

✗ ✿ ⌷ ☕ ☎

⑬ WICK FARM GARDENS
Cookbury, Holsworthy EX22 6NU. Martin & Jenny Sexton, 01409 253760. *3m E of Holsworthy. From Holsworthy take Hatherleigh Rd for 2m, L at Anvil Corner, ¹/₄ m then R to Cookbury, garden 1¹/₂ m on L.* Light lunches & home-made teas. **Adm £3.50, chd free. Sun 17, Sat 23, Sun 24, Mon 25, Sun 31 May (11.30-6). Visitors also welcome by appt.**
3-acre garden, part arranged into rooms with fernery, small ornamental pond, borders, garden statues and park surrounding small lake with island. Long border developed in 2006 with large variety of plants. All-yr interest. Plants have been selected to attract bees and butterflies. Gravel paths, gentle slopes.

  ♿ ✿ ☕ ☎ ❀

> 2-acre developing valley garden with masses of interest . . .

⑭ ◆ WILDSIDE
Green Lane, Buckland Monachorum PL20 7NP. Keith & Ros Wiley, 01822 855755, wildside.plants@virgin.net. *¹/₄ m W of Buckland Monachorum. Follow brown signs to Garden House from A386. Past Garden House, continue straight on for 0.7m. Garden 300yds past village on L.* **Adm £3.50, chd free. Garden and nursery open Thurs only, 12 Feb to 29 Oct.** For NGS: Sats 9 May; 27 June; 19 Sept (10-5). Also open **The Cider House 27 June.**
Created from field since 2004 by ex Head Gardener of The Garden House. Wide range of habitats and different plant varieties are grown in a naturalistic style, giving displays of colour throughout the season. Featured in RHS 'The Garden', 'English Garden', 'Gardens Illustrated' and National press.

✗ ✿

⑮ ◆ WINSFORD WALLED GARDEN
Halwill Junction EX21 5XT. Aileen Birks & Mike Gilmore, 01409 221477,
www.winsfordwalledgarden.com. *10m NW of Okehampton. On A3079 follow brown tourism signs from centre of Halwill Junction (1m).* **Adm £5, chd £1.50 under 14. Daily 4 Apr to 31 Oct (9.30-5, last entry).** For NGS: Suns 21 June; 19 July; 16 Aug; 13 Sept (9.30-5).

Wander in some of the best, most ornate and innovative original Victorian greenhouses in the whole of the South West! Glorious summer flower garden overflows well beyond the original Victorian walls. 3000 plant varieties. Informative exhibition. Garden guides. Featured in 'Devon Country Gardener', 'Devon Life' & 'North Devon Journal'. Electric mobility vehicle available.

  ♿ ⌷ ☕ ❀

⑫⑥ WITHLEIGH FARM
Withleigh Village, Tiverton EX16 8JG. T Matheson, 01884 253853. *3m W of Tiverton. On B3137, 10yds W of 1st small 30mph sign on L, entrance to drive by white gate.* Cream teas. **Adm £3.50, chd free (share to Arthritis Research & Cancer Research).** Sat 9, Sun 10 May (2-5). **Visitors also welcome by appt.**
Peaceful undisturbed rural setting with valley garden, 25yrs in making; stream, pond and waterside plantings; bluebell walk under canopy of mature oak and beech; wild flower meadow, primroses and daffodils in spring: wild orchids in June. Dogs on leads please.

✿ ☕ ☎

WOLVERHOLLOW
See Dorset.

⑫⑦ WOOD BARTON
Kentisbeare EX15 2AT. Mr & Mrs Richard Horton, 01884 266285. *8m SE of Tiverton, 3m E of Cullompton. 3m from M5 J28. Take A373 Cullompton to Honiton rd. After 2m turn L signed Bradfield & Willand on Horn Rd for 1m, turn R at Xrds. Farm drive ¹/₂ m on L. Bull on sign.* Home-made teas. **Adm £3, chd free (share to Action Medical Research).** Sun 12, Mon 13 Apr (2-5); Mon 4, Tue 5 May (2-5.30). **Visitors also welcome by appt for groups of 20 or less.**
2-acre arboretum planted 58yrs ago with species trees on S-facing slope. Magnolias, two davidia, azaleas, camellias, rhododendrons, acers; several ponds and water feature. Autumn colour.

  ♿ ✗ ✿ ☕ ☎

⑫⑧ YONDER HILL
Shepherds Lane, Colaton Raleigh EX10 0LP. Judy McKay & Eddie Stevenson, 07864 055532. *3m N of Budleigh Salterton. On B3178 between Newton Poppleford and Colaton Raleigh, take turning signed to Dotton, then immed R into small lane. ¹/₄ m, 1st house on R. Ample parking.*

Adm £2.50, chd £1. Every Sun 22 Mar to 25 Oct incl; Fri 10 Apr; Bank Hol Mons 13 Apr; 4, 25 May; 31 Aug (1-5). Visitors also welcome by appt weekdays throughout the yr. 3$\frac{1}{4}$-acre paradise started 1992. Unconventional planting. Shady walks, sunny glades, young woodland, ponds, herbaceous borders, orchard, vegetables, wildlife areas incl large wildlife pond made 2007. Several collections, many surprises. A garden with 'soul', must experience to appreciate. Tea/coffee and biscuits available, make it yourself as you like it. Picnics welcome. Featured in 'Devon Life' & local press. Wheelchair available.

Arboretum
of over
200 trees
from all over
the world . . .

Devon County Volunteers

County Organisers and Central Devon area
Edward & Miranda Allhusen, Sutton Mead, Moretonhampstead TQ13 8PW, 01647 440296, miranda@allhusen.co.uk

County Treasurer
Julia Tremlett, Bickham House, Kenn, Nr Exeter EX6 7XL, 01392 832671, jandjtremlett@hotmail.com

Publicity
Alan Davis, Paddocks, Stafford Lane, Colyford EX24 6HQ, 01297 552472, alan.davis@theiet.org

Assistant County Organisers
North East Devon Dorothy Anderson, Ashley Coombe, Ashley, Tiverton EX16 5PA, 01884 259971, dorothyanderson@uku.co.uk
Plymouth Shirley Fleming, Tanglewood, 8 Perches Close, Membland, Newton Ferrers PL8 1HZ 01752 873185
     shirleyafleming@btinternet.com
Torbay Ruth Haslam, 45 Crossley Moor Rd, Kingsteignton TQ12 3LQ, 01626 335658
North Devon Jo Hynes, Higher Cherubeer, Dolton, Winkleigh EX19 8PP, 01805 804265, hynesjo@gmail.com
Exeter Margaret Lloyd, Little Cumbre, 145 Pennsylvania Road, Exeter EX4 6DZ, 01392 258315
South Devon Jo Smith, 2 Homefield Cottage, Sherford, Kingsbridge TQ7 2AT, 01548 531618, jofrancis5@btopenworld.com
South West Devon Michael & Sarah Stone, The Cider House, Buckland Abbey, Yelverton PL20 6EZ, 01822 853285,
     michael.stone@cider-house.co.uk
East Devon Peter Wadeley, Prospect House, Lyme Road, Axminster EX13 5BH, 01297 631210, wadeley@btinternet.com

DORSET

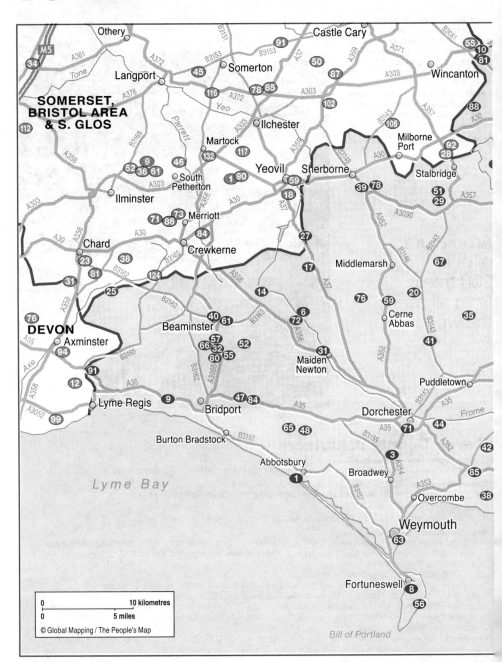

SOMERSET,
BRISTOL AREA
& S. GLOS

DEVON

Othery

Langport

Somerton

Castle Cary

Wincanton

Ilchester

Martock

South
Petherton

Ilminster

Yeovil

Sherborne

Milborne
Port

Stalbridge

Merriott

Chard

Crewkerne

Middlemarsh

Beaminster

Axminster

Maiden
Newton

Cerne
Abbas

Puddletown

Lyme Regis

Bridport

Burton Bradstock

Abbotsbury

Dorchester

Broadwey

Overcombe

Lyme Bay

Weymouth

Fortuneswell

0   10 kilometres
0   5 miles
© Global Mapping / The People's Map

Bill of Portland

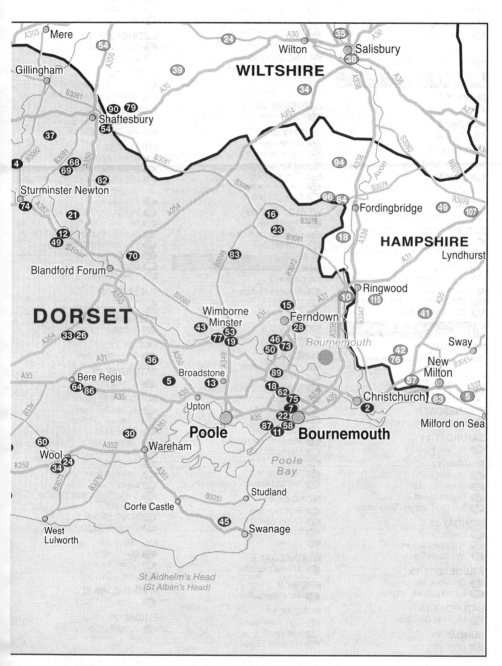

Opening Dates

February

SUNDAY 15
49 Lawsbrook

MONDAY 16
49 Lawsbrook

SUNDAY 22
72 Rampisham Manor

March

SUNDAY 1
71 Q

SUNDAY 8
27 Frankham Farm

SATURDAY 14
79 Shute Farm

SUNDAY 15
79 Shute Farm

SUNDAY 22
72 Rampisham Manor

SATURDAY 28
29 Grange Cottage
51 Manor Farm, Stourton Caundle

SUNDAY 29
29 Grange Cottage
34 Herons Mead
51 Manor Farm, Stourton Caundle
69 The Old Vicarage

April

WEDNESDAY 1
16 Cranborne Manor Garden

SUNDAY 5
10 Chiffchaffs
20 Domineys Yard

WEDNESDAY 8
23 Edmondsham House

SATURDAY 11
47 Knowle Farm

SUNDAY 12
19 Deans Court
27 Frankham Farm
34 Herons Mead
66 The Old Rectory, Netherbury

MONDAY 13
19 Deans Court
23 Edmondsham House
41 Ivy House Garden

WEDNESDAY 15
9 Chideock Manor
23 Edmondsham House

SATURDAY 18
60 Moreton Gardens

SUNDAY 19
5 Bexington

6 Broomhill
9 Chideock Manor
28 The Glade
60 Moreton Gardens
65 The Old Rectory, Litton Cheney
72 Rampisham Manor
75 46 Roslin Road South

WEDNESDAY 22
23 Edmondsham House
40 Horn Park
72 Rampisham Manor

SATURDAY 25
11 Chine View

SUNDAY 26
11 Chine View
13 Corfe Barn
18 44 Daws Avenue
22 35 Dunkeld Road
57 The Mill House
91 Wolverhollow

WEDNESDAY 29
11 Chine View
23 Edmondsham House
91 Wolverhollow

May

FRIDAY 1
2 Annalal's Gallery
45 Knitson Old Farmhouse
74 A Rosary Garden

SATURDAY 2
45 Knitson Old Farmhouse

SUNDAY 3
2 Annalal's Gallery
11 Chine View
14 Corscombe House
18 44 Daws Avenue
19 Deans Court
28 The Glade
34 Herons Mead
38 Holworth Farmhouse
41 Ivy House Garden
45 Knitson Old Farmhouse
58 10 Milner Road
66 The Old Rectory, Netherbury

MONDAY 4
4 Beech House
11 Chine View
19 Deans Court
58 10 Milner Road

WEDNESDAY 6
2 Annalal's Gallery

FRIDAY 8
2 Annalal's Gallery

SUNDAY 10
20 Domineys Yard
24 The Ferns
27 Frankham Farm

32 Hatchlands
36 Highwood Garden
42 Japanese Gardens
57 The Mill House
90 Wincombe Park

WEDNESDAY 13
2 Annalal's Gallery
53 Mayfield

FRIDAY 15
2 Annalal's Gallery
90 Wincombe Park (Evening)

SATURDAY 16
75 46 Roslin Road South
76 The Secret Garden

SUNDAY 17
4 Beech House
5 Bexington
8 Chesil Gallery & Chiswell Walled Garden
28 The Glade
36 Highwood Garden
55 Melplash Court
65 The Old Rectory, Litton Cheney
75 46 Roslin Road South
76 The Secret Garden
80 Slape Manor
89 1692 Wimborne Road

TUESDAY 19
63 'OLA'

WEDNESDAY 20
2 Annalal's Gallery

FRIDAY 22
2 Annalal's Gallery

SATURDAY 23
47 Knowle Farm

SUNDAY 24
7 6 Cawdor Road
12 Coombe Cottage
13 Corfe Barn
19 Deans Court
21 Duckdown Cottage
24 The Ferns
38 Holworth Farmhouse
49 Lawsbrook
50 Manor Farm, Hampreston
53 Mayfield
61 Mount Pleasant
66 The Old Rectory, Netherbury

MONDAY 25
4 Beech House
13 Corfe Barn
19 Deans Court

WEDNESDAY 27
2 Annalal's Gallery

FRIDAY 29
2 Annalal's Gallery

SATURDAY 30
84 Uploders Place

SUNDAY 31
22 35 Dunkeld Road
28 The Glade
34 Herons Mead
41 Ivy House Garden
54 Mayo Farm
64 The Old Post Office
86 Watendlath
91 Wolverhollow

June

TUESDAY 2
63 'OLA'

WEDNESDAY 3
54 Mayo Farm
71 Q
91 Wolverhollow

FRIDAY 5
84 Uploders Place

SATURDAY 6
16 Cranborne Manor Garden
29 Grange Cottage
43 Kingston Lacy
51 Manor Farm, Stourton Caundle

SUNDAY 7
7 6 Cawdor Road
8 Chesil Gallery & Chiswell Walled Garden
24 The Ferns
29 Grange Cottage
43 Kingston Lacy
51 Manor Farm, Stourton Caundle
53 Mayfield
64 The Old Post Office
66 The Old Rectory, Netherbury
72 Rampisham Manor
74 A Rosary Garden
86 Watendlath
89 1692 Wimborne Road

TUESDAY 9
66 The Old Rectory, Netherbury

WEDNESDAY 10
9 Chideock Manor
53 Mayfield
83 Stanbridge Mill

FRIDAY 12
45 Knitson Old Farmhouse

SATURDAY 13
45 Knitson Old Farmhouse
68 The Old School
69 The Old Vicarage
75 46 Roslin Road South

SUNDAY 14
5 Bexington
9 Chideock Manor
27 Frankham Farm
32 Hatchlands
38 Holworth Farmhouse
39 Honeycombe

42 Japanese Gardens
45 Knitson Old Farmhouse
50 Manor Farm, Hampreston
75 46 Roslin Road South
85 Warmwell House

MONDAY 15
65 The Old Rectory, Litton Cheney

TUESDAY 16
63 'OLA'

WEDNESDAY 17
6 Broomhill

THURSDAY 18
3 Ashton Farm

SATURDAY 20
31 Grovestall Farm

SUNDAY 21
3 Ashton Farm
7 6 Cawdor Road
8 Chesil Gallery & Chiswell Walled Garden
18 44 Daws Avenue
30 Greenacres
31 Grovestall Farm
55 Melplash Court
87 24a Western Avenue

WEDNESDAY 24
40 Horn Park

SATURDAY 27
70 3 Priory Gardens
81 Snape Cottage Plantsman's Garden
89 1692 Wimborne Road

SUNDAY 28
13 Corfe Barn
22 35 Dunkeld Road
34 Herons Mead
39 Honeycombe
56 Mews Cottage
62 4 Noel Road
64 The Old Post Office
70 3 Priory Gardens
81 Snape Cottage Plantsman's Garden
86 Watendlath

July

WEDNESDAY 1
2 Annalal's Gallery
39 Honeycombe

FRIDAY 3
2 Annalal's Gallery

SUNDAY 5
6 Broomhill
8 Chesil Gallery & Chiswell Walled Garden
18 44 Daws Avenue
39 Honeycombe

WEDNESDAY 8
2 Annalal's Gallery

FRIDAY 10
2 Annalal's Gallery

SUNDAY 12
5 Bexington
14 Corscombe House
26 5 Fosters Meadow
33 Hazel Lodge
35 Higher Melcombe Manor
38 Holworth Farmhouse
56 Mews Cottage
62 4 Noel Road
73 357 Ringwood Road
75 46 Roslin Road South

MONDAY 13
26 5 Fosters Meadow
33 Hazel Lodge

WEDNESDAY 15
2 Annalal's Gallery

FRIDAY 17
2 Annalal's Gallery

SUNDAY 19
2 Annalal's Gallery
8 Chesil Gallery & Chiswell Walled Garden
15 Cottesmore Farm
21 Duckdown Cottage
30 Greenacres
35 Higher Melcombe Manor
37 Hilltop
50 Manor Farm, Hampreston
85 Warmwell House

MONDAY 20
57 The Mill House (Evening)

WEDNESDAY 22
2 Annalal's Gallery
57 The Mill House (Evening)

FRIDAY 24
2 Annalal's Gallery
57 The Mill House (Evening)

SUNDAY 26
15 Cottesmore Farm
17 The Dairy House
37 Hilltop
56 Mews Cottage
64 The Old Post Office
86 Watendlath

MONDAY 27
17 The Dairy House

WEDNESDAY 29
2 Annalal's Gallery
67 The Old Rectory, Pulham
73 357 Ringwood Road

FRIDAY 31
2 Annalal's Gallery

August

SATURDAY 1
77 The Secret Garden at Serles House (Evening)

SUNDAY 2
- **2** Annalal's Gallery
- **8** Chesil Gallery & Chiswell Walled Garden
- **37** Hilltop
- **38** Holworth Farmhouse
- **67** The Old Rectory, Pulham
- **71** Q
- **77** The Secret Garden at Serles House
- **87** 24a Western Avenue

WEDNESDAY 5
- **2** Annalal's Gallery

FRIDAY 7
- **2** Annalal's Gallery

SUNDAY 9
- **5** Bexington
- **20** Domineys Yard
- **37** Hilltop
- **56** Mews Cottage

WEDNESDAY 12
- **2** Annalal's Gallery

FRIDAY 14
- **2** Annalal's Gallery

SATURDAY 15
- **68** The Old School
- **69** The Old Vicarage
- **74** A Rosary Garden

SUNDAY 16
- **10** Chiffchaffs
- **30** Greenacres
- **37** Hilltop
- **73** 357 Ringwood Road
- **77** The Secret Garden at Serles House

WEDNESDAY 19
- **2** Annalal's Gallery

FRIDAY 21
- **2** Annalal's Gallery

WEDNESDAY 26
- **2** Annalal's Gallery
- **6** Broomhill

FRIDAY 28
- **2** Annalal's Gallery

SATURDAY 29
- **77** The Secret Garden at Serles House (Evening)

SUNDAY 30
- **12** Coombe Cottage
- **19** Deans Court
- **77** The Secret Garden at Serles House

MONDAY 31
- **19** Deans Court
- **61** Mount Pleasant
- **77** The Secret Garden at Serles House

September

THURSDAY 3
- **82** Springhead

SATURDAY 5
- **19** Deans Court

SUNDAY 6
- **19** Deans Court
- **77** The Secret Garden at Serles House

FRIDAY 11
- **45** Knitson Old Farmhouse

SATURDAY 12
- **45** Knitson Old Farmhouse
- **77** The Secret Garden at Serles House (Evening)

SUNDAY 13
- **5** Bexington
- **45** Knitson Old Farmhouse
- **77** The Secret Garden at Serles House

SUNDAY 20
- **34** Herons Mead

October

WEDNESDAY 7
- **23** Edmondsham House

WEDNESDAY 14
- **23** Edmondsham House

SUNDAY 18
- **20** Domineys Yard

WEDNESDAY 21
- **23** Edmondsham House

MONDAY 26
- **82** Springhead

WEDNESDAY 28
- **23** Edmondsham House

November

SUNDAY 1
- **49** Lawsbrook

MONDAY 2
- **49** Lawsbrook

December

FRIDAY 4
- **77** The Secret Garden at Serles House (Evening)

SATURDAY 5
- **77** The Secret Garden at Serles House (Evening)

Gardens open to the public
- **1** Abbotsbury Gardens
- **10** Chiffchaffs
- **16** Cranborne Manor Garden
- **23** Edmondsham House
- **25** Forde Abbey Gardens
- **37** Hilltop
- **38** Holworth Farmhouse
- **43** Kingston Lacy
- **44** Kingston Maurward Gardens
- **46** Knoll Gardens
- **52** Mapperton Gardens
- **59** Minterne
- **60** Moreton Gardens
- **78** Sherborne Castle
- **81** Snape Cottage Plantsman's Garden
- **82** Springhead

By appointment only
- **48** Langebride House
- **88** Weston House

Also open by appointment
- **2** Annalal's Gallery
- **3** Ashton Farm
- **5** Bexington
- **6** Broomhill
- **8** Chesil Gallery & Chiswell Walled Garden
- **12** Coombe Cottage
- **20** Domineys Yard
- **28** The Glade
- **30** Greenacres
- **33** Hazel Lodge
- **34** Herons Mead
- **35** Higher Melcombe Manor
- **40** Horn Park
- **42** Japanese Gardens
- **45** Knitson Old Farmhouse
- **47** Knowle Farm
- **49** Lawsbrook
- **50** Manor Farm, Hampreston
- **53** Mayfield
- **56** Mews Cottage
- **57** The Mill House
- **61** Mount Pleasant
- **64** The Old Post Office
- **65** The Old Rectory, Litton Cheney
- **67** The Old Rectory, Pulham
- **72** Rampisham Manor
- **73** 357 Ringwood Road
- **75** 46 Roslin Road South
- **76** The Secret Garden
- **77** The Secret Garden at Serles House
- **83** Stanbridge Mill
- **86** Watendlath
- **89** 1692 Wimborne Road
- **91** Wolverhollow

The Gardens

❶ ◆ ABBOTSBURY GARDENS
nr Weymouth DT3 4LA. Ilchester
Estates, 01305 871412,
www.abbotsbury-
tourism.co.uk/gardens. *8m W of
Weymouth. From B3157 Weymouth-
Bridport, 200yds W of Abbotsbury
village.* **Please phone for opening
dates, times & adm prices.**
20 acres, started in 1760 and
considerably extended in C19. Much
recent replanting, very fine collection of
rhododendrons, camellias, azaleas.
Unique maritime micro-climate enables
a flourishing Mediterranean bank and
southern hemisphere garden to grow
rare and tender plants. In summer
there are palm trees, bananas, cannas;
ponds and streamside plantings.
Children's play area, sculpture trail,
plant sales, shop, aviaries and Colonial
tea-house.
♿ ✿ ☕

❷ ANNALAL'S GALLERY
25 Millhams Street, Christchurch
BH23 1DN. Anna & Lal Sims, 01202
567585, anna.sims@ntlworld.com.
*Town centre. Park in Saxon Square
PCP - exit to Millham St via alley at
side of church.* **Adm £2.50, chd free.
Suns 3 May, 19 July, 2 Aug; Weds,
Fris 1 May to 29 May; Weds, Fris
1 July to 28 Aug. Suns (1-5);
Weds/Fris (2-5).** **Visitors also
welcome by appt May/July/Aug.**
Enchanting 100 yr-old cottage, home
of two Royal Academy artists, with 32ft
x 12½ ft garden on 3 patio levels.
Pencil gate leads to clematis-covered
arch and small Victorian walled garden
filled with colour and scent of
honeysuckle and jasmine. Sculptures
and paintings hide among the flowers
and shrubs. Teas available at the
Ducking Stool Tea Rooms are nearby.
✖ ☎ ☎

APPLE COURT
See Hampshire.

❸ ASHTON FARM
Martinstown DT2 9HA. James &
Jenny Shanahan, 01305 889869,
jenny.shanahan@virgin.net. *3m SW
of Dorchester. From A35 take A354
towards Weymouth, after ¾ m R to
Winterborne Monkton, through gated
rd for 1½ m. After sharp R-hand bend,
L into drive to car park.* Cream teas.
**Adm £3.50, chd free. Thur 18, Sun
21 June (2-5).** **Visitors also welcome
by appt.**

Nestling below Maiden Castle this
exuberant garden, surrounded by
meadow and woodland, is largely
informal with an emphasis on attracting
wildlife. Overflowing with old-fashioned
roses, flowering shrubs and
herbaceous borders, visitors are
enticed into the walled garden or led
along secret paths, some steep, onto
pastoral views. Exhibition of paintings.
✖ ✿ ☕ ☎

AVON GLEN
See Hampshire.

❹ BEECH HOUSE
New Street, Marnhull DT10 1QA.
Linda & Peter Antell. *2m NE of
Sturminster Newton. From A30 take
B3092 signed Sturminster Newton. In
Marnhull, just past The Crown PH, 2nd
R beside church. Garden ¼ m on R,
just before Xrds.* Home-made teas.
**Adm £3, chd free. Mon 4, Sun 17,
Mon 25 May (10-5).**
Delight in discovering the intriguing
features and delectable array of flowers
in the series of garden rooms hidden in
the acre behind the house. Gravel
entrance.
♿ ✖ ✿ ☕

❺ BEXINGTON
Lime Kiln Road, Lytchett Matravers
BH16 6EL. Mr & Mrs Robin
Crumpler, 01202 622068. *5m SW of
Wimborne Minster. Opp old school at
W end of village.* Cream teas. **Adm
£2.50, chd free (share to Alzheimers
Society). Suns 19 Apr; 17 May; 14
June; 12 July; 9 Aug; 13 Sept (2-
5.30).** **Visitors also welcome by
appt.**
Colourful garden of ½ acre maintained
by owners, with mixed borders of
many interesting and unusual plants,
shrubs and trees. Bog garden of
primulas, hostas etc. Rockery,
collection of grasses and ferns, with
walkways over bog area connecting
two lawns, making a garden of interest
from spring bulbs to autumn colour.
♿ ✖ ✿ ☕ ☎

BRAEMOOR
See Hampshire.

BRAMBLE HAYES
See Devon.

❻ BROOMHILL
Rampisham DT2 0PU. Mr & Mrs D
Parry, 01935 83266. *11m NW of
Dorchester. From Yeovil take A37
towards Dorchester, 7m turn R signed*

*Evershot. From Dorchester take A37 to
Yeovil, 4m turn L A356 signed
Crewkerne; at start of wireless masts R
to Rampisham. Follow signs.* Home-
made teas June, July & Aug. **Adm £3,
chd free. Sun 19 Apr (2-6); Wed 17
June; Sun 5 July; Wed 26 Aug (2-5).
Also open Rampisham Manor 19
April, combined adm £6. Visitors
also welcome by appt May to Sept
incl.**
Delightful 1-acre garden in lovely
peaceful setting, which incorporates a
disused farmyard and paddock. Pretty
trellised entrance leads to an
abundance of island beds and borders
planted with shrubs, roses and many
unusual and interesting herbaceous
plants, giving yr-round colour. Lawns
gently slope down to large wildlife
pond and bog garden. Mown paths
take you around pond to less formal
area of mixed trees and shrubs. New
late summer border.
♿ ✖ ✿ ☕ ☎

BUCKLAND STEAD
See Hampshire.

> Hidden areas
> with ornamental
> features add to
> the garden's
> peaceful charm
> and interest . . .

❼ 6 CAWDOR ROAD
Talbot Woods, Bournemouth
BH3 7DN. David Fisher/Neil Hird. *1m
NW of Bournemouth centre. E of N
end of Glenferness Ave.* Cream teas.
**Adm £2.50, chd free. Suns 24 May;
7, 21 June (2-5).**
Secluded ⅓ acre developed by
present owners over last 12 yrs. S-
facing terrace with stone water feature.
Wide curving borders abundantly
planted with palm trees, shrubs and
perennials and sweeping lawns leading
to distant gazebo and rhododendron
and azalea beds beneath a canopy of
mature pines. Hidden areas with
ornamental features add to the
garden's peaceful charm and interest.
✖ ☕

CHERRY BOLBERRY FARM
See Somerset & Bristol.

Colour-themed cool and hot borders . . . secret garden with Mediterranean planting . . .

8 CHESIL GALLERY & CHISWELL WALLED GARDEN
Pebble Lane, Chiswell DT5 1AW. Mrs Margaret Somerville, 01305 822738, margaret@msomerville. fsnet.co.uk, www.chiswellcommunity.org. *3m N of Portland Bill. S of Weymouth. Follow signs to Portland; from Victoria Square turn R into Chiswell & immed R into Pebble Lane. Park in car park by Bluefish Restaurant.* Cream teas in Chiswell Walled Garden. **Adm £2.50, chd free (share to Chiswell Community Trust). Suns 17 May; 7, 21 June; 5, 19 July; 2 Aug (2-5). Visitors also welcome by appt.**
Small, delightful garden in lee of Chesil Bank. 2 courtyard gardens provide domestic adjunct to artists' studio. On upper level flowering plants of coastal regions have been naturalised. Information on the flora of Chesil Beach and the history of Chiswell is available with entrance ticket at Chesil Gallery. Both gardens, The Chesil Gallery and The Chiswell Walled Garden, a very successful community project, grow plants which are tolerant of extreme maritime situations. Green Pennant award winner. Partial wheelchair access in Gallery, full access in Walled Garden.
  ♿ 🐕 ❀ ☕ ☎

9 CHIDEOCK MANOR
Chideock, nr Bridport DT6 6LF. Mr & Mrs Howard Coates. *2m W of Bridport on A35. In centre of village turn N at church. The Manor is 1/4 m along this rd on R.* Home-made teas. **Adm £4, chd free. Wed 15, Sun 19 Apr; Wed 10, Sun 14 June (2-5).**
Large formal and informal gardens, some in process of development. Bog garden beside stream. Woodland and lakeside walks. Walled vegetable garden and orchard. Yew hedges and many mature trees. Lime walk. Herbaceous borders. Rose and clematis arches. Fine views.
♿ 🐕 ☕ 👒

10 ◆ CHIFFCHAFFS
Chaffeymoor, Bourton, Gillingham SP8 5BY. Mr & Mrs K R Potts, 01747 840841. *3m E of Wincanton. W end of Bourton. N of A303.* **Adm £3.50, chd free. 1st & 3rd Suns 15 Mar to 6 Sept incl Easter Sun. For NGS: Suns 5 Apr; 16 Aug (2-5).**
A garden for all seasons with many interesting plants, bulbs, shrubs, herbaceous border, shrub roses. Attractive walk to woodland garden with far-reaching views across Blackmore Vale.
🐾 ❀

11 CHINE VIEW
15a Cassel Avenue, Westbourne BH13 6JD. John & Jeannie Blay. *2m W of Bournemouth. From centre of Westbourne turn S into Alumhurst Rd, take 8th turning on R into Mountbatten Rd then 1st L into Cassel Ave.* **Adm £2.50, chd free. Sat 25, Sun 26, Wed 29 Apr; Sun 3, Mon 4 May (2-5).**
Unique Chine garden of 1/2 acre. Wooded coastal site, steeply banked and spanned by a bridge with 330 tonnes of Purbeck stone incorporated in the original construction. 2 ponds, formal lawn surrounded by clipped hedge, Palladian rotunda and sculptural pieces. Planting incl subtropical species, ferns, mature shrubs, azaleas, rhododendrons, pieris and hydrangeas together with numerous perennials. Due to steep steps and uneven paths the garden is unsuitable for the less mobile.
❀

12 COOMBE COTTAGE
Shillingstone DT11 0SF. Mike & Jennie Adams, 01258 860220, mja@bryanston.co.uk. *5m NW of Blandford. On A357 next to PO Stores on main rd. Parking advised in Gunn Lane.* **Adm £2.50, chd free. Suns 24 May; 30 Aug (2-6). Visitors also welcome by appt.**
1/3 -acre plantsman's mixed garden, delineated by walls, hedges and

arbours, with a long season of herbaceous and woody perennials, climbers, bulbs and self-seeding annuals (many unusual and subtropical, combining flower-power with bold foliage), densely packed broad borders, pots and large plant house.
❀ ☎

13 CORFE BARN
Corfe Lodge Road, Broadstone BH18 9NQ. Mr & Mrs John McDavid. *1m W of Broadstone centre. From main roundabout in Broadstone, W along Clarendon Rd 3/4 m, N into Roman Rd, after 50yds W into Corfe Lodge Rd.* Home-made teas. **Adm £2, chd free. Sun 26 Apr; Sun 24, Mon 25 May; Sun 28 June (2-5).**
2/3 acre on three levels on site of C19 lavender farm. Informal country garden with much to interest both gardeners and flower arrangers. Parts of the original farm have been incorporated in the design. A particular feature of the garden is the use made of old walls. Exhibition of paintings by local artist.
🐾 ❀ ☕

14 CORSCOMBE HOUSE
Corscombe DT2 0NU. Jim Bartos. *3 1/2 m N of Beaminster. From Dorchester A356 to Crewkerne, take 1st turn to Corscombe, R signed Church. Or A37 Yeovil to Dorchester, turn W signed Sutton Bingham/ Halstock/ Corscombe. Straight past Fox Inn, up hill, L signed Church.* Cream teas in Vicarage. **Adm £3.50, chd free. Suns 3 May; 12 July (2-5.30).**
Garden in grounds of former rectory with view of Church. Garden rooms with colour-themed cool and hot borders, sunny and shady beds, parterre, reflecting pool, part-walled vegetable garden, orchard and meadow. Secret garden with Mediterranean planting. Featured in 'GGG'.
❀ ☕

15 COTTESMORE FARM
Newmans Lane. BH22 0LW. Paul & Valerie Guppy. *1m N of West Moors. Off B3072 Bournemouth to Verwood rd. Car parking in owner's field.* Home-made teas. **Adm £3, chd free. Suns 19, 26 July (2-4.30).**
Luxuriant tropical planting; bananas, bamboos, gunneras and over 100 palms. Many rare plants incl beds dedicated to Australian and

S American species. Large herbaceous borders, grass beds and wild flower area. Fancy fowl and rare breed sheep making an acre of considerable interest.

16 ◆ CRANBORNE MANOR GARDEN
Cranborne BH21 5PP. Viscount Cranborne, 01725 517248, www.cranborne.co.uk. *10m N of Wimborne on B3078.* Adm £4, chd 50p, concessions £3.50. Weds Mar-Sept (9-5, last entry 4). For NGS: Wed 1 Apr; Sat 6 June (9-4).
Beautiful and historic garden laid out in C17 by John Tradescant and enlarged in C20, featuring several gardens surrounded by walls and yew hedges: white garden, herb and mount gardens, water and wild garden. Many interesting plants, with fine trees and avenues.

17 NEW THE DAIRY HOUSE
Behind Manor Farmhouse, Melbury Osmond, Dorchester DT2 0LS. John & Elizabeth Forrest. *6m S of Yeovil. A37, 6m S of Yeovil turn W. 1m into village, L at Xrds, park at village hall. Follow signs to garden.* Home-made teas. Adm £3, chd free. Sun 26, Mon 27 July (2-5).
1-acre S-facing garden previously a farmyard. Herbaceous borders and shrubs, good variety of garden trees, pond, productive vegetable patch and small orchard. Lovely views of surrounding countryside.

18 44 DAWS AVENUE
Wallisdown BH11 8SD. Carol & John Farrance. *3m W of Bournemouth. Going N from Wallisdown roundabout take 1st L into Canford Ave then 1st R into Daws Ave.* Home-made teas Apr, cream teas other days. Adm £2, chd free. Suns 26 Apr; 3 May; 21 June; 5 July (2-5).
Small town garden offering yr-round interest with emphasis in spring on camellias, acers and magnolias, underplanted with daphnes, hellebores, erythroniums and trilliums. Roses provide summer colour along with many rare hydrangeas and unusual perennials. Enjoy tea in the summerhouse where a view of the stream can be appreciated.

19 DEANS COURT
Deans Court Lane, Wimborne Minster BH21 1EE. Sir Michael Hanham. *¼ m SE of Minster. Just off B3073 in centre of Wimborne. Entry from Deans Court Lane - continuation of High St at junction with East St & King St over pavement & past bollard. Free parking.* Cream teas. Adm £4, chd free, senior citizens £3 (share to Friends of Victoria Hospital). Suns, Mons 12, 13 Apr; 3, 4, 24, 25 May; 30, 31 Aug; Sat 5, Sun 6 Sept. Sats (2-6), Suns (2-6), Mons (10-6).
Situated on R Allen close to town centre of Wimborne Minster. 13 acres of peaceful, partly wild gardens in ancient setting with lawns, mature specimen trees, woodland, orchard and herb garden surrounding historic house. Home to same family since 1548. Explore the country's 1st Soil Association accredited kitchen garden within C18 serpentine walls and enjoy home-made cream teas by the tranquil monastic fishpond. Organic produce from kitchen garden for sale. Tours of house and garden by prior written appointment. Gravel path, steps down to tea room.

Enjoy home-made cream teas by the tranquil monastic fishpond . . .

DICOT
See Devon.

20 DOMINEYS YARD
Buckland Newton, nr Dorchester DT2 7BS. Mr & Mrs W Gueterbock, 01300 345295, william@gueterbock.net, www.domineys.com. *11m N of Dorchester, 11m S of Sherborne. 2m E*

A352 or take B3143. Take 'no through rd' between Church & Gaggle of Geese. Entrance 100metres on L. Park & picnic in arboretum on R, 10metres before garden entrance. Home-made teas; soup lunch as well 18 Oct only. Adm £3.50, chd free. Suns 5 Apr; 10 May; 9 Aug (all 2-6); 18 Oct (12-4). Visitors also welcome by appt.
Attractive, all-seasons garden of 2½ acres, where change continues after 48 yrs. Informal, with some formality. Unusual trees; shrubs, herbaceous and bulbs. Pots and patios, fruit and vegetables. A garden to relate to come rain or shine. Small separate arboretum has matured in 14 yrs with many rarities. Gravel drive, some grass paths.

21 DUCKDOWN COTTAGE
Shaftesbury Road, Child Okeford DT11 8EQ. Richard & Sarah Mower. *6m N of Blandford. From Blandford take A350 N. Through Stourpaine village, ½ m turn L signed Child Okeford. On entering Child Okeford R at Memorial Cross signed Iwerne Minster. Garden ¾ m on L, parking 50yds past garden on R.* Home-made teas. Adm £2.50, chd free. Suns 24 May; 19 July (2-5).
Plantsman's garden on SW-facing slope overlooking open fields. Mixed cottage borders, formal areas and pretty meandering stream incorporating over 350 varieties of plants, many to encourage wildlife. Large Victorian planthouse, gravelled courtyard, raised deck terrace, kitchen garden and seating areas for quiet reflection.

22 35 DUNKELD ROAD
Talbot Woods BH3 7EW. Helga Von Ow. *1m NW of Bournemouth. Off Glenferness Ave.* Home-made teas. Adm £2.50, chd free. Suns 26 Apr; 31 May; 28 June (2-5).
Plant enthusiast's garden with many different plants offering all-yr interest. Emphasis on shrubs and trees suitable for an urban garden, also many interesting flowers and grasses. Wildlife particularly encouraged. Owners keep bees.

DURMAST HOUSE
See Hampshire.

EDGEWOOD
See Hampshire.

23 ◆ **EDMONDSHAM HOUSE**
Wimborne BH21 5RE. Mrs Julia Smith, 01725 517207. *9m NE of Wimborne. 9m W of Ringwood. Between Cranborne & Verwood. Edmondsham off B3081.* Teas Weds in April & Oct only. **House and garden adm £5, chd £1, under 5 free, garden only adm £2.50, chd 50p, under 5 free. Garden open Suns, Weds, 1 Apr to 28 Oct (2-5). House also open Weds, Apr & Oct only & Easter Sun/Mon (2-5). For NGS: Weds, 8 Apr to 29 Apr; Mon 13 Apr Weds, 7 Oct to 28 Oct (2-5).**
An historic 6-acre garden of C16 house. Interesting mature specimen trees and shrubs. Spring bulbs and blossom, autumn cyclamen. Early church, Victorian dairy and stable block, medieval grass cock pit. Walled garden with vegetables, fruit and traditional herbaceous borders planted to sustain long period of interest. Managed organically. Featured in 'The Observer'. Gravel paths.

  ♿ 🐾 ❀ ☕

Profusely planted . . . 'A lovely, secret garden' . . .

24 ● **THE FERNS**
East Burton, Wool BH20 6HE. John & Jill Redfern. *Approaching Wool from Wareham, turn R just before level crossing into East Burton Rd. Garden on R, just under a mile down this rd.* Home-made teas. **Adm £2, chd free (share to Dorset Air Ambulance). Suns 10, 24 May; 7 June (2-5).**
Profusely planted with varied herbaceous borders and shrubs. Interesting use of hard landscaping. Fruit and vegetable garden leads to small woodland garden and stream and a scene from Dorset clay-mining history. 'A lovely, secret garden' (Dorset Life & Country Gardener).

  ♿ ❀ ☕

25 ◆ **FORDE ABBEY GARDENS**
Chard TA20 4LU. Mr Mark Roper, 01460 221290, www.fordeabbey.co.uk. *4m SE of Chard.* Signed off A30 Chard-Crewkerne & A358 Chard-Axminster. Also from Broadwindsor B3164. **Gardens open daily throughout the yr (10 - last adm 4.30). For current adm prices please tel.**
30 acres, fine shrubs, magnificent specimen trees, ponds, herbaceous borders, rockery, bog garden containing superb collection of Asiatic primulas, Ionic temple, working kitchen garden supplying the restaurant. Centenary fountain, England's highest powered fountain. Enjoy England Awards for Excellence Silver Winner. Gravel paths, some steep slopes.

  ♿ ❀ ☕

FOREST LODGE
See Somerset & Bristol.

26 🆕 **5 FOSTERS MEADOW**
Winterborne Whitechurch, Blandford Forum DT11 0DW. Maureen & David Clarke. *6m SW of Blandford Forum. From A354 turn into Whatcombe Lane by tel box; approx 150yds, R over bridge into Fosters Meadows (no parking, please park sensitively in village).* **Adm £2.50, chd free. Sun 12, Mon 13 July (2-5). Also open Hazel Lodge.**
4 yr-old medium-sized level garden with gravel paths linking loose cottage-style planting. Small potager, patio, pergola, trelliswork.

  🐾 ❀

27 ● **FRANKHAM FARM**
Ryme Intrinseca DT9 6JT. Richard Earle. *3m S of Yeovil. A37 Yeovil-Dorchester; turn E; drive ¼ m on L.* **Adm £2.50, chd free. Suns 8 Mar (2-4); 12 Apr; 10 May; 14 June (2-5).**
3½ -acre garden, begun in 1960s by the late Jo Earle for yr-round interest. Perennials and roses round house and stone farm buildings. Extensive wall plantings incl roses and clematis, herbaceous borders, productive vegetable and fruit garden. Many unusual shrubs and trees, particularly hardwoods, shelter belts of trees forming woodland walks, under-planted with camellias, rhododendrons, hydrangeas and spring bulbs. Plenty to see from February onwards.

  ♿ 🐾

GANTS MILL & GARDEN
See Somerset & Bristol.

28 ● **THE GLADE**
Woodland Walk, Ferndown BH22 9LP. Mary & Roger Angus, 01202 872789. *¾ m NE of Ferndown centre. N off Wimborne Rd East, nr Tricketts Cross roundabout, Woodland Walk is a metalled but single carriageway lane with no parking bays; please park on main rd and access on foot (5 mins/330yds). Drop-off/pick-up for those with restricted mobility by arrangement only, please phone.* Home-made teas. **Adm £3, chd free. Suns 19 Apr; 3, 17, 31 May (2-5.30). Visitors also welcome by appt for groups of 20+ mid-Apr to mid-June.**
The name captures the setting. Award-winning 1¾ -acre Spring garden. Terraced lawns for lingering over tea. Woodland walks through blossom trees, wild anemones, primroses and bluebells. Extensive shrubbery incl camellia, azalea, rhododendron, kalmia. Stream and large wildlife pond with primulas, marginals, waterlilies. Bog garden, wet meadow, spring bulbs, herbaceous and mixed borders. Featured in 'Dorset Life'.

  ❀ ☕ ☎

190 GOLDCROFT
See Somerset & Bristol.

29 ● **GRANGE COTTAGE**
Golden Hill, Stourton Caundle DT10 2JP. Fleur Miles. *6m SE of Sherborne. Park at Manor Farm or The Trooper PH, walk up hill to thatched cottage on R.* Home-made teas at Manor Farm. **Adm £3.50, chd free. Sats, Suns 28, 29 Mar; 6, 7 June (2-5). Also open Manor Farm, combined adm £7.**
Come and discover the peace and tranquillity of a real cottage garden. Follow the meandering paths and find many flower borders, box and yew hedging, two ponds, topiary creatures and much more to delight you. Hellebores and spring bulbs a particular feature.

  🐾

30 ● **GREENACRES**
Bere Road, Coldharbour, Wareham BH20 7PA. John & Pat Jacobs, 01929 553821. *2½ m NW of Wareham. From roundabout adjacent to stn take Wareham-Bere Regis rd. House ½ m past Silent Woman Inn.* Cream teas. **Adm £3, chd free. Suns 21 June; 19 July; 16 Aug (2-5.30).**

Visitors also welcome by appt, 15+ incl coaches.
Approx 1-acre plantswoman's garden situated in Wareham Forest. Lawns punctuated by colourful island beds designed mainly for summer interest. Unusual perennials, shrubs and specimen trees. Themed areas and stone water feature with 2 ponds. Stumpery with collection of ferns and grasses. Bill & Ben's vegetable garden plus various breeds of poultry. Bonsai collection plus live music when possible.

Densely planted former yard . . .

③① GROVESTALL FARM
Chilfrome DT2 0HA. Mr & Mrs David Orr. *10m NW of Dorchester. From Yeovil take A37 to Dorchester. 10½ m turn R into Maiden Newton, R at T-junction and 1st R to Chilfrome. From Dorchester take A37 to Yeovil. 7m turn L into Maiden Newton, then as above. Follow signs. Caution on narrow final lane.* Home-made teas. **Adm £3, chd free. Sat 20, Sun 21 June (2-6).**
2-acre garden created around old farm buildings. Densely planted former yard, walled kitchen garden and 2 small, formal gardens linked by iris and lavender walk. The very rural setting includes a 6-acre 8 yr-old broadleaf wood with mown rides.

③② HATCHLANDS
Netherbury DT6 5NA. Dr & Mrs John Freeman. *2m SW of Beaminster. Turn R off A3066 Beaminster to Bridport Rd, signed Netherbury. Car park at Xrds at bottom of hill. 200yds up bridle path.* Home-made teas June only. **Adm £3.50, chd free. Suns 10 May; 14 June (2-6). Also open The Mill House 10 May, combined adm £5.**
Country hillside garden within 3 acres. Tall yew and box hedges bordering rose gardens, herbaceous and fuchsia beds and many hardy geraniums beneath a long Georgian brick wall. Open sloping lawns and croquet court, spring-fed pond and mature broadleaf trees.

③③ NEW HAZEL LODGE
24 Old Oak Way, Winterborne Whitechurch, Blandford Forum DT11 0TN. Brian & Pauline Roberts, 01258 881441, bb.roberts@virgin.net. *6m SW of Blandford Forum. From A354 turn into Whatcombe Lane signed Winterborne Stickland, Old Oak Way 2nd L, garden 100yds on R. Limited parking, please park sensitively in village.* Cream teas. **Adm £2.50, chd free. Sun 12, Mon 13 July (2-5). Also open 5 Fosters Meadow. Visitors also welcome by appt Mons only, May/June/July, no coaches.**
Relaxing, medium-sized garden maintained by owners. Informal colourful mixed borders of shrubs, roses, perennials, acers, azaleas, rhododendrons. Seating areas give a variety of aspects of garden.

HEDDON HALL
See Devon.

③④ HERONS MEAD
East Burton Road, East Burton, Wool BH20 6HF. Ron & Angela Millington, 01929 463872, ronamillington@btinternet.com. *6m W of Wareham on A352. Approaching Wool from Wareham, turn R just before level crossing into East Burton Rd. Herons Mead ¾ m on L.* Home-made teas. **Adm £2.50, chd free. Suns 29 Mar; 12 Apr; 3, 31 May; 28 June; 20 Sept (2-5). Visitors also welcome by appt for groups of 10+.**
Long ½ -acre garden winding through plant-filled borders, island beds, tiny orchard, kitchen garden, exuberant cottage garden with old roses, finally circling a woodland garden. Spring bulbs, hellebores, epimediums, pulmonarias and foxgloves; grasses and a riot of late-summer colour. Very wildlife friendly. Cactus collection. Teas served around painted chattelhouse.

③⑤ HIGHER MELCOMBE MANOR
Melcombe Bingham DT2 7PB. Mr M C Woodhouse & Mrs L Morton, 01258 880251. *11m NE of Dorchester. Puddletown exit on A35. Follow signs for Cheselbourne then Melcombe Bingham.* Home-made teas. **Adm £3.50, chd free. Suns 12, 19 July (12-5). Visitors also welcome by appt for groups of 20+.**

Approached through a lime avenue up private rd, the 2-acre garden is set in quiet valley surrounded by downland. Traditional English garden around C16 manor house and chapel with herbaceous beds, roses and magnificent copper beech and wonderful woodland views.

③⑥ HIGHWOOD GARDEN
Charborough Park, Wareham BH20 7EW. H W Drax Esq. *6m E of Bere Regis. Behind long wall on A31 between Wimborne & Bere Regis. Enter park by Almer lodge if travelling from W, or Blandford or Lion Lodges if travelling from E. Follow signpost to Estate Office, then Highwood Garden.* Home-made teas. **Adm £4, chd £2 (share to St Mary's Church, Almer & St Mary's Church, Morden). Suns 10, 17 May (2.30-6).**
Large woodland garden with rhododendrons and azaleas.

③⑦ ◆ HILLTOP
Woodville, Stour Provost SP8 5LY. Josse & Brian Emerson, 01747 838512, www.hilltopgarden.co.uk. *5m N of Sturminster Newton. On B3092 turn R at Stour Provost Xrds, signed Woodville. After 1¼ m thatched cottage on R.* **Adm £2, chd free. Every Thur June, July, Aug (2-6), groups welcome. For NGS: Suns 19 July to 16 Aug incl (2-6).**
During summer, the garden here at Hilltop is a gorgeous riot of colour and scent, the 250 yr-old thatched cottage barely visible amongst the greenery and flowers. Unusual and interesting annuals and perennials alongside traditional and familiar plants like phlox, roses, asters and dahlias boldly combine to make a spectacular display. Nursery open Thurs, Mar-Sept.

HINTON ADMIRAL
See Hampshire.

③⑧ ◆ HOLWORTH FARMHOUSE
Holworth, nr Owermoigne DT2 8NH. Anthony & Philippa Bush, 01305 852242, www.inarcadia-gardendesign.co.uk. *7m E of Dorchester. 1m S of A352. Follow signs to Holworth. Through farmyard with duckpond on R. 1st L after 200yds. Ignore 'no access' signs.* Teas on NGS days. **Adm £3.50, chd free. Weds (2-6) 6 May to 26 Aug incl, groups by appt, teas may be**

available on request. For NGS: Sun 3, 24 May; 14 June; 12 July; 2 Aug (2-6).

Over past 30yrs this unique and peaceful setting has been transformed into a garden with a range of styles and wide variety of features. Here you have the formal and informal, light and shade, running and still water and places to explore. Planted with a wide range of mature and unusual trees, shrubs and perennials and surrounded by stunning views. We are also experimenting with hydroponics, with emphasis on water conservation. Having at some time been the rest home for the Monks of Milton Abbey, this garden makes an ideal place for retreat. Featured in 'Dorset Gardener'. Partial wheelchair access.

  ♿ 🐕 ❀ ☕

39 HONEYCOMBE
13 Springfield Crescent, Sherborne DT9 6DN. Jean & Ted Gillingham. *From A352 (Horsecastle Lane), past Skippers PH, turn into Wynnes Rise then 1st L.* Home-made teas. **Adm £2.50, chd free. Suns 14, 28 June; Wed 1, Sun 5 July (1.30-5).**
Many varieties of clematis scramble through trees, over arches and amongst a sumptuous display of roses, underplanted with a wide variety of herbaceous perennials in colour-themed borders. Teas on the terrace. Winner Sherborne in Bloom for 'My Secret Garden'.

  ❀ ☕

40 HORN PARK
Tunnel Rd, Beaminster DT8 3HB. Mr & Mrs David Ashcroft, 01308 862212. *1½ m N of Beaminster. On A3066 from Beaminster, L before tunnel (see signs).* Home-made teas. **Adm £4, chd free. Weds 22 Apr; 24 June (2-5). Visitors also welcome by appt incl groups Tues to Thurs only, Apr to Oct, teas by arrangement.**
Large garden with magnificent view to sea. Plantsman's garden, many rare plants and shrubs in terraced, herbaceous, rock and water gardens. Woodland garden and walks in bluebell woods. Good autumn colouring. Wild flower meadow with 164 varieties incl orchids. Partial wheelchair access.

  ♿ ☕ ☎

41 IVY HOUSE GARDEN
Piddletrenthide DT2 7QF. Bridget Bowen. *9m N of Dorchester. On B3143. In middle of Piddletrenthide village, opp PO/village stores near Piddle Inn.* Home-made teas. **Adm £3, chd free. Mon 13 Apr; Suns 3, 31 May (2-5).**
Unusual and challenging ½-acre plantsman's garden set on steep hillside, with fine views. Themed areas and mixed borders, wildlife ponds, propagating garden, Mediterranean garden, greenhouses and polytunnel, chickens and bees, nearby allotment. Daffodils, tulips, violets and hellebores in quantity for spring openings. Come prepared for steep terrain and a warm welcome. Plant stall.

  🐕 ❀ ☕

42 JAPANESE GARDENS
38 Bingham's Road, Crossways DT2 8BW. Mr & Mrs Geoffrey Northcote, 01305 854538. *6m E of Dorchester. Off Dick O th' Banks Rd, & the B3390. Parking in village.* **Adm £3, chd £1. Suns 10 May; 14 June (1-5). Visitors also welcome by appt May to Sept, max 16 persons.**
Two unusual small gardens planned by designer/owner. Front garden features a green 'Turtle' island, pebble sea and contrasting yellow/blue borders. 'Sansui' and 'Moon Gate' mural paintings. Rear garden 26ft x 36ft symbolises 'River of Life' with 'Moon Waves' bridge, Torre gateway, railed paved terrace, hand-carved red granite features amid contrasting red/green foliage and flower forms. Design exhibition in garden room.

  🐕 ☎

43 ♦ KINGSTON LACY
Wimborne Minster BH21 4EA. The National Trust, 01202 883402, www.nationaltrust.org.uk. *1½ m W of Wimborne Minster. On the Wimborne-Blandford rd B3082.* **House and garden adm £10, chd £5, garden only adm £5, chd £2.50. 14 Mar to 1 Nov incl, house closed Mons, Tues. For NGS: Sat 6, Sun 7 June (10.30-6).**
43 acres of garden, 9 acres of lawn. Lime avenue, rhododendrons, azaleas and National Collection of convallarias. Parterre and sunk gardens planted with Edwardian schemes, spring and summer, incl tulips, hyacinths, begonias and heliotrope. Victorian fernery contains 35 varieties and National Collection of Anemone nemorosa. Rotunda planted with roses incl 'Bonica', 'Cardinal Hume', 'Nozomi' and 'Amber Queen'. Japanese garden restored to Henrietta Bankes' creation of 1910. Gravel paths and slopes.

  ♿ 🐕 ❀ NCCPG ☕

Green 'Turtle' island, pebble sea and contrasting yellow/blue borders . . .

44 ♦ KINGSTON MAURWARD GARDENS
Dorchester DT2 8PY. Kingston Maurward College, 01305 215003, www.kmc.ac.uk/gardens. *1m E of Dorchester. Off A35. Follow brown Tourist Information signs.* **Adm £5, chd £3, concessions £4.50. Open daily 5 Jan to 20 Dec (10-5).**
National Collections of penstemons and salvias. Classic Georgian mansion (not open) set in 35 acres of gardens laid out in C18 and C20 with 5-acre lake. Terraces and gardens divided by hedges and stone balustrades. Stone features and interesting plants. Elizabethan walled garden laid out as demonstration. Nature and tree trails. Animal park. Partial wheelchair access. Gravel paths, steep slopes (alternative, longer, routes available).

  ♿ 🐕 ❀ NCCPG ☕

45 KNITSON OLD FARMHOUSE
nr Swanage BH20 5JB. Rachel & Mark Helfer, 01929 421681, rachel@knitson.co.uk, www.knitson.co.uk. *1m NW of Swanage. 3m E of Corfe Castle. Signed L off A351 Knitson. Ample parking in yard or in adjacent field.* Cream teas. **Adm £2.50, chd 50p. Fris, Sats, Suns 1, 3 May; 12, 13, 14 June; 11, 12, 13 Sept (1-5). Visitors also welcome by appt for individuals or groups, no coaches larger than 30 seater. Cream teas/light meals available on request for group visits.**
Mature cottage garden. Herbaceous borders, rockeries, climbers, shrubs - 40 hostas. Large organic kitchen garden for self-sufficiency in fruit and vegetables incl kiwis! Many Roman and medieval Purbeck stone artefacts used in garden design, with ancient stone cottage and moon-arch as backdrops. Paving, gravel paths, slopes.

  ♿ 🐕 ❀ ☕ ☎

46 ◆ **KNOLL GARDENS**
Hampreston BH21 7ND. Mr Neil
Lucas, 01202 873931,
www.knollgardens.co.uk. 2¹/₂ m W of
Ferndown. ETB brown signs from A31.
Large car park. Adm £5.25, chd
£3.75, concessions £4.50. Tues to
Suns May to Nov incl (10-5). Other
times on website.
Exciting collection of grasses and
perennials thrives within an informal
setting of mature and unusual trees,
shrubs and pools, creating a relaxed
and intimate atmosphere.
Mediterranean-style gravel garden,
eye-catching Dragon Garden and
Decennium border planted in the
naturalistic style. Nationally acclaimed
nursery specialising in grasses and
perennials. National Collections of
pennisetum, deciduous ceanothus and
phygelius. Featured on BBC TV/radio
and in National Press and RHS 'The
Garden'. Some slopes. Gravel, grass
and bark paths.
&. ✗ ⌖ NCCPG ☕

47 **KNOWLE FARM**
Uploders, nr Bridport DT6 4NS.
Alison & John Halliday, 01308
485492,
info@knowlefarmbandb.com. 1¹/₂ m
E of Bridport. Leave A35 signed to
Uploders about 2m E of Bridport. Turn
back under A35 to reach Uploders.
Turn L at T-junction (Crown Inn on L).
Knowle Farm is 200yds on R, opp
chapel. Careful roadside parking unless
using Crown Inn (lunches served).
Home-made teas. Adm £3.50, chd
free. Sats 11 Apr; 23 May (1-6).
Visitors also welcome by appt.
1-acre informal valley garden on
3 levels with slopes and steps
bordered by R Asker in conservation
area. Tranquil setting with many restful
seating areas. Wide variety of
interesting and unusual plants.
Extensive planting around old trees
and mature shrubs. Bog garden, rose
walk, small orchard meadow, riverside
walk, kitchen garden, hens.
Plantaholic's greenhouse. Partial
wheelchair access, some steep grass
slopes.
&. ⌖ ⌂ ☕ ☎

48 **LANGEBRIDE HOUSE**
Long Bredy DT2 9HU. Mrs J
Greener, 01308 482257. 8m W of
Dorchester. S off A35, well signed. 1st
gateway on L in village. Adm £3.50,
chd free. Visitors welcome by appt.
Substantial old rectory garden with
many designs for easier management.

200-yr-old beech trees, pleached
limes, yew hedges, extensive
collections of spring bulbs, herbaceous
plants, flowering trees, shrubs and
alpines. Some steep slopes.
&. ✗ ☎

49 **NEW LAWSBROOK**
Brodham Way, Shillingstone
DT11 0TE. Clive, Faith & Gina
Nelson, 01258 860148,
cne7obl@aol.com. 5m NW of
Blandford. Follow signs to
Shillingstone on A357. Turn off
A357 at PO, continue up Gunn
Lane, 2nd junction on R, 1st house
on R (200yds). Home-made teas.
Adm £3.50, chd free. Sun 15,
Mon 16 Feb; Sun 24 May; Sun
1, Mon 2 Nov (10-2). Also open
Coombe Cottage 24 May.
Visitors also welcome by appt.
6 acres with over 200 tree species,
many mature and unusual, incl
oaks, acers and redwoods.
Herbaceous and formal borders,
wildflower and wildlife areas,
fernery. Feb: extensive snowdrops,
hellebores and bulbs. Autumn:
varied and spectacular colour.
Relaxed and friendly, good
opportunity for family walks in
wildlife/stream/meadow areas.
Children and dogs welcome. In
May, village cricket club stalls incl
tombola, cake and plant sale,
children's games. Gravel entrance,
stream area, boggy.
&. ⌖ ☕ ☎

LIFT THE LATCH
See Somerset & Bristol.

THE LITTLE COTTAGE
See Hampshire.

**MACPENNYS WOODLAND
GARDEN & NURSERIES**
See Hampshire.

50 **MANOR FARM,
HAMPRESTON**
BH21 7LX. Guy & Anne Trehane,
01202 574223. 2¹/₂ m E of Wimborne,
2¹/₂ m W of Ferndown. From Canford
Bottom roundabout on A31, take exit
B3073 Ham Lane. ¹/₂ m turn R at
Hampreston Xrds. House at bottom of
village. Home-made teas. Adm £3,
chd free. Suns 24 May; 14 June; 19
July (2-5). Visitors also welcome by
appt.
Traditional farmhouse garden designed
and cared for by 3 generations of the

Trehane family who have farmed here
for over 90yrs. Garden now being
restored and thoughtfully replanted
with herbaceous borders and rose
beds within box and yew hedges.
Mature shrubbery, water and bog
garden. Dorset hardy plant society sale
on all open days.
&. ✗ ⌖ ☕ ☎

51 **MANOR FARM, STOURTON
CAUNDLE**
Stourton Caundle DT10 2JW. Mr &
Mrs O S L Simon. 6m E of Sherborne,
4 m W of Sturminster Newton. From
Sherborne take A3030. At Bishops
Caundle, L signed Stourton Caundle.
After 1¹/₂ m, L opp Trooper Inn in
middle of village. Home-made teas.
Adm £4, chd free. Sats, Suns 28,
29 Mar; 6, 7 June (2-5). Also open
Grange Cottage, combined entry
£7.
C17 farmhouse and barns with walled
garden in middle of village. Mature
trees, shrubberies, herbaceous
borders, lakes and vegetable garden.
Lovingly created over last 40 yrs by
current owners.
✗ ☕

6 acres with over 200 tree species . . .

52 ◆ **MAPPERTON GARDENS**
nr Beaminster DT8 3NR. The Earl &
Countess of Sandwich, 01308
862645, www.mapperton.com. 6m N
of Bridport. Off A35/A3066. 2m SE of
Beaminster off B3163. House and
garden adm £8.50, chd £4, under 5s
free, garden only adm £4.50, chd £2.
Sun-Fri Mar to Oct.
Terraced valley gardens surrounding
Tudor/Jacobean manor house. On
upper levels, walled croquet lawn,
orangery and Italianate formal garden
with fountains, topiary, grottos, ponds
and herbaceous borders. Below, C17
summerhouse, fishponds, topiary and
borders. Lower garden with specimen
shrubs and rare trees, leading to
woodland and spring gardens. Partial
wheelchair access, upper levels only.
Featured in 'In Britain', 'Dorset Country
Gardener' and 'Dorset Echo'.
&. ✗ ⌖ ☕

53 MAYFIELD
4 Walford Close, Wimborne
BH21 1PH. Mr & Mrs Terry Wheeler,
01202 849838. ½ m N of Wimborne.
B3078 out of Wimborne, R into Burts
Hill, 1st L into Walford Close. Home-
made teas. **Adm £2, chd free. Wed
13, Sun 24 May; Sun 7, Wed 10
June (2-5). Visitors also welcome by
appt May/June only.**
Town garden of approx ¼ acre.
Front: formal hard landscaping planted
with drought-resistant shrubs and
perennials incl cistus, salvias and
sedum. Shady area has wide variety of
hostas. Back: contrasts with winding
beds separated by grass paths and
arches. Ferns, euphorbia, geraniums
and many other perennials. Pond and
greenhouses containing succulents.
New beds for 2009.
❀ ☕ ☎

54 MAYO FARM
Higher Blandford Road, Shaftesbury
SP7 0EF. Robin & Trish Porteous.
½ m E of Shaftesbury. On B3081
Shaftesbury to Blandford rd on
outskirts of Shaftesbury. Home-made
cream teas. **Adm £3, chd free. Sun
31 May; Wed 3 June (2-6).**
2-acre garden, with walled areas,
ponds and herbaceous borders,
which has spectacular views of
Melbury Hill and the edge of the
Blackmore Vale.
✖ ❀ ☕

55 MELPLASH COURT
Melplash DT6 3UH. Mrs Timothy
Lewis. 4m N of Bridport. On A3066,
just N of Melplash. Turn W & enter
between main gates & long ave of
chestnut trees. Home-made teas.
**Adm £4.50, chd free. Suns 17 May;
21 June (2-6).**
Gardens, originally designed by Lady
Diana Tiarks, continue to evolve and
consist of park planting, bog garden,
croquet lawn and adjacent borders.
Formal kitchen garden and herb
garden, ponds, streams and lake; new
borders and areas of interest are
added and opened up each yr.
❀ ☕

56 MEWS COTTAGE
34 Easton Street, Portland DT5 1BT.
Peter & Jill Pitman, 01305 820377,
penstemon@waitrose.com. 3m S of
Weymouth. Situated on top of the
Island, 50yds past Punchbowl Inn,
small lane on L. Park in main street &
follow signs. Home-made teas. **Adm
£2, chd free. Suns 28 June; 12, 26**

July; 9 Aug (2-5). Visitors also
welcome by appt for groups of 10+
1 June to 31 Aug.
Reorganisation complete: new paths,
new beds for National Collection of
cultivar Penstemon, also raised crevice
bed for species Penstemon which
were grown from APS seed.
Agapanthus (107+), Southern
Hemisphere and Himalayan beauties
now reside in their own bed, bordered
by another raised bed of hardy orchids.
We are delighted with the result - do
come and see. Commission pottery by
Tiffany. 2 steps to WC.
♿ ✖ ❀ **NCCPG** ☕ ☎

57 THE MILL HOUSE
Crook Hill, Netherbury DT6 5LX.
Michael & Giustina Ryan, 01308
488267,
themillhouse@dsl.pipex.com. 1m S
of Beaminster. Turn R off A3066
Beaminster to Bridport rd at signpost
to Netherbury. Car park at Xrds at
bottom of hill. Cream teas. **Adm £3.50,
chd free. Sun 26 Apr; Sun 10 May
(2-6). Evening Openings £3, chd
free, wine, Mon 20, Wed 22, Fri 24
July (5.30-8). Also open 10 May
Hatchlands, joint adm £5. Visitors
also welcome by appt for groups
of 6+.**
Several small gardens arranged round
the Mill, its stream and pond, incl
formal walled garden, terraced flower
garden, vegetable garden and mill
stream garden. Emphasis on scented
flowers, hardy geraniums, lilies, spring
bulbs, clematis and water irises.
Remaining 4 acres planted with a wide
variety of trees: magnolias, fruit trees,
acers, oaks, eucalyptus, birches,
liriodendrons, nothofagus, willows,
alders and conifers. Partial wheelchair
access. Featured on ITV West.
♿ ❀ ☕ ☎

58 10 MILNER ROAD
Westbourne BH4 8AD. Mr & Mrs
Colin Harding. 1½ m W of
Bournemouth. E of Westbourne on
Poole Rd. S at T-lights into Clarendon
Rd. Cross over Westcliff Rd into
Westovercliff Dr. 1st R, then 1st L and
1st R into Milner Rd. Home-made teas.
**Adm £3, chd free. Sun 3, Mon 4 May
(10.30-5).**
Modern clifftop garden designed and
constructed by Colin Harding in 1986
in a natural style with key formal
accents incl many natural driftwood
sculptures. Wide range of fruit and
specimen trees encl by mature holly
and rhododendron hedges.
Magnificent collection of camellias,

magnolias and azaleas underplanted
with helebores and spring bulbs.
Spinning, textiles.
♿ ✖ ☕

59 ◆ MINTERNE
Minterne Magna DT2 7AU. The Hon
Mr & Mrs Henry Digby, 01300
341370, www.minterne.co.uk. 2m N
of Cerne Abbas. On A352 Dorchester-
Sherborne rd. **Adm £4, chd free.
Open daily 1 Mar to 9 Nov (10-6).
House open for pre-booked groups
only.**
Minterne valley, landscaped in C18,
home of the Churchill and Digby
families for 350yrs. 20 acres wild
woodland gardens are laid out in a
horseshoe over 1m round. March sees
magnolias and early rhododendrons;
Japanese cherries, a profusion of
rhododendrons, azaleas and Pieris
Forrestii in April and May; many fine
specimens of Davidia Involucrata
(pocket handkerchief tree) in
May/June. Eucryphias, hydrangeas,
water plants and water lilies provide a
new vista at each turn. Sensational
autumn colouring. Some steep,
uneven paths.

60 ◆ MORETON GARDENS
Moreton, nr Dorchester DT2 8RH.
The Penny Family, 01929 405084,
www.moretondorset.co.uk. 7m E of
Dorchester. 3m W of Wool. Signed
from B3390 & 2m E of Moreton stn.
Next to Lawrence of Arabia's grave in
village of Moreton. **Adm £3.50, chd
free. Daily Mar to Oct (10-5); Weds
to Suns, Nov/Dec (10-4); Sats, Suns
Jan/Feb (10-4). For NGS: Sat 18,
Sun 19 Apr (10-5).**
A garden recreated in an old setting in
the picturesque village of Moreton.
3½ acres of lawns, mixed borders,
woodland, stream and ponds, bog
garden, pergola; summerhouse and
fountain. Spring flowers and much
more. Enjoy a picnic in the garden.
Rolled gravel paths.
♿ ✖ ❀ ☕

Several
small gardens
arranged round
the Mill . . .

61 NEW MOUNT PLEASANT
29 Chantry Lane, Newtown
DT8 3ER. Douglas Gibbs, 01308
862578,
douglas.gibbs@amstrad.com.
*½ m N from Beaminster Square.
Up Fleet St, L in 'Newtown', L
again into Chantry Lane. Car
parking in Beaminster School Car
Park just before Chantry Lane, very
short walk.* **Adm £3, chd free.**
Sun 24 May; Mon 31 Aug (2-6).
Visitors also welcome by appt
Suns only June/July/Aug/Sept £4.
¼ -acre plantsman's garden
created and looked after entirely by
owner. Divided by hedges and
walkways into smaller spaces.
Water garden, subtropical garden,
orchid house. Camellias, azaleas,
hydrangeas all in pots.
Conservatory and rain forest
leading back out into Chantry Lane
with very colourful frontage. Expect
the unexpected! Plant sale in aid of
Air Ambulance.

MULBERRY HOUSE
See Hampshire.

62 4 NOEL ROAD
Wallisdown BH10 4DP. Lesley & Ivor
Pond. *4m NE of Poole. From
Wallisdown Xrds enter Kinson Rd. Take
5th rd on R, Kingsbere Ave. Noel Rd is
first on R.* Home-made teas. **Adm
£2.50, chd free. Suns 28 June; 12
July (2-5).**
Small garden, 100ft x 30ft, with big
ideas. On sloping ground many Roman
features incl water features and temple.
Most planting is in containers. 'I also
like a big element of surprise and you
do not get more surprising than a
Roman Temple at the end of a
suburban garden' (Amateur Gardening
magazine). Several new features.
Camera is a must. Come and give us
your opinion 'Is this garden over the
top?'. Featured in 'The Private
Gardens of Dorset' ('At last a garden
with architecture...').

OAKDENE
See Hampshire.

63 'OLA'
47 Old Castle Road, Rodwell,
Weymouth DT4 8QE. Jane Uff &
Elaine Smith. *1m from Weymouth
centre. Follow signs to Portland. Off
Buxton Rd, proceed to lower end of
Old Castle Rd. Bungalow just past*

*Sandsfoot Castle ruins/gardens. Easy
access by foot off Rodwell Trail at
Sandsfoot Castle.* Home-made teas.
**Adm £3, chd free. Tues 19 May;
2, 16 June (2-5).**
Seaside garden with stunning views
overlooking Portland Harbour. 1930s-
designed garden, once part of
Sandsfoot Castle estate. Mixed
herbaceous borders, shrubs and
roses. Rockeries, fish pond,
vegetables, orchard and '7 dwarfs'
bank. Circular sunken stone walled
area with box bushes and statuary.
Lovingly restored from neglected
overgrown 'jungle'.

**64 NEW THE OLD POST
OFFICE**
North Street, Bere Regis
BH20 7LA. Mary & Ron, 01929
472508. *13m E of Dorchester,
12m W of Poole. From A31/A35
junction at Bere Regis, enter village
from Wool Rd, 1st R into North St,
50m on R.* Home-made teas. **Adm
£3, chd free. Suns 31 May; 7, 28
June; 26 July (2-6). Visitors also
welcome by appt.**
Pretty and informal village garden
of ⅓ acre made up of lawns,
herbaceous borders, kitchen
garden with raised beds and small
orchard. Shaded pergola walkway,
smart Victorian-style glasshouse,
pond and boat water feature.

Water garden, subtropical garden, orchid house . . .

**65 THE OLD RECTORY, LITTON
CHENEY**
Dorchester DT2 9AH. Mr & Mrs
Hugh Lindsay, 01308 482383,
hughlindsay@waitrose.com. *9m W of
Dorchester. 1m S of A35, 6m E of
Bridport. Small village in the beautiful
Bride Valley. Park in village and follow
signs.* Home-made teas. **Adm £4
(£2.50 Feb), chd free.** Dates to be
announced for Sat/Sun Feb
openings for snowdrops; **Sun 19
Apr; Sun 17 May; Mon 15 June**

(2-5.30). **Visitors also welcome by
appt April/May/June.**
Steep paths lead to 4 acres of natural
woodland with many springs, streams
and 2 small lakes; mostly native plants
and many primulas. (Stout shoes
recommended). Cloud-pruned boxes.
Small walled garden, partly paved,
formal layout with informal planting and
prolific quince tree. Kitchen garden,
orchard and wild flower lawn. Many
snowdrops in February. Steep paths,
no wheelchair access in woodland.

**66 THE OLD RECTORY,
NETHERBURY**
DT6 5NB. Amanda & Simon
Mehigan,
simon@netherbury.demon.co.uk. *2m
SW of Beaminster. Turn off A3066
Beaminster/Bridport rd & go over river
Brit, into centre of village & up hill. The
Old Rectory is on L opp church.*
Home-made teas. **Adm £4, chd free.
Suns 12 Apr; 3 May (2-5), Suns 24
May; 7 June (2-6). Open all day on
Tue 9 June for gps who have pre-
booked by email or writing.**
5-acre garden designed and
maintained by current owners,
surrounding rectory dating from C16
(not open). Formal areas nr house with
box-edged beds and topiary contrast
with natural planting elsewhere,
especially in bog garden, which
features large drifts of irises, bog
primulas and arum lilies. Spring bulbs
in orchard, vegetable garden, mature
ginkgo.

**67 THE OLD RECTORY,
PULHAM**
DT2 7EA. Mr & Mrs N Elliott, 01258
817595. *13m N of Dorchester. 8m SE
of Sherborne. On B3143 turn E at Xrds
in Pulham. Signed Cannings Court.*
Home-made teas 2 Aug only, teas 29
July. **Adm £4, chd free. Wed 29 July;
Sun 2 Aug (2-6). Visitors also
welcome by appt Mon-Fri only incl
groups.**
4 acres of formal and informal gardens
surround C18 rectory (not open) with
superb views. Yew hedges enclose
circular herbaceous borders with late
summer colour. Mature trees. Restored
pond and waterfall. Exuberantly-
planted terrace and purple and white
terrace beds. Box parterres. Fernery.
Pleached hornbeam circle. Ha-ha.
Shrubbery and two 5-acre woods with
mown rides. New bog garden.

68 NEW THE OLD SCHOOL

East Orchard SP7 0BA. Mr & Mrs Robert Hurlow. *On B3091 4½ m S of Shaftesbury, 3½ m N of Sturminster Newton. On Shaftesbury side of 90° bend. Drop passengers at lay-by with telephone box and park in narrow road to E Orchard, nr church.* Adm £2.50, chd free. Sats 13 June; 15 Aug (2-6). Also open **The Old Vicarage.**

Moving to Dorset from Shropshire where their garden had been opened for the NGS, owners have created in 3 yrs a new garden from a school playground. Areas of mixed planting and raised beds provide yr-round interest while preserving views across Blackmore Vale. Not suitable for wheelchairs when wet.

& &

A town garden for all seasons where every inch is used . . .

69 THE OLD VICARAGE

East Orchard, Shaftesbury SP7 0BA. Miss Tina Wright. *4½ m S of Shaftesbury, 3½ m N of Sturminster Newton. On B3091, Shaftesbury side of 90° bend. Drop passengers at lay-by with telephone box and park in narrow rd to East Orchard nr church.* Home-made teas. Adm £3.50, chd free. Sun 29 Mar; Sats 13 June; 15 Aug (2-6). Also opening **The Old School** 13 June & 15 Aug.

Wildlife-friendly, 1½ -acre garden with mixed shrub and herbaceous borders. Natural swimming pool with interesting planting incl tropical plants in regeneration zone. Stream, bog garden, rockery and wildlife pond. Feature folly, Victorian-style greenhouse and potager. Mature trees with underplanting. Spring flowers and bulbs. Not suitable for wheelchairs when wet.

& &

70 3 PRIORY GARDENS

Pimperne DT11 8XH. George & Karen Tapper. *Pimperne is 1m NE of Blandford Forum on A354 towards Salisbury. Please park sensibly in Church Rd and walk to garden. Parking for less able only in Priory Gardens.* Adm £2.50, chd free. Sat 27, Sun 28 June (2-5).

See what can be achieved in a garden just 80ft x 50ft. Imaginatively-designed garden that belies its size and surprises at every turn. Not your normal back garden plot! Roses, clematis, hardy geraniums, hemerocallis, grasses and herbaceous planting create different areas. Formal and wildlife ponds.

& &

PROSPECT HOUSE
See Devon.

71 NEW Q

113 Bridport Road, Dorchester DT1 2NH. Heather & Chris Robinson. *½ m W of Dorchester. From A35 take B3150 into Dorchester. Approx 300m W of Dorset County Hospital.* Home-made teas. Adm £3, chd free. Sun 1 Mar; Wed 3 June; Sun 2 Aug (2-4.30).

A town garden for all seasons where every inch is used to create different themed rooms by imaginative planting and original design which transport you away from hustle and bustle of the town. Incl kitchen garden, fruit trees and wild life areas.

& & &

72 RAMPISHAM MANOR

Rampisham DT2 0PT. Mr & Mrs Boileau, 01935 83060, h.boileau@btinternet.com. *11m NW of Dorchester. From Yeovil take A37 towards Dorchester, 7m turn R signed Evershot. From Dorchester take A37 to Yeovil, 4m turn L A356 signed Crewkerne; at start of wireless masts R to Rampisham. Follow signs.* Home-made teas Feb/Mar; cream teas Apr/June. Adm £3 Feb/Mar; £4 June, chd free. Suns 22 Feb; 22 Mar (2-4.30); Sun 19, Wed 22 Apr; Sun 7 June (2-5). Also open **Broomhill** 19 Apr, combined adm £6. Visitors also welcome by appt for gps of 10+ incl coaches until end June.

Mature 3+-acre garden with good bones, shapely borders and colour-

themed planting. Hidden gardens, slopes and lake walks in conservation area. Feb/Mar: Winter garden, structure, snowdrops then bulbs, magnolias and blossom. April: Blossom, tulips with earliest herbaceous. June: Fresh foliage and beds awakening. C13 church open.

& & &

73 357 RINGWOOD ROAD

Ferndown BH22 9AE. Lyn & Malcolm Ovens, 01202 896071, www.lynandmalc.co.uk. *¾ m S of Ferndown. On A348 towards Longham. Parking in Glenmoor Rd or other side rds. Avoid parking on main rd.* Home-made teas. Adm £2, chd free. Sun 12 July (11-5), Wed 29 July (2-5); Sun 16 Aug (11-5). Visitors also welcome by appt late June to early Sept.

Award-winning his and hers garden. Front in cottage style with a varied composition of perennials, lilies and many different clematis. Chosen to give a riot of colour into autumn. At rear, walk through a Moorish doorway into an exotic garden where brugmansia, cannas, oleander, banana etc come together in an eclectic design. Conservatory with bougainvillea. A garden that is loved and it shows. Ferndown Common and Nature Reserve nearby.

& & & &

74 NEW A ROSARY GARDEN

Sequoia, Brinsley Close, Sturminster Newton DT10 1AX. Heather Johnson, 01258 472392. *From Gillingham B3092 into town, 1st R after T-lights. From Shaftesbury B3091, L at T-lights onto B3092, immed R. From South, over bridge, through town square, 1st L.* Home-made teas. Adm £2.50, chd free. Fri 1 May (1.30-2.30) or by appt throughout May for Rosary only. Sun 7 June; Sat 15 Aug (2.30-5).

Newly-created 'island site' garden. Enter through the wooden gate, past vegetable and fruit gardens and leave the town behind. A 'Rosary Path' takes you through the different areas of the garden. Over 60 clematis, many entwined in roses. Many scented plants between mature trees. Garden open at 1.30 for those wishing to say the Rosary around the garden.

& &

75 46 ROSLIN ROAD SOUTH
Talbot Woods BH3 7EG. Mrs Penny
Slade, 01202 510243. *1m NW of
Bournemouth. W of N end of
Glenferness Ave in Talbot Woods area
of Bournemouth.* Home-made teas.
Adm £2.50, chd free. Sun 19 Apr;
Sat 16, Sun 17 May; Sat 13, Sun
14 June; Sun 12 July (2-5). Visitors
also welcome by appt.
Plantswoman's 1/3 -acre walled town
garden planted with many unusual and
rare plants. Sunken gravel garden with
collection of grasses, surrounded by
colourful mixed borders. Features incl
many well planted containers, raised
octagonal alpine bed, pergola leading
to enclosed patio, cutting beds and
fruit cage, greenhouses and frames.
S-facing wall especially colourful for
April and May openings.

ROUSDON COTTAGE GARDENS
See Devon.

SANDLE COTTAGE
See Hampshire.

76 THE SECRET GARDEN
The Friary, Hilfield DT2 7BE. The
Society of St Francis, 01300 341345.
*10m N of Dorchester, on A352. 1st L
after village, 1st turning on R signed
The Friary. From Yeovil turn off A37
signed Batcombe, 3rd turning on L.*
Light refreshments & teas. Adm £3,
chd free. Sat 16, Sun 17 May (2-5).
Visitors also welcome by appt.
Small woodland garden begun in
1950s then neglected. Reclamation
began in 1984. New plantings from
modern day plant hunters. Mature
trees, bamboo, rhododendrons,
azaleas, magnolias, camellias (some
camellias grown from seed collected in
China), other choice shrubs with a
stream on all sides crossed by bridges.
Stout shoes recommended.

**77 THE SECRET GARDEN AT
SERLES HOUSE**
47 Victoria Road, Wimborne
BH21 1EN. Ian Willis, 01202 880430.
*Centre of Wimborne. On B3082 W of
town, very near hospital, Westfield car
park 300yds. Off-road parking close
by.* Adm £2.50 (incl entry to part of
house), chd free (share to Wimborne
Civic Society). Suns 2, 16, 30, Mon
31 Aug; Suns 6, 13 Sept (2.30-5.30).
Evening Openings £4, wine, Sats
1, 29 Aug; 12 Sept (7-10); Fri 4, Sat 5
Dec (6.30-9.30). Visitors also

welcome by appt July to Sept.
Described by Alan Titchmarsh as one
of the 10 best private gardens in Great
Britain, this garden is for people of all
ages. The plantings fit in with over 60
relics rescued from oblivion by Ian
Willis. The Anglo-Indian conservatory,
plant-pot man, tree-house and
cannons from the Solent are highlights
of this remarkable experience. Live
piano music at all openings and
selection of quality garden sculptures
often available to purchase. Mince pies
at Christmas openings. Featured in
'Dorset County Gardener' and on local
radio. Some shallow steps and gravel.
No wheelchair access to house.

Mince pies at Christmas openings . . .

78 ◆ SHERBORNE CASTLE
New Rd, Sherborne DT9 5NR. Mr J
K Wingfield Digby, 01935 813182,
www.sherbornecastle.com. *1/2 m E of
Sherborne. On New Road B3145.
Follow brown signs to 'Sherborne
Castles' from A30 & A352.* House and
garden adm £9, chd free, senior
citizens £8.50, garden only adm
£4.50, chd free. Open daily except
Mons and Fris, 1 Apr to 1 Nov
(11-4.30).
30+ acres. A Capability Brown garden
with magnificent vistas across the
surrounding landscape, incl lake and
fine ruined castle. Herbaceous
planting, notable trees, a mixture of
ornamental planting and managed
wilderness are all linked together with
lawn and pathways providing colour
and interest throughout the seasons.
'Dry Grounds Walk'. Featured on
regional TV, 'A Tale of Two Castles'.
Gravel/grass paths and some steep
slopes, please phone for further
details.

79 SHUTE FARM
Donhead St Mary SP7 9DG. Mr &
Mrs J Douglas. *5m E of Shaftesbury.
Take A350 towards Warminster from*

*Shaftesbury. Turn R at 1st turning out
of Shaftesbury, signed Wincombe &
Donhead St Mary. At Donhead St
Mary, turn R at T-junction. 1st house
on L opp tel box.* Cream teas. Adm
£3.50, chd free. Sat 14, Sun 15 Mar
(11-4).
Cottage garden around thatched
house. Plenty to see and explore, incl
stream, pond, kitchen garden and wild
flower garden. Neat and tidy garden by
house, getting wilder as it meets the
fields. Alpacas, rare breed chickens,
ducks and bees. Magnificent views
over the Donheads.

80 SLAPE MANOR
Netherbury DT6 5LH. Mr & Mrs
Antony Hichens. *1m S of Beaminster.
Turn W off A3066 to village of
Netherbury. House 1/3 m S of
Netherbury on back rd to Bridport.*
Home-made teas. Adm £3, chd free.
Sun 17 May (2-6).
Manor with river valley garden,
extensive lawns, streams and lake.
Azaleas, magnolias, rhododendrons,
large clump *Phyllostachys nigra*
'Boryana' and specimen trees.
Lakeside walks. Slightly sloping
lawns/grass paths, some stone and
gravel paths, unfenced water features.

**81 ◆ SNAPE COTTAGE
PLANTSMAN'S GARDEN**
Chaffeymoor, Bourton, Gillingham
SP8 5BZ. Ian & Angela Whinfield,
01747 840330 (evenings),
www.snapestakes.com. *5m NW of
Gillingham. At W end of Bourton, N of
A303. Opp Chiffchaffs.* Home-made
cakes and cream teas. Adm £3, chd
free. Last 2 Suns in Feb; last
Sat/Sun in month, Mar to Aug incl
(2-5). Groups welcome. For NGS:
Sat 27, Sun 28 June (2-5).
Country garden containing exceptional
collection of hardy plants and bulbs,
artistically arranged in informal cottage
garden style, organically managed and
clearly labelled. Main interests are plant
history and nature conservation.
Specialities incl snowdrops, hellebores,
primula vulgaris cvrs, 'old' daffodils,
pulmonarias, auriculas, dianthus,
herbs, irises and geraniums. Wildlife
pond, beautiful views, tranquil
atmosphere. Gallery - photographic
prints and cards.

3 SOUTHDOWN
See Somerset & Bristol.

A quiet contemplative meander with the River Asker flowing through . . .

82 ◆ SPRINGHEAD
Mill St, Fontmell Magna SP7 0NU.
The Springhead Trust Ltd, 01747
811853,
rosalindrichards9@btinternet.com.
*4m S of Shaftesbury. From
Shaftesbury or Blandford take A350 to
Fontmell Magna. In centre of village,
turn E up Mill St, opp PH. Follow
stream up twisty, narrow lane to
Springhead on sharp bend. Large,
white thatched house attached to mill.*
**Adm £3.50, under 12s free. Mon 13
Apr, Thur 7, Tues 26 May. For NGS:
Thur 3 Sept; Mon 26 Oct (10.30-5).**
Large, atmospheric garden created
around lake on ancient site. Spring
water bubbling from beneath chalk
banks; walks, resting places, vistas
and great trees. Bird life on the water,
millrace, unusual planting of
herbaceous and shrub borders, bog
garden, rich autumn colour after hot
summers. Featured in '1001 Gardens
You Must See Before You Die'. Paths
difficult for wheelchairs in wet
conditions. One gentle incline (firm
path).
& ✿ 👄

83 STANBRIDGE MILL
nr Gussage All Saints BH21 5EP. Mr
James Fairfax, 01258 841067. *7m N
of Wimborne. On B3078 to Cranborne
150yds from Horton Inn on
Shaftesbury rd.* Cream teas & light
refreshments. **Adm £4.50, chd free.
Wed 10 June (10.30-5). Visitors also
welcome by appt for groups of 5+,
coaches permitted, please book
early to avoid disappointment.**
Hidden garden created in 1990s
around C18 water mill (not open) on R
Allen. Series of linked formal gardens
featuring herbaceous and iris borders,
pleached limes, white walk and
wisteria-clad pergola. 20-acre nature
reserve with reed beds and established
shelter belts. Grazing meadows with
wild flowers and flock of Dorset Horn
sheep. Local plants and local crafts for
sale.
& ✖ ✿ 👄 ☎

84 NEW UPLODERS PLACE
Uploders, Bridport DT6 4PF. Mrs
Venetia Ross Skinner, 01308
485653. *3m E of Bridport. From
A35 to Bridport or Dorchester take
turning for Uploders on S side of
main rd. R and R again under A35.
At Crown Inn PH (excellent food) R,
2 bends and Private Parking
notice.* Home-made teas. **Adm
£3.50, chd free. Sat 30 May; Fri
5 June (2.30-5.30).**
Old yews, cedar of Lebanon and
tulip tree form the bones of this
newish garden from a wilderness in
1993. Trees and shrubs with
unusual barks and flowers are the
main interest with rhododendrons
and camellias. A quiet
contemplative meander with the R
Asker flowing through. Wheelchair
access not easy, telephone before
visiting.
✿ 👄

85 WARMWELL HOUSE
Warmwell DT2 8HQ. Mr & Mrs H J C
Ross Skinner. *7m SE of Dorchester.
Warmwell is signed off A352 between
Dorchester & Wool. House is in centre
of village. Entrance to car park through
double gates ¼ m N on B3390.*
Home-made teas. **Adm £3.50, chd
free. Suns 14 June; 19 July (2-5).**
An old garden with a Jacobean house
(not open) set on ancient site of
Domesday building. The 1617 front
with Dutch gabelling has informal
gardens. Square Dutch garden and
maze on hill behind house. Slopes,
possibly slippery on damp/wet days,
suitable only for strong wheelchair
attendant.
& 👄

86 WATENDLATH
7 North St, Bere Regis BH20 7LA.
Peter & Carole Whittaker, 01929
471176,
carole.whittaker7@btinternet.com.
*13m W of Dorchester. From A35, A31
junction at Bere Regis. Enter village*

from the Wool rd, 1st R into North St,
200metres on R.* Home-made teas.
**Adm £3, chd free (share to Royal
British Legion Poppy Appeal). Suns
31 May; 7, 28 June; 26 July (2-6).
Visitors also welcome by appt.**
Wildlife-friendly garden of ⅓ acre,
created by people who love flowering
plants, colour and scent. Densely-
packed with herbaceous borders,
island beds, rose, vegetable and secret
garden, pond, chickens and many
containers. This diverse garden has
something for everyone, particularly
children, lots of interesting corners and
a fine view.
✖ ✿ 👄 ☎

WAYFORD MANOR
See Somerset & Bristol.

87 24A WESTERN AVENUE
Branksome Park, Poole BH13 7AN.
Mr & Mrs Peter Jackson. *3m W of
Bournemouth. ½ m inland from
Branksome Chine beach. From S end
Wessex Way (A338) take The Avenue.
At T-lights turn R into Western Rd. At
church turn R into Western Ave.*
Home-made teas. **Adm £3, chd free.
Suns 21 June; 2 Aug (2-6).**
'This secluded and magical 1-acre
garden captures the spirit of warmer
climes and begs for repeated visits'
('Gardening Which'); 'A dream of
tropical planting... like coming into a
different world' ('Amateur Gardening').
June sees the rose garden at its best
whilst herbaceous beds shine in Aug.
Italian courtyard, wall and woodland
gardens, topiary and driftwood
sculptures.
& ✿ 👄

88 WESTON HOUSE
Weston St, Buckhorn Weston
SP8 5HG. Mr & Mrs E A W Bullock,
01963 371005. *4m W of Gillingham,
3m SE of Wincanton. From A30 turn
N to Kington Magna, continue towards
Buckhorn Weston & after railway
bridge take L turn towards Wincanton.
2nd on L is Weston House.* Light
refreshments/cream teas by
arrangement. **Adm £3, chd free.
Visitors welcome by appt 1 Apr to
15 Sept, individuals and groups up
to 50.**
1½ -acre garden. Old walls host
climbers, clematis and roses. Approx
90 rose varieties throughout garden.
Mixed borders of colourful perennials,
shrubs and bulbs lead to woodland
area of shade-loving plants and
orchard incl tough perennials and
ornamental grasses. Attractive lawns

lead to wild flower areas, wildlife pond and hayfields with views of Blackmore Vale.

WHITE BARN
See Hampshire.

89 1692 WIMBORNE ROAD
Bear Cross BH11 9AL. Sue & Mike Cleall, 01202 573440. *5m NW of Bournemouth. On A341, 200yds E of Bear Cross roundabout.* Home-made teas. **Adm £2.50, chd free. Suns 17 May; Sun 7, Sat 27 June (2-5). Visitors also welcome by appt May/June only.**
Suburban garden 120ft x 50ft. Spring colour provided by rhododendrons, azaleas and acers underplanted with hellebores and woodland plants. For the summer, pergola with roses and climbers, hydrangeas and herbaceous borders. Man-made stream with waterfall runs through lawned area with primulas, ferns and gunnera. Wildlife pond.

Azaleas,
rhododendrons
and camellias
in flower . . .

90 NEW WINCOMBE PARK
Shaftesbury SP7 9AB. John & Phoebe Fortescue. *2m N of Shaftesbury. A350 Shaftesbury to Warminster, past Wincombe Business Park, 1st R signed Wincombe & Donhead St Mary. ³/₄ m on R.* Home-made teas. **Adm £3.50, chd free. Sun 10 May (2-5). Evening Opening with wine, Fri 15 May (6-8).**
Extensive mature garden within glorious parkland setting with lake below. Regeneration in progress. Azaleas, rhododendrons and camellias in flower amongst shrubs and unusual trees. Beware uneven steps and sloping lawns.

91 WOLVERHOLLOW
Elsdons Lane, Monkton Wyld DT6 6DA. Mr & Mrs D Wiscombe, 01297 560610. *4m N of Lyme Regis. 4m NW of Charmouth. Monkton Wyld is signed from A35 approx 4m NW of Charmouth off dual carriageway. Wolverhollow is next to the church.* Home-made teas. **Adm £3, chd free. Sun 26, Wed 29 Apr; Sun 31 May; Wed 3 June (11-5). Visitors also welcome by appt.**
Over 1 acre of informal garden. Lawns, with unusual summerhouse, lead past borders and rockeries to shady valley with babbling brook. Numerous paths pass wide variety of colourful and uncommon plants. An area, once field, sympathetically extends the garden with streamside planting and meadow. Must be seen. Featured in 'Dorset Life'.

Dorset County Volunteers

County Organiser & South Dorset Area
Harriet Boileau, Rampisham Manor, Dorchester DT2 0PT, 01935 83612, h.boileau@btinternet.com

County Treasurer
Michael Gallagher, 6 West Street, Chickerell, Weymouth DT3 4DY, 01305 772557, michael.gallagher1@virgin.net

Publicity & Leaflets
Howard Ffitch, Brook House, Purse Caundle, Sherborne DT9 5DY, 01963 250120, h.ffitch@btinternet.com

Assistant County Organisers
North Caroline Renner, Croft Farm, Fontmell Magna, Shaftesbury SP7 0NR, 01747 811140, jamesrenner@talktalk.net
Central East Trish Neale, Rosemary Cottage, Holway Lane, Rampisham DT2 0PX, 01935 83340, trishneale1@yahoo.co.uk
Central Wendy Jackson, Vine Cottage, Melcombe Bingham, Dorchester DT2 7PE, 01258 880720, wendyjacks@fsmail.net
West Central Jenie Corbett, Hollytree House, West Chelborough, Evershot, Dorchester DT2 0PY, 01935 83846,
  jeniecorbett@btinternet.com
South Harriet Boileau, Rampisham Manor, Dorchester DT2 0PT, 01935 83612, h.boileau@btinternet.com
South West Christine Corson, Stoke Knapp Cottage, Norway Lane, Stoke Abbott, Beaminster DT8 3JZ, 01308 868203
Bournemouth, Poole and Christchurch Penny Slade, 46 Roslin Road South, Bournemouth BH3 7EG, 01202 510243
Ferndown Mary Angus, The Glade, Woodland Walk, Ferndown BH22 9LP, 01202 872789, mary@gladestock.co.uk

DURHAM & NORTHUMBERLAND

with County Durham, Teesside & Tyne and Wear

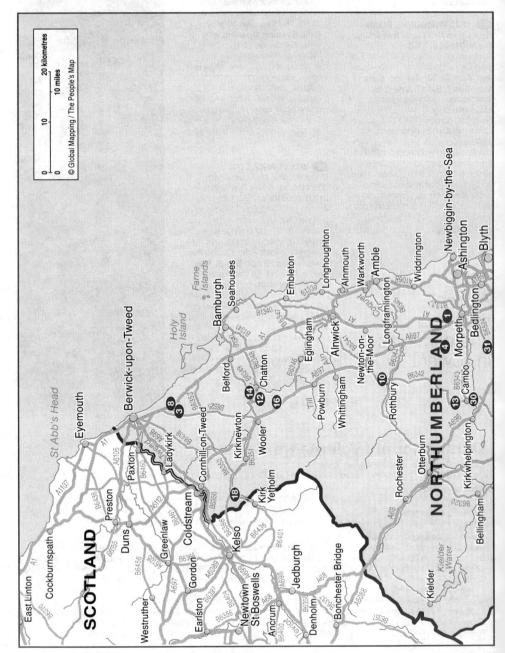

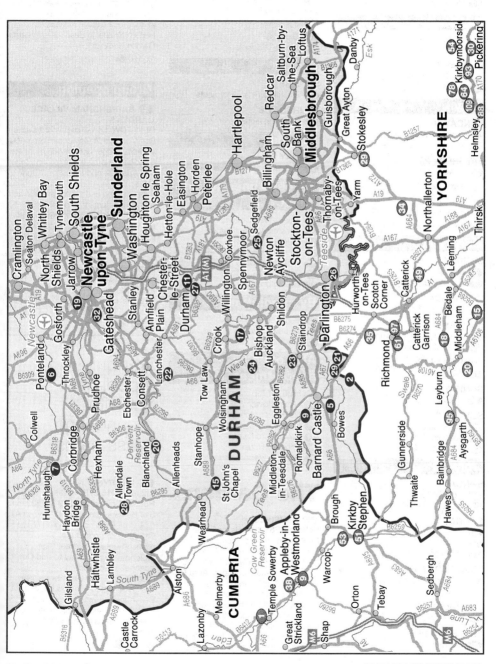

Opening Dates

March

SUNDAY 8
⑲ Moorbank Botanic Garden

April

SATURDAY 18
④ Bide-a-Wee Cottage

SUNDAY 19
㉑ The Old Vicarage, Hutton Magna
㉚ Wallington

May

SUNDAY 10
⑦ Chesters Walled Garden
⑲ Moorbank Botanic Garden

SATURDAY 23
㉒ Oliver Ford Garden

SUNDAY 24
⑯ Lilburn Tower

SUNDAY 31
㉘ Thornley House

June

SUNDAY 7
① Ashfield
② Barningham Village Gardens

WEDNESDAY 10
⑪ Crook Hall & Gardens

SUNDAY 14
⑫ Fowberry Mains Farmhouse
㉔ Ravensford Farm

THURSDAY 18
⑬ Herterton House

SUNDAY 21
⑱ Mindrum

SUNDAY 28
⑤ Browside
⑧ Cheswick House
⑳ Newbiggin House

July

SUNDAY 5
⑮ High Hill Top
㉛ Whalton Manor Gardens

SUNDAY 12
⑥ Cheeseburn Grange
⑭ Hetton House
㉗ St Margaret's Allotments

WEDNESDAY 15
⑲ Moorbank Botanic Garden
(Evening)

THURSDAY 16
⑬ Herterton House

SATURDAY 18
⑩ Cragside

㉚ Wallington

SUNDAY 19
⑨ Cotherstone Village Gardens
⑫ Fowberry Mains Farmhouse
㉕ Sedgefield Gardens

SUNDAY 26
㉙ Thorpe Gardens

August

SUNDAY 2
㉖ Smithfield Road Allotments

THURSDAY 6
⑬ Herterton House

October

SUNDAY 25
⑲ Moorbank Botanic Garden

Gardens open to the public

④ Bide-a-Wee Cottage
⑦ Chesters Walled Garden
⑩ Cragside
⑪ Crook Hall & Gardens
⑬ Herterton House
㉓ Raby Castle
㉚ Wallington

By appointment only

③ Berryburn
⑰ 10 Low Row
㉜ Woodland Cottage

Also open by appointment ☎

⑮ High Hill Top
⑯ Lilburn Tower
⑳ Newbiggin House
㉒ Oliver Ford Garden
㉔ Ravensford Farm
㉘ Thornley House
㉛ Whalton Manor Gardens

The Gardens

① ASHFIELD
Hebron NE61 3LA. Barry & Rona McWilliam. *3m N of Morpeth. 1¹/₂ m E of Heighley Gate. 1m off A1 on C130. S side of Hebron. Car park is through field gate.* Home-made teas. **Adm £3, chd free. Sun 7 June (12-5).**
Plantsman's garden, largely grown from seed. Set within 5 acres are collections of sorbus, betula and malus, beautiful hedging and remarkable alpines in full bloom from around the world. The long lawns are

bounded by herbaceous and shrub borders which contrast with the tranquil woodland set with meandering grass paths and varied under planting. Home-made teas worth making journey for. Featured in 'Morpeth Herald'. Winner in Best Summer Large Garden Competition.
 ♿ ⚘ ☕

Group opening

② BARNINGHAM VILLAGE GARDENS
DL11 7DW. *6m SE of Barnard Castle. 9m W of Scotch Corner turn S off A66 at Greta Bridge, or from A66 motel via Newsham.* Home-made teas in village hall. **Adm £4, chd free. Sun 7 June (12-5).**
Six interesting and varied gardens, and one private nursery in the beautiful village of Barningham on the edge of the Yorkshire dales. The gardens are intimate reflections of their owners style and character, the nursery has a collection of rarer cornus, holly, maple and conifer species www.plantsmancorner.co.uk. All are in a delightful setting. Featured in 'North East Life' magazine. Partial wheelchair access.
♿ ⚘ ☕

Tranquil woodland set with meandering grass paths . . .

③ BERRYBURN
Ancroft TD15 2TF. Mr & Mrs W J Rogers-Coltman, 01289 387332. *6m S of Berwick-upon-Tweed. Turn off A1 to Ancroft Mill. 2nd turning on R after 1m.* **Adm £5 (to include refreshments), chd free. Visitors welcome by appt** May to mid Oct, coaches permitted.
Created from waste land since 1981, this garden follows the course of the Berryburn as it winds through an alluvial dene past lawns, herbaceous borders, shrubs and specimen conifers.
♿ ☕ ☎

4 ◆ **BIDE-A-WEE COTTAGE**
Stanton, Morpeth NE65 8PR. Mr M
Robson, 01670 772238,
www.bideawee.co.uk. *7m NNW of
Morpeth. Turn L off A192 out of
Morpeth at Fairmoor. Stanton is 6m
along this rd.* **Adm £2.50, chd under
11 free. For opening details please
tel or see website. For NGS: Sat 18
Apr (1.30-4.30).**
Unique secret garden created over the
last 26yrs out of a small sandstone
quarry, it features rock and water.
Unusual perennials are woven within a
matrix of ferns, trees and shrubs. The
garden contains the National Collection
of centaurea, and many other plants
seldom seen.
  ♿ ✿ ❀ NCCPG

5 **BROWSIDE**
Boldron, Barnard Castle DL12 9RQ.
Mr & Mrs R D Kearton. *3m S of
Barnard Castle. On A66 3m W of
Greta Bridge, turn R to Boldron, then
proceed 1/2 m, entrance opp junction.
From Barnard Castle take A67 to
Bowes, after 2m turn L to Boldron.*
Home-made teas. **Adm £2.50, chd
free. Sun 28 June (1-5.30).**
1¼ acres with unusual water features
and large collection of conifers, wide
range of plants and imaginative stone
objects. Wonderfully tranquil seating
areas. Live music from 'Northumbrian
Pipers'.
  ♿ ❀ ☕

6 **CHEESEBURN GRANGE**
Stamfordham NE18 0PT. Mr & Mrs S
Riddell. *8m W of Newcastle upon
Tyne. From A1 take B6324 through
Westerhope, Stamfordham.
Cheeseburn is 1.8m beyond Plough
Inn on R. From Stamfordham Village
take signs to Newcastle, after approx
1m take 1st R signed Newcastle. 1st
entrance on L.* Home-made teas. **Adm
£3, chd free. Sun 12 July (2-5.30).**
Peaceful oasis just 8m from
Newcastle, this garden of approx 7
acres has been developed by present
owners in last 15yrs. Extensive lawns
with flowering cherries and bulbs in
spring surround the Dobson designed
house (not open) and chapel (open).
Mature trees and parkland views,
roses, mixed borders and parterre.
Vegetable area, fruit trees and
greenhouse in Victorian walled garden.
Woodland walk with many varieties of
birds. Featured in 'Hexham Courant' &
'Newcastle Journal'. Wheelchair
access to main paths only.
  ✿ ❀ ☕

7 ◆ **CHESTERS WALLED
GARDEN**
Chollerford NE46 4BQ. Mrs S White,
01434 681483,
www.chesterswalledgarden.co.uk.
*6m N of Hexham. Off the B6318. 1/2 m
W of Chollerford.* **Adm £3.50, chd
under 10 free. Daily (10-5) mid Mar
to end Oct, by appt in winter. For
NGS: Sun 10 May (10-5).**
Delightful 2-acre walled garden,
planted in relaxed style; wild flowers
mingle with unusual perennials and
extensive collection of herbs. Three
National Collections; marjoram,
sanguisorba and thyme, grown on
famous Thyme Bank. Roman garden;
knot garden, ponds and vegetables.
Organically run, the walled garden is a
haven for wildlife incl red squirrels.
Featured in 'The Daily Telegraph', 'Mail
on Sunday', 'Culture Magazine' &
'Garden News'.
  ♿ ✿ ❀ NCCPG

8 ◆ **CHESWICK HOUSE**
Cheswick TD15 2RL. Mr & Mrs P
Bennett. *4m S of Berwick upon
Tweed. Turn E from A1 signed
Goswick/Cheswick.* Home-made teas.
Adm £3, chd free. Sun 28 June (2-6).
Large garden incl woodland with
specimen trees, croquet lawn, formal
walled garden and woodland walk. The
garden is undergoing a restoration
programme begun in 2002 which incl
converted curling rink with pond and
raised beds. Two additional water
features will be completed this year.
Gravel paths.
  ♿ ❀ 🛏 ☕

Group opening

9 **COTHERSTONE VILLAGE
GARDENS**
DL12 9PQ. *4m NW of Barnard Castle.
On B6277 Middleton-in-Teesdale rd.*
Home-made teas. **Adm £3, chd free.
Sun 19 July (11-5).**
One of the best 20 villages in the
country. Very picturesque at the
confluence of the R Tees and Balder.
Several country gardens and
allotments open showing a wide variety
of plants and vegetables. Teas
available in naturalists garden.
Featured in 'The Sunday Times' and
8th best village in the country in
Channel 5's Property List. Some of the
gardens have good wheelchair access,
also tea venue.
  ♿ ❀ ☕

10 ◆ **CRAGSIDE**
Rothbury NE65 7PX. The National
Trust, 01669 620333,
www.nationaltrust.org.uk. *13m SW
of Alnwick. (B6341); 15m NW of
Morpeth (A697).* **House & garden
£13.20, chd £6.60, garden only £8.50,
chd £3.50. For opening details
please tel or see website. For NGS:
Sat 18 July (10.30-5).**
Formal garden in the 'High Victorian'
style created by the 1st Lord
Armstrong. Fully restored Italian
terrace, orchard house, carpet
bedding, dahlia walk and fernery.
4¹/₂ acres of rock garden with its
restored cascades. Extensive
grounds of over 1000 acres famous
for rhododendrons and beautiful
lakes.
  ✿ ☕

The gardens are intimate reflections of their owners style and character

11 ◆ **CROOK HALL & GARDENS**
Sidegate, Durham City DH1 5SZ.
Maggie Bell, 0191 384 8028,
www.crookhallgardens.co.uk. *Centre
of Durham City. Crook Hall is short
walk from Durham's Market Place.
Follow the tourist info signs. Parking
available at entrance.* **House & garden
£5.50, chd £4.50, concessions £5.
Easter 9 to 14 Apr; Suns to Weds
3 May to 30 Sept. For NGS: Wed
10 June (11-5).**
Described in Country Life as having
'history, romance and beauty'.
Intriguing medieval manor house
surrounded by 4 acres of fine gardens.
Visitors can enjoy magnificent
cathedral views from the 2 walled
gardens. Other garden 'rooms' incl the
silver and white garden, orchard, moat,
pool and maze. Limited wheelchair
access.
  ♿ ✿

12 FOWBERRY MAINS FARMHOUSE
Wooler NE71 6EN. Mr & Mrs A F McEwen. *2m W of Chatton, 3m E of Wooler. Signed between Wooler & Chatton on B6348.* Home-made teas. **Adm £3, chd free (share to Macmillan (Jun), Glendale Middle School (Jul)). Suns 14 June; 19 July (2-6).**
Artistically and lovingly created colourful 1-acre garden, developed and planted since 1999, still evolving. Relaxed country style featuring informal beds with hardy perennials, roses and shrubs, well stocked mixed herbaceous borders. Newly designed gravel beds with grasses and drought tolerant plants. Productive vegetable garden. Small wild area being developed. Featured in 'Northumberland Gazette' & 'Beswick Advertiser'.

13 ◆ HERTERTON HOUSE
Hartington NE61 4BN. Mr Frank Lawley, 01670 774278. *12m W of Morpeth. 23m NW of Newcastle. 2m N of Cambo on the B6342 signed to Hartington. Brown signs.* **Adm £3, chd free. Daily Apr to Sept (except Tue & Thur). For NGS: Thurs 18 June; 16 July; 6 Aug (1.30-5.30).**
1 acre of formal garden in stone walls around C16 farmhouse (not open). Incl small topiary garden, physic garden, flower garden, fancy garden, gazebo and nursery garden. Featured in the 'Times Magazine', 'Financial Times' & 'Amateur Gardening'.

14 NEW HETTON HOUSE
Wooler NE71 6ET. Mr & Mrs J Lovett. *2½ m N of Chatton. 4m E of Wooler, signed between Chatton & Wooler on B6348.* Home-made teas. **Adm £3, chd free (share to Holy Cross Chatton & St Peters Chillingham). Sun 12 July (2-6).**
5 acres of s-facing mature gardens. Large mixed herbaceous, rose and shrub borders. Informal, pretty paved garden. Greenhouse, productive kitchen garden, lawns with ornamental trees and shrubs. Fine views across the beautiful Glendale Valley.

15 HIGH HILL TOP
St John's Chapel DL13 1RJ. Mr & Mrs I Hedley, 01388 537952. *7m W of Stanhope. On A689. Turn L into Harthope Rd after Co-op shop in St John's Chapel. Up hill for ½ m past the Animal Hotel. Garden is next house on L.* Home-made teas. **Adm £2.50, chd free. Sun 5 July (10-4). Visitors also welcome by appt.**
See what can be achieved in an exposed garden at 1200ft. Mixed planting incls wonderful collection of sorbus, hostas, ferns, eucalyptus and candelabra primulas. Magnificent backdrop of North Pennines.

16 LILBURN TOWER
Alnwick NE66 4PQ. Mr & Mrs D Davidson, 01668 217291, davidson309@btinternet.com. *3m S of Wooler. On A697.* Home-made teas. **Adm £3.50, chd free. Sun 24 May (2-6). Visitors also welcome by appt.**
10 acres of walled and formal gardens incl conservatory and large glasshouse. Approx 30 acres of woodland with walks and pond garden. Rhododendrons and azaleas. Also ruins of Pele Tower, and C12 church. Limited wheelchair access, gravel paths.

17 10 LOW ROW
North Bitchburn, Crook DL15 8AJ. Mrs Ann Pickering, 01388 766345. *3m NW of Bishop Auckland. A689 N to Howden-Le-Wear, R up the bank before petrol stn. 1st R in village at 30mph sign.* **Adm £2. Visitors welcome by appt all year (not Tues).**
Quirky original garden with 90% grown from seeds and cuttings. Extensive views over the Wear valley. An amazing garden created without commercially bought plants or expense. Totally organic and environmentally friendly. A haven for wildlife.

18 MINDRUM
nr Cornhill on Tweed & Yetholm TD12 4QN. Mrs V Fairfax. *6m SW of Coldstream, 9m NW of Wooler. 4m N of Yetholm. 5m from Cornhill on Tweed on B6352.* Home-made teas. **Adm £3.50, chd free. Sun 21 June (2-6).**
Old-fashioned roses; rock and water garden; shrub borders. Wonderful views along Bowmont Valley. Approx 3 acres. Or more if you like to wander by river. Very limited wheelchair access, gravel and steep paths, one electric buggy available.

19 MOORBANK BOTANIC GARDEN
Claremont Road, Newcastle upon Tyne NE2 4NL. University of Newcastle. *¾ m from Newcastle Haymarket. W end of Claremont Rd, just E of Cat & Dog shelter. Shared entrance with Town Moor Superintendents Farm (blue gate). 12 mins walk up Claremont Rd from Exhibition Park entrance r'about. No parking in garden.* **Adm £2.50, chd free (share to Moorbank Garden Volunteers). Suns 8 Mar; 10 May (2-5); 25 Oct (1-4). Evening Opening wine, Wed 15 July (5-8).**
3 acre university botanic garden with collections of rare conifers, rhododendrons, sorbus, pond, perennials, herb garden, meadow. Extensive plantings under glass with tropical plants, succulents, insectivorous plants. Many original collections, originally from Kilbryde Gardens, Corbridge. Outside plantings maintained with volunteer help. Guided walks around the garden. Grass and slopes.

Magnificent collection of unusual trees . . .

20 NEWBIGGIN HOUSE
Blanchland DH8 9UD. Mrs A Scott-Harden, 01434 675005, descottharden@aol.com. *12m S of Hexham. From Blanchland village take Stanhope Rd. ½ m along narrow rd follow yellow signs up tarmac drive into car park.* **Adm £3, chd free. Sun 28 June (2-5). Visitors also welcome by appt end May, Jun & Jul, coaches permitted.**
5-acre landscaped garden at 1000ft, started in 1996 and is maturing beautifully. Old-fashioned herbaceous border, peonies, shrubs, roses, bog and wild garden incl wild rose walk. Magnificent collection of unusual trees and shrubs. Very good cafe open for teas in village. Partial wheelchair access.

21 THE OLD VICARAGE, HUTTON MAGNA

nr Richmond, N Yorkshire DL11 7HJ. Mr & Mrs D M Raw. *8m SE of Barnard Castle. 6m W of Scotch Corner on A66, Penrith direction. Signed Hutton Magna R. Continue to, and through, village. Garden 200yds past village on L, on corner of T-junction.* Home-made teas. **Adm £2.50, chd free. Sun 19 Apr (2-5.30).** S-facing garden, elevation 450ft. Plantings, since 1978, now maturing within original design contemporary to 1887 house (not open). Cut and topiary hedging, old orchard; rose and herbaceous borders featuring hellebores in profusion, with tulips and primulas. Large plant stall.

22 NEW OLIVER FORD GARDEN

Longedge Lane, Rowley DH8 9HG. Bob & Bev Tridgett, 07818 451079, bob.tridgett@hotmail.co.uk. *5m NW of Lanchester. From Castleside approx 1m S on A68 turn L to Lanchester 1/2 m on L. From Lanchester B6296 signed Satley approx 2m turn R at Woodlea Manor, garden 2.9m on R.* Home-made teas. **Adm £3, chd free. Sat 23 May (1-5). Visitors also welcome by appt.** Spectacular young woodland garden (6yrs old) containing rare acers, stewartia, betula and prunus. Some young specimen trees unlikely to be seen elsewhere in the NE. Stream and bog garden. Rock garden containing collection dwarf conifers. Profusion of spring flowers incl insect nectar bar. BBC Gardener of the Year, Silver Gilt RHS medal at Tatton Park. Some steep slopes - sensible footwear advised.

23 ◆ RABY CASTLE

Staindrop DL2 3AH. Lord Barnard, 01833 660202, www.rabycastle.com. *12m NW of Darlington, 1m N of Staindrop. On A688 8m NE of Barnard Castle.* **House & garden £9.50, chd £4, concessions £8.50, garden only £5, chd under 12 free, 12-15 £3, concessions £4. For opening details please tel or see website.** C18 walled gardens set within the grounds of Raby Castle. Designers

such as Thomas White and James Paine have worked to establish the gardens, which now extend to 5 acres, display herbaceous borders, old yew hedges, formal rose gardens and informal heather and conifer gardens. Featured in local press.

Rare acers, stewartia, betula and prunus . . .

24 RAVENSFORD FARM

Hamsterley DL13 3NH. Mr & Mrs J Peacock, 01388 488305, peacock@ravensford.eclipse.co.uk. *7m W of Bishop Auckland. From A68 at Witton-le-Wear turn off W to Hamsterley. Go through village & turn L just before tennis courts.* Home-made teas. **Adm £3, chd free. Sun 14 June (2.30-5). Visitors also welcome by appt.** A new opening date for this garden of varied areas and moods, displaying rhododendrons, irises, and a true plant-lover's range of ornamental trees, shrubs and flowers. Plants from the garden for sale. Live music in the background. Featured in 'Durham Life'. Wheelchair access only with assistance.

Group opening

25 SEDGEFIELD GARDENS

TS21 3BE. Mrs S Hannan. *12m SE of Durham. Off A689 Bishop Auckland to Hartlepool rd, 21/2 m E of junction 60 of A1(M). From Teeside take A19 N & then follow signs for A689 to Bishop Auckland. Collect a route map from Ceddesfeld Hall, Rectory Row, TS21 2AE.* Cream teas in Ceddesfeld Hall, Rectory Row. **Adm £4, chd free. Sun 19 July (1-5).** Selection of 8-10 gardens in beautiful village featuring water gardens, cottage planting and oriental display. Sedgefield boasts magnificent C13 church set on traditional village green. Winner Best Small Town - Northumbria in Bloom. Limited wheelchair access.

Allotments

26 NEW SMITHFIELD ROAD ALLOTMENTS

DL1 5UQ. Darlington Borough Council. *200 yds from main railway stn in Darlington. From clock entrance of stn turn L into Park Lane to 1st Xrd, then L into Smithfield Rd.* Cream teas. **Adm £2, chd free. Sun 2 Aug (11-4).** 24 interesting and varied allotments. Many gardeners will be on hand to answer questions incl exhibition growers. A variety of growing methods are evident on the allotments. Face painting - cut flowers for sale. Shop will be open for sale of garden sundries incl organic and conventional fertiliser.

Allotments

27 ST MARGARET'S ALLOTMENTS

Margery Lane, Durham DH1 4QG. Diocese of Durham. *From A1 take A690 to city centre/Crook. Straight ahead at T-lights after passing 4 r'abouts. Pedestrians walk up Sutton St from big roundabout at viaduct. Allotments L in Margery Lane.* Home-made teas in Antioch House, Crossgate. **Adm £2.50, chd free. Sun 12 July (2-5.30).** 5 acres of 82 allotments against the spectacular backdrop of Durham Cathedral. This site has been cultivated since the middle ages, and was saved from development 20yrs ago, allowing a number of enthusiastic gardeners to develop their plots which display a great variety of fruit, vegetables and flowers. History of site. Featured in 'Durham Times', 'Northern Echo & on regional TV. Northumbria in Bloom Gold Award.

28 THORNLEY HOUSE

Thornley Gate, Allendale, Northum NE47 9NH. Ms Eileen Finn, 01434 683255, www.thornleyhouse.co.uk. *1m W of Allendale. From Allendale town, down hill from Hare & Hound to 5th rd junction, 1m Thornley House is big house in field in front.* Light refreshments & teas. **Adm £3, chd free (share to Brook Charity for Working Animals). Sun 31 May (2-5). Visitors also welcome by appt in Aug.** Unusual 1-acre garden consisting of woodland, stream, pond, vegetable and fruit garden, rose avenue and mixed planting. A feline theme is evident throughout this child-friendly garden. Seek and find quiz is available for family fun. Maine Coon cats and ornamental animals enhance this garden. Featured in 'The Northumbrian' and 'Amateur Gardener'.

Foliage garden within a tranquil setting complemented by a trickle of water . . .

Group opening

29 THORPE GARDENS
DL12 9TU. *5m SE of Barnard Castle. 9m from Scotch Corner W on A66. Turn R at Peel House Farm Shop signed Wycliffe and Whorlton, 1m from A66.* Home-made teas. **Adm £3, chd free. Sun 26 July (2-5).**
Charming hamlet, 3 cottage gardens, one approx ¼ acre with some unusual plants. Incl Thorpe Hall, a large interesting garden in the course of development by a professional designer. Wood Carving Demonstration.

30 ◆ WALLINGTON
Cambo NE61 4AR. The National Trust, 01670 773600, www.nationaltrust.org.uk. *12m W of Morpeth. From N B6343; from S via A696 from Newcastle, 6m W of Belsay, B6342 to Cambo.* **House & garden £8.80, chd £4.40, garden only £6.10, chd £3.05. Garden daily Apr - Sept 10-7, Oct 10-6, Nov - Mar 10-4. For NGS: Sun 19 Apr; Sat 18 July (10-7).**
Walled, terraced garden with fine herbaceous and mixed borders; Edwardian conservatory; 100 acres woodland and lakes. House dates from 1688 but altered, interior greatly changed c1740; exceptional rococo plasterwork by Francini brothers. 'Ask the Gardener' general advice day.

31 WHALTON MANOR GARDENS
Whalton NE61 3UT. Mr & Mrs T R P S Norton, 01670 775205, norton@whaltonmanor.fsnet.co.uk, www.whaltonmanor.co.uk. *5m W of Morpeth.* **Adm £3.50, chd free. Sun 5 July (2-5).** Visitors also welcome by appt for groups of 10+ May to Sept.
The historic Whalton Manor, altered by Sir Edwin Lutyens in 1908, is surrounded by 3 acres of magnificent walled gardens, designed by Lutyens with the help of Gertrude Jekyll. The gardens have been developed by the Norton family since the 1920s and incls extensive herbaceous borders, 30yd peony border, rose garden, listed summerhouses, pergolas and walls, festooned with rambling roses and clematis. Some stone steps.

32 NEW WOODLAND COTTAGE
Duckpool Lane, off Market Lane, Whickham NE16 4TH. Mrs B Savage, 0191 496 0678, woodlandcott@aol.com. *2m S of Newcastle. On A1, climb ramp to metro centre drive opp direction to local rd signposted Dunston/ Whickham - bear L follow rd for ¹/₂ m. Opp Poachers Pocket on Market Lane.* **Adm £3, chd free (share to Multiple Sclerosis). Visitors welcome by appt, early summer.**
Small colourful garden packed wth many unusual plants and shrubs. Foliage garden within a tranquil setting complemented by a trickle of water. This flower arranger's garden is full of vibrant early summer colour.

Mark your diary with these special events in 2009

EXPLORE SECRET GARDENS DURING CHELSEA & HAMPTON COURT FLOWER SHOW WEEKS

Tue 19 May, Wed 20 May, Thur 21 May, Fri 22 May, Wed 8 July, Thur 9 July
Full day tours from £82 per person, 10% discount for groups
Advance booking required, telephone +44 (0)20 8693 1015 or email j.wookey@btinternet.com
Specially selected gardens in London, Essex, Kent, Hampshire and South Oxfordshire. The tour price includes transport and lunch with wine at a popular restaurant or pub.

HAMPTON COURT PALACE

Thur 2 Apr, Tue 23 June, Thur 25 June, Wed 15 July, Tue 4 Aug, Thur 10 Sept
Evening tours in the company of one of the Palace's specialist tour guides from 6.30 – 8pm
Tickets £6 per person. Advance booking required, telephone +44 (0)1483 211535 or
visit www.ngs.org.uk for more information
Gossip, scandal, murder, healing – you'll find it all within the Formal Gardens at Hampton Court Palace. Each tour will have its own unique feature whether it's the story of the Great Vine or the magic and mystery of the Maze.

FROGMORE – A ROYAL GARDEN (BERKSHIRE)

Tue 26 May 10am – 5.30pm (last admission 4pm)
Garden adm £4.50, chd free. Tickets available in advance or on the day.
Advance booking for groups and coaches, telephone
+44 (0) 1483 211535 or email orders@ngs.org.uk
A rare opportunity to explore 30 acres of landscaped garden, rich in history and beauty.

FLAXBOURNE FARM – FUN & SURPRISES (BEDFORDSHIRE)

Sun 7 June 10am – 5pm. Adm £5, chd free
No booking required, come along on the day!
Bring the whole family and have fun in this surprising and entertaining garden of 2 acres. Enjoy the large plant fair, live music, pets corner, birds of prey, dog agility show and much more.

WISLEY RHS GARDEN – MUSIC IN THE GARDEN (SURREY)

Fri 11 Sept 6 – 9pm
Adm (incl RHS members) £7, chd under 15 free
Save money on advance bookings for groups of 4 or more, telephone +44 (0)1483 211535 or
visit www.ngs.org.uk for more information
A special evening opening of this famous garden, exclusively for the NGS. Enjoy music and entertainment as you explore the gardens and the floral marquee on the first day of the Wisley Flower Show.

For further information visit www.ngs.org.uk or telephone 01483 211535

ESSEX

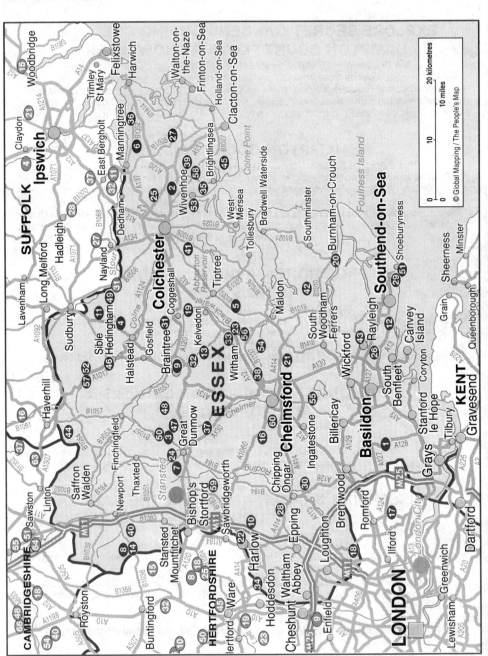

Opening Dates

March

SUNDAY 15
60 Writtle College

SUNDAY 29
25 Green Island

April

THURSDAY 2
1 Barnards Farm
19 Feeringbury Manor

FRIDAY 3
19 Feeringbury Manor

SATURDAY 4
53 Tudor Roost

SUNDAY 5
53 Tudor Roost

THURSDAY 9
1 Barnards Farm
19 Feeringbury Manor

FRIDAY 10
19 Feeringbury Manor

SUNDAY 12
45 164 Point Clear Road
51 South Shoebury Hall
53 Tudor Roost

MONDAY 13
53 Tudor Roost

THURSDAY 16
1 Barnards Farm
16 Dragons
19 Feeringbury Manor

FRIDAY 17
19 Feeringbury Manor

SUNDAY 19
28 Hobbans Farm

THURSDAY 23
1 Barnards Farm
19 Feeringbury Manor

FRIDAY 24
19 Feeringbury Manor
56 Wickham Place Farm

SATURDAY 25
41 Olivers
47 St Helens

SUNDAY 26
41 Olivers

THURSDAY 30
1 Barnards Farm
19 Feeringbury Manor

May

FRIDAY 1
19 Feeringbury Manor
56 Wickham Place Farm

SATURDAY 2
26 Greenacres
37 North End Place

SUNDAY 3
26 Greenacres
28 Hobbans Farm
37 North End Place
53 Tudor Roost
58 Woodpeckers

MONDAY 4
26 Greenacres
53 Tudor Roost
58 Woodpeckers

WEDNESDAY 6
48 Saling Hall

THURSDAY 7
1 Barnards Farm
19 Feeringbury Manor

FRIDAY 8
19 Feeringbury Manor
56 Wickham Place Farm

WEDNESDAY 13
48 Saling Hall

THURSDAY 14
1 Barnards Farm
19 Feeringbury Manor

FRIDAY 15
19 Feeringbury Manor
33 4 Millbridge Road
46 Rookwoods
56 Wickham Place Farm

SATURDAY 16
27 Hannams Hall

SUNDAY 17
27 Hannams Hall
28 Hobbans Farm

WEDNESDAY 20
48 Saling Hall

THURSDAY 21
1 Barnards Farm
16 Dragons
19 Feeringbury Manor

FRIDAY 22
19 Feeringbury Manor
56 Wickham Place Farm

SATURDAY 23
6 Chippins
26 Greenacres

SUNDAY 24
26 Greenacres
34 The Mount
53 Tudor Roost
55 West Hanningfield Hall

MONDAY 25
24 The Granary, Maysland Farm
26 Greenacres
46 Rookwoods
53 Tudor Roost

WEDNESDAY 27
48 Saling Hall

THURSDAY 28
1 Barnards Farm
19 Feeringbury Manor

FRIDAY 29
5 Casa Mia
19 Feeringbury Manor
33 4 Millbridge Road
46 Rookwoods
56 Wickham Place Farm

SATURDAY 30
47 St Helens

SUNDAY 31
13 Cressing Temple
28 Hobbans Farm
38 The Old Rectory
43 Orchard Cottage

June

WEDNESDAY 3
48 Saling Hall

THURSDAY 4
1 Barnards Farm
19 Feeringbury Manor

FRIDAY 5
19 Feeringbury Manor
23 Glen Chantry
56 Wickham Place Farm

SATURDAY 6
52 Spencers

SUNDAY 7
21 Furzelea
35 Moverons
40 The Old Vicarage
44 Parsonage House

MONDAY 8
21 Furzelea (Evening)

TUESDAY 9
32 60 Mill Lane

WEDNESDAY 10
48 Saling Hall

THURSDAY 11
1 Barnards Farm
19 Feeringbury Manor

FRIDAY 12
19 Feeringbury Manor
56 Wickham Place Farm

SATURDAY 13
- **6** Chippins
- **36** Newland Cottage

SUNDAY 14
- **6** Chippins
- **8** Clavering Gardens
- **10** 1 The Cottage
- **12** Court View
- **17** Edelweiss
- **28** Hobbans Farm
- **36** Newland Cottage
- **37** North End Place
- **45** 164 Point Clear Road

TUESDAY 16
- **53** Tudor Roost

WEDNESDAY 17
- **48** Saling Hall
- **53** Tudor Roost

THURSDAY 18
- **1** Barnards Farm
- **16** Dragons
- **19** Feeringbury Manor

FRIDAY 19
- **19** Feeringbury Manor
- **56** Wickham Place Farm

SATURDAY 20
- **33** 4 Millbridge Road
- **39** The Old School House
- **57** Willow Cottage

SUNDAY 21
- **39** The Old School House
- **50** Snares Hill Cottage
- **57** Willow Cottage

WEDNESDAY 24
- **48** Saling Hall

THURSDAY 25
- **1** Barnards Farm
- **19** Feeringbury Manor

FRIDAY 26
- **19** Feeringbury Manor
- **56** Wickham Place Farm

SATURDAY 27
- **39** The Old School House

SUNDAY 28
- **1** Barnards Farm
- **18** Fairwinds
- **24** The Granary, Maysland Farm
- **28** Hobbans Farm
- **34** The Mount
- **39** The Old School House

July

WEDNESDAY 1
- **48** Saling Hall

THURSDAY 2
- **1** Barnards Farm
- **19** Feeringbury Manor

FRIDAY 3
- **19** Feeringbury Manor
- **23** Glen Chantry
- **33** 4 Millbridge Road
- **35** Moverons
- **56** Wickham Place Farm

SATURDAY 4
- **7** Church Lodge
- **9** 352 Coggeshall Road
- **53** Tudor Roost

SUNDAY 5
- **7** Church Lodge
- **9** 352 Coggeshall Road
- **30** Little Myles
- **53** Tudor Roost

WEDNESDAY 8
- **48** Saling Hall

THURSDAY 9
- **1** Barnards Farm
- **19** Feeringbury Manor

FRIDAY 10
- **19** Feeringbury Manor
- **35** Moverons
- **56** Wickham Place Farm

SATURDAY 11
- **3** 19 Brookfields
- **6** Chippins

SUNDAY 12
- **3** 19 Brookfields
- **25** Green Island
- **28** Hobbans Farm
- **32** 60 Mill Lane
- **60** Writtle College

WEDNESDAY 15
- **48** Saling Hall

THURSDAY 16
- **1** Barnards Farm
- **16** Dragons
- **19** Feeringbury Manor

FRIDAY 17
- **19** Feeringbury Manor
- **35** Moverons
- **56** Wickham Place Farm

SUNDAY 19
- **5** Casa Mia
- **11** Court House
- **12** Court View
- **17** Edelweiss
- **43** Orchard Cottage
- **45** 164 Point Clear Road
- **51** South Shoebury Hall

WEDNESDAY 22
- **20** 4 Fernlea Road
- **42** One Brook Hall Cottages
- **48** Saling Hall

THURSDAY 23
- **1** Barnards Farm
- **19** Feeringbury Manor

FRIDAY 24
- **19** Feeringbury Manor
- **35** Moverons
- **56** Wickham Place Farm

SATURDAY 25
- **53** Tudor Roost

SUNDAY 26
- **20** 4 Fernlea Road
- **34** The Mount
- **42** One Brook Hall Cottages
- **53** Tudor Roost

WEDNESDAY 29
- **48** Saling Hall

THURSDAY 30
- **1** Barnards Farm
- **19** Feeringbury Manor

FRIDAY 31
- **19** Feeringbury Manor
- **35** Moverons
- **56** Wickham Place Farm

August

SATURDAY 1
- **29** Little Foxes

SUNDAY 2
- **29** Little Foxes

THURSDAY 6
- **1** Barnards Farm
- **16** Dragons

SATURDAY 8
- **53** Tudor Roost

SUNDAY 9
- **53** Tudor Roost

THURSDAY 13
- **1** Barnards Farm

SUNDAY 16
- **12** Court View

SUNDAY 30
- **14** Deers
- **17** Edelweiss
- **28** Hobbans Farm
- **37** North End Place
- **53** Tudor Roost

MONDAY 31
- **17** Edelweiss
- **53** Tudor Roost

September

FRIDAY 4
- **19** Feeringbury Manor
- **56** Wickham Place Farm

SATURDAY 5
- **3** 19 Brookfields
- **47** St Helens
- **52** Spencers

SUNDAY 6
- **1** Barnards Farm
- **3** 19 Brookfields
- **35** Moverons
- **44** Parsonage House

THURSDAY 10
- **19** Feeringbury Manor

FRIDAY 11
- **19** Feeringbury Manor
- **56** Wickham Place Farm

SUNDAY 13
- **12** Court View
- **25** Green Island
- **28** Hobbans Farm
- **50** Snares Hill Cottage

THURSDAY 17
- **16** Dragons
- **19** Feeringbury Manor

FRIDAY 18
- **19** Feeringbury Manor
- **56** Wickham Place Farm

SUNDAY 20
- **54** Ulting Wick

THURSDAY 24
- **19** Feeringbury Manor

FRIDAY 25
- **19** Feeringbury Manor
- **56** Wickham Place Farm

November

SUNDAY 8
- **25** Green Island

February 2010

SUNDAY 21
- **25** Green Island

Gardens open to the public

- **2** Beth Chatto Gardens
- **13** Cressing Temple
- **22** The Gibberd Garden
- **23** Glen Chantry
- **25** Green Island
- **31** Marks Hall Gardens & Arboretum
- **52** Spencers

By appointment only

- **4** Byndes Cottage
- **49** Shrubs Farm
- **59** Woolards Ash

Also open by appointment

- **1** Barnards Farm
- **3** 19 Brookfields
- **5** Casa Mia
- **6** Chippins
- **9** 352 Coggeshall Road
- **10** 1 The Cottage

- **12** Court View
- **16** Dragons
- **17** Edelweiss
- **19** Feeringbury Manor
- **20** 4 Fernlea Road
- **27** Hannams Hall
- **28** Hobbans Farm
- **33** 4 Millbridge Road
- **34** The Mount
- **35** Moverons
- **36** Newland Cottage
- **39** The Old School House
- **41** Olivers
- **42** One Brook Hall Cottages
- **43** Orchard Cottage
- **45** 164 Point Clear Road
- **46** Rookwoods
- **47** St Helens
- **48** Saling Hall
- **50** Snares Hill Cottage
- **51** South Shoebury Hall
- **53** Tudor Roost
- **54** Ulting Wick
- **56** Wickham Place Farm
- **57** Willow Cottage

The Gardens

1 BARNARDS FARM
Brentwood Road, West Horndon
CM13 3LX. Bernard & Sylvia Holmes
& The Christabella Charitable Trust,
01277 811262,
sylvia@barnardsfarm.eu,
www.barnardsfarm.eu. *5m S of
Brentwood. On A128, 1½ m S of
A127 Halfway House flyover. From the
junction continue on A128 under the
railway bridge. Garden on R just past
bridge.* Home-made teas (Suns), Light
lunches (Thurs). **Adm £5, chd free**
(share to St Francis Church, West
Horndon). Every Thurs 2 Apr to 13
Aug; (11-4.30); Suns 28 June; 6 Sept
(2-5.30). **Visitors also welcome by
appt, groups of 25+.**
A sculpture collection, incl works by
Frink, Gormley and Thomas
Heatherwick in 17 hectares of garden,
woodland and ponds. Panoramic
views from rose-covered belvedere,
Japanese, vegetable and bog gardens.
Home to the National Collection of
malus. Grass runway, aviators
welcome (PPO). The back garden
featuring a large Bramley apple tree
was completely redesigned and
replanted in 2008, introducing more
flowers and surprises. Picnickers
welcome on Thursdays. Featured on
ITV Bizarre Gardens. Wheelchair
accessible WC.

---

2 ◆ BETH CHATTO GARDENS
Elmstead Market CO7 7DB. Mrs
Beth Chatto, 01206 822007,
www.bethchatto.co.uk. *¼ m E of
Elmstead Market. On A133 Colchester
to Clacton Rd in village of Elmstead
Market.* **Adm £5, chd under 14 free.
Mons to Sats, Mar to Oct (9-5); Suns
Apr to Sept 11-5; Mons to Fris Nov
to Feb (9-4).**
6 acres of attractively landscaped
garden with many unusual plants,
shown in wide range of conditions
from hot and dry to water garden.
Famous gravel garden and woodland
garden. Disabled WC and parking.
Featured in 'Observer', 'Guardian
Weekend', 'Gardens Illustrated' and
Radio 4 Women's Hour special.

*Unusually
large pergola
festooned with
climbing roses,
clematis, jasmine
and morning
glory . . .*

3 19 BROOKFIELDS
Stebbing CM6 3SA. Trevor & Diane
Vaughan, 01371 856625. *3m NE of
Great Dunmow. Leave Gt Dunmow on
B1057, at Bran End turn R to Stebbing
Village, then 1st R into Brookfields.*
Adm £2.50, chd free (share to Helen
Rollason Heal Cancer Charity). Sats,
Suns 11, 12 July; 5, 6 Sept (1-5).
**Combined with St Helens adm £5,
5 Sept. Visitors also welcome by
appt groups 10+ anytime, coaches
permitted.**
0.6 acre tranquil site leading down to
Stebbing Brook and overlooking an
ancient meadow and farmland to the
rear. The garden features mixed
borders, limestone rock garden, gravel
area, vegetable beds, small woodland
area with several mature trees and new
plantings. Unusually large pergola
festooned with climbing roses,
clematis, jasmine and morning glory.

4 NEW BYNDES COTTAGE
CO9 2LZ. David & Margaret
MacLennan, 01787 269500,
byndes2@btinternet.com. *2m N
of Halstead on the A131. Take R
turning signed Pebmarsh & Bures.
3rd house on L before the village
round sharp bend.* **Adm £4, chd
free.** Visitors welcome by appt,
tour of garden and refreshments
incl for groups 10+. Parking for
cars and minibuses, roadside
access and nearby parking for
coaches.
Developing garden of 7 acres
adjoining thatched cottage in rural
setting. Diverse planting styles,
choice plants and habitats provide
yr-round interest. Features incl
spring bulbs, hostas, perennials
and alpine beds, shrubs,
ornamental cherries. Recently
planted 5-acre arboretum has over
50 species of malus and large
population of bee orchids. Planted
and maintained by owners drawing
on a lifetime of gardening in the
Middle East. Strong emphasis on
maintenance techniques, practical
solutions to resource conservation
and adaptation to climatic
conditions in a very dry part of the
county. Gravel parking area and
undulating grass so wheelchair and
mobility vehicle access best in dry
weather.
&. ✕ ⊗ ☎

5 CASA MIA
Rookery Lane, Great Totham,
Maldon CM9 8DF. Ted & Linda
Walker, 01621 891152. *2m S of
Tiptree. Situated in Gt Totham N,
Rookery Lane is off B1022 Maldon to
Colchester rd.* **Adm £2.50, chd free.**
Fri 29 May; Sun 19 July (1-5).
Visitors also welcome by appt,
groups 15+, June, July, Aug, tea &
cakes for groups only.
A garden on many levels split into
different areas. Scree garden, rockery
and borders with unusual perennials,
rose garden and large collection of
hemerocallis. Seating areas swathed
with climbing roses and clematis.
Winding paths lead to koi carp pond
and woodland walk with stream.
Rhododendrons, hostas, primulas,
astilbes, hydrangeas and other shade
loving plants flourish here. Tiptree
Jams famous tearoom open (2m N).
✕ ⊗ ☎

6 CHIPPINS
Heath Road, Bradfield CO11 2UZ.
Kit & Ceri Leese, 01255 870730,
ceri.leese@sky.com. *3m E of
Manningtree. On B1352, take main rd
through village. Bungalow is directly
opp primary school.* Home-made teas.
Adm £2.50, chd free. Combined with
Newland Cottage 13, 14 June, adm
£3.50. Sats 23 May; 11 July (11-5);
Sat 13, Sun 14 June; (11-6). Visitors
also welcome by appt, Apr to July
only.
Artist's garden and plantaholic's
paradise packed with interest.
Beginning with irises, herbaceous
geraniums, hostas and alliums.
Stream, wildlife pond brimming with
bog plants. Explosion of colour –
abundance of tubs, hanging baskets.
Wide borders featuring hemerocallis
and swathes of lilies. Later dahlias,
exotics (cannas, gingers, banana,
South African streptocarpus, aeonium
and agaves. Exhibition of paintings by
owner Kit Leese) (May).
&. ✕ ⊗ ☕ ☎

7 CHURCH LODGE
Park Road, Little Easton CM6 2JN.
Vivienne Crossland. *1m N of Gt
Dunmow. From Gt Dunmow, 1st
turning L on B184 to Thaxted, then R
to Little Easton Church opp the
garden.* **Adm £2.50, chd free (share
to Dunmow Catholic Church & Little
Easton C of E Church).** Sat 4, Sun 5
July (2-5).
A fun garden. Infused with vibrance
and peace which will both surprise and
delight! Many quirky corners and
interesting features - look for the
surprising stag. Fabulous hostas.
Dunmow Catholic Church & Little
Easton C of E Church.
⊗

Group opening

8 CLAVERING GARDENS
CB11 4PX. *7m N of Bishop's
Stortford. On B1038. Turn W off
B1383 at Newport.* Home-made teas
at Piercewebbs. **Combined adm £4,
chd free.** Sun 14 June (2-5).
Popular village with many C16 and
C17 timber-framed dwellings, beautiful
C14 church, village green with
thatched cricket pavilion and pitch.
New moon gate at Deers.
&. ☕

DEERS
Mr & Mrs S H Cooke. Also open
Sun 30 Aug.
(See separate entry).

PIERCEWEBBS
Mr & Mrs B R William-Powlett
Old walled garden, shrubs, lawns,
ha-ha, yew with topiary and stilt
hedges, pond and trellised rose
garden. Extensive views.

9 352 COGGESHALL ROAD
Braintree CM7 9EH. Sau Lin Goss,
01376 329753,
richiegoss@hotmail.com. *15m W of
Colchester. 10m N of Chelmsford.
From M11 J8 take A120 Colchester.
Follow A120 to Braintree r'about
(McDonalds). 1st exit into Cressing Rd
follow to T-lights. R into Coggeshall Rd.
500yds on R opp bus company.* Light
refreshments & teas, coffee & cake.
Adm £2.50, chd free. Sat 4, Sun 5
July (1.30-5). Visitors also welcome
by appt June to Sept, groups 10+,
2-3 weeks notice.
Sau Lin arrived from Hong Kong to
become enthralled with English
gardening. 'This is my little heaven',
she says of her garden which has
various themed areas, perennials,
roses and many other plants.
Japanese style mixed border garden,
fruit trees and shrubs. Various seating
and relaxing areas, fish pond with
many plants and wildlife.
Mediterranean style patio area, with old
established grape vine, passion flowers
and numerous pot plants of varying
sizes.
⊗ ☕ ☎

> Planted and
> maintained by
> owners drawing
> on a lifetime of
> gardening in the
> Middle East.
> Strong emphasis
> on maintenance
> techniques,
> practical solutions
> to resource
> conservation and
> adaptation to
> climatic
> conditions . . .

10 NEW 1 THE COTTAGE
Housham Tye, Harlow
CM17 0NY. Maria Miola & Cyril
Cleary, 01279 731352,
maria.miola@btinternet.com. *3m
outside Old Harlow. Leave J7 M11,
travel N on A414. At 4th r'about
with B183 turn R, then R at 2nd
r'about. At T-junction turn L signed
The Matchings. After 1m turn R
signed Housham Tye, High Laver &
Carters Green. Home-made teas.*
Adm £2, chd free. Sun 14 June
(2-6). Visitors also welcome by
appt.
Charming cottage garden of
approx 1/4 acre with unusual and
interesting perennials and shrubs.
Natural pond and woodland area
contrast with the gravel garden and
lawn. A selection of tree ferns,
acers and palms are also
displayed. The Gibberd Garden is
nearby.

✈ ⊛ ☕ ☎

11 NEW COURT HOUSE
Church Road, Twinstead
CO10 7NA. David & Pamela
Holland. *6m N of Halstead. From
A131 Halstead – Sudbury take turn
for Twinstead, at green turn L
signed church. Proceed 1m, past
church. Park nr black barn. Home-
made teas.* **Adm £3, chd free.**
Sun 19 July.
This romantic country garden
covers 1 acre and surrounds C17
house (not open). Features incl
ponds, specimen trees, lawns,
flower beds, sunken and gravel
gardens, grass garden plus fruit
and vegetable gardens. This is a
place of tranquillity and charm
inhabited by rare breed hens, pet
rabbits and wildlife. House is
surrounded by gravel.

♿ ⊛ ☕

12 COURT VIEW
276 Manchester Drive, Leigh-on-
Sea SS9 3ES. Ray Spencer &
Richard Steers, 01702 713221,
arjeyeski@courtview.demon.co.uk.
*4m W of Southend, off Kingswood
Chase. From A127 London: Under
A129 (Rayleigh) to next T-lights. R to
Leigh-on-Sea, at T-lights turn R. At
r'about (Old Vienna Restaurant)
straight on to dual carriageway. 3rd
turning on R into Kingswood Chase.
Straight over Bonchurch Ave, L to
Manchester Drive. From A13: 3rd rd W*

*from Somerfield (supermarket) turn N
into Kingswood Chase, R into
Manchester Drive. Home-made teas.*
Adm £3, chd free (share to
Southend Women's Aid). Suns 14
June; 19 July; 16 Aug; 13 Sept (2-6).
Visitors also welcome by appt
weekdays (12-3) June - Sept incl,
groups 10+.
Front providing colour throughout the
yr. Rear densely planted with exotic
species. Colourful patio with
insectivorous plants; shady, scented
arbour, intimate dining area, sculptural
butterfly bench overlooking pond fed
by a winding stream. Hidden beyond
bamboo is a deck with vibrant pots of
colour, meditative Buddha, vines and
vegetables.

✈ ⊛ ☕ ☎

> This is a
> place of
> tranquillity and
> charm inhabited
> by rare breed
> hens, pet
> rabbits and
> wildlife . . .

13 ◆ CRESSING TEMPLE
Witham Road, Cressing CM77 8PD.
Essex County Council, 01376
584903, www.cressingtemple.
org.uk. *3m S of Braintree. Midway
between Braintree & Witham on
B1018. Follow brown tourist signs.*
Adm £4, chd/concessions £3. 1
March to 31 Oct 10-5, last entry 4.
For NGS: Sun 31 May (10-5).
Tudor themed walled garden in tranquil
setting, featuring reconstructed
Elizabethan knot garden, forecourt,
nosegay garden, medicinal border and
fountain centrepiece. Inspired by 'A
Midsummer Night's Dream', only
plants, trees and foliage available to
the Tudor gardener are found here.
Guided tours are available on request.
Recently planted Cullen garden is lawn
with curving borders enclosed by
herbaceous plants and shrubs. Two

800 yr-old timber framed barns built by
the Knights Templar form a beautiful
backdrop to the walled garden. Visitors
can wander the 7 acres of this ancient
moated site. Garden tour at 3pm by
horticulturist. Featured in 'Essex Life'.

♿ ✈ ⊛ ☕

14 DEERS
Clavering CB11 4PX. Mr & Mrs S H
Cooke. *7m N of Bishop's Stortford.
On B1038. Turn W off B1383 (old A11)
at Newport. Home-made teas.* **Adm**
£3.50, chd free (share to Clavering
Jubilee Field). Sun 30 Aug (2-5).
Open with Clavering Gardens Sun
14 June.
9 acres. Judged by visitors to be a very
romantic garden. Shrub and
herbaceous borders; 3 ponds with
water lilies; old roses in formal garden;
pool garden; walled vegetable garden;
moon gate; field and woodland walks.
Plenty of seats to enjoy the tranquillity
of the garden. Dogs on leads.

♿ ☕

16 DRAGONS
Boyton Cross, Chelmsford
CM1 4LS. Mrs Margot Grice,
01245 248651,
mandmdragons@tiscali.co.uk.
*5m W of Chelmsford. On A1060.
1/2 m W of The Hare PH or 1/2 m E of
India Lounge.* **Adm £3, chd free.**
Thurs 16 Apr; 21 May; 18 June;
16 July; 6 Aug; 17 Sept (10-5).
Visitors also welcome by appt.
A plantswoman's 2/3 -acre garden,
planted to encourage wildlife. Superb
lawn and sumptuous colour-themed
border with striking plant
combinations, featuring specimen
plants, fernery, clematis, mature dwarf
conifers and grasses. Meandering
paths lead to ponds, patio, scree
garden and small vegetable garden.
2 summerhouses, one overlooking
stream and farmland.

✈ ⊛ ☕ ☎

17 EDELWEISS
20 Hartland Road, Hornchurch
RM12 4AD. Joan H Hogg & Pat F
Lowery, 01708 454610. *6m SW of
Brentwood. From Romford E along the
A124 past Tesco on L, turn R into
Albany Rd opp church on corner of
Park Lane on the L. Go to the bottom
of Albany Rd, humps all the way, turn L
at the end into Hartland Rd. Cream
teas.* **Adm £2, chd free. Suns 14**
June; 19 July; Sun 30, Mon 31 Aug
(3-6). Visitors also welcome by appt
June, July & Aug.

Small town garden 200ft x 25ft. Laid out to maximise small narrow plot and featuring many containers, baskets, seasonal bedding and mixed borders. Narrow access and steps not suitable for push-chairs or wheelchairs. Vegetable plot, dovecote and tiny prize-winning front garden. 'Secret Garden' with Pets' Remembrance Corner. Prize-winner - Havering in Bloom.

Path leads past children's 'fire pit' and ornamental greenhouse to decked area by the pool and woodland behind. Look out for dragons! . . .

18 FAIRWINDS
Chapel Lane, Chigwell Row IG7 6JJ. David & Sue Coates. *2m SE of Chigwell. Tube: 10 mins walk up hill from Grange Hill. Turn R at exit. Car: nr M25 J26 & North Circular. Signed Chigwell. Turning off Lambourne Rd. Park opp Chapel Lane in Lodge Close car park.* Home-made teas. **Adm £3, chd free. Sun 28 June (2-5).**
Country garden in the suburbs (200ft x 40ft). Approach by private rd to gravelled front garden. Side entrance leads to open area with large mixed borders. Path leads past children's 'fire pit' and decked area by the pool and woodland behind. Look out for dragons! Rustic fence separates wildlife pond and vegetable plot. Gravel and woodchip paths, uneven surfaces.

19 FEERINGBURY MANOR
Coggeshall Road, Feering CO5 9RB. Mr & Mrs Giles Coode-Adams, 01376 561946, sonia@coode-adams.demon.co.uk. *12m SW of Colchester. Between Coggeshall & Feering on Coggeshall Rd, 1m from Feering.* **Adm £4, chd free (share to Firstsite). Thurs, Fris, 1 Apr to 31 July; 4 Sept to 25 Sept (9-4). Visitors also welcome by appt.**
Flower beds surround house and ponds with a fascinating mix of bulbs, herbaceous, shrubs and climbers. Tulips flower under blossom in Apr/May, wild flowers and beds peak in June/July, berries and Michaelmas daisies in Sept. Sculpture, gazebo, gates and trellis designed and made by sculptor Ben Coode-Adams. Teas by request. Some steep slopes. No disabled WC.

20 4 FERNLEA ROAD
Burnham-on-Crouch CM0 8EJ. Frances & Andrew Franklin, franklins@f2s.com, www.franklins.f2s.com. *Take B1010 to Burnham-on-Crouch. Cross the railway bridge then take 4th turn on R, Hillside Rd. Fernlea Rd 2nd L, no.4 nr end of cul de sac on L.* **Adm £2.50, chd free. Combined with One Brook Hall Cottages adm £4.50. Wed 22, Sun 26 July (2-6). Visitors also welcome by appt June, July & Aug.**
Mediterranean cum Moroccan oasis on edge of riverside park. Small (50ft x 50ft) back garden with vine-covered pergola, tranquil water features, mosaics, sculptures, dense planting featuring some unusual varieties. Drought tolerant, low maintenance and with various seating areas (incl a Moroccan tent!), this garden is for relaxing in. Featured in 'Gardeners' World'.

21 FURZELEA
Bicknacre Road, Danbury CM3 4JR. Avril & Roger Cole-Jones. *4m E of Chelmsford, 4m W of Maldon. A414 to Danbury. In village centre (Eves Corner) turn S into Mayes Lane. Take R past Cricketers PH, then L into Bicknacre Rd. Parking in NT car park. Garden on R.* Home-made teas. **Adm £3, chd free. Sun 7 June (1-5). Evening Opening Mon 8 June (4-8).**
Country garden for scent and colour, approx 2/3 acre. Mixed planting of trees, shrubs, climbers, bulbs, grasses and

perennials - many scented roses. Informal planting carefully colour themed, woven between formal topiary, meandering to a thatched summerhouse on the lower circular lawn, past pond and white garden.

22 ◆ THE GIBBERD GARDEN
Marsh Lane, Gilden Way, Harlow CM17 0NA. The Gibberd Garden Trust, 01279 442112, www.thegibberdgarden.co.uk. *3m E of Harlow. Marsh Lane is a narrow turning off B183 (to Hatfield Heath), approx 2m E of junction with A414. Look for 'Gibberd Garden' brown signs on A414 & on R opp garden entrance on B183.* **House & garden £5, over 6 £1, concessions £3.50, garden only £4, chd over 6 £1, concessions £2.50. Sats, Suns, Weds, Bank Hols Apr to Sept 2-6.**
7-acre C20 garden designed by Sir Frederick Gibberd, on side of small valley. Terraces, wild garden, landscaped vistas, pools and streams, 'Roman Columns', moated log 'castle', gazebo, tree house and large collection of modern sculpture.

23 ◆ GLEN CHANTRY
Ishams Chase, Wickham Bishops CM8 3LG. Mr & Mrs W G Staines, 01621 891342, www.glenchantry.demon.co.uk. *1½ m SE of Witham. Take Maldon Rd from Witham, 1st L to Wickham Bishops. Cross narrow bridge over R Blackwater. Turn immed L up Ishams Chase by side of Blue Mills.* **Adm £3.50, chd 50p. Fris, Sats 15 May to 15 Aug. For NGS: Fris 5 June; 3 July (10-4).**
3-acre garden, emphasis on mixed borders, unusual perennials and shrub roses. Limestone rock gardens, ponds, formal specialist white garden, foliage beds with grasses and hostas. Famous adjacent specialist perennial nursery. Due to retirement of the owners 2009 will be our last yr of opening.

Drought tolerant, low maintenance . . .

24 NEW THE GRANARY, MAYSLAND FARM
Dunmow Road, Gt Easton CM6 2DH. Martin & Sue Ward. *1¹/₂ m N of Gt Dunmow on B184. R. From Saffron Waldon on B184 garden on L approx 1m past Woods Rolls Royce Garage & Gt Easton Village turning.* Home-made teas. **Adm £3.50, chd free. Mon 25 May (2-5); Sun 28 June (2-6).** Approx 1acre garden evolved over last 11yrs with a good variety of plants, shrubs and trees. Features lawn, borders and island flower beds, koi pond with waterfall and rockery. Arbour, dovecote, summerhouse and patio area – ideal for sitting to enjoy view of garden and indulge in home-made teas.

GREAT THURLOW HALL
See Suffolk.

Ideal for sitting to enjoy view of garden and indulge in home-made teas . . .

25 ◆ GREEN ISLAND
Park Road, Ardleigh CO7 7SP. Fiona Edmond, 01206 230455, www.greenislandgardens.co.uk. *3m NE of Colchester. From Ardleigh village centre, take B1029 towards Great Bromley. Park Rd is 2nd on R after level Xing. Garden is last on L.* **Adm £4, chd £1. Suns, Tues to Fris & BH Mons, 1 Feb to 30 Nov. For NGS: Suns 29 Mar; 12 July; 13 Sept; 8 Nov (10-5). 21 Feb 2010.** Professionally designed by Fiona Edmond, beautifully situated in 19 acres of woodland. Huge variety of unusual plants with lots of interest all yr with emphasis on scent and autumn colour. Stunning mixed borders, water garden, woodland walks, seaside garden, tree house, gravel garden and Japanese garden. Garden design exhibition, photographic display. 8 acres of woodland redevelopment opening 2009. Snowdrops and bluebells not to be missed. Featured in 'Country Homes & Interiors', 'Essex Lfe'.

26 NEW GREENACRES
Goldfinch Lane, Thundersley SS7 3LT. Trudy & David. *A127 towards Hadleigh or A13 towards Rayleigh, at double mini r'about at Woodmans PH turn into Hart Rd towards Thundersley Village, on bend turn into Common Approach, then R into The Common. This turns into Goldfinch Lane.* **Adm £4, chd free. Sats, Suns, Mons 2, 3, 4, 23, 24, 25 May (10-5).** Beautiful, tranquil, mature and developing 2 acre garden, set high. Large pond with bog garden, rose, clematis and wisteria walk and stunning spring time woodland path. Meandering pathways throughout, flanked by large deep borders filled with numerous amounts of flowering, trees, shrubs and perennials, many of which are rare and unusual, incl a wedding cake tree, pagoda and paulownia tree. Many of the plants seen in the garden will be available to buy. No WC available. Some gravel and woodchip paths, some steep slopes - restricted width to part of woodland walk.

17 GREENSTONE MEWS, E11
See London.

27 HANNAMS HALL
Thorpe Road, Tendring CO16 9AR. Mr & Mrs W Gibbon, 01255 830292. *10m E of Colchester. From A120 take B1035 at Horsley Cross, through Tendring Village (approx 3m) pass Cherry Tree PH on R, after ¹/₃ m over small bridge 1st house L.* **Adm £3, chd free. Sat 16, Sun 17 May (2-6). Visitors also welcome by appt no coaches.**
C17 house (not open) set in 6 acres of formal and informal gardens and grounds with extensive views over open countryside. Herbaceous borders and shrubberies, many interesting trees incl flowering paulownias. Lawns and mown walks through wild grass and flower meadows, woodland walks, ponds and stream. Walled vegetable potager and orchard.

28 HOBBANS FARM
Stoney Lane, Bobbingworth, Ongar CM5 0LZ. John & Ann Webster, 01277 890245. *10m W of Chelmsford. N of A414 between Ongar Four Wantz r'about & N Weald 'Talbot' r'about, turn R past Blake Hall. 1st farm entrance on R after St Germain's*

Church. Home-made teas. **Adm £3, chd free. Suns 19 Apr; 3, 17, 31 May; 14, 28 June; 12 July; 30 Aug; 13 Sept (2-5). Visitors also welcome by appt.**
Romantic, tranquil gardens. Herbaceous treasures, shrubs and old roses. Honeysuckle, roses, clematis clamber over trees, walls and arches. Crab apples underplanted with narcissi, unusual trees. Walk through meadows past willow and young birch to wild garden, wood, pond with bridge to ancient oak. Delicious Teas. May - blossom, bulbs, birds, bees. June - riot of roses, peonies, aquilegia, geraniums. July - clambering clematis. Sept - mellow fruitfulness, rich colours, hazy daisies, windflower and sedums.

29 LITTLE FOXES
Marcus Gardens, Thorpe Bay SS1 3LF. Mrs Dorothy Goode. *2¹/₂ m E of Southend. From Thorpe Bay stn (S-side) proceed E, take 4th on R into Marcus Ave then 2nd L into Marcus Gdns.* **Adm £2.50, chd 50p. Sat 1, Sun 2 Aug (2-5).**
This award-winning garden, close to the sea, has been described as an oasis of foliage and flowers. Secluded by trees, the ¹/₃ acre features island beds and long borders set in lawns and planted with an interesting variety of colourful hardy perennials, grasses, flowering shrubs and beautiful foliage. Many planted containers. Colour-themed areas and pretty water feature. Collection of special hostas. Tranquil garden for plant lovers. Seaside walks and views close to sea. Featured in 'Essex Life'.

30 LITTLE MYLES
Ongar Road, Stondon Massey CM15 0LD. Judy & Adrian Cowan. *1¹/₂ m SE of Chipping Ongar. Turn off A128 at Stag PH, Marden Ash, (Ongar) towards Stondon Massey. Over bridge, 1st house on R after S bend. (400yds the Ongar side of Stondon Massey Church).* Home-made teas. **Adm £3.50, chd £1. Sun 5 July (11-4).**
Romantic garden surrounded by wild flowers and grasses, set in 3 acres. Full borders, hidden features, meandering paths, pond, hornbeam pergola and stream. Herb garden, full of nectar-rich and scented herbs, used for handmade herbal cosmetics. Asian garden with pots, statues and bamboo, ornamental vegetable plot, woven willow Gothic window feature and wire elephant.

31 ◆ **MARKS HALL GARDENS & ARBORETUM**
Coggeshall CO6 1TG. Thomas Phillips Price Trust, 01376 563796, www.markshall.org.uk. *1½ m N of Coggeshall. Follow brown & white tourism signs from A120 Coggeshall by pass.* Adm £3.80, chd £1, concessions £3.20. Tues to Sun Apr to Oct (10.30-5), Fri to Sun Nov to Mar 10.30 - dusk.
The walled garden at Marks Hall is a unique blend of traditional long borders within C17 walls and 5 contemporary gardens. These combine inventive landscaping, grass sculpture and stunningly colourful mass plantings. On the opp lake bank is a millennium walk designed for winter shape, scent and colour surrounded by over 100 acres of arboretum, incl species from all continents.

&. ✕ ✿ ☕

Plenty of walks for birdwatchers through woods to Wrabness shore . . .

32 **60 MILL LANE**
Cressing CM77 8HW. Pauline & Arthur Childs. *2m S of Braintree. 15m W of Colchester, 5m N of Witham. From M11 J8 take A120 Colchester, follow A120 to Braintree r'about, then take B1018 to Witham approx ¾ m (Tye Green), turn R into Mill Lane 400yds on L. House facing you on green.* Home-made teas. Adm £2, chd free. Tue 9 June; Sun 12 July (1-5).
Small village estate garden which is a plantaholic's paradise. Very colourful, with 2 water features. Patio with pots and hanging baskets. Lover of penstemons and fuchsias. Many hostas, ferns and some unusual plants.

✕ ✿ ☕

33 **4 MILLBRIDGE ROAD**
Witham CM8 1HB. Sebastian & Andrew, 01376 503112. *A12 N exit 21 Witham, follow rd to 1st set T-lights, turn L. At T-junction turn R then 1st L Guithavon Rd, 1st L Millbridge Rd. A12 S exit 22 Witham, follow rd to 2nd set of T-lights turn R, at mini r'about turn L then 1st R Guithavon Valley, double mini r'about turn R Guithavon Rd, 1st R Millbridge Rd. Witham train stn 10 min walk.* Adm £2.50, chd free. Fris 15, 29 May; Sat 20 June; Fri 3 July (10-4.30). Visitors also welcome by appt.
Surprising small town garden 129ft x 29ft. Designed into themed areas, laid out to maximise space. Wander through Mediterranean style, British theme into oasis of tranquillity. Mixed borders, perennials, architectural foliage, bamboos and bananas all jostle for position. Large fish pond and hidden features, several seating areas to sit and contemplate.

&. ✕ ☎

34 **THE MOUNT**
Epping Road, Roydon CM19 5HT. David & Liz Davison, 077112 31555, davidandlizzy@aol.com. *2m W of Harlow in Roydon Village. W from Harlow on B181 Roydon Rd, enter Roydon Village. Pass the High St, garden approx 500yds on R. Look for a board & yellow balloons on green light bollards.* Light refreshments & teas, wine. Adm £3.50, chd free. Suns 24 May; 28 June; 26 July (11-5). Visitors also welcome by appt, groups of 10+, access for small coaches.
The Mount is a family garden designed to accommodate our dogs. Set in 8 acres. 3 acres of formal garden and 5 acres of newly planted woodland. Meadow with wide walkways winding through the trees. Designed as 8 separate areas, the formal gardens offer a wide variety of plants and shrubs with a superb G Gauge Model Railway, great for children. For disabled we can offer free use of golf buggy. Free loan of scooters and w/chairs by appt.

&. ✕ ✿ ☕ ☎

35 **MOVERONS**
Brightlingsea CO7 0SB. Lesley Orrock & Payne Gunfield, 01206 305498, lesley@moverons.com. *7m SE of Colchester. B1027. Turn R in Thorrington onto B1029 signed Brightlingsea. At old church turn R signed Moverons Farm, follow lane &*
garden signs for approx 1m. Home-made teas (Suns only). Adm £3, chd free. Sun 7 June; Fris 3 July to 31 July; Sun 6 Sept (11-5). Visitors also welcome by appt, groups of 10+, easy access & parking for coaches.
Beautiful and peaceful country garden with stunning estuary views. Redevelopment of tennis court completed with raised beds and reflection pool. Courtyard garden and mixed borders with a wide variety of planting for varied conditions – drought, sun, shade, bog and poolside. Magnificent mature native trees and of course those views.

✕ ✿ ☕ ☎

36 NEW **NEWLAND COTTAGE**
Primrose Hill, Wrabness CO11 2TZ. Bev & Mark Griggs, 01255 886116, beverleygriggs@aol.com. *5m E of Manningtree. Primrose Hill off B1352 Bradfield to Harwich rd. Turn up Primrose Hill/Rectory Rd, last white cottage on hill before LH-bend.* Home-made teas. Adm £2.50, chd free. Combined with **Chippins** adm £3.50. Sat 13, Sun 14 June (11-6). Visitors also welcome by appt 15 - 28 June only.
Quintessential English cottage garden, 1 acre designed and created by owners in different pockets. Herbaceous borders containing a wealth of plants, shrubs and trees, pond, vegetable patch and formal garden with rotunda, fruit trees and chickens. We are in the process of erecting a Victorian glasshouse. Garden backs onto Wrabness woods owned by RSPB. Plenty of walks for birdwatchers through woods to Wrabness shore. Gravel drive, nearby parking.

&. ✕ ✿ ☕ ☎

37 NEW **NORTH END PLACE**
North End CM6 3PQ. Mr & Mrs R Benbrook, www.thecountrygardener.co.uk. *3m SE of Great Dunmow. From Dunmow take A130 signed Chelmsford, after 2½ m take 2nd North End turn on L down Black Chapel Lane. 1000yds on R turn into 'private rd'.* Home-made teas & wine. Adm £4, chd free. Sat 2, Suns 3 May; 14 June; 30 Aug (1-5).

7 acres surrounding Georgian House (not open). Created over past 8yrs by owner Claire Benbrook. Mature-tree-lined drive leads you through a gate into a carriage driveway surrounded by billowing mixed borders. Walled kitchen garden, cutting garden, greenhouse, parterre, lime walk, woodland planting, topiary, white garden. Views across the Chelmer valley to church and village of Felsted. Child friendly. Exhibition & sale of Botanical Art. From car park walk available (dogs permitted) along R Chelmer (approx 1hr). Partial wheelchair access, gravel paths, gentle slopes and some steps.

♿ ✖ ❊ ☕

Drive leads you through a gate into a carriage driveway surrounded by billowing mixed borders . . .

38 THE OLD RECTORY

Boreham CM3 3EP. Sir Jeffery & Lady Bowman. *4m NE of Chelmsford. Take B1137 Boreham Village, turn into Church Rd at Red Lion PH. 1/2 m along on R opp church.* Home-made teas. **Adm £3, chd free (share to Farleigh Hospice).** Sun 31 May (2-5). 2½ -acre garden surrounding C15 house (not open). Ponds, stream, with bridges and primulas, small meadow and wood with interesting trees and shrubs, herbaceous borders and vegetable garden. Constantly being improved.

♿ ✖ ❊ ☕

39 NEW THE OLD SCHOOL HOUSE

Plough Road, Great Bentley CO7 8LD. Georgie Roberts, 01206 251865, groberts@essex.ac.uk. *6m E of Colchester. In Great Bentley at staggered junction in village, turn across the village green signed Angers Geen & the station. House, red brick Victorian on R after*

shops, next to primary school. Light refreshments & wine. **Adm £3, chd free.** Sats, Suns 20, 21, 27, 28 June (3-7). Visitors also welcome by appt, coaches permitted weekends only. Catering by arrangement.
Enclosed, formally planned garden around a long box-edged axis running from a paved and gravelled seating area at the back of the house. Within the formal structure planting is relaxed incl pots around the seating area, mixed borders (emphasis on roses), a ruin surrounded by ferns, other features incl ponds, fountains, small birch grove and French greenhouse.

✖ ☕ ☎

40 THE OLD VICARAGE

Church End, Rickling CB11 3YL. Mr & Mrs C Firmin. *5m N of Stansted Mountfitchet. B1383 towards Newport. Turn L to Rickling Green through village towards church (1½ m). Garden on rd to Wicken & Newport.* Home-made teas. **Adm £3.50, chd free.** Sun 7 June (2-5).
Early Victorian vicarage (not open) surrounded by 1½ acres of mature gardens. Old wall and well-established hedges provide shelter and excellent backdrop to large closely planted borders, filled with a mixture of shrubs, herbaceous plants and old roses. Lily pond, formal rose garden and small walled vegetable garden. Gravel driveway and paths.

♿ ✖ ❊ ☕

41 OLIVERS

Olivers Lane, Colchester CO2 0HJ. Mr & Mrs D Edwards, 01206 330575, gay.edwards@virgin.net. *3m SW of Colchester. Between B1022 & B1026. From zoo continue 1m towards Colchester. Turn R at r'about (Cunobelin Way) & R into Olivers Lane. From Colchester via Maldon Rd turn L at r'about, R into Olivers Lane.* Light refreshments & teas. **Adm £4, chd free.** Sat 25, Sun 26 Apr (2-6). Visitors also welcome by appt.
Peaceful wooded garden overlooking Roman river valley. Dramatic bedding, yew backed borders closely planted with wide variety of plants. Refreshments on terrace of C18 redbrick house (not open) overlooking lakes, lawns and meadow. Woodland with fine trees, underplanted with shrubs and carpeted with a mass of spring bulbs and bluebells.

♿ ✖ ❊ ☕ ☎

42 ONE BROOK HALL COTTAGES

Steeple Road, Latchingdon CM3 6LB. John & Corinne Layton, 01621 741680, corinne@arrow250.fsnet.co.uk. *1m from Latchingdon Church. From Maldon drive through Latchingdon to mini r'about at church taking exit towards Steeple & Bradwell. Approx 1m turn R at bungalow onto gravel drive.* Home-made teas. **Adm £2.50, chd free. Combined with 4 Fernlea Road adm £4.50.** Wed 22, Sun 26 July (2-6). Visitors also welcome by appt groups of 10+.
1/3 -acre, naturalistic organic garden on 3 levels. Mixed borders densely planted with perennials and grasses in subtle combinations. Decked area overlooking farmland with boardwalk leading to natural wildlife pond and bog garden. Formal lawn with pleached limes and box hedges. Narrow paths and steep steps - not suitable for children and people with walking difficulties. Footpath walk to R Blackwater. Featured in 'Amateur Gardening'.

✖ ❊ ☕ ☎

43 ORCHARD COTTAGE

219 Hockley Road, Rayleigh SS6 8BH. Heather & Harry Brickwood, 01268 743838, henry.brickwood@homecall.co.uk. *1m NE from town centre. Leave A127 at Rayleigh and take B1013 to Hockley. Garden opp the white & blue sign for Hockley. Park opp on grass.* Home-made teas. **Adm £3, chd free.** Suns 31 May; 19 July (11-5). Visitors also welcome by appt.
Award-winning garden of approx 3/4 acre. Lawns slowly shrinking as packed borders expand! New central bed in the front will be a mass of colour. June's main feature will be over 500 aquilegias backed up by roses, lilies and numerous other herbaceous perennials; July will see exuberant lilies, hermerocallis, agapanthus plus colour themed beds. Pond, stream with waterfalls, and many flowering shrubs. Winner of Best Garden in Rayleigh.

♿ ❊ ☕ ☎

44 PARSONAGE HOUSE

Helions Bumpstead CB9 7AD. The Hon & Mrs Nigel Turner. *3m S of Haverhill. 8m NE of Saffron Walden. From Xrds in village centre turn up Church Hill, follow rd for 1m. Park in field opp.* Home-made teas. **Adm £3.50, chd free.** Suns 7 June; 6 Sept (3-5).

C15 house (not open) surrounded by 3 acres of formal gardens with mixed borders, topiary, pond, potager and greenhouse. Further 3-acre wild flower meadow with rare trees and further 3 acres of newly-planted orchard of old East Anglian apple varieties. Featured in 'The English Garden' Rare Plants.

 ♿ ✕ ❊ ☕

45 NEW 164 POINT CLEAR ROAD

St Osyth CO16 8JB. Brian & Wendy Wickenden, 01255 821744, briwick@aol.com. *4m W of Clacton. At St Osyth Xrds follow sign for Point Clear, across lake, approx 1/2 m on R.* **Adm £2.50, chd free. Suns 12 Apr; 14 June; 19 July (11-5). Visitors also welcome by appt.**

³/₄ -acre plantsman's garden that incorporates mixed borders of some 1500 different perennials, shrubs and trees, many of which are unusual. National Collection of Corydalis. Other features incl a stream of approx 100ft leading to pond, bridges, scree beds and grasses in gravel area. Bark paths, grass areas uneven in places.

♿ ❊ **NCCPG** ☕ ☎

THE PRIORY
See Suffolk.

46 NEW ROOKWOODS

Yeldham Road, Sible Hedingham CO9 3QG. Peter & Sandra Robinson, 01787 460224, sandy1989@btinternet.com. *8m N of Halstead. Sible Hedingham on A1017 between Braintree & Haverhill. From Haverhill take 1st R almost immed after 30mph sign, turn L by gate lodge through white gates.* Home-made teas. **Adm £3, chd free. Fri 15, Mon 25, Fri 29 May (2-5.30). Visitors also welcome by appt May & June only.**

Planted 6yrs ago, this new garden shows how quickly pleached hornbeam can develop. Large mixed borders surrounded by a selection of young and mature trees. Walk through meadow to 8-acre ancient oak wood. Gravel drive from parking to garden.

♿ ✕ ❊ ☕ ☎

ROSEDALE
See Suffolk

47 ST HELENS

High Street, Stebbing CM6 3SE. Stephen & Joan Bazlinton, 01371 856495, joanbazlinton@phonecoop.coop. *3m E of Great Dunmow. Leave Gt Dunmow on B1256. Take 1st L to Stebbing, at T-junction turn L into High St, garden 2nd house on R.* Home-made teas. **Adm £3, chd free (share to Dentaid). Sats 25 Apr; 30 May; 5 Sept (11-5). Combined with 19 Brookfields adm £5, 5 Sept. Visitors also welcome by appt.**

1-acre garden, created out of a damp bat willow plantation from 1987. Sloping S-wards with springs flowing into a hidden pond crossed by 'Monet' bridge. Mature hedges create vistas of surprise as gentle paths weave through shrubs and plants blending to achieve peace and purpose in this rural idyll.

✕ ☕ ☎

Stunning natural swimming pool which is bordered by romantic cottage beds and formal bed . . .

48 SALING HALL

Great Saling, Braintree CM7 5DT. Mr & Mrs Hugh Johnson, www.salinghall.com. *6m NW of Braintree. Turn N off B1256 (old A120) between Gt Dunmow & Braintree signed Great Saling & the Bardfields. Saling Hall is at end of village on L.* **Adm £4, chd free (share to St Jame's Church, Gt Saling). Weds 6 May to 29 July (2-5). Visitors also welcome by appt, groups, weekdays only, by written application, see above.**

Plantsman's country garden of 12acres, internationally famous for its collections of rare trees and shrubs in a sylvan landscape, chronicled over the past 35yrs by Hugh Johnson in his

monthly Tradescant's Diary. 6 ponds, Temple of Pisces, menhir and many vistas make a garden of moods and surprises, beauty and strong botanical interest. House (not open) and walled flower garden dated 1699.

♿ ✕ ☎

49 SHRUBS FARM

Lamarsh CO8 5EA. Mr & Mrs Robert Erith, 01787 227520, bob@shrubsfarm.co.uk, www.shrubsfarm.co.uk. *1¼ m from Bures. On rd to Lamarsh, the drive is signed to Shrubs Farm.* Home-made teas £2.50 by arrangement. **Adm £4, chd free. Visitors welcome by appt for parties of all sizes, May to July, Sept & Oct are best months. Ample parking for cars and coaches.**

2 acres of mature and developing gardens with shrub borders, lawns, roses and trees. For walkers there are 50 acres of parkland and meadow with wild flower paths and woodland trails. Dogs on leads in this area. Much new hedgerow and tree planting incl over 50 species of oak has taken place over the past 25yrs. Superb 10m views to N and E over the Stour valley. Ancient coppice and pollard trees in the woods incl the largest goat (pussy) willow (*Salix caprea*) in England. Rare Bee orchid variety *bicolour* was found in June 2005. Wollemi pine, Norfolk pine and banana trees. Full size black rhinoceros. Display of Bronze age burial urns. Woodland paths are boggy in wet weather.

♿ ☕ ☎

50 NEW SNARES HILL COTTAGE

Duck End, Stebbing CM6 3RY. Pete & Liz Stabler, 01371 856565, lizstabler@hotmail.com. *Between Dunmow & Bardfield. 1½ m past Stebbing turning past B&T auto salvage yard on B1057.* Home-made teas. **Adm £3.50, chd free. Suns 21 June; 13 Sept (10-4). Visitors also welcome by appt.**

Our peaceful 1¼ acre garden is divided into several small areas which incl natural bog garden, apple orchard, beach garden, fern and fountain gardens, informal style flower beds. The garden has many water features incl stunning natural swimming pool which is bordered by romantic cottage beds and formal bed.

✕ ☕ ☎

51 SOUTH SHOEBURY HALL
Church Road, Shoeburyness
SS3 9DN. Mr & Mrs M Dedman,
01702 299022. *4m E of Southend-on-Sea. Enter Southend on A127 to Eastern Ave A1159 signed Shoebury. R at r'about to join A13. Proceed S to Ness Rd. R into Church Rd. Garden on L 50 metres.* Home-made teas. **Adm £3.50, chd free (share to St Andrews Church). Suns 12 Apr; 19 July (2-5). Visitors also welcome by appt.**
Delightful, 1-acre walled garden close to sea. An established garden surrounding Grade 2 listed house (not open) and bee round house. Unusual trees and shrubs. Many spring bulbs and outstanding agapanthus varieties in late July. Rose borders, dry garden areas, Mediterranean and Southern Hemisphere plants plus 30yr old geraniums. Exciting new larger borders with tulips, fritillaria and agapanthus. Featured in local press & on radio.
&♿ ✿ ☕ ☎

52 NEW ♦ SPENCERS
Great Yeldham CO9 4JG.
William & Caroline Courtauld,
01787 238175,
www.spencersgarden.net. *Just N of Gt Yeldham on Clare rd. Turn off A1017 in Gt Yeldham at Domesday Oak. Keep L (signed Clare, Belchamp St Paul). Pass 1st entrance to Spencers and 1/4 m later turn L at Spencers Lodge.* Home-made teas. **Adm £4, chd free. By appt only, for opening details please tel or see website. For NGS: Sats 6 June; 5 Sept (2-5).**
Romantic C18 walled garden laid out by Lady Anne Spencer, grand daughter of the 1st Duke of Marlborough, who also built the house (not open). Now overflowing with blooms following Tom Stuart-Smith's renovation. Supposedly oldest greenhouse in Essex. Huge tumbling wisteria, armies of 'true-blue' Lord Butler delphiniums ('Rab' lived at Spencers in the 1970s-80s), vibrant green clover garden. Set in mature grounds with many ancient trees. Victorian woodland garden below in little valley formed by young R Colne. Featured in 'Country Life' & 'The English Garden'.
&♿ ✕ ✿ ☕

4 STRADBROKE GROVE
See London.

53 TUDOR ROOST
18 Frere Way, Fingringhoe CO5 7BP.
Chris & Linda Pegden, 01206 729831,
christopher.pegden@virgin.net. *5m S of Colchester. In centre of village by Whalebone PH. Follow sign to Ballast Quay, after 1/2 m turn R into Brook Hall Rd, then 1st L into Frere Way.* Home-made teas. **Adm £3, chd free. Sat 4, Sun 5, 12, Mon 13 Apr; Suns, Mons 3, 4, 24, 25 May; Tue 16, Wed 17 June; Sats, Suns 4, 5, 25, 26 July; 8, 9, 30, Mon 31 Aug (2-5.30). Visitors also welcome by appt coaches permitted.**
An unexpected hidden colourful 1/4-acre garden. Well manicured grassy paths wind round island beds and ponds. Densely planted subtropical area with architectural and exotic plants - cannas, bananas, palms, agapanthus, agaves and tree ferns surround a colourful gazebo. Garden planted to provide yr-round colour and encourage wildlife. Many peaceful seating areas. Within 1m of Fingringhoe Wick Nature Reserve. Featured in 'Colchester Gazette'.
✿ ☕ ☎

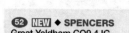

Huge tumbling wisteria, armies of 'true-blue' Lord Butler delphiniums ('Rab' lived at Spencers in the 1970s-80s) . . .

54 ULTING WICK
Maldon CM9 6QX. Mr & Mrs B Burrough, 01245 380216,
philippa.burrough@btinternet.com. *3m NW of Maldon. Take turning to Ulting (Ulting Lane) off B1019 at Langford, after 2.2m at T-junction, garden is opp.* Home-made teas. **Adm £3, chd free. Sun 20 Sept (2-5). Visitors also welcome by appt, groups of 10+. Parking space for 2 coaches.**

First autumn opening of 4 acre garden set around C16 farmhouse and barns. Many herbaceous borders incl striking pink and dramatic, dahlia filled, cutting garden. Natural pond and stream bordered by mature willows, moisture and shade loving plants. Vegetable garden with Victorian style glasshouse, 3 acre woodland planted in 2004. Walk to All Saints Ulting Church by R Chelmer, signed from garden. Church will be open for talk on its history. Featured in 'Country Living' & 'The Guardian'.
&♿ ✕ ✿ ☕ ☎

55 NEW WEST HANNINGFIELD HALL
Hall Lane, West Hanningfield CM2 8XA. Mr & Mrs M Iles. *5m S of Chelmsford. Leave A12 J16 onto B1007 (S), at Ship PH turn L into Ship Rd, after 3/4 m turn L into Hall Lane.* **Adm £3, chd free. Sun 24 May (11.30-5).**
Stunning large country garden surrounded by farmland originally developed over 30yrs ago on a sloping site and considerably extended. Altered and restocked during last 10yrs. Lawns with large borders containing shrubs, shrub roses and perennials. Features incl formal rose garden, 2 ponds, pergola, vegetable area and collection of young trees. Approx 3/4 m from Hanningfield Reservoir.
✕

56 WICKHAM PLACE FARM
Station Road, Wickham Bishops CM8 3JB. Mrs J Wilson, 01621 891282, enquiries@wickhamplacefarm.co.uk,
www.wickhamplacefarm.co.uk. *21/2 m SE of Witham. Take B1018 from Witham to Maldon. After going under A12 take 3rd L (Station Rd). 1st house on L.* Home-made teas. **Adm £3, chd free. Fris 24 Apr to 31 July; 4 Sept to 25 Sept (11-4). Visitors also welcome by appt groups 10+ & coaches, anytime.**
2-acre walled garden with huge climbers and roses. Wide borders filled by shrubs, perennials and bulbs. Renowned for stunning wisterias in May/June, one over 250ft long. 12 acres of mixed woodland, superb in Sept, incl rabbit-resistant plants and bulbs, features lovely walks. Yr-round colour; knot garden.
&♿ ✕ ✿ ☕ ☎

57 WILLOW COTTAGE

4 Stambourne Road, Great Yeldham
CO9 4RA. Mr & Mrs R Templeman,
01787 238405,
templeman431@btinternet.com.
*1m from Gt Yeldham Church. From
Braintree N on A1017. Follow sign to
Gosfield & on to Gt Yeldham. Pass
church, 1st L Stambourne Rd,
entrance 400yds on R. Home-made
teas.* **Adm £2.50, chd free.Sat 20,
Sun 21 June (2-5). Visitors also
welcome by appt May to Aug.**
Pretty cottage garden set in ⅓ acre
adjacent to farmland. Mixed borders
full of plants and shrubs that attract
birds, bees and butterflies. Enjoy the
peace and tranquillity of the Essex
countryside while having a delicious
home-made cream tea served in
delightful surroundings under flower
covered arbours and patio with
colourful pots.

58 NEW WOODPECKERS

Clacton Road, Thorrington
CO7 8JW. David & Yvonne
Pariser. *Between Colchester &
Clacton. Woodpeckers is situated
on B1027 Colchester- Clacton rd.
Park in village hall.* Home-made
teas. **Adm £3, chd free.Sun 3,
Mon 4 May (2-5).**
Attractive, immaculate 1 acre
formal style gardens surrounding
modern house (not open), featuring
yew and box topiary, herbaceous
borders and summerhouses.
Impressive Italianate koi pond set
in large patio. French inspired
gravelled orchard with soft fruit and
vegetable beds. Can you find the
fairy house.

French inspired gravelled orchard with soft fruit and vegetable beds. Can you find the fairy house . . .

59 WOOLARDS ASH

Hatfield Broad Oak CM22 7JY. Mr &
Mrs Michael Herbert, 01279 718284,
mleqh@woolardsash.fsnet.co.uk.
*5m SE of Bishop's Stortford. From
Hatfield Broad Oak follow B183 N
(towards Takeley). After ¾ m take 1st R
(signed to Taverners Green &
Broomshawbury), then 2nd R to
Woolards Ash. From Takeley, B183 S
(towards Hatfield Broad Oak). After
¾ m 1st L (signed Canfield & High
Roding), then 2nd L to Woolards Ash.*
Teas. **Adm £5, chd free.Visitors
welcome by appt Apr to July,
groups of 10+, coaches permitted.**
Peacocks, guinea fowl and bantams
roam this beautiful 3-acre garden,
divided into 5 areas by beech and yew
hedges, all set in a pastoral landscape.
The main area has 2 large subtly
planted borders of old roses, shrubs,
herbaceous plants and ha-ha with
distant views. The walled pool garden
provides a tranquil setting for mature
borders with further shrub borders,
mature trees and wild areas planted
with bulbs and old roses, small
vegetable garden.

60 WRITTLE COLLEGE

Writtle CM1 3RR, www.writtle.ac.uk.
*4m W of Chelmsford. On A414, nr
Writtle village, clearly signed.* **Adm £3,
chd free.Suns 15 Mar; 12 July
(10-4).**
Approx 15 acres; informal lawns with
naturalised bulbs in spring and wild
flowers in summer, large tree
collection, mixed shrub and
herbaceous borders, heathers and
alpines. Landscaped gardens
designed and built by students
including 'Centenary' garden and sub
tropical 'Hot 'n' Spicy' garden.
Development of new 13-acre parkland
area. Orchard meadow, recently
started on the site of an old apple
orchard. Landscaped glasshouses and
wide range of seasonal bedding
displays. Horticultural information from
Writtle College tutors.

Essex County Volunteers

County Organiser
Susan Copeland, Wickets, Langley Upper Green, Saffron Walden CB11 4RY, 01799 550553,
susan.copeland2@btinternet.com

County Treasurer
Neil Holdaway, Woodpeckers, Mangapp Chase, Burnham-on-Crouch CM0 8QQ, 01621 782137,
lindaholdaway@btinternet.com

Publicity & Assistant County Organisers
Doug Copeland, Wickets, Langley Upper Green, Saffron Walden, Essex CB11 4RY, 01799 550553,
susan.copeland2@btinternet.com
Linda Holdaway, Woodpeckers, Mangapp Chase, Burnham-on-Crouch CM0 8QQ, 01621 782137,
lindaholdaway@btinternet.com

Mark your diary with these special events in 2009

EXPLORE SECRET GARDENS DURING CHELSEA & HAMPTON COURT FLOWER SHOW WEEKS

Tue 19 May, Wed 20 May, Thur 21 May, Fri 22 May, Wed 8 July, Thur 9 July
Full day tours from £82 per person, 10% discount for groups
Advance booking required, telephone +44 (0)20 8693 1015 or email j.wookey@btinternet.com
Specially selected gardens in London, Essex, Kent, Hampshire and South Oxfordshire. The tour price includes transport and lunch with wine at a popular restaurant or pub.

HAMPTON COURT PALACE

Thur 2 Apr, Tue 23 June, Thur 25 June, Wed 15 July, Tue 4 Aug, Thur 10 Sept
Evening tours in the company of one of the Palace's specialist tour guides from 6.30 – 8pm.
Tickets £6 per person. Advance booking required, telephone +44 (0)1483 211535 or visit www.ngs.org.uk for more information
Gossip, scandal, murder, healing – you'll find it all within the Formal Gardens at Hampton Court Palace. Each tour will have its own unique feature whether it's the story of the Great Vine or the magic and mystery of the Maze.

FROGMORE – A ROYAL GARDEN (BERKSHIRE)

Tue 26 May 10am – 5.30pm (last admission 4pm)
Garden adm £4.50, chd free. Tickets available in advance or on the day.
Advance booking for groups and coaches, telephone
+44 (0) 1483 211535 or email orders@ngs.org.uk
A rare opportunity to explore 30 acres of landscaped garden, rich in history and beauty.

FLAXBOURNE FARM – FUN & SURPRISES (BEDFORDSHIRE)

Sun 7 June 10am – 5pm. Adm £5, chd free
No booking required, come along on the day!
Bring the whole family and have fun in this surprising and entertaining garden of 2 acres. Enjoy the large plant fair, live music, pets corner, birds of prey, dog agility show and much more.

WISLEY RHS GARDEN – MUSIC IN THE GARDEN (SURREY)

Fri 11 Sept 6 – 9pm
Adm (incl RHS members) £7, chd under 15 free
Save money on advance bookings for groups of 4 or more, telephone +44 (0)1483 211535 or visit www.ngs.org.uk for more information
A special evening opening of this famous garden, exclusively for the NGS. Enjoy music and entertainment as you explore the gardens and the floral marquee on the first day of the Wisley Flower Show.

For further information visit www.ngs.org.uk or telephone 01483 211535

GLOUCESTERSHIRE

(for South Gloucestershire see Somerset, Bristol Area & S Glos)

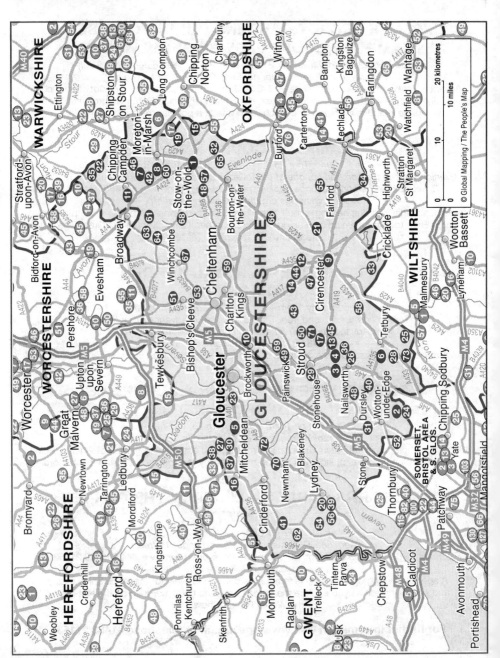

Opening Dates

January

SUNDAY 25
- 27 Home Farm

February

SUNDAY 8
- 27 Home Farm
- 69 Trench Hill

MONDAY 9
- 47 The Old Rectory, Duntisbourne Rous

SUNDAY 15
- 69 Trench Hill

SUNDAY 22
- 34 Kempsford Manor

March

SUNDAY 1
- 34 Kempsford Manor

SUNDAY 8
- 20 Green Cottage
- 34 Kempsford Manor

MONDAY 9
- 47 The Old Rectory, Duntisbourne Rous

SUNDAY 15
- 20 Green Cottage
- 27 Home Farm
- 34 Kempsford Manor
- 51 Pear Tree Cottage

SUNDAY 22
- 20 Green Cottage

April

SUNDAY 5
- 1 Abbotswood
- 23 Highnam Court
- 27 Home Farm
- 43 Misarden Park
- 46 The Old Chequer
- 62 South Lodge

SUNDAY 12
- 6 Beverston Castle
- 34 Kempsford Manor
- 36 Lammas Park
- 69 Trench Hill

MONDAY 13
- 6 Beverston Castle
- 42 Mill Dene Garden
- 69 Trench Hill

WEDNESDAY 15
- 39 Lydney Park Spring Garden

SUNDAY 19
- 41 Meadow Cottage
- 51 Pear Tree Cottage

- 64 Stanway Fountain & Water Garden
- 65 Stone House

MONDAY 20
- 35 Kiftsgate Court

SUNDAY 26
- 7 Blockley Gardens
- 27 Home Farm
- 34 Kempsford Manor
- 46 The Old Chequer

MONDAY 27
- 47 The Old Rectory, Duntisbourne Rous

May

SUNDAY 3
- 17 Eastcombe, Bussage and Brownshill Gardens
- 23 Highnam Court
- 34 Kempsford Manor
- 56 Ramblers
- 62 South Lodge

MONDAY 4
- 17 Eastcombe, Bussage and Brownshill Gardens
- 34 Kempsford Manor

SUNDAY 10
- 12 Cerney House Gardens
- 19 Grange Farm
- 54 Priors Mesne

TUESDAY 12
- 39 Lydney Park Spring Garden

WEDNESDAY 13
- 15 Daylesford House

SATURDAY 16
- 4 Bell Gardens

SUNDAY 17
- 20 Green Cottage
- 34 Kempsford Manor
- 41 Meadow Cottage
- 51 Pear Tree Cottage
- 54 Priors Mesne
- 66 Stowell Park

SATURDAY 23
- 28 Hookshouse Pottery

SUNDAY 24
- 20 Green Cottage
- 28 Hookshouse Pottery
- 34 Kempsford Manor
- 73 Westonbirt School Gardens

MONDAY 25
- 28 Hookshouse Pottery
- 34 Kempsford Manor
- 47 The Old Rectory, Duntisbourne Rous
- 73 Westonbirt School Gardens

TUESDAY 26
- 28 Hookshouse Pottery
- 62 South Lodge

WEDNESDAY 27
- 28 Hookshouse Pottery
- 38 Lower Farm House

THURSDAY 28
- 28 Hookshouse Pottery

FRIDAY 29
- 28 Hookshouse Pottery

SATURDAY 30
- 5 Berrys Place Farm
- 28 Hookshouse Pottery
- 37 Longhope Gardens

SUNDAY 31
- 5 Berrys Place Farm
- 11 Campden House
- 20 Green Cottage
- 28 Hookshouse Pottery
- 37 Longhope Gardens
- 40 The Matara Garden

June

WEDNESDAY 3
- 20 Green Cottage
- 38 Lower Farm House
- 48 Owlpen Manor
- 69 Trench Hill

SATURDAY 6
- 29 Humphreys End House
- 45 The Old Chapel

SUNDAY 7
- 7 Blockley Gardens
- 20 Green Cottage
- 23 Highnam Court
- 26 Holcombe Glen Cottage
- 29 Humphreys End House
- 31 Hunts Court
- 33 Kemble Mill
- 45 The Old Chapel
- 46 The Old Chequer
- 56 Ramblers
- 59 Sandywell Gardens
- 64 Stanway Fountain & Water Garden

MONDAY 8
- 45 The Old Chapel

TUESDAY 9
- 45 The Old Chapel

WEDNESDAY 10
- 20 Green Cottage
- 45 The Old Chapel
- 69 Trench Hill

THURSDAY 11
- 45 The Old Chapel

FRIDAY 12
- 45 The Old Chapel

SATURDAY 13
⑶ Atcombe Court
⒀ Chalford Gardens
⒁ Cotswold Farm
㊺ The Old Chapel

SUNDAY 14
⒀ Chalford Gardens
⒁ Cotswold Farm
⒇ Green Cottage
㉛ Hunts Court
㊺ The Old Chapel
(51) Pear Tree Cottage

MONDAY 15
㊺ The Old Chapel

TUESDAY 16
㊺ The Old Chapel

WEDNESDAY 17
⒅ Eyford Gardens
⒇ Green Cottage
㊺ The Old Chapel
(57) Rockcliffe
(69) Trench Hill

THURSDAY 18
㊺ The Old Chapel

FRIDAY 19
㊺ The Old Chapel

SATURDAY 20
㊲ Longhope Gardens
㊺ The Old Chapel

SUNDAY 21
⒇ Green Cottage
㉕ Hodges Barn
㊱ Lammas Park
㊲ Longhope Gardens
㊸ Misarden Park
㊺ The Old Chapel
㊿ Paulmead
(55) Quenington Gardens
(59) Sandywell Gardens
(62) South Lodge
(63) Stanton Gardens
(66) Stowell Park
(71) Wells Cottage

MONDAY 22
㉕ Hodges Barn

WEDNESDAY 24
⒅ Eyford Gardens
㊽ Owlpen Manor
(57) Rockcliffe
(61) Snowshill Manor & Garden
(69) Trench Hill

SATURDAY 27
⑸ Berrys Place Farm

SUNDAY 28
⑸ Berrys Place Farm
⑼ 25 Bowling Green Road
⑽ Brockworth Court
㉜ Icomb Place
㊹ Moor Wood

MONDAY 29
⑼ 25 Bowling Green Road

July

FRIDAY 3
㉘ Hookshouse Pottery (Evening)

SATURDAY 4
⒃ Delves Cottage

SUNDAY 5
⑼ 25 Bowling Green Road
⒃ Delves Cottage
㉑ Herbs for Healing
㉓ Highnam Court
(68) Temple Guiting Manor

MONDAY 6
⑼ 25 Bowling Green Road

WEDNESDAY 8
㊽ Owlpen Manor
(57) Rockcliffe

SATURDAY 11
⑷ Bell Gardens
⒃ Delves Cottage

SUNDAY 12
⑼ 25 Bowling Green Road
⒃ Delves Cottage
㊶ Meadow Cottage
(60) Sezincote

MONDAY 13
⑼ 25 Bowling Green Road

SATURDAY 18
㉑ Herbs for Healing
㉒ Hidcote Manor Garden

SUNDAY 19
⑼ 25 Bowling Green Road
(69) Trench Hill

MONDAY 20
⑼ 25 Bowling Green Road

WEDNESDAY 22
㊽ Owlpen Manor

SUNDAY 26
⑽ Brockworth Court

August

SUNDAY 2
㉓ Highnam Court

WEDNESDAY 5
㊽ Owlpen Manor

SUNDAY 9
㉞ Kempsford Manor

WEDNESDAY 12
㊽ Owlpen Manor

SUNDAY 16
⑻ Bourton House Garden
㉞ Kempsford Manor

MONDAY 17
㉟ Kiftsgate Court

THURSDAY 20
㉑ Herbs for Healing

SUNDAY 23
㉞ Kempsford Manor

SUNDAY 30
㉞ Kempsford Manor
㊶ Meadow Cottage
(58) Rodmarton Manor
(69) Trench Hill

MONDAY 31
㉞ Kempsford Manor

September

SUNDAY 6
㉓ Highnam Court
㉛ Hunts Court
㉞ Kempsford Manor

SUNDAY 13
㉛ Hunts Court
(69) Trench Hill
(72) Westbury Court Garden

SUNDAY 27
㊵ The Matara Garden

October

SUNDAY 4
(67) Sudeley Castle Gardens & Exhibitions

January 2010

SUNDAY 31
㉗ Home Farm

February

SUNDAY 7
(69) Trench Hill

SUNDAY 14
㉗ Home Farm
(69) Trench Hill

Gardens open to the public

⑿ Cerney House Gardens
㉑ Herbs for Healing
㉒ Hidcote Manor Garden
㉛ Hunts Court
㉞ Kempsford Manor
㉟ Kiftsgate Court
㊴ Lydney Park Spring Garden
㊵ The Matara Garden
㊷ Mill Dene Garden
㊸ Misarden Park
㊽ Owlpen Manor
㊾ Painswick Rococo Garden
(58) Rodmarton Manor
(60) Sezincote
(61) Snowshill Manor & Garden
(64) Stanway Fountain & Water Garden
(65) Stone House
(67) Sudeley Castle Gardens & Exhibitions
(72) Westbury Court Garden
(73) Westonbirt School Gardens

By appointment only

- **2** Alderley Grange
- **24** Hillesley House
- **30** Huntley Manor
- **52** Pemberley Lodge
- **53** Pigeon House
- **70** Upper Merton House

Also open by appointment

- **6** Beverston Castle
- **7** Box & Waterside Cottage, Blockley Gardens
- **8** Bourton House Garden
- **9** 25 Bowling Green Road
- **14** Cotswold Farm
- **16** Delves Cottage
- **19** Grange Farm
- **27** Home Farm
- **29** Humphreys End House
- **34** Kempsford Manor
- **36** Lammas Park
- **37** Longhope Gardens
- **44** Moor Wood
- **46** The Old Chequer
- **51** Pear Tree Cottage
- **59** Sandywell Gardens
- **62** South Lodge
- **69** Trench Hill

The Gardens

1 ABBOTSWOOD
Stow-on-the-Wold GL54 1EN. Mr R Scully. *1m W of Stow-on-the-Wold. On B4068 nr Lower Swell or B4077 nr Upper Swell.* Home-made teas. **Adm £4, chd free. Sun 5 Apr (1.30-6).** Massed plantings of spring bulbs, heathers, flowering shrubs and rhododendrons in dramatic, landscaped hillside stream gardens; fine herbaceous planting in elegant formal gardens with lily pond, terraced lawn and fountain created by Sir Edwin Lutyens.
&. ☕

2 ALDERLEY GRANGE
Alderley GL12 7QT. The Hon Mrs Acloque, 01453 842161. *2m S of Wotton-under-Edge. Turn NW off A46 Bath to Stroud rd, at Dunkirk. L signed Hawkesbury Upton & Hillesley. In Hillesley follow sign to Alderley.* Light refreshments & teas if requested in advance. **Adm £3.50, chd free. Visitors welcome by appt June only.** Walled garden with fine trees, old fashioned roses; herb gardens and aromatic plants.
&. ✗ ☎

Two small adjoining hillside gardens with spectacular views over the Golden Valley . . .

ASTHALL MANOR
See Oxfordshire.

3 NEW ATCOMBE COURT
South Woodchester. GL5 5ER. John Peach. *2m S of Stroud, take turning off A46 signed South Woodchester, Frogmarsh Mill (NOT turning signed South Woodchester, The Ram).* **Adm £3.50, chd free. Sat 13 June (2-6).** 12-acre grounds around C17 house (not open) with later Regency front. Delightful views over valley with lakes, mature trees and paddocks. Terraced herbaceous borders, lawns, extensive shrubberies, cutting garden mostly annuals. New long peony border. Woodland walk through beechwood.
✗

BARTON HOUSE
See Warwickshire & part of West Midlands.

Group opening

4 NEW BELL GARDENS
Burleigh GL5 2PU. *3m E of Stroud. Off A419. Turn S up Brimscombe Hill signed Burleigh and Minchinhampton. Parking on common.* Home-made teas at Bell Cottage. **Combined adm £2.50, chd free. Sats 16 May; 11 July (2-6).**

Two small adjoining hillside gardens with spectacular views over the Golden Valley. Limited parking nearby or on Minchinhampton Common, 300m uphill walk. Not suitable for those with walking difficulties. Small children must be closely supervised.
✗ ❀ ☕

NEW THE BELL
Jayne Morriss
Chelsea medal winner flower arranger's garden. Terraced on several levels with many different areas incl herbaceous and shrub borders, slate area and a hosta collection in pots. Many steps and winding bark paths.

NEW BELL COTTAGE
Molly Stewart
Cottage garden with sundeck, great for enjoying tea, cake and the view! Productive raised beds for organic vegetables. Planted containers for summer interest.

5 BERRYS PLACE FARM
Churcham GL2 8AS. Anne Thomas. *6m W of Gloucester. A40 towards Ross. Turning R into Bulley Lane at Birdwood.* Home-made & cream teas. **Adm £3, chd free. Sats, Suns 30, 31 May; 27, 28 June (11-6).** Country garden, approx 1 acre, surrounded by farmland and old orcharding. Lawns and mixed herbaceous borders with some old roses. Formal kitchen garden and rose arbour leading to lake and summerhouse with a variety of water lilies and carp. All shared with peacocks and ducks.
&. ✗ ❀ ⊨ ☕

6 BEVERSTON CASTLE
nr Tetbury GL8 8TU. Mrs A L Rook, 01666 502219, ejarook1@btinternet.com. *2m W of Tetbury. On A4135 rd to Dursley between Tetbury & Calcot Xrds.* Home-made teas. **Adm £3.50, chd under 14 free, seniors £2.50. Sun, Mon 12, 13 Apr (2.30-5). Visitors also welcome by appt.** Overlooked by romantic C12-C17 castle ruin (not open), overflowingly planted paved terrace leads from C18 house (not open) across moat to sloping lawn with spring bulbs in abundance, and full herbaceous and shrub borders. Large walled kitchen garden and greenhouses, orchids.
❀ ☕ ☎

Old watermill with pond and brook . . . cottage flower garden, wild flower meadow . . .

Group opening

7 BLOCKLEY GARDENS
GL56 9DB. *3m NW of Moreton-in-Marsh. Take A44 either from Moreton or Broadway and follow signs to Blockley.* Home-made teas at The Manor House 26 April, Box & Waterside Cottage 7 June. **Combined adm £8, chd free.** Suns 26 Apr; 7 June (2-6).
Popular Cotswold hillside village with great variety of high quality gardens; some walking necessary and some gardens not safe for small children. Bus provided. Free car park at St George's Hall.

BOX & WATERSIDE COTTAGE
Patricia Milligan-Baldwin, 01386 700364,
pmbaldwin@btopenworld.com. Not open Sun 26 April. Visitors also welcome by appt.
The gardens of each cottage are interlinked with complementary planting, drystone walls, water features - bordering Blockley Brook.

4 THE CLEMENTINES
Kathy Illingworth. Not open Sun 26 April.
Hillside garden on several levels with views over Cotswold countryside. Features a range of herbaceous perennials and shrubs, pond and stream, deck, lawned area and meadow with wild flowers.

COLEBROOK HOUSE
Lower Street. Not open Sun 26 April.
3-acres of garden where two streams converge. On different levels and divided into discrete areas with some formal structure (box, yew etc) with selection of unusual trees, lawns, herbaceous borders and a wild area.

3 THE DELL
Ms E Powell. Not open Sun 26 April.
Very small garden situated on the side of Blockley Brook. Restricted entry.

4 THE DELL
Viola & Bernard Stubbs. Not open Sun 26 April.
Fairly small garden, sloping down to Blockley Brook.

GRANGE COTTAGE
Mill Lane. Alison Heitmann. Not open Sun 26 April.
Mature terraced gardens, with interest from May to Oct. Mixture of traditional and contemporary, from lush perennial plantings to cool green spaces.

HOLLYROSE HOUSE
3 The Clementines. Mr & Mrs Peter Saunders. Not open Sun 26 April.
Small terraced garden.

NEW MALVERN MILL
Mr & Mrs J Bourne
Old watermill with pond and brook, kitchen garden and orchard, cottage flower garden, wild flower meadow and rare breed sheep.

THE MANOR HOUSE
George & Zoe Thompson. *Next to church*
April, daffodils and a wonderful view are the garden's main assets. June, top garden with lawn, roses, lavender and pergola. Lower garden beneath listed wall terraced with borders, box hedging and lawn leading to brook. Separate vegetable and herb garden with espaliered and cordoned fruits.

◆ MILL DENE GARDEN
School Lane. Mr & Mrs B S Dare
(See separate entry).

THE OLD CHEQUER
Mr & Mrs Linley
(See separate entry).

THE OLD SILK MILL
Mr & Mrs A Goodrick-Clarke. Not open Sun 26 April.
Old mill garden divided by brook to form picturesque millpond and race. Herbaceous walk, water garden and formal herb garden. Gravel paths, steep slopes. Unfenced water.

PEAR TREES
Mrs J Beckwith
Entrance at rear. Long narrow garden with dry shade-tolerant planting leading to open sunny lawn surrounded by mixed beds of roses, clematis and herbaceous plants.

PORCH HOUSE
Mr & Mrs C Johnson. Not open Sun 26 April.
Centrally located village garden with countryside views. Pear tree walk, knot garden and mixed borders.

SHEAFHOUSE COTTAGE
Mrs Jennifer Lidsey. Not open Sun 7 June.
Small cottage garden. Pond and rural views at rear.

8 BOURTON HOUSE GARDEN
Bourton-on-the-Hill GL56 9AE. Mr & Mrs R Paice, 01386 700754, www.bourtonhouse.com. *2m W of Moreton-in-Marsh. On A44.* Light lunches & teas. **Adm £5.50, chd free.** Sun 16 Aug (10-5).
Surrounding a delightful C18 Cotswold manor house (not open) and C16 tithe barn, this exciting 3-acre garden positively fizzes with ideas. Featuring flamboyant borders, imaginative topiary, profusions of herbaceous borders and exotic plants and, not least, a myriad of magically planted pots; a plantsman's paradise. Group visits by arrangement. May to July, Sept to Oct, groups of 20+. (not for NGS). Some gravel paths; 70% wheelchair access.

9 25 BOWLING GREEN ROAD
Cirencester GL7 2HD. Fr John & Susan Beck, 01285 653778, sjb@beck-hems.org.uk. *On NW edge of Cirencester. Take A435 to Spitalgate/Whiteway T-lights, turn into The Whiteway (Chedworth turn) then*

1st L into Bowling Green Rd to No 25 on R of rd bend. Please respect neighbours' driveways, no pavement parking. **Adm £2.50, chd free. Suns 28 June, 5, 12, 19 Jul (2-5). Mons 29 June; 6, 13, 20 July (11-4). Visitors also welcome by appt end June to end July, groups welcome.**
Mount an expedition to meander amidst pergolas, pots, pools and paths and muse on myriads (400+) of delightful, daring and different daylilies, (incl Rosy Rhinos and Blushing Jellyfish), vying for space with countless curvaceous clematis, romantic roses, graceful grasses, friendly frogs, hopeful hostas, priceless perennials and sylph-like lawns. Featured on BBC Gardeners' World and in 'Cheltenham Echo / Glos Citizen'.

🕸 ☎

⑩ BROCKWORTH COURT
Brockworth GL3 4QU. Mr & Mrs Tim Wiltshire. *6m E of Gloucester; 6m W of Cheltenham. From A46 Stroud/ Cheltenham off A417 turn into Mill Lane. At T-junction turn R, L, R. Garden next to St George's Church - Court Rd. From Ermin Rd, follow signs to Churchdown and church.* Home-made teas. **Adm £4, chd free. Suns 28 June; 26 July (2-5).**
Historic manor house (not open) once belonged to Llanthony Priory. CPRE award-winning restored C13 tithe barn. Garden has recently undergone much restoration work with new borders. Dew pond with Monet bridge leading to island summerhouse, carp and water lilies. Mostly farmhouse style planting. Organic kitchen garden. Views of Coopers and Crickley Hills. Arts & crafts. Vintage tractors. Jet Age Museum. Featured in 'Cotswold Life'.

♿ 🕸 ☕

⑪ CAMPDEN HOUSE
Chipping Campden GL55 6UP. The Hon Philip & Mrs Smith. *¹/₂ m SW of Chipping Campden. Entrance on Chipping Campden to Weston Subedge rd, approx ¹/₄ m SW of Campden, 1¹/₄ m drive.* Home-made teas. **Adm £3.50, chd free. Sun 31 May (2-6).**
2 acres featuring mixed borders of plant and colour interest around house and C17 tithe barn (neither open). Set in fine parkland in hidden valley with lakes and ponds. Woodland walk, vegetable garden. Steep slopes.

♿ ☕

⑫ ◆ CERNEY HOUSE GARDENS
North Cerney GL7 7BX. Sir Michael & Lady Angus. *4m NW of Cirencester. On A435 Cheltenham rd. Turn L opp Bathurst Arms, past church up hill, pillared gates on R.* Home-made teas. **Adm £4, chd £1. Tues, Weds, Fris & Suns Jan to end of July (10-5). For NGS: Sun 10 May (10-4).**
Romantic walled garden filled with old-fashioned roses and herbaceous borders. Working kitchen garden, scented garden, well-labelled herb garden, Who's Who beds and genera borders. Spring bulbs in abundance all around the wooded grounds. Bothy pottery. Now open from Jan for snowdrops and hellebores. Gravel paths and some inclines.

♿ ✕ 🕸 ☕

Group opening

⑬ CHALFORD GARDENS
Chalford Vale GL6 8PN. *4m E of Stroud; 9m from Cirencester. On A419 Stroud to Cirencester. Gardens are high above Chalford Vale & reached on foot by steep climb from car park on main rd or from High St.* **Combined adm £4, chd free. Sat, Sun 13, 14 June (2-5).**
Hillside village with many quaint lanes, S-facing. Canal walk. Exhibition of oil paintings in Old Chapel Studio by professional artists.

THE OLD CHAPEL
Marle Hill. F J & F Owen
(See separate entry).
✕

THANET HOUSE
High Street. Jennifer & Roger Tann. *Off A419 Stroud - Cirencester. On Chalford Vale High St nr PO*
Streamside multi-level garden with Italian flavour; a ruin, pond, packhorse bridge and (former) textile industry connections.

CHASTLETON GARDENS
See Oxfordshire.

CONDERTON MANOR
See Worcestershire.

⑭ COTSWOLD FARM
nr Duntisbourne Abbots, Cirencester GL7 7JS. Mrs Mark Birchall, 01285 821857. *5m NW of Cirencester. Off the old A417. From Cirencester turn L signed Duntisbourne Abbots Services, then immed R & R again into underpass. Private drive straight ahead. From Gloucester turn L signed Duntisbourne Abbots Services. Pass services; private drive on L.* Home-made teas. **Adm £4, chd free (share to A Rocha). Sat, Sun 13, 14 June (12-5). Visitors also welcome by appt.**
Cotswold garden in lovely position overlooking quiet valley on different levels with terrace designed by Norman Jewson in 1938; shrubs and trees, mixed borders, snowdrops, alpine border, shrub roses and 'bog garden'. Croquet and toys for children on lawn. Walled kitchen garden. Family day out. Wildlife trail, quiz, pond dipping, bring picnic. Native orchids, 100s wild flower species, Roman snails etc. Glos Wildlife Trust and other groups.

🕸 ☕ ☎

⑮ DAYLESFORD HOUSE
Daylesford GL56 0YG. Sir Anthony & Lady Bamford. *5m W of Chipping Norton. Off A436. Between Stow-on-the-Wold & Chipping Norton.* Light refreshments & teas at Daylesford Farm Shop. **Adm £4, chd free. Wed 13 May (2-5).**
Magnificent C18 landscape grounds created 1790 for Warren Hastings, greatly restored and enhanced by present owners. Lakeside and woodland walks within natural wild flower meadows. Large walled garden planted formally, centred around orchid, peach and working glasshouses. Trellised rose garden. Collection of citrus within period orangery. Secret Garden with pavilion and formal pools. Very large garden with substantial distances to be walked. Uneven gravel paths.

♿ ✕ ☕

Countless curvaceous clematis, romantic roses, graceful grasses, friendly frogs, hopeful hostas, priceless perennials . . .

16 NEW DELVES COTTAGE
Wigpool, Mitcheldean GL17 0JN. David & Hazel Ballard, 01594 543288. *1½ m NW of Mitcheldean. From Mitcheldean turn L by church into Mill End. ½ m up hill turn R signed Wigpool. After ½ m take 1st L. Follow NGS signs.* Home-made teas. **Adm £3, chd free. Sats, Suns 4, 5, 11, 12 July (2-5). Visitors also welcome by appt.**
1-acre of woodland tranquillity. Mature trees and shrubs give a backdrop of colour and texture to large mixed borders of smaller shrubs and perennials incl many hardy geraniums. New ponds with developing bog areas and marginal planting, deck, boardwalk and garden room. View the garden from the owl seat.

DYRHAM PARK
See Somerset & Bristol.

Group opening

17 EASTCOMBE, BUSSAGE AND BROWNSHILL GARDENS
GL6 7DS. *3m E of Stroud. 2m N of A419 Stroud to Cirencester rd on turning signed to Bisley & Eastcombe.* Home-made teas at Eastcombe Village Hall. **Combined adm £4, chd free (share to Cotswold Care Hospice, Cobalt Unit Appeal & Acorns Children's Hospice). Sun, Mon 3, 4 May (2-6).**
A group of gardens, large and small, set in a picturesque hilltop location. Some approachable only by foot. (Exhibitions may be on view in village hall). Please park considerately in villages. NCCPG plant sale.

22 BRACELANDS
Eastcombe. Mrs O M Turner
Large ex-council house garden with borders, pond and large vegetable garden.

BYWAYS
6 Velhurst Drive, Brownshill. Joy Elias
Level garden with lawn, water feature, small courtyard. Raised beds, mature trees and shrubs. Gravel drive.

1 HIDCOTE CLOSE
Eastcombe. Mr & Mrs J Southall
An evolving small back garden with circular lawn, raised beds and patio. Structural planting with emphasis on leaf shape and textures, perennials, with seasonal additions. Containers and palette of gravel, pebbles and wood for flexibility.

12 HIDCOTE CLOSE
Eastcombe. Mr & Mrs K Walker
Estate garden with pond feature, deck areas, greenhouse, pergola and arbour, raised vegetable beds and well-stocked with shrubs.

HIGHLANDS
Dr Crouch's Road, Eastcombe. Helen Wallis
Small cottage-style, plantlover's garden.

HOLT END
Bussage. Maurice & Jackie Rutter
Hillside, woodland edge, spring garden. Gravel & bark paths, slopes.

1 THE LAURELS
The Street, Eastcombe. Andrew & Ruth Fraser
Terraced garden on several levels joined by flights of steps with herbaceous borders, shrubs, small pond and terraced vegetable garden, largely reconstructed by present owners.

NEW MIDDLEGARTH
Bussage. Helen & Peter Walker
Traditional Cotswold garden, terraced with mixed flowers and vegetables. Beautiful views of Toadsmoor Valley. Not suitable for those with mobility difficulties.

NEW NYDENE
Wells Rd, Eastcombe. Derek & Felicity Halsey
Last summer we began to rejuvenate our worn out hillside garden. We wanted to add interest using shape and colour to combine different spaces with artistic features hidden amongst the greenery.

ROSE COTTAGE
The Street, Eastcombe. Mrs Juliet Shipman
Secret walled garden planted with old fashioned roses and cottage garden plants. Steep terraces give wonderful views over Lypiatt Park.

SILVERTREES
Manor Farm Lane, Eastcombe. Mr & Mrs Adcock
Garden divided into four parts consisting of two lawned areas each with a selection of trees and mixed borders, two dry shingled areas with ponds, rockery plants grasses and acers.

WOODVIEW
Wells Road, Eastcombe. Julian & Eileen Horn-Smith
Terraced with pretty views over the Toadsmoor Valley. Covering a hillside, this garden is unsuitable for those with walking difficulties.

View the garden from the owl seat . . .

Group opening

18 EYFORD GARDENS
Upper Slaughter GL54 2JN. *3m W of Stow on the Wold. On the B4068 (formerly A436), between Lower Swell & Naunton.* **Combined adm £5, chd £1 (share to Canine Partners). Weds 17, 24 June (10-5).**
2 gardens near to each other, just outside village.

EYFORD HOUSE
Mrs C A Heber-Percy. *Stone Lodge on R, with white iron gates & cattle grid*
1½-acre sloping N garden, ornamental shrubs and trees. Laid out originally by Graham Stuart Thomas, 1976. West garden and terrace, red border, walled kitchen garden, two lakes with pleasant walks and views (boots needed). Holy well.

EYFORD KNOLL

Mrs S Prest. *At Xrds turn R for Cotswold Farm Park, entrance 400yds on R* Cottage garden, with C18 fountain from Faringdon House, gardens redesigned 10yrs ago by Lady Aird.

FROGS NEST
See Worcestershire.

GADFIELD ELM HOUSE
See Worcestershire.

19 GRANGE FARM
Evenlode, nr Moreton-in-Marsh GL56 0NT. Lady Aird, 01608 650607, meaird@aol.com. *3m N of Stow-on-the-Wold. E of A429 Fosseway & 1½ m from Broadwell.* Light refreshments & home-made teas. **Adm £3, chd free. Sun 10 May (10-5).** Visitors also welcome by appt May to July.
From the rose covered house, past the lawn and herbaceous borders to the water garden and ancient apple trees spreading over spring bulbs in May this garden is full of yr-round interest. Vegetable garden, sunken garden and yew circle and shady tranquil places to sit.

20 GREEN COTTAGE
Redhill Lane, Lydney GL15 6BS. Mr & Mrs F Baber, www.peony-ukgardeners.co.uk. *¼ m SW of Lydney. Approaching Lydney from Gloucester, keep to A48 through Lydney. Leaving Lydney turn R into narrow lane at de-limit sign. Garden 1st R. Shady parking.* Home-made teas (Suns May & June only). **Adm £3, chd free. Suns 8, 15, 22 Mar (1-4); 17, 24, 31 May; Weds 3, 10, 17 Suns 7, 14, 21 June (2-5).**
1½ -acre country garden planted for seasonal interest and wildlife. Mature trees, stream, duckpond and bog garden. Developing woodland area planted with ferns, hellebores, daphnes and other shade lovers. Cottage garden. Wide range of herbaceous peonies, incl National Collection of rare Victorian and Edwardian lactiflora cultivars (best in June), early peonies May. Featured on ITV 'Wild Gardens'. Not suitable for wheelchairs at March openings due to location of hellebores.

HELLENS
See Herefordshire.

21 NEW ◆ HERBS FOR HEALING
Claptons Lane (behind Barnsley House Hotel), Barnsley GL7 5EE. Davina Wynne-Jones, 07773 687493, www.herbsforhealing.net. *4m NE of Cirencester. From Cirencester, take B4425 to Barnsley. Turn R after Barnsley House Hotel and R again at the dairy barn. Follow signs to end of farm track, garden on L with parking in field.* **Adm £3, chd free. Weds May to mid Sept (10-3). For NGS: Sun 5, Sat 18 July; Thur 20 Aug (2-6).**
Not a typical NGS garden, rural and naturalistic. Davina, the daughter of Rosemary Verey, has created a unique nursery, specialising in medicinal herbs and a tranquil organic garden in a secluded field where visitors can enjoy the beauty of the plants and learn more about the properties and uses of medicinal herbs. Educational tours offered on NGS days. Wide variety of herbs for sale. Group visits by arrangement. Featured in 'Country Living'.

22 ◆ HIDCOTE MANOR GARDEN
Hidcote Bartrim, Chipping Campden, nr Mickleton GL55 6LR. The National Trust, 01386 438333, www.nationaltrust.org.uk/hidcote. *4m NE of Chipping Campden. Off B4081, close to the village of Mickleton.* **Adm £9, chd £4.50. Sats, Suns 28 Feb to 8 Mar. 14 Mar to 1 Nov daily (not Thurs, Fri) (10-5). Daily July and Aug. For NGS: Sat 18 July (10-5).**
One of England's great gardens, 10½-acre Arts and Crafts masterpiece created by Major Lawrence Johnston. Series of outdoor rooms, each with a different character and separated by walls and hedges of many different species. Many rare trees and shrubs, outstanding herbaceous borders and unusual plant species from all over the world. Presentations by NGS Garden Careership Students.

HIGH GLANAU MANOR
See Gwent.

23 HIGHNAM COURT
Highnam GL2 8DP. Roger Head. *2m W of Gloucester. Leave Gloucester on A40 towards Ross on Wye. DO NOT take Newent turning, but proceed to next big Highnam roundabout. Take R exit for Highnam Court entrance directly off roundabout.* Light refreshments & teas. **Adm £4, chd free (share to Highnam Church). Suns 5 Apr; 3 May; 7 June; 5 July; 2 Aug; 6 Sept (11-5).**
40 acres of Victorian landscaped gardens surrounding magnificent Grade I house (not open), set out by the artist Thomas Gambier Parry. Lakes, shrubberies and listed Pulhamite water gardens with grottos and fernery. Exciting ornamental lakes, and woodland areas. Extensive 1-acre rose garden and many features incl wood carvings. Gravel paths. Steps to refreshment / toilet areas.

24 HILLESLEY HOUSE
Hillesley, nr Wotton-under-Edge GL12 7RD. Jeremy Walsh, Stewart (Head Gardener), 07971 854260, haggis@info.com. *3m from Wotton-under-Edge. On rd to Hawkesbury Upton & A46 from Wotton-under-Edge.* Light refreshments & teas on request. **Adm £3.50, chd free.** Visitors welcome by appt. **Please call or email.**
4 acres of walled, secret and open garden, plus vegetable garden and small arboretum (with stunning views of Gloucestershire). Unusual topiary. Rose beds and borders.

Lawn and herbaceous borders to the water garden and ancient apple trees spreading over spring bulbs in May . . .

Cotswold stone walls act as host to climbing and rambling roses, clematis, vines and hydrangeas . . .

25 HODGES BARN
Shipton Moyne GL8 8PR. Mr & Mrs N Hornby. *3m S of Tetbury. On Malmesbury side of village.* **Adm £5, chd free. Sun, Mon 21, 22 June (2-6).**
Very unusual C15 dovecote converted into family home (not open). Cotswold stone walls act as host to climbing and rambling roses, clematis, vines, hydrangeas, and together with yew, rose and tapestry hedges create formality around house. Mixed shrub and herbaceous borders, shrub roses; water garden; woodland garden planted with cherries, magnolias and spring bulbs. Also open for NGS, adjoining garden of **Hodges Farmhouse** by kind permission of Mrs Clive Lamb.
&

26 HOLCOMBE GLEN COTTAGE
Minchinhampton GL6 9AJ. Christine & Terry Sharpe. *1m E of Nailsworth. From Nailsworth take Avening Rd B4014. Turn L at Weighbridge Inn. Turn L 100yds into Holcombe Glen. 1st house on L. From Minchinhampton 1¼ m via Well Hill or New Rd.* Light refreshments & teas. **Adm £3, chd free (share to Smile). Sun 7 June (11-5).**
3 acres incl springs and ponds. Small waterfalls feed river and stream, giving bog and meadow areas full of wildlife and wild flowers. Above these, terraced walled garden for vegetables and herbaceous plants.
&

27 HOME FARM
Huntley GL19 3HQ. Mrs T Freeman, 01452 830209, torill@ukgateway.net. *4m S of Newent. On B4216 ½ m off A40 in Huntley travelling towards Newent.* **Adm £2.50, chd free. Suns 25 Jan; 8 Feb; 15 Mar; 5, 26 Apr (2-5); Suns 31 Jan; 14 Feb 2010. Visitors also welcome by appt end Jan to end April.**
Set in elevated position with exceptional views. 1m walk through woods and fields to show carpets of spring flowers. Enclosed garden with fern border, sundial and heather bed. White and mixed shrub borders. Stout footwear advisable in winter.
☎

28 HOOKSHOUSE POTTERY
Hookshouse Lane, Tetbury GL8 8TZ. Lise & Christopher White. *2½ m WSW of Tetbury. From Tetbury take A4135 towards Dursley, then take 2nd L signed Leighterton. Hookshouse Pottery is 1½ m on R.* Home-made teas. **Adm £2.50, chd free. Daily Sat 23 May to Sun 31 May (11-6). Evening Opening £4, wine, Fri 3 July (6-9).**
A combination of dramatic open perspectives and intimate corners. Borders, shrubs, woodland glade, water garden with treatment ponds (unfenced) and flowform cascades. Kitchen garden with raised beds and orchard. Sculptural features. Run on organic principles. Pottery showroom with handthrown wood-fired pots incl frostproof garden pots. Art & craft exhibition incl garden sculptures (May 23-31 only). Featured on BBC2 Open Gardens. Gravel car park, alternative access on request.
& ✿ ☕

29 HUMPHREYS END HOUSE
Randwick, nr Stroud GL6 6EW. Pat & Jim Hutton, 01453 765401, pathutton@gps-footpaths.co.uk. *2m NW of Stroud. M5 J13, follow signs to Cashes Green & Randwick. At Townsend, turn R. Parking, look for signs.* Cream teas. **Adm £2.50, chd free. Sat, Sun 6, 7 June (2-6). Visitors also welcome by appt.**
Different areas of contrasting mood and interesting planting surrounding listed C16 farmhouse (not open). A wildlife friendly garden. Pond area, old roses, grasses and organic vegetables. Art exhibition nearby.
✿ ☕ ☎

30 HUNTLEY MANOR
Huntley GL19 3HQ. Prof Tim Congdon & Mrs Dorianne Congdon. *4m S of Newent. Newent Lane. On B4216 ½ m off A40 in Huntley travelling towards Newent.* **Adm £5, chd free. Visitors welcome by appt, apply in writing to Mrs D Congdon.**
Park-like grounds surround the gothic 'French Château' style house (open by arrangement) built in 1862 by S S Teulon. Informal beds of mature shrubbery and rare specimen trees (tulip tree reputed to be tallest in the country after Kew), intersperse with sweeping lawns down to lake. Woodland walk with giant redwoods; exotic waterfowl and peacocks roam the grounds. Walled garden with rare breed hens and alpacas. Harp concerts in the grounds by Venetia Congdon by arrangement.
& ✕ ☎

31 ◆ HUNTS COURT
North Nibley GL11 6DZ. Mr & Mrs T K Marshall, 01453 547440, huntscourt@tiscali.com. *2m NW of Wotton-under-Edge. From Wotton B4060 Dursley rd turn R in North Nibley at Black Horse; fork L after ¼ m.* Home-made teas (NGS days). **Adm £3.50, chd free. Tues to Sats all yr (2-5) not Good Fri & Aug. For NGS: Suns 7, 14 June; 6, 13 Sept (2-6).**
A plant lover's garden with unusual shrubs, 450 varieties old roses, large collection of penstemons and hardy geraniums in peaceful 2½ -acre garden set against tree-clad hills and Tyndale monument. Mini-arboretum. House (not open) possible birthplace of William Tyndale. Picnic area.
& ✕ ✿ ☕

32 ICOMB PLACE
Icomb, nr Stow-on-the-Wold GL54 1JD. T L F Royle. *2m S of Stow. After 2m on A424 Burford Rd turn L to Icomb village.* Home-made teas. **Adm £5, chd £2 (share to Deus Laudamus Trust). Sun 28 June (2-6).**
Gardens were laid down in first decade of C20 and consist of ponds, water garden and 100 yr-old natural woodland. Potager with pergola added by the present owners. One of the first gardens opened under the NGS. Unfenced paths through the woodland area are not suitable for the elderly, infirm and unsupervised children. Steep slopes & paths.
& ✕ ☕

33 KEMBLE MILL
nr Somerford Keynes, Cirencester GL7 6ED. Vittoria & Simon Thornley, www.kemblemill.com. *5m S of Cirencester. From A419 (Cotswold Water Park exit), go W towards Ashton Keynes. Follow spine rd for 2m. Go over Xrds & after 1.5m turn R on lane signed Old Mill Farm. 1st house on R.* Home-made teas. **Adm £3, chd free. Sun 7 June (2-5).**
C16 watermill (house not open) on banks of infant Thames. Formal, walled

garden with rose arches and pond. Kitchen and fruit garden; plantation of mixed trees; cottage garden; island garden bordered by mill race with apple orchard and woodland walk. 8-acre field with chickens. Playground. Featured in 'Gloucester Echo'.

34 ◆ **KEMPSFORD MANOR**
High Street, Kempsford GL7 4EQ. Mrs Z I Williamson, 01285 810131, www.kempsfordmanor.co.uk. *3m S of Fairford. Take A419 from Cirencester or Swindon. Kempsford is signed 10m (approx) from each. The Manor is in the centre of village.* **Adm £3.50, chd free.** See website or tel for opening times. Group visits by arrangement. For NGS: Suns 22 Feb; 1, 8, 15 Mar; 12, 26 Apr; Sun 3, Mon 4, Sun 17, 24, Mon 25 May; Suns 9, 16, 23, 30, Mon 31 Aug; Sun 6 Sept (2-5). Early spring garden with variety of bulbs incl snowdrop walk along old canal. Peaceful, expansive summer garden for relaxation, adjacent to cricket field, croquet and outdoor games for children. Occasional plant sales; frequently classical or jazz music; games and quizzes for children. Gravel paths. Canal walk unsuitable for wheelchairs.

KENCOT GARDENS
See Oxfordshire.

35 ◆ **KIFTSGATE COURT**
nr Chipping Campden GL55 6LN. Mr & Mrs J G Chambers, 01386 438777, www.kiftsgate.co.uk. *4m NE of Chipping Campden. Adjacent to Hidcote NTGarden. 1m E of B4632 & B4081.* **Adm £6.50, chd £2.** Open May to July daily (not Thur & Fri) (12-6). April and Sept Suns, Mons, Weds. Aug daily not (Thurs & Fris) (2-6). **For NGS:** Mons 20 Apr; 17 Aug (2-6). Magnificent situation and views; many unusual plants and shrubs; tree peonies, hydrangeas, abutilons, species and old-fashioned roses, incl largest rose in England, *Rosa filipes* 'Kiftsgate'. Steep slopes & steps.

36 ◆ **LAMMAS PARK**
Cuckoo Row, Minchinhampton GL6 9HA. Mr P Grover, 01453 886471. *4m SE of Stroud. From Market Sq down High St for 100yds, turn R at Xrds. After 300yds turn L, Lammas Park 100yds on L.* Home-made teas. **Adm £3, chd free.** **Suns 12 Apr; 21 June (12-5).** Visitors also welcome by appt all-yr. 2½ acres around Cotswold Arts and Crafts style house (not open). Herbaceous borders, pleached lime allée, wild garden, alpines, restored C17 'hanging gardens' with tunnel. Superb views.

Group opening

37 **NEW** **LONGHOPE GARDENS**
Longhope GL17 0LL. Annie Frost. 01452 830717, frostiesuk@msn.com. *10m W of Gloucester. 6m E of Ross on Wye. Take Longhope turn off A40 into Church Road. Park by church.* Home-made teas. **Combined adm £3, chd free.** Sats (11-5), Suns (2-6) 30, 31 May; 20, 21 June. Visitors also welcome by appt. Small village in a valley with wonderful views. C12 church. Two small gardens with cottage planting. Both gardens also open by appointment.

NEW **3 CHURCH ROAD**
Rev Clive & Mrs Linda Edmonds
Newly- developed cottage garden with connecting rooms containing a large collection of hardy geraniums, other herbaceous plants and grasses. Small vegetable plot with hens and stunning views to May Hill.

NEW **COURT LEET**
Annie & Gary Frost
Small, evolving garden on several levels with steps. Around C17 listed house (not open). Lovely countryside views. Exuberant cottage-style planting with a mix of traditional favourites and unusual varieties. 100+ roses. A plantsman's garden.

38 **LOWER FARM HOUSE**
Cliffords Mesne GL18 1JT. Gareth & Sarah Williams. *2m S of Newent. From Newent follow signs to Cliffords Mesne & Birds of Prey Centre (1½ m). Approx ½ m beyond 'Centre', turn L at Xrds, signed Kents Green. Garden 150yds down hill on bend. Car park (limited if wet).* Home-made teas. **Adm**

£3, chd free. Weds 27 May; 3 June (2-6). 2-acre garden, incl woodland, stream and large natural lily pond with rockery and bog garden. Herbaceous borders, pergola walk, terrace with ornamental fishpond, kitchen and herb garden; many interesting and unusual trees and shrubs. Gravel paths & grass.

Herbaceous borders, pleached lime allée, wild garden, alpines, restored C17 'hanging gardens' . . .

39 ◆ **LYDNEY PARK SPRING GARDEN**
Lydney GL15 6BU. The Viscount Bledisloe, 01594 842844, mrjames@phonecoop.coop. *½ m SW of Lydney. On A48 Gloucester to Chepstow rd between Lydney & Aylburton. Drive is directly off A48.* **Adm £4, chd 50p.** Suns, Weds & BH Mons 29 Mar to 7 June. **For NGS:** Wed 15 Apr; Tue 12 May (10-5). Spring garden in 8-acre woodland valley with lakes, profusion of rhododendrons, azaleas and other flowering shrubs. Formal garden; magnolias and daffodils (April). Picnics in deer park which has fine trees. Important Roman Temple site and museum. Teas in family dining room (otherwise house not open).

MARSHFIELD GARDENS
See Somerset & Bristol.

40 ◆ THE MATARA GARDEN
Kingscote GL8 8YA. Herons Mead
Ltd, 01453 861050,
www.matara.co.uk. *5¹/₂ m NW of
Tetbury. On A4135 towards Dursley. At
the Hunters Hall Inn turn R into
Kingscote village. Enter Park at 1st
gate on R.* Adm £4, chd under 14
free, concessions £3. May to Sept
Tues & Thurs. Teas NGS days only.
For NGS: Suns 31 May; 27 Sept
(1-5).
A unique meditative garden alive with
inspiration from around the world.
Labyrinths, medicine wheel, ponds,
sculptures and walled ornamental herb
garden. Developing Eastern woodland
walk and wild flower meadow. Matara
is a spiritual garden dedicated to the
full expression of the human spirit. All
set within a 28-acre parkland.

41 MEADOW COTTAGE
59 Coalway Road, Coalway, nr
Coleford GL16 7HL. Mrs Pamela
Buckland. *1m SE of Coleford. From
Coleford take Lydney & Chepstow Rd
at T-lights in town. Turn L after police
stn, signed Coalway & Parkend.
Garden on L ¹/₂ m up hill opp layby.*
Adm £2.50, chd free. Suns 19 Apr;
17 May; 12 July; 30 Aug (2-6).
¹/₃ -acre cottage garden, a plantaholic
craftworker's creation with shrubs,
perennials, spring bulbs in colourful
borders and interlinking garden rooms.
Lawned area. Gravel paths leading to
small pond with waterfall and bog
garden. Vegetable garden in raised
beds. Gravel garden with grasses,
bamboos and pots and containers in
abundance.

42 ◆ MILL DENE GARDEN
School Lane, Blockley GL56 9HU.
Mr & Mrs B S Dare, 01386 700457,
www.milldenegarden.co.uk. *3m NW
of Moreton-in-Marsh. From A44, follow
brown signs from Bourton-on-the-Hill,
to Blockley. 1¹/₃ m down hill turn L
behind village gates. Parking for 8 cars.
Coaches by appoint.* Adm £5, chd £1,
concessions £4.75. 1 April to 9 Oct
Weds to Fris (10.30-5 last entry
4pm.) Sats (9.30-12) Closed 12-18
Jul. 12 Oct to 31 Oct (3.30-7.30) for
new garden lighting. Check website
for special events. For NGS: Mon 13
Apr (2-5).
This garden of 2¹/₂ acres surrounds a
Cotswold stone water-mill and is set in
a tiny steep sided valley. It seems to
have evolved naturally in English

'country garden' style. A millpond,
stream, grotto, potager and trompe
l'oeil all contribute to the owner's
design for surprise, concealment,
scent, colour and, above all, fun.
'Scratch & sniff' herb garden with rills.
Featured in 'Period House', 'The
English Garden' & 'Gardening Which'.
Limited wheelchair access; gravel
paths & steep slopes. Please ring
ahead to reserve disabled parking.

Spring bulbs in colourful borders and interlinking garden rooms . . .

43 ◆ MISARDEN PARK
Misarden GL6 7JA. Major M T N H
Wills, 01285 821303,
www.misardenpark.co.uk. *6m NW of
Cirencester. Follow signs off A417 or
B4070 from Stroud.* Adm £4, chd
free. Tues, Weds, Thurs 1 Apr to 30
Sept (9.30-5). For NGS: Suns 5 Apr;
21 June (2-6).
Essentially formal, dating from C17,
magnificent position overlooking the
Golden Valley. Walled garden with long
mixed borders, yew walk leading to a
lower lawn with rill and summerhouse.
Aboretum with spring bulbs en masse.
Climbing roses and rose walk linking
parterre. Silver and grey border, blue
border and scented border. Blue/gold
walkway below house. Disabled
parking at front of house on NGS days.

44 MOOR WOOD
Woodmancote GL7 7EB. Mr & Mrs
Henry Robinson, 01285 831397,
henry@moorwood.fslife.co.uk. *3¹/₂ m
NW of Cirencester. Turn L off A435 to
Cheltenham at North Cerney, signed
Woodmancote 1¹/₄ m; entrance in
village on L beside lodge with white
gates.* Adm £3, chd free. Sun 28
June (2-6). Visitors also welcome by
appt.
2 acres of shrub, orchard and wild
flower gardens in isolated valley
setting. Holder of the National
Collection of rambler roses.

45 THE OLD CHAPEL
Marle Hill, Chalford Vale GL6 8PN.
F J & F Owen. *4m E of Stroud. On
A419 to Cirencester. Above Chalford
Vale, steep climb from car park on
main rd, up Marle Hill.* Adm £3, chd
free. Daily Sat 6 June to Sun 21
June (2-5). Also open with Chalford
Gardens 13, 14 June (2-5).
1-acre Victorian chapel garden on
precipitous hillside. A tiered tapestry of
herbaceous borders, formal potager,
small orchard, pond and
summerhouse and old roses all laid out
on terraced S-facing Marle Cliff.
Exhibition of landscape and natural
history oil paintings. Featured in many
publications incl 'Gardens Illustrated',
'Times' & 'Telegraph'.

46 THE OLD CHEQUER
Draycott, nr Blockley GL56 9LB. Mr
& Mrs H Linley, 01386 700647,
g.f.linley1@btinternet.com. *2m NE of
Moreton-in-Marsh. Nr Blockley.* Home-
made teas. Adm £3, chd free. Sun 5,
Apr (12-4.30). Also open Blockley
Gardens 26 April & 7 June. Visitors
also welcome by appt, Apr to Aug.
A natural garden, created by owner,
set in 2 acres of old orchard with
original ridge and furrow. Emphasis on
spring planting but still maintaining yr-
round interest. Kitchen garden/soft
fruit, herbaceous and shrubs in island
beds. Croquet lawn, unusual plants,
alpines and dry gravel borders.

THE OLD CORN MILL
See Herefordshire.

**47 THE OLD RECTORY,
DUNTISBOURNE ROUS**
Duntisbourne Rous GL7 7AP.
Charles & Mary Keen,
mary@keengardener.com. *4m NW of
Cirencester. From Daglingworth NW of
Cirencester take rd to the
Duntisbournes; or from A417 from
Gloucester take Duntisbourne Leer
turning.* Adm £3.50, chd free. Mons
9 Feb; 9 Mar; 27 Apr; 25 May (11-5).
Garden in an exceptional setting made
by designer and writer Mary Keen.
Subject of many articles and Telegraph
column. Designed for atmosphere, but
collections of galanthus, hellebores,
auriculas and half hardies - especially
dahlias - are all features in their season.
Plants for sale occasionally.

OVERBURY COURT
See Worcestershire.

48 NEW ◆ OWLPEN MANOR
GL11 5BZ. Lady Mander, 01453
860261, www.owlpen.com. *4m E
of Dursley. From the B4066 at Uley
follow signs to Owlpen by the Old
Crown PH.* **Adm £3.75, chd
£1.75.** *May to Sept Tues, Thurs,
Suns (12-5).* For NGS: Weds 3,
24 June; 8, 22 July; 5, 12 Aug
(12-5).
Owlpen Manor (not open) is one of
the most romantic Tudor manor
houses in England. Set in a remote
and picturesque wooded valley, the
formal garden contains topiary
yews, box parterres, old roses and
mill pond walk. The estate contains
lovely walks through beech woods.

Discover the horticultural treasures . . .

49 ◆ PAINSWICK ROCOCO GARDEN
Painswick GL6 6TH. Painswick
Rococo Garden Trust, 01452
813204, www.rococogarden.org.uk.
*¼ m N of Painswick. ½ m outside
village on B4073.* **Adm £5.50, chd
£2.75, concessions £4.50.** *Daily 10
Jan to 31 Oct (11-5).*
Unique C18 garden from the brief
Rococo period, combining
contemporary buildings, vistas, ponds,
kitchen garden and winding woodland
walks. Anniversary maze.

50 PAULMEAD
Bisley GL6 7AG. Judy & Philip
Howard. *5m E of Stroud. On S edge
of Bisley at head of Toadsmoor Valley
on top of Cotswolds. Garden & car
park well signed in Bisley village.
Disabled can be dropped off at garden
prior to parking car.* **Adm £3.50, chd
free. Combined with Wells Cottage
£4.50.** Sun 21 June (2-6).
Approx 1-acre landscaped garden
constructed in stages over last 20yrs.
Terraced in three main levels: natural
stream garden; formal herbaceous and
shrub borders; yew and beech
hedges; formal vegetable garden;
lawns; summerhouse with exterior
wooden decking by pond and
thatched roof over well head. Unusual
tree house.

51 ◆ PEAR TREE COTTAGE
58 Malleson Road, Gotherington
GL52 9EX. Mr & Mrs E Manders-
Trett, 01242 674592. *4m N of
Cheltenham. From A435, travelling N,
turn R into Gotherington 1m after end
of Bishop's Cleeve bypass at garage.
Garden on L approx 100yds past
Shutter Inn.* **Adm £3, chd free.** Suns
15 Mar; 19 Apr; 17 May; 14 June
(2-5). Visitors also welcome by appt.
Mainly informal country garden approx
½ -acre with pond and gravel garden,
grasses and herbaceous borders,
trees and shrubs surrounding lawns.
Wild garden and orchard lead to
greenhouses, herb and vegetable
gardens. Spring bulbs and early
summer perennials and shrubs
particularly colourful.

52 ◆ PEMBERLEY LODGE
Churchend Lane, Old Charfield
GL12 8LJ. Rob & Yvette
Andrewartha, 01454 260885. *3½ m
SW of Wotton-under-Edge. Off B4058
from Wotton-under Edge through
Charfield Village. At top of Charfield
Hill, turn L. 2m from M5 J14, at Xrds
on B4509 go straight across into
Churchend Lane.* **Adm £4, chd free.**
Visitors welcome by appt. Groups of
10+. Advance booking only.
Small private garden designed and
planted in 2002 by Lesley Rosser.
Densely planted for all-yr interest,
maturing well. Incorporates trees,
shrubs, perennials, grasses, water,
gravel and hard landscaping to give an
informal peaceful feel. Roof garden.

53 ◆ PIGEON HOUSE
Southam Lane, Southam GL52 3NY.
Mrs Dee Taylor, 01242 529342,
dee@stita.co.uk. *3m NE of
Cheltenham. Off B4632 toward
Winchcombe. Parking adjacent to
Southam Tithe Barn.* **Adm £3, chd
free.** Visitors welcome by appt,
March to Sept, coaches permitted.
2-acre garden surrounding Cotswold
stone manor (not open) of medieval
origin. Small lake with island and
separate water garden with linked
pools featuring water margin and bog
plants. Extensive lawns on several
levels; wide range of flowering shrubs
and borders designed to create a
multitude of vistas; woodland area with
shade-loving plants and many spring
bulbs.

54 PRIORS MESNE
Aylburton, Lydney GL15 6DX. Mr &
Mrs Brian Thornton. *3m NW of
Lydney. At the George PH in Aylburton
take St Briavels rd off A48. Go up hill
for 2m to T-junction. Turn sharp L, go
down hill for approx 200 metres. Turn
R into entrance marked Priors Mesne
private rd. Go to end of drive 300
metres through auto gate.* **Adm £3.50,
chd free (share to Gloucestershire
Community Foundation).** Suns 10,
17 May (2-6).
Approached down an avenue of
mature lime trees, this large terraced
garden enjoys distant views over deer
park to Severn Estuary and Cotswolds
beyond. Collection of rhododendrons,
azaleas, magnolias and cornus set
amongst three magnificent copper
beeches, water feature and woodland
walk through bluebells.

Group opening

55 QUENINGTON GARDENS
nr Fairford GL7 5BW. *8m NE of
Cirencester. Home-made teas at The
Old Rectory.* **Combined adm £4, chd
free.** Sun 21 June (2-5.30).
A rarely visited Coln Valley village
delighting its infrequent visitors with
C12 Norman church and C17 stone
cottages (not open). An opportunity to
discover the horticultural treasures
behind those Cotswold stone walls
and visit 3 very different but charming
gardens incorporating everything from
the exotic and the organic to the
simple cottage garden; a range of
vistas from riverside to seclusion.
Sculpture exhibition at The Old
Rectory.

BANK VIEW
Victoria Road. Mrs J A Moulden
Terraced garden with wonderful
views over the R Coln.

THE OLD RECTORY, QUENINGTON
Mr & Mrs D Abel Smith
On the banks of the mill race and
the R Coln, this is an organic
garden of variety. Mature trees,
large vegetable garden,
herbaceous, shade, pool and bog
gardens. Finalist in Perfect Old
Rectory competition.

YEW TREE COTTAGES
Victoria Road. Mr J Lindon
Quintessential cottage garden.

56 RAMBLERS

Lower Common, Aylburton, nr Lydney GL15 6DS. Jane & Leslie Hale. *1¹/₂ m W of Lydney. Off A48 Gloucester to Chepstow Rd. From Lydney through Aylburton, out of de-limit turn R signed Aylburton Common, ³/₄ m along lane.* Home-made teas. **Adm £3, chd free. Suns 3 May; 7 June (2-6).**
Peaceful medium-sized country garden with informal cottage planting, herbaceous borders and small pond looking through hedge 'windows' onto wild flower meadow. Front woodland garden with shade-loving plants and topiary. Large productive vegetable garden. Apple orchard.

🗡 ⊕ ☕

Looking through hedge 'windows' onto wild flower meadow . . .

57 ROCKCLIFFE

nr Lower Swell GL54 2JW. Mr & Mrs Simon Keswick. *2m SW of Stow-on-the-Wold. 1¹/₂ m from Lower Swell. On B4068. From Stow-on-the-Wold to Cheltenham go through Lower Swell. Climb hill staying on B4068. Converted barn on L. Round corner & start dropping down hill. Rockcliffe halfway down on R.* Home-made teas. **Adm £4, chd free (share to Kate's Home Nursing). Weds 17, 24 June; 8 July (10-5).**
Large traditional English garden of 8-acres incl pink, white and blue gardens, herbaceous border, rose terrace; walled kitchen garden and orchard; greenhouses and original stone dovecot with pathway of topiary birds leading up through orchard to it.

🗡 ☕

58 ◆ RODMARTON MANOR

Cirencester GL7 6PF. Mr & Mrs Simon Biddulph. *5m NE of Tetbury. Off A433. Between Cirencester & Tetbury.* **House and garden £7, chd £3.50. Garden only £4, chd £1. Weds & Sats May to Sept (2-5). For NGS: Sun 30 Aug (2-5).**
The 8-acre garden of this fine Arts and Crafts house is a series of outdoor rooms each with its own distinctive character. Leisure garden, winter

garden, troughery, topiary, hedges, lawns, rockery, containers, wild garden, kitchen garden, magnificent herbaceous borders. Snowdrop collection.

⅃ 🗡 ☕

SALFORD GARDENS

See Oxfordshire.

Group opening

59 SANDYWELL GARDENS

nr Whittington, Cheltenham GL54 4HF, 01242 820606, shirley.sills@tesco.net. *5m E of Cheltenham. On A40 between Whittington & Andoversford.* Home-made teas at Barn House. **Combined adm £4, chd free. Suns 7, 21 June (11-5). Visitors also welcome by appt 6 June to 10 July. Coaches permitted. Groups of 10+.**
Two vibrant, plant-packed, complementary walled gardens, totalling 3¹/₄ acres and featuring areas both traditional and contemporary. Mature trees, varied borders, secret corners, lawns, water features, walkways, avenues and vistas.

🗡 ⊕ ☕ ☎

BARN HOUSE

Shirley & Gordon Sills
Plantaholic designer's own 2¹/₂ - acre walled garden. Maintained by owners. Exuberantly planted for form, scent and colour. Herbaceous, roses, climbers, shrubs, trees, lawns, hedges, structures, formal and informal water features. Featured in 'Gloucester Echo'.

GARDEN COTTAGE

Charles Fogg & Gilly Bogdiukiewicz
Peaceful ³/₄ -acre cottage garden with four interconnecting walled areas of different character and separate levels. Borders, lawns, gravel areas, pergolas and patios. Also stone, marble and raised water features, urns, tubs, baskets and greenhouse.

🗡

60 ◆ SEZINCOTE

nr Moreton-in-Marsh GL56 9AW. Mr & Mrs D Peake, 01386 700444, www.sezincote.co.uk. *3m SW of Moreton-in-Marsh. From Moreton-in-Marsh turn W along A44 towards Evesham; after 1¹/₂ m (just before Bourton-on-the-Hill) take turn L, by*

stone lodge with white gate. **Adm £5, chd £1.50. House tours and teas Thurs, Fris, BH, May to Sept (2.30-6). Closed Dec. For NGS: Sun 12 July (2-6).**
Exotic oriental water garden by Repton and Daniell with lake, pools and meandering stream, banked with massed perennials. Large semi-circular orangery, formal Indian garden, fountain, temple and unusual trees of vast size in lawn and wooded park setting. House in Indian manner designed by Samuel Pepys Cockerell. Gravel paths & steep slopes.

⅃ 🗡 ☕

61 ◆ SNOWSHILL MANOR & GARDEN

nr Broadway WR12 7JU. The National Trust, 01386 852410, snowshillmanor@nationaltrust.org.uk. *2¹/₂ m S of Broadway. Off A44 bypass into Broadway village.* **House and Garden £8.50, chd £4.30. Garden only £4.60, chd £2.30. Weds, Suns & BH Mons 14 March to 1 Nov. For NGS: Wed 24 June (11-5).**
An Arts & Crafts inspired terraced hillside garden in which only organic methods are used. Highlights incl tranquil ponds, old roses, quirky objects and herbaceous borders rich in plants of special interest. Working kitchen garden.

🗡 ⊕

62 SOUTH LODGE

Church Road, Clearwell, Coleford GL16 8LG. Andrew & Jane MacBean, 01594 837769. *2m S of Coleford. Off B4228. Follow signs to Clearwell. Garden on L of castle driveway.* Home-made teas. **Adm £2.50, chd free. Sun 5 Apr (2-5); Sun 3 May (12-4), Tue 26 May (2-6); Sun 21 June (11-5). Visitors also welcome by appt May & June. Evenings & weekends only. Groups of 10+.**
2-acre, organic garden on a sloping site formerly part of Clearwell Castle in the Royal Forest of Dean. Surrounded by high stone walls with views accross the countryside. Vegetable garden, fernery, large herbaceous borders, wildlife and formal ponds, wild flower patch, variety of trees incl fruit trees. Early season colour provided by masses of bulbs and in summer by roses, clematis and perennials. Sun 3 May only, teas in village hall & Church Flower Festival. Featured in 'Glos Citizen'.

🗡 ⊕ ☕ ☎

SPECIAL PLANTS
See Somerset & Bristol.

Group opening

63 STANTON GARDENS
nr Broadway WR12 7NE. *3m SW of Broadway. Off B4632, between Broadway (3m) & Winchcombe (6m).* Home-made teas at selected gardens and Burland Hall. **Adm £5, chd free. Sun 21 June (2-6).**
One of the most picturesque and unspoilt C17 Cotswold villages with many gardens to explore (20 expected in 2009) ranging from charming cottage to large formal gardens which should appeal to visitors of all tastes. More formal gardens have wheelchair access while the Burland Hall has disabled facilities.
⚘ ⊛ ☕

64 ◆ STANWAY FOUNTAIN & WATER GARDEN
nr Winchcombe GL54 5PQ. Lord Neidpath, 01386 584469, www.stanwayfountain.co.uk. *9m NE of Cheltenham. 1m E of B4632 Cheltenham to Broadway rd or B4077 Toddington to Stow-on-the-Wold rd.* **House and garden adm £6, chd £1.50, concessions £4.50, garden only adm £4, chd £1, concessions £3. Tues & Thurs, June to Aug (2-5). For NGS: Suns 19 Apr; 7 June (2-5).**
20 acres of planted landscape in early C18 formal setting. The restored canal, upper pond and 165ft high fountain have re-created one of the most interesting baroque water gardens in Britain. Striking C16 manor with gatehouse, tithe barn and church. Britain's highest fountain at 300ft, the world's highest gravity fountain.

65 ◆ STONE HOUSE
Wyck Rissington GL54 2PN. Mr & Mrs Andrew Lukas, 01451 810337, www.stonehousegarden.co.uk. *3m S of Stow-on-the-Wold. Off A429 between Bourton-on-the-Water & Stow-on-the-Wold. Last house in village behind high bank on R.* **Adm £4, chd free. For NGS: Sun 19 Apr (2-6).**
2 acres full of unusual bulbs, shrubs and herbaceous plants. Crab apple walk, rose borders, herb and water garden, meadow walk. Visits also by arrangement (not for NGS) 1 Mar to 1 Oct. Plantswoman's garden with yr-round interest.
⚘ ✕ ⊛

66 STOWELL PARK
Northleach GL54 3LE. The Lord & Lady Vestey. *8m NE of Cirencester. Off Fosseway A429 2m SW of Northleach.* Home-made teas. **Adm £5, chd free (share to church 17 May; British Legion 21 June). Suns 17 May; 21 June (2-5).**
Magnificent lawned terraces with stunning views over Coln Valley. Fine collection of old-fashioned roses and herbaceous plants, with pleached lime approach to C14 house (not open). Two large walled gardens containing vegetables, fruit, cut flowers and range of greenhouses. Long rose pergola and wide, plant-filled borders divided into colour sections. Open continuously for 45 years. Plant Sale 17 May only.
✕ ☕

67 ◆ SUDELEY CASTLE GARDENS & EXHIBITIONS
Winchcombe GL54 5JD. Lord & Lady Ashcombe & Henry & Mollie Dent Brocklehurst, 01242 602308, www.sudeleycastle.co.uk. *8m NE of Cheltenham. On B4632 (A46) or 10m from J9 M5. Bus service operates between Winchcombe & Cheltenham or Broadway.* **House & gardens adm £7.20, chd £4.20, concessions £6.20. 10 April to 31 Oct (10.30-5). For NGS: Sun 4 Oct (10.30-5).**
Magnificent gardens work themselves seamlessly around castle buildings. Individual gardens incl Queen's Garden with old-fashioned roses, annuals and herbs; examples of fine topiary incl Tudor Knot Garden; exotic plantings in the Secret Garden and autumn colour throughout gardens. A fine collection of rare and colourful pheasants create added interest.
⚘ ✕ ⊛ ☕

68 TEMPLE GUITING MANOR
Temple Guiting, nr Stow-on-the-Wold GL54 5RP. Mr S Collins. *7m from Stow-on-the-Wold. From Stow-on-the-Wold take B4077 towards Tewkesbury. On descending hill bear L to village (signed) ½ m. Garden in centre of village on R.* Home-made teas. **Adm £3, chd free. Sun 5 July (2-6).**
Recently designed formal contemporary gardens to Grade I listed historic manor house (not open) in Windrush Valley. Designed by Jinny Blom, gold medal winner Chelsea Flower Show 2007. New for 2009, small courtyard garden to newly converted manor barns.
✕ ⊛ ☕

69 TRENCH HILL
Sheepscombe GL6 6TZ. Celia & Dave Hargrave, 01452 814306, celia.hargrave@btconnect.com. *1½ m E of Painswick. On A46 to Cheltenham after Painswick, turn R to Sheepscombe. Approx 1½ m (before reaching village) turn L by telegraph poles, Trench Hill at top of lane.* Home-made teas. **Adm £3, chd free. Suns 8, 15 Feb (11-4); Sun 12, Mon 13 Apr; (11-6); Weds 3, 10, 17, 24 June (2-6); Suns 19 July; 30 Aug; 13 Sept (11-6); Sun 7, 14 Feb 2010. Visitors also welcome by appt.**
Approx 3 acres set in small woodland with panoramic views. Variety of herbaceous and mixed borders, rose garden, extensive vegetable plots, wild flower areas, plantings of spring bulbs with thousands of snowdrops and hellebores, woodland walk, 2 small ponds, waterfall and larger conservation pond. Interesting wooden sculptures. Run on organic principles. Most of the garden wheelchair accessible. Disabled parking close to house.
⚘ ✕ ⊛ ☕ ☎

Plantings of spring bulbs with thousands of snowdrops and hellebores . . .

70 UPPER MERTON HOUSE
High Street, Newnham-on-Severn GL14 1AD. Roger Grounds & Diana Grenfell, 01594 517146, diana@uppermerton.co.uk. *Halfway between Chepstow & Gloucester on A48. Restricted parking outside house or along service rd parallel to High St between library & Dean Rd. Parking also available at village car park.* **Adm £2.50, chd 50p. Visitors welcome by appt Tues, Weds, Thurs 2, 3, 4 June 7, 8, 9 July, 4, 5, 6 Aug (2-5).**
Small, recently created, formal but exuberantly planted, town garden. Collection of hostas, daylilies, ferns, ornamental grasses, palms and many unusual plants displayed to benefit from different levels, incl stone steps, courtyards and terrace. National Collection of miniature hosta. Refreshments at The Lower George Café, High St.
✕ NCCPG ☎

Lawns and
herbaceous
borders.
Collection of
grasses. Formal
pond area.
Rambling roses
on rope
pergola . . .

71 WELLS COTTAGE
Wells Road, Bisley GL6 7AG. Mr &
Mrs Michael Flint. *5m E of Stroud.
Garden & car park well signed in Bisley
village. Garden lies on S edge of village
at head of Toadsmoor Valley, above
A419.* **Adm £3.50, chd free.
Combined with Paulmead £4.50.
Sun 21 June (2-6).**
Just under an acre. Terraced on
several levels with beautiful views over
valley. Much informal planting of trees
and shrubs to give colour and texture.
Lawns and herbaceous borders.
Collection of grasses. Formal pond
area. Rambling roses on rope pergola.
Vegetable garden with raised beds.
Plant sale at Paulmead.

**72 ◆ WESTBURY COURT
GARDEN**
Westbury-on-Severn GL14 1PD. The
National Trust, 01452 760461,
www.nationaltrust.org.uk. *9m SW of
Gloucester. On A48.* **Adm £4.20, chd
£2.10. Weds to Suns 12 Mar to Oct
(10-5) except July & Aug, daily (10-
5). For NGS: Sun 13 Sept (10-5).**

Formal Dutch-style water garden,
earliest remaining in England; canals,
summerhouse, over 100 species of
plants grown in England, and recreated
vegetable plots, growing crops all from
before 1700.

WESTON MEWS
See Herefordshire.

**73 ◆ WESTONBIRT SCHOOL
GARDENS**
GL8 8QG. Westonbirt School, 01666
881338,
doyle@westonbirt.gloucs.sch.uk. *3m
SW of Tetbury. Opp Westonbirt
Arboretum, on A433 (follow brown
tourist information signs).* **Adm £3.50,
chd £2. Thur to Sun 21 Mar to 12
April; 9 July to 30 Aug; 22 Oct to 1
Nov, (11-4). For NGS: Sun, Mon 24,
25 May (2-4).**
22 acres. Former private garden of
Robert Holford, founder of Westonbirt
Arboretum. Formal Victorian gardens
incl walled Italian garden, terraced
pleasure garden, rustic walks, lake,
statuary and grotto. Rare, exotic trees
and shrubs. Beautiful views of
Westonbirt House, now Westonbirt
School, not open. Gravel paths.

**WHICHFORD & ASCOTT
GARDENS**
See Warwickshire & part of West
Midlands.

WHITCOMBE HOUSE
See Worcestershire.

WHITEHILL FARM
See Oxfordshire.

WOODPECKERS
See Warwickshire & part of West
Midlands.

Gloucestershire County Volunteers

County Organiser
Norman Jeffery, 28 Shrivenham Road, Highworth, Swindon SN6 7BZ, 01793 762805, normjeffery28@aol.com

County Treasurer
Graham Baber, 11 Corinium Gate, Cirencester GL7 2PX, 01285 650961, grayanjen@onetel.com

Booklet Coordinator
John Sidwell, Lavender Down, Cheltenham Road, Painswick, Stroud GL6 6SJ, 01452 814244, john@johnsidwell.plus.com

Assistant County Organisers
Barbara Adams, Warners Court, Charfield, Wotton under Edge GL12 8TG, 01454 261078, adams@waitrose.com
Pamela Buckland, Meadow Cottage, 59 Coalway Road, Coalway, Coleford GL16 7HL, 01594 833444
Trish Jeffery, 28 Shrivenham Road, Highworth, Swindon SN6 7BZ, 01793 762805, trishjeffery@aol.com
Valerie Kent, 9 Acer Close. Bridewell Green, Nr Burford, Oxon OX18 4XE, 01993 823294
Stella Martin, Dundry Lodge, France Lynch, Stroud GL6 8LP, 01453 883419, martin@franlyn.fsnet.co.uk
Shirley & Gordon Sills, Barn House, Sandywell Park, Whittington, Cheltenham GL54 4HF, 01242 820606, shirley.sills@tesco.net

Mark your diary with these special events in 2009

EXPLORE SECRET GARDENS DURING CHELSEA & HAMPTON COURT FLOWER SHOW WEEKS

Tue 19 May, Wed 20 May, Thur 21 May, Fri 22 May, Wed 8 July, Thur 9 July
Full day tours from £82 per person, 10% discount for groups
Advance booking required, telephone +44 (0)20 8693 1015 or email j.wookey@btinternet.com
Specially selected gardens in London, Essex, Kent, Hampshire and South Oxfordshire. The tour price includes transport and lunch with wine at a popular restaurant or pub.

HAMPTON COURT PALACE

Thur 2 Apr, Tue 23 June, Thur 25 June, Wed 15 July, Tue 4 Aug, Thur 10 Sept
Evening tours in the company of one of the Palace's specialist tour guides from 6.30 – 8pm
Tickets £6 per person. Advance booking required, telephone +44 (0)1483 211535 or
visit www.ngs.org.uk for more information
Gossip, scandal, murder, healing – you'll find it all within the Formal Gardens at Hampton Court Palace. Each tour will have its own unique feature whether it's the story of the Great Vine or the magic and mystery of the Maze.

FROGMORE – A ROYAL GARDEN (BERKSHIRE)

Tue 26 May 10am – 5.30pm (last admission 4pm)
Garden adm £4.50, chd free. Tickets available in advance or on the day.
Advance booking for groups and coaches, telephone
+44 (0) 1483 211535 or email orders@ngs.org.uk
A rare opportunity to explore 30 acres of landscaped garden, rich in history and beauty.

FLAXBOURNE FARM – FUN & SURPRISES (BEDFORDSHIRE)

Sun 7 June 10am – 5pm. Adm £5, chd free
No booking required, come along on the day!
Bring the whole family and have fun in this surprising and entertaining garden of 2 acres. Enjoy the large plant fair, live music, pets corner, birds of prey, dog agility show and much more.

WISLEY RHS GARDEN – MUSIC IN THE GARDEN (SURREY)

Fri 11 Sept 6 – 9pm
Adm (incl RHS members) £7, chd under 15 free
Save money on advance bookings for groups of 4 or more, telephone +44 (0)1483 211535 or
visit www.ngs.org.uk for more information
A special evening opening of this famous garden, exclusively for the NGS. Enjoy music and entertainment as you explore the gardens and the floral marquee on the first day of the Wisley Flower Show.

For further information visit www.ngs.org.uk or telephone 01483 211535

HAMPSHIRE

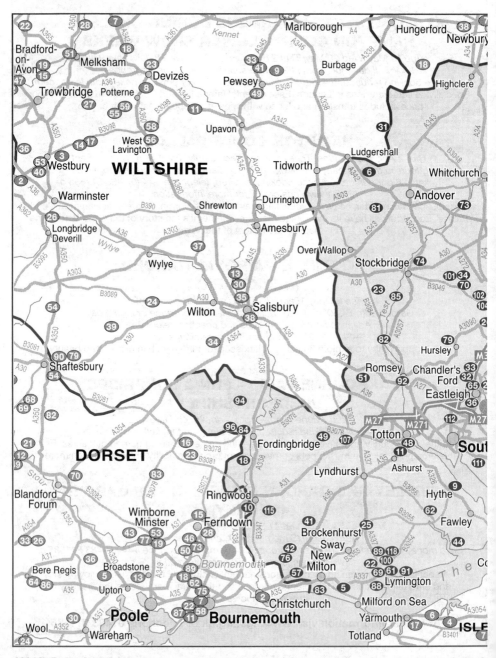

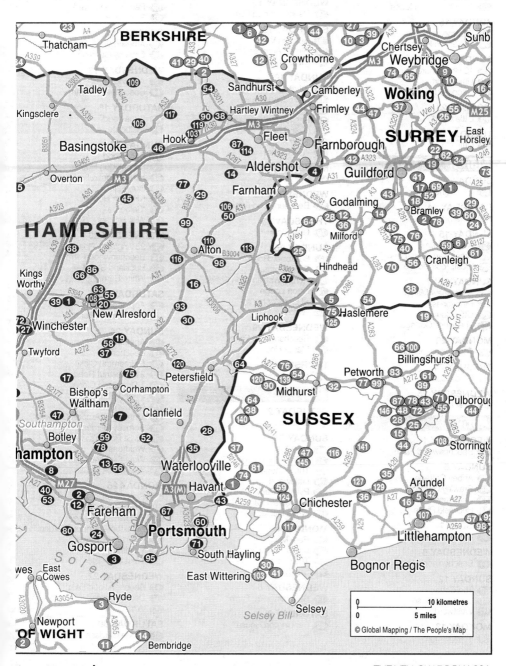

Opening Dates

February

SATURDAY 7
- 20 Brandy Mount House

SUNDAY 15
- 19 Bramdean House
- 39 The Down House

SUNDAY 22
- 26 12 Christchurch Road
- 70 Little Court
- 72 Litton Lodge

MONDAY 23
- 70 Little Court

TUESDAY 24
- 70 Little Court

March

SUNDAY 1
- 53 Heathlands

SATURDAY 14
- 9 Atheling Villas

SUNDAY 15
- 9 Atheling Villas
- 19 Bramdean House
- 110 Westbrook House

SUNDAY 22
- 6 Appleshaw Manor
- 47 Flintstones
- 70 Little Court
- 116 The White Cottage

MONDAY 23
- 116 The White Cottage

TUESDAY 24
- 70 Little Court

WEDNESDAY 25
- 14 Beechenwood Farm

April

WEDNESDAY 1
- 14 Beechenwood Farm

SUNDAY 5
- 1 Abbey Cottage
- 34 Crawley Gardens
- 53 Heathlands
- 54 Heckfield Place

TUESDAY 7
- 34 Crawley Gardens

WEDNESDAY 8
- 14 Beechenwood Farm

SUNDAY 12
- 32 The Cottage
- 41 Durmast House
- 112 Westward

MONDAY 13
- 32 The Cottage

- 82 Mottisfont Abbey & Garden
- 112 Westward

WEDNESDAY 15
- 14 Beechenwood Farm

SATURDAY 18
- 9 Atheling Villas
- 58 Hinton Ampner
- 98 'Selborne'

SUNDAY 19
- 9 Atheling Villas
- 19 Bramdean House
- 87 Old Thatch
- 94 St Christopher's
- 98 'Selborne'
- 100 Spinners
- 108 Weir House

MONDAY 20
- 100 Spinners

WEDNESDAY 22
- 14 Beechenwood Farm

THURSDAY 23
- 70 Little Court

SUNDAY 26
- 2 80 Abbey Road
- 16 Berry Cottage
- 61 Hordle Walhampton School
- 72 Litton Lodge
- 94 St Christopher's
- 106 Walbury

WEDNESDAY 29
- 14 Beechenwood Farm
- 77 Manor House

THURSDAY 30
- 77 Manor House

May

SATURDAY 2
- 71 Littlewood

SUNDAY 3
- 15 Bere Mill
- 21 6 Breamore Close
- 32 The Cottage
- 71 Littlewood
- 91 Pylewell Park
- 93 Rotherfield Park
- 117 White Gables

MONDAY 4
- 15 Bere Mill
- 21 6 Breamore Close
- 32 The Cottage
- 97 Sandy Slopes

WEDNESDAY 6
- 14 Beechenwood Farm

SATURDAY 9
- 88 Pennington House

SUNDAY 10
- 34 Crawley Gardens
- 62 The House in the Wood
- 88 Pennington House
- 91 Pylewell Park

TUESDAY 12
- 9 Atheling Villas
- 34 Crawley Gardens

WEDNESDAY 13
- 9 Atheling Villas
- 14 Beechenwood Farm

SATURDAY 16
- 42 Edgewood
- 98 'Selborne'

SUNDAY 17
- 42 Edgewood
- 52 Hambledon House
- 57 Hinton Admiral
- 59 Holywell
- 64 Kimpton House
- 98 'Selborne'
- 108 Weir House

WEDNESDAY 20
- 4 23 Anglesey Road
- 14 Beechenwood Farm
- 22 Buckland Stead
- 115 White Barn

SATURDAY 23
- 8 Appletrees
- 25 21 Chestnut Road

SUNDAY 24
- 8 Appletrees
- 13 Beechcroft
- 21 6 Breamore Close
- 25 21 Chestnut Road
- 40 7 Downland Close
- 68 Linden Barn
- 79 Merdon Manor
- 81 Monxton & Amport Gardens
- 92 Romsey Gardens
- 95 28 St Ronan's Avenue
- 107 Waldrons
- 109 West Silchester Hall
- 110 Westbrook House

MONDAY 25
- 13 Beechcroft
- 21 6 Breamore Close
- 40 7 Downland Close
- 81 Monxton & Amport Gardens
- 92 Romsey Gardens
- 107 Waldrons
- 109 West Silchester Hall

WEDNESDAY 27
- 14 Beechenwood Farm
- 37 Dean House
- 115 White Barn

SATURDAY 30
- 50 Froyle Gardens

SUNDAY 31
- (16) Berry Cottage
- (47) Flintstones
- (50) Froyle Gardens
- (78) Meon Orchard
- (97) Sandy Slopes

June

MONDAY 1
- (47) Flintstones

TUESDAY 2
- (105) The Vyne

WEDNESDAY 3
- (14) Beechenwood Farm
- (22) Buckland Stead
- (115) White Barn

FRIDAY 5
- (28) Clibdens

SATURDAY 6
- (11) Barhi
- (28) Clibdens
- (36) The Daisy House
- (48) The Fountains

SUNDAY 7
- (11) Barhi
- (28) Clibdens
- (31) Conholt Park
- (36) The Daisy House
- (48) The Fountains
- (66) Lake House
- (73) Longparish Gardens
- (103) Tylney Hall Hotel

MONDAY 8
- (73) Longparish Gardens

TUESDAY 9
- (47) Flintstones (Evening)
- (66) Lake House

WEDNESDAY 10
- (14) Beechenwood Farm
- (115) White Barn

FRIDAY 12
- (98) 'Selborne' (Evening)

SATURDAY 13
- (9) Atheling Villas
- (25) 21 Chestnut Road
- (36) The Daisy House
- (40) 7 Downland Close
- (42) Edgewood
- (98) 'Selborne'

SUNDAY 14
- (9) Atheling Villas
- (12) 19 Barnwood Road
- (16) Berry Cottage
- (17) Blackdown House
- (25) 21 Chestnut Road
- (33) Cranbury Park
- (36) The Daisy House
- (40) 7 Downland Close
- (42) Edgewood
- (65) 53 Ladywood
- (83) Mulberry House

MONDAY 15
- (65) 53 Ladywood
- (85) The Old Rectory, Houghton

WEDNESDAY 17
- (22) Buckland Stead
- (37) Dean House
- (69) The Little Cottage
- (115) White Barn

FRIDAY 19
- (18) Braemoor

SATURDAY 20
- (36) The Daisy House
- (58) Hinton Ampner
- (120) Wrens Farm

SUNDAY 21
- (10) Avon Glen
- (18) Braemoor
- (19) Bramdean House
- (31) Conholt Park
- (35) Crookley Pool
- (36) The Daisy House
- (38) Dipley Mill
- (59) Holywell
- (67) 60 Lealand Road
- (74) Longstock Park Water Garden
- (84) Oakdene
- (110) Westbrook House (Evening)
- (120) Wrens Farm

TUESDAY 23
- (10) Avon Glen

WEDNESDAY 24
- (34) Crawley Gardens
- (115) White Barn

THURSDAY 25
- (34) Crawley Gardens

SATURDAY 27
- (24) 2 Carisbrooke Road

SUNDAY 28
- (10) Avon Glen
- (24) 2 Carisbrooke Road
- (30) Colemore House Gardens
- (39) The Down House
- (40) 7 Downland Close
- (41) Durmast House
- (68) Linden Barn
- (82) Mottisfont Abbey & Garden
- (83) Mulberry House
- (84) Oakdene

MONDAY 29
- (30) Colemore House Gardens
- (40) 7 Downland Close

July

WEDNESDAY 1
- (22) Buckland Stead
- (69) The Little Cottage
- (115) White Barn

Oakdene listings:
- (84) Oakdene
- (85) The Old Rectory, Houghton
- (98) 'Selborne'

FRIDAY 3
- (18) Braemoor
- (29) The Coach House (Evening)
- (102) Treeside

SATURDAY 4
- (29) The Coach House
- (102) Treeside
- (111) Weston Allotments

SUNDAY 5
- (18) Braemoor
- (29) The Coach House
- (43) Emsworth Gardens
- (46) Fir Trees
- (64) Kimpton House
- (102) Treeside
- (103) Tylney Hall Hotel
- (111) Weston Allotments
- (117) White Gables

TUESDAY 7
- (9) Atheling Villas
- (46) Fir Trees

WEDNESDAY 8
- (9) Atheling Villas
- (37) Dean House
- (115) White Barn

SATURDAY 11
- (42) Edgewood
- (104) Ulvik

SUNDAY 12
- (2) 80 Abbey Road
- (42) Edgewood
- (45) Farleigh House
- (90) The Priors Farm
- (96) Sandle Cottage
- (104) Ulvik
- (109) West Silchester Hall
- (114) Whispers
- (119) 1 Wogsbarne Cottages

MONDAY 13
- (104) Ulvik

TUESDAY 14
- (104) Ulvik

WEDNESDAY 15
- (115) White Barn

THURSDAY 16
- (23) The Buildings

SATURDAY 18
- (58) Hinton Ampner
- (82) Mottisfont Abbey & Garden
- (105) The Vyne

SUNDAY 19
- (12) 19 Barnwood Road
- (19) Bramdean House
- (23) The Buildings
- (34) Crawley Gardens
- (37) Dean House
- (60) The Homestead
- (67) 60 Lealand Road
- (80) Michaelmas
- (95) 28 St Ronan's Avenue
- (99) Shalden Park House

MONDAY 20
(80) Michaelmas

TUESDAY 21
(34) Crawley Gardens

WEDNESDAY 22
(22) Buckland Stead
(69) The Little Cottage
(115) White Barn

FRIDAY 24
(18) Braemoor
(27) Christchurch Road Gardens (Evening)

SATURDAY 25
(112) Westward

SUNDAY 26
(16) Berry Cottage
(18) Braemoor
(27) Christchurch Road Gardens
(78) Meon Orchard
(96) Sandle Cottage
(112) Westward
(116) The White Cottage

MONDAY 27
(116) The White Cottage

WEDNESDAY 29
(115) White Barn

FRIDAY 31
(87) Old Thatch (Evening)

August

SATURDAY 1
(95) 28 St Ronan's Avenue (Evening)
(98) 'Selborne'

SUNDAY 2
(37) Dean House
(55) Hill House
(89) Pilley Hill Gardens
(96) Sandle Cottage
(98) 'Selborne'

MONDAY 3
(98) 'Selborne'

TUESDAY 4
(55) Hill House

WEDNESDAY 5
(89) Pilley Hill Gardens

THURSDAY 6
(86) The Old Rectory, Swarraton

SATURDAY 8
(104) Ulvik

SUNDAY 9
(16) Berry Cottage
(86) The Old Rectory, Swarraton
(104) Ulvik
(109) West Silchester Hall
(118) Willows

MONDAY 10
(104) Ulvik

TUESDAY 11
(104) Ulvik

WEDNESDAY 12
(69) The Little Cottage

FRIDAY 14
(18) Braemoor

SUNDAY 16
(18) Braemoor
(19) Bramdean House
(63) The Hyde

TUESDAY 18
(63) The Hyde

WEDNESDAY 19
(118) Willows

THURSDAY 20
(23) The Buildings

SATURDAY 22
(113) Wheatley House

SUNDAY 23
(23) The Buildings
(53) Heathlands
(67) 60 Lealand Road
(89) Pilley Hill Gardens
(113) Wheatley House

WEDNESDAY 26
(89) Pilley Hill Gardens

SATURDAY 29
(51) Gilberts Nursery

SUNDAY 30
(1) Abbey Cottage
(49) Fritham Lodge
(51) Gilberts Nursery
(118) Willows

MONDAY 31
(1) Abbey Cottage
(51) Gilberts Nursery
(52) Hambledon House
(118) Willows

September

WEDNESDAY 2
(69) The Little Cottage
(118) Willows

SUNDAY 6
(16) Berry Cottage
(63) The Hyde
(78) Meon Orchard

TUESDAY 8
(63) The Hyde

SUNDAY 13
(19) Bramdean House
(45) Farleigh House
(54) Heckfield Place
(87) Old Thatch
(108) Weir House

THURSDAY 17
(23) The Buildings

SATURDAY 19
(58) Hinton Ampner

SUNDAY 20
(23) The Buildings
(29) The Coach House
(93) Rotherfield Park
(103) Tylney Hall Hotel

WEDNESDAY 23
(4) 23 Anglesey Road

February 2010

SUNDAY 7
(39) The Down House

SUNDAY 14
(19) Bramdean House

SUNDAY 21
(70) Little Court

MONDAY 22
(70) Little Court

TUESDAY 23
(70) Little Court

Gardens open to the public

(3) Alverstoke Crescent Garden
(5) Apple Court
(19) Bramdean House
(44) Exbury Gardens & Steam Railway
(58) Hinton Ampner
(76) Macpennys Woodland Garden & Nurseries
(82) Mottisfont Abbey & Garden
(100) Spinners
(105) The Vyne

By appointment only

(7) Appletree House
(56) 2 Hillside Cottages
(75) Longthatch
(101) Tanglefoot

Also open by Appointment

(2) 80 Abbey Road
(4) 23 Anglesey Road
(9) Atheling Villas
(10) Avon Glen
(11) Barhi
(12) 19 Barnwood Road
(13) Beechcroft
(14) Beechenwood Farm
(15) Bere Mill
(16) Berry Cottage
(18) Braemoor
(21) 6 Breamore Close
(22) Buckland Stead
(23) The Buildings
(29) The Coach House
(31) Conholt Park
(32) The Cottage

35 Crookley Pool
40 7 Downland Close
41 Durmast House
42 Edgewood
43 23 New Brighton Road, Emsworth Gardens
47 Flintstones
48 The Fountains
49 Fritham Lodge
50 2 Colthouse Lane, Froyle Gardens
52 Hambledon House
55 Hill House
60 The Homestead
63 The Hyde
65 53 Ladywood
66 Lake House
68 Linden Barn
69 The Little Cottage
70 Little Court
73 Longmead House, Longparish Gardens
78 Meon Orchard
79 Merdon Manor
83 Mulberry House
84 Oakdene
86 The Old Rectory, Swarraton
92 4 Mill Lane, Romsey Gardens
94 St Christopher's
95 28 St Ronan's Avenue
96 Sandle Cottage
98 'Selborne'
104 Ulvik
106 Walbury
107 Waldrons
108 Weir House
109 West Silchester Hall
112 Westward
113 Wheatley House
115 White Barn
116 The White Cottage
118 Willows
120 Wrens Farm

The Gardens

1 ABBEY COTTAGE
Itchen Abbas SO21 1BN. Patrick Daniell, www.abbeycottage.org.uk. 2½ m W of Alresford. On B3047 between Kingworthy and Alresford, ½ m E of the Trout Inn at Itchen Abbas. Home-made teas. **Adm £3, chd free. Sun 5 Apr; Sun 30, Mon 31 Aug (12-5).**
This 1½ -acre organic garden, on alkaline soil, is a fine garden by any standards. Inside the C18 walls of an old kitchen garden there are enclosures, on different levels, which together create an inspirational garden. The adjoining meadow contains specimen trees, an orchard, spring bulbs, summer wild flowers and a plantation of native trees.

    🚻 🐕 ❀ ☕

2 80 ABBEY ROAD
Fareham PO15 5HW. Brian & Vivienne Garford, 01329 843939, vgarford@aol.com. 1m W of Fareham. From M27 J9 take A27 E towards Fareham for approx 2 m. At top of hill (past Titchfield gyratory) turn L at T-lights into Highland Rd. Turn 4th R into Blackbrook Rd. Abbey Rd 4th turning on L. Home-made teas. **Adm £2.50, chd free. Suns 26 Apr; 12 July (11-5). Visitors also welcome by appt.**
Small garden with extensive collection of herbs and unusual plants of botanical and historical interest, many of which are for sale. Formal box edging provides structure for the more relaxed planting. Interesting use of containers, and other ideas for small gardens. Two small ponds and tiny meadow area attract wide range of butterflies and other wildlife. Garden trails for children. Living willow seat, trained grapevine. Art exhibition by local artist.

    🐕 ❀ ☕ ☎

Three into one small garden does go . . .

3 ◆ ALVERSTOKE CRESCENT GARDEN
Crescent Road, Gosport PO12 2DH. Gosport Borough Council, 02392 586403, www.angleseyville.com. 1m S of Gosport. From A32 & Gosport follow signs for Stokes Bay. Continue alongside bay to small roundabout, turn L into Anglesey Rd. Crescent Garden signed 50yds on R. **Adm by donation. Open daily all yr.**
Restored Regency ornamental garden, designed to enhance fine Crescent (Owen 1826). Trees, walks and flowers lovingly maintained by community/Council partnership. Garden's considerable local historic interest highlighted by impressive restoration and creative planting of adjacent St Mark's churchyard. Worth seeing together. Heritage, history and horticulture: a fascinating package (see website). Plant sale Mon 25 May. Winner Green Flag Award (Civic Trust) and Green Heritage Site Award in conjunction with St Mark's churchyard. Gravel paths, limited wheelchair access in churchyard.

    ♿

4 23 ANGLESEY ROAD
Aldershot GU12 4RF. Adrian & Elizabeth Whiteley, 01252 677623. On E edge of Aldershot. From A331 take A323 towards Aldershot. Keep in R-hand lane, turn R at T-lights into North Lane, then immed L into Lower Newport Rd. Round bend turn immed R into Newport Rd, 1st R into Wilson Rd. Round L-hand bend turn immed R into Roberts Rd, Anglesey Rd 1st on L. Please park considerately in local rds. **Adm £2.50, chd free. Weds 20 May; 23 Sept (2-6). Visitors also welcome by appt.**
Three into one small garden does go. Mediterranean at the front, shady fernery down the side and urban jungle round the back. Trees, shrubs and bold perennials give a feeling of maturity and seclusion. Generous geometric beds house many unusual specimens, both hardy and tender, regularly rearranged for best effect.

    🐕 ❀ ☕ ☎

5 ◆ APPLE COURT
Hordle Lane, Hordle, Lymington SO41 0HU. Charles & Angela Meads, 01590 642130, www.applecourt.com. 4m W of Lymington. From A337 between Lymington & New Milton, turn into Hordle Lane at Royal Oak at Downton Xrds. **Adm £4, chd free. Fris, Sats, Suns & B Hol Mons 1 Mar to 31 Oct (10-5).**
1½ -acre formally designed and exuberantly planted sheltered walled garden. Theatrical white garden, extensive ornamental grass plantings, subtropical borders. 70 metre hosta walk. International display gardens of day lilies, fern walk, Japanese-style garden with koi pond. Featured on Solent Radio and in 'Hampshire Life' & 'Hampshire View'.

    ♿ 🐕 ❀ 🛏 ☕

6 APPLESHAW MANOR
nr Andover SP11 9BH. Mr & Mrs Patrick Walker. 5m NW of Andover. Take A342 Andover to Marlborough rd. Turn to Appleshaw 1m W of Weyhill. Fork L at playing field, on R after ½ m, nr church. Disabled parking by house. Home-made teas. **Adm £3, chd free (share to St Peter in the Wood Church, Appleshaw). Sun 22 Mar (2-5).**
7-acre walled mature gardens, incl wide lawns, wood garden, arboretum, kitchen garden and pond. Carpets of spring bulbs and notable yew and beech hedges.

    ♿ 🐕 ❀ ☕

❼ APPLETREE HOUSE

Station Road, Soberton SO32 3QU.
Mrs J Dover, 01489 877333. *10m N of Fareham. A32 N to Droxford, at Xrds turn R B2150. Turn R under bridge into Station Rd, garden 1m. Parking in lay-by 300yds or in rd.* Light refreshments. **Adm £2.50, chd free. Visitors welcome by appt, no coaches.**
Very popular, small romantic woodland garden with many varieties of clematis climbing through richly planted beds as well as over obelisks and arches. Meandering paths lead to views of the meadow beyond, and sitting areas afford vistas across the garden. The design belies the actual size: 40ft x 100ft.

🐾 ✿ ☕ ☎

❽ APPLETREES

267 Botley Rd, Burridge SO31 1BS.
Kath & Ray Butcher. *From A27 take A3051 Park Gate to Botley, on L after 1¹/₂ m. From Botley take A3051, Appletrees is 2m on R.* **Adm £3, chd free. Sat 23, Sun 24 May (2-5).**
Flower arranger's ¹/₃ -acre garden densely planted with perennials, good foliage. Large patio with sinks and containers. Many winding paths with seats, small pond and waterfall.

🐾

❾ ATHELING VILLAS

16 Atheling Road, Hythe,
Southampton SO45 6BR. Mary & Peter York, 02380 849349, athelingvillas@mac.com. *7m E of Lyndhurst. Leave M27 J2, follow A326 signed Hythe and Fawley. Go across all roundabouts until Dibden roundabout (¹/₂ m after Marchwood Priory Hospital). Turn L towards Hythe. After Shell garage, Atheling Road is 2nd L.* Home-made teas. **Adm £2.50, chd free (share to The Children's Society). Sats, Suns 14, 15 Mar; 18, 19 Apr; Tue 12, Wed 13 May; Sat 13, Sun 14 June; Tue 7, Wed 8 July (2-5). Visitors also welcome by appt, dates and numbers by agreement.**
'Winding paths, archways, shrubberies, dry weather planting, shady nooks, and sunny flower beds. A garden for all seasons, with surprises around every corner' (Waterside Herald). ¹/₃ acre with less usual trees and shrubs; species bulbs; wall-trained fruit; several seating areas; self-guide leaflet and children's quiz. Teas in gardener's cottage.

🐾 ✿ ☕ ☎

❿ NEW AVON GLEN

Hurn Lane, Ringwood
BH24 2AG. Sue & Mike Sismey, 01425 479176. *¹/₂ m W of Ringwood. From Ringwood take A31 (W) past car park, church and Texaco garage (¹/₂ m). Immediately take slip rd to Verwood and Matchams. Before bridge turn L to Matchams, Avon Glen 200yds on R.* Home-made teas. **Adm £3, chd free (share to The Heal Project). Sun 21, Tue 23, Sun 28 June (2-5.30). Visitors also welcome by appt.**
Our sheltered small garden incl the drive and terraced bank is an excellent example of shrub planting. In spring, snowdrops, crocuses, primroses and bluebells carpet the ground under mature trees, azaleas, magnolia and camellias, whilst herbaceous borders bring a mass of colour in summer. Look carefully around the pond and you may see the resident frog! Wheelchair access to lower part of garden only.

♿ 🐾 ☕ ☎

In spring, snowdrops, crocuses, primroses and bluebells carpet the ground under mature trees . . .

⓫ BARHI

27 Reynolds Dale, Ashurst,
Southampton SO40 7PS. Ms F Barnes, 02380 860046, fbarnes@barhi.net, www.barhi.net/garden. *6m W of Southampton. From M27, J2 take A326 to Fawley. At 4th roundabout L into Cocklydown Lane. At mini roundabout L into Ibbotson Way. 1st L into Reynolds Dale and follow signs.* Home-made teas. **Adm £2.50, chd free. Sat 6, Sun 7 June (2-5). Also open nearby The Fountains. Visitors also welcome by appt.**
Compact 'modern cottage' garden shared with lively Springer Spaniels,

designed around a chambered nautilus spiral. No lawn, so lots of space for plants. The dense planting, meandering paths, secluded pergola, raised formal pond and feature patio have led visitors to describe the garden as 'Tardis-like'. Our dogs will be in the garden on open days.

♿ 🐾 ☕ ☎

⓬ 19 BARNWOOD ROAD

Fareham PO15 5LA. Jill & Michael Hill, 01329 842156, thegarden19@btinternet.com. *1m W of Fareham. From M27 J9 take A27 towards Fareham. At top of hill past Titchfield Mill PH turn L at T-lights into Highlands Rd. Take 4th R into Blackbrook Rd, Meadow Bank 4th turn on R. Barnwood Rd is off Meadow Bank. Please consider the neighbours when parking.* Home-made teas. **Adm £2.50, chd free. Suns 14 June; 19 July (11-5). Visitors also welcome by appt.**
Step through the gate to an enchanting garden designed for peace with an abundance of floral colour and delightful features. Greek-style courtyard leads to natural pond with bridge and bog garden, complemented by a thatched summerhouse and jetty, designed and built by owners. Secret pathways, mosaic seating area and hexagonal greenhouse. Gold Medal winner Plantsman's Garden, Fareham in Bloom.

🐾 ✿ ☕ ☎

⓭ BEECHCROFT

Hundred Acres Road, Wickham,
Fareham PO17 6HY. Maggie & David Smith, 01329 835122, maggie@gladehouse.co.uk. *5m N of Fareham, 1¹/₂ m E of Wickham. From A32 at Wickham take B2177 E. Turn 1st L after 1¹/₂ m into Hundred Acres Rd, Beechcroft approx ¹/₄ m on R over brow of hill.* Home-made teas. **Adm £2.50, chd free. Sun 24, Mon 25 May (11-5). Visitors also welcome by appt May to July.**
Challenging 1-acre plot developed over the last 6yrs. Main garden has generous borders with wide variety of trees, shrubs and perennials, 2 wildlife ponds and greenhouse. Steeply-sloping wild flower bank with fruit trees and coppiced willows descends to natural pond and bog garden and rises to orchard and large fruit/vegetable cage. Wheelchair access to main part of garden only.

♿ ✿ ☕ ☎

14 BEECHENWOOD FARM
Odiham RG29 1JA. Mr & Mrs M
Heber-Percy, 01256 702300,
beechenwood@totalise.co.uk. *5m
SE of Hook. Turn S into King St from
Odiham High St. Turn L after cricket
ground for Hillside. Take 2nd turn R
after 1½ m, modern house ½ m.*
Home-made teas. **Adm £3.50, chd
free.** Every Wed 25 Mar to 10 June
(2-5). **Visitors also welcome by appt
Apr to June only, no coaches. Small
groups and individuals welcome.**
2-acre garden in many parts. Lawn
meandering through woodland with
drifts of crocus, daffodils, hyacinths,
tulips and bluebells. Rose pergola with
steps, pots with spring bulbs and later
aeoniums. Fritillary and cowslip
meadow. Walled herb garden with pool
and exuberant planting incl alliums and
angelica. Orchard incl white garden
and hot border. Large greenhouse and
vegetable garden. Rock garden
extending to grasses, ferns and
bamboos. Shady walk to belvedere
with views over farmland. 8-acre copse
of native species with grassed rides.
Quality plant sales. Gravel drive.
  ♿ ✿ ☕ ☎

15 BERE MILL
London Road, Whitchurch
RG28 7NH. Rupert & Elizabeth
Nabarro, 01256 892210,
rnabarro@aol.com. *9m E of Andover,
12m N of Winchester. In centre of
Whitchurch, take London Rd at
roundabout. Up hill 1m, turn R 50yds
beyond The Gables on R. Drop-off
point for disabled at garden.* Home-
made teas. **Adm £4, chd free** (share
to The Smile Train). Sun 3, Mon
4 May (1.30-5.30). **Visitors also
welcome by appt, Fris only,
minimum 10 visitors.**
Garden created since 1993 around the
1712 mill (not open) where Portals first
made bank notepaper. Set by the R
Test and carrier streams, a large
lozenge-shaped site, loosely fashioned
on a Japanese stroll garden.
Herbaceous and Mediterranean beds;
replanted walled orchard and
vegetable garden; wisteria garden and
lake with Japanese tea-house.
Extensively planted with bulbs; irises a
speciality. Modern sculpture. Unfenced
and unguarded rivers and streams.
  ♿ ✿ ☕ ☎

16 BERRY COTTAGE
Church Road, Farringdon, nr Alton
GU34 3EG. Mrs P Watts, 01420
588318. *3m S of Alton off A32. Turn L
at Xrds, lst L into Church Rd. Follow rd
past Masseys Folley, 2nd house on R
opp church.* Cream teas. **Adm £2.50,
chd free.** Suns 26 Apr; 31 May; 14
June; 26 July; 9 Aug; 6 Sept (2.30-6).
**Visitors also welcome by appt June
to Aug, for groups of 10+.**
Small organic cottage garden with all-
yr interest. Spring bulbs, roses,
clematis and herbaceous borders.
Pond and bog garden. Shrubbery and
small kitchen garden. Featured in
'Amateur Gardening'.
  ♿ ☕ ☎

**17 NEW BLACKDOWN
HOUSE**
Blackdown Lane, Upham
SO32 1HS. Mr & Mrs Tom
Sweet-Escott. *5m SE of
Winchester. 1m N of Upham, best
accessed from Morestead Rd Xrds
with Longwood Dean Lane.* Home-
made teas. **Adm £3, chd free.**
Sun 14 June (2-6).
A family garden in the making.
2009 will be the 2nd year of the
100m long, colourful herbaceous
border set against a flint wall. There
is a 12yr-old wild flower meadow to
meander through, a part-walled
kitchen garden, orchard and family
garden. In all, the garden covers
approx 5 acres. Jacob sheep and
alpacas in the parkland.
  ✗ ☕

BORDER COTTAGE
See Berkshire.

18 BRAEMOOR
Bleak Hill, Harbridge, Ringwood
BH24 3PX. Tracy & John Netherway
& Judy Spratt, 01425 652983,
jnetherway@btinternet.com. *2½ m S
of Fordingbridge. Turn off A338 at
Ibsley. Go through Harbridge village to
T-junction at top of hill, turn R for ¼ m.*
Cream teas. **Adm £3, chd free.** Fris,
Suns 19, 21 June; 3, 5, 24, 26 July;
14, 16 Aug (2-5.30). **Visitors also
welcome by appt June to Aug,
coaches permitted.**
In the pretty hamlet of Harbridge, this
¾ -acre garden is brimming with bold,
colourful planting and interesting areas.
Cottage garden herbaceous borders
contrast with beach-themed gravel. A
little stream runs by the lawn to a
pond. Two greenhouses house
collections of cacti and carnivorous
plants. Vegetables and bantam
chickens. Small adjacent nursery.
Featured in 'Hampshire Life'.
  ✗ ✿ ☕ ☎

19 ◆ BRAMDEAN HOUSE
Bramdean SO24 0JU. Mr & Mrs H
Wakefield, 01962 771214. *4m S of
Alresford. In centre of village on A272.*
Adm £3.50, chd free. For NGS: Suns
15 Feb; 15 Mar; 19 Apr; 21 June; 19
July; 16 Aug; 13 Sept (2-5); 14 Feb
2010.
Traditional 6-acre garden on chalk,
famous for mirror-image herbaceous
borders. Carpets of bulbs, especially
snowdrops, in the spring. Very many
unusual plants incl collection of old-
fashioned sweet peas. 1-acre kitchen
garden featuring prizewinning
vegetables, fruit and flowers. Group
visits by arrangement, not weekends,
£5 per person.
  ♿ ✗ ✿ ☕

> Cottage garden
> herbaceous
> borders contrast
> with beach-
> themed gravel. A
> little stream runs
> by the lawn to a
> pond . . .

20 BRANDY MOUNT HOUSE
Alresford SO24 9EG. Caryl &
Michael Baron,
www.brandymount.co.uk. *nr
Alresford centre. From centre, 1st R in
East St before Sun Lane. Please leave
cars in Broad St or stn car park.*
Home-made teas. **Adm £3, chd free.**
Sat 7 Feb (11-4).
1-acre, informal plantsman's garden.
Spring bulbs, hellebores, species
geraniums. National Collections of
snowdrops and daphnes. European
primulas, expanding collection of dwarf
narcissi, herbaceous and woodland
plants. 2 new raised beds to display
early spring bulbs. New small
collections of ferns in the shady part of
the garden. Wheelchair access must
be supervised.
  ♿ ✿ NCCPG ☕

21 6 BREAMORE CLOSE
Eastleigh SO50 4QB. Mr & Mrs R
Trenchard, 02380 611230,
dawndavina@tiscali.co.uk. *1m N of
Eastleigh. M3 J12, follow signs to
Eastleigh. Turn R at roundabout into
Woodside Ave, then 1st L into
Broadlands Ave (park here). Breamore
Close 3rd on L.* Home-made teas.
**Adm £2.50, chd free. Suns, Mons 3,
4, 24, 25 May (1-5.30). Visitors also
welcome by appt in May & June
only, for groups of 10+.**
Delightful 1/2 -acre plant lover's garden
designed with coloured foliage and
unusual plants, giving a pleasing
tapestry effect of texture and colour.
Many different hostas displayed in
pots. The peaceful garden is laid out in
distinctive planting themes with many
seating areas to sit and contemplate.
Over 60 clematis scramble up fences,
through roses and over a pergola
which displays a magnificent wisteria
(flowers 3ft-4ft long) in late spring.
Small gravel area.

   ♿ ✕ ✿ ☕ ☎

22 BUCKLAND STEAD
Sway Road, nr Lymington
SO41 8NN. Valerie & John Woolcott,
01590 673465,
valwoolcott@ukonline.co.uk. *1m N
of Lymington town centre. Off A337.
Pass Toll House Inn, 1st L into Sway
Rd. After 300yds, at sharp R-hand
bend, turn L into Buckland Granaries
entrance. Follow signs to garden.* Light
refreshments & teas. **Adm £2.50, chd
free. Weds 20 May; 3, 17 June; 1,
22 July (2-5). Also open The Little
Cottage 17 June, 1, 22 July. Visitors
also welcome by appt.**
Two gardens in one: 'His and Hers'.
Tranquil 1/4 acre designed and
maintained by owners. His: formal
rose garden with lavender edging filling
the air with fragrance. Shady walk
through 'neutral zone' to Hers: less
formal with colour themes using
herbaceous perennials and grasses.
Winding paths, archways, pergola and
water features. Featured on BBC
Breakfast TV.

   ♿ ✕ ✿ ☕ ☎

23 THE BUILDINGS
Broughton, Stockbridge SO20 8BH.
Dick & Gillian Pugh, 01794 301424.
*3m W of Stockbridge. NGS yellow
signs 2m W of Stockbridge off A30, or
6m N of Romsey off B3084.* Home-
made teas. **Adm £3, chd free. Thurs,
Suns 16, 19 July; 20, 23 Aug; 17, 20
Sept (2-5). Visitors also welcome by
appt.**

A 'dry' garden, and the wettest
summer for years! Yet 'original and
dramatic', 'very special planting',
'amazing colour sense', 'such textures
and movement' are some of the kind
compliments received during our first
year of opening. All this on the thin
chalk soil and wide open spaces of the
Hampshire downland. Featured in
'Amateur Gardening'.

   ♿ ✕ ✿ ☕ ☎

Two gardens in one: 'His and Hers' . . .

24 2 CARISBROOKE ROAD
Gosport PO13 0HQ. Chris & Norma
Matthews. *3m S of Fareham. Exit
M27 J11 signed Fareham Central.
Follow A32, Gosport. Take fork at
Newgate Lane signed Lee-on-Solent.
At 3rd roundabout 1st exit B3334
signed Rowner. L at T-lights, 1st house
on R.* Home-made teas. **Adm £3, chd
free. Sat 27, Sun 28 June (10-4).**
1/3 -acre cottage-style garden
developed by owners over 20yrs.
Shrubs, herbaceous perennials, gravel
and alpine gardens give yr-round
interest. Raised organic kitchen
garden. Interesting colourful baskets
and containers with plants propagated
by owners. Wildlife area and garden,
birds enthusiastically encouraged.
Fishpond and miniature wildlife pond.
Baskets, pots and plants for sale.
Winner of 2 Gold Awards in Gosport in
Bloom for Best Back Garden & for
Newcomers.

   ✿ ☕

25 21 CHESTNUT ROAD
Brockenhurst SO42 7RF. Iain & Mary
Hayter. *4m S of Lyndhurst. S on A337
to Brockenhurst, take R fork B3055,
Grigg Lane, opp Careys Manor Hotel.
Garden 500yds from junction via 2nd L
Chestnut Rd and 2nd L again for no
21. Parking limited; please use village
car park nearby.* Home-made teas.
**Adm £3, chd free. Sats, Suns 23, 24
May; 13, 14 June (Sats 11-5, Suns
2-6).**
From pastels to hots, this colourful
garden has sunny and shady areas
and a secret kitchen and wild flower
garden which mix with formal and
casual areas. American irises in May,
followed by roses and climbers which
adorn a circular pergola. Raised deck
over a wildlife pond accompany further

water features in this 1/3 -acre garden.
New small courtyard for shade lovers.
Finalist Daily Mail National Garden
Competition.

   ♿ ✕ ✿ ☕

26 12 CHRISTCHURCH ROAD
Central Winchester SO23 9SR. Iain
& Penny Patton. *Leave centre of
Winchester by Southgate St, 1st R into
St James Lane, 3rd L into Christchurch
Rd.* Light refreshments & home-made
teas. **Adm £2.50, chd free. Sun 22
Feb (11-4). Also open Litton Lodge.
Opening with Christchurch Road
Gardens 24, 26 July.**
Small town garden with strong design
enhanced by exuberant planting and
all-yr interest. Winter-flowering shrubs,
bulbs and hellebores. 2 water features
incl slate-edged rill bordered by
climbers. Small front garden designed
to be viewed from the house.

   ✕ ✿ ⊨ ☕

Group opening

**27 CHRISTCHURCH ROAD
GARDENS**
Central Winchester SO23 9SR.
*Leave centre of Winchester by
Southgate St, 1st R into St James
Lane, 3rd L into Christchurch Rd, 1st L
into Compton Rd.* Home-made teas.
**Combined adm £5, chd free.
Evening Opening, wine, Fri 24 July
(6-8). Sun 26 July (11-5).**
Two small walled gardens, 200yds
apart, in central Winchester.

   ✕ ✿ ☕

12 CHRISTCHURCH ROAD
Iain & Penny Patton
(See separate entry).

NEW 4 COMPTON ROAD
Mrs Anthea Fortescue
Developed over 5yrs, densely
planted and filled with the owner's
favourite planting of unusual
foliage and sculptured form,
together with subtle blending of
colours.

28 CLIBDENS
Chalton PO8 0BG. Michael &
Jacqueline Budden. *6m S of
Petersfield. Turn L off A3M at
Horndean then directly R over
motorway to Chalton. Clibdens is 1st
turning on L in village, directly before
Chalton village sign.* Home-made teas
and wine. **Adm £3.50, chd free. Fri 5,
Sat 6, Sun 7 June (11.30-5).**
1-acre walled garden surrounded by

farmland with fine views to Windmill Hill. Chalk garden with 4 rooms of lawn, shrubs and herbaceous plants. Terrace with stone pots of agapanthus, box, lavender and yew topiary. Gravel garden, stump garden and wildlife pond. Rose garden with oak posts and rope arches. All beautifully gardened and maintained.

29 THE COACH HOUSE

South Warnborough RG29 1RR. John & Sarah Taylor, 01256 862782, johntaylormw@hotmail.com. *5m N of Alton on B3349. In the middle of village opp village shop/post office. Car parking in lay-by opp.* Home-made teas Sat, Suns only. **Adm £3, chd free. Sat 4, Sun 5 July; Sun 20 Sept (2-6). Evening Opening £4.50, wine, Fri 3 July (5-9). Visitors also welcome by appt.**
³/₄ acre of semi-walled garden almost entirely given over to plantings of perennials and grasses in a naturalistic and informal style. Gravel planting and deep generous beds with an emphasis on height and proximity to plants. Featured on BBC TV Gardeners' World. NGS Gold Medal winner Channel 5 'I own Britain's Best Home and Garden'.

30 COLEMORE HOUSE GARDENS

Colemore, Alton GU34 3RX. Mr & Mrs Simon de Zoete. *5m S of Alton. Take turning to Colemore (Shell Lane) off A32, just S of E Tisted.* Home-made teas. **Adm £3.50, chd free. Sun 28, Mon 29 June (2-6).**
Situated in beautiful unspoilt country, 2¹/₂ acres with wide variety of unusual plants. Yew and box hedges, mixed herbaceous and shrub borders, yellow and blue garden, rose walk and excellent lawns. Garden is being constantly developed and incl spectacular water rill, swimming pool garden and the creation of a wild flower, tree and shrub area. Many different roses, salvias, penstemons and tender plants and bulbs. Extensive new planting of trees and shrubs.

Will you be our 8,000th visitor and receive free entry, tea & cake? . . .

31 CONHOLT PARK

Hungerford Lane, nr Chute SP11 9HA. Conholt Park Estate, 07917 796826. *7m N of Andover. Turn N off A342 Andover to Devizes rd at Weyhill Church. Go 5m N through Clanville & Tangley Bottom. Turn L at Conholt ¹/₂ m on R, just off Chute causeway. A343 to Hurstbourne Tarrant, turn to and go through Vernham Dean, next turn L signed Conholt.* Home-made teas. **Adm £3.50, chd free. Suns 7, 21 June (2-5). Visitors also welcome by appt in June & July only, coaches permitted.**
10 acres surrounding Regency house (not open), with mature cedars. Rose, 'Calor', Shakespeare, fern dell, winter and secret gardens. Restored 1¹/₂ - acre walled garden with vegetable and flower cartwheels, berry wall, orchard, Ladies' Walk and large (3,000sq m) foot-shaped maze with viewing platform.

32 THE COTTAGE

16 Lakewood Road, Chandler's Ford SO53 1ES. Hugh & Barbara Sykes, 02380 254521. *2m NW of Eastleigh. Leave M3 at J12, follow signs to Chandler's Ford. At King Rufus on Winchester Rd, turn R into Merdon Ave, then 3rd rd on L.* Home-made teas. **Adm £2.50, chd free. Suns, Mons 12, 13 Apr; 3, 4 May (2-6). Visitors also welcome by appt in Apr & May.**
³/₄ acre. Azaleas, bog garden, camellias, dogwoods, erythroniums, free-range bantams, greenhouse grapes, honey from our bees, irises, jasmines, kitchen garden, landscaping began in 1950, maintained by owners, new planting, osmunda, ponds, quiz for children, rhododendrons, smilacina, trilliums, unusual plants, viscum, wildlife areas, eXuberant foliage, yr-round interest, zantedeschia. Will you be our 8,000th visitor and receive free entry, tea & cake?

33 CRANBURY PARK

Otterbourne, nr Winchester SO21 2HL. Mr & Mrs Chamberlayne-Macdonald. *3m NW of Eastleigh. Main entrance on old A33 between Winchester and Southampton, by bus stop at top of Otterbourne Hill. Entrances also in Hocombe Rd, Chandler's Ford and next to church in Otterbourne.* Home-made teas. **Adm £4, chd free (share to All Saints Church, North Baddesley). Sun 14 June (2-6).**
Extensive pleasure grounds laid out in late C18 and early C19 by Papworth; fountains, rose garden, specimen trees and pinetum, lakeside walk and fern walk. Family carriages and collection of prams will be on view, also photos of King George VI, Eisenhower and Montgomery reviewing Canadian troops at Cranbury before D-Day. Disabled toilets.

Group opening

34 CRAWLEY GARDENS

nr Winchester SO21 2PU. *5m NW of Winchester. Off A272 or A3049 Winchester to Stockbridge rd. Parking at top of village nr church or in Littleton Rd.* Home-made teas at Village Hall. **Combined adm: £4 in Apr, £5 in May, June & July, chd free. Suns, Tues 5, 7 Apr; 10, 12 May (2-5.30); Wed 24, Thur 25 June (1.30-6); Sun 19, Tue 21 July (2-5.30).**
Exceptionally pretty small village with thatched houses, C14 church and village pond. The gardens comprise an interesting variety of character and style. Many other good front gardens visible from the road. Featured on Meridian TV.

BARN COTTAGE

Jane & Kenneth Wren. Not open April, May or July dates.
³/₄ -acre landscaped garden surrounds a converted barn. Painted trellising divides a courtyard garden into 3 areas where viticella clematis, roses and jasmine scramble and bee-loving plants abound.

BAY TREE HOUSE

Julia & Charles Whiteaway. Not open April or May dates.
Contemporary garden created during the last 6yrs. Features incl a rill, pleached lime square, large borders, potager and fruit trees with wild flowers. Gravel drive and path.

NEW GABLE COTTAGE
Patrick Hendra & Ken Jones.
Not open April, May or June
dates.
Cottage garden with waterfalls.

LITTLE COURT
Prof & Mrs A R Elkington. Not
open July dates.
(See separate entry).
&

PAIGE COTTAGE
Mr & Mrs T W Parker. Not open
May, June or July dates.
1 acre of traditional English
country garden incl grass tennis
court (not open) and walled
Italian-style swimming pool (not
open); spring garden with large
variety of bulbs and wild flowers.
&

TANGLEFOOT
Mr & Mrs F J Fratter. Not open
April dates.
(See separate entry).
&

36 NEW THE DAISY HOUSE
241 Passfield Avenue, Eastleigh
SO50 9ND. Kit & Diann Grafton.
*1m SW of Eastleigh. M3 J13, R
towards Eastleigh, follow signs to
airport; at Xrds R into Passfield
Ave. Or from M27 J5, L to Sports
Grounds, R at mini roundabout, L
at next mini roundabout into
Passfield Ave.* Home-made teas &
light refreshments. **Adm £3, chd
free. Sats, Suns 6, 7, 13, 14, 20,
21 June (1-5.30).**
English country garden with a
difference, fresh and exciting!
Lovingly tended and artistically
created 1/5 -acre garden with
impressive, innovative and inspiring
'cloud-formation' pruning of
numerous shrubs and trees. A rose
haven, giving an air of informality
with an overall enchanting
atmosphere.
🐕 ⊛ ☕

38 DIPLEY MILL
Dipley RG27 8JP. Miss Rose & Mr J
P McMonigall. *2m NE of Hook. Turn E
off B3349 at Mattingley (1½ m N of
Hook) signed Hartley Wintney, West
Green and Dipley. Dipley Mill ½ m on L
just over bridge.* Home-made teas.
**Adm £3, chd free (share to St
Michael's Hospice). Sun 21 June
(2-6).**
An adventure awaits as you wander by
the meandering streams surrounding
this Domesday Book listed mill! Explore
a grotto, scented, fuchsia and Indian
gardens, a hothouse, ornamental
courtyard and theatrical rose collection.
Or just escape into wild meadows.
Featured on Channel 5 'I Own Britain's
Best Home & Garden'.
🐕 ⊛ ☕

39 NEW THE DOWN HOUSE
Itchen Abbas SO21 1AX. Jackie
& Mark Porter. *6m E of
Winchester. On B3047, coming
from Winchester, 5th house on R
after Itchen Abbas village sign.*
Home-made teas. **Adm £2.50,
chd free (share to PCaSO). Suns
15 Feb (12-4), 28 June (2-6). 7
Feb 2010.**
2-acre garden developed by
owners since 2001, laid out in
rooms overlooking Itchen Valley,
adjoining the Pilgrim's Way, with
walks through a large meadow to
the river. Carpet of snowdrops
and crocus, plus borders of
coloured stems in winter. Roped
rose garden, hot borders, wildlife
pond and shady places in summer.
Pleached hornbeams, yew-lined
avenues, woodland nut and
orchard walk. Working vineyard.
& ☕

Carpet of snowdrops and crocus, borders of coloured stems in winter. Roped rose garden, hot borders, shady places in summer . . .

35 CROOKLEY POOL
Blendworth Lane, Horndean
PO8 0AB. Mr & Mrs Simon Privett,
02392 592662. *5m S of Petersfield.
2m E of Waterlooville, off A3. From
Horndean village go up Blendworth
Lane between bakery and hairdresser.
Entrance 200yds before church on L
with white railings.* Home-made teas.
**Adm £4, chd free. Sun 21 June
(2-5.30). Visitors also welcome by
appt.**
This very warm garden where tender
plants thrive is built around 1930s
swimming pool. The borders burst with
colour. In the pool garden, Californian
tree poppies have escaped and make
a forest of flowers around the pool.
Free-range bantams stroll through the
kitchen garden's formal borders. Well
stocked greenhouses. Organic garden,
animals. Flower paintings on show.
Featured in 'Petersfield Post'.
& 🐕 ⊛ ☕ ☎

37 DEAN HOUSE
Kilmeston SO24 0NL. Mr P H R
Gwyn,
www.deanhousegardens.co.uk. *5m
S of Alresford. Via village of Cheriton or
off A272 signed at Cheriton Xrds.*
Cream teas. **Adm £4, chd free. Weds
27 May; 17 June; 8 July (10-4). Suns
19 July; 2 Aug (12-5).**
The 9 acres have been described as 'a
well-kept secret hidden beside the
elegant facade of its Georgian
centrepiece' with mixed and
herbaceous borders, symmetrical rose
garden, pond garden, working walled
garden and glasshouses, sweeping
lawns, York stone and gravel pathways
and many young and mature trees and
hedges. Gravel paths.
& 🐕 ⊛ ☕

40 7 DOWNLAND CLOSE
Locks Heath, nr Fareham
SO31 6WB. Roy & Olwen Dorland,
01489 571788,
roydorland@hotmail.co.uk. *3m W of
Fareham. Leave M27 J9 (Whitely).
Follow A27 on Southampton Rd to
Park Gate. L into Locks Rd, 3rd R into
Meadow Ave, 2nd L into Downland
Close.* Home-made teas. **Adm £2.50,
regret not suitable for small children.
Sun 24, Mon 25 May; Sat 13, Suns
14, 28, Mon 29 June (11-5). Visitors
also welcome by appt from May to
July.**
Visit this beautiful and inspirational 45ft
x 45ft plantsman's garden, packed
with ideas for the 'modest-sized' plot.

Many varieties of hardy geraniums, hostas, heucheras, shrubs, ferns and other unusual perennials, weaving a tapestry of harmonious colour. Attractive water feature, plenty of seating areas and charming summerhouse. Gold Medal Plantsman's Back Garden, Fareham in Bloom.

41 DURMAST HOUSE

Burley BH24 4AT. Mr & Mrs P E G Daubeney, 01425 402132, philip@daubeney.co.uk. *5m SE of Ringwood. Off Burley to Lyndhurst rd, nr White Buck Hotel. Cream teas.* **Adm £3, chd free (share to Delhi Commonwealth Womens' Assn Clinic). Suns 12 Apr; 28 June (2-5). Visitors also welcome by appt.**
Commissioned in 1907 by Miss Baring, a cousin of Miss Jekyll, Durmast is a Gertrude Jekyll garden with contrasting hot and cool colour borders, a formal rose garden edged with lavender shaped like 2 halves of a diamond and an Edwardian long herbaceous border. Many old trees, a Victorian rockery, orchard and azalea borders. Listed in Hampshire Register of Historic Gardens.

42 NEW EDGEWOOD

175 Burley Road, Bransgore, Christchurch BH23 8DE. Teresa Knight, 01425 672754, robinteresa75@hotmail.com. *3m S of Burley. From Bransgore village take Burley rd towards Burley for 1m. Cream teas.* **Adm £2.50, chd free (share to Southampton Hospital Charity). Sat, Suns 16, 17 May; 13, 14 June; 11, 12 July (2-5). Visitors also welcome by appt May to Aug for groups of 10+.**
Our 1½ -acre working cottage garden is in a delightful wooded setting which incl our own woodland walk with broad sweeping paths. Several structures all covered in roses or clematis; paved path leads across the lawn to the vegetable patch. Beyond lies the summerhouse with its secret garden, a productive greenhouse and polytunnel. Orchard and long herbaceous border, thence to the kitchen garden with its hens. Finish with a scrumptious home-made tea!

Group opening

43 NEW EMSWORTH GARDENS

PO10 7PR. *7m W of Chichester, 2m E of Havant. Take A259 W of Chichester, follow signs to Emsworth roundabout N of town centre.* Home-made teas. **Combined adm £4, chd free. Sun 5 July (2-6).**
2 complementary gardens close to the centre of Emsworth, an historic fishing and sailing village on Chichester Harbour with numerous pubs, small local museums and walks along foreshore and around mill pond.

NEW 7 BEACON SQUARE

Annette & Michael Wood. *½ m W of Emsworth Village. From Emsworth village, take A259 towards Havant. Take 3rd L (Warblington Rd). After about 200yds, turn L into Seafields, R at end of rd, garden around corner on L*
Award winning, medium sized, densely planted garden with S facing herbaceous borders and N facing 'white' border. Fruit trees, small vegetable area and pond. Owner awarded Silver Medal for Small Garden at Hampton Court.

NEW 23 NEW BRIGHTON ROAD

Lucy Doherty, 01243 376161, lucywatson100@hotmail.com. *From main Emsworth roundabout go N for 1m (signed Rowlands Castle) under railway bridge and flyover, immediately on L up slope.* **Visitors also welcome by appt, groups of 10+.**
Eclectic mix of plants and ornaments in 200ft long, narrow garden. Ranging from full sun to full shade, the informal planting maximises the available space. A large number of containers, a wildlife pond, greenhouse, shady reading area and mixed borders give yr-round interest. Unusual plants and unusual garden for the plantsperson.

44 ◆ EXBURY GARDENS & STEAM RAILWAY

Southampton SO45 1AZ. Edmund de Rothschild, 023 8089 1203, www.exbury.co.uk. *16m S of Southampton. 4m Beaulieu. Exbury 20mins M27 J2.* **Adm £8, chd £1.50, concessions £7.50. Family £18.50. Open daily 7 Mar to 8 Nov (10-5).**
Created by Lionel de Rothschild in the 1920s, the gardens are a stunning vision of his inspiration offering 200 acres of natural beauty and horticultural variety. Woodland garden with world-famous displays of rhododendrons, azaleas, camellias and magnolias. Rock garden, exotic garden, herbaceous gardens, ponds, cascades, river walk and seasonal trails. Superb autumn colour, incl National Collection of Nyssa and Oxydendrum. Steam railway (wheelchair accessible) and Summer Lane Garden are popular favourites. Free wheelchair loan.

> # Gertrude Jekyll garden . . . a formal rose garden edged with lavender shaped like 2 halves of a diamond . . .

45 FARLEIGH HOUSE

Farleigh Wallop, nr Basingstoke RG25 2HT. The Earl & Countess of Portsmouth. *3m SE of Basingstoke. Off B3046 Basingstoke to Preston Candover rd. Cream teas in Barn 100yds down lane.* **Adm £4.50, chd free. Suns 12 July, 13 Sept (2-5).**
Contemporary garden of great tranquillity designed by Georgia Langton, surrounded by wonderful views. 3-acre walled garden in three sections: ornamental potager, formal rose garden and wild rose garden. Greenhouse full of exotics, serpentine yew walk, contemplative pond garden and lake with planting for wildlife. Approx 10 acres and 1 hour to walk around.

46 NEW FIR TREES
**Bexmoor, Old Basing RG24 7BT.
Jan & John Mabbott.** *1¹/₂ m E of
Basingstoke. M3, J6, follow A339
towards Basingstoke, turn R at 1st
roundabout signed A30 Hook, L
after 40mph sign into Park Lane,
1st L at T-lights, R at T junction.
Garden 150yds on L, opp church.
Park in The Street.* Home-made
teas. **Adm £3, chd free. Sun 5,
Tue 7 July (2-5.30).**
Just under ¹/₂ acre inspiring
garden, recently transformed by
owners from overgrown orchard
(photographs on show). Stone
terrace leads onto lawn with
various themed herbaceous
borders. Perennials, shrubs, rose-
covered pergolas, acers, old apple
trees. Large organic vegetable
garden and solar powered
rainwater system.

47 FLINTSTONES
**Sciviers Lane, Durley SO32 2AG.
June & Bill Butler, 01489 860880,
j.b.butler@hotmail.co.uk.** *5m E of
Eastleigh. From M3 J11 follow signs
for Marwell Zoo. From B2177 turn R
opp Woodman PH. From M27 J7
follow signs for Fair Oak then Durley,
turn L at Robin Hood PH.* Teas March,
home-made teas May/June. **Adm £3,
chd free (share to Durley Church &
Camphill Village Trust). Suns 22 Mar
(2-5); 31 May; Mon 1 June (2-6);
Evening Opening £4.50, wine, Tue
9 June (6.30-8.30). Visitors also
welcome by appt Mar to Oct.**
Garden of great tranquillity. All yr
pleasing tapestry effect of contrasting
and blending foliage and flowers.
Plantswoman's garden developed from
a field on fertile acid clay. Large
perennial plant collections, especially
hardy geraniums. Interesting island
beds to wander round and explore.
Wheelchair access only when dry.

48 THE FOUNTAINS
**34 Frampton Way, Totton SO40 9AE.
Mrs J Abel, 023 8086 5939.** *5m W of
Southampton. M271 J3 onto A35
Totton bypass for lm to roundabout.
Circle roundabout and return up A35.
Immed L into Rushington Ave, then
follow signs.* Home-made teas. **Adm
£2.50, chd free (share to Naomi
House Children's Hospice). Sat 6,
Sun 7 June (2-5). Also open nearby
Barhi. Visitors also welcome by
appt.**

Unusually shaped ¹/₄ -acre garden
bordered by hedges and filled with a
variety of fruit trees, soft fruit cordons
and espaliers. Trellis covered in
rambling roses and clematis.
Plantswoman's garden designed for
continual interest with vegetable plot,
wildlife ponds and chickens. 'Cottage
garden meets the Good Life' - a
garden to relax in and enjoy.

49 FRITHAM LODGE
**Fritham SO43 7HH. Mr & Mrs
Christopher Powell, 02380 812650,
chris.powell@ddblondon.com.** *6m N
of Lyndhurst. 3m NW of M27 J1
Cadnam. Follow signs to Fritham.*
Cream teas. **Adm £3, chd free. Sun
30 Aug (2-5). Visitors also welcome
by appt.**
Set in heart of New Forest in 18 acres;
with 1-acre old walled garden round
Grade II listed C17 house (not open)
originally one of Charles II hunting
lodges. Parterre of old roses, potager
with wide variety of vegetables, herbs
and fruit trees, pergola, herbaceous
and blue and white mixed borders,
ponds, walk across hay meadows to
woodland and stream, with ponies,
donkeys, rare breed Poitou donkeys
and rare breed hens.

Large organic vegetable garden and solar powered rainwater system . . .

Group opening

50 FROYLE GARDENS
GU34 4LJ. *5m NE of Alton. Access to
Lower Froyle from A31 between Alton
& Farnham, at Bentley. Follow signs
from Lower Froyle to Upper Froyle.*
Home-made teas at Froyle Village Hall.
**Combined adm £5, chd free. Sat 30,
Sun 31 May (2-6).**
'The Village of Saints'. Maps given to
all visitors. Large display of richly
decorated antique church vestments in
local church.

**BRAMLINS
Lower Froyle. Mrs Anne Blunt**
Informally planted to harmonise
with surrounding countryside and
to provide variety of material for
nationally-known flower arranger.
Wild flowers in small orchard.
Conservatory with unusual plants.
Gravel drive.

**2 COLTHOUSE LANE
West End Farm, Upper Froyle.
Susan & Tony Goodsell, 01420
525272. Visitors also welcome
by appt in June & July.**
Cottage garden full of colour.
Vegetables, fruit, greenhouses
and several interesting features.
Chickens and vintage tractors.

**THE COTTAGE
Lower Froyle. Mr & Mrs Carr**
Not only plants, but a collection of
animals frequently associated with
a true cottage garden.

**NEW DAY COTTAGE
Lower Froyle. Mr Nick
Whines**
Pretty C18 cottage garden of
¹/₃ acre. Courtyard with
outbuildings and greenhouse,
wildlife pond, mixed borders with
grasses, vegetable plot. Small wild
flower meadow with country views.

**THE OLD SCHOOL
Upper Froyle. Nigel & Linda
Bulpitt**
Mature and revamped garden,
mainly perennials with climbing
roses and shrubs. Small wild area
making a foil between garden and
countryside.

**WALBURY
Lower Froyle. Ernie & Brenda
Milam**
(See separate entry).

**WARREN COTTAGE
Lower Froyle. Mrs A A
Robertson**
Garden surrounds C18 cottage
(not open). Many interesting plants
and lovely views.

51 NEW GILBERTS NURSERY
Dandysford Lane, Sherfield English, nr Romsey SO51 6DT. Nick & Helen Gilbert. *Midway between Romsey and Whiteparish on A27, in Sherfield English village. From Romsey 4th turn on L, just before small petrol stn on R, visible from main rd.* **Adm £2.50, chd free. Sat, Sun, Mon 29, 30, 31 Aug (11-5).**
This may not be a garden but do come and be amazed by the sight of over 300 varieties of dahlias in our dedicated 1½-acre field. The blooms are in all colours, shapes and sizes and can be closely inspected from wheelchair-friendly hard grass paths. An inspiration for all gardeners. Nursery open all yr.

52 HAMBLEDON HOUSE
Hambledon PO7 4RU. Capt & Mrs David Hart Dyke, 02392 632380. *8m SW of Petersfield, 5m NW of Waterlooville. In village centre.* Home-made teas. **Adm £3, chd free. Sun 17 May; Mon 31 Aug (2-5). Visitors also welcome by appt.**
2-acre partly walled plantsman's garden for all seasons. Large borders filled with wide variety of unusual shrubs and imaginative plant combinations. Large collection of salvias, hardy geraniums and ornamental grasses. Hidden, secluded areas reveal surprise views of garden and village rooftops. Featured in 'Hampshire Life'.

53 HEATHLANDS
47 Locks Road, Locks Heath, nr Fareham SO31 6NS. John & Josephine Burwell. *5m W of Fareham. From M27 J9, go W on A27 towards Southampton. After 1m in Parkgate (just after pelican crossing) turn L into Locks Rd. No. 47 is 1m down on R.* Home-made teas. **Adm £3, chd free. Suns 1 Mar; 5 Apr; 23 Aug (2-5).**
This peaceful 1-acre garden has 7 very different areas. It is a green garden but with many seasonal flowers. Even when the openings are only a few weeks apart, each is very different. Many of our regulars try never to miss an opening. Children are welcome and enjoy the wandering paths and the quizzes.

54 HECKFIELD PLACE
Heckfield RG27 0LD. Heckfield Place Ltd. *9m S of Reading. 4½ m NW of Hartley Wintney on B3011.* Cream teas. **Adm £5, chd free. Sun 5 Apr; Sun 13 Sept (10-4.30).**
75 acres of Georgian/Victorian pinetum/arboretum with lakes, walled garden and herbaceous borders, in the process of very extensive restoration. Some trees are notable for their size and age and are documented. Historic garden demonstration.

55 HILL HOUSE
Old Alresford SO24 9DY. Mrs W F Richardson, 01962 732720. *1m W of Alresford. From Alresford 1m along B3046 towards Basingstoke, then R by church.* Home-made teas. **Adm £3, chd free. Sun 2, Tue 4 Aug (1.30-5). Visitors also welcome by appt mid-July to mid-Aug only.**
Traditional English 2-acre garden, established 1938, divided by yew hedge. Large croquet lawn framing the star of the garden, the huge multi-coloured herbaceous border. Impressive dahlia bed and butterfly-attracting sunken garden in lavender shades. Prolific old-fashioned kitchen garden with hens and bantams both fluffy and large. Small Dexter cows, possibly with calves.

Children are welcome and enjoy the quizzes . . .

56 2 HILLSIDE COTTAGES
Trampers Lane, North Boarhunt PO17 6DA. John & Lynsey Pink, 01329 832786. *5m N of Fareham. 3m E of Wickham. From A32 at Wickham take B2177 E. Trampers Lane 2nd on L (approx 2m). Hillside Cottages approx ½ m on L.* **Adm £2.50, chd free. Visitors welcome by appt.**
This 1½ -acre garden, on gently rising ground, contains so much of interest for plantspeople. Many rare and unusual specimens are shown off in sweeping borders in a tranquil setting. The National Collection of salvias is well displayed, all colours, sizes and growing habits. Something for everyone and an ideal venue for a group visit from summer through to October.

57 NEW HINTON ADMIRAL
Christchurch BH23 7DY. MEM Ltd. *On N side of A35, ¾ m E of Cat & Fiddle PH.* **Adm £5, chd free (share to Naomi House Children's Hospice). Sun 17 May (1-4.30).**
Magnificent 20-acre garden (within a much larger estate) now being restored and developed. Mature plantings of deciduous azaleas and rhododendrons amidst a sea of bluebells. Wandering paths lead through rockeries and beside ponds and a stream with many cascades. Orchids appear in the large lawns. The 2 walled gardens are devoted to herbs and wild flowers and a very large greenhouse. The terrace and rock garden were designed by Harold Peto. No refreshments, but picnics may be taken in the orchard.

58 ◆ HINTON AMPNER
Alresford SO24 0LA. The National Trust, www.nationaltrust.org.uk. *3½ m S of Alresford. S on A272 Petersfield to Winchester rd.* **House & Garden £7.10, chd £3.55. Garden only £6.10, chd £3. Mid Mar to end Oct. Days & times vary according to season; please phone or see website for details. For NGS: Sats 18 Apr; 20 June; 18 July; 19 Sept (11-5).**
12 acres; C20 shrub garden designed by Ralph Dutton. Strong architectural elements using yew and box topiary; spectacular views. Bold effects using simple plants, restrained and dramatic bedding. Orchard with spring wild flowers and bulbs within formal box hedges; magnolia and philadelphus walks. Dell garden made from chalk pit. Shrub rose border dating from 1950s. Walled garden now restored.

59 HOLYWELL
Swanmore SO32 2QE. Earl & Countess of Clarendon. *12m SE of Winchester. On A32 S of Droxford between Droxford and Wickham.* Home-made teas. **Adm £4, chd free. Suns 17 May; 21 June (2-6).**
Large garden in rural woodland and lakeside setting. Colourful organic kitchen garden, greenhouse, borders, roses, trees and shrubs. Pergola walk. Mature woodland garden with many acid-loving specimens.

60 THE HOMESTEAD

Northney Road, Hayling Island PO11 0NF. Stan & Mary Pike, 02392 464888. *3m S of Havant. From A27 Havant/Hayling Island roundabout, travel S over Langstone Bridge & turn immed L into Northney Rd. 1st house on R after Langstone Hotel.* Home-made teas. **Adm £3, chd free. Sun 19 July (1.30-5.30). Visitors also welcome by appt.**

1-acre garden developed and maintained by owners. Features incl pleached lime walk, pergola, arbour and ponds. Lawn surrounded by herbaceous beds and shrub borders with additional alpine beds and interesting trees. Small walled garden contains trained fruit trees, formal herb garden and vegetables.

61 HORDLE WALHAMPTON SCHOOL

Beaulieu Road, Lymington SO41 5ZG. Hordle Walhampton School Trust Ltd. *1m E of Lymington. From Lymington follow signs to Beaulieu (B3054) for 1m & turn R into main entrance at 1st school sign 200yds after reaching top of hill.* **Adm £4, chd free (share to St John's Church). Sun 26 Apr (2-6).**

97-acre grounds of C18/19 manor (not open). Landscape: naturalistic derived from styles of: early C18 formal, English and late C18 picturesque (influenced by Capability Brown); early C19 picturesque/Gothic; late C19/early C20 Italianate revival (influence of Peto); early C20 Arts and Crafts (Mawson's designs). Features: lakes, canal, mount, banana house, shell grotto, vistas and views of IOW. Guided tours. Gravel paths, lakes and ponds, grassy slopes.

62 THE HOUSE IN THE WOOD

Beaulieu SO42 7YN. Victoria Roberts. *8m NE of Lymington. Leaving the entrance to Beaulieu motor museum on R (B3056) take the next R turn signed Ipley Cross. Take 2nd gravel drive on RH-bend, approx 1/2 m.* Cream teas. **Adm £3.50, chd free. Sun 10 May (2-6).**

Peaceful 12-acre woodland garden with continuing progress and improvement. New areas and streams have been developed and good acers planted among mature azaleas and rhododendrons. Used in the war to train the Special Operations Executive. 'A magical garden to get lost in' and popular with bird-watchers.

63 THE HYDE

Old Alresford SO24 9DH. Sue Alexander, 01962 732043. *1m W of Alresford. From Alresford 1m along B3046 towards Basingstoke. House in centre of village, opp village green.* Home-made teas. **Adm £3, chd free. Suns, Tues 16, 18 Aug; 6, 8 Sept (1.30-5). Visitors also welcome by appt in Aug & early Sept, coaches permitted.**

Tucked away behind an old field hedge, a delightful 3/4 -acre garden created by the owner to attract wildlife and reflect her flower arranging passion for colour and texture. Flowing borders contain an abundant mixture of perennials, half-hardies, annuals, grasses and shrubs. Interesting planting for shady areas. Featured in 'The English Garden'. Short gravel drive at entrance.

KENT HOUSE
See Sussex.

A magical garden to get lost in . . .

64 KIMPTON HOUSE

Lower Durford Wood, nr Petersfield GU31 5AS. Mr & Mrs Christopher Napier. *1 1/2 m NE of Petersfield. B2070 N of Petersfield towards Rake. Pass A272 junction to Midhurst. 1/2 m further on turn R into white gates marked 'Durford Wood, Lower Wood only'. Kimpton House 1/2 m on R.* **Adm £3, chd free. Suns 17 May; 5 July (2-5).**

10 acres of gardens with panoramic views of S Downs. Large traditional herbaceous and shrub borders with topiary in a formal setting. Contemporary tropical garden where temperatures regularly reach 110°F. Formal French garden of pleaching and topiary. Herb garden. Woodland areas. Water features and wild flower butterfly meadow.

65 53 LADYWOOD

Eastleigh SO50 4RW. Mr & Mrs D Ward, 023 8061 5389, sueatladywood@btinternet.com. *1m N of Eastleigh. Leave M3 J12. Follow signs to Eastleigh. Turn R at roundabout and into Woodside Ave, then 2nd R into Bosville. Ladywood 5th on R. Park in Bosville.* Home-made teas (Sun only). **Adm £3, chd free. Sun 14 (11-5), Mon 15 June (2-5). Visitors also welcome by appt Apr, June & July for groups of 10+.**

This lovely garden, only 45ft x 45ft, is full of ideas and creative ways of using every available space to grow over 2000 different plants. Clever uses of numerous unusual foliage plants enhance the flower borders throughout the seasons. Pond garden and tiny shade garden are created using trellis onto which many climbers are grown. In 2009 Sue will be doing the floral design and display for Hardy Plant Society at Chelsea Flower Show.

66 LAKE HOUSE

Northington SO24 9TG. Lord Ashburton, 01962 734293. *4m N of Alresford. Off B3046. Follow English Heritage signs to The Grange, then directions.* Home-made teas. **Adm £4, chd free. Sun 7, Tue 9 June (1-5.30). Visitors also welcome by appt.**

2 large lakes in Candover Valley set off by mature woodland with waterfalls, abundant bird life, long landscaped vistas and folly. 1 1/2 -acre walled garden, mixed borders, long herbaceous border, rose pergola leading to moon gate. Formal kitchen garden, flowering pots, conservatory and greenhouses. Picnicking by lakes.

67 60 LEALAND ROAD

Drayton, Portsmouth PO6 1LZ. Mr F G Jacob. *2m E of Cosham. Old A27 (Havant Rd) between Cosham & Bedhampton.* **Adm £2, chd free. Suns 21 June; 19 July; 23 Aug (1-5).**

Prizewinning garden with a difference, created by the owner since 1969. Plants from around the world incl palms, yuccas, echiums and cannas. Designed for maximum effect with lily ponds and rockery. Incl collection of bamboos and grasses, also cacti and other exotics in greenhouse.

Drifts of colours using classic cottage garden plants alongside contemporary species . . .

68 LINDEN BARN
Church Barns, Church Bank Road, East Stratton SO21 3XA. Terry & Vanessa Winters, 01962 774778, terry.winters@lindenbarn.co.uk, www.lindenbarn.co.uk. *8m N of Winchester. 1m off A33 Basingstoke to Winchester rd, signed to East Stratton. Opp village church.* **Adm £3, chd free. Sun 24 May (1-6); Sun 28 June (11-6). Visitors also welcome by appt May, June & July, £4 per person, chd free.**

1/3 -acre garden created from old farmyard in 2001. Flowing herbaceous planting contained within topiary hedging with emphasis on structure and colour combinations. Gravel and paved paths, seating areas and many interesting vistas. Planting scheme creates drifts of colours using classic cottage garden plants alongside contemporary species. Specimen trees create woodland escape against backdrop of village church. Plants for sale, June only. Finalist Daily Mail Garden Competition. Featured in many lifestyle and gardening magazines.

69 THE LITTLE COTTAGE
Southampton Road (A337), Lymington SO41 9GZ. Peter & Lyn Prior, 01590 679395. *1m N of Lymington town centre. On A337 opp Toll House Inn.* **Adm £2.50. Weds 17 June; 1, 22 July; 12 Aug; 2 Sept (2-5). Also open Buckland Stead 17 June, 1, 22 July. Visitors also welcome by appt 17 June to 2 Sept only.**
Garden of unique and artistic design using unusual and interesting plants arranged to form pictures with arches, arbours and urns in secret rooms. Each room is hidden from the next and contrasts sharply in style and colour to stimulate, calm, excite or amaze, incl an outrageous black and white garden. A few steps and narrow archways.

70 LITTLE COURT
Crawley, nr Winchester SO21 2PU. Prof & Mrs A R Elkington, 01962 776365, elkslc@tiscali.co.uk. *5m NW of Winchester. Off A272 or B3049, in Crawley village; 300yds from either village pond or church.* Home-made teas. **Adm £3.50 (Feb £3), chd free. Sun 22, Mon 23, Tue 24 Feb (2-4.30); Sun 22, Tue 24 Mar; Thur 23 Apr (2-5.30); Sun 21, Mon 22, Tue 23 Feb 2010. Opening with Crawley Gardens 5, 7 Apr; 10, 12 May; 24, 25 June. Visitors also welcome by appt Apr to Sept, groups welcome, weekdays only.**
3-acre traditional English country garden, also very sheltered. Old walls with climbers, many perennials for all seasons set off by fine lawns. Carpets of naturalised spring bulbs. Productive kitchen garden. Quiz for children. Grass labyrinth and a tree house which appeals to all ages, with glorious views over rolling countryside. A very peaceful place.

71 LITTLEWOOD
West Lane, Hayling Island PO11 0JW. Mr & Mrs Steven Schrier. *3m S of Havant. From A27 Havant/Hayling Island junction, travel S for 2m, turn R into West Lane and continue 1m. House set back from rd in wood. Disabled should drive to very top of drive.* Home-made teas. **Adm £3, chd free. Sat 2, Sun 3 May (11-5).**
2 1/2 -acre woodland garden surrounded by fields and near sea, protected from sea winds by multi-barrier hedge. Rhododendrons, azaleas, camellias and many other shrubs. Woodland walk to full size tree house. Features incl pond, bog garden, house plants, summerhouse and many places to sit outside and under cover. Dogs on leads and picnickers welcome.

72 LITTON LODGE
Clifton Road, Winchester SO22 5BP. Dr & Mrs J Theaker. *After passing city Westgate, cross railway bridge and take 2nd rd on R up hill, signed Clifton Rd.* Home-made bread & soup in Feb, home-made teas in Apr. **Adm £2.50 (Feb), £3 (Apr), chd free (share to Emmaus House & Damien Centre). Suns 22 Feb (1.30-3.30); 26 Apr (2-5). Also open 22 Feb 12 Christchurch Rd.**
A tranquil 1/2 -acre garden overlooking the city, with traditional and exotic

species flourishing in the flint-walled microclimate. Unusual scented winter shrubs, hellebores and bulbs are succeeded by colour-themed borders with uncommon perennials. Featured on Meridian TV.

Group opening

73 LONGPARISH GARDENS
nr Andover SP11 6PZ. *7m E of Andover. Off A303. To village centre on B3048. Parking at Lower Mill only, except for disabled.* Home-made teas. **Combined adm £6, chd free. Sun 7, Mon 8 June (2-6).**
Small beautiful village on R Test with many thatched cottages.

LONGMEAD HOUSE
John & Wendy Ellicock, 01264 720386, jhe777@googlemail.com. **Visitors also welcome by appt, May to July for groups of 10+.**
2 1/2 -acre organic and wildlife garden. Large, hedged vegetable garden with deep beds, polytunnel, fruit cage and composting area. Fish pond, wildlife pond. Wild flower meadow. Herbaceous and shrub borders, woodland walk. Conservatory and greenhouse.

LOWER MILL
Mill Lane. Mrs K-M Dinesen
Spacious garden with enormous variety of design and planting incl newly laid out formal bed, courtyard and water garden. Tranquil natural walks beside the R Test. Approx 15 acres.

74 LONGSTOCK PARK WATER GARDEN
nr Stockbridge SO20 6JF. Leckford Estate Ltd, part of John Lewis Partnership, www.longstockpark.co.uk. *4m S of Andover. From A30 turn N on to A3057; follow signs to Longstock.* Home-made teas. **Adm £5, chd £1. Sun 21 June (2-5).**
Famous water garden with extensive collection of aquatic and bog plants set in 7 acres of woodland with rhododendrons and azaleas. A walk through park leads to National Collections of *Buddleja* and *Clematis viticella*; arboretum, herbaceous border.

75 LONGTHATCH
Lippen Lane, Warnford SO32 3LE.
Peter & Vera Short, 01730 829285,
peter.short1@homecall.co.uk. *12m N
of Fareham. On A32, turn R from N or
L from S at George & Falcon PH. After
100yds turn R at T-junction, continue
for 1/4 m; thatched C17 house on R.*
Adm £3, chd free. Visitors welcome
by appt, no coaches, groups of 10
or fewer.
31/2 acres, plantsman's garden on R
Meon. Rare trees and shrubs. Fine
lawns, herbaceous borders, island
beds and bog gardens. Spring-fed
ponds, woodland area with hellebores,
primulas and shade-loving plants.
Partial wheelchair access.

♿ ✕ ✿ ☎

**76 ◆ MACPENNYS WOODLAND
GARDEN & NURSERIES**
Burley Road, Bransgore,
Christchurch BH23 8DB. Mr & Mrs T
M Lowndes, 01425 672348,
www.macpennys.co.uk. *6m S of
Ringwood, 5m NE of Christchurch.
Midway between Christchurch &
Burley. From A35, at Xrds by The
Crown Bransgore turn R & proceed
1/4 m. From A31 (towards
Bournemouth) L at Picket Post, signed
Burley, then R at Burley Cross. Garden
on L after 2m.* Adm by donation.
Daily all yr (9-5, Sun 10-5) closed
Christmas & New Year period.
12 acres; 4-acre gravel pit converted
into woodland garden with many
unusual plants. Offering interest all yr
but particularly in spring and autumn.
Large Gold & Sir James Scott Cup for
Best in Class of shrubs & trees at New
Forest Show.

♿ ✿

MALT HOUSE
See Sussex.

77 MANOR HOUSE
Church Street, Upton Grey
RG25 2RD. Rosamund Wallinger. *6m
S of Basingstoke. In Upton Grey on hill
by church. Parking in field opp church.*
Home-made teas. Adm £5, chd
under 8 free. Wed 29, Thur 30 Apr
(9-4).
Gertrude Jekyll's 1908 garden for Arts
and Crafts figure Charles Holme. Copy
of her plans on display. 5-acre garden
incl tennis and bowling lawns, rose
garden, herbaceous borders, dry stone
walls, orchard and kitchen garden.
Wild garden holds some of Miss
Jekyll's original daffodils, a pond,
shrubs, trees and wild flowers. Old

Emperor and Empress daffodils in
flower. Prizewinner 'I own Britain's Best
Home & Garden'.

✕ ✿ ☕

78 MEON ORCHARD
Kingsmead, N of Wickham
PO17 5AU. Doug & Linda Smith,
01329 833253,
doug.smith@btinternet.com. *5m N of
Fareham. From Wickham take A32 N
for 11/2 m. Turn L at Roebuck Inn.
Continue 1/2 m.* Home-made teas.
Adm £3, chd free. Suns 31 May; 26
July; 6 Sept (2-6). Visitors also
welcome by appt, groups of 15+
only, coaches welcome.
11/2 -acre garden designed and
constructed by current owners. An
exceptional range of rare, unusual and
architectural plants incl National
Collections of Eucalyptus,
Podocarpaceae & Araliaceae. Much
use made of dramatic foliage plants
from around the world, both hardy and
tender, big bananas, huge taros, tree
ferns, cannas, hedychiums and palms.
Streams and ponds, combined with an
extensive range of planters, complete
the display. Owners available to answer
questions. Plant sale of the exotic and
rare Sun 6 Sept. Featured in RHS 'The
Garden'.

♿ ✿ NCCPG ☕ ☎

A variety of
tall plants for a
tall lady! . . .

79 MERDON MANOR
Hursley SO21 2JJ. Mr & Mrs J C
Smith, 01962 775215/281,
vronk@bluebottle.com. *5m SW of
Winchester. From A3090 Winchester
to Romsey rd, turn R at Standon to
Slackstead; proceed 11/2 m.* Home-
made teas. Adm £3.50, chd free. Sun
24 May (2-6). Visitors also welcome
by appt for any number at any time,
but only by arrangement.
5 acres with panoramic views;
herbaceous border, water lilies, large
wisteria; selection of roses; fruit-
bearing lemon trees and small secret
walled water garden. Ha-ha and black
Hebridean (St Kilda) sheep.

♿ ✕ ✿ ☕ ☎

80 NEW MICHAELMAS
2 Old Street, Hill Head, Fareham
PO14 3HU. Ros & Jack Wilson.
*41/2 m S of Fareham. From M27,
J9 take A 27 signed Fareham. After
approx 3m at gyratory follow
B3334 to Gosport. After 21/4 m at
2nd roundabout in Stubbington go
straight over, signed Hill Head.
Approx 500yds turn R into Bells
Lane. 1m pass Osborne View PH,
next R is Old Street.* Home-made
teas. Adm £2.50, chd free. Sun
19, Mon 20 July (2-5).
Very cheerful, colourful small
garden with the 'wow' factor. A
variety of tall plants for a tall lady!
Many are grown from seed or
cuttings. Small vegetable garden,
greenhouse, garden room, pot-
grown vegetables and flowers.
100yds from beach and 1/4 m from
Titchfield Haven Nature Reserve.
Cup winner at West Dean for best
tasting tomato.

✕ ✿ ☕

Group opening

**81 MONXTON & AMPORT
GARDENS**
SP11 8AW. *3m W of Andover.
Between A303 & A343; parking in
field on L in Chalkpit Lane.* Cream
teas at village hall. Combined adm £4,
chd free. Sun 24, Mon 25 May
(2-5.30).
Monxton and Amport are two pretty
villages with many thatched cottages
and linked by Pill Hill Brook.

♿ ✕ ✿ ☕

NEW BRIDGE COTTAGE
Jenny Burroughs
2-acre garden that has evolved
over the last 6yrs. Trout stream
and lake, the banks planted
informally with drifts of colour.
Large potager and fruit cage.
Small mixed orchard. Arboretum
with specimen trees. A haven
wildlife. Potager paths not
suitable for wheelchairs.

HUTCHENS COTTAGE
Mr & Mrs R A Crick
3/4 -acre cottage garden with
interesting scented plants: old
roses, clematis, shrubs incl
daphnes, mature trees, small
orchard; mixed thyme patch
and kitchen garden with
developed compost and leaf
mould systems.

WHITE GABLES

Mr & Mrs D Eaglesham
Cottage-style garden of 1/3 acre, leading down to Pill Hill Brook. Interesting trees, incl a young giant redwood, and shrubs, old roses and herbaceous plants.

---

82 ◆ MOTTISFONT ABBEY & GARDEN

Romsey SO51 0LP. The National Trust, 01794 340757, www.nationaltrust.org.uk. *4½ m NW of Romsey. From A3057 Romsey to Stockbridge turn W at sign to Mottisfont. 6 wheelchairs & battery car service available at garden.* Adm £8, chd £4 (June £9, chd £4.50). Opening days & times vary according to season; please phone or see website for details. For NGS: Mon 13 Apr (11-5); Sun 28 June (11-8.30); Sat 18 July (11-5).
Built C12 as Augustinian priory, now house of some note. 30-acre landscaped garden incl spring or 'font', from which house derives its name, magnificent ancient trees and walled gardens with National Collection of over 300 varieties of old roses. Tranquil walks in grounds, along the R Test and in the glorious countryside of the estate. Guided walks with Head Gardener.
  ♿ ✗ ❀ NCCPG ☕ 🌿

83 MULBERRY HOUSE

7 Moorland Avenue, Barton-on-Sea, New Milton BH25 7DB. Rosemary & John Owen, 01425 612066, rojowen@btinternet.com. *6m W of Lymington. From the A337 (S of New Milton), going W, take L turn into Barton Court Ave and 4th R into Moorland Ave.* Home-made teas. Adm £2.50, chd free (share to Oakhaven Hospice). Suns 14, 28 June (2-5). Visitors also welcome by appt.
Pretty family garden of 1/4 acre with old-fashioned and modern roses; a scramble of clematis; traditional fruit trees incl medlar, mulberry and quince, plus hazel and cob nuts; good selection of hardy geraniums, and herb and vegetable areas. Late summer colour with a number of viticella clematis, salvias and penstemons. Relaxed, organic garden with much native planting to attract insect and bird life. Productive hens in an Egloo. Mason bee nests and chickens. Art studio open. Limited wheelchair access, some narrow paths.
  ♿ ✗ ❀ ☕ 📞

Traditional flint and cob walled garden with prolific old-fashioned roses . . .

84 OAKDENE

Sandleheath, Fordingbridge SP6 1PA. Shirley & Chris Stanford, 01425 652133, christopher.stanford@homecall.co.uk. *1½ m W of Fordingbridge. Adjacent to St Aldhelm's Church.* Cream teas. Adm £3.50, chd free. Suns 14, 21, 28 June (2-5.30). Visitors also welcome by appt.
Think of a picture postcard country garden with its croquet lawn, rose garden and herbaceous borders; think of lavender, clipped box and the scent of 400 roses, an orchard with hens foraging under apple, pear and plum trees and with resident white doves murmuring by a children's village shop. Add a mature walled kitchen garden with an abundance of vegetables, soft fruits and flowers for cutting, then enter a tea garden to enjoy in Joe Swift's words 'the best tea in Hampshire'. This is Oakdene, a joy for everyone.
  ♿ ✗ ❀ ☕ 📞

85 THE OLD RECTORY, HOUGHTON

Church Lane, Houghton, Stockbridge SO20 6LJ. Mr & Mrs Richard Priestley. *2m S of Stockbridge. From Stockbridge take minor rd S signed to Houghton (2m). Turn R by war memorial (opp Boot Inn) into Church Lane. Garden 200yds on R before church.* Home-made teas. Adm £3, chd free. Sun 14 June (2-5), Mon 15 June (2-6).
Fine views of the church and Test Valley from this 4-acre village garden. Traditional flint and cob walled garden with prolific old-fashioned roses. Mixed herbaceous borders, rockery, herb potager with pond, yew and thuja hedges, rolling lawns. Teas in the attractive yellow and blue pool garden. Gravel paths.
  ♿ ✗ ❀ ☕

86 THE OLD RECTORY, SWARRATON

SO24 9TQ. Pam & Peter Davidson. *4m N of Alresford. Follow B3046 N from Alresford to Swarraton, or from A33 turn at dual carriageway to Northington, then R at T-junction. Parking in field.* Home-made teas. Adm £3, chd free. Thur 6, Sun 9 Aug (2-6). Visitors also welcome by appt for groups of 10+ in Aug only, by written application.
Interesting, well designed 2-acre garden enveloped by 13 acres of Glebe land. Courtyard garden with topiary alongside thatched barn. Subtle combinations of perennials and unusual annuals, raised in Victorian-style greenhouse, cascade down terraced beds with flint walls. Mature trees, long traditional border, young orchard, vegetable corner. Woodland walk through Parsons Belt with old beeches and countryside views. Alpacas. Unfenced ponds.
  ♿ ❀ ☕ 📞

87 OLD THATCH

Sprats Hatch Lane, Winchfield, Hook RG27 8DD. Jill Ede. *3m W of Fleet. From A287 Odiham to Farnham rd turn N to Dogmersfield. L by Queens Head PH and L opp Barley Mow PH. From Winchfield stn car park turn R towards Dogmersfield and after 1.3m R opp Barley Mow. Follow signs for parking and disabled access.* Home-made teas. Adm £3, chd free. Suns 19 Apr; 13 Sept (2-5). Candlelit Evening Opening £5, wine, Fri 31 July (7-10).
'Chocolate box' thatched cottage, featured on film and TV and evolving smallholding alongside the Basingstoke Canal (unfenced). A succession of spring bulbs, a profusion of wild flowers, perennials and home-grown annuals pollinated by our own bees and fertilised by the donkeys, who await your visit. Lambs in Apr, donkey foals in summer. Arrive by boat! Surrey & Hants Canal Soc may have trips on their narrow boat 'John Pinkerton' to coincide with opening days. Contact Marion Gough 01962 713564. For private boat owners, slipway at The Barley Mow 1/2 m E of Old Thatch.
  ♿ ✗ ❀ ☕

88 PENNINGTON HOUSE

Ridgeway Lane, Lymington SO41 8AA. Sue Stowell & John Leach. *1½ m S of Lymington. S on A337 from Lymington approx 1/3 m to Pennington roundabout. Turn L into*

Ridgeway Lane. At L bend, continue straight on for 1/3 m until Chequers PH. Turn R immed by post box into private drive. Home-made teas (weather permitting). **Adm £3.50, chd free (share to Oakhaven Hospice Trust).** Sat 9, Sun 10 May (2-4.30). 7 acre garden created around 1910 and entirely organic for the last 16yrs. Substantial rockery of mature acers. Stream and pond. Italian sunken garden, rose garden, organic 1/2-acre walled Victorian kitchen garden in full use. Magnificent wisteria on the house. Some gravel paths.

Ancient lichen-covered trees with semi-wild underplanting . . .

Group opening

89 NEW PILLEY HILL GARDENS nr Lymington SO41 5QF. Off A337 Lymington to Brockenhurst rd. 2m N of Lymington, 21/2 m S of Brockenhurst, turn into Rope Hill for Pilley, Boldre and Spinners. Go 1m via Boldre Bridge, up Pilley Hill. Also signed from B3054 Beaulieu to Lymington road. Gardens approx 80yds apart. Spinners woodland garden open nearby (not Suns). Cream teas at Willows. **Combined adm £5, chd free.** Suns, Weds 2, 5, 23, 26 Aug (2-5). The setting is a typical New Forest village which boasts the oldest and one of the prettiest New Forest pubs, the Fleur-de-Lys, the Red Lion and nearby (1/2 m) C11 church.

NEW PILLEY HILL COTTAGE Stephanie & Sandy Glen Cottage garden surrounding Georgian house (not open). Ancient lichen-covered trees with semi-wild underplanting; sunny herbaceous borders and lawn; wildlife ponds and bog-loving perennials; oak-framed greenhouse and pergolas. Paths leading into every nook and cranny.

NEW TREVIN COTTAGE Mr & Mrs M Clague. Not open Wed dates. A gem of a small garden, with orchard, herbaceous borders and climbers. Features include a vegetable plot, wildlife pond and some unusual trees and plants. Many places to sit and enjoy the views and statuary.

NEW WILLOWS Elizabeth & Martin Walker (See separate entry).

---

90 THE PRIORS FARM Reading Road, Mattingley RG27 8JU. Mr & Mrs Miles Hudson. 11/2 m N of Hook. On B3349 Reading Rd. Parking on green just N of Leather Bottle PH. Entrance by gate on green parking area. Home-made teas. **Adm £3, chd free.** Sun 12 July (2-5). Old barns, C15 granary and old goatery give great atmosphere to this 31/2 -acre garden of mixed borders, with cedar and other mature trees. Attractive rose garden, bog garden, herb garden, orchard and other old roses and shrubs, enhanced by statuary. Delicious teas served in swimming pool area. Gravel drive.

91 PYLEWELL PARK Lymington SO41 5SJ. Lord Teynham. 2m E of Lymington. Beyond IOW car ferry. **Adm £4, chd free.** Sun 3, 10 May (2-5). Very large garden of botanical interest, dating from 1900. Fine trees, flowering shrubs, rhododendrons, with walk beside the lakes and seashore.

Group opening

92 ROMSEY GARDENS SO51 8EU. All within walking distance of Romsey Abbey, clearly signed. Car parking by King John's Garden. Home-made teas at King John's Garden. **Combined adm £4, chd free.** Sun 24, Mon 25 May (11-5.30). Small attractive market town with notable Norman C12 Abbey, backdrop to 4 Mill Lane. No hills and all shops within walking distance.

KING JOHN'S GARDEN Church Street. Friends of King John's Garden & Test Valley Borough

Listed C13 house (not open). Historic garden planted with material available up to 1700. Award-winning Victorian garden and North Courtyard with water features. Some gravel paths.

THE LAKE HOUSE 64 Mill Lane. David & Lorraine Henley. At bottom of Mill Lane 41/2 acres, part garden, part meadow, part lake. Wonderful views from all aspects. Tranquillity just 5 mins from Romsey town centre. Spot the kingfishers if you're lucky!

4 MILL LANE Miss J Flindall, 01794 513926. Visitors also welcome by appt. Garden suitable for artists; groups of 10-15 at any time by prior arrangement. Small, long, floriferous town garden. S-facing. Backdrop Romsey Abbey; original sculpture and attractive hard landscaping. Featured in 'Wiltshire Society'.

93 ROTHERFIELD PARK East Tisted, Alton GU34 3QE. Sir James & Lady Scott. 4m S of Alton on A32. Home-made teas. **Adm £3, chd free.** Suns 3 May; 20 Sept (2-5). Take some ancient ingredients: ice house, ha-ha, lime avenue; add a walled garden, fruit and vegetables, trees and hedges; set this 12-acre plot in an early C19 park (picnic here from noon) with views to coin clichés about. Mix in a bluebell wood in May and apple-picking in September. Gravel or grass paths, reasonable wheelchair access.

94 ST CHRISTOPHER'S Whitsbury, Fordingbridge SP6 3PZ. Christine Southey & David Mussell, 01725 518404. 31/2 m NW of Fordingbridge. In village centre, 200yds down from Cartwheel PH. Cream teas & home-made cakes in village hall. **Adm £3, chd free.** Suns 19, 26 Apr (2-5.30). **Visitors also welcome by appt for groups of 20+.** Tranquil 3/4 -acre long, sloping garden with superb views. Alpines in S-facing scree bed with unusual bulbs, incl dwarf iris, tulips and narcissi, and alpine troughs. In spring, wild banks of bluebells and primroses, fern bed with erythronium, hellebores and anemone blanda. Many spring shrubs incl mimosa. Pond and bog gardens full of primula, a conservatory with many unusual plants. In summer, 25ft rambling roses, beds of delphiniums, perennial geraniums, eremurus and many herbaceous treasures. Fruit and vegetable garden and several secret seating areas. Enjoy the garden, have a lovely cream tea, then walk to look at bluebells and foals; walks can be 15 or 50 mins. England at its best in springtime!

95 28 ST RONAN'S AVENUE
Southsea PO4 0QE. Mr I Craig, 02392 787331, ian.craig93@ntlworld.com, www.28stronansavenue.co.uk. *Turn into St Ronan's Rd from Albert Rd at junction opp Trinity Methodist Church. St Ronan's Ave is a cul-de-sac off St Ronan's Rd. Alternatively, follow signs to seafront and then follow yellow NGS signs from canoe lake and Eastern Parade. Park at Craneswater School.* Home-made teas. **Adm £2.50, chd free (share to Craneswater School). Suns 24 May; 19 July (2-6). Evening Opening £3.50, wine, Sat 1 Aug (4-8). Visitors also welcome by appt.** Town garden 145ft x 25ft. Contains many architectural and tender plants including king protea, hedychium, bananas, wild flower area, bog garden and dry garden. Recycled items have been used to create sculptures.

SANDHILL FARM HOUSE
See Sussex.

96 SANDLE COTTAGE
Sandleheath, Fordingbridge SP6 1PY. Peter & Yo Beech, 01425 654638, peter@sandlecottage.com, www.sandlecottage.com. *2m W of Fordingbridge. Turn R at Sandleheath Xrds. Entrance 50yds on L. Ample field parking.* Home-made teas. **Adm £3, chd free (share to Fordingbridge URC). Sun 12 July with Sandleheath Band; Suns 26 July; 2 Aug (1.30-5.30). Visitors also welcome by appt in July only for groups of 25+, coaches welcome.** We invite you to our 3 acres to stroll through the walled garden, well-stocked with vegetables, relax to the sound of the fountain in the sunken garden, tiptoe across the manicured lawn to relax in the summerhouse within its own cottage garden. Explore the woodland walk, visit the productive greenhouses and discover the waterfall. Find fabulous fuchsias,

admire the sweet peas (best on 12 July) and enjoy the formal beds of annuals and dahlias (best on 2 Aug). Question & answer session with the owners. Double trophy winner at national sweet pea championships.

97 SANDY SLOPES
Honeysuckle Lane, Headley Down GU35 8EH. Mr & Mrs R Thornton. *6m S of Farnham. From A3 take B3002 through Grayshot, on to Headley Down. Turn L at mini roundabout by garage, down hill to 2nd turning L, bungalow 3rd drive on R. From Headley village take B3002 towards Grayshot, after S bend on to sharp L bend up hill to Honeysuckle Lane on R. Parking very limited.* Home-made teas. **Adm £2.50, chd £1. Mon 4, Sun 31 May (2-6).** Sloping and partly terraced plantsman's and garden lecturer's garden with many special features incl woodland with rhododendrons, camellias, meconopsis, primulas and other seasonal plants. Stream and pool, herbaceous mixed shrub borders. Rock gardens. Many trees and unusual plants within about 1/4 acre. Not suitable for those with walking difficulties; steep slopes and steps.

Double trophy winner at national sweet pea championships. .

98 'SELBORNE'
Caker Lane, East Worldham, Alton GU34 3AE. Brian & Mary Jones, 01420 83389, mary.trigwell-jones@virgin.net. *2m SE of Alton. On B3004 at Alton end of East Worldham opp The Three Horseshoes PH (please note, NOT in the village of Selborne). Parking signed.* Home-made teas. **Adm £2.50, chd free (share to St Mary's Church May & June, Tafara Mission Zimbabwe Aug). Sats, Suns 18, 19 Apr; 16, 17 May (2-5). Evening Opening, wine, Fri 12 June (6-8). Sat, Sun 13, 14 June; Sat 1, Sun 2, Mon 3 Aug (2-6). Visitors also welcome by appt late Apr to early Aug.**

A garden of surprises. 1/2 -acre mature garden with old established orchard of named varieties. Meandering paths provide changing vistas across farmland. Mixed borders feature a large collection of hardy geraniums and other herbaceous plants and shrubs. Soft fruit garden, containers, metal and stone sculpture and summerhouses. Listen to birdsong as you enjoy tea in the dappled shade of the orchard, or in the conservatory. Book stall. Sandpit and garden quizzes for children. Some narrow paths may be slippery when wet.

99 SHALDEN PARK HOUSE
The Avenue, Shalden GU34 4DS. Michael D C C Campbell. *41/2 m NW of Alton. B3349 from Alton or J5 M3 onto B3349. Turn W at Golden Pot PH marked Herriard, Lasham, Shalden. Entrance 1/4 m on L.* Light refreshments & home-made teas. **Adm £3, chd free (share to Hampshire & IOW Community Foundation). Sun 19 July (2-5).** 4-acre garden surrounded by woodland, redesigned in 2005/6 by Georgia Langton. Extensive views. Herbaceous borders. Walled kitchen garden and glasshouses. Early stage arboretum. We are working on a new planting design around the pond. Early picnics welcome.

100 ◆ SPINNERS
Spinners, School Lane, Boldre SO41 5QE. Andrew & Victoria Roberts, 01590 673347, www.spinnersgarden.co.uk. *11/2 m N of Lymington. Signed off A337 Brockenhurst to Lymington rd (do not follow sign to Boldre Church).* Cream teas Sun 19 Apr only. **Adm £3.50, chd free (Tues to Sats, 1 Apr to 14 Sept (10-5). For NGS: Sun 19, Mon 20 Apr (2-6).** Peaceful woodland garden on a slope overlooking the Lymington river valley. Azaleas, rhododendrons, magnolias, camellias and other rare shrubs interplanted with a wide variety of choice woodland and groundcover plants. Particularly good in spring are the erythroniums and trilliums and other rarities such as michelias. Free wheelchair entry to part of garden.

SWALLOWFIELD HORTICULTURAL SOCIETY
See Berkshire.

101 TANGLEFOOT
Crawley, nr Winchester SO21 2QB.
Mr & Mrs F J Fratter, 01962 776243,
fred@tanglefoot-
house.demon.co.uk. *5m NW of
Winchester. Private lane beside
entrance to Crawley Court (Arqiva).
Drop-off & disabled parking only at
house, parking in field 50m.* **Adm £3,
chd free. Opening with Crawley
Gardens** 10, 12 May; 24, 25 June;
19, 21 July. **Visitors welcome by
appt, summer only.**
Approx ¹/₂ acre on chalk, designed and
developed by owners, with mature
shrubs and a wide variety of
herbaceous plants, incl British natives.
Features incl colour-themed
herbaceous and mixed borders, raised
lily pond, herb wheel and wild flower
area. Magnificent Victorian boundary
wall protects trained top fruit and
compact productive kitchen garden
and greenhouse.
 ♿ ✕ ✽ ☎

**THRIVE'S TRUNKWELL GARDEN
PROJECT**
See Berkshire.

102 TREESIDE
New Road, Littleton SO22 6QR. Mr
& Mrs Alan Lyne. *2m NW of
Winchester. Between B3049 and
B3420 (A272) off Main Rd, Littleton,
near and on same side as the Running
Horse. Park on grass verge in New Rd.*
Home-made teas. **Adm £2.50, chd
free. Fri 3, Sat 4, Sun 5 July (1-5).**
¹/₃ acre, 6 seating areas for different
times of the day. 2 unusual water
features. Original raised beds for
vegetables. Fruit cage, divided
greenhouse and cold frames. Split
ponds, young and established wild
flower areas with increasing plant and
insect species. Mainly shrubs with
flowers highlighting key areas. Quiz for
children. Short gravel drive.
 ♿ ✕ ✽ ☕

TROTTON OLD RECTORY
See Sussex.

103 TYLNEY HALL HOTEL
Ridge Lane, Rotherwick RG27 9AZ.
The Manager, www.tylneyhall.com.
*3m NW of Hook. From M3 J5 via A287
& Newnham, M4 J11 via B3349 &
Rotherwick.* Cream teas. **Adm £3, chd
free. Suns 7 June; 5 July; 20 Sept
(10-5).**
Large garden of 66 acres with
extensive woodlands and fine vistas
being restored with new planting. Fine
avenues of wellingtonias;

rhododendrons and azaleas; Italian
garden; lakes, large water and rock
garden, dry stone walls originally
designed with assistance of Gertrude
Jekyll.
 ✕ ✽ ☕

104 ULVIK
114 Harestock Road, Winchester
SO22 6NY. Mr & Mrs G G Way,
01962 852361. *1m N of Winchester.
5th house on L in Harestock Rd off
A3049 (old A272).* Cold drinks. **Adm
£2.50, chd free. Sat 11 to Tues 14
July incl: Sat 8 to Tues 11 Aug incl
(1-5). Visitors also welcome by appt
June to Aug, afternoons preferred.**
Completely enclosed hedged garden
of ¹/₂ acre designed to create
interesting and unfolding views and
sinuous shapes with many nooks and
crannies. Fairly naturalistic planting of
mixed herbaceous borders, large
variety of shrubs, many ornamental
grasses, prairie-style border, small
vegetable area, pond, wooded areas
for shade-loving plants and features to
encourage wildlife. Fun sculptures and
children's discovery quiz.
 ♿ ✕ ☎

Exclusive tour of formal garden with Garden Steward, with Cream tea . . .

105 ◆ THE VYNE
Sherborne St John RG24 9HL. The
National Trust, 01256 883858,
www.nationaltrust.org.uk. *4m N of
Basingstoke. Between Sherborne St
John & Bramley. From A340 turn E at
NT signs.* **Garden adm £5.50, chd
£2.75. Gardens 14 Mar to 28 Oct,
Sats to Weds (11-5). For NGS: Tue 2
June Special NGS Event:
Exclusive tour of formal garden
with Garden Steward, with
Cream tea** £7.50 bookable in
advance only, limited numbers
(3.15-5); Sat 18 July (11-5).
A good mix of garden areas including
C18 landscape, Edwardian-style
summerhouse garden, and a walled
garden which incl new glasshouse and
vegetable plots. Vegetables grown by
gardeners from the charity Thrive.
Featured in Local Press.
 ♿ ✕ ✽ ☕

106 WALBURY
Lower Froyle, Alton GU34 4LJ. Ernie
& Brenda Milam, 01420 22216,
walbury@uwclub.net. *5m NE of
Alton. Access to Lower Froyle from
A31 between Alton and Farnham at
Bentley. Walbury nr village hall where
parking available.* Home-made teas.
**Adm £2.50, chd free. Sun 26 Apr
(2-5). Opening with Froyle Gardens**
30, 31 May. **Visitors also welcome
by appt Apr to July.**
Cottage garden atmosphere with small
pond. Lower area is a small, formal,
colour-themed garden, informally
planted with many unusual plants.
Many spring bulbs and alpine house.
 ♿ ✽ ☕ ☎

107 WALDRONS
Brook SO43 7HE. Major & Mrs J
Robinson, 02380 813367. *4m N of
Lyndhurst. On B3079 1m W from J1
M27. 1st house L past Green Dragon
PH & directly opp Bell PH.* Home-
made teas. **Adm £2.50, chd free. Sun
24, Mon 25 May (2-5). Visitors also
welcome by appt in May & June.**
Visitors have always been pleasantly
surprised when they visit our well cared
for 1-acre garden hidden behind a high
hedge. We have interesting mixed
herbaceous beds for yr-round interest,
raised gravel and kitchen garden,
brick-based greenhouse and textile
exhibition in our new garden room
converted from an old stable block.
 ♿ ✕ ☕ ☎

108 WEIR HOUSE
Abbotstone Road, Alresford
SO24 9DG. Mr & Mrs G Hollingbery,
01962 736493,
ghollingbery@mac.com. *¹/₂ m N of
Alresford. From Alresford down Broad
St (B3046) past Globe PH. Take 1st L,
signed Abbotstone. Park in signed
field.* Teas 17 May only. **Adm £5, chd
free. Suns 19 Apr; 17 May; 13 Sept
(2-5). Visitors also welcome by appt
May & Sept for groups of 10+.**
Spectacular riverside garden.
Contemporary vegetable and cut
flower garden incorporating many
different crops, surprising uses for
scaffolding and painters' ladders and
sculpture by Mark Merer. Children can
use the playground at their own risk.
The rose/swimming pool garden will be
reopened for the 2009 season.
Featured in 'Gardeners' World Design
Special'. Most areas wheelchair
accessible.
 ♿ ✽ ☕ ☎

109 WEST SILCHESTER HALL

Silchester RG7 2LX. Mrs Jenny Jowett, 0118 970 0278. *7m N of Basingstoke. 7m S of Reading, off A340 (signed from centre of village).* Home-made teas. **Adm £3, chd free. Sun 24, Mon 25 May; Suns 12 July; 9 Aug (2.5.30). Visitors also welcome by appt May to Aug, for groups of 10+ only, coaches permitted.**

This much loved 2-acre garden has fascinating colour combinations, inspired by the artist owners. Herbaceous borders crammed with rare and unusual plants, very good clematis, pots full of half hardies, wild pond garden and self-supporting kitchen garden with lovely view across to field of grazing cattle. Studio open with exhibition of botanical and landscape paintings, cards and prints by owners. Large plant sale. Gravel drive.

 ♿ ✿ ☕ ☎

Please phone us if you can't make a Wednesday, we'd love to see you. . .

110 WESTBROOK HOUSE

Holybourne, nr Alton GU34 4HH. Mr Andrew Lyndon-Skeggs. *Turn off A31 at roundabout immed to NE of Alton towards Holybourne & Alton. 1st R to Holybourne. 1st L up Howards Lane. Entrance on R. Or B3349 from Odiham, turn L at Golden Pot PH (2m before Alton). After ½ m 1st R downhill into Holybourne, R at church, garden 300yds on L.* Light refreshments & teas. **Adm £2.50, chd free. Suns 15 Mar (2-4); 24 May (2-5). Evening Opening, wine, Sun 21 June (6-8).**

3-acre garden designed and evolved over the past 30yrs by the present owner, with the benefit of existing mature trees such as a magnificent Gingko biloba. Though not a 'room garden' as such, the garden has nevertheless been planned with different areas each with its own character, ranging from formal mixed borders to orchard, stream and village pond. May be plants for sale.

🐕 ☕

Allotments

111 WESTON ALLOTMENTS

Newtown Road, Woolston SO19 9HX. *3m E of Southampton City Centre. Leave M27 J8, follow signs for Hamble-le-Rice. At Windhover roundabout, take 2nd exit past Tesco into Hamble Lane B3397. R into Portsmouth Rd, 1m L at 2nd mini roundabout into Upper Weston Lane, 2nd L into Newtown Rd. Allotments opp phone box. Disabled parking only at allotments, other parking on public rd.* Home-made teas. **Adm £2.50, chd free. Sat 4, Sun 5 July (2-5).**

Many allotments packed with salad crops, vegetables, fruit and flowers for floral art are available to wander around. Also various greenhouses, polytunnels and fruit cages with more unusual plant varieties. Come and get tips to get you started! One plot holds Hampshire Federation of Horticultural Societies Trophy for Best Allotment.

🐕 ✿ ☕

112 WESTWARD

11 Ridgemount Avenue, Bassett, Southampton SO16 7FP. Jan & Russ Smith, 02380 767112, russjsmith@btinternet.com. *3m N of Southampton city centre. From end of M3 J14 continue down A33 to 2nd roundabout and head back to M3. Ridgemount Ave 2nd on L.* Home-made teas. **Adm £3, chd free. Sun 12, Mon 13 Apr; Sat 25, Sun 26 July (1.30-4.30). Visitors also welcome by appt.**

Very colourful ¼ -acre garden with diverse selection of planting. Early spring: many bulbs, hellebores and irises. Summer: lilies, fuchsias, heucheras and acers. Many baskets and containers full of summer colour. Hosta border, vegetable garden, summerhouse, clear pond with koi and goldfish. Waterfall and wildlife pond. Large collection of cacti and succulents.

 ♿ ✿ ☕ ☎

113 WHEATLEY HOUSE

between Binsted and Kingsley GU35 9PA. Mr & Mrs Michael Adlington, 01420 23113, mikeadlington36@tiscali.co.uk. *4m E of Alton, 5m SW of Farnham. From Alton follow signs to Holybourne & Binsted. At end of Binsted turn R signed Wheatley. ¾ m down lane on L. From Farnham/Bordon on A325 take*

turn signed Binsted at Buckshorn Oak. *1½ m turn L signed Wheatley.* Home-made teas. **Adm £3, chd free. Sat 22, Sun 23 Aug (1.30-5.30). Visitors also welcome by appt, groups of 10+, coaches permitted.**

Magnificent setting with panoramic views over fields and forests. Sweeping mixed borders, shrubberies and grasses. 1½ acres, designed by artist-owner. The colours are spectacular. 'White & black' border. Varied selection of local crafts and paintings for sale in old barn.

 ♿ 🐕 ✿ ☕ ☎

114 WHISPERS

Chatter Alley, Dogmersfield RG27 8SS. Mr & Mrs John Selfe. *3m W of Fleet. Turn N to Dogmersfield off A287 Odiham to Farnham rd. Turn L by Queen's Head PH.* Home-made teas. **Adm £3, chd free (share to Samantha Dickson Brain Tumour Trust). Sun 12 July (12-5).**

Visitors have said you could spend all day discovering new plants in these 2 acres of manicured lawns surrounded by large borders of colourful shrubs, trees and long flowering perennials. Astromerias and salvias a speciality. Wild flower area, water storage system greenhouse, kitchen garden and unique living sculptures add to the attraction. Spectacular waterfall cascades over large rock slabs and magically disappears below the terrace. A garden not to be missed! Gravel paths & slopes.

 ♿ 🐕 ✿ ☕

115 WHITE BARN

Woodend Road, Crow Hill, Ringwood BH24 3DG. Marilyn & Barrie Knight, 01425 473527, bandmknight@btinternet.com. *2m SE of Ringwood. From Ringwood take B3347 towards Winkton & Sopley. After 1m turn L immed after petrol stn into Moortown Lane, proceed 1m, Woodend Rd, a gravel rd on L by pillar box.* **Adm £3, chd free. Every Wed 20 May to 29 July (10.30-5). Visitors also welcome by appt for individuals and groups.**

Tranquil ¾ -acre country garden full of unusual plants in harmonious colours. 250+ clematis and many roses attract birds, butterflies and bees. Shapes and structures help the garden to blend with the house and surrounding views. Please phone us if you can't make a Wednesday, we'd love to see you.

 ♿ 🐕 ☕ ☎

116 THE WHITE COTTAGE
35 Wellhouse Road, Beech, Alton
GU34 4AQ. Mr & Mrs P Conyers,
01420 89355. *2m N of Alton. Leave
Alton on Basingstoke Rd A339. After
approx 1m turn L to Medstead &
Beech. Wellhouse Rd is 2nd on R.
Parking at village hall at bottom of rd,
limited parking at house.* Adm £2.50,
chd free. Suns, Mons 22, 23 Mar; 26,
27 July (2-5). Visitors also welcome
by appt.
1-acre garden with a wide range of
shrubs and plants. Large collection of
hellebores and bulbs in spring.
Herbaceous borders with plenty of
late-summer colour. Pebble area with
fountain for display of sun-loving
plants. Greenhouses, soft fruit area,
conservatory with exotics and scree
bed. Grass paths, some slopes.

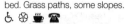

117 WHITE GABLES
Breach Lane, Sherfield-on-Loddon
RG27 0EU. Terry & Brian
Raisborough. *5m N of Basingstoke.
From Basingstoke follow A33 towards
Reading for approx 5m. Breach Lane is
unmade lane immed before Sherfield-
on-Loddon roundabout on R. Limited
parking for disabled by house. Main
parking in 2 free signed car parks in
main village. Short walk to garden.*
Home-made teas. Adm £3, chd free.
Suns 3 May; 5 July (1-5).
Plantaholic's paradise of ⅓ acre
created by owner since 1997.
Interesting themed areas containing
massed planting of tropical plants,
unusual shrubs, perennials and roses.
Oriental border with arbour, raised
banana bed, gravel garden with 3
small ponds, conifer bed, tropical
border, numerous tender plants in pots
on patio. Raised vegetable garden,

cottage garden planting with rose,
jasmine and honeysuckle arches.
Spring bulbs, camellias and
rhododendrons in pots. Large hosta
collection.

118 NEW WILLOWS
Pilley Hill, Boldre, nr Lymington
SO41 5QF. Elizabeth & Martin
Walker, 01590 677415,
elizabethwalker@boldre.
wanadoo.co.uk. *Off A337
Lymington to Brockenhurst rd. 2m
N of Lymington, 2½ m S of
Brockenhurst, turn into Rope Hill
for Pilley, Boldre and Spinners. Go
1m via Boldre Bridge, up Pilley Hill.
Garden at school sign. Also signed
from B3054 Beaulieu to Lymington
road. Spinners woodland garden
open nearby (not Suns).* Cream
teas. Adm £3, chd free. Sun 9,
Wed 19, Sun 30, Mon 31 Aug;
Wed 2 Sept (2-5). Also open with
Pilley Hill Gardens Suns, Weds
2, 5, 23, 26 Aug. Visitors also
welcome by appt July to Sept,
for groups of 10+.
Exciting new garden started in
2003 around established trees and
small stream. Dam and pond built
2005; waterlilies, bog gardens,
surrounded by bamboos, gunnera,
palms and dogwoods. Traditional
borders planted 2006/7 and exotic
Ruby Border in 2008. New shrub
border planned for winter 2008.
Watch this garden develop.
Photographic display of
construction of dam, pond and
walls. Some steep slopes to upper
garden.

Watch this garden develop . . .

119 1 WOGSBARNE COTTAGES
Rotherwick RG27 9BL. Mr R & Miss
S Whistler. *2½ m N of Hook. M3 J5,
M4 J11, A30 or A33 via B3349.*
Home-made teas. Adm £3, chd free.
Sun 12 July (2-5.30).
Traditional cottage garden with a 'roses
around the door' look, much
photographed, seen on calendars,
jigsaws and in magazines. Mixed
flower beds and borders. Vegetables
grown in abundance. Ornamental
pond and alpine garden. Views over
open countryside to be enjoyed whilst
you take afternoon tea on the lawn.
Small vintage motorcycle display
(weather permitting). Some gravel
paths.

120 WRENS FARM
Lower Bordean GU32 1ER. Major &
Mrs R A Wilson, 01730 263983. *4m
W of Petersfield, 3m E of W Meon Hut.
From A3 take A272 towards
Winchester. After 3m turn R at small
Xrds with bicycle symbol on sign, then
immed R again.* Home-made teas.
Adm £2.50, chd free. Sat 20, Sun 21
June (2-6). Visitors also welcome by
appt June & July only.
Plantsman's garden in former farmyard
setting. Mixed and herbaceous
borders. Gravel beds focus on plants
for hot, dry conditions. Mediterranean-
type terrace with vine-covered pergola
and sun-loving plants. Many unusual
plants, stunning atmosphere.

Hampshire County Volunteers

County Organiser
and Central West area Patricia Elkington, Little Court, Crawley, Winchester SO21 2PU, 01962 776365, elkslc@tiscali.co.uk

County Treasurer
Fred Fratter, Tanglefoot, Crawley, Winchester SO21 2QB, 01962 776243, fred@tanglefoot-house.demon.co.uk

Assistant County Organisers
Central East Sue Alexander, The Hyde, Old Alresford, Alresford SO24 9DH, 01962 732043, suegreenhouse@hotmail.co.uk
North East Rosie & David Darrah, Avenue Cottage, Main Road, Bentley, Farnham GU10 5JA, 01420 23225, dtdarrah@msn.com
North Cynthia Oldale, Yew Tree Cottage, School Lane, Bentley, Farnham GU10 5JP, 01420 520438
North West Carol Pratt, 10 Catherine's Walk, Abbotts Ann, Andover SP11 7AS, 01264 710305, carolacap@yahoo.co.uk
East Linda Smith, Meon Orchard, Kingsmead, Wickham PO17 5AU, 01329 833253, doug.smith@btinternet.com
West Christopher Stanford, Oakdene, Sandleheath, Fordingbridge SP6 1TD, 01425 652133, christopher.stanford@homecall.co.uk
South Barbara Sykes, The Cottage, 16 Lakewood Road, Chandlers Ford SO53 1ES, 02380 254521, barandhugh@aol.com
South West Sybil Warner, Birch Wood House, New Forest, Cadnam, Southampton SO40 2NR, 02380 813400,
  sybilwarnerhome@aol.com

Mark your diary with these special events in 2009

EXPLORE SECRET GARDENS DURING CHELSEA & HAMPTON COURT FLOWER SHOW WEEKS

Tue 19 May, Wed 20 May, Thur 21 May, Fri 22 May, Wed 8 July, Thur 9 July
Full day tours from £82 per person, 10% discount for groups
Advance booking required, telephone +44 (0)20 8693 1015 or email j.wookey@btinternet.com
Specially selected gardens in London, Essex, Kent, Hampshire and South Oxfordshire. The tour price includes transport and lunch with wine at a popular restaurant or pub.

HAMPTON COURT PALACE

Thur 2 Apr, Tue 23 June, Thur 25 June, Wed 15 July, Tue 4 Aug, Thur 10 Sept
Evening tours in the company of one of the Palace's specialist tour guides from 6.30 – 8pm
Tickets £6 per person. Advance booking required, telephone +44 (0)1483 211535 or
visit www.ngs.org.uk for more information
Gossip, scandal, murder, healing – you'll find it all within the Formal Gardens at Hampton Court Palace. Each tour will have its own unique feature whether it's the story of the Great Vine or the magic and mystery of the Maze.

FROGMORE – A ROYAL GARDEN (BERKSHIRE)

Tue 26 May 10am – 5.30pm (last admission 4pm)
Garden adm £4.50, chd free. Tickets available in advance or on the day.
Advance booking for groups and coaches, telephone
+44 (0) 1483 211535 or email orders@ngs.org.uk
A rare opportunity to explore 30 acres of landscaped garden, rich in history and beauty.

FLAXBOURNE FARM – FUN & SURPRISES (BEDFORDSHIRE)

Sun 7 June 10am – 5pm. Adm £5, chd free
No booking required, come along on the day!
Bring the whole family and have fun in this surprising and entertaining garden of 2 acres. Enjoy the large plant fair, live music, pets corner, birds of prey, dog agility show and much more.

WISLEY RHS GARDEN – MUSIC IN THE GARDEN (SURREY)

Fri 11 Sept 6 – 9pm
Adm (incl RHS members) £7, chd under 15 free
Save money on advance bookings for groups of 4 or more, telephone +44 (0)1483 211535 or
visit www.ngs.org.uk for more information
A special evening opening of this famous garden, exclusively for the NGS. Enjoy music and entertainment as you explore the gardens and the floral marquee on the first day of the Wisley Flower Show.

For further information visit www.ngs.org.uk or telephone 01483 211535

HEREFORDSHIRE

Opening Dates

February

THURSDAY 5
23 Ivy Croft

THURSDAY 12
23 Ivy Croft

THURSDAY 19
23 Ivy Croft

THURSDAY 26
23 Ivy Croft

March

SUNDAY 15
49 Wilton Castle on the Wye

SUNDAY 29
36 Perrycroft
48 Whitfield

MONDAY 30
30 Moors Meadow

April

SUNDAY 5
6 Brobury House Gardens
26 Lower Hope

FRIDAY 10
33 The Old Corn Mill

MONDAY 13
33 The Old Corn Mill

SUNDAY 19
1 Aulden Farm
23 Ivy Croft

SUNDAY 26
7 Caves Folly Nursery
25 Longacre

MONDAY 27
30 Moors Meadow

May

SATURDAY 2
20 Holme Lacy House Hotel

SUNDAY 3
20 Holme Lacy House Hotel
36 Perrycroft
39 Rhodds Farm
49 Wilton Castle on the Wye

MONDAY 4
33 The Old Corn Mill

TUESDAY 5
20 Holme Lacy House Hotel

THURSDAY 7
20 Holme Lacy House Hotel

SATURDAY 9
20 Holme Lacy House Hotel

SUNDAY 10
20 Holme Lacy House Hotel

48 Whitfield

TUESDAY 12
20 Holme Lacy House Hotel
38 The Rambles

WEDNESDAY 13
24 The Long Barn

THURSDAY 14
4 Berrington Hall
20 Holme Lacy House Hotel
24 The Long Barn

FRIDAY 15
24 The Long Barn

SATURDAY 16
18 Hill House Farm
20 Holme Lacy House Hotel

SUNDAY 17
3 Batch Cottage
14 Hardwick House
18 Hill House Farm
19 The Hollies
20 Holme Lacy House Hotel

TUESDAY 19
12 The Griggs
20 Holme Lacy House Hotel
38 The Rambles

WEDNESDAY 20
24 The Long Barn

THURSDAY 21
20 Holme Lacy House Hotel
24 The Long Barn

FRIDAY 22
24 The Long Barn

SATURDAY 23
20 Holme Lacy House Hotel
29 Monnington Court

SUNDAY 24
7 Caves Folly Nursery
20 Holme Lacy House Hotel
25 Longacre
26 Lower Hope
27 Luston & Moreton Gardens
29 Monnington Court

MONDAY 25
27 Luston & Moreton Gardens
29 Monnington Court
33 The Old Corn Mill

TUESDAY 26
20 Holme Lacy House Hotel
38 The Rambles

WEDNESDAY 27
24 The Long Barn

THURSDAY 28
20 Holme Lacy House Hotel
24 The Long Barn

FRIDAY 29
15 Hellens
24 The Long Barn

SATURDAY 30
15 Hellens (Day & Evening)
20 Holme Lacy House Hotel

SUNDAY 31
1 Aulden Farm
3 Batch Cottage
8 Glan Arrow
20 Holme Lacy House Hotel
23 Ivy Croft

June

MONDAY 1
30 Moors Meadow

TUESDAY 2
20 Holme Lacy House Hotel
38 The Rambles

WEDNESDAY 3
24 The Long Barn

THURSDAY 4
20 Holme Lacy House Hotel
24 The Long Barn

FRIDAY 5
24 The Long Barn

SATURDAY 6
12 The Griggs
20 Holme Lacy House Hotel
28 Middle Hunt House
43 Tarrington Court (Evening)

SUNDAY 7
2 The Bannut
10 The Great House
20 Holme Lacy House Hotel
28 Middle Hunt House
44 Upper Tan House
49 Wilton Castle on the Wye

MONDAY 8
44 Upper Tan House

TUESDAY 9
20 Holme Lacy House Hotel
38 The Rambles

WEDNESDAY 10
24 The Long Barn

THURSDAY 11
20 Holme Lacy House Hotel
24 The Long Barn

FRIDAY 12
24 The Long Barn

SATURDAY 13
20 Holme Lacy House Hotel
40 Shieldbrook
47 Weston Mews

SUNDAY 14
20 Holme Lacy House Hotel

22 Hundred Bank
35 The Orchards
40 Shieldbrook

TUESDAY 16
12 The Griggs
20 Holme Lacy House Hotel
38 The Rambles

WEDNESDAY 17
24 The Long Barn

THURSDAY 18
20 Holme Lacy House Hotel
24 The Long Barn

FRIDAY 19
24 The Long Barn

SATURDAY 20
20 Holme Lacy House Hotel
45 The Vine

SUNDAY 21
6 Brobury House Gardens
7 Caves Folly Nursery
9 Grantsfield
20 Holme Lacy House Hotel
25 Longacre
32 Old Chapel House
36 Perrycroft

TUESDAY 23
20 Holme Lacy House Hotel
38 The Rambles

WEDNESDAY 24
24 The Long Barn

THURSDAY 25
20 Holme Lacy House Hotel
24 The Long Barn

FRIDAY 26
16 Hereford Cathedral Gardens
24 The Long Barn

SATURDAY 27
12 The Griggs
20 Holme Lacy House Hotel
31 Netherwood Manor
50 Wolferlow House

SUNDAY 28
1 Aulden Farm
20 Holme Lacy House Hotel
23 Ivy Croft
50 Wolferlow House

TUESDAY 30
20 Holme Lacy House Hotel
38 The Rambles

July

WEDNESDAY 1
24 The Long Barn

THURSDAY 2
20 Holme Lacy House Hotel
24 The Long Barn

FRIDAY 3
24 The Long Barn

SATURDAY 4
20 Holme Lacy House Hotel

SUNDAY 5
11 Grendon Court
20 Holme Lacy House Hotel
49 Wilton Castle on the Wye

MONDAY 6
30 Moors Meadow

TUESDAY 7
12 The Griggs
20 Holme Lacy House Hotel
38 The Rambles

WEDNESDAY 8
24 The Long Barn

THURSDAY 9
20 Holme Lacy House Hotel
24 The Long Barn

FRIDAY 10
24 The Long Barn

SATURDAY 11
20 Holme Lacy House Hotel

SUNDAY 12
2 The Bannut
20 Holme Lacy House Hotel
26 Lower Hope
51 Woodview

TUESDAY 14
12 The Griggs
20 Holme Lacy House Hotel
38 The Rambles

WEDNESDAY 15
24 The Long Barn

THURSDAY 16
20 Holme Lacy House Hotel
24 The Long Barn

FRIDAY 17
24 The Long Barn

SATURDAY 18
20 Holme Lacy House Hotel

SUNDAY 19
20 Holme Lacy House Hotel
39 Rhodds Farm
51 Woodview

TUESDAY 21
12 The Griggs
20 Holme Lacy House Hotel
38 The Rambles

WEDNESDAY 22
24 The Long Barn

THURSDAY 23
20 Holme Lacy House Hotel
24 The Long Barn

FRIDAY 24
24 The Long Barn

SATURDAY 25
18 Hill House Farm
20 Holme Lacy House Hotel

SUNDAY 26
18 Hill House Farm
20 Holme Lacy House Hotel
35 The Orchards

TUESDAY 28
12 The Griggs
20 Holme Lacy House Hotel
38 The Rambles

WEDNESDAY 29
24 The Long Barn

THURSDAY 30
20 Holme Lacy House Hotel
24 The Long Barn

FRIDAY 31
24 The Long Barn

August

SATURDAY 1
20 Holme Lacy House Hotel

SUNDAY 2
20 Holme Lacy House Hotel
37 The Picton Garden
49 Wilton Castle on the Wye

MONDAY 3
30 Moors Meadow

TUESDAY 4
20 Holme Lacy House Hotel
38 The Rambles

WEDNESDAY 5
24 The Long Barn

THURSDAY 6
20 Holme Lacy House Hotel
24 The Long Barn

FRIDAY 7
24 The Long Barn

SATURDAY 8
20 Holme Lacy House Hotel

SUNDAY 9
20 Holme Lacy House Hotel
37 The Picton Garden

TUESDAY 11
20 Holme Lacy House Hotel
38 The Rambles

WEDNESDAY 12
24 The Long Barn

THURSDAY 13
20 Holme Lacy House Hotel
24 The Long Barn

FRIDAY 14
24 The Long Barn

SATURDAY 15
17 Hergest Croft Gardens
20 Holme Lacy House Hotel
28 Middle Hunt House

SUNDAY 16
2 The Bannut
20 Holme Lacy House Hotel

28 Middle Hunt House
37 The Picton Garden

TUESDAY 18
20 Holme Lacy House Hotel
38 The Rambles

WEDNESDAY 19
24 The Long Barn

THURSDAY 20
20 Holme Lacy House Hotel
24 The Long Barn

FRIDAY 21
24 The Long Barn

SATURDAY 22
20 Holme Lacy House Hotel

SUNDAY 23
20 Holme Lacy House Hotel
37 The Picton Garden

TUESDAY 25
20 Holme Lacy House Hotel
38 The Rambles

WEDNESDAY 26
24 The Long Barn

THURSDAY 27
20 Holme Lacy House Hotel
24 The Long Barn

FRIDAY 28
24 The Long Barn

SATURDAY 29
20 Holme Lacy House Hotel
50 Wolferlow House

SUNDAY 30
1 Aulden Farm
19 The Hollies
20 Holme Lacy House Hotel
23 Ivy Croft
37 The Picton Garden

September

TUESDAY 1
20 Holme Lacy House Hotel
38 The Rambles

WEDNESDAY 2
24 The Long Barn

THURSDAY 3
20 Holme Lacy House Hotel
24 The Long Barn

FRIDAY 4
24 The Long Barn

SATURDAY 5
20 Holme Lacy House Hotel

SUNDAY 6
20 Holme Lacy House Hotel
22 Hundred Bank
46 Weston Hall

MONDAY 7
30 Moors Meadow

TUESDAY 8
20 Holme Lacy House Hotel
38 The Rambles

THURSDAY 10
20 Holme Lacy House Hotel

SATURDAY 12
20 Holme Lacy House Hotel
33 The Old Corn Mill

SUNDAY 13
11 Grendon Court
20 Holme Lacy House Hotel
33 The Old Corn Mill
37 The Picton Garden

TUESDAY 15
20 Holme Lacy House Hotel
38 The Rambles

THURSDAY 17
20 Holme Lacy House Hotel

SATURDAY 19
17 Hergest Croft Gardens
20 Holme Lacy House Hotel
37 The Picton Garden

SUNDAY 20
20 Holme Lacy House Hotel
23 Ivy Croft

TUESDAY 22
20 Holme Lacy House Hotel

THURSDAY 24
20 Holme Lacy House Hotel

SATURDAY 26
20 Holme Lacy House Hotel

SUNDAY 27
20 Holme Lacy House Hotel

TUESDAY 29
20 Holme Lacy House Hotel
37 The Picton Garden

October

SUNDAY 4
26 Lower Hope

SATURDAY 17
37 The Picton Garden

SUNDAY 18
37 The Picton Garden

SUNDAY 25
25 Longacre

February 2010

THURSDAY 4
23 Ivy Croft

THURSDAY 11
23 Ivy Croft

THURSDAY 18
23 Ivy Croft

THURSDAY 25
23 Ivy Croft

Gardens open to the public

1 Aulden Farm
2 The Bannut
4 Berrington Hall
6 Brobury House Gardens
13 Hampton Court
15 Hellens
16 Hereford Cathedral Gardens
17 Hergest Croft Gardens
23 Ivy Croft
28 Middle Hunt House
30 Moors Meadow
37 The Picton Garden
42 Staunton Park

By appointment only

5 Brilley Court
21 Hope End House
34 The Old Quarry
41 Shucknall Court

Also open by appointment ☎

3 Batch Cottage
7 Caves Folly Nursery
9 Grantsfield
12 The Griggs
18 Hill House Farm
19 The Hollies
25 Longacre
26 Lower Hope
33 The Old Corn Mill
34 The Old Quarry
35 The Orchards
38 The Rambles
40 Shieldbrook
43 Tarrington Court
44 Upper Tan House
46 Weston Hall
47 Weston Mews
48 Whitfield
51 Woodview

A sea of flowering grasses make a highlight . . .

The Gardens

❶ ◆ AULDEN FARM

Aulden, Leominster HR6 0JT. Alun & Jill Whitehead, 01568 720129, www.auldenfarm.co.uk. *4m SW of Leominster. From Leominster take Ivington/Upper Hill Rd. ³/₄ m after Ivington Church, turn R (signed Aulden), garden 1m on R. From A4110 signed Ivington, take 2nd R (approx ³/₄ m), garden ³/₄ m on L. Teas at Ivy Croft (NGS days only).* **Adm £3, chd free, combined with Ivycroft adm £5, chd free (NGS days). Tues & Thurs Apr to Aug, Thurs Mar & Sept 10-5. For NGS: Suns 19 Apr; 31 May; 28 June; 30 Aug (2-5.30).**

Informally planted country garden and nursery surrounding old farmhouse. 3 acres planted with wildlife in mind. Numerous iris incl ditch containing ensatas, sibiricas by natural pond. Hemerocallis with grasses and kniphofias for added zing. Emphasis on structure and form with a hint of quirkiness. Garden started from scratch in 1997, feels mature but still evolving. Home-made ice-cream NGS days only.

✕ ❀ ☕

❷ ◆ THE BANNUT

Bringsty WR6 5TA. Daphne & Maurice Everett, 01885 482206, www.bannut.co.uk. *2¹/₂ m E of Bromyard. On A44 Worcester Rd, ¹/₂ m E of entrance to National Trust, Brockhampton.* **Adm £4, chd £1.50. Weds, Sats, Suns & Bank Hols 10 Apr to 30 Sept. For NGS: Suns 7 June; 12 July; 16 Aug (12.30-5).**

3 acres of formal and informal gardens, with much to enjoy throughout the seasons and lovely views to the Malvern Hills. Manicured hedges divide colourful garden rooms, which incl a yellow and white garden, romantic arbour garden, secret garden and unusual knot garden. Spectacular heather gardens, woodland garden, many unusual and interesting trees and shrubs. Featured in RHS Garden Finder.

ᗑ ❀ ☕

❸ BATCH COTTAGE

Almeley HR3 6PT. Jeremy & Elizabeth Russell, 01544 327469. *16m NW of Hereford. 2m off A438-A4111 to Kington, turn R at Eardisley.* **Cream teas. Adm £3.50, chd free. Suns 17, 31 May (2-5.30). Visitors also welcome by appt Apr to Sept.**

Established unregimented, conservation-oriented garden of some 2¹/₂ acres with streams and large pond, set in a natural valley, surrounded by woodland and orchard. Over 360 labelled trees and shrubs, mixed borders, fern and bog beds, wild flower bank, stumpery, woodland walk and wooden sculptures.

ᗑ ✕ ❀ ☕ ☎

❹ ◆ BERRINGTON HALL

Leominster HR6 0DW. The National Trust, 01568 615721, www.nationaltrust.org.uk. *3m N of Leominster. On A49, signed. Buses: Midland Red (W) 92, 292 alight Luston 2m.* **Adm £5.20, chd £2.60. Sats to Weds 9 Mar to 30 Nov 11-5. For NGS: Thur 14 May (12-4).**

Extensive views over Capability Brown park; formal garden; wall plants, unusual trees, camellia collection, herbaceous plants, wisteria. Woodland walk, rhododendrons, walled garden with historic apple collection. Potting shed with old garden implements on display.

ᗑ ✕ ❀ ☕

BIRTSMORTON COURT

See Worcestershire.

❺ ◆ BRILLEY COURT

Whitney-on-Wye HR3 6JF. Mr & Mrs David Bulmer, 01497 831467. *6m NE of Hay-on-Wye. 5m SW of Kington. 1¹/₂ m off A438 Hereford to Brecon rd signed to Brilley.* **Adm £3, under 12 chd free. Visitors welcome by appt groups, coaches & individuals.**

3-acre garden, walled, ornamental kitchen garden. Spring tulip collection, summer rose and herbaceous borders. 7-acre wild valley stream garden. Limited wheelchair access.

ᗑ ✕ ☎

❻ ◆ BROBURY HOUSE GARDENS

Brobury by Bredwardine HR3 6BS. Keith & Pru Cartwright, 01981 500229, www.broburyhouse.co.uk. *10m W of Hereford. S off A438 signed Bredwardine & Brobury. Garden 1m L before bridge. Teas NGS days only.* **Adm £3, chd £1. Open daily all yr 10-5 or dusk if earlier. For NGS: Suns 5 Apr; 21 June (11-5).**

5 acres of gardens, set on the banks of an exquisitely beautiful section of the R Wye, offer the visitor a delightful combination of Victorian terraces with mature specimen trees, inspiring water features, architectural planting and woodland areas. Redesign and development is ongoing. Bring a picnic, your paint brushes, binoculars and linger awhile. Wheelchair users, strong able-bodied assistant advisable.

ᗑ ᗌ ☕

❼ CAVES FOLLY NURSERY

Evendine Lane, Colwall WR13 6DY. Wil Leaper & Bridget Evans, 01684 540631, bridget@cavesfolly.com, www.cavesfolly.com. *1¹/₄ m NE of Ledbury. B4218. Between Malvern & Ledbury. Evendine Lane, off Colwall Green. Car parking at Caves Folly.* **Home-made teas. Combined with Longacre adm £3.50, chd free. Suns 26 Apr; 24 May; 21 June (2-5). Visitors also welcome by appt for group visits. Refreshments & talk on organic gardening can be provided.**

Organic nursery and display gardens. Specialist growers of herbaceous, alpines, grasses, vegetable and herb plants, all grown organically. This is not a manicured garden! It is full of drifts of colour and wild flowers and a haven for wildlife. Childrens wildlife trail. Grass and gravel paths.

ᗑ ✕ ❀ ᗌ ☕ ☎

❽ GLAN ARROW

Eardisland HR6 9BW. Christopher & Lotty James. *5m W of Leominster on B4529. Cross bridge & immediately turn sharp L up driveway.* **Home-made teas. Adm £3, chd free. Sun 31 May (2-6).**

4-acre English riverside garden with herbaceous borders, roses, bog garden leading to small lake and potager. Gravel courtyard at entrance.

ᗑ ✕ ☕

Drifts of colour and wild flowers and a haven for wildlife. Childrens wildlife trail . . .

9 GRANTSFIELD

nr Kimbolton, Leominster HR6 0ET. Colonel & Mrs J G T Polley, 01568 613338. *3m NE of Leominster. A49 N from Leominster, A4112 turn R & follow signs. No parking for coaches - drop & collect visitors in village; (minibus acceptable). A44 W to Leominster. Turn R at Drum Xrds (notice up).* Home-made teas. **Adm £3, chd free (share to Hamnish Village Hall), combined with Old Chapel House adm £5. Sun 21 June (2-5.30). Visitors also welcome by appt 19 Apr to 30 Sept.**

Contrasting styles in gardens of old stone farmhouse; wide variety of unusual plants, trees and shrubs, old roses, climbers, herbaceous borders, superb views. 1½ -acre orchard and kitchen garden with flowering and specimen trees and shrubs. Spring bulbs.

10 THE GREAT HOUSE

Dilwyn HR4 8HX. Tom & Jane Hawksley, www.thegreathousedilwyn.co.uk. *7m W of Leominster. A44 from Leominster joining A4112 (signed Brecon). Turn L into Dilwyn village. House on RH-side opp village green.* Home-made teas. **Adm £3, chd free. Sun 7 June (2-5).**

1½ -acre all-yr garden, designed and created by owners over the last 10yrs. Spring bulbs, traditional rose gardens, yew and beech hedging, raised knot garden, decorative stone and brickwork. 40ft reflecting pool and pleached hornbeams lining the drive all add interest to this country garden which is fronted by wonderful C18 wrought iron gates. Gravel paths.

11 NEW GRENDON COURT

Upton Bishop HR9 7QP. Mark & Kate Edwards. *3m NE of Ross-on-Wye. M50 J3 towards Hereford. Follow B4224 to Hereford past Moody Cow PH, down hill, up otherside, 1st gate on L. From Ross A40, B449, at Xrds, R to Upton Bishop, 100yds on L.* **Adm £4.50, chd free. Suns 5 July; 13 Sept (3-6).**

A contemporary garden designed by Tom Stuart-Smith. Planted on 2 levels, a clever collection of mass planted perennials and grasses of different heights, texture, and colour give all-yr round interest.

The upper walled garden with a sea of flowering grasses make a highlight. Views of pond and valley walk. Some steep grass slopes.

12 THE GRIGGS

Newton St Margarets HR2 0QY. John & Bridget Biggs, 01981 510629, www.artaura.co.uk/thegriggs. *14m SW of Hereford. Take B4348 to Vowchurch, turn L, signed Michaelchurch Escley, continue for 2½ m, then follow NGS signs. Signs will be posted locally for those approaching from Longtown & Ewyas Harold.* Home-made teas. **Adm £3.50, chd free (share to Community Action, Nepal). Tues 19 May; 16 June, Sats 6, 27 June; Tues 7 July to 28 July (2-6). Visitors also welcome by appt May - July incl.**

Located in a remote scenic setting between the Golden Valley and the Black Mountains, a floriferous country garden of 1½ acres, managed organically and incl extensive mixed borders, over 60 old roses, wild flower meadows, wildlife pond and large productive kitchen garden. A garden to lose oneself in. Some gravel paths.

Walled garden with historic pear trees . . .

13 ◆ HAMPTON COURT

Hope-under-Dinmore HR6 0PN. Hampton Court Trading Ltd, 01568 797777, www.hamptoncourt.org.uk. *5m S of Leominster. On A417, 500yds from junction with A49.* **For details please tel or see website.**

Exciting mix of new and old gardens within the grounds of C15 castle. Work started to rebuild gardens in 1996. Newly restored formal walled garden, herbaceous borders, Dutch garden, sunken garden with waterfall and thatched hermitage and organic kitchen garden. Featured in Herefordshire & Worcestershire Life - Best Garden.

14 HARDWICK HOUSE

Pembridge, Leominster HR6 9HE. Mr & Mrs D J Collins. *6m W of Leominster. Between Eardisland & Pembridge. Take A44 from Leominster, 1m before Pembridge, turn up lane signed Bearwood & Hardwick. Drive entrance 250yds up lane, over cattlegrid between stone pillars.* **Adm £3.50, chd free. Sun 17 May (11-6).**

Large garden with extensive lawns, colourful shrubberies and ornamental trees. Fine views over unspoilt countryside. Ponds with collection of waterfowl. Teas available locally.

15 ◆ HELLENS

Much Marcle HR8 2LY. PMMCT, 01531 660504, info@hellensmanor.com. *6m from Ross-on-Wye. 4m SW of Ledbury, off A449.* **Adm £2.50, chd free. For opening details please tel or email. For NGS: Fri 29 May (2-5). Afternoon & Evening Opening** wine, Sat 30 May (2-5 & 6-7.30).

In the grounds of Hellens Manor House, the gardens are being gently redeveloped to reflect the C17 ambience of the house. Incl a rare octagonal dovecot. 2 knot gardens and yew labyrinth, lawns, herb and kitchen gardens; short woodlands and pond walk. Longer walk to Hall Wood, site of SSI.

16 NEW ◆ HEREFORD CATHEDRAL GARDENS

HR1 2NG. Dean of Hereford Cathedral, 01432 374202, visits@herefordcathedral.org. *Centre of Hereford. Approach rds to The Cathedral are signed.* **Combined adm £5, chd free. Weds & Sats, June to Aug - tours 2.30pm. Group bookings by appt. For NGS: Fri 26 June (11-3.45).**

Guided tours of a courtyard garden, atmospheric cloisters garden enclosed by C15 buildings. The vicar's garden, the planting having ecclesiastical connections. The dean's private riverside garden and the bishop's private garden with fine trees, vegetable and cutting garden, outdoor chapel for meditation in a floral setting. Guided tours at regular intervals.

Group opening

17 ◆ HERGEST CROFT GARDENS

Kington HR5 3EG. Mr W L Banks, 01544 230160, www.hergest.co.uk. 1/2 m W of Kington. 1/2 m off A44 on Welsh side of Kington. Turn L at Rhayader end of bypass; then 1st R; gardens 1/4 m on L. **Adm £6, chd free. Week days in Mar; daily 28 Mar to 1 Nov. For NGS: Sats 15 Aug; 19 Sept (12-5.30).**
4 gardens for all seasons, from spring bulbs to spectacular autumn colour, incl spring and summer borders, roses, brilliant azaleas and old-fashioned kitchen garden growing unusual vegetables. Brightly coloured rhododendrons 30ft high grow in Park Wood. Over 60 champion trees in one of the finest collections of trees and shrubs in the British Isles. Limited wheelchair access.

& ✿ NCCPG ☕

18 HILL HOUSE FARM

Knighton LD7 1NA. Simon & Caroline Gourlay, 01547 528542, simon@maryvalefarms.co.uk. 4m SE of Knighton. S of A4113 via Knighton (Llanshay Lane, 3m) or Bucknell (Reeves Lane, 3m). Home-made teas. **Adm £3, chd free. Sats, Suns 16, 17 May; 25, 26 July (2-5.30). Visitors also welcome by appt.**
S-facing 5-acre hillside garden developed over past 40yrs with magnificent views over unspoilt countryside. Herbaceous area amongst magnificent mature oak trees, extensive lawns and paths surrounded by roses, shrubs and specimen trees. Sloping paths to Oak Pool 200ft below house. Transport available from bottom of garden if needed.

✗ ☕ ☎

19 THE HOLLIES

Old Church Road, Colwall WR13 6EZ. Margaret & Graham White, 01684 540931, mandgwhite@dsl.pipex.com. 3m SW of Malvern. Take B4218 past Old Court Nursery, (Picton), turn R into Old Church Rd. Hollies 250yds on R. Drop off at garden, parking at Coca Cola Enterprises Ltd on B4218 (nr junction). Home-made teas. **Adm £3, chd free. Suns 17 May; 30 Aug (2-5.30). Visitors also welcome by appt Feb to Oct, individuals & groups.**
Hardy planter's 1/2 -acre garden developed over the last 14yrs from a plot containing mature trees but little

else. Continually evolving beds containing a wide mixture of shrubs, bulbs and perennials planted to provide interest throughout the yr. A gently sloping site with views toward the Malvern Hills. Some gravel paths.

& ✿ ☕ ☎

20 NEW HOLME LACY HOUSE HOTEL

Holme Lacy. HR2 6LP. Bourne Leisure Ltd, 01432 870870, www.warnerleisurehotels.co.uk. 5m SE of Hereford. From Hereford B4399, from Gloucester B4215, then B4224, from Ledbury A438 signed from Holme Lacy Village. **House & garden £5, chd free, garden only £3, chd free. Historic House Tours, Tues, Thurs, Sats 11am please tel. Tues, Thurs, Sats, Suns 2 May to 29 Sept; (11-30-5.30, Suns 2-5.30).**
The gardens were conceived on a very bold scale in 'The Grand Manner' and is Herefordshire's only surviving example of such gardens. Battlement gardens, ancient yew hedging, formal Italian gardens with ponds. Herbaceous borders, walled garden with historic pear trees. New walled garden project for 2009. Partial wheelchair access.

& ✗ 🛏 ☕ ✿

Oriental poppies in June . . .

21 HOPE END HOUSE

Hope End, Wellington Heath HR8 1JQ. Mrs P J Maiden, 01531 635890, sharonmaiden@btinternet.com, www.hopeendhouse.com. 2m NE of Ledbury. Home-made teas. **Adm £3, chd free. Visitors welcome by appt, garden & parkland open Apr - Sept, please tel for directions.**
5 acres of mature country house gardens, with extensive herbaceous borders, parkland trees, sweeping lawns and glorious spring colours. Explore the wild flower glade, Japanese, and productive gardens or extend your visit to a fabulous bluebell wood, taking in wonderful long-reaching views S to Eastnor and the Malvern Hills.

✿ 🛏 ☕ ☎

22 NEW HUNDRED BANK

Little Cowarne HR7 4RH. Pat Johnstone & Gill Sanders. 6m SW of Bromyard. On A465, 1/2 m S of Stoke Lacy turn R signed Pencombe/Ullingswick. Garden past Three Horseshoes PH, L at bend signed Little Cowarne Church. Home-made teas. **Adm £2.50, chd free. Suns 14 June; 6 Sept (2-5).**
Idyllic 1/3 acre designer garden with stunning views. Eclectic mix of subtropical, herbaceous and architectural plants hot and cold coloured borders. Oriental poppies in June. Grasses, pools, water features, vegetables, lawn, vine covered sitting area and many pots. Inspiring ideas, incl stained glass features from resident artist.

✗ ✿ ☕

23 ◆ IVY CROFT

Ivington Green, Leominster HR6 0JN. Sue & Roger Norman, 01568 720344, www.ivycroft.freeserve.co.uk. 3m SW of Leominster. From Leominster take Ryelands Rd to Ivington. Turn R at church, garden 3/4 m on R. From A4110 signed Ivington, garden 13/4 m on L. **Adm £3, chd free, combined with Aulden Farm adm £5 (NGS openings Apr to Aug). Every Thurs Apr - Sept 9-4. For NGS: Thurs 5 Feb to 26 Feb; Suns 19 Apr; 31 May; 28 June; 30 Aug; 20 Sept (2-5.30); 2010 Thurs 4 Feb to 25 Feb.**
Garden created since 1997 surrounds C17 cottage (not open) in 4 acres of rich grassland. Plant lovers' garden designed for all-yr interest. Raised beds, mixed borders, trees, alpines, troughs, formal vegetable garden framed by trained fruit trees; collections of ferns, willows and snowdrops.

✗ ✿ ☕

LLANTHONY AND DISTRICT GARDENS

See Gwent.

24 THE LONG BARN

Eastnor HR8 1EL. Fay & Roger Oates. 2m E of Ledbury. On A438 Ledbury to Tewkesbury rd. From Ledbury take Malvern rd & turn R after 11/4 m towards Eastnor-Tewkesbury. Roger Oates Studio 3/4 m along rd, on LH-side. Situated behind the design studio of Roger Oates Design Co. Parking in car park. **Adm £2.50, chd free (share to The Gloucester MS Information Therapy Centre). Weds,**

Thurs, Fris 13 May to 4 Sept; (10-5). Garden with strong design structure in an idyllic setting of Eastnor parkland. Dense and natural planting of mixed perennials and herbaceous plants selected for the owners pleasure with texture and fragrance paramount. The Garden is an enclosed 1/3 -acre, set within a 3-acre orchard. Roger Oates Design Studio shop, showing own range of rugs and interior fabrics with contemporay lighting accessories, modern garden pots and books.

25 LONGACRE
Evendine Lane, Colwall Green WR13 6DT. Mr D M Pudsey, 01684 540377, davidpudsey@onetel.com. *3m S of Malvern. Off Colwall Green. Off B4218. Car parking at Caves Folly Nursery.* Home-made teas at Caves Folly (not Oct). **Adm £2, chd free, Combined with Caves Folly adm £3.50, (not 25 Oct). Suns 26 Apr; 24 May; 21 June; 25 Oct (2-5). Visitors also welcome by appt.**
3-acre garden-cum-arboretum developed since 1970. Island beds of trees and shrubs, some underplanted with bulbs and herbaceous perennials, present a sequence of contrasting pictures and views through the seasons. There are no 'rooms' - rather long vistas lead the eye and feet, while the feeling of spaciousness is enhanced by glimpses caught between trunks and through gaps in the planting. Over 50 types of conifer provide the background to maples, rhododendrons, azaleas, dogwoods, eucryphias etc. Featured on TV Gardeners World.

26 LOWER HOPE
Ullingswick HR1 3JF. Mr & Mrs Clive Richards, 01432 820557. *5m S of Bromyard. From Hereford take A465 N to Bromyard. After 6m turn L at Burley Gate on A417 signed Leominster. Approx 2m take 3rd turning on R signed Lower Hope & Pencombe, 1/2 m on LH-side.* Home-made teas. **Adm £3, chd £1. Suns 5 Apr; 24 May; 12 July; 4 Oct (2-5). Visitors also welcome by appt.**
5-acre garden facing S and W. Herbaceous borders, rose walks and gardens, laburnum tunnel, Mediterranean garden, bog gardens. Lime tree walk, lake landscaped with wild flowers; streams; ponds. Conservatories and large glasshouse

with exotic species orchids incl colourful butterflies, bougainvilleas. Prizewinning herd of pedigree Hereford cattle, flock of pedigree Suffolk sheep.

Group opening

27 NEW LUSTON & MORETON GARDENS
HR6 0DP. *3m N of Leominster. B4361, S end of Luston. Follow signs to The Nest.* Home-made teas at The Nest. **Combined adm £5, chd free. Sun 24, Mon 25 May (2-5).**
3 gardens, 2 small side by side, part of barn conversion on edge of Luston: 1 large garden round old yeoman's house (not open) in Moreton Hamlet. Eye Manor (1681), C12 church and Berrington Hall NT part of parish. Wild flower meadow, plants & WC at The Nest.

THE NEST
Moreton, Eye. Sue Evans & Guy Poulton. *Follow signs from Upper Court, or 1m W of A49 at Ashton, 4m N of Leominster*
Classic cottage garden 1 acre surrounding 1530s timber framed house (not open). Summer garden with water features, pond, waterfall, Mediterranean plants, ferns, potager, scree and gravel gardens. Canal remnant and wild flower meadow with rare orchids. Some gravel, assistance available.

NEW 2 UPPER COURT
Luston. Fred & Sue Cherrill
First of 2 immaculate bijou gardens, lawns, herbaceous borders with cottage perennials. Scree area, patio with pots. Through gate, patio with rockery to back lawn, steps to arbour with clematis, play area and gipsy caravan. Partial wheelchair access, to front garden only.

NEW 3 UPPER COURT
Luston. Jane Cooper & Anthony Batson
Opp garden gate, bank with shrubs, ferns, rhododendrons, roses. Garden with small lawn surrounded by shrubs, roses and herbaceous plants, roses climb the house, wisteria and clematis adorn the pergola.

28 NEW ◆ MIDDLE HUNT HOUSE
Walterstone, Hereford HR2 0DY. Trustees of Monnow Valleys Arts Centre & Rupert Otten, 01873 860359, www.monnowvalleyarts.org. *4m W of Pandy. 17m S of Hereford, 10m N of Abergavenny. A465 to Pandy, L towards Longtown, turn R at Clodock Church, 1m on R.* Disabled parking available. **Gallery & garden £5, chd £2.50, garden only £3, chd £1.50. For details please tel or see website. For NGS: Sats, Suns 6, 7 June; 15, 16 Aug (2-6).**
2 acre modern garden with outstanding views, surrounding stonebuilt farmhouse, converted gallery barn and artist's studio. Plants inspired by Piet Oudoulf using swathes of herbaceous plants and grasses. Sensory, vegetable and Japanese gardens, and hornbeam alley. Special features: birches under planted with irises (June) and Echinacea (Aug). Exhibitions of work by Ardizzune family members (June), and of the Sir Christopher Bland collection of work by Eric Gill (Aug).

Wild flower meadow with rare orchids . . .

29 MONNINGTON COURT
Monnington-on-Wye, Hereford HR4 7NL. Mr & Mrs Bulmer, www.monnington-morgans.co.uk. *9m W of Hereford. S off A438. Monnington-on-Wye. Lane to village & Monnington Court.* Teas & barbecue. **House & garden £7, chd £3.50, garden £5.50, chd £3 (share to Riding for the Disabled). Sat 23 to Mon 25 May; (10-7).**
25 acres, lake, river, cider press, sculpture garden (Mrs Bulmer is sculptor Angela Conner). Famous mile-long avenue of pines and yews, favourite of Sir John Betjeman and in Kilvert's Diary. Foundation Farm of British Morgan Horse, who are living replicas of statues in Trafalgar Square. C13 Moot Hall, C15 and C17 house. Sculpture garden. Horse and Carriage display 3.30pm. Featured in local press & radio.

30 ◆ **MOORS MEADOW**
Collington HR7 4LZ. Ros Bissell,
01885 410318,
www.moorsmeadow.co.uk. *4m N of
Bromyard, on B4214. Turn L up lane,
over two cattle grids turn R.* **Adm £4,
chd £1** 3-16yrs. For details please
tel or use website. For NGS: Mons
30 Mar; 27 Apr; 1 June; 6 July;
3 Aug; 7 Sept (11-5).
Captivating organic 7-acres
overlooking Kyre Valley, many rarely
seen trees, shrubs, flowers, ferns,
grasses and bulbs. A little 'formal', a lot
of 'ordered chaos', to 'bring your own
machete'. Full of inspiration, ideas,
intriguing features, myriad wildlife,
something to surprise and fascinate all
yr. Eccentric plantswomen, artist
blacksmith some days. Featured in
'Country Living'.
🐕 ✿

31 **NETHERWOOD MANOR**
Tenbury Wells WR15 8RT. Lord &
Lady Clifton. *5m N of Bromyard.
¹/₂ way between Bromyard & Tenbury
Wells on B4214. Signed from rd in
Stoke Bliss.* Home-made teas. **Adm
£5, chd free.** Sat 27 June (2-5).
Well established garden centred on
medieval dovecote, with parkland
backdrop. Several distinct areas, each
with own interest, incl walled garden
with herbaceous borders, 'wilderness'
garden, gravel garden and ponds
(unfenced). Other areas in development,
wide variety of unusual shrubs and
trees. Children very welcome.
🐕 ✿ ☕

32 **OLD CHAPEL HOUSE**
Kimbolton, Leominster HR6 0HF.
Stephen & Penny Usher & Audrey
Brown. *2m NE of Leominster. A49 N
from Leominster. A4112 into
Kimbolton. Garden on R at bottom of
hill. From Tenbury Wells S A4112 6m
Kimbolton. Park in village hall car park
5mins walk, please follow signs.
Disabled parking at garden.* Home-
made teas. **Adm £3, chd free,
combined with Grantsfield adm £5.**
Sun 21 June (2-5).
S-facing 1-acre garden. Devastated by
the floods in July 2007. Major
reconstruction works now completed
with new planting schemes. Mill stream
and mill race developed into a wildlife
garden. Potager and cutting garden for
flower arranger. Formal box parterre
with old roses and lavender walk.
Croquet lawn with gazebo and
herbaceous borders.
♿ 🐕 ✿ ☕

33 **THE OLD CORN MILL**
Aston Crews HR9 7LW. Mrs Jill
Hunter, 01989 750059. *5m E of Ross-
on-Wye. A40 Ross to Gloucester. Turn
L at T-lights at Lea Xrds onto B4222
signed Newent. Garden ¹/₂ m on L.
Parking for disabled down drive.*
Home-made teas. **Adm £2.50, chd
free.** Fri 10, Mon 13 Apr; Mon 4, 25
May; Sat 12, Sun 13 Sept (11-5).
Visitors also welcome by appt all yr
for individuals & small groups,
coaches permitted, photographers
& artists most welcome.
Surrounding the Award Winning
converted C18 Mill (not open) this
valley garden has been designed to
merge into the surrounding fields.
Massed banks and borders provide
colour all yr while streams, ponds,
meadows and native trees support a
variety of wildlife. Wild daffodils,
common spotted orchids and primulas
are spring highlights. Featured 'GGG'.
🐕 ✿ ☕ ☎

Famous mile-long avenue of pines and yews . . .

34 **THE OLD QUARRY**
Almeley Road, Eardisley HR3 6PR.
John & Anne Davis, 01544 327264,
old.quarry@virgin.net. *16m NW of
Hereford. ³/₄ m off A438-A4111 to
Kington, turn R at Eardisley.* **Adm £3,
chd free.** Visitors welcome by appt.
Gently-sloping garden of 2¹/₂ acres,
laid out in the 1930s now being
renovated and developed for yr-round
interest. Terraces and old quarry
gardens with rhododendrons and
mature trees, parterre, vegetable
garden and herbaceous beds. Far-
reaching views of Black Mountains and
Hay Bluff.
🐕 ☎ ▣

35 **THE ORCHARDS**
Golden Valley, Bishops Frome, nr
Bromyard WR6 5BN. Mr & Mrs
Robert Humphries, 01885 490273,
theorchards.humphries@btinternet.c
om. *14m E of Hereford. A4103 turn L
at bottom of Fromes Hill, through*
*village of Bishops Frome on B4214.
Turn R immed after de-regulation signs
along narrow track for 250yds. Park in
field by garden.* Home-made teas.
Adm £3, chd free. Suns 14 June;
26 July (2-6). Visitors also welcome
by appt.
1-acre garden designed in areas on
various levels. 15 water features incl
Japanese water garden and tea house,
Mediterranean area, rose garden with
rill, also aviary. Large rose, clematis,
fuchsia and dahlia collections. Seating
areas on all levels. New projects every
yr.
🐕 ✿ ☕ ☎

36 **PERRYCROFT**
Jubilee Drive, Upper Colwall
WR13 6DN. Gillian & Mark Archer.
*Between Malvern & Ledbury. From
A449 Malvern to Ledbury rd, take
B4232 at British Camp (Jubilee Drive).
Garden 1m on L. Park in Gardiners
Quarry car park on R (pay & display),
short walk to garden.* **Adm £3, chd
free.** Suns 29 Mar; 3 May; 21 June
(12-4).
10-acre garden and woodland on
upper slopes of Malvern Hills with
magnificent views. Arts and Crafts
house (not open), garden partly
designed by CFA Voysey. Ongoing
restoration, walled garden, yew
hedges, spring bulbs, natural wild
flower meadows, ponds (unfenced),
bog garden, gravel and grass walks.
Some steep and uneven paths.
🐕 ☕

37 ◆ **THE PICTON GARDEN**
Old Court Nurseries, Colwall
WR13 6QE. Mr & Mrs Paul Picton,
01684 540416,
www.autumnasters.co.uk. *3m W of
Malvern. On B4218 (Walwyn Rd) N of
Colwall Stone. Turn off A449 from
Ledbury or Malvern.* **Adm £3.50, chd
free.** Fris to Suns in Aug, 2.30-5;
daily 1 Sept to 10 Oct 2-5. For NGS:
Suns 2 Aug to 30 Aug (2.30-5); Sun
13, Sat 19, Tue 29 Sept; Sat 17, Sun
18 Oct (2-5).
1¹/₂ acres W of Malvern Hills. A myriad
of late summer perennials in Aug. In
Sept and Oct huge, colourful borders
display The National Collection of
Michaelmas daisies; backed by
autumn colouring trees and shrubs.
Many unusual plants to be seen, incl
bamboos, ferns and acers. Raised
beds, silver garden and centenary
garden. Featured in 'The English
Garden'.
🐕 ✿ NCCPG

38 THE RAMBLES

Shelwick, Hereford HR1 3AL. Shirley & Joe Fleming, 01432 357056, joe.eff@virgin.net. *E of Hereford at A4103/A465 r'about take Sutton St Nicholas/Bodenham rd, after 1m under railway bridge turn L signed Shelwick, under another bridge. The Rambles is behind 1st house on L.* **Adm £3, chd free. Tues 12 May to 15 Sept (2-5). Visitors also welcome by appt, May to Sept, garden clubs welcome.**
Plantaholics 1/3-acre garden packed with a wide range of interesting plants, colour themed borders, large covered shade area, and water feature. Many pots with tender plants.

39 NEW RHODDS FARM

Lyonshall HR5 3LW. Richard & Cary Goode. *1m E of Kington. From A44 take small turning S just E of Penrhos Hotel, 1m E of Kington. Continue 1m garden straight ahead.* Home-made teas. **Adm £3, chd £1. Suns 3 May; 19 July (2-6).**
The garden began in 2004 and is still a work in progress. The site is challenging with difficult soil and steep banks rising to overhanging woodland, incls mixed borders, courtyard, gravel garden, several ponds, wild flower meadow and woodland walks with wonderful bluebells in spring. Plant interest throughout the yr.

40 SHIELDBROOK

Kings Caple HR1 4UB. Sue & Oliver Sharp, 01432 840670, www.shieldbrooksculpturegarden.co.uk. *7m S of Hereford. Take A49 from Hereford or Ross. Take 1st rd signed to Hoarwithy (there are 3). Go past New Harp PH on R, then next R over R Wye. Up the hill take 2nd R into Kings Caple, down hill over Xrds then Shieldbrook 1/2 m on L.* Home-made teas. **Adm £4, chd free. Sat 13, Sun 14 June (2-5). Visitors also welcome by appt.**
1-acre country garden planted for yr-round interest featuring grasses, shrubs and perennials. Rose garden and orchard, healing garden with pond and rockery. Sculpture garden of local sculptor's work is of special interest, many on display. Stream runs through the garden and there are many secret corners. Garden managed organically. Featured in 'Hereford Times'. Some gravel.

41 SHUCKNALL COURT

Hereford HR1 4BH. Mr & Mrs Henry Moore, 01432 850230, cessa.moore@btconnect.com. *5m E of Hereford. On A4103, signed (southerly) Weston Beggard.* **Adm £5, chd free. Visitors welcome by appt.**
Tree peonies in May. Large collection of species, old-fashioned and shrub roses. Mixed borders in old walled farmhouse garden. Wild garden, small stream garden, vegetables and fruit. Featured in 'Herefordshire Life'. Partial wheelchair access.

42 ◆ STAUNTON PARK

Staunton-on-Arrow HR6 9LE. Susan Fode, 01544 388556, www.stauntonpark.co.uk. *3m N of Pembridge. From Pembridge (on A44) take rd signed Presteigne, Shobdon. After 3m look out for red phone box on R. Staunton Park is 150yds on L. Do not go to Staunton-on-Arrow.* **Adm £3, chd free. Thurs only 14 May to Thur 10 Sept (11-5).**
10-acre garden and grounds incl drive with stately wellingtonias, rose garden, separate kitchen garden, large, very colourful mixed borders and Victorian rock garden, lake and lakeside walk with views. Specimen trees incl mature monkey puzzle, gigantic liriodendron, *Davidia involucrata, Ginkgo bilobas* and several ancient oaks.

43 TARRINGTON COURT

Tarrington HR1 4EX. Mr & Mrs K C Jago, 01432 890632, catherine@cirenenergy.com, www.simplesite.com/tarringtoncourt. *7m W of Ledbury, 7m E of Hereford. Tarrington Village on A438. Follow signs from Tarrington Arms. Park as directed at community hall. Only disabled parking at house.* **Adm £5, chd free. Evening Opening** wine, Sat 6 June (5.30-8.30). **Visitors also welcome by appt, groups of 15+.**
C16 timber framed farmhouse (not open), set in 5-acre mature garden. Newly designed features incl Venetian black and white garden, Mediterranean, cutting, hot, courtyard, Gothic rose and kitchen gardens. Arboretum, turf mounds, orangery, woodland, orchard and vineyard, unusual statuary and design features. For 2009: Physic garden and folly, or Japanese tea garden and cherry orchard. Ledbury Choral Society. Wine and canapes in the Cider House. Children's quiz. Featured in 'Daily Telegraph' & on BBC Gardeners World, BBC Hereford & Worcester. Slight slope in places.

TAWRYN
See Powys.

44 UPPER TAN HOUSE

Stansbatch HR6 9LJ. James & Caroline Weymouth, 01544 260574, james.weymouth@btinternet.com, www.uppertanhouse.com. *4m W of Pembridge. Off A44 in Pembridge, signed Shobdon & Presteigne.* Home-made teas. **Adm £3, chd free. Sun 7,**

Ponds to sit by, space to relax and reflect taking in the views . . .

Mon 8 June (2-5). **Visitors also welcome by appt.**
S-facing garden sloping down to Stansbatch brook in idyllic spot. Deep herbaceous borders with informal and unusual planting, pond and bog garden, informal vegetable garden framed by yew hedges and espaliered pears. Reed beds, wild flower meadow with orchids in June. Good autumn colour and diverse wildlife.

✈ ⊛ ☕ ☎

45 NEW THE VINE
Tarrington HR1 4EX. Mr & Mrs R J Price. *Between Hereford & Ledbury on A438. Follow signs for Tarrington Arms on A438. Park as directed. Disabled parkng only at house.* Home-made teas at Lady Emily Community Hall, a stones throw away from the garden. **Adm £4, chd free. Sat 20 June (2-5, last entry 4).**
Mature, traditional garden in peaceful setting with stunning views of the surrounding countryside. Consisting of various rooms with mixed and herbaceous borders. Secret garden in blue/yellow/white, croquet lawn with C18 summer house, temple garden with ponds, herb and nosegay garden, vegetable/cutting/soft fruit garden around greenhouse on the paddock. Live music by local brass band. Gentle slopes and gravel paths.

♿ ✖ ☕

An abundance of sweetly scented old fashioned roses . . .

THE WALLED GARDEN
See Powys.

46 WESTON HALL
Weston-under-Penyard HR9 7NS. Mr P & Miss L Aldrich-Blake, 01989 562597. *1m E of Ross-on-Wye. On A40 towards Gloucester. Parking in field with entrance off lane ¼ m before house.* **Adm £4, chd free. Sun 6 Sept (11-5). Visitors also welcome by appt.**
6 acres surrounding Elizabethan house (not open). Large walled garden with herbaceous borders, vegetables and fruit, overlooked by Millennium folly. Lawns with both mature and recently planted trees, shrubs with many unusual varieties. Ornamental ponds and small lake. Traditional country house garden, but evolving after 4 generations in the family.

♿ ✖ ⊛ ☕ ☎

47 WESTON MEWS
Weston-under-Penyard HR9 7NZ. Ann Rothwell & John Hercock, 01989 563823. *Going towards Gloucester on A40, continue approx 100yds past the Weston Cross PH and turn R into grey brick-paved courtyard.* Light refreshments & teas. **Adm £3, chd free. Sat 13 June (11-5). Visitors also welcome by appt.**
Walled ex-kitchen garden divided by yew and box hedges. Traditional in style and planting with large herbaceous beds and borders at different levels. Broad range of plants incl roses. Enclosed garden with sundial. Large vine house.

♿ ✖ ☕ ☎

48 WHITFIELD
Wormbridge HR2 9BA. Mr & Mrs Edward Clive, 01981 570202, tboyd@globalnet.co.uk. *8m SW of Hereford. On A465 Hereford to Abergavenny rd.* Home-made teas. **Adm £3.50, chd free (share to Friends of Dore Abbey). Suns 29 Mar; 10 May (2-5). Visitors also welcome by appt.**
Parkland, wild flowers, ponds, walled garden, many flowering magnolias (species and hybrids), 1780 ginkgo tree, 1½ m woodland walk with 1851 redwood grove. Picnic parties welcome.

⊛ ☕ ☎

49 NEW WILTON CASTLE ON THE WYE
Ross on Wye HR9 6AD. Alan & Suzie Parslow, www.wiltoncastle.co.uk. *½ m NW of Ross on River Wye. Take the Ross rd at Wilton r'about on M50/A40/A449 trunk rd. Immed turn L opp petrol garage, down lane. Castle entrance behind Castle Lodge Hotel.* Home-made teas. **Adm £3.50, chd free. Suns 15 Mar; 3 May; 7 June; 5 July; 2 Aug (11-5).**
The romantic ruins of a restored C12 castle and C16 manor house (not open) form the perfect backdrop for herbaceous borders, roses entwined around mullion windows, an abundance of sweetly scented old fashioned roses, gravel gardens and shrubberies. The 2 acre gardens are surrounded by a dry moat which leads down to the river Wye with swans, ducks, kingfishers etc. The restored castle will be open for viewing. No access to dry moat area, a few steps into towers, disabled WC.

♿ ✖ ⊛ ☕

50 NEW WOLFERLOW HOUSE
Wolferlow HR7 4QA. Stuart & Jill Smith. *5m N of Bromyard. Off B4203 or B4214.* Home-made teas. **Adm £3, chd free. Sat 27, Sun 28 June; Sat 29 Aug (11-5).**
Surrounded by farmland this former Victorian Rectory is set within formal and informal gardens with planting to attract wildlife. Walks through the old orchard (now being newly planted) and ponds to sit by, space to relax and reflect taking in the views of borrowed landscape. Gravel paths.

♿ ✖ ⊛ ☕

51 WOODVIEW
Great Doward, Whitchurch HR9 6DZ. Janet & Clive Townsend, 01600 890477, clive.townsend5@homecall.co.uk. *6m SW of Ross-on-Wye, 4m NE of Monmouth. A40 Ross/Monmouth. At Whitchurch follow signs to Symonds Yat West. Then signs to Dowards Park Campsite. Take uneven forest track, 1st L, garden 2nd on L. Parking at house.* Light refreshments & teas. **Adm £3, chd free. Suns 12, 19 July (2-5). Visitors also welcome by appt June**

to Aug, groups max 40 (no access for coaches).
Formal and informal gardens approx 2 acres in woodland setting. Herbaceous borders, hosta collection, mature trees, shrubs and seasonal bedding. Gently sloping lawns. Statuary and found sculpture, local limestone, rockwork and pools. Woodland garden, wild flower meadow and indigenous orchids. Croquet, clock golf and garden games. Featured in local press & on BBC Hereford & Worcester.

Many flowering magnolias (species and hybrids), 1780 ginkgo tree, 1$\frac{1}{2}$ m woodland walk with 1851 redwood grove . . .

Herefordshire County Volunteers

County Organiser
Rowena Gale, Bachefield House, Kimbolton, Leominster HR6 0EP, 01568 61585, rowena@jimgale.eclipse.co.uk

County Treasurer
Mr Michael Robins, Newsholme, 77 Bridge Street, Ledbury HR8 2AN, 01531 632232

Publicity
Mrs Sue Evans, The Nest, Moreton, Eye, nr Leominster HR6 0DP, 01568 614501, sue@thenest99.freeserve.co.uk

Assistant County Organisers
Dr J A F Evans, 7 St Margaret's Road, Hereford HR1 1TS, 01432 273000, antliz@talktalk.net
Sue Londesborough Brighton House, St Margarets, Vowchurch HR2 0JU, 01981 510148, susanlondesborough@firenet.uk.net
Mrs Gill Mullin, The White House, Lea, Ross-on-Wye HR9 7LQ, 01989 750593, gill@longorchard.plus.com
Mr Graham Spencer, 4 Nightingale Way, Hereford HR1 2NQ, 01432 267744, gramy.spencer@virgin.net
Penny Usher Old Chapel House, Kimbolton, Leominster HR6 0HF, 01568 611688, pennyusher@totalise.co.uk

HERTFORDSHIRE

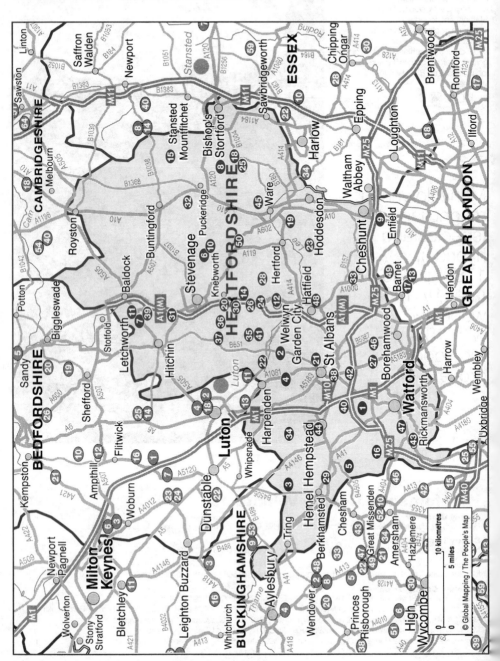

Opening Dates

March

SATURDAY 14
9 Capel Manor Gardens

SUNDAY 15
9 Capel Manor Gardens

SUNDAY 22
46 The Walled Garden

April

SUNDAY 5
37 St Paul's Walden Bury

SUNDAY 19
24 28 Mill Lane

May

SUNDAY 3
1 The Abbots House
29 Patchwork
34 Ragged Hall

SUNDAY 10
2 Amwell Cottage
23 The Manor House

SUNDAY 17
19 Jenningsbury Gardens
21 19 Lancaster Road
49 West Lodge Park

FRIDAY 22
46 The Walled Garden (Evening)

SUNDAY 24
16 Great Sarratt Hall
33 Queenswood School
45 Thundridge Hill House

SUNDAY 31
25 Moor Place
38 Saint Stephens Avenue Gardens
39 Scudamore

June

FRIDAY 5
11 10 Cross Street (Evening)
14 The End House (Day & Evening)

SATURDAY 6
35 2 Ruins Cottage

SUNDAY 7
11 10 Cross Street
13 207 East Barnet Road
14 The End House
15 Furneaux Pelham Hall
30 Plummers Farm
35 2 Ruins Cottage (Evening)

SATURDAY 13
10 Croft Cottage

SUNDAY 14
8 Bromley Hall
10 Croft Cottage
17 13 Greenhill Park

41 Shaw's Corner

MONDAY 15
8 Bromley Hall

SUNDAY 21
3 Ashridge
26 1 Nathans Close
40 Serge Hill Gardens
50 Woodhall Park

FRIDAY 26
46 The Walled Garden (Evening)

SUNDAY 28
6 Benington Lordship
22 Mackerye End Gardens
28 106 Orchard Road
47 Waterdell House

July

SATURDAY 4
32 The Pump House

SUNDAY 5
1 The Abbots House
32 The Pump House

SUNDAY 12
21 19 Lancaster Road
24 28 Mill Lane
42 14 Spooners Drive

WEDNESDAY 15
36 Rustling End Cottage

FRIDAY 17
48 West Garden at Hatfield House

SUNDAY 19
36 Rustling End Cottage

WEDNESDAY 22
36 Rustling End Cottage

THURSDAY 23
43 Stresa (Evening)

FRIDAY 24
4 2 Barlings Road (Evening)
36 Rustling End Cottage (Evening)

SUNDAY 26
4 2 Barlings Road
12 35 Digswell Road
31 The Priory

FRIDAY 31
46 The Walled Garden (Evening)

August

SATURDAY 1
44 9 Tannsfield Drive

SUNDAY 9
44 9 Tannsfield Drive

FRIDAY 14
7 44 Broadwater Avenue (Evening)

SUNDAY 16
5 The Barn
7 44 Broadwater Avenue

SUNDAY 23
29 Patchwork

FRIDAY 28
43 Stresa (Evening)

SUNDAY 30
1 The Abbots House

September

SUNDAY 13
27 45 Oakridge Avenue

October

SUNDAY 4
36 Rustling End Cottage

SUNDAY 11
12 35 Digswell Road

SATURDAY 17
9 Capel Manor Gardens

SUNDAY 18
9 Capel Manor Gardens

SUNDAY 25
49 West Lodge Park

Gardens open to the public

6 Benington Lordship
9 Capel Manor Gardens
18 Hopleys
20 Knebworth House Gardens
37 St Paul's Walden Bury
41 Shaw's Corner
46 The Walled Garden
48 West Garden at Hatfield House

Also open by appointment ☎

1 The Abbots House
8 Bromley Hall
12 35 Digswell Road
13 207 East Barnet Road
27 45 Oakridge Avenue
28 106 Orchard Road
29 Patchwork
43 Stresa
44 9 Tannsfield Drive
45 Thundridge Hill House
47 Waterdell House
49 West Lodge Park

Peaceful
water and bog
gardens . . .

The Gardens

1 THE ABBOTS HOUSE
10 High Street, Abbots Langley
WD5 0AR. Peter & Sue Tomson,
01923 264946,
peter.tomson@btinternet.com. *5m
NW of Watford. Exit J20 on M25. Take
A4251 signed Kings Langley. R at 1st
r'about (Home Park Industrial Estate).
R at T-junction. Follow rd, under
railway bridge and the yellow signs will
become apparent. Free parking in
village car park.* Home-made teas.
**Adm £3.50, chd free (share to
Friends of St Lawrence Church).
Suns 3 May; 5 July; 30 Aug (2-5).
Visitors also welcome by appt.**
1³/4 -acre garden with interesting trees,
shrubs, mixed borders, sunken
garden, pond, wild flower meadow,
conservatory. Exotic garden. A garden
of 'rooms' with different styles and
moods. Many half-hardy plants. Plants
propagated from the garden. Gravel
paths.
  👟 ❀ ☕ ☎

2 AMWELL COTTAGE
Amwell Lane, Wheathampstead
AL4 8EA. Colin & Kate Birss. *¹/2 m S
of Wheathampstead. From St Helens
Church, Wheathampstead turn up
Brewhouse Hill. At top L fork (Amwell
Lane), 300yds down lane, park in field
opp.* Home-made teas. **Adm £3, chd
free. Sun 10 May (2-5).**
Well established garden of approx
2¹/2 acres and C17 cottage (not open).
Large orchard of mature apples, plums
and pear laid out with paths. Stone
seats with views, yew hedges, roses
and woodland pond. Access from
main gravel drive to grass paths.
  ☕

3 ASHRIDGE
Berkhamsted HP4 1NS. Ashridge
(Bonar Law Memorial) Trust,
www.ashridge.org.uk. *3m N of
Berkhamsted. A4251, 1m S of Little
Gaddesden.* Cream teas. **Adm £3.50,
chd free, concessions £2. Sun 21
June (2-6).**
The gardens at Ashridge cover 190
acres and form part of the Grade II*
Registered Landscape of Ashridge
Park. Based on designs by Humphry
Repton in 1813 which were modified
by Jeffry Wyatville, the gardens are
made up of a number of small
gardens, as well as a large lawn area
leading to avenues of trees affording
views out to the old parkland. House
not open. Paths lead to many features

within the formal gardens, areas of
parkland not accessible to
wheelchairs.
  ☕

4 2 BARLINGS ROAD
Harpenden AL5 2AN. Liz & Jim
Machin. *1m S of Harpenden. Take
A1081 S from Harpenden, after 1m
turn R into Beesonend Lane, bear R
into Burywick to T-junction, turn R into
Barlings Rd.* **Adm £2.50, chd free.
Evening Opening wine, Fri 24 July
(5-9); Sun 26 July (2-5).**
Peaceful, mature and secluded. This
compact plantswomen's garden
contains a formal pond surrounded by
borders and island beds packed with
unusual perennials and shrubs.
Colourful courtyard with unusual water
feature plus shaded gold and silver
corner, entered through a honeysuckle
arch, complete the picture.
👟

> Roses with
> clematis and
> honeysuckle,
> wild flower
> meadow and
> pond with small
> orchard . . .

5 THE BARN
Stoney Lane, Bovingdon HP3 0LY.
Richard Daynes & Lorraine Donnelly.
*3m SW of Hemel Hempstead. At lower
end of Bovingdon High St turn into
Church St, Bull PH on corner, car park
60yds on L, short walk to garden.*
Home-made teas. **Adm £3, chd free.
Sun 16 Aug (2-6).**
Medium-sized garden around
converted agricultural building in
16 acres. Garden divided into
rooms; roses along with clematis,
honeysuckle, topiary, water features
and woodland. Wild flower meadow
and pond along with small orchard.
👟 ☕

BARNET GARDENS
See London.

6 ◆ BENINGTON LORDSHIP
nr Stevenage SG2 7BS. Mr & Mrs R
R A Bott, 01438 869668,
www.beningtonlordship.co.uk. *5m E
of Stevenage. In Benington Village,
signs off A602. Next to church.* **Adm
£4, chd under 12yrs free, 12-16yrs
£2. For opening details, please tel or
see website. For NGS: Sun 28 June
(12-6).**
7-acre garden incl historic buildings,
kitchen garden, lakes, roses.
Spectacular herbaceous borders,
unspoilt panoramic views.
👟 ☕

7 44 BROADWATER AVENUE
Letchworth Garden City SG6 3HJ.
Karen & Ian Smith. *¹/2 m SW
Letchworth town centre. A1(M) J9
signed Letchworth. Straight on at 1st
three r'abouts, 4th r'about take 4th exit
then R into Broadwater Ave.* Home-
made teas. **Adm £3, chd free.
Evening Opening wine, Fri 14 Aug
(6-9); Sun 16 Aug (1-5).**
Town garden in the Letchworth Garden
City conservation area that
successfully combines a family garden
with a plantswoman's garden. Out of
the ordinary, unusual herbaceous
plants and shrubs. Attractive front
garden designed for yr-round interest.
☕

8 BROMLEY HALL
Standon, Ware SG11 1NY. Julian &
Edwina Robarts, 01279 842422,
edwina.robarts@btinternet.com,
www.bromley-hall.co.uk. *6m W of
Bishop's Stortford. On Standon to
Much Hadham rd.* Home-made teas
(Sun), Tea (Mon). **Adm £4, chd free.
Sun 14 (2-5.30), Mon 15 June (11-5).
Visitors also welcome by appt for
groups of 10+.**
Mature 4¹/2 -acre garden surrounding
C16 farmhouse (not open). It is both an
architectural and a plantsman's garden
with an immaculate kitchen garden.
Good use has been made of walls and
hedges to shelter borders filled with a
mixture of shrubs, foliage plants and
unusual perennials. Mown paths
through rough grass reveal glimpses of
countryside beyond. Petanque court.
Access over gravel.
  👟 ❀ ☕ ☎

9 ◆ CAPEL MANOR GARDENS
Bullsmoor Lane, Enfield, Middlesex
EN1 4RQ. Capel Manor Charitable
Corporation, 08456 122122,
www.capelmanorgardens.co.uk. *2m
from Cheshunt. 3 mins from junction

M25/A10. **Adm £6, chd £3, concessions £5. For other dates please tel or see website. For NGS: Sats, Suns 14, 15 Mar; 17, 18 Oct (10-6).**
30 acres of historical and modern theme gardens, Japanese garden, large Italian style maze, rock and water features. Walled garden with rose collection and woodland walks. Also trial gardens run by 'Gardening Which?' together with small model gardens, incl new front gardens designed to inspire and provide ideas. National Collection of Sarcococca.

   NCCPG

Letchworth Garden City exhibition cottage of 1905 . . .

10 CROFT COTTAGE
9 Church Green, Benington SG2 7LH. Richard Arnold-Roberts & Julie Haire. *4m E of Stevenage. A1M J7. A602 Hertford, L at 6th r'bout, down short hill to mini r'about, straight across (Broadwater Lane). Through Aston to Xrds (1½ m). Straight across. Cottage on R after 1½ m opp church.* **Adm £3, chd free. Sat 13, Sun 14 June (1-5).**
C16 cottage (not open) with small but extensively planted garden divided by hedges and tall shrubs into several different areas. Many varigated and colourful-leafed shrubs and perennials. Mixed border devoted to shades of blue, pink and white. Euphorbia and hosta collection. Small pool with gold fish, water feature and seat. Rose and clematis shaded arbour with view over fields. Small Japanese maple garden with pool, chairs and table overlooking C13 church. Gravel paths.

11 NEW 10 CROSS STREET
Letchworth Garden City SG6 4UD. Renata Hume, www.cyclamengardens.com. *nr town centre. From A1(M) J9 signed Letchworth, across 2 r'abouts, R at 3rd, across next 3 r'abouts L into Nevells Rd, 1st R into Cross St.* **Adm £2.50, chd free. Evening Opening** wine, **Fri 5 June (6-9). Sun 7 June (12-5).**

A small front cottage garden leads to a Letchworth Garden City exhibition cottage of 1905. The back garden is informally laid out within a coherent design dictated by the gently sloping plot. Trees, shrubs, grasses and herbaceous perennials combine to create interest in the different areas of the garden. Lily pond, small pond for wildlife, well-stocked greenhouse and apple walk with a selection of old varieties, all held in balance by 3 formal lawns.

12 35 DIGSWELL ROAD
Welwyn Garden City AL8 7PB. Adrian & Clare de Baat, 01707 324074, adrian.debaat@ntlworld.com. *½ m N of Welwyn Garden City centre. From the Campus r'about in centre of City take N exit just past public library into Digswell Rd. Over the White Bridge, 200yds on L.* Home-made teas (July). **Adm £3, chd free. Suns 26 July (2-5.30); 11 Oct (2-5). Visitors also welcome by appt June to Oct.**
Mature trees and high hedges surround town garden of ⅓ acre. Piet Oudolf-inspired naturalistic borders with tall perennials and grasses surround lawn. Beyond, grass paths link island beds and contemporary planting gives way to the exotic and succulent border, leading finally to a jungle garden with unusual tender plants. Ornamental grasses and seedheads particular feature in Oct. Plants for sale (July). Featured on BBC Open Gardens. Grass paths, gentle slopes.

13 207 EAST BARNET ROAD
New Barnet EN4 8QS. Margaret Chadwick, 020 8440 0377, magg1ee@hotmail.com. *M25 J24 then A111 to Cockfosters. Underground stations High Barnet or Cockfosters. On bus route 184, 307 & 326.* Home-made teas. **Adm £2, chd free. Sun 7 June (2-5). Visitors also welcome by appt.**
Delightful example of minute courtyard garden 25ft x 30ft. High fences are covered with clematis, honeysuckle and passion flowers, roses and vines scramble over an arch above a seat. Small pond with goldfish and water plants. Many interesting and unusual plants, mainly in pots.

14 THE END HOUSE
15 Hangmans Lane, Welwyn AL6 0TJ. Sarah Marsh. *2m NE of Welwyn. A1 J6 over 2 r'abouts turn R at next r'about onto B197 for approx 1½ m towards Knebworth. Turn L into Cannonfield Rd after 1m car park on L. Short woodland walk to garden. Disabled parking only at garden.* Home-made teas & wine. **Adm £3, chd free. Late afternoon & Evening Opening** Fri 5 June (4-9); **Sun 7 June (2-6).**
Plantswoman's peaceful ½ acre woodland garden which incls jungle walk, tropical planting, bog and dell garden, pond and various water features. Archway to secret garden. Designer bantams and Moroccan treehouse. Interesting and inspirational. Featured on BBC2 Open Gardens.

15 FURNEAUX PELHAM HALL
Buntingford SG9 0LB. Mr & Mrs A Brunner. *From A10 at Puckeridge take B1368. Turn R through Braughing village. Approx 3m, turn L Furneux Pelham. From A120 Little Hadham, take Albury rd. Approx 3m, turn L Furneux Pelham. Car parking in field by Hall Gardens.* Home-made teas. **Adm £3.50, chd free. Sun 7 June (2-6).**
Lovely C16 hall (not open), once lived in by Lord Monteagle of Guy Fawkes fame. Walled herbaceous garden; lake with ornamental waterfowl, islands and bridges. Peaceful water and bog gardens. Vegetable garden and greenhouses.

16 GREAT SARRATT HALL
Sarratt, Rickmansworth WD3 4PD. Mr H M Neal. *5m N of Rickmansworth. From Watford N via A41 (or M1 J5) to Kings Langley; left (W) to Sarratt; garden is 1st on R after village sign.* Home-made cream teas. **Adm £4, chd free (share to The Courtauld Institute of Art). Sun 24 May (2-6).**
4 acres. Herbaceous and mixed shrub borders; pond, moisture-loving plants and trees; walled kitchen garden; rhododendrons, magnolias, camellias; new planting of specialist conifers and rare trees.

17 13 GREENHILL PARK
Barnet EN5 1HQ. Sally & Andy Fry. *1m S of High Barnet. 1m S of High Barnet tube stn. Take 1st L after Odeon Cinema, Weaver PH on corner. Buses: 34, 234, 263, 326, 84.* Home-

made teas. **Adm £3, chd free. Sun 14 June (2-6).**
An oasis in suburbia. Approx 1/4 -acre. Colourful herbaceous borders, wildlife pond, summer house, shady fern garden. Series of rustic arches link main garden to path through wildlife-friendly secret garden, incorporating tree fern collection, acers, stumpery and architectural plants. New this year Victorian plant house and hidden courtyard vegetable garden. A garden of many parts with a range of planting ideas to acknowledge differing situations.

18 ◆ **HOPLEYS**
High Street, Much Hadham SG10 6BU. Aubrey & Jan Barker, 01279 842509, www.hopleys.co.uk. *5m W of Bishop's Stortford. On B1004. M11 (J8) 7m or A10 (Puckeridge) 5m via A120. 50yds N of Bull PH in centre of Much Hadham.* **Donations. Open every Mon, Wed to Sat (9-5), Sun (2-5) Mar to Oct.**
4 acres of constantly developing garden; trees, shrubs, herbaceous and grasses; island beds with mixed planting in parkland setting; pond.

THE HYDE WALLED GARDEN
See Bedfordshire.

Group opening

19 **JENNINGSBURY GARDENS**
Hertford Heath SG13 7NS. *1m SE of Hertford towards Hertford Heath. From A414 between A10 & Hertford take B1197, to Hertford Heath & Haileybury College, (Foxholes r'about, Lancaster Mercedes garage) 1/2 m on RH-side at post and rail fencing.* Home-made teas. **Combined adm £4.50, chd free. Sun 17 May (2-5.30).**

FAR END BARN
4 Jenningsbury Court. Mr & Mrs Richard Conyers
S-facing family garden running down to moat from rear of barn conversion.

JENNINGSBURY
Hertford Heath. Barry & Gail Fox
Approx 3 acres of wild flower meadow designed by Julie Toll; moat, ponds and borders created to attract wildlife. Approx 1 acre formal, mixed planting surrounds C17 farmhouse (not open).

---

20 ◆ **KNEBWORTH HOUSE GARDENS**
Knebworth SG3 6PY. The Hon Henry Lytton Cobbold, 01438 812661, www.knebworthhouse.com. *28m N of London. Direct access from A1(M) J7 at Stevenage. Stn, Stevenage 3m.* **For opening details & admission, please tel or see website.**
Historic home of Bulwer Lytton, Victorian novelist and statesman. Knebworth's magnificent gardens were laid out by Lutyens in 1910. Lutyens' pollarded lime avenues, Gertrude Jekyll's herb garden, the restored maze, yew hedges, roses and herbaceous borders are key features of the formal gardens with peaceful woodland walks beyond. Gold garden, green garden, brick garden, walled vegetable and herb garden.

21 **NEW** **19 LANCASTER ROAD**
St Albans AL1 4EP. Pauline & Michael Foers. *1/2 m N of St Albans city centre. From city centre take A1081 towards Harpenden then B651 towards Sandridge, after 100yds turn R into Sand Pit Lane, take 5th on L into Lancaster Road.* Home-made teas. **Adm £2.50, chd free. Suns 17 May; 12 July (2-5).**
This medium-sized well-stocked garden has unusual trees, shrubs and herbaceous perennials. Displaying the owners' interest in coloured foliage. An all-yr round, plantsperson's garden. Small terrace with pots.

Ancient
900 year old
John of Gaunt
oak . . .

Group opening

22 **MACKERYE END GARDENS**
Harpenden AL5 5DR. *1m E of Harpenden. A1 J4, follow signs Wheathampstead then Luton. Gardens on R. M1 J10 follow Lower Luton Rd (B653) to Cherry Tree Restaurant. Turn L follow signs to Mackerye End.* Teas. **Combined adm £5, chd free. Sun 28 June (2-5).**
Small hamlet between Batford and Porters End.

EIGHTACRE
Mr & Mrs S Cutmore
2-acre garden incl shrub and herbaceous beds, wildlife pond, raised vegetable beds, greenhouse and orchards.

HOLLYBUSH COTTAGE
Mr & Mrs Prosser
Well established cottage garden around this listed house (not open).

MACKERYE END FARM
Mr & Mrs A Clark
3-acre garden in grounds of restored, listed C16 farmhouse (not open) with extensive new mixed borders, yew hedge and large pond, rose garden and fountain. Rear borders lead to old mulberry tree, small arboretum, laurels, orchard with various fruit trees and well-house.

MACKERYE END HOUSE
Mr & Mrs G Penn
1550 Grade 1 manor house (not open) set in 11 acres of gardens and park. Front garden set in framework of formal yew hedges with long border. Victorian walled garden now divided into smaller sections; path maze; cutting garden; quiet garden. W garden enclosed by pergola walk of old English roses and vines. Plants for sale.

23 **NEW** **THE MANOR HOUSE**
Bayford SG13 8PU. Mr & Mrs David Latham. *3m SW of Hertford, off B158.* Home-made teas. **Adm £4, chd free. Sun 10 May (2-5).**
Large old established garden. Natural ornamental lake, many specimen trees and unusual shrubs. Walled garden, spring bulbs. Ancient 900yr old John of Gaunt oak. Gravel paths.

24 NEW 28 MILL LANE

Welwyn AL6 9ET. Stan & Cindy Andrews. *Centre of Welwyn. From A1(M) J6 follow signs to Welwyn (NOT Welwyn Garden City). Parking in Lockley's Drive car park. Garden next to The White Horse PH.* **Adm £2.50, chd free. Suns 19 Apr; 12 July (12-5.30).** Courtyard style plantsman and artists paved garden. Mature magnolia, decorative box, clematis, hostas, roses, small woodland area with hellebores and spring bulbs, ferns, shrubs, containers and hanging baskets. A great little garden. Artist's studio open on request.

25 MOOR PLACE

Much Hadham SG10 6AA. Mr & Mrs B M Norman. *5m W of Bishop's Stortford. Entrance either at war memorial or at Hadham Cross.* Home-made teas. **Adm £4, chd free. Sun 31 May (2-5.30).** 2 C18 walled gardens. Herbaceous borders. Large area of shrubbery, lawns, hedges and trees. 2 ponds. Approx 10 acres.

&. ✗ ❀ ☕

26 NEW 1 NATHANS CLOSE

Welwyn AL6 9QB. Margaret & Roger Bardell. *A1(M) J6, over 2 r'abouts, turn L onto B656 towards Codicote. Take 1st R, then 3rd R. Parking in Blakes Way.* Home-made teas. **Adm £3, chd free. Sun 21 June (2-6).** Constantly evolving, plant enthusiast's garden with island beds, densely-planted borders, pond and gravel areas. Much wildlife interest amid many unusual plants. Enjoy also walk around adjoining Danesbury Nature Reserve with lovely views over local countryside!

✗ ☕

Wildlife interest amid many unusual plants . . .

27 45 OAKRIDGE AVENUE

Radlett WD7 8EW. Leonora & Edgar Vaughan, 01923 854650. *1m N of central Radlett. Off A5183, Watling St. From S, through Radlett Village last turning on L.* Cream teas. **Adm £3, chd free (share to National Council Conservation Plants & Gardens). Sun 13 Sept (2-6).** Visitors also welcome by appt Sat afternoons 3-5. No coaches. Tranquil country garden on the edge of a working farm. Emphasis on late summer colour and wide range of choice planting. Small pond and vegetable patch. Unusual plants for sale all home grown.

&. ✗ ❀ ☕ ☎

28 106 ORCHARD ROAD

Tewin AL6 0LZ. Linda Adams, 01438 798147, alannio@btinternet.com, www.tewinvillage.co.uk. *3m N of Welwyn Garden City. Take B1000 between Hertford & Welwyn Garden City signed Tewin. In village stay on L past the Rose & Crown PH on to Upper Green Road towards Burnham Green. Pass Plume of Feathers PH. Tewin Orchard 200yds on L. Park in field opp.* Home-made teas. **Adm £3.50, chd free. Sun 28 June (2-6).** Visitors also welcome by appt May to Sept incl. Spacious garden behind listed modern movement house (not open). Elements of 1935 garden - lawns, lily pond, topiary, maze, colourful beds and borders. Productive fruit and vegetable cage. Orchard part of the Hertfordshire Millennium orchard. Unusual trees and shrubs. Peaceful country setting and beautiful views. Front garden features rabbit-resistant plants. Light Years' Dance group from Hertford will make guest appearances.

&. ❀ ☕ ☎

29 PATCHWORK

22 Hall Park Gate, Berkhamsted HP4 2NJ. Jean & Peter Block, 01442 864731. *3m W of Hemel Hempstead. Entering E side of Berkhamsted on A4251, turn L 200yds after 40mph sign.* Light refreshments & teas. **Adm £2.50, chd free. Suns 3 May; 23 Aug (2-5).** Visitors also welcome by appt, March to Oct. 1/4 -acre garden with lots of yr-round colour, interest and perfume, particularly on opening days. Sloping site with background of colourful trees, rockeries, two small ponds, patios, shrubs and trees, spring bulbs, herbaceous border, roses, bedding,

fuchsias, dahlias, patio pots and tubs galore and hanging baskets. Seating and cover from the elements.

❀ ☕ ☎

30 PLUMMERS FARM

Sally Deards Lane, nr Welwyn AL6 9UE. Mrs Helena Hodgins. *1m N of Welwyn. On B656 turn R signed Rabley Heath & Potters Heath follow lane for 1m. Turn L into Sally Deards Lane, Plummers Farm on R approx 1/4 m.* Wine. **Adm £3, chd free. Sun 7 June (2-6).** Large country garden, beautifully maintained with large open sunny borders, planted in the contemporary style, aromatic garden and shady mixed borders. Oak pergola planted with wisteria and late flowering clematis viticella bissects the garden. New walled vegetable garden 2009 and small wild flower meadow establishing. Gravel path under pergola.

&. ✗ ❀

31 THE PRIORY

Little Wymondley SG4 7HD. John & Ann Hope. *1m W of Stevenage. A1(M) J8, exit to Little Wymondley, then 1st R Priory Lane. Garden approx 1/2 m on R.* Light refreshments & cream teas. **Adm £3.50, chd free. Sun 26 July (11-5).** C16 priory (not open) surrounded by newly planted 2 acre garden within the confines of the moat, part of which remains filled. 4 acres parkland with many interesting new trees. Teas in magnificent tythe barn overlooking moat and bog garden. Formal kitchen garden. Colourful borders filled with half hardy annuals and herbaceous plants.

&. ✗ ☕

32 THE PUMP HOUSE

Coles Park, Westmill SG9 9LT. Lord & Lady Carter of Coles. *3m S of Buntingford. Off A10, leave Westmill heading for Dane End & follow rd for approx 1m. Park on L, then drive in front of lodge through gate posts for Coles Park.* Home-made teas. **Adm £4, chd free. Sat 4, Sun 5 July (2-6).** Part of the landscaped park and pleasure gardens for Coles Park (now demolished). The gardens incl lavender walk, double herbaceous border and fine collection of old cedars. Extensive lawns and splendid views over parkland. Gravel paths and gravel access to garden.

&. ✗ ❀ ☕

33 QUEENSWOOD SCHOOL

Shepherds Way, Brookmans Park, Hatfield AL9 6NS. *3m N of Potters Bar. From S: M25 J24 signed Potters Bar. In 1/2 m at lights turn R onto A1000 signed Hatfield. In 2m turn R onto B157. School is 1/2 m on R. From N: A1000 from Hatfield. In 5m turn L onto B157.* Light refreshments & teas. **Adm £3, chd £1.50. Sun 24 May (11-6).** 120 acres of informal gardens and woodlands. Rhododendrons, fine specimen trees, shrubs and herbaceous borders. Glasshouses. Fine views to Chiltern Hills. Picnic area. Some gravel paths.

 ఈ ✗ ⊕ ☕

34 RAGGED HALL

Gaddesden Row, nr Hemel Hempstead HP2 6HJ. Mr & Mrs Anthony Vincent. *4m N of Hemel Hempstead. Take A4146 to Water End. Turn R up hill for 2m, turn R at T-junction. House is 3rd L past Chequers PH.* Teas. **Adm £3.50, chd free. Sun 3 May (2-5.30).** Garden of 1 1/2 acres. Lovely spring garden. Stunning mixed borders. Some unusual plants. Pond garden and cutting garden. Potager with vegetables and flowers. Tulips in May. Featured in Saturday FT (potager).

 ఈ ✗ ⊕ ☕

RECTORY FARM HOUSE
See Cambridgeshire.

ROSE COTTAGE
See Buckinghamshire.

35 NEW 2 RUINS COTTAGE

Ayot St Lawrence AL6 9BU. Sally Trendell. *4m S of Welwyn. A1(M) J6 follow signs to Welwyn, Codicote (B656) then Ayot St Lawrence (Shaws Corner NT).* Home-made teas. **Adm £3, chd free (share to The Ayot St Lawrene Old Church Preservation Trust). Sat 6 June (12-5). Afternoon & Early Evening Opening** wine, **Sun 7 June (4-7).** Nestling adjacent to C12 church ruins this is a cottage garden with an eccentric twist. Incorporating many unusual reclaimed architectural pieces and featuring a stunning tree deck straight 'Out of Africa' with magnificent pastoral views towards the Palladian Church. Recline in an antique day bed amidst tree ferns. Imaginative and inspirational. Ayot St Lawrence

35th annual Art Show in nearby Pallidian Church. Winner - Britains Most Imaginative Sensory Garden by Response Charity as Featured in Financial Times. Wheelchair access to lower levels only, gravel paths.

 ఈ ✗ ☕

36 RUSTLING END COTTAGE

Rustling End, nr Codicote SG4 8TD. Julie & Tim Wise, 01438 821509, juliewise@f2s.com, www.rustlingend.com. *1m N of Codicote. From B656 turn L into '3 Houses Lane' then R to Rustling End. House is 2nd on L.* **Adm £3.50, chd free. Weds, Suns 15, 19, 22 July; 4 Oct (12-5). Evening Opening** wine, Fri 24 July (5-9). Attractive C18 cottage (not open) surrounded by fields and woodland. Meander through our wild flower meadow to a romantic cottage garden with contemporary planting. N-facing shady borders behind crinkly crankly hedges feature a softly shaped box parterre. Topiary hedges and reflecting pool emphasise the simple space of the French garden; late flowering deep mixed borders and planting throughout the garden emphasising texture and colour. Winner of NGS Gold Award on Channel 5's I Own Britains Best Home & Garden.

 ✗ ⊕

Recline in an antique day bed amidst tree ferns . . .

37 ◆ ST PAUL'S WALDEN BURY

Hitchin SG4 8BP. Simon & Caroline Bowes Lyon, 01438 871218, spw@boweslyon.demon.co.uk. *5m S of Hitchin. On B651; 1/2 m N of Whitwell.* **Adm £3.50, chd 50p, concessions £3. Suns 26 April; 17 May. By appt adm £6. For NGS: Sun 5 Apr (2-7).** Formal woodland garden, covering 60 acres, laid out 1730. Grade 1 listed. Long rides lined with clipped beech hedges lead to temples, statues, lake, ponds, and outdoor theatre. Seasonal displays of snowdrops, daffodils, cowslips, irises, magnolias, rhododendrons, and lilies. Wild flower areas. Childhood home of the late Queen Mother.

 ఈ ☕

Group opening

38 NEW SAINT STEPHENS AVENUE GARDENS

St Albans AL3 4AD. *1 1/2 m S of St Albans City Centre. From A414/M10 r'about, take A5183 (Watling St). At double mini-r'about by St Stephens's Church/King Harry PH take B4630 Watford Rd. St Stephens Ave is 1st R after 400ydsl.* **Combined adm £3, chd free. Sun 31 May (2-6).** Two gardens of similar size and aspect, developed in totally different waysl.

 ✗ ⊕ ☕

NEW 30 ST STEPHENS AVENUE
Carol & Roger Harlow
Gravel front garden with planting tolerant of dry conditions. The back garden is divided into sections by clipped box to provide a formal framework for herbaceous planting, irises, geraniums, alliums, tulips. A continuously developing gardenl.

NEW 20 STEPHENS AVENUE
Heather & Peter Osborne
175ft x 40ft garden planted for yr round colour and fragrance. Winding paths lead through mixed borders with unusual perennials. Wildlife pond, shade and 'hot' beds. Patio containers, conservatory, climbers on fences and arches.

39 NEW SCUDAMORE

1 Baldock Road, Letchworth Garden City SG6 3LB. Michael & Sheryl Hann. *1m S of Letchworth Garden City centre. A1(M) J9 signed to Letchworth on A505. At 2nd r'about turn L towards Hitchin, still on A505. After 1m, house on L between Muddy Lane & Letchworth Lane.* Home-made teas. **Adm £3, chd free (share to Garden House Hospice). Sun 31 May (1-5).** 1/3 acre garden surrounding early C17 cottages that were converted and extended in 1920s to form current house (not open). Family garden of mature trees, mixed herbaceous borders with shrubs, pond and stream, wet bed, wild garden and orchard/vegetable area. Many sculptures add interest to the garden. Family quiz.

 ఈ ⊕ ☕

Group opening

⓵ SERGE HILL GARDENS
WD5 0RY. ½ m E of Bedmond.
Home-made teas at Serge Hill.
Combined adm £6, chd free (share to Herts Garden Trust & Tibet Relief Fund). Sun 21 June (2-5).
In Bedmond, turn into Serge Hill Lane by white tin church. Follow signs which will take you down the drive to Serge Hill. From Chiswell Green, take Chiswell Green Lane by the Three Hammers PH. Follow signs to Bedmond. The gardens are ½ m up hill after crossing M1.

THE BARN
Tom Stuart-Smith & family
2 contrasting areas, enclosed courtyard, recently redesigned with paved area and above ground tanks of water, more open area laid out within a formal framework comprising wide range of herbaceous perennials and shrubs tolerant of generally dry conditions. Area of naturalistic planting, 5 acre wild flower meadow.

SERGE HILL
Kate Stuart-Smith
Regency house (not open) in parkland setting with fine kitchen garden of ½ acre, large greenhouse with vegetables. Range of unusual wall plants, mixed border, long mixed border, an outside stage and ship.

⓶ ◆ SHAW'S CORNER
Ayot St Lawrence AL6 9BX. The National Trust, 01438 820307, www.nationaltrust.org.uk. 2m NE of Wheathampstead. At SW end of village, approx 2m from B653 (A1 J4 - M1 J10). Signed from B653 (Shaw's Corner/The Ayots). House & garden £5.20, chd £2.60, garden only £2, chd free. Weds to Suns & Bank Hols Mons Mar to Oct. For NGS: Sun 14 June (12-5.30).
Approx 3½ acres with richly planted borders, orchard, small meadow, wooded areas and views over the Hertfordshire countryside. Historical garden, belonging to George Bernard Shaw from 1906 until his death in 1950. Hidden among the trees is the revolving summerhouse where Shaw retreated to write. Music provided Madrigal Singers.

⓸ NEW 14 SPOONERS DRIVE
St Albans AL2 2HL. Richard & Lynne Wilson. 2m S of St Albans. At r'about, S end of M10 take A5183 signed Radlett, 2nd R int Park St Lane & continue into Tippendale Lane, L into Spooners Drive. Home-made teas. Adm £2.50, chd free. Sun 12 July (2-5).
A very interesting town garden of approx 150ft x 30ft. Large patio with numerous tubs and an eclectic mix of planting. Mixed borders with a gravel/tropical area, all with different planting style and constantly evolving to provide yr round interest. Water features incl 3000gal koi pond. Numerous trees all dominated by 130ft lime tree.

⓹ STRESA
126 The Drive, Rickmansworth WD3 4DP. Roger & Patt Trigg, 01923 774293, patt.trigg@tiscali.co.uk. 1m NW of Rickmansworth. From M25 J18 take A404 towards Rickmansworth for 200yds, turn R into The Clump, then 1st L into The Drive. From Rickmansworth take A404 toward Amersham for approx ⅓ m, L into Valley Road, 1st L into The Drive. Light refreshments, wine & nibbles. Adm £5, chd free. Evening Openings Thur 23 July; Fri 28 Aug (6-9.30). Visitors also welcome by appt late May - early Sept, groups of 12+.
Approx ½ acre plantsman's garden. The front garden is a sunny part-gravel area of alpines, Mediterranean plants, borderline-hardiness plants, dogwoods and collection of grasses. Small woodland area leads to rear garden which features continually evolving borders of perennials and shrubs incl hostas, heucheras, euphorbias, rhododendrons and other shade-loving plants. Astilbes and phlox highlight the summer display; conservatory features sub-tropical plants. (Plant-identifying map and list is available for visitors). Large plant sale (July).

⓺ 9 TANNSFIELD DRIVE
Hemel Hempstead HP2 5LG. Peter & Gaynor Barrett, 01442 393508, tterrabjp@ntlworld.com. 1m NE of Hemel Hempstead town centre. Approx 2m W of J8 on M1 take A414 straight over 2 r'abouts. 1st R Leverstock Green Rd into High St Green, L at Ellingham Rd. R at Orchard Close, L at Tannsmore Close leading to Tannsfield Drive. Home-made teas. Adm £2.50, chd free. Sat 1, Sun 9 Aug (11-5). Visitors also welcome by appt, June to Sept only, £3 per person.
A truly interesting small town garden. 50ft x 25ft plot has been imaginatively laid out and creatively planted. Wide variety of grasses, ferns, clematis, fuchsias and ornamental trees feature in densely planted flower beds which incl shade and gravel planting, mini orchard and water features. Featured on 3 Counties Radio.

Water features incl 3000 gallon koi pond. Numerous trees all dominated by 130ft lime tree . . .

⓻ THUNDRIDGE HILL HOUSE
Cold Christmas Lane, Ware SG12 0UE. Mr & Mrs Christopher Melluish, 01920 462500, c.melluish@btopenworld.com. 2m NE of Ware. ¾ m from The Sow & Pigs PH off the A10 down Cold Christmas Lane, crossing new bypass. Cream teas. Adm £3.50, chd free. Sun 24 May (2-5.30). Visitors also welcome by appt anytime.
Well-established garden of approx 2½ acres; good variety of plants, shrubs and roses, attractive hedges. Fast developing 'yellow only' bed is a feature. Several delightful places to sit. Wonderful views in and out of the garden with fine views down to the Rib Valley. A most popular garden to visit. Plant stall.

46 ◆ **THE WALLED GARDEN**
Radlett Lane, Shenley WD7 9DW.
Shenley Park, 01923 852629,
www.shenleypark.co.uk. *5m S of St
Albans. 2m S of M25 J22, 1m E of
Radlett on Radlett to Shenley rd. At the
edge of Shenley Village.* **Adm £3, chd
free. For opening details, please tel
or see website. For NGS: Sun 22
Mar (12-5). Evening Openings** wine,
Fris 22 May; 26 June; 31 July (6-9).
2 acre C16 walled garden. Uniquely
designed ornamental garden with
terracing on 3 levels, and
amphitheatre. Mature planting, ancient
fruit trees, interesting features. Fine
views over adjacent countryside. 3
working Victorian greenhouses with
plants sales.

♿ ✿ ☕

Enjoy the
peaceful west
garden's
scented garden
and fountains.
View the famous
knot garden
adjoining the
Tudor Old
Palace . . .

47 **WATERDELL HOUSE**
Little Green Lane, Croxley Green
WD3 3JH. Mr & Mrs Peter Ward,
01923 772775,
pmjward@btinternet.com. *1 1/2 m NE
of Rickmansworth. M25, J18, direction
Rickmansworth to join A412 towards
Watford. From A412 turn L signed
Sarratt, along Croxley Green, fork R
past Coach & Horses, cross Baldwins
Lane into Little Green Lane, then L at
top.* Home-made teas. **Adm £4, chd
free. Sun 28 June (2-5.30). Visitors
also welcome by appt.**
1 1/2 -acre walled garden
systematically developed over
more than 50yrs by present
owner/gardener: mature and young
trees, topiary holly hedge, herbaceous
borders, modern island beds of
shrubs, old-fashioned roses, grasses
and pond gardens.

♿ 🐕 ✿ ☕ ☎

48 ◆ **WEST GARDEN AT
HATFIELD HOUSE**
AL9 5NQ. The Marquess of
Salisbury, 01707 287010,
www.hatfield-house.co.uk. *Opp
Hatfield Stn, 21m N of London, M25
J23. 7m A1(M) J4 signed off A414 &
A1000.* **Adm £6, chd £4.50. Wed -
Sun & BH Mons; Easter to end Sept.
For NGS: Fri 17 July (11-5.30).**
Dating from C17, the garden at
Hatfield House has evolved into a
gardeners' paradise. Enjoy the
peaceful west garden's scented
garden and fountains. View the famous
knot garden adjoining the Tudor Old
Palace. Delightful formal gardens
planted for yr round colour and
interest.

♿ 🐕 ☕

49 **WEST LODGE PARK**
Cockfosters Road, Hadley Wood
EN4 0PY. Beales Hotels, 020 8216
3904, headoffice@bealeshotels.
co.uk. *2m S of Potters Bar. On A111.
J24 from M25 signed Cockfosters.*
Home-made teas. **Adm £3, chd free.
Suns 17 May (2-5); 25 Oct (1-4).
Visitors also welcome by appt.**
10-acre Beale Arboretum consists of
over 700 varieties of trees and shrubs,
incl National Collection of Hornbeam
cultivars, with a good selection of
conifers, oaks, maples and mountain
ash. A network of paths has been laid
out, and most specimens are labelled.
2 rare Wollemi pines. Limited access
by gravel paths.

♿ 🐕 NCCPG 🏠 ☕ ☎

WIMPOLE HALL
See Cambridgeshire.

50 **WOODHALL PARK**
Watton-at-Stone SG14 3NF. Mr &
Mrs Ralph Abel Smith,
www.woodhallestate.co.uk. *4m N of
Hertford. 6m S of Stevenage, 4m NW
of Ware. Main lodge entrance to
Woodhall Park is on A119, Hertford to
Stevenage, between villages of
Stapleford & Watton-at-Stone.* Home-
made teas. **Adm £4, chd free. Sun 21
June (12-5.30).**
Mature 4-acre garden created out of
surrounding parkland in 1957 when
C18 stable block was converted (not
open). Special features: courtyard,
climbing and shrub roses, herbaceous
and mixed borders, kitchen garden
and areas to sit with unspoilt views.
Grassland park full of mature trees incl
ancient oak and hornbeam, traversed
by river and lake. Visitors welcome to
walk and picnic in the park. Gravel
paths.

♿ 🐕 ✿ ☕ ✿

Hertfordshire County Volunteers

County Organiser
Edwina Robarts, Bromley Hall, Standon, Ware SG11 1NY, 01279 842422, edwina.robarts@btinternet.com

County Treasurer
Virginia Newton, South Barn, Kettle Green, Much Hadham SG10 6AE, 01279 843232, vnewton@southbarn.net

Assistant County Organisers
Michael Belderbos, 6 High Elms, Hatching Green, Harpenden AL5 2JU, 01582 712612
Marigold Harvey, Upwick Hall, Little Hadham, Ware SG11 2JY, 01279 771769, marigold@upwick.com
Gail Fox, Jenningsbury, London Road, Hertford SG13 7NS, 01992 583978, foxgail@fox06.wanadoo.co.uk
Rösli Lancaster, Manor Cottage, Aspenden, Buntingford SG9 9PB, 01763 271711
Jan Marques, Cockhamsted, Braughing, Ware SG11 2NT, 01279 771312, cockhamsted@freeuk.com
Sarah Marsh, 15 Hangmans Lane, Welwyn AL6 0TJ, 01438 714956, sarahkmarsh@hotmail.co.uk
Christopher Melluish, Thundridge Hill House, Cold Christmas Lane, Ware SG12 0UF, 01920 462500, c.melluish@btinternet.com
Karen Smith, 44 Broadwater Avenue, Letchworth Garden City SG6 3HJ, 01462 673133, hertsgardeningangel@googlemail.com
Julie Wise, Rustling End Cottage, Rustling End, Nr Codicote SG4 8TD, 01438 821509, juliewise@f2s.com

Mark your diary with these special events in 2009

EXPLORE SECRET GARDENS DURING CHELSEA & HAMPTON COURT FLOWER SHOW WEEKS

Tue 19 May, Wed 20 May, Thur 21 May, Fri 22 May, Wed 8 July, Thur 9 July
Full day tours from £82 per person, 10% discount for groups
Advance booking required, telephone +44 (0)20 8693 1015 or email j.wookey@btinternet.com
Specially selected gardens in London, Essex, Kent, Hampshire and South Oxfordshire. The tour price includes transport and lunch with wine at a popular restaurant or pub.

HAMPTON COURT PALACE

Thur 2 Apr, Tue 23 June, Thur 25 June, Wed 15 July, Tue 4 Aug, Thur 10 Sept
Evening tours in the company of one of the Palace's specialist tour guides from 6.30 – 8pm
Tickets £6 per person. Advance booking required, telephone +44 (0)1483 211535 or
visit www.ngs.org.uk for more information
Gossip, scandal, murder, healing – you'll find it all within the Formal Gardens at Hampton Court Palace. Each tour will have its own unique feature whether it's the story of the Great Vine or the magic and mystery of the Maze.

FROGMORE – A ROYAL GARDEN (BERKSHIRE)

Tue 26 May 10am – 5.30pm (last admission 4pm)
Garden adm £4.50, chd free. Tickets available in advance or on the day.
Advance booking for groups and coaches, telephone
+44 (0) 1483 211535 or email orders@ngs.org.uk
A rare opportunity to explore 30 acres of landscaped garden, rich in history and beauty.

FLAXBOURNE FARM – FUN & SURPRISES (BEDFORDSHIRE)

Sun 7 June 10am – 5pm. Adm £5, chd free
No booking required, come along on the day!
Bring the whole family and have fun in this surprising and entertaining garden of 2 acres. Enjoy the large plant fair, live music, pets corner, birds of prey, dog agility show and much more.

WISLEY RHS GARDEN – MUSIC IN THE GARDEN (SURREY)

Fri 11 Sept 6 – 9pm
Adm (incl RHS members) £7, chd under 15 free
Save money on advance bookings for groups of 4 or more, telephone +44 (0)1483 211535 or
visit www.ngs.org.uk for more information
A special evening opening of this famous garden, exclusively for the NGS. Enjoy music and entertainment as you explore the gardens and the floral marquee on the first day of the Wisley Flower Show.

For further information visit www.ngs.org.uk or telephone 01483 211535

ISLE OF WIGHT

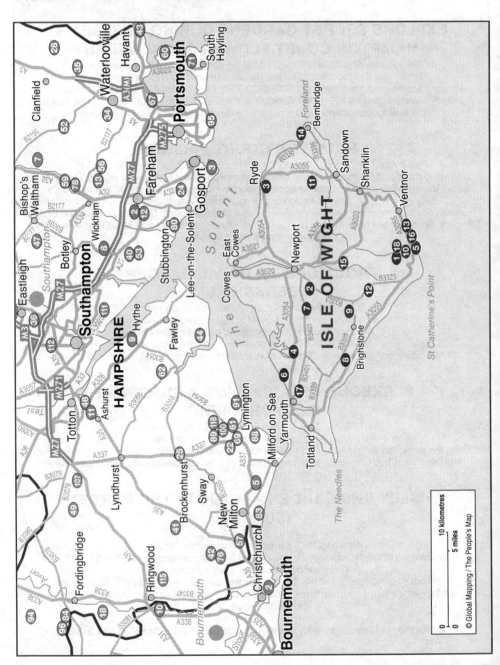

Opening Dates

April

THURSDAY 9
(14) Pitt House

SUNDAY 12
(9) Northcourt Gardens

May

SUNDAY 17
(18) Whitwell Village

SUNDAY 24
(2) Badminton

SUNDAY 31
(7) Meadowsweet
(11) Nunwell House

June

SATURDAY 6
(3) Blenheim House

SUNDAY 7
(3) Blenheim House

SUNDAY 14
(10) Northern Star
(12) The Old Rectory

SATURDAY 20
(15) Rookley Manor

SUNDAY 21
(15) Rookley Manor

TUESDAY 30
(8) Mottistone Manor Garden

July

SATURDAY 4
(1) Ashknowle House

SUNDAY 5
(1) Ashknowle House

SUNDAY 12
(17) Thorley Manor

SUNDAY 26
(13) Pelham House

August

SUNDAY 9
(16) The Shute

SUNDAY 16
(4) Crab Cottage

THURSDAY 20
(14) Pitt House

Gardens open to the public

(8) Mottistone Manor Garden
(11) Nunwell House

By appointment only

(5) Haddon Lake House
(6) Highwood

Also open by appointment ☎

(4) Crab Cottage
(7) Meadowsweet
(12) The Old Rectory

The Gardens

(1) ASHKNOWLE HOUSE
Whitwell PO38 2PP. Mr & Mrs K Fradgley. *4m W of Ventnor. From Ventnor rd turn for Ashknowle Lane next to Old Rectory. Lane is unmade. Car parking in village but field parking available, except when wet.* **Adm £3.50, chd free. Sat 4, Sun 5 July (1-4).**
A variety of features to explore in the grounds of this Victorian house. Mature and young woodlands, borders, wildlife pond and other water features. The well-maintained kitchen garden is highly productive and boasts a wide range of fruit and vegetables grown in cages, tunnels, glasshouses and raised beds. Children's woodland trail.
✕ ✿ ☕

Artists' garden fantasy . . . exploring the decorative qualities and long term effects of pattern making, colour and form . . .

(2) BADMINTON
Clatterford Shute, Carisbrooke PO30 1PD. Mr & Mrs G S Montrose. *1½ m SW of Newport. Free parking in Carisbrooke Castle car park. Public footpath to Millers Lane in corner of car park leads down to garden, approx 200yds. Parking for disabled can be arranged; please telephone prior to opening.* Home-made teas. **Adm £3, chd free. Sun 24 May (2-5).**
One-acre garden on sheltered S- and W-facing site with good vistas. Planted for all-yr interest with many different shrubs, trees and perennials to give variety, structure and colour. Natural stream and pond being developed alongside kitchen garden.
✿ ☕

(3) NEW BLENHEIM HOUSE
Spencer Road (use Market St entrance), Ryde PO33 2NY. David Rosewarne & Magie Gray. *Market St entrance behind Ryde Town Hall/Theatre.* **Adm £2.50, chd free. Sat 6, Sun 7 June (1-5).**
Artists' garden fantasy, developed over 6yrs, exploring the decorative qualities and long term effects of pattern making, colour and form in both hard and soft landscaping. This 116ft x 30ft plot uses many ideas, plants and materials from our Chelsea Silver Medal entry 'A Garden for All Seasons'.
✕ ☕

(4) CRAB COTTAGE
Mill Road, Shalfleet PO30 4NE. Mr & Mrs Peter Scott, 01983 531319, mencia@btinternet.com. *3½ m E of Yarmouth. Turn past New Inn into Mill Rd. Please park before going through NT gates. Entrance is first on L, less than 5 mins walk.* Home-made teas. **Adm £3, chd free. Sun 16 Aug (11-5). Visitors also welcome by appt.**
Lovely views over Newtown Creek and Solent. 1¼ acres of gravelly soil exposed to the Westerlies. Walled garden with herbaceous borders leading to terraced sunken garden with ornamental pond and pavilion planted with exotics, tender shrubs and herbaceous perennials. Mixed rose borders. Croquet lawn leading to grass path through wild flower meadow and flowering shrubs to waterlily pond and woodland walk. Featured in 'County Press'. Gravel paths.
♿ ✿ ☕ ☎

5 HADDON LAKE HOUSE

Old Park Road, St Lawrence PO38 1XR. Phillippa & Stephen Lambert, 01983 855151, www.lakehousedesign.co.uk. *2m SW of Ventnor. Turn off Undercliff Drive (A3055) into Old Park Rd and follow signs for 'IOW Glass Studio'. Garden opp IOW Glass car park. Park off rd in front of Haddon Lake House.* **Adm £5, chd free. Visitors welcome by appt in Aug for groups of 6-20, chd 12+yrs. Guided tour only.**
Newly-restored Victorian garden dating from 1832, formerly part of the Old Park estate. A site of contrasts with contemporary borders contrasting with formal walled potager. Major features are $1/3$ -acre lake with gravity-fed fountain and gravelled perimeter path. Featured on Channel 5 'I own Britain's Best Home & Garden', and in 'Amateur Garden' and 'Country Living'.

6 HIGHWOOD

Cranmore PO41 0XS. Mr & Mrs Cooper, 01983 760550, ross.cooper@virgin.net. *2m E of Yarmouth on A3054. 2m from Yarmouth, turning on LH-side, opp bus shelter, unmade rd.* **Adm £3, chd free. Visitors welcome by appt.**
We welcome visitors all yr to our unforgiving clay garden (boots necessary in inclement weather!). Approx $2\frac{1}{2}$ acres of garden on a 10-acre S-facing slope, incl pond, borders of shrubs and perennials and oak copse full of interesting 'woodlanders'.

7 MEADOWSWEET

5 Great Park Cottages, off Betty-Haunt Lane, Carisbrooke PO30 4HR. Gunda Cross, 01983 529930. *4m SW of Newport. From A3054 Newport to Yarmouth rd turn L at crossroads Porchfield-Calbourne into Betty-Haunt Lane, over bridge and into lane on R. Parking along L side on grass verge, past Meadowsweet.* Home-made teas. **Adm £3, chd free. Sun 31 May (11-4). Visitors also welcome by appt May to Aug for groups of 10+.**
From windswept barren 2-acre cattle field to developing tranquil country garden. Natural, mainly native, planting and wild flowers. Cottagey front garden, herb garden, orchard, fruit cage and large pond. The good life and haven for wildlife!

8 ◆ MOTTISTONE MANOR GARDEN

Mottistone PO30 4ED. The National Trust, 01983 714302, www.nationaltrust.org.uk. *8m SW Newport on B3399 between Brighstone & Brook.* **Adm £3.85, chd £1.95. 15 Mar to 1 Nov, Suns to Thurs (11-5). For NGS: Tue 30 June (11-5).**
Magical garden planted to allow for climate change, with mirrored herbaceous borders, formal rose garden, kitchen garden, wild flower banks and unusual trees. The garden surrounds an Elizabethan manor house in a sheltered valley. All plantings organically maintained.

9 NORTHCOURT GARDENS

Main Road, Shorwell PO30 3JG. Mrs C D Harrison, Mr & Mrs J Harrison. *4m SW of Newport. On entering Shorwell from Carisbrooke, entrance on R, immed after rustic footbridge.* Home-made teas. **Adm £4, chd £1. Sun 12 Apr (1-5).**
15-acre garden surrounding Jacobean Manor House incl bathhouse, walled kitchen garden, stream, terraces, magnolias and camellias. Subtropical planting. New broadwalk along jungle garden. No wheelchair access to tea room. Some steep and slippery paths.

10 NEW NORTHERN STAR

Hunts Road, St Lawrence, Ventnor PO38 1XT. Richard & Hazel Russell. *2m W of Ventnor. From Ventnor take A3055. Follow signs for glassworks down Old Park Rd, turn R into Hunts Rd. Limited parking in Hunts Rd & Old Park Rd.* Teas. **Adm £3, chd free. Sun 14 June (11-5).**
Situated in the heart of Undercliff, gardens of approx 1 acre within sylvan setting. Mixed borders with shrubs, perennials and annuals, planted within garden rooms. Inspiration has been drawn from Christopher Lloyd's plantings. Small vegetable plot and fruit area recently added.

11 ◆ NUNWELL HOUSE

Coach Lane, Brading PO36 0JQ. Colonel & Mrs J A Aylmer, 01983 407240. *3m S of Ryde. Signed off A3055 in Brading into Coach Lane.* **Adm £3, chd under 12 free. For NGS: Sun 31 May (2-5).**
5-acres of beautifully set formal and shrub gardens with Cornus *kousa* and old-fashioned shrub roses prominent. Exceptional Solent views from the terraces. Small arboretum laid out by Vernon Russell Smith and walled garden with herbaceous borders. House (not open) developed over 5 centuries and full of architectural interest.

12 THE OLD RECTORY

Kingston Road, Kingston PO38 2JZ. Derek & Louise Ness, 01983 551701, louise@warders.freeserve.co.uk, www.kingstonrectorygarden.co.uk. *8m S of Newport. On entering Shorwell from Carisbrooke, take L turn at mini roundabout towards Chale (B3399). Follow rd until you see Kingston sign, house 2nd on L after this. Park in adjacent field.* Home-made teas. **Adm £3, chd free. Sun 14 June (2-5). Visitors also welcome by appt, please phone or email in advance.**
Country garden with developing formal structure. Areas of interest incl the ornamental walled kitchen garden, orchard, formal and wildlife ponds. A wonderfully scented collection of old and English roses is complemented by borders planned with colour, fragrance and texture in mind.

> Gardens of approx 1 acre within sylvan setting . . . Inspiration has been drawn from Christopher Lloyd's plantings . . .

13 NEW **PELHAM HOUSE**
Seven Sisters Road, St
Lawrence PO38 1UY. Steve &
Dee Jaggers. *1½ m W of Ventnor.
A3055 Undercliff Road from
Ventnor to Niton, ½ m past
Botanical Gardens, on R, Seven
Sisters Road & St Lawrence Village
Hall (free parking opp), house 3rd
on R. Home-made teas at St
Lawrence village hall from 12pm.*
**Adm £3, chd free. Sun 26 July
(11-5).**
1-acre hidden away in heart of the
Undercliff, stunning sea views,
private access into Pelham Woods.
Planted for all-yr interest with trees,
shrubs, perennials and raised fish
pond. Sloping lawns lead to
tropical 'Nippa' hut from
Philippines surrounded by exotic
plants and tree ferns.
✕ ✿ ☕

14 **PITT HOUSE**
Love Lane, Bembridge PO35 5NF.
Mr L J Martin. *In Bembridge, pass
Co-op Stores & take 1st L into Love
Lane. Continue down lane (5 min walk)
as far as bend; Pitt House is on L.
Enter tall wrought iron gates. By car
enter Ducie Ave 1st L before Co-op.
Pitt House at bottom on R. Parking in
Ducie Ave and Trelawny Way. Light
refreshments & home-made teas.* **Adm
£2.50, chd free. Thurs 9 Apr; 20 Aug
(1-5).**
Approx 4 acres with varied aspects
and beautiful sea views. A number of
sculptures dotted around garden; also
Victorian greenhouse, mini waterfall
and 4 ponds. Summer bedding display
and hanging baskets. Gravel paths,
accessible grass areas.
♿ ✕ ☕

15 **ROOKLEY MANOR**
Niton Road, Rookley PO38 3NR. Mr
M Eastwood & Mr M von Brasch.
*Enter Niton Rd from Rookley village.
Manor is 8th house on R. Home-made
teas.* **Adm £2.50, chd free. Sat 20,
Sun 21 June (11-4) with music.**
Beautiful, mature 1-acre garden
surrounding a Georgian manor house
(not open). A romantic, well maintained
garden with ancient trees. Features incl
exotics, ferns, rose varieties, camellias,
echiums and a pond. A real treat for
plant lovers and people who
appreciate relaxed, considered spaces
with horticultural interest. Art exhibition
of Island artist Marius von Brasch. Live
music - harp with Anna Sacchini.
✕ ✿ ☕

Sea views
from the
windy terrace,
cottage-style
planting and
vegetable plot
in the lower,
sheltered
area . . .

16 NEW **THE SHUTE**
Seven Sisters Road, St
Lawrence PO38 1UZ. Mr & Mrs
C Russell. *Half way along Seven
Sisters Rd, opp bottom of St
Lawrence Shute. No parking in
drive. Parking in Fishers Rd or
Twining Rd (almost opp) or nr
village hall in Undercliffe Drive (a
steep but pleasant walk). Home-
made teas.* **Adm £3, chd free.
Sun 9 Aug (11-5).**
About ½ acre overlooking the sea.
Formerly part of a large Victorian
garden, the current owners are
attempting to restore it after a
period of neglect. Sea views from
the windy terrace, cottage-style
planting and vegetable plot in the
lower, sheltered area, also a
greenhouse and tropical bed.
✕ ☕

17 **THORLEY MANOR**
Yarmouth PO41 0SJ. Mr & Mrs
Anthony Blest. *1m E of Yarmouth.
From Bouldnor take Wilmingham Lane.
House ½ m on L. Home-made teas.*
**Adm £3, chd free. Sun 12 July
(2.30-5).**
Delightful informal gardens of over 3
acres surrounding Manor House (not
open). The long-neglected water
garden has been fully restored.
Charming walled garden for tea.
Eccentric head gardener.
✕ ✿ ☕

Group opening

18 NEW **WHITWELL VILLAGE**
PO38 2PP. *4m W of Ventnor.
Close to villages of Godshill and
Niton. Parking signed for field
parking at Strathwell Park if
conditions permit. Alternative
parking along walking route also in
Kemming Rd, Bannock Rd and
Strathwell Crescent. Home-made
teas at Whitwell church &
Stockbridge Manor.* **Combined
adm £4.50, chd free. Sun 17 May
(12-5).**
Whitwell was probably named after
the white (pure) well that was visited
by many on pilgrimages during
medieval times. Now a well
dressing and blessing occurs every
summer. Six more old water stands
can be seen around the village. The
lovely Church of St Mary and St
Radegund dates back to the C12.
Many buildings date back to the
C15 and The White Horse Inn
claims to be the oldest inn on the
Island. The R Yar runs through the
village and can be seen in one of
the gardens to be visited. Whitwell
has many bridleways and footpaths
and is frequented by many walkers.
The gardens of this walk are very
varied in both size and theme. Entry
tickets can be purchased at the
church and at any of the gardens
opening. Village maps given to all
visitors. Plant Fayre.
✿ ☕

NEW **MISTRAL**
Joy Morgan
Small bungalow garden with
wonderful view. Mostly lawn
and specimen shrubs, secluded
gravel garden.

NEW **THE OLD COACH
HOUSE**
Tom Smith
Truly a garden for all seasons. A
monolith granite standing stone
from Bodmin Moor overlooking
the E Yar within a circle of mature
trees is a unique feature.

NEW **PARK COTTAGE**
Mr & Mrs D Hussey
Triangular plot bordered on one
side by stream. 2 small ponds to
encourage indigenous species
and solar driven water feature.
Vegetables, fruits and various
borders. Badgers, foxes and red
squirrels are occasional visitors.
♿ ✕

NEW SAXONS
Rhys & Nicola Nigh
Created over 14yrs on sloping ground, spread over 3 terraced levels, this ½-acre garden has 3 ponds and unusual trees and shrubs in borders providing yr-round interest and attracting much wildlife.

NEW STOCKBRIDGE MANOR
Mr & Mrs R Austin
Manor dates back to 1560 with an old world garden, complete with babbling brook, very old period stone bridge and large fish pond and fountain.

NEW 13 STRATHWELL CRESCENT
Mr & Mrs G Cole
Small well tended garden with shrubs, herbaceous borders, lawns, ponds, various pots, seasonal planting.

NEW WATERDINE
David Denness
Informal terraced garden with some drystone walls. Divided into separate rooms, it comprises lawns, patios and decking with trees, shrubs, perennials and annual flowers. Also a fish pond and vegetable plot.

The gardens of this walk are very varied in both size and theme . . .

Isle of Wight County Volunteers

County Organiser
Jennie Fradgley, Ashknowle House, Ashknowle Lane, Whitwell, Ventnor, Isle of Wight PO38 2PP, 01983 730805, jenniemf805@yahoo.co.uk

Assistant County Organisers
Sukie Hillyard, Spithead House, Seaview Lane, Seaview, Isle of Wight PO34 5DG, 01983 875163
Sally Parker, Beach House, The Duver, Seaview, Isle of Wight PO34 5AJ, 01983 612495, sallyparkeriow@btinternet.com
Maggie Smee, 45 Bannock Road, Whitwell, Ventnor, Isle of Wight PO38 2RB, 01983 731084, itsmee@uwclub.net

Mark your diary with these special events in 2009

EXPLORE SECRET GARDENS DURING CHELSEA & HAMPTON COURT FLOWER SHOW WEEKS

Tue 19 May, Wed 20 May, Thur 21 May, Fri 22 May, Wed 8 July, Thur 9 July
Full day tours from £82 per person, 10% discount for groups
Advance booking required, telephone +44 (0)20 8693 1015 or email j.wookey@btinternet.com
Specially selected gardens in London, Essex, Kent, Hampshire and South Oxfordshire. The tour price includes transport and lunch with wine at a popular restaurant or pub.

HAMPTON COURT PALACE

Thur 2 Apr, Tue 23 June, Thur 25 June, Wed 15 July, Tue 4 Aug, Thur 10 Sept
Evening tours in the company of one of the Palace's specialist tour guides from 6.30 – 8pm
Tickets £6 per person. Advance booking required, telephone +44 (0)1483 211535 or
visit www.ngs.org.uk for more information
Gossip, scandal, murder, healing – you'll find it all within the Formal Gardens at Hampton Court Palace. Each tour will have its own unique feature whether it's the story of the Great Vine or the magic and mystery of the Maze.

FROGMORE – A ROYAL GARDEN (BERKSHIRE)

Tue 26 May 10am – 5.30pm (last admission 4pm)
Garden adm £4.50, chd free. Tickets available in advance or on the day.
Advance booking for groups and coaches, telephone
+44 (0) 1483 211535 or email orders@ngs.org.uk
A rare opportunity to explore 30 acres of landscaped garden, rich in history and beauty.

FLAXBOURNE FARM – FUN & SURPRISES (BEDFORDSHIRE)

Sun 7 June 10am – 5pm. Adm £5, chd free
No booking required, come along on the day!
Bring the whole family and have fun in this surprising and entertaining garden of 2 acres. Enjoy the large plant fair, live music, pets corner, birds of prey, dog agility show and much more.

WISLEY RHS GARDEN – MUSIC IN THE GARDEN (SURREY)

Fri 11 Sept 6 – 9pm
Adm (incl RHS members) £7, chd under 15 free
Save money on advance bookings for groups of 4 or more, telephone +44 (0)1483 211535 or
visit www.ngs.org.uk for more information
A special evening opening of this famous garden, exclusively for the NGS. Enjoy music and entertainment as you explore the gardens and the floral marquee on the first day of the Wisley Flower Show.

For further information visit www.ngs.org.uk or telephone 01483 211535

KENT

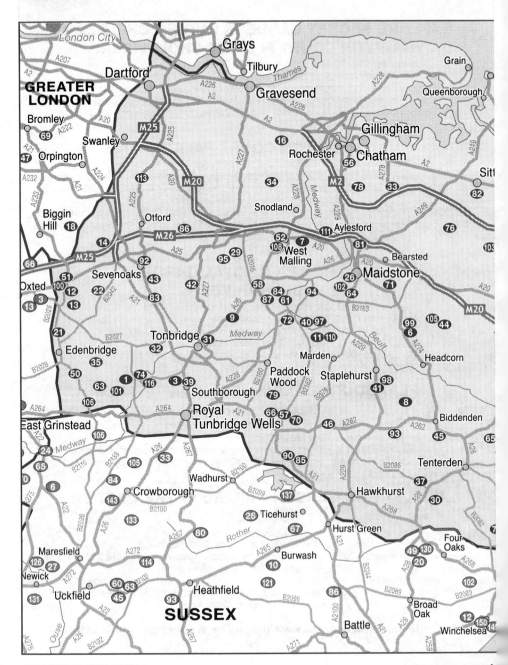

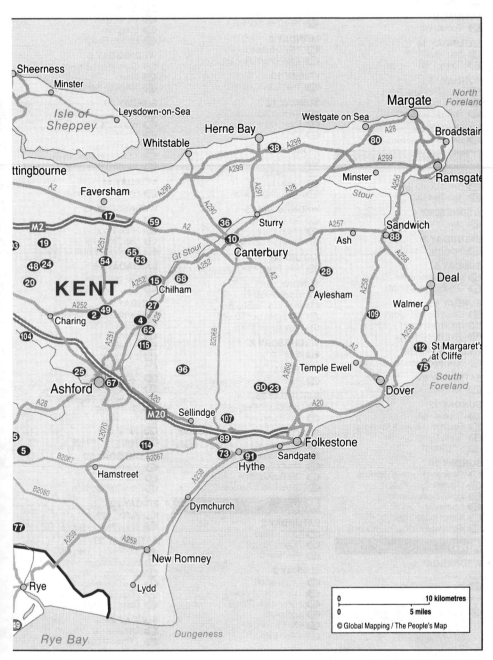

Sheerness
Minster
Isle of Sheppey
Leysdown-on-Sea
Whitstable
Herne Bay
Westgate on Sea
Margate
North Foreland
Broadstairs
A28
80
A299
38
A299
A299
Minster
A256
Ramsgate
ttingbourne
A2
Faversham
A299
M2
17
59
A290
A291
36
Sturry
Stour
A257
Sandwich
88
Ash
Deal
19
A251
54
55 53
10
Canterbury
28
A253
48 24
Gt Stour
A252
20
KENT
A252
15
68
Chilham
A252
2 49
27
Aylesham
A28
A256
109
Walmer
Charing
A251
4
62
A2
112
St Margaret's at Cliffe
104
115
96
75
South Foreland
25
B2068
A260
Temple Ewell
67
A20
60 23
Dover
Ashford
A28
M20
Sellindge
107
A20
5
89
Folkestone
5
114
73
91
Sandgate
Hythe
B2067
A259
Hamstreet
B2080
Dymchurch
77
A259
A259
New Romney
Rye
Lydd
Rye Bay
Dungeness
49

0 ───────── 10 kilometres
0 ───────── 5 miles
© Global Mapping / The People's Map

Opening Dates

February

SATURDAY 7
- 85 Rogers Rough

SUNDAY 8
- 85 Rogers Rough

SATURDAY 14
- 97 Southover
- 99 Spring Platt

SUNDAY 15
- 56 190 Maidstone Road
- 58 Mere House
- 99 Spring Platt

THURSDAY 19
- 9 Broadview Gardens

March

SUNDAY 1
- 29 Great Comp Garden
- 116 Yew Tree Cottage

WEDNESDAY 4
- 116 Yew Tree Cottage

SATURDAY 7
- 116 Yew Tree Cottage

SUNDAY 8
- 28 Goodnestone Park Gardens
- 29 Great Comp Garden

SUNDAY 15
- 29 Great Comp Garden
- 100 Squerryes Court
- 116 Yew Tree Cottage

WEDNESDAY 18
- 116 Yew Tree Cottage

SATURDAY 21
- 116 Yew Tree Cottage

SUNDAY 22
- 17 Copton Ash
- 25 Godinton House & Gardens
- 29 Great Comp Garden
- 110 Whitehurst

SUNDAY 29
- 25 Godinton House & Gardens
- 27 Godmersham Park
- 29 Great Comp Garden
- 49 Laurenden Forstal
- 58 Mere House
- 101 Stonewall Park

April

WEDNESDAY 1
- 43 Knole
- 116 Yew Tree Cottage

SATURDAY 4
- 116 Yew Tree Cottage

SUNDAY 5
- 16 Cobham Hall
- 36 Highlands
- 37 Hole Park
- 98 Spilsill Court
- 116 Yew Tree Cottage

MONDAY 6
- 88 The Salutation
- 93 Sissinghurst Garden

FRIDAY 10
- 75 The Pines Garden

SUNDAY 12
- 17 Copton Ash
- 21 Edenbridge House
- 53 Longacre

MONDAY 13
- 17 Copton Ash
- 53 Longacre
- 58 Mere House
- 72 Parsonage Oasts

WEDNESDAY 15
- 30 Great Maytham Hall
- 57 Marle Place
- 116 Yew Tree Cottage

SATURDAY 18
- 116 Yew Tree Cottage

SUNDAY 19
- 5 Boldshaves
- 24 Frith Old Farmhouse
- 55 Luton House
- 116 Yew Tree Cottage

WEDNESDAY 22
- 37 Hole Park

THURSDAY 23
- 83 Riverhill House Gardens

SATURDAY 25
- 8 1 Brickwall Cottages
- 63 Old Buckhurst

SUNDAY 26
- 7 Bradbourne House and Gardens
- 8 1 Brickwall Cottages
- 59 Mount Ephraim
- 63 Old Buckhurst
- 87 St Michael's Gardens

May

SATURDAY 2
- 64 Old Orchard
- 85 Rogers Rough
- 116 Yew Tree Cottage

SUNDAY 3
- 20 Eagleswood
- 21 Edenbridge House
- 39 Honnington Farm
- 53 Longacre
- 64 Old Orchard
- 85 Rogers Rough

SUNDAY 5
- 101 Stonewall Park
- 116 Yew Tree Cottage

MONDAY 4
- 17 Copton Ash
- 39 Honnington Farm
- 53 Longacre
- 85 Rogers Rough

WEDNESDAY 6
- 30 Great Maytham Hall
- 43 Knole
- 116 Yew Tree Cottage

SUNDAY 10
- 24 Frith Old Farmhouse
- 36 Highlands
- 53 Longacre
- 55 Luton House
- 81 11 Raymer Road
- 89 Sandling Park

MONDAY 11
- 22 Emmetts Garden

WEDNESDAY 13
- 33 25 Hanover Drive
- 57 Marle Place
- 63 Old Buckhurst
- 74 Penshurst Place

SATURDAY 16
- 63 Old Buckhurst
- 116 Yew Tree Cottage

SUNDAY 17
- 2 Beech Court Gardens
- 4 Bilting House
- 12 Charts Edge
- 37 Hole Park
- 46 Ladham House
- 53 Longacre
- 63 Old Buckhurst
- 79 Puxted House
- 87 St Michael's Gardens
- 94 Smiths Hall
- 103 Torry Hill
- 104 Tram Hatch
- 116 Yew Tree Cottage

WEDNESDAY 20
- 21 Edenbridge House
- 84 Rock Farm
- 116 Yew Tree Cottage

FRIDAY 22
- 45 Kypp Cottage
- 47 212 Langley Way

SATURDAY 23
- 8 1 Brickwall Cottages
- 45 Kypp Cottage
- 47 212 Langley Way
- 67 One Dering Road
- 84 Rock Farm
- 85 Rogers Rough

SUNDAY 24
- 5 Boldshaves
- 8 1 Brickwall Cottages

(19) Doddington Place
(32) Hall Place
(45) Kypp Cottage
(47) 212 Langley Way
(53) Longacre
(62) Olantigh
(67) One Dering Road
(85) Rogers Rough

MONDAY 25
(17) Copton Ash
(45) Kypp Cottage
(53) Longacre
(67) One Dering Road
(75) The Pines Garden
(85) Rogers Rough

TUESDAY 26
(45) Kypp Cottage

FRIDAY 29
(41) Iden Croft Herb Gardens
(45) Kypp Cottage

SATURDAY 30
(10) Canterbury Cathedral Gardens
(41) Iden Croft Herb Gardens
(45) Kypp Cottage
(63) Old Buckhurst
(111) Wickham Lodge

SUNDAY 31
(6) Boyton Court
(10) Canterbury Cathedral Gardens
(18) Cottage Farm
(45) Kypp Cottage
(63) Old Buckhurst
(95) Sotts Hole Cottage

June

TUESDAY 2
(45) Kypp Cottage

WEDNESDAY 3
(43) Knole
(45) Kypp Cottage
(63) Old Buckhurst
(116) Yew Tree Cottage

THURSDAY 4
(45) Kypp Cottage
(77) Primrose Cottage

FRIDAY 5
(45) Kypp Cottage
(77) Primrose Cottage

SATURDAY 6
(39) Honnington Farm
(45) Kypp Cottage
(51) Little Gables
(67) One Dering Road
(77) Primrose Cottage
(114) Wyckhurst
(116) Yew Tree Cottage

SUNDAY 7
(18) Cottage Farm
(20) Eagleswood
(21) Edenbridge House
(23) The Farm House

(34) Haydown
(39) Honnington Farm
(45) Kypp Cottage
(51) Little Gables
(60) Mounts Court Farmhouse
(67) One Dering Road
(77) Primrose Cottage
(79) Puxted House
(103) Torry Hill
(108) West Malling Gardens
(114) Wyckhurst
(116) Yew Tree Cottage

MONDAY 8
(93) Sissinghurst Garden

TUESDAY 9
(45) Kypp Cottage

WEDNESDAY 10
(30) Great Maytham Hall
(45) Kypp Cottage

THURSDAY 11
(45) Kypp Cottage

FRIDAY 12
(18) Cottage Farm (Evening)
(45) Kypp Cottage

SATURDAY 13
(45) Kypp Cottage
(63) Old Buckhurst
(67) One Dering Road
(70) Orchard End
(85) Rogers Rough
(114) Wyckhurst

SUNDAY 14
(11) Chainhurst Cottage Gardens
(12) Charts Edge
(18) Cottage Farm
(40) Hunton Gardens
(45) Kypp Cottage
(57) Marle Place
(61) Nettlestead Place
(66) Old Tong Farm
(67) One Dering Road
(70) Orchard End
(81) 11 Raymer Road
(85) Rogers Rough
(86) St Clere
(104) Tram Hatch
(107) West Court Lodge
(112) Windy Ridge
(114) Wyckhurst

TUESDAY 16
(45) Kypp Cottage

WEDNESDAY 17
(11) Chainhurst Cottage Gardens (Evening)
(18) Cottage Farm
(21) Edenbridge House (Evening)
(45) Kypp Cottage
(63) Old Buckhurst
(66) Old Tong Farm
(106) Upper Pryors (Day & Evening)
(116) Yew Tree Cottage

THURSDAY 18
(45) Kypp Cottage

FRIDAY 19
(41) Iden Croft Herb Gardens
(45) Kypp Cottage

SATURDAY 20
(41) Iden Croft Herb Gardens
(45) Kypp Cottage
(67) One Dering Road
(116) Yew Tree Cottage

SUNDAY 21
(5) Boldshaves
(14) Chevening
(18) Cottage Farm
(32) Hall Place
(37) Hole Park
(45) Kypp Cottage
(49) Laurenden Forstal
(52) Little Went
(63) Old Buckhurst
(67) One Dering Road
(68) The Orangery
(80) Quex Gardens
(110) Whitehurst
(113) The World Garden at Lullingstone Castle
(116) Yew Tree Cottage

MONDAY 22
(110) Whitehurst

TUESDAY 23
(45) Kypp Cottage
(110) Whitehurst

WEDNESDAY 24
(45) Kypp Cottage
(84) Rock Farm
(110) Whitehurst

THURSDAY 25
(45) Kypp Cottage

FRIDAY 26
(45) Kypp Cottage

SATURDAY 27
(44) Knowle Hill Farm (Evening)
(45) Kypp Cottage
(84) Rock Farm

SUNDAY 28
(2) Beech Court Gardens
(4) Bilting House
(18) Cottage Farm
(31) 115 Hadlow Road
(33) 25 Hanover Drive
(36) Highlands
(45) Kypp Cottage
(63) Old Buckhurst
(87) St Michael's Gardens
(92) Sevenoaks Allotments
(94) Smiths Hall
(98) Spilsill Court

TUESDAY 30
(45) Kypp Cottage

July

WEDNESDAY 1
- 43 Knole
- 45 Kypp Cottage
- 57 Marle Place
- 84 Rock Farm
- 116 Yew Tree Cottage

THURSDAY 2
- 45 Kypp Cottage

FRIDAY 3
- 45 Kypp Cottage

SATURDAY 4
- 15 Chilham Castle
- 38 9 Holmscroft Road
- 45 Kypp Cottage
- 67 One Dering Road
- 84 Rock Farm
- 116 Yew Tree Cottage

SUNDAY 5
- 38 9 Holmscroft Road
- 67 One Dering Road
- 105 Ulcombe Place
- 115 Wye Gardens
- 116 Yew Tree Cottage

WEDNESDAY 8
- 13 Chartwell
- 84 Rock Farm

THURSDAY 9
- 54 Lords

SATURDAY 11
- 26 The Godlands
- 67 One Dering Road
- 84 Rock Farm

SUNDAY 12
- 12 Charts Edge
- 16 Cobham Hall
- 23 The Farm House
- 54 Lords
- 60 Mounts Court Farmhouse
- 63 Old Buckhurst
- 67 One Dering Road
- 104 Tram Hatch

WEDNESDAY 15
- 33 25 Hanover Drive
- 63 Old Buckhurst
- 116 Yew Tree Cottage

FRIDAY 17
- 41 Iden Croft Herb Gardens

SATURDAY 18
- 41 Iden Croft Herb Gardens
- 42 Ightham Mote
- 67 One Dering Road
- 71 Otham Gardens
- 78 14 & 16 Prince Charles Avenue
- 90 Scotney Castle
- 116 Yew Tree Cottage

SUNDAY 19
- 19 Doddington Place
- 63 Old Buckhurst
- 67 One Dering Road

- 69 Orchard Cottage
- 78 14 & 16 Prince Charles Avenue
- 91 Sea Close
- 103 Torry Hill
- 112 Windy Ridge
- 116 Yew Tree Cottage

WEDNESDAY 22
- 80 Quex Gardens
- 88 The Salutation

FRIDAY 24
- 47 212 Langley Way

SATURDAY 25
- 47 212 Langley Way
- 51 Little Gables
- 70 Orchard End

SUNDAY 26
- 36 Highlands
- 47 212 Langley Way
- 51 Little Gables
- 63 Old Buckhurst
- 68 The Orangery
- 70 Orchard End
- 82 Riddles Road Allotments
- 95 Sotts Hole Cottage

WEDNESDAY 29
- 63 Old Buckhurst

August

SATURDAY 1
- 38 9 Holmscroft Road
- 45 Kypp Cottage
- 63 Old Buckhurst
- 67 One Dering Road
- 116 Yew Tree Cottage

SUNDAY 2
- 31 115 Hadlow Road
- 38 9 Holmscroft Road
- 45 Kypp Cottage
- 63 Old Buckhurst
- 67 One Dering Road
- 116 Yew Tree Cottage

WEDNESDAY 5
- 43 Knole
- 116 Yew Tree Cottage

FRIDAY 7
- 45 Kypp Cottage

SATURDAY 8
- 45 Kypp Cottage

SUNDAY 9
- 3 Bidborough Gardens
- 45 Kypp Cottage
- 50 Leydens

MONDAY 10
- 93 Sissinghurst Garden

FRIDAY 14
- 45 Kypp Cottage

SATURDAY 15
- 45 Kypp Cottage
- 116 Yew Tree Cottage

SUNDAY 16
- 2 Beech Court Gardens
- 45 Kypp Cottage
- 116 Yew Tree Cottage

WEDNESDAY 19
- 116 Yew Tree Cottage

FRIDAY 21
- 45 Kypp Cottage

SATURDAY 22
- 45 Kypp Cottage

SUNDAY 23
- 45 Kypp Cottage
- 49 Laurenden Forstal
- 109 West Studdal Farm

WEDNESDAY 26
- 100 Squerryes Court

FRIDAY 28
- 45 Kypp Cottage

SATURDAY 29
- 45 Kypp Cottage

SUNDAY 30
- 31 115 Hadlow Road
- 45 Kypp Cottage
- 53 Longacre

MONDAY 31
- 45 Kypp Cottage
- 53 Longacre
- 75 The Pines Garden

September

WEDNESDAY 2
- 21 Edenbridge House
- 116 Yew Tree Cottage

SATURDAY 5
- 63 Old Buckhurst
- 70 Orchard End
- 116 Yew Tree Cottage

SUNDAY 6
- 9 Broadview Gardens
- 63 Old Buckhurst
- 70 Orchard End
- 116 Yew Tree Cottage

SATURDAY 12
- 15 Chilham Castle
- 111 Wickham Lodge

SUNDAY 13
- 21 Edenbridge House
- 24 Frith Old Farmhouse
- 28 Goodnestone Park Gardens
- 91 Sea Close
- 112 Windy Ridge

WEDNESDAY 16
- 116 Yew Tree Cottage

SATURDAY 19
- 116 Yew Tree Cottage

SUNDAY 20
- 5 Boldshaves
- 19 Doddington Place

The Gardens

ARDEN LODGE
See Surrey.

1 ABBOTSMERRY BARN
Salmans Lane, Penshurst TN11 8DJ. Margaret & Keith Wallis, 01892 870900, abbotsmerry@aol.com, www.abbotsmerry.co.uk. *5m W of Tonbridge. Off B2176 in direction Leigh: 200yds N of Penshurst turn L, 1m down narrow lane with speed ramps.* Adm £4, chd free. Visitors welcome by appt at most times from beginning of Mar to mid June, incl groups. Please phone out of gardening hours. Garden developed over 25yrs on a 7^1/$_2$ -acre undulating S-facing slope to take advantage of existing features and differing planting conditions. Cheerful display of bulbs and blossom in spring followed by a wide variety of flowers and foliage provided by herbaceous plants and roses, complemented by bulbs, shrubs and trees.

2 ◆ BEECH COURT GARDENS
Challock TN25 4DJ. Mr & Mrs Vyvyan Harmsworth, 01233 740735, www.beechcourtgardens.co.uk. *5m N of Ashford, Faversham 6m, Canterbury 9m. W of Xrds A251/A252, off the Lees.* Adm £5, chd £1, concessions £4.30. Apr to Oct Sat to Thur (10.30-5.30), Suns (12-5.30). Closed Fris. For NGS: Suns 17 May; 28 June; 16 Aug; 18 Oct (12-5.30). Informal woodland garden surrounding medieval farmhouse (not open). Spring bulbs, rhododendrons, azaleas and viburnums give superb spring colour; climbing roses, summer borders and hydrangeas follow; fine collection of trees incl acers give autumn colour. Extensive lawns, meandering paths and surprising vistas. Picnic area. Limited wheelcair access when very wet.

Group opening

3 NEW BIDBOROUGH GARDENS
TN4 0XB. *3m N of Tunbridge Wells, between Tonbridge and Tunbridge Wells W of A26. Take B2176 Bidborough Ridge signed to Penshurst. Take 1st L into Darnley Drive, then 1st R into St Lawrence Ave. Toilets by the Village Hall.* Light refreshments & teas at Long Barn, 24 St Lawrence Ave. Combined adm £3.50, chd

free (share to Brain Tumour UK).
Sun 9 Aug (11-5).
The Bidborough gardens are
situated in a small village at the
heart of which are the Hare &
Hounds PH (book in advance for
lunch), St Lawrence church, garage,
village store and primary school. It
is a thriving community with many
well-supported clubs, incl a very
active Garden Association! There is
a recreation ground where cricket
and stoolball matches are regularly
played, a bowling green, tennis
court and children's play area. In
the surrounding countryside there
are several local walks meandering
through The Birchwood with its lake
and glade, or over the 'Camp Field'
to nearby Southborough Common.
The 3 gardens are all owner-
designed and very different, each
reflecting personal taste, ideas and
uses. Exhibition of pet portraits and
water colours by local artist.

❀ ☕

NEW BOUNDES END
2 St Lawrence Avenue. Mr &
Mrs M Marks, 01892 542233,
carole.marks@btinternet.com.
Visitors also welcome by appt
July & Aug for groups of 10-20.
Young garden, designed by
owners, an usually-shaped
1/3-acre plot formed from 2 triangles
of land. Front garden featuring
raised beds, and the main garden
divided into a formal area with
terrace, pebble bed and pergolas,
and an informal area in a woodland
setting with interesting features and
specimen trees. Plenty of places
to sit and enjoy the garden.

♿ ☎

NEW 1 ST LAWRENCE AVENUE
Mr & Mrs C Mauduit
Owner-designed front garden of
gravel-terraced borders, with
interesting use of a difficult site.
Steps lead to the rear family
garden with lawn surrounded by
mature trees, shrubs, herbaceous
borders and 2 ponds. Small area
still under construction.

NEW 23 WOODLAND WAY
William & Gillian Long
Refurbished in the last 5yrs, this
garden, packed with interest,
contains lawns and wide borders
planted with acers and many
unusual herbaceous and tropical
plants. Spacious formal terrace
with pergola covered in fruiting
vines. Greenhouse and herbs.

Fragrance fills the air . . .

④ BILTING HOUSE
nr Ashford TN25 4HA. Mr John Erle-
Drax, 020 7629 5161,
jdrax@marlboroughfineart.com. *5m
NE of Ashford. A28, 9m from
Canterbury. Wye 1½ m.* Home-made
teas. **Adm £3.50, chd free. Suns 17
May; 28 June (2-6). Visitors also
welcome by appt.**
6-acre garden with ha-ha set in
beautiful part of Stour Valley. Wide
variety of rhododendrons, azaleas and
ornamental shrubs. Woodland walk
with spring bulbs. Mature arboretum
with new planting of specimen trees.
Rose garden and herbaceous borders.
Conservatory.

♿ ✕ ❀ ☕ ☎

⑤ BOLDSHAVES
Woodchurch, nr Ashford TN26 3RA.
Mr & Mrs Peregrine Massey, 01233
860302, masseypd@hotmail.co.uk.
*Between Woodchurch & High Halden.
From A28 towards Ashford, turn R at
village green in High Halden. 2nd R,
Redbrook St, towards Woodchurch,
before R on unmarked lane. After ½ m
R through brick entrance. Ignore oast
house on L, follow signs to car park.*
Home-made teas. **Adm £4, chd free
(share to Kent Minds). Suns 19 Apr;
24 May; 21 June; 20 Sept (2-4).
Visitors also welcome by appt last
Sun of month for groups of 8+,
minibuses but no coaches please.**
7-acre garden with a number of new
features being developed. Partly
terraced, S-facing, with ornamental
trees and shrubs, walled garden,
herbaceous borders, bluebell walks,
woodland and ponds. Featured in
'Kent Life' & 'GGG'. Grass paths.

♿ ✕ ❀ ☕ ☎

⑥ BOYTON COURT
Sutton Valence ME17 3BY. Richard
& Patricia Stileman, 01622 844065,
richstileman@aol.com. *5m SE of
Maidstone. Turn off A274 at Kings
Head & go through Sutton Valence.
Leaving chapel/art centre on R go
½ m to Xrds. Turn R, garden 200yds
on L.* Home-made teas. **Adm £4, chd
free. Sun 31 May (2-6). Visitors also
welcome by appt.**

3- acre garden on S edge of
greensand ridge affording spectacular
views over the Weald. Garden falls in
series of slopes and terraces through
which water from a natural spring has
been harnessed to create ponds and
other water features. Large mixed
borders and several intimate areas
featuring yew, box, Austin roses,
irises, lavender, perennial geraniums,
sedums etc.

♿ ✕ ⊨ ☕ ☎

⑦ BRADBOURNE HOUSE AND GARDENS
East Malling ME19 6DZ. East
Malling Trust for Horticultural
Research,
www.bradbournehouse.org.uk. *4m
NW of Maidstone. Entrance is E of
New Rd, which runs from Larkfield on
A20 S to E Malling.* Home-made teas.
**Adm £3.50, chd free. Sun 26 Apr
(2-5).**
The Hatton Fruit Garden consists of
demonstration fruit gardens of
particular interest to amateurs, in
walled former kitchen garden and incl
intensive forms of apples and pears.
Members of staff will be available for
questions. Interactive scientific exhibits,
plant and produce sales. Viewing of
Bradbourne House also provided.
Children's quiz, string quartet and
medieval instruments. Featured in
'Kent Messenger'.

♿ ✕ ❀ ☕

BRAEKENAS
See Surrey.

⑧ 1 BRICKWALL COTTAGES
Frittenden TN17 2DH. Mrs Sue
Martin, 01580 852425,
sue.martin@talktalk.net. *6m NW of
Tenterden. E of A229 between
Cranbrook & Staplehurst & W of A274
between Biddenden & Headcorn. Park
in village & walk along footpath opp
school.* Home-made teas. **Adm £2,
chd free. Sats, Suns 25, 26 Apr; 23,
24 May (2-5.30). Visitors also
welcome by appt.**
True cottage garden, small but
crammed with unusual plants. Some
beds are colour-themed: a yellow
border and the bed in front of the
pleached limes have a mix of silver,
white and deep red plants. Fragrance
fills the air from philadelphus, Eleagnus
'Quicksilver' among others. Fruit trees
and raised vegetable beds. Geums are
everywhere, the National Collection
keeps growing! They are at their best in
late May.

♿ ❀ NCCPG ☕ ☎

9 ◆ **BROADVIEW GARDENS**
Hadlow College, Hadlow TN11 0AL.
Hadlow College, www.hadlow.ac.uk.
*4m NE of Tonbridge. On A26 9m SW
of Maidstone.* **Adm £2.50, chd free.
Gardens open all yr 10-4. For NGS:
Thur 19 Feb; Sun 6 Sept (10-4); Thur
18 Feb 2010.**
10 acres of ornamental planting in
attractive landscape setting; 100 meter
double long border, island beds with
mixed plantings, lakes and water
gardens; series of demonstration
gardens incl Italian, oriental and
Suttons vegetable garden. National
Collections of *Anemone japonica* and
hellebores. In Feb only exhibition on
hellebores and the NCCPG; tours of
garden and hellebore collection
available. Featured on Radio Kent.

Group opening

10 ◆ **CANTERBURY CATHEDRAL
GARDENS**
CT1 2EP, www.canterbury-
cathedral.org. *Canterbury Cathedral
Precincts. Enter Precincts by main
Christchurch gate.* **No access for cars:
please use park & ride and public car
parks.** Gardens will be signed within
Precincts. **Combined Cathedral and
NGS gardens ticket £11,**
concessions **£10. Precinct pass
holders £4. Sat 30 May (11-5), Sun
31 May (2-5).**
Five Canonical gardens all set against
the magnificent backdrop of
Canterbury Cathedral, plus the
Medicinal Herb Garden, Water Tower
Garden, Memorial Garden and
Campanile Mound.

ARCHDEACONRY 29 THE
PRECINCTS
The Archdeacon, Sheila Watson
³/₄ -acre medieval walled garden
incl the historic mulberry tree in
the former Cellarer's Hall. The
garden is under renovation, mixing
architectural planting with the
more traditional elements of the
former design and introducing
new varieties and approaches to
planting. Gravel paths and uneven
surfaces.

THE DEANERY
The Dean
Large garden of over 1 acre with
small orchard and 'wild' area,
lawns, herbaceous border and
vegetable garden.

15 THE PRECINCTS
Canon & Mrs E Condry
Large walled garden bounded on
one side by the City Wall. Large
herbaceous bank. A little more
formal, in keeping with the
historical house. Gravel paths.

19 THE PRECINCTS
Canon Irvine
Small enclosed garden with a view
dominated by the Cathedral.

22 THE PRECINCTS
Canon Clare Edwards
Front garden planted to attract
birds and insects. Back garden a
very small walled 'secret' garden.
Gravel paths.

Group opening

11 **CHAINHURST COTTAGE
GARDENS**
Chainhurst, Marden TN12 9SU,
01622 820654/820483. *6m S of
Maidstone, 3m N of Marden. From
Marden proceed along Pattenden
Lane; at T-junction turn L, follow signs
to Chainhurst. In Chainhurst take 2nd
turning on L. From Maidstone take
A229. At Stile Bridge Inn fork R, then
1st R until NGS signs appear.* Home-
made teas. **Combined adm £4, chd
free. Sun 14 June (2-5.30). Evening
Opening £4.50, wine, Wed 17 June
(6-8.30).** Visitors also welcome by
appt at both gardens, June only.
Rural hamlet surrounded by arable
farmland. Featured in 'Kent Life'.

1 CHAINHURST COTTAGES
Audrey & John Beeching
Informal cottage garden; at the
front gravel area with mixed
grasses and water feature
alongside blue, white and yellow
border. To the side, meadow
planted with various trees and
enclosed by hedge of native
species. To the rear of the
cottage, mixed borders,
summerhouse, paved terrace, lily
pond and vegetable patch with
fruit and flowers for cutting.
Wheelchair access to all but
vegetable garden.

3 CHAINHURST COTTAGES
Heather & Richard Scott
Garden surrounding Kent peg tiled
cottage. At front small herb
garden edged with clipped box.
Side steps lead down to borders
of silver and burgundy planting,
greenhouse and vegetable beds.
Rear garden features rose and

wisteria covered pergola, rose
garden, potting shed and gravel
area surrounded by garden wall.
🛏

CHARDLEIGH COTTAGE
See Surrey.

Medieval walled garden with the historic mulberry tree in the former Cellarer's Hall . . .

12 ◆ **CHARTS EDGE**
Westerham TN16 1PL. Mr & Mrs J
Bigwood, 07833 385169,
pignmix@blueyonder.co.uk,
www.chartsedgegardens.co.uk.
*¹/₂ m S of Westerham, 4m N of
Edenbridge. On B2026 towards
Chartwell.* **Adm £3.50, chd free. Suns
& Fris mid Apr to mid Sept. For
NGS: Suns 17 May; 14 June; 12 July
(2-5).**
7-acre hillside garden being restored
by present owners; large collection of
rhododendrons, azaleas and
magnolias; specimen trees and newly-
planted mixed borders; many rare
plants; majority of plants labelled;
Victorian folly; walled fruit garden; rock
garden. Water gardens and cascade.
Rainbow borders and rill. Fine views
over N Downs.

13 ◆ **CHARTWELL**
Mapleton Road, nr Westerham
TN16 1PS. The National Trust, 01732
866368, www.nationaltrust.org.uk.
*4m N of Edenbridge. 2m S of
Westerham. Fork L off B2026 after
1¹/₂ m.* **House & garden £11.80, chd
£5.90. Garden only £5.90, chd £2.95.
Weds to Suns all yr, Tues to Suns
July & Aug. Please phone 01732
866368 or visit website for further
details. For NGS: Wed 8 July (11-5).**
12-acre informal gardens on hillside
with glorious views over Weald of Kent.
Water garden and lakes together with
red-brick wall built by Sir Winston
Churchill, former owner of Chartwell.
Avenue of golden roses given by Sir
Winston's children on his golden
wedding anniversary runs down the
centre of a productive kitchen garden.

14 CHEVENING
nr Sevenoaks TN14 6HG. **The Board of Trustees of the Chevening Estate.** *4m NW of Sevenoaks. Turn N off A25 at Sundridge T-lights on to B2211; at Chevening Xrds 1½ m turn L.* Home-made teas. **Adm £4, chd £1. Sun 21 June (2-5).**
27 acres with lawns and woodland garden, lake, maze, formal rides, parterre. Flower Festival in neighbouring St Botolph's Church. Gravel paths, unfenced lake.
&. ⊗ ☕

15 ◆ CHILHAM CASTLE
Chilham CT4 8DB. **Mr & Mrs Wheeler, 01227 733100, www.chilham-castle.co.uk.** *6m SW of Canterbury. Follow signs for car park and gardens entrance from A252, ½ m from Chilham village towards Charing, signed on L. Village Hall/Chilham Park. Car park & entrance at top of hill.* **Adm £4, chd/concessions £3. 1 Mar for spring bulbs, then second Tue of month, Apr to Sept (10-3). For NGS: Sats 4 July; 12 Sept (2-5).**
Garden surrounding Jacobean mansion (not open) leads onto C17 terraces with herbaceous borders comprehensively restored and designed by Lady Mary Keen and Pip Morrison. Topiary frames the magnificent views with lake walk below. Extensive kitchen and cutting garden beyond spring bulb filled Quiet Garden. Established trees and ha-ha lead onto park.
⊗ ☕

16 ◆ COBHAM HALL
Cobham DA12 3BL. **Mr N G Powell (Bursar), 01474 823371, www.cobhamhall.com.** *5m N of Rochester. 8m E of M25 J2. Take A2 to exit signed Cobham, Shorne, Higham. Disregard Sat Nav directions to Lodge Lane; entrance to Cobham Hall on Brewers Rd 100m S of A2.* **House & garden £5.50, chd/concessions £4.50. Garden only £2.50, chd free. Open many dates, please phone for details. For NGS: Suns 5 Apr; 12 July (2-5).**
Beautiful Grade I listed Elizabethan mansion in 142 acres, Grade 2* listed landscape by Humphry Repton at end C18. Herbaceous borders, formal parterres, C17 and C18 garden walls, yew hedges, lime avenue. Parkland with veteran trees (cedars, oaks, planes, ginkgos, chestnuts, walnuts, cherries) with naturalised daffodils,

snowdrops, crocus and bluebells. Garden follies' restoration completed 2007, wooded areas cleared for return to woodland glades and parkland vistas. Film location for 'Wild Child'. Limited wheelchair access; video available for disabled, please phone ahead.
&. ☕

COLUMCILLE
See London.

Special interest in woodland flowers, snowdrops and hellebores . . .

17 COPTON ASH
105 Ashford Road, Faversham ME13 8XW. **Drs Tim & Gillian Ingram, 01795 535919.** *½ m S of Faversham. On A251 Faversham to Ashford rd, opp E-bound J6 with M2.* Home-made teas. **Adm £2.50, chd free. Sun 22 Mar (12-5); Sun 12, Mon 13 Apr; Mons 4, 25 May (2-5.30). Visitors also welcome by appt.**
Garden grown out of a love and fascination with plants from an early age. Contains very wide collection incl many rarities and newly introduced species raised from wild seed. Special interest in woodland flowers, snowdrops and hellebores with flowering trees and shrubs of spring. Wide range of drought-tolerant plants. Raised beds with choice alpines and bulbs.
&. ✕ ⊗ ☕ ☎

18 COTTAGE FARM
Cacketts Lane, Cudham TN14 7QG. **Phil & Karen Baxter, 01959 532506, karen@cottagefarmturkeys.co.uk.** *5m NW of Sevenoaks, 4m SW of Orpington. Sign for Cudham from Green-Street-Green roundabout on A21. 3m into village, turn L past*

garage. 2nd block cottages on R. Entrance through working farmyard. Home-made teas. **Adm £4.50, chd free (share to Harris HospisCare). Sun 31 May; Suns, Wed 7, 14, 17, 21, 28 June (1.30-5.30), (Sun 21 June followed by BBQ, extra £5). Evening Opening** £7, cheese & wine, **Fri 12 June (7-9.30). Visitors also welcome by appt in June & July only.**
Cottage garden. No lawns! Intimate and individual style. Approx 1 acre. Self-sufficient vegetable and fruit gardens, with raised beds growing vegetables for exhibition. Tropical garden, cut flower garden, fernery, greenhouses with tender and tropical fruits and flowers; rose-covered pergolas and wildlife ponds. Created and maintained by owner. BBQ following 21 June opening, from 5pm. Fit wheelchair pusher required.
&. ⊗ ⊨ ☕ ☎

19 ◆ DODDINGTON PLACE
nr Sittingbourne ME9 0BB. **Mr & Mrs Richard Oldfield, www.doddingtonplacegardens. co.uk.** *6m SE of Sittingbourne. From A20 turn N opp Lenham or from A2 turn S at Teynham or Ospringe (Faversham), all 4m.* **Adm £4.50, chd £1. Suns & Bank Hol Mons Easter to end Sept (2-5). For NGS: Suns 24 May; 19 July; 20 Sept (2-5).**
10-acre garden, landscaped with wide views; trees and clipped yew hedges; woodland garden with azaleas and rhododendrons; Edwardian rock garden recently renovated (not wheelchair accessible); formal garden with mixed borders. Gothic folly.
&. ☕

20 EAGLESWOOD
Slade Road, Warren Street, Lenham, Maidstone ME17 2EG. **Mike & Edith Darvill.** *Going E on A20 nr Lenham, L into Hubbards Hill for approx 1m then 2nd L into Slade rd. Garden 150yds on R.* Light refreshments. **Adm £3.50, chd free (share to Demelza House Children's Hospice). Suns 3 May; 7 June (11-5).**
1½ -acre plantsman's garden situated high on N Downs, developed over the past 21yrs. Wide range of trees and shrubs (many unusual), herbaceous material and woodland plants grown to give yr-round interest. Some gravel, grass paths may be slippery when wet.
&. ✕ ⊗ ☕

21 ◆ **EDENBRIDGE HOUSE**
Edenbridge TN8 6SJ. Mrs M T
Lloyd, 01732 862122,
dg.lloyd@btinternet.com. *1¹/₂ m N of
Edenbridge. Nr Marlpit Hill, on B2026.*
Teas on NGS days. **Adm £3.50, chd
free. Tues, Weds & Thurs, Apr to
Sept (2-5). For NGS: Suns, Weds:
12 Apr; 3, 20 May; 7 June; 2,
13 Sept (Suns 2-6, Weds 1-5).
Evening Opening, £4.50, wine,
17 June (6-9). Also open 17 June
(1-9) Upper Pryors.**
House part C16 (not open). 5-acre
garden laid out in 1930s as a series of
rooms, with herbaceous and mixed
borders, old-fashioned and shrub
roses, alpines, ornamental trees and
shrubs, water and gravel gardens,
orchard and wildlife pond, kitchen
garden and greenhouses; many
unusual plants.

& ❀ ☕

Terraced lawns
lead through
herbaceous
borders, rose
garden and
formal lily pond
to intimate Italian
Garden . . .

22 ◆ **EMMETTS GARDEN**
Ide Hill TN14 6AY. The National
Trust, 01732 868381,
www.nationaltrust.org.uk. *5m SW of
Sevenoaks. 1¹/₂ m S of A25 on
Sundridge-Ide Hill Rd. 1¹/₂ m N of Ide
Hill off B2042.* **Adm £6.40, chd
£1.60. Sats to Weds 14 Mar to
1 Nov (11-5). For NGS: Mon 11 May
(11-5).**
5-acre hillside garden, with the highest
tree top in Kent, noted for its fine
collection of rare trees and flowering
shrubs. The garden is particularly fine
in spring, while a rose garden, rock
garden and extensive planting of acers
for autumn colour extend the interest
throughout the season.

& ❀ ☕

23 NEW **THE FARM HOUSE**
Acrise Place, nr Folkestone
CT18 8JX. Winfried & Hilary
Richter. *5¹/₂ m NW of Folkestone.
From A260 Folkestone to
Canterbury rd, turn L at Swingfield
(Densole) opp Black Horse PH, 1m
towards Elham & Lyminge. Parking
close to St Martin, Acrise.* Home-
made teas at Mounts Court
Farmhouse, also open. **Adm £3,
chd free. Suns 7 June; 12 July
(2-5).**
1¹/₂ acres designed by Debbie
Jolley. Formal area with pond close
to house (C18, not open) with
potager-style rose borders gives
way to large mixed borders with
all-yr interest. Large pond, uncut
grass and mown paths in
woodland, developing orchard and
wild flower area. Many roses incl
species and scramblers.

❀

24 NEW **FRITH OLD
FARMHOUSE**
Frith Road, Otterden, Faversham
ME13 0DD. Drs Gillian & Peter
Regan, 01795 890556,
peter.regan@virgin.net. *¹/₂ m off
Lenham to Faversham rd. From
A20 E of Lenham turn up
Hubbards Hill, follow signs to
Eastling. After 4m turn L signed
Newnham, Doddington. From A2
in Faversham, turn S towards
Brogdale and continue through
Painters Forstal and Eastling. Turn
R 1¹/₂ m beyond Eastling.* **Adm
£3.50, chd free. Suns 19 Apr; 10
May; 13 Sept (11-5). Visitors also
welcome by appt Apr to Sept,
for groups of up to 50, coaches
permitted.**
Plantsman's garden developed
over 30yrs containing a very wide
range of unusual plants. Special
interest in bulbs (spring and
autumn) and woodland plants (e.g.
erythroniums and trilliums).
Interesting perennials, together
with trees and shrubs chosen for
yr-round appeal. Decorative raised-
bed vegetable garden. Scree area
under development for alpines.

✗ ❀ ☕ ☎

25 ◆ **GODINTON HOUSE &
GARDENS**
Godinton Lane, Ashford TN23 3BP.
Godinton House Preservation Trust,
01233 632652, www.godinton-
house-gardens.co.uk. *1¹/₂ m W of
Ashford. M20 J9 to Ashford. Take A20

towards Charing and Lenham, then
follow brown tourist signs.* **House &
garden £7, chd under 16 free.
Garden only £4, chd under 16 free.
Gardens daily 1 Mar to 1 Nov.
House Fris to Suns 10 Apr to 4 Oct.
For NGS: Suns 22, 29 Mar (2-5.30).**
13 acres designed in 1900 by Reginald
Blomfield to complement the
magnificent Jacobean house. Famous
for its vast, enclosing yew hedge with
views over ancient parkland. Terraced
lawns lead through herbaceous
borders, rose garden and formal lily
pond to intimate Italian Garden and
large walled garden with delphiniums,
fruit, vegetables, cut flowers and new
iris border. Early in the yr, the Wild
Garden is a mass of daffodils, fritillaries,
other spring flowers. Featured on BBC
Gardeners' World, Meridian News & in
'The English Garden'.

& ✗ ❀ ☕

26 **THE GODLANDS**
Straw Mill Hill, Tovil, Maidstone
ME15 6XB. The Kent Fire & Rescue
Service, 01662 692121,
media.mailbox@kent.fire-uk.org,
www.kent.fire-uk.org/about us. *1m
S of Maidstone. From Maidstone town
centre follow signs to Tovil, turn L after
Woodbridge Drive up Straw Mill Hill,
towards Kent Fire HQ (2nd on L).*
Home-made teas. **Adm £3, chd free
(share to Dandelion Trust for
Children). Sat 11 July (12.30-5.30).
Visitors also welcome by appt, last
weekend in month, May to Aug.
Groups of 15+, coaches permitted.**
3 acres of grounds laid out in the
1890s around an Arts & Crafts style
house (not open). Substantial
replanting and work over the last 4yrs.
Mature specimen trees and shrubs.
Terrace, rockery and woodland paths
with rock features. An office with
unusual appeal. Gravel paths and
steep grassed slopes. Woodland paths
not wheelchair-accessible.

& ☕

27 **GODMERSHAM PARK**
Godmersham CT4 7DT. Mr John B
Sunley. *5m NE of Ashford. Off A28,
midway between Canterbury &
Ashford.* Home-made teas. **Adm £4,
chd free. Sun 29 Mar (1-5).**
Associations with Jane Austen. Early
Georgian mansion (not open) in
beautiful downland setting, 24 acres of
formal and landscaped gardens,
topiary, rose beds, herbaceous borders
and superb daffodils in restored
wilderness. Deep gravel paths.

& ❀ ☕

28 ◆ GOODNESTONE PARK GARDENS

Wingham CT3 1PL. Margaret, Lady FitzWalter, 01304 840107, www. goodnestoneparkgardens.co.uk. *6m SE of Canterbury. Village lies S of B2046 from A2 to Wingham. Brown tourist signs off B2046.* **Adm £5, chd (6-16) £1, concessions £4.50. 15 Feb to 22 Mar, Suns only. 24 Mar to 2 Oct, Tues to Fris (11-5), Suns & BH Mons (12-5). For NGS: Mon 8 Mar; Sun 13 Sept (12-5).**
10-12 acres with good trees, woodland garden, snowdrops, spring bulbs and walled garden with old-fashioned roses. Connections with Jane Austen who stayed here. 2 arboretums planted in 1984 and 2001, gravel garden. Picnics allowed.

♿ ✖ ★ ☕

29 ◆ GREAT COMP GARDEN

Comp Lane, Platt, nr Borough Green TN15 8QS. Great Comp Charitable Trust, 01732 886154, www.greatcomp.co.uk. *7m E of Sevenoaks. A20 at Wrotham Heath, take Seven Mile Lane, B2016; at 1st Xrds turn R; garden on L ½ m.* **Adm £5, chd £1. Daily 1 Apr to 31 Oct (11-5). For NGS: Suns 1, 8, 15, 22, 29 Mar; 1 Nov (11-5).**
Skilfully designed 7-acre garden of exceptional beauty. Spacious setting of well-maintained lawns and paths lead visitors through plantsman's collection of trees, shrubs, heathers and herbaceous plants. Good autumn colour. Early C17 house (not open). Magnolias, hellebores and snowflakes are great feature in spring. A great variety of perennials in summer incl salvias, dahlias and crocosmias.

♿ ✖ ★ ☕

30 GREAT MAYTHAM HALL

Maytham Road, Rolvenden TN17 4NE. The Sunley Group. *3m from Tenterden. Maytham Rd off A28 at Rolvenden Church, ½ m from village on R.* **Adm £4, chd free. Weds 15 Apr; 6 May; 10 June (2-5).**
Lutyens-designed gardens famous for having inspired Frances Hodgson Burnett to write 'The Secret Garden' (pre-Lutyens). Parkland, woodland with bluebells. Walled garden with herbaceous beds and rose pergola. Pond garden with mixed shrubbery and herbaceous borders. Interesting specimen trees. Large lawned area with far-reaching views. Featured on BBC TV during Chelsea Week.

✖

Indigenous and unusual trees, orchard, ponds, vineyard (wine available) and meadowland with many varieties of wild orchids . . .

31 115 HADLOW ROAD

Tonbridge TN9 1QE. Mr & Mrs Richard Esdale, 01732 353738. *1½ m N of Tonbridge stn. Take A26 from N end of High St signed Maidstone, house 1m on L in service rd.* **Adm £3, chd free. Suns 28 June; 2, 30 Aug (2-6). Visitors also welcome by appt.**
⅓ -acre unusual terraced garden with large collection of modern roses, island herbaceous border, many clematis, hardy fuchsias, heathers, grasses, hostas, phormiums, and ferns, shrub borders, alpines, annuals, kitchen garden and pond; well labelled.

✖ ☕ ☎

32 HALL PLACE

Leigh TN11 8HH. The Lady Hollenden. *4m W of Tonbridge. From A21 Sevenoaks to Tonbridge, B245 to Hildenborough, then R onto B2027 through Leigh & on R.* Home-made teas. **Adm £5, chd £2. Suns 24 May; Sun 21 June (2-6).**
Large outstanding garden with 11-acre lake, lakeside walk crossing over picturesque bridges. Many rare and interesting trees and shrubs.

♿ ☕

33 25 HANOVER DRIVE

Wigmore, Gillingham ME8 0RF. Joan & Fred Jepson. *3m S of Gillingham. From M2 J4 A278, 1st roundabout 3rd exit to Wigmore. R at roundabout into Wigmore Rd, L at roundabout into Bredhurst Rd, 3rd R into Georgian Way, 1st L Hanover Drive.* Light refreshments. **Adm £3, chd free (share to Medway Macmillan Cancer Support). Wed 13 May; Sun 28 June; Wed 15 July (2-4).**
Developed and maintained by owners for 35yrs believing the garden to be an extension of the house. Enter through a small courtyard leading to the main garden. Lawn, trees, ponds and herbaceous mixed borders. 3 small secret gardens and plenty of seating to enjoy this secluded garden.

♿ ✖ ★ ☕

HARCOURT HOUSE

See London.

34 HAYDOWN

Great Buckland, Luddesdown DA13 0XF. Dr & Mrs I D Edeleanu, 01474 814329. *6m W of Rochester. 4m S of A2. Take turning for Cobham, at war memorial straight ahead down hill, under railway bridge to T-junction. Turn R, after 200yds take L fork, follow narrow lane for 1½ m. Entrance on L.* Light refreshments, wine & home-made teas. **Adm £4, chd free (share to Rotary Club of Northfleet). Sun 7 June (11-5). Visitors also welcome by appt May to Aug, no coaches, groups of 10 or less.**
9-acre garden on North Downs created over the past 36yrs. Formerly scrubland, it now incl woodland of indigenous and unusual trees, orchard, ponds, vineyard (wine available) and meadowland with many varieties of wild orchids. Haven for wildlife, incl badgers. Conducted garden tours. Featured on ITV and in 'Kent Messenger'.

★ ☕ ☎

35 ◆ HEVER CASTLE & GARDENS

nr Edenbridge TN8 7NG. Broadland Properties Ltd, 01732 865224, www.hevercastle.co.uk. *3m SE of Edenbridge. Between Sevenoaks & East Grinstead off B2026. Signed from J5 & J6 of M25, A21, A264.* **House & garden £12, chd £6.50, Senior £10. Garden only £9.50, chd £5.80, Senior £8. Family ticket available. Opening days and times vary according to season; please phone or visit website for details.**
Romantic double moated castle, the childhood home of Anne Boleyn, set in 30 acres of formal and natural landscape. Topiary, Tudor herb garden, magnificent Italian gardens with classical statuary, sculpture and fountains. 38-acre lake, yew and water mazes. Walled rose garden with over 3000 roses, 110 metre-long herbaceous border. Partial wheelchair access.

♿ ✖ ★ ☕

36 HIGHLANDS
Hackington Close, St Stephen's,
Canterbury CT2 7BB. Dr & Mrs B T
Grayson, 01227 765066,
terrygrayson@supanet.com. *1m N of
Canterbury. At the foot of St Stephen's
Hill, 200yds N of Archbishops School,
on rd to Tyler Hill & Chestfield. Car
parking on St Stephen's Hill Rd or
Downs Rd, opp Hackington Close or
nearby side sts.* Home-made teas.
**Adm Apr & May £3, June & July £4,
chd free. Suns 5 Apr; 10 May (2-5);
28 June; 26 July (11-5). Visitors also
welcome by appt.**
2-acre peaceful garden, set in S-facing
bowl, with sweeps of narcissus in
spring and island beds of herbaceous
perennials, roses, azaleas, acers,
hydrangeas, hebes and other shrubs.
Many conifer and broad-leafed trees,
incl plantation of ornamental trees. Two
ponds, small alpine bed and hanging
gardens feature.
⎣ ✕ ☕ ☎

37 ◆ HOLE PARK
Rolvenden, Cranbrook TN17 4JB.
Mr & Mrs E G Barham, 01580
241344, www.holepark.com. *4m SW
of Tenterden. Midway between
Rolvenden & Benenden on B2086.*
**Adm £5, chd 50p. Weds & Thurs Apr
to end Oct, also Suns & BH Mons,
Easter to end June, Suns in Oct.
New bluebell spectacular 12 Apr to
10 May, daily 11-6. For NGS: Sun
5 Apr (2-6), Wed 22 Apr Bluebell
Spectacular (11-6); Suns 17 May;
21 June; 11 Oct (2-6).**
First opened in 1927. 15-acre garden
surrounded by parkland with beautiful
views, yew hedges, large lawns and
specimen trees. Walled gardens, pools
and mixed borders combine with
bulbs, rhododendrons and azaleas.
Massed bluebells in woodland walk,
standard wisterias, orchids in flower
meadow and glorious autumn colours
make this a garden for all seasons.
⎣ ✕ ✿ ☕

**38 NEW 9 HOLMSCROFT
ROAD**
Beltinge, Herne Bay CT6 6PE.
Shirley Davis, 01227 373352,
artenvision@msn.com. *2m E of
Herne Bay. E of Herne Bay take
A299 Thanet Way towards
Margate. Turn off at Beltinge, L at
roundabout over bridge and R
towards Beltinge. Pass PH on L, at
pedestrian crossing Holmscroft Rd
is next on R. Extended car park at
end of village.* Light refreshments &
cream teas. **Sats, Suns 4, 5 July;
1, 2 Aug (11-5). Visitors also
welcome by appt for groups of
10+.**
The garden shows a passionate
and fanatical love of plants, which
is evident in this small, open,
square garden. A variety of shrubs,
ornamental trees, flower borders,
Bonsai, plus at least 300 containers,
make for a breathtaking sight. Take
time not to miss anything. Within
walking distance of the sea.
⎣ ✿ ☕ ☎

> At least 300
> containers,
> make for a
> breathtaking
> sight . . . take
> time not to miss
> anything . . .

39 HONNINGTON FARM
Vauxhall Lane, Southborough,
Tunbridge Wells TN4 0XD. Mrs Ann
Tyler, 07780 800790,
sianburgess@gmail.com,
www.honningtonfarmgardens.co.uk.
*Between Tonbridge and Tunbridge
Wells, E of A26 signed Honnington
Equestrian Centre.* Light lunches &
cream teas. **Adm £4, chd free. Sun 3,
Mon 4 May; Sat 6, Sun 7 June (11-
4). Visitors also welcome by appt at
any time for groups of 10+, coaches
welcome. Please see Farm website
for primrose and bluebell walk
dates.**
6-acre garden, its heavy clay soil
enriched yearly and producing a wide
range of habitats, incl water and bog
gardens, primrose and bluebell walks.
Wildlife promotion a priority. Natural
swimming pool in wild flower meadow.
Gravel garden under development.
Rose and clematis walkways, rockery,
lakes and water features. Large
herbaceous beds, some with New
Zealand influence. Wonderful views.
Sculptures exhibited by our local
sculptor.
✕ ✿ ☕ ☎

Group opening

40 HUNTON GARDENS
ME15 0SE. *6m S of Maidstone. Via
B2163 turn S down Hunton Hill and
West St. Or via Yalding into Vicarage
Rd. Gardens and car parks signed.
Maps available. Gardens accessible
from either of the 2 car parks via public
footpath across fields, 15 mins walk.*
Home-made teas at Queen Anne
House. **Combined adm £3.50, chd
free. Sun 14 June (11-5).**
Small spread-out village with quiet
lanes and church. Limited wheelchair
access.
✕ ☕

NEW THE OLD STABLES
Tim & Jenny Backshall
Natural theme garden around
converted stables. Contemporary
design with views over
surrounding farmland. Curved
features emphasised through
mass planting of perennials and
flowing waves of grasses,
providing intense interest through
all seasons.

NEW QUEEN ANNE HOUSE
Mr & Mrs J Scott
Typical cottage garden of approx
1 acre, 4yrs old, on gentle S-
facing slope. Many choice roses
and herbaceous borders of mixed
planting. Splendid views of the
Weald. Fruit and vegetable area.
Croquet lawn and wildlife area.

SOUTHOVER
David & Anke Way
(See separate entry).
⎣

**41 ◆ IDEN CROFT HERB
GARDENS**
Frittenden Road, Staplehurst
TN12 0DH. Mr Philip Haynes, 01580
891432, www.uk-herbs.com. *9m S of
Maidstone. Brown tourist signs on
A229 just S of Staplehurst.* **Adm £4,
chd free, concessions £3. All yr Mon
to Fri (9-5), Weekends Mar to Sept
(11-5). For NGS: Fris, Sats, 29, 30
May; 19, 20 June; 17, 18 July (9-5).**
Mature themed herb gardens incl
culinary, medicinal, household and
Shakespearean are linked by paths
that lead to the Victorian walled garden
with its serene atmosphere and
sweeping herbaceous borders.
NCCPG collections of mentha,
origanum and nepeta on display. New
for 2009: Raised organic vegetable
beds and restored sensory garden.
⎣ NCCPG ☕

42 ◆ IGHTHAM MOTE

Ivy Hatch TN15 0NT. The National Trust, 01732 810378, www.nationaltrust.org.uk. *6m E of Sevenoaks. Off A25, 2½ m S of Ightham. Buses from rail stns Sevenoaks or Borough Green to Ivy Hatch, ½ m walk to Ightham Mote.* **Adm £10.40, chd £5.20. 14 Mar to 1 Nov Thur to Mon (10.30-5). For NGS: Sat 18 July (10.30-5, last entry 4.30).** 14-acre garden and moated medieval manor c1320, first opened for NGS in 1927. North lake and woodland gardens, ornamental pond and cascade created in early C19. Orchard, enclosed, memorial, vegetable and cutting gardens all contribute to the famous sense of tranquillity. Free guided tours of garden; garden team on hand giving tips and advice.

& ✗ ✿ ☕

Mediterranean terrace with marble fountain, fish, and pergola with vines . . .

43 ◆ KNOLE

Sevenoaks TN15 0RP. The Lord Sackville & The National Trust, 01732 462100, www.nationaltrust.org.uk. *½ m SE of Sevenoaks. Stn: Sevenoaks.* **House & Garden £12, chd £6. Garden only £2, chd £1. House 7 Mar to 1 Nov, Gardens 1 Apr to 30 Sept. Opening days and times vary according to season; please phone or visit website for details. For NGS: Weds 1 Apr; 6 May; 3 June; 1 July; 5 Aug (11-4, last entry 3.30).** Pleasance, deer park, landscape garden and herb garden. The garden commands the most beautiful view of the house and visitors can witness the changing seasons in the garden from early spring to late autumn.

& ✗ ✿ ☕

44 KNOWLE HILL FARM

Ulcombe ME17 1ES. The Hon Andrew & Mrs Cairns, 01622 850240, elizabeth.cairns@btinternet.com. *7m SE of Maidstone. From M20 J8 follow A20 towards Lenham for approx 2m. Turn R to Ulcombe. After 1½ m, 1st L, ½ m 2nd R Windmill Hill. Past Pepper Box PH, ½ m 1st L. R at T-junction.* **Adm £4, chd free. Evening Opening,** wine, Sat 27 June (5-8). Sun 20 Sept (12-6), home-made teas. **Visitors also welcome by appt May to Sept.** 1½ -acre garden created over last 25yrs on S-facing slope of North Downs with spectacular views. Mixed borders contain Mediterranean and tender plants, roses, lavenders, verbenas, salvias and grasses. Pool and rill enclosed within small walled garden planted mainly with white flowers. Easy-care planting around entrance. Mini vegetable and herb garden. Wheelchair users please phone in advance to arrange gravel-free access.

& ✗ ✿ ☕ ☎

45 KYPP COTTAGE

Woolpack Corner, Biddenden TN27 8BU. Mrs Zena Grant, 01580 291480. *5m N of Tenterden. 1m S of Biddenden on A262 at junction with Benenden Rd.* Home-made teas. **Adm £2.50, chd free (share to All Saints Church, Biddenden). Fri 22 May to Tue 26 May incl; Fri 29, Sat 30, Sun 31 May. All June not Mons. Wed 1 to Sat 4 July incl. Every Fri, Sat & Sun in Aug, Mon 31 Aug (Mons to Sats 11-5, Suns 2-6). Visitors also welcome by appt in June & Aug for groups of 10+, coaches & evening appointments welcome.** Not for the tidy-minded! Open for over 30 yrs, this small, romantic, natural garden gently reveals its treasures. Knowledgeable owner has fine plant collection including rare hydrangeas and Eucryphia Nymansay. Roses and clematis entwine and cascade from trees. Paths ramble through dense fern and geranium ground cover to summerhouse and part-pond.

✗ ☕ ☎

46 LADHAM HOUSE

Goudhurst TN17 1DB. Mr Guy Johnson. *8m E of Tunbridge Wells. On NE of village, off A262. Through village towards Cranbrook, turn L at The Chequers PH. 2nd R into Ladham Rd, main gates approx 500yds on L.* Light refreshments & teas. **Adm £4, chd £1. Sun 17 May (2-5).** 10 acres with rolling lawns, fine specimen trees, rhododendrons, camellias, azaleas, shrubs and magnolias. Arboretum. Spectacular twin mixed borders; ha-ha; fountain and bog gardens. Fine view. Edwardian rockery reopened but inaccessible to wheelchairs.

& ✗ ☕

47 212 LANGLEY WAY

West Wickham BR4 0DU. Fleur, Cliff & William Wood, fleur.wood@ntlworld.com. *1½ m SW of Bromley. At junction of A232 (Croydon to Orpington rd) with the B265 T-lights, turn N into Baston Road. At mini roundabout junction with B251 turn L into Pickhurst Lane. Follow rd to Pickhurst PH, then lst L into Langley Way.* Light refreshments, home-made teas & wine. **Adm £3, chd free (share to National Hospital Development Foundation). Fris, Sats, Suns 22, 23, 24 May; 24, 25, 26 July (11-5.30). Visitors also welcome by appt for groups of 10+, Mar to Sept, coaches permitted. Lunches by arrangement.** Not your average suburban back garden! Enter through old oak door under brick arch into cool white courtyard garden. In contrast, fiery Mediterranean terrace with marble fountain and fish, and pergola with vines. Natural cottage garden, a tree house in jungle garden, vegetable area with raised beds, greenhouses, fruit trees and chickens. Everything grown organically with emphasis on wildlife. Narrow paths, rear of garden not wheelchair accessible.

& ✗ ✿ ☕ ☎

48 LARCH COTTAGE

Seed Road, nr Doddington ME9 0NN. Tony & Lesley Bellew, 01795 886016, lesleybellew@yahoo.co.uk. *2½ m S of Doddington, 9m S of Sittingbourne. From A2 nr Ospringe to Newnham turn L by church, 2½ m S along Seed Rd. From A20 nr Lenham proceed to Warren St. At Harrow turn N, follow signs for Newnham along Slade Rd, approx 1½ m. From Doddington village follow signs up Hopes Hill (opp butcher). Teas by arrangement.* **Adm £3, chd free. Visitors welcome by appt.** 3-acre garden on N Downs. Contrasting areas incl knot garden, woodland and rhododendrons, colour-themed mixed borders, ponds and secret garden.

& ✗ ✿ ☕ ☎

49 LAURENDEN FORSTAL

Blind Lane, Challock TN25 4AU. Mrs M Cottrell. *6m N of Ashford. Close to junction of A251 & A252, access from both. All parking in field off village hall car park behind house.* Home-made teas. **Adm £3, chd under 10 free. Suns 29 Mar; 21 June; 23 Aug; 4 Oct (2-6).**

2-acre garden with woodland and rhododendrons, around part C14 house (not open). Rose walk and extensive yew hedging framing lawns and borders. Partly walled rose garden overlooking large wildlife pond; courtyard white garden. Vegetable garden with raised beds, living willow shelter with earth seat overlooking pond. Featured in GGG & 'Kent Life'.

  👤 ✿ ☕

50 LEYDENS
Edenbridge TN8 5NH. Mr Roger Platts, www.rogerplatts.co.uk. *1m S of Edenbridge. On B2026 towards Hartfield (use Nursery entrance & car park).* Home-made teas. **Adm £3.50, chd free. Sun 9 Aug (12-5).**
Private garden of garden designer, nursery owner and author who created the NGS Garden at Chelsea in 2002, winning Gold and Best in Show. Garden at Leydens started in 1999/2000 and under constant development, featuring a wide range of shrubs and perennials. Plenty of planting ideas, several water features, plants clearly labelled and fact sheet available. Wild flower meadow and adjacent nursery, display and propagation beds.

  👤 ✖ ✿ ☕

51 LITTLE GABLES
Holcombe Close, Westerham TN16 1HA. Peter & Elizabeth James. *Centre of Westerham. Off E side of London Rd A233, 200yds from The Green. Please park in public car park.* Home-made teas. **Adm £3, chd free. Sats, Suns 6, 7 June; 25, 26 July (2-5).**
3/4 -acre plant lover's garden extensively planted with a wide range of trees, shrubs, perennials etc, incl many rare ones. Collection of climbing and bush roses and clematis. Large pond with fish, water lilies and bog garden. Fruit and vegetable garden. Large greenhouse.

  ✖ ☕

52 LITTLE WENT
106 High Street, West Malling ME19 6NE. Anne Baring, 01732 843388. *5m W of Maidstone. In middle of West Malling opp car park; entry through gates marked.* Home-made teas. **Adm £3, chd under 12 free. Sun 21 June (11-5.30). Visitors also welcome by appt in June & July only for groups of 10+.**
Long narrow secret garden, fish ponds, aviary with lovebirds,

conservatory, gravel garden and parterre. Lavender garden and statues. Exhibition and sale of paintings.

  👤 ✖ ✿ ☕ 🐕 ☎

53 LONGACRE
Selling ME13 9SE. Dr & Mrs G Thomas, 01227 752254. *5m SE of Faversham. From A2 (M2) or A251 follow signs for Selling, passing White Lion on L. 2nd R & immed L, continue for 1/4 m. From A252 at Chilham, take turning signed Selling at Badgers Hill Garden Centre. L at 2nd Xrds, next R, L & then R.* Home-made teas. **Adm £3, chd free. Sun 12, Mon 13 Apr; Suns 3, 10, 17, 24 May, Mons 4, 25 May; Sun 30, Mon 31 Aug (2-5). Visitors also welcome by appt.**
Plantsman's garden with wide variety of interesting plants, gravel garden and raised vegetable beds. We aim to have colour and interest throughout spring and summer using bulbs, annuals and many containers with cannas, eucomis, *Arundo donax*, etc. Conservatory displays range of tender plants. New Mediterranean garden.

  ✖ ✿ ☕ 🐕 ☎

Restored Victorian 40ft greenhouse with orchid collection . . . collection of interesting chickens . . .

54 LORDS
Sheldwich, Faversham ME13 0NJ. Jane Wade. *4m S of Faversham. From A2 or M2 take A251. 1/2 m S of Sheldwich church find entrance lane on R side adjacent to wood.* **Adm £3, chd free. Thur 9, Sun 12 July (2-5.30). Visitors also welcome by appt for groups of 10+ in early July by written application.**
C18 walled garden with organic vegetables, Mediterranean herb terrace, rose walk and flowery mead under fruit trees. Old specimen trees incl 100ft tulip tree, yew hedges, lawns, cherry orchard grazed by Jacob sheep, ponds and woodland walk.

  ✖ ☎

55 LUTON HOUSE
Selling ME13 9RQ. Sir John & Lady Swire. *4m SE of Faversham. From A2 (M2) or A251 make for White Lion, entrance 30yds E on same side of rd.* **Adm £3, chd free. Suns 19 Apr; 10 May (2-6). Visitors also welcome by appt, small groups of up to 20 in spring. Please apply in writing.**
6 acres; C19 landscaped garden; ornamental ponds; trees underplanted with azaleas, camellias, woodland plants. Hellebores, spring bulbs, magnolias, cherries, daphnes, halesias, maples, Judas trees and cyclamen. Depending on the weather, those interested in camellias, early trees and bulbs may like to visit in late Mar/early Apr before 1st opening date.

  ✖ ☎

56 190 MAIDSTONE ROAD
Chatham ME4 6EW. Dr M K Douglas, 01634 842216. *1m S of Chatham on A230.* **Adm £2, chd free. Sun 15 Feb (2-4.30). Visitors also welcome by appt.**
Informal 1/4 -acre garden; herbaceous borders on either side of former tennis court; scree garden and pool; many snowdrops and other spring bulbs. Doll's house (1/12 scale model of house) may also be viewed.

  ✖ ✿ ☎

57 ◆ MARLE PLACE
Brenchley TN12 7HS. Mr & Mrs Gerald Williams, 01892 722304, www.marleplace.co.uk. *8m SE of Tonbridge. From A21 Kippings Cross roundabout take B2160 to Matfield, R to Brenchley, then follow brown tourist signs. From A21 Forstal Farm roundabout take B2162 Horsmonden rd and follow signs.* **Adm £5, chd £1, concessions £4.50. Combined adm with Old Tong Farm Sun 14 June £6.50. Fris to Mons Apr to Sept (10-5). For NGS: Weds 15 Apr; 13 May; 1 July; Sun 14 June (10-5.30).**
Victorian gazebo, plantsman's shrub borders, walled scented garden, Edwardian rockery, herbaceous borders, bog and kitchen gardens. Woodland walks, mosaic terrace, artists' studios and gallery with contemporary art. Autumn colour. Restored Victorian 40ft greenhouse with orchid collection. C17 listed house (not open). Collection of interesting chickens.

  👤 ✖ ✿ ☕

58 MERE HOUSE
Mereworth ME18 5NB. Mr & Mrs Andrew Wells. *7m E of Tonbridge. From A26 turn N on to B2016 & then into Mereworth village. 3¹/₂ m S of M20/M26 J, take A20, then B2016 to Mereworth.* Home-made teas. **Adm £3, chd free. Sun 15 Feb (2-5); Sun 29 Mar; Mon 13 Apr; Sun 18 Oct (2-5.30); Sun 14 Feb 2010.**
6-acre garden with C18 lake. Snowdrops, daffodils, lawns, herbaceous borders, ornamental shrubs and trees with foliage contrast and striking autumn colour. Woodland walk and major tree planting and landscaping. New park and lake walk.
&. ⊛ ☕

59 ◆ MOUNT EPHRAIM
Hernhill, Faversham ME13 9TX. Mrs M N Dawes, Mr & Mrs E S Dawes, 01227 751496, www.mountephraimgardens.co.uk. *3m E of Faversham. From end of M2, then A299 take slip rd 1st L to Hernhill, signed to gardens.* **Adm £4.50, chd £3, groups £4. 12 Apr to end Sept, Weds, Thurs, Sats, Suns & Bank Hols (12-5). For NGS: Suns 26 Apr; 27 Sept (12-5).**
Herbaceous border; topiary; daffodils and rhododendrons; rose terraces leading to small lake. Rock garden with pools; water garden; young arboretum. Rose garden with arches and pergola planted to celebrate the millennium. Magnificent trees. Grass maze. Superb views over fruit farms to Swale estuary.
⊛ ☕

60 MOUNTS COURT FARMHOUSE
Acrise, nr Folkestone CT18 8LQ. Graham & Geraldine Fish, 01303 840598, graham.s.fish @btinternet.com. *6m NW of Folkestone. From A260 Folkestone to Canterbury rd, turn L at Swingfield (Densole) opp Black Horse Inn, 1¹/₂ m towards Elham & Lyminge, on N side.* Home-made teas. **Adm £3, chd free. Suns 7 June; 12 July (2-5). Also open The Farm House, Acrise Place. Visitors also welcome by appt.**
1¹/₂ acres surrounded by open farmland; variety of trees, shrubs, grasses and herbaceous plants; pond and bog garden. 20,000 gallon rainwater reservoir waters garden and keeps pond topped up; compost heats to 170° for fast turnover.
&. ✗ ⊛ ☕ ☎

Ornamental shrubs and trees with foliage contrast and striking autumn colour . . .

61 NETTLESTEAD PLACE
Nettlestead ME18 5HA. Mr & Mrs Roy Tucker, www.nettlesteadplace.co.uk. *6m W/SW of Maidstone. Turn S off A26 onto B2015 then 1m on L, next to Nettlestead Church.* Home-made teas. **Adm £5, chd free. Suns 14 June (2-5.30); 4 Oct (2-5).**
C13 manor house in 10-acre plantsman's garden. Large formal rose garden. Large herbaceous garden of island beds with rose and clematis walkway leading to garden of China roses. Fine collection of trees and shrubs; sunken pond garden, terraces, bamboos, glen garden, acer lawn. Young pinetum adjacent to garden. Sculptures. Wonderful open country views. Gravel paths. Sunken pond garden not wheelchair accessible at water level.
&. ☕

62 OLANTIGH
Olantigh Road, Wye TN25 5EW. Mr & Mrs J R H Loudon. *10m SW of Canterbury, 6m NE of Ashford. Turn off A28 to Wye. 1m from Wye on Olantigh rd towards Godmersham.* **Adm £3, chd free. Sun 24 May (2-5).**
Edwardian garden in beautiful 20-acre setting; wide variety of trees; river garden; rockery; shrubbery; herbaceous border; extensive lawns; tree sculpture and woodland walks. This is a simply beautiful garden. Sorry, no teas, but please feel free to bring your own.
✗

63 ◆ OLD BUCKHURST
Markbeech, nr Edenbridge TN8 5PH. Mr & Mrs J Gladstone, 01342 850825, www.oldbuckhurst.co.uk. *4m SE of Edenbridge. B2026, at Queens Arms PH turn E to Markbeech. In approx 1¹/₂ m, 1st house on R after leaving Markbeech. Parking in paddock if dry.*

Adm £3, chd free. For NGS: Sats, Suns, Weds: 25, 26 Apr; 13, 16, 17, 30, 31 May; 3, 13, 17, 21, 28 June; 12, 15, 19, 26, 29 July; 1, 2 Aug; 5, 6 Sept (11-5).
1-acre partly-walled cottage garden around C15 listed farmhouse with catslip roof (not open). Shrubs, clematis, climbing and shrub roses, anemones, astilbes, campanulas, eryngiums, day lilies in May, July/Aug, hardy geraniums, grasses, iris, jasmine, lilies, peonies, poppies, penstemons, wisteria, fruit and vegetables. Yr-round interest using structure, texture, scent and colour. WC. Groups welcome by arrangement. Featured on Radio Kent, in 'Garden Answers' & 'Traumgarten'.
✗ ⊛

64 OLD ORCHARD
56 Valley Drive, Loose, Maidstone ME15 9TL. Mike & Hazel Brett, 01622 746941, mandh.brett@tiscali.co.uk. *2¹/₂ m S of Maidstone. From Maidstone on A229, turn R into Lancet Lane, 1st L into Waldron Drive then 1st R into Valley Drive. Property at end of cul-de-sac. Access also from Old Loose Hill via footpath between bus stop and allotments.* **Adm £2.50, chd free (share to National Talking Newspapers & Magazines). Sat 2, Sun 3 May (11-5). Visitors also welcome by appt.**
Secluded garden with S-facing rear acre overlooking conservation area. Meandering grass paths around informal island beds containing usual and unusual trees, shrubs and perennials. Numerous alpines, bulbs, dwarf irises, and dwarf shrubs in extensive rockeries, screes, raised beds and troughs with woodland plants in shadier areas. Small arboretum for foliage, form and colour.
&. ✗ ⊛ ☕ ☎

65 OLD PLACE FARM
High Halden TN26 3JG. Mr & Mrs Jeffrey Eker, 01233 850202, jeffreyeker@tiscali.co.uk. *10m SW of Ashford. From A28, centre of village, take Woodchurch Rd (opp Chequers PH) for ¹/₂ m.* Home-made teas by prior arrangement. **Adm £5, chd free. Visitors welcome by appt for individuals & groups, also evening visits.**
4-acre garden, mainly designed by Anthony du Gard Pasley, surrounding period garmhouse (not open) and buildings, with paved herb garden and parterres, small lake, ponds, lawns, mixed borders, cutting garden and

potager, old shrub roses, foliage plants and specimen trees. Two bridges leading to woodland and fields. Wild flower meadow. New woodland topiary garden, a whimsical creation, inspired by Séricourt. Tulips, blossom and bluebells a special feature in April and May. Featured in 'Topiarius', 'Daily Mail' & 'GGG'.

66 OLD TONG FARM

Tong Road, Brenchley TN12 7HT. Simon Toynbee, 01892 723552, toynbee@aol.com. *6m E of Tunbridge Wells. 1¹/₂ m S of Brenchley village. From A21 going S, past B2160, turn L into Cryals Rd. After 2m R into Tong Rd, house is 800yds on L. Or exit Brenchley village on rd to Horsmonden. Turn R, Fairmans Lane leads to Tong Rd. Parking in orchard 300yds S of property, enter property through wood.* Home-made teas 14 June only. **Adm £3, chd free. Combined adm with Marle Place Sun 14 June £6.50. Sun 14, Wed 17 June (12-6).** Visitors also welcome by appt 10, 24 June; 1, 8, 15 July (no refreshments).

4-acre terraced garden around pre-Tudor farmhouse (not open) with mixed borders, rose garden, nuttery, pond, meadow and small organic vegetable garden. Other features incl trees, formal circular lawn, sunken herb garden with varieties of sweet peas. Emphasis on tamed informality and non-regimented approach. Featured in 'Gardens Monthly'. Visitors in wheelchairs must be dropped off at main gate.

67 ONE DERING ROAD

Ashford TN24 8DB. Mrs Claire de Sousa Barry, 07979 816104, nazgulnota-bene@ntlworld.com. *Town centre. Just off Hythe Rd nr Henwood roundabout. Short walk from pay and display car park located just past fire stn in Henwood Rd. Please do not park in Doring Rd.* Fairtrade tea, coffee & delicious home-made cakes June onwards. **Adm £3, regret children not admitted. Sat 23, Sun 24, Mon 25 May; Sats, Suns 6, 7, 13, 14, 20, 21 June; 4, 5, 11, 12, 18, 19 July; 1, 2 Aug (2-5).** Visitors also welcome by appt for groups of 10+, no coaches, teas by arrangement.

Plantsperson's romantic town garden with optimum use of space. Successional planting for yr-round interest. Pittosporum, robinia, crinodendron, cardiocrinum.

Cascading roses, clematis, jasmine, honeysuckle, delphiniums, arisaemas, trilliums, uvularias, camellias and rhododendrons. A host of other unusual plants. Visitors say: 'inspiring, exceptional, all the senses are alive in this garden'. Featured on GMTV nationwide weather forecast, BBC Radio Kent & in 'Kent Life'. Please note: no WC.

68 THE ORANGERY

Mystole, Chartham CT4 7DB. Rex Stickland & Anne Prasse, rex@mystole.fsnet.co.uk. *5m SW of Canterbury. Turn off A28 through Shalmsford Street. After 1¹/₂ m at Xrds turn R down hill. Keep straight on, ignoring rds on L (Pennypot Lane) & R. Ignore drive on L signed 'Mystole House only' & at sharp bend in 600yds turn L into private drive signed Mystole Farm.* Home-made teas. **Adm £3, chd free. Suns 21 June; 26 July (1-6).** Visitors also welcome by appt.

1¹/₂ -acre gardens around C18 orangery, now a house (not open). Front gardens, established well-stocked herbaceous border and large walled garden with a wide variety of shrubs and mixed borders. Splendid views from terraces over ha-ha and paddocks to the lovely Chartham Downs. Water features and very interesting collection of modern sculptures set in natural surroundings.

Small village with eclectic mix of gardening styles and sizes . . .

69 ORCHARD COTTAGE

3 Woodlands Road, Bickley, Bromley BR1 2AD. Mrs J M Wall. *1¹/₂ m E of Bromley. About 400yds from the A222. From Bickley Park Rd turn into Pines Rd, then 1st R into Woodlands Rd, No 3 is 1st house on L.* Home-made teas. **Adm £2.50, chd free (share to Diabetes UK). Sun 19 July (2-5).**

Attractive, colourful and varied ¹/₃ -acre garden, compartmentalised and themed, with many interesting and unusual herbaceous plants and shrubs. Incl areas of scree beds, troughs and pots with alpines and other specialist plants.

70 ORCHARD END

Cock Lane, Spelmonden Road, Horsmonden TN12 8EQ. Mr & Mrs Hugh Nye, 01892 723118. *8m E of Tunbridge Wells. From A21 going S turn L at roundabout towards Horsmonden on B2162. After 2m turn R into Spelmonden Rd, ¹/₂ m to top of hill, R into Cock Lane. Garden 50yds on R.* Light refreshments & home-made teas. **Adm £3.50, chd free. Sats, Suns 13, 14 June; 25, 26 July; 5, 6 Sept (11-5.30).** Visitors also welcome by appt.

Classically English garden on 1¹/₂ -acre sloping site, landscaped 13yrs ago by owners' garden designer son. Divided into rooms with linking vistas. Incl hot borders, cottage and white gardens, exotics with pergola, raised summerhouse overlooking lawns and drive planting. Formal fish pond with bog garden. Ornamental vegetable and fruit areas. Wildlife orchard. Small display and sale of local artists' work.

Group opening

71 OTHAM GARDENS

nr Maidstone ME15 8RS. *4m SE of Maidstone. From A20 or A274 follow signs for Otham or Stoneacre, 1m. Parking restricted to official car parks except for disabled visitors at Stoneacre.* Light refreshments at Otham Village Hall. **Combined adm £3.50, chd free. Sat 18 July (11-5).** Small village with eclectic mix of gardening styles and sizes. Village map available for all visitors.

ASHLEY

White Horse Lane, Otham, Maidstone. Susan & Roger Chartier

Front garden developed into a parterre, leading to surprisingly large rear garden with many unusual perennials. Pond with bridge, kitchen garden. New dry garden and collection of 50 pelargoniums.

BEEHIVE COTTAGE

Linda & John Middleton

S-facing garden with interesting planting. Contemporary water feature and small vegetable garden.

GREENHILL HOUSE

Hugh & Susan Vaux

Established garden with mixed borders, roses, shrubs, parterre, alpine bed and mini vegetable garden. Splendid views.

THE LIMES
Mrs Annette Stephens
Well-established garden,
herbaceous borders, kitchen
garden, wild garden and artist's
garden.

◆ **STONEACRE**
Graham Fraser & Richard Nott &
The National Trust, 01622
862871. (Open Sats 11-6).
C15 half timber frame hall house,
surrounded by herbaceous
borders, orchard, wild areas,
courtyard, many unusual plants,
spring bulbs and topiary. All-yr
colour. Featured in 'The English
Garden'.
&

OXTED PLACE GARDENS
See Surrey.

Adjacent, long and narrow town gardens of different styles . . .

72 PARSONAGE OASTS
Hampstead Lane, Yalding
ME18 6HG. Edward & Jennifer
Raikes, 01622 814272. *6m SW of
Maidstone. On B2162 between Yalding
village & stn, turn off at Anchor PH over
canal bridge, continue 100yds up lane.
House and car park on L.* Cream teas.
Adm £2, chd free. Easter Mon
13 Apr (2-5.30). Visitors also
welcome by appt.
³/4 -acre riverside garden with walls,
shrubs, daffodils, spectacular
magnolia. Unfenced river bank. Gravel
paths and a few shallow steps.
& ♣ ☕ ☎

73 PEDLINGE COURT
Pedlinge, Saltwood CT21 4JJ. Mr &
Mrs J P Scrivens, 01303 269959.
*¹/2 m W of Hythe. Top of hill, on A261
from Hythe up hill signed M20 &
Ashford opp sign 'Pedlinge'. From
Newingreen 1m opp sign 'Hythe
twinned with....'.* Adm £3.50 (share to
Cats Protection). Visitors welcome
by appt mid May to mid July, for
small groups.
1¹/2 -acre garden with a profusion of
interesting plants around C14
farmhouse (not open), birthplace of the
orchid foxglove 'Saltwood Summer'.

Wide variety of cottage garden plants,
ferns, old shrub roses, medicinal and
culinary herbs with a backdrop of trees
and shrubs incl topiary. Featured in
'Kentish Express'.
♣ ❀ ☎

74 ◆ PENSHURST PLACE
Penshurst TN11 8DG. Viscount De
L'Isle, 01892 870307,
www.penshurstplace.com. *6m NW
of Tunbridge Wells. SW of Tonbridge
on B2176, signed from A26 N of
Tunbridge Wells.* House & garden
£8.50, chd £5.50. Garden only £7,
chd £5. Weekends from 28 Feb,
daily 28 Mar to 1 Nov, gardens
10.30-6, house 12-4. For NGS: Wed
13 May (10.30-6, last entry 4.45).
10 acres of garden dating back to
C14; garden divided into series of
rooms by over a mile of clipped yew
hedge; profusion of spring bulbs:
herbaceous borders; formal rose
garden; famous peony border.
Woodland trail. All-yr interest. Toy
museum.
& ♣ ❀ ☕

75 ◆ THE PINES GARDEN
St Margaret's Bay CT15 6DZ. St
Margaret's Bay Trust, 01304 851737,
www.baytrust.org.uk. *4¹/2 m NE of
Dover. Approach village of St
Margaret's-at-Cliffe off A258
Dover/Deal rd. Continue through village
centre & down Bay Hill. Signed just
before beach.* Adm £3, chd 50p,
concessions £2.50. Garden open all
yr (10-5), not Christmas Day. Phone
or see website for museum and
tearoom information. For NGS: Fri
10 Apr; Mons 25 May; 31 Aug (10-5).
Adjacent to cliff walks and beach, this
mature garden offers a mixture of open
undulating parkland, trees, shrubs and
secluded areas. Lake, waterfall, grass
labyrinth, roundhouse shelter, famous
Oscar Nemon statue of Winston
Churchill. Chalk-constructed
conference centre with grass-covered
roof. Special family-friendly events led
by Rippledown Environmental
Education Centre exploring the garden
and its wildlife. Access for disabled,
ample seating, picnics.
&

76 PLACKETTS HOLE
Bicknor, nr Sittingbourne ME9 8BA.
Mr & Mrs D P Wainman, 01622
884258, aj@aj-
wainman.demon.co.uk. *5m S of
Sittingbourne. W of B2163. Bicknor is
signed from Hollingbourne Hill & from*

*A249 at Stockbury Valley. Placketts
Hole is midway between Bicknor &
Deans Hill.* Light refreshments by
arrangement. Adm £3.50. Visitors
welcome by appt May to Sept,
regret no coaches owing to single
track road.
Mature 3-acre garden in Kent
Downland valley incl herbaceous
borders, rose and herb gardens, small
kitchen garden and informal pond
intersected by walls, hedges and
paths. Many unusual plants, trees and
shrubs provide colour and interest from
spring to autumn. Some gravel paths
and short steep slopes.
& ♣ ❀ ☕ ☎

77 PRIMROSE COTTAGE
Rose Hill, Wittersham, Tenterden
TN30 7HE. Jenny & Michael Clarke,
01797 270820,
greenfingers@kent.uk.net. *6m S of
Tenterden. Signed off B2082 1m E of
centre of Wittersham at highest point
of Isle of Oxney.* Adm £2.50, chd free
(share to Arcadia Animal Welfare).
Thur 4 to Sun 7 June incl (2-5).
Visitors also welcome by appt.
Joyful jumble of cottage garden plants,
many unusual. Rose pergola walk, well
and water feature. Vegetable garden in
blocks for easy maintenance. A
peaceful garden maintained by
owners. Sorry, no teas, but you are
welcome to picnic in our field.
& ♣ ❀ ☎

**78 NEW 14 & 16 PRINCE
CHARLES AVENUE**
Walderslade, Chatham
ME5 8EX. Mrs Penn & Mrs
Roser. *From M2 J3 turn L to
Walderslade. L from roundabout
into Robin Hood Lane. R at small
roundabout into Princes Ave, 3rd R
into Prince Charles Ave.* Home-
made teas. Adm £3, chd free
(share to Kent Autistic Trust). Sat
18, Sun 19 July (10-4).
Adjacent, long and narrow town
gardens of different styles. Number
14 is an English country garden
with many unusual plants, small
pond with water feature and rose
garden. Number 16 has been
designed by senior citizens aiming
for low maintenance and minimum
outlay with the use of pots and
containers, resulting in a garden
with a difference. Pond with large
Koi fish.
❀ ☕

79 PUXTED HOUSE

Brenchley Road, Brenchley TN12 7PB. Mr P J Oliver-Smith, pjospux@aol.com. *6m SE of Tonbridge. From A21, 1m S of Pembury turn N onto B2160, turn R at Xrds in Matfield signed Brenchley. 1/4 m from Xrds stop at 30mph sign at village entrance.* Cream teas 17 May only, no teas in June. **Adm £3, chd free. Suns 17 May; 7 June (2-6).** Visitors also welcome by appt.

1 1/2 acres, planted with scented and coloured foliage shrubs selected to ensure yr-long changing effects. Meandering gravel paths lead from the alpine garden via herbaceous borders and croquet lawn with its thyme terrace to formal rose garden and thereafter swing amongst oriental woodland plants and bamboos about a lily pond. Large glasshouse protects many Australasian shrubs and cacti. Gravel paths and grass.

80 ◆ QUEX GARDENS

Quex Park, Birchington CT7 0BH. Quex Museum Trust, 01843 842168, www.quexmuseum.org. *3m W of Margate. 10m NE of Canterbury. A28 towards Margate, then rd to Acol to Quex Park. Follow signs for Quex Museum, Quex Park.* **House & garden £7, chd/concessions £5. Garden £2, chd/concessions £1.50. 1 Apr to 29 Oct, Suns to Thurs (11-5). Nov to Mar Suns only (1-3.30). For NGS: Sun 21 June; Wed 22 July (11-5).**
15 acres of woodland and gardens with fine specimen trees unusual on Thanet, spring bulbs, wisteria, shrub borders, old figs and mulberries, herbaceous borders. Victorian walled garden with cucumber house, long glasshouses, cactus house, fruiting trees. Peacocks, dovecote, woodland walk, wildlife pond, children's maze, croquet lawn, picnic grove, lawns and fountains.

81 11 RAYMER ROAD

Penenden Heath, Maidstone ME14 2JQ. Mrs Barbara Badham. *From M20 J6 at Running Horse roundabout take Penenden Heath exit along Sandling Lane. At T-lights turn into Downsview Rd and follow signs.* Home-made teas. **Adm £3, chd free. Suns 10 May; 14 June (11-5).**
Compact garden with lovely views of North Downs. Divided into different areas containing wide range of plants, shrubs, fruit and vegetables for yr-round interest. Large strawberry tree, apple arch, wisteria, magnolias, azaleas, tulips, roses, hardy geraniums, peonies and foxgloves. Minarette fruit trees underplanted with wild flowers. Raised vegetable beds, small pond.

Allotments

82 RIDDLES ROAD ALLOTMENTS

Sittingbourne ME10 1LF. Sittingbourne Allotment and Gardeners' Society. *1/2 m S of Sittingbourne. At A2/A249 junction turn E off roundabout towards Sittingbourne. After approx 1m turn R into Borden Lane, just after Coniston Hotel. Riddles Rd 2nd L after approx 1/2 m.* Light refreshments. **Adm £2.50, chd free. Sun 26 July (11-4).**
The site, with 100+ plots, is exceptionally well maintained and plot holders practise many horticultural methods to grow crops of vegetables, fruit and flowers, incl show-winning produce, such as roses, daffodils, dahlias and chrysanthemums, and soft fruit. Come and talk to the plot holders, and buy home-made drinks, cakes, jams, and of course some of the freshly-picked fruit and vegetables. Featured on Radio Kent & in local press.

83 ◆ RIVERHILL HOUSE GARDENS

Sevenoaks TN15 0RR. The Rogers Family, jane@riverhillgardens.co.uk. *2m S of Sevenoaks on A225.* **Adm £3.50, chd 50p. Suns & Bank Hol weekends, mid Mar to end June (11-5). For NGS: Thur 23 Apr (11-5).**
Mature hillside garden with extensive views; specimen trees, sheltered terraces with roses and rare shrubs; bluebell wood with rhododendrons and azaleas. Primrose meadow. Picnics allowed. Unsuitable for wheelchairs but users may have free access to the tea terrace - on the level and with views across the garden.

84 ROCK FARM

Gibbs Hill, Nettlestead ME18 5HT. Mrs S E Corfe, 01622 812244. *6m W of Maidstone. Turn S off A26 onto B2015, then 1m S of Wateringbury turn R up Gibbs Hill.* **Adm £4, chd free (share to St Mary the Virgin, Nettlestead). Weds, Sats 20, 23 May; 24, 27 June; 1, 4, 8, 11 July (11-5).** Visitors also welcome by appt.

2-acre garden set around old Kentish farmhouse (not open) in beautiful setting; created with emphasis on all-yr interest and ease of maintenance. Plantsman's collection of shrubs, trees and perennials for alkaline soil; extensive herbaceous border, vegetable area, bog garden and plantings around two large natural ponds. Starred garden in GGG.

Come and talk to the plot holders . . .

85 ROGERS ROUGH

Chicks Lane, Kilndown TN17 2RP. Richard & Hilary Bird, 01892 890554, richardbird@rogersrough.demon.co.uk. *10m SE of Tonbridge. From A21 2m S of Lamberhurst turn E into Kilndown; take 1st R down Chick's Lane until rd divides.* Home-made teas. **Adm £4, chd free. Sat, Sun 7, 8 Feb Snowdrop Weekend (11-4); Sats, Suns, Mons 2, 3, 4, 23, 24, 25 May; Sat 13, Sun 14 June Geranium Weekend (11-5.30).** Visitors also welcome by appt Apr to July, coaches permitted.
Garden writer's 1 1/2 -acre garden, divided into many smaller gardens containing herbaceous borders, rock gardens, shrubs, small wood and pond. Very wide range of plants, incl some unusual ones. Extensive views. Snowdrop Weekend 7, 8 Feb, Geranium Weekend 13, 14 June. Featured on TV and press.

86 ST CLERE

Kemsing TN15 6NL. Mr & Mrs Ronnie Norman. *6m NE of Sevenoaks. Take A25 from Sevenoaks toward Maidstone; 1m past Seal turn L signed Heaverham & Kemsing. In Heaverham take rd to R signed Wrotham & W Kingsdown; in 75yds straight ahead marked private rd; 1st L & follow rd to house.* Home-made teas. **Adm £4, chd 50p. Sun 14 June (2-5.30).**
4-acre garden, full of interest. Formal terraces surrounding C17 mansion (not open), with beautiful views of the Kent countryside. Herbaceous and shrub borders, productive kitchen and herb gardens, lawns and rare trees.

Group opening

87 ST MICHAEL'S GARDENS
East Peckham TN12 5NH. *5m NE of Tonbridge, 5m SW of Maidstone. On A26 at Mereworth roundabout take S exit (A228 Paddock Wood). After 1½ m turn L into Roydon Hall Rd. Gardens ½ m up hill on L. From Paddock Wood A228 towards West Malling. 1m after roundabout with Wheelbarrow turn R into Roydon Hall Rd.* Home-made teas. **Combined adm £4, chd free (share to Friends of St Michael's Church). Suns 26 Apr; 17 May; 28 June (2-5).** Victorian house, cottage garden and cottage yard. Crafts at Cuckoo Cottage, jewellery, cards & encaustic prints. No wheelchair access to St Michael's Cottage.

CUCKOO COTTAGE
Mr Gavin Walter & Mrs Emma Walter
Born from a desire to add life and colour to a derelict and shady yard, a slate scree base is used with pots and containers.

ST MICHAEL'S COTTAGE
Mr Peter & Mrs Pauline Fox
Garden designed so it cannot be seen all at once. Traditional cottage garden with collection of lavenders, hostas, clematis, shrubs, ferns, heathers and wildlife area.

ST MICHAEL'S HOUSE
Brigadier & Mrs W Magan
Grey stone old vicarage with yew topiary hedges surrounding flower beds planned in coordinated colours. Lovely display of tulips followed by splendid irises, then a mass of roses from red-hot to old soft colours. Wonderful views from the meadow.

88 ◆ THE SALUTATION
Knightrider Street, Sandwich CT13 9EW. Mr & Mrs Dominic Parker, 01304 619919, www.the-salutation.com. *In the heart of Sandwich. Turn L at Bell Hotel and into Quayside car park. Entrance on far R-hand corner of car park.* **Adm £4.50, chd £3, family £14. Open all yr, not Thurs. For NGS: Mon 6 Apr (10-4); Wed 22 July (10-5); Sat 10 Oct (10-4).** 3½ acres of ornamental and formal gardens designed by Sir Edwin Lutyens and Gertrude Jekyll in 1911

surrounding Grade I listed house. Designated historic park and garden. Lake, white, yellow, spring, woodland, rose, kitchen, vegetable and herbaceous gardens. Designed to provide yr-round changing colour. Featured on TV Country Lives with Chris Beardshaw.

89 SANDLING PARK
Hythe CT21 4HN. The Hardy Family. *1½ m NW of Hythe. Entrance off A20 only. From M20 J11 turn E onto A20. Entrance ¼ m.* Home-made teas. **Adm £4, chd free (share to Saltwood Church). Sun 10 May (10-5).** 25-acre woodland garden with an extensive collection of trees and shrubs with rhododendrons, azaleas, magnolias and other interesting plants that also relish acid soil. Regret not suitable for wheelchairs.

90 ◆ SCOTNEY CASTLE
Lamberhurst TN3 8JN. The National Trust, 01892 893820, www.nationaltrust.org.uk. *6m SE of Tunbridge Wells. On A21 London-Hastings, brown tourist signs. Bus: (Mon to Sat) Tunbridge Wells-Wadhurst, alight Lamberhurst Green.* **House & Garden £8.50, chd £4.25. Garden only £6.50, chd £3.50. Opening dates & times vary according to season. Please visit website for details. For NGS: Sat 18 July (11-5.30, house closes 5).** Picturesque landscape garden, created by the Hussey family in the 1840s surrounding moated C14 Castle. Picnic area by car park in walled garden. Some steep slopes.

91 SEA CLOSE
Cannongate Road, Hythe CT21 5PX. Major & Mrs R H Blizard, 01303 266093. *½ m from Hythe. Towards Folkestone (A259), on L. Signed.* Light refreshments. **Adm £3, chd free (share to Royal Signals Benevolent Fund). Suns 19 July; 13 Sept (2-5). Visitors also welcome by appt for any number.** Handsome 1914 house (not open) in well-designed 1-acre cottage-style garden overlooking Channel. Many tender and unusual plants and shrubs provide monthly-changing scenario. En route for continent? Shuttle terminal 3m, Dover 15m. Probably last formal opening days, visitors welcome by appt.

Allotments

92 SEVENOAKS ALLOTMENTS
Allotment Lane, off Quaker Hall Lane, Sevenoaks TN13 3TX. Sevenoaks Allotment Holders Assn, www.sevenoaksallotments.co.uk. *Quaker Hall Lane is off A225, St John's Hill. Site directly behind St John's Church.* Light refreshments & home-made teas. **Adm £3, chd free. Sun 28 June (10-5).** The Association self-manages 11½ acres of productive allotment gardens situated in the heart of the town. A wide cross-section of allotment owners grow a massive variety of flowers, fruit and vegetables using a number of different techniques. Gardeners cite healthy produce, exercise and relaxation in a beautiful open space as reasons to rent a plot. Scarecrow competition. Featured on Radio Kent. Hilly site with some steep slopes.

Many tender and unusual plants and shrubs provide monthly-changing scenario . . .

93 ◆ SISSINGHURST GARDEN
Sissinghurst TN172AB. The National Trust, 01580 710700, www.nationaltrust.org.uk. *16m E of Tunbridge Wells. On A262 1m E of village. Bus: Arriva Maidstone-Hastings, alight Sissinghurst 1¼ m. Direct bus Tue, Fri & Sun. Stn: Staplehurst. Ring for details.* **Adm £9.80, chd £4.90. Telephone or see website for regular opening dates and times. For NGS: Mons 6 Apr; 8 June; 10 Aug; 5 Oct (11- last entry 5).** Garden created by the late Vita Sackville-West and Sir Harold Nicolson. Spring garden, herb garden, cottage garden, white garden, rose garden. Tudor building and tower, partly open to public. Moat. Exhibition on history of the garden and property in the oast buildings.

94 SMITHS HALL
Lower Road, West Farleigh
ME15 0PE. Mr S Norman, 01622
814106, leebrayshaw@hotmail.com.
*3m W of Maidstone. A26 towards
Tonbridge, turn L into Teston Lane
B2163. At T-junction turn R onto
Lower Rd B2010. Opp Tickled Trout
PH.* Light refreshments & home-made
teas. **Adm £4, chd free (share to The
Dandelion Trust). Suns 17 May;
28 June (11-5). Visitors also
welcome by appt.**
3-acre formal and informal garden.
Bluebell woodland walk leading to
newly-designed 9-acre parkland, incl
native woodland, wild flower meadow,
and American tree species. Garden
surrounds Queen Anne house (not
open). Long formal herbaceous
borders, rose garden, rose walk,
sunken water garden, peony border
and walled garden.
&♿ ✿ ☕ ☎

95 SOTTS HOLE COTTAGE
Crouch Lane, Borough Green
TN15 8QL. Mr & Mrs Jim Vinson. *7m
E of Sevenoaks. Crouch Lane runs SE
from A25 between Esso garage &
Black Horse PH, garden at bottom of
2nd hill, approx 3/4 m.* Home-made
teas. **Adm £3, chd free (share to
Heart of Kent Hospice). Suns 31
May; 26 July; 20 Sept (11-6).**
6 acres of landscaped cottage garden
relying entirely on the threat of visitors
to motivate the owners to maintain it.
We look forward to seeing you.
✖ ☕

96 SOUTH HILL FARM
Hastingleigh TN25 5HL. Sir Charles
Jessel, 01233 750325. *41/2 m E of
Ashford. Turn off A28 to Wye, go
through village & ascend Wye Downs.
In Brabourne turn R at Xrds marked
Brabourne & South Hill, then 1st L. Or
from Stone St (B2068) turn W opp
Stelling Minnis, follow signs to
Hastingleigh. Continue towards Wye &
turn L at Xrds marked Brabourne &
South Hill, then 1st L.* **Adm £4, incl
tea & biscuits, chd free. Visitors
welcome by appt mid-June to mid-
July only, groups of 10+, coaches
permitted.**
2 acres high up on N Downs, C17/18
house (not open). Old walls, ha-ha,
formal water garden; old and new
roses, unusual shrubs, perennials and
foliage plants.
&♿ ✖ ☕ ☎

97 SOUTHOVER
Grove Lane, Hunton, Maidstone
ME15 0SE. David & Anke Way,
01622 820876,
anke@away2.wanadoo.co.uk. *6m S
of Maidstone. Turn W from A229 to
B2163. At Xrds past Coxheath turn L
down Hunton Hill, past church to
school, then R into Grove Lane. Or
from Yalding War Memorial follow
Vicarage Rd into Hunton to school,
then L into Grove Lane.* Refreshments
by arrangement for groups of 10+.
**Adm £3.50, chd free. Sat 14 Feb (11-
4). Open with Hunton Gardens Sun
14 June. Also open Sat 14 Feb
Spring Platt. Visitors also welcome
by appt 5 Jan to 1st week Mar for
snowdrops, also in 2010.**
Plant enthusiasts' 0.5ha garden in a
rural setting with good countryside
views. A garden of gardens which
surround the C15 house. Many varied
features creating diversity and contrast
and providing homes for a wide range
of plants incl small bulbs and unusual
perennials, snowdrops a speciality,
producing interest in early spring.
Plants sometimes available. Partial
wheelchair access, ground very soft
when wet.
&♿ ✖ ☕ ☎

Saturday 14,
Sunday 15
February . . .
soup, bread &
teas, all home-
made . . .

98 SPILSILL COURT
Frittenden Road, Staplehurst
TN12 0DJ. Mrs Doonie Marshall. *8m
S of Maidstone. To Staplehurst on
A229 (Maidstone to Hastings). From S
enter village, turn R immed after
garage on R & just before the 30mph sign,
into Frittenden Rd; garden 1/2 m on L.
From N go through village to 40mph
sign, immed turn L into Frittenden Rd.*
April, tea/coffee & biscuits all day.
June, tea/coffee 11-1, cream teas
2.30-4.30. **Adm £2, chd 50p. Suns 5
Apr; 28 June (11-5).**

Approx 4 acres of garden, orchard and
paddock; series of gardens incl blue,
white and silver; roses; lawns; shrubs,
trees and ponds. Small private chapel.
Jacob sheep and unusual poultry.
&♿ ✖ ✿ ☕

99 NEW SPRING PLATT
Boyton Court Road, Sutton
Valence ME17 3BY. Carolyn
Millen. *5m SE of Maidstone. From
A274, turn L at Kings Head PH into
Sutton Valence centre. Through
village with chapel on R, after 1/2 m
turn R at Xrds. 1st house
(bungalow) on R opp Boyton
Court.* Soup, bread & teas, all
home-made. **Adm £3.50, chd
free. Sat 14, Sun 15 Feb (11-4).
Also open Sat 14 Feb
Southover.**
1-acre garden under development
with panoramic views over the
Weald. Raised beds with over 70
varieties of snowdrops, borders
with spring bulbs, extensive
rockeries and a croquet lawn.
&♿ ✿ ☕ ☕

100 ◆ SQUERRYES COURT
Westerham TN16 1SJ. Mrs John
Warde, 01959 562345,
www.squerryes.co.uk. *1/2 m W of
Westerham. Signed from A25.* **House
& garden £7, chd £4, concessions
£6.50. Garden only £4.50, chd £2.50,
concessions £4. Weds, Suns & Bank
Hol Mons, 1 Apr to end Sept. House
not open NGS days.** For NGS: **Sun
15 Mar (12-4); Wed 26 Aug (11.30-5).**
15 acres of garden, lake and woodland
surrounding beautiful C17 manor
house. Lovely throughout the seasons
from the spring bulbs to later-flowering
borders. Cenotaph commemorating
General Wolfe. Lawns, yew hedges,
ancient trees, parterres, azaleas, roses
and borders add to the peaceful
setting. Film location for The Boat that
Rocked.
&♿ ✿ ☕

101 STONEWALL PARK
Chiddingstone Hoath, nr
Edenbridge TN8 7DG. Mr & Mrs
Valentine Fleming. *4m SE of
Edenbridge. Via B2026. Halfway
between Markbeech & Penshurst.*
Home-made teas. **Adm £4, chd free.
Car with 4 adults £14. (Share to
Sarah Matheson Trust & St Mary's
Church). Suns 29 Mar; 3 May
(1.30-5).**

Romantic woodland garden in historic setting featuring species rhododendrons, magnolias, azaleas, a range of interesting trees and shrubs, wandering paths and lakes. Parkland with cricket ground, Victorian walled garden with herbaceous borders and vegetable garden backed by 100 yr-old espalier pear trees. Sea of wild daffodils in March.

102 TIMBERS
Dean Street, East Farleigh, nr Maidstone ME15 0HS. Mrs Sue Robinson, 01622 729568, suerobinson.timbers@googlemail.com. *2m S of Maidstone. From Maidstone take B2010 to East Farleigh. Opp The Bull turn into Vicarage Lane, then L into Forge Lane and L into Dean St. Garden 50yds on R, park through gates in front of house.* Home-made teas. **Adm £3, chd free.** Visitors welcome by appt Apr to July for groups of 8+, coaches permitted.
5-acre garden, well stocked with unusual hardy plants, annuals and shrubs designed with flower arranger's eye. Formal areas comprising parterre, pergola, herbaceous, vegetables, fruit, lawns and mature specimen trees surrounded by 100yr-old Kentish cobnut plat, wild flower meadow and woodland.

TITSEY PLACE GARDENS
See Surrey.

103 TORRY HILL
Frinsted/Milstead ME9 0SP. The Lord & Lady Kingsdown, 01795 830258, lady.kingsdown@btinternet.com. *5m S of Sittingbourne. From M20 J8 take A20 (Lenham). At roundabout by Ramada Inn turn L Hollingbourne (B2163). Turn R at Xrds at top of hill (Wormshill). Thereafter Wormshill-Frinsted-Doddington (not suitable for coaches), then Torry Hill & NGS signs. From M2 J5 take A249 towards Maidstone, first L and L again (Bredgar-Milstead), then Torry Hill and NGS signs.* Home-made teas. **Adm £3, chd free (share to St Dunstan's Church). Suns 17 May; 7 June; 19 July (2-5).** Visitors also welcome by appt, written applications preferred.
8 acres; large lawns, specimen trees, flowering cherries, rhododendrons, azaleas and naturalised daffodils; walled gardens with lawns, shrubs, herbaceous borders, rose garden incl shrub roses, wild flower areas and

vegetables. Extensive views to Medway and Thames estuaries. Shallow steps to main gardens and rose garden. No wheelchair access to rose garden but can be viewed from pathway.

104 TRAM HATCH
Charing Heath TN27 0BN. Mrs P Scrivens, www.tramhatchgardens.co.uk. *10m NW of Ashford. A20 turn towards Charing railway stn. Continue on Pluckley Rd over motorway, 1st R signed Barnfield to end. Turn L, follow lane past Barnfield, Tram Hatch on L.* Home-made teas. **Adm £3.50, chd free. Suns 17 May; 14 June; 12 July (1.30-5).**
C14 manor house with tithe barn (not open) set in 3 acres of formal garden with the Great River Stour edging its boundary. Vegetable and fruit garden, orchard, rose garden, new gravel garden and 2 large ponds, one with ornamental wildfowl. Large variety of plants and trees, some unusual. The gardens are managed organically. Featured in 'Kent Life'.

105 ULCOMBE PLACE
Ulcombe Hill, nr Maidstone ME17 1DN. Gina & Dale Jennings, 01622 842019. *7m SE of Maidstone, 3m N of Headcorn. From A274 or A20, follow rd to Ulcombe church and park in church car park.* Light refreshments & home-made teas. **Adm £4, chd free. Sun 5 July (2-6).** Visitors also welcome by appt.
3 acres of informal gardens around C13 house (not open) on the Greensand Way. Walled garden, herbaceous borders, wide variety of interesting trees and shrubs. Views across the Weald.

106 UPPER PRYORS
Butterwell Hill, Cowden TN8 7HB. Mr & Mrs S G Smith. *4½m SE of Edenbridge. From B2026 Edenbridge-Hartfield, turn R at Cowden Xrds & take 1st drive on R.* Home-made teas. **Adm £3.50, chd free. Day £3.50 (1-6) & Evening Opening £4.50, wine, Wed 17 June (6-9). Also open 6-9 Edenbridge House 6-9.**
10 acres of country garden surrounding C16 house with herbaceous colour, magnificent lawns, water gardens and wooded/field areas.

107 NEW WEST COURT LODGE
Postling Court, The Street, Postling, nr Hythe CT21 4EX. Mr & Mrs John Pattrick. *2m NW of Hythe. From M20 J11 turn S onto A20. Immed 1st L. After ½ m on bend take rd signed Lyminge. 1st L into Postling.* Home-made teas. **Adm £3, chd free. Sun 14 June (1-5).**
S-facing 1-acre walled garden at the foot of the N Downs, designed in 2 parts: main lawn with sunny borders and romantic woodland garden. C11 Postling Church open.

Group opening

108 WEST MALLING GARDENS
ME19 6NE. *On A20, nr J4 of M20. Tickets, map and list of gardens available from Brome House, 148 High St (next to St Mary's Church). Parking available in town car park or railway stn car park. Follow the yellow signs.* Home-made teas at Brome House from 2-5pm. **Combined adm £5, chd free (share to St Mary's Church). Sun 7 June (12-5.30).**
West Malling is an attractive small market town with some fine buildings. Most of the gardens are within walking distance of the High Street. Some wheelchair access. For further information please phone 01732 521268.

Victorian walled garden with herbaceous borders and vegetable garden backed by 100 year-old espalier pear trees . . .

Plantsman's garden . . . with extensive views over country and sea. . .

109 WEST STUDDAL FARM
West Studdal, nr Dover CT15 5BJ.
Mr Peter Lumsden. *4m SW of Deal.
6m N of Dover halfway between Eastry
& Whitfield. Take A256 from A2. At 1st
roundabout turn S signed Studdal. At
top of hill turn R, entrance 1/4 m by
yellow cottage.* Home-made teas.
**Adm £3, chd free. Sun 23 Aug
(2-5.30).**
Medium-sized garden around old
farmhouse (not open) set by itself in
small valley; herbaceous borders,
roses and fine lawns protected by old
walls and beech hedges. Teas served
in 12-sided folly.

110 WHITEHURST
Chainhurst TN12 9SU. John & Lyn
Mercy, 01622 820616. *6m S of
Maidstone, 3m N of Marden. From
Marden stn turn R into Pattenden Lane
& under railway bridge; at T-junction
turn L; at next fork bear R to Chainhurst,
then 2nd turning on L.* Home-made
teas. **Adm £4, chd £1. Sun 22 Mar;
Sun 21 June to Wed 24 June incl;
Sun 4 Oct to Wed 7 Oct incl (2-5).**
Visitors also welcome by appt.
1 1/2 acres of romantic, rather wild
garden with many delightful and
unexpected features. Victorian spiral
staircase leads to a treetop walk; water
tumbles down stone steps to a rill and
on to several ponds; tunnels of yew
and dogwood; walled rose garden;
courtyards and lawns. Ever-popular
and changing exhibition of miniature
porcelain and root dwellings. Miniature
porcelain demonstrations and sales,
donations to NGS.

111 WICKHAM LODGE
The Quay, High Street, Aylesford
ME20 7AY. Cherith & Richard
Bourne, www.wickhamlodge.co.uk.
*3m NW of Maidstone. Off High St on
riverbank, turning into The Quay by
Chequers PH. Park in village car park.*
Light refreshments & cream teas. **Adm
£3.50, chd free (share to St Peter &
St Paul's Church). Sats 30 May; 12
Sept (11-4).**

Every corner of this walled and
terraced 1/2 -acre plot has been used to
create 14 inspirational small gardens
that could be picked up and recreated
anywhere. Journey from productive
kitchen gardens to formal Tudor, from
Japanese to funky banana foliage.
Endless surprises are here in
abundance. Featured in 'Amateur
Gardening' & 'Kent Life'.

112 WINDY RIDGE
Victory Road, St Margarets-at-Cliffe
CT15 6HF. Mr & Mrs D Ryder, 01304
853225, www.gardenplants-
nursery.co.uk. *4 1/2 m NE of Dover.
From Duke of York roundabout on A2 N
of Dover follow A258 signed Deal. Take
3rd rd on R (Station Rd), then 3rd rd on
L (Collingwood Rd). Continue onto
unmade track & follow signs (approx
1/2 m). Telephone for map.* Home-made
teas. **Adm £2.50, chd free. Suns 14
June; 19 July; 13 Sept (2-6).**
Plantsman's garden on top of chalk hill,
with extensive views over open country
and sea. Island beds of shrubs and
perennials (many rare). Large collection
of penstemon and salvia. Wildlife pond.
Gravel seating area and viewpoint.
Additional 2/3 -acre extension to garden
incl shrub and kniphofia border. Small
specialist nursery.

113 ◆ THE WORLD GARDEN AT
LULLINGSTONE CASTLE
Eynsford DA4 0JA. Guy Hart Dyke,
01322 862114,
www.lullingstonecastle.co.uk. *1m
from Eynsford. M25 J3, signs to
Brands Hatch then Eynsford. In
Eynsford turn R at church over ford
bridge. Follow lane under viaduct, with
Lullingstone Roman Villa on R, to
private rd sign, follow signs for World
Garden via Gatehouse.* Refreshments
Fris, Sats & Suns. **Adm £6, chd £3
(5-15), concessions £5.50. Easter to
Sept, Fris & Sats 12-5, Suns & Bank
Hol Mons (2-6). See website for
further details. For NGS: Sun
21 June (12-5).**
Interactive world map of plants laid out
as a map of the world within a walled
garden. The oceans are your pathways
as you navigate the world in 1 acre.
You can stroll around Mt Everest, sip
water from an Asian waterfall, see
Ayers Rock and walk alongside the
Andes whilst reading intrepid tales of
plant hunters. Discover the origins of
plants - you'll be amazed where they
come from!

114 WYCKHURST
Mill Road, Aldington TN25 7AJ. Mr &
Mrs C Older, 01233 720395,
cdo@rmfarms.co.uk. *4m SE of
Ashford. Leave M20 at J10, on A20
travel 2m to Aldington turning; turn R
at Xrds; proceed 1 1/2 m to Aldington
village hall. Turn R and immed L by
Walnut Tree. Take rd down Forge Hill
signed to Dymchurch, after 1/4 m turn R
into Mill Rd.* Home-made teas. **Adm
£3.50, chd free. Sats, Suns, 6, 7, 13,
14 June (11-dusk).Visitors also
welcome by appt in June only.**
C16 cottage (not open). 1-acre cottage
garden in romantic setting with unusual
topiary; extensive views across
Romney Marsh; continually developing
garden. Featured in GGG.

Group opening

115 WYE GARDENS
TN25 5BJ. *3m NE of Ashford. From
A28 take turning signed Wye. Bus:
Ashford to Canterbury via Wye. Train:
Wye stn.* Home-made teas.
**Combined adm £4, chd free. Sun 5
July (2-6).**
4 unusual gardens in historic village.
Start at centre of village.

3 BRAMBLE CLOSE
Bramble Lane. Dr M & Mrs D
Copland
A very wild garden planted in
1989. Wild flower meadow, pond
and ditches, mown paths, native
copse and hedges buzzing with
wildlife - a unique experience.
Research work on effect on
wildlife being carried out.

CUMBERLAND COURT
Church Street. Mr & Mrs F
Huntington
An exciting courtyard garden
created in 1999 from asphalt car
park. Densely planted with wide
range of unusual plants. Water
feature and unique artefacts. New
garden room.

KENT HOUSE
Scotton Street. Canon A & Mrs
E Ramsey
Small narrow garden divided into
5 very different areas, incl shade,
lawn and herbaceous, vegetables
and semi-wild.

MISTRAL
Oxenturn Road. Dr & Mrs G Chapman
Garden developed, in part, on site of old hard tennis court. 250 species of botanical interest incl white and alpine gardens. All plants labelled. Mini outdoor theatre recently added.

&. |=|

---

116 YEW TREE COTTAGE
Penshurst TN11 8AD. Mrs Pam Tuppen, 01892 870689. *4m SW of Tonbridge. From A26 Tonbridge to Tunbridge Wells, join B2176 Bidborough to Penshurst rd. 2m W of Bidborough, 1m before Penshurst. Utterly unsuitable for coaches. Please phone if needing advice for directions.* Light refreshments. **Adm £2, chd free.**
Weds, Sats & Suns, first and third week of each month, Mar to Sept incl. Please see diary section for exact dates. Visitors also welcome by appt.
Small, romantic, hillside cottage garden with steep entrance. Lots of seats and secret corners, full of unusual plants - hellebores, spring bulbs, old roses, many special perennials. Small pond; something to see in all seasons. Created and maintained by owner. Please visit throughout long opening period to ease pressure on small garden. Featured in 'Period Living'.

Kent County Volunteers

County Organiser
Felicity Ward, Hookwood House, Shipbourne TN11 9RJ, 01732 810525, hookwood1@yahoo.co.uk

County Treasurer
Stephen Moir, Little Worge Barn, Willingford Lane, Brightling, E Sussex TN32 5HN, 01424 838136, moirconsult@btinternet.com

Publicity
Claire Tennant-Scull, Wellington House, Oaks Road, Tenterden, Kent TN30 6RD, 01580 766694, claire@tennant-scull.com

Radio
Jane Streatfeild, Hoath House, Chiddingstone Hoath, Edenbridge, Kent TN8 7DB, 01342 850362, jane@hoath-house.freeserve.co.uk

Leaflet distribution
Susan Moir, Little Worge Barn, Willingford Lane, Brightling, E Sussex TN32 5HN, 01424 838136, moirconsult@btinternet.com

Assistant County Organisers
Marylyn Bacon, Ramsden Farm, Stone-cum-Ebony, Tenterden, Kent TN30 7JB, 01797 270300, streakybacon@kent.uk.net
Clare Barham, Hole Park, Rolvenden, Cranbrook TN17 4JB, 01580 241386, clarebarham@holepark.com
Virginia Latham, Stowting Hill House, Ashford TN25 6BE, 01303 862881, vjlatham@hotmail.com
Caroline Loder-Symonds, Denne Hill Farm, Womenswold, Canterbury CT4 6HD, 01227 831203, cloder_symonds@hotmail.com
Ingrid Morgan Hitchcock, 6 Brookhurst Gardens, Southborough, Tunbridge Wells TN4 0NA, 01892 528341, ingrid@morganhitchcock.co.uk
Elspeth Napier, 53 High Street, East Malling, Kent ME19 6AJ, 01732 522146, elspeth@cherryvilla.demon.co.uk

Mark your diary with these special events in 2009

EXPLORE SECRET GARDENS DURING CHELSEA & HAMPTON COURT FLOWER SHOW WEEKS

Tue 19 May, Wed 20 May, Thur 21 May, Fri 22 May, Wed 8 July, Thur 9 July
Full day tours from £82 per person, 10% discount for groups
Advance booking required, telephone +44 (0)20 8693 1015 or email j.wookey@btinternet.com
Specially selected gardens in London, Essex, Kent, Hampshire and South Oxfordshire. The tour price includes transport and lunch with wine at a popular restaurant or pub.

HAMPTON COURT PALACE

Thur 2 Apr, Tue 23 June, Thur 25 June, Wed 15 July, Tue 4 Aug, Thur 10 Sept
Evening tours in the company of one of the Palace's specialist tour guides from 6.30 – 8pm
Tickets £6 per person. Advance booking required, telephone +44 (0)1483 211535 or visit www.ngs.org.uk for more information
Gossip, scandal, murder, healing – you'll find it all within the Formal Gardens at Hampton Court Palace. Each tour will have its own unique feature whether it's the story of the Great Vine or the magic and mystery of the Maze.

FROGMORE – A ROYAL GARDEN (BERKSHIRE)

Tue 26 May 10am – 5.30pm (last admission 4pm)
Garden adm £4.50, chd free. Tickets available in advance or on the day.
Advance booking for groups and coaches, telephone
+44 (0) 1483 211535 or email orders@ngs.org.uk
A rare opportunity to explore 30 acres of landscaped garden, rich in history and beauty.

FLAXBOURNE FARM – FUN & SURPRISES (BEDFORDSHIRE)

Sun 7 June 10am – 5pm. Adm £5, chd free
No booking required, come along on the day!
Bring the whole family and have fun in this surprising and entertaining garden of 2 acres. Enjoy the large plant fair, live music, pets corner, birds of prey, dog agility show and much more.

WISLEY RHS GARDEN – MUSIC IN THE GARDEN (SURREY)

Fri 11 Sept 6 – 9pm
Adm (incl RHS members) £7, chd under 15 free
Save money on advance bookings for groups of 4 or more, telephone +44 (0)1483 211535 or visit www.ngs.org.uk for more information
A special evening opening of this famous garden, exclusively for the NGS. Enjoy music and entertainment as you explore the gardens and the floral marquee on the first day of the Wisley Flower Show.

For further information visit www.ngs.org.uk or telephone 01483 211535

LANCASHIRE

with Liverpool, Merseyside & Greater Manchester

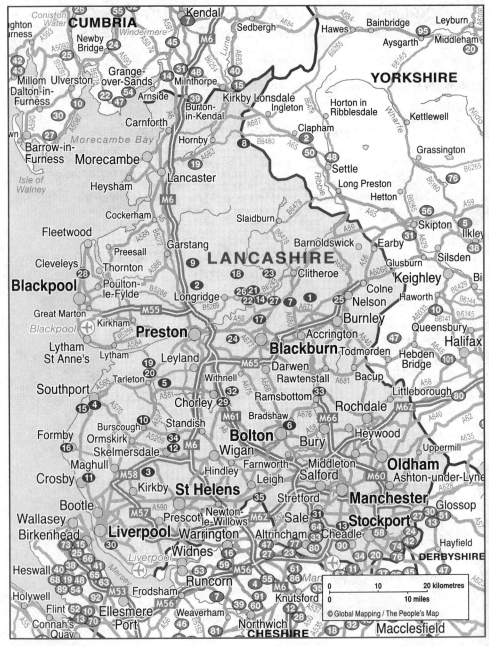

Opening Dates

February

SUNDAY 15
35 Weeping Ash

SUNDAY 22
35 Weeping Ash

April

SUNDAY 19
35 Weeping Ash

May

SUNDAY 3
6 Bridge House
29 The Ridges

MONDAY 4
6 Bridge House

SATURDAY 9
32 The Stones & Roses Garden

SUNDAY 10
2 The Barn on the Green
32 The Stones & Roses Garden

SUNDAY 17
10 Crabtree Lane Gardens
23 Manor Farm

SUNDAY 24
5 Bretherton Gardens
8 Clearbeck House
17 Greenacre

MONDAY 25
8 Clearbeck House

SUNDAY 31
11 Crosby Hall

June

SATURDAY 6
3 Barrow Nook Gardens
25 Montford Cottage
26 1 New Row Cottages

SUNDAY 7
1 Aureol House
3 Barrow Nook Gardens
25 Montford Cottage
26 1 New Row Cottages

SUNDAY 14
7 Casa Lago
10 Crabtree Lane Gardens
13 Didsbury Gardens
21 Huntingdon Hall

SUNDAY 21
8 Clearbeck House
12 Cypress House
15 Foxbury
24 Mill Barn & Primrose Cottage
34 Tudor House

SATURDAY 27
14 Dutton Hall

SUNDAY 28
8 Clearbeck House
14 Dutton Hall
20 Hesketh Bank Village Gardens
24 Mill Barn & Primrose Cottage

July

SATURDAY 4
18 Harrison-De-Moss

SUNDAY 5
2 The Barn on the Green
4 Birkdale Village Gardens
18 Harrison-De-Moss
33 The Stubbins Three

SATURDAY 11
31 Southlands

SUNDAY 12
1 Aureol House
5 Bretherton Gardens
16 Freshfield Gardens
30 Sefton Park Gardens
31 Southlands

SATURDAY 18
32 The Stones & Roses Garden

SUNDAY 19
4 Birkdale Village Gardens
32 The Stones & Roses Garden
33 The Stubbins Three
35 Weeping Ash

SATURDAY 25
17 Greenacre

August

SATURDAY 8
22 Lower Dutton Farm

SUNDAY 9
21 Huntingdon Hall
22 Lower Dutton Farm

SUNDAY 16
5 Bretherton Gardens

FRIDAY 28
27 The Old Zoo Garden

SUNDAY 30
6 Bridge House
27 The Old Zoo Garden
29 The Ridges

MONDAY 31
6 Bridge House

September

SUNDAY 6
7 Casa Lago

SATURDAY 19
32 The Stones & Roses Garden

SUNDAY 20
32 The Stones & Roses Garden
35 Weeping Ash

February 2010

SUNDAY 14
35 Weeping Ash

SUNDAY 21
35 Weeping Ash

Gardens open to the public

5 Hazelwood, Bretherton Gardens
9 Cobble Hey Farm & Gardens
29 The Ridges

By appointment only

19 Hawthornes Nursery Garden
28 6 Queensbury Road

Also open by appointment ☎

2 The Barn on the Green
4 10 Meadow Avenue, Birkdale Village Gardens
4 14 Saxon Road, Birkdale Village Gardens
5 Hazel Cottage, Bretherton Gardens
10 79 Crabtree Lane, Crabtree Lane Gardens
10 81 Crabtree Lane, Crabtree Lane Gardens
12 Cypress House
15 Foxbury
17 Greenacre
20 31 Becconsail Lane, Hesketh Bank Village Gardens
20 Wedgwood, Hesketh Bank Village Gardens
24 Mill Barn & Primrose Cottage
26 1 New Row Cottages
31 Southlands
32 The Stones & Roses Garden

The Gardens

1 NEW **AUREOL HOUSE**
off Pendle Street East, Sabden BB7 9EQ. Hazel & Rowland Lansdell. *3m E of Whalley. Leave M6 J31 take A59 to Clitheroe, after approx 12m turn R at r'about signed A671 Burnley, after 1st set of T-lights take L sign to Sabden. On entering village take 1st R Watt St, next L Pendle St East. Parking nearby.* **Adm £3, chd free.** Suns 7 June; 12 July (11-4).
Secluded 1 acre garden below Pendle hill in the beautiful Ribble Valley. 4 distinct areas, English,

Italianate, Japanese and woodland. Many interesting features, bridged pond with fish and cascade, temple, sculptures, wide variety of mature trees, shrubs, old fashioned roses, herbaceous borders and walled herb garden.

2 NEW THE BARN ON THE GREEN
Silk Mill Lane, Inglewhite PR3 2LP. Arthur & Vivienne Massey-Fairhurst, 01995 641008, vivs@zoom.co.uk. *9m N of Preston, 6.2m E of Garstang. From M55, take A6 towards Garstang for 2½ m. At Roebuck PH turn R into Bilsborrow Lane for 2½ m to Hamlet of Inglewhite. 1st R just before The Green. Garden on immed R next to Green Man PH where you can park, parking also available at Inglewhite Chapel just past PH & garden.* Adm £3.50, chd free (share to Rotary). Suns 10 May; 5 July (11.30-5). Visitors also welcome by appt Apr, June, July for groups 10+.
This delightful 1¼ acre garden, overlooking stunning scenery guides the visitor through a series of rooms, some secluded and secretive others allowing panoramic views. A vast array of plants, trees, bushes, bulbs, roses, hostas, water lilies, vegetables, pond, river bed and much more. Too much for you to miss. Gravel paths.

Group opening

3 BARROW NOOK GARDENS
Bickerstaffe L39 0ET. *5m SW of Ormskirk. From M58, J3 to Southport (A570) to T-lights at Stanley Gate PH, turn L into Liverpool Rd, then 1st L into Church Rd, then Hall Lane, approx 1m into Barrow Nook Lane.* Cream teas. Combined adm £3.50, chd free. Sat 6, Sun 7 June (1-5).
Barrow Nook Gardens are 3 neighbouring gardens of very different styles within a short walking distance, set in rural surroundings.

BARROW NOOK FARM
Cynthia & Keith Moakes
½ acre country garden overlooking fields with mature trees, shrubs, roses and many old favourite

perennials, wildlife pond and bog garden. Pergola leads to orchard with soft and stoned fruit. Homemade jams for sale.

18 BARROW NOOK LANE
Paul & Sheila Davies
Small diverse garden, rockery, water feature, herbs, island beds, herbaceous borders, pergola, fruit trees and raised vegetable beds. Garden started from scratch 13yrs ago and still being developed. Gravel paths.

26 BARROW NOOK LANE
Gary Jones
Low maintenance garden for people with limited time and budget who appreciate outdoor living, dining and relaxing. Garden incls pathways, ponds, water features, BBQ area, pergola, lawns and other works in progress.

Series of rooms, some secluded and secret . . .

Group opening

4 BIRKDALE VILLAGE GARDENS
PR8 2AX, www.birkdalevillagegardens.co.uk. *1m S of Southport. Off A565 Southport to Liverpool rd. 4th on L after r'about, opp St James Church. By train short walk from Birkdale Stn, exit L for Saxon Rd & R for Liverpool Rd.* Home-made teas. Combined adm £4, chd free (share to Macmillan Cancer Support & Northmeols Carriage Driving Group). Suns 5, 19 July (10.30-5.30).
An expanding group of gardens open in 2 groups of 3, some within easy walking distance of the attractive Victorian village of Birkdale. Maps available at each location.

FOXBURY
Pam & Richard James. Not open 5 July. Also open Sun 21 June. (See separate entry).

NEW 100 LIVERPOOL ROAD
Ralph & Pat Gregson. *¼ m from Birkdale Village.* Not open 5 July. ¼ acre flower arrangers garden with well-maintained lawns and hedges. Well stocked herbaceous borders, water feature, patio, sun-house and pergola.

NEW 10 MEADOW AVENUE
John & Jenny Smith. *S on A5267 through Birkdale Village, L at T-lights, continue past 1 zebra Xing, just before next turn R into Warwick St, then 2nd L.* Not open 19 July. Visitors also welcome by appt June & July, groups 10+.
Surprisingly large family garden with many different features incl pergola, Japanese garden, water features, mature plants and mixed bedding, Creative use of reclaimed materials throughout. Some gravel paths.

14 SAXON ROAD
Margaret & Geoff Fletcher, 01704 567742. *1m S of Southport, off A565 Southport to Liverpool Rd. 4th rd on L after r'about opp St James Church.* Visitors also welcome by appt June to Aug, groups 10+.
¼ -acre walled garden transformed over 13 yrs into an exciting mix of secret areas, informal beds and water features, accessed by bark and gravel paths. A collection of 12 water butts disguised with creative use of plant material. Developing redesigned front garden.

19 SAXON ROAD
Marie O'Neill & Linus Birtles. Not open 19 July.
Open for the 2nd year, garden of a Victorian house (not open) with mixed borders, mature trees and large lawn. Recently built period style walled garden and orangery with trained fruit trees, vegetable and flower beds. Gravel path.

Group opening

5 BRETHERTON GARDENS
PR26 9AN. *8m SW of Preston. Between Southport & Preston, from A59, take B5247 towards Chorley for 1m. Gardens off North Rd (B5248) & South Rd (B5247).* Home-made teas at Congregational Church mid-way.

Combined adm £3.50, chd free.
Suns 24 May; 12 July; 16 Aug (12-5).
Two gardens 1m apart in this
attractive, spacious village with a
conservation area at its heart. Maps
available at each garden.

HAZEL COTTAGE
6 South View, Bamfords Fold.
John & Kris Jolley, 01772
600896, jolley@johnjolley.
plus.com. Visitors also welcome
by appt.
Plant and wildlife lovers' garden
developed from Victorian
subsistence plot. Series of themed
spaces delights the senses and the
intellect. Courtyard ponds, mixed
borders, kitchen garden, Yorkshire
and Lancashire beds, meadow
and orchard.

◆ HAZELWOOD
North Road. Jacqueline Iddon &
Thompson Dagnall, 01772
601433,
www.jacquelineiddonhardyplants.
co.uk. Adm £2.50, chd free.
Weds 6 May to 12 Aug 1-5.
1½ acre garden and hardy plant
nursery, originally orchard, now has
gravel garden with silver and
variegated foliage plants, shrubs,
herbaceous borders and large
stream-fed pond with woodland
walk. Sculpture and Victorian fern
house. Newly completed oak-
framed, brick summerhouse and
traditional log cabin as sculpture
gallery. Jacqueline will give a flower
arranging demonstration at
2.30pm and Thompson Dagnall
will give a demonstration of wood
sculpture at 3.30pm. Winner of
Large Gold Medal, Southport
Flower Show.

6 **NEW** **BRIDGE HOUSE**
Bolton Road, Bradshaw
BL2 3EU. Glenda & Graham
Ostick. *2m NE of Bolton. On A676
to Ramsbottom. In Bradshaw half
way between 'Latino Lounge'
Restaurant and The Crofters PH.*
Cream teas. **Adm £2.50, chd free
(share to Fort Alice - Bolton
Women's Aid). Suns, Mons 3, 4
May; 30, 31 Aug (2-6).**
An impressive and beautiful garden
of more than 1 acre created by
2 dedicated gardeners over many
years. Spring interest in bulbs,
azaleas and some unusual shrubs

and trees, 2 ponds. Summer,
herbaceous borders, challenging
'wild area'. Views across meadow
and brook, extensive lawns and
prolific vegetable garden. Garden
for all seasons, not to be missed.
Wild area inaccessible to
wheelchairs.

7 **CASA LAGO**
1 Woodlands Park, Whalley
BB7 9UG. Carole Anne Cronshaw &
Stephen Powers. *2½ m S of
Clitheroe. Leave M6 J31, take A59
towards Clitheroe. 9m take 2nd exit at
r'about for Whalley. After 2m reach
village, straight on at mini r'about, turn
1st R Woodlands Park Drive, 1st L
Woodlands Park. Garden 25yds on L.
Parking available in village car parks
(300yds) or nearby.* **Adm £2.50, chd
free. Suns 14 June, 6 Sept (1-5).**
This small garden is tightly packed with
interest. Within its limited space. 2 fish
ponds, tree ferns, acers, bamboos,
grasses, bananas and succulents.
Interesting features incl black limestone
wall, the owner makes distinctive
garden furniture and ornaments from
naturally felled Ribble Valley trees.
Teeming with ideas to inspire. Featured
in 'Lancashire Life'.

Garden for all seasons, not to be missed . . .

8 **CLEARBECK HOUSE**
Mewith Lane, Higher Tatham
LA2 8PJ. Peter & Bronwen Osborne.
*13m NE of Lancaster. Signed from
Wray (M6 J34, A683, B6480) & Low
Bentham.* Home-made teas & light
refreshments. **Adm £2.50, chd free.
Suns 24 May, 21, 28 June, Mon 25
May (11-5).**
'A surprise round every corner' is the
most common response as visitors
encounter fountains, streams, ponds,
sculptures, boathouses and follies:
(Rapunzel's tower, temple, turf maze,
walk-through pyramid). 2-acre wildlife
lake attracts many species of insects
and birds. Planting incl herbaceous
borders, grasses, bog plants and
many roses. Artist's studio open in
garden. Children's quiz available.
Featured in 'GGG' & 'WI Life', Radio
Lancashire. Mainly grass paths.

9 **◆ COBBLE HEY FARM &
GARDENS**
Claughton-on-Brock PR3 0QN. Mr &
Mrs D Miller, 01995 602643,
www.cobblehey.co.uk. *4m S of
Garstang. Leave M6 at J32 or 33. Take
brown sign from A6 nr Bilsborough.
Claughton is 2m E, up Butt Hill Lane,
2nd farm rd on L.* **Adm £4, chd £2.50,
concessions £3.50. Open Thurs to
Mons Feb 1 to 24 Dec 10.30-4.30.
Closed Mon until Easter from Oct.**
3-acre hillside garden on working farm.
Mature beds of hardy herbaceous
perennials; over 200 species of phlox,
primulas and hellebores; natural
streams with stone banks. Woodland
and colour-themed garden, prairie and
potterage under development.
Featured on Granada Go West.

Group opening

10 **CRABTREE LANE GARDENS**
Burscough L40 0RW, 01704 893239.
*3m NE of Ormskirk. Follow A59
Preston - Liverpool rd to Burscough.
From N before 1st bridge turn R into
Redcat Lane - brown sign Martin
Mere. From S pass through village over
2nd bridge, then L into Redcat Lane,
after ¾ m turn L into Crabtree Lane.
Gardens by level Xing.* Home-made
teas at 79 Crabtree Lane. **Combined
adm £3, chd free. Suns 17 May, 14
June (1-5).**
Featured in 'Lancashire Life', Radio
Lancashire.

79 CRABTREE LANE
Sandra & Peter Curl, 01704
893713,
petercurl@btinternet.com.
Visitors also welcome by appt.
¾ acre year round garden
comprising many established and
contrasting hidden areas. Patio
surrounded by shrubs and new
alpine bed. Colour themed
herbaceous beds, island beds with
conifers and shrubs. Rose garden,
2 ponds, pergola covered by
wisteria. Spring garden and new
'derelict, dry stone bothy'.

81 CRABTREE LANE
Prue & Barry Cooper, 01704
893239. Visitors also welcome
by appt.
Medium sized garden with 6ft wall,
pond, water features, old fashioned
rockery, vine covered pergola,
trompe l'oeils. Central gazebo with

climbers and other plants. Beds containing some shrubs, but mostly herbaceous plants. Arches with clematis and roses.

⑪ CROSBY HALL
Back Lane, Little Crosby, Liverpool L23 4UA. Mark & Suzanne Blundell. *8m N of Liverpool. From church in Little Crosby take Back Lane. Entrance ¼ m on R.* Light refreshments & teas. **Adm £4, chd free (share to Crosby Hall Educational Trust).** Sun 31 May (2-5).
4-acre garden, originally designed by John Webb circa 1815, set in parkland of 120-acre estate. Many fine trees, rhododendrons and azaleas. Special features in this developing garden incl Victorian stone archway, decorative walled garden, espalier pears and wisteria, new orchard and Zen garden. Gravel paths throughout.

  ♿ 🐕 ⚘ ☕

6 suburban gardens from a courtyard to a country-style garden . .

⑫ CYPRESS HOUSE
Higher Lane, Dalton, nr Wigan WN8 7RP. David & Coleta Houghton, 01257 463822, www.cypresshousegarden.com. *5m E of Ormskirk. M6 J27. Follow A5209 in direction of Ormskirk. Proceed to 1st mini-r'about E of Newburgh, turn L onto Higher Lane. Garden 1m on R.* Home-made teas. Combined with **Tudor House** adm £4, chd free. Sun 21 June (1-6). Visitors also welcome by appt.
3/4 -acre garden, exposed and overlooking the West Lancashire plain. Mixed informal plantings which incl shrubs and trees, conifers, acers, hostas, heucheras, herbaceous and grasses. Many rare and unusual plants. Large rockery and water feature. Alpine and vine house. 1/4 -acre young arboretum with rare and unusual trees. Feature in 'Lancashire Life' & Lancashire 'Design & Living'.

🐕 ⚘ ☕ ☎

Group opening

⑬ NEW DIDSBURY GARDENS
South Manchester M20 6TQ. *5m S of Manchester City Centre. From M60 J5 follow signs to Northenden. Turn R at T-lights onto Barlow Moor Rd & into Didsbury centre. From M56 follow A34 to Didsbury Village centre. Parking on road near each garden.* Home-made teas at 88 Atwood Road. **Combined adm £4, chd free.** Sun 14 June (12-5).
We are 6 suburban gardens reflecting diversity in design planting from a tiny gem of a courtyard to a beautifully elegant country-style garden. Didsbury it's self an attractive S Manchester suburb retaining much of its village atmosphere. All gardens are walkable from centre. Maps available at each garden. Disabled WC & WCs nr library.

  ♿ 🐕 ⚘ ☕

NEW ATWOOD COTTAGE
88 Atwood Road. Roland & Sheila Fairbrother. *off Parrs Wood Rd*
Surprisingly large s-facing rear garden with all-yr round colour. Patio with pond, several lawns with packed borders, punctuated by sculptural and architectural plant focal points. Interesting pot bed/plant bank.

NEW 86 ATWOOD ROAD
Les & Shirley Berry. *off Parrs Wood Rd*
Entry via no.88. Patio area with pots facing curved lawn and path leading to chalet and shaded back of garden. To the sides are borders packed with perennials, shrubs, climbers and ornamental trees.

NEW 23 CRANMER ROAD
Christine Clarke. *Off Wilmslow Rd, then Fog Lane*
Long, narrow plot, designed with contrasting trees and shrubs, to conceal awkward shape. Lawn, hard landscaping, granite water feature and natural brook. Feature roses, acers and herbaceous borders.

NEW 33 DANESMOOR ROAD
Edwina Dyson. *off Palatine Rd*
Peaceful courtyard oasis, small but incorporating differing areas, water feature, arch, seating and range of pots. Mixed planting with a cool palette and variety of shrubs.

GROVE COTTAGE
8 Grenfell Road. Sue & David Kaberry. *off Barlow Moor Rd*
Small suburban garden divided into 4 areas. Fountain, pergola and dining area with mirrors and bamboos. Unusual plants and many roses.

NEW MOOR COTTAGE
Grange Lane. William Godfrey. *Off Wilmslow Rd*
Echium pinnata entwined with Cardiocrinum giganteum. 'Rambling Rector' cascading over log shed, a Buff Beauty' rose peering through Cotinus coggygria in the herbaceous borders - just some of the delights of this walled garden.

⑭ DUTTON HALL
Gallows Lane, Ribchester PR3 3XX. Mr & Mrs A H Penny. *2m NE of Ribchester. Signed from B6243 & B6245.* Home-made teas. **Adm £3.50, chd free.** Sat 27, Sun 28 June (1-5).
A fine collection of old-fashioned roses in a developing garden with extensive views over Ribble Valley. More formal garden at front within attractive setting of C17 house (not open). Orangery with interesting range of conservatory plants. Sculpture exhibition.

🐕 ⚘ ☕

⑮ FOXBURY
47 Westbourne Road, Birkdale PR8 2HY. Pam & Richard James, 01704 569251, richjame@aol.com. *2m S of Southport. Off A565 Southport to Liverpool rd. Turn R at 2nd T-lights after r'about, turn L at end, house on L.* Home-made teas. **Adm £2.50, chd free.** Sun 21 June (11-5.30). Combined with **Birkdale Village Gardens** 19 July, adm £4. Visitors also welcome by appt June to Aug, groups 10+.
1/2 acre suburban garden just inland from dunes and famous golf course of Birkdale. Very low lying. Mature pine trees shelters water feature. Mixed beds and newly planted trees are interspersed through a well maintained lawn. Mature shrubs and hedges shelter this developing garden from off-shore winds, giving a peaceful atmosphere.

🐕 ⚘ ☕ ☎

Group opening

16 NEW FRESHFIELD GARDENS

L37 1PB. *6m S of Southport. From A565 (Crosby to Southport Rd) take B5424 signed Formby, at Grapes PH mini r'about turn R into Green Lane, Woodlands is 500yds on R. For Gorse Way follow Green Lane right round & take 3rd on R into Victoria Rd, continue over level Xing to end, turn L into Larkhill Lane, Gorse Way 1st on L.* **Combined adm £2.50, chd free. Sun 12 July (10.30-4.30).**
2 suburban gardens on sandy soil nr to NT nature reserve, home to the red squirrel.

NEW 2 GORSE WAY
Brenda & Ray Doldon
Completely redesigned by the present owners this 5yr old, s-facing split level, enclosed garden features sunken garden, pergola, pond and beach area, lawn and paths leading to colour themed herbaceous beds. Partial wheelchair access.

NEW WOODLANDS
46 Green Lane. Ken & Rita Carlin
Leafy suburban, shady front garden with mature trees under preservation leading to oblong rear garden, with cottage style colourful borders, small pond and plenty of seating areas to relax and view.

Packed with inspirational ideas in reclaimed stone . . .

17 GREENACRE
157 Ribchester Road, Clayton-le-Dale BB1 9EE. **Dorothy & Andrew Richards, 01254 249694.** *3½ m N of Blackburn. Leave M6 J31. Take A59 towards Clitheroe. In 7m at T-lights turn R towards Blackburn along 36245. Garden ½ m on RH-side. Park nearby or at Salesbury Memorial Hall, 500yds on RH-side. Disabled parking nearby.* **Adm £3, chd free (share to Vitalise). Sun 24 May; Sat 25 July 1.30-5).** Visitors also welcome by

appt May, June, July & early Sept, groups of 14 to 25.
Peaceful 1-acre garden on edge of Ribble Valley. Broad sweep of lawn with 11 beds incl white, gravel and sculpture. Emphasis on colour, yellow leaved and variegated plants. Vegetable and cutting garden with raised beds and separate fruit areas. Visitor information by flowerbeds. A continually evolving plant collector's garden with a stunning view as you enter. Featured in 'Clitheroe Advertiser'.

18 NEW HARRISON-DE-MOSS

Moss Lane, Chipping, nr Preston PR3 2TR. Sue & Peter Harrison. *From Longridge go to Chipping Village centre. At T-junction turn R for Clitheroe, after 1m turn R into Leagram Organic Cheese Dairy to park. 500yd walk down tree lined lane to garden.* Tea & wine. **Adm £3, chd free. Sat 4, Sun 5 July (1.30-5).**
Nestling in the foothills of the Forest of Bowland ¾ acre packed with inspirational ideas in reclaimed stone. Stone sofa, cobbled ½ moongate, 3 water features, 2 pergolas. Arbour, unusual trees, plants and climbers everywhere. Stunning views in every direction. Organic kitchen garden with raised beds and herb wheel. Across the lane opp the house, is an RSPB nature reserve. Featured in 'Amateur Gardening'.

19 HAWTHORNES NURSERY GARDEN
Marsh Road, Hesketh Bank PR4 6XT. Mr & Mrs R Hodson, 01772 812379, richardhaw@talktalk.net, www.hawthornes-nursery.co.uk. *10m SW of Preston. From Preston take A59 towards Liverpool. Turn R at T-lights for Tarleton. Through Tarleton Village into Hesketh Bank. Large car park at Station Rd/Shore Rd. WC.* **Adm £2.50, chd free.** Visitors welcome by appt June, July, Aug.
1-acre plant lover's garden. Intensively planted borders and beds with 150 old-fashioned shrub and climbing roses, over 200 clematis. (Rare and unusual herbaceous and viticella clematis. National Collection of viticellas). Interplanted with dramatic collection of hardy geraniums, phlox, aconitums, lythrums and heleniums for

later colour. Adjoining nursery. Featured in Lancashire Life', 'Garden News', 'Gardens Monthly', 'GGG'.

Group opening

20 HESKETH BANK VILLAGE GARDENS
PR4 6RQ. *10m SW of Preston. From Preston take A59 towards Liverpool, then turn R at T-lights for Tarleton village. Straight through Tarleton to Hesketh Bank.* Teas. **Combined adm £3.50, chd free. Sun 28 June (12-5).** Free minibus between gardens. Maps available at each garden.

31 BECCONSALL LANE
Mr & Mrs J Baxter, 01772 813018. Visitors also welcome by appt.
Cottage-style garden with pond, white and green beds and semi-woodland walk. Organic garden. Hot bed.

74 CHAPEL ROAD
Mr & Mrs T Iddon
Compact colourful garden. Wide variety of plants. Pond, arbour and gazebo. Dunscar Garden Centre Competition Winner.

11 DOUGLAS AVENUE
Mr & Mrs J Cook
Large established garden with lawns, mature trees, topiary, box wheel, mixed herbaceous borders and naturalised areas, with pond. Limited wheelchair access.

155 STATION ROAD
Mr & Mrs G Hale
Large garden with lawns; cottage-style herbaceous borders. Summerhouse and pond.

WEDGWOOD
Shore Road. Mr & Mrs D Watson, 01772 816509, heskethbank@aol.com. Visitors also welcome by appt, June & July only.
A garden which has been developed into diverse planting areas. These incl gravel, woodland, herbaceous, formal pond, lawns, large glasshouse, orchard with meadow and colour-themed parterre rainbow-garden.

21 HUNTINGDON HALL
Huntingdon Hall Lane, Dutton
PR3 2ZT. Mr & Mrs J E Ashcroft. *6m
NE of Preston. Leave M6 J31. Take
A59 towards Clitheroe, turn L at 1st
T-lights to Ribchester along B6245.
After bridge over R Ribble take next R
up Gallows Lane. T-junction turn L.
Next R into Huntingdon Hall Lane.*
Home-made teas & wine. **Adm £3,
chd free. Suns 14 June, 9 Aug (11-6).**
C17 house (not open) in glorious
countryside. Garden features incl:
formal layout with pleached limes,
developing herbaceous beds,
woodland walk, terraced pond, many
unusual plants.

♿ 🐕 ❀ ☕

**22 NEW LOWER DUTTON
FARM**
Gallows Lane, Dutton PR3 3XX.
Mr R Robinson. *1½ m NE of
Ribchester. Leave M6 J31. Take
A59 towards Clitheroe, turn L at T-
lights towards Ribchester. Signed
from B6243 & B6245.* Light
refreshments & teas. **Adm £3.50,
chd free. Sat 8, Sun 9 Aug (1-5).**
Traditional long Lancashire
farmhouse and barn (not open),
with 1½ acre garden. Formal
gardens nr house with mixed
herbaceous beds and shrubs,
sweeping lawns leading to wildlife
area and established large pond
and small woodland with eclectic
mix of trees and plants. Lawns
may be difficult in very wet weather.

♿ ❀ ☕

23 NEW MANOR FARM
Chipping Road, Chaigley
BB7 3LS. Michael & Liz Bell. *3m
W of Clitheroe. Take B6243 from
Clitheroe, 2nd R after Edisford
bridge, next L signed Chipping,
over Hodder bridge, 1st R 20
metres.* **Adm £4, chd free. Sun
17 May (11-5).**
Nestling by the R Hodder in
picturesque and imposing setting,
country garden 1.7 acres featuring
ancient sycamore. Mediterranean
garden with olive tree, 50ft pergola
with developing herbaceous beds,
large pond, established shrubs.
Interesting hard landscaping with
use of home grown oak, sweeping
lawns and winding gravel paths.

🐕 ☕

**24 MILL BARN & PRIMROSE
COTTAGE**
Goosefoot Close, Samlesbury
PR5 0SS. Chris Mortimer & Susan
Childs, 01254 853300,
chris@millbarn.net. *6m E of Preston.
From M6 J31 2½ m on A59/A677
B/burn. Turn S. Nabs Head Lane, then
Goosefoot Lane.* Cream teas. **Adm £3,
chd free. Suns 21, 28 June (1-5).
Visitors also welcome by appt June
& July. Groups of 5+.**
Tranquil terraced garden along the
banks of R Darwen. A garden on many
levels, both physical and
psychological. Flowers, follies and
sculptures engage the senses on
moving up from the semi formal to the
bucolic. Primrose Bank (adjacent) is a
relaxed garden, sensitively controlled,
which is subtly changed year by year.
Partial, steps limit access.

♿ ❀ 🛏 ☕ ☎

25 MONTFORD COTTAGE
Cuckstool Lane, Fence, nr Burnley
BB12 9NZ. Craig Bullock & Tony
Morris. *4m N of Burnley. From J13
M65, take A6068 (signs for Fence) & in
2m turn L onto B6248 (signs for
Brierfield). Proceed down hill for ½ m
(past Forest PH). Entrance to garden
on L, with limited car park further down
hill.* Cream teas. **Adm £3, chd 50p.
Sat 6, Sun 7 June; (2-6).**
Well established 1-acre walled garden,
with recent projects synthesizing with
mature plantings to enhance this
plantsman's collection. The
artist/photographer/floral designer has
created a garden with individual
identity. Many seats and shelters
provide the opportunity to relax and
soak up the atmosphere.

♿ ❀ ☕

**26 NEW 1 NEW ROW
COTTAGES**
Clitheroe Road, Knowle Green,
Longridge PR3 2YS. Harry &
Jean Procter, 01254 878447. *8m
E of Clitheroe, 8m W of Preston.
From South leave M6 J31a. Follow
B6243 for approx 6m, New Row
on L. From North leave M6 J32
turn N follow B5269 to Longridge,
join B6243 to New Row.* Home-
made teas. **Adm £2.50, chd free.
Sat 6, Sun 7 June (1-5). Visitors
also welcome by appt groups
10 - 25, June to Aug.**
Glorious views and garden of 3
parts: cottage garden overflowing
with plants, greenhouse with vine
and small vegetable garden. 2nd

quiet woodland area with mature
trees. 3rd developing wildlife
meadow with pond and recently
planted traditional Lancashire field
hedge.

♿ ❀ ☕ ☎

Recently planted traditional Lancashire field hedge . . .

27 THE OLD ZOO GARDEN
Cherry Drive, Brockhall Village
BB6 8AY. Gerald Hitman. *5m N
Blackburn. Leave M6 J31, take A59
Clitheroe approx 10m. Follow signs for
Old Langho & Brockhall Village. Just
prior to Blackburn r'about (junction
A666) follow signs to The Old Zoo.
Partial access for wheelchairs & prams.*
Light refreshments & teas. **Adm £5,
chd free. Fri 28, Sun 30 Aug (11-4).**
15 acres. The Old Zoo garden is
constructed with pleasure in mind;
it encloses figurative sculpture,
16 varieties of Lancashire apples,
water courses, unusual planting and
very unusual earth workings. The size
and speed with which The Old Zoo has
been constructed has made it one of
the North's premier gardens, with its
acclaim growing by the week.

☕

**28 NEW 6 QUEENSBURY
ROAD**
Thornton-Cleveleys FY5 1SW.
Don Knight, 01253 869390. *3m N
of Blackpool. From M55 J3 head
for Fleetwood (A585), at 2nd
r'about turn L towards Cleveleys.
In centre turn L (keeping tram
tracks on R) & head for Blackpool.
At 1st R, cross over tracks & head
back towards Fleetwood. Turn 1st
L.* **Visitors welcome by appt for
groups max 16.**
This small garden, approx 30ft x
30ft, has been meticulously
designed on an oriental theme with
a 6000 gal koi pond built with slate
incls waterfall and large koi carp.
Bonsai trees, Japanese stone
lanterns and Mediterranean style
barbecue are also incorporated.
Owner will give a talk on designing
Bonsai trees from garden centre
material.

♿ 🐕 ☎

29 ◆ THE RIDGES
Cowling Road, Limbrick, Chorley
PR6 9EB. Mr & Mrs J M Barlow,
01257 279981, www.bedbreakfast-
gardenvisits.com. *2m SE of Chorley.
J27 M6 or J8 M61 approaching
Chorley on A6, follow signs for Chorley,
then signs for Cowling & Rivington.
From A6 S turn R at 1st r'about, R at
Morrison's. Up Brooke St, take
Cowling Brow, approx 1/4 m garden on
RH-side.* Adm £3, chd free. Bank
Hols, 4, 24, 25 May; 31 Aug 11-5;
Weds June & July 11-7. For NGS:
Suns 3 May; 30 Aug (11-5).
3 acres. Incl old walled kitchen garden,
cottage-style; herbaceous borders;
natural garden with stream, ponds.
Living arch leads to large formal lawn,
surrounded by natural woodland.
Shrub borders and trees with
contrasting foliage. Walled area planted
with scented roses and herbs. Paved
area with grasses. Wall feature with
Italian influence. New woodland walk
and wild flower garden. Classical music
played throughout open days.
⬤ ❀ 🛏 ☕

Group opening

30 SEFTON PARK GARDENS
Liverpool L8 3SA. *3m S of Liverpool
city centre. From end of M62 take
A5058 Queens Drive ring rd through
Allerton to Sefton Park and follow
signs. Park roadside in Sefton Park.
Tickets at all venues and gardens.*
Light refreshments & teas in Palm
House. Combined adm £5, chd free.
Sun 12 July (12-5).
Two large and one small interesting city
gardens and nearly 100 allotments
open. Rare and unusual plants for sale,
musical entertainment and
refreshments in the restored Victorian
Sefton Park Palm House. Featured in
'Liverpool Daily Post' & 'Lancashire
Life'.
☕

PARKMOUNT
38 Ullet Road. Jeremy Nicholls
Developing garden with mixed
borders, woodland paths,
moroccan patio, some surprises
and many rare plants in one of
Liverpool's old merchant houses
overlooking Sefton Park.
🐾 ❀

SEFTON PARK ALLOTMENTS
Greenbank Drive. Sefton Park
Allotments Society. *Next door to
Sefton Park cricket club*
Nearly 100 individually tended fruit
and vegetable plots with a wide
variety of produce. This year there
will be a Produce Show on Open
Day and visitors can vote for the
best vase of flowers and basket of
vegetables. The site has featured in
national TV and film productions -
see the 'Bread' shed where Li-low
Lil held her trysts on plot 89.
Featured in 'Kitchen Garden'/
NAGT Best Community Allotment
Project, Highly Commended (joint
4th).
🐾

NEW SEFTON VILLA
14 Sefton Park. Patricia Williams
Small walled Victorian garden,
many mature and unusual trees
and shrubs give garden a secluded
and tranquil atmosphere.
Conservatory, patio, raised pool,
brick pergolas, lawn with mixed
borders, enclosed Japanese style
garden with bamboos.
🐾 ❀ 🛏

VICE CHANCELLOR'S GARDEN
12 Sefton Park Road. University
of Liverpool, Vice-Chancellor Sir
Howard & Lady Sheila Newby,
Gardener Mr Brian Farrington
Collection of old shrub roses,
formal terrace, grape vine, shrub
borders and large weeping ash.
Gravel paths.
⬤

Refreshments in the restored Victorian Sefton Park Palm House . . .

31 SOUTHLANDS
12 Sandy Lane, Stretford M32 9DA.
Maureen Sawyer & Duncan
Watmough, 0161 283 9425,
moe@southlands12.com,
www.southlands12.com. *3m S of
Manchester. Sandy Lane (B5213) is
situated off A5181 (A56) 1/4 m from
M60 J7.* Home-made teas. Adm £3,
chd free (share to Christie Hospital
NHS Trust). Sat 11, Sun 12 July (1-

6). Visitors also welcome by appt 1
June to end of Aug. Guided tour for
groups of 10+.
Artist's 1/4-acre town garden making
full use of structures and living screens
to create a number of intimate gardens
each with its own theme incl courtyard,
Mediterranean, ornamental, woodland
and organic kitchen gardens with large
glasshouse. Many exotics and unusual
herbaceous perennials, 2 ponds and
water feature. Moss garden. Featured
in All Things Bright and Beautiful. Live
jazz twice daily (weather permitting).
Exhibition of art work derived from the
garden.
⬤ 🐾 ❀ ☕ ☎

32 THE STONES & ROSES GARDEN
White Coppice Farm, White
Coppice, nr Chorley PR6 9DF.
Raymond & Linda Smith, 01257
277633,
stonesandroses@btinternet.com,
www.stonesandroses.org. *3m NE of
Chorley. J8 M61. A674 to Blackburn.
3rd R to Heapey & White Coppice.
Parking next to garden.* Adm £2.50,
chd free. Sats, Suns 9, 10 May; 18,
19 July; 19, 20 Sept (2-5). Visitors
also welcome by appt.
Still developing 3-acre garden where
the cows used to live. Sunken garden,
500 roses, fountains, waterfalls,
stonework, rockery, herbaceous,
stumpery. Colour themed planting, fruit
tree walk down to dewpond with jetty.
Wildflower planting. Gravel paths.
⬤ ❀ ☕ ☎

Group opening

33 NEW THE STUBBINS THREE
BL0 0SD. *4m N of Bury. Exit at J1
M66 turn R onto A56 signed
Ramsbottom, continue straight
until yellow NGS signs.* Coffee &
home-made teas at 1 School
Court. Combined adm £2.50, chd
free. Suns 5, 19 July (12-5).
A fine opportunity to see 3 different
examples of how to make small
gardens into attractive areas. Water
features, mixed planting, unusual
ornamentation, mirror, statuary and
much more besides. Craft stall.
🐾 ☕

NEW 1 EAST VIEW
Robert Townsend
Tropical style garden with many
interesting features, incl small
Japanese garden.

NEW NUTWOOD
3 School Court. Sheila Sherris
Small traditional garden with lawn,
borders of mixed planting incl
shrubs, clematis, sweetpeas,
delphiniums, lupins and other
perennials. Variety of hanging
baskets, troughs and containers.

NEW TREVINIA
**1 School Court. Trevor & Lavinia
Tod**
A garden inspired by the painter
Rex Whistler, unusual features
complemented with shrubs, conifer
and perennials. House (not open) is
surrounded by flower filled pergola
where you can enjoy refreshments.

34 TUDOR HOUSE
Higher Lane, Dalton, nr Wigan
WN8 7RP. Steve & Dorothy Anders.
*5m E of Ormskirk. M6 J27 follow
A5209 direction of Ormskirk, at 1st
mini r'about E of Newburgh turn L into
Higher Lane, garden 1.2m on L.*
Cream teas. **Combined with
Cypress House adm £4, chd free.
Sun 21 June (1-6).**
Set in 1½ acres with panoramic views
stretching to the Fylde coast this
garden has many interesting features
incl a bridge over dry stone bed,
rockery and many grasses. Small folly
with clematis and grape vine. Many
unusual shrubs amongst interesting
landscape.

 ♿ 🐕 ☕

35 WEEPING ASH
Bents Garden & Home, Warrington
Road, Glazebury WA3 5NS. John
Bent, 01942 266300,
www.bents.co.uk. *15m W of
Manchester. Located next to Bents
Garden & Home, just off the East
Lancs rd A580 at Greyhound r'about*

*nr Leigh. Follow brown 'Garden
Centre' signs.* Light refreshments &
teas at Bents Garden Centre next to
garden. **Adm £2, chd free. Suns 15,
22 Feb; 19 Apr; 19 July; 20 Sept
(11-4.30); 2010 14, 21 Feb.**
Created by retired nurseryman and
photographer John Bent, Weeping Ash
is a garden of all-year interest with a
beautiful display of early snowdrops.
Broad sweeps of colour lend elegance
to the sweeping garden, where
herbaceous perennials over spill their
boundaries and lawns are framed with
an eclectic mix of foliage, flowers and
form to create simply stunning visual
sensations. Featured in 'Visit
Cheshire's Gardens of Distinction.
Limited wheelchair access.
♿ 🐕 ☕

Water features,
mixed planting,
unusual
ornamentation,
mirror, statuary
and much more
besides . . .

Lancashire, Merseyside, Greater Manchester & surrounding areas County Volunteers

County Organisers
Ray & Brenda Doldon, 2 Gorse Way, Formby, Merseyside L37 1PB, 01704 834253, ray@doldon.plus.com

County Treasurer
Ray Doldon, 2 Gorse Way, Formby, Merseyside L37 1PB, 01704 834253, ray@doldon.plus.com

Publicity
Christine Ruth, 15 Princes Park Mansions, Croxteth Road, Liverpool L8 3SA, 0151 727 4877, caruthchris@aol.com
Lynn Kelly, 48 Bedford Road, Birkdale PR8 4HJ, 01704 563740, lynn-kelly@hotmail.co.uk

Assistant County Organisers
Margaret & Geoff Fletcher, 14 Saxon Road, Birkdale, Southport, Merseyside PR8 2AX, 01704 567742,
  geoffwfletcher@hotmail.co.uk
Phil & Mel Gibbs 12 Bowers Avenue, Davyhulme, Urmston M41 5TG, 01674 79243, melphil@freeuk.com
Dorothy & Andrew Richards, Greenacre, 157 Ribchester Rd, Clayton-Le-Dale, Blackburn BB1 9EE, 01254 249694,
  andrewfrichards@talk21.com

Mark your diary with these special events in 2009

EXPLORE SECRET GARDENS DURING CHELSEA & HAMPTON COURT FLOWER SHOW WEEKS

Tue 19 May, Wed 20 May, Thur 21 May, Fri 22 May, Wed 8 July, Thur 9 July
Full day tours from £82 per person, 10% discount for groups
Advance booking required, telephone +44 (0)20 8693 1015 or email j.wookey@btinternet.com
Specially selected gardens in London, Essex, Kent, Hampshire and South Oxfordshire. The tour
price includes transport and lunch with wine at a popular restaurant or pub.

HAMPTON COURT PALACE

Thur 2 Apr, Tue 23 June, Thur 25 June, Wed 15 July, Tue 4 Aug, Thur 10 Sept
Evening tours in the company of one of the Palace's specialist tour guides from 6.30 – 8pm
Tickets £6 per person. Advance booking required, telephone +44 (0)1483 211535 or
visit www.ngs.org.uk for more information
Gossip, scandal, murder, healing – you'll find it all within the Formal Gardens at Hampton Court
Palace. Each tour will have its own unique feature whether it's the story of the Great Vine or the
magic and mystery of the Maze.

FROGMORE – A ROYAL GARDEN (BERKSHIRE)

Tue 26 May 10am – 5.30pm (last admission 4pm)
Garden adm £4.50, chd free. Tickets available in advance or on the day.
Advance booking for groups and coaches, telephone
+44 (0) 1483 211535 or email orders@ngs.org.uk
A rare opportunity to explore 30 acres of landscaped garden, rich in history and beauty.

FLAXBOURNE FARM – FUN & SURPRISES (BEDFORDSHIRE)

Sun 7 June 10am – 5pm. Adm £5, chd free
No booking required, come along on the day!
Bring the whole family and have fun in this surprising and entertaining garden of 2 acres. Enjoy
the large plant fair, live music, pets corner, birds of prey, dog agility show and much more.

WISLEY RHS GARDEN – MUSIC IN THE GARDEN (SURREY)

Fri 11 Sept 6 – 9pm
Adm (incl RHS members) £7, chd under 15 free
Save money on advance bookings for groups of 4 or more, telephone +44 (0)1483 211535 or
visit www.ngs.org.uk for more information
A special evening opening of this famous garden, exclusively for the NGS. Enjoy music
and entertainment as you explore the gardens and the floral marquee on the first day of
the Wisley Flower Show.

For further information visit www.ngs.org.uk or telephone 01483 211535

LEICESTERSHIRE & RUTLAND

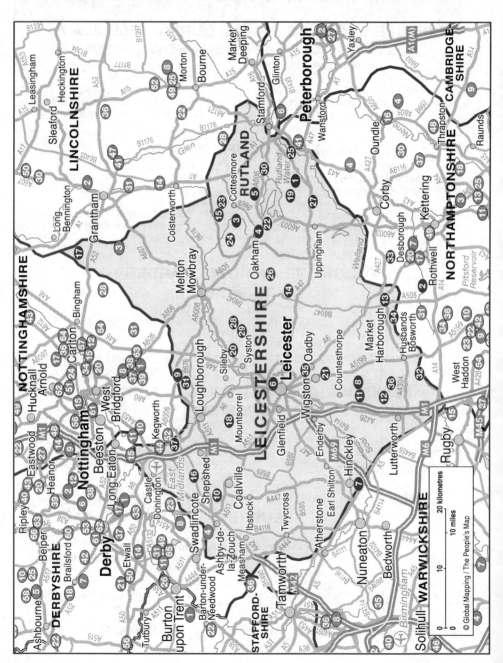

Opening Dates

March

SUNDAY 1
17 The Homestead

SUNDAY 15
5 Barnsdale Gardens
13 Hammond Arboretum

SUNDAY 29
27 The Park House

April

SUNDAY 5
18 Long Close
22 Mirwood

SUNDAY 26
23 The Old Hall

May

SUNDAY 3
4 Barleythorpe Gardens
7 Burbage Gardens

MONDAY 4
7 Burbage Gardens

SUNDAY 10
9 Cradock Cottage
37 Whatton Gardens

SUNDAY 17
3 Ashwell House
6 Belgrave Hall Museum & Gardens
21 Mill House

WEDNESDAY 20
34 Thorpe Lubenham Hall

SUNDAY 24
12 Gilmorton Gardens

WEDNESDAY 27
12 Gilmorton Gardens (Evening)

SUNDAY 31
18 Long Close

June

WEDNESDAY 3
2 Arthingworth Garden
33 Stoke Albany House

SUNDAY 7
30 Prebendal House
36 Walton Gardens

WEDNESDAY 10
2 Arthingworth Garden
33 Stoke Albany House
36 Walton Gardens

SUNDAY 14
12 Gilmorton Gardens
24 The Old Vicarage
32 South Kilworth Gardens

WEDNESDAY 17
2 Arthingworth Garden
33 Stoke Albany House

THURSDAY 18
6 Belgrave Hall Museum & Gardens (Evening)

SUNDAY 21
27 The Park House
31 Ridgewold Farm

WEDNESDAY 24
2 Arthingworth Garden
19 Lyndon Gardens (Evening)
31 Ridgewold Farm
33 Stoke Albany House

SUNDAY 28
8 Coldor
11 Farmway
14 Hedgehog Hall
25 The Old Vicarage

July

WEDNESDAY 1
2 Arthingworth Garden
33 Stoke Albany House

SUNDAY 5
16 Hill Park Farm
32 South Kilworth Gardens
37 Whatton Gardens

WEDNESDAY 8
2 Arthingworth Garden
33 Stoke Albany House

SUNDAY 12
1 Acre End
7 Burbage Gardens

WEDNESDAY 15
2 Arthingworth Garden
8 Coldor
11 Farmway
33 Stoke Albany House

SATURDAY 18
26 Owston Gardens

SUNDAY 19
21 Mill House

WEDNESDAY 22
2 Arthingworth Garden

SUNDAY 26
35 University of Leicester 'Harold Martin' Botanic Garden

WEDNESDAY 29
2 Arthingworth Garden

August

SUNDAY 2
8 Coldor
11 Farmway

SUNDAY 23
29 Pine House

SUNDAY 30
22 Mirwood

October

SUNDAY 11
13 Hammond Arboretum

SUNDAY 25
5 Barnsdale Gardens

Gardens open to the public

5 Barnsdale Gardens
6 Belgrave Hall Museum & Gardens
37 Whatton Gardens

By appointment only

10 The Dairy
15 Hill House
20 1700 Melton Road
28 Parkside

Also open by appointment ☎

1 Acre End
2 Bosworth House, Arthingworth Garden
4 Dairy Cottage, Barleythorpe Gardens
7 7 Hall Rd, Burbage Gardens
8 Coldor
11 Farmway
12 Tudor Cottage, Gilmorton Gardens
12 Ulverscroft Close, Gilmorton Gardens
14 Hedgehog Hall
17 The Homestead
18 Long Close
21 Mill House
22 Mirwood
23 The Old Hall
24 The Old Vicarage
29 Pine House
31 Ridgewold Farm
32 Croft Acre, South Kilworth Gardens
32 Oak Tree House, South Kilworth Gardens
33 Stoke Albany House

All organically managed to encourage wildlife . . .

The Gardens

1 ACRE END
The Jetties, North Luffenham
LE15 8JX. Jim & Mima Bolton,
01780 720906, mmkb@mac.com.
*7m SE of Oakham. Via Manton & Edith
Weston, 7m SW of Stamford via
Ketton. 2m off A47 through Morcott
village.* Light refreshments & teas at
North Luffenham Community Centre.
Adm £3.50, chd free (share to St
John The Baptist Church, N
Luffenham). Sun 12 July (11-5).
Visitors also welcome by appt mid
Jun to mid Aug, groups welcome.
1-acre garden, imaginatively designed
and intensively planted, incl knot
garden, oriental courtyard garden,
mixed borders, circular lawn with island
beds, herb and scented garden.
Working fruit and vegetable garden,
long herbaceous border and woodland
garden. Many unusual trees, shrubs,
herbaceous perennials and tender
exotics in containers. All organically
managed to encourage wildlife. Studio
Art Exhibition (share to NGS). Wildlife
wood carvings. Featured in 'The
English Garden'. Mainly grass paths &
lawns, some gravel.

2 ARTHINGWORTH GARDEN
LE16 8JT. *6m S of Market
Harborough. From Market Harborough
via A508, at 4m L to Arthingworth.
From N'pton on A508 turn R just after
Kelmarsh at bottom of hill. Follow to
village turn L on to Oxenden Rd then
2nd R.* Adm £2, chd free. Weds 3,
10, 17, 24 June; 1, 8, 15, 22, 29 July
(2-5).

BOSWORTH HOUSE
Arthingworth. Mrs C Irving-Swift,
01858 525202,
irvingswift@btinternet.com.
Visitors also welcome by appt.
1½ acre of lawns, herbaceous
borders, little orchard, small
spinney, vegetable patch. A few
magnificent old trees and rose bed.
Panoramic views.

Featured on BBC2 'Gardeners' World' . . .

3 ASHWELL HOUSE
Ashwell, nr Oakham LE15 7LW. Mr &
Mrs S D Pettifer. *3m N of Oakham.
Via B668 towards Cottesmore, then L
for Ashwell.* Light refreshments & teas.
Adm £3, chd free. Sun 17 May (1.30-
5.30).
Over 21yrs of opening this 1½ -acre
walled vicarage garden dates back to
1812. Against background of ancient
trees; front lawns are bordered by
interesting shrubs and plants with
classical summer pavilion. The formal
swimming pool garden leads to
traditional planting of vegetables and
fruit. Willow making display by John
Shone.

Group opening

4 BARLEYTHORPE GARDENS
Barleythorpe, Nr Oakham LE15 7EQ.
*1m from Oakham on A6006 towards
Melton Mowbray. Car park in Pasture
Lane 1st turn L in Barleythorpe by
phone box. Please park in field on L
not on lane.* Home-made teas.
Combined adm £3, chd free (share
to East Midlands Accident Care
Scheme). Sun 3 May (2-5).

DAIRY COTTAGE
Pasture Lane, Barleythorpe. Mr
& Mrs W Smith, 01572 759848.
Visitors also welcome by appt
May only.
Cottage-style garden at rear with
interesting and unusual shrubs and
spring bulbs. Paved/walled garden
to front (with pond) and lime
hedge. Separate semi-formal
orchard. Gravel access from car
park.

THE LODGE
Pasture Lane. Dr & Mrs T J Gray
Mixed flowers within walled
garden, ½ lawn and part-walled
kitchen garden. Small stretch of
gravel path between lawned area
and vegetable garden.

8 MANOR LANE
Barleythorpe. Richard Turner
Water and woodland. Flowering
shrubs, large weeping trees, small
lake and woodland walk. Children
must be supervised at all times.

Group opening

5 ◆ BARNSDALE GARDENS
The Avenue, Exton, nr Oakham
LE15 8AH. Nick & Sue Hamilton,
01572 813200,
www.barnsdalegardens.co.uk. *3m E
of Oakham. Turn off A606 at Barnsdale
Lodge Hotel then 1m on L.* Adm £6,
chd £2, concessions £5 (share to
NGS). For NGS: Suns 15 Mar; 25 Oct
(9-5).
8 acres of individual gardens used by
the late Geoff Hamilton for BBC TV
'Gardeners' World'. Wide variety of
ideas and garden designs for all-yr
interest. Enjoyed by gardeners and
non-gardeners alike. Featured on
BBC2 'Gardeners' World', Award
Winning Garden Designs, Chelsea,
Gardeners' World Live, Hampton Court
& Harrogate.

6 ◆ BELGRAVE HALL MUSEUM & GARDENS
Church Road off Thurcaston Road,
Belgrave, Leicester LE4 5PE.
Leicester City Council, 0116 2666
590, www.leicester.gov.uk/museums
- for other open dates. *1½ m N of
Leicester. From A6/A563 junction at
Redhill roundabout take A6030
Loughborough Rd towards city, signed
Outdoor Pursuits Centre. Turn R at 1st
T-lights and L at Talbot PH.* Teas in
May. Refreshments in June. Adm
£2.50, chd free. For NGS: Sun
17 May (1-4). Evening Opening
Thur 18 June (6-9).
Historic Grade II listed garden. House
and walled garden date from 1709.
Includes formal garden, herbaceous
garden, rose walks, Victorian
evergreen garden, rock and water
garden, botanic beds, herb border,
woodland garden. Alpine, temperate
and tropical glasshouses with wide
collection of plants incl banana. The
Handkerchief tree 'Davida Involucrata'
usually produces a spectacular display
of white bracts in May.

BERTIE ROAD GARDENS
See Warwickshire & part of West
Midlands.

BLUEBELL ARBORETUM
See Derbyshire.

Colour themed borders with alliums . . . small bluebell woodland with mature trees . . .

Group opening

7 BURBAGE GARDENS
LE10 2LR. *1m S of Hinckley. From M69 J1, take B4109 signed Hinckley. 1st L after 2nd r'about into Sketchley Manor Estate then 1st R, 1st L. All gardens within walking distance.* Home-made teas at 6 Denis Road (May), 13 Hall Road (July). **Combined adm £3, chd free (May). £2 (July). Sun 3, Mon 4 May; (1-5); Sun 12 July (1-5).**
A pleasant West Leicestershire village.

6 DENIS ROAD
Mr & Mrs D A Dawkins. *Sketchley Manor Est.* **Not open 12 July.**
Small garden designed to appear much larger with wide range of plants incl hardy geraniums, ferns, hostas, foliage plants, species clematis, hellebores and spring bulbs. Alpines in sinks. Large collection of snowdrops.

7 HALL ROAD
Don & Mary Baker, 01455 635616. *Sketchley Manor Est.* **Not open 12 July.**
Medium-sized garden; mixed borders; foliage plants; good mixture of shrubs. Hellebores and spring bulbs, collection of snowdrops. Hostas, hardy geraniums and unusual perennials; pond. Late summer colour.

13 HALL ROAD
Mr & Mrs G A & A J Kierton. *Sketchley Manor Est.* Decorative medium-sized flower garden, incoporating pool and waterfall, herbaceous borders, central lawn, scree garden, 2 patios, pergola, summer house; greenhouse and small fountain. Abundance of summer colour. Winner of 'Burbage in Bloom' Front & Rear gardens.

CALKE ABBEY
See Derbyshire.

8 COLDOR
4 Arnesby Lane, Peatling Magna, Leicester LE8 5UN. Colin & Doreen Shepherd, 01162 478407. *9m S of Leicester. 2m W of Arnesby on A5199. Arnesby Lane is opp Cock Inn, Peatling Magna. Garden is on private drive 100yds from Cock Inn. Parking on Main St.* Home-made teas 28 Jun & 5 Jul only. **Adm £2, chd free (share to Coping with Cancer). Combined with Farmway adm £3. Sun 28 June (11-5); Wed 15 July (2-5); Sun 2 Aug (11-5).** Visitors also welcome by appt June to mid August.
1/4 acre garden with immaculate lawns, mixed herbaceous and shrub borders. Small pond and water feature. Patio with many plants in containers. Garden nursery, plants for sale. Feature in 'Leicester & Rutland Life' magazine.

THE COTTAGE
See Derbyshire.

9 NEW CRADOCK COTTAGE
74 Brook Street, Wymeswold LE12 6TU. Mike & Carol Robinson. *3m NE of Loughborough. On A6006 between Melton and Kegworth.* Home-made teas. **Adm £2.50, chd free. Sun 10 May (1-6).**
3/4 -acre S facing country garden developed over the last 7 years. 3/4 -acre meadow beyond with attractive views of the village and countryside. Colour themed borders with alliums. Small bluebell woodland with mature trees. Formal vegetable garden. Display and stall by garden retailers 'The Worm That Turned'.

10 THE DAIRY
Moor Lane, Coleorton LE67 8FQ. Mr & Mrs J B Moseley, 01530 834539. *2m E of Ashby De La Zouch. Moor Lane is off A512 200yds W of Peggs Green roundabout.* **Adm £2.50, chd free.** Visitors welcome by appt June & July only, groups of 10+, coaches can be accommodated.
Approx 1/2 -acre of mature trees, shrubs and herbaceous borders containing many unusual and architectural plants. Herb garden, fragrant roses, pergola, Japanese garden and dry area with grasses and agaves. The separate 'rooms' of the garden create surprises around every corner. Summer flowering plants create a riot of colour in June and July.

11 FARMWAY
Church Farm Lane, Willoughby Waterleys LE8 6UD. Eileen Spencer, 0116 2478321, eileenfarmway9@msn.com. *9m S of Leicester. From Leicester take A426. L at t-lights at Dunton Bassett x-rds. Follow signs to Willoughby. From M1 J20 take A426 through Lutterworth. R at t-lights at Dunton Bassett x-rds. Park in main street.* Light refreshments & teas at Willoughby Village Hall 2 Aug only. **Adm £2, chd free. Combined with Coldor adm £3. Sun 28 June (11-5); Wed 15 July (2-5); Sun 2 Aug (11-5).** Visitors also welcome by appt Mid June end of Aug.
W-facing, 1/4 -acre garden on gentle slope with views across Leicestershire. Mature plant lover's garden, closely planted with a wide variety of shrubs, herbaceous perennials, roses and clematis. Many varieties of lavender. Two ponds, vegetable garden, herbs and extensive collection of containers. Good for late summer colour.

Group opening

12 GILMORTON GARDENS
Nr Lutterworth LE17 5LY. *12m S of Leicester. 4m from J20 of M1. Proceed through Lutterworth town centre. Turn R at police stn. Follow signs to Gilmorton. From Leicester follow A426 towards Lutterworth. At Dunton Bassett turn L signed to Gilmorton. Also A5199 Leicester/Northampton Rd via Bruntingthorpe signed Gilmorton.* Light refreshments & teas in village hall (teas only Weds). **Combined adm £3, chd free. Also combined with South**

Kilworth Gardens Sun 14 June adm £5. Suns 24 May; 14 June (11-6). Evening Opening Wed 27 May (2-8).
Gilmorton, Saxon origin, listed in Domesday survey. Examples of mud walled, thatched cottages (1500s), a motte (1100s), and brick cottages dating from 1710. Church (will be open), of Norman origin, was extensively rebuilt in 1860. Notable are its reredos and fine examples of Kempe stain glass windows.

MOATFIELD
Church Lane. Mr & Mrs R P Morgan. Not open Sun 14 June.
Garden around barn conversion next to church started in 1995. Lawns, climbers, roses, unusual shrubs, flower borders and raised beds for acid loving plants in original walled farmyard area. Field with large natural pond, collection of trees; rowans, birches, hollies etc, and old moat area. Open views of countryside. Gravel entrance.

TUDOR COTTAGE
Main Street. Mr & Mrs Dolby. Visitors also welcome by appt June - Aug. With group gardens only.
Interesting cottage garden with unusual 'quirky' features. Parterre.

ULVERSCROFT CLOSE
Ashby Road. Mr & Mrs M J Maddock, 01455 553226, michael.maddock@care4free.net, www.maddock-garden.co.uk. Visitors also welcome by appt June - Aug. Coaches permitted.
1/2 -acre garden on two levels. Upper level features conservatory, courtyard, tree-lined paved walkway. Lower level has pond, bog garden and stream situated in colourful herbaceous and shrub borders hosting over 120 clematis. Formal kitchen garden.

GRANBY GARDENS
See Nottinghamshire.

---

13 NEW HAMMOND ARBORETUM
The Robert Smyth School, Burnmill Road, Market Harborough LE16 7JG. *From the High Street, follow signs to The Robert Smyth School via Bowden Lane to Burnmill Road. Park in the first entrance on the left.* Adm £3, chd free. Suns 15 Mar; 11 Oct (2-5).
A site of 2.4-acres containing an unusual collection of trees and shrubs, many from Francis Hammond's original planting dating from 1913 to 1936 whilst headmaster of the school. Species from America, China and Japan with malus and philadelphus walks and a moat. Guided walks and walk plans available. Display of photographs, drawings and pressed leaves of the trees and shrubs throughout the seasons. Original records of planting and history of Francis Hammond. Featured in Harborough in Bloom and Britain in Bloom. Open access to hard paths, grassed areas with difficulty.

14 NEW HEDGEHOG HALL
Loddington Road, Tilton on the Hill LE7 9DE. Janet & Andrew Rowe, 0116 2597339. *8m W of Oakham. 2m N of A47 on the B6047 between Melton & Market Harborough. Turn between church and pub in Tilton towards Loddington and follow signs.* Home-made teas. Adm £3, chd free. Sun 28 June (11-5). Visitors also welcome by appt mid June - mid Aug. Groups of 10+.
1/2 -acre organically managed plant lover's garden. Steps leading to three stonewalled terraced borders filled with shrubs, perennials and bulbs. Lavender walk, herb border, spring garden, colour themed long border and serpentine island bed packed with campanulas, astrantias, sangui sorbas roses, clematis and many more. Sheltered walled courtyard filled with hostas, ferns and wisteria. Hot terraced borders. Cake stall.

---

15 HILL HOUSE
18 Teigh Road, Market Overton LE15 7PW. Brian & Judith Taylor, 01572 767337. *6m N of Oakham. Beyond Cottesmore, 5m from A1 via Thistleton, 10m E from Melton Mowbray via Wymondham.* Adm £2, chd free. Visitors welcome by appt for groups of 10+, June to September.
Owner-maintained plant enthusiasts' garden consisting mainly of mixed beds designed to provide colour and interest from mid-June to the end of Sept. The emphasis is on architectural plants and unusual hardy and tender perennials. Ornamental pond. Referred to in 'The Good Gardens Guide'.

16 HILL PARK FARM
Dodgeford Lane, Belton, Loughborough LE12 9TE. John & Jean Adkin. *6m W of Loughborough. Dodgeford Lane off B5324 bet Belton & Osgathorpe.* Home-made teas. Adm £2.50, chd free. Sun 5 July (11-5).
Medium-sized garden to a working farm with wonderful views over Charnwood Forest. Herbaceous borders, rock garden; many planted stone troughs and pergola with clematis and roses.

HOLYWELL HALL
See Lincolnshire.

17 THE HOMESTEAD
Normanton-by-Bottesford NG13 0EP. John & Shirley Palmer, 01949 842745. *8m W of Grantham. From A52. In Bottesford turn N, signed Normanton; last house on R before disused airfield. From A1, in Long Bennington follow signs S to Normanton, 1st house on L.* Home-made teas. Adm £2, chd free. Sun 1 Mar (1-5). Visitors also welcome by appt.
3/4 -acre informal plant lover's garden. Vegetable garden, small orchard, woodland area, many hellebores, snowdrops and single peonies and salvias. Collections of hostas and sempervivums. National Collection of heliotropes.

KILSBY GARDENS
See Northamptonshire.

Francis Hammond's original planting dating from 1913 to 1936 . . .

The village is one of the few south facing villages in Rutland and is mainly traditional stone . . .

18 LONG CLOSE
Main St, Woodhouse Eaves
LE12 8RZ. John & Pene Oakland,
01509 890376. *4m S of
Loughborough. Nr M1 J23. From A6,
W in Quorn. Tickets at time of visit from
Gift Shop opp. If shop closed tickets at
garden.* Home-made teas 5 Apr & 31
May only. Adm £4, chd 50p. Suns 5
Apr (1-5), plant market; 31 May (2-6).
Also daily Tues to Sats & BH
weekends, Apr to July, Sept to mid
Oct. Also group visits by
appointment. Catering by
arrangement.
5-acres spring bulbs, rhododendrons,
azaleas, camellias, magnolias, many
rare shrubs, mature trees, lily ponds;
terraced lawns, herbaceous borders,
potager in walled kitchen garden,
penstemon collection, wild flower
meadow walk. Winter, spring, summer
and autumn colour, a garden for all
seasons. Plants for sale. 5 April plant
market, 6 stalls.

Group opening

19 NEW LYNDON GARDENS
Post Office Lane, Lyndon,
Oakham LE15 8TZ. *South Shore,
Rutland Water. Between Oakham
& Uppingham (A6003), S Shore of
Rutland water, 1/2 m from Manton/
Edith Weston Rd.* Combined adm
£3.50, chd free (share to Derbs,
Leics & Rutland Air Ambulance).
Evening Opening, wine, Wed
24 June (5-8.30).
Two adjoining gardens in the
delightful and secluded village of
Lyndon, largely owned by the
Conant Family, who have occupied
Lyndon Hall since it was built in
1667. The village is one of the few
south facing villages in Rutland and
is mainly traditional stone. Small
C12 church will be open. Visit the
Community Kitchen Garden on the
way.

NEW PARSONS ORCHARD
Post Office Lane, Lyndon.
Sarah & Mike Peck
1/2 -acre south facing village
garden, in a beautiful setting.
Mixed borders, shrubs,
herbaceous, scented/old
fashioned roses, integrated herb
and vegetable garden, peaceful
corners.

NEW THE POST HOUSE
Post Office Lane, Lyndon.
Pauline & Clive Pitts
Small, stylish, contemporary
garden with delightful rural views
to the rear of recently constructed
stone cottage. Planting designed
with emphasis on foliage and
year round interest. Some gravel.

THE MALTINGS
See Northamptonshire.

20 1700 MELTON ROAD
Rearsby LE7 4YR. Mrs Hazel Kaye,
01664 424578. *6m NE of Leicester.
On A607.* Adm £2, chd free. Visitors
welcome by appt.
In spring hellebores, early flowering
shrubs and daffodils feature. In autumn
Michaelmas daisies, colchicum and
shrubs with colourful berries and
foliage. 1 1/2 acres planted for yr-round
interest. National Collection of
Tradescantia (Andersoniana Group),
best in early June. Grass paths.

21 MILL HOUSE
118 Welford Road, Wigston,
Leicester LE18 3SN. Mr & Mrs P
Measures, 01162 885409. *4m S of
Leicester. 1m S of Wigston, on main
old A50.* Light refreshments & teas.
Adm £1.80, chd free. Suns 17 May;
19 July (11-5). Visitors also welcome
by appt June/July. Groups of 10+.
Walled town garden; extensive plant
variety. Unusual and interesting design
features incorporating planting,
bygones and memorabilia. A genuine
journey back in time.

22 MIRWOOD
69a Brooke Road, Oakham
LE15 6HG. Kevin & Kate O'Brien,
01572 755535. *200yds from town
centre. Turn into Mill St at roundabout
opp library at X-roads/T-lights. Parking
available in Brooke Rd car park (free on
Sun). Garden 200yds on RH-side.*

Light refreshments & teas. Adm £3,
chd free (share to Melton & Rutland
MS Society). Suns 5 Apr; 30 Aug
(1-6). Visitors also welcome by appt.
3/4 -acre garden containing large
collection of rare and unusual shrubs
and trees. Seasonal formal beds,
recently built folly, vegetable garden,
yr-round interest particularly with
spring bulbs.

NASEBY GARDENS
See Northamptonshire.

23 THE OLD HALL
Main Street, Market Overton
LE15 7PL. Mr & Mrs Timothy Hart,
01572 767145,
stefa@hambleton.co.uk. *6m N of
Oakham. Beyond Cottesmore; 5m
from A1 via Thistleton. 10m E from
Melton Mowbray via Wymondham.*
Teas & cream teas. Adm £3.50, chd
free (share to Macmillan Cancer
Support). Sun 26 Apr (2-6). Visitors
also welcome by appt £4 entry.
Garden is set on a southerly ridge
overlooking Catmose Vale. Garden
now on four levels with stone walls and
yew hedges dividing the garden up in
to enclosed areas with herbaceous
borders, shrubs, and young and
mature trees. In 2006 the lower part of
garden was planted with new shrubs
to create a walk with mown paths.
Terrace and lawn give a great sense of
space, enhancing the view. Lots of
gravel. Lower garden has steep, mown
grass paths.

THE OLD POLICE STATION
See Derbyshire.

24 THE OLD VICARAGE
Whissendine LE15 7HG. Prof Peter
& Dr Sarah Furness, 01664 474549,
shfdesign@pathology.plus.com,
www.pathology.plus.com/garden/.
*5m N of Oakham. Whissendine village
is signed from A606 between Melton
Mowbray & Oakham. Head for church
- very visible tower. The Old Vicarage is
adjacent, higher up the hill. Main
entrance on opp side, 1st L on Station
Rd; alternative entrance from
churchyard. Maps available on
website.* Home-made teas at the
church. Adm £2.50, chd free. Sun
14 June (1-5.30). Visitors also
welcome by appt.
2/3 -acre packed with variety. Walled
terrace with mature olive trees, formal
fountain and raised beds backed by
small gothic orangery burgeoning with

tender plants. Herbaceous borders surround main lawn. Wisteria tunnel leads to orchard filled with naturalised bulbs. Hidden 'white walk' overflowing with unusual plants. Much more... Beautiful C14th church - a real 'village cathedral'. Featured in 'Rutland and Leicestershire Life'. Gravel drive, some steps.

♿ 🐶 ✿ ☕ ☎

25 NEW THE OLD VICARAGE
27 Church Road, Ketton PE9 3RD. Mr & Mrs R C Bell. *4m W of Stamford. Ketton lies 4m W of A1 at Stamford on the A6121, Church Rd runs S from A6121 to the A43 at Collyweston.* **Adm £2.50, chd free. Sun 28 June** (2-6).
Stone walls and mature hedging divide the 1½ -acres into areas with different functions and form. Lawns are bordered by herbaceous and shrub planting, swimming pool garden leads to River Chater and a tranquil area beside a fountain and several specimen trees.

♿ 🐶 ✿ ☕

Group opening

26 NEW OWSTON GARDENS
Owston, nr Oakham LE15 8DH. *7m W of Oakham. Car park in field in middle of village.* Light refreshments. **Combined adm £3.50, chd free. Evening Opening** Sat 18 July (5-8).
Rural farming village surrounding church, on site of C12 abbey and fish ponds. Dogs allowed on lead. Church open.

☕

NEW BRICKYARD FARM
Owston. Dr & Mrs John Merrill. *Top of village on Main St* Garden created over the last 20 years. Herbaceous borders, rose garden, alpine and conifer walk, large vegetable garden, wild flower area and small arboretum. Unfenced pool, children welcome but must be supervised at all times. Dogs on leads. Steps, gravel paths, and a steep slope.

NEW LITTLE BUTT
Owston. Mrs Louise Hammond. *Bottom of village opp church* Evolving garden of different areas incl orchard, ponds, long

herbaceous tunnel, kitchen garden and new paved courtyard based on Islamic traditions. Dogs on leads.

27 THE PARK HOUSE
Glaston Park, Spring Lane, Glaston LE15 9BW. Sheila & Stuart Makings. *6m S of Oakham on A47. 2m E of A6003 Uppingham roundabout travelling on A47 towards Peterborough.* Teas at Glaston Village Hall. **Adm £3, chd free. Suns** 29 Mar (1-5); 21 June (2-6).
4 acres approx of historic parkland, formerly part of grounds of Glaston Hall. Informal walks incl extensive lime arbour. Serpentine yew hedge, mature trees, medieval ha-ha and fish ponds. Herbaceous borders, traditional rose garden. Rural views, wildlife friendly. Wild wood walk. Carpets of spring bulbs, hellebores and shrubs. Ornamental wildfowl. Some gravel paths, sloping grounds. Unfenced water, children welcome but must be supervised at all times.

♿ ✿ ☕

Rural farming village surrounding church, on site of C12 abbey and fish ponds . . .

28 PARKSIDE
6 Park Hill, Gaddesby LE7 4WH. Mr & Mrs D Wyrko, 01664 840385, david.wyrko1@btinternet.com. *8m NE of Leicester. From A607 Rearsby bypass turn off for Gaddesby. L at Cheney Arms. Garden 400yds on R.* Home-made teas. **Adm £3, chd free. Visitors welcome by appt** April to July. Any size group welcome.
1¼ -acre garden and woodland in

process of re-development from original planting. Mature trees and shrubs, together with informal mixed borders, planted to encourage wildlife and provide a family friendly environment. Newly created vegetable and fruit area together with garden pond. Many spring bulbs and hellebores in a woodland setting.

🐶 ✿ ☕ ☎

PIECEMEAL
See Nottinghamshire.

29 PINE HOUSE
Gaddesby LE7 4XE. Mr & Mrs T Milward, 01664 840213. *8m NE of Leicester. From A607, turn off for Gaddesby.* Home-made teas. **Adm £3, chd free. Sun** 23 Aug (11-5). **Visitors also welcome by appt** May-Sept. Groups 10+. Coaches permitted.
2-acre garden with fine mature trees, woodland walk, and water garden. Herb and potager garden and wisteria archway to Victorian vinery. Pleached lime trees, mixed borders with rare and unusual plants and rock garden; new gravel garden and terracotta pot garden. Interesting topiary hedges and box trees.

🐶 ✿ ☕ ☎

30 PREBENDAL HOUSE
Empingham LE15 8PS. Mr & Mrs J Partridge. *5m E of Oakham. 5m W of Stamford. On A606.* Home-made teas. **Adm £3.50, chd free. Sun** 7 June (2-5).
House (not open) built in 1688; summer palace for the Bishop of Lincoln. 4-acre garden incl herbaceous borders, water garden, topiary and kitchen gardens.

✿ ☕

31 RIDGEWOLD FARM
Burton Lane, Wymeswold, Loughborough LE12 6UN. Robert & Ann Waterfall, 01509 881689. *5m SE of Loughborough. Off Burton Lane between A6006 & B676.* Home-made teas. **Adm £2.50, chd free. Sun** 21 June (2-6), **Afternoon & Evening Opening** Wed 24 June (3-9). **Visitors also welcome by appt.**
Planted in the last 8 years, 1½ -acre garden set in open countryside, specimen trees, copses, lawns with a good deal of mixed hedging. Rose garden, shrubs, borders, orchard, kitchen garden with water feature and natural pond around the house.

✿ ☕ ☎

Walled grey garden; nepeta walk arched with roses, parterre with box and roses . . .

Group opening

32 SOUTH KILWORTH GARDENS
Nr Lutterworth LE17 6DX. *15m S of Leicester. From M1 J20, take A4304 towards Market Harborough. At Walcote turn R, signed South Kilworth.* Home-made teas at Croft Acre. **Combined adm £3, chd free. Suns 14 June (11-6); 5 July (11-5). Combined with Gilmorton Gardens Sun 14 June combined adm £5.** Small village tucked away in SW corner of Leicestershire, with excellent views over Avon valley and Hemplow hills.

CROFT ACRE
The Belt. Colin & Verena Olle, 01858 575791, colin.olle@tiscali.co.uk. *At White Hart PH take rd signed North Kilworth. The Belt is a bridleway 250yds on R. Parking on North Rd.* **Visitors also welcome by appt June to mid July.**
1-acre garden, herbaceous borders, island beds, wide selection of shrubs and perennials. Rose and wisteria pergolas, ponds and small stream. Rose garden with unusual water sculpture. Yin Yang landscape. Vegetable garden. Summerhouse and garden room seating areas for quiet contemplation.

OAK TREE HOUSE
North Road. Pam & Martin Shave. *From centre of village take rd to N Kilworth. 300yds down North Rd on RH-side (just after bridleway, The Belt).* **Visitors also welcome by appt contact Croft Acre.**
Newly created garden of 2/3 acre. Formal layout with greenhouse, ornamental vegetable plot, pond and herbaceous borders. Patio with numerous pots and hanging baskets. Arched pergola with roses and clematis, leading to gravel patio. Access to pond & greenhouse via steps.

33 STOKE ALBANY HOUSE
Stoke Albany LE16 8PT. Mr & Mrs A M Vinton, 01858 535227. *4m E of Market Harborough. Via A427 to Corby; turn to Stoke Albany; R at the White Horse (B669); garden 1/2 m on L.* **Adm £3.50, chd free (share to Marie Curie Cancer Care). Wed 3, 10, 17, 24 June; Wed 1, 8, 15 July (2-4.30). Visitors also welcome by appt June to July, Tues & Weds for groups only.**
4-acre country-house garden; fine trees and shrubs with wide herbaceous borders and sweeping striped lawn. Good display of bulbs in spring, roses June and July. Walled grey garden; nepeta walk arched with roses, parterre with box and roses. Mediterranean garden. Heated greenhouse, potager with topiary, water feature garden and sculptures. Featured in 'Leicestershire & Rutland Life Magazine'.

34 THORPE LUBENHAM HALL
Lubenham LE16 9TR. Sir Bruce & Lady MacPhail. *2m W of Market Harborough. From Market Harborough take 3rd L off main rd, down Rushes Lane, past church on L, under old railway bridge and straight on up private drive.* Cream teas. **Adm £3, chd free (share to Leicestershire Air Ambulance). Wed 20 May (10-5).**
15 acres of formal and informal garden surrounded by parkland and arable. Many mature trees. Traditional herbaceous borders and various water features. Large wild flower meadow and ha ha wall. Rose and lavender beds circling large pond. Walled pool garden with raised beds. Ancient moat area along driveway. Gravel paths & some steep slopes.

35 UNIVERSITY OF LEICESTER 'HAROLD MARTIN' BOTANIC GARDEN
'The Knoll', Glebe Road, Oadby LE2 2NA. University of Leicester. *11/2 m SE of Leicester. On outskirts of city opp race course.* Light refreshments & teas. **Adm £2, chd free. Sun 26 July (11-4).**
16-acre garden incl grounds of Beaumont Hall, The Knoll, Southmeade and Hastings House. Wide variety of ornamental features and glasshouses laid out for educational purposes.

Group opening

36 WALTON GARDENS
LE17 5RP. *4m NE of Lutterworth. M1 exit 20 and, via Lutterworth follow signs for Kimcote and Walton, or from Leicester take A5199. After Shearsby turn R signed Bruntingthorpe. Follow signs.* Home-made teas at Orchards. **Combined adm £3, chd free. Sun 7, Wed 10 June (11-5).**
Small village in South Leicestershire. Village maps given to all visitors.

THE MEADOWS
Mowsley Lane. Mr & Mrs Falkner
Plantsman's garden, with emphasis on wildlife friendly flowers. Two ponds, conservatory with unusual plants and many plants in containers. A collection of unusual plants, shrubs and roses developing every year.

ORCHARDS
Hall Lane. Mr & Mrs G Cousins. **Visitors also welcome by appt June to Aug.**
In this garden all the leaves are green (no varigated, gold or purple). Many rare flowering plants. Extensive use of grasses. Views of the countryside. 'Quite unlike any other garden (RHS Garden Finder). Featured in 'The Garden'.

SANDYLAND
Hall Lane. Martin & Linda Goddard
Gently sloping cottage garden with attractive rural views. Herbaceous plants, shrubs, containers, terraced garden, pond and kitchen garden.

In this garden all the leaves are green (no varigated, gold or purple) . . .

37 ◆ **WHATTON GARDENS**
nr Loughborough LE12 5BG. Lord &
Lady Crawshaw, 01509 842225,
whattho@tiscali.co.uk. *4m NE of
Loughborough. On A6 between
Hathern & Kegworth; 2¹/₂ m SE of J24
on M1.* **Adm £3, chd free. Mar-Oct,
Sun-Fri 11-4. For NGS: Suns 10
May; 5 July (11-5).**
Dating from the 1800, 15 acres of
varied nooks and crannies, from formal
rose garden, arboretum with many fine
trees, large traditional herbaceous
borders, ponds, many shrubs. Large
variety of spring bulbs. Described by
many visitors as one of East Midlands
unknown treasures. Featured in
'Leicester & Rutland Life' Magazine.

Leicestershire & Rutland County Volunteers

County Organiser Leicestershire
John Oakland, Long Close, Woodhouse Eaves, Loughborough LE12 8RZ, 01509 890376

County Treasurer Leicestershire
Martin Shave, Oak Tree House, North Road, South Kilworth
Lutterworth, LE17 6DU, 01455 556633, martinshave@kilworthaccountancy.co.uk

Publicity Leicestershire
Jacqui Fowler, 37 Barrow Road, Quorn, Loughborough LE12 8DH, 07958 490631, jacqui.fowler@btopenworld.com

Assistant County Organisers Leicestershire
Colin Olle, Croft Acre, The Belt, South Kilworth, Lutterworth LE17 6DX, 01858 575791, colin.olle@tiscali.co.uk
Sue Milward, Pine House, Gaddesby LE7 4XE, 01664 840213

County Organiser Rutland
Jennifer Wood, Townsend House, Morcott Road, Wing, Nr Oakham LE15 8SA, 01572 737465, rdavidwood@easynet.co.uk

County Treasurer Rutland
David Wood, Townsend House, Morcott Road, Wing, nr Oakham LE15 8SA, 01572 737465, rdavidwood@easynet.co.uk

Publicity Rutland
Michael Peck, Parsons Orchard, Post Office Lane, Lyndon, Nr Oakham LE15 8TX, 01572 737248

Assistant County Organiser Rutland
Rose Dejardin, 5 Top Street, Wing, Nr Oakham LE15 8SE, 01572 737557

Mark your diary with these special events in 2009

EXPLORE SECRET GARDENS DURING CHELSEA & HAMPTON COURT FLOWER SHOW WEEKS

Tue 19 May, Wed 20 May, Thur 21 May, Fri 22 May, Wed 8 July, Thur 9 July
Full day tours from £82 per person, 10% discount for groups
Advance booking required, telephone +44 (0)20 8693 1015 or email j.wookey@btinternet.com
Specially selected gardens in London, Essex, Kent, Hampshire and South Oxfordshire. The tour price includes transport and lunch with wine at a popular restaurant or pub.

HAMPTON COURT PALACE

Thur 2 Apr, Tue 23 June, Thur 25 June, Wed 15 July, Tue 4 Aug, Thur 10 Sept
Evening tours in the company of one of the Palace's specialist tour guides from 6.30 – 8pm
Tickets £6 per person. Advance booking required, telephone +44 (0)1483 211535 or visit www.ngs.org.uk for more information
Gossip, scandal, murder, healing – you'll find it all within the Formal Gardens at Hampton Court Palace. Each tour will have its own unique feature whether it's the story of the Great Vine or the magic and mystery of the Maze.

FROGMORE – A ROYAL GARDEN (BERKSHIRE)

Tue 26 May 10am – 5.30pm (last admission 4pm)
Garden adm £4.50, chd free. Tickets available in advance or on the day.
Advance booking for groups and coaches, telephone
+44 (0) 1483 211535 or email orders@ngs.org.uk
A rare opportunity to explore 30 acres of landscaped garden, rich in history and beauty.

FLAXBOURNE FARM – FUN & SURPRISES (BEDFORDSHIRE)

Sun 7 June 10am – 5pm. Adm £5, chd free
No booking required, come along on the day!
Bring the whole family and have fun in this surprising and entertaining garden of 2 acres. Enjoy the large plant fair, live music, pets corner, birds of prey, dog agility show and much more.

WISLEY RHS GARDEN – MUSIC IN THE GARDEN (SURREY)

Fri 11 Sept 6 – 9pm
Adm (incl RHS members) £7, chd under 15 free
Save money on advance bookings for groups of 4 or more, telephone +44 (0)1483 211535 or visit www.ngs.org.uk for more information
A special evening opening of this famous garden, exclusively for the NGS. Enjoy music and entertainment as you explore the gardens and the floral marquee on the first day of the Wisley Flower Show.

For further information visit www.ngs.org.uk or telephone 01483 211535

LINCOLNSHIRE

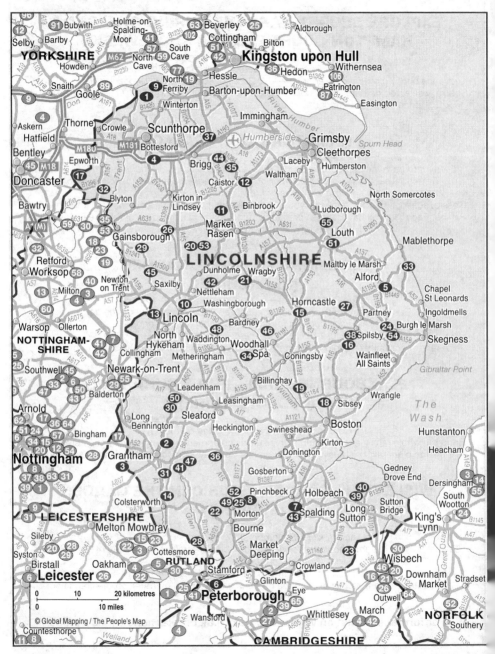

Opening Dates

February
SATURDAY 21
- 8 21 Chapel Street

SUNDAY 22
- 8 21 Chapel Street
- 21 Goltho House

SATURDAY 28
- 44 Pinefields

March
SUNDAY 1
- 44 Pinefields

THURSDAY 5
- 8 21 Chapel Street

SUNDAY 15
- 13 Doddington Hall Gardens

April
SUNDAY 5
- 20 The Garden House
- 53 West Barn

FRIDAY 10
- 14 Easton Walled Gardens

SUNDAY 12
- 31 Little Ponton Hall

MONDAY 13
- 8 21 Chapel Street

SUNDAY 19
- 6 Burghley House Private South Gardens
- 22 Grimsthorpe Castle
- 38 The Old Rectory

SUNDAY 26
- 55 Woodlands

May
SUNDAY 3
- 32 38 Low Street

SUNDAY 10
- 47 South Lodge

SATURDAY 16
- 54 Willow Cottage

SUNDAY 17
- 39 The Old Vicarage
- 46 2 School House
- 48 Station House
- 54 Willow Cottage

SUNDAY 24
- 16 Fen View
- 21 Goltho House
- 33 Marigold Cottage
- 38 The Old Rectory
- 55 Woodlands

SATURDAY 30
- 5 Brightlands

June (first col cont.)
SUNDAY 31
- 5 Brightlands
- 34 Martin Gardens
- 52 10 Wendover Close

June
FRIDAY 5
- 25 Haconby Hall (Evening)
- 49 Walters Cottage (Evening)

SATURDAY 6
- 19 Frog Hall Cottage

SUNDAY 7
- 18 Fishtoft Drove Gardens
- 25 Haconby Hall
- 29 Kexby House
- 49 Walters Cottage

WEDNESDAY 10
- 41 The Orchards

THURSDAY 11
- 28 Holywell Hall

SATURDAY 13
- 48 Station House

SUNDAY 14
- 1 Alkborough and Burton Stather Gardens
- 10 The Coach House
- 23 Guanock House
- 30 Les Allées
- 36 The Moat

MONDAY 15
- 3 Belvoir Castle

WEDNESDAY 17
- 13 Doddington Hall Gardens

THURSDAY 18
- 22 Grimsthorpe Castle

SATURDAY 20
- 43 68 Pennygate

SUNDAY 21
- 43 68 Pennygate
- 47 South Lodge

MONDAY 22
- 3 Belvoir Castle

SATURDAY 27
- 2 Belton House

SUNDAY 28
- 9 Cliff House
- 32 38 Low Street
- 48 Station House

July
WEDNESDAY 1
- 20 The Garden House (Evening)
- 53 West Barn (Evening)

SUNDAY 5
- 19 Frog Hall Cottage

WEDNESDAY 8
- 50 Washdyke Farm

SUNDAY 12
- 39 The Old Vicarage
- 40 Old White House
- 45 73 Saxilby Road

WEDNESDAY 15
- 51 68 Watts Lane

SATURDAY 18
- 2 Belton House
- 5 Brightlands
- 7 39 Cathedral Drive
- 43 68 Pennygate

SUNDAY 19
- 5 Brightlands
- 7 39 Cathedral Drive
- 17 Field House Farm
- 43 68 Pennygate
- 46 2 School House
- 48 Station House

SATURDAY 25
- 4 Bottesford Gardens

SUNDAY 26
- 4 Bottesford Gardens
- 11 Cobwebs
- 35 Mill Farm

August
SUNDAY 9
- 24 Gunby Hall
- 27 Harrington Hall
- 51 68 Watts Lane

SATURDAY 15
- 5 Brightlands
- 43 68 Pennygate

SUNDAY 16
- 5 Brightlands
- 37 Old Quarry Lodge
- 43 68 Pennygate

SUNDAY 23
- 55 Woodlands

SATURDAY 29
- 51 68 Watts Lane

SUNDAY 30
- 11 Cobwebs

September
THURSDAY 3
- 8 21 Chapel Street

SATURDAY 5
- 26 Hall Farm

SUNDAY 6
- 26 Hall Farm

SATURDAY 19
2 Belton House

SUNDAY 20
47 South Lodge

SUNDAY 27
55 Woodlands

October

SUNDAY 4
45 73 Saxilby Road
8 21 Chapel Street

February 2010

SATURDAY 27
8 21 Chapel Street

SUNDAY 28
8 21 Chapel Street

Gardens open to the public

2 Belton House
3 Belvoir Castle
6 Burghley House Private South Gardens
13 Doddington Hall Gardens
14 Easton Walled Gardens
20 The Garden House
22 Grimsthorpe Castle
24 Gunby Hall
26 Hall Farm

By appointment only

12 The Crocosmia Gardens
15 15 Elmhirst Road
42 Overbeck

Also open by appointment ☎

5 Brightlands
7 39 Cathedral Drive
8 21 Chapel Street
11 Cobwebs
25 Haconby Hall
29 Kexby House
33 Marigold Cottage
34 Labourers Cottage, Martin Gardens
36 The Moat
37 Old Quarry Lodge
38 The Old Rectory
39 The Old Vicarage
43 68 Pennygate
46 2 School House
47 South Lodge
50 Washdyke Farm
51 68 Watts Lane
54 Willow Cottage
55 Woodlands

The Gardens

Group opening

1 **ALKBOROUGH AND BURTON STATHER GARDENS**
DN15 9JW. *9m N of Scunthorpe. 12m W of Humber Bridge. Follow brown signs from A1077 for Julian's Bower.* Home-made teas at Alkborough Methodist Chapel. **Combined adm £3, chd free. Sun 14 June (1-6).**
Attractive villages, both within conservation areas. Alkborough is noted for the turf maze, known as Julian's Bower. Situated on the escarpment, it overlooks the confluence of the Humber, Trent and Ouse. Fine church and chapel. Burton Stather is 3m S of Alkborough and 1m from Normanby Park. WC at Alkborough Methodist Chapel.
☕

CHARNWOOD
Front Street, Alkborough. Dave & Pam Batty
An imaginative garden created out of a former stackyard. Lawned area with attractive trees and shrubs, leading through a stepped archway to a productive fruit and vegetable area. Many varieties of flowering plants.

HOLLY COTTAGE
5 Normanby Road, Burton upon Stather. Ms Patricia Brown. *3m S of Alkborough. Take Walcott Rd through to Tee Lane. Turn R into Burton Stather village & follow rd (B1430) to end of High St. Garden entrance via path bet 36 High St & 7 Normanby Rd*
Small cottage garden with colourful informal planting in raised borders enclosing 150yr old end cottage with original outbuildings. Wildlife pond area with ferns and grasses. Raised lawn with herbaceous border. Seating areas. Owner knows every plant.

NEW 7 HUTESON LANE
Mrs Irene Thomas
Small and stylish. This garden provides total relaxation, the planting perfectly in tune with the hard landscaping. The ultimate in low maintenance.
🐾

RAVENDALE
Front Street, Alkborough. Avis & John Ablott
Fruit and flowers intermingle in true cottage style. Paved secluded areas, with container planting. Walk through pergola to grassed area, leading to island beds and wildlife pond, finally reaching organic vegetable plot. Limited access to walled garden.
♿ ❀

ASKHAM GARDENS
See Nottinghamshire.

2 ♦ **BELTON HOUSE**
Grantham NG32 2LS. The National Trust, 01476 566116. *3m NE of Grantham. On A607 Grantham to Lincoln rd. Easily reached & signed from A1 (Grantham N junction).* **House & garden £10, chd £6, garden only £8, chd £4.75. Open daily Wed to Sun 14 Mar to 1 Nov. For NGS: Sats 27 June (11-5.30); 18 July; 19 Sept (10.30-5.30).**
Belton House gardens include formal Italian and Dutch areas with informal gardens that are an inspiration to all gardeners. These 35 acres to the north of the house are a popular attraction in their own right. Orangery by Sir Jeffrey Wyatville. Wheelchair users, please ask at ticket kiosk for recommended route.
♿ 🐾 ❀

3 ♦ **BELVOIR CASTLE**
Grantham NG32 4DQ. The Duke & Duchess of Rutland, 01476 871002, www.belvoircastle.com. *9m from Grantham. Follow brown heritage signs for Belvoir Castle on A52, A1, A607.* **House & garden £12, concession £10, chd £6, chd £3, concessions £5. For details please tel or see website. For NGS: Mons 15, 22 June (11-5).**
English Heritage Grade 2 garden. Secluded in steep woodland 1/2 m from castle. A haven of tranquillity created around original moss house. Magical hillside setting in natural amphitheatre with fresh water springs. Many mature specimen trees and shrubs ensure all-yr colour. Rhododendrons, azaleas, naturalised daffodils, primroses and bluebells. Tallest bird cherry (90ft) and yew tree (93ft) in British Isles. Flat shoes essential. Rose garden with sculpture exhibition. Some steep paths. 🐾
♿ 🐾

The ultimate in low maintenance . . .

Group opening

④ NEW BOTTESFORD GARDENS
Bottesford, Scunthorpe DN16 3TG. *S of Scunthorpe. A159 Scunthorpe to Messingham rd.* Teas at 280A Messingham Rd. **Combined adm £3, chd free. Sat 25, Sun 26 July (1-5).**
Bottesford is a small town on S side of Scunthorpe adjoining open countryside. Bottesford Beck walks, C12 St Peters-ad-Vinicula Church, Templars Bath spring and St Johns Ragwell; Bulls Field with its mature trees is on the way to the Wheatfield allotment site. These productive allotments are set out in a bed and grass path system giving full access.

NEW 24 MERRYWEATHER COURT
Richard Low & Russell Chant. *Turn off A159 Scunthorpe to Messingham rd onto Valley View Drive. 2nd R onto Baldwin Ave then 1st L. Please park on Valley View Drive*
Unusual, small (150ft) wedge-shaped garden developed over 27 yrs. Wide range of perennials, climbers, topiary, summerhouse, arbour, water feature and seating areas.

NEW 280A MESSINGHAM ROAD
Mrs Ann Brumpton
Large garden with lawns surrounded by summer bedding, pots and water feature. Pond with waterfall, stocked with many fish, sited under thatched gazebo. Small orchard leading to vegetable garden with greenhouse and summerhouse.

⑤ NEW BRIGHTLANDS
1 Bilsby Road, Alford LN13 9EW. Pauline & John Clues, 01507 463989, www.freewebs.com/brightlands. *9m NE of Spilsby. 12m NW of Skegness, 6m SW of Sutton-on-Sea. In Alford, R at junction on A1111 to Sutton-on-Sea. Garden 1st on L, (free car parks 100yds next to Co-op store and South Market Sq 200yds).* Home-made teas. **Adm £2, chd free (share to Alford First Responders). Sats, Suns 30,**

31 May; 18, 19 July; 15, 16 Aug (11-4.30). Visitors also welcome by appt in July & Aug, groups of 10+ & coaches by advanced appt (10 days).
Award-winning recently designed garden of approx 3/4 acre surrounding C17 old hangman's cottage (not open). Split into different areas offering well stocked borders and island beds. Small and large ponds, woodland walk with view of working windmill. Courtyard garden, vegetable garden and greenhouses. Many interesting features, old yew trees, acers, architectural and unusual plants, ferns, grasses and containers. Seating areas. Working windmill - opp open. Featured on local radio. Alford & District Hort Soc Best Large Garden. Short gravel drive, some slopes and steps.

Enjoy the scented climbing roses and honeysuckle on the pergola . . .

⑥ NEW ◆ BURGHLEY HOUSE PRIVATE SOUTH GARDENS
Burghley Park, Stamford PE9 3JY. Burghley House Preservation Trust, 01780 752451, www.burghley.co.uk. *1m E of Stamford. From Stamford follow signs to Burghley via B1443.* **House and Garden adm £11.30, chd £5.60, Concessions £9.90, Garden only adm £6.50, chd £3.15. Open daily 21 Mar to 30 Oct (11-5). See website or tel for full details. For NGS: Sun 19 Apr (11-5). Adm to the Private South Gardens £3.50, chd £2, concessions £3.**
On 19 April the Private South Gardens at Burghley House will open for the NGS with spectacular spring flowers and the opportunity to enjoy Capability Brown's famous lake and temple folly. Entry to the Private South Gardens via Orangery. The Garden of Surprises, Sculpture Garden and house are open as normal. Regular adm prices apply.

⑦ NEW 39 CATHEDRAL DRIVE
Spalding PE11 1PQ. Mr & Mrs John Mepham, 01775 725291. *1m W of Spalding. Take A151 towards Bourne. Turn R onto Park Rd immed after railway Xing. Then 1st L onto Pennygate, 1st R into Woolram Wygate, 2nd R into Lincoln Way, R into Cathedral Drive.* Light refreshments & teas. **Adm £2, chd free. Sat 18, Sun 19 July (1-5). Visitors also welcome by appt 6 to 31 July only.**
Medium-sized town garden filled with perennials and annuals to supply a rainbow of colours. Ornamental trees, path leading to second garden and patio.

⑧ 21 CHAPEL STREET
Hacconby, Bourne PE10 0UL. Cliff & Joan Curtis, 01778 570314. *3m N of Bourne. A15, turn E at Xrds into Hacconby.* Home-made teas. **Adm £2, chd free. Sat 21, Sun 22 Feb; Thur 5 Mar; Mon 13 Apr; Thur 3 Sept, Sun 4 Oct (11-5 Feb, Apr, Sept) (2-6 Mar, Oct); 2010 Sat 27, Sun 28 Feb. Visitors also welcome by appt anytime.**
Cottage garden overflowing with plants for yr-round interest; special interest alpines, bulbs, herbaceous. Early opening for hellebores and snowdrop collection. Asters for late opening.

⑨ NEW CLIFF HOUSE
Main Street, Whitton DN15 9LJ. Sue & Sam Dron. *10m N of Scunthorpe, 11m W of Humber Bridge. Follow signs for West Halton and Whitton from A1077. Last house on L before village hall.* Home-made teas at the village hall. **Adm £2.50, chd free. Sun 28 June (1-6).**
Approx 1/2 acre of informal country garden created over the past 24yrs from a potato field. Paved courtyard and box hedging with yew walk; intimate circular sundial garden; mature herbaceous borders and splendid views across Humber to Yorkshire Wolds. Enjoy the scented climbing roses and honeysuckle on the pergola. Native woodland area, small vegetable plot and orchard.

10 THE COACH HOUSE
1A Hereward Street, Lincoln
LN1 3EW. Jo & Ken Slone,
www.bruntswoldcoachhouse.co.uk.
*Central Lincoln. Coming off the A46 N
circular take B1226 to Newport.
150yds from Radio Lincs turn into
Rasen Lane, then take 1st R into
Hereward St.* Light refreshments &
home-made teas. **Adm £2.50, chd
free. Sun 14 June (11-5).**
Small courtyard garden behind
Victorian town house, 5mins walk from
historic quarter of Lincoln. Brimming
with unusual plants, climbers and
sculpture. Many plants grown in
containers for versatility,
complemented by summer bedding.
No on site parking. Use Bail area car
parks or roads in vicinity. Tiny gravel
area.

11 COBWEBS
Moor Road, North Owersby, Market
Rasen LN8 3PR. Ms Pauline Gass,
01673 828254,
cobwebshouse@lineone.net. *4½ m
N of Market Rasen. Turn off A46 at
North Owersby sign. Garden 200yds
on R.* Home-made teas. **Adm £2.50,
chd free. Suns 26 July; 30 Aug
(11-5). Visitors also welcome by
appt groups 10+, June to Sept,
coaches welcome.**
Mature cottage garden extending to
two thirds of an acre amid open
countryside. Many large herbaceous
borders crammed with unusual and
colourful perennials and grasses. Steps
leading to patio and pergola clothed in
clematis and wisteria. Wildlife pond.
Nursery offering many of the plants
grown in the garden. New dahlia bed.

**12 NEW THE CROCOSMIA
GARDENS**
9 North Street, Caistor LN7 6QU.
Mr M A Fox, 01472 859269,
crocosmia@tiscali.co.uk,
www.simplesite.com/crocosmia.
*On Caistor High St, follow signs for
Town Hall car park. Garden next to
car park.* Light refreshments &
teas. **Adm £2.50, chd free.
Visitors welcome by appt from
25 July to 6 Sept, small groups
welcome.**
Small terraced cottage garden full
of some unusual cottage garden
plants plus the National Collection
of crocosmia.

**13 ◆ DODDINGTON HALL
GARDENS**
Lincoln LN6 4RU. Claire & James
Birch, 01522 694308,
www.doddingtonhall.com. *5m W of
Lincoln. Signed clearly from A46
Lincoln bypass & A57, 3m.*
Refreshments at farm shop. Booking
advisable 01522 688581. **House &
garden £7.75, chd £3.75, garden
only £5, chd £2.75. For details
please tel or see website. For NGS:
Sun 15 Mar (11-4); Wed 17 June
(12-5).**
5 acres of romantic walled and wild
gardens. Pageant of naturalised spring
bulbs and scented shrubs from Feb to
May. Spectacular iris display late
May/early June in box-edged parterres
of West Garden. Sumptuous
herbaceous borders throughout
summer; extraordinary ancient
chestnut trees; turf maze; temple of the
winds. Fascinating walled Kitchen
Garden growing for popular farm shop
and cafe. Very much a family-owned
and run garden. Variety of surfaces:
gravel, grass. Can get muddy. Electric
buggy available for free hire, booking
advisable. Sensory tours of house &
gardens for visually impaired visitors.

**14 ◆ EASTON WALLED
GARDENS**
Easton NG33 5AP. Sir Fred & Lady
Cholmeley, 01476 530063,
www.eastonwalledgardens.co.uk.
*7m S of Grantham. 1m off A1 N of
Colsterworth roundabout. Follow
village signposts via B6403.* **Adm
£5, chd £1. For details please tel or
see website. For NGS: Fri 10 Apr
(11-4).**
12 acres of forgotten gardens
undergoing extensive renovation. Set in
parkland with dramatic views. C16
garden with Victorian embellishments.
Italianate terraces; yew tunnel;
snowdrops and cut flower garden.
David Austin roses, iris, daffodil and
sweet pea collections. Please wear
sensible shoes suitable for country
walking. Daffodil collection in flower.
Lincolnshire Visitor Attraction of the
Year, National Treasure Award. For
wheelchair & disabled access please
see website.

15 15 ELMHIRST ROAD
Horncastle LN9 5AT. Sylvia
Ravenhall, 01507 526014,
john.ravenhall@btinternet.com. *From
A158 Lincoln Rd turn into*

*Accommodation Rd, go to end, turn L
into Elmhirst Rd. No 15 approx 80yds
on L.* Light refreshments & teas. **Adm
£2, chd free. Visitors welcome by
appt 25 May-2 Aug. Individuals or
groups, coaches. Evening visits
welcome.**
Plantswoman's long and narrow town
garden with beds and borders of
mainly herbaceous plants combined
with climbers, shrubs and small trees.
Variety of hostas are grown in
containers and in the ground. Winding
paths with shallow steps give varied
access to all areas.

Features including willow dome, reclining turf figures, pond . . .

16 FEN VIEW
Fen Lane, East Keal PE23 4AY. Mr &
Mrs Geoffrey Wheatley. *2m SW of
Spilsby. Park at The Old Rectory, path
to Fen View.* Teas at The Old Rectory.
**Combined adm with The Old
Rectory, East Keal £4, chd free.
Sun 24 May (11-5).**
Sloping secluded ½ -acre garden re-
developed by owners over last 5yrs to
reflect their interest in gardening for
wildlife. Designed around a number of
different themed areas, ponds, vistas,
sculptures and plenty of seating.

17 NEW FIELD HOUSE FARM
Field Lane, Wroot DN9 2BL. Sue
Dare & Joan Wilson. *5m W of
Epworth. M180 J2, S on A161 to
Epworth.* Home-made teas. **Adm
£3, chd free. Sun 19 July (11-5).**
1-acre garden designed by garden
designer Sue Dare. ¼ m of paths
lead around exuberant borders
overflowing with colourful
perennials and grasses. Features
incl willow dome, reclining turf
figures, pond, productive organic
vegetable garden, garden
sculpture, prairie style planting,
small woodland area. Many places
to sit and relax. Display of garden
irrigation by Wroot Water Co.

Group opening

⑱ FISHTOFT DROVE GARDENS
Frithville, Boston PE22 7ES. *3m N of Boston, 1m S of Frithville. Unclassified rd. On W side of the West Fen Drain. Easy parking.* Home-made teas. **Combined adm £3, chd free (share to Pilgrim Heart & Lung Fund).** Sun 7 June (12-5).
A relaxed and welcoming atmosphere awaits visitors of all ages at these two garden oases nestling in open fenland within easy reach of historic Boston. Featured on Radio Lincolnshire.

BARLEY END COTTAGE
Andy & Yvonne Mathieson.
100yds W of Holly House
¼-acre traditional cottage garden, very informal. Relaxed mixture of borders, shrubs, vegetables, natural areas, with some quirky features. Elevated view from garden balcony gives a birdseye perspective.

HOLLY HOUSE
Sally & David Grant
Approx 1-acre informal mixed borders, scree beds, old sinks with alpines and steps leading down to large pond with cascade and stream. Small woodland area. Quiet garden with water feature. Extra 2½ acres devoted to wildlife with dewpond. Interviewed on Radio Lincolnshire. Some gravel paths, steep slopes.

⑲ FROG HALL COTTAGE
Langrick Road, New York LN4 4XH. Kathy Wright. *B1192 2m S of New York Xrds. 3½m N of Langrick Bridge.* Home-made teas. **Adm £2.50, chd free.** Sat 6 June; Sun 5 July (2-5).
¾ acre garden. Patio with many unusual plants, stream, courtyard-style patio, large gravelled area with raised beds and an arbour, again planted for interest. Lawned area with large island beds, unfenced pond. Classic-style garden planted with roses, shrubs and perennials, small paved terrace.

⑳ ◆ THE GARDEN HOUSE
Saxby, Lincoln LN8 2DQ. Chris Neave & Jonathan Cartwright, 01673 878820, www.thegardenhousesaxby.co.uk. *8m N of Lincoln; 2¼ m E of A15.* Teas *(Apr)*. **Combined with West Barn Adm £3.50, chd £1.** For details please tel or see website. For NGS: Sun 5 Apr (10-4). **Evening Opening** wine, Wed 1 July (6-9).
7-acre landscaped garden packed with interest. Yew hedging and walls enclose magical garden rooms full of roses and herbaceous plants. Long terrace, Dutch, pergola and obelisk gardens link to a lavender walk. Large natural damp garden. Dry garden leading onto hillside planted with rarer trees overlooking a large reflective pond. Native woodland areas, prairie and wild flower meadow planted with massed bulbs. Wonderful views. Adjacent to C18 classical church. 'Welcome to Spring' (Apr), 'Roses and Wine' (July).

㉑ ◆ GOLTHO HOUSE
Goltho LN8 5NF. Mr & Mrs S Hollingworth, www.golthogardens.com. *10m E of Lincoln. On A158, 1m before Wragby. Garden on LH-side (not in Goltho Village).* Light refreshments & home-made teas. **Adm £3, chd free.** Suns 22 Feb (10-3); 24 May (10-4).
4½-acre garden started in 1998 but looking established with long grass walk flanked by abundantly planted herbaceous borders forming a focal point. Paths and walkway span out to other features incl nut walk, prairie border, wild flower meadow, rose garden and large pond area. Snowdrops, hellebores and shrubs for winter interest.

㉒ ◆ GRIMSTHORPE CASTLE
Bourne PE10 0LY. Grimsthorpe & Drummond Castle Trust, 01778 591205, www.grimsthorpe.co.uk. *3m NW of Bourne. 8m E of A1 on A151 from Colsterworth junction.* **Castle & garden £9, concessions £8, chd £3.50, garden only £4, chd £2, concessions £3.50.** Suns to Thurs June to Sept. For NGS: Sun 19 Apr; Thur 18 June (11-6).
15 acres of formal and woodland gardens incl bulbs and wild flowers. Formal gardens encompass fine topiary, roses, herbaceous borders and unusual ornamental kitchen garden.

㉓ ◆ GUANOCK HOUSE
Guanock Gate, Sutton St Edmund PE12 0LW. Mr & Mrs Michael Coleman. *16m SE of Spalding. From village church turn R, cross rd, then L Guanockgate. Garden at end of rd, RH-side.* Light refreshments & home-made teas. **Adm £2, chd free.** Sun 14 June (1.30-5).
Former home of garden designer Arne Maynard. 5 acres. Herbaceous border, knot garden, rose garden and lime walk. Orchard, walled kitchen garden, Italian garden. Guanock House is a C16 manor house built in the flat fens of S Lincs.

Elevated view from garden balcony gives a birdseye perspective . . .

㉔ ◆ GUNBY HALL
Spilsby PE23 5SS. The National Trust/Mrs Claire Ayres, 07870 758876, www.gunbyhall.ic24.net. *2½ m NW of Burgh-le-Marsh. 7m NW of Skegness. On A158. Signed off Gunby roundabout.* **Adm £4, chd £2, family £10.** For details please tel or see website. For NGS: Sun 9 Aug (10-5).
7 acres of formal and walled gardens; old roses, herbaceous borders; herb garden; kitchen garden with fruit trees and vegetables. Greenhouses, carp pond and sweeping lawns. Tennyson's 'Haunt of Ancient Peace'. House built by Sir William Massingberd 1700. Featured on local radio.

㉕ NEW HACONBY HALL
Haconby PE10 0UY. Mr & Mrs J F Atkinson, 01778 570790, atkinson.je@btconnect.com. *3m N of Bourne. ¾ m E of A15 in Haconby village.* Home-made teas. **Combined with Walters Cottage adm £4, chd free. Evening Opening** wine, Fri 5 June (5-9). Sun 7 June (11-5). Visitors also welcome by appt for groups of 40+, also coaches, Apr to Sept.
Large country garden surrounding Jacobean House (not open). Numerous informal borders of trees, shrubs, roses and unusual perennials.

26 ◆ HALL FARM
Harpswell, Gainsborough DN21 5UU. Pam & Mark Tatam, 01427 668412, www.hall-farm.co.uk. *7m E of Gainsborough. On A631. 1½ m W of Caenby Corner.* Light refreshments & home-made teas. **Adm £3, chd free. For NGS: Sat 5, Sun 6 Sept (10-5).**
1½ -acre garden with mixed borders of trees, shrubs, old roses and unusual perennials. Sunken garden, pond, courtyard garden, walled gravel garden and orchard. Short walk to old moat and woodland. Free seed collecting in garden Sept 5 & 6. Large plant nursery.

&. ✕ ⊗ ☕

Paths, pergolas, arches and secret trails make the garden magical . . .

27 HARRINGTON HALL
Harrington, Spilsby PE23 4NH. Mr & Mrs David Price, www.harringtonhallgardens.co.uk. *6m NW of Spilsby. Turn off A158 (Lincoln-Skegness) at Hagworthingham, 2m to Harrington.* **Adm £3, chd free (share to South Ormsby Group of Parishes).** Sun 9 Aug (2-5).
Approx 6-acre Tudor and C18 walled gardens; incl 3 walled gardens; herbaceous borders, croquet lawn leading to viewing terrace, Tennyson's High Hall Garden in 'Maud'. Organic kitchen garden, shrub borders, roses and wildlife pond. Gravel paths.

&. ⊗ ☕

HOLMES VILLA
See Nottinghamshire.

28 HOLYWELL HALL
Holywell PE9 4DT. Mr & Mrs R Gillespie. *8m N of Stamford. From A1 signed Clipsham. Through Clipsham then turn R to Holywell. Entrance to Hall 2m on L.* **Adm £3.50, chd 50p. Thur 11 June (2-5).**
The beautiful gardens at Holywell are among the most handsome and historically interesting in S Lincolnshire. Nestled in a vale they are laid out on a broad S-facing slope overlooking C18 lake. Numerous water features, walled vegetable garden, stunning

herbaceous borders, chapel, fishing temple and orangery. Wild flower meadow. New colourful flower garden created by Head Gardener Brian Oldman in 2007.

THE HOMESTEAD
See Leicestershire & Rutland.

29 KEXBY HOUSE
Gainsborough DN21 5NE. Herbert & Jenny Whitton, 01427 788759, jenny.whitton@btinternet.com. *12m NNW of Lincoln. 6m E of Gainsborough. On B1241, outskirts of Kexby village.* Light refreshments & home-made teas. **Adm £4, chd free. Sun 7 June (11-5). Visitors also welcome by appt.**
Approx 5 acres of gardens which have evolved over last 100yrs. Long herbaceous borders, unusual plants, wildlife pond and bog garden, scree gardens and all-white border, wild flower area. New perennial prairie-style meadow. New greenhouse and ornamental vegetable garden. Plant, book and card stalls.

&. ⊗ ☕ 🍴

30 LES ALLÉES
12 Frieston Road, Caythorpe NG32 3BX. Alan & Marylyn Mason. *8m N of Grantham. From Grantham A607 towards Lincoln. L turn to Caythorpe village, immed L again into Frieston Rd. No 12 300yds ahead.* Home-made teas. **Adm £3, chd free. Sun 14 June (2-6).**
A plantsman's garden created by Alan Mason, TV gardener and garden designer. Ornamental potager, woodland walk, specimen trees and shrubs, Italian avenue of cypresses. Pond; large mixed borders; tree house; subtropical border. A garden of different styles and atmospheres which link seamlessly. Avenues and allées lead round the garden.

&. ✕ ☕

31 LITTLE PONTON HALL
Grantham NG33 5BS. Mr & Mrs Alastair McCorquodale. *2m S of Grantham. ½ m E of A1 at S end of Grantham bypass.* Home-made teas. **Adm £3.50, chd free. Sun 12 Apr (2-5).**
3 to 4-acre garden. Spacious lawns with cedar tree over 200yrs old. Many varieties of old shrub roses and clematis; borders and young trees. Stream, spring blossom and hellebores; bulbs and river walk. Formal walled kitchen garden and listed dovecote. Victorian

greenhouses with many plants from exotic locations. Featured in local/national press & on TV & radio. Disabled car park and WC.

&. ⊗ ☕

32 NEW 38 LOW STREET
Haxey, Doncaster DN9 2LE. Mr & Mrs S Bowman. *10m NW of Gainsborough. A161 to Haxey. Situated on A161 midway between war memorial & Kings Arm PH. Please park in village.* Light refreshments. **Adm £2.50, chd free. Suns 3 May; 28 June (1-5.30).**
½ -acre garden developed over 20yrs, consisting of front rockery, hostas and herbaceous borders. To rear, peaceful garden surrounded by 10ft Leylandii hedge with trellis draped with various climbers. Fish pond, wildlife pond leading to orchard and vegetable plot.

&. ✕ ☕

33 MARIGOLD COTTAGE
Hotchin Road, Sutton-on-Sea LN12 2JA. Stephanie Lee, 01507 442151, marigoldlee@btinternet.com. *From High St facing sea, turn R at Corner House Café, along Furlong's Rd past playing fields, round bend, into Hotchin Rd. Garden 2nd on L.* Home-made teas. **Adm £2.50, chd free. Sun 24 May (11-6). Visitors also welcome by appt.**
½ -acre seaside garden containing a large variety of unusual hardy perennials. Paths, pergolas, arches and secret trails make the garden magical. Features incl Japanese bed, planting schemes to excite the palette. Courtyard with wheelchair friendly raised beds and newly developed area for 2009.

&. ⊗ ☕ ☎

Group opening

34 MARTIN GARDENS
LN4 3QY. *15m SE of Lincoln. On B1191. 4m W of Woodhall Spa. Martin Gardens on main rd. Parking on roadside. Blankney Barff garden signed off B1189.* Home-made teas. **Combined adm £3.50, chd 50p. Sun 31 May (11-5).**
4 gardens, diverse in size and features. Superb fenland views.

☕

49 HIGH STREET

Helen & Laurie Whittle. *Opp Royal Oak PH*
Wildlife-friendly, organic and environmentally low impact, with long flowering season of nectar and berry-rich species. 2 ponds, mixed native hedging and established dry garden. Herbaceous perennials, cottage border and drought-tolerant species. All plants for sale are peat free.

HOLMDALE HOUSE

High Street. Ian Warden & Stewart MacKenzie
1-acre plantsman's garden started March 2000, surrounding Victorian farmhouse and barns (not open). Informal mixed borders planted to reflect owners' interest in unusual hardy plants, especially good foliage and variegated leaf forms. Collection of hostas, large pond, courtyard gardens and nursery. Newly acquired 1/2 acre under development with white garden, pickery, grasses bed and woodland area.

LABOURERS COTTAGE

Blankney Barff. Mrs Linda Brighty. 01526 378669, linda.brightly2@btinternet.com. *Signed off B1189 between Metheringham & Martin.* **Visitors also welcome by appt.**
1850s cottage in approx 3 acres. 2 ponds, bog garden, borders and beds of mixed plantings, hedged rose garden, various trees, vegetable and fruit garden. Over past 10 yrs we have changed a meadow into a wildlife-friendly garden.

NEW 10 MOOR LANE

Gill Hills
Traditional cottage garden with many unusual plants. Large pond provides a haven for wildlife and is surrounded by colourful grasses and perennials. Trellises and arches provide support for a variety of climbing plants.

35 NEW MILL FARM

Grasby DN38 6AQ. Mike & Helen Boothman. *3m NW of Caistor on A1084.* Home-made teas. **Adm £2.50, chd free (share to St Andrew's Hospice, Grimsby). Sun 26 July (11-5).**
Approx 3 1/2 -acre hill-top garden with panoramic views, developed over the last 5yrs. Plantsman's garden with a wealth of perennials, shrubs and trees in formal and informal settings. Continually evolving with features incl the remains of a windmill, wildlife ponds and vegetable beds. Particularly colourful in July.

36 THE MOAT

Newton, Sleaford NG34 0ED. Mr & Mrs Mike Barnes, 01529 497462. *Off A52 halfway between Grantham & Sleaford. In Newton village, opp church. Please park sensibly in village.* Home-made teas. **Adm £3, chd free. Sun 14 June (11-5). Visitors also welcome by appt.**
2 1/2 -acre country garden, formerly a farmyard, now 7yrs old. Island mixed beds, natural pond, courtyard garden with topiary and many interesting trees and plants.

37 OLD QUARRY LODGE

15 Barnetby Lane, Elsham, nr Brigg DN20 0RB. Mel & Tina Welton, 01652 680309. *6m S of Humber Bridge. Leave M180 at J5. Drive past 'Little Chef' into Elsham village. Old Quarry Lodge is 1st house on R on entering village.* Light refreshments & home-made teas. **Adm £2.50, chd free. Sun 16 Aug (10.30-5). Visitors also welcome by appt June to Aug, large groups welcome.**
Approx 1/2 -acre sloping garden with formal and informal features. Abundant borders and island beds with architectural focal points, Mediterranean influence in parts. Highly imaginative garden with exciting mixture of the flamboyant and the quintessentially 'English'. Featured in 'Amateur Gardening'. Prize Winner - Large Garden catergory N Lincs. Gravel drive, sloping site.

38 THE OLD RECTORY

East Keal PE23 4AT. Mrs Ruth Ward, 01790 752477. *2m SW of Spilsby. Off A16. Turn into Church Lane by PO.* Light refreshments & home-made teas. **Combined adm with Fen View £4, chd free, 24 May. Suns 19 Apr (2-5) £3; 24 May (11-4.30).** Visitors also welcome by appt for individuals and groups; teas by arrangement.
Beautifully situated, with fine views, rambling cottage garden on different levels falling naturally into separate areas, with changing effects and atmosphere. Steps, paths and vistas to lead you on, with seats well placed for appreciating special views and plant combinations or relaxing and enjoying the peace. New dry border.

39 THE OLD VICARAGE

Low Road, Holbeach Hurn PE12 8JN. Mrs Liz Dixon-Spain, 01406 424148. *2m NE of Holbeach. Turn off A17 N to Holbeach Hurn, past post box in middle of village, 1st turn R into Low Rd. Old Vicarage on R approx 400yds.* Home-made teas. **Adm £3, chd free. Combined with The Old White House, Holbeach Hurn £4, chd free (12 July). Suns 17 May (2-5); 12 July (12-5). Visitors also welcome by appt.**
2 acres of gardens with mature trees, old grass tennis court and croquet lawns surrounded by borders of shrubs, roses, herbaceous; informal areas incl pond and bog garden, wild flowers, grasses and bulbs, shrub roses and herb garden in old paddock area. Environmentally maintained and fun for kids too. Treasure Hunt for children 17 May.

40 OLD WHITE HOUSE

Holbeach Hurn PE12 8JP. Mr & Mrs A Worth. *2m N of Holbeach. Turn off A17 N to Holbeach Hurn, follow signs to village, go straight through, turn R after Rose & Crown at Baileys Lane.* Home-made teas. **Combined with The Old Vicarage, Holbeach Hurn £4, chd free. Sun 12 July (12-5).**
1 1/2 acres of mature garden, featuring herbaceous borders, roses, patterned garden, herb garden and wild garden with small pond. Walled kitchen garden.

Large pond provides a haven for wildlife . . .

41 THE ORCHARDS
Old Somerby, nr Grantham
NG33 4AG. Mrs P Dean. *3m E of Grantham. In School Lane, Old Somerby.* Home-made teas. **Adm £3, chd free.** Afternoon & Evening Opening wine, Wed 10 June (2-8). Yew trees dominate this 1 acre village garden created from scratch in last 10yrs on site of old farm steddings. Mixed borders, pond, bog garden, fruit and vegetable area. Large lawn for sporting grandchildren. Some gravel.
&. ✕ ✿ ☕

42 OVERBECK
46 Main Street, Scothern LN2 2UW.
John & Joyce Good, 01673 862200,
john.good4@btinternet.com. *4m E of Lincoln. Scothern is signed from A46 at Dunholme & A158 at Sudbrooke. Overbeck is at E end of Main St.* **Adm £2, chd free.** Visitors welcome by appt May to Sept. Individuals, groups and/or coaches. Tea 50p.
Approx 1/2 acre garden in quiet village. Long herbaceous borders and colour-themed island beds with some unusual perennials. Hosta border, gravel bed with grasses, fernery, trees, numerous shrubs and climbers and large prolific vegetable and fruit area. Two thirds of garden suitable for wheelchairs. Ground rises steeply to vegetable & fruit area.
&. ✕ ☕ ☎

Old Station
Master's house in
1/4 acre gardens
by railway . . .

43 68 PENNYGATE
Spalding PE11 1NN. Mr & Mrs Carroll, 01775 767554. *1m W of Spalding. Take A151 towards Bourne. Turn R onto Park Rd immediately after rail crossings. Then 1st L onto Pennygate. No 68 on L.* **Adm £2.50, chd free.** Sats, Suns 20, 21 June; 18, 19 July; 15, 16 Aug (1-5). Visitors also welcome by appt.
A plantsperson's garden consisting of island beds and borders. Stocked with unusual plants, large pond, waterfall, rockery and bog garden. Well stocked nursery. Featured in 'Garden News', 'Lincolnshire Today' and local papers.
&. ✕ ✿ ☎

44 NEW PINEFIELDS
Smithy Lane, Bigby, Barnetby
DN38 6ER. Reg & Madeleine Hill. *Bigby is on A1084. 5m Caistor, 4m Brigg. Turn into Bigby Village off A1084. House at top of Smithy Lane junction with Main St.* **Adm £2, chd free.** Sat 28 Feb; Sun 1 Mar (11-5).
3/4 -acre country garden with lots of interest. A paved terrace leads on to shrub/herbaceous beds packed with plants, many unusual. Clipped box and gravel area, half circle pergola and wildlife garden. Early spring starts with hellebores incl some Ashwood doubles and anemone centred varieties. One step up to garden.
&. ✿ ☕

ROSELEA
See Nottinghamshire.

45 73 SAXILBY ROAD
Sturton by Stow LN1 2AA. Charles & Tricia Elliott. *9m NW of Lincoln. On B1241. Halfway between Lincoln & Gainsborough.* Home-made teas. **Adm £2.50, chd free.** Suns 12 July; 4 Oct (11-5).
Extensively cultivated plot planted in a cottage garden style and mainly devoted to a wide selection of summer and autumn flowering perennials and late season grasses. Shrub borders with some unusual shrubs and small trees chosen to give early interest in leaf colour and shape and to produce good autumn colour. Large display of tender fuchsias in July. Small hardy plant nursery. Art Exhibition.
✿ ☕

46 2 SCHOOL HOUSE
Stixwould, nr Woodhall Spa
LN10 5HP. Andrew & Sheila Sankey, 01526 352453. *1 1/2 m N of Woodhall Spa. From roundabout in Woodhall Spa, take rd to Bardney past Petwood Hotel. Follow rd for 1 1/2 m and at sharp RH bend turn off L into Stixwould. Garden is on main rd opp red phone box.* **Adm £2, chd free.** Suns 17 May; 19 July (2-5). Visitors also welcome by appt Apr to Sept.
1/4 -acre garden, redesigned in Oct 1994 by owners in cottage garden style, to incl front garden with unusual perennials, shrubs, herb garden, small turf maze, and cobbled stream.
✕ ✿ ☕ ☎

47 SOUTH LODGE
Ropsley NG33 4AS. Nicholas Turner, 07936 325805,
russ@designs2gardens.com. *4m E of Grantham. From Grantham take Ropsley turn off A52. Proceed along Long Lane. Garden 1m R on R.* Home-made teas. **Adm £3, chd free (share to Ropley Church).** Suns 10 May; 21 June; 20 Sept (2-5). Visitors also welcome by appt May to Oct for groups of 10+.
Enjoy the extensive tulip displays along with other spring wonders in May. Early summer the garden is a kaleidoscope of colour with the roses and herbaceous borders at their most splendid. The borders are no less florific in Sept as the mellow colours of autumn brighten the shortening days.
&. ✕ ✿ ☕ ☎

SQUIRREL LODGE
See Nottinghamshire.

48 STATION HOUSE
Station Road, Potterhanworth,
Lincoln LN4 2DX. Carol & Alan Harvey. *6m S of Lincoln. B1178 immed on L under railway bridge before reaching Potterhanworth village.* **Adm £2, chd free.** Sun 10 May; Sat 13, Suns 28 June; 19 July (1-5).
Old Station Master's house in 1/4 acre gardens by railway embankment, a haven for wildlife. Very informal style with mixed borders, lawns and 2 tiny ponds. Collection of old memorabilia and 'quirky' accessories. Garden owners keen ornithologists. Small book stall. Featured in local press & on local radio.
&. ☕

49 WALTERS COTTAGE
6 Hall Road, Haconby, nr Bourne PE10 0UY. Ivan & Sadie Hall. *3m N of Bourne A15. Turn E at Xrds to Haconby. Turn R at Hare & Hounds PH.* Home-made teas. **Combined with Haconby Hall adm £4, chd free.** Evening Opening wine, Fri 5 June (5-9). Sun 7 June (11-5).
Country cottage garden of over 1/4 of an acre developed over the past 6yrs. Various themed areas. Walled garden with hornbeam allée, topiary and rill. Woodland area with wildlife pond and plants. Sunken garden. Long herbaceous borders, lawns and collection of hostas. Garden is well-stocked with many interesting and rare plants with added features.
✕ ✿ ☕

50 WASHDYKE FARM
Lincoln Road, Fulbeck NG32 3HY.
Anna Greenhalgh, 01400 272880,
gary.greenhalgh@treasuretransport.
co.uk. *10m N of Grantham; 15m S of
Lincoln. On A607 in dip opp Washdyke
Lane.* Cream teas & wine. **Adm £3,
chd free. Wed 8 July (2-7).** Visitors
also welcome by appt from 7 June
to 12 July, incl coach parties &
groups of 10+.
Approx 2 acres with meandering paths
leading to interesting features with
contrasting moods. Lawns with
cottage-style mixed borders; attractive
waterside planting alongside stream;
wildlife pond and woodland walk with
mature trees.
🐕 ☕ ☎

51 68 WATTS LANE
Louth LN11 9DG. Jenny & Rodger
Grasham, 01507 601004/07977
318145. *½ m S of Louth town centre.
Watts Lane off B1200 Louth to
Mablethorpe rd. Turn by pedestrian
lights and Londis shop.* Home-made
teas. **Adm £2, chd free** (share to
Louth and District Hospice). **Wed 15
July (11-6); Sun 9, Sat 29 Aug (12-5).**
Visitors also welcome by appt 15
July to 6 Sept, coaches permitted.
Blank canvas of ⅓ acre. Developed
over 12yrs into lush, colourful, tropical
to traditional plant packed haven. A
whole new world on entering from
street. Generous borders, raised
tropical island, long hot tropical border,
ponds, water features, summerhouse,
conservatory with grapevine, cutting
garden and secluded seating along
garden's journey. Grass pathways.
♿ 🐕 ☕ ☎

56 WELL CREEK ROAD
See Norfolk.

52 10 WENDOVER CLOSE
Rippingale PE10 0TQ. Chris & Tim
Bladon. *5½ m N of Bourne.
Rippingale is signed on the A15. On
entering village at the Rippengale /
Kirby Underwood Xrd, Wendover
Close is 1st turning on L. Garden at
end of the close.* Home-made teas.
Adm £2, chd free. Sun 31 May (11-5).
Peaceful village garden of approx ½ an
acre containing usual and unusual
herbaceous plants, shrubs and trees of
general and specialist interest in a
secluded situation. Approx 30yds from
main entrance to garden is gravel.
♿ 🐕 ☕

53 WEST BARN
Saxby, Lincoln LN8 2DQ. Mrs E
Neave. *8m N of Lincoln; 2¼ m E of
A15.* Light refreshments & cream teas.
Combined with **The Garden House**
adm £3.50, chd £1. **Sun 5 Apr (10-5).
Evening Opening** wine, **Wed 1 July**
(6-9).
Formal walled courtyard garden with
loggia, box hedging, shrub roses,
climbers and herbaceous planting.
Water feature and pots with seasonal
planting.
♿ 🐕 ☕

54 NEW WILLOW COTTAGE
Gravel Pit Lane, Burgh-le-Marsh
PE24 5DW. Bob & Karen Ward,
01754 811450. *6m W of
Skegness. S of Gunby roundabout
on A158, take 1st R signed Bratoft
and Burgh-le-Marsh. 1st R again
onto Bratoft Lane. L at T-junction,
parking on R 25yds.* Home-made
teas. **Adm £2, chd free. Sat 16,
Sun 17 May (1-5).** Visitors also
welcome by appt.
A transformation: weeds to
willows, nettles to nymphs!

Naturally planted, therapeutic
haven. Undulating walkways
around shallow dug ponds leading
to peaceful spots for reflection.
Springtime riotous exuberance
tempered by the English cottage
style.
🐝 ☕ ☎

55 WOODLANDS
Peppin Lane, Fotherby, Louth
LN11 0UW. Ann & Bob Armstrong,
01507 603586,
annbobarmstrong@uwclub.net,
www.woodlandsplnts.co.uk. *2m N of
Louth. On A16. Leave bypass (A16)
signed Fotherby. Woodlands is
situated nr far end of Peppin Lane, a
no through rd, running E from village
centre. No parking at garden. Please
park on RH verge opp allotments and
walk (approx 250yds) to garden.*
Home-made teas. **Adm £2.50, chd
free. Suns 26 Apr; 24 May; 23 Aug;
27 Sept (11-5).** Visitors also
welcome by appt.
Mature woodland garden being further
developed by the present owners.
Packed with rare and unusual
perennials, shrubs, ferns and climbers.
Meandering paths lead to surprises
around every corner. In contrast, the
planting nearer the house takes
advantage of the more open aspect
but is equally interesting. Award
winning professional artist's
studio/gallery open to visitors. Plant
nursery featured in RHS Plantfinder.
🐕 🐝 ☕ ☎

Transformation:
weeds to
willows . . .

Lincolnshire County Volunteers

County Organiser
Susie Dean, The Orchards, Old Somerby, Grantham NG33 4AG, 01476 565456

County Treasurer
Peter Sandberg, Croft House, Ulceby DN39 6SW, 01469 588330, peter.sandberg@tiscali.co.uk

Publicity
Erica McGarrigle, Corner House Farm, Little Humby, Grantham NG33 4HW, 01476 585909, colinmcgarrigle@tiscali.co.uk

Leaflet Coordinator
Lucy Dawes, The Grange, Bulby, Bourne PE10 0RU, 01778 591220

Assistant County Organisers
Ursula Cholmeley, The Dower House, Easton, Grantham NG33 5AP, 01476 530063, eastonwalledgardens.co.uk
Sally Grant, Holly House, Fishtoft Drove, Boston PE22 7ES, 01205 750486
Lizzie Milligan-Manby, Wykeham Hall Farm, East Wykeham, Ludford, Market Rasen LN8 6AU, 01507 313286,
lizzie@milliganmanby.plus.com
Chris Neave, The Garden House, Saxby, Market Rasen LN8 2DQ, 01673 878820, jonland@btinternet.com
Margaret Sandberg, Croft House, Ulceby DN39 6SW, 01469 588330, peterhsandberg@hotmail.com

LONDON

HERTFORDSHIRE

BUCKINGHAMSHIRE

BERKSHIRE

SURREY

EN2
EN4
Enfield
EN5
Barnet
Southgate
N21
N20
N14
EN
HA7 HA8 NW7
Edgware
N12 N11
N13
Wood
Green
HA6
HA5
HA3
NW4
Finchley
N3
N10
N22
Hendon
N2
N8
Harrow
HA1
NW9
NW11
N6
N4
N19
HA9
Hampstead
N7
N5
Ruislip
HA4 HA2
HA0 Wembley
NW2
NW3
NW5
N1
Northolt
NW10
NW6
Islington
Uxbridge
UB10
UB5 UB6
NW8
NW1
Hillingdon
UB8
UB4
W10
W9
Bayswater
WC1 EC1
West Drayton
UB1 W7 W13
Ealing
W12 W11
W2 W1
LOND
Southall
W5 W3
W8
Westminster
SE1
UB3 UB2
Hammersmith W14
W6
Battersea
UB7
Brentford TW8
W4
SW1
SE11 SE17
TW5
TW7
TW9
SW13
SW6
SW8
SE5
Hounslow
TW6
London
Heathrow
TW4 TW3
Richmond
SW14
Wandsworth
SW11
SW9
SE24
TW14
TW1
SW15
SW18
SW4
Dulwich
Feltham
TW2
TW10
SW12
SW2
Twickenham
Wimbledon
SW17
SE27
TW13
Teddington
SW19
SW16
TW12 TW11
KT2
Hampton
SW20
CR4
Mitcham
CR7
KT8 KT1
Kingston
KT3
SM4
KT5
CR8
KT7 KT6
KT4
Croydon
KT9
SM3
SM1
Sutton
SM6
Purley
SM2
SM5
Coulsdon
CR5
Berkshire
River Thames

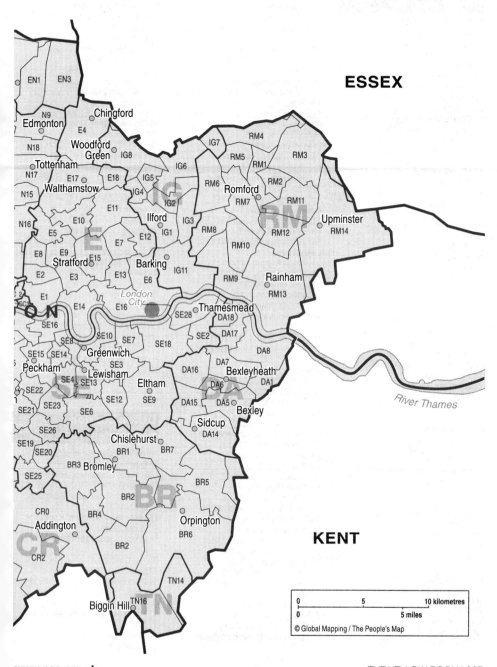

ESSEX

KENT

EN1 EN3
N9
Edmonton
Chingford
N18
E4
Woodford Green
Tottenham
IG8
N17
E17
E18
IG5
Walthamstow
IG4
N15
E11
IG2
N16
E10
Ilford
IG3
E5
E7
E12
IG1
E8
E9
E15
E2
Stratford
E13
IG11
E1
E3
Barking
E6
E14
E16
SE16
SE28
Thamesmead
SE8
SE10
SE7
SE18
SE2
Greenwich
SE3
SE15 SE14
Lewisham
Eltham
Peckham
SE13
SE9
SE4
SE22
SE12
SE21
SE23
SE6
SE26
Chislehurst
SE19
BR1 BR7
SE20
BR3 Bromley
SE25
BR5
BR2
CR0
BR4
Orpington
Addington
BR6
CR2
BR2
TN14
Biggin Hill TN16

RM4
IG7
RM5
RM1
RM3
IG6
RM6
RM2
Romford
RM7
RM11
RM8
Upminster
RM12
RM14
RM10
RM9
Rainham
RM13
London City
DA18
DA17
DA8
DA7
DA16
Bexleyheath
DA6
DA1
DA15
DA5
Bexley
Sidcup
DA14

River Thames

London gardens listed by postcode

Inner London postcodes

E & EC London
Lower Clapton Gardens, E5
42 Latimer Road, E7
Albion Square & London Fields, E8
46 Lavender Grove, E8
53 Mapledene Road, E8
12 Bushberry Road, E9
128 Cadogan Terrace, E9
9 Coopersale Road, E9
11 Coopersale Road, E9
17 Greenstone Mews, E11
13 Redbridge Lane West, E11
24 Brunswick Street, E17
60 Brunswick Street, E17
47 Maynard Road, E17
17 Stanhope Road, E17
Waltham Forest Register Office, E17
Amwell Gardens Group, EC1
Charterhouse, EC1
The Inner Temple Garden, EC4

N, NW
37 Alwyne Road, N1
1 Battlebridge Court
13 College Cross, N1
De Beauvoir Gardens, N1
Islington Gardens Group 1, N1
Islington Gardens Group 2, N1
Malvern Terrace Gardens, N1
66 Abbots Gardens, N2
40 Bancroft Avenue, N2
The Bungalow, N2
East Finchley Cottage Gardens, N2
15 Lytton Close, N2
7a New Oak Road, N2
2 Stanley Road, N2
44 Cholmeley Crescent, N6
51 Cholmeley Crescent, N6
4 The Grove, N6
7 The Grove, N6
2 Millfield Place, N6
3 The Park, N6
Southwood Lodge, N6
1a Hungerford Road, N7
62 Hungerford Road, N7
Penn Road Gardens, N7
90 St George's Avenue, N7
5 New Road, N8
5 Cecil Road, N10
16 Cecil Road, N10
15 Dukes Avenue, N10
46 Dukes Avenue, N10
6 Methuen Park, N10
12 Rookfield Avenue, N10
5 St Regis Close, N10
27 Wood Vale, N10
33 Wood Vale, N10
Golf Course Allotments, N11
71 Fallowcourt Avenue, N12

15 Norcott Road, N16
39 Arundel Gardens, N21
23 Myddleton Gardens, N21
Alexandra Park Gardens N22
Railway Cottages, N22
Gloucester Crescent Gardens, NW1
The Holme, NW1
Regents College's Garden, NW1
Royal College of Physicians Garden, NW1
121 Anson Road, NW2
64 Blenheim Gardens, NW2
10 Hoveden Road, NW2
72 Tanfield Avenue, NW2
208 Walm Lane, The Garden Flat, NW2
180 Adelaide Road, NW3
17 Belsize Lane, NW3
6 Emerald House, NW3
Fenton House, NW3
Little House A, NW3
1 Lower Merton Rise, NW3
5 Greville Place, NW6
116 Hamilton Terrace, NW8
170 Doyle Gardens, NW10
Asmuns Hill Gardens, NW11
4 Asmuns Hill, NW11
113 Corringham Road, NW11
48 Erskine Hill, NW11
157 Hampstead Way, NW11
5 Heathgate, NW11
5 Hillcrest Avenue, NW11
94 Oakwood Road, NW11
5 Turner Drive, NW11
5 Wildwood Rise, NW11
86 Willifield Way, NW11
91 Willifield Way, NW11

S, SE & SW London
Downings Roads Moorings Barge Gardens, SE1
The Garden Museum, SE1
Lambeth Palace, SE1
35 Camberwell Grove, SE5
34 Grove Park, SE5
Roots and Shoots, SE11
41 Southbrook Road, SE12
Centre for Wildlife Gardening, SE15
Choumert Square, SE15
71 Central Hill, SE19
13 Gipsy Hill, SE19
21a Waldegrave Road, SE19
49 Alleyn Park, SE21
118 Court Lane, SE21
Dulwich Village Gardens, SE21
14 Frank Dixon Way, SE21
North House, SE21
97 South Croxted Road, SE21
174 Peckham Rye, SE22
22 Scutari Road, SE22
Sydenham Garden, SE23
Tewkesbury Lodge Garden Group, SE23
82 Wood Vale, SE23
5 Burbage Road, SE24
20 Rollscourt Avenue, SE24
South London Botanical Institute, SE24

99 Stradella Road, SE24
Stoney Hill House, SE26
15a Sydenham Hill, SE26
Ardlui Gardens, SE27
24 Chestnut Road, SE27
10A The Pavement, SE27
Eccleston Square, SW1
40 Holmewood Road, SW2
38 Killieser Avenue, SW2
16 Lanercost Road, SW2
Chelsea Physic Garden, SW3
51 The Chase, SW4
17 Crescent Lane, SW4
The Hurlingham Club, SW6
Natural History Museum Wildlife Garden, SW7
225a Brixton Road, SW9
28 Old Devonshire Road, SW12
2 Western Lane, SW12
12 Westmoreland Road, SW13
96 East Sheen Avenue, SW14
5 Garden Close, SW15
66 Woodbourne Avenue, SW16
18 Littleton Street, SW18
28 Multon Road, SW18
97 Arthur Road, SW19
123 South Park Road, SW19
Southside House, SW19

W London
Mill Hill Road Gardens, W3
Redwing, W3
Stone (Zen) Garden, W3
The Orchard, W4
All Seasons, W5
23 Woodville Road, W5
Chiswick Mall Gardens, W4
Edwardes Square, W8
57 St Quintin Avenue, W10
29 Addison Avenue, W11
12 Lansdowne Road, W11
8 Lansdowne Walk, W11
27 St James Avenue, W13

Outer London postcodes

Harcourt House, Bromley, BR1
36 Downs Hill, Bromley, BR3
Columcille, Chislehurst, BR7
Elm Tree Cottage, South Croydon, CR2
55 Warham Road, South Croydon, CR2
17 Valley View Gardens, Kenley, nr Purley, CR8
Myddelton House Gardens, Enfield, EN2
Barnet Gardens, Barnet, EN5
7 Byng Road, Barnet, EN5
54 Ferndown, Northwood Hills, HA6
23 Links Way, Northwood, HA6
Hornbeams, Stanmore, HA7
4 Stradbroke Grove, Buckhurst Hill, IG9
The Watergardens, Kingston-upon-Thames, KT2

The Wych Elm Public House,
Kingston-upon-Thames, KT2
52A Berrylands Road, Surbiton, KT5
Fishponds House, Surbiton, KT6
Little Lodge, Thames Ditton, KT7
10 Arnison Road, East Molesey, KT8
Hampton Court Palace, Hampton,
KT8
239a Hook Road, Chessington, KT9
Old Palace Lane Allotments,
Twickenham, TW1
7 St George's Road, Twickenham,
TW1
Whitton CRC, Whitton, TW2
Osterley Park and House, Isleworth,
TW7
Kew Green Gardens, Kew, TW9
Leyborne Park Gardens, Kew, TW9
Richmond Riverside, Richmond, TW9
Trumpeters' House, Richmond, TW9
31 West Park Road, Kew, TW9
Ham House and Garden, Richmond,
TW10
Ormeley Lodge, Richmond, TW10
Petersham House, Petersham, TW10
Petersham Lodge, Petersham, TW10
St Michael's Convent, Richmond,
TW10
18 Cranmer Road, Hampton Hill,
TW12
Hampton Hill Gardens, Hampton Hill,
TW12

Opening Dates

February

SUNDAY 15
Myddelton House Gardens

April

THURSDAY 2
Hampton Court Palace (Evening)
(Pre-booking essential)

SUNDAY 5
Chelsea Physic Garden, SW3
7 The Grove, N6

SUNDAY 19
Edwardes Square, W8
Natural History Museum Wildlife
Garden, SW7
72 Tanfield Avenue, NW2

SUNDAY 26
5 Burbage Road, SE24
36 Downs Hill
8 Lansdowne Walk, W11
Malvern Terrace Gardens, N1
Myddelton House Gardens
St Michael's Convent
Southside House, SW19

May

SUNDAY 3
16 Cecil Road, N10
5 St Regis Close, N10
Southwood Lodge, N6
The Watergardens

MONDAY 4
Petersham Lodge
Waltham Forest Register Office, E17

WEDNESDAY 6
51 The Chase, SW4 (Evening)

THURSDAY 7
Fenton House, NW3 (Evening)

SATURDAY 9
The Garden Museum, SE1

SUNDAY 10
49 Alleyn Park, SE21
51 The Chase, SW4
Eccleston Square, SW1
Elm Tree Cottage
13 Gipsy Hill, SE19
2 Millfield Place, N6
23 Myddleton Gardens, N21
The Orchard, W4
90 St George's Avenue, N7
Southside House, SW19
15a Sydenham Hill, SE26
2 Western Lane, SW12

SATURDAY 16
Hampton Hill Gardens
Stone (Zen) Garden, W3

SUNDAY 17
66 Abbots Gardens, N2
39 Arundel Gardens, N21
15 Dukes Avenue, N10
46 Dukes Avenue, N10
Hampton Hill Gardens
Kew Green Gardens
7a New Oak Road, N2
3 The Park, N6
22 Scutari Road, SE22
Stone (Zen) Garden, W3
Stoney Hill House, SE26
31 West Park Road
91 Willifield Way, NW11
33 Wood Vale, N10

SATURDAY 23
Tewkesbury Lodge Garden Group,
SE23 (Evening)

SUNDAY 24
39 Arundel Gardens, N21
Chiswick Mall Gardens, W4
5 Garden Close, SW15
Leyborne Park Gardens
23 Links Way
Myddelton House Gardens
94 Oakwood Road, NW11
Tewkesbury Lodge Garden Group,
SE23

MONDAY 25
Leyborne Park Gardens

WEDNESDAY 27
12 Lansdowne Road, W11

SATURDAY 30
The Hurlingham Club, SW6
Lambeth Palace, SE1

SUNDAY 31
35 Camberwell Grove, SE5
Columcille
118 Court Lane, SE21
34 Grove Park, SE5
5 Heathgate, NW11
Islington Gardens Group 1, N1
Little Lodge
Lower Clapton Gardens, E5
20 Rollscourt Avenue, SE24
97 South Croxted Road, SE21
South London Botanical Institute,
SE24
5 Turner Drive, NW11

June

WEDNESDAY 3
Whitton CRC

THURSDAY 4
Fenton House, NW3 (Evening)

SATURDAY 6
18 Littleton Street, SW18
Richmond Riverside (Evening)
Roots and Shoots, SE11

SUNDAY 7
Albion Square & London Fields, E8
37 Alwyne Road, N1
Ardlui Gardens, SE27
97 Arthur Road, SW19
64 Blenheim Gardens, NW2
Centre for Wildlife Gardening, SE15
44 Cholmeley Crescent, N6
Choumert Square, SE15
East Finchley Cottage Gardens, N2
48 Erskine Hill, NW11 (Day & Evening)
71 Fallowcourt Avenue, N12
5 Greville Place, NW6
4 The Grove, N6
7 The Grove, N6
40 Holmewood Road, SW2
239a Hook Road
10 Hoveden Road, NW2
Islington Gardens Group 2, N1
16 Lancrost Road, SW2
Osterley Park and House
174 Peckham Rye, SE22
Petersham House
Roots and Shoots, SE11
7 St George's Road
41 Southbrook Road, SE12
2 Stanley Road, N2
208 Walm Lane, The Garden Flat,
NW2 (Day & Evening)
12 Westmoreland Road, SW13

WEDNESDAY 10
239a Hook Road (Evening)
13 College Cross, N1 (Evening)

SUNDAY 14
17 Belsize Lane, NW3
24 Chestnut Road, SE27
17 Crescent Lane, SW4
De Beauvoir Gardens, N1
Elm Tree Cottage
Fishponds House
14 Frank Dixon Way, SE21
5 Hillcrest Avenue, NW11
1a Hungerford Road, N7
62 Hungerford Road, N7
Little House A, NW3
123 South Park Road, SW19
15 Norcott Road, N16
North House, SE21
Penn Road Gardens, N7
4 Stradbroke Grove
Trumpeters' House

TUESDAY 16
Charterhouse, EC1 (Evening)

WEDNESDAY 17
5 Hillcrest Avenue, NW11 (Evening)
2 Millfield Place, N6 (Evening)

SATURDAY 20
The Holme, NW1
Regents College's Garden, NW1
7 St George's Road (Evening)

SUNDAY 21
Amwell Gardens Group, EC1
5 Burbage Road, SE24
Dulwich Village Gardens, SE21
5 Garden Close, SW15
116 Hamilton Terrace, NW8
The Holme, NW1
1 Lower Merton Rise, NW3
6 Methuen Park, N10
28 Old Devonshire Road, SW12
Ormeley Lodge
Regents College's Garden, NW1
Royal College of Physicians Garden, NW1
27 St James Avenue, W13
99 Stradella Road, SE24
17 Valley View Gardens
2 Western Lane, SW12

TUESDAY 23
Hampton Court Palace (Evening)
(Pre-booking essential)

WEDNESDAY 24
28 Old Devonshire Road, SW12 (Evening)

THURSDAY 25
Hampton Court Palace (Evening)
(Pre-booking essential)

SUNDAY 28
4 Asmuns Hill, NW11
24 Brunswick Street, E17
60 Brunswick Street, E17
12 Bushberry Road, E9
5 Cecil Road, N10
113 Corringham Road, NW11

15 Lytton Close, N2
47 Maynard Road, E17
5 St Regis Close, N10

July

SATURDAY 4
Ham House and Garden

SUNDAY 5
The Bungalow, N2
9 Coopersale Road, E9
11 Coopersale Road, E9
5 Garden Close, SW15
47 Maynard Road, E17
Natural History Museum Wildlife Garden, SW7
Old Palace Lane Allotments
Railway Cottages, N22
Sydenham Garden, SE23

SATURDAY 11
All Seasons, W5
27 Wood Vale, N10

SUNDAY 12
All Seasons, W5
121 Anson Road, NW2
40 Bancroft Avenue, N2
71 Central Hill, SE19
Elm Tree Cottage
Gloucester Crescent Gardens, NW1
Mill Hill Road Gardens, W3
13 Redbridge Lane West, E11
57 St Quintin Avenue, W10
72 Tanfield Avenue, NW2
5 Wildwood Rise, NW11
27 Wood Vale, N10
82 Wood Vale, SE23
66 Woodbourne Avenue, SW16

WEDNESDAY 15
Hampton Court Palace (Evening)
(Pre-booking essential)
86 Willifield Way, NW11 (Evening)

SUNDAY 19
180 Adelaide Road, NW3
52A Berrylands Road
128 Cadogan Terrace, E9
Downings Roads Moorings Barge Gardens, SE1
36 Downs Hill
116 Hamilton Terrace, NW8 (Evening)
157 Hampstead Way, NW11
Harcourt House
2 Western Lane, SW12
86 Willifield Way, NW11

SATURDAY 25
42 Latimer Road, E7

SUNDAY 26
29 Addison Avenue, W11
10 Arnison Road
Barnet Gardens
42 Latimer Road, E7
10A The Pavement, SE27
57 St Quintin Avenue, W10
5 St Regis Close, N10

August

SUNDAY 2
180 Adelaide Road, NW3
Asmuns Hill Gardens, NW11
13 Gipsy Hill, SE19
47 Maynard Road, E17
The Wych Elm Public House

TUESDAY 4
Hampton Court Palace (Evening)
(Pre-booking essential)

SATURDAY 8
225a Brixton Road, SW9

SUNDAY 9
Alexandra Park Gardens N22
10 Arnison Road (Evening)
Elm Tree Cottage
Gloucester Crescent Gardens, NW1
12 Rookfield Avenue, N10
55 Warham Road

SATURDAY 15
The Holme, NW1
Regents College's Garden, NW1

SUNDAY 16
The Holme, NW1
Regents College's Garden, NW1

SUNDAY 23
7a New Oak Road, N2

SUNDAY 30
28 Multon Road, SW18
23 Woodville Road, W5

September

FRIDAY 4
21a Waldegrave Road, SE19 (Evening)

SUNDAY 6
7 Byng Road
24 Chestnut Road, SE27 (Evening)
54 Ferndown
Golf Course Allotments, N11

THURSDAY 10
Hampton Court Palace (Evening)
(Pre-booking essential)

SUNDAY 13
6 Methuen Park, N10

October

SUNDAY 4
The Inner Temple Garden, EC4

SUNDAY 18
The Watergardens

Gardens open to the public

Chelsea Physic Garden, SW3
Fenton House, NW3
The Garden Museum, SE1
Ham House and Garden
Hampton Court Palace

Myddelton House Gardens
Natural History Museum Wildlife
　Garden, SW7
Osterley Park and House
Roots & Shoots, SE11

By appointment only

51 Cholmeley Crescent, N6
170 Doyle Gardens, NW10
96 East Sheen Avenue, SW14
6 Emerald House, NW3
17 Greenstone Mews, E11
Hornbeams
38 Killieser Avenue, SW2
5 New Road, N8
17 Stanhope Road, E17

Also open by Appointment

1 Battlebridge Court
17 Belsize Lane, NW3
225a Brixton Road, SW9
60 Brunswick Street, E17
5 Burbage Road, SE24
12 Bushberry Road, E9
35 Camberwell Grove, SE5
16 Cecil Road, N10
51 The Chase, SW4
44 Cholmeley Crescent, N6
13 College Cross, N1
Columcille
118 Court Lane, SE21
18 Cranmer Road
158 Culford Road, De Beauvoir
　Gardens, N1
36 Downs Hill
46 Dukes Avenue, N10
Elm Tree Cottage
16 Eyot Gardens, Chiswick Mall
　Gardens, W4
54 Ferndown
69 Gloucester Crescent
70 Gloucester Crescent
5 Greville Place, NW6
7 The Grove, N6
116 Hamilton Terrace, NW8
Harcourt House
5 Hillcrest Avenue, NW11
40 Holmewood Road, SW2
239a Hook Road
1a Hungerford Road, N7
The Hurlingham Club, SW6
8 Lansdowne Walk, W11
46 Lavender Grove, E8
Lingard House, Chiswick Mall
　Gardens, W4
Little Lodge
18 Littleton Street, SW18
23 Links Way
53 Mapledene Road, E8
47 Maynard Road, E17
6 Methuen Park, N10
28 Multon Road, SW18
23 Myddleton Gardens, N21
21 Northchurch Terrace, De Beauvoir
　Gardens, N1

94 Oakwood Road, NW11
28 Old Devonshire Road, SW12
3 The Park, N6
10A The Pavement, SE27
Redwing, W3
12 Rookfield Avenue, N10
58 Rushmore Road, Lower Clapton
　Gardens, E5
7 St George's Road
1 & 3 St Helena Terrace, Richmond
　Riverside
57 St Quintin Avenue, W10
5 St Regis Close, N10
Southwood Lodge, N6
2 Stanley Road, N2
4 Stradbroke Grove
15a Sydenham Hill, SE26
72 Tanfield Avenue, NW2
21a Waldegrave Road, SE19
Waltham Forest Register Office, E17
2 Western Lane, SW12
33 Wood Vale, N10

The Gardens

66 ABBOTS GARDENS, N2
East Finchley N2 0JH. Stephen &
Ruth Kersley. *Tube: East Finchley, 6
mins walk from rear exit along the
Causeway (pedestrian) to East End Rd,
2nd L into Abbots Gdns. Buses: 143
stop at Abbots Gdns on East End Rd.
102, 263 & 234 stop on East Finchley
High Rd.* Home-made teas. **Adm
£2.50, chd free. Sun 17 May (2-5.30).
Also open 7a New Oak Rd.**
Designed for tranquillity and all-yr
interest, this 4yr old S-facing garden
(20m x 10m) uses plant form, colour,
texture and strong underlying
asymmetrical geometry, to create a
calming yet dramatic environment with
grasses, herbaceous perennials,
ornamental shrubs and trees, water
features and a discreet vegetable plot.
Garden is enhanced by hanging fused
glass pieces and a mosaic created by
Ruth. Stephen studied garden design
at Capel Manor.

29 ADDISON AVENUE, W11
W11 4QS. David & Shirley
Nicholson. *No entry for cars from
Holland Park Ave, approach via
Norland Square & Queensdale Rd.
Tube: Holland Park & Shepherds Bush.
Buses: 31, 94, 148, 295.* **Adm £2.50,
chd free. Sun 26 July (2-6). Also
open 57 St Quintin Ave.**
Garden designed to be at its peak in
July and August. Unusual wall shrubs,
itea, schizophragma, clerodendrum,
surround beds of colourful perennials,

phlox, monarda, agastache,
eupatorium. A pear tree dominates the
central lawn and a giant *Euonymus
japonicus*, over 150yrs old, amazes all
who see it.

180 ADELAIDE ROAD, NW3
Swiss Cottage NW3 3PA. Simone
Rothman,
simonerothman@ukonline.co.uk.
*Tube: Swiss Cottage, 100yds. Buses:
13, 46, 82, 113 on Finchley Rd; 31 &
C11 on Adelaide Rd. 50yds from
Marriott Hotel, Winchester Rd.* Home-
made teas. **Adm £2.50, chd free.
Suns 19 July; 2 Aug (3-5).**
Enchanting S-facing walled garden
25ft x 30ft, with numerous densely
planted containers on gravel, profuse
and colourful. Roses, climbers and
topiary. Stylish front garden with lawn,
shrubs and topiary.

Group opening

**ALBION SQUARE & LONDON
FIELDS, E8**
E8 4ES. *2m N of Liverpool St stn
(mainline & tube). 1m S of
Dalston/Kingsland stn (mainline).
Buses: 67, 149, 242, 243, alight
Downham Rd. By car approach from
Queenbridge Rd northbound, turning L
into Albion Drive leading to Albion
Square.* Home-made teas. **Combined
adm £5, chd free. Sun 7 June (2-5).**

　15 ALBION DRIVE
　Izi Glover & Michael Croton
　46 LAVENDER GROVE
　Richard Sharp & Mark Forrest
　(See separate entry)

　NEW 84 LAVENDER GROVE
　Ann Pauleau

　NEW 36 MALVERN ROAD
　Kath Harris

　53 MAPLEDENE ROAD
　Tigger Cullinan
　(See separate entry)

Five hidden gardens in the historic
Albion Square area. Highlights incude a
formal walled garden, a long family
garden, a herb garden, mature trees,
pretty country garden planting and
meadow. Children will enjoy the pond
and tree house. With a backdrop of
Victorian houses and a Victorian
Gothic church, come and explore this
peaceful corner of E London.

Group opening

NEW ALEXANDRA PARK GARDENS N22
N22 7BG. *Tube: Bounds Green or Wood Green, then bus 15 mins. Mainline: Alexandra Palace 3 mins. Buses: 184, W3 alight at junction of Alexandra Park Rd & Palace Gates Rd.* Home-made teas at 272 Alexandra Park Rd. **Combined adm £3.50, chd free.** Sun 9 Aug (2-6). **Also open 12 Rookfield Ave.**

NEW 272 ALEXANDRA PARK ROAD
Clive Boutle & Kate Tattersall

NEW 278 ALEXANDRA PARK ROAD
Gail & Wilf Downing

NEW 289 ALEXANDRA PARK ROAD
Julie Littlejohn

NEW 300 ALEXANDRA PARK ROAD
Paul Cox & Bee Peak

On the site of the original Alexandra Park estate are four gardens to enjoy: the surprisingly long rear garden of a 1920s house backing onto deer enclosure and three exuberant contrasting front gardens. The back garden retains many pre-war features incl an Anderson Shelter rock garden, crazy paving and venerable trees as well as a tree house, greenhouse and wildlife-friendly eclectic planting. The three front gardens all provide colour and interest for the community and are brilliant examples of how much can be achieved in a very small space. There is a profusion of colour in pots, while tall plants hide a secret hidden from the street. One steeply-sloping front garden has a semi-tropical theme, with a rill running through a riverbed rockery, disappearing under the path and dropping into a pool surrounded by beautiful stones.

ALL SEASONS, W5
97 Grange Road, Ealing W5 3PH. Dr Benjamin & Mrs Maria Royappa. *Tube: walking distance Ealing Broadway.* Home-made teas. **Adm £3, chd free.** Sat 11, Sun 12 July (1-6). Garden designed and planted by owners. Features incl ponds, pergolas, Japanese gardens, tropical house for orchids and exotics, aviaries, recycled features, composting and rain water harvesting, orchard, kiwi, grape vines, architectural and unusual plants, collections incl ferns, bamboos, conifers and cacti.

🐕 ❀ ☕

NEW 49 ALLEYN PARK, SE21
Dulwich SE21 8AT. Celia Randell. *Mainline: W Dulwich. ½ m from A205.* Home-made teas. **Adm £3, chd free.** Sun 10 May (2-6). **Also open 13 Gipsy Hill & 15a Sydenham Hill.** Romantic garden of ⅓ acre featuring unusual mature trees and shrubs and contemporary sculpture. The natural planting is within a formal structure and was designed with children and other wildlife in mind. Unfenced pond.

🐕 ☕

37 ALWYNE ROAD, N1
N1 2HW. Mr & Mrs J Lambert. *Buses: 38, 56, 73, 341 on Essex Rd; 4, 19, 30, 43 on Upper St, alight at Town Hall; 271 on Canonbury Rd, A1. Tube: Highbury & Islington.* Home-made teas. **Adm £2.50, chd free.** Sun 7 June (2-6).
The New River curves around the garden, the trees and sky are big, you could be in the country. Clipped box, holly and yew keep things in order while pots reclaim space for colour. Hidden formal garden; old-fashioned roses along the river. Shelter if it rains. Plants for sale are carefully chosen for all seasons: agapanthus for summer; cyclamen, liriope and aconites for autumn; iris for winter, and more. Wheelchairs possible only with own assistant for 3 entrance steps.

♿ 🐕 ❀ ☕

Group opening

AMWELL GARDENS GROUP, EC1
South Islington EC1R 1YE. *Tube: Angel, 5 mins walk. Buses: 19, 38 Rosebery Ave; 30, 73 Pentonville Rd.* Home-made teas. **Combined adm £5, chd free.** Sun 21 June (2-5.30).

NEW 11 CHADWELL STREET
Andrew Post & Mary Aylmer

24 MYDDELTON SQUARE
Professor Diana Leonard

27 MYDDELTON SQUARE
Sally & Rob Hull

LLOYD SQUARE
Lloyd Square Garden Committee. *Through gate opp 7 Lloyd Square*

NEW RIVER HEAD
Myddelton Passage. The Residents.

The Amwell Gardens Group is in a secluded corner of Georgian Clerkenwell. Contrasting gardens incl Lloyd Square, a mature space with drifting borders in the centre of the Lloyd Baker Estate, creating a natural space and calm haven in this inner city setting. Nearby are the gardens surrounding the historic New River Head, where a stylish fountain and pergola have replaced the outer pond where the 400 yr-old New River distributed fresh water to London. In Myddelton Square, a rooftop oasis (65 steps) with views of chimney pots, the Post Office Tower and Sadler's Wells contrasts with small, lushly planted courtyard gardens in this elegant terraced setting. Some wheelchair access.

🐕 ☕

NEW 121 ANSON ROAD, NW2
Cricklewood NW2 4AH. Helen Marcus. *Tube: Willesden Green, or Cricklewood, Thameslink 10 mins walk. Buses: 226, Golders Green to Ealing, stops outside the door; 16, 32, 189, 245, 260, 266, 316 to Cricklewood Broadway, then consult A-Z.* Home-made teas. **Adm £2.50, chd free.** Sun 12 July (2-5.30). **Also open 72 Tanfield Ave, NW2.**
Helen Marcus's 3rd garden for the NGS. 100ft x 40ft divided into flower garden, lawn surrounded by mixed borders and pergola with seating, deeply planted with

Rill running through a riverbed rockery, disappearing under the path and dropping into a pool . . .

shrubs, climbers and many traditional cottage garden plants to contrast form and texture in drifts of colour for yr-round interest. Vegetable garden in development. Plans incl wild flower area and mini-orchard.

Group opening

ARDLUI GARDENS, SE27

West Norwood SE27 9HL. *Mainline stns: West Norwood, Tulse Hill or West Dulwich. Buses: 2, 68, 196, 322, 468 to W Norwood High St, then 5 mins walk. Street parking available.* Home-made teas at Idmiston Rd and light refreshments at Towton Rd. **Combined adm £4, chd free. Sun 7 June (2-5). Also open 40 Holmewood Rd, SW2 & 16 Lanercost Road, SW2.**

45 IDMISTON ROAD
David Aitman & Marianne Atherton

37 TOWTON ROAD
Josie Slade. *Access to garden via garage on Ardlui Road*

Two London gardens separated by a few metres but very different in scale and style. One uses a tiny space with skill and imagination and the other uses a far larger London space more classically with lawns, trees and parterre. **45 IDMISTON ROAD** is a tranquil 100ft S-facing garden on 2 levels: upper level parterre with architectural plants, patio roses, alliums, lavender, clematis; lower level with ancient apple trees on beds of geraniums, shady beds of thalictrum, eryngium and brunnera. All approached through a wisteria- and laburnum-clad pergola. **37 TOWTON ROAD** (featured in 'Amateur Gardening') has a delightful small back garden, 20ft x 20ft, with decking and pergola with climbing roses and akebia. Beautiful rambling rose. Flower beds packed with an abundance of perennials and semi-hardy plants. Central circle, gravel, stepping stones, millstone pond, colourful baskets, potted hosta collection. A city garden to relax in. Picture postcards of gardens for sale.

10 ARNISON ROAD
East Molesey KT8 9JJ. David Clarke. *1/2 m from Hampton Court. Towards East Molesey via Bridge Rd, Arnison Rd 3rd on R.* Light refreshments & teas. **Adm £2.50, chd free. Sun 26 July (1-6). Evening Opening £3.50, chd free, wine, Sun 9 Aug (6-10).** Medium-sized garden with natural planting designed to attract wildlife and insects. Large collection of fragrant lilies. Restful koi pond with waterfall, to sit and contemplate and possibly feed the fish. Borders and island beds packed with colour, a garden to tickle the senses.

97 ARTHUR ROAD, SW19
SW19 7DP. Tony & Bella Covill. *Wimbledon Park tube, then 200yds up hill on R.* Light refreshments. **Adm £3, chd free. Sun 7 June (2-6).** 1/3-acre garden of an Edwardian house. Garden established for more than 20yrs and constantly evolving with a large variety of plants and shrubs. It has grown up around several lawns with pond and fountains. Abundance of wildlife and a bird haven. A beautiful place with much colour, foliage and texture.

Two Arts and Crafts gardens in the Artisan's Quarter of Hampstead Garden Suburb . . .

39 ARUNDEL GARDENS, N21
Winchmore Hill N21 3AG. Julie Floyd. *Mainline stn: Winchmore Hill, then approx 7 mins walk. Turn along Hoppers Rd, Arundel Gardens 3rd on L. Tube/bus: Southgate tube, then W9 Hoppa bus along Hoppers Rd.* Home-made teas. **Adm £2.50, chd free. Suns 17, 24 May (2-6).** 100ft x 30ft town garden planted informally with unusual shrubs, climbers and herbaceous plants. Arbour, water features and conservatory with a collection of cacti and succulents.

Group opening

ASMUNS HILL GARDENS, NW11
Hampstead Garden Suburb NW11 6ES. *Close to Finchley Rd & N Circular. Tube: Golders Green then bus H2 to Willifield Green or buses 82, 102, 460 to Temple Fortune, then 2 mins walk along Hampstead Way. Asmuns Hill 2nd on L.* Home-made teas. **Combined adm £4.50, chd free. Sun 2 Aug (2-5.30).**

NEW 23 ASMUNS HILL
Christopher & Wendy Parry

25 ASMUNS HILL
Ms Lorraine Wilder

Two Arts and Crafts gardens in the Artisan's Quarter of Hampstead Garden Suburb, these adjacent plots are lovely traditional cottage gardens and a true breath of country style in the urban jungle. **23 ASMUNS HILL** is a charming suburb garden, 150ft x 30ft, with borders crammed with traditional herbaceous perennials and annuals. In August, the dahlias are spectacular. Potted acers, some over 30yrs old, line the path to the well-stocked greenhouse, past old apple trees laden with fruit. **25 ASMUNS HILL** has densely planted beds brimming with colour and texture, mature trees and a York stone terrace which enhances the historic Arts and Crafts house. A grassy track leads past a vegetable parterre to a secret orchard at the end of this 1/2 -acre country garden.

4 ASMUNS HILL, NW11
Hampstead Garden Suburb NW11 6ET. Peter & Yvonne Oliver. *Close to Finchley Rd & N Circular. Tube: Golders Green then bus H2 to Willifield Green or buses 82, 102, 460 to Temple Fortune, then 2 mins walk along Hampstead Way, Asmuns Hill 2nd on L.* **Adm £3, chd free. Sun 28 June (2-5.30). Also open 113 Corringham Rd & 15 Lytton Close.** Award-winning Arts & Crafts cottage garden in artisan's quarter of Hampstead Garden Suburb. Many clematis and other climbers both front and back. Pond, patio, herbaceous bed, shade area. Succulents, acers and other plants in pots and containers. Sculptures and objets trouvés. 1st prize Hampstead Horticultural Society competition (medium sized). Photo in 'Evening Standard' NGS feature.

NEW 40 BANCROFT AVENUE, N2

Hampstead Garden Suburb N2 0AS. Carmen Gould. *Tube: East Finchley, turn R into Bishops Ave, then 1st L or Golders Green tube, then H2 bus to Market Place, then 5 mins walk.* Home-made teas. **Adm £3, chd free. Sun 12 July (2-5.30).**

A pebble-strewn path lined with boulders and planted with exotic Mediterranean trees and shrubs leads into an elegant, lushly planted oasis of calm. This plantswoman's garden, designed for yr-round interest with rare subtropical trees, shrubs, grasses and bamboos, evokes the spirit of warmer climes with a majestic black tree fern and the unusual water feature by the patio at the end of the garden.

Group opening

BARNET GARDENS

EN5 1EJ. *Tube: Midway between High Barnet and Totteridge & Whetstone stns, 20 mins walk. Buses: 34, 234, 263, 326, alight at junction of Great North Rd, Cherry Hill and Lynsdown Ave.* Teas at Cherry Hill & wine at 45 Great North Rd. **Combined adm £3, chd free. Sun 26 July (1-5.30).**

10 CHERRY HILL
Graham & Jean Shaddick

45 GREAT NORTH ROAD
Ron & Miriam Raymond

10 CHERRY HILL won 2nd prize in the Barnet in Bloom competition for best front gardens with its modern, colourful front garden. The 60ft x 18ft back garden is immaculately maintained and planted for maximum colour impact. 45 GREAT NORTH ROAD, 1st prize winner in the Barnet in Bloom competition for best front gardens, has an 80ft x 80ft cottage-style front garden with a wide variety of unusual plants. The rear garden consists of tiered beds, a small pond and features an extensive variety of well-planted tubs and specialist begonias, as well as interesting collections of origanums, ferns and begonias.

NEW 1 BATTLEBRIDGE COURT

Wharfdale Road. N1 9UA. Mike Jackson, 020 7833 2173, michaeljackson215@blueyonder.co.uk. *Tube/Bus: Kings Cross.* **Open with Islington Gardens Group 1 Sun 31 May. Visitors also welcome by appt.**

35ft x 17ft plantsman's garden maximising use of sun and shade. Peat block terracing up to canal basin. Adjacent communal gardens also being developed, see naturalised terrapins living between the houseboats. An oasis of peace and tranquillity only 2 mins from Kings Cross.

17 BELSIZE LANE, NW3

Hampstead NW3 5AD. Maureen Michaelson & Ivan Fiser, 020 7435 0510, mm@maureenmichaelson.com. *Tube: Belsize Park, 5 mins or Finchley Rd 15 mins. Mainline stn: Hampstead Heath 10 mins. Buses: C11, 168 & 268 stop opp Royal Free Hospital off corner of Belsize Lane; 13, 46, 82 & 113 all 10 mins.* **Adm £3, chd free. Sun 14 June (2-6). Also open Little House A. Visitors also welcome by appt.**

Newly-created garden (autumn 2006) rapidly establishing, with backdrop of mature trees. Irregularly shaped plot gradually reveals design of different moods and all-yr colour and texture. Pergolas with many climbers; small pond; unusual plants; container planting. Curved beds for dry, shady, woodland planting; edible beds for fresh food. Sculptural installations and work of contemporary artists. incl stunning ceramic pots.

Evokes the spirit of warmer climes with a majestic black tree fern . . .

52A BERRYLANDS ROAD

Surbiton KT5 8PD. Dr Tim & Mrs Julia Leunig. *A3 to Tolworth; A240 (dir Kingston) for approx 1m, then R into Berrylands Rd (after Fire Stn). 52A is on R after Xrds.* Home-made teas. **Adm £2.50, chd free. Sun 19 July (2.30-5.30).**

Professionally designed and planted T-shaped garden. Lawn and patio surrounded by lavender, cistus, albizia, tetrapanax, abutilon, roses and ginger. Natural wooded area under copper beech arranged around pond, stream and waterfall with eucalyptus, bamboo, tree fern, gunnera etc. Hidden jungle climbing frame and tiny allotment make it one for all the family. Featured on Alan Titchmarsh Show and in 'The Independent'.

64 BLENHEIM GARDENS, NW2

NW2 4NT. Claudia Kerner. *5 mins walk from Willesden Green tube. Buses: 260, 266, 460 to corner of Walm Lane & Anson Rd.* **Adm £2.50, chd free. Sun 7 June (2-5). Also open 10 Hoveden Rd & 208 Walm Lane.**

Mixed shrubs, roses, climbers and perennials informally planted to give a lush and dense effect. Garden is organically maintained. Pergola area with wildlife pond. Small, shady hideaway. Courtyard with statue and containers. Recent changes incl more grasses to achieve a natural, soft appearance and patio pots with long-lasting displays of acers, palm trees and bamboos.

225A BRIXTON ROAD, SW9

SW9 6LW. Deborah Nagan & Michael Johnson, 020 7735 8250, deborah@deborahnagan.orangehome.co.uk. *Tube: Oval or Brixton. Buses: 3, 59, 133, 159. Brixton Rd is the A23; 225a is on E side, next to Mostyn Rd.* Home-made teas & wine. **Adm £3, chd free. Sat 8 Aug (2-8). Visitors also welcome by appt for individuals and groups of up to 10.**

New garden to complement modern extension. Basement level with pool and upper level of metal raised beds. Mixed vegetable, fruit and perennial planting in 'rusty' colour palette. A modern urban oasis. Children must be supervised around pond and steps.

NEW 24 BRUNSWICK STREET, E17
E17 9NB. Mr Martyn Cox. *8 mins walk from Walthamstow Central mainline/tube towards Walthamstow village.* Home-made teas. **Adm £2, chd free. Sun 28 June (10-5). Also open 60 Brunswick St & 47 Maynard Rd.**
A tiny front garden of shade-loving woodlanders leads to a 30ft x 15ft S-facing plot crammed full of hundreds of plants, incl 20 types of fruit. A garden writer's urban sanctuary, every inch of space has been put to good use. Lots of storage and recycling ideas. Green roof, borders, patio, greenhouse with exotics and covered deck.

60 BRUNSWICK STREET, E17
E17 9NB. Henry Burgess, 020 8520 7377. *8 mins walk from Walthamstow Central mainline/tube towards Walthamstow village.* Home-made teas. **Adm £2, chd free. Sun 28 June (10-5). Also open 24 Brunswick Street & 47 Maynard Rd.** Visitors also welcome by appt.
Quickly maturing garden packed with head-height interest. Winding path leads through imposing planting, past raised beds, finishing under a secluded pergola. Vine, fig and vegetables. Lots to see in an untypical London terrace garden.

THE BUNGALOW, N2
15 Elm Gardens. N2 0TF. Paul Harrington & Patsy Joseph. *Tube: E Finchley, then East End Rd for ³/₄ m, R into Church Lane, 1st L Elm Gardens. Bus: 143 to Five Bells PH, then 2 mins walk; 263 to E Finchley Library, then 5 mins walk up Church Lane.* Home-made teas. **Adm £2.50, chd free. Sun 5 July (2-6).**
Mediterranean cottage-style front garden crammed with tender exotics: aloes, beschorneria, manettia, melaleucas and a 12ft high tetrapanax. Side garden an array of ferns under a canopy of climbing trachelospermum and mandevilla. Leafy rear garden. Thalia dealbata which flowered in 2005 takes centre stage in a small pond, also home for 2 terrapins.

> A garden writer's urban sanctuary, every inch of space has been put to good use . . . . lots of storage and recycling ideas . . .

---

5 BURBAGE ROAD, SE24
SE24 9HJ. Crawford & Rosemary Lindsay, 020 7274 5610, rl@rosemarylindsay.com, www.rosemarylindsay.com. *Nr junction with Half Moon Lane. Herne Hill and N Dulwich mainline stns, 5 mins walk. Buses: 3, 37, 40, 68, 196, 468.* Home-made teas Apr. **Adm £3, chd free. Suns 26 Apr; 21 June (2-5). Also open 21 June 99 Stradella Rd.** Visitors also welcome by appt Apr/May/June, coaches permitted.
Garden of member of The Society of Botanical Artists. 150ft x 40ft with large and varied range of plants. Herb garden, herbaceous borders for sun and shade, climbing plants, pots, terraces, lawns. Gravel areas to reduce watering. See our website for what the papers say.

12 BUSHBERRY ROAD, E9
Bushberry Vale E9 5SX. Molly St Hilaire, 020 8985 6805. *Mainline stn: Homerton, then 5 mins walk. Buses: 26, 30, 388, alight last stop in Cassland Rd.* Home-made teas. **Adm £1.50, chd free. Sun 28 June (2-5). Visitors also welcome by appt.**
Petite courtyard garden with water feature. Rambling roses, jasmine, vine and clematis cover the overarching pergola.

---

7 BYNG ROAD
High Barnet EN5 4NW. Mr & Mrs Julian Bishop. Home-made teas. **Adm £2.50, chd free (share to Barnet Hospital Special Care Baby Unit). Sun 6 Sept (2-5).**
Plantaholic heaven, packed with unusual flowers, incl many salvias, rudbeckias and crocosmias. Organic garden divided into different sections - bright 'hot' coloured area and more subdued planting through an arch. Tropical border. Experimental Piet Oudolf-inspired front garden with sanguisorbas, persicarias, helianthus and contrasting yellows. Many pots full of pampered treasures. Featured in 'Hertfordshire Life'.

NEW 128 CADOGAN TERRACE, E9
Hackney E9 5HP. William Dowden. *Silverlink stn: Hackney Wick. Cadogan Terrace runs parallel to A102M, along edge of Victoria Park, enter by St Mark's Gate.* Teas at Top of the Morning PH, proceeds to NGS. **Adm £2, chd free. Sun 19 July (2-6).**
A tranquil yet exotic garden. Your journey begins at the Regent's Canal. You enter the upper level with its gazebo surrounded by roses, hibiscus and lavatera. You move through the middle level with its shrub borders, and finally enter the courtyard with its sunken pool. Journey's end. Exhibition of wood art. Adjacent nursery.

35 CAMBERWELL GROVE, SE5
SE5 8JA. Lynette Hemmant & Juri Gabriel, 020 7703 6186, juni@jurigabriel.com. *From Camberwell Green go down Camberwell Church St. Turn R into Camberwell Grove.* Cold drinks & biscuits. **Adm £2.50, chd free. Sun 31 May (12-6). Also open 20 Rollscourt Ave.** Visitors also welcome by appt, coaches welcome, max 30 people.
120ft x 20ft garden with backdrop of St Giles Church. Evolved over 23yrs into country-style garden brimming with colour and overflowing with pots. In June spectacular roses swamp the artist's studio and festoon an old iron staircase.

CAPEL MANOR GARDENS
See Hertfordshire

NEW 16 CECIL ROAD, N10
N10 2BU. Jilayne Rickards,
07801 946878,
studio@jilaynerickards.com.
*Tube: Bounds Green or East
Finchley, then bus 102, 299 to St
Andrew's Church, Alexandra Park
Rd. Look for signs, 2 mins walk.*
**Adm £2, chd free. Sun 3 May
(2-6). Also open 5 St Regis
Close. Visitors also welcome by
appt, groups welcome at most
times of year.**
Garden designer's own garden
appears at first glance a romantic
painting. 3 levels are linked
together by strong structural
planting. Perennials weave
through, with interest at each
season. Designed on a subtle
colour palette, the garden is
atmospheric and interesting from
all angles, even in winter. Steps
may be unsuitable for infirm or
very young.

🐕 ☎

Spectacular in spring, 1500 tulips bloom among irises and tree peonies . . .

---

5 CECIL ROAD, N10
Muswell Hill N10 2BU. Ben Loftus.
*Just off Alexandra Park Rd between
Muswell Hill & N Circular Rd, off
Roseberry Rd.* **Adm £2.50, chd free.
Sun 28 June (2-5). Also open 5 St
Regis Close.**
Garden designer's sloping garden with
unusual small trees, shrubs and
perennials. Garden office with green
roof of bulbs etc.

🐕

---

71 CENTRAL HILL, SE19
SE19 1BS. Sue Williams. *Stns: Gipsy
Hill & Crystal Palace. On Central Hill,
midway between Harold Rd &
Rockmount Rd, is narrow, unmade
road. Proceed to bottom of this and
garden is through cast iron gates. No
parking in lane.* Home-made teas.
**Adm £3, chd free. Sun 12 July (2-5).
Also open 82 Wood Vale.**
Hidden away at end of unmade track
lies this 1/4 -acre 'secret garden'.
Formerly a Victorian nursery, the
garden is now an eclectic mix of large
traditional herbaceous beds and
structural Mediterranean planting. A
wildlife pond and formal pond and
numerous objects of C19 architectural
salvage provide further interest.

🐕 ☕

**CENTRE FOR WILDLIFE
GARDENING, SE15**
28 Marsden Road, Peckham
SE15 4EE. The London Wildlife
Trust, www.wildlondon.org.uk. *Stn:
East Dulwich, 10 mins walk. Behind
Goose Green, between Ondine &
Oglander Rds.* Light refreshments &
teas. **Adm £3, chd free. Open Tues,
Weds, Thurs & Suns 10.30-4.30,
closed 2 weeks Christmas.** For
NGS: **Sun 7 June (12-4). Also open
174 Peckham Rye.**
Inspirational community wildlife garden.
Hedges, ponds and meadows
complement beds brimming with
herbs, cottage garden plants and wild
flowers. Yr-round interest. Organic
vegetable beds, wild flower nursery
and tree scheme, beehives. Visitor
Centre with wildlife gardening displays
and advice, workshops and children's
craft activities. Picnic and family
areas. Green Pennant Award. Gravel
paths.

♿ ❀ ☕

CHARTERHOUSE, EC1
Charterhouse Square EC1M 6AN.
*Buses: 4, 55. Tube: Barbican. Turn L
out of stn L into Carthusian St & into
square. Entrance through car park.*
**Evening Opening £5, chd free,
wine, Tue 16 June (6-9).**
Enclosed courtyard gardens within the
grounds of the historic Charterhouse,
which dates back to 1347. 'English
Country Garden' style featuring roses,
ancient mulberry trees and small pond.
Various garden herbs found here are
still used in the kitchen today. Buildings
not open. Gravel paths.

♿ 🐕 ☕

NEW 51 THE CHASE, SW4
SW4 0NP. Mr Charles
Rutherfoord & Mr Rupert Tyler,
020 7627 0182,
mail@charlesrutherfoord.net. *Off
Clapham Common Northside.
Tube: Clapham Common. Buses:
137, 452.* Light refreshments.
**Adm £2.50, chd free. Evening
Opening Wed 6 May (6-8). Sun
10 May (2-6). Visitors also
welcome by appt.**
Member of the Society of Garden
Designers, Charles has created the
garden over 20yrs using 15 different
species of trees. Spectacular in
spring, 1500 tulips bloom among
irises and tree peonies. Narrow
paths lead to a mound surrounded
by acanthus and topped by a large
steel sculpture. Rupert's geodetic
dome shelters seedlings, succulents
and subtropicals.

🐕 ☕ ☎

◆ **CHELSEA PHYSIC GARDEN,
SW3**
66 Royal Hospital Road. SW3 4HS.
Chelsea Physic Garden self-funding
charity, 020 7352 5646 ext 30,
m.manager@ chelseaphysicgarden.
co.uk, www.chelseaphysicgarden.
co.uk. *Tube: Sloane Square (10 mins).
Bus: 170. Parking Battersea Park
(charged). Entrance in Swan Walk
(except wheelchairs).* **Adm £8, chd £5.
1st & 2nd weekends in Feb (11-4);
1 Apr to 30 Oct, Weds Thur, Fri (12-5),
Sun (12-6).** For NGS: **Sun 5 Apr (12-6).**
Oldest Botanic Garden in London.
3¾ acres; medicinal and herb garden,
perfumery border; family order beds;
historical walk, glasshouses. Cool
fernery and Robert Fortune's tank
pond. Guided and audio tours.

♿ 🐕 ❀ ☕

---

24 CHESTNUT ROAD, SE27
West Norwood SE27 9LF. Paul
Brewer & Anne Rogerson. *Stns:
West Norwood or Tulse Hill. Buses:
2, 68, 196, 322, 432, 468. Off S end of
Norwood Rd, nr W Norwood
Cemetery.* Home-made teas. **Adm
£1.50, chd free (share to Sound
Minds). Sun 14 June (2-5). Evening
Opening £3, wine, Sun 6 Sept (6-9).**
Well-stocked front garden. Compact
rear garden with patios, decking, pond
and unusual gazebo in recycled wood.
Lush planting with gunnera, vintage
ferns, bamboos and banana. Lots of
pots. Penguin. Featured in 'House
Beautiful'.

🐕 ☕

CHEVENING
See Kent

Group opening

CHISWICK MALL GARDENS, W4
W6 9TN. *Tube: Stamford Brook.
Buses: 27, 190, 267 & 391 to Young's
Corner from Hammersmith through St
Peter's Sq under A4 to river. By car A4
westbound turn off at Eyot Gdns S,
then R into Chiswick Mall.* Teas at 16
Eyot Gardens. **Adm £2 each garden,
chd free. Sun 24 May** (2-6).

EYOT COTTAGE
Mrs Peter Trumper

16 EYOT GARDENS
Ms Dianne Farris
(☎ 020 8741 1370)

LINGARD HOUSE
Rachel Austin
(☎ 020 8747 1943)

SWAN HOUSE
Mr & Mrs George Nissen

A unique group of riverside houses and
gardens situated in an unspoilt quiet
backwater. With a beautiful river
frontage, **EYOT COTTAGE** has two
interconnecting gardens, one an old
walled garden with many unusual white
plants, the other a terrace garden with
imaginative use of old stones and
pavers. The small town garden at 16
EYOT GARDENS is planted to
complement the Victorian house, the
back garden showing what can be
done with a small space, by using the
walls for yr-round interest. **LINGARD
HOUSE**'s walled garden is divided into
a brick courtyard and terrace with
huge acacia tree; formal lawn with
miniature pond and water-spout and
wild garden with ancient apple trees,
climbing roses and beehive. At **SWAN
HOUSE** see an informal walled garden,
herbaceous border, fruit trees, small
vegetable garden and a tiny
greenhouse. Also a small wild flower
area, 2 ponds and a rill.

---

44 CHOLMELEY CRESCENT, N6
N6 5HA. Mrs Patrizia Gutierrez,
07850 756784,
yulia@gardenshrink.com. *Tube:
Highgate. Buses: 43, 134.* Home-
made teas, light refreshments & wine.
Adm £2.50, chd free. Sun 7 June
(2-6.30). **Visitors also welcome by
appt.**

Contemporary family garden designed
by Chelsea medal winner, Yulia Badian.
Hardwood decking extends the living
space. A boardwalk through 3 arches
leads to summerhouse with green roof.
Gabion baskets planted and filled with
slate form an unusual retaining wall.
Immaculate lawn. Low maintenance
planting gives yr-round colour and
scent.

51 CHOLMELEY CRESCENT, N6
Highgate N6 5EX. Ernst
Sondheimer, 020 8340 6607,
ernst@sondheimer.fsnet.co.uk.
*Between Highgate Hill & Archway Rd,
off Cholmeley Park. Tube: Highgate.*
Adm £2, chd free. Visitors welcome
by appt.
Approx 1/6 -acre garden with many
alpines in screes, peat beds, tufa,
troughs and greenhouse; shrubs,
rhododendrons, camellias, magnolias,
pieris, ceanothus etc. Clematis, bog
plants, roses, primulas, tree ferns.
Water features. Garden on steep slope
with many steps and narrow paths.
☎

Prize-winning, paved garden behind a peaceful Georgian terrace . ..

CHOUMERT SQUARE, SE15
SE15 4RE. The Residents. *Via
wrought iron gates off Choumert
Grove. Peckham Rye mainline stn is
visible from the gates, & buses galore
(12, 36, 37, 63, 78, 171, 312, 345)
less than 10 mins walk. Car park
2 mins.* Light refreshments, home-
made teas & wine. **Adm £2.50, chd
50p (share to St Christopher's
Hospice). Sun 7 June** (1-6).
About 46 mini gardens with maxi-
planting in a Shangri-la situation that
the media has described as a 'Floral
Canyon', which leads to small
communal 'secret garden'. Art, craft
and home-made produce stalls and
live music. Delicious refreshments.
Gardens and village fête in one! Silver-
Gilt award, Southwark in Bloom.
Featured on BBC TV Gardeners'
World.

13 COLLEGE CROSS, N1
N1 1YY. Diana & Stephen Yakeley,
diana@yakeley.com. *Tube: Highbury
& Islington. Buses: 19, 73, 277.* **Adm
£3, chd free. Evening Opening,**
wine, Wed 10 June (6-8). Also open
with **Islington Gardens Group 2**
Sun 7 June. **Visitors also welcome
by appt May to July only.**
Arisaemas, huge tetrapanax leaves,
ferns, hostas and many unusual
plants create form and texture in a
designer's green and white oasis.
Black slate bench and glass
balustrade provide contemporary
design interest in a prize-winning,
paved garden behind a peaceful
Georgian terrace.

COLUMCILLE
9 Norlands Crescent, Chislehurst
BR7 5RN. Nancy & Jim Pratt, 020
8467 9383,
nancyandjim@btinternet.com. *Off
A222 turn into Cricket Ground Rd, then
1st R into Norlands Cres, approx 1/2 m
from Chislehurst BR stn. Buses: 162 or
269, Bank House stop.* Home-made
teas. **Adm £3, chd free. Sun 31 May**
(2-5). **Visitors also welcome by appt
May to Sept.**
Small garden featuring Japanese
sanctuary, influenced by Zen tradition,
incl water feature, lanterns, traditional
Japanese plants and garden shed
transformed into a tea house. Also
cottage garden section with colourful
display of roses, digitalis, lupins,
peonies and delphiniums, especially in
June; day lilies July, dahlias Aug and
Sept.

**NEW 9 COOPERSALE ROAD,
E9**
Homerton, Hackney E9 6AU.
Alistair & Isobel Siddons. *5 mins
Homerton overground. Buses:
236, 242, 276 within 3 mins walk.*
Cream teas. **Adm £1.50, chd
free. Sun 5 July** (2-6). Also open
11 Coopersale Rd.
A little haven in Hackney. A
complete re-design began when
the current owners moved here in
mid-2007. Testing showed the soil
to be wildly alkaline and practically
devoid of nutrients. Maturing trees
and shrubs incl a specimen exotic
Acca *sellowiana*. Small but distinct
zones make the most of varying
aspects and soil types. Little
wildlife garden.

NEW 11 COOPERSALE ROAD, E9

Homerton, Hackney E9 6AU. S Bourne. *5 mins Homerton overground. Buses: 236, 242, 276 within 3 mins walk.* **Adm £1.50, chd free. Sun 5 July (2-6). Also open 9 Coopersale Rd.** Mature garden planted mainly with shrubs to encourage wildlife and for easy maintenance. A green oasis in a busy urban area.

113 CORRINGHAM ROAD, NW11

Hampstead Garden Suburb NW11 7DL. Veronica Clein. *Tube: Golders Green, then 10mins walk. Entrance to courtyard between 101 & 117 Corringham Rd (Hampstead Way end). Buses: 13, 82, 102, 113, 460 to Golders Geen.* Home-made teas. **Adm £3, chd free. Sun 28 June (2-6). Also open 4 Asmuns Hill & 15 Lytton Close.** Garden designer and plantswoman's garden created since 2005 behind a house situated in listed Arts and Crafts courtyard. The formal garden is profusely planted with perennials, unusual annuals and shrubs with an emphasis on painterly colour combinations. Dry shade woodland garden, wildlife pond, sculptured figure, potager, greenhouse and lavishly planted containers.

NEW 118 COURT LANE, SE21

SE21 7EA. Margaret Evison, 020 8693 2254. *Nr Dulwich Village. Mainline: N Dulwich, then 10mins walk. Buses: 12, 37, 176, P4. Ample parking.* Home-made teas. **Adm £2.50, chd free. Sun 31 May (2-5.30). Visitors also welcome by appt Apr to Sept, weekends only.** Front garden planned to give yr-round interest with white and green foliage. 180ft rear garden backs onto Dulwich Park and emphasises owner's interest in unusual plants. Terrace area, wide herbaceous borders, scented area and newly-established wildlife garden with pond.

The planting is intended to cope with the attentions of a small dog . . .

18 CRANMER ROAD

Hampton Hill TW12 1DW. Bernard Wigginton, 020 8979 4596. *4m from Twickenham/Kingston-upon-Thames. Between A312 (Uxbridge Rd) & A313 (Park Rd). Bus: 285 from Kingston stops at end of rd. Stn: Fulwell 15 mins walk.* **Adm £2.50, chd free. Open with Hampton Hill Gardens Sat 16, Sun 17 May. Visitors also welcome by appt May and June only.** Medium-sized garden with herbaceous and exotics borders. WW2 air raid shelter transformed as rockery, water garden with azaleas, helianthemums and foliage plants. Containers with seasonal planting complete this interesting and colourful all-yr garden with a backdrop of St James's Church spire. Wheelchair access to main lawn only.

17 CRESCENT LANE, SW4

SW4 9PT. Paddy & Sue Sumner. *Near junction of Abbeville Rd and Crescent Lane, NOT in one-way part of Crescent Lane.* Home-made teas & wine. **Adm £2, chd free. Sun 14 June (3-6).** Long garden, opening into a square lawn, surrounded by roses, shrubs and trees with a pond, backed by a yew hedge. The design is unusual and the planting predominantly focuses on blue and white and is intended to be robust enough to cope with the attentions of a small dog. Featured in Clapham Society Newsletter.

Group opening

DE BEAUVOIR GARDENS, N1

N1 4HU. *Tube: Highbury & Islington then buses 30 or 277 from St Paul's Rd; or Angel tube then 38 or 73 bus. Cars via Southgate Rd, park in Northchurch Rd or via Kingsland & Downham Rd.* Home-made teas at 158 Culford Rd. **Combined adm £3.50, or £2 each garden, chd free. Sun 14 June (2-6).**

158 CULFORD ROAD

Gillian Blachford
(☎ 020 7254 3780, gmblachford@ btopenworld.com)

21 NORTHCHURCH TERRACE

Ms Nancy Korman
(☎ 020 7249 4919 n.korman@lse.ac.uk)

Two mature gardens in a leafy enclave of period houses (both also welcome visitors in June by appt). The small town garden at **158 CULFORD ROAD** is long and narrow, with a romantic feel. Winding path and herbaceous borders, incl shrubs, small trees, perennials and many unusual plants. The walled 30ft x 75ft town garden at **21 NORTHCHURCH TERRACE** has a formal feel, with deep herbaceous borders, pond, fruit trees, pergola, patio pots and herb beds.

DOWNINGS ROADS MOORINGS BARGE GARDENS, SE1

31 Mill Street. SE1 2AX. Mr Nicholas Lacey. *Close to Tower Bridge & Design Museum. Mill St off Jamaica Rd, between London Bridge & Bermondsey stns, Tower Hill also nearby. Buses: 47, 188, 381, RV1.* Home-made teas. **Adm £3, chd free (share to RNLI). Sun 19 July (2-5).** Series of 7 floating barge gardens connected by walkways and bridges. Gardens have an eclectic range of plants for yr-round seasonal interest. Marine environment: suitable shoes and care needed. Not suitable for small children.

36 DOWNS HILL

Beckenham BR3 5HB. Marc & Janet Berlin, 020 8650 9377, janetberlin@hotmail.com. *1m W of Bromley. 2 mins from Ravensbourne mainline stn nr top of Foxgrove Rd.* Home-made teas. **Adm £2.50, chd free. Suns 26 Apr; 19 July (2-5). Also open 19 July Harcourt House, just down the rd. Visitors also welcome by appt.** Long, 2/3 -acre E-facing, award-winning garden sloping steeply away from house. Ponds, water courses and sheltered patio area with many tender unusual plants and hundreds of pots. Wooded area, dense planting of trees, shrubs and flowers. Raised beds, paths and patio areas. Alpine house, bulbs in pots. Display of auriculas in April.

170 DOYLE GARDENS, NW10
Kensal Rise/Willesden NW10 3SU.
James Duncan Mattoon, 020 8961
6243. *Tube: Kensal Green, up College
Rd, L into Liddell Gdns which
becomes Doyle Gdns.* **Visitors
welcome by appt at any time.**
Professional plantsman's private
fantasy garden with an impossibly
tropical theme: musa, trachycarpus,
yucca, puya, plumbago, grasses.
Garden 95% organic and incl many
native and introduced wild flowers to
help create a natural effect and
promote wildlife. Frog and newt pond,
log piles and over 350 plant species,
living with slugs and snails! Featured
on BBC2 Open Gardens.

15 DUKES AVENUE, N10
N10 2PS. Vivienne Parry. *Short walk
from main Muswell Hill roundabout.
Buses: 43, 134, alight Muswell Hill
Broadway or 7 from Finsbury Park.
Tube: Highgate, then bus 43 or 134.*
Home-made teas. **Adm £2.50, chd
free. Sun 17 May (2-5). Also open
46 Dukes Ave & 33 Wood Vale.**
Mediterranean-style gravel front garden
in silver, lilacs, pinks and blues. Small
back garden crammed with wide
variety of plants, many unusual. Large
plant sale including rarer salvias and
other plants for dry, sunny sites.
Featured in 'The English Garden'.

46 DUKES AVENUE, N10
Muswell Hill N10 2PU. Judith Glover,
0208 444 9807,
www.judithglover.com. *Short walk
from main Muswell Hill roundabout.
Tube: Highgate then bus 43 or 134 to
Muswell Hill Broadway or bus 7 from
Finsbury Park.* Light refreshments.
**Adm £3, chd free. Sun 17 May (2-6).
Also open 15 Dukes Ave & 33
Wood Vale.** Visitors also welcome
by appt May & June only.
Designer and botanical illustrator's
country-style garden described as
being 'just on the right side of
controlled chaos'. Organic, curvy beds
with foxgloves, aquilegias, irises and
valerian anchored with clipped
evergreens. Topiary, grasses and
driftwood throne from the medal-
winning garden Judith designed for the
Chelsea Flower Show in 2003. Open
studio, wine, soft drinks & nibbles.
Featured in 'The English Garden' &
'Ideal Home' magazines.

DULWICH VILLAGE GARDENS, SE21
SE21 7BJ. *Mainline: N Dulwich or W
Dulwich then 10-15 mins walk. Tube:
Brixton then P4 bus passes both
gardens. Street parking.* Home-made
teas. **Combined adm £4.50, chd free
(share to Macmillan, Local Branch).
Sun 21 June (2-5).**

103 DULWICH VILLAGE
Mr & Mrs N Annesley

105 DULWICH VILLAGE
Mr & Mrs A Rutherford

2 Georgian houses with large
gardens, 2 mins walk from Dulwich
Picture Gallery and Dulwich Park.
103 DULWICH VILLAGE is a
'country garden in London' with a
long herbaceous border, lawn, pond,
roses and fruit and vegetable garden.
105 DULWICH VILLAGE is a very
pretty garden with many unusual
plants, lots of old-fashioned roses, an
ornamental pond and water garden.

EAST FINCHLEY COTTAGE GARDENS, N2
N2 8JJ. *Tube: East Finchley 12 mins
walk. Bus: 263 to library, turn L into
Church Lane, R into Trinity Rd. Car:
turn into Trinity Rd from Long Lane, off
Church Lane.* **Combined adm £3,
chd free. Sun 7 June (2-5). Also
open 2 Stanley Rd.**

399 LONG LANE
Jonathan Maitland

20 TRINITY ROAD
Jane Meir

22 TRINITY ROAD
J Maitland

Three very different cottage gardens,
creating densely-planted intimate
spaces filled with exuberant and varied
planting in beds and pots. In one,
cottage garden plants mingle happily
with elegant ferns and grasses. A
majestic black bamboo towers over
pots of dainty annuals and a giant
trachycarpus palm falls over a feathery
tamarix. In another 1960s crazy paving
fast is disappearing to accommodate
new planting. There are ponds and
places to sit and relax.

96 EAST SHEEN AVENUE, SW14
SW14 8AU. Alex Clarke, 020 8876
5152, alexclarke43@btinternet.com.
*Buses: 33, 367 along Upper Richmond
Rd W, alight end of East Sheen Ave.*
**Adm £3, chd free. Visitors welcome
by appt in Aug only, for groups of
10+.**
70ft x 30ft garden, recently
redesigned to incl an interesting stream
water feature. Many tender and
unusual plants providing yr-round
interest, vibrant colour, shape and
texture. Shed with green roof. At end
of garden are hidden, established and
very well maintained allotments, also
open. Featured in 'Amateur
Gardening'.

ECCLESTON SQUARE, SW1
SW1V 1NP. Roger Phillips & the
Residents,
www.rogerstreesandshrubs.com.
*Off Belgrave Rd nr Victoria stn, parking
allowed on Suns.* Home-made teas.
**Adm £3.50, chd free. Sun 10 May
(2-5).**
Planned by Cubitt in 1828, the 3-acre
square is subdivided into mini-gardens
with camellias, iris, ferns and
containers. Dramatic collection of
tender climbing roses and 20 different
forms of tree peonies. National
Collection of ceanothus incl more than
70 species and cultivars. Notable
important additions of tender plants
being grown and tested. Gravel paths.
Award for Best Garden Square in
Westminster.

EDWARDES SQUARE, W8
W8 6HL. Edwardes Square Garden
Committee. *Tube: Kensington High St
& Earls Court. Buses: 9, 10, 27, 28,
31, 49 & 74 to Odeon Cinema.
Entrance in South Edwardes Square.*
Home-made teas. **Adm £3, chd free.
Sun 19 Apr (12-5).**
One of London's prettiest secluded
garden squares. 3½ acres laid out
differently from other squares, with
serpentine paths by Agostino Agliothe,
Italian artist and decorator who lived at
no.15 from 1814-1820, and a beautiful
Grecian temple which is traditionally
the home of the gardener. Romantic
rose tunnel winds through the middle
of the garden. Good displays of bulbs
and blossom.

Species pelargoniums and exotic aeoniums compete with breathtaking views across London . . .

ELM TREE COTTAGE
85 Croham Road, South Croydon
CR2 7HJ. Wendy Witherick &
Michael Wilkinson, 020 8681 8622.
*2m S of Croydon. Off B275 from
Croydon, off A2022 from Selsdon, bus
64.* **Adm £2.50. Suns 10 May; 14
June; 12 July; 9 Aug (1-4.30). Also
open 9 Aug 55 Warham Road.
Visitors also welcome by appt.**
Cottage garden transformed into an
oasis of sharp gardening. Agaves,
grasses, yuccas, olives, kniphofia, iris,
alliums, phormiums, phlomis, figs.
Topiary boxwood, taxus and much
more. Designed to be drought-
tolerant/low maintenance. Not suitable
for those unsteady on their feet and
beware spikes of 50 varieties of agave!
Regret no children. Finalist Daily Mail
Garden of the Year. Featured in 'The
Independent' and 'House Beautiful'.

6 EMERALD HOUSE, NW3
1c King Henry's Road, Primrose Hill
NW3 3QP. Dr Catherine Horwood
Barwise, 020 7483 2601,
cbarwise@gmail.com,
www.emerald-house.co.uk. *Tube:
Chalk Farm, 5 mins walk. Buses: 31,
168, 393 or C11, 24, 27, 274 (10
mins).* **Adm £3, chd free. Visitors
welcome by appt July & Aug for
groups of 5-15.**
Stunning S-facing L-shaped roof
terrace garden stuffed with unusual
shrubs, tender perennials, clematis and
succulents, chosen to cope with
extreme weather conditions. Raised
trays and tubs of alpines surround
water feature topped with wind-swept
hanging baskets of echeverias and
sempervivums. Species pelargoniums
and exotic aeoniums compete with
breathtaking views across London.

**NEW 48 ERSKINE HILL,
NW11**
Hampstead Garden Suburb
NW11 6HG. Mrs Marjorie Harris.
*Close to North Circular and A1.
Tube: Golders Green. Circular Hail
& Ride bus H2 from Golders
Green passes door (ask for
Denman Drive). 8-10 minute walk
from Finchley Road (buses 82,
102, 460 to Temple Fortune)
or from Falloden Way (bus 102
to The Market Place, then H2 -
S side only).* **Day & Evening
Opening Sun 7 June (2-6pm
£2.50, chd free; 6-8pm £4 with
wine & nibbles, chd free).**
Bird-friendly, pesticide-free garden
wrapped around artisan's cottage
in Hampstead Garden Suburb.
Perennials, shrubs, roses,
clematis, *Cotinus* Grace. Lawn
shaded by large apple tree and
flowering cherry. Terrace with
many pots and containers. Brick-
paved area with 4 raised beds,
incl tiny box-edged organic herb
and vegetable patch. Some single
steps and narrow paths.

71 FALLOWCOURT AVENUE, N12
Finchley N12 0BE. Yasuko & John
O'Gorman. *7 mins walk from West
Finchley stn, between Ballards Lane &
Finchley High Rd. Buses: 82, 125, 263
& 460 to Finchley Memorial Hospital.*
Home-made teas & light refreshments.
**Adm £2, chd free. Sun 7 June
(2-5.30).**
Well maintained 120ft x 30ft S-facing
plot. Densely planted garden of trees,
shrubs and perennials, at its first peak
in May/June. Sunlit borders and
shaded area with an intimate patio at
rear, not immediately visible from the
house. Many Japanese varieties: tree
peonies, maples, magnolias, cherry
blossoms, azaleas, hydrangeas,
hostas and irises.

◆ FENTON HOUSE, NW3
Hampstead Grove. NW3 6RT. The
National Trust.
www.nationaltrust.org.uk. *300yds
from Hampstead tube. Entrances: top
of Holly Hill & Hampstead Grove.* For
NGS: **Evening Openings** £3.50, chd
£1.50, wine, Thurs 7 May; 4 June
(6.30-8.30).
Timeless 1½-acre walled garden, laid
out on three levels, containing
imaginative plantings concealed by
yew hedges. The herbaceous borders

give yr-round interest while the brick-
paved sunken rose garden provides a
sheltered hollow of scent and colour.
The formal lawn area contrasts with the
rustic charm of the kitchen garden and
orchard. Vine house. In spring, good
borders and underplanted orchard.

54 FERNDOWN
Northwood Hills HA6 1PH. David &
Ros Bryson, 020 8866 3792,
davidbryson@sky.com. *Tube:
Northwood Hills 5 mins walk. R out of
stn, R down Briarwood Drive then 1st
R.* Home-made teas. **Adm £3, chd
free. Sun 6 Sept (11-5). Visitors also
welcome by appt.**
Unusual collection of exotics, cacti and
Australasian plants. Palm trees, tree
ferns and bananas set in an original
design. Elevated deck overlooks the
garden underplanted with rare ferns
and aroids. Featured in 'Garden
News'.

FISHPONDS HOUSE
Fishponds Park, 219 Ewell Road,
Surbiton KT6 6BE. Robert Eyre-
Brook. *1m from Tolworth junction on
A3 towards Kingston on A240. House
in middle of The Fishponds, a public
park bordered by Ewell Rd, Browns
Rd, King Charles Rd & Hollyfield Rd.
House is behind the main pond. Park
in neighbouring rds. No vehicle
access to park other than for
disabled; disabled access from Ewell
Rd.* Home-made teas. **Adm £2.50,
chd free. Sun 14 June (2-5).**
Large garden, part formal, part
terrace, with adjoining woodland
overlooking a large duck pond. Partly
redesigned by Andy Sturgeon and
filled with structural plants and
grasses. Visitors could visit the park
for a picnic before garden opening.
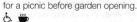

14 FRANK DIXON WAY, SE21
SE21 7ET. Frank & Angie Dunn.
*Mainline: W Dulwich. From Dulwich
Village pass Dulwich Gallery on R,
Frank Dixon Way (private rd) 500m on
L.* Home-made teas. **Adm £3, chd
free. Sun 14 June (2-5). Also open
North House.**
Large family garden surrounded by
mature trees, low maintenance shrub
borders and annual plantings. Lawns.
Sit-on railway around the garden for
children's rides.

5 GARDEN CLOSE, SW15

SW15 3TH. Vivien Fowler & Tom Jestico. ½ m E of Roehampton. Off Portsmouth Rd, 10 mins walk from the Green Man PH, via Wildcroft Rd, Putney Hill. **Adm £2.50, chd free. Suns 24 May; 21 June; 5 July (11-5).**
¼ -acre walled garden which serves as backdrop to architect's all-glass house. Oriental inspiration with black bamboos, and swathes of box, hebe, lavender and rhododendrons. Ponds and timber decks surround house. New planting. House and garden open.

◆ THE GARDEN MUSEUM, SE1

Lambeth Palace Road. SE1 7LB, 020 7401 8865, www.museumgardenhistory.org. Tube: Lambeth North, Vauxhall, Waterloo. Buses: 507 Red Arrow from Victoria or Waterloo mainline & tube stns, also 3, 77, 344; alight Lambeth Palace. **Adm £6, chd free (share to Garden Museum). For NGS: Sat 9 May (10.30-5).**
Reproduction C17 knot garden with period plants, topiary and box hedging. Wild garden in front of graveyard area; drought planting at front entrance. Historic tools, information displays, changing exhibitions, shop and café housed in former church of St-Mary-at-Lambeth.

13 GIPSY HILL, SE19

Crystal Palace SE19 1QG. Jon & Eils Digby-Rogers. Stn: Gipsy Hill. Bus: 322 from Clapham Junction via Herne Hill goes up Gipsy Hill, Crystal Palace buses within walking distance. Light refreshments & teas. **Adm £3, chd free. Suns 10 May; 2 Aug (2-7). Also open 10 May 15a Sydenham Hill & 49 Alleyn Park.**
Secluded town garden, 17m x 17m, protected by high brick wall and steep shrub-covered bank. York stone terraced areas with many coloured glazed and terracotta pots. Wide variety of different shrubs, climbers and perennials for yr-round colour. Wisteria-covered oak-framed pergola, summerhouse, large blown glass and copper fountain, all providing outside rooms for the home.

A shed on castors . . .

Group opening

GLOUCESTER CRESCENT GARDENS, NW1

Camden Town NW1 7EG. Tube: Camden Town 2 mins, Mornington Crescent 10 mins. Limited metered parking in Oval Rd. **Combined adm £3.50, chd free. Suns 12 July; 9 Aug (2-5.30).**

NEW 69 GLOUCESTER CRESCENT
Sandra Clapham
(☎ 020 7485 5764)

70 GLOUCESTER CRESCENT
Lucy Gent & Malcolm Turner
(☎ 020 7485 6906,
l-gent@tiscali.co.uk)

Two neighbouring gardens (both welcoming visitors at other times by appointment) in a street well-known for its literary and musical connections. Ursula Vaughan Williams lived at no. 69 and Mrs Charles Dickens at no.70. Unexpected oases of calm and plant interest, 1 min from Camden Lock. **69 GLOUCESTER CRESCENT** is an ingenious and welcoming cottage garden, a treat behind front wall and gate. Roses, perennials, annuals and a bed of tomatoes, plus the odd self-seeder. **70 GLOUCESTER CRESCENT** meets the challenges of space and shade constraints, plus a warm microclimate, with by versatile planting. All-yr interest, with a climax of colour in August, incl a miniature pomegranate.

Allotments

GOLF COURSE ALLOTMENTS, N11

Winton Avenue N11 2AR. GCAA/Haringey, www.gcaa.pwp.blueyonder.co.uk. Tube: Bounds Green approx 1km. Buses: 102, 184, 299 to Sunshine Garden Centre, Durnsford Rd. Then Bidwell Gardens (on foot through park) to Winton Ave. Gate opp junction with Blake Rd. Light refreshments & home-made teas. **Adm £2.50, chd free. Sun 6 Sept (1-4).**
Large, long-established allotment with over 200 plots maintained by culturally diverse community growing a wide variety of flowers, fruit and vegetables - some working towards organic cultivation. Picturesque corners and charming sheds. Annual show, produce sale, home-made jellies, jams, chutneys, books and teas. Bric-a-brac. Tour of plots and exhibits of prize winning fruit & vegetables. Some gravel paths, rough ground in places.

NEW 17 GREENSTONE MEWS, E11

Wanstead E11 2RS. Mr & Mrs S Farnham, 07761 476651, farnhamz@yahoo.co.uk. Tube: Snaresbrook or Wanstead, 5 mins walk. Bus: 101, 308 to Wanstead High St. **Adm £2.50, chd free. Visitors welcome by appt for 4-8 visitors.**
Tiny squarish (20ft x 17ft) paved garden on one level with small iron veranda. Planting incl mature bottlebrush, tree peony, climbers and plants grown from cuttings, with 2 strawberry trees providing height. Use of reclaimed material incl bath buried in the ground, enjoyed by koi and goldfish. Vegetables in pots and hanging baskets cultivated with tools stored in a shed on castors.

Two neighbouring gardens in a street well-known for its literary and musical connections . . .

5 GREVILLE PLACE, NW6

NW6 5JP. Dr & Mrs T Laub, renee@laub.co.uk. Tube: Kilburn Park. Buses 16 & 98 to Kilburn High Rd, 139 & 189 to Boundary Rd. Home-made teas. **Adm £3, chd free. Sun 7 June (2-5.30). Visitors also welcome by appt for groups of 8+, June, July & Sept.**
Recently created garden, establishing fast. Large front garden with herbaceous planting. Behind the house a stream links two ponds and meanders through a woodland garden. Good collection of ferns and many unusual plants. Interesting Victorian pots.

34 GROVE PARK, SE5
Camberwell SE5 8LG. Christopher & Philippa Matthews. 1/2 m S of Camberwell. *Stn: Peckham Rye, 10mins walk. Buses: all to Camberwell Green. Access to Grove Park by car either from Chadwick Rd or top of Camberwell Grove.* Home-made teas. **Adm £3, chd free. Sun 31 May (2-5.30).** Also open **35 Camberwell Grove.**
120ft x 40ft garden started in 2006, designed for yr-round flowers. Large colour-themed beds with abundant perennials, old English roses, alliums, echiums, cardoons and climbers. Secret wood at end of garden (limited access). Packed 50ft S-facing front garden, best described as organised chaos.

4 THE GROVE, N6
Highgate Village N6 6JU. Polly & Daisy Stenham. *The Grove is between Highgate West Hill & Hampstead Lane. Tube: Archway or Highgate. Buses: 143, 210, 271 to Highgate Village from Archway, 214 from Camden Town.* **Adm £2.50, chd free. Sun 7 June (2-5.30).** Also open **7 The Grove.**
Delightful two-tiered garden. Formal upper garden with a mixture of Mediterranean and traditional plants and flowers; Cooper's Burmese rose and wildlife pond with fountain. Woodland area; hidden garden, greenhouse, laburnum tunnel and silver pear arch in bottom garden.

7 THE GROVE, N6
Highgate Village. N6 6JU. Mr Thomas Lyttelton, 07713 638161. *For directions see 4 The Grove.* Home-made teas. **Adm £2.50, chd free. Suns 5 Apr; 7 June (2-5.30).** Also open **7 June 4 The Grove.** Visitors also welcome by appt.
1/2 acre designed for max all-yr interest with its variety of conifers and other trees, ground cover, water garden, vistas, 19 paths, surprises. Exceptional camellias in April. Wheelchair access to main lawn only; some very narrow paths.

◆ HAM HOUSE AND GARDEN
Ham, Richmond TW10 7RS. The National Trust, 020 8940 1950, www.nationaltrust.org.uk. *Mid-way between Richmond & Kingston. W of A307 on Surrey bank of R Thames.*

Follow National Trust signs. **House & garden £9.90, chd £5.50, family £25.30. Garden only £3.30, chd £2.20, family £8.80. Opening days & times vary according to season;** please phone or visit website for details. For NGS: **Sat 4 July (11-6).**
The beautiful C17 gardens incl Cherry Garden, featuring lavender parterres flanked by hornbeam arbours; S terrace with clipped yew cones, hibiscus and pomegranate trees; eight grass plats; maze-like wilderness; C17 orangery with working kitchen garden and licensed café and terrace.

116 HAMILTON TERRACE, NW8
NW8 9UT. Mr & Mrs I B Kathuria, 020 7625 6909,
gkathuria@hotmail.co.uk. *Tubes: Maida Vale, 5 mins walk, St John's Wood, 10 mins walk. Buses: Maida Vale 16, 98, Abbey Rd 139, 189, Finchley Rd 13, 113.* Home-made teas. **Adm £2.50, chd free (share to St Mark's Church Repair Appeal). Sun 21 June (2-6). Evening Opening £4, chd free, wine, Sun 19 July (5-9).** Visitors also welcome by appt.
Lush front garden full of dramatic foliage with a water feature and tree ferns. Large back garden of different levels with Yorkshire stone paving, many large terracotta pots and containers, water feature and lawn. Wide variety of perennials and flowering shrubs, many unusual, and subtropical plants, succulents, acers, ferns, hebes, climbers, roses, fuchsias and prizewinning hostas. Packed with colour and rich foliage of varied texture. 1st prize All London Garden Society (Back Gardens).

157 HAMPSTEAD WAY, NW11
Hampstead Garden Suburb NW11 7YA. Richard & Carol Kemp. *1m N of Golders Green. Tube: Golders Green, then H2 bus to Hampstead Way junction with Willifield Way.* **Adm £2.50, chd free. Sun 19 July (2-5.30).** Also open **86 Willifield Way.**
100ft split-level SW-facing cottage garden containing a wealth of colourful and informally planted hardy perennials and succulents, against a backdrop of interesting shrubs. Designed for all-yr interest. Undergoing gradual modification to cope with local environmental and climate change.

NEW ◆ HAMPTON COURT PALACE
East Molesey KT8 9AU. Historic Royal Palaces, 0870 751 5175, www.hrp.org.uk. *Well signed.* Adm £6. For NGS: **Pre-booking essential** Thur 2 Apr; Tue 23 June, Thur 25 June; Wed 15 July; Tue 4 Aug; Thur 10 Sept (6.30-8). Special evening tours of the Formal Gardens, incl the new Heraldic Tudor Courtyard Garden, with specialist talks. **Please visit www.ngs.org.uk for information & bookings, or phone 01483 211535.**
The finest surviving Anglo-Dutch gardens in Europe, best demonstrated by the restored Privy Garden and the Orangery Gardens of William III. As well as these wonderful garden reconstructions, visitors can enjoy a riot of colour all spring and summer, with beds and borders planted with thousands of bulbs, followed by summer annuals and perennials, famous since Victorian times. New Heraldic Tudor Courtyard Garden will open June 2009 to celebrate the 500th Anniversary of the succession of Henry VIII to the English throne. Seasonal plant sales

  NCCPG

Special tours of the Formal Gardens, and the new Heraldic Tudor Courtyard Garden . . .

Group opening

HAMPTON HILL GARDENS
Hampton Hill TW12 1DW. *4m from Twickenham/Kingston-upon-Thames. Between A312 (Uxbridge Rd) and A313 (Park Rd). Bus: 285 from Kingston stops at end of rd. Stn: Fulwell 15 mins walk.* Home-made teas & wine. **Combined adm £5, chd free. Sat 16, Sun 17 May (2-6).**

NEW 12 CRANMER ROAD
Peter & Jean Jennings

18 CRANMER ROAD
Mr B Wigginton
(☎ see separate entry)

NEW 76 PARK ROAD
Mrs Margaret Gawler. *On the corner of Park Rd and Cranmer Rd, 5 mins from 12 and 18 Cranmer Rd*

Three gardens of diverse interest in an attractive West London suburb. Tickets from 18 Cranmer Rd only, teas at 12 Cranmer Rd and wine at 76 Park Rd. **12 CRANMER ROAD** offers several seating areas for refreshment and relaxation, from the patio with container planting to the large lawn surrounded by herbaceous and native shrubs. A magnificent pink rhododendron leads the eye to a beautiful 'black locust' acacia tree and the hidden world of the garden has wild flowers among the trees. **18 CRANMER ROAD** (see separate entry) with its WW2 air raid shelter transformed as rockery and water garden is an interesting and colourful all-yr garden with a backdrop of St James's Church spire. **76 PARK ROAD** is an imaginative and surprising grand Victorian garden with York stone paths leading to lawned garden with magnificent Lebanese cedar, weeping willow, rambling roses, exotic border planting, bamboos, cordylines, tree ferns and unusual shrubs. Tiered fountain and large glasshouse, and a rondavel which blends with the garden's tranquil ambience.

HARCOURT HOUSE
Grasmere Road, Bromley BR1 4BB. Freda Davis, 07958 534074, fredagdavis@aol.com, www.fredasgarden.co.uk. *1½ m W of Bromley. WD buses 208, 227 to junction of Highland Rd.* Light refreshments. **Adm £2.50, chd free. Sun 19 July (2-5). Also open 36 Downs Rd**, just down the rd. Visitors also welcome by appt June to Sept, coaches permitted or groups of 10+.
Colourful Victorian garden wrapped around large Victorian house. Winding pathways, fern garden, Hercules secret garden, water features, many statues, unusual objects incl French antique lampposts placed among planted areas. Dozens of pots, many hanging baskets, large conservatory in the Victorian style.

NEW 5 HEATHGATE, NW11
Hampstead Garden Suburb NW11 7AR. Patricia Larsen. *Tube: Golders Green, then 12 mins walk. Bus: H2 to Heathgate.* Light refreshments & teas. **Adm £2.50, chd free (combined adm with 5 Turner Drive £4). Sun 31 May (2-6).**
Set in a stunning borrowed treescape on the edge of Hampstead Heath, this 45ft x 25ft Arts and Crafts garden has lavishly planted traditional herbaceous borders with newly installed contemporary features. Handmade greetings cards of flowers from the artist's garden. Wheelchairs will need help up steps.

Imaginative and surprising grand Victorian garden with York stone paths leading to lawned garden with magnificent Lebanese cedar . . .

5 HILLCREST AVENUE, NW11
NW11 0EP. Mrs R M Rees, 020 8455 0419, ruthmrees@aol.com. *1m N of Golders Green. Hillcrest Ave is off Bridge Lane. Buses: 82, 102, 460 to Temple Fortune. Tube: Golders Green or Finchley Central. Walk down Bridge Lane.* Home-made teas. **Adm £2, chd free. Sun 14 June (2-6). Evening Opening £3, wine & light refreshments, Wed 17 June (5-9).** Visitors also welcome by appt.
Small labour-saving traditional back garden; rockery, fish pond, conservatory, tree ferns, secluded patio. Urban jungle front garden with drought-resistant plants, traditional back garden. Chairlift available from decking to main garden. Featured in 'Garden News'.

THE HOLME, NW1
Inner Circle, Regents Park. NW1 4NT. Lessee of The Crown Commission. *5 mins from Baker St in Regents Park. Opp Rose Garden. Tube: Regents Park or Baker St, over York bridge then L at Inner Circle. Buses 13, 18, 27, 30, 74, 82, 113, 139, 159, 274.* **Adm £3.50, chd free. Sats, Suns 20, 21 June; 15, 16 Aug (2.30-5.30). Also open Royal College of Physicians 21 June & Regents College Garden** (all dates).
4-acre garden filled with interesting and unusual plants. Sweeping lakeside lawns intersected by islands of herbaceous beds. Extensive rock garden with waterfall, stream and pool. Formal flower garden with unusual annual and half hardy plants, sunken lawn, fountain pool and arbour. Teas available in nearby Rose Garden. Gravel paths.

NEW 40 HOLMEWOOD ROAD, SW2
Brixton Hill SW2 3RR. Judith Colquhoun & Ian Owings, 020 8674 3697, judithcolquhoun09@hotmail.co.uk. *1m N of Brixton, 1m W of Tulse Hill. Mainline & tube to Brixton, train to Tulse Hill. Buses: P2, 45, 59, 118, 133, 137, 159, 250, 333. No entry from Brixton Hill. Parking on Holmewood Gdns.* Light refreshments, teas & wine. **Adm £2, chd free. Sun 7 June (2-5). Also open Ardlui Gardens, SE27.** Visitors also welcome by appt for max 12, no coaches.
Small S-facing urban garden planted principally for shade. Many woodland plants incl pulmonaria, wild garlic, euphorbias, anemone, digitalis, ferns, astrantias and actaea combine in a loose structure. A modern deck is bordered by sun-loving perennials and shrubs, incl rambling rose, olive tree, potted bamboos and species pelargoniums. Exhibition of artwork by owners. 2 steps to house, one in garden, assistance given.

239A HOOK ROAD
Chessington KT9 1EQ. Mr & Mrs D St Romaine, 020 8397 3761, derek@gardenphotolibrary.com. *4m S of Kingston. A3 from London, turn L at Hook underpass onto A243 Hook Rd. Garden approx 300yds on L. Parking opp in park. Buses: K4, 71, 465 from Kingston & Surbiton to North Star PH.* **Adm £2.50, chd free. Sun 7 June (2-6). Evening Opening £3.75, wine, Wed 10 June (8-10.15). Visitors also welcome by appt.**
Garden photographer's garden. A contemporary flower garden, entertaining area, gravel garden, herbaceous borders, fernery, pond and rose tunnel. Traditional potager with over 25 varieties of fruit and 50+ varieties of vegetables and herbs. Special twilight opening to show how garden lighting can effectively transform a garden at night.

HORNBEAMS
Priory Drive, Stanmore HA7 3HN. Dr & Mrs R B Stalbow, 020 8954 2218, barbara@bstalbow.wanadoo.co.uk. *5m SE of Watford. Tube: Stanmore. Priory Drive private rd off Stanmore Hill (A4140 Stanmore-Bushey Heath Rd).* Home-made teas. **Adm £3, chd free. Visitors welcome by appt, groups welcome.**
All-season garden cottage in ½ acre designed by plantaholic owner. Winter-flowering scented shrubs, snowdrops, aconites, species tulips. Colourful containers, ornamental potager, formal pool. Muscat grape shades conservatory. Learn how to utilise borrowed landscape in an enclosed space. A sunny day in winter is a joy. Come and see!

10 HOVEDEN ROAD, NW2
NW2 3XD. Ian Brownhill & Michael Hirschl. *Tube: Kilburn or Willesden Green. Buses: 16, 32, 189, 226, 245, 260, 266 & 316 to Cricklewood Broadway, then consult A-Z.* **Adm £2.50, chd free. Sun 7 June (2-6). Also open 64 Blenheim Gdns & 208 Walm Lane.**
70ft x 25ft award-winning urban garden. Stylish deck with pergola and fish pond leads into attractive circular paved area surrounded by box hedging and deeply planted borders. Shade area at the end of the garden features gazebo. No access for wheelchairs or prams.

1A HUNGERFORD ROAD, N7
N7 9LA. David Matzdorf, davidmatzdorf@blueyonder.co.uk. *Tube: Caledonian Rd, 6 mins walk. Buses: 29 & 253 to Hillmarton Rd stop in Camden Rd; 17, 91 & 259 to last stop in Hillmarton Rd; 10 to York Way at Market Rd & 274 to junction of Market Rd & Caledonian Rd.* **Adm £2, chd 50p. Sun 14 June (12-6). Also open 62 Hungerford Rd & Penn Rd Gardens. Visitors also welcome by appt May to Oct, no more than 4 visitors. Private visits get access to entire 'green roof'.**
Unique eco-house with walled, lush front garden planted in modern-exotic style. Front garden densely planted with palms, acacia, ginger lilies, brugmansias, bananas, euphorbias and yuccas. Floriferous 'green roof' resembling scree slope planted with agaves, aloes, cacti, bromeliads, alpines, sedums, mesembryanthemums, bulbs, grasses and aromatic herbs - access via ladder only to part of roof (for safety reasons, can be seen from below). Garden and roof each 50ft x 18ft. Featured on Gardeners' World.

Winter-flowering scented shrubs, snowdrops, aconites, species tulips . . . a sunny day in winter is a joy . . .

62 HUNGERFORD ROAD, N7
N7 9LP. John Gilbert & Lynne Berry. *Directions as 1a Hungerford Rd.* **Adm £2, chd free. Sun 14 June (2-6). Also open 1a Hungerford Rd & Penn Rd Gardens.**
Densely planted mature town garden at rear of Victorian terrace house which has been designed to maximise space for planting and create several different sitting areas, views and moods. Arranged in a series of paved rooms with a good range of perennials, shrubs and trees. Professional garden designer's own garden.

THE HURLINGHAM CLUB, SW6
Ranelagh Gardens, Fulham SW6 3PR, 020 7471 8209, ellen.wells@hurlinghamclub.org.uk, www.hurlinghamclub.org.uk. *Main gate at E end of Ranelagh Gardens. Tube: Putney Bridge (110yds).* Light refreshments, teas & wine. **Adm £5, chd free. Sat 30 May (11-4). Visitors also welcome by appt.**
Rare oppportunity to visit this 42-acre jewel with many mature trees, 2-acre lake with water fowl, expansive lawns and a river walk. Capability Brown and Humphry Repton were involved with landscaping. The gardens are renowned for their roses, herbaceous and lakeside borders, shrubberies and stunning bedding displays. The riverbank is a haven for wildlife with native trees, shrubs and wild flowers.

NEW THE INNER TEMPLE GARDEN, EC4
Crown Office Row, Inner Temple. EC4Y 7HL. The Honourable Society of the Inner Temple. *Use Tudor St gate on Tudor St, wheelchair access via disabled entrance.* **Adm £3, chd free. Sun 4 Oct (12.30-4).**
3-acre garden lying between the river and Fleet St with sweeping lawns, many unusual trees, and spectacular herbaceous borders showing late-flowering perennials at their peak in Oct, together with exotic displays of salvias and annual bedding. The courtyards of the Temple and its famous C12 church are adjacent. Featured in national press.

Group opening

ISLINGTON GARDENS GROUP 1, N1
N1 1BE. *Tube: Kings Cross or Angel. Buses: 17, 91, 259 to Caledonian Rd.* Home-made teas at 36 Thornhill Square. **Combined adm £6 or £2 each garden (Barnsbury Wood £1.50), chd free. Sun 31 May (2-6).**

BARNSBURY WOOD
Islington Council. *Off Crescent Street, N of Thornhill Square*

NEW 1 BATTLEBRIDGE COURT
Wharfdale Road. Mike Jackson (☎ See separate entry)

44 HEMINGFORD ROAD
Dr Peter Willis

36 THORNHILL SQUARE
Anna & Christopher McKane

Walk through Islington's Georgian streets and squares to these contrasting gardens, ranging from an informal country-style garden to urban gardens packed with flowers. At **BARNSBURY WOOD** wild flower borders lead to Islington's hidden secret. A place of peace and relaxation, the borough's only site of mature woodland and one of London's smallest nature reserves. Wildlife gardening advice and information available. **44 HEMINGFORD ROAD** is a surprisingly lush, country-style garden in the city with interesting trees, shrubs, perennials, lawns and pond in a very small space. Matured over 30 yrs in symbiosis with honey fungus. **36 THORNHILL SQUARE** has old roses, hardy geraniums, clematis and alliums in curved beds giving a country garden atmosphere in this 120ft long garden. Small bonsai collection. Many unusual perennials propagated for sale. Some wheelchair access at Barnsbury Wood. Also visit the plantsman's garden at **1 BATTLEBRIDGE COURT** (see separate entry) and see naturalised terrapins living between the nearby houseboats in an oasis of peace and tranquillity only 2 mins from Kings Cross.

 ⚗ ☕

Group opening

ISLINGTON GARDENS GROUP 2, N1
N1 1YY. *Tube: Highbury & Islington. Buses: 19, 73, 277.* **Combined adm £5 or £2 each garden, chd free.** Sun 7 June (2-6).

🆕 **29 CANONBURY PARK NORTH**
Jamie Longstaff,
www.29cpn.com.

8 COLLEGE CROSS
Anne Weyman & Chris Bulford

13 COLLEGE CROSS
Diana & Stephen Yakeley
(☎ see separate entry)

Come to Islington, once home to Lenin and Blair and now home to Boris, to see a group of diverse gardens behind the Georgian facades. From a mature walled garden combining city elegance with cottage garden charm, to designer foliage with glass and slate, to hot borders and a lavender walk, each offers a different perspective on urban gardening. Nearby Upper St provides retail therapy and restaurants to suit all political persuasions.

Group opening

KEW GREEN GARDENS
TW9 3AH. *NW side of Kew Green. Tube: Kew Gardens. Mainline stn: Kew Bridge. Buses: 65, 391. Entrance via towpath.* Home-made teas at Church Hall. **Combined adm £5, chd free.** Sun 17 May (2-6).

65 KEW GREEN
Giles & Angela Dixon

69 KEW GREEN
Mr & Mrs John Godfrey

71 KEW GREEN
Mr & Mrs Jan Pethick

73 KEW GREEN
Donald & Libby Insall

Four long gardens behind a row of C18 houses on the Green, close to the Royal Botanic Gardens. These gardens feature the profusely-planted and traditional borders of a mature English country garden, and contrast formal gardens, terraces, lawns laid out around tall, old trees with wilder areas with a nuttery, woodland and meadow planting. One has an unusual architect-designed summerhouse, while another offers the surprise of a modern planting of espaliered miniature fruit trees.

 ☕

38 KILLIESER AVENUE, SW2
SW2 4NT. Mrs Winkle Haworth, 020 8671 4196,
winklehaworth@hotmail.com.
Mainline stn: Streatham Hill, 5 mins walk. Buses: 133, 137, 159 to Telford Ave. Killieser Ave 2nd turning L off Telford Ave. **Adm £3.50.** Visitors welcome by appt **Apr to July, min 5, coaches permitted.**
Densely-planted, romantic, 90ft x 28ft garden divided into four distinct areas. Unusual perennial plants and shrubs provide the backbone. Miniature cascade, wall fountain, Gothic seating arbour and gravel garden with drought-tolerant plants. Rose-filled parterre provides a formal element and stunning tulip display in spring.

🌾 🛏 ☎

LAMBETH PALACE, SE1
SE1 7JU. The Church Commissioners,
www.archbishopofcanterbury.org.
Mainline stn & tube: Waterloo. Tube: Westminster, Lambeth North & Vauxhall, all about 10 mins walk. Buses: 3, C10, 76, 77, 77a, 344. Entry to garden on Lambeth Palace Rd (not at gatehouse). Home-made teas. **Adm £3.50, chd free.** Sat 30 May (2-5.30). Lambeth Palace garden is one of the oldest and largest private gardens in London. Site occupied by Archbishops of Canterbury since end C12. Formal courtyards with historic white fig (originally planted 1555). Parkland-style garden with mature trees, woodland and native planting, pond, hornbeam allée. Also formal rose terrace, summer gravel border, chapel garden and beehives. Beekeepers in attendance. Gravel paths.

♿ ⚗ ☕

🆕 **16 LANERCOST ROAD, SW2**
SW2 3DN. Melinda Hilliard. *Stn: Tulse Hill, 5 mins. Lanercost Rd runs parallel to the S Circular; enter from Hillside Rd or Probyn Rd.* **Adm £2.50, chd free.** Sun 7 June (2-5).
Self-seeding plants are welcomed in this informal, S-facing garden, so it's never going to be immaculate. The design incorporates family needs, incl a shed and compost heaps, whilst the planting features both inherited shrubs and newer styles, such as cannas and grasses. Also newly-planted shady area.

🌾 ☕

Come to Islington, once home to Lenin and Blair and now home to Boris, to see a group of diverse gardens behind the Georgian facades . . .

Every planting opportunity maximised through a colourful abundance of baskets, climbers, shrubs and fruit trees . . .

12 LANSDOWNE ROAD, W11

W11 3LW. **The Lady Amabel Lindsay.** *Turn N off Holland Park Ave nr Holland Park stn or W off Ladbroke Grove halfway along. Buses: 12, 88, GL 711, 715. Bus stop & tube: Holland Park, 4 mins.* **Adm £3, chd free. Wed 27 May (2-6).** Medium-sized fairly wild garden; borders, climbing roses, shrubs; mulberry tree 200yrs old.

8 LANSDOWNE WALK, W11

W11 3LN. **Nerissa Guest, 020 7229 3661, nmguest@waitrose.com.** *Tube: Holland Park, then 2 mins walk N. Buses: 94, 148.* Home-made teas. **Adm £2.50, chd free. Sun 26 Apr (2-6). Visitors also welcome by appt.** Medium-sized garden owned by plantaholic with diverse passions! All-yr interest peaking with specialist collection of camellias in spring and choice salvias in autumn. Emphasis on foliage, texture and scent with unusual and eclectic mix of exotic, herbaceous and grasses entwined with many clematis. Containers incl Pseudopanax *ferox*, Metrosideros *excelsa*, Woodwardia *radicans* and echiums. Access path slippery when wet.

42 LATIMER ROAD, E7

Forest Gate E7 0LQ. **Janet Daniels.** *8 mins walk from Forest Gate or Wanstead Park stn. From Forest Gate cross to Sebert Rd, then 3rd rd on L.* Home-made teas. **Adm £2.50, chd free. Sat 25, Sun 26 July (11-5).** Plantaholic's garden, 90ft x 15ft, behind terraced house, with every planting opportunity maximised through a colourful abundance of baskets, climbers, shrubs and fruit trees. Raised koi carp pond. 4 steps down to secret garden, 70ft x 40ft, with exuberant mixed borders, wildlife pond with gunnera and small green oasis lawn with arbour. Featured on BBC, ITV, BBC Radio and in local press.

46 LAVENDER GROVE, E8

E8 3LS. **Richard Sharp & Mark Forrest, 07943 715003, rsharp@clapton.hackney.sch.uk.** *2m N of Liverpool St stn (mainline & tube). 1m S of Dalston/Kingsland stn (mainline). Buses: 67, 149, 242, 243, alight Downham Rd. By car approach from Queenbridge Rd northbound, turning L into Albion Drive leading to Albion Square.* **Open with Albion Square & London Fields Sun 7 June (2-5). Visitors also welcome by appt, small groups.** Small garden behind terraced Victorian house packed with fruit trees, vine fruit and perennial flowers. Bulbs bloom in spring, followed by dahlias and echinacea in mid-summer.

Group opening

NEW LEYBORNE PARK GARDENS

Kew TW9 3HA. *Stn: Kew Gardens, 5 mins walk. Buses: 65 to Kew Gardens, Victoria Gate, 391 to to Kew Gardens stn.* Home-made teas at Fiveways. **Combined adm £5, chd free. Sun 24, Mon 25 May (2-5).**

NEW FIVEWAYS
Mr & Mrs Alan Britten

NEW 64 LEYBORNE PARK
Mrs Lindie White

38 LEYBORNE PARK
Ann & Alan Sandall

Three gardens in strikingly contrasted styles, close to one another and within easy reach of Royal Botanic Gardens, Kew. Tickets from 38 Leyborne Park only. **FIVEWAYS** is the mature and surprisingly large and private garden of Victorian cottage character. It features late spring flowers with flowering shrubs and large trees around an irregular lawn, with some narrow paths (partial wheelchair access).

38 LEYBORNE PARK's long narrow garden is maturing with its owners. Some trendy bits: blue shed, finds from skips, bananas. Then the urge to do that bit less: extended terrace, pots, statuesque shrubs, collection of peonies. A plantaholic trying to simplify - without success! **64 LEYBORNE PARK** is a family garden with lawn and mixed beds. Also a potager and hidden vegetable plot.

NEW 23 LINKS WAY

Northwood HA6 2XA. **Jackie Simmonds, 01923 824180, jackiesdesk@gmail.com.** *5m S of Watford, 15m NW of Central London. Close to A40 & M25 off A404. Tube: Northwood Metropolitan Line, stn 25 mins walk.* Light refreshments & teas. **Adm £3, chd free. Sun 24 May (2-7). Visitors also welcome by appt.** $2/3$-acre, artist's garden with rhododendrons and azaleas, sweeping lawn, herbaceous border of perennials, annuals and shrubs; stunning Magnolia grandiflora. 6 ponds, 3 stocked with fish, the others within beautiful rock garden with alpines and acers. Display of award-winning artist's paintings with garden painting demo possible, weather permitting.

LITTLE HOUSE A, NW3

16A Maresfield Gardens, Hampstead NW3 5SU. **Linda & Stephen Williams.** *5 mins walk Swiss Cottage or Finchley Rd tube. Off Fitzjohn's Ave and 2 doors away from Freud Museum (signed).* Light refreshments & teas. **Adm £3, chd free. Sun 14 June (2-6). Also open 17 Belsize Lane.** 1920s Arts & Crafts house (not open) built by Danish artist Arild Rosenkrantz. Award-winning front and rear garden set out formally with water features, stream and sculpture. Unusual shrubs and perennials, many rare, incl *Paeonia rockii* and *Dicksonia fibrosa*. Wide collections of hellebores, hostas, toad lilies, acers, clematis and astrantia. Featured in Hampstead & Highgate Express.

LITTLE LODGE
Watts Road, Thames Ditton
KT7 0BX. Mr & Mrs P Hickman, 020
8339 0931. *2m SW of Kingston.
Mainline stn Thames Ditton 5 mins. A3
from London; after Hook underpass
turn L to Esher; at Scilly Isles turn R
towards Kingston; after 2nd railway
bridge turn L to Thames Ditton village;
house opp library after Giggs Hill
Green.* Home-made teas. **Adm £3,
chd free (share to Cancer
Research). Sun 31 May (11.30-5.30).
Visitors also welcome by appt.**
Partly walled informal flower garden
filled with shrubs and herbaceous
plants that create an atmosphere of
peace. Small secret garden; terracotta
pots; stone troughs and sinks; roses;
clematis; topiary; very productive
parterre vegetable garden.

Victorian
terraced house
garden, designed
by present
owners to
provide seclusion
for humans and
wildlife . . .

**NEW 18 LITTLETON STREET,
SW18**
SW18 3SY. Ian & Cathy Shaw,
020 8944 6048,
garden@shawc.demon.co.uk.
*Stn: Earlsfield, 10 mins walk.
Buses: 44, 77, 270 along Garratt
Lane.* Home-made teas. **Adm
£2.50, chd free. Sat 6 June
(2-6).Visitors also welcome by
appt in June & July, Sat pm
only.**
Victorian terraced house garden,
designed by present owners to
provide seclusion for humans and
wildlife, with colour, scent and
structure all yr and to be tolerant
of changing climates. Densely
planted in every available space,
incl roses, perennials, grasses,
ferns, flowering shrubs, herbs,
acer, cherry and euonymus.
Miniature wildlife pool and lily
bowl.

Group opening
LOWER CLAPTON GARDENS, E5
E5 0RL. *Tube: Bethnal Green, then
bus 106, 254, or Manor House, then
bus 253, 254, alight Lower Clapton
Rd. By car: leave Lower Clapton Rd by
Millfields or Atherden Rd, R into
Rushmore Rd and follow signs.* Home-
made teas & cakes at 58 Rushmore
Rd. **Combined adm £5, chd free.
Sun 31 May (2-6).**

8 ALMACK ROAD
Mr Philip Lightowlers

99 POWERSCROFT ROAD
Rose Greenwood

58 RUSHMORE ROAD
Annie Moloney
(☎ 07989 803196,
anniemoloney58@yahoo.co.uk.
*If driving, entry to Rushmore Rd
via Atherden or Millfields Rd only*

Lower Clapton is an area of Victorian
villas on terraces that lead down to the
R Lea. A varied group of gardens is
open, each reflecting their owner's
taste and providing tranquillity in an
otherwise hectic area of East London.
8 ALMACK ROAD is a long walled
garden in 2 rooms: the first has a
yellow and blue theme, with lawn,
shrubs and water feature; the second
a sunny garden with brick paths,
tropical foliage, succulents and a
secluded seating area.
99 POWERSCROFT ROAD's small
town garden is on 3 levels featuring a
decked balcony, running water over
rock and a thatched gazebo, while the
garden at **58 RUSHMORE ROAD** is
on two levels: the lower level 2m x 3m,
with lots of pots and wall fountain;
upper level 3m x 4m reached by spiral
staircase, with many subtropical
plants. Visitors are also welcome by
appt.

1 LOWER MERTON RISE, NW3
NW3 3RA. Mr & Mrs Paul Findlay.
*Between Swiss Cottage & Chalk
Farm, Primrose Hill.* Home-made
teas. **Adm £3, chd free. Sun 21
June (2-6).**
Approx ¼ acre. Cottage-style garden
with herbaceous borders, lawns and
roses. A sunken courtyard with
cascade, pergolas and winding paths
link the different areas.

15 LYTTON CLOSE, N2
Hampstead Garden Suburb N2 0RH.
Edwin & Toni Fine. *In the heart of
Hampstead Garden Suburb. Tube:
Golders Green, then H2 bus to corner
of Linden Lea and Lytton Close.*
Home-made teas. **Adm £3, chd free.
Sun 28 June (2-6).Also open
4 Asmuns Hill & 113 Corringham
Rd.**
Stunning formal garden, 120ft x 60ft,
planted for yr-round interest with
emphasis on texture and contrasting
forms. Wide terrace with integral
fishpond and fernery overlooks 60ft
herbaceous border guarded by
windsock seagulls set in impeccable
lawns and leading to children's garden
with playhouse and giant sunflowers.
Pots of over 50 ornamental grasses
line the eastern border, the whole
surrounded by mature trees. Winner
Best Garden, Hampstead Garden
Suburb in Bloom.

Group opening
MALVERN TERRACE GARDENS,
N1
N1 1HR. *Approach from S via
Pentonville Rd into Penton St, then
into Barnsbury Rd. From N via
Thornhill Rd opp Albion PH. Tube:
Angel, Highbury & Islington, Kings X.
Buses: 19, 30 to Upper St, Town Hall
or 17, 91 from Kings X to Caledonian
Rd (Richmond Ave).* Home-made
teas. **Adm £3, chd free. Sun 26 Apr
(2-5.30).**
Group of unique 1830s London terrace
houses built on the site of Thomas
Oldfield's dairy and cricket field.
Cottage-style gardens in cobbled cul-
de-sac. Music and plant stall.

53 MAPLEDENE ROAD, E8
E8 3JW. Tigger Cullinan, 020 7249
3754, tiggerine8@blueyonder.co.uk.
*2m N of Liverpool St stn (mainline &
tube). 1m S of Dalston/Kingsland stn
(mainline). Buses: 67, 149, 242, 243,
alight Downham Rd. By car approach
from Queenbridge Rd northbound,
turning L into Albion Drive leading to
Albion Square.* **Open with Albion
Square & London Fields** Sun
**7 June (2-5).Visitors also welcome
by appt June to mid-Aug, small
groups only.**
90ft x 15ft N-facing garden, divided in
3, crammed with plants, largely grown
from cuttings, chosen for their

contrasting leaves and colour combinations. Boundaries smothered in roses, clematis and other climbers. Featured in 'Easteight' magazine.

47 MAYNARD ROAD, E17
Walthamstow E17 9JE. Don Mapp, 020 8520 1565, don.mapp@gmail.com, www.donsgarden.co.uk. *10 mins walk from Walthamstow (central stn). Bus to Tesco on Lea Bridge Rd then walk through Barclay Path, or bus W12 to Addison Rd. Turn R to Beulah Path.* Adm £2.50, chd free. Suns 28 June; 5 July; 2 Aug (11-6). **Also open 28 June 24 & 60 Brunswick St.** Visitors also welcome by appt June to Aug after 12 noon.
Plant collector's paradise. An eclectic mix of exotic plants in a 40ft x 16ft space, entered via a densely planted front garden.

Meandering paths lead from courtyard to greenhouse, lawn with long border, pond with stream, orchard, oriental garden . . .

6 METHUEN PARK, N10
Muswell Hill N10 2JS. Yulia Badian, 07850 756784, yulia@gardenshrink.com. *Tube: Highgate, then bus 43, 134 to Muswell Hill Broadway, 3rd on L off Dukes Ave or Finsbury Park tube then W7 bus.* Home-made teas & wine. Adm £2.50, chd free. Suns 21 June; 13 Sept (2-6.30). Visitors also welcome by appt.
Contemporary family garden designed by Chelsea medal winner. Hardwood decking extends the living space. Across the formal pond the beach grows into a path. An arch doubles as a swing. Flowing curves and unique planting create an enchanting peaceful space. Tree house provides hours of entertainment. Sonic installation. 'The Green Man' glass sculpture by Max Jaquard.

Group opening

MILL HILL ROAD GARDENS, W3
Acton W3 8JE. *Tube: Acton Town, turn R, Mill Hill Rd 3rd on R.* Home-made teas. **Combined adm £6, chd free (share to Chicken Shed). Sun 12 July (2-6).**

41 MILL HILL ROAD
Marcia Hurst

65 MILL HILL ROAD
Ms Anna Dargavel

REDWING
69 Mill Hill Road. Mr & Mrs M Temple
(☎ see separate entry)

Three gardens in one road encourage wildlife with ponds, a mound and and a huge range of plants to attract insects. The owner at **41 MILL HILL ROAD** describes herself as a compulsive plantaholic. The 120ft x 40ft garden features a hot gravel garden with unusual plants, lawn with herbaceous border and lavender hedge and a raised terrace with topiary. **65 MILL HILL ROAD** is a typically long narrow London garden, paved, with borders and planted with fruit trees and shrubs. It is wildlife-friendly with ponds and flowers to which bees and other insects are attracted. Frogs and dragonflies abound. Visit **REDWING** (see separate entry) for a secluded, contemplative wildlife-friendly garden with its 'Lavender Halt' pavilion.

2 MILLFIELD PLACE, N6
N6 6JP. *Off Highgate West Hill, E side of Hampstead Heath. Buses: C2, C11 or 214 to Parliament Hill Fields.* Home-made teas (Sun). Adm £2.50, chd free. Sun 10 May (2-6). **Evening Opening** £3.50, chd free, wine, Wed 17 June (5.30-9).
1½-acre spring and summer garden with camellias, rhododendrons, many flowering shrubs and unusual plants. Spring bulbs, herbaceous borders, small orchard, spacious lawns. Wheelchair assistance available.

28 MULTON ROAD, SW18
Wandsworth SW18 3LH. Victoria Orr, 020 8704 0645, v.summerley@independent.co.uk, www.victoriasbackyard.co.uk. *Mainline: 10 mins walk from Earlsfield or Wandsworth Common. Buses: 219, 319 along Trinity Rd.* Home-made

teas. Adm £2.50, chd free. Sun 30 Aug (2-6). Visitors also welcome by appt.
'The planting here is strong and modern: bananas, gorgeous tetrapanax, a tree fern... and the biggest phormium I've ever seen. Vast paddle leaves of bananas splay out against a background of bamboo' (Anna Pavord). 70ft x 40ft subtropical suburban oasis, designed to defy global warming, garden pests and kids without recourse to carbon emissions, chemicals or cranial damage. Design is contemporary but not minimalist, there is lots of seating, and 3 ponds. Featured in 'The Independent'.

◆ MYDDELTON HOUSE GARDENS
Bulls Cross, Enfield EN2 9HG. Lee Valley Regional Park Authority, 01992 702200, www.leevalleypark.org.uk. *2m N of Enfield. J25 (A10) off M25 S towards Enfield. 1st T-lights R into Bullsmoor Lane, L at end along Bulls Cross.* Light refreshments & teas on NGS days only. Adm £3, chd free. Apr to Sept (10-4.30), Oct to Mar (10-3); Closed Christmas period. For NGS: Suns 15 Feb; 26 Apr; 24 May (12-4).
4 acres of gardens created by E A Bowles. Gardens feature diverse and unusual plants incl National Collection of award-winning bearded irises. Large pond with terrace, conservatory and interesting historical artefacts. A garden for all seasons, snowdrops in Feb. Green Flag Award.

NEW 23 MYDDLETON GARDENS, N21
N21 2PA, 07773 789780. *Stn: Winchmore Hill, then 10 mins walk. Off Green Dragon Lane, Winchmore Hill. Bus: 125 from Southgate Tube, or 329 from Enfield St. Parking available.* Home-made teas. Adm £3, chd free. Sun 10 May (2-6). Visitors also welcome by appt, adm £5 incl tea & biscuits.
Front garden created 2004. Large secluded back garden with mature hedges. Meandering paths lead from courtyard to greenhouse, lawn with long border, pond with stream, orchard, oriental garden, fernery and excellent compost area. All-yr interest. Some uneven paths and steps.

◆ **NATURAL HISTORY MUSEUM WILDLIFE GARDEN, SW7**
Cromwell Road. SW7 5BD, 020 7942 5011, www.nhm.ac.uk/garden. *Tube: South Kensington, 5 mins walk.* **Adm by donation. Daily 1 Apr to 31 Oct 12-5, other times by arrangement. For NGS: Suns 19 Apr; 5 July (2-5).** Set in the Museum grounds, the Wildlife Garden has provided a lush and tranquil habitat in the heart of London since 1995. It reveals a varied range of British lowland habitats, incl deciduous woodland, meadow and ponds. With over 2000 plant and animal species, it beautifully demonstrates the potential for wildlife conservation in the inner city. Meet the scientists and volunteers and learn more about the wildlife in the garden. Green Flag award winner.

NEW 7A NEW OAK ROAD, N2
N2 8LN. David Dorton. *Tube: East Finchley 15 mins walk. Bus: 263 to Oak Lane. Walk up Oak Lane, turn R into New Oak Rd. Car: turn L into Oak Lane off High Rd, then R into New Oak Rd.* Teas at 66 Abbot Gdns 17 May, wine at garden 23 Aug. **Adm £2.50, chd free. Suns 17 May; 23 Aug (2-5.30). Also open 17 May 66 Abbots Gdns.**
Graduate in landscape architecture, the owner has created a simple design in this young garden. A central path links 2 terraces, dividing 2 beds, planted to contrast and complement. Species are mirrored and mixed to add depth and interest. A real plantlover's space with touches of humour and drama.

5 NEW ROAD, N8
Crouch End N8 8TA. The Misses S & M West, 020 8340 8149. *Bus: W7 Muswell Hill to Finsbury Park or W5, alight Wolsey Rd. New Rd is cul-de-sac. Some parking rear of Health Centre, better parking Middle Lane or Park Rd.* **Visitors welcome by appt.** Traditional country garden 60ft x 24ft in heart of Crouch End, evolved over 50yrs. Small prizewinning front garden adjoins colourful conservatory leading to back garden planted for yr-round interest. Many unusual and borderline tender plants - abutilons, streptocarpus, achimenes, crinum.

Fruit trees, ornamental shrubs and trees, small pond, lawn and productive greenhouse create a delightful experience of cherished nostalgia.

15 NORCOTT ROAD, N16
Stoke Newington N16 7BJ. Amanda & John Welch. *Buses: 67, 73, 76, 106, 149, 243, 393, 476. Clapton & Rectory Rd mainline stns. One way system: by car approach from Brooke Rd which crosses Norcott Rd, garden in S half.* Home-made teas. **Adm £2.50, chd free. Sun 14 June (2-6).** Largish (for Hackney) walled back garden developed by present owners over 30yrs, with pond, long-established fruit trees, abundantly planted with a great variety of herbaceous plants. Front garden recently released from concrete.

Mirrored and mixed to add depth and interest . . . with touches of humour and drama . . .

NORTH HOUSE, SE21
93 Dulwich Village. SE21 7BJ. Vivian Bazalgette & Katharine St John-Brooks. *Dulwich Village next to Oddbins, 8 mins level walk from N Dulwich stn or 10 mins from W Dulwich stn via Belair Park. Bus P4.* Home-made teas. **Adm £2.50, chd free (share to Dulwich Helpline). Sun 14 June (2-6). Also open 14 Frank Dixon Way.**
$2/3$-acre mature garden with lawns, trees, climbing roses and flowerbeds, unusual shape, pleasant borrowed landscape. Gravel at entrance.

94 OAKWOOD ROAD, NW11
Hampstead Garden Suburb NW11 6RN. Michael Franklin, 07836 541383, mikefrank@onetel.com. *In the heart of Hampstead Garden Suburb. Tube: Golders Green. Bus: H2 to Northway.* Home-made teas. **Adm £2.50, chd free. Sun 24 May (2-5.30). Visitors also welcome by appt.**
A fine example of a typical Hampstead

Garden Suburb cottage garden. In beautiful woodland setting, divided into 2 rooms by box hedging. Arch with lawns, an old wisteria, and unusual plants. Herbaceous borders filled with colour and foliage.

28 OLD DEVONSHIRE ROAD, SW12
SW12 9RB. Georgina Ivor, 020 8673 7179, georgina@giamanagement. com. *Tube and mainline: Balham, 5 mins walk.* Cream teas. **Adm £2.50, chd free (share to Trinity Hospice). Sun 21 June (2-5.30). Evening Opening £3.50, Pimm's or Prosecco, Wed 24 June (6-8.30). Also open 21 June 2 Western Lane. Visitors also welcome by appt.**
Drought-tolerant plants thrive in the sun-drenched front garden. A pear tree dominates the secluded 45ft x 20ft rear garden, with curving lawn surrounded by planting for yr-round interest. A eucalyptus tree, Rosa 'Rambling Rector' and strawberry tree (Arbutus unedo) add height, while a balustraded wooden balcony creates another level for herbs and tender climbers. Featured in 'Wandsworth Borough News'.

Allotments

OLD PALACE LANE ALLOTMENTS
Old Palace Lane, Richmond TW1 1PG. Old Palace Lane Allotment Group. *Next to White Swan PH, through gate in wall. Mainline and tube: Richmond. Parking on meters in lane or round Richmond Green, or in Old Deer Park car park, entrance on A316 Twickenham Rd.* Home-made teas. **Adm £3, chd free. Sun 5 July (2-5).**
Secret garden in the heart of Richmond. 33 allotments on the site of Old Richmond Palace, squeezed between an ancient wall and a railway viaduct midway between Richmond Green and the river. Some resemble cottage gardens where sunflowers and sweet peas mingle haphazardly with sweetcorn and zucchini, while others sport raised beds, regimented rows of runner beans and gleaming greenhouses. Produce stall.

ORCHARD COTTAGE
See Kent

THE ORCHARD, W4
40a Hazledene Road. W4 3JB.
Vivien Cantor. *10 mins walk from Chiswick mainline & Gunnersbury tube. Close to junction of A4 & Sutton Court Rd, off Fauconberg Rd.* Home-made teas. **Adm £3, chd free. Sun 10 May (2-6).**
Informal, romantic 1/4 -acre garden with mature flowering trees, shrubs and imaginative planting in flowing herbaceous borders. Climbers, water features and fern planting in this ever-evolving garden.

✖ ❀ ☕

Best in early June when pinks and purples predominate in sunny beds, and more delicate displays in woodland . . .

ORMELEY LODGE
Ham Gate Avenue, Richmond TW10 5HB. **Lady Annabel Goldsmith.** *From Richmond Park, exit at Ham Gate into Ham Gate Ave. 1st house on R. From Richmond, A307; after 1 1/2 m, past New Inn on R, at T-lights turn L into Ham Gate Ave.* **Adm £4, chd £1. Sun 21 June (3-6).**
Large walled garden in delightful rural setting on Ham Common. Wide herbaceous borders and box hedges. Walk through to orchard with wild flowers. Vegetable garden, knot garden, aviary. Trellised tennis court with roses and climbers.

♿ ✖ ☕

◆ OSTERLEY PARK AND·HOUSE
Jersey Road, Isleworth TW7 4RB. The National Trust, 020 8232 5050, www.nationaltrust.org.uk. *4m N of Richmond. Tube: Osterley, turn L on leaving station, 1/2 m walk. Access via Thornbury Rd on N side of A4 between Gillette Corner & Osterley tube station. Follow brown tourist signs.* Car Park £3.50. **House & garden £8.40, chd £4.20. Garden only £3.70, chd £1.85. Wed to Sun & Bank Hols 4 Mar-1 Nov 11-5. For NGS: Sun 7 June (11-5).**

Rare C18 garden created by the Child family, owners of Osterley Park House, in 1770s and 1780s. The garden is currently being restored to its former glory following recent research incl the discovery in America of documents showing lists of plants to be purchased for the garden in 1788. Highlights incl the Robert Adam designed Garden House and Mrs Child's Flower Garden. Introductory talks.

♿ ✖ ❀ ☕

3 THE PARK, N6
off Southwood Lane. N6 4EU. **Mr & Mrs G Schrager,** 020 8348 3314, bunty1@blueyonder.co.uk. *3 mins from Highgate tube, up Southwood Lane. The Park is 1st on R.* Buses: 43, 134, 143, 263. Home-made teas. **Adm £2.50, chd free. Sun 17 May (2-5).** Visitors also welcome by appt at any time.
Large garden with pond and frogs, fruit trees and eclectic planting. Interesting plants for sale. Children especially welcome.

✖ ❀ ☕ ☎

10A THE PAVEMENT, SE27
Chapel Road, West Norwood SE27 0UN. **Mr Brendan Byrne,** 020 8761 5651, brendan.byrne@tiscali.co.uk. *Mainline stn: W Norwood, no trains from London Bridge on Suns. Buses: 2, 432, 468 to Knights Hill alight Norwood bus garage. Located off Ladas Rd down alleyway, L coming from Chapel Rd.* **Adm £2, chd free (share to RSPCA). Sun 26 July (10-12 & 2-5).** Visitors also welcome by appt.
Smallest garden in London. A hidden oasis behind houses and shops. Country type of garden, with cottage garden planting, mostly in containers. Shrubs, herbaceous, bedding, rare plants, herbs and some vegetables, continually changing. Of special interest to gardeners with small spaces.

❀ ☎

174 PECKHAM RYE, SE22
SE22 9QA. **Mr & Mrs Ian Bland.** *Stn: Peckham Rye. Overlooks Peckham Rye Common from Dulwich side. Reached by alley to side of house.* Home-made teas. **Adm £2.50, chd free. Sun 7 June (2.30-5.30).** Also open **Centre for Wildlife Gardening.**
100ft x 30ft rear garden originally designed by Judith Sharpe. Easy-care

and child-friendly, the garden is frequently changed but always displays a wide variety of contrasting foliage and yr-round interest. Best in early June when pinks and purples predominate in sunny beds, and more delicate displays in woodland and semi-shade borders.

♿ ✖ ❀ ☕

Group opening

PENN ROAD GARDENS, N7
N7 9RD. *Tube: Caledonian Rd. Turn L out of stn & continue N up Caledonian Rd for approx 700yds. Penn Rd is on L.* Buses: 17, 91, 259 along Caledonian Rd; 29, 253 to nearby Nags Head. Home-made teas at 23 Penn Rd, plants at 2a Penn Rd. **Combined adm £4, £2.50 each garden, chd free. Sun 14 June (2-6).** Also open **1a & 62 Hungerford Rd.**

2a PENN ROAD
Mr & & Mrs P Garvey

23 PENN ROAD
Pierre Delarue & Mark Atkinson

2a PENN ROAD: 100ft x 30ft walled garden; long, shady, side entrance border; small seaside-themed front garden. Huge variety of plants in well stocked borders. Over 60 containers. Greenhouse and small vegetable plot. Mature trees create secluded feel close to busy urban thoroughfares. **23 PENN ROAD:** 75ft x 25ft walled garden, recently redesigned incl garden studio, pond, palms and Mediterranean plants as well as English classics such as ancient fruit trees and roses. An 'overgrown minimalist alpine' front garden and leafy side passage. Plantsman's garden with emphasis on yr-round interest. Partial wheelchair access.

♿ ✖ ❀ ☕

◆ PENSHURST PLACE
See Kent

PETERSHAM HOUSE
Petersham TW10 7AA. **Francesco & Gael Boglione.** *Stn: Richmond, then 65 bus to Dysart PH. Entry to garden off Petersham Rd, through nursery. Parking very limited on Church Lane.* Light refreshments & teas at adjoining nursery. **Adm £3.50, chd free. Sun 7 June (11-4).**

Broad lawn with large topiary, generously planted double borders. Productive vegetable garden with chickens.

NEW PETERSHAM LODGE
River Lane, Richmond TW10 7AG. Princess J C Loewenstein. *Stn: Richmond, then Bus 65 to Dysart PH.* **Adm £3, chd free. Mon 4 May (11-4).** 3½-acre garden around the Georgian House, with formal borders and a knot garden with *Rosa banksiae* covering the SW facade. Numerous paths lead to semi-formal areas: small lake with Chinese bridge, temple, bluebell glade and large specimen trees. Also potager and vegetable garden.

Group opening

RAILWAY COTTAGES, N22
Alexandra Palace N22 7SL. *Tube: Wood Green, 10 mins walk. Stn: Alexandra Palace, 3 mins. Buses: W3, 184, 3 mins. Free parking in Bridge Rd, Buckingham Rd, Palace Gates Rd, Station Rd, Dorset Rd.* Home-made teas at 2 Dorset Rd. **Combined adm £3.50, chd free. Sun 5 July (2-5.30).**

15 BRIDGE ROAD
Sherry Zeffert

2 DORSET ROAD
Jane Stevens

14 DORSET ROAD
Cathy Brogan

22 DORSET ROAD
Mike & Noreen Ainger

Two front gardens of a row of railway cottages and two railway cottage back gardens. The two front gardens at 14 & **22 DORSET ROAD** show a variety of interesting planting, incl aromatic shrubs and herbs, jasmine, flax, fig, fuchsia, vines and a climbing rose, with an emphasis on sustainability and organic methods. The tranquil country-style back garden at **2 DORSET ROAD** is full of interest. Topiary and clipped box contrasts with climbing roses, jasmine and honeysuckle. Long mixed hedge and pond. Mulberry, quince, fig and apple trees and annuals chosen for scent and colour. **15 BRIDGE ROAD** (featured in 'The

English Garden') demonstrates a magical transformation from railway cottage backyard to plant lover's secluded courtyard garden. Densely planted borders, a profusion of perennials, over 40 climbers and large collection of species clematis, specimen camellias, bamboos, grasses, ferns, evergreen irises and figs. Plant list available. Steep steps, unsuitable for small children or elderly.

---

13 REDBRIDGE LANE WEST, E11
E11 2JX. Kathy Taylor, www.kathytaylordesigns.co.uk/cs_myowngarden.htm. *2 mins drive from Redbridge roundabout at N Circular/A12/M11 junction (off M11 link road towards Leytonstone). Tube: Wanstead, 5 mins walk.* Light refreshments. **Adm £3, chd free. Sun 12 July (2-6).** Small 2-roomed, S-facing garden, 14m x 6.5m, with gravel, decking, tiny lawn and raised beds. Many features of interest incl formal wildlife pond and bog garden, ceramic tile wall water feature, and pebble mosaics. Planting for yr-round interest and for sunny and shady aspects. Photography exhibition. Featured in RHS 'The Garden'. Deep pond.

REDWING, W3
69 Mill Hill Road, Acton W3 8JF. Mr & Mrs M Temple, 020 8993 6514, malcolm.temple@hotmail.co.uk. *Tube: Acton Town, turn R, Mill Hill Rd 3rd on R.* Open with **Mill Hill Gardens** Sun 12 July. Visitors also welcome by appt. Secluded, contemplative wildlife-friendly garden containing many young and mature trees. An artist-designed haven meandering from reclaimed brick patio past deep pond, native flower sculpture mound to 'Lavender Halt' pavilion and potting shed.

REGENTS COLLEGE'S GARDEN, NW1
Inner Circle, Regents Park. NW1 4NS. *Tube: Regents Park or Baker St, 5 mins walk over York Bridge & garden is L at junction with the Inner Circle. Buses: 13, 18, 27, 30, 74, 82, 113, 139, 159, 274.* Light refreshments & teas. **Adm £3, chd free. Sats, Suns 20, 21 June; 15, 16 Aug (12-5). Also**

open **The Holme (all dates) & The Royal College of Physicians 21 June.** Thought to contain the largest plane tree in London, and covering 11 acres in the heart of Regents Park, the garden has many reminders of its historic past as a botany garden (now the Secret Garden). There's a subtropical rockery with 'folly' thought to be an old ice house, and Moroccan tea garden. The extensive lawns, herbaceous borders full of unusual plants, and woody glades make it ideal for a family outing.

An artist-designed haven meandering from reclaimed brick patio to 'Lavender Halt' pavilion and potting shed . . .

Group opening

RICHMOND RIVERSIDE
Friars Lane, Richmond TW9 1NR, 020 8940 3894/020 8948 0288, christina gascoigne.com/maklouf@btinternet.com. *Tube & mainline stn: Richmond, then 5 mins walk via Richmond Green, on Friars Lane 50yds from river, just beyond car park.* **Combined adm £4.50, chd free. Evening Opening** wine, Sat 6 June (6-8). Visitors also welcome by appt, May to July only.

1 ST HELENA TERRACE
Christina Gascoigne
(☎ 020 8940 3894)

3 ST HELENA TERRACE
Raphael & Marillyn Maklouf
(☎ 020 8948 0288
maklouf@btinternet.com))

Two small secret gardens both with artist's studios, one a walled garden with water, the other showing original use of limited space with pots, plants, roses and climbing plants in abundance. Some wheelchair access. Both gardens welcome visitors from May to July.

20 ROLLSCOURT AVENUE, SE24

Herne Hill SE24 0EA. Ms Clare Checkland. *Stns: North Dulwich or Herne Hill, then less than 10 mins walk. Buses: 68 to end of road or 3, 37, 196, 322 to Herne Hill stn.* Home-made teas. **Adm £2.50, chd free. Sun 31 May (2-5).** Also open **35 Camberwell Grove & South London Botanical Institute.** Woodland garden, 90ft x 15ft, divided up with circular lawns and meandering paths with clever use of willow panels and open fencing to create an illusion of width. Ornamental trees incl Prunus *maakii*, multi-stemmed Betula *albosinensis* and magnolia are underplanted with ferns, euphorbia and Thalictrum *aquifolium*. Small vegetable /herb garden, scuptural bench and formal circular pool with fish pond.

NEW 12 ROOKFIELD AVENUE, N10

Muswell Hill N10 3TS. Andrew Barr & Joanna Ryan, 020 8245 3674. *Bottom of Muswell Hill. Tube: Highgate, 1m lovely walk through Queen's Wood. Bus: W7 from Finsbury Park stn or Muswell Hill Broadway to top of Park Rd, then walk up Etheldene Ave.* Home-made teas. **Adm £2.50, chd free. Sun 9 Aug (2-5).** Also open **Alexandra Park Gardens.** Visitors also welcome by appt, June for old roses, Sept/Oct for late flowering perennials.
Naturalistic cottage garden to complement our 1910 Arts and Crafts cottage, enclosing it on 3 levels, within a rural estate. Almost entirely replanted since purchase in 2005, following organic principles, with focus on perennials and native flora and fauna. Substantial (for London) and supposedly colour-themed herbaceous border, peaking in late summer. Many perennials propagated for sale.

◆ ROOTS AND SHOOTS, SE11

Walnut Tree Walk. SE11 6DN. Trustees of Roots and Shoots, 020 7587 1131, www.rootsandshoots.org.uk. *Tube: Lambeth North. Buses: 3, 59,159. Just S of Waterloo Stn, off Kennington Rd, 5 mins from Imperial War Museum. No car parking on site. Pedestrian entrance through small open space on Fitzalan St.* **Adm £2, chd free. Mon to Fri (10-4), not Aug. Please phone or visit website to be sure.** For NGS: **Sat 6 June & Children's Day Sun 7 June (11-4).**
$1/2$-acre wildlife garden run by innovative charity providing training and garden advice. Summer meadow, observation beehives, 2 large ponds, hot borders, Mediterranean mound, old roses and echiums. Learning centre with photovoltaic roof, solar heating, rainwater catchment, three planted roofs, one brown roof. Study room for wildlife garden. Displays of children's art and other work and exhibits from wildlife garden. Information on urban biodiversity. Children's Day on Sun 7 June with storytelling and other special activities. Limited wheelchair access, assistance available if needed.

ROYAL COLLEGE OF PHYSICIANS GARDEN, NW1

11 St Andrew's Place, Outer Circle, SE corner of Regents Park NW1 4LE. Royal College of Physicians of London, www.rcplondon.ac.uk/garden. *Tube: Great Portland St, turn L along Marylebone Rd for 100yds, R to Outer Circle, 150yds on R.* Light refreshments & teas. **Adm £3, chd free. Sun 21 June (10-5).** Also open **The Holme & Regents College Garden.**
Garden replanted between 2005 and 2007 to display plants used in conventional and herbal medicines around the world and in past centuries, and plants with historical links to physicians associated with the College. The plants are labelled and arranged by continent. Tours of the garden with explanations about the medicinal uses of the plants.

90 ST GEORGE'S AVENUE, N7

Tufnell Park N7 0AH. Ms J Chamberlain & Mr R Hamilton. *Tube: Tufnell Park, or bus 4 to Tufnell Park Rd, alight Dalmeny Rd.* **Adm £2, chd free. Sun 10 May (2-6).**
Long rear garden created 9yrs ago with trees and shrubs providing structure and yr-round interest, incl acers, Pittosporum tobira, Choisya ternata, clematis-covered pergola and two areas of lawn. Passage at side of house contains many evergreen sbrubs and hostas in pots. The front garden has won many certificates of merit and contains mostly drought-tolerant, silver-leaved Mediterranean plants set around an octagonal central bed with Magnolia stellata.

7 ST GEORGE'S ROAD

St Margarets, Twickenham TW1 1QS. Richard & Jenny Raworth, 020 8892 3713, jenny@jraworth.freeserve.co.uk, www.raworthgarden.com. *1½ m SW of Richmond. Off A316 between Twickenham Bridge & St Margarets roundabout.* Home-made teas. **Adm £3.50, chd 50p. Sun 7 June (11-5). Evening Opening £4.50, chd 50p, wine, Sat 20 June (6-8). Visitors also welcome by appt May to July for groups of 12+.**
Exuberant displays of old English roses and vigorous climbers with unusual herbaceous perennials. Massed scented crambe cordifolia. Pond with bridge converted into child-safe lush bog garden. Large N-facing luxuriant conservatory with rare plants and climbers. Pelargoniums a speciality. Sunken garden and knot garden. Featured in 'GGG' & 'Period Living'.

27 ST JAMES AVENUE, W13

Ealing W13 9DL. Andrew & Julie Brixey-Williams. *Uxbridge Rd (A206) to West Ealing; Leeland Terrace leads to St James Ave.* Home-made teas. **Adm £3, chd free. Sun 21 June (2-5).**
Small (60ft x 20ft) exotic garden, full of exuberant and dense planting, designed by Jason Payne. On several levels, the garden is dissected by a full-width butterfly-shaped pond, with a stone bridge leading to a mini-jungle. Featured in 'Ideal Home' magazine.

Substantial (for London) and supposedly colour-themed herbaceous border, peaking in late summer . . .

ST MICHAEL'S CONVENT
56 Ham Common, Richmond TW10 7JH. Community of the Sisters of the Church. *2m S of Richmond. From Richmond or Kingston, A307, turn onto the common at the Xrds nr New Inn, 100yds on the R adjacent to Martingales Close. Mainline trains to Richmond & Kingston also tube to Richmond, then bus 65 from either to Ham Common.* Home-made teas. **Adm £3, chd free.** Sun 26 Apr (2-5).
4-acre organic garden comprises walled vegetable garden, orchards, vine house, ancient mulberry tree, extensive borders, meditation and Bible gardens. Spring blossom and bulbs a feature.

57 ST QUINTIN AVENUE, W10
W10 6NZ. Mr H Groffman, 020 8969 8292. *1m from Ladbroke Grove or White City tube. Buses: 7, 70 from Ladbroke Grove stn; 220 from White City, all to North Pole Rd.* Home-made teas. **Adm £2.50, chd free.** Suns 12, 26 July (2-6.30). **Also open 26 July 29 Addison Ave.** Visitors also welcome by appt in July only.
30ft x 40ft walled garden; wide selection of plant material incl evergreen and deciduous shrubs for foliage effects. Patio area mainly furnished with bedding material, colour themed, incl topical carpet bedding display. Special features and focal points throughout. Refurbished with new plantings and special features. Celebrating the 250th Anniversary of Royal Botanic Gardens, Kew, with photographic memories of a long-serving member of gardens staff: a unique Kew experience. Silver Medal for back garden in London Garden Society Competition, First prizes for front and back gardens in Brighter Kensington & Chelsea Competition. Steps from house to patio, assistance available.

5 ST REGIS CLOSE, N10
Alexandra Park Road. N10 2DE. Ms S Bennett & Mr E Hyde, 020 8883 8540, suebearlh@yahoo.co.uk. *2nd L in Alexandra Park Rd from Colney Hatch Lane. Tube: Bounds Green or E Finchley then bus 102 or 299. Alight at St Andrew's Church on Windermere Rd. Bus: 43 or 134 to Alexandra Park Rd.* Home-made teas. **Adm £3, chd free.** Suns 3 May; 28 June; 26 July (2-7). **Also open 3 May 16 Cecil Rd, 28 June 5 Cecil Rd.** Visitors also

welcome by appt May to Oct, incl coach parties.
A cornucopia of sensual delights! Artists' garden renowned for unique architectural features and delicious cakes. Baroque temple, pagodas, oriental raku-tiled mirrored wall conceals plant nursery. Compost heap with medieval pretensions alongside American Gothic shed. Maureen Lipman's favourite garden, combining colour, humour and trompe l'oeil with wildlife-friendly ponds, waterfalls, weeping willow and lawns. Imaginative container planting and abundant borders incl exotic and native species, creating an inspirational and re-energising experience. Open ceramics studio. Featured in 'The Times' magazine.

22 SCUTARI ROAD, SE22
East Dulwich SE22 0NN. Sue Hillwood-Harris & David Hardy. *S side of Peckham Rye Park. B238 Peckham Rye/Forest Hill Rd, turn into Colyton Rd (opp Herne Tavern). 3rd on R. Bus: 63. Stn: East Dulwich.* Home-made teas. **Adm £2.50, chd free.** Sun 17 May (2-6). **Also open Stoney Hill House.**
Our pretty garden, created from astoundingly boring scratch 5yrs ago, is still work in progress, but has cottagey area, water, trees and lots of attractive shrubs. Plus palatially-housed chickens (eggs on sale for NGS funds, subject to the whim of the hens). Tea and cakes of memorable standard.

🆕 97 SOUTH CROXTED ROAD, SE21
West Dulwich SE21 8BA. Katy Bowyer. *Stns: mid-way between West Dulwich and Gipsy Hill. Bus: 3 (stops in rd). Close to junction with Church Approach.* Home-made teas. **Adm £2.50, chd free.** Sun 31 May (2.30-5).
Pretty country-style family garden 80ft x 26ft with herbaceous borders for sun and shade. Lawn divided by screen of roses, clematis and honeysuckle which then scramble through conifer, providing yr-round colour, scent and privacy. Secluded seating area, climbing plants, ferns, bamboos and patio with small raised pond.

A high deck in the trees looks over the main area of lawn, water, patio and pots . . .

SOUTH LONDON BOTANICAL INSTITUTE, SE24
323 Norwood Road. SE24 9AQ, www.slbi.org.uk. *Mainline stn: Tulse Hill. Buses: 68, 196, 322 & 468 stop at junction of Norwood & Romola Rds.* Home-made teas. **Adm £2, chd free** (share to SLBI). Sun 31 May (2-5). **Also open 20 Rollscourt Avenue.**
London's smallest botanic garden, formally laid out with paved paths. Densely planted with over 500 labelled species and many rare and interesting plants of worldwide origin incl medicinal, carnivorous, British plants and ferns. Featured in 'Country Life'.

🆕 123 SOUTH PARK ROAD, SW19
Wimbledon SW19 8RX. Susan Adcock. *Mainline & tube: Wimbledon, 10 mins; S Wimbledon tube 5 mins. Buses: 57, 93, 131, 219 along High St. Entrance in Bridges Rd (next to church hall) off South Park Rd.* Light refreshments. **Adm £2.50, chd free.** Sun 14 June (2-6).
A high deck in the trees looks over the main area of lawn, water, patio and pots. This small, harmonious L-shaped garden contains a courtyard with raised vegetable beds and pergola, and a hot tub!

41 SOUTHBROOK ROAD, SE12
Lee SE12 8LJ. Barbara & Marek Polanski. *Off Sth Circular at Burnt Ash Rd. Mainline stns: Lee & Hither Green, both 10 mins walk.* Home-made teas. **Adm £2.50, chd free.** Sun 7 June (2-5).
Large suburban garden in rural setting. Formal paving and pond to the rear divided from the main garden by a parterre with climbing roses and arbours. Large lawn with deep herbaceous borders. Sunny terrace close to house.

SOUTHSIDE HOUSE, SW19
3-4 Woodhayes Road, Wimbledon Common SW19 4RJ. Pennington Mellor Munthe Charity Trust, www.southsidehouse.com. *1m W of Wimbledon Village. House at junction of Cannizaro, Southside and Woodhayes Rds.* Cream teas. **Adm £2.50 (garden only), chd free.** Suns 26 Apr; 10 May (11-5).
Romantic country garden extending to almost 2 acres. Mature trees and hedges and a long informal canal form the structure of this unique and amusing garden. 2 grottos, 2 temples, pet cemetery, young orchard and wild flower meadow. Many of the smaller plantings are being gradually renovated. Lovely swathes of bluebells and small fernery. House open for guided tours Sats, Suns, Weds, from Easter Sat to 30 Sept. Closed Wimbledon tennis fortnight.

SOUTHWOOD LODGE, N6
33 Kingsley Place. N6 5EA. Mr & Mrs C Whittington, 020 8348 2785, suewhittington@hotmail.co.uk. *Tube: Highgate, 4 mins walk Highgate Village. Off Southwood Lane. Buses: 143, 210, 214, 271.* Home-made teas. **Adm £2.50, chd free.** Sun 3 May (2-5.30). Visitors also welcome by appt Apr to July.
Secret garden hidden behind C18 house (not open), laid out last century on steeply sloping site, now densely planted with wide variety of shrubs, climbers and perennials. Ponds, waterfall, frogs and newts. Many unusual plants are grown and propagated for sale. Toffee hunt for children.

NEW 17 STANHOPE ROAD, E17
E17 9QT. Joanne Westerby, 020 8521 9464, randj.westerby@btinternet.com. *Walthamstow Central mainline/tube, 10 mins walk. Buses: 48, 69, 97, 257, one stop from stn.* **Adm £2.50, chd free.**
Visitors welcome by appt in May and June, min 6 visitors.
Long, secluded garden, 100ft wide tapering from 25ft to 5ft. Small pond, New Zealand plants.

2 STANLEY ROAD, N2
East Finchley N2 0NB. Tudor & Hilary Spencer, 020 8883 7301, tudorspencer@hotmail.com. *Tube: East Finchley, then 10 mins walk. Bus: 143, or any bus to High Rd, then 5 mins walk.* Home-made teas. **Adm £2, chd free.** Sun 7 June (2-6). Also open **East Finchley Cottage Gardens.** Visitors also welcome by appt.
Recently transformed front and rear garden of Edwardian semi, with formal 'heron-proof' pond, central circle, and viewing platform. Densely planted to create 8 distinct areas, incorporating colourful vegetable plot, alpine bed, ferns and tree fern, bamboos and perennials. Boundaries softened with varied climbers for scent and foliage. Designed to be completely wheelchair-friendly without aesthetic compromise in hard landscape or planting. A garden for yr-round enjoyment.

Many unusual plants are grown and propagated for sale. Toffee hunt for children . . .

STONE (ZEN) GARDEN, W3
55 Carbery Avenue, Acton W3 9AB. Three Wheels Buddhist Centre, www.threewheels.org.uk. *Tube: Acton Town 5 mins walk, 200yds off A406.* **Adm £2, chd free.** Sat 16, Sun 17 May (2-5.30).
Pure Japanese Zen garden (so no flowers) with twelve large and small rocks of various colours and textures set in islands of moss and surrounded by a sea of grey granite gravel raked in a stylised wave pattern. Garden surrounded by trees and bushes

outside a cob wall. Oak-framed wattle and daub shelter with Norfolk reed thatched roof. Japanese Tea Ceremony demonstrations and talks by designer/creator of the garden. Buddha Room open to visitors.

NEW STONEY HILL HOUSE, SE26
Rock Hill. SE26 6SW. Cinzia & Adam Greaves. *Stn: Sydenham Hill, steep climb, exits in Rock Hill. Buses: to Crystal Palace or 363 along Sydenham Hill, house at end of cul-de-sac on L.* Home-made teas. **Adm £3, chd free.** Sun 17 May (2-5). Also open **22 Scutari Rd.**
Mature garden/woodland of approx 1 acre. Trees and shrubs incl oak, eucryphia, amelanchier, magnolia, azaleas and beech. Secluded green oasis in an urban setting, with lawns, terrace and mature climbers around house and some modern sculptures.

4 STRADBROKE GROVE
Buckhurst Hill IG9 5PD. Mr & Mrs T Brighten, 020 8505 2716, carol@cbrighten.fsnet.co.uk. *Between Epping & Woodford, 5m from M25 J26. Tube: Buckhurst Hill, turn R cross rd to Stradbroke Grove.* Home-made teas. **Adm £2.** Sun 14 June (2-5). Visitors also welcome by appt, June only.
Secluded garden, designed to enhance its strong sloping aspect. Central gravelled bed with grasses, shells, pots and succulents. Rose-screened vegetable and fruit garden complete with banana plant. Large lawn with good herbaceous borders.

99 STRADELLA ROAD, SE24
SE24 9HL. Chris & Ted Barry. *Off Herne Hill end of Half Moon Lane. Mainline stns: Herne Hill 5 mins walk, N Dulwich 10 mins walk. Buses: 3, 37, 68, 196, 468, P4.* Home-made teas. **Adm £2.50, chd free.** Sun 21 June (2-5). Also open **5 Burbage Road.**
40ft x 100ft plantsman's garden backed by Victorian railway viaduct with emphasis on structural plants which reflect the owners' New Zealand origins.

NEW SYDENHAM GARDEN, SE23

Holland Drive. SE23 2QJ.
Trustees of Sydenham Garden,
www.sydenhamgarden.org.uk.
*Off Queenswood Rd (free
parking), no parking in Holland
Drive, garden entrance signed.
Buses: 75, 202.* **Adm £3, chd
free. Sun 5 July (2-5).**
¾-acre garden and nature
reserve managed by community-
based charity, offering gardening
and art activities to local people
coping with serious illness and
mental ill health. Vegetable and
fruit raised beds, newly-restored
Victorian-style greenhouse, nature
reserve, pond, bird hide, borders.
Art and craft exhibition by co-
workers. Featured in RHS 'The
Garden' and local press.

NEW 15A SYDENHAM HILL, SE26

SE26 6SH. Mrs Sue Marsh, 020
8670 6017. *Nr Crystal Palace. At
Crystal Palace end of Sydenham
Hill, off mini roundabout on A212.
Stn: Sydenham Hill 10 mins walk.
Buses: to Crystal Palace and 363
along Sydenham Hill.* Home-made
teas. **Adm £3, chd free. Sun 10
May (2-5). Also open 49 Alleyn
Park & 13 Gipsy Hill.** Visitors
also welcome by appt 10 May
to 10 June.
Terraced hillside woodland garden
of over ¼ acre with
rhododendrons, azaleas, camellias,
unusual trees and shrubs and
mixed herbaceous beds. Acer
glade with spring planting. Gravel
garden with gazebo. Secret
courtyard area with pergola and
fountain. Living willow 'fedge'
screening composting area. One
area awaiting development into
stumpery with ferns.

72 TANFIELD AVENUE, NW2

NW2 7RT. Mr Orod Ohanians, 07887
853090, oohanians@yahoo.co.uk.
Tube: Neasden, then short walk.
Home-made teas & wine. **Adm £2.50,
chd free. Suns 19 Apr; 12 July (1-6).
Also open 12 July 121 Anson Rd.**
Visitors also welcome by appt.
Garden designed to be a 'mini
botanical garden', packed with many
exotic plants from China, New
Zealand, Australia, Chile, central
America, Middle East, Mediterranean,

S Africa and Britain. Plants carefully
chosen to survive, with a bit of care, in
the British climate and complemented
by rocks, pond, waterfall and bog
garden. Over 400 species of plants.

Group opening

TEWKESBURY LODGE GARDEN GROUP, SE23

Forest Hill SE23 3DE. *Off S Circular
(A205) behind Horniman Museum &
Gardens. Stn: Forest Hill, 10 mins
walk. Buses: 176, 185, 312, P4.*
Home-made teas at 53 Ringmore Rise.
**Combined adm £4.50, chd free. Sun
24 May (2-6). Evening Opening £6,
chd free, wine, Sat 23 May (6-9).**

THE COACH HOUSE
3 The Hermitage. Pat Rae

27 HORNIMAN DRIVE
Rose Agnew

53 RINGMORE RISE
Valerie Ward

30 WESTWOOD PARK
Jackie McLaren

A group of very different gardens with
spectacular views over London and
the N Downs. At **THE COACH
HOUSE** discover a sculptor's mature
courtyard and roof garden, crammed
full of unusual plants and sculptures.
Water features, wildlife interest,
vegetables and decorative plants in
containers large and small, many of
which have been fired in the artist's
kiln. Art, sculpture and plants are for
sale. **27 HORNIMAN DRIVE** has a
small, low maintenance, N-facing front
garden with shrubs creating tapestry of
green and a back garden with
emphasis on colour harmony.
Vegetable areas, greenhouse.
53 RINGMORE RISE occupies a
corner plot with a front garden inspired
by Beth Chatto's dry garden, with
stunning borders in soft mauves,
yellows and white. The rear garden is
on three levels. Large pond, patio with
pergola. **30 WESTWOOD PARK**
(featured in 'The English Garden',
'Gardeners' World' magazine, 'Homes
& Gardens' & 'Amateur Gardening') is
a garden designer's sloping creation
with herb garden, water features,
winding paths with modern elements
and unusual plant combinations.
Unusual pots and hanging baskets link
the patio and garden. Steep slopes,
regret no pushchairs.

NEW TRUMPETERS' HOUSE

Old Palace Yard, Richmond
TW9 1PD. Mrs Pamela Franklyn
and Baron & Baroness van
Dedem. *Just off Richmond
Green, 5 mins from stn.* Home-
made teas. **Adm £5, chd free.
Sun 14 June (2-5).**
Trumpeters' House is a 3-acre
garden situated between
Richmond Green and the R
Thames, surrounded by beautiful
mature trees with woodland
planting. The formal garden is
symmetrically laid out in sections
edged with box, with different
colour planting which incl iris,
peonies and roses. Potager,
croquet lawn and large pond. The
late Sarah Franklyn's garden was
planted in 1996 as a drought-
resistant garden, with various
eucalyptus, eleagnus, abutilons
and many greens contrasting with
drifts of Californian poppies and
aquilegia. Aviary with white doves
and C18 gazebo.

Eucalyptus, eleagnus, abutilons and many greens contrasting with drifts of poppies and aquilegia . . .

NEW 5 TURNER DRIVE, NW11

Hampstead Garden Suburb
NW11 6TX. Wendy & Peter
Phillips. *1m N of Golders Green.
Tube: Golders Green, H2 bus to
Turner Close or Meadway Close.*
Home-made teas. **Adm £2.50,
chd free (combined adm with
5 Heathgate £4). Sun 31 May
(2-6).**
Romantic Suburb garden backing
onto Hampstead Heath. Wide
paved terrace leads to pergola
walk with a wisteria and jasmine
arbour. Mature cercis and acacia.
Well stocked borders with azalea
and rhododendrons all set in a
beautiful tree-scape.

NEW 17 VALLEY VIEW GARDENS

Kenley CR8 5BR. Mr & Mrs Tassera. *2m S of Purley on A22 Eastbourne Rd. Parking for 500yds on either side of A22 in bays provided and on pavement. House below A22 behind hedges. Ignore final L or R turn on Sat Nav as restricted access.* **Adm £2.50, chd free. Sun 21 June (2-5).** Eclectic mix of plants and recycled materials are cleverly combined to make this multi-levelled plot as much a theatrical piece as a garden. Drama and humour abound in equal measure in this long, narrow garden.

NEW 21A WALDEGRAVE ROAD, SE19

SE19 2AL. Suzie Gibbons, suzie@flowerpowerpictures.com. *Off Anerley Rd, 1min from Crystal Palace mainline stn. Turn L outside stn then L onto Anerley Rd, next R.* **Adm £3.50. Evening Opening,** wine, Fri 4 Sept (6.30-8.30). **Visitors also welcome by appt June to Sept for groups of 10+.** Urban roof terrace, 60ft x 30ft, with Mary Poppins views, central rusty water feature and sedum roof. Simply planted with trees, grasses and verbena bonariensis. A calm oasis in the sky. Access via 2 flights of stairs, regret not suitable for children.

208 WALM LANE, THE GARDEN FLAT, NW2

NW2 3BP. Miranda & Chris Mason, www.thegardennw2.co.uk. *Tube: Kilburn. Garden at junction of Exeter Rd & Walm Lane. Buses: 16, 32, 189, 226, 245, 260, 266, 316 to Cricklewood Broadway, then consult A-Z.* Home-made teas, light refreshments & wine. **Adm £2.50, chd free. Day & Evening Opening** Sun 7 June (2-8). **Also open 10 Hoveden Rd** (2-6) & **64 Blenheim Gardens** (2-5). Large S-facing oasis of green with big sky. Meandering lawn with island beds, fishpond with fountain, curved and deeply planted borders of perennials and flowering shrubs. Shaded mini woodland area of tall trees underplanted with rhododendrons, ferns and hostas with winding path

from oriental-inspired summerhouse to secluded circular seating area. Music, plant sale & raffle prizes.

WALTHAM FOREST REGISTER OFFICE, E17

106 Grove Road, Walthamstow E17 9BY. Garden Curator, Teresa Farnham, 07761 476651, farnhamz@yahoo.co.uk. *On corner of Grove Rd & Fraser Rd. Bus to Lea Bridge Rd, Bakers Arms & 5 mins walk up Fraser Rd. Separate gates to front and rear garden.* Light refreshments & home-made teas. **Adm £1.50, chd free. Mon 4 May (12-4). Visitors also welcome by appt.** Front and rear gardens of former Victorian vicarage in Walthamstow, created using cuttings as well as plants from seed to survive drought and shallow soil, and plants that look after themselves until they are pruned! Walkway, planted with roses and passion flowers, leads to honeysuckle and clematis arbour. Mixed borders, oak and Judas tree. Low maintenance ideas for yr-round cover. Chemical-free. Hedgehogs, frogs and many bird species. Quiet area for contemplation with wild and native flowers. Book & plant sale. Advice on taking cuttings.

Urban roof terrace, 60ft x 30ft, with Mary Poppins views . . .

NEW 55 WARHAM ROAD

South Croydon CR2 6LH. Shanthee Siva. *Off A23, S of central Croydon. Mainline stn: S Croydon, or E Croydon then buses 119, 405, 455.* Home-made teas. **Adm £2.50, chd free. Sun 9 Aug (2-5). Also open Elm Tree Cottage.** Large suburban garden with wide lawn edged by sweeping borders. Planted for maximum colour with wide variety of plants, surrounded by mature trees and shrubs interspersed with some semi-tropical planting.

THE WATERGARDENS

Warren Road, Kingston-upon-Thames KT2 7LF. The Residents' Association. *1m E of Kingston. From Kingston take A308 (Kingston Hill) towards London; after about 1/2 m turn R into Warren Rd.* **Adm £3, chd £1. Suns 3 May; 18 Oct (2-4.30).** Japanese landscaped garden originally part of Coombe Wood Nursery, planted by the Veitch family in the 1860s. Approx 9 acres with ponds, streams and waterfalls. Many rare trees which, in spring and autumn, provide stunning colour. For the tree-lover this is a must-see garden. Gardens attractive to wildlife. Some steep slopes and steps.

31 WEST PARK ROAD

TW9 4DA. Anna Anderson. *By Kew Gardens Stn, on E side of railway line.* **Adm £2.50, chd free. Sun 17 May (2-6).** Modern botanical garden with an oriental twist. Emphasis on foliage and an eclectic mix of plants, reflecting pool and rotating willow screens which provide varying views or privacy. Dry bed, shady beds, mature trees and a private paved dining area with dappled light and shade.

2 WESTERN LANE, SW12

SW12 8JS. Mrs Anne Birnhak, annebirnhak@castlebalham.fsnet.co.uk, or apply in writing. *Tube: Clapham South or Balham. Wandsworth Common mainline stn. Please park in Nightingale Lane.* **Adm £3. Suns 10 May; 21 June; 19 July (3-4.30). Also open 21 June 28 Old Devonshire Rd. Visitors also welcome by appt for private groups of 10+.** Sensational, walled, tiny patio garden, 28ft x 22ft. Mature trees and shrubs grow in vast containers. 250 clematis scramble through 2000 species plants. Special features: circular wooden pergola, thundering waterfall, pots stacked in tiers and narrow walkways. An exceptional horticultural 'jungle' of scented flowers and textured plants. Featured in 'Amateur Gardening' and on GMTV. No access for wheelchairs, prams or bicycles.

12 WESTMORELAND ROAD, SW13
SW13 9RY. **Mrs Norman Moore.** *Buses: 33, 72, 209, 283, 419 to the Red Lion from Hammersmith.* **Adm £2.50, chd free (share to Myeloma UK). Sun 7 June (2-6).**
Raised stone terrace planted with choisya, wisteria, jasmine and decorative herbs. Two lower lawns, densely planted borders and pretty gazebo with solanum, golden hop, roses and clematis. Circular lawn with mulberry tree, hydrangeas, ferns and hostas. Charming bower seat and secluded potting area.

WHITTON CRC
1 Britannia Lane, off Constance Road, Whitton TW2 7JX. London Borough of Richmond. *3m W of Richmond. Mainline stn: Whitton. Bus: H22 alight at Whitton stn. No parking in Britannia Lane. Free parking in Constance Rd & surrounding streets.* Home-made teas. **Adm £2, chd free. Wed 3 June (11-3).**
Narrow 180ft organic garden maintained by staff and people with learning disabilities whose day centre occupies the remainder of the site. The cottage-style planting has produced a mass of colour and scent with a lavender and fuchsia bed, mixed borders, butterfly garden, wildlife pond and raised bed of shrubs and roses. Winner Richmond in Bloom.

5 WILDWOOD RISE, NW11
Hampstead Garden Suburb NW11 6TA. **Ms Judy Green.** *Tube: Golders Green, then H2 bus to Wildwood Rd. Off Wildwood Rd, last house on L.* Home-made teas. **Adm £3, chd free. Sun 12 July (2-6).**
Stunningly beautiful garden on the edge of Hampstead Heath. Architectural planting with some interesting clipped trees, especially the 'cloud' bay tree. Good selection of unusual and decorative shrubs and perennials throughout the yr.

86 WILLIFIELD WAY, NW11
Hampstead Garden Suburb NW11 6YJ. **Diane Berger.** *1m N of Golders Green. Tube: Golders Green, then H2 bus to Willifield Way.* Teas (Sun only). **Adm £2.50, chd free. Sun 19 July (2-5.30). Evening Opening £4, chd free, wine, Wed 15 July (6-9). Also open 19 July 157 Hampstead Way.**

Mature trees and hedges frame this 80ft x 50ft award-winning cottage garden, a plantsman's delight, densely planted with interesting perennials, trees and shrubs. Features incl pergola walk draped in roses and clematis leading to secret, shady decked patio; herbaceous and hot borders and terraced pond area.

Contemporary garden designed by Christopher Bradley-Hole. A jigsaw of perennial and grass bays with a range of views offering interest for plantsmen, designers and children . . .

91 WILLIFIELD WAY, NW11
Hampstead Garden Suburb NW11 6YH. **Ms Karen Grant.** *Off Finchley Rd, nr N Circular. Tube: Golders Green. Buses: H2 to Willifield Green or 82, 102, 460 to Temple Fortune.* Home-made teas. **Adm £2.50, chd free. Sun 17 May (2-5).**
Windows and doors are framed by topiaried pyracantha. Re-creation of an Elizabethan knot garden with 4 box-edged beds densely planted for yr-round interest. Dovecote, mosaic floor, sink troughs with alpines and succulents.

27 WOOD VALE, N10
N10 3DJ. **Mr & Mrs A W Dallman.** *Muswell Hill 1m. A1 to Woodman PH; signed Muswell Hill. From Highgate tube, take Muswell Hill Rd, sharp R into Wood Lane leading to Wood Vale.* Home-made teas. **Adm £2.50, chd 50p, under 5 free. Sat 11, Sun 12 July (1.30-6).**

³/₄ -acre garden, 300ft long, abounding with surprises. Herbaceous borders, shrubbery, pond and a new feature every yr. Once inside you would think you were in the countryside. Seating for over 90 people, with shady areas and delicious home-made teas. Every effort is made to make our visitors welcome.

33 WOOD VALE, N10
N10 3DJ. **Mona Abboud, 020 8883 4955, monaabboud@hotmail.com.** *Tube: Highgate, 10 mins walk. Buses: W3, W7 to top of Park Rd.* **Adm £2, chd free. Sun 17 May (2-6). Also open 15 & 46 Dukes Ave.** Visitors also welcome by appt.
Very long garden entered via steep but safe staircase. Unusual trees and Mediterranean shrubs with emphasis on shapes, textures and foliage colour. Garden on two levels, the first more formal with a centrepiece fountain, the second meandering, leading to mixed borders and camomile seat.

82 WOOD VALE, SE23
SE23 3ED. **Nigel & Linda Fisher.** *Off S Circular Rd. Mainline stn: Forest Hill. Buses: 176, 185, 363 & P13. Ample street parking.* Home-made teas. **Adm £3, chd free. Sun 12 July (2-5). Also open 71 Central Hill.**
Large 90ft x 180ft contemporary garden designed by Christopher Bradley-Hole. A jigsaw of perennial and grass bays with a range of views offering yr-round interest for plantsmen, designers and children. Starred garden in 'GGG'.

66 WOODBOURNE AVENUE, SW16
SW16 1UT. **Brian Palmer & Keith Simmonds.** *Enter from Garrads Rd by Tooting Bec Common (by car only).* Cream teas. **Adm £2.50, chd free. Sun 12 July (1-6).**
Garden designer's garden, constantly evolving. Cottage-style front garden 40ft x 60ft containing roses and herbaceous plants with a subtropical twist with bananas and palms. Rear garden approx 40ft x 80ft with recently added features, shrubs, trees and gazebo, creating a tranquil oasis in an urban setting. 14th yr of opening in 2009.

23 WOODVILLE ROAD, W5
Ealing W5 2SE. John & Julia
Argyropoulos,
www.cooltropicalplants.com.
*Tube/mainline: Ealing Broadway, then
approx 200m N. Easy unrestricted
parking in nearby rds.* Home-made
teas. **Adm £3, chd free.** Sun 30 Aug
(2-7).
120ft walled garden featuring a mixture
of stunning tender and hardy exotics.
These magnificent beauties cloak the
garden which encompasses 3 levels
and 2 ponds. Big leaves, giant
grasses, ferns, meat-eaters and spiky
things all come together evoking a
strange and faraway land. Featured in
'The Guardian'.

◆ **THE WORLD GARDEN AT
LULLINGSTONE CASTLE**
See Kent.

**NEW THE WYCH ELM PUBLIC
HOUSE**
93 Elm Road, Kingston-upon-
Thames KT2 6HT. Janet Turnes,
020 8546 3271. *Stn: Kingston,
10min walk. 8min walk Kingston
Gate, Richmond Park.* Teas for
NGS. **Adm £2.50, chd free.** Sun
2 Aug (noon to closing time).
Prize-winning floriferous garden
famed for its brilliant colourful
display from eaves to pavement.
Back garden features pampered
exotic plants creating a
Mediterranean atmosphere. Many
unusual species lovingly tended
by plantaholic licensee. Cool,
shady corner and hot colours on
the terrace. Pergola, festooned
with exotic climbers, protects
banana and other tender plants.
1st prize Fuller, Smith & Turner
Gardens Competition.

Prize-winning floriferous garden
famed for its brilliant colourful display
from eaves to pavement. Many
unusual species lovingly tended by
plantaholic licensee . . .

London County Volunteers

County Organiser
Penny Snell, Moleshill House, The Fairmile, Cobham, Surrey KT11 1BG, 01932 864532, pennysnellflowers@btinternet.com

County Treasurer
Richard Raworth, 7 St George's Road, St Margarets, Twickenham TW1 1QS, 07831 476088, raworth.r@blueyonder.co.uk

Assistant County Organisers
Outer W London Rita Armfield, 45 Tudor Road, Hampton TW12 2NG, 020 8941 3315, rita@tudor45.plus.com
NW London Susan Bennett & Earl Hyde, 5 St Regis Close, Alexandra Park Road, Muswell Hill, London N10 2DE,
    020 8883 8540, suebearlh@yahoo.co.uk
SW London Joey Clover, 13 Fullerton Road, London SW18 1BU, 020 8870 8740, joeyclover@dsl.pipex.com
Hampstead Anne Crawley, 116 Willifield Way, London NW11 6YG, 020 8455 7618, annecrawley@waitrose.com
SE London Gillian Davies, 32 Chestnut Road, London SE27 9LF, 020 8670 8916, cag.davies@btinternet.com
E London Teresa & Stuart Farnham, 17 Greenstone Mews, London E11 2RS, 07761 476651, farnhamz@yahoo.co.uk
Hackney Izi Glover, 15 Albion Drive, London E8 4LX, 020 7683 0104, glover@gayhurst.hackney.sch.uk
SE & Outer London Winkle Haworth, 38 Killieser Avenue, London SW2 4NT, 020 8671 4196, winklehaworth@hotmail.com
Islington Anna McKane, 36 Thornhill Square, London N1 1BE, 020 7609 7811, a.r.mckane@city.ac.uk
W London, Barnes & Chiswick Jenny Raworth, 7 St George's Road, St Margarets, Twickenham TW1 1QS, 020 8892 3713,
    jenny@jraworth.freeserve.co.uk
Highgate, St John's Wood & Holland Park Sue Whittington, Southwood Lodge, 33 Kingsley Place, London N6 5EA,
    020 8348 2785, suewhittington@hotmail.com

Mark your diary with these special events in 2009

EXPLORE SECRET GARDENS DURING CHELSEA & HAMPTON COURT FLOWER SHOW WEEKS

Tue 19 May, Wed 20 May, Thur 21 May, Fri 22 May, Wed 8 July, Thur 9 July
Full day tours from £82 per person, 10% discount for groups
Advance booking required, telephone +44 (0)20 8693 1015 or email j.wookey@btinternet.com
Specially selected gardens in London, Essex, Kent, Hampshire and South Oxfordshire. The tour price includes transport and lunch with wine at a popular restaurant or pub.

HAMPTON COURT PALACE

Thur 2 Apr, Tue 23 June, Thur 25 June, Wed 15 July, Tue 4 Aug, Thur 10 Sept
Evening tours in the company of one of the Palace's specialist tour guides from 6.30 – 8pm
Tickets £6 per person. Advance booking required, telephone +44 (0)1483 211535 or
visit www.ngs.org.uk for more information
Gossip, scandal, murder, healing – you'll find it all within the Formal Gardens at Hampton Court Palace. Each tour will have its own unique feature whether it's the story of the Great Vine or the magic and mystery of the Maze.

FROGMORE – A ROYAL GARDEN (BERKSHIRE)

Tue 26 May 10am – 5.30pm (last admission 4pm)
Garden adm £4.50, chd free. Tickets available in advance or on the day.
Advance booking for groups and coaches, telephone
+44 (0) 1483 211535 or email orders@ngs.org.uk
A rare opportunity to explore 30 acres of landscaped garden, rich in history and beauty.

FLAXBOURNE FARM – FUN & SURPRISES (BEDFORDSHIRE)

Sun 7 June 10am – 5pm. Adm £5, chd free
No booking required, come along on the day!
Bring the whole family and have fun in this surprising and entertaining garden of 2 acres. Enjoy the large plant fair, live music, pets corner, birds of prey, dog agility show and much more.

WISLEY RHS GARDEN – MUSIC IN THE GARDEN (SURREY)

Fri 11 Sept 6 – 9pm
Adm (incl RHS members) £7, chd under 15 free
Save money on advance bookings for groups of 4 or more, telephone +44 (0)1483 211535 or
visit www.ngs.org.uk for more information
A special evening opening of this famous garden, exclusively for the NGS. Enjoy music and entertainment as you explore the gardens and the floral marquee on the first day of the Wisley Flower Show.

For further information visit www.ngs.org.uk or telephone 01483 211535

NORFOLK

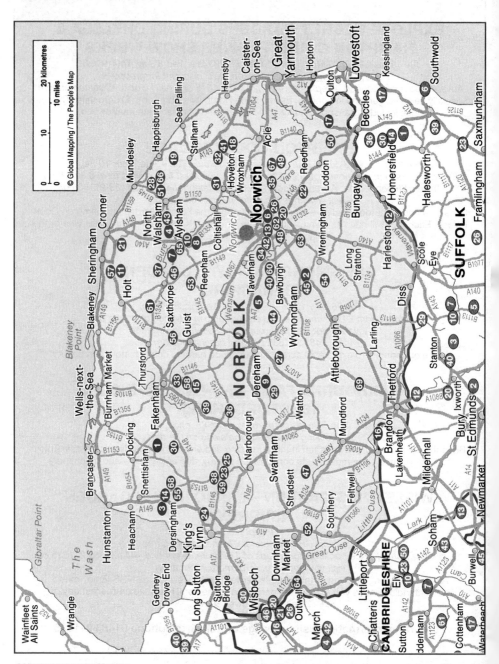

Opening Dates

February

SUNDAY 8
- (1) Bagthorpe Hall
- (36) Lexham Hall

March

SUNDAY 29
- (23) Gayton Hall

April

SUNDAY 5
- (16) Desert World Gardens

SUNDAY 12
- (24) Grasmere
- (69) Wretham Lodge

MONDAY 13
- (24) Grasmere
- (69) Wretham Lodge

SUNDAY 19
- (9) Bradenham Hall
- (59) Spinney Lodge

SATURDAY 25
- (19) East Ruston Old Vicarage

SUNDAY 26
- (14) Croft House

May

SUNDAY 3
- (49) Plovers Hill

MONDAY 4
- (43) The Old Cottage
- (66) Witton Hall

SUNDAY 10
- (10) Burgh House
- (17) Devils End
- (29) Holme Hale Hall
- (37) Mannington Hall
- (51) Rivermount

WEDNESDAY 13
- (36) Lexham Hall

SUNDAY 17
- (10) Burgh House
- (32) How Hill Farm
- (36) Lexham Hall
- (52) Ryston Hall
- (57) Sheringham Park

FRIDAY 22
- (31) Hoveton Hall Gardens

SUNDAY 24
- (8) Bolwick Hall
- (12) Conifer Hill
- (24) Grasmere

MONDAY 25
- (24) Grasmere
- (50) Raveningham Hall

SUNDAY 31
- (15) Derwen
- (41) The Mowle
- (46) Oulton Hall
- (57) Sheringham Park
- (58) 'Sol'

June

SUNDAY 7
- (3) 11 Bank Road
- (45) Old Sun House
- (54) Sallowfield Cottage

SUNDAY 14
- (4) Beck House
- (18) The Dutch House
- (25) Great Barn Farm
- (38) Manor Farmhouse
- (63) Summer Cottage

SATURDAY 20
- (64) 56 Well Creek Road

SUNDAY 21
- (22) The Garden in an Orchard
- (39) Manor House Farm
- (40) 4 Mill Road
- (42) North Lodge
- (47) Oxburgh Hall Garden & Estate
- (60) Spring Grove
- (64) 56 Well Creek Road

SUNDAY 28
- (5) The Birches
- (6) Bishop's House
- (27) High House Gardens

July

SUNDAY 5
- (2) Banhams Barn
- (16) Desert World Gardens
- (30) Houghton Hall Walled Garden
- (43) The Old Cottage
- (44) The Old Rectory
- (62) Strangers Hall

SUNDAY 12
- (13) 7 Connaught Road
- (33) 6 Jarvis Drive
- (42) North Lodge

SATURDAY 18
- (7) Blickling Hall
- (21) Felbrigg Hall

SUNDAY 19
- (4) Beck House
- (47) Oxburgh Hall Garden & Estate
- (49) Plovers Hill
- (65) West Lodge
- (67) Woodland View

SUNDAY 26
- (9) Bradenham Hall
- (53) Salle Park

August

SUNDAY 2
- (29) Holme Hale Hall

SUNDAY 9
- (49) Plovers Hill
- (56) Severals Grange
- (67) Woodland View

SUNDAY 16
- (11) Chestnut Farm
- (20) The Exotic Garden
- (26) Hawthorn House
- (34) Jungle Garden

SUNDAY 30
- (17) Devils End

September

SUNDAY 6
- (31) Hoveton Hall Gardens
- (48) The Plantation Garden

SATURDAY 12
- (22) The Garden in an Orchard

SUNDAY 13
- (22) The Garden in an Orchard

SUNDAY 20
- (27) High House Gardens

WEDNESDAY 23
- (36) Lexham Hall

SUNDAY 27
- (9) Bradenham Hall
- (37) Mannington Hall

October

SATURDAY 3
- (19) East Ruston Old Vicarage

Gardens open to the public

- (7) Blickling Hall
- (9) Bradenham Hall
- (19) East Ruston Old Vicarage
- (20) The Exotic Garden
- (21) Felbrigg Hall
- (30) Houghton Hall Walled Garden
- (31) Hoveton Hall Gardens
- (37) Mannington Hall
- (47) Oxburgh Hall Garden & Estate
- (48) The Plantation Garden
- (50) Raveningham Hall
- (55) Sandringham Gardens
- (56) Severals Grange
- (57) Sheringham Park
- (61) Stody Lodge
- (62) Strangers Hall

By appointment only

- (28) Hill Cottage
- (35) Lake House
- (68) Woodwynd

Also open by appointment ☎

④ Beck House
⑤ The Birches
⑧ Bolwick Hall
⑪ Chestnut Farm
⑭ Croft House
⑯ Desert World Gardens
⑱ The Dutch House
㉓ Gayton Hall
㉙ Holme Hale Hall
㊴ Manor House Farm
㊶ The Mowle
㊸ The Old Cottage
㊺ Oulton Hall
㊾ Plovers Hill
㊴ Sallowfield Cottage
㊽ 56 Well Creek Road
㊿ Woodland View

The Gardens

❶ BAGTHORPE HALL
Bagthorpe PE31 6QY. Mr & Mrs D Morton. 3¹/₂ m N of East Rudham, off A148. At King's Lynn take A148 to Fakenham. At East Rudham (approx 12m) turn L by Cat & Fiddle PH. 3¹/₂ m into hamlet of Bagthorpe. Farm buildings on L, wood on R, white gates set back at top. Home-made teas and soup. **Adm £3.50, chd free. Sun 8 Feb (11-4).**
Snowdrops carpeting woodland walk, snowdrop walk. Homemade organic soups, cakes & tea.
♿ ⊛ ⮕ ☕

❷ NEW BANHAMS BARN
Browick Road, Wymondham NR18 9RB. Mr C Cooper & Mrs J Harden. 1m E of Wymondham. A11 from Attlebrough, exit signed Mulbarton. R at r'about, cross bridge over A11. Immed take farm track on R opp rd signed E Carleton/Ketteringham. A11 from Norwich, exit signed Mulbarton, L at r'about, then as above. Home-made teas. **Adm £3, chd free. Sun 5 July (11-5 last entry 4).**
1-acre lawned garden with all-yr round interest. Specimen trees, parterre, terrace, well stocked borders, large pond and kitchen garden are the main features. In July hemerocallis, roses and extensive herbaceous border are at their best. (Enjoy home-made teas on the walled terrace overlooking the garden).
♿ ⚔ ⊛ ☕

❸ NEW 11 BANK ROAD
Dersingham PE31 6HW. David & Ruth Mountain. 8m NE of King's Lynn A149 N then B1440 into Dersingham. Bank Rd is 3rd L exit (by recreation ground). Home-made teas. **Adm £4, chd free. Sun 7 June (11-4).**
Small ¹/₄ -acre landscaped garden with interesting features. Pond, shrubbery, island beds, rock garden, Mediterranean area, seating. Collection of favourite and unusual plants incl bearded iris, heucheras, hostas, ferns. 6-acre allotment site, reputedly one of the best kept in Norfolk, will be open for viewing, adjacent to the garden.
⊛ ☕

❹ BECK HOUSE
Bridge Road, Colby, nr Aylsham NR11 7EA. Hazel & Tony Blackburn, 01263 733167 (evenings). 14m N of Norwich. Take B1145 from N Walsham to Aylsham, after 3¹/₂ m turn R into Bridge Rd opp Banningham Bridge Old Garage, next to school (Colby). Home-made teas. **Adm £3, chd free. Suns 14 June; 19 July (11-5). Visitors also welcome by appt.**
1¹/₂ acres, packed borders of unusual perennials, shrubs and trees, large natural pond and paths through wild areas with lovely views across the river. S-facing front garden with drought-loving plants; sit and enjoy the tranquil views on the many seats provided. Featured in 'Amateur Gardening'. Gravel drive, assistance given if needed.
♿ ⚔ ⊛ ☕ ☎

❺ NEW THE BIRCHES
Mattishall Road, East Tuddenham, Dereham NR20 3LY. Terry & Viv Eagling, 01603 880668. 8m W of Norwich. Off A47, 1m after Norwich Southern bypass, turn L to E Tuddenham. Garden on R 20yds from village hall & car park, available fr NGS day. Home-made teas & wine. **Adm £3, chd free (share to East Tuddenham Village Hall). Sun 28 June (12-5). Visitors also welcome by appt.**
¹/₂ acre garden. Walled patio dining area with pergola. Archway to herbaceous borders of roses, shrubs and herbs. Pathways to hidden seating areas. Greenhouse, orchard, garden room (serving refreshments). Gateway to 1-acre organic allotment. Complete display of soft fruit and vegetables. Set aside featuring wild grasses, flowers for wildlife nesting. Gravel driveway and grass paths.
♿ ☕ ☎

Set aside featuring wild grasses, flowers for wildlife nesting . . .

❻ BISHOP'S HOUSE
Bishopgate, Norwich NR3 1SB. The Bishop of Norwich. City centre. Entrance opp Law Courts on Bishopgate on N side of Cathedral (not through The Close). Through Archway on R. Public car parking nearby. No parking at Bishop's House. Home-made teas. **Adm £3, chd free. Sun 28 June (2-5).**
4-acre walled garden dating back to C12. Extensive lawns with specimen trees. Borders with many rare and unusual shrubs. Spectacular herbaceous borders flanked by yew hedges. Rose beds, meadow labyrinth, kitchen garden, woodland walk and long border with hostas and bamboo walk. Popular plant sales area. Gravel paths.
♿ ⚔ ⊛ ☕

❼ ◆ BLICKLING HALL
Aylsham NR11 6NF. The National Trust, 01263 738030, www.nationaltrust.org.uk/blickling. 15m N of Norwich. 1¹/₂ m NW of Aylsham on N side of B1354. **House and Garden Adm £9.75, chd £4.85, Garden only Adm £6.50, chd £3.25. Weds to Suns & BH Mons Mar to Oct. For NGS: Sat 18 July (10.15-5.15).**
Large garden, orangery, crescent lake, azaleas, rhododendrons, herbaceous borders. Historic Jacobean house. New wilderness area project taking shape. Special opening of kitchen garden. Gravel path, powered vehicles to loan, adapted toilet facilities.
♿ ⚔ ⊛ ☕

8 BOLWICK HALL
Marsham NR10 5PU. Mr & Mrs G C Fisher, 01263 732131, www.bolwick.com. 1/2 m S of Aylsham. On A140 towards Aylsham, take 1st R past Plough PH at Marsham, then next R onto private rd to front of Hall. Home-made teas. **Adm £3, chd free. Sun 24 May (1-5). Visitors also welcome by appt.**
Landscaped gardens and park, attributed to Humphry Repton, surrounding late Georgian hall (not open) and stable block. Collection of mature trees, woodland walks around stream and mill pond, as well as more recently planted borders and working vegetable garden.
  🚫 🐕 🛏 ☕ ☎ 🏡

9 ◆ BRADENHAM HALL
Bradenham IP25 7QP. Chris & Panda Allhusen, 01362 687243/687279, www.bradenhamhall.co.uk. 6m E of Swaffham. 5m W of East Dereham off A47. Turn S signed Wendling & Longham. 1m turn S signed Bradenham, 2m. **Garden only £4, chd free. 2nd & 4th Suns June to Sept. For NGS: Suns 19 Apr; 26 July; 27 Sept (2.30-5).**
A garden for all seasons. Flower gardens, formally designed and richly planted, formal rose gardens, paved garden, unusual climbers, herbaceous and shrub borders, traditional kitchen gardens with 2 glasshouses. Arboretum of over 800 different trees, all labelled. Massed daffodils in spring. A delight and an education.
  🚫 🐕 ✿ ☕

10 NEW BURGH HOUSE
Burgh Road, Aylsham NR11 6AT. Mr & Mrs R Burr. 11m N of Norwich. Off A140 between Norwich & Cromer, 250 metres E of Aylsham Town Sq. Free public car park in Burgh Rd almost opp the garden entrance. Disabled parking only at Burgh House. Light refreshments & home-made teas. **Adm £3, chd free. Sun 10, 17 May (12-6).**
4 acre mixed deciduous woodland walk. Bluebells, ponds, free range fowl, large rookery. Once part of Aylsham Manor garden; slow project to uncover its history and reclaim paths etc. Home-made pizza lunches (french wood-fired oven) 12-2pm, teas 2-5.
  🐕 ✿ ☕

11 CHESTNUT FARM
West Beckham NR25 6NX. Mr & Mrs John McNeil Wilson, 01263 822241, john@mcneil-wilson.freeserve.co.uk. 2 1/2 m S of Sheringham. Mid-way between Holt & Cromer. 1m S off the A148 at the Sheringham Park entrance. Sign post indicates 'By Rd to W Beckham'. Chestnut Farm located behind the village sign. Lots of free parking, WC. Light refreshments & teas. **Adm £3, chd free. Sun 16 Aug (11-5). Visitors also welcome by appt Feb to Sept. Coaches permitted. Open for groups.**
In August come and enjoy the exuberance of summer, including herbaceous borders, summer flowering trees and shrubs spread over 3 acres. Year round interest. Aconites in January, snowdrops (over 60 varieties) in February, to autumn crocus and colchicums in September followed by winter berries. New plants and ideas are constantly added. 2008 saw extension to woodland, so for 2009 there will be more ferns and ariods. Radio coverage. Local paper. May be difficult following heavy rain.
  🚫 ✿ ☕ ☎

12 NEW CONIFER HILL
Low Road, Starston IP20 9NT. Mr & Mrs Richard Lombe Taylor. 1m NE of Harleston. B1134 from Pulham Xrds. Off A140 or B1134 from Harleston on A143. Home-made teas. **Adm £3.50, chd free. Sun 24 May (11-5).**
The house (1881) with its formalormal terrace of rose beds and lavender is set in mature 3 1/2 acre garden surrounded by woodland, unusual trees and flowering shrubs, fern, stump walk and interesting pinetum in a quarry. Of particular interest is the kitchen garden with double border and contemporary yew roundel with its tactile sculpture.
  🚫 🛏 ☕

13 NEW 7 CONNAUGHT ROAD
Norwich NR2 3BP. Mr & Mrs Peter Salt. 1.2m W of Norwich City centre. Turn L off A1074 (Dereham Rd), 200yds before Bowthorpe Rd, garden on R 50yds up. Buses: 16, 19, 20, 21, 22 stop St Phillips Rd. On-street parking. **Adm £2.50, chd free. Adm £4. Sun 12 July (11-5). Combined with North Lodge.**
Small town-garden bordered by wall and evergreen shrubs, with lush varied planting in cottage garden style. Ornamental and fruit trees. Different areas of paving with planters, of box hedging, punctuated with clipped trees. To the rear a stepped terrace with shade plants, standard hollies and laurels. Conservatory.
  🐕 ☕

14 CROFT HOUSE
111 Manor Road, Dersingham PE31 6YW. Walter & Jane Blaney, 01485 544733. 8m NE of King's Lynn. Take A149 N from King's Lynn then B1440 into Dersingham. At T-lights turn R into Chapel Rd. In 1/2 m bear R into Manor Rd. Croft House opp church car park. Park in adjacent rds & church hall car park. Cream teas in adjacent church hall. **Adm £3, chd free. Sun 26 Apr (1-5). Visitors also welcome by appt.**
In this 2 1/2 -acre garden, adjcent to Sandringham Estate, paths meander through shady woodland containing secluded gardens in clearings, each with its special character and hidden surprises. Lawns punctuated by formal shrub and herbaceous beds, ponds, water features, statuary, and many unusual plants make this a special and memorable garden. Plants for sale supplied by Gold Medal winning nursery.
  🚫 🐕 ✿ ☕

Yew roundel with its tactile sculpture . . .

15 DERWEN
Whissonsett Road, Colkirk NR21 7NL. Alan & Maureen Piggott. 2m S of Fakenham. Between B1146 & A1065 (Colkirk not signed from A1065), follow NGS signs. Home-made teas. **Adm £4, chd free. Sun 31 May (11-5). Combined with Sol.**
Herbaceous borders, shrubs, fruit trees, ponds, gravel garden, vegetable plots, unusual plants and shrubs, lawned areas. 2 greenhouses, chickens. Gravel driveway, some narrow paths.
  🚫 🐕 ✿ ☕

16 DESERT WORLD GARDENS
Santon Downham IP27 0TU. Mr &
Mrs Barry Gayton, 01842 765861.
*4m N of Thetford. On B1107 Brandon
2m.* Light refreshments & teas. **Adm
£3, chd free.** Suns 5 Apr; 5 July (10-
5). **Visitors also welcome by appt.**
1¼ acres plantsman's garden,
specialising in tropical and arid plants,
hardy succulents - sempervivums,
hanging gardens of Babylon
(plectranthus). Main garden - bamboos,
herbaceous primula theatre, spring/
summer bulbs, particularly lilies. Over
70 species and varieties of magnificent
magnolias. View from roof garden.
Radio Cambridge gardener.
Glasshouses cacti/succulents 12500,
viewing by appt only on a different day.
Plant clinic - identifications with
demonstrations on request. Featured
in 'Garden News' Besotted Gardener,
Hardy Plant Society 'Borderline Plants'.
✖ ⊛ ☕ ☎

3½ -acre garden created by the owners set in old orchard . . .

17 DEVILS END
Church Lane, Haddiscoe NR14 6PB.
Peter Manthorpe. *7m SW of Gt
Yarmouth. Nr junction of A143 &
B1136. Park in Haddiscoe Church car
park, accessed from B1136. Short
walk to garden.* Home-made teas in
church. **Adm £3.50, chd free.** Suns
10 May (11-5.30); 30 Aug (1-6).
Romantic, 1-acre enthusiasts garden
laid out on S-facing slope with some
steep steps. Contains parterre, topiary,
woodland walks, pond, potager and
colour-themed borders. Many
interesting plants. Village Church &
Local History Exhibition (Aug only).
Featured in 'The English Garden' &
'Country Life'.
✖ ⊛ ☕

18 THE DUTCH HOUSE
Ludham NR29 5NS. Mrs Peter
Seymour, 01692 678225. *5m W of
Wroxham. B1062 Wroxham to
Ludham 7m. Turn R by Ludham village
church into Staithe Rd. Garden ¼ m
from village.* Home-made teas. **Adm
£3.50, chd free.** Sun 14 June (2-5).
**Visitors also welcome by appt June
only, groups 10+ adm £6, coaches
welcome.**

Long, narrow garden of approx 2½
acres leading through marsh and wood
to Womack Water. Designed and
planted originally by the painter
Edward Seago and recently replanted
by the present owner. Access to
Womack Water limited due to steep
bridge and uneven paths. Further replanting in hand. Wheelchair access
possible but difficult, terrace, cobbles
and steps.
♿ ✖ ☕ ☎

**19 ♦ EAST RUSTON OLD
VICARAGE**
East Ruston NR12 9HN. Alan Gray &
Graham Robeson, 01692 650432,
www.e-ruston-
oldvicaragegardens.co.uk. *3m N of
Stalham. Turn off A149 onto B1159
signed Bacton, Happisburgh. After 2m
turn R 200yds N of East Ruston
Church (ignore sign to East Ruston).*
**Adm £6, chd £1. Weds, Fris, Sats,
Suns & Bank Hol Mons Mar to Oct.**
For NGS: Sats 25 Apr; 3 Oct (2-
5.30).
20-acre exotic coastal garden incl
traditional borders, exotic garden,
desert wash, sunk garden, topiary,
water features, walled and
Mediterranean gardens. Many rare and
unusual plants, stunning plant
combinations, wild flower meadows,
old-fashioned cornfield, vegetable and
cutting gardens.
♿ ✖ ⊛ ☕

EUSTON HALL
See Suffolk.

20 ♦ THE EXOTIC GARDEN
126 Thorpe Road, Thorpe, Norwich
NR1 1UL. Mr Will Giles, 01603
623167, www.exoticgarden.com. *Off
A47. New entrance & car park via side
entrance of Alan Boswell Insurance
126 Thorpe Rd next to DEFRA. Approx
½ m from Thorpe railway stn.* **Adm
£4.50, chd free. Suns 14 June to 25
Oct.** For NGS: Sun 16 Aug (1-5).
Exotic city garden covering approx 1
acre on a S-facing hillside incl new
½ -acre garden. In high summer the
garden is a riot of colour among
towering architectural plants such as
cannas, bananas, aroids, palms etc
giving the garden a truly subtropical
feel, especially with its use of
houseplants as bedding. New
xerophytic garden (desert garden).
Featured in & on various TV
programmes & publications, weekly
column on Exotic Gardens in (EDP).
✖ ⊛ ☕

21 ♦ FELBRIGG HALL
Cromer NR11 8PR. The National
Trust, 01263 837444,
www.nationaltrust.org.uk. *2½ m SW
of Cromer. S of A148; main entrance
from B1436.* **House & garden £7.90,
chd £3.70, garden only £3.70, chd
£1.60. For details please tel or see
website.** For NGS: Sat 18 July
(11-5).
Large pleasure gardens; mainly lawns
and shrubs; orangery with camellias;
large walled garden restored and
restocked as fruit, vegetable, herb and
flower garden; vine house; dovecote;
dahlias; National Collection of
Colchicum; wooded parks. 1 electric
and 2 manual wheelchairs available.
NGS sponsored trainee will be giving
guided walks 12noon & 2pm. Felbrigg
Church Flower Festival (church in park).
Featured in Kitchen Garden Magazine
& on BBC Radio Norfolk.
♿ ✖ ⊛ [NCCPG] ☕

**22 THE GARDEN IN AN
ORCHARD**
Mill Road, Bergh Apton NR15 1BQ.
Mr & Mrs R W Boardman. *6m SE of
Norwich. Off A146 at Hellington Corner
signed to Bergh Apton. Down Mill Rd
300yds.* Home-made teas. **Adm £3,
chd free.** Sun 21 June; Sat 12, Sun
13 Sept (11-6).
3½ -acre garden created by the
owners set in old orchard. Many rare
plants set out in an informal pattern of
wandering paths. ½ acre of wild flower
meadows, many bamboos, species
roses and Michaelmas daisies. 9
species of eucalyptus. A plantsman's
garden. Garden sculpture. Botanical
Embroidery Exhibition. Grass paths
may be difficult when wet.
♿ ⊛ ☕

23 GAYTON HALL
Gayton PE32 1PL. The Earl &
Countess of Romney, 01553 636259.
*6m E of King's Lynn. On B1145; R on
B1153. R down Back St 1st entrance
on L.* Home-made teas. **Adm £4, chd
free (share to St Nicholas Church,
Gayton).** Sun 29 Mar (12-5). **Visitors
also welcome by appt.**
20-acre water garden, with over 2m of
paths. Lawns, woodland, lakes,
streams and bridges. Many unusual
trees and shrubs. Spring bulbs and
autumn colour. Traditional and
waterside borders. Primulas, astilbes,
hostas, lysichitums, gunneras and
many more. Gravel paths.
♿ ☕ ☎

24 GRASMERE
57 Ullswater Avenue, South Wootton PE30 3NJ. Steve & Elsa Carden. *4 NE of King's Lynn. On A149 King's Lynn by-pass follow signs Hunstanton/Sandringham until reaching Knights Hill Hotel, turn L towards N & S Wootton/docks. After 1/2 m turn L into Sandy Lane, rd bears L and becomes Ullswater Ave at T-junction, turn L garden on R by metal gates.* **Adm £3, chd free. Suns, Mons 12, 13 Apr; 24, 25 May (2-6).**
0.2-acre garden generously planted plantsperson's organic garden, with many acid-loving plants incl camellias, acers and azaleas, unusual shrubs and plants for almost yr-round scent/structure. Lots of underplanting, grasses and phormiums. Tender plants and hidden rooms create an 'Aladdin's Cave' garden. Agave and succulent collection. Tearooms available 5mins drive away. Limited wheelchair access.
&. ⚲

25 NEW GREAT BARN FARM
Gayton Thorpe PE32 1PN. *7m E of King's Lynn. On B1145, R onto B1153, 1st L to Gayton Thorpe, continue through village towards B1145, last house on L.* Home-made teas. **Adm £4 (share to Gayton & Thorpe PCC). Sun 14 June (12-5). Combined with Manor Farm.**
Established farmhouse garden going through transitional phase. Long established herbaceous borders and kitchen garden. Fruit cage and small orchard area. Newly planted low maintenance bed for yr round interest. Established pond and patio. Children's lawn. Woodland garden with den. Child friendly. Limited wheelchair access, some gravel paths. Moderately sloping garden.
&. ☕

26 NEW HAWTHORN HOUSE
22 Cotman Road, Norwich NR1 4AF. Mr & Mrs R Palmer. *Central Norwich. 1/2 m E of Norwich Rail Stn. Off 126 Thorpe Rd next to Defra via the side entrance, behind (The Exotic Garden) car park of Alan Boswell Insurance.* **Adm £2.50, chd free. Sun 16 Aug (1-5).**
Multi-level terraced hillside 1-acre garden. Substantial, impressive topiary, artistically managed shrubs

and fine mature trees with sweeping paths leading to striking vistas within the garden and beyond. The garden has a varied feel combining formal and woodland area. Steep slopes and steps.
⚲

27 HIGH HOUSE GARDENS
Blackmoor Row, Shipdham IP25 7PU. Mr & Mrs F Nickerson. *6m SW of Dereham. Take the airfield or Cranworth Rd off A1075 in Shipdham. Blackmoor Row is signed.* Home-made teas. **Adm £3.50, chd free. Suns 28 June; 20 Sept (2-5.30).**
Plantsman's garden with colour-themed herbaceous borders with extensive range of perennials. Box-edged rose and shrub borders. Woodland garden, pond and bog area. Newly planted orchard and vegetable garden. Wildlife area. Glasshouses.
&. ⚲ ✿ ☕

28 HILL COTTAGE
School Road, Edingthorpe NR28 9SY. Shirley Gilbert, 01692 403519, shirley@ flandershouse.demon.co.uk. *3m NE of North Walsham. Off B1150 halfway between North Walsham and Bacton, leave main rd at Edingthorpe Green and continue straight towards Paston for 3/4 m. Cottage on L at top of hill. Parking in adjacent field.* Visitors welcome by appt **groups welcome, adm £5 incl garden tour & refreshments.**
Cottage garden, approx 1/4 acre, surrounding former farm workers' cottages. Organically cultivated, never watered and densely planted with both traditional and unusual varieties of drought resistant climbers, shrubs, perennial and annuals. Fruit, vegetable and herb gardens, greenhouse and pond. A real butterfly and wildlife paradise. Small nursery. Member of Norfolk Cottage Garden Society. Featured on BBC2 Gardeners World, Cottage Garden Special.
&. ⚲ ✿ ☕ ☎

29 HOLME HALE HALL
Holme Hale IP25 7ED. Mr & Mrs Simon Broke, 01760 440328, broke@freenet.co.uk. *6m E of Swaffham, 8m W Dereham. Exit A47 King's Lynn/Norwich rd at Necton Garden Centre. Continue through Necton village and Holme Hale village approx 1 1/2 m. At T-junction turn L, Hall*

gates on L immed after Low Common Rd. Home-made teas. **Adm £4.50, chd free. Suns 10 May; 2 Aug (12-6). Visitors also welcome by appt.**
The garden is noted for its spring display of over 3000 tulips, historic wisteria and mid and late summer flowering. Contemporary walled kitchen garden and front garden designed and planted in 2000 by Chelsea winner Arne Maynard. The garden incorporates large herbaceous borders, trained fruit, vegetables and traditional greenhouse.
&. ⚲ ✿ ☕ ☎

Woodland garden with den . . .

30 ♦ HOUGHTON HALL WALLED GARDEN
New Houghton, King's Lynn PE31 6UE. The Marquess of Cholmondeley, 01485 528569, www.houghtonhall.com. *11m W of Fakenham. 13m E of King's Lynn. Signed from A148.* **House & garden £8.80, chd £3.50, family £22, garden only £6, chd £2.50, family £15. Weds, Thurs, Suns & Bank Hol Mons, 12 Apr to 30 Sept. For NGS: Sun 5 July (11.30-5.30).**
Superbly laid-out 5-acre walled garden divided by clipped yew hedges into 'garden rooms', incl large mixed kitchen garden. Magnificently colourful 120m double herbaceous border. Rose parterre with over 120 varieties. Fountains, incl 'Waterflame' by Jeppe Hein, glasshouse, statues, rustic temple and croquet lawn. Media coverage. 2 mobility scooters available. Gravel and grass paths.
&. ⚲ ✿ ☕

31 ♦ HOVETON HALL GARDENS
nr Wroxham NR12 8RJ. Mr & Mrs Andrew Buxton, 01603 782798, www.hovetonhallgardens.co.uk. *8m N of Norwich. 1m N of Wroxham Bridge. Off A1151 Stalham Rd - follow brown tourist signs.* **Adm £5, chd £2.50, wheelchairs & carers £3. 12 Apr to 14 Sept, Weds, Thurs, Fris, Suns, BH Mon. For NGS: Fri 22 May; Sun 6 Sept (10.30-5).**
15-acre gardens and grounds featuring daffodils, azaleas, rhododendrons and hydrangeas in woodland. Mature walled herbaceous garden, and

redesigned walled kitchen garden. Water plants and lakeside walk. Woodland and gravel paths. Early C19 house (not open).

 ♿ ✕ ◈ ☕

32 HOW HILL FARM
Ludham NR29 5PG. Mr P D S Boardman. *2m W of Ludham. On A1062; then follow signs to How Hill. Farm garden S of How Hill.* **Adm £3, chd free. Sun 17 May (1-5).**
2 pretty gardens around house, 3rd started 1968 leading to 3-acre Broad dug 1978 with views over R Ant and Turf Fen Mill. About 10 acres incl Broad, 4 ponds, site of old Broad with 5ft Tussock sedges, about an acre of indigenous ferns under oak and alder. Paths through rare conifers, rhododendrons, azaleas, ornamental trees, shrubs, bamboos and herbaceous plants. Collection of holly species and varieties.

☕

33 6 JARVIS DRIVE
Colkirk NR21 7NG. Geoff Clark & Jenny Filby. *2m S of Fakenham. From Fakenham take B1145 towards Dereham. Through Pudding Norton then 1st R (signed Byway to Colkirk). Follow lane into village, Jarvis Drive is opp The Crown PH. Drop-off & pick-up only in Jarvis Drive (narrow cul-de-sac). Please park in field opp or if wet, surrounding rds or The Crown PH (Sun lunch bookable).* Home-made teas. **Adm £3, chd free. Sun 12 July (1-5).**
A heaven for plant lovers! Over 300 varieties of shrubs and perennials create spectacular borders bursting with colour. Large vegetable and fruit garden, wild flower areas and many other features provide interest to all visitors. Full planting plans available and owners happy to advise. Gravel front drive.

 ♿ ✕ ◈ ☕

34 JUNGLE GARDEN
Tollhouse Road, Norwich NR5 8QF. Jon Kelf. *2m W of Norwich. Off A1074 Dereham Rd nr the ring rd, on LH-side travelling away from the city just past Kwik Fit & Gatehouse PH. Limited off street parking available.* **Adm £2.50, chd free. Sun 16 Aug (1-5).**
Small town garden approx 26ft x 60ft with 5 levels of decking surrounded by dense, lush exotic planting, over 200 different and unusual types of plants incl palms, bamboos, bananas, gingers, cannas and more. Featured on BBC & ITV.

35 LAKE HOUSE
Postwick Lane, Brundall NR13 5LU. Mr & Mrs Garry Muter, 01603 712933. *5m E of Norwich. On A47; take Brundall turn at r'about. Turn R into Postwick Lane at T-junction.* **Visitors welcome by appt all yr, coaches welcome.**
2 acres of water gardens set among magnificent trees in steep cleft in river escarpment. Informal flower beds with interesting plants; naturalist's paradise; unsuitable for young children or the infirm. Stout shoes advisable. Beautiful lake - shore restoration. Featured on BBC TV The Flying Gardener.

◈ ☎

36 LEXHAM HALL
nr Litcham PE32 2QJ. Mr & Mrs Neil Foster. *2m W of Litcham. 6m N of Swaffham off B1145.* Light refreshments & teas (Feb), Home-made teas (May). **Adm £4, chd free. Sun 8 Feb (11-4); Wed 13, Sun 17 May; Wed 23 Sept (11-5).**
Fine C17/C18 Hall (not open). Parkland with lake and river walks. Formal garden with terraces, yew hedges, roses and mixed borders. Traditional kitchen garden with crinkle crankle wall. Extensive collection of scented, winter flowering shrubs and woods, carpeted with snowdrops. 3-acre woodland garden with azaleas, rhododendrons, camellias, spring bulbs, and fine trees. Dogs on leads welcome Feb only. Featured in 'Gardens Illustrated', 'Country Life'.

✕ ◈ ☕

37 ◆ MANNINGTON HALL
nr Saxthorpe/Corpusty NR11 7BB. The Lord & Lady Walpole, 01263 584175, www.manningtongardens.co.uk. *18m NW of Norwich. 2m N of Saxthorpe via B1149 towards Holt. At Saxthorpe/Corpusty follow sign posts to Mannington.* **Adm £5, chd free, concessions £4. Suns May to Sept (12-5), Weds, Thurs, Fris June to Aug (11-5). For NGS: Suns 10 May; 27 Sept (12-5).**
20 acres feature shrubs, lake, trees and roses. History of the Rose display and period gardens. Borders. Sensory garden. Extensive countryside walks and trails. Moated manor house and Saxon church with C19 follies. Wild flowers and birds.

 ♿ ✕ ◈ ☕

38 [NEW] MANOR FARMHOUSE
PE32 1QR. Alistair Beales. *6m E of King's Lynn. Signed from B1145 and B1153.* Home-made teas. **Adm £4, chd free. Sun 14 June (12-5). Combined with Great Barn Farm.**
Colourful cottage garden created in 2001 on 1/2 -acre plot ruined by major building work to house. Small gravel garden added 2002, courtyard garden and conservatory 2006. Garden changes constantly as owner progresses from non gardener to garden fanatic. Gravel paths, ramps provided on steps.

 ♿ ☕

> Garden changes constantly as owner progresses from non gardener to garden fanatic . . .

39 MANOR HOUSE FARM
Wellingham PE32 2TH. Robin & Elisabeth Ellis, 01328 838227, www.manor-house-farm.co.uk. *7m from Fakenham, 8m from Swaffham, 1/2 m off A1065 N of Weasenham. Garden is beside the church.* Home-made teas. **Adm £3.50, chd free. Sun 21 June (2-6). Visitors also welcome by appt.**
Charming 4-acre garden surrounds an attractive farmhouse. Many interesting features. Formal quadrants with obelisks. 'Hot Spot' with grasses and gravel. Small arboretum with specimen trees, pleached lime walk, vegetable parterre and rose tunnel. Unusual 'Taj' garden with old-fashioned roses, tree peonies, lilies and pond. Small herd of Formosan Sika deer. Featured in local press.

✕ 🏨 ☕ ☎

40 NEW 4 MILL ROAD

Marlingford NR9 5HL. Mrs Jean Austen. *6m W of Norwich. A47 to B1108 Watton Rd junction, 3rd on R. Bear R past mill & garden on R after village hall, (parking) before The Bell. From Easton, opp Des Amis.* Teas at Spring Grove. **Adm £4, chd free (share to St Mary's PC Marlingford).** Sun 21 June (11-5). Combined with **Spring Grove.**

This small peaceful 5yr-old garden has a modern interpretation of the classic garden, designed to draw your eye past the formality of the box-edged rooms and linking paths to the water meadows beyond. Colour-themed borders, Japanese garden, wisteria arch, pleached limes, fruit, vegetables and wildlife pond. Plenty of places to sit and enjoy. Two shallow steps, handrail.

41 THE MOWLE

Staithe Road, Ludham NR29 5NP. Mrs N N Green, 01692 678213, ann@mowlegreen.fsnet.co.uk. *5 W of Wroxham. B1062 Wroxham to Ludham 7m. Turn R by Ludham village church into Staithe Rd. Garden 1/4 m from village.* Home-made teas. **Adm £3.50, chd free.** Sun 31 May (1.30-5.30). Visitors also welcome by appt anytime, please call first.

Approx 2¹/₂ acres running down to marshes. The garden incl several varieties of catalpa. Japanese garden and enlarged wildlife pond with bog garden. A special border for gunnera as in Aug 2008 we were given full National Collection statues.

🔥 ✖ ✿ NCCPG ☕ ☎

42 NORTH LODGE

Bowthorpe Road, Norwich NR2 3TN. Bruce Bentley & Peter Wilson. *1¹/₂ m W of Norwich City Centre. In Bowthorpe Rd off Dereham Rd, turn after 150 metres L through cemetery gates (opp end of Bond St) to North Lodge. Parking restricted, can park outside gates. FirstBus services 16, 19, 20, 21, 22 and Connect service 5 stop at Dereham Rd - Bowthorpe Rd junction.* Home-made teas. **Adm £2.50, chd free.** Sun 21 June (11-5). **Adm £4** Sun 12 July (11-5). Combined with **7 Connaught Road.**

Town garden 0.1 acre to Victorian Gothic Cemetery Lodge (not open),

created from barren, challenging triangular plot over past 10yrs. Strong structure and attention to internal vista incl Gothic conservatory, formal pond, pergola, and classical-style summerhouse. Predominantly herbaceous planting. Adjacent associated historic parkland cemetery also worth a visit. Featured in 'Eastern Daily Press'.

✖ ☕

43 THE OLD COTTAGE

Colby Corner, nr Aylsham NR11 7EB. Stuart Clarke, 01263 734574, enchanting@talktalk.net, www.enchantinggardens.co.uk. *14m N of Norwich. Take B1145 from Aylsham to N Walsham. After 3¹/₂ m turn L opp Banningham Bridge Inn Garage onto Bridge Rd. Pass Colby school on R & continue straight, following Colby Corner sign. Garden on the L, parking by the poly tunnel.* Home-made teas. **Adm £4, chd free (share to Arthritis Research Campaign).** Mon 4 May; Sun 5 July (10-5). Visitors also welcome by appt.

The garden created by Judith Clarke is being redeveloped following her death in April 2008. The work will take approx 2yrs to produce a lower maintenance garden. Visitors are being invited to see the progress and purchase plants that are being removed. May for perennials ad shrubs, July for exotic plants.

🔥 ✖ ✿ 🛏 ☕ ☎

44 THE OLD RECTORY

Stone Lane, Brandon Parva NR9 4DL. Mr & Mrs S Guest. *9m W of Norwich. Leave Norwich on B1108 towards Watton, turn R at sign for Barnham Broom. L at T-junction, stay on rd approx 3m until L next turn to Yaxham. L at Xrds, house on R.* Home-made teas. **Adm £3.50, chd free.** Sun 5 July (11-4).

4-acre, mature, predominantly shrub garden planted by previous owner. Walkways with pergolas covered with climbing plants lead to large lawn surrounded by boldly planted borders. This leads to an area of woodland with grass paths and pond. Walled garden and further lawns complete the garden.

45 OLD SUN HOUSE

Damgate, Wymondham NR18 0BH. Leonie Woolhouse. *At T-lights on B1172 at edge of Wymondham turn to*

town centre. Immed turn L, follow main st, 50 metres past market cross, turn L into car park. From top of car park down Chandlers Hill turn R then L into Damgate. Home-made teas. **Adm £3, chd free. Also open Sallowfield Cottage.** Sun 7 June (11-5).

Plantsperson's and artist's garden, approx 1¹/₃acres, borders, mature trees, river frontage, old roses, bog garden, fruit trees, wild flower meadow, new mini arboretum. Hens, shrubs, ferns, interesting out-buildings. Colour and interest at all times of yr. Gravel drive, lawn and woodchip paths.

🔥 ✖ ✿ ☕

Peaceful 5 year-old garden has a modern interpretation of the classic garden . . .

46 OULTON HALL

Oulton, Aylsham NR11 6NU. Clare & Bolton Agnew. *4m W of Aylsham. From Aylsham take B1354. After 4m Turn L for Oulton Chapel, Hall 1/2 m on R. From B1149 (Norwich/Holt rd) take B1354, next R, Hall 1/2 m on R.* Home-made teas. **Adm £4, chd free.** Sun 31 May (11-5). Visitors also welcome by appt, by written application.

C18 manor house (not open) and clocktower set in 6-acre garden with lake and woodland walks. Chelsea designer's own garden - herbaceous, Italian, bog, water, wild, verdant, sunken and parterre gardens all flowing from one tempting vista to another. Developed over 15yrs with emphasis on structure, height and texture, with a lot of recent replanting. Silver Gilt medal - RHS Award Chelsea Show.

🔥 ✖ ✿ ☕ ☎

47 ◆ OXBURGH HALL GARDEN & ESTATE

Oxborough PE33 9PS. The National Trust, 01366 328258, www.nationaltrust.org.uk. *7m SW of Swaffham. At Oxborough on Stoke*

Ferry rd. **House & Garden £7.45, chd £3.90. Garden only £3.90, chd £2.25. Sats to Weds 14 Mar to 1 Nov, daily in Aug (11-5).** For NGS: Suns 21 June; 19 July (11-5). Hall and moat surrounded by lawns, fine trees, colourful borders; charming parterre garden of French design. Orchard and vegetable garden. Woodland walks. A garden steward is on duty on open days to lead 4 free tours throughout the day. Sun 21 June Boys & Their Toys model displays; 19 July Archaeological display. Gravel paths.

    ♿ ✕ ✿

48 ◆ THE PLANTATION GARDEN
4 Earlham Road, Norwich NR2 3DB. Plantation Garden Preservation Trust, 01603 219630, www.plantationgarden.co.uk. *Nr St John's R C Cathedral. Parking available at Black Horse PH Earlham Rd (please notify).* Teas Suns end Apr to end Sept. **Adm £3, chd free. Daily dawn till dusk.** For NGS: Sun 6 Sept (2-5). 3-acre Victorian town garden created 1856-97 in former medieval chalk quarry. Undergoing restoration by volunteers. Remarkable architectural features incl 60ft Italianate terrace, unique 30ft Gothic fountain, re-built Gothic alcove, rustic bridge and summerhouse. Surrounded by mature trees. Beautifully tranquil atmosphere.

    ♿ ✕ ✿ ☕

49 ● PLOVERS HILL
Buckenham Road, Strumpshaw NR13 4NL. Jim & Jan Saunt, 01603 714587, jamessaunt@hotmail.com. *9m E of Norwich. Off A47 at Brundall continuing through to Strumpshaw village. Turn R 300yds past PO, then R at T-junction. Plovers Hill is 1st on R up the hill.* Home-made teas. **Adm £3, chd free (share to How Hill Educational Trust).** Suns 3 May (11-5); Adm £4.50 Suns 19 July; 9 Aug (11-5). Visitors also welcome by appt. Combined with **Woodland View.**
1-acre garden of contrasts, small C18 house (not open) with RIBA award winning orangery. Formal lawn hedged with yew and lesser species, huge mulberry, gingko, liquidambar and Japanese bitter orange, herbaceous borders with a range of varied plants and spring bulbs. Kitchen garden with orchard and soft fruits. Garden sculpture. New water feature. Some shallow steps.

    ♿ ☕ ☎

Delightful, fully productive Victorian kitchen garden with original vine houses . . .

50 ◆ RAVENINGHAM HALL
Raveningham NR14 6NS. Sir Nicholas Bacon, www.raveningham.com. *14m SE of Norwich. 4m from Beccles off B1136.* **Adm £4, chd free, concessions £3. Mon-Fri, Easter to end Aug (11-4); Bank Hols Suns, Mons (2-5).** For NGS: Mon 25 May (2-5). Traditional country house garden with an interesting collection of herbaceous plants and shrubs. Restored Victorian conservatory and walled kitchen garden. Newly planted arboretum, lake and herb garden. Contemporary sculpture.

    ♿ ✿

REDGRAVE GARDENS
See Suffolk.

51 ● RIVERMOUNT
Hall Lane, Knapton NR28 9SW. Mrs E Purdy. *2m NE North Walsham. B1150 through North Walsham towards Bacton. 2nd turning on L after Blue Bell PH & pond. Ample parking.* Home-made teas. **Adm £3, chd free.** Sun 10 May (2-5). Traditional style garden. Brick terrace, sloping lawn to woodland garden. Herbaceous borders enclosed by climbing rose trellis. Paved kitchen garden with herb garden and old-fashioned rose beds. Many unusual and species plants and bulbs. Orchard and wild flower meadow walk. New azalea and shrub bed in woodland area, new planting at the bottom of the garden following tree felling and lopping. Not brilliant for wheelchairs but manageable with assistance. Gravel paths and narrow brick paths.

    ♿ ✕ ✿ ☕

52 ● RYSTON HALL
PE38 0AA. Mr & Mrs Piers Pratt. *1m S of Downham Market. Turn off A10 S of Downham Market, signed Ryston.* Home-made teas. **Adm £4, chd free.** Sun 17 May (2-6). 6-acre garden with azaleas and rhododendrons; rock garden and rare trees; walled kitchen garden and woodland walk. Ketts Oak Tree (300yds).

    ♿ ✿ ☕

53 ● SALLE PARK
Salle, Norwich NR10 4SF. Sir John White, www.salleestategardens.com. *1m N of Reepham. Off B1145, between Cawston & Reepham.* Home-made teas. **Adm £4, chd free.** Sun 26 July (12-5). Very varied estate gardens consisting of delightful, fully productive Victorian kitchen garden with original vine houses, double herbaceous borders, display glasshouse, ice house, orchard and wild flowers. Formal Georgian pleasure gardens with yew topiary, rose gardens, all-yr round interest shrubs beds, lawns, specimen trees and exotically planted orangery. Featured in 'Country Life'. Gravel and bark paths, gentle slopes.

    ♿ ✿ ☕

54 ● SALLOWFIELD COTTAGE
Wattlefield Road, Wymondham NR18 9PA. Caroline Musker, 01953 605086, www.sallowfieldcottage.co.uk. *2m S of Wymondham. Leave A11 signed Wymondham & Spooner Row. Turn R for Spooner Row, into village straight over Xrds at Boars PH. At T-junction take L, after 1¹/₂ m, grey barrels on L. Disabled parking near the house.* Home-made teas. **Adm £3, chd free. Also open Old Sun House.** Sun 7 June (12-5). Visitors also welcome by appt.
1-acre garden with large pond, lots of clematis, old roses, herbaceous plants and wooded area. Views toward Wymondham Abbey across what used to be Wymondham deer park. Some gravel paths, but mostly grass.

    ♿ 🛏 ☕ ☎

55 ◆ SANDRINGHAM GARDENS
Sandringham PE35 6EN. Her Majesty The Queen, 01553 612908, www.sandringhamestate.co.uk. *6m NW of King's Lynn. By gracious permission, the House, Museum & Gardens at Sandringham will be open.* **House & garden £10, concessions £8, chd £5, garden only £6.50, chd £3.50, concessions £5.50. Daily 11 Apr to 1 Nov (garden 10.30-5) (house 11-4.45).**

NORFOLK

60 acres of formal gardens, woodland and lakes, with rare plants and trees. Donations are given from the Estate to various charities. Gravel paths, long distances - please tel for details.

56 ◆ SEVERALS GRANGE
Holt Road, Wood Norton NR20 5BL. Jane Lister, 01362 684206, www.hoecroft.co.uk. 8m S of Holt, 6m E of Fakenham. 2m N of Guist on LH-side of B1110. Guist is situated 5m SE of Fakenham on A1067 Norwich rd. Adm £2.50, chd free. Thurs to Suns 1 Apr to 17 Oct (Donations to NGS) 10-4. For NGS: Sun 9 Aug (2-5). This 18yr-old garden has evolved from a bare field and is a perfect example of how colour, shape and form can be created by the use of foliage plants, from large shrubs to small alpines. Movement and lightness is achieved by interspersing these plants with a wide range of ornamental grasses, which are at their best in late summer. Short gravel path at entrance which can be avoided by using an alternative route.

57 ◆ SHERINGHAM PARK
Upper Sheringham NR26 8TL. The National Trust, 01263 820550, www.nationaltrust.org.uk. 2m SW of Sheringham. Access for cars off A148 Cromer to Holt Rd, 5m W of Cromer, 6m E of Holt, signs in Sheringham town. Adm £4 per car, coaches free (must book). Daily (dawn til dusk), refreshment kiosk (11-5). For NGS: Suns 17, 31 May (dawn to dusk). 50 acres of species rhododendron, azalea and magnolia. Also numerous specimen trees incl handkerchief tree. Viewing towers, waymarked walks, sea and parkland views. Special walkway and WCs for disabled. Park open dawn to dusk all year.

58 'SOL'
Whissonsett Road, Colkirk NR21 7NJ. Rod & Marjorie Diaper. 2m S of Fakenham. Between B1146 & A1065 Colkirk not signed from A1065. Follow NGS signs. Home-made teas. Adm £4, chd free. Sun 31 May (11-5). Combined with Derwen. Large front garden set to lawns and various flower beds, patio area, greenhouse and summerhouse. Some narrow paths.

59 NEW SPINNEY LODGE
Winch Road, Gayton PE32 1QP. Mr & Mrs Peter Grant. 6m E of King's Lynn. R at Winch Road, 200yds on R past Back Street junction. Blue badge parking only, all others at Bridge House, Winch Road as signed. Home-made teas. Adm £3.50, chd free. Sun 19 Apr (11-4). Approx 2-acre smallholding transformed by owners in 8 yrs into landscaped gardens with existing unusual trees and shrubs. Bounded with stream and divided into formal and informal areas with shrubbery, boardwalk with large wildlife pond, woodland walk and a Victorian raised bed vegetable garden. WC.

60 NEW SPRING GROVE
Mill Road, Marlingford NR9 5HL. Mr & Mrs J Barnes. 6m W of Norwich. Leave A47 B1108 Watton junction, then 3rd R, down into Marlingford. Garden on R after village hall. Parking at village hall. Home-made teas. Adm £4, chd free (share to St Mary's PC Marlingford). Sun 21 June (11-5). Combined with 4 Mill Rd. Spring Grove's pleasing garden of ⅓ - acre backs onto water meadows. Large mixed borders have a good stock of herbaceous perennial plants, shrubs and large mature trees. Gently stroll along the meandering gravel paths and stop at the fish pond.

61 ◆ STODY LODGE
Melton Constable NR24 2ER. Mrs Ian MacNicol, 01263 860572, www.stodyestate.co.uk. 16m NW of Norwich, 3m S of Holt. Off B1354. Signed from Melton Constable on Holt Rd. Adm £4.50, chd under 12 free. For opening details please tel or see website. Donation to NGS. Spectacular gardens having one of the largest concentrations of rhododendrons and azaleas in East Anglia with both Japanese water gardens and formal garden. Stunning walks and vistas are enhanced by a large variety of mature trees, magnolias, acers and cedars. Daffodils in early May give way to carpets of bluebells.

62 NEW ◆ STRANGERS HALL
Charing Cross, Norwich NR2 4AL, 01603 667229, www.museums.norfolk.gov.uk. City Centre. At the city end of St Benedicts Street, just past Hog in Armour PH. Nearest parking - St Andrews car park. Adm £3, chd free. House & garden Weds & Sats 10.30-4.30 all-yr. For NGS: Sun 5 July (11-4). ¼ acre hidden behind Strangers' Hall, home of the wealthy merchants and mayors of C16 & C17 provides an unexpected peaceful oasis in a busy city. This urban garden offers glimpses of history with small herb beds, abutting the Eastern window of a C14 church, knot garden and borders with historic roses. Crafts and traditional garden games for children. Morning coffee & afternoon tea.

A 'Tardis' created from an old apple orchard in 2000, behind a pink cottage . . .

63 NEW SUMMER COTTAGE
High Common, Swardeston NR14 8DL. Richard & Deidre Cave. 4m S of Norwich. Take B1113 out of Norwich, turn R at Swardeston Village sign, down Short Lane, then L round bend on unmade rd to High Common. Park on edge of cricket pitch or by village hall. Home-made teas. Adm £3, chd free. Sun 14 June (11-5). A 'Tardis' created from an old apple orchard in 2000, behind a pink cottage. 5 small gardens in ⅓ -acre linked by brick, grass and gravel paths, featuring wild flowers with pond and summerhouse. Formal English borders, intimate sundial retreat, model kitchen garden and walled area with bamboos. Possibly cricket match on High Common.

64 56 WELL CREEK ROAD
Outwell PE14 8SA. Tim Meakin &
Nick Bergamaschi, 01945 774064.
*6m W of Downham Market. 2m W of
Nordelph on A1122. Take bridge on L
immed after 'Middle Level Main Drain'
sign, 3rd house, approx 100metres
from bridge.* Teas. **Adm £3.50, chd
free. Sat 20, Sun 21 June (11-5).**
Visitors also welcome by appt, max
30, no coaches.
Well stocked plantsman's garden of
¾ acre. Planted with emphasis on form
and foliage with wide use of salvaged
natural materials for structural interest.
Many unusual plants, and particular
use made of collections of grasses,
hebes, hederas and heucheras. Island
beds, shaded areas, gravel garden,
ponds and vegetable garden.

65 WEST LODGE
Aylsham NR11 6HB. Mr & Mrs
Jonathan Hirst. *¼ m NW of Aylsham.
Off B1354 Blickling Rd out of Aylsham,
turn R down Rawlinsons Lane, garden
on L.* Home-made teas. **Adm £3.50,
chd free. Sun 19 July (12-5).**
9-acre garden with lawns, splendid
mature trees, rose garden, well-
stocked herbaceous borders,
ornamental pond, magnificent C19
walled kitchen garden (maintained as
such). Georgian house (not open) and
outbuildings incl a well-stocked
toolshed (open) and greenhouses.

WHITE HOUSE FARM
See Suffolk.

66 WITTON HALL
nr North Walsham NR28 9UF. Sally
Owles. *3½ m from North Walsham.
Off B1150 halfway between North
Walsham & Bacton. Take R fork to
Bacton Woods picnic area, driveway
200yds on L.* Light refreshments &

home-teas. **Adm £3, chd free. Mon 4
May (11-5).**
A natural woodland garden. Walk past
the handkerchief tree and wander
through carpets of English bluebells,
rhododendrons and azaleas. Stunning
views over farmland and to the sea.
Wheelchair access difficult on soft
ground.

67 WOODLAND VIEW
2 Woodland View, Norwich Road,
Strumpshaw NR13 4NW. Mike &
Gillian Page, 01603 712410,
skyview@clara.co.uk. *8m E of
Norwich. Off A47 at Brundall carry on
through Brundall St toward
Strumpshaw. Garden on R 200yds
after Strumpshaw Church at rear of
Pages Garage.* **Adm £3, chd free,
£4.50. Suns 19 July; 9 Aug (11-5).**
Combined with **Plovers Hill.**
Visitors also welcome by appt July
& Aug.
3-acre conservation area comprising
woodland walk and formal garden with
large pond. Woodland planted in 1993
with pond and borders commenced in
2004. Dragonflies, butterflies, birds and
wildlife abound. Separate wheelchair
access, grass paths, some slopes and
small gravel area.

68 WOODWYND
6 Dodds Hill Road, Dersingham
PE31 6LW. Mr & Mrs D H Dingle,
01485 541218. *8m NE of King's Lynn.
¾ m N of Sandringham House. Take
B1440 from Sandringham & continue
into Dersingham. Turn R into Dodds Hill
Rd just past the Feathers Hotel.* Teas
by arrangement. **Adm £3.50, chd
free. Visitors welcome by appt Thur
16 to Sun 19 July only.**
Dry gravel garden, S-facing terrace
features contemporary design garden
room. Sweeping lawns, island beds,

and borders. Steps and pathways
wind through dell to meandering
brook. Fine mature trees create
dappled canopy above informal
naturalistic planting of lush vegetation.
Encompassed by Sandringham's Royal
Woodland. Dersingham Church Flower
Festival 16 to 19 July. Steep slopes in
dell.

3-acre
conservation
area comprising
woodland walk
and formal
garden . . .
dragonflies,
butterflies, birds
and wildlife
abound . . .

69 WRETHAM LODGE
East Wretham IP24 1RL. Mr Gordon
Alexander. *6m NE of Thetford. A11 E
from Thetford, L up A1075, L by village
sign, R at Xrds then bear L.* Teas in
Church. **Adm £3, chd free. Sun 12,
Mon 13 Apr (11-5).**
In spring masses of species tulips,
hellebores, fritillaries, daffodils and
narcissi; bluebell walk. In June
hundreds of old roses. Walled garden,
with fruit and interesting vegetable
plots. Mixed borders and fine old trees.
Double herbaceous borders. Wild
flower meadows.

Norfolk County Volunteers

County Organisers
Fiona Black, The Old Rectory, Ridlington, North Walsham NR28 9NZ, 01692 650247, blacks7@email.com
Anthea Foster, Lexham Hall, King's Lynn PE32 2QJ, 01328 701341, antheafoster@lexhamestate.co.uk

County Treasurer
Neil Foster, Lexham Hall, King's Lynn PE32 2QJ, 01328 701288, neilfoster@lexhamestate.co.uk

Publicity
Annette Bowler, 260 Aylsham Road, Norwich NR3 2RG, 01603 301110, annette.bowler@ntlworld.com

Assistant County Organisers
Panda Allhusen, Bradenham Hall, Bradenham, Thetford IP25 7QP, 01362 687243/687279, panda@bradenhamhall.co.uk
Stephanie Powell, Creake House, Wells Road, North Creake, Fakenham NR21 9LG, 01328 730113, stephaniepowell@creake.com
Jim & Jan Saunt, Plovers Hill, Buckenham Road, Strumpshaw NR13 4NL, 01603 714587, jamessaunt@hotmail.com

Mark your diary with these special events in 2009

EXPLORE SECRET GARDENS DURING CHELSEA & HAMPTON COURT FLOWER SHOW WEEKS

Tue 19 May, Wed 20 May, Thur 21 May, Fri 22 May, Wed 8 July, Thur 9 July
Full day tours from £82 per person, 10% discount for groups
Advance booking required, telephone +44 (0)20 8693 1015 or email j.wookey@btinternet.com
Specially selected gardens in London, Essex, Kent, Hampshire and South Oxfordshire. The tour price includes transport and lunch with wine at a popular restaurant or pub.

HAMPTON COURT PALACE

Thur 2 Apr, Tue 23 June, Thur 25 June, Wed 15 July, Tue 4 Aug, Thur 10 Sept
Evening tours in the company of one of the Palace's specialist tour guides from 6.30 – 8pm
Tickets £6 per person. Advance booking required, telephone +44 (0)1483 211535 or
visit www.ngs.org.uk for more information
Gossip, scandal, murder, healing – you'll find it all within the Formal Gardens at Hampton Court Palace. Each tour will have its own unique feature whether it's the story of the Great Vine or the magic and mystery of the Maze.

FROGMORE – A ROYAL GARDEN (BERKSHIRE)

Tue 26 May 10am – 5.30pm (last admission 4pm)
Garden adm £4.50, chd free. Tickets available in advance or on the day.
Advance booking for groups and coaches, telephone
+44 (0) 1483 211535 or email orders@ngs.org.uk
A rare opportunity to explore 30 acres of landscaped garden, rich in history and beauty.

FLAXBOURNE FARM – FUN & SURPRISES (BEDFORDSHIRE)

Sun 7 June 10am – 5pm. Adm £5, chd free
No booking required, come along on the day!
Bring the whole family and have fun in this surprising and entertaining garden of 2 acres. Enjoy the large plant fair, live music, pets corner, birds of prey, dog agility show and much more.

WISLEY RHS GARDEN – MUSIC IN THE GARDEN (SURREY)

Fri 11 Sept 6 – 9pm
Adm (incl RHS members) £7, chd under 15 free
Save money on advance bookings for groups of 4 or more, telephone +44 (0)1483 211535 or
visit www.ngs.org.uk for more information
A special evening opening of this famous garden, exclusively for the NGS. Enjoy music and entertainment as you explore the gardens and the floral marquee on the first day of the Wisley Flower Show.

For further information visit www.ngs.org.uk or telephone 01483 211535

NORTHAMPTONSHIRE

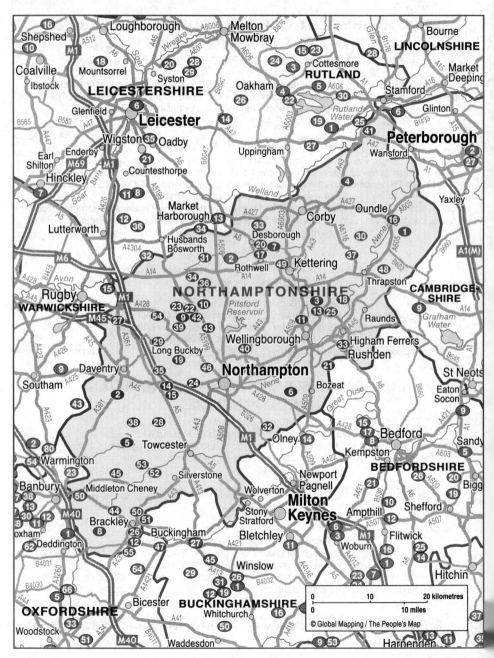

Opening Dates

February

SUNDAY 15
11 Dolphins
42 Rosemount

SUNDAY 22
3 Beech House
21 Greywalls

March

SUNDAY 15
37 The Old Rectory, Sudborough

April

SATURDAY 11
31 The Maltings

SUNDAY 12
31 The Maltings

MONDAY 13
18 Great Addington Manor
31 The Maltings

SUNDAY 19
15 Flore Spring Gardens

SATURDAY 25
23 Guilsborough Spring Gardens

SUNDAY 26
23 Guilsborough Spring Gardens

May

SUNDAY 3
12 Evenley Wood Garden
19 Great Brington Gardens

MONDAY 4
12 Evenley Wood Garden

TUESDAY 5
9 Coton Manor Garden

SUNDAY 10
20 Greenway
43 Spratton Gardens

SATURDAY 16
22 Guilsborough & Hollowell May Gardens

SUNDAY 17
22 Guilsborough & Hollowell May Gardens

SUNDAY 24
50 Turweston Gardens

THURSDAY 28
20 Greenway (Evening)

SUNDAY 31
2 Badby and Newnham Gardens
8 Charlton Gardens
16 Foxtail Lilly
44 Steane Park

June

SUNDAY 7
13 Finedon Gardens

---

38 Preston Capes Gardens
41 Rosebriar

THURSDAY 11
25 67-69 High Street

SATURDAY 13
31 The Maltings
37 The Old Rectory, Sudborough
48 Titchmarsh House

SUNDAY 14
1 Armston Lodge
27 Kilsby Gardens
31 The Maltings
45 Sulgrave Gardens
49 Top Lodge
51 Turweston House
52 Wappenham Gardens

WEDNESDAY 17
47 Tile House Farm (Evening)

THURSDAY 18
25 67-69 High Street (Evening)

SATURDAY 20
14 Flore Gardens

SUNDAY 21
7 Cedar Farm
14 Flore Gardens
24 Harpole Gardens
29 Long Buckby Gardens
34 Naseby Gardens

SATURDAY 27
32 The Menagerie

SUNDAY 28
13 Finedon Gardens
28 Litchborough Gardens
53 Weedon Lois & Weston Gardens

July

SUNDAY 5
47 Tile House Farm
54 West Haddon Gardens

SATURDAY 11
31 The Maltings

SUNDAY 12
31 The Maltings
39 Ravensthorpe Gardens

SATURDAY 18
5 Canons Ashby House
30 Lyveden New Bield

SUNDAY 19
4 Bulwick Gardens
6 Castle Ashby Gardens

SUNDAY 26
10 Cottesbrooke Hall Gardens
17 Froggery Cottage
53 Weedon Lois & Weston Gardens

August

SUNDAY 2
40 Roseanns Rose Garden

SATURDAY 29
35 The Old Rectory, Brockhall

SUNDAY 30
35 The Old Rectory, Brockhall

Gardens open to the public

5 Canons Ashby House
6 Castle Ashby Gardens
9 Coton Manor Garden
10 Cottesbrooke Hall Gardens
12 Evenley Wood Garden
30 Lyveden New Bield
32 The Menagerie
37 The Old Rectory, Sudborough
44 Steane Park

By appointment only

26 Hill Grounds
33 71 Midland Road
36 The Old Rectory, Haselbech
46 Thimble Hall
55 Woodchippings

Also open by appointment ☎

3 Beech House
7 Cedar Farm
14 The Old Bakery, Flore Gardens
16 Foxtail Lilly
17 Froggery Cottage
19 The Old Rectory, Great Brington Gardens
22 Dripwell House, Guilsborough & Hollowell May Gardens
22 Gower House, Guilsborough & Hollowell May Gardens
25 67-69 High Street
27 Hunt House, Kilsby Gardens
28 Kiln Cottage, Litchborough Gardens
29 45 Brington Road, Long Buckby Gardens
29 Mill House, Long Buckby Gardens
31 The Maltings
35 The Old Rectory, Brockhall
38 City Cottage, Preston Capes Gardens
38 Old West Farm, Preston Capes Gardens
38 Village Farm, Preston Capes Gardens
39 Mill House, Ravensthorpe Gardens
39 Ravensthorpe Nursery, Ravensthorpe Gardens
41 Rosebriar
42 Rosemount
43 Dale House, Spratton Gardens

43 Mulberry Cottage, Spratton Gardens
45 West End
47 Tile House Farm
48 Titchmarsh House
49 Top Lodge
53 Home Close, Weedon Lois & Weston Gardens
53 Old Barn, Weedon Lois & Weston Gardens
54 Rivendell, West Haddon Gardens
54 West Cottage & 45 West End, West Haddon Gardens

The Gardens

1 NEW ARMSTON LODGE
Armston PE8 5PR. Mr & Mrs R Ashby. *3m S of Oundle off A605. Turn off A605 at Barnwell, signed Polebrook. Armston is on this rd, 1m.* Cream teas & wine. **Adm £3, chd free (share to Polebrook Church). Sun 14 June (11-6).**
Farmhouse has wonderful views of the Nene Valley. Garden mainly created for the conservation of wildlife. Large pond and woodland, informal gardens, re-claimed cherry orchard and a young tree plantation. Woods not suitable for wheelchairs or infirm.
&♿ ❀ ☕

ARTHINGWORTH GARDENS
See Leicestershire & Rutland.

AVON DASSETT GARDENS
See Warwickshire & part of West Midlands.

See Leicestershire & Rutland.

Group opening

2 BADBY AND NEWNHAM GARDENS
Daventry NN11 3AR. *3m S of Daventry. E side of A361.* Home-made teas. **Combined adm £3.50, chd free. Sun 31 May (2-6).**
Maps provided for visitors.
☕

HILLTOP
Church Street. David & Mercy Messenger
Large organic cottage-style with packed borders and climbers rambling through trees. 3 acres, many different levels and views, mature hedges and trees dividing the garden into sections. Very quiet and peaceful and in the biased opinion of the owners 'a bit of magic'.

THE LILACS
School Lane. Matthew and Ruth Moser
Medium sized walled cottage garden partly terraced, lawn, mixed borders, vegetables and orchard. 14 steps to main garden.

THE OLD HOUSE
Malcolm & Marigold MacGregor.
Opposite Badby Church
A medium-sized enclosed garden with fine views over Badby woods. Secluded courtyard, mostly stone-raised beds, densely planted with many traditional herbaceous plants and roses.
❀

SHAKESPEARES COTTAGE
Sarah & Jocelyn Hartland-Swann
Small garden surrounding C18 thatched cottage, reclaimed by present owners after some years of neglect. Raised stone beds, sloping lawn to rear, mixed borders. Flagstone, terracotta and gravelled seating areas with colourful pots.
❀

TRIFIDIA
Church Hill. Dr & Mrs C M Cripps
Medium-sized country garden with internal yew and beech hedges enclosing mixed borders. Some interesting plants, clipped yews, shady border, pond, vegetable garden and conservatory.

Garden mainly created for the conservation of wildlife . . .

3 BEECH HOUSE
73 Church Street, Burton Latimer NN15 5LU. Mr & Mrs Nicholas Loake, 01536 723593, gloake@mac.com. *4m S of Kettering. From High St turn into Church St by War Memorial, Beech House on L 100yds past church.* Home-made teas. **Adm £2.50, chd free. Sun 22 Feb (10-4). Visitors also welcome by appt for groups 8+.**
Semi-formal garden with winter/spring

interest. Clipped box and yew hedging frame borders containing over 150 cultivars of snowdrops plus hellebores etc.
&♿ ❀ ☕ ☎

Group opening

4 BULWICK GARDENS
Corby NN17 3DZ. *10m SW of Stamford. 1/2 m off A43.* Cream teas at Bulwick Hall. **Combined adm £3, chd free. Sun 19 July (2-5).**
Unspoilt Northamptonshire stone conservation village. Interesting C14 church and PH.
❀ ☕

BULWICK HALL
Mr & Mrs G T G Conant
Formal terraced 8-acre walled garden leading to river and island. Double herbaceous borders, holly walk ending at attractive C17 wrought iron gates. C19 orangery and C17 arcade, large kitchen garden, fine mature trees, topiary, peacocks. (House not open).
&♿ ❀

19 CHURCH LANE
David Haines
Small cottage garden with fruit trees and vegetables, courtyard and water features.

THE SHAMBLES
12 Main Street. Roger Glithero
Herbaceous plants, many containers, vegetable garden with fruit and original village well, lawns, hedges and stone walls. Steep slopes.
&♿

5 ◆ CANONS ASHBY HOUSE
Daventry NN11 3SD. The National Trust, 01327 8610044, canonsashby@national trust.org.uk. *12m NE of Banbury, 9m S of Daventry. On unclassified rd between B4525 and A5. Follow NT signs.* **House and Garden £7.95, chd £3.95, Garden only £2.95, chd £1.75.** Visit website or phone for details. For NGS: Sat 18 July (11-5).
Formal gardens of London and Wise style enclosed by walls. Gate piers from 1710, fine topiary, axial arrangement of paths and terraces, wild flowers, old varieties of fruit trees and herb border. Phase 1 of a 5yr plan to restore gardens to designs of 1880-1900. New beds with bedding schemes. Home of the Dryden family since C16, Manor House 1550.
&♿ ❀ ❀ ☕

6 ◆ **CASTLE ASHBY GARDENS**
Northampton NN7 1LQ. Earl Compton, 01604 695200, www.castleashbygardens.co.uk. *6m E of Northampton. 1½ m N of A428; turn off between Denton & Yardley Hastings.* **Adm £5, chd £4.50, under 10 free, concessions £4.50. Apr-Sept (10-5.30), Oct & Mar (10-4.30). For NGS: Sun 19 July (11-5).**
25 acres within a 10,000 acre estate of both formal and informal gardens, incl Italian gardens with orangery and arboretum with lakes, all dating back to the 1860s.

7 **CEDAR FARM**
Copelands Road, Desborough NN14 2QD. Mr & Mrs R Tuffen, 01536 763992, thetuffenfamily@aol.com. *6m N of Kettering, 5m S of Market Harborough, from A6. Signed from centre of Desborough.* Home-made teas. **Adm £3, chd free. Sun 21 June (2-6). Visitors also welcome by appt.**
2-acre garden with a further 8 acres. Secret garden with roses and clematis. Avenue of mature limes. Large colour planted borders filled with unusual plants and shrubs. Large mirror pond, wildlife ponds, vegetables. Massed snowdrops and spring bulbs, wonderful autumn colour, small arboretum. Featured in 'The English Garden', 'Homes and Antiques', 'Garden News' and NFU 'Countryside Magazine'.

Group opening

8 **CHARLTON GARDENS**
Banbury OX17 3DR. *7m SE of Banbury, 5m W of Brackley. From B4100 turn off N at Aynho, or from A422 turn off S at Farthinghoe.* Home-made teas. **Combined adm £4, chd free. Sun 31 May (2-6).**
Well preserved stone village, off road parking, lunch at pub. A selection of gardens, large and small, several open for the first time.

THE COTTAGE
Lady Juliet Townsend
Flowering shrubs, raised cottage garden, lawns, woodland walk, stream and lakes.

NEW **ELLESMERE**
Brackley Road. Wendy & Rod Cone
Small, mainly dry gravel garden developed from new over 5yrs. Grasses, bamboos and perennials designed for low maintenance with patio, water feature, summer house and decked dining area.

HOLLY HOUSE
Miss Alice Townsend
Walled garden with beautiful views. Kitchen garden. C18 house, not open.

HOME FARM HOUSE
Mrs N Grove-White
Paved courtyard with tubs, containers and climbers. Walled garden with roses and clematis, herbaceous border and fruit garden.

WALNUT HOUSE
Sir Paul & Lady Hayter
Large garden behind C17 farmhouse. Colour themed borders, separate enclosures with beech and yew hedges. Orchard with wild flowers, old fashioned vegetable garden. Wilderness (in C18 sense), archery lawn. Created since 1992. Some gravel.

100 CHURCH GREEN ROAD
See Buckinghamshire.

COLDOR
See Leicestershire & Rutland.

9 ◆ **COTON MANOR GARDEN**
Guilsborough NN6 8RQ. Mr & Mrs Ian Pasley-Tyler, 01604 740219, www.cotonmanor.co.uk. *10m N of Northampton, 11m SE of Rugby. From A428 & A5199 follow tourist signs.* **Adm £5, chd £2, concessions £4.50. Tues to Sats, 31 Mar-3 Oct. Suns in April & May. BH weekends. For NGS: Tue 5 May (12-5.30).**
10-acre garden set in peaceful countryside with old yew and holly hedges, extensive herbaceous borders containing many unusual plants, rose, water, herb and woodland gardens, famous bluebell wood, wild flower meadow. Adjacent specialist nursery with over 1000 plant varieties propagated from the garden. Featured in 'The English Garden'.

10 ◆ **COTTESBROOKE HALL GARDENS**
Cottesbrooke NN6 8PF. Mr & Mrs A R Macdonald-Buchanan, 01604 505808, www.cottesbrookehall.co.uk. *10m N of Northampton. Signed from J1 on A14. Off A5199 at Creaton, A508 at Brixworth.* **House & Garden £8, chd £3.50, concessions, £6.50, Garden only £5.50, chd £2.50, concessions £4.50. Phone or see website for open days & times. For NGS: Sun 26 July (2-5.30) House not open.**
Award winning gardens by Geoffrey Jellicoe, Dame Sylvia Crowe and James Alexander Sinclair. Formal gardens and terraces surround Queen Anne house with extensive vistas onto the lake and C18 parkland containing many mature trees. Wild and woodland gardens a short distance from the formal areas. Contact admin for disabled access.

COWPER & NEWTON MUSEUM GARDENS
See Buckinghamshire.

Orchard with wild flowers, old fashioned vegetable garden. Wilderness (in C18 sense) . . .

11 **DOLPHINS**
Great Harrowden NN9 5AB. Mr & Mrs R C Handley. *2m N of Wellingborough. 5m S of Kettering on A509.* Light refreshments & teas. **Adm £2.50, chd free. Sun 15 Feb (10-4).**
2-acre country garden surrounding old stone house (not open). Lge drifts of snowdrops and several smaller groups in variety. Abundant hellebores, shrubs and trees for winter interest. Very free draining with beech hedges and firm gravel paths.

12 ◆ EVENLEY WOOD GARDEN
Brackley NN13 5SH. Timothy
Whiteley, 01280 703329,
www.evenleywoodgarden.co.uk. ³/₄
m S of Brackley. A43, turn L to Evenley
straight through village towards
Mixbury, 1st turning L. **Adm £5, chd
£1. Phone or see website for
opening times & dates.** For NGS:
Sun 3, Mon 4 May (11-6).
This 60 acre woodland is a
plantsman's garden with a huge
variety of plants all of which are
labelled. Mainly trees, shrubs, bulbs
and lilies. Many magnolias, azaleas,
rhododendrons and camellias.

FARMWAY
See Leicestershire & Rutland.

Group opening

13 FINEDON GARDENS
NN9 5JN. 2m NE of Wellingborough.
6m SE Kettering, A6/A510 junction.
Home-made teas at 67- 69 High St.
Combined adm £2.50, chd free.
Suns 7, 28 June (2-6).
The village has a varied history dating
from Roman times and evolving
through farming, ironstone mining,
shoe and leather manufacturing. An
ancient parish church with a collection
of 'green men' and many other
historical buildings. The gardens are
different - everything from vegetables
to flowers on show. Local History
Society adjacent to 67/69 High St.

67-69 HIGH STREET
Mary & Stuart Hendry
(See separate entry).

INDEGARDEN
24 Albert Road. Ray & Honor
Parbery
Approx 50ft with borders of
annuals and perennials, pots and
containers, a walk through pergola,
greenhouse with cacti, period dolls
house and gypsy caravan. Seating
on patio and in summer house.

4 IRTHLINGBOROUGH ROAD
Jenny & Roger Martin
Small front garden and encl rear
garden with raised beds, fish pond
and containers, which is reached
through the rear garden at No 8
thanks to their kind permission.

WELLS COTTAGE
11 Thrapston Rd. John & Gillian
Ellson
¹/₅ -acre cottage garden with lawns
and mixed borders, gravel and
paved seating areas with planters
and water features. Pergola, rose
arches, summer house and tree
house. Mixed vegetable plot, soft
fruit and apple trees.

An ancient parish church with a collection of 'green men' and many other historical buildings . . .

Group opening

14 FLORE GARDENS
NN7 4LQ. 7m W of Northampton. 5m
E of Daventry. On A45. Lunches &
home-made teas. **Combined adm £4,
chd free (share to Flore PCC).** Sat
20, Sun 21 June (11-6).
Part of the established (46th) Village
Flower and Garden Festival. Maps
provided at official car park, signed.

BERTHAS PATCH
17 Collins Hill. Claire and Gary
Ryan
Family garden with perennial and
bedding areas and an established
secret woodland. The garden is on
three different levels around a main
lawn. Help provided with steps.

BLISS LANE NURSERY
Geoff & Chris Littlewood
Mature garden behind plant
nursery, full of surprises. Secluded,
peaceful, gorgeous views
overlooking the Nene valley,
packed with perennial plants,
shrubs and shrub roses. Access to
most areas via concrete farm road.

24 BLISS LANE
John & Sally Miller
Cottage garden filled with a mixture
of shrubs, flowers, herbs and
vegetables. Victorian-style
greenhouse and summer house.
Lots of pots.

17 THE CRESCENT
Lindsey Butler & Edward
Atkinson
Cottage style garden full of colour
and fragrance. Mixed floral borders
blend with patios and seating
areas. Unique hand built summer
house.

THE CROFT
John & Dorothy Boast
Cottage garden of about ¹/₃ acre.
Informally planted with good
structure incl several seating
areas. Planted for all-yr interest
with many perennials, shrubs, trees
and small area for fruit, vegetables
and herbs. Help provided with
gravel paths.

THE GARDEN HOUSE
The Avenue. Edward & Penny
Aubrey-Fletcher
Walled former kitchen garden
restructured in the 90s into 4
rooms, the main three separated
by swagged wisteria and a double
row of hornbeam arches. Planting
largely informal. It is still evolving.
Gravel paths OK. Gravel drive less
easy.

THE OLD BAKERY
John Amos & Karl Jones, 01327
349080, yeolbakery@aol.com.
Visitors also welcome by appt
June & July.
Maturing village garden designed in
2000 to incorporate terraces and
practical spaces for both pleasure
and relaxation. Planting ranges
from the exotic to the unusual
especially planting for shady sites.
C19 gazebo houses a unique and
growing collection of marble
crowned Queen-Empresses with
their rose and clematis namesakes.
Vegetable garden. Featured on
'Gardeners World'.

31 SPRING LANE
Margaret Clarke
Small constantly changing garden.
Another area has been cleared
this year to create a new
archway planted with shade loving
plants.

33 SPRING LANE
Rosemary Boyd
Small garden with herbaceous
flower beds, fruit trees and a
vegetable and herb area.

STONE COTTAGE
John & Pat Davis
Informal cottage garden set in approx 1/5 acre arranged over several levels with patio, lawn, pond, small fruit and vegetable area. New garden room.

Group opening

⑮ FLORE SPRING GARDENS
NN7 4LQ. *7m W of Northampton. 5m E of Daventry on A45.* Home-made teas in Chapel School Room. **Combined adm £3.50, chd free.** Sun 19 Apr (2-6). Map provided at the official car park, signed.

BLISS LANE NURSERY
Chris & Geoff Littlewood
Colourful display of spring bulbs with unusual shrubs, with drifts of daffodils and tulips in the borders. Views over the quiet, peaceful Nene valley. Access to most areas via concrete farm road.

NEW 24 BLISS LANE
John & Sally Miller
Cottage garden planted with a mixture of flowers, fruit, herbs and vegetables. Pots of bulbs and seasonal plants. Victorian style greenhouse.

THE CROFT
Kings Lane. John & Dorothy Boast
1/3 -acre well structured garden with informal planting incl a large variety of bulbs, perennials, shrubs and mature trees. Help given with gravel paths.

3 MEADOW FARM CLOSE
Eric & Jackie Ingram
Woodland garden planted with shade tolerant perennials. Spring planting around the house.

4 MEADOW FARM CLOSE
Bob & Lynne Richards
Small garden densely planted for yr-round colour. Particularly pretty in spring.

OAKLANDS
Martin & Rose Wray
Medium sized garden planted for spring colour with bulbs and shrubs under a canopy of mature oak trees.

⑯ NEW FOXTAIL LILLY
41 South Road, Oundle PE8 4BP. Tracey Mathieson, 01832 274593, tracey@mathieson4727.freeserve.co.uk. *1m town centre. From A605 at Barnwell Xrds take Barnwell Rd, 1st R to South Rd.* **Adm £3, chd free.** Sun 31 May (10-5). Visitors also welcome by appt.
A cottage garden where perennials and grasses are grouped creatively together amongst gravel paths, complementing one another to create a natural look. Some unusual plants and quirky oddities create a different and colourful informal garden. Lots of flowers for cutting, shop in barn. Featured in 'Garden News'.

Unusual plants and quirky oddities create a different and colourful informal garden . . .

⑰ FROGGERY COTTAGE
85 Breakleys Road, Desborough NN14 2PT. Mr John Lee, 01536 760002, johnlee@froggerycottage85.fsnet.co.uk. *6m N of Kettering. 5m S of Market Harborough.* Signed off A6 & A14. Lunches & home-made teas. **Adm £2, chd free.** Sun 26 July (11.30-6). Visitors also welcome by appt in groups 10+.
3/4 -acre plantsman's garden full of rare and unusual plants. National Collection of 435 varieties of penstemons incl dwarfs and species. Artefacts on display incl old ploughs and garden implements. Workshops during day. Featured in 'Garden News' and on BBC Look East Garden of the Week.

GILMORTON GARDENS
See Leicestershire & Rutland.

⑱ GREAT ADDINGTON MANOR
Great Addington NN14 4BH. Mr & Mrs G E Groome. *7m SE of Kettering. Junction 11, A510 exit off A14 signed Finedon & Wellingborough. Turn 2nd L* to the Addingtons. Home-made teas. **Adm £3, chd 5+ £1.** Mon 13 Apr (2-5). 4 1/2 -acre manor gardens with terrace, lawns, mature trees, mulberry, yew hedges, pond and spinney, spring daffodils.

Group opening

⑲ GREAT BRINGTON GARDENS
NN7 4JJ. *7m NW of Northampton. Off A428 Rugby Rd. 1st L turn past main gates of Althorp.* Coffee & lunches at Reading Room. Home-made teas at Church. **Combined adm £3.50, chd free.** Sun 3 May (11-5).
Tickets (maps and programmes) at Church, Reading Room and free car park. 7 gardens of great variety signed in village. Small attractive stone and thatch village with Spencer and Washington connections and C12 church. Local history exhibition & plant stalls.

BEARD'S COTTAGE
Captain Bill Bellamy
1/2 -acre of lawns, shrubs and herbaceous borders. Large orchard with maturing bluebells and primroses in three small copses. Steep gravel path between 2 gardens.

8 BEDFORD COTTAGES
Anne & Bob Billingsby
Long sloping N-facing garden with outstanding views. Designed, created and maintained by the owners. Many shrubs and herbaceous plants for all-yr interest.

BRINGTON LODGE
Peter & Jenny Cooch
3/4 -acre, partly walled, beautiful mature garden overlooking the Althorp Estate.

THE OLD RECTORY
Mr & Mrs R Thomas, 01604 770727, jewelbrington@hotmail.com. Visitors also welcome by appt April-Sept.
3-acre garden with mature trees, yew hedging, formal rose garden, vegetable garden, flower borders and 1/3 acre orchard, secret garden. Gravel paths but all level.

RIDGWAY HOUSE
Mr & Mrs R Steedman
1½ -acres. A blend of more formal areas, inc 2 rose gardens and orchard, and less formal herbaceous borders, many spring flowering shrubs and bulbs. Gravel paths.
&. 🐕 🗙

ROSE COTTAGE
David Green & Elaine MacKenzie
Small cottage garden continues to evolve with the acquisition of the 'new' garden next door. Shady woodland area and pond garden incl a patio/dining area, water features and a small sensory garden.

THE STABLES
Mrs A George
Small cottage garden containing shrubs, herbaceous plants and climbers. Compact and unusual shape with water feature and summer house. Small step.
&.

---

20 GREENWAY
Pipewell Road, Desborough NN14 2SN. Robert Bass. *6m NW of Kettering, 5m SE of Market Harborough. On B576. 150 metres E of Pipewell Rd railway bridge and Travis Perkins builders' yard.* Home-made teas. **Adm £2, chd free. Sun 10 May (2-6). Evening Opening wine, Thur 28 May (6-9).**
Constantly evolving arboretum style garden set in 1/3 acre with over 80 acers (Japanese maple cultivars) in containers and open planting. Many garden structures, water features, statuary and containers to provide year round interest. Recent additions incl gothic folly with fernery and a viewing platform. Covered seating areas for contemplation.
&. ⊛ 🍵

21 GREYWALLS
Farndish NN29 7HJ. Mrs P M Anderson. *2½ m SE of Wellingborough. A609 from Wellingborough, B570 to Irchester, turn to Farndish by cenotaph. House adjacent to church.* Light refreshments & teas. **Adm £3, chd free (share to St Katherine's Church). Sun 22 Feb (12-4).**
2-acre mature garden surrounding old vicarage (not open). Over 100 varieties of snowdrops, drifts of hardy cyclamen and hellebores. Alpine house and raised alpine beds. Water features and natural ponds with views over open countryside.
&. 🗙 ⊛ 🍵

Drifts of hardy cyclamen and hellebores . . .

Group opening

22 GUILSBOROUGH & HOLLOWELL MAY GARDENS
NN6 8PY. *10m NW Northampton, 5m S of junction 1 on A14. Between A5199 and A428.* Home-made teas at Dripwell House. **Combined adm £4, chd free. Sat 16, Sun 17 May (1-5).**
3 plantsman's gardens with azaleas, shrubs, woodland, alpines and many rare and unusual plants. 2 small hilltop village gardens and a large garden down a terraced N-facing slope. Wild flowers, vegetable gardens and orchards. Ponds, a bog garden and use of natural springs featured.
⊛ 🍵

DRIPWELL HOUSE
Mr J W Langfield & Dr C Moss, 01604 740755/740140, cattimoss@aol.com. Visitors also welcome by appt in May & June, combined with Gower House.
3-acre mature garden. Many fine trees and shrubs on partly terraced slope. Rock garden, herbaceous borders, herb, wild flower and vegetable gardens, soft fruit and apple orchard. Unusual shrubs, rhododendrons and azaleas in woodland garden.☎

GOWER HOUSE
Peter & Ann Moss, 01604 740755. Visitors also welcome by appt in May & June, combined with Dripwell House.
Plantsman's garden with perennials, orchids, wild flowers and alpines packed into a small cottage type garden. Soft fruit and vegetable garden shared with Dripwell. Many seating areas designed for elderly relatives.
🗙 ☎

ROSEMOUNT
Mr & Mrs J Leatherland
(See separate entry).

Group opening

23 GUILSBOROUGH SPRING GARDENS
NN6 8PT. *10m NW of Northampton. 10m E of Rugby. Between A5199 & A428. Parking in field at Guilsborough House.* Light refreshments & teas at Four Acres. **Combined adm £4, chd free. Sat 25, Sun 26 Apr (1-5).**
Village set in beautiful rolling countryside. 7 gardens of different styles most with wonderful views and plenty of room to sit and relax. Come early - there's a lot to see. Maps provided. Parking at Guilsborough House.
⊛ 🍵

FOUR ACRES
Mark & Gay Webster
In the family for over 60yrs. Venerable old shrubs and conifers wth recent plantings of bulbs and spring flowers for an exhuberant display. Productive potager and trained fruit trees aid self-sufficiency. Long gravel drive.
&.

THE GATE HOUSE
Mike & Sarah Edwards
Small multi-level encl cottage garden with pond and encl well stocked borders with flowers, shrubs, vegetables, fruit and trees. Some steps, but help available.

GUILSBOROUGH HOUSE
Mr & Mrs John McCall
Country garden, terraces, lawns and hedges and mature trees with emphasis on texture and form. Plenty of room and shade for picnic in field - improved access. In celebration of becoming OAPs we have a new tree planting project.
&.

NORTOFT GRANGE
Sir John & Lady Lowther
We are fanatical gardeners! With glorious borders, fantastic views, a wildflower meadow, a pond where you can feed large carp and a well stock plant stall, you will not be disappointed.
⊛

OAK DENE
Mr & Mrs A Darker
Small encl cottage garden with interesting trees and a variety of foliage. Vast array of plants, grasses and flowers for yr-round colour. A good example of what can be achieved in a small space.
&. 🗙

THE OLD HOUSE
Richard & Libby Seaton Evans
1-acre of lawns, herbaceous borders, spring flowers and walled kitchen garden. Additional woodland with wild flowers, paddocks and a wonderful view, enhanced by llamas, mares and foals.

THE OLD VICARAGE
John & Christine Benbow
1½ -acre garden revitalised over the past 6 years. Colourful herbaceous borders with spring bulbs, especially tulips. Woodland areas, small pond, walled vegetable garden leading down to orchard in meadow.

HAMMOND ARBORETUM
See Leicestershire & Rutland.

Wall sculptures and other artifacts together with a small water feature . . .

24 HARPOLE GARDENS
NN7 4BX. 4m W Northampton. On A45 towards Weedon. Turn R at The Turnpike Hotel into Harpole. Home-made teas at The Close. **Combined adm £4, chd free. Sun 21 June (12-6).**
Village maps given to all visitors.

NEW BRYTTEN-COLLIER HOUSE
James & Lucy Strickland
Partly walled S-facing garden with herbaceous borders and many climbing roses and clematis.

THE CLOSE
Michael Orton-Jones
Old-fashioned English country garden with large lawns, herbaceous borders and mature trees. Stone house (not open).

74 LARKHALL LANE
Mr & Mrs J Leahy
Medium-sized informal garden with a wide variety of plants, shrubs, some mature trees, climbers, alpines, grasses, small pond and a variety of pots. 1 step from patio, 1 path unsuitable, others paved.

19 MANOR CLOSE
Caroline & Andy Kemshed
40yds ◊ 10yds flower arranger's garden on an estate, cultivated by present owners since 1975.

17 MANOR CLOSE
Irene & Ian Wilkinson
Small, well stocked garden with lawns, gravel areas, pond and mixed borders.

MILLERS
Mr & Mrs M Still
Old stone farmhouse (not open) with 1 acre of lawns and mixed borders, mainly shrubs, some mature trees, good views overlooking the farm and strawberry field.

NEW THE OLD DAIRY
David & Di Ballard
Walled secret garden based on 2 intersecting part circles. Small trees and shrubs are interspersed with cottage garden planting, wall sculptures and other artifacts together with a small water feature. Access 70cms wide, 10cms step.

25 67-69 HIGH STREET
Finedon NN9 5JN. Mary & Stuart Hendry, 01933 680414, hendrymary@hotmail.com. 6m SE Kettering, junction A6 & A510. **Adm £2.50, chd free. Evening Openings** wine, Thurs 11, 18 June (5-9). **Visitors also welcome by appt Feb to Sept, groups 4+.**
Constantly evolving, ⅓ -acre rear garden of C17 cottage (not open). Mixed borders, obelisks and containers, kitchen garden and herb bed. Rope border, spring garden, snowdrops and hellebores, late summer borders. Also open with Finedon Gardens. Featured in 'Garden News'.

26 HILL GROUNDS
Evenley NN13 5RZ. Mr & Mrs C F Cropley, 01280 703224, cropleyhg@hotmail.co.uk. 1m S of Brackley. On A43, turn L into Evenley. R off Church Lane. Visitors welcome by appt.
Plantsman's garden of 2 acres, surrounded by C19 200yd yew hedge. Planted for yr-round interest. Bulbs, terrace, rose pergola, double herbaceous borders. Many rare and less hardy plants grown. Millennium 'arborette'. Cuttings & seedlings as they come.

HILLESDEN HOUSE
See Buckinghamshire.

27 KILSBY GARDENS
CV23 8XP. 5m SE of Rugby. 6m N of Daventry on A361. On A428 turn R on B4038 through village. Home-made teas at and in aid of Kilsby Village Hall. **Combined adm £3.50, chd free.** Sun 14 June (1-5).
On Watling St and close to the famous Kilsby Railway Tunnel. Compact village with numerous listed houses, historic church, village school and 2 pubs. Pleasantly rural with good ridge and furrow fields around. Gardens open vary from yr to yr. A friendly welcome awaits you. Embroidery exhibition at village hall.

HUNT HOUSE
Lulu Harris, 01788 823282, luluharris@hunthouse. fsbusiness.co.uk. Visitors also welcome by appt.
English country gardens within gardens. Lawn, gravel paths, cottage borders, herbaceous and herb borders, patio gardens. Spring delight. Ramp to main garden, some gravel and cobbles.

NEW 12 MAIN ROAD
Mrs S Cornes
Long narrow garden transformed by landscaping in spring 2008. Creation of curved herbaceous borders with shrubs and perennials giving colour all yr. Pergola arches with climbers, mature fruit trees, raised vegetable beds, pond.

PYTCHLEY HOUSE
Mr & Mrs T F Clay
Garden downsized to ½ -acre and being developed and re-shaped. 2 ponds, one a C19 reservoir discovered while creating a new herbaceous bed. Linked lawns with island beds. Vegetables in deep beds, fruit trees and soft fruit.

RAINBOW'S END
7 Middle Street. Mr & Mrs J Madigan
Small garden, large pond, quirky features.

NEW YADRAN
10 Rugby Road. Mr & Mrs L Widdicombe
Medium-sized country garden with open aspect, mature trees and shrubs. Well stocked herbaceous borders, secluded courtyard, seating area, small water feature, climbing roses and colourful pots.

Group opening

28 LITCHBOROUGH GARDENS
NN12 8JH. *10m SW of Northampton, nr Towcester. Please use car park nr village green. Maps provided.* Home-made teas. **Combined adm £4, chd free (share to Baptist Church).** Sun 28 June (2-6).
A small attractive ironstone village with conservation area, listed buildings and C13 church.

ABBOTS LEA
M Cronin
Lawn with surrounding flower beds.

BRUYERE COURT
Mr M Billington
3 acres of landscaped garden. Lawns, 2 ornamental lakes with rock streams and fountain, shrubs, rhododendrons, azaleas and herbaceous borders, old-fashioned roses, ornamental trees and conifers.

THE HALL
Mr & Mrs A R Heygate
Large garden with open views of parkland, laid to lawns and borders with clipped hedges. Extensive woodland garden with specimen trees and shrubs. Walks wind through this area and around the lakes. No wheelchair access to woodland glade, gravel paths.

NEW THE HOSTELRY
John & Anna Prior
Small front courtyard with patio and planted area and the back garden under development.

NEW THE HOUSE ON THE GREEN
Keith & Jackie Ellis
⅓ -acre cottage garden with well, summerhouse, water feature, variety of trees, roses and shrubs, vegetables and soft fruit, walled herb garden and patio.

NEW KILN COTTAGE
Mr & Mrs Graham & Sarah Hobbs, 01327 831318, sandg.hobbs@btinternet.com. Visitors also welcome by appt.
Complete redesign over the last 18 months. Arbour, hot tub, herb and cottage beds plus hopefully a shepherd's hut. All development by owners and friends. Various levels and steps.

2 KILN LANE
Anna Steiner
Flag like sculptures capturing natural elements of the garden, wind, shadows and movement. A green garden with oak tree and willows.

4 KILN LANE
Mr & Mrs Linnell
300yr-old cottage (not open) with modern cottage garden. Developed over 10yrs following levelling, terracing and hard landscaping incl the construction of 2 ponds, retaining existing trees and shrubs.

NEW THE LIME HOUSE
Mr & Mrs L Skinner
Very pretty small cottage garden.

ORCHARD HOUSE
Mr & Mrs B Smith
Landscape architects' country garden surrounding listed building (not open) designed for low maintenance. Orchard, pools, conservatory and working pump.

NEW THE ROSARY
Mr & Mrs G J Lugar-Mawson
Terraced mixed garden to an C18 village house with some work still in progress. Several stone steps.

TIVY FARM
Mr & Mrs J Pulford
Lawn sloping down to large wildlife pond surrounded by beautiful trees. Patio with lovely pots and containers.

51 TOWCESTER ROAD
Mr Norman Drinkwater
Small council house garden featuring lawns, shrubs, rockery and productive vegetable garden.

Attractive ironstone village with conservation area . . .

Group opening

29 LONG BUCKBY GARDENS
NN6 7RE. *8m NW of Northampton, midway between A428 & A5. 6 gardens in village close to Square, WC and parking. Mill House at junction of A428 and Long Lane, 1m distant with parking.* Home-made teas at 45 Brington Road. **Combined adm £3.50, chd free.** Sun 21 June (1-6).
One large garden in the countryside outside the village, 1 medium-sized and 5 small gardens in the village. Small gardens have a variety of layout and planting with 3 on sloping sites. The 7 incl organic gardens, shrub beds, perennials annual bedding, a wide range of water features and garden structures, wildlife areas and fruit and vegetables.

NEW ASHMORE HOUSE
24 East Street. Mike Greaves & Sally Sokoloff
Small encl garden with formal lawn, pool, mixed borders and unusual iron well-head separated by yew hedge from informal area with narrow gravel path, tree arbour and wildlife pond. Topiary and stilt-hedge developing. Narrow gravel paths.

45 BRINGTON ROAD
Derick & Sandra Cooper, 01327 843762. Visitors also welcome by appt.
1/3 -acre organic village garden designed to create haven of peace and harmony, home to unusual wildlife. Features incl rose walk, 4 varied water features, Victorian-style greenhouse and summerhouse surrounded by box-edged raised vegetable plots. All constructed from reclaimed materials. Army field kitchen which fed 2nd WW troops from France to Belgium. Vegetables for sale.

NEW 11 HARBIDGES LANE
Mr & Mrs J & L Huxtable
Small secluded garden on 3 levels. Fishpond with waterfall, flower beds, shrubs, wild garden for butterflies and wildlife. No parking in lane.

7 HIGH STACK
Tiny & Sheila
Cottage garden on 2 levels, established over 7 yrs. Mixed borders, vegetables and fruit, pond, patio and seating area. Gravelled front garden with perennial planting.

MILL HOUSE
Long Lane. Ken and Gill Pawson, 01604 770103, gill@gpplanning.co.uk. Visitors also welcome by appt.
Over 1 acre in open countryside. Large fruit and vegetable plot with some old and rare varieties. Owner is Heritage Seed Library Guardian. Orchard, pergola, pond, grasses, hot garden, borders and shady areas. Foundations of East Haddon Windmill.

NEW 10 TEBBITT CLOSE
Molly Brown
Sloping garden with mixed shrubs and perennial plants, varying textures and foliage. Steep ramp beside house, help needed, owner willing.

TORESTIN
10 Lime Ave. June Ford
1/3 -acre mature garden divided into 3 separate areas incorporating water features, rockeries and pergolas. Interesting perennials, clematis and roses.

38 LOW STREET
See Lincolnshire.

30 ♦ LYVEDEN NEW BIELD
Oundle PE8 5AT. The National Trust, 01832 205358, www.@nationaltrust.org.uk. 5m SW of Oundle, 3m E of Brigstock. Signed off A427 & A6116. Adm £4, chd free. Wed to Sun, Mar-Nov. For NGS: Sat 18 July (10.30-5).
One of England's oldest garden landscapes, abandoned in 1605 after family involvement in the Gunpowder Plot, Lyveden still retains original terraces, prospect mounts, canals and the impressive garden lodge built to symbolise the Tresham's catholic faith. Recently replanted 5-acre orchard of pre-C17 tree varieties.

31 THE MALTINGS
10 The Green, Clipston LE16 9RS.
Mr & Mrs Hamish Connell, 01858 525336, j.connell118@btinternet.com. 4m S of Market Harborough, 9m W of Kettering, 10m N Northampton. From A14 take junction 2, A508 N. After 2m turn L for Clipston. 2 houses away from Old Red Lion. Cream teas. Adm £3, chd free. Mon 13 Apr (11-6) Sats, Suns 11 & 12 April, 13 & 14 June; 11 &12 July. Sats (1-6), Suns (11-6). Visitors also welcome by appt for groups 10+ all yr. Meals at village PH.
3/4 acre sloping plantsman's garden designed for all year interest by the present owner over more than 10 years. Many unusual plants, shrubs, old and new trees. Over 50 different clematis, wild garden walk, spring bulb area, over 20 different species roses, 2 ponds connected by a stream, bog garden, many different fruits and vegetables. Home made cake stall. Swing & slide for children. Wheelchair access difficult, older people may need a little help.

32 ♦ THE MENAGERIE
Newport Pagnell Road, Horton NN7 2BX. Mr A Myers, 01604 870710. 6m S of Northampton. 1m S of Horton. On B526, turn E at lay-by, across field. Adm £5, chd £1.50, concessions £4. For NGS: Sat 27 June (2-6).
Newly developed gardens set around C18 folly, with 2 delightful thatched arbours. Recently completed large formal walled garden with fountain, used for vegetables, fruit and cutting flowers. Recently extended exotic bog garden and native wetland area. Also

rose garden, shrubberies, herbaceous borders and wild flower areas.

MIDDLETON CHENEY GARDENS
See Oxfordshire.

33 NEW 71 MIDLAND ROAD
NN10 9UJ. Mrs Shirley Jackson, 01933 386710. 4m E Wellingborough. From Rushden High Street turn into Station Rd, R to Midland Rd. Light refreshments & teas. Adm £3, chd free. Visitors welcome by appt from June to August, 2-4.30, not Mon or Wed.
Unusual shaped terraced house garden extended by demolishing factory leaving 8ft high wall. Collection of clematis, Japanese maples, hemerocallis, hostas, bonsai and many plants packed to give a colourful effect. Summerhouse overlooks a pond containing many Koi carp to give a restful aspect.

Pre-war Austin 7 cars on show . . .

Group opening

34 NEW NASEBY GARDENS
NN6 6DE. 9m E of M1, M6, A14 Junction. 5m S Market Harborough on A508. R turn signed Naseby, 3m. Home-made teas at village hall. Combined adm £4, chd free. Sun 21 Jun (1-6).
An historic battle villlage set in lovely rolling countryside and the site of the source of the R Avon. Several interesting Victorian and earlier buildings, monuments and viewing platforms relating to the famous battle of 1645.

NEW 44 HIGH STREET
Pat & Robin Oldfield
3/4 -acre mature garden with an outlook over open fields. Formerly the gardens of 4 Victorian workers cottages, it incl lawns, cottage garden borders and a gravel garden. Pre-war Austin 7 cars on show.

NEW NEWHALL FARM
Scott & Julie Westaway
Large cottage style garden with
unusual herbaceous plants.

NEW 3 NEWLANDS
Pete & Roz Bradshaw
Victorian cottage garden with
perennial borders, pond and
original well.

NEW NOW & THEN
Mr & Mrs S L Booth
Cottage garden with large
perennial border and ornamental
vegetable areas.
✈ ✿

**35 THE OLD RECTORY,
BROCKHALL**
NN7 4JY. Mrs J Quarmby, 01327
340280,
jane.quarmby@tqtraining.co.uk. *2m
E of Weedon towards Flore. In village,
as you enter from Flore, opp church.*
Home-made teas. **Adm £4, chd free.
Sat 29, Sun 30 Aug (2-5.30). Visitors
also welcome by appt for groups
10+.**
4¹/₂ -acres being restored by the
owners. Large sweeping lawns, very
colourful flower cutting garden, newly
created shady planting area, ¹/₂ -acre
working kitchen garden, arboretum,
pool garden, herbaceous borders,
wildlife area and free range chickens.
Concert on Saturday evening.

wildlife ponds and wonderful views over unspoilt countryside . . .

**36 THE OLD RECTORY,
HASELBECH**
Cottesbrook Road. NN6 9LJ. Mr &
Mrs P C Flory, 01604 686432. *12m N
of Northampton. L turn off A508 just S
of A14 junction, 2m to village. A14
junction 2, take A508 towards
Northampton. 1st R to Haselbech.*
Home-made teas. **Adm £3.50, chd
free (share to St Michaels Church).
Visitors welcome by appt, incl
coaches.**

1-acre garden set in 9 acres, incl tree
plantations, with glorious unspoilt
views, surrounding Georgian rectory
(not open). Old walled garden,
herbaceous borders, rose garden with
clipped box hedge, yew and beech
hedges. Small potager vegetable
garden and interesting bog garden.
Lovely planted terrace area overlooking
lawn, ha-ha and magnificent trees.
Overlooking farmland and totally
unspoilt views. One steep slope, some
gravel paths.

**37 ♦ THE OLD RECTORY,
SUDBOROUGH**
NN14 3BX. Mr & Mrs A Huntington,
01832 733247,
info@oldrectorygardens.co.uk. *8m
NE of Kettering. Exit 12 off A14. Village
just off A6116 between Thrapston &
Brigstock.* Home-made teas. **Adm £4,
chd free (share to All Saints Church
15 March). Tues, Mar-Sept, groups
welcome. For NGS: Sun 15 Mar (2-
6); Sat 13 June (10-6) in conjunction
with Marie Curie.**
Classic 3-acre country garden with
extensive herbaceous borders of
unusual plants. Magnolias and cornus
in spring, containers of bulbs and large
plantings of tulips and daffodils, early
rare hellebores. Formal rose circle and
box edged potager designed by
Rosemary Verey, woodland walk and
pond alongside Harpers Brook. Some
gravel paths.

Group opening

38 PRESTON CAPES GARDENS
NN11 3TF. *6m SW of Daventry. 13m
NE of Banbury. 3m N of Canons
Ashby.* Lunches & home-made teas.
**Combined adm £4, chd free. Sun 7
June (12-5).**
Unspoilt rural village in the
Northamptonshire uplands. Local
sandstone houses and cottages,
Norman Church. Village maps for all
visitors.
✈ ☕

CITY COTTAGE
Mr & Mrs Gavin Cowen, 01327
361603. Visitors also welcome
by appt in June, groups 10+.
Mature garden in the middle of an
attractive village. Walled
herbaceous border, newly planted
rose beds, flowering shrubs and
wisteria.

LADYCROFT
Mervyn & Sophia Maddison
Contemporary garden, planted
since 2005 for yr-round interest, on
exposed site with fine views.
Gravel drive.
♿

LANGDALE HOUSE
Michael & Penny Eves
1-acre country garden with far-
reaching views designed and
maintained by the owners. Foliage
plants for sun and shade,
herbaceous border, semi-formal
wildlife pond planted with mainly
native species and Mediterranean
gravel bed. No access to small
woodland but can be viewed from
above.

NORTH FARM
Mr & Mrs Tim Coleridge
Rural farmhouse garden
maintained by owners.
Outstanding view towards Fawsley
and High Wood.

OLD WEST FARM
Mr & Mrs Gerard Hoare, 01327
361263, claire.hoare@virgin.net.
³/₄ m E of Preston Capes. Visitors
also welcome by appt in June,
groups 10+.
Rural 2-acre garden. Borders of
interesting and unusual plants,
roses and shrubs. Woodland area
underplanted with shrubs.
Exposed site with shelter planting,
maintained by the owners without
help, so designed for easy upkeep.
Small raised vegetable gardenl.

VILLAGE FARM
Trevor & Julia Clarke, 01327
361263. Visitors also welcome
by appt in June, July, Aug. Book
2 weeks in advance.
Large garden on steeply sloping
site. Interesting trees and shrubs,
3 large wildlife ponds and
wonderful views over unspoilt
countryside. Rare breed cattle, Old
English Longhorns. Steep slopes
limits wheelchairs.

**WEST ORCHARD FARM
HOUSE**
Mr & Mrs Nick Price
1-acre informal garden with
outstanding views. Renovated
completely by Caroline Price and
replanted with shrubs and
herbaceous plants.

PRIORS MARSTON MANOR GARDEN

See Warwickshire & part of West Midlands.

Group opening

39 NEW RAVENSTHORPE GARDENS

NN6 8ES. *7m NW of Northampton. Signed from A5199 and the A428.* Home-made teas at village hall. **Combined adm £4, chd free. Sun 12 July (2-6).** Attractive villlage in Northamptonshire uplands near to Ravensthorpe reservoir which has bird watching and picnic opportunities. 5 very different gardens, some well established, one in the process of development. Disabled WC at village hall.

MILL HOUSE

Ken and Gill Pawson, 01604 770103, gill@gpplanning.co.uk. Visitors also welcome by appt. Over 1-acre in open countryside. Large vegetable and fruit area with some old and rare varieties. Owner is Heritage Seed Library Guardian. Orchard, pergola, pond, grasses, hot garden, borders and shady area. Foundations of windmill.

NEW THE OLD FORGE HOUSE

Brian & Anna Guest
Long sloping garden with southerly aspect. Rose garden and long borders in the 2nd season of development. Courtyard and small natural woodland walk.

NEW QUIET WAYS

Russ & Sally Barringer
Approx 1/3 -acre. Garden has evolved to encourage wildlife with natural pond as shelter and feeding for birds and hedgehogs, work in progress for kitchen garden and outdoor room with woodburner. Many shrubs and herbaceous borders.

NEW RAVENSTHORPE NURSERY

Mr & Mrs Richard Wiseman, 01604 770548. Visitors also welcome by appt except Mondays.

Approx 3/4 -acre garden planted with many unusual shrubs and herbaceous perennials over the last 20yrs to reflect the wide range grown in the nursery. Shrub rose border and beautiful views.

NEW TORCH HILL BUNGALOW

Bill Saunders
1-acre low maintainance relaxing lawn area dotted with specimen trees. Large spring fed wildlife pond and interesting shrubbery surrounded by natural hedges and views over open countryside.

Pretty field with sheep, ducks and hens . . .

40 NEW ROSEANNS ROSE GARDEN

55 The Grove, Moulton NN3 7UE. Peter Hughes, Roseanne Hughes, Irene Kay, Mary Morris. *3m N Northampton on A43. Into village centre, pass St Peter & Paul Church. L at T junction, 80yds on L.* Light refreshments & teas. **Adm £3, chd free. Sun 2 Aug (11-5).** Mature garden set mostly to roses, over 350 bushes, many different. Several main enclosed areas, fish ponds, gazebos, arbours with rose covered arches, several small and unusual trees incl small pine trees.

41 ROSEBRIAR

83 Main Road, Collyweston PE9 3PQ. Jenny Harrison, 01780 444389. *On A43 3 1/2 m SW of Stamford. 3 doors from pub.* **Adm £3, chd free (share to Hearing Dogs). Sun 7 June (11-6).** Visitors also welcome by appt.
The garden, which is on quite a steep slope, contains a variety of areas with alpine and grass beds, water feature with stream and bog garden, surrounded by herbaceous and shrub borders lavishly planted with exciting combinations, linked by gravel paths, patios and original sculptures.

42 ROSEMOUNT

Church Hill, Hollowell NN6 8RR. Mr & Mrs Leatherland, 01604 740354. *10m NW of Northampton, 5m S junction 1 A14. Between A5199 and A428.* **Adm £2, chd free. Sun 15 Feb (11-4).** Visitors also welcome by appt from Feb to Aug, groups 10+.
1/2 -acre plantsman's garden. Unusual plants and shrubs, alpine garden, fish pond, small collections of clematis, camellias and abutilons. Snowdrops, hellebores and spring bulbs. Unusual varieties for sale. Also open with **Guilsborough and Hollowell May Gardens.**

SOUTH KILWORTH GARDENS

See Leicestershire & Rutland.

CROFT ACRE

See Leicestershire & Rutland.

Group opening

43 SPRATTON GARDENS

NN6 8HL. *6 1/2 m NNW of Northampton. From Northampton on A5199 turn L at Holdenby Rd for Spratton Grange Farm, after 1/2 m turn L up long drive. For other gardens turn R at Brixworth Rd. Car park signed.* Refreshments & teas at St Andrews Church. **Combined adm £4, chd free. Sun 10 May (12-5).** Attractive village with many C17 ironstone houses and C12 church. Tickets and maps at gardens.

NEW DALE HOUSE

Fiona & Chris Cox, 01604 846458, cjcatdalehouse@aol.com. Visitors also welcome by appt Home-made teas.
3-acre village garden incl ha-ha and small wood. Ancient Holm Oak, prolific wisteria, roses and lavender. Pretty field with sheep, ducks and hens. Children welcome.

NEW FORGE COTTAGE

Daniel Bailey & Jo Lawrence
Newly established cottage style garden completely redesigned and replanted by new owners with a family in mind.

THE GRANARY
Stephanie Bamford & Mark Wilkinson
Semi-formal courtyard garden with circular pond, walled rear garden with circular lawn, mixed shrub and flower borders, archways through to small orchard. Some shallow steps.

11 HIGH STREET
Philip & Frances Roseblade
Small and compact, making full use of a difficult shape. Neat hedging and topiary.

MULBERRY COTTAGE
Michael & Morley Heaton, 01604 846032. Visitors also welcome by appt from April to July, groups 10+, £2.50 ea, refreshments available.
1/2 -acre part cottage-style. Feature mulberry tree, lawns, herbaceous, rose and shrub borders, shady planting and water features.☎

SPRATTON GRANGE FARM
Dennis & Christine Yardy
2-acre garden in an elevated position with superb country views, courtyard, parterre and large walled area with mature borders. A naturally fed pond with bog garden leading to a small spinney.

THE STABLES
Pam & Tony Woods
A plant lover's garden of approx 3/4 -acre with trees and a wide variety of shrubs and herbaceous perennials in areas of differing character, scree planting, rockery, stream, ponds, pergola and vegetable garden.

WALTHAM COTTAGE
Norma & Allan Simons
Small cottage garden that has evolved over the years with some interesting features.

The vine and clematis covered pergola is a haven for sundowners . . .

44 ♦ STEANE PARK
NN13 6DP. Lady Connell, www.steanepark.co.uk. 2m from Brackley towards Banbury. On A422, 6m E of Banbury. **Adm £4.50, chd free under 5. For NGS: Sun 31 May (11-5).**
Beautiful trees in 80 acres of parkland, old waterway and fishponds, 1620 church in grounds. The gardens are constantly being remade and redesigned in sympathy with old stone house and church. Limited access for wheelchairs.

STOKE ALBANY HOUSE
See Leicestershire & Rutland.

Group opening

45 SULGRAVE GARDENS
Banbury OX17 2RP. 8m NE of Banbury. Just off B4525 Banbury to Northampton rd, 7m from J11 off M40. Home-made teas at The Cottage. **Combined adm £4, chd free.** Sun 14 June (2-6).
Small historic village with lovely stone houses, C14 church and C16 manor house, home of George Washington's ancestors. Award winning community owned and run village shop.

CHURCH COTTAGE
Church Street. Hywel & Ingram Lloyd
1/2 -acre garden with shrubs, trees, rambling roses and pond. Mixed planting for colour, form and scent throughout the yr. Good range of shade tolerant plants, developing wild area. Fine view.

NEW EAGLE HOUSE
Gillie Clegg
Attractive walled garden replanted in 2008 providing herbaceous borders with seasonal shrubs and colourful perennials. Patio attracts the morning sun, the vine and clematis covered pergola is a haven for sundowners.

THE HERB SOCIETY GARDEN AT SULGRAVE MANOR
The Herb Society
Formal gardens, created in the 1920s by Sir Reginald Blomfield, with orchard, parterre, lawns and herbaceous borders. The Manor hosts the National Garden of The Herb Society with themed beds.

MILL HOLLOW BARN
David Thompson
7-acre garden with different levels and aspects, being developed for all-yr interest and to house a wide range of plants. Water gardens, shrubberies, herbaceous borders and gravel garden. Newly planted arboretum with rare and interesting trees.

NEW SUNNYMEAD
Bob & Jean Bates
Mature, restful 1/4 -acre garden set on 3 sides of the house. Mature trees, shrubs and traditionally planted borders and lawns, being updated by the present owners.

THREEWAYS
Alison & Digby Lewis
Old cottage garden on 2 levels enclosed by stone walls. Mainly herbaceous perennial planting with old roses, clematis and white wisteria on walls. Various fruit trees and bushes, container grown vegetables.

THE WATERMILL
Mr & Mrs A J Todd
Contemporary garden set around C17 watermill and pond. Extensive mixed planting in borders and gravel, winding stream, new woodland and pathways. Designed by James Alexander Sinclair. Featured in 'House & Garden'.

46 NEW THIMBLE HALL
601 Harlstone Road. NN5 6NU. Mrs Maureen Basford, 01604 751208. 4m W of Northampton on A428. 1 1/2 m from Lower Harlestone, 3 1/2 m Althorp. Home-made teas. **Adm £3.50 (share to S Midlands Barn Owl Conservation).** Visitors welcome by appt in June, July, Aug for groups max 20.
Small garden divided into small rooms with some unusual plants. Wildlife pond, barn owls on display, garden shop. Sorry, no children under 12yrs. Narrow gravel paths.

THORPE LUBENHAM HALL
See Leicestershire & Rutland.

47 NEW TILE HOUSE FARM

Fulwell Rd, Finmere MK18 4AS. Peter & Buzzy Lepper, 01280 848358, www.tilehouseplants.co.uk. *4m E Brackley, 4m W of Buckingham. From A421 through Finmere on Fulwell Rd to Westbury. From A422 towards Finmere follow daisy sign.* Home-made teas. **Adm £3, chd free. Sun 5 July (2-6). Evening Opening** wine, Wed 17 June (6-9). **Visitors also welcome by appt.**

³/₄ -acre farmhouse garden with a cottage garden atmosphere. Herbaceous beds, kitchen garden with raised beds, pond and gravel garden. Adjacent nursery. Partial wheelchair access.

Unspoilt rural stonebuilt village and church with C13 tower and unusual C17 clock . . .

48 TITCHMARSH HOUSE

Chapel Street. NN14 3DA. Sir Ewan & Lady Harper, 01832 732439, jenny.harper@church-schools.com. *2m N of Thrapston. 6m S of Oundle. Exit A14 at A605 junction, Titchmarsh signed as turning to E.* Light refreshments & teas at village fete. **Adm £3, chd free. Sat 13 June (12-5). Visitors also welcome by appt from April to 15 June.**

4¹/₂ -acres extended and laid out since 1972. Cherries, magnolias, herbaceous, irises, shrub roses, range of unusual shrubs, walled borders and ornamental vegetable garden. Village Fete Day.

49 TOP LODGE

Violet Lane, Glendon NN14 1QL. Glenn & Anne Burley, 01536 511784. *3m NW of Kettering. Take A6003 to Corby, off r'about W of Kettering turn L onto Glendon Rd, signed at T-lights, approx 2m L into Violet Lane.* Cream teas. **Adm £3, chd free. Sun 14 June (2-5.30). Visitors also welcome by appt in June & July.**

1¹/₂ -acre garden which is full of pleasant surprises around every corner. Large collection of plants, some rare and unusual shrubs plus a good selection of climbing roses and clematis. Woodland area, pond with stream and waterfalls, gravel, secluded garden and a children's garden. Access mostly on grass.

Group opening

50 TURWESTON GARDENS

Brackley NN13 5JY. *A43 from M40 J10. On Brackley bypass turn R on A422 towards Buckingham, ¹/₂ m turn L signed Turweston.* Cream teas at Versions Farm. **Combined adm £3.50, chd free. Sun 24 May (2-5.30).** Charming unspoilt stone built village in a conservation area near the head of the R Great Ousel.

NEW SPRING VALLEY

Mr & Mrs A Wildish
1-acre terraced garden leading to formal and informal ponds, bog garden, herbaceous borders and vegetable garden. Wheelchairs view garden from terrace.

TURWESTON MILL

Mr & Mrs Harry Leventis
5-acre beautifully designed garden making full use of the mill stream with water garden waterfall and wildlife ponds. Lawns with lovely trees and herbaceous borders and newly designed kitchen garden with raised beds.

VERSIONS FARM

Mrs E T Smyth-Osbourne
3-acre plantsman's garden. Wide-range of unusual plants, shrubs and trees. Old stone walls, terraces, old-fashioned rose garden, pond. Conservatory. Part of the garden has been re-designed with pergola and small water garden designed by Anthony Barry.

51 NEW TURWESTON HOUSE

NN13 5JX. Mr & Mrs C Allen. *On A43 from M40 J10. On Brackley bypass turn R on A422 towards Buckingham. ¹/₂ m turn L signed Turweston.* Home-made teas. **Adm £3, chd free. Sun 14 June.**

5 acres of gardens which feature magnificent old beech trees, walled flower, herb and vegetable gardens. Less formal areas incl woodland walk around the lake. Gravel paths and some steep slopes.

Group opening

52 NEW WAPPENHAM GARDENS

NN12 8SJ. *4m W of Towcester, 6m N of Brackley, 8m E of Banbury.* Home-made teas. **Combined adm £4, chd free. Sun 14 June (2-5.30).** Unspoilt stonebuilt village and church with C13 tower and unusual C17 clock. Village map for all visitors.

NEW COTTONWOOD

Margaret & David Bradshaw
Wildlife friendly garden which has been extended and developed over 17 yrs. 2 ponds, lawns, borders and vegetable plot.

NEW HOME FARM

Mr & Mr Robert Tomkinson
Mature walled garden with borders of unusual and interesting plants, roses and shrubs. Small arboretum and orchard planted in 1999. Pond with ducks, conservatory and vegetable garden. Outstanding unspoilt views.

NEW PITTAMS FARM

Hilary and John Wickham
Medium sized informal garden that has evolved over many years. Mixed borders, roses, fruit and vegetables, small herb bed encl by box hedging, container planting. Pretty setting on the edge of the village adjacent to pastureland. Some narrow grass paths.

NEW STONE COTTAGE

Diane & Brian Watts
S-facing cottage garden on alkaline soil. Mixed shrub and flower borders, paved terrace,

lawns, mature silver birch underplanted with shade tolerant woodland plants and bulbs. Small courtyard with acid-loving shrubs.

NEW WAPPENHAM MANOR
Mr & Mrs Fordham
1½ -acre garden laid out to lawns with formal vegetable garden and herbaceous border. Pleached lime walk and formal pond.

Small orchard with . . . wildlife area and native hedgerows . . .

Group opening

53 WEEDON LOIS & WESTON GARDENS
NN12 8PL. *6m N of Brackley. 8m W of Towcester. Off A43.* Cream teas 28 June at Weston Community Project, 26 July Weston Lois Church.
Combined adm £4, chd free (share to 28 June St Katherine House).
Suns 28 June; 26 July (2-5.30).
Two adjacent villages in S Northants with a handsome medieval church in Weedon Lois. The extension churchyard contains the graves of the poets Dame Edith Sitwell and her brother Sacheveral who lived in Weston Hall. Weston has some fine stone houses incl Armada House, Weston Hall and a cluster of village centre farmhouses.

NEW 27 HIGH STREET
Mr & Mrs John Jarman. Not open 26 July.
A quintessentially cottage garden offering self seeded mixed borders, rear terraced garden giving open views to the village and field beyond. Small orchard with designated wild life area and native hedgerows. Some steep steps.

HOME CLOSE
Clyde Burbidge, 01327 860097. Visitors also welcome by appt in June & July.
2-acre garden estabished over last 10 yrs. Informal cottage garden surrounding stone barn conversion. Meadow, ponds and small spinney, vegetable garden,

herbaceous borders. Living willow arbour. Gravel paths, some steps.

LOIS WEEDON HOUSE
Sir John & Lady Greenaway. *7m W of Towcester. On the eastern edge of village. Last entrance on R going E towards Wappenham.* **Not open 26 July.**
Large garden with terraces and fine views, lawns, pergola, water garden, mature yew hedges, pond.

OLD BARN
Mr & Mrs John Gregory, 01327 860577, irisgregory@tiscali.co.uk. Visitors also welcome by appt in June & July.
Small plantsman's garden surrounding C18 barn overlooked by medieval church. Over 26yrs the garden has matured and reflects the owner's enthusiasm for hardy plants incl collections of campanula, euphorbia, geranium, clematis and roses. Unusual collection of perennial violas grown in clay pots.

NEW THE WILDE HOUSE GARDEN
Mrs Sara Wilde. Not open 26 July.
Award winning family garden established over last 5yrs. ¼ -acre incl formal courtyard with unusual waterfall feature and pond, tree ferns, vegetable garden and mature orchard with a naturally fed pond and wildlife area. Part of garden still under renovation. Gravel paths, some steps.

Group opening

54 WEST HADDON GARDENS
NN6 7AY. *10m NW of Northampton. Off A428 between Rugby & Northampton, 4m E of M1 J18. Village now bypassed.* Light refreshments & teas at West Cottage. **Combined adm £3.50, chd free. Sun 5 July (2-6).**
A traditional village, predominantly brick but some local stone and thatch, plus modern housing estates. A few shops, PHs with restaurants and a well preserved church and chapel. Tickets and maps at all gardens, 3 of which are large and 6 small.

CLOVER COTTAGE
Helen & Stephen Chown
Walled cottage garden with terraces, cobbles, gravel, pots and decking. Very sunny sheltered space with a lovely lemon tree, orange bush.

THE CROWN COURTYARD
Mark Byrom
Public House courtyard with C16 outbuildings decorated with hanging baskets, containers and cascading flora.

NEW 16 FIELD CLOSE
Andy & Bev French
Small low maintenace garden of a 1960s property with numerous shrubs and containers, decked area and small pond.

LIME HOUSE
Lesley & David Roberts
½ -acre walled garden with rockeries, herbaceous borders, walk-through shrubbery, rose beds, croquet lawn. Summerhouse, patio with greenhouse and a variety of garden statues and ornaments.

NEW 2 PARNELL CLOSE
Jane & Brian Cartlidge
⅕ -acre 5yr old garden in modern development with cottage style borders, shrubs, vegetables, fruit trees, greenhouse and lawn. Remains of 400yr old hedge on part of boundary.

RIVENDELL
Ewen & Sandy Maclean, 01788 510523, smaclean@hotmail.com. Visitors also welcome by appt.
Medium-sized family garden with lawns, mixed borders and pond.

TOWNLEY BARN
Kate & Richard Tilt
1-acre organic garden with wild flower meadow, kitchen garden, stream, waterfall, pond, shrubs, flowers and peaceful inner courtyard. Beautiful views over meadow.

WESLYAN COTTAGE
Arnie & Gillean Stensones
Small densely planted walled garden on various levels where lush plants and climbers jostle for space. Summer house smothered with clematis.

WEST COTTAGE & 45 WEST END

Geoff & Rosemary Sage, 01788 510334, geoffsage@aol.com. Visitors also welcome by appt in July & Aug.

1-acre of mixed borders, lawns, ponds, lawn tennis court, kitchen garden and greenhouses with straw bale cultivation. Wildlife and wild flower garden inhabited by frogs, toads, hedgehogs, grass snakes, great crested newts, woodpeckers, spotted flycatchers and more.

Wildlife and wild flower garden inhabited by frogs, toads, hedgehogs, grass snakes . . .

55 WOODCHIPPINGS

Juniper Hill NN13 5RH. Richard Bashford & Valerie Bexley, 01869 810170. *3m S of Brackley, 3m N J10 M40. Off A43, S of Croughton r'about take L turn, 1/2 m to Juniper Hill.* **Adm £3, chd free. Visitors welcome by appt from Feb to 30 June, individuals & groups.**

1/3 -acre plantsman's garden surrounding stone cottage. Densely and abundantly planted for colour and scent. Snowdrops, hellebores and woodland garden in spring. Vibrant perennials in hot borders in summer. Planting especially for insects. Narrow paths may be unsuitable for infirm or very young. Small nursery.

For Northumberland please see Durham & Northumberland page 222

Northamptonshire County Volunteers

County Organiser
Annabel Smyth-Osbourne Versions Farm, Turweston, Brackley NN13 5JY, 01280 702412, annabelso@aol.com

County Treasurer
Michael Heaton, Mulberry Cottage, Yew Tree Lane, Spratton NN6 8HL, 01604 846032, ngs@mimomul.co.uk

Publicity
Ingram Lloyd, The Old Forge, Sulgrave, Banbury OX17 2RP, 01295 760678, ingramlloyd@dial.pipex.com

Assistant County Organisers
David Abbott, Wroxton Lodge, Church Hill, Finedon, Wellingborough NN9 5NR, 01933 680363, d_j_abbott@btinternet.com
Ruth Dashwood, Farthinghoe Lodge, Farthinghoe, Brackley NN13 5NX, 01295 710377, rmdashwood@aol.com
Philippa Henmann, The Old Vicarage, Broad Lane, Evenley, Brackley NN13 5SF, 01280 702409, philippaheumann@andreas-heumann.com
Gay Webster, Four Acres, The Green, Guilsborough NN6 8PT, 01604 740 203, egwebster16@hotmail.com

NOTTINGHAMSHIRE

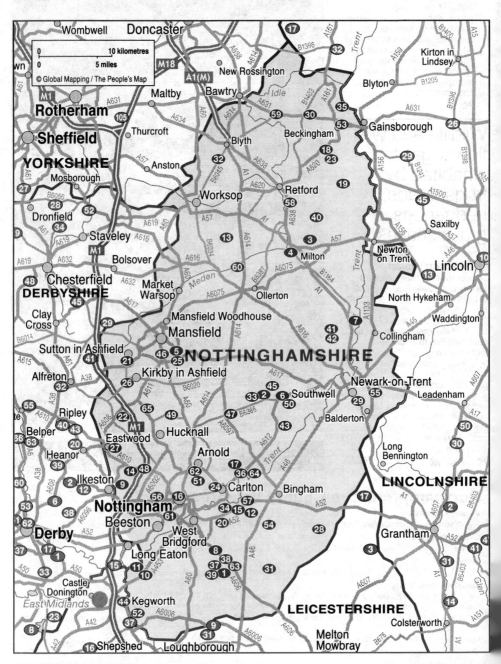

Opening Dates

February
SUNDAY 8
- (4) The Beeches

March
SUNDAY 1
- (4) The Beeches

SUNDAY 29
- (55) Roselea

April
SUNDAY 12
- (22) Felley Priory

WEDNESDAY 15
- (63) The White House

SUNDAY 19
- (2) Ashdene

SUNDAY 26
- (4) The Beeches
- (43) Old Mill House

May
SUNDAY 3
- (2) Ashdene
- (16) Darby House

MONDAY 4
- (14) 7 Collygate
- (27) Gorene

SUNDAY 10
- (25) The Garden House
- (30) Gringley Gardens
- (61) University of Nottingham Gardens

SATURDAY 16
- (7) Carlton Walled Garden Nursery

SUNDAY 17
- (17) Dumbleside
- (36) 61 Lambley Lane
- (39) 17 Main Street
- (42) Norwell Nurseries
- (55) Roselea
- (58) Squirrel Lodge

THURSDAY 21
- (63) The White House

SUNDAY 24
- (49) Papplewick Hall
- (64) Woodpeckers

MONDAY 25
- (35) Holmes Villa
- (52) Piecemeal
- (64) Woodpeckers

TUESDAY 26
- (52) Piecemeal

SUNDAY 31
- (6) Bishops Manor

- (18) Eastfield House
- (23) The Ferns
- (26) Gardeners Cottage
- (45) The Old Vicarage

June
SUNDAY 7
- (29) The Grange Hotel
- (37) 1 Lyncombe Gardens
- (38) 6 Lyncombe Gardens
- (44) The Old Police House
- (47) Oxton Gardens
- (62) 6 Weston Close

FRIDAY 12
- (63) The White House

SATURDAY 13
- (63) The White House (Evening)

SUNDAY 14
- (3) Askham Gardens
- (7) Carlton Walled Garden Nursery
- (8) Cherry Tree House
- (21) Eynord
- (28) Granby Gardens
- (63) The White House

WEDNESDAY 17
- (3) Askham Gardens (Evening)

SATURDAY 20
- (33) Holbeck Lodge (Evening)

SUNDAY 21
- (10) 54 Church Lane
- (11) 59 Church Lane
- (14) 7 Collygate
- (31) Hall Farm Cottage
- (33) Holbeck Lodge
- (40) Nether Headon Gardens
- (45) The Old Vicarage

SATURDAY 27
- (60) Thoresby Hall Hotel & Spa

SUNDAY 28
- (1) 29 Ash Grove
- (41) Norwell Gardens
- (54) Redland House
- (65) Woodside Cottage

July
WEDNESDAY 1
- (41) Norwell Gardens (Evening)
- (60) Thoresby Hall Hotel & Spa

SUNDAY 5
- (9) 41 Church Lane
- (29) The Grange Hotel
- (45) The Old Vicarage (Evening)
- (48) 20 The Paddocks
- (51) 48 Penarth Gardens

WEDNESDAY 8
- (15) Cornerstones (Evening)
- (48) 20 The Paddocks (Evening)

SATURDAY 11
- (60) Thoresby Hall Hotel & Spa

SUNDAY 12
- (5) 335 Berry Hill Lane
- (15) Cornerstones
- (24) Fuchsia View
- (53) Primrose Cottage
- (59) Sunnyside Cottage
- (63) The White House

WEDNESDAY 15
- (57) 125 Shelford Road (Evening)
- (60) Thoresby Hall Hotel & Spa

THURSDAY 16
- (24) Fuchsia View (Evening)
- (43) Old Mill House (Evening)

SATURDAY 18
- (13) Clumber Park Walled Kitchen Garden

SUNDAY 19
- (43) Old Mill House
- (46) Orchard House
- (65) Woodside Cottage

THURSDAY 23
- (50) Park Farm

SATURDAY 25
- (60) Thoresby Hall Hotel & Spa

SUNDAY 26
- (19) The Elms
- (50) Park Farm
- (52) Piecemeal

WEDNESDAY 29
- (60) Thoresby Hall Hotel & Spa

THURSDAY 30
- (24) Fuchsia View (Evening)

August
SATURDAY 1
- (60) Thoresby Hall Hotel & Spa

SUNDAY 2
- (24) Fuchsia View
- (56) 55 Russell Avenue

WEDNESDAY 5
- (60) Thoresby Hall Hotel & Spa

SUNDAY 9
- (7) Carlton Walled Garden Nursery
- (12) Clarence House
- (15) Cornerstones
- (20) Elms Farm

WEDNESDAY 12
- (12) Clarence House (Evening)

SUNDAY 16
- (44) The Old Police House
- (61) University of Nottingham Gardens

SUNDAY 23
52 Piecemeal
58 Squirrel Lodge

SUNDAY 30
4 The Beeches
26 Gardeners Cottage

September

SUNDAY 6
29 The Grange Hotel

SUNDAY 13
45 The Old Vicarage
52 Piecemeal
63 The White House

SUNDAY 27
34 Holme Pierrepont Hall

February 2010

SUNDAY 7
4 The Beeches

SUNDAY 28
4 The Beeches

Gardens open to the public

7 Carlton Walled Garden Nursery
13 Clumber Park Walled Kitchen Garden
22 Felley Priory
29 The Grange Hotel
32 Hodsock Priory Gardens
34 Holme Pierrepont Hall
42 Norwell Nurseries

Also open by appointment ☎

2 Ashdene
4 The Beeches
9 41 Church Lane
10 54 Church Lane
11 59 Church Lane
14 7 Collygate
15 Cornerstones
16 Darby House
17 Dumbleside
19 The Elms
20 Elms Farm
24 Fuchsia View
25 The Garden House
27 Gorene
35 Holmes Villa
45 The Old Vicarage
46 Orchard House
48 20 The Paddocks
51 48 Penarth Gardens
52 Piecemeal
55 Roselea
57 125 Shelford Road
59 Sunnyside Cottage
62 6 Weston Close
63 The White House
64 Woodpeckers
65 Woodside Cottage

The Gardens

1 29 ASH GROVE
Keyworth NG12 5DH. Lynn & Gary Longworth. *8m SE of Nottingham. Turn off A606 Melton Rd. Signed Plumtree/Keyworth. Drive through Plumtree under railway bridge. Turn L at Keep L sign onto Nicker Hill, R onto Wolds Dr, 2nd L past the shops to Beech Ave. 2nd R into Ash Grove.* Home-made teas. **Adm £2.50, chd free (share to Oasis Breast Cancer Trust). Sun 28 June (1-5).**
Plantswoman's garden of generous size with a huge range of plants. Many climbers on fences, house walls, a pergola and any other support available. The plants in herbaceous borders jostle for position with shrubs and trees. Exotics both in the ground and in pots. Numerous hanging baskets. Large pond with fish.
✈ ❀ ☕

2 ASHDENE
Radley Road, Halam NG22 8AH. Glenys & David Herbert, 01636 812335, david@herbert.newsurf.net. *1m W of Southwell. From B6386 in Halam village 300yds past church.* Home-made teas. **Adm £3, chd free (share to Halam Church). Suns 19 Apr; 3 May (1-5.30). Visitors also welcome by appt.**
Many mature trees incl magnificent walnut (200yrs), paulownia (50yrs) and mulberry. Japanese-style garden incl mature spiral yew. Species and scented rose and woodland gardens. Many clematis, hebes. Newly-planted Bible garden.
♿ ❀ ☕ ☎

A variety of
pleasant
English village
gardens with
a flower festival
in church . . .

3 ASKHAM GARDENS
Markham Moor NG22 0RP. *6m S of Retford. On A638, in Rockley village turn E to Askham.* Home-made teas. **Combined adm £3.50, chd free (share to St Nicholas Church, Askham). Sun 14 June (2-6). Evening Opening, wine, Wed 17 June (6-9).**
A variety of pleasant English village gardens with a flower festival in church. Vintage tractor display.
☕

DOVECOTE COTTAGE
Town Street. Mrs C L Slack
Traditional English cottage garden incl roses on the wall.
♿ ✈

FERN LEA
Top Street. Mr G Thompson & Miss N Loy
Small ornamental garden with lawns and borders at different levels.

MANOR LODGE
Town Street. Mr & Mrs K Bloom
Large garden with spreading lawns, gazebo and summerhouses.
♿

NURSERY HOUSE
Top Street. Mr & Mrs D Bird
Secluded and very private garden, with every plant meticulously labelled; waterfall and well-stocked pond. Deep gravel at front.
♿ ❀

4 THE BEECHES
The Avenue, Milton, Tuxford, Newark NG22 0PW. Margaret & Jim Swindin, 01777 870828. *1m S A1 Markham Moor. Exit A1 at Markham Moor, take Walesby sign into village (1m). From Main Street, L up The Avenue.* Soup, rolls & teas (Feb, March). Home-made teas (April, Aug). **Adm £3, chd free. Suns 8 Feb, 1 Mar; (11-4); 26 Apr; 30 Aug (2-5.30). 7, 28 Feb 2010. Visitors also welcome by appt Feb, Mar, Apr & Sept.**
1-acre all seasons garden well stocked with colourful, desirable plants incl over 200 varieties of snowdrops, and spring bulbs. Herbaceous areas incl over 50 different clematis and a wild flower meadow. Raised beds with organically grown fruit and vegetables. Many autumn species and grasses are at

their best in our Aug opening. Lovely views over open countryside. Newcastle Mausoleum (adjacent) open to view in Apr & Aug openings.

 ⛿ 🏵 ☕ ☎

5 NEW 335 BERRY HILL LANE
Berry Hill Lane, Mansfield NG18 4JB. Sheila Whalley. *2m S of Mansfield. Berry Hill Lane joins A60 Nottingham Road and goes through to A614 Southwell Road opposite the Oak Tree PH.* Light refreshments & teas. **Adm £2.50, chd free (share to Air Ambulance). Sun 12 July (1-5).** Large mature garden with trees, shrubs and several herbaceous borders. Water features, statuary and oriental garden. Terraced steps lead down to a large patio and summerhouse. Seating throughout. Short sloping bank to the lower garden.

⛿ 🏵 ☕

6 BISHOPS MANOR
Bishops Drive, Southwell NG25 0JR. The Rt Reverend George Cassidy, Bishop of Southwell. *Centre of Southwell, end of Bishops Dr on S side of Minster.* Teas in Minster Café. **Adm £3, chd free. Sun 31 May (2-5).** House built into part of old medieval palace of the Archbishops of York. Ruins form delightful enclosed garden, lawns and 4-seasons tree garden in unusual setting. Large garden with Edwardian layout, includes herb knot garden and other features. Gravel paths.

⛿ ☕

7 NEW ♦ CARLTON WALLED GARDEN NURSERY
Carlton-on-Trent, Newark NG23 6LP. Paul & Suzanne Beech. *6m N of Newark. 300yds from A1. Leave A1 signed Carlton heading E to give way to Great North Road. Straight over, following wall and signs for car park.* Light refreshments & teas. **Adm £2.50, chd free. For NGS: Sat 16 May; Suns 14 June; 9 Aug (10-5).** 1½ -acre restoration project for former kitchen garden of Carlton Hall. 'Hot' long border, 'dry riverbed' of grasses and bamboo. Herb and vegetable maze in a square of old fruit trees. Many

shade loving and woodland plants, hundreds of diverse perennials in island beds. Some gravel paths.

⛿ ☕

8 CHERRY TREE HOUSE
Church Hill, Plumtree, Nottingham NG12 5ND. Drs H & C Lewis. *6m SE of Nottingham. Enter Plumtree from A606, 100yds down hill from church.* Cream teas, cake stall. **Adm £2, chd free. Sun 14 June (2-5). Also open The White House.**
A truly romantic ¼ -acre garden with an exuberant mass of flowers, winding streams, narrow paths and overflowing borders. Wildlife pond and an island with wild flowers. Small woodland area with tree ferns and woodland plants. Clipped box and secluded corners with seating. Some bridges may be slippery if wet.

🏵 ☕

Drifts of grasses and plants mingle in a soft and naturalistic form . . .

9 NEW 41 CHURCH LANE
Cossall Village NG16 2RW. W B Spittal, 0115 9328551. *3m W of Nottingham. J26 M1 take A610 (W). 1st L, A6096 then Awsworth - Cossall. L to Cossall village. Or from A609 Trowell, take lane signed Cossall.* Home-made teas. **Adm £2.50, chd free. Sun 5 July (12-5). Visitors also welcome by appt Jun & Jul. Groups of 5-30.**
A cottage garden with secluded front garden set with colourful perennials and shrubs. Rear garden has curved lawn paths, mixed borders and beds immaculately planted. Lovely displays of geraniums, crocosmia and day lilies. A conveniently placed summerhouse for viewing the garden and a small vegetable patch fits in nicely.

🏵 ⛿ ☕ ☎

10 54 CHURCH LANE
Thrumpton NG11 0AW. Carol & Mike Staves, 0115 983 0720, stavesmc@btinternet.com. *7m SW of Nottingham. Thrumpton is off A453 between Nottingham & J24 of M1. From Nottingham 1st R signed Thrumpton approx 2m after Crusader PH in Clifton. In ½ m R, No 54 is ½ m on R. From M1 approx 3m along A453 turn L just after power station. 1st R then L in ½ m. No 54 is ½ m on R.* Home-made teas at 59 Church Lane. **Combined adm with 59 Church Lane £2.50, chd free. Sun 21 June (2-6). Visitors also welcome by appt.** Herbaceous borders overflowing with shrubs, perennials and many different types of roses wandering through trees, fences and shrubs. Larger front garden is tiered on two levels and has patio area at front. Back garden has beautiful views stretching for miles, with two further patio areas, plus water feature.

⛿ 🏵 ☕ ☎

11 59 CHURCH LANE
Thrumpton, Nottingham NG11 0AW. Valerie & John Collins, 0115 983 0533. *7m SW of Nottingham. See 54 Church Lne for directions.* Teas. **Combined adm £2.50 with 54 Church Lane, chd free. Sun 21 June (2-6). Visitors also welcome by appt.**
Two different styles of garden here. Drifts of grasses and plants mingle in a soft and naturalistic form creating an unusual gravel front garden with pond and waterfall. Overflowing with herbaceous perennials, shrubs and trees, the back garden is artistically arranged with an eye for colour and form. Small wild flower patch and woodland with a rural landscape beyond complete this 'garden with a view'.

⛿ 🏵 ☕ ☎

12 CLARENCE HOUSE
Cropwell Road, Radcliffe on Trent NG12 2JG. Pam & Greg Stevens. *1m S of A52/A46 junction (Saxondale r'about). From A52 Radcliffe on Trent follow signs to Cropwell Butler. From A46 follow signs to Radcliffe on Trent down Cropwell Rd.* Home-made teas. **Adm £3, chd free. Sun 9 Aug (1-6). Evening Opening £4, wine, Wed 12 Aug (5-9).**
Sunny, ½ -acre flower garden of curves and circles. Paths meander from one secluded seating area to another. Arbour, pergola, bridge, pond,

raised deck and summerhouse surrounded by colourful well maintained borders. Created by a gardener with a passion for flowers and an obsession for perfection.

✖ ✿ ☕

⑬ ◆ CLUMBER PARK WALLED KITCHEN GARDEN
Clumber Park, Worksop S80 3AZ. The National Trust, 01909 476592, www.nationaltrust.org.uk. *4m S of Worksop. From main car park follow directions to the Walled Kitchen Garden. Turn L up Cedar Ave to wrought iron gates.* **Adm £5 per vehicle. £3 adm to Walled Kitchen Garden. See website for other opening times. For NGS: Sat 18 July (10-6).**
Beautiful 4-acre walled kitchen garden, growing unusual and old varieties of vegetables, fruit trees, herbs and ornamentals, incl the magnificent recently extended 400ft long double herbaceous borders. 450ft long glasshouse (the longest owned by the National Trust), with grape vines, peaches, nectarines and figs. Museum of gardening tools. Featured in press. Gravel paths & slopes. Self drive mobility scooters available free of charge, pre-booking advisable 01909 544911.

&

COBWEBS
See Lincolnshire.

⑭ 7 COLLYGATE
Swingate, Kimberley NG16 2PJ. Doreen Fahey & John Arkinstall, 0115 919 2690. *6m W of Nottingham. From M1 J26 take A610 towards Nottingham. L at next island on B600 into Kimberley. At Sainsbury's mini island take L. L at top. Park on this rd in 500yds. Collygate on R.* Home-made teas. **Adm £2.50, chd free (share to Oasis Breast Cancer Trust). Mon 4 May; Sun 21 June (1-5). Visitors also welcome by appt May to Sept.**
Delightful garden created by serious plant addicts tucked away at the end of a short narrow lane in Swingate. It greets you with an impact of unexpected colour and delights you with the variety and sensitivity of the planting. A peaceful backwater in an urban setting.

& ✖ ✿ ☕ ☎

7 COLLYGATE
See Nottinghamshire.

⑮ CORNERSTONES
15 Lamcote Gardens, Radcliffe-on-Trent, Nottingham NG12 2BS. Judith & Jeff Coombes, 0115 845 8055, judith.coombes@ntlworld.com, www.cornerstonesgarden.co.uk. *4m E of Nottingham. From A52 take Radcliffe exit at the RSPCA junction, then 2nd L just before hairpin bend.* Home-made teas. **Adm £3, chd free. Suns 12 July; 9 Aug (2-5.30). Evening Opening £4, wine, Wed 8 July (6-9). Visitors also welcome by appt July to mid-Aug for groups 10+, coaches permitted.**
Plant lover's garden, approaching ½ an acre. Flowing herbaceous borders, containing rare and unusual plants, provide a wealth of colour and interest, whilst an abundance of produce is grown in the unique vegetable/fruit garden. Bananas, palms, olive border, fernery, fish pond, summerhouse, greenhouse and areas for relaxation. New for 2009 - bog garden. Some bark paths and unfenced ponds.

& ✖ ✿ ☕ ☎

THE DAIRY
See Leicestershire & Rutland.

⑯ DARBY HOUSE
10 The Grove, Southey Street, Nottingham NG7 4BS. Jed Brignal, 07960 065042. *¾ m NE of city centre take A610, turn R into Forest Rd, first L into Southey St.* **Adm £2, chd free. Sun 3 May (2-5). Visitors also welcome by appt, groups of 10+.**
Unusual city garden designed and developed by artist owner is a tranquil oasis in unlikely location. Victorian walled garden with ponds, waterfall, gazebos and a fairy-tale shady area surrounded by mature trees. House (1849) and garden provide temporary home and sanctuary for actors, writers, dancers and other creative visitors. Artists work on view. Ceramics & bespoke lanterns for sale. Rare and unusual plants for sale.

✿ ☎

DODDINGTON HALL GARDENS
See Lincolnshire.

⑰ DUMBLESIDE
17 Bridle Road, Burton Joyce NG14 5FT. Mr & Mrs P Bates, 0115 931 3725. *5m NE of Nottingham. In Burton Joyce turn off A612, Nottingham to Southwell Rd into Lambley Lane. Bridle Rd is an impassable looking rd to the R off Lambley Lane. Car parking easiest*

beyond garden. **Combined adm with 61 Lambley Lane £3.50, chd free. Sun 17 May (2-6). Visitors also welcome by appt.**
2 acres of varied habitat. Natural spring and stream planted with primulas, fritillaries and fine specimen shrubs. A small meadow is being developed with large variety of bulbs and wild flowers planted and seeded into grass. 60yd mixed border. Ferns are an important feature in spring, cyclamen in Aug and Sept and through the winter.

& ✿ ☎

⑱ NEW EASTFIELD HOUSE
Gainsbrough Road, North Wheatley, Retford DN22 9BH. Jon & Zoe Isaacs. *On A620 between Retford & Gainsborough, 250yds past N Wheatley village on L heading towards Gainsborough.* Home-made teas. **Combined with The Ferns adm £3, chd free (share to St Peter's & St Paul's Church). Sun 31 May (12-5).**
Enjoy a 2-acre country garden with mature trees set to lawn. Large, well stocked pond with fountain, waterfall and rockery. Long perennial and shrub borders. Play area for children. Kitchen garden, greenhouse, and chickens.

& ✿ ☕

Delightful garden created by serious plant addicts tucked away at the end of a short narrow lane . . .

⑲ THE ELMS

Main Street, North Leverton
DN22 0AR. Tim & Tracy Ward, 01427
881164, Tracy@wardt2.fsnet.co.uk.
*5m E of Retford, 6m SW of
Gainsborough. From Retford town
centre take the rd to Leverton for 5m,
into North Leverton with
Habblesthorpe.* Adm £2.50, chd free.
Sun 26 July (2-6). Visitors also
welcome by appt.
This small garden is very different,
creating an extension to the living
space. Inspiration comes from
tropical countries, giving a
Mediterranean feel. Palms and
bananas, along with other exotics,
create drama, and yet make a
statement true to many gardens,
that of peace and calm. North
Leverton Windmill will be open for
visitors.

⑳ ELMS FARM

Bassingfield, Nottingham
NG12 2LG. Philip & Jane Parker,
0115 981 4899. *2m SE of Trent
Bridge, Nottingham. Off A52 Lings Bar
Rd to Tollerton, Bassingfield 1st L.*
Home-made teas. Adm £2.50, chd
free. Sun 9 Aug (2-6). Visitors also
welcome by appt.
Garden developed in the last 16yrs,
approx 2 acres. Unusual trees, shrubs
and herbaceous plants in island beds
and borders. Large pond and stream.
Plenty of seating areas. Annual bed
display.

㉑ EYNORD

Church Hill, Sutton-in-Ashfield
NG17 1EW. Peter & Judy Ford.
*3m E of J28 M1. From M1 A38 into
Sutton town centre. Garden opp
public swimming baths. A60 into
Nottingham, Ravenshead A6014 to
Sutton town centre.* Home-made teas.
Adm £2.50, chd free (share to
Rotary International). Sun 14 June
(2-5).
Classic 1930s town house with its one
third of an acre, recently restored
garden, displaying well-stocked
borders surrounding immaculate
lawns. Countless tender specimens in
pots, a decked-over air-raid shelter,
leading to a clematis and akebia
pergola with adjacent fruit garden.
Interesting cacti collection. Peaceful
garden hidden away in a busy town
centre.

㉒ ◆ FELLEY PRIORY

Underwood NG16 5FJ. The Hon Mrs
Chaworth Musters, 01773 810230.
*8m SW of Mansfield. Off A608 ½ m W
M1 J27.* Adm £3, chd free. Tues,
Weds & Fris (9-1) all yr. Every 2nd &
4th Wed (9-4); every 3rd Sun (10-4)
March-Oct. For NGS: Sun 12 Apr
(10-4).
Garden for all seasons with yew
hedges and topiary, snowdrops,
hellebores, orchard of daffodils,
herbaceous borders and old-fashioned
rose garden. There are pergolas, a
medieval garden, a small arboretum
and borders filled with unusual trees,
shrubs, plants and bulbs. The grass-
edged pond is planted with primulas,
bamboo, iris, roses and eucomis.
Magnificent orchard of old fashioned
daffodils.

㉓ NEW THE FERNS

Low Pasture Lane DN22 9DQ.
Keith & Flicky Hebdon. *Off A620
between Retford & Gainsborough.
Enter N Wheatley at Sun Inn PH.
Follow Low Street for ½ m. L
signed sports field opp PO. Park at
Village Hall.* Home-made teas at
Eastfield House. Combined with
Eastfield House adm £3, chd
free. Sun 31 May (12-5).
Cottage garden of 1-acre, retrieved
from woodland 10yrs ago. Sloping
site incl pond, stream, ferns and
bog garden. Model train set
meanders through 'rooms'. Rose
garden, statuary, oriental poppies
and paeonies in borders. Disabled
parking at adjacent property.

FIELD HOUSE FARM
See Lincolnshire.

㉔ FUCHSIA VIEW

9 Winster Avenue, off Cromford
Avenue, Carlton NG4 3RW. Mr & Mrs
J Thorp, 0115 911 5734,
thorpjb@hotmail.com. *4m N of
Nottingham. Follow the Carlton Rd into
Carlton. Turn L at Tesco past police
stn. Over the mini island, pass the
cemetery up Cavendish Rd. R into
Cromford Ave. 1st L into Winster Ave
or from Mapperley, down Westdale
Lane & R onto Cavendish Road & L
onto Cromford or Buxton Ave where
parking is advisable.* Home-made teas.
Adm £2.50, chd free. Suns 12 July;
2 Aug (11-5). Evening Opening £4,
wine, Thurs 16, 30 July (6-9). Visitors
also welcome by appt.

The abundance of colour in this garden
is achieved by the dense planting of
roses and 150 varieties of fuchsias incl
many standards, with a supporting
cast of mixed perennials, penstemons
and hanging baskets. 5 patio areas
give a panoramic view over Carlton
while enjoying a strawberry scone or
home-made cake. In the evening enjoy
the chef's canapés with a glass of
wine. Featured on BBC TV.

㉕ THE GARDEN HOUSE

Chatsworth Drive, Mansfield
NG18 4QX. Mrs V A & Mr P M Jelley,
07812 202425. *1m S of Mansfield.
Approaching Mansfield on A60 from
Nottingham, with West Notts College
in view turn R into Newark
Rd/Litchfield Lane. On L-hand bend
turn R into Chatsworth Drive.* Home-
made teas. Adm £2.50, chd free. Sun
10 May (12-4). Visitors also welcome
by appt.
Plantaholic's organically maintained
terraced garden of approx 1000sq yds.
All-yr round interest. Lawn on two
levels. Rill, stream, pond. Magnolias,
camellias, rhododendrons, tree
paeonies. In excess of 100 newly
planted clematis for winter, spring,
summer and autumn colour. Some
steps.

Model train
set meanders
through
'rooms' . . .

㉖ GARDENERS COTTAGE

Rectory Lane, Kirkby in Ashfield
NG17 8PZ. Martin & Chris Brown.
*1m W of Kirkby. From the A38, take
the B6018 towards Kirkby in Ashfield.
Straight across mini island. Rectory
Lane (no parking) is at the side of St
Wilfrid's Church, on Church St.* Home-
made teas. Adm £3, chd free. Suns
31 May; 30 Aug (1-5).
Garden makeovers take, it seems, only
days. The one at Gardener's Cottage
was started in late 2000 and is still
happening! From a barren 45-degree
slope with a few old apple trees, it is
now a mature garden that boasts
features and plant collections arranged
by perfectionists, that will give
satisfaction and inspiriation to all who
visit.

27 GORENE
20 Kirby Road, Beauvale Estate, Newthorpe NG16 3PZ. Gordon & Irene Middleton, 01773 788407. *5m NE of Nottingham. From M1 J26 take A610 (Eastwood & Kimberley bypass) exit Langley Mill (not Eastwood). At island turn R to Eastwood to 1st set of T-lights. Keep L down Mansfield Rd, turn R at bollards (Greenhills Rd). Turn R at the 7th rd - Kirby Rd.* Adm £2, chd free. Mon 4 May (1-5). Visitors also welcome by appt April to Aug. Groups of 4 to 30.
Small but intensely packed garden which is a delight to garden lovers. Incs water feature, secret garden and aviary. Apart from our main open day, when the garden is very pretty, it is forever changing throughout the season and we would like to encourage private visits from April to August.

Group opening

28 NEW GRANBY GARDENS
NG13 9PS. *14m E of Nottingham, 2m off A52 signed Granby.* Home-made teas at Newbray House. Combined adm £4.50, chd free (share to Sightsavers International). Sun 14 June (2-6).
3 large, beautiful, diverse gardens in the tranquil vale of Belvoir village of Granby.

MANOR FARM HOUSE
Plungar Road. Brenda & Philip Straw. *Next to church*
¹/₃ -acre garden surrounding grade II listed C18 farmhouse. Cottage garden style planting with climbing roses, hardy geraniums, delphiniums, white garden, yellow corner, daisy steps and mixed borders. Church wall, brick outbuildings and old walnut tree provide perfect backdrop for this plant enthusiasts' garden.

NEWBRAY HOUSE
Church Street, Granby. Shirley & Stan Taylor. *2m off A52 signed Granby*
With views towards Belvoir Castle, this 2-acre garden has been developed to complement the attractive Victorian house. Strong structure is overlaid by imaginative planting. Many unusual plants are found in large herbaceous beds full of colour and interest over a long season. Ponds, gravel, herb and vegetable areas. Scented roses and wisteria climb pergolas and walls. Picnics in the orchard.

NEW WOODBINE COTTAGE
Old Forge Lane. Erika & Stuart Humphreys
A garden of 2 halves; a partly walled, densely-planted cottage garden with unusual herbaceous perennials and old roses, melds into the orchard and ornamental pond garden which has many specimen trees. Lawns, gravel access.

29 NEW ♦ THE GRANGE HOTEL
73 London Rd, Newark NG24 1RZ. Tom & Sandra Carr, 01636 703399, www.grangenewark.co.uk. *¹/₄ m E of Newark town centre. On B6326 (London Rd) opp Newark Cemetary and Polish War Graves.* Adm £3, chd free. For NGS: Suns 7 June; 5 July; 6 Sept (1-5).
A series of colourful town gardens with Victorian influence. Different areas of formal and informal design, sun and deep shade borders, herb garden and a mass of colourful planters, hold interest yr-round. Rose arch and sweet peas. Winner Newark in Bloom Best Large Garden.

Group opening

30 GRINGLEY GARDENS
Gringley-on-the-Hill, Doncaster DN10 4SF. Mrs S Round. *On A631 between Bawtry & Gainsborough. Approach Gringley on A631. From dual carriageway there is signage into village. Parking is on streets of village.* Light refreshments & teas in Village Hall. Combined adm £3, chd free (share to Gringley-on-the-Hill WI). Sun 10 May (1.30-5).
Picturesque North Nottinghamshire village with panoramic views over the surrounding countryside from Beacon Hill and other vantage points around the village. 800yr old church open.

APPLETON HOUSE FARM
Finkell Street. Mr & Mrs R Round
Peaceful S-facing farmhouse garden in rooms, partly walled with Victorian gazebo. Formal canal pond garden, mixed borders, secret garden. Vegetable plot containing some old HDRA varieties; all gardened organically.

GRINGLEY HALL
Ian & Dulce Threlfall, 01777 817262. Visitors also welcome by appt.
1¹/₂ -acre walled country garden on dry sandy hill. Several colour-themed mixed borders densely planted. Spring woodland garden. Dry/Mediterranean garden, many climbing roses, secluded pond area. Potager and summer fruit area.

THE SUMMER HOUSE
High Street. Helena Bishop
A charming English garden, lovingly planted with outstanding views framed by overflowing borders. The romantic rose garden, wildflower meadow and white border are maturing and the water garden with stream makes a stunning focal point.

VICARAGE COTTAGE
High Street. John & Susan Taylor
Tucked in by The Summer House and opposite the local inn, this small cottage and delightful little garden will make those who dream of retirement think it's heaven.

3 large, beautiful, diverse gardens in the tranquil vale of Belvoir village of Granby . . .

31 HALL FARM COTTAGE
Hall Lane, Kinoulton NG12 3EF. Mrs Bel Grundy. *8m SE of West Bridgford. Kinoulton is off A46 just N of intersection with A606. Into village to T-junction with PH on L. Cottage at end of lane on L.* **Adm £2.50, chd free (share to Macmillan Cancer Support). Sun 21 June (2-5).** Plantaholic's small cottage garden. A masterclass in the positioning and management of plants which have to move if they don't behave! New 'Pebble' water feature. Collection of home-grown bonsai demonstrates attention to detail and the quality of 'plants for sale' ensures that Bel has no escape from her addiction.
&

HARDWICK HALL
See Derbyshire.

HILL PARK FARM
See Leicestershire & Rutland.

32 ◆ HODSOCK PRIORY GARDENS
Blyth, Worksop S81 0TY. Sir Andrew & Lady Buchanan & Mr George Buchanan (Hodsock Priory Trust), 01909 591204, www.hodsockpriory.com. *2m from A1(M) at Blyth. 4m N of Worksop off B6045, Blyth-Worksop rd approx 2m from A1. Well signed.* **Adm £4.50, chd £1. Daily 31 Jan to 2 Mar (10-4, last adm).** 5-acre private garden on historic Domesday site. Sensational winter garden plus snowdrop wood. Many fragrant winter flowering shrubs, trees, hellebores and bulbs. Some gravel. Wood NOT suitable for wheelchairs if wet. Some gravel paths. Wheelchairs with small front wheels may find it difficult.

33 NEW HOLBECK LODGE
Manor Fields, Halam NG22 8DU. Paul & Jane Oakley. *1m W of Southwell. From B6386 in Halam village 350yds past church, R into Manor Fields. Parking on Radley Rd.* Home-made teas at The Old Vicarage. **Adm £3.50, chd free. Sat, Sun 20, 21 June. Evening Opening £3.50, wine, Sat 20 June (6-9). Combined adm with The Old Vicarage 21 June (1-5.30), £4.50.** Lovely garden created from scratch to complement house built in 2001,

this ½-acre area has been selectively planted to blend in with open countryside and bordering beck. Wild plants, herbaceous beds, shrubs, ferns, vegetable garden, rose pergolas, spectacular Constance Spry, Maigold and the Generous Gardener and containers form an interesting and varied environment. Some steep slopes.

34 ◆ HOLME PIERREPONT HALL
Holme Pierrepont, Nottingham NG12 2LD. Mr & Mrs Robin Brackenbury, 0115 933 2371, www.holmepierreponthall.com. *5m E of Nottingham. From Nottingham A52 E-bound, follow signs for National Watersports Centre. Continue 1m past main entrance. House on L next to church. Park outside church.* **House and garden adm £5, chd £1.50, garden only adm £3, chd £1. Mons, Tues, Weds Feb to Mar; Sun 8 Mar. For NGS: Sun 27 Sept (2-5).** In the courtyard the romantic summer planting gives way to the fiery tones of autumn from dahlias and crocosmias. The sharpness of the newly clipped yews in the East Garden, contrasts with the more relaxed feel of the new autumn border with grasses and late flowering perennials in shades of purple and gold. Featured in 'Nottingham Evening Post' & on Central TV.
&

35 HOLMES VILLA
Holmes Lane, Walkeringham, nr Gainsborough DN10 4JP. Peter & Sheila Clark, 01427 890233, clarkshaulage@aol.com. *4m NW of Gainsborough. A620 from Retford or A631 from Bawtry/Gainsborough & A161 to Walkeringham then towards Misterton. Follow yellow signs for last mile.* Home-made teas. **Adm £2, chd free. BH Mon 25 May (1-5). Visitors also welcome by appt.** 1¾-acre plantsman's interesting and inspirational garden; surprises around every corner with places to sit and ponder, gazebos, arbours, ponds, hosta garden, unusual perennials and shrubs for flower arranging. Lots of ideas to copy.
&

THE HOMESTEAD
See Leicestershire & Rutland.

Created from scratch in 2001 . . . selectively planted to blend in with open countryside and bordering beck . . .

KEXBY HOUSE
See Lincolnshire.

36 61 LAMBLEY LANE
Burton Joyce NG14 5BG. Mr & Mrs R B Powell. *6m N of Nottingham. In Burton Joyce turn off A612 Nottingham to Southwell Rd into Lambley Lane.* **Combined adm with Dumbleside £3.50, chd free. Sun 17 May (2-6).** Approx ¾-acre of spring flowering shrubs, plants and bulbs. Mixed borders, greenhouse and terrace, cacti, vegetable garden. Colourful display of azaleas and camellias. Steep drive to entrance.
&

LONG CLOSE
See Leicestershire & Rutland.

37 NEW 1 LYNCOMBE GARDENS
Keyworth. NG12 5FZ. Doris & Ian McGowan. *6m S of Nottingham. Take the A606 through Tollerton and follow signs for Keyworth or off A52 ring road and through Plumtree. At Nicker Hill, turn L. R at Wolds Drive and 1st R into Lyncombe Gardens.* Light refreshments & wine. **Adm £2.50, chd free. Sun 7 June (2-5.30). Combined opening 6 Lyncombe Gardens.** Interesting and pleasant garden full of mixed plants, perennials, roses and evergreens. Pond, water features, pathway and archways. A variety of vegetables, salads and fruits grown in containers and a small greenhouse. Garden quiz.

38 6 LYNCOMBE GARDENS

Keyworth. NG12 5FZ. Mr J Walton. *6m S of Nottingham. See 1 Lyncombe Gardens for directions.* Home-made teas. **Adm £2.50, chd free. Sun 7 June (2-5). Combined with 1 Lyncombe Gardens.**

All-yr round garden with mature borders consisting of herbaceous shrubs, roses and clematis with many other features.

39 17 MAIN STREET

Keyworth NG12 5AA. Graham & Pippa Tinsley. *7m S of Nottingham. Follow signs to Keyworth from A60 or A606 and head for the church. Garden about 50yds past the Co-op on L. Some parking on Main St. Car parking at village hall and public car park on Bunny Lane.* Home-made teas. **Adm £3, chd free. Sun 17 May (1-5).**
The old gardens and paddock behind the farmhouse have been developed over 30yrs to give a peaceful haven near the centre of a busy village. Full of unexpected views and hidden places. Nicely maturing trees incl cedars and chestnuts. Yew hedges, ponds, secret rose garden and a turf mound. Access to garden via gravel yard & path. Some steps & slopes.

Group opening

40 NETHER HEADON GARDENS

DN22 0RQ. *4m SE of Retford. 4m from Markham Moor r'about.* Home-made teas at Mill Hill Farm. **Combined adm £3, chd free (share to Bassetlaw Hospice). Sun 21 June (2-5).**
Nether Headon is a tiny hamlet adjacent to Headon village and the three gardens are on Greenspotts Road, all within easy walking distance of each other.

GREENSPOTTS

Mr & Mrs Dolby
Old roses and clematis. Pond and wildlife area. Herbaceous border and vegetable area.

HEADON MANOR

Mrs & Mrs John Ogle
1-acre garden formal to the front

with a more romantic rear garden. Pond in process of renovation, orchard and small vegetable patch.

MILL HILL FARM

Rosie & Nigel Greenhalgh
Large farmhouse garden, patio area. New herbaceous borders, shrubbery and rockeries. Open view of surrounding countryside.

Group opening

41 NORWELL GARDENS

NG23 6JX. *6m N of Newark. Off A1 at Cromwell turning, take Norwell Rd at bus shelter.* Home-made teas in village hall, wine at Norwell Nurseries. **Combined adm £3, chd free. Sun 28 June (2-5). Evening Opening £3.50, wine, Wed 1 July (6.30-9).**
Beautiful 'hidden away' village with parish church of St Lawrence having notable C15 clerestory and views over water meadows. The gardens are an eclectic mix of design and planting, providing inspiration for all. The inclusion of the Parish Gardens means 27 new gardeners from Norwell and surrounding villages have the opportunity to show their expertise on many plots that in 2007 were underwater in summer floods. The beautiful Medieval Church of St Laurence will be open. Adult and child heritage trails through village.

CHERRY TREE HOUSE

5 Foxhall Close. Mr & Mrs S Wyatt
5 yr-old garden with many innovative features selected to dramatise the orientation of the 4 faces of the garden. Formal box front garden with decorative mulches and water-saving installations. Decking, water features, lush plantings, seating areas, architectural screens and colourful schemes.

NORWELL NURSERIES

Andrew & Helen Ward
(See separate entry).

NORWELL PARISH GARDENS

Norwell Parish Council
Norwell Parish Gardens are the equivalent to allotments. 27 allotment holders on a range of

plot sizes. Fruit, vegetables and flowers are grown by both young and older gardeners. Grass paths only.

THE OLD MILL HOUSE, NORWELL

Main Street. Mr & Mrs M Burgess
Front garden with shrubs, old roses and mixed herbaceous borders with lots of new planting. Walled back garden with interesting water feature and wildlife pond. Extensive planting of shade and sun-loving plants.

YEW TREE FARM

Susan Brown & Chris Dobbs
1½ m out of Norwell, nr tel box in Norwell Woodhouse
Recently-established country cottage garden with herbaceous perennial borders and shrubs. Summerhouse, seating areas and archways, small vegetable plot and herb knot garden. Gravel drive.

Fruit, vegetables and flowers are grown by both young and older gardeners . . .

42 ◆ NORWELL NURSERIES

Woodhouse Road, Norwell NG23 6JX. Andrew & Helen Ward, 01636 636337, www.norwellnurseries.co.uk. *6m N of Newark. Turn off A1 at Cromwell turning, take rd to Norwell at bus stop.* **Adm £2, chd free. Daily (10-5) except Sats & Tues from 1 Mar to 2● Oct. Closed Aug.** For NGS: **Sun 17 May (2-5).**
A treasure trove of over 2000 different beautiful, rare and unusual plants set out in ¾ -acre plantsman's garden inc woodland with orchids and cardiocrinums, specimen grasses.

Large alpine and scree area, bell garden with penstemons and dierama, and new pond with bog gardens. Extensive herbaceous borders, hot beds and sumptuous colour-themed beds. Featured in 'Garden News'. Gravel drive.

An eclectic mix! . . .

43 NEW OLD MILL HOUSE
NG14 7FN. Mr & Mrs Langley. 11m SW of Newark. Taking A612 from Nottingham (towards Southwell) enter Thurgarton Village, R signed Bleasby. Garden up lane on L, approx 1m out of Thurgarton. Home-made teas. **Adm £3, chd free. Suns 26 Apr; 19 July (2-5). Evening Opening £3.50, wine, music, Thur 16 July (6-9).**
1-acre hillside garden under development. Glorious views across Trent Valley. Spring bulbs and summer colour in various tubs, baskets and borders. Working kitchen garden with stocked glass houses. Naturalistic copses, hosta glade, rose walk, knot garden, green-themed pond area and yews - an eclectic mix! Orchard available for picnic (July). Local craft/produce on display/for sale. Grass slopes, some narrow entrances and gravel. Help available. Steps and York stone slippery when wet.

44 NEW THE OLD POLICE HOUSE
69 Derby Road, Kegworth DE74 2EN. Val & Paul Blyth. 10m S of Nottington. 6m N of Loughborough. From A453 on M1 J24 r'about take 1st exit signed A6 Loughborough/Kegworth. ½m from J24 on R opp Londis garage. A6 from Loughborough, through village on L opp garage. Home-made teas. **Adm £2, chd free. Suns 7 June; 16 Aug (12-5).** Welcome. Our garden is ⅓ acre which we have transformed from a blank canvas to a garden bursting with colour and a few surprises. Old fashioned urns overflow with flowers. Designed in 3 sections, each area has something different, with mature bushes, shrubs, and flowers throughout. Many seats to relax and enjoy tea and home-made cakes. Fun quiz for children.

45 THE OLD VICARAGE
Halam Hill, Halam Village, nr Southwell NG22 8AX. Mrs Beverley Perks, 01636 812181/07977 920833, perks.family@talk21.com. 1m W of Southwell. On approach to Halam village down hill on LH-side or from A614 through Farnsfield & Edingley villages over Xrds in Halam, last house on RH-side. Home-made teas. **Adm £3, chd free. Suns 31 May (1-5.30); 21 June, 13 Sept (1-5). Evening Opening £4, wine, music, Sun 5 July (5-8). Combined adm with Holbeck Lodge 21 June (1-5.30), £4.50. Visitors also welcome by appt June & July. Groups of 15+, coaches welcome.**
Plantsman's garden of 2 acres surrounded by woodland and fields, begun 12yrs ago from nothing. Benefits from undulating landscape incorporating design, texture, colour, unusual plants and trees. Peaceful rooms, nooks, crannies, borrowed views of hills and farmland. A children's haven. Just lovely and very welcoming. Delicious cakes to add to enjoyment on new terraces. Church and churchyard nearby open - abundant bird & wildlife. Featured in 'Nottingham Post'. Steps, lawn, & gravel - assistance available.

46 ORCHARD HOUSE
High Oakham Road, Mansfield NG18 5AJ. Mr & Mrs Michael Bull, 01623 623884. S side of Mansfield. High Oakham Rd joins the A60-Nottingham Rd at junction with Forest Rd and Waverley Rd, leading to Atkin Lane at the western end. Home-made teas. **Adm £2.50, chd free. Sun 19 July (1-5). Visitors also welcome by appt June & July. Groups of 10-30.** This mature garden is one of Mansfield's treasures in a quiet and secluded area. Diverse colourful planting of shrubs, herbaceous borders and specimen trees. Clever use of water, statuary and other unique features enhance this garden, providing interest for discerning gardeners throughout the summer. Twice featured on local BBC TV.

Group opening

47 OXTON GARDENS
NG25 0SS. 4m SW of Southwell. From B6386 turn into Oxton village (Blind Lane). Home-made teas at Crows Nest Cottage. **Combined adm £4, chd free. Sun 7 June (1.30-5).** An interesting selection of lovely wildlife-friendly gardens.

CROWS NEST COTTAGE
Forest Road. Joan Arnold & Tom Heinersdorff. From B6386 turn R into Oxton village (Blind Lane). At T-junction turn R into Forest Rd. Garden is approx 200yds on R A bird-friendly, colourful mature garden wrapped round the cottage. Large wildlife ponds, streams and waterfalls now well-established. Enjoy clematis, peonies, fuchsia and some unusual shrubs and plants. Unfenced ponds, deep water.

HOME FARM COTTAGE
Blind Lane, Oxton. Pauline & Brian Hansler. From B6386 turn into Oxton village (Blind Lane). Home Farm Cottage is on L opp Green Dragon PH, immed before T-junction
Each corner of this magical cottage garden offers a new and exciting experience. At every turn, from the hidden alpine garden, through the imaginative stumpery and woodland grotto to the selection of unusual plants, it reveals a horticultural heaven.

OAKWOOD COTTAGE
Forest Road, Oxton. Tracey & Paul Akehurst. At T-junction turn R onto Forest Rd. Oakwood Cottage is immed on RH-side up a gravel drive (no parking)
Both a wind tunnel, and a frost pocket, this secluded cottage garden proves that a small space should never limit the imagination. Abundant planting and clever use of recycled materials provides continual interest throughout the year.

ROMAN WAY
Blind Lane. Corby & Lewie Lewington. *Roman Way is on R next to Green Dragon PH, immed before T-junction*
With a mixture of paved, lawned and planted areas, this unusual small corner plot has been lovingly developed over the last few years; its tranquillity provides the perfect antidote to busy living.

48 20 THE PADDOCKS
Nuthall NG16 1DR. Mr & Mrs Bowness-Saunders, 0115 938 4590, alex.bowness@ntlworld.com. *5m NW of Nottingham. From M1 J26, A610 towards Nottingham. At 1st roundabout take B600 towards Kimberley. Paddocks is 2nd rd on L after Three Ponds PH. Parking in cul-de-sac restricted, please park on main rd or on L as you enter The Paddocks.* Home-made teas. **Adm £3, chd free. Sun 5 July (1-5). Evening Opening £3.50, wine, Wed 8 July (6-9).** Visitors also welcome by appt.
Fun garden shared with children and dogs which unlike oil and water do mix in this unusual combination of interesting gardens. Many inspirational ideas incl beach, well, living willow structures, ponds, mature trees, herbaceous borders and vegetables. A gardener's playground not to be missed (200 x 80ft). Featured in 'The Mail on Sunday'.

Spectacular views to The Minster Cathedral . . .

49 PAPPLEWICK HALL
Papplewick NG15 8FE. Mr & Mrs J R Godwin-Austen, www.papplewickhall.co.uk. *7m N of Nottingham. N end of Papplewick village on B683, off the A60. Parking at Hall.* Home-made teas. **Adm £3, chd free (share to St James's Church). Sun 24 May (2-5).**
This mature 8-acre established garden, mostly shaded woodland, abounds with rhododendrons, hostas, ferns, and spring bulbs. Featured in 'Nottinghamshire Today'.

50 NEW PARK FARM
Crink Lane, Southwell NG25 0TJ. Dr & Mrs Ian Johnston. *1m SE of Southwell. A612 out of Southwell towards Newark, take rd to Fiskerton and 200yds up hill turn R into Crink Lane.* **Adm £3, chd free (share to Campaign to Protect Rural England - Notts branch). Thur 23, Sun 26 July (2-6).**
3-acre garden for gardeners and nature lovers. Extensive borders with large varieties of plants, shrubs and trees planned to excite the eye. Woodland garden, oak arches with roses, long flower borders, large wild flower meadow, pond and ha-ha complement the garden with spectacular views across fields to The Minster Cathedral.

51 48 PENARTH GARDENS
Sherwood Vale, Nottingham NG5 4EG. Josie & Geoff Goodlud, 0115 9609067. *Approx 2¹/₂ m N of Nottingham city centre off B684 (Woodborough Rd). From city, turn L into Woodthorpe Rd, after Millennium Garage, L again (Penarth Rise). L again to Penarth Gardens (No 48).* Light refreshments. **Adm £2.50, chd free. Sun 5 July (12-5). Visitors also welcome by appt in July for groups of 10+.**
One of Nottingham city's hidden gems is to be found in the unlikely setting of a small back garden in Sherwood Vale, but it will please and surprise both by its planting and bold design. Its setting is amongst dense housing packed into the old Nottingham brickworks quarry, the overgrown face of which is steadily being transformed into an extension to a densely packed garden.

52 PIECEMEAL
123 Main Street, Sutton Bonington, Loughborough LE12 5PE. Mary Thomas, 01509 672056, admet123@btinternet.com. *2m SE of Kegworth (M1 J24). 6m NE of Loughborough. Almost opp St Michael's Church.* **Adm £2.50, chd free. Mon 25, Tue 26 May; Suns 26 July; 23 Aug; 13 Sept (2-6). Visitors also welcome by appt June to Aug inclusive. Max 10 per visit.**
Plant enthusiast's garden in tiny, sheltered courtyard enabling extensive and amazing collection of shrubs, perennials and climbers to thrive in

over 300 containers. Many unusual and not fully hardy, and a number from the southern hemisphere (list available). Busy herbaceous borders. Plants with distinctive foliage and colourful colour combinations provide interest from spring to autumn. Fern-filled well. Conservatory overflowing with tender specimens.

53 NEW PRIMROSE COTTAGE
16 Bar Road North, Beckingham DN10 4NN. Terry & Brenda Wilson, 01427 848852. *8m N of Retford. Off A631, main island off Beckingham bypass into village, L to village green, L to Bar Road.* Teas at village hall opp Sunnyside Cottage. **Combined with Sunnyside Cottage adm £3, chd free. Sun 12 July (2-6).**
Old fashioned cottage garden. Walled harbaceous border, well stocked shrubbery. Many old roses, feature pergola, vegetable garden, summerhouse. Plant nursery on village green.

54 REDLAND HOUSE
Main Street, Cropwell Butler NG12 3AB. Shelagh Barnes. *Cropwell Butler lies to the E of Nottingham, off A52, signed to village. Cross A46 after 1¹/₂ m. ¹/₂ m on, garden on R.* Home-made teas. **Adm £3, chd free. Sun 28 June (11-5).**
A larger than average garden nurtured under a flower arranger's eye is underway. The garden created is of mixed planting with yr-round interest, colour, texture, form and diverse species. Maturing design features give it an established feel; it is still a garden to watch!. Gravel paths, paved and grass slopes.

RIDGEWOLD FARM
See Leicestershire & Rutland.

55 ROSELEA
40 Newark Road, Coddington NG24 2QF. Bruce & Marian Richmond, 01636 676737, richmonds@roselea47.fsnet.co.uk. *1¹/₂ m E of Newark. Leave A1 signed Coddington, 100yds from junction S; 300yds from junction N.* Home-made teas. **Adm £2, chd free (share to**

Newark Parkinsons Group). **Suns 29 Mar; 17 May (11-5)**. Visitors also welcome by appt.
Picturesque plantsman's garden. Mixed borders, shrubs, roses, clematis and geraniums. Many unusual plants. Hostas and ferns in pots. Small alpine area. Pergolas covered with climbers. Compost area. Places to sit and ponder. Come and enjoy home-made cakes and teas. Wheelchair access only to front garden.

56 **NEW** **55 RUSSELL AVENUE**
Wollaton NG8 2BN. **John Munns & Janet Wood.** *2m W of Nottingham. From Nottingham city centre take A609 towards Ilkeston. Approx 2m turn R at Wheelhouse PH then bear left onto Russell Ave.* Light refreshments & teas. **Adm £2.50, chd free. Sun 2 Aug (2-5.30).**
Medium sized S-facing surburban garden with a definite cottage garden feel. Surrounded by mature trees, the garden has pretty borders overflowing with perennial and annual plants. Gravel garden with grasses and hostas.

73 SAXILBY ROAD
See Lincolnshire.

57 **125 SHELFORD ROAD**
Radcliffe on Trent NG12 1AZ. **John & Elaine Walker,** 0115 911 9867. *4m E of Nottingham. From A52 follow signs to Radcliffe. In village centre take turning for Shelford (by Co-op). Approx ¾ m on LH-side.* **Evening Opening £4,** chd free, wine/soft drink, **Wed 15 July (6-9).** Visitors also welcome by appt for groups of 10+, coaches permitted.
Just under ½ an acre designed for overall effect of colour, texture and movement, incorporating many unusual varieties especially hardy perennials and grasses. Front garden is formal in layout with packed borders incl hot and cool colour-themed beds and prairie-style borders planted for late summer colour. Back is based on flowing curves with informal planting and incl gazebo, pond, bog garden and jungle area with turf dragon. 'A stunning garden', Monty Don. 'Back garden is truly spectacular', Prof David Stevens. Mirror sculptures and artwork by owner feature in the garden - some

items for sale on open days. Featured in 'Garden News' and 'Nottingham Evening Post'.

58 **SQUIRREL LODGE**
2 Goosemoor Lane, Retford DN22 7JA. **Peter & Joan Whitehead,** 01777 705474. *1m S of Retford. Travelling S out of Retford on A638, last R turn before railway bridge.* Home-made teas. **Adm £2.50, chd free. Suns 17 May; 23 Aug (2-5).**
Journey a little further north in the County and you will be rewarded by a garden that has been skilfully crafted into a corner plot. Some is in deep shade but the variety will both delight and please as will the welcome and the teas. Venture into Mr McGregors garden and find Peter Rabbit!. Occasional artist at work.

Mirror sculptures and artwork by owner feature in the garden . . .

---

59 **NEW** **SUNNYSIDE COTTAGE**
High Street, Everton DN10 5AU. **Mrs Anne Beeby,** 01777 817170, anne.beeby@sky.com. *7m N of Retford. Everton - on the Bawtry to Gainsborough Rd A631. L to High Street opposite Sun Inn. Garden opposite village hall on High Street.* Cream teas at village hall. **Combined with Primrose Cottage adm £3, chd free. Sun 12 July (2-6).** Visitors also welcome by appt.
⅓ -acre s-facing secluded cottage garden designed to incorporate areas of different planting schemes and features which include roses, perennials. acers, a pond and some unusual foliage plants and trees.

60 **NEW** **THORESBY HALL HOTEL & SPA**
Thoresby Park, nr Ollerton NG22 9WH. **Thoresby Hall Hotel & Spa,** 01623 821000, www.warnerleisurehotels.co.uk. *N of Nottingham. From A1 exit at r'about signed A614 Nottingham - Leicester. After 4m at the next r'about take exit signed Thoresby Hall Hotel. Entrance 1m on L.* **Adm £3.50. Gardens open only by guided tour Sats 1pm, Weds 10.30. Sats, Weds 27 June; 1, 11, 15, 25, 29 July; 1, 5 Aug.**
Thoresby Hall gardens are famous for their beauty. Set in 50-acres of Sir Humphry Repton designed gardens, featuring a Grade 1 listed victorian rose garden with rare species. Gravel paths.

61 **UNIVERSITY OF NOTTINGHAM GARDENS**
University Park, Nottingham NG7 2RD, www.nottingham.ac.uk/estate/ friends. *1½ m W of Nottingham city centre. We suggest visitors arrive at the north entrance which is on the A52 adjacent to the QMC roundabout. The event is based at the Millennium Garden which is on University Park and well signed within the campus. No buses within campus on Sunday.* **Adm £2.50, chd free. Suns 10 May; 16 Aug (2-5).**
University Park has many beautiful gardens incl the award-winning Millennium Garden with its dazzling flower garden, timed fountains and turf maze. Visitors in late spring will see extensive plantings of bulbs throughout the park incl in our Jekyll Garden. During summer the walled garden will be alive with exotic plantings. In total 300 acres of landscape and gardens. Winner of the Green Flag Award, Britain in Bloom Best University College, Best Public Park, Best Flower Border.

62 **NEW** **6 WESTON CLOSE**
Woodthorpe NG5 4FS. **Diane & Steve Harrington,** 0115 9857506, di.harrington@lycos.co.uk. *3m N of Nottingham city centre. From city centre, A60 Mansfield Road. After Sherwood shops turn R at T-lights by Woodthorpe Park. 2nd L into Grange Road. R into The Crescent, R into Weston Close.*

Park in The Crescent. Home-made teas. **Adm £2.50, chd free. Sun 7 June (1-5). Visitors also welcome by appt weekends in July, groups of 8+.**
Medium sized garden created over 16 yrs from bare clay plot, taking advantage of a substantial upward slope to create a full, varied yet relaxed display in 3 separate areas. Mixed borders, scented roses, clematis, hostas, fuchsias, summer bedding in pots, small vegetable plot.

WHATTON GARDENS
See Leicestershire & Rutland.

63 THE WHITE HOUSE
Nicker Hill, Keyworth NG12 5EA. Tony & Gillian Hill, 0115 937 2049, gillyplants@aol.com. 8m SE of Nottingham. From A606 at Stanton-on-the-Wolds turn into Browns Lane beside petrol station. Follow rd 1½ m into Stanton Lane becoming Nicker Hill. Light refreshments & teas. Teas at Cherry Tree House 14 Jun. **Adm £2, chd free. Wed 15 Apr; Thur 21 May (2-5); Fri 12 (11-2), Suns 14 June, 12 July, 13 Sept (2-5). Evening Opening** £2, wine, Sat 13 June (6-8.30). **Also open Cherry Tree House, Sun 14 June. Visitors also welcome by appt groups 10+. Coaches permitted.**
Retired garden designers ¾ -acre garden with lawns, gravel, pergolas, seats, views and raised pond. Large packed beds with informal planting. Very floriferous/colourful throughout the seasons. April, pulmonarias, epimediums, spring bulbs. Late May/Jun spectacular crinodendron, iris, poppies, roses, cistus. Late summer/autumn big flowering spectacle. Specialist nursery on site.

Bog garden and sunken area below ha-ha, newly created and planted to tempt the eye onwards towards ancient well . . .

64 NEW WOODPECKERS
35 Lambley Lane, Burton Joyce NG14 5BG. Lynn Drake & Mark Carr, 01159 313237, lynn.drake@virgin.net. 6m N of Nottingham. In Burton Joyce, turn off A612 (Nottm/Southwell rd) into Lambley Lane, garden on L. Home-made teas. **Adm £3, chd free (share to Meningitis Trust). Sun 24, Mon 25 May (12.30-5). Visitors also welcome by appt,mini coach access only.**
4 acres of mature woodland and formal gardens with spectacular views over the Trent Valley. Over 300 rhododendrons and azaleas. Balustraded terrace for teas or pimms. Glade with 200 yr-old cedars overlooking ponds, waterfalls and croquet lawn. Bog garden and sunken area below ha-ha, newly created and planted to tempt the eye onwards towards ancient well. Slopes, unfenced ponds, some uneven pathways.

65 WOODSIDE COTTAGE
Hucknall Road, Newstead Village NG15 0BD. Ivan & Jean Kirby, 0115 963 1137. 2m N of Hucknall. From Hucknall take A611 towards Mansfield/M1. Turn R T-lights signed Newstead Village. Cottage 200m on L. From Mansfield/M1 J27 proceed towards Hucknall. Turn L at T-lights signed Newstead Village. Cottage 200m on L. Off road parking 250m. Drop off point. No on road parking. Home-made teas. **Adm £2.50, chd free (share to Nottingham Oasis Breast Cancer Trust). Suns 28 June; 19 July (1-5). Visitors also welcome by appt July to Aug, groups of 10 - 25 max.**
Country garden of ½ an acre set against a woodland backdrop. Lawns with borders of coloured foliage, conifers and shrubs interlaced with herbaceous plants. Climbing roses and clematis-clad pergola. Gravel planting. Paths with dry stone walls lead to rock garden, with converted well and millstone water features. Silver birch spinney and specimen trees together with wood and stone ornaments make up a developing garden. Gravel paths.

Nottinghamshire County Volunteers

County Organiser
Georgina Denison, 27 Campden Hill Road, London W8 7DX, 020 7937 0557. campden27@aol.com
County Treasurer
Michael Bull, Orchard House, High Oakham Road, Mansfield, NG18 5AJ, 01623 623884, mabull@tiscali.co.uk
Publicity
Barry Cope, 196 Tamworth Road, Sawley, Long Eaton, NG10 3GS, 01149 728309, the_copes@hotmail.com
Assistant County Organisers
Anne Bull, Orchard House, High Oakham Road, Mansfield NG18 5AJ, 01623 623884. mabull@tiscali.co.uk
Ann Henstock, 4 Lytham Drive, Edwalton, Nottingham NG12 4DQ, 0115 9235679, Annhenstock@aol.com
Beverley Perks, The Old Vicarage, Halam Hill, Halam NG22 8AX, 01636 812181, perks.family@talk21.com
Dulce Threlfall, Gringley Hall, Gringley on the Hill, Doncaster DN10 4QT, dulce@gringleyhall.fsnet

Mark your diary with these special events in 2009

EXPLORE SECRET GARDENS DURING CHELSEA & HAMPTON COURT FLOWER SHOW WEEKS

Tue 19 May, Wed 20 May, Thur 21 May, Fri 22 May, Wed 8 July, Thur 9 July
Full day tours from £82 per person, 10% discount for groups
Advance booking required, telephone +44 (0)20 8693 1015 or email j.wookey@btinternet.com
Specially selected gardens in London, Essex, Kent, Hampshire and South Oxfordshire. The tour price includes transport and lunch with wine at a popular restaurant or pub.

HAMPTON COURT PALACE

Thur 2 Apr, Tue 23 June, Thur 25 June, Wed 15 July, Tue 4 Aug, Thur 10 Sept
Evening tours in the company of one of the Palace's specialist tour guides from 6.30 – 8pm
Tickets £6 per person. Advance booking required, telephone +44 (0)1483 211535 or
visit www.ngs.org.uk for more information
Gossip, scandal, murder, healing – you'll find it all within the Formal Gardens at Hampton Court Palace. Each tour will have its own unique feature whether it's the story of the Great Vine or the magic and mystery of the Maze.

FROGMORE – A ROYAL GARDEN (BERKSHIRE)

Tue 26 May 10am – 5.30pm (last admission 4pm)
Garden adm £4.50, chd free. Tickets available in advance or on the day.
Advance booking for groups and coaches, telephone
+44 (0) 1483 211535 or email orders@ngs.org.uk
A rare opportunity to explore 30 acres of landscaped garden, rich in history and beauty.

FLAXBOURNE FARM – FUN & SURPRISES (BEDFORDSHIRE)

Sun 7 June 10am – 5pm. Adm £5, chd free
No booking required, come along on the day!
Bring the whole family and have fun in this surprising and entertaining garden of 2 acres. Enjoy the large plant fair, live music, pets corner, birds of prey, dog agility show and much more.

WISLEY RHS GARDEN – MUSIC IN THE GARDEN (SURREY)

Fri 11 Sept 6 – 9pm
Adm (incl RHS members) £7, chd under 15 free
Save money on advance bookings for groups of 4 or more, telephone +44 (0)1483 211535 or
visit www.ngs.org.uk for more information
A special evening opening of this famous garden, exclusively for the NGS. Enjoy music and entertainment as you explore the gardens and the floral marquee on the first day of the Wisley Flower Show.

For further information visit www.ngs.org.uk or telephone 01483 211535

OXFORDSHIRE

Opening Dates

February

SATURDAY 14
74 Waterperry Gardens

SUNDAY 15
57 Ramsden House

March

SUNDAY 1
44 Lime Close

SUNDAY 22
70 Trinity College
73 Wadham College

SUNDAY 29
45 Lingermans

April

WEDNESDAY 1
81 Woolstone Mill House

SUNDAY 5
3 Ashbrook House
24 Epwell Mill
42 Kingston Bagpuize House
46 Magdalen College
53 The Old Rectory, Coleshill

TUESDAY 7
65 Stansfield

WEDNESDAY 8
81 Woolstone Mill House

SUNDAY 12
58 St Hugh's College

MONDAY 13
10 Brook Cottage
41 Kencot Gardens

WEDNESDAY 15
81 Woolstone Mill House

WEDNESDAY 22
81 Woolstone Mill House

SUNDAY 26
12 Broughton Grange
27 Garsington Manor
79 Wick Hall & Nurseries
80 Wildwood

WEDNESDAY 29
81 Woolstone Mill House

May

TUESDAY 5
65 Stansfield

WEDNESDAY 6
81 Woolstone Mill House

SUNDAY 10
1 Adderbury Gardens

WEDNESDAY 13
81 Woolstone Mill House

SATURDAY 16
29 Greys Court

SUNDAY 17
34 Hollyhocks
35 Holywell Manor
51 Monks Head
59 Salford Gardens
66 Steeple Aston Gardens
75 Wayside

WEDNESDAY 20
81 Woolstone Mill House

SUNDAY 24
5 Barton Abbey
16 Charlbury Gardens

MONDAY 25
63 Sparsholt Manor

WEDNESDAY 27
81 Woolstone Mill House

SUNDAY 31
19 Church Farm Field
24 Epwell Mill
25 Evelegh's
31 Headington Gardens
76 Westwell Manor

June

TUESDAY 2
65 Stansfield

WEDNESDAY 3
81 Woolstone Mill House

SATURDAY 6
33 Hill Court

SUNDAY 7
12 Broughton Grange
21 East Hagbourne Gardens
33 Hill Court
44 Lime Close

MONDAY 8
34 Hollyhocks (Evening)
51 Monks Head (Evening)

WEDNESDAY 10
2 All Saints Convent & St Johns Home
81 Woolstone Mill House

SATURDAY 13
48 Manor House

SUNDAY 14
4 Asthall Manor
8 Blewbury Manor
9 Brize Norton Gardens
14 Broughton Poggs & Filkins Gardens
22 East Hanney Gardens
26 14 Farndon Road
34 Hollyhocks
39 Iffley Gardens
47 Manor Farm

48 Manor House
51 Monks Head
54 The Old Vicarage
60 Sibford Gower Gardens
69 Thame Gardens
77 Wheatley Gardens

WEDNESDAY 17
54 The Old Vicarage
81 Woolstone Mill House

SUNDAY 21
6 Blenheim Palace
7 Blewbury Gardens
13 Broughton Grounds Farm
30 Hazelford Cottage
50 Middleton Cheney Gardens
72 Upper Chalford Farm

WEDNESDAY 24
81 Woolstone Mill House

SUNDAY 28
23 Eaves Cottage
40 Keble College
64 Springhill House
78 Whitehill Farm

July

WEDNESDAY 1
81 Woolstone Mill House

THURSDAY 2
71 University of Oxford Botanic Garden

SUNDAY 5
12 Broughton Grange
81 Woolstone Mill House

TUESDAY 7
65 Stansfield

WEDNESDAY 8
81 Woolstone Mill House

SUNDAY 12
1 Adderbury Gardens
17 Chastleton Gardens
61 Somerville College
72 Upper Chalford Farm
73 Wadham College

WEDNESDAY 15
81 Woolstone Mill House

SUNDAY 19
15 Chalkhouse Green Farm

WEDNESDAY 22
81 Woolstone Mill House

SATURDAY 25
49 Merton College Oxford Fellows' Garden

SUNDAY 26
11 Broughton Castle
70 Trinity College

WEDNESDAY 29
81 Woolstone Mill House

August

SUNDAY 2
⑫ Broughton Grange

TUESDAY 4
㊿ Stansfield

WEDNESDAY 5
㉛ Woolstone Mill House

WEDNESDAY 12
㉛ Woolstone Mill House

SUNDAY 16
① Adderbury Gardens

WEDNESDAY 19
㉛ Woolstone Mill House

SUNDAY 23
㉘ Greenfield Farm

WEDNESDAY 26
㉛ Woolstone Mill House

SUNDAY 30
㊱ Radcot House
㉞ Springhill House

MONDAY 31
⑩ Brook Cottage

September

TUESDAY 1
㊿ Stansfield

WEDNESDAY 2
㉛ Woolstone Mill House

SUNDAY 6
③ Ashbrook House
⑲ Church Farm Field
㉔ Epwell Mill
㊷ Kingston Bagpuize House
㊝ The Old Rectory, Coleshill

WEDNESDAY 9
㉛ Woolstone Mill House

SUNDAY 13
㉒ East Hanney Gardens
㊸ Lady Margaret Hall

WEDNESDAY 16
㉛ Woolstone Mill House

SUNDAY 20
㉗ Garsington Manor
㊱ Radcot House
㊹ Waterperry Gardens

WEDNESDAY 23
㉛ Woolstone Mill House

WEDNESDAY 30
㉛ Woolstone Mill House

Gardens open to the public

⑥ Blenheim Palace
⑩ Brook Cottage
⑪ Broughton Castle
㉙ Greys Court
㊷ Kingston Bagpuize House
㊻ Magdalen College
㊾ Merton College Oxford Fellows' Garden
㉛ University of Oxford Botanic Garden
㊹ Waterperry Gardens

By appointment only

⑱ Chivel Farm
⑳ Clock House
㉜ Hearns House
㊱ Home Close
㊲ Home Farm
㊳ Homeland
㊿ The Old Vicarage, Bledington
㊽ South Newington House
㊼ Swalcliffe Lea House
㊽ Tadmarton Manor

Also open by appointment

① Fairfield, Adderbury Gardens
① Placketts, Adderbury Gardens
⑮ Chalkhouse Green Farm
⑲ Church Farm Field
㉔ Epwell Mill
㉘ Greenfield Farm
㉛ 40 Osler Road, Headington Gardens
㊹ Lime Close
�51 Monks Head
㊼ Old Church House
㊼ The Old Vicarage
㊱ Radcot House
㊽ St Hugh's College
㊾ Old Rectory, Salford Gardens
㊾ Willow Tree Cottage, Salford Gardens
㊽ Springhill House
㊿ Stansfield
㊻ Primrose Cottage, Steeple Aston Gardens
㊼ Upper Chalford Farm
㊷ Wayside
㊼ The Manor House, Wheatley Gardens
㊼ The Studio, Wheatley Gardens
㊽ Whitehill Farm
㉛ Woolstone Mill House

The Gardens

Group opening

① ADDERBURY GARDENS
OX17 3LS. *3m S of Banbury. J10 M40, onto A43 signed Northampton, then A4260 to Adderbury, or A4260 S from Banbury.* Home-made teas at The Institute or Church House depending on weather. **Combined adm £5, chd free (share to Katharine House Hospice).** Suns 10 May (£4); 12 July (£5); 16 Aug (£3) (2-6). Attractive Hornton stone village with a fine church. Village maps given to all visitors. The two gardens open on 16 Aug are full of late summer colour.
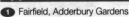

BERRY HILL HOUSE
Berry Hill Road. Mr & Mrs J P Pollard. *Off A4260 signed Milton, Bloxham, W Adderbury.* **Not open 12 July & 16 Aug.**
2 acres; mature trees and lawns with countryside views; features separate garden areas linked together informally in a tranquil setting; many unusual plant varieties; kitchen garden and orchard.

CROSSHILL HOUSE
Manor Road. Mr & Mrs Gurth Hoyer Millar. **Not open 10 May & 16 Aug.**
Georgian house (not open) surrounded by 4-acre classic Victorian walled gardens and grounds with ha-ha.

FAIRFIELD
Cross Hill Road. Mr & Mrs Mike Adams, 01295 810109. **Not open 10 May.** Visitors also welcome by appt.
This exquisite, tiny, paved garden is a tapestry of beautiful plants and a patchwork of colour, interwoven with a selection of unusual and interesting clematis and climbers. Notable for late summer colour.
☎

The two gardens open on 16 August are full of late summer colour . . .

HOLLY BANK
Berry Hill Road. Malcolm & Erica Brown. Not open 12 July & 16 Aug.
Interesting re-development of one third of an acre garden with island beds which include a variety of trees, shrubs, bulbs and herbaceous plants.

HOME FARM HOUSE
Manor Road. Mr & Mrs J V Harper. Not open 12 July & 16 Aug.
2 acres; lawns, mature trees and shrubs, landscaped paddock, carp pond and flower borders.

NEW THE OLD VICARAGE
Church Lane. M Boyd, Head Gardener. Not open 10 May & 16 Aug.
C18 vicarage (not open) with wide sweep of front garden limited by yew hedge. Walled garden to side. Large rear garden stretching out from ha-ha to small lake with flood-meadows beyond. Unusual plants and trees. Japanese maple plantation.

PLACKETTS
High Street. Dr D White. Nr Church. Visitors also welcome by appt jointly with Fairfield.
Queen Anne cottage (not open); 0.2-acre walled garden, sheltered gravel courtyard. Main garden exposed and sunny with views. Many tulips, euphorbias, primulas, anemones. Numerous clematis, roses and lilies. Notable for late summer colour.

NEW SORBROOK MANOR
Cross Hill Road. Mr & Mrs Robin Thistlethwayte. Not open 10 May & 16 Aug.
3-acres of lawns, ornamental trees and shrubs gently sloping down to Sor Brook.

2 ALL SAINTS CONVENT & ST JOHNS HOME
St Mary's Road, East Oxford OX4 1RU. Society of All Saints Sisters of the Poor. 1m E of Oxford. Bus 1 or 5 from Queen St along Cowley Rd. Alight at Manzil Way, cross Cowley Rd, 1st turn R into Leopold St,

then 1st L into St Mary's Rd and 1st gateway on L. Adm £3, chd free (share to St Johns Home). Wed 10 June (2-5).
Approx 2-acre garden with lawns, mature trees, shrubberies, mixed herbaceous and shrub borders. Vegetable garden; secluded quiet garden and wild flower meadow which includes many common spotted orchids. Comper Chapel open. Uneven lawns and small unfenced pond.

3 ASHBROOK HOUSE
Blewbury OX11 9QA. Mr & Mrs S A Barrett. 4m SE of Didcot. Turn off A417 in Blewbury into Westbrook St. 1st house on R. Home-made teas. Adm £3, chd free. Suns 5 Apr; 6 Sept (2-6).
The garden where Kenneth Grahame read 'Wind in the Willows' to local children and where he took inspiration for his description of the oak doors to Badger's House. Come and see - you may catch a glimpse of Toad and friends in this 3½ -acre chalk and water garden. Plant sale April only.

4 ASTHALL MANOR
Asthall, nr Burford OX18 4HW. Rosanna Taylor, www.onformsculputre.co.uk. 3m E of Burford. At roundabout between Witney & Burford on A40, take turning to Minster Lovell. Turn immed L (signed to Asthall). At bottom of hill, follow avenue of trees and look for car park signs. Adm £4, chd free. Sun 14 June (2-6).
6-acres of garden surround this C17 manor house (not open) once home to the Mitford family and overlooking the Windrush Valley. The gardens designed by I & J Bannerman in 1998, offer a "beguiling mix of traditional and contemporary" (GGG). Exuberant borders. sloping box parterres.

5 BARTON ABBEY
Steeple Barton OX25 4QS. Mr & Mrs P Fleming. 8m E of Chipping Norton. On B4030, ½ m from junction of A4260 & B4030. Home-made teas. Adm £4, chd free. Sun 24 May (2-5).
15-acre garden with views from house (not open) across sweeping lawns and picturesque lake. Walled garden with colourful herbaceous borders, separated by established yew hedges and espalier fruit, contrasts with more informal woodland garden paths with

vistas of specimen trees and meadows. Working glasshouses and fine display of fruit and vegetables.

Come and see - you may catch a glimpse of Toad and friends in this 3½ -acre chalk and water garden . . .

6 ◆ BLENHEIM PALACE
Woodstock OX20 1PX. His Grace the Duke of Marlborough, 01993 811091, www.blenheimpalace.com. 8m N of Oxford. Bus: 20 Oxford-Chipping Norton, alight Woodstock. Adm £4, chd £2, concessions £3. Please visit website for opening dates/times. For NGS: Sun 21 June (10-6).
Blenheim Gardens, originally laid out by Henry Wise, include the formal Water Terraces and Italian Garden by Achille Duchêne, Rose Garden, Arboretum, and Cascade. The Secret Garden offers a stunning garden paradise for all seasons. Blenheim Lake, created by Capability Brown and spanned by Vanburgh's Grand Bridge, is the focal point of over 2,000 acres of landscaped parkland. The Pleasure Gardens complex includes the Herb and Lavender Garden and Butterfly House. Other activities incl the Marlborough Maze, putting greens, adventure play area, giant chess and draughts. Some gravel but tarmac route available.

The view
from the gate
draws you
into this
natural cottage
garden . . .

Group opening

⑦ BLEWBURY GARDENS
OX11 9QB. *4m SE of Didcot. On A417. Follow yellow signs for car parks.* Home-made teas. Teas at St Michael's Church for the church, teas at Hall Barn for NGS. **Adm £4, chd free. Sun 21 June (2-6).**
6 gardens in a charming downland village. 4 of the 5 gardens featured in 'Rachel's Flower Hour' Gardeners' World Special. The gardens were also filmed for Rachel de Thame's 'The Changing Face of the Cottage Garden'.

ABNERS
Joyce Gilbert
The view from the gate draws you into this natural cottage garden. Joyce is President of the Village Produce Association and has stocked many Blewbury gardens over the years.

CHAPMANS
Jenny Craig
1/2 -acre garden with listed house (not open) and stream. Informal cottage beds with established and new herbaceous planting featuring some unusual plants. Gravel entrance and gentle slopes.

GREEN BUSHES
Phil Rogers
A garden created by Rhon (died 2007), a true plant lover, developed around a C16 cottage (not open). Large range of plants grown in a variety of settings; colour-themed borders, ponds and poolside planting, alpine troughs, ferns, pleached limes and roses.

HALL BARN
Malcolm & Deirdre Cochrane
Garden and paddocks extend to 4 acres with traditional herbaceous borders and a kitchen garden. Special features include a quality croquet lawn, C16 dovecote, a thatched cob wall and clear chalk streams.

NOTTINGHAM FEE HOUSE
Mrs Carolyn Anderson
Newly planted garden surrounding timber-framed house (not open). 1/3 acre. Gravel paths, clipped boxes, perennials and shrubs.

STOCKS
Norma & Richard Bird
Around this early cruck-constructed thatched cottage (not open), a densely planted collection of lime-tolerant herbaceous perennials offers tiers of colour throughout the year.

---

⑧ BLEWBURY MANOR
Blewbury OX11 9QJ. Mr & Mrs M R Blythe. *4m SE of Didcot. Turn off A417 in Blewbury into Westbrook St, after 1/3m bear R at sign to village hall (car parking in school car park & in village hall car park). Continue into Berry Lane & house is 20yds on L.* Home-made teas. **Adm £4, chd £2 (5-16 yrs). Sun 14 June (2-6).**
Part C17 Manor House (not open) with moat set in a garden of about 10 acres. Features incl a parterre; flower garden, herbaceous and mixed borders; pergola; decorative vegetable and herb garden; stream planting and woodland area; lake and sunken gravel garden surrounded by hornbeam allées. Large traditional courtyard with late season flowering borders.

Group opening

⑨ BRIZE NORTON GARDENS
OX18 3NN, 01993 846386. *3m SW of Witney. Brize Norton village, S of A40, or on Burford Rd.* Home-made teas at Elderbank Hall & Lingermans. **Combined adm £3.50, chd free (share to St Britius Church, Brize Norton Brownies & Brize Norton over 60s). Sun 14 June (1-6).**
Pretty village. Church open with Flower

Festival. Teas by WI in Elderbank Hall. Large recreation ground for picnics. Ice creams and plants available for NGS. Coaches welcome but should telephone first to arrange parking.

BARNSTABLE HOUSE
Manor Road. Mr & Mrs P Butcher
C17 converted Cotswold stone barn (not open) with Mediterranean-style patio and planting. Courtyard garden with lawn surrounded by tightly packed borders against a backdrop of lime trees.

10 CHICHESTER PLACE
David & Claire Harrison.
Small garden with a wide variety of plants incl herbs, clematis, roses, bog plants and lots more. Come and see what you can fit in a small place.

17 CHICHESTER PLACE
Mr & Mrs Howard
Family garden with decking and barbeque areas, borders and water feature. Seating area and conservatory.

CHURCH FARM HOUSE
Philip & Mary Holmes
A garden designed with seating areas at different levels and viewpoints and including herb garden, rockery, water features, mixed borders, pergola, gazebo, greenhouse and pool enclosure with bougainvillea and oleanders.

NEW THE COTTAGE
Mr & Mrs Griffin
Approx 1/3 acre lawn, mature borders, roses and a vegetable patch. White border and a rose tunnel. Gravel drive.

16 DAUBIGNY MEAD
Bob & Margaret Watts
Garden is loosely based on room system, divided into various sections. Contains many shrubs. Water feature. Stream runs the length of garden. Back lawn is home to a guinea pig. Small step.

2 ELM GROVE
Mr & Mrs Brian De'ath
Garden of medium size, front, side and rear areas. Patio, front and rear ponds with stream. Pergola with mixed climbers, borders with mixed herbaceous plants and shrubs, variety of ornamental trees and large lawned areas.

GAYLYN
Burford Road. Benita Wallace
1/3-acre garden, with mature trees, herbaceous borders, roses and lawns.

GRANGE FARM
Burford Road. Mr & Mrs Mark Artus
Family garden in rural setting with croquet lawn, stream and 3 paddocks containing C14 dovecot, vegetable garden, children's play area, fruit trees, pheasant enclosure and wide walkable paths mowed through meadow.

LINGERMANS
Burford Road. Mrs E Dobson.
Follow signs for Foxbury Farm. Approx 2m from village (See separate entry).

MIJESHE
Elm Grove. Mr & Mrs M Harper
Established garden with many areas of interest incl herbaceous borders, patios, fruit trees and many features.

🆕 3 MINSTER ROAD
James & Sarah Jane Gillies
Medium sized front and rear garden. Young pear and apple cordon partitioning vegetable garden. Lawn, patio area, pond and a variety of shrubs and flowers.

PAINSWICK HOUSE
Carterton Road. Mr & Mrs T Gush
Approx 3/4 -acre mature garden; old apple trees; herb garden; vegetable garden, new pond area, herbaceous borders and friendly chickens.

🆕 ROSEDALE
Burford Road. Mr & Mrs S Finlayson
1/2 acre of gardens comprising fruit and vegetable plots, terraced lawns with surrounding borders filled with mature shrubs, herbaceous plants and ornamental grasses. Semi-wild area with pond plus free range chicken and guinea pigs. Gravel drive.

SCHOOL GARDEN
Station Road. Brize Norton Primary School
Flowers; vegetables; beautiful pond area; sound garden, willow dome and quiet area. All created and maintained with the help of the school children, all produced organically.

Family garden in rural setting with croquet lawn, stream and wide walkable paths mowed through meadow . . .

🔟 ◆ BROOK COTTAGE
Well Lane, Alkerton OX15 6NL. Mrs David Hodges, 01295 670303, www.brookcottagegarden.co.uk. *6m NW of Banbury. 1/2 m off A422. Follow signs in village.* **Adm £5, chd free, concessions £4. Mon-Fri 13 Apr to 31 Oct (9-6). For NGS: Mons 13 Apr; 31 Aug (9-6).**
4-acre hillside garden formed since 1964. Wide variety of trees, shrubs and perennials in areas of differing character. Water gardens, gravel garden, colour coordinated borders. Over 200 shrub and climbing roses. Many clematis; interesting throughout season. Limited wheelchair access.

⑪ ◆ BROUGHTON CASTLE
nr Banbury OX15 5EB. The Lord Saye & Sele, 01295 262624, www.broughtoncastle.com. *2 1/2 m SW of Banbury. On Shipston-on-Stour rd (B4035).* **House and garden adm £6.50, concession £5.50, chd £2.50, garden only adm £3, chd £1, concessions £2. For NGS: Sun 26 July (2-5).**
1 acre; shrubs, herbaceous borders, walled garden, roses, climbers seen against background of C14-C16 castle surrounded by moat in open parkland.

⑫ BROUGHTON GRANGE
Wykham Lane, Broughton OX15 5DS. *1/4 m out of village. From Banbury take the B4035 to village of Broughton. At the Seye & Sele Arms PH turn L up Wykham Lane (one way). Follow rd out of village along lane for 1/4 m. Entrance on R.* **Teas. Adm £6, chd free. Suns 26 Apr; 7 June; 5 July; 2 Aug (10-5).**
An impressive 25 acres of gardens and light woodland in an attractive Oxfordshire setting. The centrepiece is a large terraced walled garden created by Tom Stuart-Smith in 2001. Vision has been used to blend the gardens into the countryside. Good early displays of bulbs followed by outstanding herbaceous planting in summer. Formal and informal areas combine to make this a special site incl newly laid arboretum with many ongoing projects.

⑬ BROUGHTON GROUNDS FARM
North Newington OX15 6AW. Mr & Mrs Andrew Taylor. *3m from Banbury. 3m off B4035 through North Newington. Leave Banbury on Shipston Rd, B4035. Turn R to N Newington, follow rd signed Shutford. On L 3/4 m signed B & B.* **Home-made teas. Adm £2.50, chd free. Combined with Hazelford Cottage. Sun 21 June (2-5).**
One of the few farms to achieve recognition under the 'High Level Stewardship Scheme'. You will see rare wild flowers, grasses and wildlife in an area set in an 18-acre meadow. Also includes an old mill race and views of the deserted (1914) village of Hazelford. An area 'species rich'.

Dramatically combining local materials with modern planting . . .

Group opening

⑭ BROUGHTON POGGS & FILKINS GARDENS
GL7 3JH. *3m N of Lechlade. 5m S of Burford.* Home-made teas in Filkins village hall. **Combined adm £4, chd free. Sun 14 June (2-5.30).**
Two beautiful Cotswold stone villages. Gardens of widely varied scale and character. Village maps will be available, donation invited. Communally-run village shop (ices etc). Swinford Museum of Cotswold tools and artefacts. Woollen weavers.
☕

BROUGHTON HALL
Broughton Poggs. Karen & Ian Jobling
Formal walled garden, together with less formal grounds; ha-ha and views out to Thames valley; medieval carp pond; Roman well.
& ❀

BROUGHTON POGGS MILL
Charles Payne & Avril Inglis. *On B4477 as it crosses Broadwell Brook, between Filkins & Broughton Poggs*
Contemporary garden, with newly-formed linked 'rooms' in a traditional Cotswold watermill setting, dramatically combining local materials with modern planting.

DOLPHIN HOUSE
Filkins, Lechlade. J M Moir
A garden to encourage wildlife.

FILKINS FARMHOUSE
Filkins. Mr & Mrs Bristow
Traditional walled farmhouse garden. Lawns, borders, rose trellis, orchard. Gravel paths.
&

FILKINS HALL
Filkins Hall Residents
Open last year for the first time. House (not open) partly rebuilt 1912. Grand landscape setting now under rejuvenation: lawns, ha-ha, venerable trees, shrubs, herbaceous borders, wall shrubs: parkland pasture beyond. Gravel drive & paths.
&

LITTLE PEACOCKS
Filkins. Colvin & Moggridge
Garden made by Brenda Colvin 1956 onwards, very strong structure from walls and colours and textures of foliage.
&

THE MILLER'S COTTAGE
Luke Bailey
Small garden yet with several character areas; eccentric plan form defined by beech hedge; lawn, miniature flowery borders, shrubs, small trees. An object lesson in what can be done with a smaller garden.

NO 1 COACH HOUSE
Filkins Hall, Filkins. Mrs Elizabeth Gidman
Small, intensive, semi-formal walled garden of many elements: terrace, pool, pergola, seats, form and texture of plants, grey plants.
�

PIP COTTAGE
Filkins. G B Woodin
Village house garden - formal in front; lawn, hedges and a view at the back.
& ✕

POGGS COTTAGE
Broughton Poggs. Phil & Helen Dunmall
A young reworking of an older garden: patio, lawn, island beds, mature shrubs, raised organic vegetable beds, soft fruit.
&

ST PETER'S HOUSE
Filkins. John Cambridge
Large garden of lawns and trees, herbaceous borders, rose garden, sunken paved garden with pool. Gravel paths and driveway.
&

BURROW FARM
See Buckinghamshire.

⑮ CHALKHOUSE GREEN FARM
nr Kidmore End RG4 9AL. Mr & Mrs J Hall, 01189 723631. *2m N of Reading, 5m SW of Henley-on-Thames. Situated between A4074 & B481. From Kidmore End take Chalkhouse Green Rd. Follow yellow signs.* Home-made teas. **Adm £3, chd free. Sun 19 July (2-6). Visitors also welcome by appt.**
1-acre garden and open traditional farmstead. Herbaceous borders, herb garden, shrubs, old-fashioned roses, trees incl medlar, quince and mulberries, walled ornamental kitchen garden. New cherry orchard. Rare breed farm animals incl an ancient breed of British White cattle, Suffolk Punch & Percheron horses, donkeys, Berkshire pigs, piglets, goats, chickens, ducks and turkeys. Vintage farm machinery displays. Farm trail and donkey rides, vintage tractor trailer rides. Swimming in covered pool, plant stall. Explore WW2 Air Raid Shelter and exhibits. Majority of garden wheelchair accessible, some uneven paving.
& ✕ ❀ ☕ ☎

Group opening

⑯ CHARLBURY GARDENS
OX7 3PP. *6m SE of Chipping Norton.* Teas at Charlbury Memorial Hall. **Combined adm £4, chd free. Sun 24 May (2-6).**
Large Cotswold village on B4022 Witney-Enstone Rd.
☕

GOTHIC HOUSE
Mr & Mrs Andrew Lawson. *In Church St, nr Bell Hotel*
1/3-acre walled garden, designed for sculpture display and colour association. New area of planted squares replaces lawn. False perspective, pleached lime walk, trellis, terracotta containers. Gravel paths.
& ✕ ❀

HEATHFIELD
Browns Lane. Helen & Trevor Jones. *In Browns Lane between Spendlove car park & The Bull*
1/2-acre walled garden. Mixed borders, with a variety of interesting plants, have been created by the owners over the last nine years, around newly designed landscape features and existing trees. Some gravel paths.
& ❀

LYDBROOK
Crawborough. **Aija & Christopher Hastings.** *Close to centre of Charlbury on rd from the Playing Close*
A typical long 1930s garden that has been divided into a number of rooms including patios, lawns and a small pond. Planting incl some exotic species such as tree ferns, bananas and bamboos.

THE PRIORY GARDEN
Church Lane, Charlbury. **Dr D El Kabir & Colleagues.** *White gate off St Mary's church yard*
1 acre of formal terraced topiary gardens with Italianate features. Foliage colour schemes, shrubs, parterres with fragrant plants, old roses, water features, sculpture and inscriptions aim to produce a poetic, wistful atmosphere. Arboretum of over 3 acres borders the R Evenlode and incl wildlife garden and pond. Gravel path/ drive at entrance.

CHARLTON GARDENS
See Northamptonshire.

Group opening

17 CHASTLETON GARDENS
Chastleton GL56 0SZ. *4m NW of Chipping Norton. 3m SE of Moreton-in-Marsh on A44.* Cream teas. Combined adm £5, chd free. Sun 12 July (2-6).
2 very different gardens: Prue Leith's 5-acre garden with views, lake, Cotswold terraces (one red), rose tunnel, woods, vegetable and flower parterres and Chastleton House, Jacobean manor house with topiary and parkland. Please note it is 1m between gardens. Both properties have car parks.

CHASTLETON GLEBE
Prue Leith
5 acres, old trees, terraces (one all red); small lake, island; Chinese-style bridge, pagoda; formal vegetable garden; views; rose tunnel. Vegetable and flower parterres. Gravel paths and access to grass areas dependent on weather.

◆ CHASTLETON HOUSE
The National Trust. *From A436 off A44. Car park 270yds from garden*

3-acre garden with a typical Elizabethan/Jacobean layout, ring of fascinating topiary at its heart. At Chastleton House (not open) the rules of modern croquet were codified in 1866. Croquet lawn survives.

---

18 CHIVEL FARM
Heythrop OX7 5TR. **Mr & Mrs J D Sword,** 01608 683227, rosalind.sword@btinternet.com. *4m E of Chipping Norton. Off A361 or A44.* Adm £3.50. Visitors welcome by appt.
Beautifully designed country garden, with extensive views, designed for continuous interest. Colour-schemed borders with many unusual trees, shrubs and herbaceous plants. Small formal white garden. Conservatory.

19 CHURCH FARM FIELD
Church Lane, Epwell OX15 6LD. **Mr V D & Mrs D V D Castle,** 01295 788473. *7¹/₂ m W of Banbury on N side of Epwell.* Adm £2, chd free. Suns 31 May; 6 Sept (2-6). **Also open Epwell Mill.** Visitors also welcome by appt.
Woods; arboretum with wild flowers (planting started 1992); over 150 different trees and shrubs in 4¹/₂ acres. Paths cut through trees for access to various parts.

20 CLOCK HOUSE
Coleshill SN6 7PT. **Denny Wickham & Peter Fox,** 01793 762476, denny.ambrose@virgin.net. *3¹/₂ m SW of Faringdon. On B4019.* Adm £2.50, chd free. Visitors welcome by appt.
Rambling garden on hilltop overlooking NT parkland and Vale of the White Horse. On the site of Coleshill House, burnt down in 1952, the floor plan has been laid out as a garden with lavender and box 'walls' and gravel 'rooms' full of self-sown butterfly-attracting flowers. Exuberant, not too tidy, garden with unusual plants; walled garden; vegetables.

CUDDINGTON GARDENS
Thame. See Buckinghamshire.

DAYLESFORD HOUSE
See Gloucestershire North & Central.

These allotments are a focal point of the village . . . some luxuriant clumps of rhubarb . . .

Group opening

21 EAST HAGBOURNE GARDENS
OX11 9LN. *1¹/₂ m SE of Didcot. On B4016 Didcot-Blewbury. Follow signs to car park.* Sun 7 June (2-6).
An exceptionally pretty downland village which has frequently won awards for 'Best Kept Village'. A variety of gardens incl allotments. C11/12 church open for visitors and award-winning wildflower meadow attached to cemetery. Scarecrow trail round village.

FLETCHERS
19 Main Rd. OX11 9LN. Charlie & Alison Laing
Garden 'under development'. New planting within old framework. Several garden 'rooms' inc formal area, vegetable garden, stream and orchard. Newly planted white and peony beds.

THE GABLES
20 Main Rd. OXLL 9LN. Mr & Mrs C Booth
C16 house (not open) with classic English garden designed to complement the house. Herbaceous borders set out in colour groupings.

5 HIGGS CLOSE
Mrs Jenny Smith
Colourful garden, part-walled with a bit of everything: herbaceous borders, mixed shrub screen, vegetable patch, small pond, greenhouse, lawns.

KINGSHOLM
5 Main Rd. OX11 9LN.
Mr & Mrs John Lawson
Partly Elizabethan, partly C17 house (not open) with medieval (circa 1450) origins. $3/4$ -acre garden with topiary in box and yew. Herbaceous and shrub borders; water garden; rockery. Short wooded walk. Short gravel path to lawn.

MANOR FARM
Manor Farm Lane. Mr & Mrs R W Harries
2-acre garden, water surrounds the main house (not open) in the form of a moat and full use has been made of this feature. Mixed borders. Well planted vegetable plot incl peaches, plums, pears and apples.

TUDOR HOUSE ALLOTMENTS
Main Road. Penny Kisby & Craig Barfoot
Alongside a thatched barn, these allotments are a focal point of the village. As well as seasonal fruit, vegetables and some luxuriant clumps of rhubarb, there are many varieties of iris, tulips, roses and dahlias.

Group opening

22 NEW EAST HANNEY GARDENS
OX12 0HJ. *3m out of Wantage on A338 towards Oxford. Turn into E Hanney off A338 opp La Fontana Restaurant, keep red telephone box on L & continue 200yds down road, turn L into Halls Lane & Philberds & car park are on R.* Home-made teas. **Combined adm £5, chd free** (share to Sorbell Howe Hospice). **Suns 14 June; 13 Sept (2-6).**
Character filled village with many thatched and timber framed cottages. Ancient church with Norman features and monumental brasses (W Hanney) and good village pubs. Pretty walk between Philberds Manor (car park), Lower Mill and Jasmine Cottage along the willow-lined bank of the Letcombe Brook, with timeless views over water meadows.

JASMINE COTTAGE
Main Street, East Hanney. Gill & David Parry. *4m NE of Wantage.* Small $1/5$ -acre S-facing garden attached to C17 thatched cottage (not open). Developed over last 13yrs by a plantaholic and her willing helper, both with busy lives. Herbaceous borders, trees and shrubs enclosing different areas for yr-round interest. Cordon fruit trees, vegetable patch and terrace.

NEW LOWER MILL
Halls Lane Robert & Maryrose Hodgson
Atmospheric garden, designed by Jinny Blom, planted in silt from the Letcombe Brooke, which borders it. Featured in 'Dream Gardens', 'The English Garden', 'Gardens Illustrated' & 'Sunday Telegraph'. Steps up into the garden but can be seen from the terrace.

PHILBERD'S MANOR
Halls Lane. Robert & Maryrose Hodgson
$1^1/2$ acres of peaceful garden surrounding newly restored C17 house (after fire in 2006 - Google Maryrose Hodgson). Perennial borders and restored terrace and herb garden.

Atmospheric garden by Jinny Blom, planted in silt from the Letcombe Brooke. . .

23 NEW EAVES COTTAGE
Cropredy Lane, Williamscot OX17 1AD. Ken & Sandra Atack. *3m NE of Banbury. From J11 M40 take A361 to Daventry. After 3m L into Williamscot. Eaves Cottage on L at the end of the village.* Home-made teas. **Adm £2.50, chd free** (share to Pancreatic Cancer UK). **Sun 28 June (2-5).**

Cottage garden set in 1-acre of C17th house with SE facing sloped aspect. Planted for yr-round interest with many different shrubs, trees and herbaceous borders. Pond, stream and bog area with natural planting. Newly cultivated large vegetable and fruit area.

24 EPWELL MILL
nr Banbury OX15 6HG. Mrs William Graham & Mrs David Long, 01295 788242. *7m W of Banbury. Between Shutford & Epwell.* **Adm £2, chd free. Suns 5 Apr; 31 May; 6 Sept (2-6).** Also open **Church Farm Field, Epwell** 31 May & 6 Sept. Visitors also welcome by appt.
Medium-sized peaceful garden, interestingly landscaped in open country, based around former watermill with terraced pools. Spring bulbs in April, azaleas in May and early autumn colour in September. White double border.

25 EVELEGH'S
High Street, Long Wittenham, nr Abingdon OX14 4QH. Dr & Mrs C S Ogg. *3m SE of Didcot. Evelegh's is next to The Plough PH, Long Wittenham.* Home-made teas in village hall. **Adm £3.50, chd free. Sun 31 May (2-6).**
$3/4$ -acre garden leading through areas of different characters to River Thames. Well stocked with many unusual shrubs, bulbs and perennials, incl collections of old bush roses, delphiniums, tree and herbaceous peonies, iris and clematis.

EVENLEY WOOD GARDEN
See Northamptonshire.

26 14 FARNDON ROAD
OX2 6RT. Mrs Judith Lane. *$3/4$ m N of Oxford city centre. Off Woodstock Rd. $1/4$ m N of Radcliffe infirmary.* **Adm £3, chd free. Sun 14 June (2-6).**
Professionally designed long narrow town garden with visual impact. Formal layout divided into 'rooms' by yew hedges. Restrained planting and colour scheme - box, bay, ivies, roses, peonies. Designed for privacy. Featured in 'The Sunday Times' & 'The English Garden'.

27 GARSINGTON MANOR
28 Southend, Garsington, nr Oxford
OX44 9DH. Mrs R Ingrams. *3m SE of
Oxford. N of B480. 1¹/₂ m S of
Wheatley.* Home-made teas. **Adm £4,
chd free. Suns 26 Apr; 20 Sept (2-5).**
C17 Manor house of architectural,
literary and musical interest (not open).
Early monastic fish ponds, water
garden, dovecote c1700. Lake and
flower parterre, Italianate terrace and
loggia and Italian statues laid out by
Philip and Lady Ottoline Morrell c1915-
1923. Gravel paths, steps, steep
slopes.

28 GREENFIELD FARM
Christmas Common, nr Watlington
OX49 5HG. Andrew & Jane Ingram,
01491 612434,
ingram@greenfieldfarm.fsnet.co.uk.
*4m from J5 of M40, 7m from Henley.
J5 M40; A40 towards Oxford for ¹/₂ m;
turn L signed Christmas Common.
³/₄ m past Fox & Hounds. Turn L at
'Tree Barn' sign.* **Adm £3, chd free
(share to Farm Wildlife Advisory
Group). Sun 23 Aug (2-4). Visitors
also welcome by appt.**
10-acre wild flower meadow,
surrounded by woodland, established
14 yrs ago under the Countryside
Stewardship Scheme. Traditional
Chiltern chalkland meadow in beautiful
peaceful setting with 80 species of
perennial wild flowers and grasses.
Chiltern Gentian expected to be
flowering in abundance. ¹/₂ m walk
from parking area. Opportunity to
return via typical Chiltern beechwood.

29 ◆ GREYS COURT
Rotherfield Greys, Henley-on-
Thames RG9 4PG. The National
Trust, 01491 628529,
greyscourt@nationaltrust.org.uk. *2m
W of Henley-on-Thames. Signed from
Nettlebed taking B481. Direct route
from Henley-on-Thames town centre
unsigned for NT): follow signs to
Badgemore Golf Club towards
Rotherfield Greys, about 3m out of
Henley.* **House & Garden Adm £5,
chd £2.50. Weds to Suns 1 April to
27 Sept (12-5), last adm 4.30pm. For
NGS: Sat 16 May (12-5).**
acres amongst which are the ruined
walls and buildings of original fortified
manor. Rose, cherry, wisteria and white
gardens; lawns; kitchen garden; ice
house; Archbishop's maze. Tudor
house (open) with C18 alterations on
te of original C13 house fortified by

Lord Grey in C14. Donkey wheel and
tower. A band plays during the
afternoon. Tours of garden on the day.
Gravel paths throughout garden.
Gentle slopes. Cobbles in places.

**30 NEW HAZELFORD
COTTAGE**
Sandfine Road, Broughton
OX15 6AP. Anna Fryer & Norman
Filleul. *³/₄ m W of Broughton
Castle. 2m SW of Banbury on the
B4035. Turn R and proceed
through N Newington. After 1m
turn L. At gated road follow NGS
signs to top of hill.* Teas at
Broughton Grounds Farm. **Adm
£2.50, chd free. Combined with
Broughton Grounds Farm.** Sun
21 June (2-5).
Very small cottage garden
surrounding a C19 shepherd's
cottage and barn (not open).
Mostly herbaceous plants, shrubs,
roses, violas and pinks.
Greenhouse and small wildlife
pond. Very pretty views.

Group opening

31 HEADINGTON GARDENS
Old Headington, Oxford OX3 9BT.
*2m E from centre of Oxford. After T-
lights, centre of Headington, towards
Oxford, 2nd turn on R into Osler Rd.
Gardens at end of rd in Old
Headington.* **Combined adm £3.50,
chd free (share to Ruskin College).**
Sun 31 May (2-5).
Attractive village of Saxon origin hidden
within the bounds of Oxford.

37 ST ANDREWS ROAD
Judith & David Marquand.
*Driveway to 37 lies between 33 &
35 St Andrew's Rd*
Two small, well planted linked
gardens against a backdrop of
neighbours' mature trees. Planted
to provide all-yr interest.

THE COACH HOUSE
The Croft, Headington. Mr & Mrs
David Rowe. *After T-lights in
centre of Headington, 2nd turn on
R towards Oxford into Osler Rd. R
again off Osler Rd*
Two linked gardens of differing
character: one laid to lawn with
formal hedges, flower beds and

small woodland area; the other a
sunny courtyard with ponds on two
levels, a gravel garden, a new
parterre and sculpture. Some
gravel paths.

40 OSLER ROAD
Oxford. Mr & Mrs N Coote,
01865 767680,
nicholas@coote100.freeserve.
co.uk. *2m E from centre of Oxford.
Off London Rd, ³/₄ m inside ring rd.
After T-lights in centre of
Headington towards Oxford, 2nd
turn on R, Osler Rd.* **Visitors also
welcome by appt.**
Richly planted town garden,
²/₃ acre, now into its fourth
decade, with majestic trees, clear
structure, abundant flowers,
whitewashed walls, shutters,
mosaic paths, cypresses and a
multitude of pots borrowing the
'panache' of Italy.

STOKE COTTAGE
Stoke Place. Steve & Jane
Cowls. *End of Osler Rd to St
Andrew's Rd to Stoke Place*
Mature trees and old stone walls
provide a framework for a linked
series of paths and flower beds
containing many contrasting
shrubs and plants which give an
atmosphere of seclusion.

Multitude of pots borrowing the 'panache' of Italy . . .

32 HEARNS HOUSE
Gallows Tree Common RG4 9DE.
John & Joan Pumfrey, 0118 972
2848. *5m N of Reading, 5m W of
Henley. From A4074 turn E at Cane
End.* Light refreshments & teas. **Adm
£3.50, chd free. Visitors welcome by
appt, unsuitable for coaches.**
2-acre garden in woodland setting

provides shady walks. Design and planting ideas for small as well as larger gardens. Good foliage, single colour planting and innovative hard landscaping abound. Black spiral garden contrasts with the new vibrant hot bed in its crinkle-crankle setting. Wide variety of hardy plants incl many new varieties, chosen and propagated for yr-round interest in the garden and nursery. National Collection of Brunnera and Omphalodes. Special events incl garden related study days and arts events. Phone for details or visit NGS website.

 ♿ ✿ **NCCPG** 🚫 ☎

33 HILL COURT
Tackley OX5 3AQ. Mr & Mrs Andrew C Peake. 9m N of Oxford. Turn off A4260 at Sturdy's Castle. Home-made teas. **Adm £2.50, chd free. Sat 6, Sun 7 June** (2-6).
Walled garden of 2 acres with yew cones at top of terrace as a design feature by Russell Page in the 1960s. Terraces incl silver, pink and blue plantings, white garden, herbaceous borders, shrubberies, orangery. Many rare and unusual plants. Entry incl History Trail with unique geometric fish ponds (1620), C17 stables, pigeon house, C18 lakes, ice house (not suitable for wheelchairs). Local crafts and plants for sale. Music. Gravel paths, steep slopes, paving.

♿ 🐕 ✿ ☎

HILLCREST
See Buckinghamshire.

HILLESDEN HOUSE
See Buckinghamshire.

34 HOLLYHOCKS
North Street, Islip, nr Kidlington OX5 2SQ. Avril Hughes. 3m NE of Kidlington. From A34 - exit Bletchingdon/Islip. B4027 direction Islip, turn L into North St. Home-made teas at Hollyhocks 14 June, Monkshead May & 8 June. **Adm £2.50, chd free. Combined adm with Monkshead, Bletchingdon £4. Suns 17 May; 14 June** (2-6). **Evening Opening Mon 8 June** (5.30-8.30).
Plantaholic's small Edwardian garden brimming with yr-round interest. Divided into areas with herbaceous borders, roses, clematis, shade and woodland planting, alpine troughs as well as lots of pots around the house.

🐾 ☕

35 HOLYWELL MANOR
Manor Road, Oxford OX1 3 UH. Balliol College Graduate Centre. 1m E of Carfax. In town centre. Corner of Manor Rd & St Cross Rd off Longwall. Light refreshments & teas. **Adm £2, chd free. Sun 17 May** (2-5).
Garden of approx 1 acre, not normally open to the public. Imaginatively laid out 50yrs ago around horse chestnut to give formal and informal areas. Mature ginkgo avenue, spinney with spring flowers and bulbs. Basketry demonstration. Gravel paths, uneven paving. Unfenced pond.

♿ 🐾 ✿ ☕

Mature ginkgo avenue, spinney with spring flowers and bulbs . . .

36 HOME CLOSE
Southend, Garsington OX44 9DH. Ms M Waud & Dr P Giangrande, 01865 361394. 3m SE of Oxford. Southend. N of B480. Opp Garsington Manor. Teas by arrangement. **Adm £3.50, chd free. Visitors welcome by appt 1 Apr to 30 Sept.**
2-acre garden with listed house (not open) and granary. Trees, shrubs and perennials planted for all-yr effect. Terraces, walls and hedges divide the garden into ten distinct areas to reflect a Mediterranean interest.

🐾 ☎

37 HOME FARM
Balscote OX15 6JP. Mr Godfrey Royle, 01295 738194. 5m W of Banbury. 1/2 m off A422. **Adm £3, chd free. Visitors welcome by appt.**
C17 house and barn (not open), 1/2 -acre plant lover's peaceful garden giving yr-round interest with unusual plants, coloured foliage, flowering shrubs, bulbs and perennials created by garden owners over 20yrs in an informal way. Two lawns give a feeling of spaciousness and a small terrace has views of surrounding countryside.

♿ 🐾 ☕ ☎

38 **NEW** HOMELAND
Middle Lane, Balscote OX15 6JP. Mrs Pat Jesson, 01295 738640, r.jesson@btinternet.com. 5m W of Banbury. From Banbury on A422 pass through Wroxton. After 1 1/2 m turn L down hill into Balscote. Middle Lane runs at rear of church. **Adm price on application. Visitors welcome by appt.**
2/3 -acre garden with herbaceous borders, rockeries, fruit and vegetable section and varied collection of trees. Positioned at rear of church - itself worth a visit. Village has a nature reserve dedicated to bird life, developed from an old quarry.

🐾 ☎

Group opening

39 IFFLEY GARDENS
Iffley Village OX4 4ET. 2m S of Oxford. Within Oxford's ring rd, off A4158 from Magdalen Bridge to Littlemore roundabout. Map provided at each garden. Home-made teas. **Combined adm £4, chd free. Sun 14 June** (2-6).
Secluded old village with renowned Norman church, featured on cover of Pevsner's Oxon guide. Short footpath from Mill Lane leads to scenic Iffley Lock and Sandford to Oxford towpath.

☕

15 ABBERBURY ROAD
Allen & Boglarka Hill
Variety of beds planted over the last 10yrs in different styles featuring many shrubs, climbers, and perennials.

🐾

65 CHURCH WAY
Mrs J Woodfill
Small English cottage garden with a few Californian plants.

🐾 ✿

NEW 86 CHURCH WAY
Helen Beinart
A long, narrow 200ft garden with views towards fields and R Thames. The garden is accessed via steep steps and slopes gently through a series of rooms. Herbaceous borders, fruit and vegetable areas. The garden is predominantly shady and has many shade loving plants.

🐾

122 CHURCH WAY
Sir John & Lady Elliott
Small secluded cottage-style garden with trees, shrubs, roses and herbaceous plants behind listed house (not open) with view of church tower.
  🚫 🐕

NEW 6 FITZHERBERT CLOSE
Tom & Eunice Martin. *Opp The Tree Hotel*
Delightful, small professionally designed Japanese-style garden featuring Japanese maples, miniature pines, evergreen shrubs and ornamental grasses set off by areas of paving, stepping stones, water feature and groundcover plants. Numbers limited to 10.
  🚫 🐕

NEW THE MALT HOUSE
Mr & Mrs R Potts
A significant large 2-acre garden on several levels falling away to water meadow, small lake and river bank. Various areas incl shrubs, roses, herbaceous border and fine specimen trees.
🐕

THE THATCHED COTTAGE
2 Mill Lane. Mr & Mrs Foreman.
Delightful 3/4 -acre garden tucked behind C17 village house (not open). Range of specimen trees and plants in terracing; water features, formal gardens and water meadow with Thames frontage.
🐕

40 KEBLE COLLEGE
Parks Road. OX1 3PG.
www.keble.ox.ac.uk/about/gardens.
Central Oxford. On Parks Rd. S of University Parks & opp University Museum. Home-made teas (3-5).
Adm £3, chd free. Sun 28 June (2-6).
Dramatic lawned quads (4½ acres) with recently completed, flowery, modern planting by Sarah Ewbank. Warden's private garden, in the style of Russell Page, is open. The College chapel, containing the 'Light of the World' painting and the college hall (Oxford's longest!) are both open to visitors. No wheelchair access to Warden's garden; one small garden pebbled but both gardens can be viewed from suitable vantage points.
🚫 🐕 ☕

2-acre garden, lovingly designed for a peaceful atmosphere . . .

KEMPSFORD MANOR
See Gloucestershire North & Central.

Group opening

41 KENCOT GARDENS
Kencot, nr Lechlade GL7 3QT. *5m NE of Lechlade. E of A361 between Burford & Lechlade.* Home-made teas.
Combined adm £3, chd free. Mon 13 Apr (2-6).
Charming Cotswold village with interesting Norman church, beautifully decorated with flowers for Easter.

THE ALLOTMENTS
Amelia Carter Trust
Six plots containing vegetables, fruit and flowers, with emphasis on organic gardening.

DE ROUGEMONT
Mr & Mrs D Portergill
1/2 -acre garden with mature trees, shrubs and container plants, soft fruits, apples, pears, spring bulbs and flowers, vegetables, beds for perennials, fuchsias, conifers and heathers, herb garden with box hedging, well, greenhouse with vines. Sloped gravel drive, help available.
🚫

IVY NOOK
Mrs G Cox
Cottage garden with rockeries, shrubs and mixed borders providing yr-round colour. Well-stocked pond with waterfall. 150yr-old apple tree.
🚫

KENCOT HOUSE
Mr & Mrs Andrew Patrick
Well-established 2-acre garden, lovingly designed for a peaceful atmosphere. Interesting trees (incl gingko) and shrubs. Quantities of various daffodils and other spring bulbs, roses: over 50 different

---

clematis. Interesting carved C13 archway adds to the attractions.
🚫

MANOR FARM
Mr & Mrs J R Fyson
2-acre garden. Naturalised daffodils, fritillaries, wood anemones in mature orchards, incl quince, medlar and mulberry; pleached lime walk, pergola with rambling gallica roses. Pair of resident geese, 2 alpacas and small flock of bantams patrol the paddock. C17 listed house, not open.
🚫 ❀

NEW WELL HOUSE
Mr & Mrs I J Morrison
Attractive garden in 1/3 acre. Lawns, mature trees and hedges. Wildlife pond with waterfall. Island beds and mixed borders providing yr round interest. Semi enclosed patio with dry stone wall, rockeries and container planting. Gravel entrance driveway.
🚫

42 ♦ KINGSTON BAGPUIZE HOUSE
Kingston Bagpuize, nr Abingdon OX13 5AX. Mrs Francis Grant, 01865 820259,
www.kingstonbagpuizehouse.org.uk.
5m W of Abingdon. In Kingston Bagpuize just off A415, 1/4 m S of A415/A420. **House and garden adm: adult £5, concessions £4.50, chd £2.50, garden only adm £3, chd free. Open many days throughout the year. Please phone or visit website for details.** For NGS: Suns 5 Apr; 6 Sept (2-5).
Notable collection of unusual trees, incl magnolias, shrubs, perennials and bulbs, incl snowdrops, providing yr-round interest and colour. Large mixed borders, interesting summer flowering trees and shrubs. Some gravel paths.
🚫 🐕 ❀ ☕

43 LADY MARGARET HALL
Norham Gardens, Oxford OX2 6QA. Principal & Fellows of Lady Margaret Hall. *1m N of Carfax. From Banbury Rd, R at T-lights into Norham Gdns.* Home-made teas. **Adm £2.50, chd free. Sun 13 Sept (2-5.30).**
Lots of late flowering perennials, grasses and dahlias. Many fine trees and a river walk. 10 acres in all.
🐕 ❀ ☕ 🍽

44 LIME CLOSE
**35 Henleys Lane, Drayton,
Abingdon OX14 4HU. M C de
Laubarede,
mail@mclgardendesign.com.** *2m
S of Abingdon. Henleys Lane is off
main rd through Drayton.* Cream teas.
**Adm £3.50, chd free (share to
CLIC Sargent). Suns 1 Mar; 7 June
(2-5.30). Visitors also welcome by
appt.**
Plantsman's 3-acre mature garden with
rare trees, shrubs, perennials and
bulbs. Mixed borders, raised beds,
pergola, unusual topiary and shade
borders. Herb garden designed by
Rosemary Verey. Listed C16 house
(not open). New cottage garden
designed by owner, a professional
garden designer, focusing on colour
combinations and an iris garden with
over 100 varieties of tall bearded irises.
Many winter bulbs, hellebores and
shrubs.

Terrace with rose and vine covered pergola around lily pond . . .

45 LINGERMANS
**Burford Road, Brize Norton
OX18 3NZ. Mrs E Dobson.** *3m SW of
Witney; 3m SE of Burford. Turn off A40
1m W of roundabout at end of Witney
bypass, signed Brize Norton.
Lingermans ¾ m on L. From Brize
Norton take Burford Road 1½ m on R.*
Teas. **Adm £3, chd free. Sun 29 Mar
(2-5).**
Masses of spring bulbs - snowdrops,
aconites, different daffodils, narcissi,
hellebores, flowering spring shrubs,
trees. All in 1 acre with lawns, mature
trees, herbaceous borders, sunken
dry gravel with pergola, scented
border, wildlife areas with frog pond,
secret garden, vegetable and fruit
areas.

46 ◆ MAGDALEN COLLEGE
**Oxford OX1 4AU. 01865 276000,
www.magd.ox.ac.uk.** *Entrance in
High St.* **Adm £4, chd £3,
concessions £3. Open daily (1-6 or
dusk if earlier), 12 noon July to Sept.
For NGS: Sun 5 Apr (1-6).**

60 acres incl deer park, college lawns,
numerous trees 150-200yrs old,
notable herbaceous and shrub
plantings; Magdalen meadow, where
purple and white snake's-head
fritillaries can be found, is surrounded
by Addison's Walk, a tree-lined circuit
by the R Cherwell developed since the
late C18. Ancient herd of 60 deer. Steel
sculpture commissioned to celebrate
550th anniversary by Turner prize-
winning artist Mark Wallinger. Called Y
and 10m high in the form of a tree, it is
situated in Bat Willow Meadow.
Contact Porters' Lodge on arrival for
access.

47 MANOR FARM
**Minster Lovell OX29 0RR. Lady
Parker, 01993 775728.** *1½ m W of
Witney. Off B4047 rd between
Witney/Burford. Follow sign opp White
Hart down to R Windrush, 100yds over
bridge turn R at Old Swan & up village
street. Manor Farm is last house on R
before continuing to Crawley. Parking:
enter at end of 1st field towards
Crawley if approaching from village.
Drive back across field to enter close
to garden. No parking in village.* Home-
made teas. **Adm £3.50, chd free. Sun
14 June (2-5).**
6-acre garden of C15 farmhouse (not
open) with open access to adjoining
Minster Lovell Hall ruins. Old shrub and
climbing roses, fish ponds, herbaceous
and lawns. Old barns within garden
area. Grasses area.

48 NEW MANOR HOUSE
**Manor Farm Road, Dorchester-
on-Thames OX10 7HZ. Mr & Mrs
S Broadbent.** *8m SSE of Oxford.
Off A4074, signs from village
centre. Parking on recreation
ground (500yds). Disabled parking
at house.* Home-made teas at
Abbey tea room (open 2.30-5).
**Adm £3, chd free. Sat, Sun 13,
14 June (2-5).**
2-acre traditional garden in
beautiful setting around Georgian
house (not open) and medieval
abbey. Spacious lawn leading to
riverside copse of towering black
poplars from which there are fine
views of Dorchester Abbey. Terrace
with rose and vine covered pergola
around lily pond. Colouful
herbaceous borders, small orchard
and vegetable garden. Gravel
paths, some kerbs.

**THE MANOR HOUSE,
HAMBLEDEN
See Buckinghamshire.**

49 ◆ MERTON COLLEGE
**OXFORD FELLOWS' GARDEN
Merton Street, Oxford OX1 4JD,
07923 652029,
garden@admin.merton.ox.ac.uk.**
*Merton Street runs parallel to High
Street.* **Adm £3, chd free. For NGS:
Sat 25 July (2-5).**
Ancient mulberry, said to have
associations with James I. Specimen
trees, long mixed border, recently-
established herbaceous bed. View of
Christ Church meadow.

Group opening

50 MIDDLETON CHENEY GARDENS
OX17 2NP. *3m E of Banbury. From
M40 J11 follow A422, signed
Middleton Cheney. Map available at all
gardens.* Home-made teas at Peartree
House. **Combined adm £5, chd free.
Sun 21 June (1-6).**
Large village with a diversity of
gardens. Also open, late C13 church
with Pre-Raphaelite stained glass and
William Morris ceiling.

**CHURCH COTTAGE
12 Church Lane. David & Sue
Thompson**
Entry to private back garden
through rear garden of 8 Church
Lane. Typical English cottage
garden-style with 'Mediterranean'
influences. Public front garden by
church path, yellow and white
themed borders.

**8 CHURCH LANE
Mr & Mrs Style**
Cottage garden in the process
of being renovated since 2005.
Mixed borders, vegetable and
fruit area, pergola and small
pond.

**15 CHURCH LANE
Dr Jill Meara**
A series of open spaces incl
cottage garden, vegetable patch,
orchard area and field ending in a
stream.

5 LONGBURGES
Mr & Mrs D Vale
Small SW-facing garden on three levels with patios, ponds, lawn and planting. Collection of acers predominate with herbaceous, mixed and spring borders. Small container-grown fruit and herb patio.

38 MIDWAY
Margaret & David Finch
Small front garden. Back garden with mixed borders and shrubs. Water feature with pond and waterfall and other interesting features. A plant lover's garden.

PEARTREE HOUSE
Roger & Barbara Charlesworth
A garden of varying styles and hidden corners with an emphasis on the ever-changing sound and sight of water.

2 QUEEN STREET
Lynn Baldwin
Be prepared for close encounters with plants in this small but very intensively planted garden.

14 QUEEN STREET
Brian & Kathy Goodey
Mature cottage garden that has evolved through family use. 'Rooms' in a rectangle where there is always room for an extra plant. Children's animal trail quiz.

NEW 35 STANWELL LEA
Jo & Bernie Jennings
A place to relax and reflect. A small enclosed garden. Home to two Labradors.

27 STANWELL LEA
Frank & Jane Duty
Cottage garden with surprises. Water feature and penstemon collection.

51 MONKS HEAD
Weston Road, Bletchingdon OX5 3DH. Sue Bedwell, 01869 350155. *Approx 4m N of Kidlington. From A34 take B4027 to Bletchingdon, turn R at Xrds into Weston Rd.* Home-made teas. **Adm £2.50, chd free. Combined with Hollyhocks, Islip £4. Suns 17 May; 14 June (2-6). Evening Opening Mon 8 June (5.30-8.30).** Visitors also welcome by appt all yr. £2 groups 10+; £3 groups of under 10.
Plantaholics' garden for all-yr interest. Bulb frame and alpine area, greenhouse.

52 OLD CHURCH HOUSE
Priory Road, Wantage OX12 9DD. Dr & Mrs Dick Squires, 01235 762785. *Situated next to Parish Church nr Wantage market square.* Light refreshments & teas at Vale & Downland Centre, Church Street. **Adm £2, chd free. Daily Apr to Oct (10.30-4.30).** Visitors also welcome by appt.
Unusual town garden running down to the Letcombe Brook. Much interest with different levels, follies, water, mature trees and many special plants.

53 THE OLD RECTORY, COLESHILL
SN6 7PR. Sir George & Lady Martin. *3m SW of Faringdon. Coleshill (NT village) is on B4019.* Home-made teas. **Adm £2, chd free. Suns 5 Apr; 6 Sept (2-5).**
Medium-sized garden; lawns and informal shrub beds; wide variety shrubs, incl old-fashioned roses, 50yr-old standard wisteria. Distant views of Berkshire and Wiltshire Downs. House (not open) dates from late C14.

THE OLD RECTORY FARNBOROUGH
See Berkshire.

54 NEW THE OLD VICARAGE
Aston Rowant, Watlington OX49 5ST. Julian & Rona Knight, 01844 351315, jknight652@aol.com. *Between Chinnor and Watlington. From M40 J6, take B4009 towards Chinnor and Princes Risborough. After 1m L signed 'Aston Rowant village only'.* Home-made teas 14 Jun only on village green. **Adm £3, chd free. Sun 14, Wed 17 June.** Visitors also welcome by appt, groups of 10+.
Romantic, 1¾-acre vicarage garden lovingly rejuvenated and enjoyed by the present family. Centered around a croquet lawn surrounded by beds brimming with shrubs and herbaceous plants, hot bed and roses. Lushly planted pond leading through a pergola overflowing with roses and clematis to a tranquil green garden. Small vegetable and cutting garden. Village fete Sun 14 June. Grass paths.

55 THE OLD VICARAGE, BLEDINGTON
Main Street, Bledington, Chipping Norton OX7 6UX. Sue & Tony Windsor, 01608 658525, tony.windsor@tiscali.co.uk. *6m SW of Chipping Norton. 4m SE of Stow-on-the-Wold. On the main st, B4450, through Bledington. NOT next to church.* Visitors welcome by appt.
1½-acre garden attached to late Georgian (1843) vicarage (not open). Rose garden with over 350 David Austin roses, borders of hardy perennials, small pond and paddock with shrubs and beds. Garden is on gentle slope but quite hard work.

56 RADCOT HOUSE
Radcot OX18 2SX. Robin & Jeanne Stainer, 01367 810231, rstainer@radcothouse.co.uk. *1¼ m S of Clanfield. On A4095 between Witney & Faringdon, 200yds N of Radcot bridge.* Teas. **Adm £4, chd free. Suns 30 Aug; 20 Sept (2-6).** Visitors also welcome by appt.
Started in 2000, with many recent developments. Dramatic planting nearer the house, shady areas, formal pond, wood, fruit and vegetable cages. Convenient seating at key points enables relaxed observation

Vicarage garden lovingly rejuvenated and enjoyed by the present family . . .

and reflection. Extensive use of grasses and unusual perennials. Featured on Radio Oxford.

57 RAMSDEN HOUSE
Akeman Street, Ramsden OX7 3AX. **Laura Sednaoni.** *Off B4022 midway Charlbury/Witney. Middle of Ramsden, adjacent to church. Parking at house, please do not park in village.* Home-made teas. **Adm £3, chd free (share to KULINKA). Sun 15 Feb (2-5).** Waves of snowdrops through 2-acre Victorian garden, originally planted 1862. Many mature trees and shrubs. Present owner now restoring Victorian wild garden. Too boggy for wheelchairs if wet.

58 ST HUGH'S COLLEGE
St Margaret's Road, Oxford OX2 6LE, 01865 274900, john.brooke@st-hughes.ox.ac.uk. *1m N of city centre. Entry to the garden via Canterbury Road between Banbury rd and Woodstock rd.* Home-made teas. **Adm £2.50, chd free. Sun 12 Apr (2.30-5.30). Visitors also welcome by appt.** Springtime garden, well planted with a variety of flowering bulbs, fine trees, shrub borders and herbaceous plantings in a 14-acre site with plenty of interest throughout the yr in a relaxed and informal setting. A peaceful oasis between 2 busy roads.

Group opening

59 NEW SALFORD GARDENS
OX7 5YN. *2m W of Chipping Norton. Off A44 Oxford-Worcester Rd.* Teas in village hall. **Combined adm £4, chd free. Sun 17 May (2-5).** Small Cotswold village with attractive church.

NEW JUNIPERS
Lower End. Mr M Edmunds
Small family garden, cottage-style herbaceous borders and shrubs.

MANOR FARM
Mrs P G Caldin
Small mature well-stocked garden.

OLD RECTORY
Mr & Mrs N M Chambers, 01608 643969. **Visitors also welcome by appt.**
1½ acres mainly enclosed by walls. Yr-round interest, with some unusual plants in mixed borders, many old roses, small orchard and vegetable garden.

NEW STONE CROSS
Lower End. John Grantham
Village garden. Rose pergolas, mixed perennials in borders and beds, small vegetable patch. Partial wheelchair access, gravel drive.

WILLOW TREE COTTAGE
Chapel Lane. Mr & Mrs J Shapley, 01608 642478, john.shapley@virgin.net. **Visitors also welcome by appt April to Aug incl.**
Small walled twin gardens with shrub and herbaceous borders, many clematis; one garden created from old farmyard with large alpine garden. Small grass beds. Plantsman's garden with many interesting plants.

Group opening

60 SIBFORD GOWER GARDENS
OX15 5RX. *7m W of Banbury. Nr the Warwickshire border, S of B4035, in centre of village nr Wykham Arms PH.* Home-made teas at Temple Mill (garden not open for NGS). **Combined adm £3, chd under 12s free. Sun 14 June (2-6).** Small village with charming thatched houses and cottage gardens. Four very different gardens, all packed full of interest. Village pond has a flock of Indian Runner ducks who love to be visited.

BUTTSLADE HOUSE
Temple Mill Road (also known as Colony Road). Mrs Diana Thompson
Intriguingly designed garden with many rooms. Areas of formal and informal planting. ⅓-acre packed with plants. Roses a speciality.

CARTER'S YARD
Sue & Malcolm Bannister. *Use entrance up steps next to Wykham Arms*
Newly designed cottage garden, small vegetable area with espaliered apples and pears, exciting new planting round house.

GOWERS CLOSE
Judith Hitching & John Marshall
Garden writer's cottage garden, tucked behind a wisteria clad thatched house (not open). Box parterre, herb garden, clipped yew hedges, rose smothered pergola and bosky borders in purples and pinks, small kitchen garden.

THE MANOR HOUSE
Temple Mill Road. Michael Donovan & Alison Jenkins
Combination of well established garden and charming extensive patio area provides romantic setting for rambling thatched Manor House (not open).

61 SOMERVILLE COLLEGE
Woodstock Road, Oxford OX2 6HD. *½ m E of Carfax Tower. Enter from the Woodstock Rd, S of the Radcliffe Infirmary.* **Adm £2.50, chd free (share to Friends of Oxford Botanic Garden). Sun 12 July (2-6).** Approx 2 acres, robust college garden planted for yr-round interest. Formal bedding, colour-themed and vibrant old-fashioned mixed herbaceous borders.

Rose
smothered
pergola and
bosky borders
in purples and
pinks . . .

62 SOUTH NEWINGTON HOUSE
Barford Road, South Newington
OX15 4JW. Mr & Mrs John Ainley,
01295 721207,
rojoainley@btinternet.com. *6m SW
of Banbury. South Newington is
between Banbury and Chipping
Norton, on A361; take lane signed The
Barfords, 200yds on L.* **Adm £3, chd
free. Visitors welcome by appt all yr.
Coaches welcome. No group too
small.**
This enchanting 3-acre garden
changes seamlessly through every
season. Spring heralds hellebores and
carpets of spring bulbs. Rambler roses
and wisteria adorn the walls of the
house and parterre. Mixed borders of
great depth and colour inspire and thrill
the visitor. The organic kitchen garden
and orchard supply the house.

✖ ⚞ ☎

63 SPARSHOLT MANOR
nr Wantage OX12 9PT. Sir Adrian &
Lady Judith Swire. *3¹/₂ m W of
Wantage. Off B4507 Ashbury Rd.* Teas
in village hall. **Adm £2, chd free.** Mon
25 May (2-6).
Lakes and wildfowl; ancient boxwood,
wilderness and summer borders.
Wheelchair access to part of garden.

&. ✿ ☕

64 NEW SPRINGHILL HOUSE
Main Street, Hethe OX27 8ES.
Mrs Penny Jacoby, 01869
277971. *4m N of Bicester. L off
A4421 N from Bicester. Follow
signs to Hethe.* Home-made teas.
Adm £3, chd free. Suns 28 June;
30 Aug (2-5.30). **Visitors also
welcome by appt May to Sept.**
A secret 1³/₄ -acre garden
cascading down a slope to a
delightfully planted extensive pond.
The walled garden area is heavily
planted with many varieties of
plants. There are over 200 roses, a
Mediterranean garden incl many
tender and exotic plants (no
wheelchair access), a vegetable
garden and small arboretum. True
plantswoman's garden. Limited
wheelchair access.

&. ✿ ☕ ☎

65 STANSFIELD
49 High Street, Stanford-in-the-Vale
SN7 8NQ. Mr & Mrs David Keeble,
01367 710340. *3¹/₂ m SE of
Faringdon. Park in street.* Home-made
teas. **Adm £3, chd free.**

Tues 7 Apr; 5 May; 2 June; 7 July; 4
Aug; 1 Sept (10-5). **Visitors also
welcome by appt, please telephone
first.**
1¹/₄ -acre plantsman's garden on
alkaline soil. Wide variety of unusual
trees, shrubs and hardy plants. New
labelling system almost completed.
Scree, damp garden, copse
underplanted with woodlanders. Flower
arrangers' and drought resistant plants.
Guided tours if wished.

✖ ✿ ☕ ☎

Group opening

66 STEEPLE ASTON GARDENS
OX25 4SP. *14m N of Oxford, 9m S of
Banbury. ¹/₂ m E of A4260.* Home-
made teas in village hall. **Combined
adm £4.50, chd free.** Sun 17 May
(1-6).
Beautiful stone village bordering
Cherwell valley; interesting church and
winding lanes with a variety of
charming stone houses and cottages.
Map available at all gardens.

✿ ☕

ACACIA COTTAGE
Jane & David Stewart. *Southside
- limited parking possible*
Approx ¹/₂ -acre garden within high
stone walls. Herbaceous border,
decked and paved area around
Edwardian summerhouse and old
stone barns. Box edged parterre
with white planting in a courtyard
setting.

&.

KRALINGEN
Fenway. Mr & Mrs Roderick
Nicholson. *Possible to park on
Fenway, with care. Large car park
at Steeple Aston Village Hall*
2-acre informal garden created
over many yrs by present owners.
Many varieties of interesting trees
and shrubs and mixed borders
lead down to the tranquil
woodland/water/bog garden, with
candelabra primulas, bluebells,
golden saxifrage, fernery etc. Slope
is hard work for wheelchairs.

&.

THE LONGBYRE
Mr Vaughan Billings. *Park at
village hall*
Hornton stone house (not open) in
¹/₄ acre. Garden constructed in old
orchard. Water feature, mixed
perennials, shrubs, tubs on
different levels.

&.

PRIMROSE COTTAGE
North Side. Richard & Daphne
Preston, 01869 340512,
richard.preston5@btopenworld.
com. *Parking in North Side is
limited, park at village hall.* **Visitors
also welcome by appt May to
July. Groups of 10+. Light
refreshments on request.**
Former walled kitchen garden of
approx 1 acre on southerly
elevation. Shrubs, herbaceous
borders, ponds, glasshouses and
large vegetable plot. Many features
designed and constructed by the
owners. Garden offering interest
throughout the yr.

☎

TOUCHWOOD
No 2 Nizewell Head. Gary Norris.
Heyford Road
Small cottage garden with ponds
on 2 levels. Truly astonishing array
of plants and colour crammed into
this small space, with view to lovely
countryside beyond.

NEW WILLOW COTTAGE
The Dickerage off Heyford Rd.
Mrs Joy Vivian. *Opp White Horse
PH*
Closely planted ¹/₂ -acre garden
evolved over 25yrs with many
mature specimen trees presenting
a canopy of interwoven foliage,
colour and texture. Several
discretely interlinked garden rooms,
a fish pond with large koi and
many pots.

Many mature
specimen
trees presenting
a canopy of
interwoven
foliage,
colour and
texture . . .

67 SWALCLIFFE LEA HOUSE
Swalcliffe Lea OX15 6ET. Jeffrey &
Christine Demmar, 01295 788278.
*6m W of Banbury. Off the B4035. At
Lower Tadmarton, turn (as posted) to
Swalcliffe Lea & Shutford.Turn L, single
track road. Bear R at fork, 250 yds to
entrance, take 1st drive on L.* **Adm
£2.50, chd free. Visitors welcome by
appt.**
Mature terraced garden with densely
planted mixed borders; pergola, herb
garden, vegetable garden and orchard.
Two informal ponds. Stream and small
woodland. Range of specimen trees,
many varieties of clematis and other
herbaceous plants. Some slopes and
uneven steps. 2 unfenced ponds.

68 TADMARTON MANOR
Upper Tadmarton OX15 5TD. Mr &
Mrs R K Asser, 01295 780212. *5m
SW of Banbury. On B4035.* **Adm £3,
chd free. Visitors welcome by appt.**
Old-established 2½ -acre garden;
beautiful views of unspoilt countryside;
great variety of perennial plants and
shrubs; tunnel arbour; C15 barn and
C18 dovecote. Agapanthus bed (Aug);
bank of autumn cyclamen; stilted
hornbeam hedge. Wildlife pond. Tree
sculptures.

Group opening

69 THAME GARDENS
Thame. 0X9 3LS. *½ m E of Thame
centre. From M40 J7/8 follow signs to
Thame.* **Home-made teas at Pots 'n'
Rocks. Combined adm £3.50, chd
free (share to Children with
Leukaemia). Sun 14 June (2-6).**
Three very different town gardens
within the boundary of a delightful old
market town of east Oxfordshire. Map
available at each garden.

NEW 143 CHINNOR ROAD
Mrs D Metcalf. *On B4445
Chinnor Rd, close to dog-leg over
bridge on outskirts of Thame*
A heavily planted natural garden
with mature shrubs, perennials
and a well-stocked pond, divided
into rooms with restful seating
areas. Well designed around a
large walnut tree.

12 PARK TERRACE
Maggie & Colin Sear. *From centre
of Thame follow signes for Chinnor
(B4445). At junction with*

*Postcombe Road (B4012), Park
Terrace is on R, opp Shell garage.
Coming from centre of Thame,
park on Station Approach, L off
B4012, signed Postcombe.*
Small quiet oasis at end of cul-de-
sac. Husband's fine gravel and
grass garden at front. Back garden
designed and created by keen
plantswoman. Shrubs and plants
chosen for foliage and long
flowering period to provide interest
and variety throughout the year.
Attractive water feature.

POTS 'N' ROCKS
18 Willow Road. Mrs K M Pease.
*Park in public car park opp
entrance to Waitrose. Up Lashlake
rd, opp Waitrose. Willow Rd 2nd
on R.*
Quirky and unique small garden
with an amazing range of plants in
pots and hanging baskets - tender
tropical to bonsai. For children and
keen observers there are
numerous hidden animals and
features to be found and counted
as well as a small 9 hole putting
green. Very child friendly.

70 TRINITY COLLEGE
Oxford OX1 3BH. Dr C R Prior,
Garden Master. *Central Oxford.
Entrance in Broad St.* **Cream teas Mar.
Home-made teas July. Adm £2, chd
free. Suns 22 Mar; 26 July (2-5).**
Historic main College Gardens with
specimen trees incl aged forked
catalpa, spring bulbs, fine long
herbaceous border and handsome
garden quad originally designed by
Wren. President's Garden surrounded
by high old stone walls, mixed borders
of herbaceous, shrubs and statuary.
Fellows' Garden: small walled terrace,
herbaceous borders; water feature
formed by Jacobean stone heraldic
beasts. Award-winning lavender
garden and walk-through rose
arbour.

TURWESTON MILL
See Northamptonshire.

TURWESTON HOUSE
See Northamptonshire.

TYTHROP PARK
See Buckinghamshire.

More species of plants per acre than anywhere else on earth . . .

**71 ◆ UNIVERSITY OF OXFORD
BOTANIC GARDEN**
Rose Lane, Oxford OX1 4AZ.
University of Oxford, 01865 286690,
www.botanic-garden.ox.ac.uk. *1m S
of Oxford city centre. Bottom of High
Street in central Oxford, on the banks
of the R Cherwell by Magdalen Bridge
& opp Magdalen College Tower.*
**Adm £3, chd free, conc £2.50. See
website for other opening times. For
NGS: Evening opening Thur 2 July
(6-8).**
The Botanic Garden contains more
species of plants per acre than
anywhere else on earth. These plants
are grown in 7 glasshouses, water and
rock gardens, large herbaceous
border, walled garden and every
available space. In total there are over
6,000 different plants to see. National
Collection of Euphorbia. Gravel paths.
NCCPG

72 UPPER CHALFORD FARM
between Sydenham & Postcombe
OX39 4NH. Mr & Mrs Paul Rooksby,
01844 351320. *4½ m SE of Thame.
M40 J6, then A40. At Postcombe turn
R signed Chalford (turn L if on A40
from Oxford direction). After 1 mile on
LH-side at 1st telegraph pole. (House
is half way between Sydenham and
Postcombe).* **Home-made teas. Adm
£3, chd free. Suns 21 June; 12 July
(2-5.30). Visitors also welcome by
appt groups of 10+.**
Jacobean farmhouse garden brimming
with old roses, shrubs and perennials.
Huge black pine and unusual trees.
Sundial garden and conservatory with
vine and plumbagos. Spring garden
with early snowdrops and narcissi
followed by cherry blossom all
overlooking a natural pond cascading
into a shady stream lined with damp-
loving plants. Native woodland area,
paddock, donkeys and bantams.
Location for 'Midsomer Murders'.

VERSIONS FARM
See Northamptonshire.

73 WADHAM COLLEGE

Oxford OX1 3PN. **The Warden & Fellows.** *Central Oxford. Parks Road.* **Adm £3, chd free** (share to Sobell House Hospice). **Sun 22 Mar (2-5); Sun 12 July (2-6).**
5 acres, best known for trees, spring bulbs and mixed borders. In Fellows' main garden, fine ginkgo and *Magnolia acuminata*; bamboo plantation; in Back Quadrangle very large *Tilia tomentosa* 'Petiolaris'; in Mallam Court white scented garden est 1994; in Warden's garden an ancient tulip tree; in Fellows' private garden, Civil War embankment with period fruit tree cultivars, recently established shrubbery with unusual trees and ground cover amongst older plantings.

Spectacular views overlooking Burford and Windrush valley . . .

74 ◆ WATERPERRY GARDENS

Waterperry, Wheatley OX33 1JZ. **Mrs P Maxwell, Secretary, 01844 339226, www.waterperrygardens.co.uk.** *9m E of Oxford. M40 J8 from London (turn off Oxford-Wheatley, first L to Wheatley, follow brown rose symbol). J8a from Birmingham (turn R Oxford-Wheatley over A40, first R Wheatley, follow brown rose symbol. We are 2½ m N of Wheatley.* **Adm £5.45 (£3.50 Feb), chd £3.65 (£3.30 Feb), concessions £4.35 (£3.50 Feb). Open yr-round 10-5. Closed between Christmas & New Yr. For NGS: Sat 14 Feb (10-5); Sun 20 Sept (10-5.30).**
The gardens at Waterperry are quite simply an inspiration. 8 acres of landscaped gardens include a rose and formal knot garden, water lily canal, riverside walk and one of the finest purely herbaceous borders in the country. Quality plant centre, teashop, art gallery, museum and Saxon church. National Collection of Kabschia Saxifrages. Featured in 'The English Garden' and on Gardeners' World. Riverside walk may be difficult when wet.

75 WAYSIDE

82 Banbury Road, Kidlington OX5 2BX. **Margaret & Alistair Urquhart, 01865 460180, alistairurquhart@ntlworld.com.** *5m N of Oxford. On the RH-side of A4260 travelling N through Kidlington.* **Adm £2.50, chd free. Sun 17 May (1-6). Visitors also welcome by appt May to July only.**
¼ -acre garden with wide variety of plants and mature trees; mixed borders with hardy geraniums, clematis and bulbs. Conservatory, greenhouse and fern house with tender plants. Woodland garden with unusual species of tree ferns and extensive collection of hardy ferns; drought resistant planting in gravel garden.

76 WESTWELL MANOR

nr Burford OX18 4JT. **Mr & Mrs T H Gibson.** *2m SW of Burford. From A40 Burford-Cheltenham, turn L ½ m after Burford roundabout on narrow rd signed Westwell. Unspoilt hamlet with delightful church.* **Adm £5, chd free** (share to St Mary's Church, Westwell). **Sun 31 May (2.30-6).**
6 acres surrounding old Cotswold manor house (not open), knot garden, potager, shrub roses, herbaceous borders, topiary, earth works, moonlight garden, rills and water garden. Some unprotected water. Some surfaces slippery in wet weather, stone and wood.

Group opening

77 WHEATLEY GARDENS

Wheatley OX33 1XX. *5m E of Oxford. Leave A40 at Wheatley, turn into High St. Gardens at W end of High St.* Cream teas. **Combined adm £4, chd free. Sun 14 June (2-6).**
Three adjoining gardens in the historic coaching village of Wheatley. Access from the High St, the original Oxford to London Rd, before it climbs onto the Shotover plain.

BREACH HOUSE GARDEN

Liz Parry. *Entrance via The Manor House*
1-acre garden with coppiced hazel wood. Main established area with extensive shrubs and perennials, also a more contemporary reflective space with a wild pond.

THE MANOR HOUSE

High Street. **Mr & Mrs Edward Hess, 01865 875022.** Visitors also welcome by appt.
1½ -acre garden of Elizabethan manor house (not open). Formal box walk; herb garden, cottage garden with rose arches and a shrubbery with old roses. A romantic oasis in this busy village. 2 shallow steps, Gravel entrance.

THE STUDIO

S & A Buckingham, 01865 876526. *Access via The Manor House.* **Visitors also welcome by appt.**
Cottage-style walled garden developed from previous farm yard. Herbaceous borders, climbing roses and clematis, shrubs, vegetable plot and fruit trees.

WHICHFORD & ASCOTT GARDENS

See Warwickshire & part of West Midlands.

78 WHITEHILL FARM

Widford nr Burford OX18 4DT. **Mr & Mrs Paul Youngson, 01993 823218, a.youngson@virgin.net.** *1m E of Burford. From A40 take turn signed Widford. Follow signs to Whitehill Farm Nursery.* Teas. **Adm £3, chd free. Sun 28 June (2-6). Visitors also welcome by appt.**
2 acres of hillside gardens and woodland with spectacular views overlooking Burford and Windrush valley. Informal plantsman's garden being continuously developed in various areas. Herbaceous and shrub borders, ponds and bog area, old-fashioned roses, ground cover, ornamental grasses, bamboos and hardy geraniums.

79 WICK HALL & NURSERIES

Audlett Drive, Radley OX14 3NF. **Mr & Mrs P Drysdale.** *2m NE of Abingdon. Between Abingdon & Radley.* Home-made teas. **Adm £2.50, chd 50p. Sun 26 Apr (2-5).**
Approx 10 acres lawns and wild garden; topiary; pond garden; rockeries; walled garden enclosing knot garden; young arboretum. Early C18 house (not open), barn and greenhouses, large display of old horticultural and agricultural tools.

80 WILDWOOD

Farnborough OX17 1EL. Mr & Mrs M Hart. *5m N of Banbury, 8m S of Southam. On A423 at Oxon/Warwicks border. Next to Farnborough Garden Centre. Home-made teas.* **Adm £2.50, chd free. Sun 26 Apr (2-6).**
Delightful ¹/₂ -acre garden in the country set amongst mature trees and shrubs providing a haven for wildlife. Garden is stocked with many unusual plants and shrubs and also contains interesting rustic garden features, many of which are made by the owner. Willow weaving demonstration and items for sale.

WOOLLEY PARK
See Berkshire.

Delightful garden in the country set amongst mature trees and shrubs providing a haven for wildlife . . .

81 WOOLSTONE MILL HOUSE

Woolstone, nr Faringdon SN7 7QL. Mr & Mrs Anthony Spink, 01367 820219, spinkos@btinternet.com. *7m W of Wantage. 7m S of Faringdon. Woolstone is a small village off B4507 below Uffington White Horse Hill. Home-made teas.* **Adm £4, chd free. Weds, 1 Apr to 30 Sept (2-5); Sun 5 July (2-6). Visitors also welcome by appt.**
1¹/₂ -acre garden in pretty hidden village. Stream runs through garden. Large mixed herbaceous and shrub circular border bounded by yew hedges. Small gravel, cutting, kitchen and bog gardens. Topiary. Medlars and old-fashioned roses. Tree house with spectacular views to Uffington White Horse and White Horse Hill. C18 mill house and barn, not open.

Oxfordshire County Volunteers

County Organiser
John Ainley, South Newington House, South Newington, Nr Banbury, OX15 4JW, 01295 721207, rojoainley@btinternet.com

County Treasurer
David White, Placketts, High Street, Adderbury, Banbury OX17 3LS, 01295 812679, david.white@doctors.org.uk

Publicity & North West Oxon
Priscilla Frost, 27 Ditchley Road, Charlbury, Chipping Norton OX7 3QS, 01608 810578, info@oxconf.co.uk

Leaflet Coordinator
Catherine Pinney, Pond House, Pyrton, Watlington OX49 5AP, 01491 612638

Assistant County Organisers
North   Roberta Ainley, South Newington House, South Newington, Nr Banbury OX15 4JW, 01295 721207, rojoainley@btinternet.com
North   Lynn Baldwin, 2 Queen Street, Middleton Cheney, Banbury OX17 2NP, 01295 711205, baldwinlynn@aol.com
West   Graham & Rosemary Lenton, The Old School, 25A Standlake Road, Ducklington, Witney OX29 7UR, 01993 899033, grahamlenton@btopenworld.com
South   Diana Gordon, Oaklea House, 41a Netherton Road, Appleton, Abingdon OX13 5JZ, 01865 865450
East   Charles & Lyn Sanders, Uplands, Old Boars Hill, Oxford OX1 5JF, 01865 739486, sandersc4@hotmail.com
South West   Marina Hamilton-Baillie, Rectory House, Church Green, Stanford in the Vale SN7 8HU, 01367 710486, marina_hamilton_baillie@hotmail.com

Mark your diary with these special events in 2009

EXPLORE SECRET GARDENS DURING CHELSEA & HAMPTON COURT FLOWER SHOW WEEKS

Tue 19 May, Wed 20 May, Thur 21 May, Fri 22 May, Wed 8 July, Thur 9 July
Full day tours from £82 per person, 10% discount for groups
Advance booking required, telephone +44 (0)20 8693 1015 or email j.wookey@btinternet.com
Specially selected gardens in London, Essex, Kent, Hampshire and South Oxfordshire. The tour price includes transport and lunch with wine at a popular restaurant or pub.

HAMPTON COURT PALACE

Thur 2 Apr, Tue 23 June, Thur 25 June, Wed 15 July, Tue 4 Aug, Thur 10 Sept
Evening tours in the company of one of the Palace's specialist tour guides from 6.30 – 8pm
Tickets £6 per person. Advance booking required, telephone +44 (0)1483 211535 or
visit www.ngs.org.uk for more information
Gossip, scandal, murder, healing – you'll find it all within the Formal Gardens at Hampton Court Palace. Each tour will have its own unique feature whether it's the story of the Great Vine or the magic and mystery of the Maze.

FROGMORE – A ROYAL GARDEN (BERKSHIRE)

Tue 26 May 10am – 5.30pm (last admission 4pm)
Garden adm £4.50, chd free. Tickets available in advance or on the day.
Advance booking for groups and coaches, telephone
+44 (0) 1483 211535 or email orders@ngs.org.uk
A rare opportunity to explore 30 acres of landscaped garden, rich in history and beauty.

FLAXBOURNE FARM – FUN & SURPRISES (BEDFORDSHIRE)

Sun 7 June 10am – 5pm. Adm £5, chd free
No booking required, come along on the day!
Bring the whole family and have fun in this surprising and entertaining garden of 2 acres. Enjoy the large plant fair, live music, pets corner, birds of prey, dog agility show and much more.

WISLEY RHS GARDEN – MUSIC IN THE GARDEN (SURREY)

Fri 11 Sept 6 – 9pm
Adm (incl RHS members) £7, chd under 15 free
Save money on advance bookings for groups of 4 or more, telephone +44 (0)1483 211535 or
visit www.ngs.org.uk for more information
A special evening opening of this famous garden, exclusively for the NGS. Enjoy music and entertainment as you explore the gardens and the floral marquee on the first day of the Wisley Flower Show.

For further information visit www.ngs.org.uk or telephone 01483 211535

SHROPSHIRE

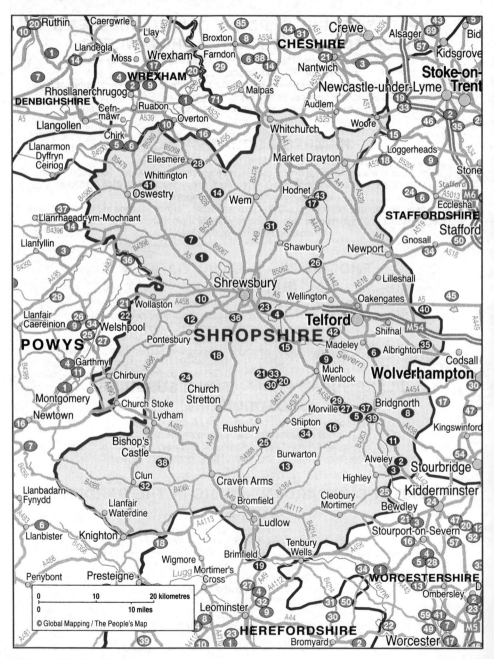

Opening Dates

April

SUNDAY 5
30 Preen Manor

TUESDAY 14
32 Radnor Cottage

TUESDAY 21
7 Brownhill House

SUNDAY 26
31 Preston Hall

May

FRIDAY 1
43 Wollerton Old Hall

SUNDAY 3
14 Gate Cottage
35 Swallow Hayes

MONDAY 4
25 Millichope Park

TUESDAY 5
7 Brownhill House

SUNDAY 10
28 Oteley
42 Windy Ridge

TUESDAY 12
32 Radnor Cottage

SUNDAY 17
1 Adcote School

TUESDAY 19
7 Brownhill House

FRIDAY 22
43 Wollerton Old Hall

SUNDAY 24
6 Brockton Court
14 Gate Cottage
38 Walcot Hall

MONDAY 25
38 Walcot Hall

TUESDAY 26
32 Radnor Cottage

THURSDAY 28
30 Preen Manor

SUNDAY 31
16 Heath House
23 Longner Hall
24 Marehay Farm
35 Swallow Hayes

June

TUESDAY 2
7 Brownhill House

WEDNESDAY 3
12 Edge Villa

SUNDAY 7
1 Adcote School
8 Chyknell
9 The Cottage
17 Hodnet Hall Gardens
27 Morville Hall Gardens

FRIDAY 12
10 Cruckfield House

SATURDAY 13
41 Whittington Village Gardens

SUNDAY 14
16 Heath House
18 Holly Grove
37 30 Victoria Road
39 8 Westgate Villas
41 Whittington Village Gardens

TUESDAY 16
7 Brownhill House

SUNDAY 21
3 Applecross House
19 Holmcroft
26 Moortown

THURSDAY 25
30 Preen Manor

SUNDAY 28
13 Field House

July

WEDNESDAY 1
40 Weston Park

SUNDAY 5
5 Bridgwalton House
29 Poplar Cottage Farm

TUESDAY 7
7 Brownhill House

SUNDAY 12
2 Ancoireán
42 Windy Ridge

SATURDAY 18
11 Dudmaston Hall Gardens

TUESDAY 21
7 Brownhill House

SUNDAY 26
20 Jessamine Cottage
21 Laurel Cottage
33 Rose Villa
36 Valducci Flower & Vegetable Gardens

THURSDAY 30
30 Preen Manor

August

SUNDAY 2
12 Edge Villa

SUNDAY 9
42 Windy Ridge

SUNDAY 30
20 Jessamine Cottage

September

SUNDAY 6
2 Ancoireán
42 Windy Ridge

TUESDAY 8
7 Brownhill House

SATURDAY 12
15 Harnage Farm

SUNDAY 13
3 Applecross House

October

SUNDAY 4
30 Preen Manor

November

SATURDAY 7
4 Attingham Park

Gardens open to the public

4 Attingham Park
11 Dudmaston Hall Gardens
20 Jessamine Cottage
40 Weston Park
43 Wollerton Old Hall

By appointment only

22 Little Heldre
34 Ruthall Manor

Also open by appointment ☎

2 Ancoireán
3 Applecross House
5 Bridgwalton House
6 Brockton Court
7 Brownhill House
10 Cruckfield House
12 Edge Villa
14 Gate Cottage
18 Holly Grove
19 Holmcroft
21 Laurel Cottage
28 Oteley
30 Preen Manor
31 Preston Hall
32 Radnor Cottage
35 Swallow Hayes
36 Valducci Flower & Vegetable Gardens
38 Walcot Hall
42 Windy Ridge

The Gardens

ABERNANT
See Powys.

1 ADCOTE SCHOOL
Little Ness SY4 2JY. Adcote School Educational Trust Ltd. *8m NW of Shrewsbury. Via A5, turn off NE follow signs to Little Ness.* Home-made teas. **Adm £4, chd free.** Suns 17 May; 7 June (2-5).
26 acres; fine trees incl beeches, tulip trees, oaks (American and evergreen), atlas cedars, wellingtonia etc. Rhododendrons, azaleas; landscaped garden. House (part shown) designed by Norman Shaw RA; Grade I listed building. Gravel paths, some slopes.
✿ ✖ ✪ ☕

2 NEW ANCOIREÁN
24 Romsley View, Alveley WV15 6PJ. Judy & Peter Creed, 01746 780504, peter@creedpd.freeserve.co.uk. *6m S Bridgnorth off A442 Bridgnorth to Kidderminster rds. N from Kidderminster, turn L just after Royal Oak PH, S from Bridgnorth turn R after Squirrel PH. Take 3rd turning R into Romsley View after 50yds bear R & follow NGS signs to bottom of rd, last house in the corner on R.* Home-made teas. **Adm £3, chd free.** Suns 12 July; 6 Sept (1-5). **Visitors also welcome by appt from mid May to mid Sept.**
Natural garden layout on several levels, developed over 30yrs, with a large variety of plants and shrubs. Water features, wooded area with bog garden containing numerous varieties of ferns and hostas. Large selection of plants and bird boxes for sale. Close to Severn Valley Park and Dudmaston Hall NT.
✖ ✪ ☕ ☎

3 APPLECROSS HOUSE
Alveley, Bridgnorth WV15 6NB. Mary & Colin Wells, 01746 780313, mary@marywells.com. *6m S of Bridgnorth. Alveley off A442 Bridgnorth to Kidderminster rds. N from Kidderminster, turn L just after the Royal Oak PH. S from Bridgnorth, turn R after the Squirrel PH follow NGS signs.* Home-made teas. **Adm £3, chd free.** Suns 21 June; 13 Sept (1-5). **Visitors also welcome by appt.**
2 acre garden divided into several

small areas, developed from paddocks since 1995. Features incl ponds, pergolas, vegetable garden, orchard, dovecote and collection of contemporary sculpture. Large range of trees, shrubs and herbaceous plants. Outstanding view of Clee Hills and only 1/2 m from award winning Severn Valley Country Park. Featured in 'Shropshire Life'. Some gravel paths.
✿ ✖ ✪ ☕ ☎

4 ◆ ATTINGHAM PARK
Shrewsbury SY4 4TP. The National Trust, 01743 708162, www.nationaltrust.org.uk. *4m SE of Shrewsbury. From M54 follow A5 to Shrewsbury then B4380 to Atcham.* Gardens only £4.20, chd £2.20. For times & dates of opening, please tel or see website. For NGS: Sat 7 Nov (9-5).
Attingham Park (house not open) is a landscape park designed by Humphry Repton. There are attractive walks through the grounds and along the river. There are also extensive walks through the woodland and deer park. The walled garden has recently been re-cultivated producng fresh fruit and vegetables. Autumn colour. Mobility buggys and wheelchairs available to loan free of charge.
✿ ✪ ☕

Wooded area with bog garden containing numerous varieties of ferns and hostas . . .

BIRCH TREES
See Staffordshire & part of West Midlands.

BODYNFOEL HALL
See Powys.

5 BRIDGWALTON HOUSE
Telegraph Lane, Morville WV16 5NP. Mary Bower, 01746 714401. *1m from Bridgnorth. Off A458 Shrewsbury to Bridgnorth, nr Morville. Signed on the day.* Home-made teas. **Adm £3.50, chd free.** Sun 5 July (2-6). **Visitors also welcome by appt.**
1 1/4 acres plantsmans award winning garden with many unusual trees and shrubs. Collections of daphnes and peonies with oriental design at the garden. Wonderful views. All year

interest with garden rooms, exuberant planting of herbaceous shrubs and bulbs, highly praised by Roy Lancaster. Featured in 'Shropshire' magazine, 'Express & Star', 'Shropshire Star'.
✿ ✖ ✪ ☕ ☎

6 BROCKTON COURT
Brockton TF11 9LZ. Mr & Mrs H Meynell. *5m S Telford. From Shifnal A4169 Bridgnorth rd for 2m then B4379 for 1m. In Brockton fork R for Coalport. From Bridgnorth A442 for Telford 8m Sutton Maddock Garage, continue on A442 towards Telford for 1/2 m, turn R signed Brockton. Brockton Court is 1st house on L.* Home-made teas. **Adm £3, chd free.** Sun 24 May (2.30-5.30). **Visitors also welcome by appt.**
Approx 2 acres herbaceous and mixed borders, bedding, roses, hanging and ornamental tubs, shrubs, arboretum, fruit and vegetables. Cascade water feature with flower/shrub border surround. Cottage garden with greenhouses and cacti. Featured in 'Shropshire Star'. Gravel paths.
✿ ✖ ✪ ☕ ☎

7 BROWNHILL HOUSE
Ruyton XI Towns SY4 1LR. Roger & Yoland Brown, 01939 261121, brownhill@eleventowns.co.uk, www.eleventowns.co.uk. *10m NW of Shrewsbury. On B4397.* Home-made teas. **Adm £3, chd free.** Tues 21 Apr; 5, 19 May; 2, 16 June; 7, 21 July; 8 Sept (1.30-5). **Visitors also welcome by appt May to Aug.**
Unusual and distinctive hillside garden (over 600 steps) bordering R Perry. Great variety of plants and styles from laburnum walk and formal terraces to woodland paths, plus large kitchen garden. Over 100 varieties of plants for sale, proceeds to NGS. Featured in 'Shropshire Life'.
✖ ✪ 🛏 ☕ ☎

8 CHYKNELL
Bridgnorth WV15 5PP. Mr & Mrs W S R Kenyon-Slaney. *5m E of Bridgnorth. Between Claverley & Worfield. Signed off A454 Wolverhampton to Bridgnorth & A458 Stourbridge to Bridgnorth.* Home-made teas. **Adm £3, chd free.** Sun 7 June (2-6).
5 acres of magnolias, rhododendrons, azaleas, roses and herbaceous plants; interesting shrubs and fine trees in tranquil park setting. Formal structure of hedged compartments designed by Russell Page in 1951. Hungry light soil susceptible to drought.
✖ ✪ ☕

CIL Y WENNOL
See Powys.

⑨ THE COTTAGE
2 Farley Dingle, Much Wenlock
TF13 6NX. Mr & Mrs P D Wight. *2m
E of Much Wenlock. On A4169 Much
Wenlock to Telford rd. At the end of the
dead end lane, opp the road signed
Wyke. Parking is limited.* Home-made
teas. **Adm £3, chd free.** Sun 7 June
(11-5).
Cottage garden of 2 acres, set at the
end of a small valley, enclosed by
woodland. Natural stream surrounded
by hostas, ferns, shrubs and
perennials, meanders through the
garden. The sides of the valley have
been terraced to create an
amphitheatre. Steps, bridges and
paths abound. Children under 16yrs
must be supervised. Featured in & on
BBC 'Gardeners' World', Radio
Shropshire, 'Shropshire Star'.
✖ ✿ ☕

⑩ CRUCKFIELD HOUSE
Ford SY5 9NR. Mr & Mrs G M
Cobley, 01743 850222. *5m W of
Shrewsbury. A458, turn L towards
Shoothill.* Home-made teas. **Adm
£4.50, chd £1.** Fri 12 June (2-6).
**Visitors also welcome by appt June
& July only, groups of 25+.**
4-acre romantic S-facing garden,
formally designed, informally and
intensively planted with substantial
variety of unusual herbaceous plants.
Nick's garden, with many species trees
and shrubs, surrounds a large pond
with bog and moisture-loving plants.
Ornamental kitchen garden with pretty
outbuildings. Rose and peony walk.
Courtyard fountain garden and an
extensive shrubbery. Extensive
clematis collection. Large rockery and
lily pond.
✖ ✿ ☕ ☎

CWMLLECHWEDD FAWR
See Powys.

CWM-WEEG
See Powys.

DINGLE NURSERIES & GARDEN
See Powys.

**⑪ ◆ DUDMASTON HALL
GARDENS**
Quatt, nr Bridgnorth WV15 6QN. The
National Trust, 01746 780866,
dudmaston@nationaltrust.org.uk.
*4m SE of Bridgnorth. On A442,
between Bridgnorth & Kidderminster.*
**Adm £3, chd free. Garden; Sun to
Wed, 1 Apr to 30 Sept, (12-6).**

House; Tues, Wed, Sun, 1 Apr to 30
Sept (2-5). For NGS: Sat 18 July
(12-6).
9 acres with a good mixture of
herbaceous borders, rose border,
rockery with lavender, erigeron and
caryopteris. Wide range of large and
small trees incl *Cornus kousa*,
complemented by modern sculptures
and terraced lawn. Lake side and
woodland walks. Musical interludes by
string quartet. Some steep slopes in
garden but alternative paths available.
✖ ✖ ✿ ☕

⑫ EDGE VILLA
Edge, nr Yockleton SY5 9PY. Mr &
Mrs W F Neil, 01743 821651,
bill@billfneil.fsnet.co.uk. *6m from
Shrewsbury. From A5 take either A488
signed to Bishops Castle or B4386 to
Montgomery for approx 6m then follow
NGS signs.* Coffee & home-made teas.
Adm £3, chd free. Wed 3 June (10-
1); Sun 2 Aug (2-5.30). **Visitors also
welcome by appt groups of 10+,
cars or small coaches only.**
2-acres nestling in South Shropshire
hills. Self-sufficient vegetable plot.
Chickens in orchard. Large
herbaceous borders. Dewpond
surrounded by purple elder, irises,
candelabra primulas and dierams.
Large selection of fragrant roses.
Comprehensive plant stall. Teas in
sheltered courtyard. Some gravel
paths.
✖ ✖ ✿ ☕ ☎

⑬ FIELD HOUSE
Clee St Margaret SY7 9DT. Dr & Mrs
John Bell. *8m NE of Ludlow. Turning
to Stoke St Milborough & Clee St
Margaret, 5m from Ludlow, 10m from
Bridgnorth along B4364. Through
Stoke St Milborough to Clee St
Margaret. Ignore R turn to Clee Village.
Field House on L.* Home-made teas.
Adm £3, chd free. Sun 28 June (2-6).
1-acre garden created since 1982 for
yr-round interest. Mixed borders; rose
walk; pool garden; herbaceous
borders. Lovely views, in a tranquil rural
setting with donkeys, sheep and
ducks.
✖ ✖ ✿ ☕

⑭ GATE COTTAGE
Cockshutt SY12 0JU. G W
Nicholson & Kevin Gunnell, 01939
270606. *10m N of Shrewsbury. On
A528. At Cockshutt take rd signed
English Frankton. Garden 1m on R.
Parking in adjacent field.* Teas. **Adm
£3, chd free.** Suns 3, 24 May (1-5).

Visitors also welcome by appt.
2 acres of informal mixed plantings of
trees, shrubs, herbaceous plants of
interest to flower arrangers and
plantsmen. Pool, rock garden and
informal pools. Large collection of
hostas; old orchard with roses, incl
items of unusual growth or colour. New
plantings of meconopsis and arum lilies
together with gravel garden and prarie
planted grasses.
✿ ☕ ☎

Iris and lilies, secret garden with rill . . .

GLANSEVERN HALL GARDENS
See Powys.

⑮ HARNAGE FARM
Cound SY5 6EJ. Mr & Mrs Ken
Cooke. *8m SE of Shrewsbury. On
A458. Turn to Cound 1m S of Cross
Houses. Harnage Farm 1m, bearing L
past church.* Home-made teas. **Adm
£3, chd free (share to Country Air
Ambulance Trust).** Sat 12 Sept
(12-5).
1/2 -acre farm house garden.
Herbaceous plants and shrubs, small
raised vegetable plot. Good autumn
colour and extensive views over
Severn Valley and 15 min walk through
fields to conservation wood and wildlife
pool.
♿ ✖ ☕

⑯ NEW HEATH HOUSE
Lightwood WV16 6UL. Margaret
Bill. *5m W of Bridgnorth. From
Bridgnorth bypass take B4364 to
Ludlow, fork R after 1.2m, signpost
'Middleton Priors', garden 2.9m on
L.* Home-made teas. **Adm £3, chd
free.** Suns 31 May; 14 June (2-5).
Over 1-acre, natural pond with
primulas, iris and lilies, secret
garden with rill. Mixed herbaceous
and shrub borders, orchard and
vegetable garden. Long border
with mixed planting leading to
country views.
♿ ✖ ✿ ☕

HEATH HOUSE
See Staffordshire & part of West Midlands.

17 HODNET HALL GARDENS
nr Market Drayton TF9 3NN. Mr & The Hon Mrs Heber-Percy, 01630 685786 (Secretary), www.hodnethallgardens.org. 5½ m SW of Market Drayton. 12m NE Shrewsbury. At junction of A53 & A442. Light refreshments. **Adm £4.50, chd £2. Sun 7 June (12-5).**
60-acre landscaped garden with series of lakes and pools; magnificent forest trees, great variety of flowers, shrubs providing colour throughout season. Unique collection of big-game trophies in C17 tearooms. Kitchen garden. For details please see website.

🚫 ♨

25 metre pergola walkway with many varieties of clematis and roses . . .

18 HOLLY GROVE
Church Pulverbatch SY5 8DD. Peter & Angela Unsworth, 01743 718221. 6m S of Shrewsbury. Midway between Stapleton & Church Pulverbatch. From A49 follow signs to Stapleton & Pulverbatch. Home-made teas. **Adm £3.50, chd free. Sun 14 June (2-6). Visitors also welcome by appt.**
3-acre garden set in S Shropshire countryside. Yew and beech hedges enclosing 'rooms', box parterres, pleached limes, vegetable garden, rose and herbaceous borders containing many rare plants. New arboretum, lake and wild flower meadows. Opportunity to see rare White Park cattle and Soay sheep. Featured in 'Country Life' Magazine.

🚫 ✈ ✿ ♨ ☎

19 HOLMCROFT
Wyson Lane, Brimfield, nr Ludlow SY8 4NW. Mr & Mrs Michael Dowding, 01584 711743, www.anenglishcottageonline.com. 4m S of Ludlow. 6m N of Leominster. From Ludlow or Leominster leave A49 at Brimfield sign. From Tenbury Wells turn L when A456 meets A49, then 1st L into Brimfield. Home-made teas. **Adm £3, chd free. Sun 21 June (2-**

5.30). Visitors also welcome by appt June & July. No coaches. Groups of 10-20.
C17 thatched cottage, set in ¾ -acre garden with spectacular views set amongst a series of terraced gardens. Herb partier, sunken garden, camomile bank, gravel garden and willow tunnel. Kitchen garden, woodland trail and new rose walk and stumpery. Twice semi-finalist in Shropshire Star 'Garden of the Year'. Third in 'Shropshire Star' Gardener of the Year.

🚫 ✈ ✿ ♨ ☎

20 ♦ JESSAMINE COTTAGE
Kenley SY5 6NS. Lee & Pamela Wheeler, 01694 771279, www.stmem.com/jessamine-cottage. 6m W of Much Wenlock. Signed from B4371 Much Wenlock to Church Stretton rd and from A458 Shrewsbury to Much Wenlock rd at Harley. **Adm £3, chd £1. Thurs, Suns & Bank Hols, 1 May - 31 Aug. For NGS: Suns 26 July; 30 Aug (2-6).**
3-acre garden. Mature wildlife pond; large wild flower meadow; mixed island beds; lime avenue; large kitchen garden; parterre; stream and woodland. Rose garden and ornamental trees, large range of attractive perennials and shrubs provide all season colour.

🚫 ✈ ♨

21 NEW LAUREL COTTAGE
Ruckley, Acton Burnell SY5 7HR. Mark & Judy Freeman, 01694 731458, markjudefreeman@gmail.com. 9m S/SE of Shrewsbury. From A5 bypass take A458 exit Much Wenlock, Bridgnorth Rd, turn R immed after A5 slip rd (Pitchford, Acton Burnell), continue approx 8m through Acton Burnell village to Cross Roads, continue straight ahead to Ruckley/Causeway Wood, 1¼ m. House opp junction to Langley Chapel. Teas. **Combined with Rose Villa adm £4, chd free. Sun 26 July (2-5). Visitors also welcome by appt.**
A cottage garden of approximately ⅓ -acre set in a little known, peaceful Shropshire Valley. The garden is terraced and landscaped into rooms of mixed herbaceous planting. A 25m pergola walkway with many varieties of clematis and roses, leads to a summerhouse with outstanding views across the valley.

✈ ✿ ♨ ☎

22 LITTLE HELDRE
Buttington SY21 8TF. Peter & Gillian Stedman, 01938 570457, p.stedman317@btinternet.com. 12m W of Shrewsbury. Off A458. From Welshpool take A458 Shrewsbury rd for 3m, turn R into Heldre Lane. From Shrewsbury turn L past Little Chef at Trewern into Sale Lane, follow signs. Home-made teas. **Adm £2.50, chd free. Visitors welcome by appt, groups or individuals, 1 Apr to 30 Sept, not suitable for coaches.**
1¾ -acre garden on steep N-facing hillside. Yr round colour, unusual plants and shrubs. Hard landscaping, terraced herbaceous borders, moon gate, stepped pergola, wood sculptures. Wooded dingle with stream, bog garden, fantastic views across Severn to Berwyn Mountains. Spring bulbs and alpines, followed by rhododendrons, azaleas, flowering shrubs, candelabra primroses. Productive vegetable plot.

✈ ♨ ☎

23 LONGNER HALL
Atcham, Shrewsbury SY4 4TG. Mr & Mrs R L Burton. 4m SE of Shrewsbury. From M54 follow A5 to Shrewsbury, then B4380 to Atcham. From Atcham take Uffington rd, entrance ¼ m on L. Home-made teas. **Adm £4, chd free. Sun 31 May (2-5).**
A long drive approach through parkland designed by Humphry Repton. Walks lined with golden yew through extensive lawns, with views over Severn Valley. Borders containing roses, herbaceous and shrubs, also ancient yew wood. Enclosed walled garden containing mixed planting, garden buildings, tower and game larder. Short woodland walk around old moat pond. Some gravel paths and gentle slopes, woodland walk not suitable for wheelchairs.

🚫 ✈ ♨

MAESFRON HALL AND GARDENS
See Powys.

24 MAREHAY FARM
Gatten, Ratlinghope SY5 0SJ. Stuart & Carol Buxton, 01588 650289. 6½ m W of Church Stretton. 6m S of Pontesbury, 9m NNE of Bishops Castle. 1½ m from 'The Bridges' Xrds & the intersection of the Longden, Pulverbatch & Bishops Castle rd and the minor rd from Church Stretton to the Stiperstones. Home-made teas. **Adm £3, chd free. Sun 31 May (11-6). Visitors also welcome by appt, mid May to mid July.**

In 1982 a building society surveyor reported 'there is no garden and at this height (1100ft), elevation and aspect there never will be!' Since 1990, on heavy boulder clay a 1½ acre woodland/water garden evolved, with primulas, hostas, iris, damp/shade tolerant perennials. Rhododendrons, azaleas, various conifers, trees, roses and shrubs complementing the location. Runner up 'Shropshire Star' Garden of the year 2008. Wheelchairs with assistance, some gravel.

MILL COTTAGE
See Powys.

25 MILLICHOPE PARK
Munslow SY7 9HA. Mr & Mrs L Bury, 01584 841234, sarah@millichope.com. *8m NE of Craven Arms. From Ludlow (11m) turn L off B4368, ¾ m out of Munslow.* Home-made teas. **Adm £4, chd free. Mon 4 May (2-6).**
13-acre garden with lakes, woodland walks, fine specimen trees, wild flowers and herbaceous borders, good autumn colour.

26 MOORTOWN
nr Wellington TF6 6JE. Mr David Bromley. *8m N of Telford. 5m N of Wellington. Take B5062 signed Moortown 1m between High Ercall & Crudgington.* **Adm £4, chd £1.00. Sun 21 June (2-5.30).**
Approx 1-acre plantsman's garden. Here may be found the old-fashioned, the unusual and even the oddities of plant life, in mixed borders of 'controlled' confusion.

Group opening

27 MORVILLE HALL GARDENS
nr Bridgnorth WV16 5NB. *3m W of Bridgnorth. On A458 at junction with B4368.* Home-made teas at Morville Hall. **Combined adm £5, chd free (share to Morville Church). Sun June (2-5).**
A varied and interesting group of gardens that immediately surround a beautiful Grade 1 listed mansion (house not open).

THE COTTAGE
Mr & Mrs Begg
Pretty walled cottage garden with good climbers, informal vegetable area with soft fruit bushes. Good lawn and small fish pond with kettle feature.

THE DOWER HOUSE
Dr Katherine Swift
1½ -acre sequence of gardens in various historical styles designed to tell the history of Morville Hall from medieval times to the present, incl turf maze, cloister garden, Elizabethan knot garden, Edwardian fruit and vegetable garden, C18 canal garden, wild garden. Featured on BBC Radio 4, Book of the Week, 'The Morville Hours - the Story of a Garden'.

1 THE GATEHOUSE
Mr & Mrs Rowe
½ -acre walled garden comprising formal and woodland areas with colour-filled herbaceous borders.

2 THE GATEHOUSE
Mrs G Medland
A garden in transition. Cottage garden with colourful borders.

MORVILLE HALL
Dr & Mrs J C Douglas & The National Trust
4-acre garden in fine setting, incl box parterre, mature shrub borders, pond garden and medieval stewpond.

SOUTH PAVILION
Mr & Mrs B Jenkinson
Walled courtyard garden with a collection of hebes, cistus and roses, incl wall covering *R.banksiae Lutea.*

---

28 OTELEY
Ellesmere SY12 0PB. Mr & Mrs R K Mainwaring, 01691 622514. *1m SE of Ellesmere. Entrance out of Ellesmere past Mere, opp Convent nr to A528/495 junction.* Home-made teas. **Adm £3, chd free. Sun 10 May (2-6). Visitors also welcome by appt for groups of 10+, coaches permitted.**
10 acres running down to Mere, incl walled kitchen garden; architectural features; many interesting trees, rhododendrons and azaleas, incl wild woodland walk, views across Mere to Ellesmere Church. Wheelchairs only if dry. Some gravel paths and slopes.

29 POPLAR COTTAGE FARM
Morville, nr Bridgnorth WV16 4RS. Elizabeth & Barry Bacon. *¾ m NW of Morville. On A458.* Teas available at Bridgwalton House. **Adm £2.50, chd free (share to Morville Church Building Trust). Sun 5 July (2-6).**
⅓ -acre flower arranger's garden with yr-round interest. Different soil textures and micro-climate allow for varied planting in a series of exciting 'rooms' - many unusual plants. Recently restored gipsy caravan to view.

POWIS CASTLE GARDEN
See Powys.

30 PREEN MANOR
Church Preen SY6 7LQ. Mrs Ann Trevor-Jones, 01694 771207. *6m W of Much Wenlock. Signed from B4371.* Home-made teas. **Adm £4, chd 50p 5-16yrs. Suns 5 Apr, 4 Oct (2-5); Thurs 28 May; 25 June; 30 July; (2-6). Visitors also welcome by appt, June & July only, groups of 10+.**
6-acre garden on site of Cluniac monastery and Norman Shaw mansion. Kitchen, chess, water and wild gardens. Fine trees in park; woodland walks. Developed over last 30yrs with changes always in progress. Produce stall (Apr,Oct), Harvest Thanksgiving in church adjacent to garden (Oct). Featured in 'Country Life'.

Recently restored gipsy caravan to view . . .

31 PRESTON HALL
Preston Brockhurst SY4 5QA. C C & L Corbet, 01939 220312, corbetleil@btinternet.com. *8m N of Shrewsbury. On A49.* Cream teas. **Adm £3, chd free. Sun 26 Apr (2-5). Visitors also welcome by appt by arrangement, small groups, coaches permitted.**
Garden around stone Cromwellian house (not open). Interesting perennials, tulips, trees and shrubs. Good walk around meadow, woodland walk, cutting garden and courtyard garden. Grass paths.

Fine views of Sir William Chambers' Clock Towers, with lake and hills . . .

32 RADNOR COTTAGE
Clun SY7 0JA. Pam & David
Pittwood, 01588 640451. *7m W of
Craven Arms. 1m E of Clun on B4368.*
Home-made teas. **Adm £3, chd free
(share to Link Romania). Tues 14
Apr; 12, 26 May (2-6). Visitors also
welcome by appt April - mid June.**
2 acres on S-facing slope, overlooking
Clun Valley. Wide variety of garden
habitats all densely planted. Incl sunny
terracing with paving and dry-stone
walling; alpine troughs; cottage garden
borders; damp shade for white flowers
and gold foliage; pond, stream and
bog garden; orchard; rough grass with
naturalised bulbs and wild flowers.

ROSE COTTAGE
See Powys.

33 NEW ROSE VILLA
Ruckley, Acton Burnell SY5 7HR.
John & Margaret Westhead.
**Combined adm with Laurel
Cottage adm £4, chd free. Sun
26 July (2-5).**
Sloping fruit and vegetable garden
which has been managed
organically for 26 years by present
owners. Wildlife is encouraged by
maintaining original mixed hedges,
welcoming wild flowers and having
a small pond with solar powered
waterfall. Next door to Laurel
Cottage.

ROWAN
See Powys.

34 RUTHALL MANOR
Ditton Priors WV16 6TN. Mr & Mrs G
T Clarke, 01746 712608,
clarke@ruthall.orangehome.co.uk.
*7m SW of Bridgnorth. Ruthall Rd
signed nr garage.* **Adm £2.50, chd
free. Visitors welcome by appt, May
to August - any number.**
1-acre garden with ha-ha and old
horse pond planted with water and
bog plants. Rare specimen trees.
Designed for easy maintenance with
lots of ground cover and unusual
plants. New gravel art garden and
dryer climate adaptions. New features
being added year by year.

35 SWALLOW HAYES
Rectory Road, Albrighton WV7 3EP.
Mrs P Edwards, 01902 372624,
patedwards70@btinternet.com. *7m
NW of Wolverhampton. M54 exit 3.
Rectory Rd to R, 1m towards
Wolverhampton off A41 just past
Wyevale Garden Centre.* Home-made
teas. **Adm £3, chd free. Suns 3, 31
May (2-6). Visitors also welcome by
appt, coaches permitted all year.
Any number of visitors.**
2 acres planted since 1968 with
emphasis on all-yr interest and ease of
maintenance. National Collections of
Hamamelis and Russell lupins. Nearly
3000 different plants, many labelled.
Trees, shrubs, herbaceous, bulbs,
groundcover and ferns. Children's trail.
Some gravel paths.

TAN-Y-LLYN
See Powys.

**36 VALDUCCI FLOWER &
VEGETABLE GARDENS**
Vicarage Road Site, Meole Brace
SY3 0NR. Luigi Valducci, 07921
368968, valbros@btconnect.com.
*2m W of Shrewsbury. Meole Brace
Garden & Allotment Club. On A5 exit at
Dobbies r-about, direction Shrewsbury.
Follow sign for Nuffield Hospital, opp
hospital Stanley Lane, follow Stanley
Lane until you reach Vicarage Rd. Car
park on R, garden on L.* Light
refreshments & teas. **Adm £3, chd
free. Sun 26 July (12-5). Visitors also
welcome by appt.**
1200 sq yds of gardens and allotments
containing 4 greenhouses, orchard and
site of National Collection of
Brugmansias (Angel's Trumpets) with
over 80 varieties. An Italian style of
gardening focusing on vegetables and
flowers with a European feel.

37 30 VICTORIA ROAD
Bridgnorth WV16 4LF. Mr & Mrs
Parker. *A458 Bridgnorth bypass, take
rd into Bridgnorth at Ludlow Rd
r'about signed town centre. At T-
junction (pay & display parking B/N
council offices) turn R into Victoria Rd,
Victoria Rd, no. 30 on L.* Teas at 8
Westgate Villas. **Combined with
8 Westgate Villas adm £4, chd
free. Sun 14 June (2-5.30).**

Town garden facing SW. Walled formal
area, lawn with herbaceous borders,
quiet sitting area, pond, summerhouse
and large patio with containers.
Emerging perennials show the promise
of summer. New exotic area, New smal
fern area, 20 clematis. In attractive
market town on R Severn with cliff
railway between High and Low Town.
Severn Valley steam railway and
Thomas Telford Church.

38 WALCOT HALL
Lydbury North SY7 8AZ. Mr & Mrs
C R W Parish, 01588 680570,
maria@walcothall.com,
www.walcothall.co.uk. *4m SE of
Bishop's Castle. B4385 Craven Arms
to Bishop's Castle, turn L by Powis
Arms, in Lydbury North.* Home-made
teas. **Adm £3.50, chd free. Sun 24,
Mon 25 May (1.30-5.30). Visitors
also welcome by appt for groups of
15+, throughout the year.**
Arboretum planted by Lord Clive of
India's son, Edward. Cascades of
rhododendrons, azaleas amongst
specimen trees and pools. Fine views
of Sir William Chambers' Clock
Towers, with lake and hills beyond.
Walled kitchen garden; dovecote; meat
safe; ice house and mile-long lakes.
Outstanding ballroom where excellent
teas are served. Russian wooden
church, grotto and fountain now
complete and working; tin chapel.
Beautiful borders and rare shrubs.
Grass paths. Not all areas accessible
but main garden area and ballroom for
teas are.

THE WERN
See Powys.

39 8 WESTGATE VILLAS
Salop Street, Bridgnorth WV16 4QX
Bill & Marilyn Hammerton. *From
A458 Bridgnorth bypass, take rd into
Bridgnorth at Ludlow Rd r'about
signed town centre. At T-junction (pay
& display parking at B/N council offices
here) turn R, garden 100 yds on L just
past entrance to Victoria Rd.* Home-
made teas. **Combined with 30
Victoria Road adm £4, chd free.
Sun 14 June (2-5.30).**
Town garden having formal Victorian
front garden with box hedging and
water feature to complement house.
Back garden has shade border, lawn,
small knot garden and orchard
together with a strong oriental
influence, incl Japanese style teahous
and zen garden. New path in Chinese

style. Bridgnorth is an attractive market town on the R Severn with cliff railway between high and low town, Severn Valley steam railway and Thomas Telford Church.

WESTLAKE FISHERIES & CAMPING
See Powys.

40 ◆ WESTON PARK
Weston-under-Lizard, Shifnal TF11 8LE. The Weston Park Foundation, 01952 852100, www.@weston-park.com. *6m E of Telford. Situated on A5 at Weston-under-Lizard. J12 M6 & J3 M54.* House & garden £8, chd £5.50, concessions £7, garden only £5, chd £3, concessions £4.50. For opening dates & times please tel or see website. For NGS: Wed 1 July (11-6).
Capability Brown landscaped gardens and parkland. Formal gardens restored to original C19 design, rose garden and long border together with colourful adjacent Broderie garden. New yew hedge maze and orchard in the walled garden.
&

Mature trees and shrubs in woodland. Ponds and environmentally friendly wild flower areas . . .

Group opening

41 WHITTINGTON VILLAGE GARDENS
nr Oswestry SY11 4EA. *2½ m NE of Oswestry. Daisy Lane & Top St, Whittington. Turn off B5009 150yds NW of church into Top St. Car parking at Whittington Castle (charge) & Top St.* Home-made teas at Greystones, Daisy Lane. **Adm £3, chd free. Sat 13, Sun 14 June (12-5).**
Opening off Daisy Lane, adjacent gardens. Cottage, featuring pots brimful of colour, an old garden being remodelled. Modern family garden for leisure bordered by plant packed beds. On larger plots, kitchen gardens, mature trees and shrubs in woodland. Ponds and environmentally friendly wild flower areas. Kinnerton Morris Dancers on Sunday at approx 3pm.

42 WINDY RIDGE
Church Lane, Little Wenlock, Telford TF6 5BB. George & Fiona Chancellor, 01952 507675, fionachancellor@btinternet.com, www.gardenschool.co.uk. *2m S of Wellington. Follow signs for Little Wenlock from the north (junction7, M54) or east (off A5223 at Horsehay). Park at 'The Huntsman' PH in centre of village.* Home-made teas. **Adm £3.50, chd free. Suns 10 May; 12 July; 9 Aug; 6 Sept (12-5). Visitors also welcome by appt.**
Multi Award-winning ⅔ acre village garden highly praised by Roy Lancaster with a strong design and exuberant planting. Surprising features, winding paths to explore and quiet corners to linger in, to appeal to all generations. 1000 species of plants (mostly labelled) with plant list available. Winner of 'Daily Mail' National Garden Competition.
& ✕ ✿ ☕ ☎

43 ◆ WOLLERTON OLD HALL
Wollerton, Market Drayton TF9 3NA. Leslie & John Jenkins, 01630 685760, www.wollertonoldhallgarden.com. *4m SW of Market Drayton. On A53 between Hodnet & A53-A41 junction. Follow brown signs.* **Adm £5, chd £1. Fris, Suns, BH; Good Friday to Sept. For NGS: Fris 1, 22 May (12-5).**
4-acre garden created around C16 house (not open). Formal structure creates variety of gardens each with own colour theme and character. Planting is mainly of perennials, the large range of which results in significant collections of salvias, clematis, crocosmias and roses. Lunches provided. Head gardener's tour 1 May. Featured on 'I own Britain's Best Home & Garden' Channel 5. All formal areas easily accessible.
& ✕ ✿ ☕

WOODHILL
See Powys.

Shropshire County Volunteers

SOMERSET, BRISTOL AREA
& South Gloucestershire incl Bath

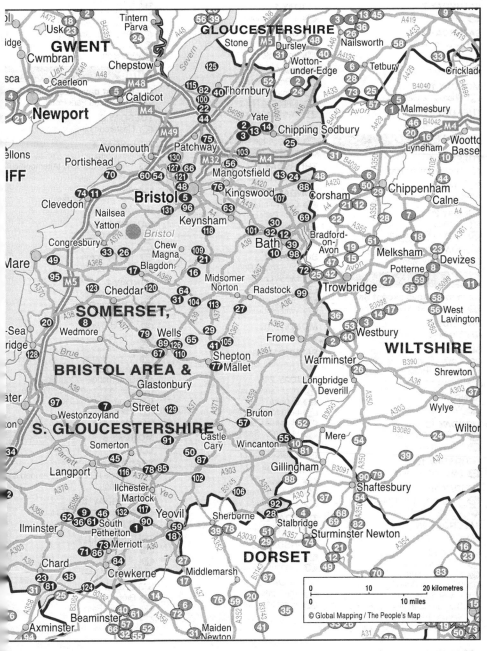

Opening Dates

February

SUNDAY 1
- 100 Rock House

SATURDAY 7
- 46 East Lambrook Manor Gardens

SATURDAY 14
- 104 Sherborne Garden

SUNDAY 15
- 104 Sherborne Garden

MONDAY 16
- 104 Sherborne Garden

TUESDAY 17
- 104 Sherborne Garden

March

TUESDAY 3
- 68 Hestercombe Gardens

SUNDAY 15
- 104 Sherborne Garden

SUNDAY 29
- 51 Fairfield
- 101 Saltford Farm Barn

MONDAY 30
- 85 Lytes Cary Manor

April

Open most days except Sat
- 72 Homewood Park Hotel

SATURDAY 4
- 114 Stowleys

SUNDAY 5
- 31 Coley Court & Rose Cottage
- 38 Cricket House and Gardens
- 39 Crowe Hall

SUNDAY 12
- 124 Wayford Manor

MONDAY 13
- 47 Elworthy Cottage
- 124 Wayford Manor

THURSDAY 16
- 47 Elworthy Cottage

SUNDAY 19
- 62 Hangeridge Farmhouse
- 106 3 Southdown

SATURDAY 25
- 129 Westbrook House

SUNDAY 26
- 48 Emmaus House
- 63 Hanham Court
- 70 25 Hillcrest Road
- 84 Lower Severalls
- 109 Stanton Court Nursing Home
- 123 Watcombe

May

Open most days except Sat
- 72 Homewood Park Hotel

FRIDAY 1
- 18 1 Braggchurch

SATURDAY 2
- 18 1 Braggchurch
- 84 Lower Severalls

SUNDAY 3
- 18 1 Braggchurch
- 25 Camers
- 78 Kingsdon Nursery Garden
- 124 Wayford Manor

MONDAY 4
- 62 Hangeridge Farmhouse
- 124 Wayford Manor

THURSDAY 7
- 55 Forest Lodge

SUNDAY 10
- 37 Court House
- 98 Prior Park Landscape Garden

SATURDAY 16
- 73 Springdale

SUNDAY 17
- 70 25 Hillcrest Road
- 89 Milton Lodge
- 106 3 Southdown
- 73 Springdale
- 123 Watcombe

MONDAY 18
- 73 Springdale

SATURDAY 23
- 71 Hinton St George Gardens

SUNDAY 24
- 4 Aller Farmhouse
- 50 Esotera
- 52 Farndon Thatch
- 64 Harptree Court
- 71 Hinton St George Gardens
- 93 Olive Cottage
- 124 Wayford Manor

MONDAY 25
- 50 Esotera
- 52 Farndon Thatch
- 93 Olive Cottage

TUESDAY 26
- 126 Wellfield Barn

THURSDAY 28
- 47 Elworthy Cottage
- 74 Jasmine Cottage

SATURDAY 30
- 36 The Cottage
- 88 Marshfield Gardens

SUNDAY 31
- 19 4 Brendon View
- 36 The Cottage
- 48 Emmaus House
- 77 Kilver Court
- 78 Kingsdon Nursery Garden
- 84 Lower Severalls
- 88 Marshfield Gardens
- 94 Orchard Wyndham
- 122 Vellacott

June

Open most days except Sat
- 72 Homewood Park Hotel

TUESDAY 2
- 68 Hestercombe Gardens

THURSDAY 4
- 6 Ash Cottage
- 54 1 Fernlea Gardens (Afternoon & Evening)
- 74 Jasmine Cottage
- 119 Triscombe Nurseries
- 123 Watcombe

SATURDAY 6
- 10 Barrow Castle
- 49 14 Eskdale Close
- 59 190 Goldcroft
- 87 Maple House

SUNDAY 7
- 10 Barrow Castle
- 19 4 Brendon View
- 33 Congresbury Gardens
- 58 Gardd Owen
- 59 190 Goldcroft
- 82 The Lintels
- 87 Maple House
- 89 Milton Lodge
- 99 Roadmenders Cottage
- 109 Stanton Court Nursing Home
- 115 Sunnyside Cottage
- 122 Vellacott
- 131 The Wycke

MONDAY 8
- 59 190 Goldcroft (Evening)

TUESDAY 9
- 54 1 Fernlea Gardens (Afternoon & Evening)

WEDNESDAY 10
- 102 Self Realization Meditation Healing Centre Garden

THURSDAY 11
- 6 Ash Cottage
- 74 Jasmine Cottage
- 118 Tranby House

SATURDAY 13
- 22 Brook Farm
- 43 Dyrham Park
- 44 The East Barn
- 129 Westbrook House

SUNDAY 14
- **7** Ashcott Gardens
- **16** Bishop Sutton Gardens
- **22** Brook Farm
- **25** Camers
- **29** Church Farm House
- **39** Crowe Hall
- **43** Dyrham Park
- **44** The East Barn
- **58** Gardd Owen
- **62** Hangeridge Farmhouse
- **84** Lower Severalls
- **97** Penwood Farm
- **106** 3 Southdown
- **124** Wayford Manor
- **127** West Bristol Gardens

WEDNESDAY 17
- **54** 1 Fernlea Gardens

THURSDAY 18
- **21** 1 Bromley Villas (Evening)
- **55** Forest Lodge
- **74** Jasmine Cottage
- **107** Special Plants

FRIDAY 19
- **5** 22 Ambra Vale (Evening)
- **46** East Lambrook Manor Gardens (Evening)

SATURDAY 20
- **5** 22 Ambra Vale (Evening)
- **26** Cedar House

SUNDAY 21
- **13** Beech House
- **26** Cedar House
- **28** Cherry Bolberry Farm
- **29** Church Farm House
- **52** Farndon Thatch
- **58** Gardd Owen
- **66** Henleaze Gardens
- **91** Northfield House
- **92** 35 Old Station Gardens
- **96** 22 Parson Street
- **97** Penwood Farm
- **111** Stogumber Gardens
- **130** 18 Woodgrove Road

MONDAY 22
- **52** Farndon Thatch

THURSDAY 25
- **47** Elworthy Cottage
- **74** Jasmine Cottage
- **122** Vellacott

SATURDAY 27
- **61** Greenmantle
- **114** Stowleys

SUNDAY 28
- **1** Abbey Farm
- **56** 29 Four Acre Avenue
- **58** Gardd Owen
- **61** Greenmantle
- **65** Haydon Lodge Farm
- **93** Olive Cottage
- **96** 22 Parson Street
- **122** Vellacott

MONDAY 29
- **1** Abbey Farm

TUESDAY 30
- **1** Abbey Farm

July

Open most days except Sat
- **72** Homewood Park Hotel

THURSDAY 2
- **74** Jasmine Cottage

SATURDAY 4
- **27** The Chalet

SUNDAY 5
- **30** 9 Church Road
- **32** 45A Combe Park
- **46** East Lambrook Manor Gardens
- **48** Emmaus House
- **53** Fernhill
- **62** Hangeridge Farmhouse
- **70** 25 Hillcrest Road
- **95** 3 Palmer's Way
- **96** 22 Parson Street

MONDAY 6
- **46** East Lambrook Manor Gardens

WEDNESDAY 8
- **53** Fernhill

THURSDAY 9
- **74** Jasmine Cottage
- **118** Tranby House

FRIDAY 10
- **5** 22 Ambra Vale (Evening)

SATURDAY 11
- **5** 22 Ambra Vale (Evening)
- **73** Springdale

SUNDAY 12
- **28** Cherry Bolberry Farm
- **30** 9 Church Road
- **32** 45A Combe Park
- **34** Coombe Gardens
- **40** Daggs Allotments
- **76** 28 Kensington Road
- **89** Milton Lodge
- **92** 35 Old Station Gardens
- **96** 22 Parson Street
- **73** Springdale
- **116** Sutton Hosey Manor
- **130** 18 Woodgrove Road

MONDAY 13
- **73** Springdale
- **132** Yews Farm

TUESDAY 14
- **132** Yews Farm

THURSDAY 16
- **11** Barum
- **47** Elworthy Cottage
- **74** Jasmine Cottage
- **107** Special Plants

SATURDAY 18
- **9** Barrington Court

36 The Cottage
42 Dunster Castle Gardens
85 Lytes Cary Manor
90 Montacute House
117 Tintinhull

SUNDAY 19
- **20** Brent Knoll Gardens
- **29** Church Farm House
- **36** The Cottage
- **76** 28 Kensington Road
- **95** 3 Palmer's Way
- **122** Vellacott
- **125** Wayside
- **128** West Huntspill Gardens

THURSDAY 23
- **11** Barum
- **74** Jasmine Cottage

SATURDAY 25
- **15** Binham Grange Gardens
- **73** Hooper's Holding
- **86** Mallards

SUNDAY 26
- **35** Cothay Manor Gardens
- **38** Cricket House and Gardens
- **73** Hooper's Holding
- **76** 28 Kensington Road
- **86** Mallards

MONDAY 27
- **23** 20 Bubwith Road

TUESDAY 28
- **15** Binham Grange Gardens

THURSDAY 30
- **11** Barum
- **74** Jasmine Cottage

August

Open most days except Sat
- **72** Homewood Park Hotel

SUNDAY 2
- **21** 1 Bromley Villas
- **25** Camers
- **53** Fernhill
- **62** Hangeridge Farmhouse

MONDAY 3
- **23** 20 Bubwith Road

TUESDAY 4
- **54** 1 Fernlea Gardens (Afternoon & Evening)

WEDNESDAY 5
- **53** Fernhill
- **113** Ston Easton Park

THURSDAY 6
- **70** 25 Hillcrest Road
- **74** Jasmine Cottage

FRIDAY 7
- **83** Little Yarford Farmhouse (Evening)

SATURDAY 8
- **83** Little Yarford Farmhouse

SUNDAY 9
83 Little Yarford Farmhouse

MONDAY 10
83 Little Yarford Farmhouse

TUESDAY 11
23 20 Bubwith Road
83 Little Yarford Farmhouse

WEDNESDAY 12
105 Somerfoss

THURSDAY 13
74 Jasmine Cottage

SUNDAY 16
29 Church Farm House
105 Somerfoss
118 Tranby House

MONDAY 17
23 20 Bubwith Road

WEDNESDAY 19
105 Somerfoss

THURSDAY 20
12 Bath Priory Hotel
107 Special Plants

SATURDAY 22
61 Greenmantle

SUNDAY 23
13 Beech House
47 Elworthy Cottage
57 Gants Mill & Garden
61 Greenmantle
77 Kilver Court
105 Somerfoss

MONDAY 24
23 20 Bubwith Road

September

Open most days except Sat
72 Homewood Park Hotel

TUESDAY 1
23 20 Bubwith Road

WEDNESDAY 2
113 Ston Easton Park

THURSDAY 3
47 Elworthy Cottage

MONDAY 7
23 20 Bubwith Road

SUNDAY 13
14 Beechwell House
110 Stoberry Garden
121 University of Bristol Botanic Garden
122 Vellacott

THURSDAY 17
107 Special Plants

SATURDAY 19
84 Lower Severalls

SUNDAY 20
122 Vellacott

SUNDAY 27
38 Cricket House and Gardens

October

MONDAY 5
85 Lytes Cary Manor

THURSDAY 15
107 Special Plants

SUNDAY 25
119 Triscombe Nurseries

January 2010

SUNDAY 31
100 Rock House

Gardens open to the public

9 Barrington Court
15 Binham Grange Gardens
35 Cothay Manor Gardens
38 Cricket House and Gardens
39 Crowe Hall
42 Dunster Castle Gardens
43 Dyrham Park
46 East Lambrook Manor Gardens
47 Elworthy Cottage
57 Gants Mill & Garden
63 Hanham Court
68 Hestercombe Gardens
77 Kilver Court
84 Lower Severalls
85 Lytes Cary Manor
89 Milton Lodge
90 Montacute House
98 Prior Park Landscape Garden
102 Self Realization Meditation Healing Centre Garden
104 Sherborne Garden
107 Special Plants
113 Ston Easton Park
117 Tintinhull
121 University of Bristol Botanic Garden

By appointment only

2 Algars Manor
3 Algars Mill
8 Badgers' Acre
17 Bourne House
24 Cadwell Hill Barn
41 Darkey Pang Tso Gang
45 East End Farm
60 16 Gordano Gardens
67 Henley Mill
69 Hill Lodge
75 Jens Gardyn
79 Kites Croft
80 Knoll Cottage
81 Lift The Latch

103 Serridge House
112 Stoke St Mary Gardens
120 Ubley Hill Farm House

Also open by appointment ☎

1 Abbey Farm
4 Aller Farmhouse
11 Barum
14 Beechwell House
18 1 Braggchurch
20 Copse Hall, Brent Knoll Gardens
21 1 Bromley Villas
25 Camers
26 Cedar House
28 Cherry Bolberry Farm
29 Church Farm House
30 9 Church Road
32 45A Combe Park
33 Oakside, Congresbury Gardens
33 Yeo Meads, Congresbury Gardens
36 The Cottage
53 Fernhill
54 1 Fernlea Gardens
55 Forest Lodge
58 Gardd Owen
59 190 Goldcroft
61 Greenmantle
62 Hangeridge Farmhouse
73 Hooper's Holding
74 Jasmine Cottage
78 Kingsdon Nursery Garden
83 Little Yarford Farmhouse
91 Northfield House
92 35 Old Station Gardens
93 Olive Cottage
95 3 Palmer's Way
96 22 Parson Street
97 Penwood Farm
99 Roadmenders Cottage
100 Rock House
101 Saltford Farm Barn
105 Somerfoss
110 Stoberry Garden
122 Vellacott
123 Watcombe
124 Wayford Manor
126 Wellfield Barn
127 4 Haytor Park, West Bristol Gardens
127 18 Queens Gate, West Bristol Gardens
129 Westbrook House
132 Yews Farm

The Gardens

① ABBEY FARM
Montacute TA15 6UA. Mr & Mrs G Jenkins, 01935 823572, abbeygj@dsl.pipex.com. *4m from Yeovil. Follow A3088, take slip rd to Montacute, turn L at T-junction into village. Turn R between Church & King's Arms (no through rd).* Home-made teas. **Adm £3.50, chd free. Sun 28, Mon 29, Tue 30 June (2-5.30). Visitors also welcome by appt.**
2½ acres of mainly walled gardens on sloping site, provide the setting for Cluniac medieval Priory gatehouse. Interesting plants incl roses, shrubs, grasses, clematis. Herbaceous borders, white garden, gravel garden. Small arboretum. Pond for wildlife - frogs, newts, dragonflies. Fine mulberry, walnut and monkey puzzle trees. Seats for resting. No wheelchair access in gravel garden or white garden. Steep slope.
  🚻 ⊕ ☕ ☎

Small town garden with romantic feel . . .

② ALGARS MANOR
Station Road, Iron Acton BS37 9TB. Dr & Mrs J M Naish, 01454 228372, johnnaish@msn.com. *9m N of Bristol. 3m W of Yate/Chipping Sodbury. Turn S off Iron Acton bypass B4059, past village green, 200yds, then over level Xing (Station Rd).* **Visitors welcome by appt for entrance to both Algars Manor & Algars Mill gardens, groups & garden clubs particularly welcome. Combined adm £4, chd free.**
2 acres of woodland garden beside R Frome, mill stream, native plants mixed with collections of 60 magnolias and 70 camellias, eucalyptus and other unusual trees and shrubs. Mar/Apr camellias, magnolias; Apr/May/June rhododendrons, azaleas; Oct autumn colours. Limited wheelchair access, gravel paths, some steep slopes.
  ☎

③ ALGARS MILL
Station Road, Iron Acton BS37 9TD. Mr & Mrs John Wright, 01454 228373, marilyn@algarsmill.plus.com. *9m N of Bristol. 3m W of*

Yate/Chipping Sodbury. (For directions see Algars Manor). **Visitors welcome by appt (see Algars Manor). Combined adm £4, chd free.**
2-acre woodland garden bisected by R Frome; spring bulbs, shrubs; very early spring feature (Feb-Mar) of wild Newent daffodils. 300-400yr-old mill house (not open) through which millrace still runs.
  & ☎

④ ALLER FARMHOUSE
nr Williton TA4 4LY. Mr & Mrs Richard Chandler, 01984 633702. *7m E of Minehead, 1m S of Williton. From A358 (½ m S of Williton) opp garage, through Sampford Brett, then Capton; curve R, down hill to Aller Fat bottom.* Home-made teas. **Adm £3, chd free. Sun 24 May (2-5.30). Visitors also welcome by appt April/May/June, max 25, no coaches.**
2-3 acres. Hot, dry, sunny, S-facing, surrounded by pink stone walls and sub-divided into 5 separate compartments by same. 'Cliff Garden' is old 3-sided quarry. Old magnolias, figs, Judas, etc; newer acacias; many unusual and/or tender plants incl eremurus in variety, cantua and protea. The garden is now 16yrs old. Featured in 'Exmoor Magazine'. Easy access only to cliff garden and lower garden, i.e. 2 out of 5 compartments.
  🚻 ⊕ ☕ ☎

⑤ NEW 22 AMBRA VALE
Clifton Wood, Bristol BS8 4RW. Joyce Poole. *Off A4 Hotwells Rd nr Holy Trinity Church. Very limited parking. Entrance in Ambrose Rd next to Ambrose Villas.* **Evening Openings £3.50, chd free, wine, Fris, Sats 19, 20 June; 10, 11 July (6-9).**
Part-walled small town garden with romantic feel. Informal planting incl grasses, ferns, exotics, fig and vine. Plenty of hidden corners for restive contemplation with a glass of wine.
  🚻

⑥ NEW ASH COTTAGE
Shurton, Bridgwater TA5 1QF. Barbara & Peter Oates. *8m W of Bridgwater. From A39 nr Holford, follow signs to Stogursey then to Shurton. From A39 at Cannington*

follow signs to Hinkley Point then Shurton. Home-made teas. **Adm £3.50, chd free. Thurs 4, 11 June (2-5.30).**
Tranquil cottage garden in rural area, approx ⅔ acre, wrapping around 3 sides of early C16 cottage (not open). Colour-themed borders and flowerbeds, with raised 40ft border reached by steps from either end. Natural stream with planted banks runs through garden. Children must be supervised at all times. Some gravel paths.
  & 🚻 ⊕ ☕

Group opening

⑦ ASHCOTT GARDENS
TA7 9QB. *3m W of Street on A39. Turn opp Ashcott Inn into Middle St. At T-junction turn R to car park at village hall.* Home-made teas. **Combined adm £5, chd free. Sun 14 June (2-5.30).**
A pleasant and friendly village situated in the Polden Hills. Many activities take place each week in Ashcott, from short mat bowls to an art group. We look forward to welcoming visitors to our NGS Open Gardens.
  🚻 ⊕ ☕

CHERRY ORCHARD
17 Chapel Hill. Geoff & Sue Wilton
Wildlife-friendly garden, various perennials/shrubs. Archway with stone and gravel paths. Lawns, patio area, tubs incl geraniums, fuchsias. Lily/fish pond, waterfall, vegetable plot, several fruits. Majestic Bramley tree sheltering rear of property.
  🚻

HOLLY TREE COTTAGE
Chapel Hill. Robin & Denise Wale
Quiet garden, set in middle of village, with peaceful combination of new and mature planting.
  &

NEW 5 KINGS LANE
Pam Burge
Well-established garden. Lawns, herbaceous borders, shrubs, trees and tubs. Magnificent views, facing South over fields and hills.
  & 🚻

MANOR HOUSE
11 Middle Street. Peter & Daphne Willis

1/4-acre garden with mixed shrub and herbaceous planting, small pond and bog areas with some hardy and tender exotics. Water feature and gravel garden planted with grasses. Pergola divides ornamental areas from vegetable and fruit garden, grown on raised beds.

22 MIDDLE STREET
Mary & David Adkins

1/2-acre garden developed over past 8yrs. Bank, heathers, rockery plants, ground cover. Waterfall tumbling down into pond. Long herbaceous border, rose walk, shady area, vegetable garden, wild area with trees and shrubs. Gravel entrance.

MILLGREEN
3 Station Road. Ruth & Gus Wans

1 acre reclaimed from a field in the last 16yrs. Predominance of shrub borders, incl perennial planting and rose beds. Large areas of grass, small pond. Productive vegetable garden in raised beds and large polytunnel. Varied selection of trees.

TREMERRYN
Middle Street. Mr & Mrs Hemmings

Small but colourful garden. One steep slope.

8 BADGERS' ACRE
New Road, Stone Allerton BS26 2NW. Lucy Hetherington & Jim Mathers, 01934 713159. *3m SW of Cheddar. Please call for directions.* Adm £2.50, chd free. Visitors welcome by appt 1 April to 31 Aug incl.
1-acre garden. Colour-themed mixed shrub and herbaceous borders. Secret Walk with shade-loving plants. Pond and colourful rockery. Semi-circular tulip and allium bed surrounded by box hedge and pergola with climbing roses, clematis and passionflower. Vegetable potager with raised brick beds and pergola draped in rambling roses and clematis.

9 ◆ BARRINGTON COURT
Ilminster TA19 0NQ. The National Trust, 01460 241938, barringtoncourt@nationaltrust.org.uk. *5m NE of Ilminster. In Barrington village on B3168.* Adm £8.60, chd £3.70, family £20.70. Mar to Oct daily (not Weds) (11-5.30, last adm 5). For NGS: Sat 18 July (11-5.30).
Well known garden constructed in 1920 by Col Arthur Lyle from derelict farmland (the C19 cattle stalls still exist). Gertrude Jekyll suggested planting schemes for the layout. Paved paths with walled rose and iris, white and lily gardens, large kitchen garden.

10 NEW BARROW CASTLE
Rush Hill, Bath BA2 2QR. Peter Hawkins, www.barrowcastle.co.uk. *3m SW of Bath. 2.3m from A4 Globe Roundabout on A3062 (Rush Hill). 1/2 m beyond Hilliers garden centre on R.* Home-made teas, wine. Adm £3.50, chd free. Sat 6, Sun 7 June (2-6).
Victorian garden set in 37 acres of fields with commanding views towards the Mendips, Bristol and Wales. Incl 2/3 acre of walled garden, large enneagram herb garden, orchard, terraced lawns, woodlands and animals (goats, cows, horses, hens, guinea fowl, fish). Garden incl Woodland Trust's Sirius Wood, one of the Trafalgar Woods opened in 2005. Steep slopes.

11 BARUM
50 Edward Road, Clevedon BS21 7DT. Marian & Roger Peacock, 01275 341584, barum@blueyonder.co.uk, www.barum.pwp.blueyonder.co.uk. *12m W of Bristol. M5 J20, follow signs to pier, continue N, past Walton Park Hotel, turn R at St Mary's Church. Up Channel Rd, over Xrds, turn L into Edward Rd at top.* Adm £2.50, chd free. Thurs 16, 23, 30 July (2-5). Visitors also welcome by appt for groups of 10+.
Informal 1/3 acre plantsman's garden, reclaimed by the owners from years of neglect. Now crammed with shrubs and perennials from around the world, incl tender and exotic species using the clement coastal climate and well-drained soil. The vegetable patch uses a no-tread bedding system growing several tender crops.

12 BATH PRIORY HOTEL
Weston Road, Bath BA1 2XT. Jane Moore, Head Gardener. *Close to centre of Bath. From Bath centre take Upper Bristol Rd, turn R at end of Victoria Park & L into Weston Rd.* Home-made teas. Adm £2.50, chd free. Tues 21 Apr; Thur 20 Aug (2-5).
3-acre walled garden. Main garden has croquet lawn, herbaceous borders and dell with snowdrops and spring bulbs in April. Adjoining garden has summer meadow and woodland borders with specimen trees. Formal pool surrounded by roses leads to stone gazebo overlooking the vegetable garden which supplies the restaurant. Late summer colour August.

Victorian garden set in 37 acres of fields . . .

13 BEECH HOUSE
Yate Road, Iron Acton BS37 9XX. John & Hazel Williams. *9m N of Bristol, 3m W of Yate. From A432, Badminton Rd, turn into B4059 - Stover Rd. Garden opp entrance to Beeches Industrial Estate. From B4059, Iron Acton bypass exit at roundabout for Yate Station.* Cream teas. Adm £3, chd free. Suns 21 June; 23 Aug (1-5).
Well laid-out garden of approx 1 acre, maturing since 1980. Many level paths intertwine between borders of mixed shrubs, roses, herbaceous and rockery areas. Fish pond, mini arboretum, kitchen garden, orchard with chickens, fernery, productive greenhouse adapted from Victorian pigsty, 1/2 m walk along R Frome. Some gravel paths. R walk not accessible by wheelchair users.

14 BEECHWELL HOUSE
51 Goose Green, Yate BS37 5BL. Tim Wilmot, 07768 443318, www.beechwell.com. *1m NE of Bristol. From centre of Yate (Shopping & Leisure Centre) or Station Rd B4060, turn N onto Church Rd. After 1/2 m turn L onto Greenways Rd then immed R onto continuation of Church Rd. Goose Green starts after 200yds. After 100yds take R-fork, garden 100yds on L.* Cream teas & light refreshments. Adm £3, chd free. Sun 13 Sept (1-6). Visitors also welcome by appt for groups of 10+.

Enclosed, level, subtropical garden created over last 19yrs and filled with exotic planting, incl palms (over 12 varieties), tree ferns, yuccas, agaves and succulent bed, phormiums, bamboos, bananas, aroids and other 'architectural planting'. Wildlife pond and koi pond. C16 40ft deep well. Rare plant raffle every hour.

A welcome awaits you in the 6 gardens . . .

15 ◆ BINHAM GRANGE GARDENS
Old Cleeve, Minehead TA24 6HX. Stewart & Marie Thomas, 01984 640056, www.binhamgrange.co.uk. *4m E of Dunster. Take A39 for Minehead, R at Xrds after Washford to Blue Anchor, past Old Cleeve, garden on L.* **Adm £3, chd free. Open daily except Feb. For NGS: Sat 25, Tues 28 July (2-6).**
Relatively new garden set in 300 acres of farmed Somerset countryside with extensive views. Parterre garden to the front of house, Italian-style garden, pergola, island beds, cutting and vegetable garden. Plants for the senses working with the seasons. Gravel paths.

Group opening

16 BISHOP SUTTON GARDENS
Avon BS39 5UP. *10m W of Bath. Village on A368 Bath to Weston-super-Mare, nr Chew Valley Lake. Turn off main rd at Red Lion PH, into Sutton Hill Rd. Park in rd. 2 gardens on A368.* Home-made teas, wine. **Combined adm £4.50, chd free. Sun 14 June (2-6).**
A welcome awaits you in the 6 gardens. Whether you aspire to large or small scale gardening, examples can be found in the village. Delicious cream teas - even a glass of wine - to fortify you en route. Something for everyone from plant varieties and different planting schemes to back-saving ideas. Wild areas, secret areas, gardening on a spoil heap, creative hard landscaping softened by time, statues, simple-to-make water feature ideas - it is all here!

CEDAR VALE
Sutton Hill Road. Mr & Mrs D Thompson
1/4 -acre garden with bed of heathers and conifers, variety of herbaceous plants and peat bed containing rhododendrons and azaleas. Screened vegetable area, waterfall, 2 ponds with bog plants and various grasses. Pergola. Rose beds in front.

NEW 1 CHURCH COTTAGE
Church Lane. Sharon Gillen
Variety of many pots, containers of various colourful blooms and plump filled hanging baskets.

DENBY
Church Lane. Malcolm Hunt
Created on spoil heap of colliery waste and shale. Dramatic water feature and stunning gazebo. Extensively planted and designed for minimum maintenance.

NEW PEMBROKE
3 Northwick Gardens. David & Yvonne Young
Pretty, medium-sized cottage garden with yr-round interest. Ornamental wildlife pond with varied water planting. Secluded sitting area and gazebo, collection of hostas, roses, clematis and ornamental grasses. Patio area containing tubs and hanging baskets.

TRUFFLES
Church Lane. Heather Clewett
1 1/2 acres. Formal and semi-natural. Little secret valley and small stream, amphitheatre, 2 wildlife ponds, wild flower meadow. New 1/4 -acre kitchen garden with 21x4ft waist-high oak beam beds. Some gravel and grass paths, quite steep tarmac drive.

NEW 42 WOODCROFT
Ann & Mervyn Williams. *On A368 past Butchers Arms PH on R, car parking opp house*
Good average-sized garden. Mixed planting, small vegetable area with container planting and greenhouse. Interesting focal points with water features. Rose arch with cottage-style planting at front.

17 BOURNE HOUSE
Bourne Lane, Burrington BS40 7AF. Mr & Mrs C Thomas, 01761 462494, bourne.thomas@tiscali.co.uk. *12m S of Bristol. N of Burrington. Turn off A38 signed Blagdon-Burrington; 2nd turning L.* Home-made teas. **Adm £3.50, chd free. Visitors welcome by appt, max 24, no coaches.**
5 acres, 2 paddocks. Stream with waterfalls and lily pond; pergola; mature trees and shrubs. Mixed borders; large area hardy cyclamen and rose bed. Spring bulbs.

18 1 BRAGGCHURCH
93 Hendford Hill, Yeovil BA20 2RE. Veronica Sartin, 01935 473841/471508. *Walking distance of Yeovil centre. Approaching Yeovil on A30 from The Quicksilver Mail PH roundabout, go halfway down Hendford Hill, 1st driveway on R. Roadside parking at Southwoods (next R down hill) and Public Car Park at bottom of Hendford Hill.* Home-made teas. **Adm £3, chd free. Fri 1, Sat 2, Sun 3 May (2-6). Visitors also welcome by appt.**
Old garden of undulating lawns and mature trees evolving, since May 2002, to semi-wild, nature-friendly, woodland garden with a few surprises within the new planting. Tree house, swing, dancing figures, anderson shelter, pond, willow weaving, retreat.

19 4 BRENDON VIEW
Crowcombe TA4 4AG. Chris Hayes. *9m NW of Taunton. Off A358 signed Crowcombe. Garden opp turning for Hagleys Green.* **Adm £2, chd free. Suns 31 May; 7 June (2-5.30).**
Plantsman's garden, S-facing with views of the Quantock Hills. Subtropical planting, mixed herbaceous borders. Vegetables. Over 600 species of cacti and other succulents in 2 greenhouses, many in flower in May & June.

Group opening

20 BRENT KNOLL GARDENS
TA9 4DF. *2m N of Highbridge. Off A38 & M5 J22.* Cream teas. **Combined adm £5, chd free. Sun 19 July (2-6).**
The distinctive hill of Brent Knoll, an iron age hill fort, is well worth climbing 449ft for the 360 degree view of the surrounding hills, including Glastonbury

Tor and 'levels'. The lovely C13 church is renowned for its bench ends.

ANVIL COTTAGE
Brent Street. Jean Owen
Many ideas for a small garden.

COPSE HALL
Mrs S Boss & Mr A J Hill, 01278 760301, susan.boss@gmail.com.
Visitors also welcome by appt.
The S-facing Edwardian house (not open) on the lower slopes of the Knoll sits above 3 terraces with borders and lawns below. Ha-ha, wild area and pond with Great Crested newts, crinkle crankle walled kitchen garden with heritage vegetables, kiwi fruit, feijoas and wall-trained fruit. New track (Monkey Rd) up hill beyond house with new planting of trees and shrubs. Partial wheelchair access.

NEW DOLPHIN COTTAGE
Church Lane. Colin Townsend
Rejuvenated old garden to Victorian cottage.

Gently winding paths lead you to a surprise round every corner . . .

21 1 BROMLEY VILLAS
Bromley Road, Stanton Drew BS39 4DE. Mr & Mrs S Whittle, 01275 331311, judith.chubb.rills@qfruit.co.uk. 7m S of Bristol. From A37 Chelwood roundabout take A368 towards Chew Valley Lake. 2nd turning on R. Follow car park signs. Park only in designated car park. Strictly no parking on Bromley Rd. Home-made teas. **Adm £3, chd free.** Sun 2 Aug (2-6). **Evening Opening £4.50,** wine, Thur 18 June (6-9). Visitors also welcome by appt June/July/Aug.
A lawnmower's nightmare! A garden maturing nicely, just like its owners. Rose arches, rills, fruit and figs, sculptured mounds, fire pit, monolith and menagerie. Just under an acre of interesting things to see.

22 NEW BROOK FARM
Lower Tockington Rd, Tockington BS32 4LE. Dr & Mrs James Mulvein. 2m NW of Almondsbury. Off A38, N of Almondsbury, down Fernhill, signed Olveston and Tockington. Garden on R after 30mph sign at entrance to Tockington. Parking available. Home-made teas. **Combined adm £3, chd free.** Sat 13, Sun 14 June (2-5.30). Opening with **The East Barn.**
1/2 -acre garden beside Tockington Mill, partially walled, with herbaceous borders, roses, shrubs and trees. Patio area beside small pond and bog garden.

23 NEW 20 BUBWITH ROAD
Chard TA20 2BN. Paul & Barbara Blackburn. A30 or A358 to Chard. At T-lights surrounded by 2 churches, school and garage, take Axminster rd (A358), L at mini R-about into Milfield Rd, next R. Garden on L before 2nd R turn. From Axminster, pass police stn on L before mini R-about, R into Milfield Rd. **Adm £2, chd free.** Mon 27 July; Mon 3, Tue 11, Mons 17, 24 Aug; Tue 1, Mon 7 Sept (11-4).
Surprising oasis for a small young garden just 4 yrs old yet full of perennials, shrubs, herbaceous plants, trees, lawn area, deck, arches and containered acers. To the rear, gently winding paths lead you to a surprise round every corner. At front, unusual parking incorporated into cottage-style planting.

24 CADWELL HILL BARN
West Littleton SN14 8JE. John & Elizabeth Edwards, 01225 891122. 8m N of Bath. 1/2 m on Marshfield side of W Littleton. **Adm £2, chd free.** Visitors welcome by appt July only. Interestingly-designed garden. Pleached lime walk, Italianate garden with several small enclosures.

25 CAMERS
Old Sodbury BS37 6RG. Mr & Mrs A G Denman, 01454 322430, dorothydenman@camers.org. 2m E of Chipping Sodbury. Entrance in Chapel Lane off A432 at Dog Inn.

Home-made teas. **Adm £4, chd free.** Suns 3 May; 14 June; 2 Aug (2-5.30). Visitors also welcome by appt Feb to Oct for groups of 15+.
Elizabethan farmhouse (not open) set in 4 acres of garden and young woodland with spectacular views over Severn Vale. Garden full of surprises divided into range of formal and informal areas planted with very wide range of species to provide yr-round interest. Parterre, topiary, Japanese garden, bog shade and prairie areas, waterfalls, white and hot gardens, woodland walks. Some steep slopes.

CASTLE HILL
See Devon.

26 CEDAR HOUSE
High Street, Wrington BS40 5QD. Jenny Denny, 01934 863375, hamishdenny@wrington.eclipse.co. uk. 12m S of Bristol on A38. Follow sign for Wrington after airport & on reaching village, garage on L. T-junction turn R up hill. House on L. Parking in village (or at house by arrangement). Cream teas. **Adm £3, chd free.** Sat 20, Sun 21 June (11-5). Visitors also welcome by appt June/July.
Mature formal garden with specimen trees, lawns, walled herbaceous borders, rose beds, mixed borders, hosta and hydrangea beds. Wildflower orchard, pond fed by warm springs and sculpture park. Exhibition of art, ceramics and sculpture. Flower and plant sale.

27 THE CHALET
52 Charlton Road, Midsomer Norton BA3 4AH. Sheila & Chris Jones. 1/2 m from centre of Midsomer Norton. Just off A367. Past the White Post Inn towards Radstock, turn L immed after next mini R-about into Charlton Rd. Disabled parking only at house. Home-made teas. **Adm £2, chd free (share to HCPT The Pilgrimage Trust/N Somerset Jumbulance Group).** Sat 4 July (2-5).
Covering 1 acre, garden contains lots of interest with plenty of lawns, mixed borders, vegetable garden and 80yr-old rotating cedar shingle summerhouse. Topiary is slowly becoming a feature. A quiet, relaxing garden next to a busy rd, it is shared by Orchard Lodge (52a), the next generation of the family.

28 CHERRY BOLBERRY FARM

Furge Lane, Henstridge BA8 0RN.
Mrs Jenny Raymond, 01936 364321,
marysmclean@btinternet.com. *6m E
of Sherborne. In centre of Henstridge,
turn R at small Xrds signed Furge
Lane. Continue straight on to farm.*
Home-made teas. **Combined adm
£3, chd free. Suns 21 June; 12 July
(2-6). Combined with 35 Old
Station Gardens.** Visitors also
welcome by appt June/July.
30 yr-old, owner-designed 1-acre
garden planted for yr-round interest
with wildlife in mind. Colour-themed
island beds, shrub and herbaceous
borders, unusual perennials, old roses
and specimen trees. Vegetable and
flower cutting garden, greenhouses,
nature ponds. Wonderful extensive
views.

  ♿ ✿ 🛏 ☕ ☎

29 CHURCH FARM HOUSE

Turners Court Lane, Binegar
BA3 4UA. Susan & Tony Griffin,
01749 841628,
smgriffin@beanacrebarn.co.uk. *4m
NE of Wells. On A37 Binegar (Gurney
Slade), at George Inn, follow sign to
Binegar. 1m past PH and church to
Xrds at Binegar Green, turn R,
300metres, turn R. From Wells B3139,
4m turn R signed Binegar. 1m to Xrds.
Turn L, 300metres turn R.* **Adm £3,
chd free. Suns 14, 21 June; 19 July;
16 Aug (11-5).** Visitors also welcome
by appt May to Aug incl.
See what can be achieved on top of
the Mendips! Walled garden with
contemporary cottage garden style
planting. Colour wheel design
continues to be fine-tuned. Growth of
'the smallest prairie in the west' is
amazing! Opening dates reflect colour
and interest throughout seasons.
Seating to enjoy views of garden,
church and hills beyond. Featured in
local press. Gravel forecourt, 2 shallow
steps.

  ♿ ✖ ✿ 🛏 ☎

Pond and waterfall surrounded by grasses . . .

30 NEW 9 CHURCH ROAD

Weston BA1 4BT. Jane &
Bernard Rymer, 01225 427377.
*2m NW of city centre. Follow signs
for Royal United Hospital in
Weston. Continue N for 1/4 m, R
just before zebra crossing into
Weston High St, L at war
memorial. Next L just before
Lucklands Rd/Old Crown PH. No
parking in Church Rd.* Home-made
teas & light refreshments.
**Combined adm £3.50, chd free.
Suns 5, 12 July (1-5). Combined
with 45A Combe Park.** Visitors
also welcome by appt for
individuals or groups.
1/3 -acre informal garden tucked
away in city suburb with colour-
themed shrubs and herbaceous
plants, ferns and annual planting
which can be viewed from
numerous sitting areas and paths
meandering through the borders.
Recently-planted walled garden
with pond and waterfall surrounded
by grasses and mixed planting with
adjacent rose garden and alpine
bed.

  ♿ ✿ ☕ ☎

Group opening

31 COLEY COURT & ROSE COTTAGE

Smithams Hill, East Harptree
BS40 6BY. Home-made teas at Rose
Cottage, cream teas at New Manor
Farm Shop, N Widcombe. **Combined
adm £4, chd free. Sun 5 Apr (2-5).**

  ✖ ☕

COLEY COURT
Coley. Mrs M J Hill. *1m E of East
Harptree. From A39 at Chewton
Mendip take B3114 for 2m. Well
before E Harptree turn R at sign
Coley and Hinton Blewett*
Early Jacobean house (not open).
1-acre garden, stone walls, spring
bulbs; 1-acre old mixed orchard.

  ✖ ✿

ROSE COTTAGE
Smithams Hill. Bev & Jenny
Cruse. *From B3114 turn into High
St in East Harptree. L at Clock
Tower and immed R into Middle St,
continue up hill for 1m. From
B3134 take East Harptree turning
opp Castle of Comfort, continue for
1 1/2 m. Car parking in field opp
cottage*
1-acre hillside cottage garden with
panoramic views over the Chew

Valley. Garden is carpeted with
primroses, spring bulbs and
hellebores and is bordered by
stream and established mixed
hedges. Wildlife area and pond in
field next to car park.

  ✖

32 45A COMBE PARK

Weston, Bath BA1 3NS. Stephen
Brook, 01225 428288. *1 1/2 m W of city
centre. Follow signs for Royal United
Hospital in Weston. Garden 10metres
from main hospital entrance.*
**Combined adm £3.50, chd free.
Suns 5, 12 July (1-5). Combined with
9 Church Road.** Visitors also
welcome by appt for individuals or
groups, no coaches.
Walled town garden creatively
landscaped on 3 levels with raised
borders of colour-schemed perennials.
Grasses, phormiums, acers and vine-
covered pergola lead to fernery with
large tree ferns. Pond with wooden
walkway, small central lawn and
secluded seating areas. Featured in
'Amateur Gardening'. Some steps.

  ✖ ✿ ☎

Group opening

33 CONGRESBURY GARDENS

BS49 5EX. *8m N of Weston-super-
Mare. 13m S of Bristol on A370. At
T-lights in Congresbury head E signed
Churchill - Cheddar. From A38, take
B3133 to Congresbury.* Morning
coffee/tea/cakes at Fernbank/Yeo
Meads; afternoon tea/cakes at
Moorway/Middlecombe Nurseries.
**Combined adm £5, chd free.
Sun 7 June (10.30-5).**

  ♿ ✖ ✿ ☕

FERNBANK
High Street. Simon & Julia Thyer.
*100yds along High St from Ship &
Castle*
Informal garden of approx 1/3 acre,
tucked away behind Victorian
house (not open). Patio with
hundreds of potted plants, jungle-
like conservatory, kitchen garden
with picturesque greenhouse and
potting shed, 2 ponds, mature
copper beech, small
Mediterranean courtyard. Narrow
paths. Free range bantams.

  ✖

MIDDLECOMBE NURSERY
Wrington Rd. Nigel J North,
www.middlecombenursery.
co.uk. *On the edge of*

Congresbury, on the Bristol side,
turn to Wrington along the
Wrington Rd off the A370 Weston
to Bristol rd. Garden 200yds on L
Series of gardens, lovely country
setting, woods bordering 3-acre
nursery site. Different styles and
features, excellent shrub borders
and beds in sweeping lawn area
alongside delightful fish pond.
Surrounding patio gardens and
water features ensure an enjoyable
visit. Dogs on leads. Nigel North is
a regular contributor to gardening
programmes on BBC Radio Bristol.

NEW MOORWAY
30 The Causeway. Brian & Julie
Gosling. *1/3-acre well-established*
flower garden and family sized
vegetable plot with mature trees,
overlooking village cricket field.
Wheelchair access to flower
garden only.

OAKSIDE
Paul Laws, 01934 832052.
200yds along High St from Ship &
Castle. **Visitors also welcome by**
appt.
25m x 25m. Tropical garden
packed with unusual plants.
Bananas, elephant ears, daturas,
cannas, bamboo, agaves, konjac
acers. Various sitting areas,
decking, pergolas, water features,
doves.

3 SILVER MEAD
Terry & Geraldine Holden. *Approx*
1/2 m along High St from Ship &
Castle, R into Silver St, 1st L into
Silver Mead
Approx 1/3 acre manicured
shrub/herbaceous borders and
trees developed over past 22yrs
from farmland. Two 'hot'
Mediterranean-type patios, water
features, pots, lavender walk.
Organic vegetable plot.
Uninterrupted views of Mendips.
Short steep slope to main part of
garden.

YEO MEADS
Debbie Fortune & Mark
Hayward, 01934 832904,
mark.hayward@sky.com. 150yds
along High St from Ship & Castle
PH on L. **Visitors also welcome**
by appt.
11/4 acres, formally laid out in C17
incl 350yr-old Cedar of Lebanon

tree which fell in 2007 but survives
as a feature, Atlas Blue cedar,
300+ yr-old oak, 150 yr-old lime,
many more with large growths of
mistletoe. Lead-lined pond with rill
plus Victorian pond. Topiarised
golden cypresses set off by darker
copper beech behind, octagonal
thatched summerhouse. Vegetable
garden, orchard, herbaceous
borders, rockeries. Featured on
BBC Points West.

Group opening

34 COOMBE GARDENS
TA2 8RE. *6m S of Bridgwater, 4m N of*
Taunton. Off A38, well signed. Ample
parking. Cream teas. **Combined adm**
£3, chd free. Sun 12 July (2-6).
Two gardens in a hamlet.

COOMBE QUARRY
West Monkton. Miss Patricia
Davies-Gilbert
Cottage garden with quarry walk.
Roses and other shrubs,
vegetables and animals. Partial
wheelchair access, quarry walk
inaccessable.

COOMBE WATER
Coombe. Mr & Mrs M K Paul
Cottage garden with stream and
pond in a small valley.

35 ◆ COTHAY MANOR
GARDENS
Greenham, nr Wellington TA21 0JR.
Mr & Mrs Alastair Robb, 01823
672283, www.cothaymanor.co.uk.
5m SW of Wellington. At M5 J26 or 27
take direction Exeter or Wellington
respectively. Approx 4m take direction
Greenham. After 1m follow tourist
signs. In lane keep always L. Car park
1m. Brown signs on A38 approx 4m W
of Greenham. **Adm £5.30, chd £2.50.**
Weds, Thurs, Suns, Easter to Sept
incl (11-6). For NGS: Sun 26 July (2-6).
Few gardens are as evocatively
romantic as Cothay. Laid out in 1920s
and replanted in 1990s within the
original framework, Cothay
encompasses a rare blend of old and
new. Plantsman's paradise set in 12
acres of magical gardens. Gravel
paths.

Topiarised golden cypresses set off by darker copper beech behind . . .

36 THE COTTAGE
Water Street, Barrington TA19 0JR.
Maureen & Tony Russell, 01460
52012. *5m NE of Ilminster. In*
Barrington village on B3168, approx
100yds from entrance to Barrington
Court. **Adm £1.50, chd free. Sats,**
Suns 30, 31 May; 18, 19 July (1-5).
Also open Barrington Court 18 July.
Visitors also welcome by appt.
Small cottage garden with
summerhouse, ponds and vegetable
garden.

37 COURT HOUSE
East Quantoxhead TA5 1EJ. Lady
Luttrell. *12m W of Bridgwater. Off*
A39; house at end of village past duck
pond. Home-made teas. **Adm £4, chd**
free. Sun 10 May (2-5).
Lovely 5-acre garden; trees, shrubs,
many rare and tender; herbaceous and
3-acre woodland garden. Views to sea
and Quantocks.

38 NEW CRICKET HOUSE
AND GARDENS
Nr Chard TA20 4DD. Warner
Leisure Hotels, 01460 30111,
www.warnerleisurehotels.co.uk.
3m E of Chard. On A303, Cricket
St Thomas Wildlife Park signed
from M3, M4, M5. **Adm £3.50.**
Suns 5 Apr; 26 July; 27 Sept
(10-4).
The grounds were designed by a
student of Capability Brown.
Mixture of mature trees in beautiful
setting along valley next to wildlife
park. Newly-planted rose gardens
and selection of borders. Worth
visiting at any time of yr. Sorry, no
children in house and garden.
Some gravel paths and steep
slopes.

39 ◆ CROWE HALL
Bath BA2 6AR. Mr John Barratt,
01225 310322. *1m SE of Bath. L up
Widcombe Hill, off A36, leaving White
Hart on R. Limited parking.* **Adm £4,
chd £1. For NGS: Suns 5 Apr; 14
June (2-6).**
Large varied garden; fine trees, lawns,
spring bulbs, series of enclosed
gardens cascading down steep
hillside. Italianate terracing and Gothic
Victorian grotto contrast with park-like
upper garden. Dramatic setting, with
spectacular views of Bath. Lovely
walks through the fields along mown
grass paths.

40 DAGGS ALLOTMENTS
High Street, Thornbury BS35 2AW.
Park in free car park off Chapel St.
Cream teas. **Adm £3, chd free. Sun
12 July (2-5).**
Situated in historic town on edge of
Severn Vale. 105 plots, all in cultivation,
many organic, incl vegetables, soft
fruit, herbs and flowers for cutting.
Narrow, steep, grass paths between
plots.

41 ◆ DARKEY PANG TSO GANG
High Street, Oakhill BA3 5BT.
Chrissy & Graham Price, 01749
840795,
solidjelly@darkeypang.org.uk. *3m N
of Shepton Mallet. Off A367 in Oakhill
High St opp converted chapel.* **Adm
£3, chd free. Visitors welcome by
appt May/June.**
1/4 -acre garden creatively designed
and landscaped by owners since
1981. Crammed with trees, shrubs,
herbaceous and climbers, the garden
is an adventure along winding paths
with a lushness of greens and leaf
combinations linking wild and
cultivated areas with grotto, terraces,
pergola, wildlife pond and bog garden
with the recently-discovered cave
being a major feature.
☎

**42 ◆ DUNSTER CASTLE
GARDENS**
Dunster TA24 6SL. The National
Trust, 01643 821314,
www.nationaltrust.org.uk. *3m SE of
Minehead. NT car park approached
direct from A39 Minehead to
Bridgwater rd, nr to A396 turning. Car
park charge to non-NT members.*
Tearooms nearby. **House and garden
adm £8.60, chd £4.20, family £20.50,
garden only adm £4.80, chd £2.20,**

family £11.80. Opening times vary;
please phone or visit website for
details. For NGS: Sat 18 July (11-
4.30).
Hillside woodland garden surrounding
fortified mansion, previously home to
the Luttrell family for 600yrs. Terraced
areas, interlinked by old carriage drives
and paths, feature tender plants.
National Collection of Arbutus
(Strawberry Tree). Fine views over polo
lawns and landscape with C18
features. Gravel paths and steep
slopes.
占 ⋈ ⊛ **NCCPG**

43 ◆ DYRHAM PARK
Bath SN14 8ER. The National Trust,
01179 372501
*12m E of Bristol. 8m N of Bath.
Approached from Bath to Stroud rd
(A46), 2m S of Tormarton interchange
with M4 exit 18.* **House and garden
adm £10.50, chd £5.25, garden only
adm £4.20, chd £2.10. For opening
dates and times, please visit
www.nationaltrust.org.uk/
dyrhampark. For NGS: Sat 13, Sun
14 June (11-5).**
Situated on W side of C17 Mansion
House. Ongoing development plan of
constant change in layout incl
herbaceous borders, yew hedging and
paths flowing to ponds and cascades.
C18 orangery traditionally used for
citrus plants, magnificent views. Steep
slopes in park, cobbles in courtyard.
占 ⋈ ⊛ ☕

> The garden is
> an adventure
> along winding
> paths with a
> lushness of
> greens and leaf
> combinations
> linking wild
> and cultivated
> areas . . .

44 NEW THE EAST BARN
Lower Tockington Rd,
Tockington BS32 4LE. Mr & Mrs
John Crossley. *2m NW of
Almondsbury. Off A38, down
Fernhill signed Olveston &
Tockington. Garden on R on bend
after 30mph sign. Off-street parking
at adjoining property.* Teas at Brook
Farm. **Combined adm £3, chd
free. Sat 13, Sun 14 June (2-
5.30). Opening with Brook Farm.**
1/4 -acre 3 yr-old cottage-style
garden overlooking open fields.
Level site on what was once farm
buildings. Gravel paths.
占 ⋈

45 NEW EAST END FARM
Pitney, Langport TA10 9AL. Mrs
A M Wray, 01458 250598. *Please
telephone for directions.* **Visitors
welcome by appt June only, no
groups.**
Timeless small garden of old roses
in herbaceous borders set
amongst ancient farm buildings.
占 ⋈ ☎

**46 ◆ EAST LAMBROOK MANOR
GARDENS**
East Lambrook TA13 5HH. Mike &
Gail Werkmeister, 01460 240328,
www.eastlambrook.com. *2m N of
South Petherton. Off A303 at South
Petherton. Follow brown East
Lambrook Manor Gardens and flower
signs from A303 or Martock.* **Adm
£3.50, chd free. Open most days
Feb - Oct, phone or visit website for
details. For NGS: Sat 7 Feb; Sun 5,
Mon 6 July (10-5). Evening
Opening Fri 19 June (6-9).**
One of England's best loved privately
owned gardens created by the late
Margery Fish. Her natural gift for
combining old-fashioned and
contemporary plants in a relaxed and
informal manner has created a garden
of immense beauty and charm. Now
Grade I listed, the garden is renowned
as the premier example of the English
cottage gardening style and is noted for
its specialist collections of snowdrops
and hardy geraniums. Snowdrops Feb.
June/July openings art exhibition in
Malthouse Gallery by local watercolour
artist Moish Sokal. Featured on BBC
Gardeners' World and in RHS 'The
Garden' and 'Amateur Gardening'.
Partial wheelchair access only. Narrow
paths and steps.
占 ⋈ ⊛ ☕

Home-made preserves and craft items for sale . . .

47 ◆ **ELWORTHY COTTAGE**
Elworthy, Taunton TA4 3PX. Mike & Jenny Spiller, 01984 656427, www.elworthy-cottage.co.uk. *12m NW of Taunton. On B3188 between Wiveliscombe & Watchet.* **Adm £2.50, chd free. Thurs, Fris, Apr to Aug (10-4). Please phone for other times. For NGS: Mon 13 Apr, Thurs 16 Apr; 21, 28 May; 25 June; 16 July; Sun 23 Aug; Thur 3 Sept. Suns, Mons (2-5), Thurs (10-4).**
1-acre plantsman's garden in tranquil setting. Island beds, scented plants, clematis, unusual perennials and ornamental trees and shrubs to provide yr-round interest. In spring, pulmonarias, hellebores and more than 100 varieties of snowdrops. Planted to encourage birds, bees and butterflies, lots of birdsong. Wild flower areas, decorative vegetable garden, living willow screen. Stone ex privy and pigsty feature. Adjoining nursery.
✕ ⊕

48 **EMMAUS HOUSE**
Clifton Hill, Bristol BS8 1BN. Sisters of La Retraite, www.emmaushouse.org.uk. *From Clifton Downs down to Clifton Village to bottom of Regent St on R. Opp Saville Place at top of Hensmans Hill.* Light refreshments & teas. **Adm £3, chd free. Suns 26 Apr; 31 May; 5 July (11-4).**
1½ acres with Victorian walled kitchen garden, also fruit, formal herb and Zen gardens. Rose and herbaceous borders, lawns, secret garden with summerhouse. Courtyard garden with original stone watercourse. Ponds with fountains and fine views towards Dundry. Recently excavated remains of old coach house in wild garden. Partial wheelchair access only, garden on different levels.
♿ ✕ ⊕ ⊨ ☕

49 **14 ESKDALE CLOSE**
Weston-Super-Mare BS22 8QG. Janet & Adrian Smith. *1½ m E of WSM town centre. J21 M5, 1½ m (B3440) towards WSM town centre. L at chevrons into Corondale Rd, 1st R*

into Garsdale Rd. Park halfway along and take footpath beside no. 37. Home-made teas. **Adm £2,50, chd free. Sat 6 June (2-5.30).**
Interestingly-planned, natural style cottage garden with all-yr interest. Fish pond with seating areas, lawn, patio, rockery with conifers, Heidi playhouse with secrets. Wisteria archway leading to productive vegetable, herb and fruit garden. Home-made preserves and craft items for sale.
♿ ✕ ⊕ ☕

50 **NEW** **ESOTERA**
Foddington nr Babcary TA11 7EL. Andrew & Shirley Harvey. *6m E of Somerton, 6m SW of Castle Cary. Signs to garden off A37 Ilchester to Shepton Mallet and B3153 Somerton to Castle Cary.* Cream teas. **Adm £3, chd free. Sun 24, Mon 25 May (11-5).**
2-acre established informal country garden housing 3 wildlife ponds of various sizes with moorhens and ducks in residence. Large prairie border and others with flourishing shrubs and herbaceous planting. Young wood underplanted with bluebells and meadow walk with shepherd's hut. Mature trees, boxed topiary and new courtyard. Mostly wheelchair access. Children must be supervised near ponds.
♿ ✕ ⊕ ☕

51 **FAIRFIELD**
nr Stogursey TA5 1PU. Lady Gass. *7m E of Williton. 11m W of Bridgwater. From A39 Bridgwater to Minehead rd turn N; garden 1½ m W of Stogursey on Stringston rd.* No coaches. Teas. **Adm £3, chd free. Sun 29 Mar (2-5).**
Woodland garden with bulbs, shrubs and fine trees; paved maze. Views of Quantocks and sea.
♿ ✕ ⊕ ☕

52 **NEW** **FARNDON THATCH**
TA19 9JA. Bob & Jane St John Wright. *3m N of Ilminster. From Ilminster take B3168 to Langport. Through Puckington village, last house on L. No parking at house, directions on arrival.* Home-made teas. **Adm £2.50, chd free. Suns, Mons 24, 25 May; 21, 22 June; Suns (11-5), Mons (2-5).**
C16 thatched cottage (not open) with 1-acre garden in the making.

Outstanding views with fine trees, mixed borders and banks, lawns, formal rose garden, vegetable garden and areas of natural tranquillity.
✕ ⊕ ⊨ ☕

53 **FERNHILL**
nr Wellington TA21 0LU. Peter & Audrey Bowler, 01823 672423, peter@bowler1934.fsnet.co.uk. *3m W of Wellington. On A38, White Ball Hill. Past Beam Bridge Hotel stay on A38 at top of hill, follow signs on L into garden & car park.* Home-made teas. **Adm £2.50, chd free. Sun 5, Wed 1 July; Sun 2, Wed 5 Aug (2-5). Visitors also welcome by appt June/July/Aug for groups of 10+, no coaches in car park.**
Mature wooded garden in approx 2 acres with rose, herbaceous, shrub and mixed borders, all unique in colour and content. Interesting octagonal pergola; alpine and bog garden with waterfalls and pools leading to shady arbour, banks of hydrangeas mid-summer. Fine views over ha-ha to Blackdowns and Mendips. No wheelchair access to water garden.
♿ ✕ ⊕ ☕ ☎

54 **NEW** **1 FERNLEA GARDENS**
Easton-in-Gordano BS20 0JF. Sandy & Dyck Willis, 01275 373957. *5m W of Bristol, 1m E of J19 M5. A397 towards Bristol, L at 1st turning to Easton-in-Gordano/Pill. Past Kings Arms PH, past football field/church hall, R after 100yds.* Cream teas 17 June, teas other days. **Adm £2.50, chd free. Wed 17 June (2-5). Afternoon & Evening Openings Thur 4 June (5-8.30); Tue 9 June (4-9); Tue 4 Aug (5-8.30). Visitors also welcome by appt May/June/July max 15.**
We did it ourselves, we would like to show you how. ¼ -acre garden designed to be low maintenance. Gravel, woodchip, chapel/cloister/brick paving, small grass area. Mature trees, bamboo, heathers, clematis, roses, numerous other shrubs and perennials. 4 ponds, weir, 4ft waterfall, decking, pergolas and many sitting areas. Helpful advice on 'having a go', progress photographs.
♿ ☕ ☎

55 FOREST LODGE
Pen Selwood BA9 8LL. Mr & Mrs
James Nelson, 07974 701427,
lucyn2002@aol.com. 1½ m N of
A303, 3m E of Wincanton. Leave A303
at B3081 (Wincanton to Gillingham rd),
up hill to Pen Selwood, L towards
church. ½ m, garden on L. Adm
£2.50, chd free. Thurs 7 May;
18 June (2-5). Visitors also welcome
by appt.
3-acre mature garden with many
camellias and rhododendrons in May.
Lovely views towards Blackmore Vale.
Part formal with pleached hornbeam
allÈe and rill, part water garden with
lake. Unusual trees. Wonderful roses in
June. Featured on BBC2 Open
Gardens.
  ❀ ⊛ ☕ ☎

FOSSLEIGH
See Devon.

**56 [NEW] 29 FOUR ACRE
AVENUE**
Downend, Bristol BS16 6PD.
Anne & Lyndon Heal. NE Bristol.
From A4174 ring road take A432
towards Downend (Willy Wicket R-
about), after ⅔ m R into Four Acre
Rd, immed L into Four Acre Ave,
1st bungalow on R. Home-made
teas. Adm £2.50, chd free. Sun
28 June (2-5.30).
Large colourful garden all-yr round
suburban garden transformed with
good architecture. Over 50
clematis, numerous climbers,
densely-planted borders with
perennials, unusual plants, shrubs
and trees. Tropical plants, large
ornamental fish pond, red bed and
wicker moon window. Small
productive vegetable patch,
ornamental grasses. Recently
revamped border. Owners
plantaholics.
❀ ☕

57 ◆ GANTS MILL & GARDEN
Bruton BA10 0DB. Alison & Brian
Shingler, 01749 812393,
www.gantsmill.co.uk. ½ m SW of
Bruton. From Bruton centre on Yeovil
rd, A359, under railway bridge, 100yds
uphill, fork R down Gants Mill Lane.
Mill & garden adm £6, chd £1,
garden only adm £4, chd £1. 2nd &
4th Suns, 15 May to end Sept. For
NGS: Sun 23 Aug (2-5).
½-acre garden. Clematis, rose arches
and pergolas; streams, ponds, bog

garden; brick circle, grasses in gravel;
garden sculpture exhibition; riverside
walk to the top weir; colour-themed
planting with many iris, oriental
poppies, delphiniums, day lilies,
dahlias; also vegetable, soft fruit and
cutting flower garden. The garden is
overlooked by the historic watermill,
also open on NGS day. Featured in
'Country Gardener'.
  ⛪ ☕

58 GARDD OWEN
16 Owen Street, Wellington
TA21 8JY. Carole & Tim Lomas,
01823 664180,
carole.lomas@phonecoop.coop.
From centre of Wellington follow signs
to Sports Centre (B3187) for ½ m.
R along Seymour St opp Dolphin PH,
next L. Home-made teas. Adm £2.50,
chd free (share to All Saints Church,
Rockwell Green). Suns, 7, 14, 21, 28
June (2-5). Visitors also welcome by
appt June only.
Inspirational small garden comprising
formal, rose and wild gardens, potager
garden and pergola with a profusion of
roses. Managed organically for the
benefit of wildlife.
❀ ☕ ☎

59 190 GOLDCROFT
Yeovil BA21 4DB. Eric & Katrina
Crate, 01935 475535,
eric@ericcrate.orangehome.co.uk.
Take A359 from R-about by Yeovil
College, then 1st R. Home-made teas.
Adm £2.50, chd free. Sat 6, Sun 7
June (2-5). Evening Opening Mon
8 June (4-8). Visitors also welcome
by appt individuals or groups.
¼ acre. Colour-themed shrub and
herbaceous borders and island beds,
rose garden, raised pond, seaside
deck, fernery, hosta walk, greenhouse
surrounded by silver bed, vegetable
garden designed for the visually
impaired and greenhouse. Many
mature shrubs and trees and sensory
features. Featured in 'Gardening
Which'.
❀ ⊛ ☕ ☎

60 16 GORDANO GARDENS
Easton-in-Gordano BS20 0PD. Mr &
Mrs Milsom, 01275 373463. 5m W of
Bristol. J19 M5 Gordano Services,
head towards Bristol, L Easton-in-
Gordano, ½ m. Church car park on L,
walk through field directly behind scout
hut. Adm £2.50, chd free. Visitors
welcome by appt July only, no
coaches.
Cottage-style garden 80ft long with

many pretty and unusual features incl
decked area, natural pond with
waterfall, grasses and herbaceous
plants.
❀ ☎

61 GREENMANTLE
6 Water Street. TA19 0JR. Colin & Jill
Leppard, 01460 54434. Approx
250yds from entrance to Barrington
Court. Light refreshments & teas. Adm
£2.50, chd free. Sats, Suns 27, 28
June; 22, 23 Aug (11-5). Visitors also
welcome by appt.
1-acre wildlife/cottage garden, moving
through large traditional herbaceous
(butterfly) borders with water features,
pergola and vegetable garden into
orchard/coppice incorporating various
wildlife habitats incl meadow, wildlife
pond and living willow features. Partial
wheelchair access. 2 large unfenced
ponds, one deep.
  ☕ ☎

Tropical plants, large ornamental fish pond, red bed and wicker moon window . . .

62 HANGERIDGE FARMHOUSE
Wrangway TA21 9QG. Mrs J M
Chave, 01823 662339. 2m S of
Wellington. 1m off A38 bypass signed
Wrangway. 1st L towards Wellington
Monument over mway bridge 1st R.
Home-made teas. Adm £2.50, chd
free. Sun 19 Apr; Mon 4 May; Suns
14 June; 5 July; 2 Aug (11-5).
Visitors also welcome by appt.
Informal, relaxing, 30 yr-old family
garden set under Blackdown Hills.
Seats to enjoy views across Somerset
landscape. Atmospheric mix of
herbaceous borders, mixed rockeries
and newly-created oriental garden, this
lovingly-designed and still-evolving
garden contains wonderful flowering
shrubs, heathers, mature trees,
rambling climbers and bulbs in season.
Content and design belie its 1-acre
size.
  ❀ ⊛ ☕ ☎

63 ◆ HANHAM COURT

BS15 3NT. Julian & Isabel Bannerman, www.hanhamcourt.co.uk. *5m E of Bristol centre. Old Bristol Rd A431 from Bath, through Wilsbridge, L down Court Farm Rd for 1m, L down Ferry Rd at St Stephens Green, before Chequers PH.* **Adm £5, chd £3.50. Fri to Mon, 10 Apr to 31 Aug. For NGS: Sun 26 Apr (11-4.30).**
The garden designers Julian & Isabel Bannerman are still developing this rich mix of bold formality, water, woodland, orchard, meadow and kitchen garden with emphasis on scent, structure and romance, set amid a remarkable cluster of manorial buildings between Bath and Bristol. Winners of Garden of the Year HHA award for their design at Houghton Hall, Norfolk. Their work features regularly in the press. Steep slopes, some steps.

♿ ✕ ✿ ☕

64 HARPTREE COURT

East Harptree BS40 6AA. Mrs Richard Hill & Mr & Mrs Charles Hill. *8m N of Wells. A39 Bristol rd to Chewton Mendip, then B3114 to E Harptree, gates on L. From Bath, A368 Weston-super-Mare rd to W Harptree.* Cream teas. **Adm £3, chd free. Sun 24 May (2-6).**
Spacious garden designed when the house was built in 1797. Two ponds linked by a romantic waterfall and a stream, flanked by large trees. Lily pond and formal garden. Pleached limes. Walled garden with herbaceous borders, fruit trees and other fruits.

♿ ✿ ⛺ ☕

65 NEW HAYDON LODGE FARM

Haydon Drove, nr Wells BA5 3EH. Jane Clisby. *2m NE of Wells. From Wells take B3139 to the Horringtons. After 2m, L for Sole Retreat Reflexology, garden 50yds on L.* Home-made teas and premium ice cream stall. **Adm £3, chd free. Sun 28 June (11-5).**
It is a challenge to garden at 1000ft on the Mendip Hills. AONB close to the cathedral city of Wells. Peaceful garden of 1/3 acre in cottage garden style with 9 differing areas incl fernery, sun terrace and swimming pool, water feature and pool, therapy garden, vegetable plot and hidden meditation garden.

♿ ✿ ☕

9 differing areas including fernery, pool, therapy garden . . .

Group opening

66 NEW HENLEAZE GARDENS

BS9 4RS. *3½ m N of Bristol city centre. (Please see individual gardens for directions).* Home-made teas at Montroy Cl, cream teas at Glenwood Rd. **Combined adm £3, chd free. Sun 21 June (2-6).** Partial wheelchair access (7 steps to garden at Glenwood Rd but garden can be viewed from upper patio).

♿ ✕ ✿ ☕

NEW 6 GLENWOOD ROAD

BS10 5HQ. Pat & Graham Thomas. *A4018 Westbury Rd across Durdham Down then B4056 Henleaze Rd. At junction Henleaze Rd/Southmead Rd, mini R-about 2nd exit Lake Rd then 1st R*
NE-facing woodland garden with shrubs, herbaceous borders, rock garden, fishpond and lawn. Stream at bottom and very large Sequoia tree!

✕ ✿

NEW 16 MONTROY CLOSE

BS9 4RS. Sue & Rod Jones. *On B4056 continue past all shops, R into Rockside Dr (opp Eastfield Inn). Up hill, across Xrds into The Crescent, Montroy Close 3rd on L*
Large S-facing informal garden on corner plot. Stream-fed pond with pebble beach, pergola and seating area. Lawn with curving flowerbeds incl fernery, shrubs, perennials, climbers, small rock gardens. Unusual partitioned greenhouse with alpine bench. Hanging baskets and many pots, a profusion of fuchsias.

♿ ✕ ✿

67 HENLEY MILL

Wookey BA5 1AW. Peter & Sally Gregson, 01749 676966, millcottageplants@tiscali.co.uk, www.millcottageplants.co.uk. *2m W of Wells. Off A371. Turn L into Henley Lane, driveway 50yds on L.* **Adm £3, chd free. Visitors welcome by appt May to Sept, incl coaches and groups.**
2½ acres beside R Axe. Traditional and unusual cottage plants informally planted in formal beds with roses, hydrangea borders, shady 'folly garden' and late summer borders with grasses and perennials. Ornamental kitchen garden. Rare Japanese hydrangeas.

♿ ✕ ☎

68 ◆ HESTERCOMBE GARDENS

Cheddon Fitzpaine TA2 8LG. Mr P White, Hestercombe Gardens Trust, 01823 413923, www.hestercombe.com. *4m N of Taunton. Follow tourist signs.* **Adm £7.90, chd £3, concessions £7.10. Daily all yr (closed Xmas Day) (10-5, 5.30 winter). For NGS: Tues 3 Mar (10-5.30); 2 June (10-6).**
Georgian landscape garden designed by Coplestone Warre Bampfylde, Victorian terrace/shrubbery and stunning Edwardian Lutyens/Jekyll formal gardens together make up 40 acres of woodland walks, temples, terraces, pergolas, lakes and cascades. Gravel paths, some steep slopes.

♿ ✿ ☕

69 HILL LODGE

Northend, Batheaston BA1 8EN. Susan & Sydney Fremantle, 01225 852847. *4m NE of Bath. Turn N in Batheaston village up steep, small rd signed Northend & St Catherine. Hill Lodge ¾ m on L. Parking in courtyard for disabled, frail & elderly.* **Adm £3.50, chd free. Visitors welcome by appt all yr, individuals and groups, no coaches.**
3-acre country garden used for work experience by horticultural students because of variety of features incl stream, small wildlife lake, 2 ponds, bog garden, herbaceous borders, alpine bed, rose/clematis pergola, small cottage garden, vegetable garden, orchard, coppice and hill with trees and view. Small lake with nesting waterfowl. Some steep slopes, avoidable.

♿ ✕ ✿ ☕ ☎

70 25 HILLCREST ROAD
Redcliffe Bay, Portishead
BS20 8HN. Colin & Molly Lewis.
$2^1/_2$ m from Portishead. Take Nore Rd
S out of Portishead centre for $2^1/_2$ m.
Past Feddon Village (old Nautical
School). Hillcrest Rd is 1st L. Home-
made & cream teas. **Adm £2.50, chd
free. Suns 26 Apr; 17 May; 5 July;
Thur 6 Aug (1-6).**
Sloping garden with 3 terraces; bottom
- a lawn, middle - a formal garden with
central fountain and extensively
planted, top - a large patio with
wisteria-covered pergola and
spectacular water feature. Front
garden is a riot of colour.

Group opening

**71 HINTON ST GEORGE
GARDENS**
TA17 8SA. 3m N of Crewkerne. N of
A30 Crewkerne-Chard; S of A303
Ilminster Town Rd, at R-about signed
Lopen & Merriott, then R to Hinton St
George. Home-made teas. **Combined
adm £5, chd free. Sat 23, Sun 24
May (2-5).**
Pretty village with thatched Hamstone
houses and C15 church. Country seat
of the Earls of Poullett for 600yrs until
1973.

ARKARINGA
69 West Street. Bel Annetts.
Access through passage on L
This long, narrow sloping garden
was planned to avoid the
rectangular and to provide contrast
in colour, texture, shape and habit
in the planting (both vertically and
horizontally) yr-long. Church view
enhances effect. Steep steps, no
handrail. Easier exit by gate at rear.

HOOPER'S HOLDING
45 High Street. Ken & Lyn
Spencer-Mills
(See separate entry).

MALLARDS
Gas Lane. Captain & Mrs T
Hardy
(See separate entry).

NEW RUSSETS
Lopen Road. Jean & Eric
Burgess
Secluded $1/_2$ -acre garden raised
above adjoining rd on edge of
village. Wildlife and bird friendly.
Variety of herbaceous perennials,
shrubs, trees incl fruit. Small
vegetable plot.

HOLCOMBE COURT
See Devon.

72 HOMEWOOD PARK HOTEL
Abbey Lane, Hinton Charterhouse
BA2 7TB. Homewood Park Hotel,
www.homewoodpark.co.uk. 6m S of
Bath. Just off A36 Warminster rd,
before village of Hinton Charterhouse.
**Adm £3, chd free. Sun to Fri, Apr to
Sept (11-5) subject to availability
due to business commitments,
please phone first (01225 723731).**
Set in 10 acres of formal and informal
gardens, incl circular rose garden and
large herbaceous borders, rolling lawns
and cut flower garden. Also large
parkland with mature trees. The
gardens have won awards 6 times in
the Bath in Bloom Flower Show. Gravel
paths, large front lawn, gentle slopes.

73 HOOPER'S HOLDING
45 High Street, Hinton St George
TA17 8SE. Ken & Lyn Spencer-Mills,
01460 76389,
kenlyn@devonrex.demon.co.uk. 3m
N of Crewkerne. (see directions for
Hinton St George Gardens). Home-
made teas. **Opening with Mallards,
combined adm £3, chd free. Sat 25,
Sun 26 July (2-5). Also opening with
Hinton St George Gardens 23, 24
May. Visitors also welcome by appt
up to mid-Aug.**
$1/_3$ -acre garden in colour
compartments; lily pool; azaleas, rare
herbaceous and shrubby plants, many
exotics. Pedigree cats. Garden
mosaics developing. Gravel paths but
help at hand.

A subtropical treat to delight the sense and revive the spirit . . .

74 JASMINE COTTAGE
26 Channel Road, Clevedon
BS21 7BY. Margaret & Michael
Redgrave, 01275 871850,
margaret@bologrew.demon.co.uk,
www.bologrew.pwp.blueyonder.co.uk.

12m W of Bristol. M5 J20. From
Clevedon seafront travel N (0.8m), via
Wellington Terrace follow winding rd to
St Mary's Church, R into Channel Rd,
approx 100yds on L. Bus stop nr
church - 824, X24 & X25. **Adm £2.50,
chd free. Thurs only 28 May to 13
Aug (11-4).** Visitors also welcome by
appt June to Aug.
Closely-planted garden of $1/_3$ acre with
hedged rooms. Familiar perennials and
shrubs are interplanted with annuals,
bulbs and tender perennials for a feast
of colour, form and scent. Around 50
varieties of the genus salvia are grown.
Pergolas and fences are covered with
climbers - wisterias, schisandra,
solanum, roses, clematis, maurandyas
and rhodochiton. Featured in 'Amateur
Gardening'. RHS recommended
garden.

75 NEW JENS GARDYN
4 Wroxham Dr, Little Stoke
BS34 6EJ. Jennifer & Gary
Ellington, 01454 610317. 5m N of
Bristol city centre. From Cribbs
Causeway Rabout go S on A38.
Over next Rabout, L into Stoke
Lane, 4th L into Braydon Ave, 1st L
into Wroxham Drive. Home-made
teas. **Adm £3.50, chd free.
Visitors welcome by appt
June/July, max 6, incl 2 evening
viewings to enjoy the tranquility
of the garden.**
'Small garden...... big ideas'!
Growing over 70 varieties of
culinary, medicinal and aromatic
herbs and many scented shrubs.
Our fern gully, stream and goldfish
pond are wildlife friendly. Densely-
planted tree ferns, bananas,
bamboos, palms, grasses and
exotics make this a subtropical
treat to delight the sense and
revive the spirit. Home-made
produce for sale.

76 28 KENSINGTON ROAD
St George, Bristol BS5 7NB. Mr
Grenville Johnson & Mr Alan Elms,
0117 949 6788,
www.victorianhousegarden.pwp.
blueyonder.co.uk. $2^1/_2$ m E of Bristol
City centre. Take A420 in direction of
St George towards Kingswood &
Chippenham Rd. At Bell Hill St George,
turn into Kensington Rd. Entrance to
garden in Cromwell Rd at side of
house. **Adm £3.50, chd free. By appt
only Suns, 12, 19, 26 July (1-5).**

Award-winning, small courtyard town house garden on 2 decked levels with Italianate classical features incorporating temple folly ruin, exotic and S-hemisphere gardens. Woodland stumpery and wildlife pond all add to the romantic atmosphere. The planting scheme is luscious and exotic with vibrant colour theming. Max 5 adults can be accommodated. Featured on BBC Gardeners' World and local TV and radio and in 'Homes and Antiques' magazine.

🐾 ☎

77 NEW ◆ KILVER COURT
Kilver St, Shepton Mallet BA4 5NF. Roger Saul, 01749 340416, www.kilvercourt.com. *Shepton Mallet. Directly off A37, opp Gaymer Cider factory.* **Adm £3.50, chd free. Garden open all yr Tues - Sun (10-4), Sharpham Park shop open daily (9.30-5.30). For NGS: Suns 31 May; 23 Aug (10-4).**
Created in 1800s and restored in 1960s by the Showering family, who commissioned Charles Whiteleg to recreate his gold medal winning Chelsea garden. Millpond, boating lake, herbaceous borders and parterre with the most stunning feature being the Grade II listed viaduct built for the Somerset and Dorset railway. Partial wheelchair access, some uneven and gravel paths.

♿ ❀ ☕

Wander down winding paths to rockery where cypress-like columnars and yuccas lend a Mediterranean air . . .

78 KINGSDON NURSERY GARDEN
Somerton TA11 7LE. Patricia Marrow, 01935 840232. *2m SE of Somerton. Off B3151 Ilchester rd. From Ilchester roundabout on A303 follow NT signs to Lytes Cary; L opp gates, 1/2 m to Kingsdon. Drive through village, nursery signs on L, gate.* Home-made teas. **Adm £3.50, chd free. Suns 3, 31 May (2-7). Visitors also welcome by appt all yr.**
2-acre plantsman's garden with lovely plants to see. Large nursery. Selection of trees, shrubs and herbaceous and rock plants for sale. Knowledgeable gardener to help with new or established gardens.

♿ ❀ ☕ ☎

79 KITES CROFT
Westbury-sub-Mendip BA5 1HU. Dr & Mrs W I Stanton, 01749 870328. *5m NW of Wells. On A371 Wells to Cheddar rd, follow signs from Westbury Cross.* **Adm £2.50, chd free. Visitors welcome by appt 1 Apr to 30 Sept, max 30, no coaches, refreshments available.**
2-acre sloping garden planted for colour throughout season with fine views to Glastonbury Tor. Wander down winding paths to rockery where cypress-like columnars and yuccas lend a Mediterranean air, pass ponds and lawn to densely-planted mixed borders, shrubs and perennials. Fruit trees incl figs, walnut and mulberry. In the wood primroses, bluebells and cyclamen thrive.

❀ ☕ ☎

80 KNOLL COTTAGE
Stogumber TA4 3TN. Elaine & John Leech, 01984 656689, john@knoll-cottage.co.uk, www.knoll-cottage.co.uk. *3m SE of Williton. From Taunton take A358 towards Minehead. After 11m turn L to Stogumber. In centre of Stogumber, R towards Williton. After 1/3 m, R up narrow lane, follow signs for parking.* Home-made teas. **Adm £3, chd free. Visitors welcome by appt. Also open with Stogumber Gardens Sun 21 June.**
2-acre garden started from fields in 1998. Extensive mixed beds with shrubs, perennials and annuals. Over 80 different roses. Woodland area incl many different rowans, hawthorns and birches. Pond, vegetable and fruit area.

♿ ❀ 🛏 ☕ ☎

81 LIFT THE LATCH
Blacklands Lane, Forton, Chard TA20 2NF. Pauline & David Wright, 01460 64752. *11/2 m S of Chard. Blacklands Lane is off B3162 at E end of Forton from Chard.* **Adm £2.50, chd free. Visitors welcome by appt all yr incl groups up to 50.**
Pretty cottage garden bordered by small stream. Large wildlife pond and raised fish pond. Wide variety of evergreens, giving yr-round interest. Particularly colourful rhododendrons, azaleas and acers in spring and vivid autumn colours from many trees and shrubs such as rhus, liquidambar and cornus, but interesting 365 days of the yr.

♿ 🐾 ☎

82 THE LINTELS
Littleton-on-Severn BS35 1NS. Mr & Mrs Ernest Baker. *10m N of Bristol, 31/2 m SW of Thornbury. From old Severn Bridge on M48 take B4461 to Alveston. In Elberton, take 1st L to Littleton-on-Severn. 4th house 100yds past Field Lane.* **Adm £2, chd free. Sun 7 June (1-5). Also open Sunnyside Cottage.**
Small cottage-type garden in front of house with good variety of herbaceous plants. Main attraction Japanese garden at rear with waterfall, koi carp, stream, teahouse. Gravel paths.

♿

83 LITTLE YARFORD FARMHOUSE
Yarford, Kingston St Mary TA2 8AN. Brian Bradley, 01823 451350, yarford@ic24.net. *31/2 m N of Taunton. From Taunton on Kingston St Mary rd. At 30mph sign turn L at Parsonage Lane. Continue 11/4 m W, to Yarford sign. Continue 400yds. Turn R up concrete rd. Park on L.* Cream teas (except eve), light refreshments also 10/11 Aug. **Adm £3.50, chd free. Sat 8, Sun 9 Aug (2-6), Mon 10, Tue 11 Aug (11-5). Evening Opening £10, wine, music, Fri 7 Aug (6-8.30). Visitors also welcome by appt, no large coaches.**
This unusual garden embraces a C17 house (not open) overgrown with a tapestry of climbing plants. The 3 ponds exhibit a full compliment of aquatic gems. The special draw is an array of unusual trees all exemplifying shape, colour and form. The 3 acres are a delight to both artist and plantsman. Some slopes.

♿ 🐾 ❀ ☕ ☎

Collections of unusual plants, shrubs and interesting features . . .

84 ♦ **LOWER SEVERALLS**
Crewkerne TA18 7NX. Mary Pring,
01460 73234,
www.lowerseveralls.co.uk. 1½ m NE
of Crewkerne. Signed off A30
Crewkerne to Yeovil rd or A356
Crewkerne to A303. **Adm £3, chd £1.**
Tues, Weds, Fris, Sats 3 Mar to 31
July & Sept. For NGS: Sun 26 Apr;
Sat 2, Sun 31 May; Sun 14 June; Sat
19 Sept; Sats (10-5), Suns (2-5).
3-acre plantsman's garden beside early
Hamstone farmhouse. Herbaceous
borders and island beds with
collections of unusual plants, shrubs
and interesting features incl dogwood
basket, wadi, scented garden. Green
roofed building. Nursery specialises in
herbs, geraniums and salvias. Grass
paths.

85 ♦ **LYTES CARY MANOR**
Kingsdon TA11 7HU. National Trust,
01458 224471,
www.nationaltrust.org.uk. 3m SE of
Somerton. Signed from Podimore R-
about at junction of A303, A37, take
A372. **House and garden adm £7.35,**
chd £3.70, family £18.40, garden
only adm £5.25, chd £2.65. Sats to
Weds, 14 Mar to 1 Nov. For NGS:
Mon 30 Mar; Sat 18 July; Mon 5 Oct
(11-4.30).
Garden laid out in series of rooms with
many contrasts, topiary, mixed borders
and herbal border based on famous
C16 Lytes Herbal, which can be seen
in house. Workshops available: Spring
planting and garden tasks 30 Mar;
Seed collecting and cuttings from the
garden incl tour with Head Gardener
18 July; Autumn lawn maintenance
demonstration and practical workshop
5 Oct. Booking essential.

86 **MALLARDS**
Gas Lane. TA17 8RX. Capt & Mrs T
Hardy. 3m N of Crewkerne. See
directions for Hinton St George
gardens. **Opening with Hoopers**
Holding, combined adm £3, chd
free. Sat 25, Sun 26 July (2-5). Also
opening with Hinton St George

Gardens 23/24 May.
Small garden surrounding bungalow
with lovely views. Mixture of shrubs
and herbaceous plants in beautiful
peaceful setting. Wheelchair access to
front garden only.
  &

87 **MAPLE HOUSE**
South Barrow, Yeovil BA22 7LN. Mr
& Mrs P K Shaw & Mrs E Verrinder.
6m SW of Castle Cary. Off A359 but
best approached from Sparkford.
Garden is 2m N of Sparkford. Follow rd
sign to South Barrow & Lovington opp
Haynes Publishers, then NGS sign.
Adm £3, chd free. Sat 6, Sun 7 June
(2-6).
Gently sloping 5-acre site with fine view
to Glastonbury Tor and Mendips.
Developing garden begun in 1996,
with lake, shrubberies, lawns, mown
paths, pergola. 4-acre wild flower
meadow (Somerset Wildlife site and
private nature reserve) with mature and
recently planted hedges, small wood of
native trees and shrubs. Pond; garden
around house with alpine bed and
herbaceous borders. Conservation a
priority. Some sloping grass paths,
possibly slippery in wet weather.

Group opening

88 **MARSHFIELD GARDENS**
Marshfield SN14 8LR. 7m NE of
Bath. From Bath A46 to Cold Ashton
Roundabout, turn R onto A420.
Marshfield 2m. From M4 J18, turn R
onto A46 and L at Cold Ashton
Roundabout. Light lunches & home-
made teas at 111 High Street from 12
noon. **Combined adm £4.50, chd**
free. Sat 30, Sun 31 May (1-5).
5 gardens in large, interesting village.
Please note, Marshfield Gardens will be
taking a break in 2010 but hope to be
back in 2011. Guided walks in and
around village. Meet in Market Place
10.30am, walking boots advised.

MONTAGU HOUSE
1 Old School Court. Mr & Mrs
David Dodd. Off E end of High Str,
turn R before Old School into Weir
Lane. Opp Weir Cottage.
Started in 2006. Grass, gravel,
flower borders, box trees and
espaliered apple trees. Old dry
stone walls form 2 sides.
Wonderful view across fields.
Approx 100 sq yds.

4 OLD SCHOOL COURT
Mrs Jenny Wilkinson
Small courtyard garden with
cottage-style planting showing the
use of mixed planting in a small
space. Many clematis, roses and
other climbers on walls, arches and
pergola. Narrow path and small
garden restrict visitor numbers at
any one time.

WEIR COTTAGE
Weir Lane. Ian & Margaret
Jones. Opp Old School Court
Approx ¼ -acre walled garden
divided into terraces. S-facing,
open aspect. Lawn, borders and
vegetable garden with raised
beds.

43 HIGH STREET
Linda & Denis Beazer. Continue
on from Weir Cottage, entrance
from Weir Lane.
Walled garden with terraced
potager and companion planting
leading to lawned area with shrubs
and herbaceous borders and
pond. New for 2009,
summerhouse with green sedum
roof.
✖

111 HIGH STREET
Joy & Mervyn Pierce. Bristol end
of village.
Large garden and paddock, split
into many areas. Pond,
summerhouse, many seating
places, vegetable garden, walnut
tree planted by owner 49 yrs ago.
Quiet, relaxing garden.

89 ♦ **MILTON LODGE**
Wells BA5 3AQ. Simon Tudway
Quilter, 01749 672168,
www.miltonlodgegardens.co.uk.
½ m N of Wells. From A39 Bristol-
Wells, turn N up Old Bristol Rd; car
park first gate on L. **Adm £4, chd**
under 14 free. Tues, Weds, Suns &
Bank Hols, Easter to 31 Oct (2-5).
For NGS: Suns 17 May; 7 June; 12
July (2-5).
Mature Grade II listed terraced garden
with outstanding views of Wells
Cathedral and Vale of Avalon. Mixed
borders, roses, fine trees. Separate
7-acre arboretum.

90 ♦ MONTACUTE HOUSE
Montacute TA15 6XP. The National Trust, 01935 823289, www.nationaltrust.org.uk. *4m W of Yeovil. NT signs off A3088 & A303.* House and garden adm £10, chd £4.70, garden only adm £6, chd £3. Daily, not Tues, 14 Mar to 1 Nov. For NGS: Sat 18 July (11-6).
Magnificent Elizabethan house with contemporary garden layout. Fine stonework provides setting for informally planted mixed borders and old roses; range of garden features illustrates its long history.

&♿ ✖ ✿ ☕

91 NORTHFIELD HOUSE
Barton Rd, Barton St David TA11 6BJ. Mr & Mrs D R Clarke, 01458 223203, donaldclarke0@gmail.com. *4m E of Somerton. From A37 Lydford traffic lights take B3153 Somerton rd. In Keinton Mandeville, turn R into Barton Rd, 100yds before derestriction sign. From Somerton take B3153 Castle Cary rd. In Keinton Mandeville, turn L into Barton Rd, 100yds after 30mph sign. House 250yds on L immed beyond Barton St David sign.* Home-made teas. Adm £3, chd free. Sun 21 June (2-5). Visitors also welcome by appt.
2 acres of semi-formal gardens, orchard and ponds with splendid views over Somerset levels to Glastonbury Tor and Mendips. Main features are rose arbour, nepeta beds and Shona sculptures. Large pond, children should be supervised.

&♿ ☕ ☎

Stunning garden with rich and versatile planting . . . Inspiration for the garden has been drawn from foreign travel . . .

92 35 OLD STATION GARDENS
Henstridge, Templecombe BA8 0PU. Mary McLean, 01963 364321, marysmclean@btinternet.com. *6m E of Sherborne, 9m W of Shaftesbury on A30. Signage from A30 T-lights at Henstridge and at rd end.* Home-made teas. Combined adm £3, chd free. Suns 21 June; 12 July (2-6). Combined with **Cherry Bolberry Farm.** Visitors also welcome by appt June/July.
Small owner-designed plantaholic's garden. Many exotics mixed with roses, clematis and herbaceous. Raised beds, pergolas, patio and pond. Floriferous and abundant planting with added spring underplanting of bulbs to give extra interest. Bonsai collection of native and exotic trees. Partial wheelchair access.

&♿ ✖ ✿ ☕ ☎

93 OLIVE COTTAGE
Langley Marsh, Wiveliscombe TA4 2UJ. Mrs Frankie Constantine, 01984 624210. *1m NW of Wiveliscombe. From Taunton take B3227 to Wiveliscombe. Turn R at T-lights. At Square turn R past White Hart & continue 1m. Olive Cottage on R before Three Horseshoes PH.* Home-made teas. Adm £2.50, chd free (share to St Margarets Hospice). Sun 24, Mon 25 May; Sun 28 June (2-6). Visitors also welcome by appt.
An informal cottage garden of about 2/3 acre created by the owner for over 30yrs. Small pond, bog garden and new rockery, together with shrubs, perennials, climbers and trees create colour and interest throughout the yr. Productive kitchen garden and 2 greenhouses where many of the plants are raised. Gravel paths, short slope, unfenced pond.

&♿ ✿ ☕ ☎

94 ORCHARD WYNDHAM
nr Williton TA4 4HH. The Trustees. *7m SE of Minehead. 16m Taunton. In Williton A39 Minehead rd. L opp agricultural machines showroom signed Bakelite Museum, follow lane past church to lodge, long drive to house.* Adm £3, chd free. Sun 31 May (2-5.30).
Garden of historic house (not open) in parkland setting: woods, interesting old trees, borders, rose walk, small lake, wild garden. Gravel paths.

✖

95 3 PALMER'S WAY
Hutton, Weston-super-Mare BS24 9QT. Mary & Peter Beckett, 01934 815110, macbeckett@tiscali.co.uk. *3m S of Weston-super-Mare. From A370 (N or S) follow signs to Hutton. L at PO, 1st L into St Mary's Rd, 2nd R to car park (signed). Garden 2 mins walk. Very limited disabled parking at garden (L off St Mary's Rd and L into Palmer's Way).* Home-made teas. Adm £2.50, chd free. Suns 5, 19 July (2-5.30). Visitors also welcome by appt, Weds in July only.
Plantsman's garden described as 'an informal tapestry' of plants with sculpture and found objects. Redeveloped rockery and borders. Even more hardy geraniums and perennials added to our unusual collection. Minarette fruit trees, herbs in knot garden. Wildlife ponds, gravel bed, Japanese area, 'Secret Corner'. Home-made teas amongst the bougainvilleas. Conserves made from locally grown fruit. Craft items for sale. Steps, some steep, limited access if very wet.

&♿ ✖ ✿ ☕ ☎

96 NEW 22 PARSON STREET
Bedminster BS3 5PT. Andrew Tyas, 07725 832615, annieandy22@yahoo.co.uk. *2m S of Bristol City centre. From Redcliffe area, take A38 through Bedminster into West St, L into Parson St, over bridge towards traffic lights. Garden just before junction with Bedminster Rd and Parson St, nr Mansfield St.* Cream teas. Adm £2, chd free. Suns 21, 28 June; 5, 12 July (10-4). Visitors also welcome by appt.
Stunning, compact cottage-style garden with rich and versatile planting. Heavily planted with herbaceous perennials, unusual shrubs, clematis, exotic perennials such as echiums, banksia and protea. Inspiration for the garden has been drawn from foreign travel. Front garden: rose garden with yew hedging, over twenty varieties of roses. Wildlife and flower photography on sale, all images taken in garden by owner. 'Best Front Garden in South Bristol' award. Gravel paths.

&♿ ✖ ☕ ☎

97 PENWOOD FARM
Parchey, Chedzoy, nr Bridgwater
TA7 8RW. Mr & Mrs E F W Clapp,
01278 451631,
clapppauline@aol.com. 3½ m E of
Bridgwater. Take A39 from Bridgwater.
Bridge over M5, turn sharp R into
Chedzoy Lane. At T-junction in village
turn L. Pass church approx ¾ m.
Penwood Farm facing sharp LH-bend.
From Stawell off Glastonbury rd, cross
bridge over King's Sedgemoor Drain
(Parchey River). 1st house on L.
Home-made teas. Adm £2.50, chd
free (share of plant sales to Chedzoy
Playing Field Association). Suns 14,
21 June (2-5). Visitors also welcome
by appt June & 1st week July only,
coaches permitted.
Plant lover's garden approx ¾ acre.
Terrace, patio, pergola, gravel, rock,
water and kitchen gardens. Hundreds
of different roses - old, 'new' English
and modern; collections of clematis,
hosta, penstemon, shrubs and
herbaceous perennials, unusual plants
and trees. Japanese-style bridge over
sunken garden with water lilies.
Vegetable and cutting garden. Teas in
tractor shed where, for a few years
now, a family of swallows tend their
brood, oblivious to our visitors.

98 ♦ PRIOR PARK LANDSCAPE GARDEN
Ralph Allen Drive, Bath BA2 5AH.
The National Trust, 01225 833422,
www.nationaltrust.org.uk. 1m S of
Bath. Visitors are advised to use public
transport as there is no parking at Prior
Park or nearby, except for disabled
visitors. Telephone 01225 833422 for
'How to get there' leaflet. Adm £5.25,
chd £2.95. Daily, not Tues, 14 Feb to
30 Oct (11-5.30). Sats, Suns 31 Oct
to 31 Jan 2010 (11-dusk). Last adm
1 hr before closing. For NGS: Sun
10 May (11-5.30).
Beautiful and intimate C18 landscape
garden created by Bath entrepreneur
Ralph Allen (1693-1764) with advice
from the poet Alexander Pope and
Capability Brown. Sweeping valley with
magnificent views of city, Palladian
bridge and lakes. Wilderness
restoration, completed in 2007,
involved reinstating the Serpentine
Lake, Cascade and Cabinet to their
former glory. See drifts of wild garlic
carpeting the woodlands. We offer
visitors the opportunity to take same
wild garlic home with a fact/recipe
sheet. Featured on radio and TV.

PRIORY HOUSE
See Wiltshire.

99 NEW ROADMENDERS COTTAGE
Town Barton, Norton-St-Philip
BA2 7LN. Dr Michael & Mrs
Barbara Lutterloch, 01373
834214,
barbaralutterloch@dsl.pipex.co.
uk. 8m SE of Bath. At junction of
B3110 & A366. Park in The
George or Fleur de Lys Inn car
park. Walk 44yds up A366, past
Old Police House then immed R
into Town Barton. Home-made
teas. Adm £3, chd free. Sun
7 June (2-5.30). Visitors also
welcome by appt.
¾ -acre cottage garden
surrounding listed house in very
pretty conservation village.
Vegetable potager, mixed
herbaceous borders, small rose
garden, new hosta area. Mature
trees incl cedrus deodara,
magnolia, majestic beech, yew
hedging. All complemented by
local stone walls, paths and
edging. Ancient village with much
historical interest. C14 church,
village mead with playground
facilities. Stunning C13 PH believed
to be the oldest licensed PHs in
the country.

100 ROCK HOUSE
Elberton BS35 4AQ. Mr & Mrs John
Gunnery, 01454 413225. 10m N of
Bristol. 3½ m SW Thornbury. From Old
Severn Bridge on M48 take B4461 to
Alveston. In Elberton, take 1st turning L
to Littleton-on-Severn & turn immed R.
Adm £2.50, chd free (share to St
Johns Church, Elberton). Suns 1
Feb 2009; 31 Jan 2010 (11-4).
Visitors also welcome by appt.
1-acre walled garden undergoing
improvement. Pond and old yew tree,
mixed borders, cottage garden plants
and developing woodland.

101 SALTFORD FARM BARN
565a Bath Road, Saltford BS31 3JS.
Eve Hessey, 01225 873380,
eve.hessey@blueyonder.co.uk. 6m
W of Bath. On A4 between Bath &
Bristol, Saltford Farm Barn is at Bath
end of village. Parking arrangements
will be signed - busy A4 not suitable for
parking. Home-made teas, crafts.
Adm £3, chd free. Sun 29 Mar (2-5).

Visitors also welcome by appt.
1-acre garden with 5 main separate
gardens. Ornamental vegetable garden
with trained fruit trees contained within
scented hedges of lavender, rosemary
and box. Woodland garden with
seasonal shrubs and trees
underplanted with spring bulbs,
hellebores, ferns, foxgloves and alpine
strawberries. Garden of reflection
depicting owner's life in New Zealand
and England, labyrinth, meadow,
orchard and Mediterranean garden.
Some gravel paths.

Cottage garden in very pretty conservation village . . .

102 NEW ♦ SELF REALIZATION MEDITATION HEALING CENTRE GARDEN
Laurel Lane, Queen Camel
BA22 7NU. SRMH Charitable
Trust, 01935 850266,
www.selfrealizationcentres.org.
6m NE of Yeovil. A359 S from
Sparkford R-about (on A303) to
Queen Camel. Garden 100yds off
High St, R after school and before
Hair Studio. Park opp school in
field, disabled parking at SRMH
centre. Adm £4, chd free,
concessions £2. Open 7 Mar
(12-6) (Wellbeing Day) & 2 May
(2-6) (Garden Day with
Minstrels), also by appointment.
For NGS: Wed 10 June (2.30-6).
Peaceful 3-acre garden with varied
vistas, trees, lawns and new
Mediterranean area, surrounding
spiritual retreat and training centre.
Stunning herbaceous borders and
fragrant old roses around C17
farmhouse (not open). Oriental
garden and koi pond (by
arrangement). Wildflower tumps,
pond, waterfall, maze, herb beds
and meditation room garden.
Accompanied children only. Ask on
arrival for wheelchair accessible
routes avoiding gravel paths, steps
and uneven flagstones.

103 SERRIDGE HOUSE
Henfield Road, Coalpit Heath
BS36 2UY. Mrs J Manning, 01454
773188. *9m N of Bristol. On A432 at
Coalpit Heath T-lights (opp church),
turn into Henfield Rd. R at PH, 1/2 m
small Xrds, house with iron gates on
corner.* Cream teas. **Adm £4 incl
cream tea or wine (eve), chd free.**
Visitors welcome by appt July/Aug
only, groups of 10+.
2 1/2 -acre garden with mature trees,
heather and conifer beds, island beds
mostly of perennials, woodland area
with pond. Colourful courtyard with old
farm implements. Lake views and
lakeside walks. Unique tree carvings.
& ✗ ☕ ☎

104 ◆ SHERBORNE GARDEN
Litton, Radstock BA3 4PP. Mr & Mrs
John Southwell, 01761 241220. *15m
S of Bristol. 15m W of Bath, 7m N of
Wells. On B3114 Litton to Harptree rd,
1/2 m past The Kings Arms. Car park in
field.* **Adm £3.50, chd free.** Mons
only June/July (11-5), individuals
and groups other days by appt. For
NGS: Daily Sat 14 Feb to Tue 17
Feb; Sun 15 Mar (11-3).
4 1/2 -acre gently sloping garden of
considerable horticultural interest.
Small pinetum, giant grasses area,
woodland garden and 3 linked ponds
with bridges. Collections of hollies,
ferns, Asian wild roses with hybrids
and climbing species, all well labelled,
hemerocallis, water lilies and unusual
trees and shrubs. Open for NGS
Feb/Mar for snowdrops, hellebores
and daffodils. Picnic area.
& ☕

105 SOMERFOSS
Bath Road, Oakhill BA3 5AG. Ewan
& Rosemary Curphey, 01749
840542, ecurphey@aol.com. *3m N of
Shepton Mallet. From Oakhill School
1/4 m N on A367. Parking in lay-by on
R.* Home-made teas. **Adm £3, chd
free.** Weds, Suns 12, 16, 19, 23 Aug
(2-6). Visitors also welcome by appt
June/July/Aug for groups of 10+,
small coaches only.
2-acre garden hidden in peaceful
valley, distinctly different areas for
planting allow for yr-round colour and
interest. Natural rocky outcrops with
bulbs, shrubs, climbers. Borders and
island beds with unusual perennials
and grasses. Damp meadow with
native orchids. Large decks with pots
set off unusual 1970s house (not
open). Some steep slopes and steps.
✗ ⊛ ☕ ☎

106 3 SOUTHDOWN
Milborne Port Rd, Charlton
Horethorne DT9 4NQ. Pippa Hill.
*4 1/2 m NE of Sherborne. From
Sherborne, B3145 towards
Wincanton, at Charlton Horethorne 1st
R to Milborne Port Rd. From
Wincanton, follow signs to Sherborne,
Milborne Port Rd on L after church.*
Home-made teas. **Adm £2.50, chd
free.** Suns 19 Apr; 17 May; 14 June
(11-5).
Long garden with meandering curves
leading towards views across fields.
Mixed planting using many old
favourites planted into gravel and
amongst shrubs with one or two
rarities. Many hidden surprises, garden
full of sculptures, large and small,
some easier to find than others.
Sculpture on show and for sale.
✗ ☕

Natural rocky outcrops with bulbs, shrubs, climbers . . .

107 ◆ SPECIAL PLANTS
Nr Cold Ashton SN14 8LA. Derry
Watkins, 01225 891686,
www.specialplants.net. *6m N of Bath
on A46. From Bath on A46, turn L into
Greenways Lane just before
roundabout onto A420.* Home-made
teas. **Adm £4, chd free.** Weds July
to Sept (11-5). For NGS: Thurs
18 June; 16 July; 20 Aug; 17 Sept;
15 Oct (11-5).
Architect-designed 3/4 -acre hillside
garden with stunning views. Started
autumn 1996. Exotic plants. Gravel
gardens for borderline hardy plants.
Black and white (purple and silver)
garden. Vegetable garden and orchard.
Hot border. Lemon and lime bank.
Annual, biennial and tender plants for
late summer colour. Spring-fed ponds.
Bog garden. Woodland walk. Allium
alley. Free list of plants in garden.
Adjoining nursery, open Mar through
Oct.
✗ ⊛ ☕

112 SPRINGDALE
EX14 9RF. Graham & Ann Salmon
On Devon/Somerset border. Please
see Devon entry.

**109 NEW STANTON COURT
NURSING HOME**
BS39 4ER. *5m S of Bristol. From
Bristol on A37, R onto B3130
signed Chew Magna. 1.4m, L at
old thatched toll house into
Stanton Drew, 1st property on L.*
Cream teas. **Adm £2.50, chd free.**
Suns 26 Apr; 7 June (2-5).
2 acres of formal gardens around
grade II listed Stanton Court.
Mature trees, soft fruit/vegetables,
extensive herbaceous borders with
many interesting plants. Garden
designed by Mary Payne MBE and
maintained by Judith Chubb
Whittle. At its best in June and
during spring bulb display in Apr.
& ☕

110 STOBERRY GARDEN
Stoberry Park, Wells BA5 3LD.
Frances and Tim Young, 01749
672906, stay@stoberry-park.co.uk.
*1/2 m N of Wells. From Bristol - Wells
on A39, L into College Rd and immed
L through Stoberry Park.* **Adm £3.50,
chd free.** Evening Opening wine,
Sun 13 Sept (2-8). Visitors also
welcome by appt for groups of 10+.
With breathtaking views over Wells and
the Vale of Avalon, this 6-acre family
garden planted sympathetically within
its landscape provides a stunning
combination of vistas accented with
wildlife ponds, water features,
sculpture, 1 1/2 -acre walled garden,
sunken garden, gazebo, potager, lime
walk. Colour and interest in every
season; spring bulbs, irises, roses,
acer glade, salvias. Linger a little longer
and enjoy a completely different
experience as the walled garden is lit
from dusk to dark. Featured in 'Garden
Answers' and local press.
✗ ⊛ 🛏 🏡 ☎

Group opening

111 STOGUMBER GARDENS
TA4 3SZ. *11m NW of Taunton. On
A358. Sign to Stogumber, W of
Crowcombe.* Home-made teas.
Combined adm £4, chd free.
Sun 21 June (2-6).
6 delightful gardens of interest to
plantsmen in lovely village at edge of
Quantocks.
☕

BRAGLANDS BARN
Simon & Sue Youell,
www.braglandsbarn.com.
200metres after Stogumber stn.
Light refreshments & teas.

Adm £2.50, chd free
2-acre garden created since 1995 on site that contains areas of waterlogged clay and well-drained sand. Herbaceous borders, shrubs and trees with many rare and unusual plants. Pond and bog garden.

  ♿ ✖ ❀

BROOK HOUSE
Brook Street. Dr & Mrs J Secker-Walker. *Next to car park*
Enclosed partially-walled garden. Terraced patio area, lawn, mixed borders leading to small bog garden by brook and meadow with recently-restored wildlife pond.

  ♿ ✖

CRIDLANDS STEEP
Mrs A M Leitch
Large and interesting garden with cider apple orchard. Hidden paths leading to secret garden.

  ❀

NEW FAIRLANDS
3 Hill St. Mrs B Simms
Densely-planted small cottage garden with pond and rockery.

  ♿

KNOLL COTTAGE
Elaine & John Leech
(See separate entry).

  ♿ ❀

POUND HOUSE
Mr & Mrs B Hibbert. *Opp car park*
Old orchard on terraced sloping site, garden started 2000. Young trees, shrub borders, herbaceous plants, rockery, organic vegetable garden and courtyard with climbing plants and herbs.

Group opening

⑫ STOKE ST MARY GARDENS
TA3 5BY. *2¹/₂ m SE of Taunton. From M5 J25 take A358 S towards Ilminster. Turn 1st R after 1¹/₂ m. 1st R in Henlade then 1st L signed Stoke St Mary. Car parking in village hall car park, no parking at either garden.* Tea and cake. **Combined adm £3, chd free. Visitors welcome by appt May to Sept incl, groups of 10+.**
Village nestles below beautiful backdrop of Stoke Hill. The 2 gardens lie between C13 church (with stained glass windows by the renowned Patrick Reyntiens) and popular Half

Moon Inn. Playground at nearby Village Hall for parents with young children. Featured in 'Somerset Life' and local press and on local radio.

  ✖ ☕ ☎

FYRSE COTTAGE
Miss S Crockett, 01823 442556.
Secluded cottage garden with an oriental flavour. ¹/₂ acre of lush planting with stream, pond, pergola and lots of sculptures and Chinese pots. Birch avenue leading to ¹/₂ -acre wildlife area.

  ✖

TUCKERS FARMHOUSE
Rebecca Pow & Charles Clark, 01823 443816, rebecca@powproductions.tv
Family garden in lovely rural location. Formal/cottage-style extending to natural with wildlife. Jekyll-style border and 'busy persons' gravel/grass border. Topiary, exotic planting in courtyard and pear tree avenue. Kids cricket pitch. Fruit garden and raised bed vegetable garden developed for TV series. Borders devised for BBC 'Gardeners' World' magazine and vegetable garden for 'Kitchen Garden' magazine.

  ♿ ✖

⑬ NEW ◆ STON EASTON PARK
von Essen Hotels, Ston Easton BA3 4DF, 01761 241631, www.stoneaston.co.uk. *On A37 between Bath and Wells. Entrance to Park from main rd through village.* **Adm £3.50, chd free. Every Wed 6 May to 30 Sept (10.30-4). For NGS: Weds 5 Aug; 2 Sept (10.30-4).**
A hidden treasure in the heart of the Mendips. Walk through the historic 30 acres of Repton landscape alongside R Norr to the productive, walled, Victorian kitchen garden. Also visit newly-restored octagonal rose garden, stunning herbaceous border, numerous colourful flowerbeds, fruit cage and orchard. Many gravel paths, 2 steep slopes.

  ♿ ❀ ☕

⑭ STOWLEYS
Bossington Lane, Porlock TA24 8HD. Rev R L Hancock. *NE of Porlock. Off A39. 6m W of Minehead.* Cream teas. **Adm £2, chd free. Sats 4 Apr; 27 June (2-6).**

Medium-sized garden, approx 2 acres with magnificent views across Porlock Bay and Bristol Channel. Roses, unusual tender plants incl leptospermum, drimys and embothrium. Plant sale June only.

  ♿ ❀ ☕

Jekyll-style border and 'busy persons' gravel and grass border. Topiary, exotic planting in courtyard. . .

⑮ SUNNYSIDE COTTAGE
Littleton-on-Severn BS35 1NR. Harold & Hesta Knapp. *11m N of Bristol, 3¹/₂ m SW of Thornbury. From old Severn Bridge on M48 take B4461 to Alveston. In Elberton, take 1st L to Littleton-on-Severn. Carry on into The Village past the Old School. Sunnyside Cottage opp Evangelical Church.* **Adm £2, chd free. Sun 7 June (1-5). Also open The Lintels.**
Approx ¹/₂ acre of mixed perennial borders, water feature, shrubs, vegetables, also far-reaching views. Over 60 different roses and 30 clematis, several wisterias and a Blue Atlas cedar.

  ♿ ✖

⑯ SUTTON HOSEY MANOR
Long Sutton TA10 9NA. Roger Bramble. *2m E of Langport, on A372. Gates N of A372 at E end of Long Sutton.* Home-made teas. **Adm £3.50, chd £2. Sun 12 July (2.30-6).**
3 acres, of which 2 walled. Lily canal through pleached limes leading to amelanchier walk past duck pond; rose and juniper walk from Italian terrace; Judas tree avenue; *Ptelea* walk. Ornamental potager. Drive-side shrubbery. Music by The Sinfonia of Westminster directed by John Wilson.

  ♿ ✖ ❀ ☕

117 ◆ TINTINHULL
nr Yeovil BA22 8PZ. The National Trust, 01935 823289, www.nationaltrust.org.uk. *5m NW of Yeovil. Tintinhull village. Signs on A303, W of Ilchester.* Adm £5.60, chd £2.90. Weds to Suns & BH Mons, 14 Mar to 1 Nov. For NGS: Sat 18 July (11-5).
C17 and C18 house (not open). Famous 2-acre garden in compartments, developed 1900 to present day, influenced by Hidcote; many good and uncommon plants.

118 TRANBY HOUSE
Norton Lane, Whitchurch BS14 0BT. Jan Barkworth. *5m S of Bristol. 1/2 m S of Whitchurch. Leave Bristol on A37 Wells Rd, through Whitchurch village, 1st turning on R signed Norton Malreward.* Home-made teas. Adm £3, chd free. Thurs 11 June; 9 July (12-4); Sun 16 Aug (2-5).
1 1/4 -acre well-established informal garden, designed and planted to encourage wildlife. Wide variety of trees, shrubs and flowers; ponds and wild flower meadow.

119 TRISCOMBE NURSERIES
West Bagborough TA4 3HG. Stuart Parkman, www.triscombenurseries.co.uk. *8m Taunton, 15m Minehead. On A358, signed between villages of W Bagborough and Crowcombe.* Adm £2.50, chd free. Thur 4 June (2-5); Sun 25 Oct (1-4).
Private arboretum planted since 1986 in lovely location overlooking fields up to the Quantocks (AONB & SSSI). Acers, Japanese azaleas, oak, coccinea splendens, conifers. Parrotia, cornus chinensis and more, underplanted incl cowslips. 10% of plant sales to NGS on open days.

120 UBLEY HILL FARM HOUSE
Ubley Drove, Blagdon BS40 7XN. Peter Gilraine, 01761 462663, peter.gilraine@btinternet.com. *2m SE of Blagdon. From A38 (20m S of Bristol) at Churchill traffic lights, turn L onto A368 to Blagdon, 2m turn R onto B3134 (Burrington Combe), proceed to top of hill, 3m. Ubley Drove on L. 1/2 m down this no-through-rd, garden at end on R.* Home-made teas/light refreshments. Adm £3, chd free.
Visitors welcome by appt June/July/Aug.

1-acre garden set in secluded spot on top of Mendips with far-reaching views over Severn Estuary and Chew Valley. Rich and varied areas from full sun to deep shade containing many specimen plants. Sit awhile in our courtyard garden and take in the almost subtropical splendour before climbing terraced rockeries to view wildlife pond and waterfall. Wild flower meadows and mass blooming of orchids in June. A plantsman's delight.

Ruin under construction . . .

121 ◆ UNIVERSITY OF BRISTOL BOTANIC GARDEN
Bristol BS9 1JB, 0117 3314912, www.bris.ac.uk/Depts/BotanicGardens. *1/4 m W of Durdham Downs. By car from city centre, proceed across Downs towards Stoke Bishop, crossing T-lights at edge of Downs. Stoke Park Rd, 1st turning R off Stoke Hill. Parking opp in Churchill Hall Car Park.* Adm £4.50, chd free (share to Friends of Bristol University Botanic Garden). Weds, Thurs, Fris, Suns, Apr to Nov (10-4.30) plus some special Sat openings, please see website for latest details. For NGS: Sun 13 Sept (2-5).
Exciting contemporary Botanic Garden with organic flowing network of paths which lead visitors through collections of Mediterranean flora, rare natives, useful plants (incl European and Chinese herbs) and those that illustrate plant evolution. Large floral diversity, displays illustrating pollination/flowering plant evolution. Glasshouses, home to Giant Amazon Waterlily, tropical fruit and medicinal plants, orchids and cacti. Free tours illustrating how the garden has been developed and used. Exhibitions. Featured on BBC Points West. Winner Britain in Bloom SW for best use of indigenous plants.

122 VELLACOTT
Lawford, Crowcombe TA4 4AL. Kevin & Pat Chittenden, 01984 618249, pat@chitdn.freeserve.co.uk. *9m NW of Taunton. Off A358, signed Lawford.* Home-made teas. Adm £2.50, chd free. Sun 31 May; Sun 7, Thur 25, Sun 28 June; Suns 19 July; 13, 20 Sept (1-5). Visitors also welcome by appt.
1-acre cottage garden with splendid panoramic views. Mixed herbaceous and shrub borders, grasses, alpines and ponds. A collection of trees, mainly betula and sorbus grown for bark and berries. Ornamental vegetable garden and other interesting features - ruin under construction.

123 WATCOMBE
92 Church Road, Winscombe BS25 1BP. Peter & Ann Owen, 01934 842666, peter.o@which.net. *2m NW of Axbridge. From Axbridge, A371 to A38 N. Turn R up hill then next L into Winscombe Hill. After 1m reach The Square. Pink house on L after further 150yds down hill.* Cream teas. Adm £3, chd free. Suns 26 Apr; 17 May; Thur 4 June (2-5.30). Visitors also welcome by appt Apr to Aug incl.
3/4 -acre mature Italianate garden with colour-themed, informally planted mixed borders. Topiary, box hedging, lime walk, pleached hornbeams, orchard, vegetable plot, 2 small formal ponds, many unusual trees and shrubs. Shallow steps nr house.

124 WAYFORD MANOR
Crewkerne TA18 8QG. Mr & Mrs Robin Goffe, 01460 73253, robingoffe@btinternet.com. *3m SW of Crewkerne. Turning N off B3165 at Clapton; or S off A30 Chard to Crewkerne rd.* Cream teas. Adm £3, chd £1. Sun 12, Mon 13 Apr; Sun 3, Mon 4, Suns 24 May; 14 June (2-5). Visitors also welcome by appt.
The mainly Elizabethan manor (not open) mentioned in C17 for its 'fair and pleasant' garden was redesigned by Harold Peto in 1902. Formal terraces with yew hedges and topiary have fine views over W Dorset. Steps down between spring-fed ponds past mature and new plantings of magnolia, rhododendron, maples, cornus and, in season, spring bulbs, cyclamen, giant echium. Primula candelabra, arum lily, gunnera around lower ponds. Featured in 'The Lady' & 'Gardens Illustrated'.

⑫⑤ WAYSIDE
Shepperdine Road, Oldbury Naite
BS35 1RJ. Peter & Belinda Orford.
4m NW of Thornbury. From A38 follow
signs to Oldbury Power Station then
signs to Hill & Shepperdine. R at Xrds,
then L into Shepperdine Rd, 3rd L.
Home-made teas. **Adm £3, chd free**
(share to Diabetes UK). Sun 19 July
(2-5).
²/₃ -acre country garden with
ornamental pond, Mediterranean
plants, Italianate garden, undulating
lawns bordered by mature shrubs,
collection of acers, paddock, raised
beds, herb corner, 3 patios,
summerhouse. Some gravel paths.
&. ✕ ✿ ☕

This year a
living roof adds
an exciting new
dimension to
already plant-
packed beds,
secret paths
and spaces . . .

⑫⑥ WELLFIELD BARN
Walcombe Lane, Wells BA5 3AG.
David & Virginia Nasmyth, 01749
675129, david.nasmyth@talktalk.net.
1/2 m N of Wells. From A39 Bristol to
Wells rd turn R at 30mph sign into
Walcombe Lane. Entrance at 1st
cottage on R, parking signed. Home-
made teas. **Adm £3, chd free. Tue**
26 May (11-6). Visitors also welcome
by appt, coaches permitted (max
29 seater on site, larger coaches
car park 1/2 m).
1¹/₂ -acre gardens, made by owners
over the past 12yrs from concrete
farmyard. Ha-ha, wonderful views,
pond, lawn, mixed borders, grass
walks and interesting young trees.
Structured design integrates house
with landscape. New areas under
development.
&. ✿ ☕ ☎

Group opening

⑫⑦ NEW WEST BRISTOL
GARDENS
BS9 2LR. *3m NW of Bristol city*
centre. Please see individual
gardens for directions. Home-
made teas at 159 Westbury Lane.
Combined adm £5, chd free. Sun
14 June (2-6).
✕ ✿ ☕

4 HAYTOR PARK
Bristol BS9 2LR. Mr & Mrs C J
Prior, 01179 856582. *Edge of*
Coombe Dingle. From A4162 Inner
Ring Rd between A4 Portway &
A4108 Falcondale Rd, take turning
into Coombe Bridge Ave, Haytor
Park is 1st turning L. No parking in
Haytor Park. Visitors also
welcome by appt Apr to Sept
only, £3.50 incl tea and cake.
This year a living roof adds an
exciting new dimension to already
plant-packed beds, secret paths
and spaces, flower-covered arches
and wildlife pools. Rest a moment
in this peaceful place where the
boundaries blur and the dragon still
lurks!
✕ ✿ ☎

18 QUEENS GATE
Stoke Bishop BS9 1TZ. Sheila &
Eric White, 01179 626066,
sheilaericwhite@yahoo.co.uk.
From M5 J17, follow A4018 (Bristol
West) to Westbury-on-Trym. At
village centre join Stoke Lane, go
over T-lights, past shops to T-
junction. Turn R for 500yds then L
at mini-roundabout & immed R into
Druid Stoke Ave. Access lane on R
between 20 & 22. No
parking/access via Queens Gate.
Visitors also welcome by appt,
teas by arrangement.
All-yr garden with adjoining
woodland garden of betula, sorbus
and alnus. Various design features
and numerous unusual plants and
trees, grasses and containers.
Good variety of bulbs in spring,
selection of clematis in summer
and autumn. Colour-themed
borders, pergola and small
Japanese garden. Gravel area and
alterations to other areas for ease
of maintenance.
&. ✕ ✿ ☎

159 WESTBURY LANE
Coombe Dingle BS9 2PY.
Maureen Dickens. *2m from J18*
M5. L A4162/Sylvan Way,
B4054/Shirehampton Rd, R to

Westbury Lane. 1st house on R
Gently sloping garden. Large patio
at rear, walled beds, pond and
many other features. Some
common and unusual plants with
successional planting to give
colour throughout yr. Closely
planted in owner's style. From
patio, garden is seen through
rambler and other climber-covered
wooden archways. Garden now
coming into shape and changing
rapidly as plants fill out. Wheelchair
access to front garden and back
patio only.
✕ ✿

Group opening

⑫⑧ WEST HUNTSPILL GARDENS
Highbridge TA9 3SD. *1m S of*
Highbridge. Off M5 at J22. Follow A38
towards Bridgwater through
Highbridge into West Huntspill. R at
Orchard PH into Church Rd. 1st & 2nd
L, ltd parking on rd. Home-made teas.
Combined adm £3, chd free (share
to Childrens Hospice South West).
Sun 19 July (2-5.30).
Sprawling rural village with 2 churches,
village hall, village green with old pump,
school and 4 PHs, one C14.
☕

JOYCE & PETES
12 Grange Road. Joyce & Pete
Wrigglesworth
Small garden with much interest
incl shrubs, perennials, annuals,
small pond, ferns, small vegetable
patch, carnivorous plants, shingle
and grass areas.
✕ ✿

PATS
3 Sunny Close. Mrs Pat Boult
Large colourful garden with
herbaceous border 60ftx15ft with
other mixed borders of shrubs and
plants, lawn, shingle and patio
areas with pots of colourful plants,
raised vegetable area leading to
main garden through arch.
✕ ✿

⑫⑨ WESTBROOK HOUSE
West Bradley BA6 8LS. Keith
Anderson and David Mendel, 01458
850604, andersonmendel@aol.com.
4m E of Glastonbury. From A361 at W
Pennard follow signs to W Bradley
(2m). **Adm £3, chd free (share to**
West Bradley Church). Sats 25 Apr;

13 June (11-5). Visitors also welcome by appt.
1½ acres of formal gardens with mixed shrub/herbaceous borders; 2 acres of newly-planted orchard and meadows with spring flowers and species roses.

130 **NEW** **18 WOODGROVE ROAD**
Henbury BS10 7RE. Peter & Ruth Whitby.
4m N of Bristol. M5 J17, follow B4018, R at 4th R-about signed Blaise Castle. R opp Blaise Castle car park - rd next to Avon riding centre. Light refreshments & teas. **Adm £2.50, chd free.**
Suns 21 June; 12 July (2-5). Medium-sized garden divided into 3 sections. Traditional flower garden with Bonsai display and small wildlife pond. Cottage garden with greenhouse and plant sale area. Small orchard with dwarf fruit trees and small vegetable garden. Peter's art studio open for sale of watercolour and oil paintings. Gravel to main garden.

131 **NEW** **THE WYCKE**
61 Long Ashton Road, Long Ashton BS41 9HW. John & Linda Leigh.
3m SW of Bristol. A370 from Bristol then B3128 (Clevedon). After 0.6m, L into Long Ashton Rd. Follow for 0.9m. Home-made teas. **Adm £3, chd free. Sun 7 June (2-6).**
½-acre, partly-walled private garden with varied planting incl flowering shrubs, sprawling perennials and clipped evergreens. Pergola and arches adorned with roses and clematis. Attractive to both adults and children with ceramic sculptures, ponds and treehouse. Organic kitchen garden.

132 **YEWS FARM**
East Street, Martock TA12 6NF. Louise & Fergus Dowding, 01935 822202, fergus.dowding@btinternet.com.
Midway between Yeovil and Langport. Turn off main str through village at Market House, onto East Str, past PO, garden 150yds on R between Nag's Head and White Hart. Home-made teas. **Adm £4, chd free. Mon 13, Tue 14 July (2-6). Visitors also welcome by appt for groups of 15+ May/June/July.**
1 acre of theatrical planting. Outsized plants in jungle garden incl 14ft high echium. Sculptural planting for height, shape, leaf and texture. Self-seeded gravel garden, box and bay ball border, espalier apples, cloud pruning. Working organic kitchen garden feeds growing family. Hens, pigs and orchard.

Sculptural planting for height, shape, leaf and texture . . .

Bristol Area County Volunteers

County Organiser
Su Mills, 3 Over Court Mews, Over Lane, Almondsbury BS32 4DG, 01454 615438, susanlmills@gmail.com

County Treasurer
Richard Bennett, Rook Farm, Oldbury-on-Severn, BS35 1PL, 01454 412281, eileen.richard@btopenworld.com

Leaflets & Publicity
Jean Damey, 2 Hawburn Close, Brislington, Bristol BS4 2PB, 0117 9775587, jddamey@hotmail.com

Assistant County Organisers
Angela Conibere, Christmas Cottage, Church Rd, Oldbury-on-Severn BS35 1QA, 01454 413828, aeconibere@hotmail.com
Sue Etherington, 28 High Str, Wickwar GL12 8NP, 01454 294432, sue.etherington@talktalk.net
Graham Guest, The Caves, Downside Road, Backwell BS48 3DH, 01275 472393, gandsguest@btinternet.com
Margaret Jones, Weir Cottage, Weir Lane, Marshfield, Chippenham SN14 8NB, 01225 891229, weircott@3disp.co.uk
Eileen Mantell, Rook Farm, Oldbury-on-Severn BS35 1PL, 01454 412281, eileen.richard@btopenworld.com
Jane Perkins, Woodland Cottage, Oldbury-on-Severn BS35 1PL, 01454 414570, jane.perkins@simtec.ltd.uk

Somerset County Volunteers

County Organiser
Lucy Hetherington, Badgers Acre, Stone Allerton, Axbridge BS26 2NW, 01934 713159, lucyhetherington@btinternet.com

County Treasurer
David Bull, Greenfield House, Stone Allerton, Nr Axbridge BS26 2NH, 01934 712609

Leaflet Distribution
Alan Hughes, Dodhill Firs, Nailsbourne, Taunton TA2 8AT, 01823 451633, dodhill@hotmail.com

Photographer/Talks
Andrew & Sarah Wilcox, Epworth, Kingston St. Mary, Taunton TA2 8HZ, 01823 451402, epworth2@tiscali.co.uk

Assistant County Organisers
Brian & Dilly Bradley, Little Yarford Farmhouse, Kingston St Mary, Taunton TA2 8AN, 01823 451350, yarford@ic24.net
Patricia Davies-Gilbert, Coombe Quarry, West Monkton, Taunton TA2 8RE, 01823 412187, patriciacoombequarry@tiscali.co.uk
Alison Highnam, Candleford, Fernhill, East Stour, Nr Gillingham SP8 5ND, 01747 838133, allies1@btinternet.com
Rosemary Lee, Bay House West, Bay Hill, Ilminster TA19 6AT, 01460 54117, rosemarylee@supanet.com
Diana Sprent, Watermeadows, Clapton, Crewkerne TA18 8PU, 01460 74421, sprentmead@hotmail.com
Judith Stanford, Bowden Hill Cottage, Bowden Hill, Chilcompton, Radstock BA3 4EN, 01761 420466

Mark your diary with these special events in 2009

EXPLORE SECRET GARDENS DURING CHELSEA & HAMPTON COURT FLOWER SHOW WEEKS

Tue 19 May, Wed 20 May, Thur 21 May, Fri 22 May, Wed 8 July, Thur 9 July
Full day tours from £82 per person, 10% discount for groups
Advance booking required, telephone +44 (0)20 8693 1015 or email j.wookey@btinternet.com
Specially selected gardens in London, Essex, Kent, Hampshire and South Oxfordshire. The tour price includes transport and lunch with wine at a popular restaurant or pub.

HAMPTON COURT PALACE

Thur 2 Apr, Tue 23 June, Thur 25 June, Wed 15 July, Tue 4 Aug, Thur 10 Sept
Evening tours in the company of one of the Palace's specialist tour guides from 6.30 – 8pm
Tickets £6 per person. Advance booking required, telephone +44 (0)1483 211535 or
visit www.ngs.org.uk for more information
Gossip, scandal, murder, healing – you'll find it all within the Formal Gardens at Hampton Court Palace. Each tour will have its own unique feature whether it's the story of the Great Vine or the magic and mystery of the Maze.

FROGMORE – A ROYAL GARDEN (BERKSHIRE)

Tue 26 May 10am – 5.30pm (last admission 4pm)
Garden adm £4.50, chd free. Tickets available in advance or on the day.
Advance booking for groups and coaches, telephone
+44 (0) 1483 211535 or email orders@ngs.org.uk
A rare opportunity to explore 30 acres of landscaped garden, rich in history and beauty.

FLAXBOURNE FARM – FUN & SURPRISES (BEDFORDSHIRE)

Sun 7 June 10am – 5pm. Adm £5, chd free
No booking required, come along on the day!
Bring the whole family and have fun in this surprising and entertaining garden of 2 acres. Enjoy the large plant fair, live music, pets corner, birds of prey, dog agility show and much more.

WISLEY RHS GARDEN – MUSIC IN THE GARDEN (SURREY)

Fri 11 Sept 6 – 9pm
Adm (incl RHS members) £7, chd under 15 free
Save money on advance bookings for groups of 4 or more, telephone +44 (0)1483 211535 or
visit www.ngs.org.uk for more information
A special evening opening of this famous garden, exclusively for the NGS. Enjoy music and entertainment as you explore the gardens and the floral marquee on the first day of the Wisley Flower Show.

For further information visit www.ngs.org.uk or telephone 01483 211535

STAFFORDSHIRE
& part of West Midlands

www.ngs.org.uk

Opening Dates

February

SUNDAY 22
20 Four Seasons

March

SUNDAY 22
20 Four Seasons
31 Millennium Garden

SUNDAY 29
39 23 St Johns Road

April

SUNDAY 19
43 Stonehill Quarry Garden

MONDAY 20
43 Stonehill Quarry Garden

SUNDAY 26
13 12 Darges Lane
24 Heath House
50 Yew Tree Cottage

May

SUNDAY 3
36 The Old Rectory, Clifton
Campville

SATURDAY 9
20 Four Seasons
42 Small But Beautiful

SUNDAY 10
8 Bleak House

FRIDAY 15
3 Barnswood

SATURDAY 16
20 Four Seasons
39 23 St Johns Road (Evening)

SUNDAY 17
4 The Beeches
16 Dorset House
40 The Secret Garden

WEDNESDAY 20
1 Bankcroft Farm

SATURDAY 23
30 The Magic Garden
35 The Old Dairy House

SUNDAY 24
35 The Old Dairy House
50 Yew Tree Cottage

WEDNESDAY 27
1 Bankcroft Farm

THURSDAY 28
47 The Wombourne Wodehouse

SATURDAY 30
19 10 Fern Dene

SUNDAY 31
2 Barn House
23 Hamilton House

June

WEDNESDAY 3
1 Bankcroft Farm

FRIDAY 5
11 Coley Cottage
40 The Secret Garden

SUNDAY 7
6 Birch Trees
21 The Garth
24 Heath House

WEDNESDAY 10
1 Bankcroft Farm

FRIDAY 12
49 Yarlet House

SATURDAY 13
17 The Elms

SUNDAY 14
25 High Trees
28 Lightbounds
33 Moss Cottage
41 Shepherds Fold Gardens

WEDNESDAY 17
1 Bankcroft Farm

FRIDAY 19
39 23 St Johns Road
41 Shepherds Fold Gardens
(Evening)

SATURDAY 20
10 37 Brookfields Road

SUNDAY 21
4 The Beeches
9 The Bowers
10 37 Brookfields Road
18 Elvendell
28 Lightbounds
30 The Magic Garden
32 Moorfield

WEDNESDAY 24
1 Bankcroft Farm

SUNDAY 28
11 Coley Cottage
21 The Garth
27 The Hollies
29 Lilac Cottage
34 The Mount
40 The Secret Garden
44 Tanglewood Cottage
46 Wilkins Pleck

July

SATURDAY 4
6 Birch Trees

SUNDAY 5
7 Blackwood House Farm
22 Grafton Cottage
24 Heath House
45 The Wickets

SATURDAY 11
30 The Magic Garden
44 Tanglewood Cottage
48 Woodleighton Gardens

SUNDAY 12
8 Bleak House
11 Coley Cottage
14 4 Dene Close
18 Elvendell
48 Woodleighton Gardens
50 Yew Tree Cottage

MONDAY 13
38 15 St Johns Road (Evening)

FRIDAY 17
44 Tanglewood Cottage (Evening)

SATURDAY 18
5 Biddulph Grange Garden
42 Small But Beautiful

SUNDAY 19
9 The Bowers
22 Grafton Cottage
27 The Hollies
33 Moss Cottage
39 23 St Johns Road

SATURDAY 25
3 Barnswood
20 Four Seasons

SUNDAY 26
2 Barn House
31 Millennium Garden
46 Wilkins Pleck

August

SATURDAY 1
17 The Elms
30 The Magic Garden (Evening)
35 The Old Dairy House

SUNDAY 2
4 The Beeches
16 Dorset House
22 Grafton Cottage
25 High Trees

THURSDAY 6
33 Moss Cottage

FRIDAY 7
11 Coley Cottage
40 The Secret Garden

SATURDAY 8
20 Four Seasons
37 The Old School House

SUNDAY 9
37 The Old School House

TUESDAY 11
15 Dorothy Clive Garden

SATURDAY 15
26 133 Hillfield Lane
30 The Magic Garden (Evening)

SUNDAY 16
26 133 Hillfield Lane

TUESDAY 18
15 Dorothy Clive Garden

SUNDAY 23
23 Hamilton House

SUNDAY 30
6 Birch Trees

MONDAY 31
6 Birch Trees

September

SUNDAY 6
36 The Old Rectory, Clifton
Campville

SATURDAY 12
42 Small But Beautiful (Evening)

SATURDAY 19
5 Biddulph Grange Garden

October

SATURDAY 10
42 Small But Beautiful

SUNDAY 25
20 Four Seasons

Gardens open to the public

5 Biddulph Grange Garden
12 Consall Hall Landscape Garden
15 Dorothy Clive Garden

Also open by appointment ☎

2 Barn House
3 Barnswood
4 The Beeches
6 Birch Trees
8 Bleak House
9 The Bowers
11 Coley Cottage
13 12 Darges Lane
14 4 Dene Close
16 Dorset House
17 The Elms
18 Elvendell
21 The Garth
22 Grafton Cottage
24 Heath House
25 High Trees
27 The Hollies
30 The Magic Garden
32 Moorfield
33 Moss Cottage
34 The Mount

36 The Old Rectory, Clifton
Campville
38 15 St Johns Road
39 23 St Johns Road
40 The Secret Garden
41 Shepherds Fold Gardens
42 Small But Beautiful
44 Tanglewood Cottage
45 The Wickets
46 Wilkins Pleck
47 The Wombourne Wodehouse
50 Yew Tree Cottage

The Gardens

ALMA VILLA
See Cheshire & Wirral.

1 BANKCROFT FARM
Tatenhill DE13 9SA. Mrs Penelope
Adkins. *2m SW of Burton-on-Trent.
Branston Rd. Take Tatenhill Rd off A38
Burton-Branston flyover. 1m, 1st house
on L approaching village. Parking on
farm.* **Adm £3, chd free. Weds 20, 27
May; 3, 10, 17, 24 June (2-5).**
Lose yourself for an afternoon in our
1½ acre organic country garden.
Arbour, gazebo and many other
seating areas to view ponds and
herbaceous borders, backed with
shrubs and trees with emphasis on
structure, foliage and colour.
Productive fruit and vegetable gardens,
wildlife areas and adjoining 12 acre
native woodland walk. Picnics
welcome. Winner Best Rear Garden
'Brighter Borough', Gold award for
Best Vegetable Garden & Wildlife
Pond.

🐾 ✿

2 BARN HOUSE
Clayton Road, Newcastle-u-Lyme
ST5 4AB. Mike French, 01782
636650, frenchmike@talk21.com. *1m
S of Newcastle. ½m from exit 15 M6.
L to A519 Clayton Rd to Newcastle.
Straight over next r'about. Barn House
is on L after 80yds before pedestrian
crossing lights.* Home-made teas.
**Adm £3, chd free (share to Donna
Louise Trust). Suns 31 May; 26 July
(2-5). Visitors also welcome by appt.**
Beautiful landscaped ¾-acre garden
created by a surgeon whilst on call for
kidney transplantation. 3 ponds linked
by waterfalls and camellia walk make
this an oasis of peace in suburbia.
'Secret' garden with rockeries and
mature specimen trees and shrubs
with a potager/market garden to boot.

♿ 🐾 ✿ ☕ ☎

3 NEW BARNSWOOD
150 Hatherton Road, Cannock
WS11 1HL. Joan & John Rowley,
01543 503 407. *1m W of
Cannock. From Cannock town
centre follow signs for Penkridge,
1m from Cannock at top of New
Penkridge Rd, turn L into Sandy
Lane, pass Shoal Hill Tavern, down
hill to X-rds, turn L into Hatherton
Rd, 4th house on R.* Home-made
teas. **Adm £3, chd free. Fri 15
May; Sat 25 July (12-5). Visitors
also welcome by appt.**
Traditional tranquil large urban
garden, with lawns, mature trees,
shrubberies and herbaceous
borders. Good sized, well stocked
vegetable garden with raised beds,
large greenhouse and small
orchard. Amble through our rose
covered pergola and rest awhile in
the gazebo or on the many seating
areas around the garden. Slopes
may be slippery when wet.

♿ 🐾 ✿ ☕ ☎

> Amble through
> our rose covered
> pergola and rest
> awhile in the
> gazebo . . .

4 THE BEECHES
Mill Street, Rocester ST14 5JX. Mr &
Mrs K Sutton, 01889 590631,
joy@joy50.orangehome.co.uk. *5m N
of Uttoxeter. On B5030, turn R into
village by JCB factory. By Red Lion PH
& mini r'about take rd for Marston
Montgomery. Garden 250yds on R.*
Home-made teas. **Adm £3, chd free.
Suns 17 May; 21 June; 2 Aug (1.30-
5). Visitors also welcome by appt.**
Stroll along the sweeping driveway
planted with flowering shrubs and
island beds, containing mixed planting
of shrubs and perennials before
entering a stunning plant lover's garden
of approx ⅔ acre, enjoying views of
surrounding countryside. Formal box
garden, vibrant colour-themed
herbaceous borders, shrubs incl
rhododendrons, azaleas (looking good
in May), pools, roses, fruit trees,
clematis and climbing plants yr-round
garden. Cottage garden planting with a
surprise round every corner.

♿ 🐾 ✿ ☕ ☎

5 ◆ BIDDULPH GRANGE GARDEN

Grange Road, Biddulph ST8 7SD. The National Trust, 01782 517999, www.nationaltrust.org.uk. *3¹/₂ m SE of Congleton. 7m N of Stoke-on-Trent off the A527. Congleton to Biddulph rd.* Adm £6.75, chd £3.30. Wed to Sun 28 Feb to 2 Nov. For NGS: Sats 18 July; 19 Sept (11-5).

Exciting and rare survival of high Victorian garden extensively restored since 1988. Conceived by James Bateman, the 15 acres are divided into a number of smaller gardens designed to house specimens from his extensive plant collection. An Egyptian Court, Chinese Temple and Willow Pattern bridge, pinetum and arboretum combine to make the garden a miniature tour of the world. Talks led by gardeners.

6 BIRCH TREES

Copmere End, Eccleshall, Stafford ST21 6HH. Susan & John Weston, 01785 850448. *1¹/₂ m W of Eccleshall. On B5026, turn at junction signed Copmere End. After ¹/₂ m straight across Xrds by Star Inn.* Home-made teas. Adm £3, chd free. Sun 7 June; Sat 4 July; Sun 30, Mon 31 Aug (1.30-5.30). Also open Heath House 7 June. Visitors also welcome by appt.

Peaceful country garden with ample seating to allow visitors to enjoy the views over the 'borrowed landscape' of the surrounding countryside. Plant enthusiasts' garden, with rare and unusual varieties, designed with wildlife in mind. Herbaceous borders and island beds, water features and vegetable plot. Cedar alpine house with permanent planting. Featured in 'Sentinel'.

Wildlife pool, all designed to attract birds and butterflies …

7 BLACKWOOD HOUSE FARM

Horton ST13 8QA. Anne & Adam James. *4m W of Leek. 6m N of Stoke on Trent. A53 Stoke to Leek turn off at Black Horse PH in Endon, go to T-junction, turn R into Gratton Lane. Take 4th L (approx 2¹/₂ m) signed Lask Edge, over ford up bank, farm on L.* Home-made teas. Adm £3, chd free. Sun 5 July (2-5).

1¹/₂ acre country cottage garden with spectacular views. Large mixed borders, rockery, natural stream and koi carp pond. Grass and gravel paths through shrubs and trees. Lovely colourful wildlife garden packed with plants.

8 BLEAK HOUSE

Bagnall ST9 9JT. Mr & Mrs J H Beynon, 01782 534713. *4m NE of Stoke-on-Trent. A5009 to Milton Xrds, turn for Bagnall. 2m up hill past golf course to corner opp Bagnall Heights.* Cream teas. Adm £3, chd free. Suns 10 May; 12 July (1-5). Visitors also welcome by appt groups of 10+, coaches permitted.

1 acre on many levels. Natural stone quarry with jungle planting, pool and waterfall. Italianate terraces with canal, rose garden, white garden planted in Edwardian style around Edwardian house (not open), many unusual plants. Featured in 'Country Home & Interiors'.

BOLESWORTH CASTLE

See Cheshire & Wirral.

9 THE BOWERS

Church Lane, Standon, nr Eccleshall ST21 6RW. Maurice & Sheila Thacker, 01782 791244, metbowers@aol.com. *5m N of Eccleshall. Take A519 & at Cotes Heath turn L signed Standon. After 1m turn R at Xrds by church, into Church Lane ¹/₂ m on L.* Home-made teas. Adm £3, chd free. Suns 21 June; 19 July (1-5). Visitors also welcome by appt June & July evenings only.

Romantic multi-roomed cottage garden set in ¹/₃-acre quiet rural location. Strong colour-themed borders planted with rare and unusual perennials. Over 150 clematis, height and blossom in abundance. Water feature, collections of hardy geraniums and hostas. A colourful tranquil oasis. Winner of Stone in Bloom, Front & Back Gardens & Gardener of the Year.

10 37 BROOKFIELDS ROAD

Ipstones ST10 2LY. Pat & Pam Murray. *7m SE of Leek. From N on A523 turn on to B5053 southwards at Green Man Pub, Bottomhouse. From S on A52 turn N on to B5053 at Froghall. In the centre of Ipstone Village tight turn opp Trading Post shop into Brookfields Rd.* Home-made teas. Adm £3, chd free. Sat 20, Sun 21 June (2-6).

Organic garden with splendid views over Churnet Valley. Tranquil white garden, wildlife pond, herbaceous borders, cutting bed, vegetable garden with raised beds surrounded by natural hedges. Winding willow tunnel leads down to wild flower meadow, woodland and stream with bridge and stepping stone crossings. Good examples of dry stone walls and vernacular buildings. Children delight in the unexpected.

10 CHESTNUT WAY

See Derbyshire.

11 NEW COLEY COTTAGE

Coley Lane, Little Haywood ST18 0UU. Yvonne Branson, 01889 882715. *5m SE of Stafford. A51 from Rugeley or Weston signed Lt Haywood. ¹/₂ m from Seven Springs. A513 Coley Lane from Red Lion PH past Back Lane, 100yds on L opp red Post Box.* Teas. Adm £2.50, chd free. Fri 5, Suns 28 June; 12 July; Fri 7 Aug (2-5). Also open The Garth 28 June, The Secret Garden 5, 28 June, 7 Aug, Tanglewood Cottage 28 June. Visitors also welcome by appt.

A plant lover's cottage garden, full of subtle colours and perfume, every inch packed with plants. Clematis and old roses covering arches, many hostas and agapanthus, a wildlife pool, all designed to attract birds and butterflies. This garden has been created in 2 years from a blank canvas.

12 ◆ CONSALL HALL LANDSCAPE GARDEN

Wetley Rocks ST9 0AG. William Podmore, 01782 749994/551947, www.consallgardens.co.uk. *7m from Stoke-on-Trent, Leek & Cheadle. A52 after Cellarhead Xrds. Turn L on to A522, after ¹/₄ m turn R to Consall &*

*straight on through village. Garden
entrance* ¾ *m on R. Ample free car
park.* **Adm £5.50, chd £1.50. For
opening times, please tel or see
website.**
Beautiful secluded 70-acre landscape
garden. Easy access to many
exceptional vistas enhanced by lakes
and trees with bridges, grottoes and
follies. Covered seats enabling the
garden to be enjoyed in all weathers.

&. ⊗

13 12 DARGES LANE
**Great Wyrley WS6 6LE. Mrs A
Hackett, 01922 415064.** *2m SE of
Cannock. From A5 take A34 towards
Walsall. Darges Lane is 1st turning on
R (over brow of hill). House on R on
corner of Cherrington Drive.* **Adm
£2.50, chd free. Sun 26 Apr (2-6).
Visitors also welcome by appt.**
¼ -acre well-stocked plantsman's and
flower arranger's garden on two levels.
Foliage plants a special feature. Mixed
borders incl trees, shrubs and rare
plants giving yr-round interest. Features
constantly changing. National
Collection of lamiums. Collection of 93
clematis. The overall effect is attractive
and enticing to the plant lover. New
features for 2009.

✗ ⊗ **NCCPG** ☎

14 4 DENE CLOSE
**Penkridge ST19 5HL. David & Anne
Smith, 01785 712580.** *6m S of
Stafford. On A449 from Stafford. At far
end of Penkridge turn L into
Boscomoor Lane, 2nd L into Filance
Lane, 3rd R Dene Close. Please park
with consideration in Filance Lane.
Disabled only in Dene Close.* Home-
made teas. **Adm £2.50, chd free. Sun
12 July (11-5). Visitors also welcome
by appt, July/Aug, individuals or
groups.**
Medium-sized plant lovers' garden has
been created over 38yrs. Wide variety
of herbaceous perennials, foliage
plants; over 60 varieties of grasses, incl
miscanthus, pennisetums and
bamboos. Gravelled areas and mixed
borders, some colour themed, small
water feature. 'Rainbow border' 54ft
long with many perennials incl
achilleas, hemerocallis and heleniums.
Featured in 'Express & Star.

✗ ⊗ ☕ ☎

15 ♦ DOROTHY CLIVE GARDEN
**Willoughbridge, Market Drayton
TF9 4EU. Willoughbridge Garden
Trust, 01630 647237,
www.dorothyclivegarden.co.uk.** *3m
SE of Bridgemere Garden World. From*

*M6 J15 take A53, then A51 midway
between Nantwich & Stone, 2m from
village of Woore.* **Adm £5, chd free,
concessions £4.50. Open daily 28
Mar to 27 Sept every day. For NGS:
Tues 11, 18 Aug (10-5.30).**
12 informal acres, incl superb
woodland garden, alpine scree, gravel
garden, fine collection of trees and
spectacular flower borders. Renowned
in May when woodland quarry is
brilliant with rhododendrons. Creative
planting over last 6yrs has produced
stunning summer borders. Much to
see, whatever the season. Plant sale.
Wheelchairs can be reserved 01630
647168.

&. ⊗ ☕

Clematis-covered arches, intimate seating areas . . . creating a haven of peace and tranquillity . . .

16 DORSET HOUSE
**68 Station Street, Cheslyn Hay
WS6 7EE. Mary & David Blundell,
01922 419437,
david.blundell@talktalk.net.** *2m SE of
Cannock. J11 M6. A462 towards
Willenhall, L at island, follow rd to next
island. R into one-way system (Low
St), at T-junction L into Station Rd. A5
Bridgetown L over M6 toll rd to island,
L into Coppice Rd. At T-junction R into
Station St.* Home-made teas. **Adm £3,
chd free. Suns 17 May; 2 Aug (12-5).
Visitors also welcome by appt May,
Aug, groups of 10+, coaches
permitted.**
Inspirational ½ -acre plantaholic's
country garden giving all-yr interest.
Many unique features, wealth of
unusual rhododendrons, acers, shrubs
and perennials, planted in mixed
borders. Clematis-covered arches,
intimate seating areas, hidden corners,
water features, stream, all creating a
haven of peace and tranquillity.
Featured in local papers.

&. ✗ ⊗ ☕ ☎

17 THE ELMS
**Post Office Road, Seisdon,
Wolverhampton WV5 7HA. Mr Alec
Smith & Ms Susan Wilkinson, 01902
893482, a.smith365@btinternet.com.**

*6m W of Wolverhampton. A454
B'north rd. After Lealans Nurseries on
R, turn L at Fox PH into Fox Rd. 1m T-
junction. L at Seven Stars PH into
Ebstree Rd. Take 2nd L into Post
Office Rd (after narrow bridge). Garden
on R through large walled entrance.*
Home-made teas. **Adm £3.50, chd
free. Sats 13 June; 1 Aug (2-5).
Visitors also welcome by appt, June
& July, 10-25 visitors.**
4 acre country garden, set around
large Georgian villa. Kitchen herb
garden with roses, topiary and pots.
Tropical style walled garden enclosing
swimming pool. Variety of borders and
lawns. Ha-ha leading to open lawned
area with new and ancient trees.
Victorian bandstand, re-located from
Illfracombe pier, fully restored by
present owner. Some slopes.

&. ✗ ⊗ ☕ ☎

18 ELVENDELL
**4 Partridge Ride, The Burntwood,
Loggerheads TF9 2QX. John & Joy
Hainsworth, 01630 672269,
johndhainsworth@onetel.com.** *8m
SW of Newcastle-under-Lyme. On
Staffordshire-Shropshire borders. Turn
off A53 Newcastle to Market Drayton
rd on to Kestrel Drive nr Loggerheads
Xrds & adjacent hotel.* Home-made
teas. **Adm £3, chd free. Suns
21 June; 12 July (2-5). Visitors also
welcome by appt June/July only.**
½ -acre woodland idyll. Creative hard
landscaping, stunning glass water
cascade, rock garden waterfall, mature
tree fern grove, unusual and exotic
plants, bog garden, shrub and
herbaceous borders. Views with the
'wow' factor. Relax with a drink and
some scrumptious home-made cake.

✗ ⊗ ☕ ☎

19 10 FERN DENE
**Madeley, Crewe CW3 9ER. Martin &
Stella Clifford-Jones.** *10m W of
Newcastle under Lyme. Madeley is on
A525 between Keele/ Woore. Enter
Moss Lane next to Madeley Pool. 2nd
R, Charles Cotton Drive. At end turn R
then L into the Bridle Path, 1st R to
Fern Dene.* Home-made teas. **Adm
£3, chd free (share to Great Ormond
Street Hospital). Sat 30 May (2-5).**
Garden occupies 1 acre on sloping site
with natural springs. Designed to
encourage wildlife with several ponds,
native plants and woodland walk.
Planting incls many trees and shrubs
especially acers, cornus and salix.
Unusual features incl grass spiral and
oriental garden.

✗ ⊗ ☕

⓴ FOUR SEASONS

26 Buchanan Road, Walsall WS4 2EN. Tony & Marie Newton, www.fourseasonsgarden.co.uk. *Adjacent to Walsall Arboretum. M6 J7 take A34 Walsall. At double island take 3rd exit A4148 (signed Wolverhampton A454) onto Ring rd. Over 2 islands, at large junction turn R A461 (signed Lichfield). At 1st island take 3rd exit Buchanan Ave, R into Buchanan Rd.* Extensive parking in road or avenue. **Adm £3, chd free. Suns 22 Feb; 22 Mar; 25 Oct (2-5); Sats 9, 16 May; 25 July; 8 Aug (2-5.30).** S-facing 1/3 acre, suburban garden, gently sloping to arboretum, some steps. For all seasons and age groups. 200 acers, 350 azaleas, bright clipped conifers, shrubs provide back drop for spring bulbs, perennials, summer bedding. Many 'rooms' and themes incl contrast of red, blue and yellow. Jungle, oriental pagoda, water features. Winners 'Walsall in Bloom' Best Residential Large Rear Garden & 'Daily Mail' National Garden Competition. Featured in and on BBC Gardeners' World and local press and radio.

㉑ THE GARTH

2 Broc Hill Way, Milford, Stafford ST17 0UB. Mr & Mrs David Wright, 01785 661182. *4 1/2 m SE of Stafford. A513 Stafford to Rugeley rd; at Barley Mow turn R (S) to Brocton; L after 1/2 m.* Cream teas. **Adm £2.50, chd free. Suns 7, 28 June (2-6). Also open Coley Cottage, The Secret Garden, Tanglewood Cottage 28 June. Visitors also welcome by appt.** 1/2 acre garden of many levels on Channock Chase AONB. Acid soil loving plants. Series of small gardens, water features, raised beds. Rare trees, island beds of unusual shrubs and perennials, many varieties of hosta and ferns. Ancient sandstone caves. Featured in 'Express & Star', 'Staffordshire County Magazine' &'The Journal'.

㉒ GRAFTON COTTAGE

Barton-under-Needwood DE13 8AL. Margaret & Peter Hargreaves, 01283 713639, marpeter@talktalk.net. *6m N of Lichfield. Leave A38 for Catholme S of Barton, follow sign to Barton Green, 1/4 m on L.* Home-made teas. **Adm £3, chd free (share to Alzheimers Research Trust). Suns 5,** 19 July; 2 Aug (1.30-5.30). **Visitors also welcome by appt for groups, minimum charge £50. Coaches permitted.** Idyllic English cottage garden, with winding paths and the scent of old fashioned roses, dianthus, sweet peas, phlox, lilies. Herbaceous border with delphiniums, clematis, campanula, achillea, viola and many more unusual perennials. Textured plants, artemesia, atripex, heuchera form the basis of colour themed borders. Cottage garden annuals add to the tranquillity. Owners' particular interest is viticella clematis. Small vegetable plot. Plants propagated for sale. Featured in 'Country Homes & Interiors'. Wheelchair access to front, drive, teas & plants.

㉓ NEW HAMILTON HOUSE

Roman Grange, Roman Road, Little Aston B74 3GA. Philip & Diana Berry. *3m N of Sutton Coldfield. Follow A454 (Walsal Rd) & enter Roman Rd, Little Aston Pk. Roman Grange is 1st L after church but enter rd via pedestrian gate.* Light refreshments & teas. **Adm £3.50, chd free. Suns 31 May; 23 Aug (2-5).** 1/2 -acre N facing woodland garden in tranquil setting, making the most of challenging shade, providing haven for birds and other wild life. Large pond with stone bridge, pergolas, water features, box garden with a variety of roses and herbs. Interesting collection of rhododendrons, hostas and ferns. Music in the air and some surprises.

㉔ HEATH HOUSE

Offley Brook, nr Eccleshall ST21 6HA. Dr D W Eyre-Walker, 01785 280318. *3m W of Eccleshall. Take B5026 towards Woore. At Sugnall turn L, after 1 1/2 m turn R immed by stone garden wall. After 1m straight across Xrds.* Home-made teas & light refreshments. **Adm £3, chd free (share to Adbaston Church). Suns 26 Apr; 7 June; 5 July (2-5). Also open Birch Trees 7 June. Visitors also welcome by appt.** 1 1/2 -acre country garden of C18 miller's house in lovely valley setting, overlooking mill pool. Plantsman's garden containing many rare and unusual plants in borders, bog garden, woodland, alpine house, raised bed and shrubberies.

㉕ HIGH TREES

18 Drubbery Lane, nr Longton Park ST3 4BA. Peter & Pat Teggin, 01782 318453. *5m S of Stoke-on-Trent. Off A5035, midway between Trentham Gardens & Longton. Opp Longton Park.* Cream teas. **Adm £3, chd free (share to Douglas Macmillan Hospice). Suns 14 June; 2 Aug (2-5). Visitors also welcome by appt June & July, coaches permitted.** Very pretty secluded suburban garden with coordinated design features. Colour themed herbaceous borders planted with many unusual plants highlighting colour, texture and form for all yr interest. An ideas garden where roses intermingle with clematis, and the coolness of hostas and ferns contrast with lush summer planting.

㉖ NEW 133 HILLFIELD LANE

Burton-on-Trent DE13 0BL. Clive & Margaret Smith. *Exit A38 at Clay Mills Junction onto A5121 Derby Rd, 1st R into Hillfield Lane.* Home-made teas. **Adm £3, chd free (share to RSPCA). Sat 15, Sun 16 Aug (1.30-5).** Award winning 1/3 -acre suburban garden with water features, raised beds and vegetable garden. Many innovative features. Awarded 5 Golds in 'East Staffs in Bloom'.

Music in the air and some surprises . . .

27 THE HOLLIES
Leek Road, Cheddleton ST13 7HG.
Tim & Amanda Bosson, 01538
361079, tim_bosson@hotmail.com,
www.hollies-garden.co.uk. *2m S of
Leek. On A520. Large NGS arrow to
direct.* Cream teas. **Adm £3, chd free.
Suns 28 June; 19 July (2-8).** Visitors
also welcome by appt.
On edge of village a private walled
garden and a delight to see. Amanda
and Tim invite you to wander around
their secret oasis whilst watching their
various water features. Impressive
informal garden which features an
array of colour surrounded by shrubs
and trees. Devon Cream Teas are a
speciality for this couple from
Devonshire and the cream is sent from
Devon for the occasion. Large
marquee for inclement weather.

   🚫 🐕 ☕ 🏠

28 NEW LIGHTBOUNDS
Wood Lane, Uttoxeter
ST14 8BE. Anthony & Jenny
Phillips. *Opposite race course.
Follow signs to race course. House
is last on R opp race course, just
past speed de-restriction signs.
Car park 100yds further on.* Home-
made teas. **Adm £4, chd free.
Suns 14, 21 June (2-5).**
2-acre garden set within 4-acre
plot surrounding an Edwardian
house (not open). Created over the
past 15 yrs, a mixture of formal
and informal spaces joined by wide
green paths and incl herbaceous
borders, bamboo garden, quiet
sitting areas and bog garden. Many
unusual plants. Disabled parking
close to house. Some long shallow
slopes will require wheelchair to be
pushed rather than under
occupant's power.

   🚫 🐕 ☕

29 LILAC COTTAGE
Chapel Lane, Gentleshaw, nr
Rugeley WS15 4ND. Mrs Sylvia
Nunn, www.lilaccottagegarden.
co.uk. *5m NW of Lichfield. Approx
midway between Lichfield & Rugeley
on A51 at Longdon, turn W into
Borough Lane signed Cannock Wood
& Gentleshaw. Continue 1m to T-
junction. L for 1¹/₂ m to Gentleshaw.
From Burntwood, A5190 head N on
Rugeley Rd at Burntwood Swan island;
turn L at Xrds approx ¹/₂ m past Nags
Head PH, over Xrds to Gentleshaw.
Parking only at Cannock Wood and*

*Gentleshaw village hall. Roadside
disabled & elderly parking only at Lilac
Cottage.* Home-made teas. **Adm £3,
chd free. Sun 28 June (1.30-5).**
Plantswoman's 1-acre country garden.
At 750ft, commanding views extend
across Trent Valley. Wealth of unusual
trees, shrubs, roses and perennials
with emphasis on colour, form and
texture creating all yr interest. Wildlife
pond, bog garden, sweeping lawns,
colour themed mixed borders, vibrant
'hot' border, shady walks, 'The Dell'.
Surprise new landscaped area planned
for 2009, weather permitting!!!. Close
to ancient Iron Age Fort 'Castle Ring'
and Cannock Chase Forest, an area of
outstanding natural beauty. Perennial
plants for sale. Featured in & on BBC
Gardeners' World, 'Express & Star' &
local press. Some gravel paths.

   🚫 🐕 ❀ ☕

Bamboo garden, quiet sitting areas and bog garden . . .

30 THE MAGIC GARDEN
43 Broad Lane, Bradmore,
Wolverhampton WV3 9BW. Bob
Parker & Greg Kowalczuk, 01902
332228,
roboparker@blueyonder.co.uk. *2m
SW of Wolverhampton. 2m from town
centre on SW side. Follow signs for
Bantock House, adjacent to Bantock
Park. Broad Lane is part of B4161.
200yds from Bradmore Arms T-light.*
Home-made teas. **Adm £3, chd free.
Sats 23 May,11 July, Sun 21 June;
(1.30-5.30). Evening Openings £4,
chd free wine, Sats 1, 15 Aug (7.30-
10.30).** Visitors also welcome by
appt June to Aug, groups of 15+.
Escape the hustle and bustle of busy
urban surroundings and enter the
secure solitude of the high walled
secret garden. A magical Aladdin's
cave, full of the unexpected. Candles
flicker and lanterns glow in the evening.
Daylight is no less enchanting, with the
background is green, a plantsman's
garden, but different. Featured in 'Daily
Mail' Weekender Magazine.

   🐕 ❀ ☕ 🏠

31 MILLENNIUM GARDEN
London Road, Lichfield WS14 9RB.
Carol Cooper. *1m S of Lichfield. Off
A38 along A5206 towards Lichfield
¹/₄ m past A38 island towards Shoulder
of Mutton PH. Park in field on L.*
Home-made teas. **Adm £3.50, chd
free. Suns 22 Mar; 26 July (2-6).**
2 acre garden with many flower beds,
host of golden daffodils in March.
Millennium bridge over landscaped
water garden, leading to attractive
walks along rough mown paths
through maturing woodland, and
seasonal wild flowers, Uneven surfaces
and gravel paths.

   🚫 🐕 ☕

32 MOORFIELD
Post Lane, Endon, Stoke-on-Trent
ST9 9DU. Ian & June Sellers, 01782
504096. *4m W of Leek. 6m from
Stoke-on-Trent A53. Turn into Station
Rd over railway line, canal bridge with
lights, 1st on L opp Endon Cricket
Club.* Home-made teas. **Adm £3, chd
free. Sun 21 June (1.30-5).** Visitors
also welcome by appt.
Flower arrangers delight situated in
¹/₃ acre. This colourful garden has a
variety of different styles ranging from
herbaceous borders to areas with a
Mediterranean feel, the garden incls
many structural features such as
unusual wooden tree stumps to a
spacious summerhouse. Featured in
and on Radio & Local Paper.

   🚫 ❀ ☕ 🏠

33 MOSS COTTAGE
Moss Lane, Madeley CW3 9NQ. Liz
& Alan Forster, 01782 751366,
lizcforster@aol.com. *7m W of
Newcastle-under-Lyme. Madeley is on
A525 between Keele/Woore. Enter
Moss Lane next to Madeley pool.*
Home-made teas. **Adm £3, chd free.
Suns 14 June; 19 July; Thur 6 Aug
(1.30-5).** Visitors also welcome by
appt.
¹/₃ acre secluded and colourful cottage
style garden with mixed beds and
herbaceous borders.Small wildlife
pond and specific wildlife planting.
Small rock garden with water feature.
There are many places to sit, relax and
enjoy the flowers. A garden with
interest for the whole year. Beautifully
scented old roses, peonies, pinks and
poppies. Plant sales by
www.specialperennials.com. Featured
in & on Sky TV 'Open Gardens'.
'Britain in Bloom' Newcastle-under-
Lyme, Gold Award.

   🐕 ❀ ☕ 🏠

34 THE MOUNT
Coton, Gnosall ST20 0EQ. Andrew &
Celia Payne, 01785 822253. *8m W of
Stafford. 4m E of Newport. From
Stafford take A518 W towards
Newport/Telford. Go through Gnosall,
over canal. Garden on edge of Gnosall
Village, on LH-side of A518. Parking
approx 200yds signed up lane.* Home-
made teas. **Adm £3, chd free. Sun 28
June** (2-5.30). **Visitors also welcome
by appt July/Aug only.**
Evolving and colourful plantsman's
garden divided into different areas
covering ³/₄ -acre. Wildlife friendly with
small pond and bog area, over 70
hostas, huge Kiftsgate rose, interesting
and colourful containers combined
with some exotic planting, numerous
trees, many unusual perennials and
raised vegetable beds.

35 THE OLD DAIRY HOUSE
Trentham Park, Stoke-on-Trent
ST4 8AE. Philip & Michelle Moore.
*S edge of Stoke-on-Trent. Behind
Trentham Gardens on rd to Trentham
Church and Trentham Park Golf Club.
From A34 turn into Whitmore Rd
B5038. 1st L and follow NGS signs.*
Home-made teas. **Adm £3, chd free.
Sat 23, Sun 24 May;** (1-5); **Evening
Opening,** £4.50, wine, **Sat 1 Aug**
(6-9.30).
Grade 2 listed house (not open)
designed by Sir Charles Barry forms
backdrop to this 2-acre garden in
peaceful parkland setting. Shaded area
for rhododendrons and azaleas. Many
established trees, 'cottage garden'
area, and several long borders. Large
seating area for relaxing teas.

**36 THE OLD RECTORY,
CLIFTON CAMPVILLE**
B79 0AP. Martin & Margaret Browne,
01827 373533,
mbrowne526@aol.com. *6m N of
Tamworth. 2m W of M42 J11, in
centre of Clifton Campville. Village
signed off B5493 from Statfold or No
Man's Heath. Entrance to garden on S
side of Main St at top of hill, between
bus shelter and school.* Home-made
teas. **Adm £3, chd free. Suns 3 May;
6 Sept** (12.30-4.30). **Visitors also
welcome by appt groups (2 - 30)
welcome throughout the year, visits
tailored to your needs.**
Tranquil 2-acre garden around historic
former Rectory developed over 27yrs
by the present owners. Established
trees enhanced by a diverse range of

plants. Enjoy a garden on an ancient
site, full of colour and interest in all
seasons. Gravel and bark paths give
easy access to lawns, borders, fruit
and vegetables. Small walled garden
and gravel areas. Opportunity to visit
one of the Midland's finest mediaeval
churches. Featured in 'Staffordshire
County Magazine' & 'Lichfield
Diocesan Sound Digest'. Some gravel
paths.

Colourful containers combined with some exotic planting . . .

37 THE OLD SCHOOL HOUSE
Stowe-by-Chartley, Stafford
ST18 0LG. Keith & Wendy Jones.
*5m S of Stone. Adjacent to village hall,
7m from Stafford A51 at Weston. A518
E towards Uttoxeter. Approx 1¹/₂ m
past Amerton Farm. After approx ¹/₂ m
turn R signed Stowe (Bridge Lane). L
at T-junction past church & Cock Inn.
100yds on R.* Light lunches (Sun) &
home-made teas. **Adm £2.50, chd
free. Sat 8** (1.30-5.30), **Sun 9 Aug**
(11-5).
Informal cottage-style garden of
¹/₂ acre; developed from former school
yard. Mixed herbaceous borders; lawn
and recycled paved sitting areas;
rockery, small pond, containers.
Unexpected garden hidden from the
road creating a tranquil setting within a
small country village. Set paths and
small steps.

ORCHARD VILLA
See Cheshire & Wirral.

38 15 ST JOHNS ROAD
Pleck, Walsall WS2 9TJ. Maureen &
Sid Allen, 01922 442348,
sidallen@blueyonder.co.uk. *2m W of
Walsall. Off J10 M6. Head for Walsall
on A454 Wolverhampton Rd. Turn R
into Pleck Rd A4148 then 4th R into St
Johns Rd.* **Adm £2.50, chd free.
Evening Opening Mon 13 July**
(6-9). **Visitors also welcome by appt
June to Aug, 10 to 50, coaches
permitted.**
Long peaceful garden, small trees,
shrubs, perennials, some unusual.

Tropical area, koi pond. Visit mid June
for lush foliage and good leaf and
colour combinations. Small Japanese
style area with maples, bridge, stream,
teahouse. Walk through shady area,
with ferns, into gravel garden, pretty
planting for wildlife at best July/Aug.

39 23 ST JOHNS ROAD
Stafford ST17 9AS. Colin & Fiona
Horwath, 01785 258923,
fiona_horwath@yahoo.co.uk. *¹/₂ m S
of Stafford Town Centre. On A449.
Through entrance into private park,
therefore please park considerably.*
Home-made teas. **Adm £3, chd free.
Sun 29 Mar; Fri 19 June; Sun 19 July**
(2-5). **Evening Opening** £4, wine,
Sat 16 May (6-8.30). **Visitors also
welcome by appt.**
Town garden with a country feel
packed with interesting plants and run
organically. Many bulbs, shady walk,
herbaceous borders, wildlife pond and
bog garden. Climbers ramble over
pergolas and arches; herb garden;
rockery and raised vegetable beds.
Victorian-style greenhouse.

40 THE SECRET GARDEN
Little Haywood ST18 0UL. Derek
Higgott & David Aston, 01889
883473. *5m SE of Stafford. A51, from
Rugeley or Weston signed Little
Haywood ¹/₂ m from Seven Springs.
A513 Coley Lane from public house's
at Back Lane, R into Coley Grove.
Entrance to garden in Coley Grove.*
Home-made teas & light refreshments.
**Adm £3, chd free. Suns 17 May, 28
June; Fris 5 June; 7 Aug** (11-5).
Also open Coley Cottage 5,
28 June, 7 Aug, **The Garth,
Tanglewood Cottage** 28 June.
Visitors also welcome by appt.
Wander past the other cottage
gardens and through the evergreen
arch and there before you a fantasy for
the eyes and soul. Stunning garden
approx ¹/₂ -acre, created over the last
25yrs. Strong colour theme of trees
and shrubs, underplanted with
perennials 1000 bulbs and laced with
clematis; other features incl water,
laburnum and rose tunnel and unique
buildings. Is this the jewel in the
crown? Raised gazebo with wonderful
views over untouched meadows and
Cannock Chase. Hardy Plant Society
sale in village hall Sun 17 May.
Featured in 'Staffordshire County ' &
'Express & Star'. Gravel paths.

The evening opening with a mass of coloured lights and candles is a must for an unforgettable visit . . .

Group opening

41 SHEPHERDS FOLD GARDENS

Wildwood, Stafford ST17 4SF, 01785 660819, alison.jordan2@btinternet.com. 3m S of Stafford. Follow A34 out of Stafford towards Cannock, 2nd R onto the Wildwood Estate. Follow ring rd around, Shepherds Fold is 5th turning on L. Limited parking in cul de sac. Please use as drop off & park on ring rd. Home-made teas at no. 8, glass of wine no. 9. **Combined adm £3.50, chd free (share to Guide Dogs for the Blind). Sun 14 June (11.30-5). Evening Opening** £4.50, wine, Fri 19 June (6.30-8.30). Visitors also welcome by appt for all 3 gardens. Deceptive gardens with views over open countryside. Three very different gardens showing how similar sites can be made to look and feel individual. Fantastic home made cakes to enjoy, and a wide range of plants for sale, all propagated from the gardens.

🌼 ☕ ☎

7 SHEPHERDS FOLD
Avril & David Tooth
W-facing plant lovers' garden with many interesting features incl variety of unusual pots and water feature. Themed area with sun house.

8 SHEPHERDS FOLD
David & Janet Horsnall
Maturing S-facing garden on heavy clay. Variety of different areas and terraces. Plantsman's garden with magnificent roses, quiet areas with architectural plants and wide range of perennials. Area of wild flowers.
🌼

9 SHEPHERDS FOLD
Peter & Alison Jordan
S-facing garden on heavy clay soil. No chemicals used on garden. Informal cottage planting, interesting terraces and features, yr-round interest, unusual perennials. How to garden with help from Guide Dog puppies!
🌼

42 NEW SMALL BUT BEAUTIFUL

6 Fishley Close, Bloxwich WS3 3QA. John & Julie Quinn, 01922 475551. 1m NE of Bloxwich. Turn at side of Bloxwich Golf Club on A34, L at island, L at Spar into Fishley Lane, park on Saddlers PH (garden 5 mins walk away). Cream teas. **Adm £2.50, chd free (share to St Vincent de Paul). Sats 9 May; 18 July; 10 Oct (10-4). Evening Opening** £3.50, wine, Sat 12 Sept (7-10). Visitors also welcome by appt. This 10m x 10m garden uses every space and corner to its best potential. Mature Japanese maples complement a bridge and stunning water feature. All year round colour is achieved with little maintenance. The evening opening with a mass of coloured lights and candles is a must for an unforgettable visit. Featured in 'Garden News', & local press.

🐶 ☕ ☎

43 STONEHILL QUARRY GARDEN

Great Gate, Croxden, nr Uttoxeter ST10 4HF. Mrs Caroline Raymont, 01889 507202. 6m NW of Uttoxeter. A50 to Uttoxeter. Take B5030 to JCB Rocester, L to Hollington & Croxden Abbey. Third R into Keelings Lane & Croxden Abbey. At Great Gate, T-junction L to Stonehill. Tea & Coffee. **Adm £2.50. Sun 19, Mon 20 Apr (2-5).** 6-acre quarry garden incorporating numerous ornamental trees and shrubs (magnolias, acers, catalpa, Davidia, paeonias, azaleas) underplanted with unusual Asiatic and American woodlanders (lilies, trillium, erythroniums, paris, podophyllum, arisaemas, hellebores) bamboo 'jungle', rock garden, mixed borders. Spring bulbs and hellebores. Autumn colour of particular interest with new winter bark feature to give a 'zing' to dreary days. C12 Cistercian Abbey ruins (adm free) ½ kilometre away. Featured in & on BBC 'Gardeners' World', 'Staffs Newsletter' & other press. Regret NOT suitable for children.

♿ 🐶 🌼 ☕

44 NEW TANGLEWOOD COTTAGE

Crossheads, Colwich ST18 0UG. Dennis & Helen Wood, 01889 882857, shuritdog@hotmail.com. 5m SE of Stafford. A51 from Rugeley or Weston, signed Colwich, into village - Main Rd. Past church on L and school on R, under bridge & up hill, immed on R turn into Railway Lane (Crossheads) keep rail track to R & Abbey on L, approx ¼ m (it does lead somewhere). Park on grass as signposted. Home-made teas & cream teas. **Adm £3, chd free (share to Katherine House Hospice). Sun 28 June; Sat 11 July (11-5). Evening Opening** £4, wine, Fri 17 July (5-8.30). Also open **The Garth, Coley Cottage, The Secret Garden** 28 June. Visitors also welcome by appt June to Aug, mainly weekends & evenings. A large country cottage garden, divided into smaller areas of interest. Mixed borders, koi carp pool, tranquil seated areas, vegetables and fruit, chickens and aviary. Exotics and unusual perennials incl abutilons, daturas, dicksonias and palms. Plant lover's garden. Winners of Stafford in Bloom large back garden and Haywood's Large Garden.

🐶 ☕ ☎

45 THE WICKETS

47 Long Street, Wheaton Aston ST19 9NF. Tony & Kate Bennett, 01785 840233, ajtonyb@tiscali.co.uk. 8m W of Cannock, 10m N of Wolverhampton. From M6 J12 turn W towards Telford on A5; across A449 Gailey r'about; A5 for 1½ m; turn R signed Stretton, 150yds turn L signed Wheaton Aston; 2½ m turn L; ½ m over canal bridge; garden on R. Or Bradford Arms Wheaton Aston 2m. **Adm £2.50, chd free. Sun 5 July (1.30-5). Visitors also welcome by appt.** ⅓ -acre garden of many features, full of ideas for smaller gardens. A more open front garden is contrasted by themed areas behind the house. Pond, dry stream, clock golf, gravel beds and hanging baskets and containers. Popular and pleasant walks along Shropshire Union Canal just 25yds away.

♿ 🐶 ☎

46 WILKINS PLECK

off Three Mile Lane, Whitmore, nr
Newcastle-under-Lyme ST5 5HN.
Sheila & Chris Bissell, 01782
680351. *5m SW from Newcastle-
under-Lyme. Take A53 SW from
Newcastle-under-Lyme. At Whitmore
turn R at Mainwaring Arms PH. Signed
RH-side at Cudmore Fisheries. Please
NO Dogs in car park in field at
landowners request.* Home-made teas.
**Adm £4.50, chd free. Suns 28 June;
26 July (1.30-5).** Visitors also
welcome by appt.
5½ acres of paradise in North
Staffordshire. Featured on TV 'Open
Gardens', & in 'Country Homes &
Interiors', other publications, Garden
Retreats Calendar.

Archways,
bridges and
steps, lead to
a selection of
tranquil resting
places . . .

47 THE WOMBOURNE WODEHOUSE

Wolverhampton WV5 9BW. Mr &
Mrs J Phillips, 01902 892202. *4m S
of Wolverhampton. Just off A449 on
A463 to Sedgley.* Home-made teas.
**Adm £4, chd free. Thur 28 May
(2-5.30).** Visitors also welcome by
appt May, June & July.
18-acre garden laid out in 1750. Mainly
rhododendrons, herbaceous border,
woodland walk, water garden and over
170 different varieties of tall bearded
irises in walled kitchen garden. Partial
wheelchair access.

Group opening

48 NEW WOODLEIGHTON GARDENS

Woodleighton Grove, Uttoxeter
ST14 8BX. *SE area of Uttoxeter.
Leave town centre on B5017
Marchington Rd, ¼ m after the
turning to Racecourse, turn R into
Woodleighton Grove. Limited
parking in cul-de-sac, plenty of
parking in road before.* Home-
made teas at 9 Woodleighton
Grove. **Combined adm £3.50,
chd free. Sat 11 (11-5), Sun
12 July (1.30-5.30).**
The owners of two adjacent
properties, in a quiet cul-de-sac,
visually demonstrate very varied
and interesting approaches to the
design and planting of their above-
average sized, new development
gardens.

NEW APOLLONIA

11 Woodleighton Grove. Helen
& David Loughton
Plantaholics garden, strong
structure on several levels.
Summer house, laburnum arch,
natural stream, some steep steps.
Unusual and interesting planting
incl bamboos, tree ferns, bananas,
hostas and agaves. A place to
relax and enjoy.

NEW KARIBU

9 Woodleighton Grove. Graham
& Judy White
Unusual and distinctive garden,
set on two levels, natural stream,
summerhouse, folly and gazebo.
Informally planted with shrubs,
conifers and herbaceous.
Archways, bridges and steps,
lead to a selection of tranquil
resting places. The garden
discreetly houses a number of
artefacts. The greenhouse

contains about 300 different cacti
and succulents. Narrow paths with
steep drops. Limited wheelchair
access to top garden and
greenhouse only.

49 YARLET HOUSE

Yarlet, Stafford ST18 9SU. Mr & Mrs
Nikolas Tarling. *2m S of Stone. Take
A34 from Stone towards Stafford, turn
L into Yarlet School and L again into
car park.* Home-made teas & light
refreshments. **Adm £3, chd free
(share to Staffordshire Wildlife
Trust). Fri 12 June (1.30-4.30).**
4 acre garden with extensive lawns,
walks and herbaceous borders.
Water garden with rare lilies, putting
course and garden chess board.
Sweeping views across Trent Valley to
Sandon. Yarlet School Art Open.
Gravel paths.

50 YEW TREE COTTAGE

Podmores Corner, Long Lane, White
Cross, Haughton ST18 9JR. Clive &
Ruth Plant, 01785 282516,
pottyplantz@aol.com. *4m W of
Stafford. Take A518 W Haughton, turn
R Station Rd (signed Ranton) 1m, then
turn R at Xrds ¼ m on R.* Home-made
teas & light refreshments. **Adm £3,
chd free. Suns 26 Apr; 24 May; 12
July (2-5).** Visitors also welcome by
appt.
Cottage garden of ⅓ acre designed by
plantaholics to complement Victorian
cottage. Many unusual perennials incl
shade lovers such as meconopsis and
arisaema. Gardeners are passionate
about salvia and lathyrus. Gravel and
vegetable gardens, courtyard. Come
and sit in our new oak timbered vinery
and take tea.

Staffordshire County Volunteers

SUFFOLK

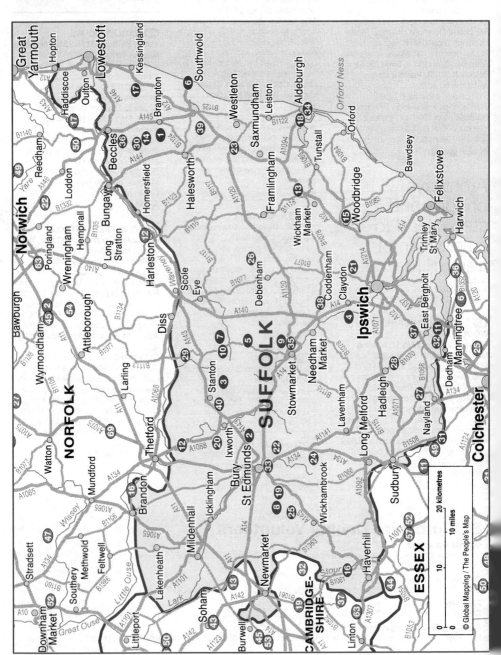

Opening Dates

February

SUNDAY 15
14 Gable House

March

SUNDAY 22
11 East Bergholt Place

SUNDAY 29
38 Woodwards

April

WEDNESDAY 1
39 Woottens

THURSDAY 2
39 Woottens

SUNDAY 5
3 The Beeches

TUESDAY 7
39 Woottens

WEDNESDAY 8
39 Woottens

THURSDAY 9
39 Woottens

SUNDAY 12
32 Rosemary

TUESDAY 14
39 Woottens

WEDNESDAY 15
39 Woottens

THURSDAY 16
39 Woottens

SATURDAY 18
4 Blakenham Woodland Garden

SUNDAY 19
4 Blakenham Woodland Garden
10 Corner Cottage
16 Great Thurlow Hall

TUESDAY 21
39 Woottens

WEDNESDAY 22
39 Woottens

THURSDAY 23
39 Woottens

SATURDAY 25
21 Larks Hill
29 Redgrave Gardens

SUNDAY 26
11 East Bergholt Place
29 Redgrave Gardens

TUESDAY 28
39 Woottens

WEDNESDAY 29
39 Woottens

THURSDAY 30
39 Woottens

May

SUNDAY 3
18 Heron House
31 Rosedale
34 Stanford House

TUESDAY 5
39 Woottens

WEDNESDAY 6
10 Corner Cottage
39 Woottens

THURSDAY 7
39 Woottens

SATURDAY 9
7 Church Farm

SUNDAY 10
7 Church Farm

TUESDAY 12
39 Woottens

WEDNESDAY 13
10 Corner Cottage
39 Woottens

THURSDAY 14
39 Woottens

SATURDAY 16
40 Wyken Hall

SUNDAY 17
27 The Priory
40 Wyken Hall

TUESDAY 19
39 Woottens

WEDNESDAY 20
10 Corner Cottage
39 Woottens

THURSDAY 21
39 Woottens

SATURDAY 23
21 Larks Hill

SUNDAY 24
20 The Kitchen Garden
33 South Hill
39 Woottens

MONDAY 25
20 The Kitchen Garden
33 South Hill
39 Woottens

TUESDAY 26
39 Woottens
39 Woottens

WEDNESDAY 27
10 Corner Cottage
39 Woottens
39 Woottens

THURSDAY 28
39 Woottens
39 Woottens

FRIDAY 29
39 Woottens

SATURDAY 30
39 Woottens

SUNDAY 31
28 Priory Hall
37 Windmill Cottage
39 Woottens

June

MONDAY 1
39 Woottens

TUESDAY 2
39 Woottens
39 Woottens

WEDNESDAY 3
39 Woottens
39 Woottens

THURSDAY 4
39 Woottens
39 Woottens

FRIDAY 5
39 Woottens

SATURDAY 6
22 The Lucy Redman School of Garden Design
36 White House Farm
39 Woottens

SUNDAY 7
2 Barton Mere
14 Gable House
39 Woottens

MONDAY 8
39 Woottens

TUESDAY 9
39 Woottens
39 Woottens

WEDNESDAY 10
39 Woottens
39 Woottens

THURSDAY 11
39 Woottens

SUNDAY 14
24 Makins Farmhouse
38 Woodwards

TUESDAY 16
39 Woottens

WEDNESDAY 17
39 Woottens

THURSDAY 18
39 Woottens

FRIDAY 19
26 Monksfield House (Evening)

SUNDAY 21
① Barracks Cottage
㉕ Millfields House
㉖ Monksfield House

TUESDAY 23
㉟ Woottens

WEDNESDAY 24
㉟ Woottens

THURSDAY 25
㉟ Woottens

SATURDAY 27
⑥ Bridge Foot Farm
⑦ Church Farm
㉑ Larks Hill

SUNDAY 28
⑥ Bridge Foot Farm
⑦ Church Farm
⑨ Columbine Hall
⑬ The Firs
⑰ Henstead Exotic Garden

TUESDAY 30
㉟ Woottens

July

WEDNESDAY 1
㉟ Woottens

THURSDAY 2
㉟ Woottens

SATURDAY 4
⑮ 12 Godfreys Wood

SUNDAY 5
㉓ Magnolia House
㉟ Stowupland Gardens

TUESDAY 7
㉟ Woottens

WEDNESDAY 8
㉟ Woottens

THURSDAY 9
㉟ Woottens

SATURDAY 11
㊳ Woodwards
㉟ Woottens

SUNDAY 12
㉚ Redisham Hall
㊳ Woodwards
㉟ Woottens

TUESDAY 14
㉟ Woottens

WEDNESDAY 15
㉟ Woottens

THURSDAY 16
㉑ Larks Hill
㉟ Woottens

SATURDAY 18
⑲ Ickworth House Park & Gardens
㉟ Woottens

SUNDAY 19
㉟ Woottens

TUESDAY 21
㉟ Woottens

WEDNESDAY 22
㉟ Woottens

THURSDAY 23
㉟ Woottens

SATURDAY 25
㉟ Woottens

SUNDAY 26
⑧ Cobbs Hall
㉟ Woottens

TUESDAY 28
㉟ Woottens

WEDNESDAY 29
㉟ Woottens

THURSDAY 30
㉟ Woottens

August

SUNDAY 2
㉛ Rosedale

TUESDAY 4
㉟ Woottens

WEDNESDAY 5
㉟ Woottens

THURSDAY 6
㉟ Woottens

TUESDAY 11
㉟ Woottens

WEDNESDAY 12
㉟ Woottens

THURSDAY 13
㉟ Woottens

SUNDAY 16
㊳ Woodwards

TUESDAY 18
㉟ Woottens

WEDNESDAY 19
⑩ Corner Cottage
㉟ Woottens

THURSDAY 20
㉟ Woottens

TUESDAY 25
㉟ Woottens

WEDNESDAY 26
㉟ Woottens

THURSDAY 27
㉟ Woottens

September

TUESDAY 1
㉟ Woottens

WEDNESDAY 2
㉟ Woottens

THURSDAY 3
㉟ Woottens

SUNDAY 6
㉖ Monksfield House

TUESDAY 8
㉟ Woottens

WEDNESDAY 9
㉟ Woottens

THURSDAY 10
㉟ Woottens

TUESDAY 15
㉟ Woottens

WEDNESDAY 16
㉟ Woottens

THURSDAY 17
㉟ Woottens

TUESDAY 22
㉟ Woottens

WEDNESDAY 23
㉟ Woottens

THURSDAY 24
㉟ Woottens

TUESDAY 29
㉟ Woottens

WEDNESDAY 30
㉟ Woottens

Gardens open to the public

④ Blakenham Woodland Garden
⑫ Euston Hall
⑲ Ickworth House Park & Gardens
㉖ Monksfield House
㊳ Woodwards
㉟ Woottens
㊵ Wyken Hall

By appointment only

⑤ Bresworth House

Also open by appointment

① Barracks Cottage
⑦ Church Farm
⑩ Corner Cottage
⑬ The Firs
⑭ Gable House
⑰ Henstead Exotic Garden
⑱ Heron House
㉑ Larks Hill
㉒ The Lucy Redman School of Garden Design
㉓ Magnolia House
㉔ Makins Farmhouse
㉘ Priory Hall
㉛ Rosedale
㉜ Rosemary
㊱ White House Farm
㊲ Windmill Cottage

The Gardens

① NEW BARRACKS COTTAGE
Bacons Green Road, Westhall IP19 8RA. Maggie & Adrian Simpson-James, 0845 391 7549, adrian@megenna.freeserve.co.uk. *4m E of Halesworth. From Bungay & Halesworth take A144. Turn E at Spexhall Xrds follow signs. From Beccles take A145, turn W at Brampton Dog follow signs. From A12 takeA145 to Beccles, turn L at Brampton Church onto B1124 follow signs.* Home-made teas. Adm £3, chd free. Sun 21 June (12-6). Visitors also welcome by appt June, July, small groups only.
This old cottage (not open) and garden nestles in the peaceful heart of Suffolk. A series of different 'rooms', incl cottage garden, rose pergola, natural pond, secret patio, potager and grass garden with surprise view. A must for rose lovers, with 60 roses. The perfect place to sit and relax on a summer's afternoon. Firm gravel and bark paths with slight slope.

& ✕ ❀ ☕ ☎

② BARTON MERE
Thurston Road, Gt Barton IP31 2PR. Mr & Mrs C O Stenderup. *4m NE of Bury St Edmunds. From Bury St Edmunds take A143 towards Ixworth. After Gt Barton turn R at Bunbury Arms PH. Continue past turnings to Pakenham & Barton Hamlet. Entrance to drive on L 100yds after Barton Hamlet sign.* Home-made teas. Adm £3, chd free. Sun 7 June (2-5.30).
C16 house (not open) with later Georgian façade, set in parkland overlooking lake (The Mere). Mainly walled gardens with roses, herbaceous borders, shrubs, large vegetable garden and conservatory. Gravel paths.

& ☕

Secret patio, potager and grass garden with surprise view . . .

③ THE BEECHES
Grove Road, Walsham-le-Willows IP31 3AD. Dr A J Russell. *11m E of Bury St Edmunds. From A143 to Diss take turning to village.* Adm £3, chd free (share to St Mary's Church, Walsham le Willows). Sun 5 Apr (2-5).
150yr-old, 3-acre garden, which incl specimen trees, pond, potager, memorial garden, lawns and variety of beds. Improvements to stream area.

&

④ ◆ BLAKENHAM WOODLAND GARDEN
Little Blakenham IP8 4LZ. Lord Blakenham, 07760 342817, blakenham@btinternet.com. *4m NW of Ipswich. Follow signs at Little Blakenham, 1m off B1113.* Adm £3, chd £1.50. 1 Mar to 30 June. For NGS: Sat 18, Sun 19 Apr (10-5).
Beautiful 6-acre woodland garden with variety of rare trees and shrubs. Chinese rocks and a landscape sculpture. Especially lovely in spring with daffodils, camellias, magnolias and bluebells followed by roses in early summer.

& ✕

⑤ BRESWORTH HOUSE
Stonham Road, Cotton IP14 4RG. Keith & Ann Bullock, 01449 780102, keith.bullockbres@tiscali.co.uk. *6m N of Stowmarket. Between B1113 & A140 close to Cotton Church.* Adm £2.50, chd free. Visitors welcome by appt, formal and informal groups, min 4 Feb to July.
Quiet 1-acre garden sheltered by mature indigenous trees. Unique water feature and recycled iron sculptures. Interesting plants, ornamental trees and shrubs, vegetable plot. A tranquil rural haven, adjacent to C14 church.

& ✕ ❀ ☎

⑥ BRIDGE FOOT FARM
Reydon, Southwold IP18 6PS. David & Susan Evan Jones. *A1095 on main rd into Southwold. Follow signs to Southwold. Honey coloured house on LH-side opp new development before Bridge Rd and bridge.* Home-made teas. Adm £2.50, chd free. Sat 27, Sun 28 June (2-5).
The garden is divided into 3 areas, gravel paths and no grass. The front garden is planted with perennials and clematis. Behind the outbuildings the area is full of climbers, geraniums etc. Within the 'L' shape of the house, replanted in 2007 are roses, and clematis on arches and trellis.

✕ ☕

CHIPPENHAM PARK
See Cambridgeshire.

⑦ NEW CHURCH FARM
Thornham Road, Gislingham IP23 8HP. Gerald & Eddie Prior, 01379 788504, g.prior@btinternet.com. *4m W of Eye. Next door to Gislingham Church. Gislingham 2½ m W of A140. 9m N of Stowmarket, 8m S of Diss.* Home-made teas. Adm £3, chd free. Sats, Suns 9, 10 May; 27, 28 June (11-4). Visitors also welcome by appt.
Mature English country garden surrounding old Suffolk farmhouse (not open) adjacent to village church. 1-acre plot incl a large fish pond, orchard and soft fruit garden, vegetables in raised beds. Shade plants and numerous mature trees and shrubs. Live Music and Art Exhibition. Featured in East Anglian Daily Times & Look East website. Some gravel and slopes.

& ❀ ☕ ☎

⑧ COBBS HALL
Great Saxham IP29 5JN. Dr & Mrs R H Soper. *4½ m W of Bury St Edmunds. A14 exit to Westley. R at Westley Xrds. L fork at Little Saxham signed Hargrave & Chevington. Approx 1½ m to sign on R turn. Mustard-coloured house 300yds on L.* Home-made teas. Adm £3, chd free (share to Gt Saxham Church). Sun 26 July (2-6).
2 acres of lawns and borders, ornamental trees, large fish/lily pond. Parterre, folly, walled kitchen garden, grass tennis court and pretty courtyard.

& ✕ ❀ ☕

⑨ COLUMBINE HALL
Stowupland IP14 4AT. Hew & Leslie Stevenson, www.columbinehall.co.uk. *1½ m NE of Stowmarket. Turn N off A1120 opp Shell garage across village green, then R at T-junction into Gipping Rd. Garden on L just beyond derestriction sign.* Home-made teas. Adm £3, chd free. Sun 28 June (2-6).
Formal gardens, designed by George Carter, surround moated medieval manor house (not open). Also, outside the moat, bog garden, Mediterranean garden, colour-themed vegetable garden, orchards and parkland.

Gardens developed since 1994 with constant work-in-progress, incl transformed farm buildings, wilderness and eyecatchers.

&. 🍵

10 CORNER COTTAGE
Rickinghall Road, Gislingham
IP23 8JJ. Trevor & Pauline Cox,
01449 781379. *5m W of Eye. Situated approx 9m N of Stowmarket or approx 2¹/₂ m S of Rickinghall on B1113.* **Adm £2.50, chd free. Sun 19 Apr; Weds 6 May to 27 May; Wed 19 Aug (11-5). Visitors also welcome by appt Apr to Aug.**
Our ³/₄ -acre garden has informal borders with shrubs (many unusual) underplanted with perennials and in spring, naturalised snakes head fritillaries, anemones and cowslips. Around the house (not open) are paved and gravelled areas with raised beds planted with shrubs and alpines.

🎽 ⊕ 🍵 ☎

11 EAST BERGHOLT PLACE
East Bergholt CO7 6UP. Mr & Mrs Rupert Eley,
ww.placeforplants.co.uk. *On B1070 towards Manningtree, 2m E of A12. Situated on the edge of East Bergholt.* Home-made teas. **Adm £3, chd free. Suns 22 Mar; 26 Apr (2-5).**
20-acre garden originally laid out at the beginning of the century by the present owner's great grandfather. Full of many fine trees and shrubs some of which are rarely seen in East Anglia. Particularly beautiful in spring when the rhododendrons, magnolias and camellias are in full flower. National Collection of deciduous euonymus. Featured on TV Chris Beardshaw - Country Matters.

🎽 ⊕ NCCPG 🍵

12 ♦ EUSTON HALL
Thetford IP24 2QW. His Grace The Duke of Grafton, 01842 766366, www.eustonhall.co.uk. *12m N of Bury St Edmunds. 3m S of Thetford on A1088.* **House & garden £6, chd £3, OAPs £5, garden only £3. For dates & opening details please tel or see website.**
Terraced lawns, herbaceous borders, rose garden, C17 pleasure grounds, lake and watermill. C18 house open; famous collection of paintings. C17 church; temple by William Kent. Shop and teas.

&. 🎽 🍵

13 NEW THE FIRS
Church Road, Marlesford
IP13 0AT. Paul & Lesley Bensley,
01728 747152,
lesleybensley@googlemail.com.
2m E of Wickham Market. On A12 travelling N from Wickham Market take L turn signed Parham. Drive past village signpost, take next L. Cream teas. **Adm £3, chd free (share to Marlesford Community Council). Sun 28 June (2-5). Visitors also welcome by appt.**
Garden in grounds of Edwardian House (not open). 2-acre country garden with mixed planting, yew hedging and small orchard. 2 acre paddock developed as a private nature reserve.

&. ⊕ 🍵 ☎

Children can you find the hidden fairies! . . .

14 GABLE HOUSE
Halesworth Road, Redisham
NR34 8NE. Mr & Mrs John Foster,
01502 575298. *5m S of Beccles. From Bungay A144 to Halesworth for 5m, turn L at St Lawrence School, 2m to Gable House.From A12 Blythburgh A145 to Beccles. At Brampton X-roads L to Station Rd. 3m on at junction is Gable House.* Soup (Feb). Ploughmans (June) & home-made teas. **Adm £3, chd free (share to St Peters Church, Redisham). Suns 15 Feb (11-4); 7 June (11-5). Visitors also welcome by appt for groups.**
1-acre garden contains a wide range of interesting plants. In Feb visitors can see over 200 varieties of snowdrops together with cyclamen, hellebore and early flowering bulbs. Wide range of summer flowering shrubs, roses and perennials providing colour for June opening. Glasshouses are well stocked with abundance of interesting plants from alpines to tender species, many for sale.

&. 🎽 ⊕ 🍵 ☎

15 NEW 12 GODFREYS WOOD
Melton, Woodbridge IP12 1QY.
Frances & Peter Grove. *8m E of Ipswich. From A12 take A1152 signed Orford, Woodbridge, Melton. 1st R Bredfield Rd, 3rd L Godfrey's Wood.* Home-made teas. **Adm £3.50, chd free. Sat 4 July (1-5).**
¹/₃ -acre incl wooded backdrop with woodland walk, mature shrubs and ferns. Extensive flower beds with cottage planting provide contrast in colour and movement. All these areas are connected by lawns. Award winning hanging baskets and tubs. Children can you find the hidden fairies! Woodbridge Flower Show.

🎽 ⊕ 🍵

16 GREAT THURLOW HALL
Haverhill CB9 7LF. Mr & Mrs George Vestey. *12m S of Bury St Edmunds, 4m N of Haverhill. Great Thurlow village on B1061 from Newmarket; 3¹/₂ m N of junction with A143 Haverhill/Bury St Edmunds rd.* Teas in church. **Adm £2.50, chd free. Sun 19 Apr (2-5).**
River walk, newly restored, and trout lake with extensive display of daffodils and blossom. Spacious lawns, shrubberies and roses. Walled kitchen garden.

&. 🍵

17 HENSTEAD EXOTIC GARDEN
Yew Cottage, Church Road, Henstead NR34 7LD. Andrew Brogan, 01502 743006/07715 876606, absuffolk@hotmail.com, www.hensteadexoticgarden.co.uk. *Equal distance between Beccles, Southwold & Lowestoft approx 5m. 1m from A12 turning after Wrentham (signed Henstead) very close to B1127.* **Adm £3, chd free. Sun 28 June (1-5). Visitors also welcome by appt.**
1-acre exotic garden featuring 60 large palms, 20+ bananas and 200 bamboo plants. 2 streams, 20ft tiered walkway leading to Thai style wooden covered pavilion. Mediterranean and jungle plants around 3 large ponds with fish and 'Suffolk's most exotic garden. Signed copies of garden owner's book for sale 'The History of the making of 'Henstead Exotic Garden'. Featured in 'Daily Telegraph', 'House & Gardens' & on BBC Gardeners World.

🎽 ⊕ ☎

18 HERON HOUSE
Priors Hill Road, Aldeburgh
IP15 5EP. Mr Jonathan Hale, 01728
452200. *Junction of Priors Hill Rd &
Park Rd*. Teas at Stanford House.
Combined with **Stanford House**
adm £4, chd free. Sun 3 May (2-5).
Visitors also welcome by appt.
2 acres with views over coastline, river
and marshes. Unusual trees,
herbaceous beds, shrubs and ponds
with waterfall in large rock garden,
stream and bog garden. Interesting
attempts to grow half hardy plants in
the coastal micro-climate.

**19 ◆ ICKWORTH HOUSE PARK
& GARDENS**
Horringer IP29 5QE. The National
Trust, 01284 735270,
www.nationaltrust.org.uk. *2m SW of
Bury St Edmunds. Ickworth is in the
village of Horringer on the A143 Bury
to Haverhill Rd*. For details please tel
or see website. For NGS: Sat 18 July
(10-4).
70 acres of garden. South gardens
restored to stylised Italian landscape to
reflect extraordinary design of the
house. Fine orangery, agapanthus,
geraniums and fatsias. North gardens
informal wild flower lawns with wooded
walk; the *Buxus* collection, great
variety of evergreens and Victorian
stumpery. New planting of cedars. The
Albana Wood, a C18 feature, initially
laid out by Capability Brown,
incorporates a fine circular walk.

KIRTLING TOWER
See Cambridgeshire.

20 THE KITCHEN GARDEN
Church Lane, Troston IP31 1EX.
Francine Raymond, www.kitchen-
garden-hens.co.uk. *8m NE of Bury St
Edmunds. Troston is signed off A143
at Gt Barton & off B1088 at Honington
& Ixworth. Garden is opp the church.
Please park in village*. Home-made
teas in the church. Adm £3, chd free.
Sun 24, Mon 25 May (2-5).
²/₃-acre country garden, catering for
family, local wildlife and flock of Buff
Orpington hens. Vegetable, fruit,
cutflower and herb gardens, wild
areas, chicken run, perennial beds
and formal yew-lined allée. Opening
in conjunction with St Mary's Church
opp housing impressive wall
paintings. Gravel path, slopes.

21 NEW LARKS HILL
Tuddenham St Martin IP6 9BY.
Mr John Lambert, 01473 785248,
jrlambert@talktalk.net. *3m NE of
Ipswich. From Ipswich take B1077
to Westerfield. Turn R for
Tuddenham St Martin at Xrds,
signed with NGS arrows to
Clopton Rd & Larks Hil*. Light
refreshments & teas. **Adm £4, chd
free. Sats 25 Apr; 23 May; 27
June (11-4); Thur 16 July (2-6).
Visitors also welcome by appt
for groups of 10+, Apr to Sept
only.**
The gardens of 8 acres comprise
woodland, field and more formal
areas, and fall away from the house
to the valley floor. A hill within a
garden and in Suffolk at that! An
interesting and beautiful site
overlooking the gentle Fynn valley
and the village beyond.

**22 THE LUCY REDMAN
SCHOOL OF GARDEN DESIGN**
6 The Village, Rushbrooke IP30 0ER.
Lucy Redman & Dominic Watts,
01284 386250,
lucy@lucyredman.co.uk,
www.lucyredman.co.uk. *3m E of
Bury St Edmunds. From A14 Bury St
Edmunds, E Sudbury exit, proceed
towards town centre. After 50yds, 1st
L exit from r'about and immed R. ³/₄ m
to T-junction, turn L, follow rd for 2m.
Before church turn R between white
houses, past brick well, thatched
house on L*. Home-made teas. Adm
£3, chd free. Sat 6 June (2-5).
Visitors also welcome by appt.
Thatched cottage surrounded by
³/₄ -acre quirky plantsman's family
garden divided into compartments
with impressive colour-coordinated
borders containing many interesting
combinations of unusual shrubs, roses,
grasses and perennials. Stone
parterre, turf tree seat, sculptures,
sedum roofed pavilion. Unusual bulb
and rhizome garden, willow igloo and
tunnel. Free range chickens and
vegetable garden. Featured in GGG.
Lucy is gardening columnist for 'EADT
Suffolk' magazine.

23 MAGNOLIA HOUSE
Yoxford IP17 3EP. Mr Mark Rumary,
01728 668321. *4m N of
Saxmundham. Centre of Yoxford on
A1120*. Adm £3, chd free. Sun 5 July
(2-6). Visitors also welcome by appt.

Small, completely walled, romantic
garden, tucked behind a pretty C18
village house (not open). Ingeniously
designed to appear larger and planted
to provide yr-round colour, scent and
horticultural interest. Contains ancient
mulberry, raised Moorish-style pool
and newly planted Victorian flower
garden.

**24 NEW MAKINS
FARMHOUSE**
Donkey Lane, Stanningfield
IP29 4RA. Elizabeth & Robert
Bradbury, 01284 827079,
robertibradbury@aol.com. *6m S
of Bury St Edmunds. A134 out of
Bury St Edmunds, at Sicklesmere
turn R towards Stanningfield, on
outskirts of village turn R down Old
Lane towards Lawshall, at bottom
of hill continue for approx ¹/₂ m,
garden on L*. Home-made teas.
Adm £3, chd free. Sun 14 June
(11-5). Visitors also welcome by
appt groups of 6+, May to Sept.
Appox 1 acre of landscaped
garden developed over the past
10yrs by present owners. The
garden is divided into several
areas. The main area has colour-
themed mixed borders with many
old roses and interesting
herbaceous plants.The garden also
includes a large natural pond,
Mediterranean garden and
enclosed courtyard. WC.

A hill within
a garden and
in Suffolk at
that! An
interesting
and beautiful
site overlooking
the gentle
Fynn valley and
the village
beyond . . .

25 NEW MILLFIELDS HOUSE

Hargrave Road, Chevington, Bury St Edmunds IP29 5QR. Mr & Mrs John Roberts. *Approaching Chevington from Hargrave on L, immed before 30mph sign.* Home-made teas. **Adm £3, chd free. Sun 21 June (2-5).**
30yr old garden developed from a green field site with mixed borders and many different, well established trees and shrubs covering approx 2½ acres, incl semi-natural water garden with a variety of iris and zantedeschia. Some gravel paths.

&. ☕

26 ◆ MONKSFIELD HOUSE

The Green, Monk Soham IP13 7EX. Kay & Richard Lacey, 01728 628449, www.k-plants.co.uk. *3m E of Debenham. 4m W of Framlingham. Off A1120 between Framsden & Earl Soham, drive through Ashfield cum Thorpe. Follow rd for 3m, turn R signed Monk Soham. Fork L at Y-junction, garden on L aftter ¾ m.* **Adm £3.50, chd free. For NGS: Evening Opening** wine & canapes, **Fri 19 June (6-8.30). Suns 21 June; 6 Sept (11-6).**
2 acre plantsman's garden comprising herbaceous and shrub borders with cottage style planting, formal parterre, meadow with native orchids. Japanese style area with unusual acers and prairie borders with a large variety of specimen grasses. Large natural pond. Bog garden with alpine planting and waterfall. ⅓ -acre woodland with tranquil walks. Visit in June to see the native orchids. Landscaping nusery open for plant sales.

&. ✿ ☕

27 THE PRIORY

Stoke-by-Nayland CO6 4RL. Mr & Mrs H F A Engleheart. *5m SW of Hadleigh. Entrance on B1068 to Sudbury (NW of Stoke-by-Nayland).* Home-made teas. **Adm £3, chd free. Sun 17 May (2-5).**
Interesting 9-acre garden with fine views over Constable countryside; lawns sloping down to small lakes and water garden; fine trees, rhododendrons and azaleas; walled garden; mixed borders and ornamental greenhouse. Wide variety of plants; peafowl. Some gravel paths.

&. ✿ ☕

28 PRIORY HALL

Benton Street, Hadleigh IP7 5AZ. Mr & Mrs A V Hilton, 01473 823185, cyndy-miles@hotmail.com, www.prioryhall.com. *11m S of Ipswich. From A12 take B1070 to Hadleigh. After 4m pass Hook Lane on R. Priory Hall is next entrance on R. From Ipswich-Sudbury A1071: through Hadleigh High St, straight over junction to Benton St. Pass Cranworth Rd on L, 50yds further to Priory Hall on L.* Cream teas. **Adm £3, chd free. Sun 31 May (3-6).** Visitors also welcome by appt.
22 acres of woods, pasture and formal gardens, with lake and water meadows incl a covered picnic area. Special interest is the knot garden and topiary; walled terrace and orchards and rose arbour. Gravel paths.

&. ✿ ☕ ☎

Group opening

29 NEW REDGRAVE GARDENS

IP22 1RR. *1m N of Botesdale, 1m S of South Lopham. B1113 - Botesdale, South Loham & Redgrave.* Light refreshments & teas in St Mary's Church. **Combined adm £3, chd free. Sat 25, Sun 26 Apr (11-5).**
Redgrave will be opening 4 gardens this spring, open all day and serving refreshments, plant sale & WC. Also the recently restored medieval church of St Mary's. Nearby are the Redgrave and Lopham Fen, home of the famous raft spider, plus award winning Little Ouse project.

✿ ☕

NEW FEN VIEW

Fen Street. Mr & Mrs Tony Bigley. *Take A143 to Botesdale then B1113 to Redgrave, drive straight through village approx ¼ m turn R at Xrds, signed Wortham/Palgrave. From A1066 Diss, Thetford Rd at South Lopham take B1113 to Redgrave at Xrds turn L, signed as before.* Informal garden with pond, herbaceous borders and woodland bed. Grasses, shrubs, trees and developing wild flower area. Vegetable garden with fruit trees and soft fruit.

✈

NEW FLINT COTTAGE

Fen Street. Julia & David Maycock. *Take A143 to Botesdale, then B1113 to Redgrave, through village past PH, approx ¼ m to Xrds. Turn R into Fen St. From A1066 take B1113 at South Lopham (opp PH) to Redgrave* Informal structured garden laid out in separate areas, incl koi pond, lawns, herbaceous borders, ornamental trees, seating areas leading to vegetable and fruit garden, small greenhouse.

✈

GREEN FARM HOUSE

The Green. Mr & Mrs Peter Holt-Wilson. *1m N of Botesdale. From A143 take B1113 to Botesdale/Redgrave. 1st turning L down lane (The Green) just after 30mph sign. From A1066 Diss/Thetford rd turn in South Lopham to Redgrave. Through village, take last lane on R (The Geen) to garden* The garden is spacious, and lovely in spring, though most of the daffodils will be over. All, the early blossom will be coming out. There is a formal garden, herbaceous beds, 2 natural ponds and interesting collection of trees. Gravel drive.

&.

NEW RED HOUSE

The Street. Bob & Margaret Hayward. *From Botesdale B1113 - Redgrave to village green, 80yds past green on R. From South Lopham take B1113 over Xrds 80yds on L before green* Large walled garden, with koi pond, herbaceous borders, interesting shrubs, orchard, a very good planting scheme throughout the garden. Gravel drive.

&. ✈

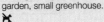

Semi-natural water garden with a variety of iris and zantedeschia . . .

30 REDISHAM HALL

Beccles NR34 8LZ. The Palgrave Brown Family. *5m S of Beccles. From A145, turn W on to Ringsfield-Bungay rd. Beccles, Halesworth or Bungay, all within 5m.* Home-made teas. **Adm £3.50, chd free. Sun 12 July** (2-6).
C18 Georgian house (not open). 5-acre garden set in 400 acres parkland and woods. Incl 2-acre walled kitchen garden (in full production) with peach house, vinery and glasshouses. Lawns, herbaceous borders, shrubberies, ponds and mature trees.

ROOKWOODS
See Essex.

31 ROSEDALE

40 Colchester Road, Bures CO8 5AE. Mr & Mrs Colin Lorking, 01787 227619, rosedale40@btinternet.com. *6m SE of Sudbury. 9m NW of Colchester on B1508. As you enter the village of Bures, garden on L. From Sudbury follow signs through village towards Colchester, garden on R as you leave village.* Home-made teas. **Adm £2.50, chd free. Suns 3 May; 2 Aug** (12-5.30). **Visitors also welcome by appt.**
Approx 1/3 -acre plantsman's garden; many unusual plants, herbaceous borders, pond, woodland area, for the Aug opening you can enjoy a superb collection of approx 60 agapanthus in full flower.

32 ROSEMARY

Rectory Hill, East Bergholt CO7 6TH. Mrs N E M Finch, 01206 298241. *9m NE of Colchester. Turn off A12 onto B1070 to East Bergholt, 1st R Hadleigh Rd, bear L at end of rd. At junction with Village St turn R, pass Red Lion PH, post office & church. Garden 100yds down from church on L.* Home-made teas. **Adm £3, chd free. Sun 12 Apr** (2-5). **Visitors also welcome by appt.**
This romantic garden, which appeals particularly to artists, has been developed over 34yrs. Planted to reveal paths and vistas. Over 100 old-fashioned roses. 2 bog beds, unusual trees, good bulbs and many unusual plants. Planted for all seasons.

33 NEW SOUTH HILL

42 Southgate Steet, Bury St Edmunds IP33 2AZ. Professor & Mrs S Gull. *Exit A14 J44, take 3rd exit off 2nd r'about into Southgate St, follow yellow signs. Opp Government offices in Southgate St, car park St Mary's Sq.* Home-made teas. **Adm £2.50, chd free. Sun 24, Mon 25 May** (11-6).
Town garden where Mr Pickwick landed in a gooseberry bush. Free-draining soil, divided into compartments in 1993, incl small maze, woodland path, herb garden and herbaceous borders. Productive compost heap and dye plants.

SPENCERS
See Essex.

34 STANFORD HOUSE

Priors Hill Road, Aldeburgh IP15 5EP. Lady Cave. *From A12 take A1094 to Aldeburgh. On approach to town go over 1st r'about then immed R into Park Rd. At tennis courts on the R turn R into Priors Hill Rd.* **Combined with Heron House adm £4, chd free. Sun 3 May** (2-5).
11/2 acres of terraced garden with waterfall, water garden and wide variety of rare plants and specimen shrubs luxuriating in mild maritime climate. Beautiful views over river marsh and sea.

Group opening

35 NEW STOWUPLAND GARDENS

IP14 4AD. *11/2 m NE of Stowmarket. Take A1120 from A14. Turn L onto Thorney Green Road, R at bus shelter just past The Retreat PH.* Teas in the church. **Combined adm £3, chd free. Sun 5 July** (12-5).
2 very different gardens situated in pretty village in mid Suffolk. Large village green.

NEW STAR ORCHARD COTTAGE

Saxham Street. Professor & Mrs Lawrence Smith
1/2 -acre cottage garden, herbaceous borders, pond, wide variety of fruit and vegetables.

NEW 2 THATCHED COTTAGE

Mr & Mrs R Cooper
Cottage garden in 3 separate parts. Koi pond, thatched summer house, aviary. Heavily planted borders with abundance of roses and clematis.

TUDOR ROOST
See Essex.

36 WHITE HOUSE FARM

Ringsfield, Beccles NR34 8JU. James & Jan Barlow, 07795 170892 Head gardener. *2m SW of Beccles. From Beccles take B1062 towards Bungay, after 11/2 m turn L, signed Ringsfield. Continue for 1m passing Ringsfield Church. Garden 300yds on L over small white railed bridge.* Home-made teas. **Adm £3, chd free. Sat 6 June** (11-4.30). **Visitors also welcome by appt.**
Fine garden of approx 30 acres with superb views over the Waveney Valley. Formal gardens and parkland with specimen trees, copses and lawns, good deal of mixed hedging. NB Beck and 2 ponds are not fenced. Limited wheelchair access to formal areas.

Town garden where Mr Pickwick landed in a gooseberry bush . . .

37 WINDMILL COTTAGE

Mill Hill, Capel St Mary IP9 2JE. Mr & Mrs G A Cox, 01473 311121. *3m SW of Ipswich. Turn off A12 at Capel St Mary. At far end of village on R after 11/4 m.* Home-made teas. **Adm £2.50, chd free. Sun 31 May** (2-5). **Visitors also welcome by appt middle of May to end of June.**
1/2 -acre plantsman's cottage-style garden. Island beds, pergolas with clematis and other climbers. Many trees and shrubs, wildlife ponds and vegetable area.

38 ◆ WOODWARDS
Blacksmiths Lane, Coddenham, Ipswich IP6 9TX. Marion & Richard Kenward, 01449 760639. *7m N of Ipswich. From A14 turn onto A140, after ¼ m turn off B1078 towards Wickham Market, Coddenham is on route. Ample parking for coaches.* **Adm £2.50, chd free. Other times by appt. For NGS: Suns 29 Mar; 14 June; Sat 11, Sun 12 July; 16 Aug (10-6).**
Award-winning, S-facing, gently sloping garden of ¾-acre, overlooking the rolling Suffolk countryside, designed and maintained by the owners for yr round colour and interest, lots of island beds, well stocked with 1000s of shrubs and perennials, vegetable plot, numerous hanging baskets and well manicured lawns. Over 11000 bulbs have been planted for our spring display and the garden is now 1½-acres with a new perennial border.

39 ◆ WOOTTENS
Blackheath Road, Wenhaston IP19 9HD. Mr M Loftus, 01502 478258, www.woottensplants.co.uk. *18m S of Lowestoft. On A12 & B1123, follow signs to Wenhaston.* **Adm £1, chd free. For NGS: Every Tues, Weds, Thurs, 1 Apr to 30 Sept; Iris field - daily Sun 24 May to Wed 10 June; Hemerocallis field - Sats, Suns only 11 July to 26 July (9.30-5).**
Small romantic garden, redesigned in 2003. Scented-leafed pelargoniums, violas, cranesbills, lilies, salvias, penstemons, primulas, etc. 2 acres of bearded iris, ¼ acre of iris sibiricas, 1 acre of hemerocallis. Wheelchair users will need assitance with access to fields.

This romantic garden, which appeals particularly to artists, has been developed over 34 years . . .

40 ◆ WYKEN HALL
Stanton IP31 2DW. Sir Kenneth & Lady Carlisle, 01359 250262, www.wykenvineyards.co.uk. *9m NE of Bury St Edmunds. Along A143. Follow signs to Wyken Vineyards on A143 between Ixworth & Stanton.* **Adm £3.50, chd free, concessions £3. Suns to Fris 1 Apr to 1 Oct. For NGS: Sat 16, Sun 17 May (2-6).**
4-acre garden much developed recently; knot and herb garden; old-fashioned rose garden, wild garden, nuttery, pond, gazebo and maze; herbaceous borders and old orchard. Woodland walk, vineyard.

Suffolk County Volunteers

County Organisers
East Patricia Short, Ruggs Hall, Raydon, Ipswich IP7 5LW, 01473 310416
West Jenny Reeve, 6a Church Walk, Mildenhall IP28 7ED, 01638 715289, j.reeve05@tiscali.co.uk

County Treasurers
East Geoffrey Cox, Windmill Cottage, Mill Hill, Capel St. Mary, Ipswich, Suffolk IP9 2JE, 01473 311121,
        gaandemcox@lineone.net
West David Reeve, 6a Church Walk, Mildenhall, Bury St. Edmunds IP28 7ED, 01638 715289,
        j.reeve05@tiscali.co.uk

Assistant County Organisers:
East Joan Brightwell, Sutherland House, 105 The Thoroghfare, Woodbridge IP12 1AS, 01394 388155
West Yvonne Leonard, Crossbills, Field Road, Mildenhall IP28 7AL, 01638 712742, yj.leonard@btinternet.com
East Joby West, The Millstone, Friars Road, Hadleigh IP7 6DF, 01473 823154

Mark your diary with these special events in 2009

EXPLORE SECRET GARDENS DURING CHELSEA & HAMPTON COURT FLOWER SHOW WEEKS

Tue 19 May, Wed 20 May, Thur 21 May, Fri 22 May, Wed 8 July, Thur 9 July
Full day tours from £82 per person, 10% discount for groups
Advance booking required, telephone +44 (0)20 8693 1015 or email j.wookey@btinternet.com
Specially selected gardens in London, Essex, Kent, Hampshire and South Oxfordshire. The tour price includes transport and lunch with wine at a popular restaurant or pub.

HAMPTON COURT PALACE

Thur 2 Apr, Tue 23 June, Thur 25 June, Wed 15 July, Tue 4 Aug, Thur 10 Sept
Evening tours in the company of one of the Palace's specialist tour guides from 6.30 – 8pm
Tickets £6 per person. Advance booking required, telephone +44 (0)1483 211535 or
visit www.ngs.org.uk for more information
Gossip, scandal, murder, healing – you'll find it all within the Formal Gardens at Hampton Court Palace. Each tour will have its own unique feature whether it's the story of the Great Vine or the magic and mystery of the Maze.

FROGMORE – A ROYAL GARDEN (BERKSHIRE)

Tue 26 May 10am – 5.30pm (last admission 4pm)
Garden adm £4.50, chd free. Tickets available in advance or on the day.
Advance booking for groups and coaches, telephone
+44 (0) 1483 211535 or email orders@ngs.org.uk
A rare opportunity to explore 30 acres of landscaped garden, rich in history and beauty.

FLAXBOURNE FARM – FUN & SURPRISES (BEDFORDSHIRE)

Sun 7 June 10am – 5pm. Adm £5, chd free
No booking required, come along on the day!
Bring the whole family and have fun in this surprising and entertaining garden of 2 acres. Enjoy the large plant fair, live music, pets corner, birds of prey, dog agility show and much more.

WISLEY RHS GARDEN – MUSIC IN THE GARDEN (SURREY)

Fri 11 Sept 6 – 9pm
Adm (incl RHS members) £7, chd under 15 free
Save money on advance bookings for groups of 4 or more, telephone +44 (0)1483 211535 or
visit www.ngs.org.uk for more information
A special evening opening of this famous garden, exclusively for the NGS. Enjoy music and entertainment as you explore the gardens and the floral marquee on the first day of the Wisley Flower Show.

For further information visit www.ngs.org.uk or telephone 01483 211535

SURREY

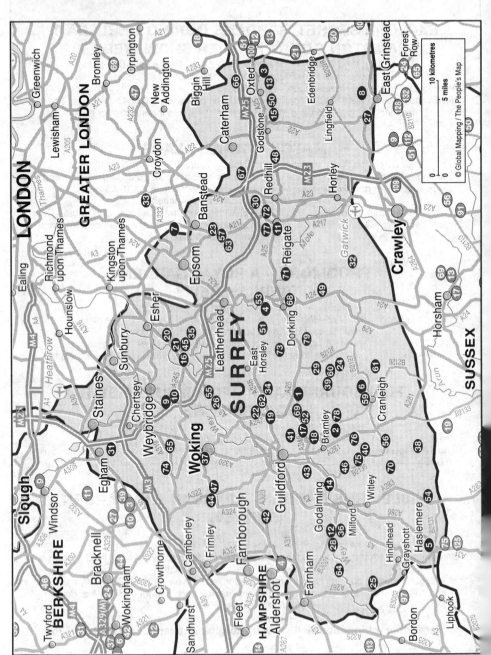

Opening Dates

February

SUNDAY 15
- (30) Gatton Park

WEDNESDAY 18
- (30) Gatton Park

March

SUNDAY 8
- (65) Timber Hill

SUNDAY 15
- (1) Albury Park

SATURDAY 28
- (76) Wintershall Manor

SUNDAY 29
- (19) Clandon Park
- (70) Vann

MONDAY 30
- (70) Vann

TUESDAY 31
- (70) Vann

April

WEDNESDAY 1
- (70) Vann

THURSDAY 2
- (70) Vann

FRIDAY 3
- (70) Vann

SATURDAY 4
- (70) Vann

SUNDAY 5
- (65) Timber Hill

SUNDAY 12
- (11) Caxton House

MONDAY 13
- (24) Coverwood Lakes

FRIDAY 17
- (78) Woodhill Manor - **Pre-booking essential**

SUNDAY 19
- (24) Coverwood Lakes
- (40) Lodkin
- (69) Vale End
- (75) Winkworth Arboretum

WEDNESDAY 22
- (57) 41 Shelvers Way
- (69) Vale End
- (78) Woodhill Manor - **Pre-booking essential**

THURSDAY 23
- (78) Woodhill Manor - **Pre-booking essential**

SATURDAY 25
- (26) Dunsborough Park
- (76) Wintershall Manor

SUNDAY 26
- (24) Coverwood Lakes
- (34) Hatchlands Park
- (46) Munstead Wood
- (57) 41 Shelvers Way

May

SUNDAY 3
- (16) Chestnut Lodge
- (24) Coverwood Lakes
- (25) Crosswater Farm
- (49) The Old Croft
- (65) Timber Hill

MONDAY 4
- (25) Crosswater Farm
- (49) The Old Croft
- (70) Vann
- (73) Walton Poor House

TUESDAY 5
- (70) Vann

WEDNESDAY 6
- (70) Vann

THURSDAY 7
- (70) Vann

FRIDAY 8
- (70) Vann

SATURDAY 9
- (20) Claremont Landscape Garden
- (70) Vann

SUNDAY 10
- (17) Chilworth Manor
- (21) The Coach House
- (24) Coverwood Lakes
- (43) Loseley Park
- (45) Moleshill House
- (54) Ramster
- (70) Vann
- (74) Westways Farm

TUESDAY 12
- (29) Fulvens Hanger

WEDNESDAY 13
- (21) The Coach House
- (29) Fulvens Hanger
- (45) Moleshill House
- (74) Westways Farm (Evening)

THURSDAY 14
- (29) Fulvens Hanger

FRIDAY 15
- (29) Fulvens Hanger

SATURDAY 16
- (8) Braekenas
- (66) Titsey Place Gardens

SUNDAY 17
- (8) Braekenas
- (39) Knowle Grange
- (46) Munstead Wood
- (53) Quinneys

MONDAY 18
- (15) Chauffeur's Flat

TUESDAY 19
- (15) Chauffeur's Flat

WEDNESDAY 20
- (15) Chauffeur's Flat

THURSDAY 21
- (15) Chauffeur's Flat

FRIDAY 22
- (15) Chauffeur's Flat

SATURDAY 23
- (15) Chauffeur's Flat

SUNDAY 24
- (15) Chauffeur's Flat
- (24) Coverwood Lakes
- (44) Memoirs
- (49) The Old Croft
- (50) Oxted Place Gardens

MONDAY 25
- (49) The Old Croft

SUNDAY 31
- (9) 40 Byfleet Road
- (23) The Copse Lodge
- (68) 6 Upper Rose Hill

June

TUESDAY 2
- (31) Great Fosters

WEDNESDAY 3
- (23) The Copse Lodge (Evening)
- (31) Great Fosters

FRIDAY 5
- (38) Howicks (Evening)
- (60) Spurfold (Evening)

SUNDAY 7
- (6) Barhatch Farm
- (42) Longer End Cottage
- (51) Polesden Lacey
- (67) Tollsworth Manor
- (70) Vann
- (73) Walton Poor House

MONDAY 8
- (70) Vann

TUESDAY 9
- (70) Vann

WEDNESDAY 10
- (6) Barhatch Farm
- (62) Stuart Cottage
- (70) Vann

THURSDAY 11
- (70) Vann

FRIDAY 12
- (10) 111 Byfleet Road (Evening)
- (70) Vann

SATURDAY 13
- ⑤ Bardsey
- ㉖ Dunsborough Park
- ㉙ Vale End (Evening)
- ⑦⓪ Vann

SUNDAY 14
- ⑤ Bardsey
- ⑩ 111 Byfleet Road
- ⑭ Charterhouse
- ⓪ Lodkin
- ㊱ The Round House
- ㊱ Square Leg Cottage

WEDNESDAY 17
- ㊱ Square Leg Cottage
- ㉙ Vale End

FRIDAY 19
- ④ Ashleigh Grange (Evening)

SATURDAY 20
- ㊅ Titsey Place Gardens

SUNDAY 21
- ④ Ashleigh Grange
- ⑫ Chandlers
- ⑱ Chinthurst Lodge
- ㊱ Hideaway House
- ㊻ Timber Hill (Evening)

MONDAY 22
- ⑮ Chauffeur's Flat

TUESDAY 23
- ⑮ Chauffeur's Flat

WEDNESDAY 24
- ④ Ashleigh Grange
- ⑮ Chauffeur's Flat
- ⑱ Chinthurst Lodge

THURSDAY 25
- ⑮ Chauffeur's Flat

FRIDAY 26
- ⑮ Chauffeur's Flat

SATURDAY 27
- ⑮ Chauffeur's Flat
- ㊳ 35 Tadorne Road
- ⑦① Vicarage Cottage

SUNDAY 28
- ⑮ Chauffeur's Flat
- ㊳ 35 Tadorne Road
- ⑦① Vicarage Cottage

July

WEDNESDAY 1
- ㊆⑧ Woodhill Manor - **Pre-booking essential**

SATURDAY 4
- ⑦⑦ Woodbury Cottage

SUNDAY 5
- ㊲ Horsell Allotments & Birch Cottage Garden
- ⑦⑦ Woodbury Cottage

THURSDAY 9
- ㊆⑧ Woodhill Manor - **Pre-booking essential**

FRIDAY 10
- ㊆⑦ Woodbury Cottage (Evening)

SATURDAY 11
- ㊷ The Old Croft

SUNDAY 12
- ⑬ Chardleigh Cottage
- ㉗ Felbridge Copse
- ㊷ The Old Croft
- ㊱ The Round House

WEDNESDAY 15
- ㉘ Foxhill

THURSDAY 16
- ㉘ Foxhill

FRIDAY 17
- ㉘ Foxhill
- ㊆⑧ Woodhill Manor - **Pre-booking essential**

SATURDAY 18
- ㊅⑥ Titsey Place Gardens

SUNDAY 19
- ㊇ 19 Oak Tree Road
- ㊐ 41 Shelvers Way
- ㊆⑨ Wotton House

THURSDAY 23
- ㊆⑧ Woodhill Manor - **Pre-booking essential**

FRIDAY 24
- ㊅② Stuart Cottage (Evening)

SATURDAY 25
- ② Appletrees

SUNDAY 26
- ② Appletrees
- ㉝ 72 Green Wrythe Lane
- ㊆③ Walton Poor House
- ㊆⑨ Wotton House

WEDNESDAY 29
- ② Appletrees (Evening)
- ㊆⑧ Woodhill Manor - **Pre-booking essential**

August

SATURDAY 1
- ㊳ 35 Tadorne Road

SUNDAY 2
- ⑯ Chestnut Lodge
- ㊽ Odstock
- ㊳ 35 Tadorne Road
- ㊆② Walnut House

WEDNESDAY 5
- ㊆② Walnut House (Evening)

FRIDAY 7
- ㊆⑧ Woodhill Manor - **Pre-booking essential**

SATURDAY 8
- ㊷ The Old Croft

SUNDAY 9
- ⑬ Chardleigh Cottage
- ㉒ Coppice
- ㊶ Long Barton
- ㊸ The Old Croft

FRIDAY 14
- ㊅⓪ Spurfold (Evening)

SATURDAY 15
- ⑤ Bardsey
- ⑦ Bethany
- ㉜ Green Lane Farm
- ㊅⑥ Titsey Place Gardens

SUNDAY 16
- ⑤ Bardsey
- ⑦ Bethany
- ㊷② Longer End Cottage

SUNDAY 23
- ㉜ Green Lane Farm

WEDNESDAY 26
- ㉓ The Copse Lodge (Evening)

SUNDAY 30
- ㉓ The Copse Lodge

MONDAY 31
- ㊅② Stuart Cottage

September

SATURDAY 5
- ⑦⑦ Woodbury Cottage

SUNDAY 6
- ⑨ 40 Byfleet Road
- ㊷② Longer End Cottage
- ㊅⑧ 6 Upper Rose Hill
- ⑦⑦ Woodbury Cottage

WEDNESDAY 9
- ⑦⑦ Woodbury Cottage

FRIDAY 11
- ㊵⑤ RHS Garden Wisley (Evening)

SATURDAY 12
- ㉖ Dunsborough Park

SUNDAY 13
- ㊴ Knowle Grange

October

SUNDAY 4
- ① Albury Park
- ㊆⑤ Winkworth Arboretum

SUNDAY 11
- ㉐ Claremont Landscape Garden

SUNDAY 18
- ㉔ Coverwood Lakes
- ㉞ Hatchlands Park

December

THURSDAY 17
- ㊆⑧ Woodhill Manor - **Pre-booking essential**

February 2010

SUNDAY 14
- 30 Gatton Park

WEDNESDAY 17
- 30 Gatton Park

Gardens open to the public

- 19 Clandon Park
- 20 Claremont Landscape Garden
- 25 Crosswater Farm
- 30 Gatton Park
- 34 Hatchlands Park
- 43 Loseley Park
- 51 Polesden Lacey
- 54 Ramster
- 55 RHS Garden Wisley
- 66 Titsey Place Gardens
- 75 Winkworth Arboretum

By appointment only

- 3 Arden Lodge
- 35 Heathside
- 52 Postford House
- 59 Spring Cottage
- 64 Tilford Cottage
- 78 Woodhill Manor

Also open by appointment

- 2 Appletrees
- 4 Ashleigh Grange
- 5 Bardsey
- 6 Barhatch Farm
- 10 111 Byfleet Road
- 18 Chinthurst Lodge
- 19 Clandon Park
- 23 The Copse Lodge
- 28 Foxhill
- 29 Fulvens Hanger
- 39 Knowle Grange
- 40 Lodkin
- 44 Memoirs
- 45 Moleshill House
- 56 The Round House
- 57 41 Shelvers Way
- 60 Spurfold
- 62 Stuart Cottage
- 68 6 Upper Rose Hill
- 69 Vale End
- 74 Westways Farm
- 77 Woodbury Cottage
- 78 Woodhill Manor

New secret garden and white water garden . . .

The Gardens

ABBOTSMERRY BARN
See Kent.

1 ALBURY PARK
Albury GU5 9BH. Trustees of Albury Estate. 5m SE of Guildford. From A25 take A248 towards Albury for 1/4 m, then up New Rd, entrance to Albury Park immed on L. Home-made teas. Adm £3.50, chd free. Suns 15 Mar; 4 Oct (2-5).
14-acre pleasure grounds laid out in 1670s by John Evelyn for Henry Howard, later 6th Duke of Norfolk. 1/4 m terraces, fine collection of trees, lake and river. Albury Park Mansion gardens also open (by kind permission of Historic House Retirement Homes Ltd. House not open). Gravel path and slight slope.

23 ANGLESEY ROAD
See Hampshire.

2 APPLETREES
Stonards Brow, Shamley Green GU5 0UY. Mr & Mrs A Hodgson, 01483 898779, thodgson@uwclub.net. 5m SE of Guildford. A281 Guildford to Horsham rd, turn L at Shalford on B2128 via Wonersh to Shamley Green. Turn R before Red Lion PH, then R into Sweetwater Lane. At top of lane turn R into Stonards Brow or follow signs to car park when entering village. From Ewhurst/Cranleigh turn L at village stores, proceed down Hullbrook Lane following signs to Longacre School car park. Adm £3, chd free. Sat 25 July (12-3 with lunchtime BBQ), Sun 26 July (2-6 with cream teas). Evening Opening £5, cheese & wine, Wed 29 July (5-8). Visitors also welcome by appt in July & Aug, for groups of not less than 15 for morning coffee, afternoon tea or evening cheese & wine.
1/4 -acre garden with many interesting features. Several small water features incl koi pond. Summerhouse, greenhouses, raised railway sleeper beds, pergolas. Shrub and perennial borders. Patio and gravel area with several colourful containers. Raised vegetable beds; jungle beds with bananas and an elevated walkway; new secret garden and white water garden. Obelisks and clematis, all on a sandy loam soil. An ideas garden.

3 ARDEN LODGE
Pastens Road, Limpsfield RH8 0RE. Mr & Mrs C Bruce-Jones, 01883 722171, chris.bruce-jones@virgin.net. 1m E of Oxted. From A25 take B269 Edenbridge Rd for 200yds. R down Brick Kiln Lane. Pastens Rd 2nd turning L, house at end of rd. Refreshments by arrangement. Adm £3.50, chd free. Visitors welcome by appt Easter to end July for groups & individuals.
2-acre garden on greensand with extensive views. Sunken garden with formal fishpond and arbour; pergola; herbaceous border; rhododendrons, azaleas and much formal and informal mixed planting with interesting trees, shrubs, roses and containers. Some gravel paths.

4 ASHLEIGH GRANGE
off Chapel Lane, Westhumble RH5 6AY. Clive & Angela Gilchrist, 01306 884613, ar.gilchrist@btinternet.com. 2m N of Dorking. From A24 at Boxhill/Burford Bridge follow signs to Westhumble. Through village & L up drive by ruined chapel (1m from A24). Home-made teas. Adm £3, chd free (share to Barnardo's). Evening Opening £4.50, wine, Fri 19 June (6-8). Sun 21, Wed 24 June (2-5.30). Visitors also welcome by appt May to July.
Sloping chalk garden on 31/2 -acre site in charming rural setting with delightful views. Many areas of interest incl rockery and water feature, raised ericaceous bed, prairie-style bank, foliage plants, woodland walk, fernery and new folly. Large mixed herbaceous and shrub borders planted for dry alkaline soil and widespread interest.

5 BARDSEY
11 Derby Road, Haslemere GU27 1BS. Maggie & David Boyd, 01428 652283, maggie.boyd@tiscali.co.uk, www.bardseygarden.co.uk. 1/4 m N of Haslemere stn. Turn off B2131 (which links A287 to A286 through town) 400yds W of stn into Weydown Rd, 3rd R into Derby Rd, garden 400yds on R. Home-made teas. Adm £3.50, chd free. Sats, Suns 13, 14 June; 15, 16 Aug (11-5). Visitors also welcome by appt June to Aug, groups of 15+ only.
Relax in this 2-acre garden in the heart of Haslemere. Wander through fragrant herb and rose parterres bordered by

lavender and box. Enjoy the herbaceous borders, raised vegetable beds and caged fruit garden. In the lower garden watch dragonflies and newts in the natural ponds.

  🚽 ✕ ❀ ☕ ☎

6 BARHATCH FARM
Barhatch Lane, Cranleigh GU6 7NG. Mr & Mrs P M Grol, 01483 277968. *2m N of Cranleigh. A281 from Guildford, L at B2128 to Cranleigh, through village, take Ewhurst Rd for 1m, turn L into Barhatch Rd which becomes Barhatch Lane. Garden 1st on R after Cranleigh Golf & Leisure Club.* Home-made teas. **Adm £3, chd free. Sun 7, Wed 10 June (11-5). Visitors also welcome by appt in June only for groups of 15+.**
Romantic 6-acre garden, created by present owners, surrounding listed Tudor farmhouse. Herbaceous borders and abundance of old roses, incl a well-established rose tunnel. A sunken walled Zen garden; new tropical walk along 'Smuggler's Lane'; pet sanctuary nestled amidst yew tree grove; wild flower and allium meadow with Tasmanian fern walk. Walled pond and ornamental pond. Some gravel paths and steps, only partial wheelchair access.

  🚽 ✕ ❀ ☕ ☎

7 BETHANY
87 Sandy Lane, South Cheam SM2 7EP. Brian & Pam West & Mr & Mrs L West. *2m W of Sutton. Approx 1m S of Cheam village, or from A217 turn into Northey Ave. At small roundabout L into Sandy Lane, then approx 100yds on L.* Home-made teas. **Adm £2.50, chd free. Sat 15, Sun 16 Aug (1-5.30).**
1/3 -acre plantsman's garden with a subtropical feel where palm trees, tree ferns, banana trees, agave and bamboo surround the wide lawn. Vibrant coloured dahlias and a large collection of cannas make this an exciting August garden. Behind pretty summerhouse is vegetable garden and greenhouses.

  ✕ ❀ ☕

BOXWOOD HOUSE
See Berkshire.

8 BRAEKENAS
West Hill Road, Dormans Park RH19 2ND. Ann & Ray Lindfield. *3m N of East Grinstead. From London on A22 turn L at T-lights in Blindley Heath - Ray Lane. In Lingfield turn R at 2nd roundabout - East Grinstead Rd. Fork L into Blackberry Lane, keep racecourse on L, turn L at bottom of hill, R into Dormans Park. Then 1st L, 1st R West Hill.* Home-made teas. **Adm £3, chd free. Sat 16, Sun 17 May (2-6).**
Created 48 yrs ago by present owners, a garden for all seasons with lovely specimen shrubs and trees, incl azaleas and camellias. Immaculate vegetable plot.

  🚽 ✕ ❀ ☕

Still a young garden but a lot of colour all year . . .

9 40 BYFLEET ROAD
New Haw, Addlestone KT15 3JX. Mrs Lyn Davis & Mr J Coxe. *1 1/2 m NW of Weybridge. From M25 J11 take A317 to Addlestone, onto A318 to White Hart PH. Turn L over New Haw canal bridge. 2nd turn R into slip rd. Parking in New Haw lock.* Home-made teas. **Adm £2.50, chd free. Suns 31 May; 6 Sept (11-5).**
An oasis in an urban setting. This 250ft long garden has individual rooms, each with its own interest. Herbaceous plants mingle with mature shrubs and trees. Kitchen garden and glasshouse lead to access path through majestic oaks onto canal towpath. Gravel path.

  🚽 ✕ ❀ ☕

10 111 BYFLEET ROAD
New Haw, Addlestone KT15 3LD. Pat & Roy Whiffin, 01932 850257, patwhiffin@ntlworld.com. *4m E of Woking. J11 M25. Take A317 towards Weybridge, 1st R onto A318, follow until Byfleet & New Haw mainline stn for parking. Garden 200yds before stn on L. Slip rd in front of house for drop-off point.* Home-made teas. **Adm £3, chd free. Evening Opening £4, wine, Fri 12 June (6-9). Sun 14 June (11-5). Visitors also welcome by appt for groups of 10+.**
220ft long garden divided into rooms with each area leading to voluptuously planted beds brimming with old English roses, peonies, iris, clematis and a varied selection of perennials, shrubs and trees. Pergola covered in climbing roses, jasmine, wisteria and honeysuckle. Many colourful pots.

  ✕ ❀ ☕ ☎

11 CAXTON HOUSE
67 West Street, Reigate RH2 9DA. Bob & Marj Bushby. *1/4 m W of Reigate. On A25 towards Dorking, approx 1/4 m W of Reigate on L. Parking on rd.* Cream teas. **Adm £3, chd free (share to Progressive Supranuclear Palsy Assoc). Sun 12 Apr (2-5).**
Large garden with wildlife wood, 3 ponds, lots of spring planting - primroses, bulbs and large collection of hellebores. New herbaceous borders and small Gothic folly built by owner.

  🚽 ✕ ❀ ☕

12 CHANDLERS
Lower Ham Lane, Elstead GU8 6HQ. Mrs Kim Budge. *From A3 Milford take B3001 to Elstead. Entering village turn 2nd R signed EVTC (tennis club). From Farnham, B3001 through village, then L after tel box signed EVTC. Park on Burford Lea recreation ground. Disabled parking use Hideaway House, Lower Ham Lane (off Broomfield).* Home-made teas. **Combined adm with Hideaway House, also open, £3.50, chd free. Sun 21 June (1-5).**
Come and enjoy a stroll around this 1/2 -acre garden brimming with exciting planting combinations, many unusual shrubs, trees, grasses, perennials and bulbs. Divided into rooms incl a picturesque potager with step-over apple trees and companion planting, woodland, and mixed borders radiating from a semi-circular slate, multi-level patio and pergola. Featured on BBC Gardeners' World. Some woodland paths inaccessible to wheelchairs.

  🚽 ❀ ☕

13 NEW CHARDLEIGH COTTAGE
Paines Hill, Limpsfield RH8 0RG. David & Morag Roulston. *5m E of Godstone. A25 at Limpsfield turn S onto B269 towards Edenbridge. 2nd R into Brick Kiln Lane, through tight double bend on Paines Hill, then 200m on L before private rd.* Home-made teas. **Adm £3, chd free. Suns 12 July; 9 Aug (2-6).**
An acre of steeply-sloping garden that has been partially terraced. Still a young garden but a lot of colour all yr from many different shrubs and herbaceous plants in a variety of borders. Many mature trees, fruit and vegetable areas and a natural stream left to nature. Children's quiz.

  ✕ ☕

⑭ CHARTERHOUSE
Hurtmore Road, Godalming GU7 2DF. *½ m N of Godalming town centre at top of Charterhouse Hill. Follow signs for Charterhouse from A3 & Godalming town centre.* Light refreshments & home-made teas. **Adm £3.50, chd free.** Sun 14 June (2.30-5).
Extensive grounds with mature trees and mixed borders around beautiful old buildings. Two historical borders planted with species available prior to 1872, based on the writings of William Robinson; several enclosed individual gardens. Headmaster's garden, originally designed by Gertrude Jekyll, with long herbaceous border, pergola, mixed borders, Lutyens summerhouse and double dry stone wall.

CHARTWELL
See Kent.

⑮ CHAUFFEUR'S FLAT
Tandridge Lane, Tandridge RH8 9NJ. Mr & Mrs Richins. *2m E of Godstone. Turn off A25 for Tandridge. Take drive on L past church. Follow arrows to circular courtyard.* Home-made teas Sats & Suns only. **Adm £3, chd free (share to Sutton & Croydon MS Therapy Centre).** Mon 18 to Sun 24 May incl; Mon 22 to Sun 28 June incl (10-5).
Enter 1-acre tapestry of magical secret gardens with magnificent views. Touching the senses, all sure-footed visitors may explore the many surprises on this exuberant escape from reality. Imaginative use of recycled materials creates an inspired variety of ideas, while wild and specimen plants reveal an ecological haven.

⑯ CHESTNUT LODGE
Old Common Road, Cobham KT11 1BU. Mr R Sawyer. *From A3 take A245 towards Cobham bearing L at 2nd roundabout onto A307. Just after Dagenham Motors turn L into Old Common Rd, Chestnut Lodge at very end.* Home-made teas. **Adm £4. Regret children under 15 not admitted.** Suns 3 May; 2 Aug (11-5).
Very interesting 5-acre garden offering unrivalled opportunity to enjoy fine specimen trees, wonderful wisteria, shrubs and rare and exotic plants at close quarters. Areas near house formally planted, while opposite is large naturalised pond, home to many waterfowl incl flamingos. Formal areas

planted round rectangular pools are complemented by bonsai and topiary which lead to an aviary walk with many fine tropical birds. Some gravel paths.
  🐕 ☕

⑰ CHILWORTH MANOR
Halfpenny Lane, Chilworth GU4 8NN. Mia & Graham Wrigley. *3½ m SE of Guildford. From centre of Chilworth village turn into Blacksmith Lane. 1st drive on R on Halfpenny Lane.* Home-made teas. **Adm £4, chd free.** Sun 10 May (11-5).
Extensive grounds of lawns and mature trees around C17/C18 manor on C11 monastic site. Substantial C18 terraced walled garden laid out by Sarah, Duchess of Marlborough, with herbaceous borders, topiary and fruit trees. Original stewponds integrated with new Japanese-themed garden and woodland garden and walk. Paddock home to alpacas. Ongoing restoration project aims to create a contemporary and practical garden sensitive to its historic context. Guildford Society Design Award (Restoration and Refurbishment).
🐕 ☕

⑱ CHINTHURST LODGE
Wonersh Common Road, Wonersh GU5 0PR. Mr & Mrs M R Goodridge, 01483 535108, michael.goodridge@ blueyonder.co.uk. *4m S of Guildford. From A281 at Shalford turn E onto B2128 towards Wonersh. Just after Wonersh sign, before village, garden on R.* Home-made teas. **Adm £3, chd free.** Sun 21, Wed 24 June (12-5.30). **Visitors also welcome by appt in June & July only.**
1-acre yr-round enthusiast's atmospheric garden, divided into rooms. Herbaceous borders, white garden, specimen trees and shrubs, gravel garden with water feature, small kitchen garden, fruit cage, 2 wells, ornamental ponds, herb parterre and millennium parterre garden.
  🐕 ✿ ☕ ☎

⑲ ◆ CLANDON PARK
West Clandon GU4 7RQ. The National Trust, 01483 222482, www.nationaltrust.org.uk. *3m E of Guildford on A247. From A3 follow signs to Ripley to join A247 via B2215.* House & Garden £8.10, chd £4. Garden only £4.10, chd £2.20. Tues to Thurs & Suns 15 Mar to 1 Nov.
For NGS: Sun 29 Mar (11-5).
Garden around the house laid out informally, apart from parterre beneath

S front. To the S a mid C18 grotto. Principal front faces parkland, laid out in the style of Capability Brown around 1770. Created in 1901, Dutch garden modelled on the pond garden at Hampton Court Palace. Large bulb field looks stunning in spring.
  🐕 ☕

Walled garden evolving to meet the challenge of light sandy soil and dry summers . . .

⑳ ◆ CLAREMONT LANDSCAPE GARDEN
Portsmouth Road, Esher KT10 9JG. The National Trust, 01372 467806, www.nationaltrust.org.uk. *1m SW of Esher. On E side of A307 (no access from A3 bypass).* Adm £6, chd £3. Apr to Oct daily 10-6. Nov to Mar (10-5) closed Mons. For NGS: Sat 9 May; Sun 11 Oct (10-6).
One of the earliest surviving English landscape gardens, begun by Vanbrugh and Bridgeman before 1720 and extended and naturalized by Kent and Capability Brown. Lake, island with pavilion; grotto and turf amphitheatre; viewpoints and avenues. Advance booking of wheelchair recommended.
  🐕 ☕

㉑ NEW THE COACH HOUSE
The Fairmile, Cobham KT11 1BG. Peter & Sarah Filmer. *2m NE of Cobham. On A307 Esher to Cobham rd next to free car park by A3 bridge, at entrance to Waterford Close.* Light refreshments. **Open with Moleshill House, combined entry £5, chd free.** Sun 10 May with Songs in the Garden & Wed 13 May (2-5).
Walled garden evolving to meet the challenge of light sandy soil and dry summers. Colourful borders with mixed shrubs and herbaceous planting, tulips and alliums. Productive vegetable plot, newly-restored original greenhouse, parterre, terrace with pots, many climbers and wall-trained fruit trees.
🐕 ☕

22 NEW COPPICE
Dedswell Drive, West Clandon
GU4 7TQ. B James. *4m E of
Guildford. On A247 between A3
and A25. From A3 leave for
Ripley/Woking, turn R to W
Clandon. From Leatherhead A246
turn R at W Clandon T-lights.
Parking at Clandon stn, limited
parking for elderly and disabled at
garden.* Home-made teas. **Adm
£3, chd free.** Sun 9 Aug (1-5).
Colourful 1½ -acre, very new,
developing garden. Large terrace
shaded by rose-covered pergola
leading on to a central path flanked
by mature apple trees. Crossing
paths with Gothic arches offer
seating from where you can enjoy
the well-stocked borders with
vibrant planting which run down
both sides of the garden. Beyond a
trellis is the kitchen garden and
buddleia trail. Wheelchair access to
main garden only.
& ✕ ⊛ ☕

23 THE COPSE LODGE
Brighton Road, Burgh Heath
KT20 6BL. Marian & Edward
Wallbank, 01737 361084,
marian.wallbank@sky.com. *6m S of
Sutton. On A217. 200yds past T-lights
at junction with Reigate Rd. Turn L into
Heathside Hotel, park in hotel car park
courtesy of hotel. Walk 80yds to
garden. Disabled parking at garden.*
Home-made teas (Suns only). **Adm
£3.50, chd free (share to Positive
Action for MS).** Suns 31 May; 30
Aug (1-6). **Evening Openings** £4,
wine, Weds 3 June; 26 Aug (6-9).
**Visitors also welcome by appt for
groups of 15+.**
Very unusual 1-acre garden with
architectural features and exciting
planting. Large Japanese garden
abounds with acers, bamboo, wisteria
and bonsai. Wander through the tea
house and emerge refreshed to enjoy
the contrast of exotic planting and
beautiful tender specimens. Potager
kitchen garden.
& ✕ ⊛ ☕ ☎

24 COVERWOOD LAKES
Peaslake Road, Ewhurst GU6 7NT.
The Metson Family,
www.coverwoodlakes.co.uk. *7m SW
of Dorking. From A25 follow signs for
Peaslake; garden ½ m beyond
Peaslake.* **Adm £5, chd £2,**
concessions £4. Mon 13 Apr, Suns
19, 26 Apr; 3, 10, 24 May (2-6);
18 Oct (11-4.30).

14-acre landscaped garden in stunning
position in the Surrey Hills with 4 lakes
and bog garden. Extensive
rhododendrons, azaleas and fine trees.
3½ -acre lakeside arboretum. Marked
trail through the working farm with
Hereford cows and calves, sheep and
horses, extensive views of the
surrounding hills.
& ✕ ⊛ ☕

25 ◆ CROSSWATER FARM
Crosswater Lane, Churt GU10 2JN.
Mrs E G Millais & Family, 01252
792698, www.rhododendrons.co.uk.
*6m S of Farnham, 6m NW of
Haslemere. From A287 turn E into
Jumps Rd ½ m N of Churt village
centre. After ¼ m turn acute L into
Crosswater Lane & follow signs for
Millais Nurseries.* **Adm £3, chd free.
Daily 1-31 May (10-5). For NGS:** Sun
3, Mon 4 May (2-5).
Idyllic 6-acre woodland garden.
Plantsman's collection of
rhododendrons and azaleas, incl rare
species collected in the Himalayas,
hybrids raised by the owners.
Everything from alpine dwarfs to
architectural large-leaved trees. Ponds,
stream and companion plantings incl
sorbus, magnolias and Japanese
acers. Trial gardens of new varieties.
Grass paths soft after rain.
& ✕ ⊛

26 DUNSBOROUGH PARK
Ripley GU23 6AL. Baron & Baroness
Sweerts de Landas Wyborgh. *6m
NE of Guildford. Entrance across
Ripley Green via The Milkway opp
Wylie & Mar.* Home-made teas. **Adm
£4, chd free.** Sats 25 Apr (12-4); 13
June; 12 Sept (11-4).
Extensive walled gardens of 6 acres
redesigned by Penelope Hobhouse
and Rupert Golby. Good structure with
much box hedging creating many
different garden rooms. Exciting long
herbaceous borders with beautiful
standard wisterias. Unusual 70ft
ginkgo hedge and ancient mulberry
tree. Atmospheric water garden
recently redesigned and restored.
Fabulous display of tulips in Apr with
10,000 bulbs and large cut flower
garden. Festival of tulips 20 to 25 &
27 to 30 April (12-4).
& ✕ ⊛ ☕

EDENBRIDGE HOUSE
See Kent.

ELM TREE COTTAGE
See London.

The formal garden was partly designed by Gertrude Jekyll in 1923 . . .

FAIRACRE
See Berkshire.

27 FELBRIDGE COPSE
Woodcock Hill, Felbridge
RH19 2RA. Paul & Martin Thomas-
Jeffreys. *1m N of E Grinstead. From
S, on A22 ¼ m N of A22/A264
junction. From N, M25 J6 8m S on
A22, approx 1m S of New Chapel
roundabout. Look out for yellow NGS
signs.* Light refreshments, cream teas
& wine. **Adm £4, chd free (share to
The Cinnamon Trust).** Sun 12 July
(12-5.30) **with music.**
Home of the celebrated London floral
designer, Paul Thomas. 2¼ -acre
Jekyll based garden wrapped around
1916 Lutyens cottage (not open).
Sunken rose garden, enclosed
courtyard garden, pair of herbaceous
long borders, kitchen garden,
woodland and meadow. Featuring
'celebrity plants' used at events, incl
hydrangeas from the Prince of Wales's
wedding. Craft stalls. Gravel paths.
& ✕ ☕

28 NEW FOXHILL
Farnham Road, Elstead
GU8 6LE. Alison & Mike Welton,
01252 703964,
aliwelton@btopenworld.com. *5m
W of Godalming, 3½ m E of
Farnham. From A3 take B3001
towards Farnham. Garden 1m past
Elstead village on R opp Donkey
PH. From Farnham take B3001
towards Godalming, garden 3½ m
on L opp PH.* Home-made teas.
Adm £3.50, chd free. Wed 15,
Thur 16, Fri 17 July (2-5). **Visitors
also welcome by appt.**
Over 4 acres incl formal gardens
and a developing woodland garden
with rhododendrons, azaleas and
primulas. The formal garden incl
herbaceous and mixed planting
and was partly designed by
Gertrude Jekyll in 1923 with hard
landscaping and an impressive
water feature.
⊛ ☕ ☎

FROYLE GARDENS
See Hampshire.

㉙ FULVENS HANGER
Fulvens, off Crest Hill, Peaslake
GU5 9PG. Anthony & Kay Jessop
Price, 01306 730421. *6m E of
Guildford. A25 to Shere. Turn R
through village and up hill. Over railway
bridge then 1st L towards Peaslake.
After village sign 3rd L opp bus shelter
into Crest Hill. 1st R into Fulvens, 2nd
L down single track lane.* Home-made
teas. **Adm £3, chd free** (share to
Tongabezi Trust School, Zambia).
Tue 12 May to Fri 15 May incl (11-5).
Visitors also welcome by appt.
Exciting new 3-acre woodland garden
in early stages of development. Lovely
bluebell walk and many recent
specimen plantings. Newly-built Huf
house sits in the middle of this
woodland haven and around the house
find contemporary, innovative planting.
Recently-dug pond gives the feeling of
a tranquil oasis. Featured on BBC TV
Open Gardens.
&⚘⊛☕☎

㉚ ◆ GATTON PARK
Rocky Lane, Merstham RH2 0TW.
Royal Alexandra & Albert School,
01737 649068,
www.gattonpark.com. *3m NE of
Reigate. 5 mins from M25 J8 (A217) or
from top of Reigate Hill, over M25 then
follow sign to Merstham. Entrance is
off Rocky Lane accessible from Gatton
Bottom or A23 Merstham.* **Adm £3.50,
chd free.** 1st Sun of each month
Feb to Oct incl (1-5). For NGS: Suns
15 Feb (11-4), Weds 18 Feb (12-4);
14, 17 Feb **2010.**
Formerly home to the Colman family (of
mustard fame), now the grounds of the
Royal Alexandra and Albert School.
Hidden gardens within historic
Capability Brown parkland. 1910
Edwardian Japanese garden restored
for Channel 4's 'Lost Gardens'.
Dramatic 1912 Pulham rock garden,
walled gardens, lakeside trail.
Restoration of gardens ongoing and
maintained by volunteers. Ivan Hick's
children's trail behind main lake.
Massed snowdrops in Feb and Mar.
Limited wheelchair access.
&⊛☕

㉛ GREAT FOSTERS
Stroude Road, Egham TW20 9UR.
The Sutcliffe Family,
www.greatfosters.co.uk. *1m S of
Egham. On A30 at T-lights opp Virginia
Water, turn down Christchurch Rd
3389. Continue over roundabout and
after railway bridge turn L at T-lights
into Stroude Rd. Great Fosters approx
³/₄ m on R.* Refreshments (not NGS).
**Adm by donation, suggested
donation £4 per person.** Tue 2,
Wed 3 June (11-8).
Within the 50-acre estate, this
wonderful and inspiring garden has
been beautifully restored over the last
13yrs. Framed on 3 sides by a Saxon
moat, the knot garden of intricate
design has fragrant beds of flowers
and herbs and is bordered by clipped
hedges and topiary. Beyond, find the
grass amphitheatre, large lake,
wisteria-draped Japanese bridge,
sunken rose garden and tranquil lily
pond. Partial wheelchair access.
&⚘⊨☕

Many containers overflowing with flowers leading to mixed borders with an explosion of late summer colour . . .

㉜ GREEN LANE FARM
Cudworth Lane, Newdigate
RH5 5BH. Mr & Mrs P Hall. *8m S of
Dorking. On A24 turn L at Beare Green
roundabout signed Newdigate. R at T-
junction in Newdigate, L at Church, R
into Cudworth Lane. Farm ¹/₄ m on R.*
Home-made teas. **Adm £3, chd free.**
Sat 15, Sun 23 Aug (2-5).
1¹/₂ -acre garden with many containers
overflowing with flowers leading to
mixed borders with an explosion of late
summer colour. Brick paths through
rose arches leading to beautiful oak
summerhouse. Gravel area with
grasses. Unique restored gypsy vardo
(caravan). Farm walk circling 3 lakes.
&⊛☕☎

㉝ 72 GREEN WRYTHE LANE
Carshalton SM5 2DP. Mrs G
Cooling. *1m E of Sutton. From
Carshalton Ponds turn N across ponds
into North St. Continue to Wrythe
Green, then 1st R into Green Wrythe
Lane.* Home-made teas. **Adm £3, chd
free.** Sun 26 July (10.30-4.30).

170ft x 50ft colourful cottage style
garden of various habitats, incl
herbaceous borders, woodland area,
wildlife pond. A plantaholic's delight,
worked organically: an oasis in
suburbia. Cover from the elements.
Painted pot stall. Featured in 'Surrey
Life' and 'Epsom & Surrey Post'.
⚘⊛

㉞ ◆ HATCHLANDS PARK
East Clandon GU4 7RT. The
National Trust, 01483 222482,
www.nationaltrust.org.uk. *4m E of
Guildford. Off A246. A3 from London,
follow signs to Ripley to join A247 & via
W Clandon to A246. From Guildford
take A25 then A246 towards
Leatherhead at W Clandon.* **House &
Garden £7, chd £3.50. Garden only
3.70, chd £1.80. Park walks 1 Apr to
31 Oct, daily (11-6); House 1 Apr to
29 Oct Tues, Weds, Thurs, Suns &
BH Mons (2-5.30). For NGS: Suns 26
Apr; 18 Oct (11-5).**
Garden and park designed by Repton
in 1800. Follow one of the park walks
to the stunning bluebell wood in spring.
In autumn enjoy the changing colours
on the long walk. S of the house a
small parterre designed by Gertrude
Jekyll in 1913 to flower in early June.
Wheelchair access to house, main
garden and driveway through park
only.
&☕

㉟ HEATHSIDE
10 Links Green Way, Cobham
KT11 2QH. Miss Margaret Arnott &
Mr Terry Bartholomew, 01372
842459, m.a.arnott@btinternet.com.
*1¹/₂ m E of Cobham. Off A245
Cobham to Leatherhead rd. From
Cobham take 4th turning L after Esso
Garage into Fairmile Lane. Straight on
at mini-roundabout over Water Lane for
¹/₂ m. Links Green Way 3rd on L.*
Home-made teas. **Adm £3, chd free.
Visitors welcome by appt at any
time.**
¹/₃ -acre terraced garden planted for yr-
round interest. Beautiful in any season.
Spring bulbs and alpines, herbaceous
borders, roses and clematis in
summer, leaf colour and berries in
autumn and winter, all set off by
harmonious landscaping with pergola,
parterre, ponds, obelisks and urns.
Many inspirational ideas.
⚘⊛☕☎

HECKFIELD PLACE
See Hampshire.

36 HIDEAWAY HOUSE
Lower Ham Lane, Elstead GU8 6HQ.
Mr & Mrs C Burridge. *For directions see entry for Chandlers.* Home-made teas. **Combined adm with Chandlers,** also open, £3.50, chd free. **Sun 21 June (1-5).**
³/₄ -acre Italianate garden with large rolling lawn interspersed with follies, ornaments and unusual archtectural plants, designed for easy maintenance. Also incl woodland area, rockery, formal and natural pond. Many exceptional pots with annual and specimen displays. Large patio area for teas.

239A HOOK ROAD
See London.

Group opening

37 HORSELL ALLOTMENTS & BIRCH COTTAGE GARDEN
GU21 4PN. *1¹/₂ m W of Woking. From Woking follow signs to Horsell, along High St, Bullbeggars Lane at Chobham end of Village. Nearest parking by Cricketers PH, Horsell Birch.* Limited parking in village. Home-made teas at Birch Cottage. **Combined adm £3, chd free. Sun 5 July (11-4).**
'War of the Worlds' village. Church with Norman keep and a number of period properties.

BIRCH COTTAGE GARDEN
5 High Street. Celia & Mel Keenan. *Entrance on High St opp Bullbeggars Lane*
Created since 1999, smallish garden designed to reflect the 400yr-old Grade II listed cottage. Active dovecote, gravel garden, shrubs and perennials, archway with climbers through to potager, developing knot garden, courtyard with containers and hanging baskets. New rill water feature.
✿

HORSELL ALLOTMENTS
Bullbeggars Lane. Horsell Allotment Assn, www. windowonwoking.org.uk/sites/ haa. *Disabled parking only on site* Large site with over 100 individual plots growing a variety of flowers, fruit and vegetables. Mixture of modern, well known, heritage and unusual vegetables, many not seen in supermarkets. Featured in 'Surrey Life'.
&. ✖

Ancient orchard underplanted with wonderful mixed wild flowers . . .

38 HOWICKS
Hurlands Lane, Dunsfold GU8 4NT. Revd & Mrs Roger ter Haar. *6m S of Godalming. Through Dunsfold village, cricket pitch on L, then next L marked Knightons Lane, Howicks and Hurlands. Howicks ³/₄ m on R.*
Evening Opening £4, wine, Fri 5 June (5-8.30).
4¹/₂ -acre garden around medieval/ Stuart beamed cottage (not open) with hedged rose garden leading to secluded walled Italian courtyard with interesting water feature. Extensive lawns and long herbaceous borders. An ancient orchard underplanted with wonderful mixed wild flowers incl spring bulbs followed by masses of orchids. Featured in 'Period Living'.
&.

KIMPTON HOUSE
See Hampshire.

39 KNOWLE GRANGE
Hound House Road, Shere GU5 9JH. Mr P R & Mrs M E Wood, 01483 202108, prmewood@hotmail.com. *8m S of Guildford. From Shere (off A25), through village for ³/₄ m. After railway bridge, continue 1¹/₂ m past Hound House on R (stone dogs on gatepost). After 100yds turn R at Knowle Grange sign, go to end of lane.* Home-made teas. **Adm £5, chd free. Suns 17 May; 13 Sept (11-5).** Visitors also welcome by appt for groups of 20+.
80-acre idyllic hilltop position. Extraordinary and exciting 7-acre gardens, created from scratch since 1990 by Marie-Elisabeth Wood, blend the free romantic style with the strong architectural frame of the classical tradition. Walk the rural one-mile Bluebell Valley Unicursal Path of Life and discover its secret allegory. Deep unfenced pools, high unfenced drops.
✖ ☕ ☎

LEYDENS
See Kent.

LITTLE GABLES
See Kent.

LITTLE LODGE
See London.

40 LODKIN
Lodkin Hill, Hascombe GU8 4JP. Mr & Mrs W N Bolt, 01483 208323, willibolt2@aol.com. *3m S of Godalming. Just off B2130 Godalming to Cranleigh rd, on outskirts of Hascombe; take narrow lane signed to garden.* Home-made teas. **Adm £3.50, chd & disabled free. Suns 19 Apr; 14 June (2-5).** Visitors also welcome by appt.
Developed over 33 yrs, this garden is now well over twice its original size and incl 110ft of mainly restored Victorian glasshouses, extensive flower borders and kitchen garden. Flowering trees, shrubs, thousands of bulbs and a natural area with pond, stream and bog garden, planned to encourage wildlife. Garden very steep in parts, so limited wheelchair access.
&. ✿ ☕ ☎

41 LONG BARTON
12 Longdown Road, Guildford GU4 8PP. Harry & Rose-Marie Stokes. *1m E of Guildford. A246 (Epsom Rd) from Guildford, after ¹/₂ m turn R into Tangier Rd. At top turn L into Warren Rd, becoming One Tree Hill. At Xrds turn sharp R into Longdown Rd, last house on R in rd.* Home-made teas. **Adm £4, chd free** (share to St Martha's Restoration Fund). **Sun 9 Aug (10-5).**
Spectacular 2-acre garden on steep slope attempts to enhance the glory of its setting in the beautiful Surrey Hills. Hundreds of Japanese maples, knot garden, cyclamen lawns, pagan love temple, specimen trees, topiaries and large formal fish pond. Wrought iron, stonework and 3 water features. Many alpines. New acer plantation. Two large flat lawns interspaced between the slopes which fall 60ft from top to bottom.
✖ ✿ ☕

42 LONGER END COTTAGE
Normandy Common Lane, Normandy GU3 2AP. Ann & John McIlwham. *4m W of Guildford on A323. At War Memorial Xrds in Normandy turn R into Hunts Hill Rd then 1st R into Normandy Common Lane.* Home-made teas. **Adm £3, chd free** (share to Brain Research Trust

(7 June) St Mark's Church, Wyke (16 Aug). Suns 7 June; 16 Aug; 6 Sept (1-6).

1½ -acre garden divided into rooms with wide variety of plants, shrubs and trees incl roses, delphiniums, tree ferns, gunnera, grasses etc. Knot garden, laburnum walk, wild flower meadow, folly and small stumpery add to the attraction of the garden. Featured in 'GGG'. Uneven drive.

& � ☕

43 ◆ LOSELEY PARK
Guildford GU3 1HS. Mr & Mrs M G More-Molyneux, 01483 304440, www.loseley-park.com. *4m SW of Guildford. Leave A3 at Compton S of Guildford, on B3000 for 2m. Signed. Guildford stn 2m, Godalming stn 3m.* **House & gardens £8, chd £4, concessions £7.50. Garden only £4.50, chd £2.25, concessions £4. Garden May to Sept, Tues to Suns & BH Mons (11-5); House May to Aug, Tues to Thurs, Suns & BH Mons (1-5). For NGS: Sun 10 May (11-5).**
Delightful 2½ -acre walled garden based on design by Gertrude Jekyll. Award-winning rose garden (over 1,000 bushes, mainly old-fashioned varieties), extensive herb garden, fruit/flower garden, white garden with fountains, and spectacular organic vegetable garden. Magnificent vine walk, herbaceous borders, moat walk, ancient wisteria and mulberry trees. Wild flower meadow. Gravel paths.

& ✺ ⊛ ☕

LOWDER MILL
See Sussex.

Knot garden, laburnum walk, wild flower meadow, folly and small stumpery add to the attraction of the garden . . .

44 MEMOIRS
Stafford Lake, Queen's Road, Bisley GU24 9AY. Mr Ted Stephens, 07780 990553, e.stephens@optichrome.com. *Approx 6m N of Guildford. A322 Guildford to Bagshot rd to Bisley, then L into Queens Rd at T-lights after Fox PH. Follow Queens Rd for just under 1m then L into unmarked track (footpath sign) and follow NGS signs.* Home-made teas. **Adm £3.50, chd free. Sun 24 May (1-6). Visitors also welcome by appt for groups of 10+.**
Interesting and varied 8-acre organic garden created by owners. Formal lawn and borders, stream, ponds, bog garden, kitchen garden, terrace garden, wildlife areas, woodland, orchard and fields with rare-breed sheep and goats, chicken and ducks. Small museum of gardening and agricultural tools with many new exhibits this yr. Sale of hand-made jewellery.

& ✺ ⊛ ☕ ☎

45 MOLESHILL HOUSE
The Fairmile, Cobham KT11 1BG. Penny Snell, 01932 864532, pennysnellflowers@btinternet.com. *2m NE of Cobham. On A307 Esher to Cobham Rd next to free car park by A3 bridge, at entrance to Waterford Close.* Home-made teas. **Combined adm with The Coach House £5, chd free. Sun 10 May with music. Wed 13 May (2-5). Visitors also welcome by appt for groups of 20+.**
Romantic garden surrounding Victorian house is constantly being replanned and replanted to meet the vagaries of the English climate. Short woodland path with shade-loving plants leads from dovecote to beehives. Informally planted colour-coordinated borders contrast with the strict formality of topiary box and garlanded cisterns. Mediterranean courtyard with bright colours and tender plants, conservatory, fountains, bog garden, pleached avenue of *Sorbus lutescens* wild flowers in rough grass, pots and many unusual features. Garden 5 mins from Claremont Landscape Garden, Painshill Park & Wisley, also adjacent excellent dog-walking woods.

✺ ⊛ ☕ ☎

46 MUNSTEAD WOOD
Heath Lane, Godalming GU7 1UN. Sir Robert & Lady Clark. *2m SE of Godalming. Take B2130 Brighton Rd towards Horsham. After 1m church on*

R, Heath Lane just after on L. Entrance to Munstead Wood 400yds on R. Parking on L of Heath Lane. Disabled parking available, ask at main gate. Home-made teas. **Adm £3, chd free (share to Meeting Point, Chorley). Suns 26 Apr; 17 May (2-5).**
This former home of Gertrude Jekyll (designed by Edwin Lutyens) is surrounded by a 10-acre restored garden incl woodland, rivers of daffodils, paths through azaleas and rhododendrons, sunken rockery, lawns, shrubbery, rose-covered pergola, tank garden, topiary box, clematis garland, borders. Doorway in bargate wall to spring and summer gardens. Primula garden behind yew hedge. Some gravel, sand and grass paths.

& ⊛ ☕

47 19 OAK TREE ROAD
Knaphill GU21 2RW. Barry & Pam Gray. *5m NW of Guildford. From A3 take A322 Bagshot Rd, continue through Worplesdon, straight over at Brookwood Xrds. 1st turning on L into Oak Tree Rd (opp Sainsbury's).* Cream teas. **Adm £2.50, chd free (share to White Lodge). Sun 19 July (11-5).**
Colourful front garden of informal bedding, baskets and containers featuring tender perennials and annuals grown by owners. Back garden (approx 80ft x 35ft) has lawn, patio, small pond, trees, shrubs and perennials for foliage, texture, scent and yr-round interest. 3 greenhouses, fruit trees and vegetables. No wasted space in this delightful garden.

✺ ☕

48 ODSTOCK
Castle Square, Bletchingley RH1 4LB. Averil & John Trott. *3m W of Godstone. Just off A25 in Bletchingley. At top of village nr Red Lion PH. Parking in village, no parking in Castle Square.* Home-made teas. **Adm £3, chd free. Sun 2 Aug (11-5).**
⅔ -acre plantsman's garden maintained by owners and developed for all-yr interest. Special interest in grasses and climbers, approx 80 at last count. Japanese features; dahlias. No-dig, low-maintenance vegetable garden. Children's quiz. Disabled parking by gate, short gravel path.

& ✺ ⊛ ☕

OLD BUCKHURST
See Kent.

49 THE OLD CROFT
South Holmwood RH5 4NT. David & Virginia Lardner-Burke, www.lardner-burke.org.uk. *3m S of Dorking. From Dorking take A24 S for 3m. Turn L at sign to Leigh-Brockham into Mill Road. 1/2 m on L, 2 free car parks in NT Holmwood Common. Follow signs for 500yds along woodland walk. Disabled and elderly: for direct access tel 01306 888224.* Cream teas. **Adm £4, chd free.** Suns, Mons 3, 4, 24, 25 May; Sats, Suns 11, 12 July; 8, 9 Aug (2-6).
'5-acre paradise garden' (Surrey Life) encompasses many diverse areas of exquisite natural beauty. Stunning and imaginative vistas; many unusual specimen trees and shrubs, stream, lake, bog gardens, woodland, roses, amazing topiary buttress hedge, elevated 'hide', tropical bamboo maze. 'Through wisteria-clad pergola experience the first magnificent view of curving lawns bordered by flowering cherries...' (SL). Glorious colour in all seasons. Visitors return again and again.

OLD THATCH
See Hampshire.

Group opening

50 OXTED PLACE GARDENS
Broadham Green, Old Oxted RH8 9PF. *1½ m S of Oxted. From A25 turn into Old Oxted High St, turn off onto Beadles Lane which becomes Hall Hill then Broadham Green Rd. Turn into Oxted Place Drive by red phone box on Broadham Green.* Home-made teas. **Combined adm £5, chd free.** Sun 24 May (10-5).
Large country house garden divided into 3 separate gardens.

OXTED PLACE
Mr & Mrs T Beckett
6 acres of Edwardian gardens designed by J Cheal. Hydraulic ram-fed water features and ponds. Mature rhododendrons, shrubs, specimen trees, bridges and ornaments. Vegetable garden. Limited wheelchair access.

OXTED PLACE EAST
Mr & Mrs John Price
Large bank of azaleas, many rhododendrons and hydrangeas; palm trees. Large lawn, woodland walks and steps, massive cedar trees. No wheelchair access to woodland walk.

OXTED PLACE WEST
Mrs G Wettern
Enclosed garden, with azaleas, rhododendrons and variety of established shrubs. Woodland views and Italian-style patio in the area of the old gardener's office.

PETERSHAM LODGE
See London.

51 ◆ POLESDEN LACEY
Great Bookham RH5 6BD. The National Trust, 01372 452048, www.nationaltrust.org.uk. *Nr Dorking, off A246 Leatherhead to Guildford rd. 1½ m S of Great Bookham, well signed.* **House & garden £11, chd £5.50. Garden only £7, chd £3.50. Times vary according to season. Please phone or see website for details.** For NGS: Sun 7 June (10-5).
30 acres formal gardens in an exceptional setting on the North Downs; walled rose garden, winter garden, lawns; magnificent views. Regency villa dating from early 1820s, remodelled after 1906 by the Hon Mrs Ronald Greville. King George VI and Queen Elizabeth the Queen Mother spent part of their honeymoon here. Mrs Greville's Rose Garden will be in full bloom. Come and learn how to make your own compost. No dogs in formal gardens.

An ancient glorious wisteria, rhododendrons and azaleas in full flower . . .

52 POSTFORD HOUSE
172 Dorking Road, Chilworth GU4 8RN. Mrs M R Litler-Jones, 01483 202657. *4m SE of Guildford. A248 Guildford to Dorking rd, garden between boundary of Chilworth and Albury.* **Adm £3, chd free.** Visitors welcome by appt in May & June only.
25 acres of woodland and formal gardens, incl rose and vegetable garden. Lovely walk along stream with rhododendrons, azaleas and established trees.

53 QUINNEYS
Camilla Drive, Westhumble RH5 6BU. Peter & Jane Miller. *1m N of Dorking. Turn L off A24 (going N) into Westhumble St, just before Boxhill roundabout. After 1/4 m, pass Boxhill and Westhumble stn & go through archway into Camilla Dr. House 3rd on L. Limited parking at garden. Parking available at Boxhill stn (3 mins walk). Coming from Leatherhead (going S) on A24 turn R just after Boxhill roundabout signed Westhumble stn. Then as above.* Home-made teas. **Adm £3, chd free.** Sun 17 May (2-6).
3 acres created at the breakup of the neighbouring estate of Camilla Lacey, incorporating some of the original cedar trees. Present owners have planted a mini arboretum, and have used the concept of 'tapestry' hedges to good effect. Also incl some rare trees and shrubs, an ancient glorious wisteria, rhododendrons and azaleas in full flower. Interesting water garden. Efforts now focussed on developing 'Jekyll' herbaceous border. Gravel drive and path.

54 ◆ RAMSTER
Chiddingfold GU8 4SN. Mr & Mrs Paul Gunn, 01428 654167, www.ramsterweddings.co.uk. *1½ m S of Chiddingfold. On A283; large iron gates on R.* **Adm £5, chd under 16 free, concessions £4.50. Daily 4 Apr to 21 June (10-5).** For NGS: Sun 10 May (10-5).
Mature woodland garden of exceptional interest with lakes, ponds and woodland walk. Outstanding collection of fine rhododendrons and azaleas in bloom in early spring with stunning varieties of camellias, magnolias and carpets of bluebells. Many rare trees and shrubs, wild flower areas, bog garden. A truly beautiful and peaceful garden. Embroidery and textile exhibition 17 to 28 Apr.

55 ◆ **RHS GARDEN WISLEY**
Woking GU23 6QB. Royal
Horticultural Society,
www.rhs.org.uk. *1m NE of Ripley. SW
of London on A3 & M25 (J10). Follow
signs.* All yr, not Christmas Day. Mon
to Fri 10-6, Sat & Sun 9-6 (Nov-Feb
4.30). Last entry 1hr before closing.
For NGS: **Special Evening
Opening with music** Fri 11 Sept
(6-9). Adm (incl RHS members) £7,
chd under 15 free (share to RHS
Wisley Garden). Reserve table for
dinner on 01483 211773.
Primary garden of the RHS and centre
of its scientific and educational
activities. Arboretum, alpine and wild
garden, rock garden, mixed borders,
model gardens, model fruit and
vegetable garden, rose garden,
orchard, trial grounds and glasshouse.
Wisley Flower Show 11-13 Sept.
  ⤶ ❀ ☕

56 **THE ROUND HOUSE**
Dunsfold Road, Loxhill GU8 4BL.
Mrs Sue Lawson, 01483 200375,
suelaw.law@btinternet.com. *4m S of
Bramley. Off A281. At Smithbrook
Kilns turn R to Dunsfold. Follow to
T-junction. Go R (B2130). After 1.2m
Park Hatch on R, enter park, follow
drive to garden.* Home-made teas.
Adm £3.50, chd free. Suns 14 June;
12 July (2-6). Visitors also welcome
by appt May to Sept, no coaches.
2½ -acre walled Victorian garden with
far-reaching views. Continuing renewal
programme since 2002. Colourful
mixed beds with perennials, roses and
interesting statuary. New water feature
and play area. Serpentine paths
between shrubs and wild flowers. 75m
lavender walk. Ornamental fish pond.
Gravel paths, steep slopes.
  ⤶ ☕ ☎

SANDY SLOPES
See Hampshire.

SHALFORD HOUSE
See Sussex.

57 **41 SHELVERS WAY**
Tadworth KT20 5QJ. Keith &
Elizabeth Lewis, 01737 210707. *6m
S of Sutton off A217. 1st turning on R
after Burgh Heath T-lights heading S.
400yds down Shelvers Way on L.*
Home-made teas. Adm £3, chd free.
Wed 22, Sun 26 Apr; Sun 19 July
(1.30-5). Visitors also welcome by
appt for groups of 10+.
½ -acre back garden of dense and
detailed planting, interesting at all

seasons, starting with a mass of spring
bulbs with over 100 varieties of
daffodils. In one part, beds of choice
perennials are interlaced by paths and
backed by unusual shrubs and mature
trees; in the other, cobbles and shingle
support grasses and special plants for
dry conditions.
⤶ ❀ ☕ ☎

In early
spring there
will be plenty
of bulbs,
specially tulips,
and by June
the roses
should be in
full glory . . .

59 **SPRING COTTAGE**
Smithwood Common Road,
Cranleigh GU6 8QN. Mr & Mrs D E
Norman, 01483 272620,
norman.springcott@btinternet.com.
*1m N of Cranleigh. From Cranleigh
cricket ground take rd signed Cranleigh
School. Garden is ¼ m N of Cranleigh
School entrance. From Guildford
A281, follow signs to Cranleigh. Turn L
immed after roundabout into
Smithwood Common Rd. Garden
1¼ m on R. Easy parking.* Adm £3,
chd free. Visitors welcome by
appt Apr to June for groups or
individuals.
We will be pleased to welcome visitors
by appointment from April to June. In
early spring there will be plenty of
bulbs, specially tulips, and by June the
roses should be in full glory.
Refreshments by arrangement plus
conducted tour of the garden.
  ⤶ 🛏 ☕ ☎

60 **SPURFOLD**
Peaslake GU5 9SZ. Mr & Mrs A
Barnes, 01306 730196,
spurfold@btinternet.com. *8m SE of
Guildford. A25 to Shere. Turn R
through Shere village & up hill. Over
railway bridge 1st L to Peaslake. In
Peaslake turn L after village stores
Radnor Rd. Approx 500yds up single
track lane to car park.* **Evening
Openings** £5, wine, Fris 5 June;
14 Aug (5-8). Visitors also welcome
by appt, groups of 12+.
Wonderful garden set in area of
outstanding natural beauty. Approx
4 acres, large herbaceous and shrub
borders, formal pond with Buddha
head from Cambodia, sunken gravel
garden with topiary box and water
feature, four terraces, beautiful lawns,
mature rhododendrons and azaleas,
woodland path, and gazebos. Garden
contains unique collection of Indian
elephants and other objets d'art.
⤶ ❀ ☎

61 **SQUARE LEG COTTAGE**
The Green, Ewhurst GU6 7RR.
Monica & Anthony Rosenberg. *3m
E of Cranleigh. Take B2127 from
obelisk at E end of Cranleigh. 2m to
Ewhurst village. Take 1st R to end then
R again. Garden opp cricket green.
Parking on green or Plough Lane.*
Home-made teas. Adm £2.50, chd
free. Sun 14, Wed 17 June (11-5).
Peaceful, romantic plantsperson's
garden of 1 acre which incl fernery,
scented roses, rose arbour and pond.
Also a small paddock with fruit trees
and pumpkin bed. Raised decorative
vegetable and herb beds, and a
greenhouse with a collection of
pelargoniums. Lots of places to sit and
have tea.
⤶ ❀ ☕

SQUERRYES COURT
See Kent.

62 **STUART COTTAGE**
Ripley Road, East Clandon
GU4 7SF. Mr & Mrs J M Leader,
01483 222689. *4m E of Guildford. Off
A246 or from A3 through Ripley until
roundabout, turn L and continue
through West Clandon until T-lights,
then L onto A246. East Clandon 1st L.*
Home-made teas. Adm £3, chd free.
Wed 10 June (2-5); **Evening
Opening with music** £5, chd free,
wine, Fri 24 July (5-8). Mon 31 Aug
(1-5.30). Visitors also welcome by
appt, groups of 20+.
½ -acre partly walled garden using

some traditional box shapes and hedging to offer formality in the otherwise informal garden of this C16 cottage. Wisteria and rose/clematis walks give shade to the S/W aspect while rosemary and lavender edge the brick paths. Unusual herbaceous plants vie for attention among cottage garden favourites. From decorative organic kitchen garden walk to small chequerboard orchard. Featured in 'The English Garden' & GGG.

SUNNINGDALE PARK
See Berkshire.

63 35 TADORNE ROAD
Tadworth KT20 5TF. **Dr & Mrs J R Lay.** *6m S of Sutton. On A217 to large roundabout, 3m N of M25 J8. Take B2220 signed Tadworth. Tadorne Rd 2nd on R.* Home-made teas served in plant-filled conservatory. **Adm £2.50, chd free.** Sats, Suns 27, 28 June; 1, 2 Aug (1.30-5.30).
$1/3$-acre hedged garden with colourful herbaceous borders, shrubby island beds, rose and clematis-covered pergola leading to secluded seating area, potager-style vegetable plot, soft fruit, woodland corner and a varied patio display. Gravel drive at entrance.

Pantiled water cascade and newly-created gravel gardens . . .

64 TILFORD COTTAGE
Tilford Road, Tilford GU10 2BX. **Mr & Mrs R Burn,** 01252 795423, rodburn@tiscali.co.uk, www.tilfordcottagegarden.co.uk. *3m SE of Farnham. From Farnham stn along Tilford Rd. Tilford Cottage opp Tilford House. Parking by village green.* Teas & wine by arrangement. **Adm £5, chd free.** Visitors welcome by appt May to July & Sept, for groups of 4+, coaches permitted.
Artist's garden designed to surprise, delight and amuse. Formal planting, herb and knot garden. Numerous examples of topiary combine beautifully with the wild flower river

walk. Japanese and water gardens, hosta beds, rose, apple willow arches, treehouse and fairy grotto all continue the playful quality especially enjoyed by children. Some steep slopes; wheelchair access possible to all but herb garden.

65 TIMBER HILL
Chertsey Road, Chobham GU24 8JF. **Mr & Mrs Nick Sealy.** *4m N of Woking. $2^{1}/_{2}$ m E of Chobham and $1/_{3}$ m E of Fairoaks aerodrome on A319 (N side). $1^{1}/_{4}$ m W of Ottershaw, J11 M25.* Excellent home-made refreshments. **Adm £3.50, chd free.** Sun 8 Mar (10.30-4); Suns 5 Apr; 3 May (11-4.30). **Evening Opening** £6, wine & light refreshments, Sun 21 June (6-8.30).
Still a smallholding where sheep graze with their lambs, this 15-acre garden consists of park and woodland, gradually being restored, with fine specimens of oaks, liquidambar and liriodendron. Early witchhazel walk and plantings of oak, beech, cherry and acers. Many camellias, magnolias and azaleas shelter under banks of rhododendron ponticum. Drifts of narcissi, daffodils and other spring bulbs, shrub and ground cover borders. Bluebells in early May, rambling roses in old apple trees in June. Good help for wheelchair users and elderly.

66 ◆ TITSEY PLACE GARDENS
Titsey Hill, Oxted RH8 0SD. **The Trustees of the Titsey Foundation,** 01273 715359, www.titsey.org. *3m N of Oxted. A25 between Oxted & Westerham. Follow brown signs from A25 at Limpsfield.* **House & garden £7. Garden only £4.50, chd £1.** Easter Mon (gardens only), then 13 May to 30 Sept, Weds & Suns & B Hols (1-5). For NGS: Sats 16 May; 20 June; 18 July; 15 Aug (1-5). Garden only on these days. Car park & picnic area open from 12.
One of the largest surviving estates in Surrey. Magnificent ancestral home and gardens of the Gresham family since 1534. Walled kitchen garden restored early 1990s. Golden Jubilee rose garden. Etruscan summer house adjoining picturesque lakes and fountains. 15 acres of formal and informal gardens in idyllic setting within the M25. Setting for feature on Darwin narrated by David Attenborough.

67 TOLLSWORTH MANOR
Rook Lane, Chaldon CR3 5BQ. **Carol & Gordon Gillett.** *2m W of Caterham. From Caterham-on-the-Hill, take B2031 through Chaldon. 300yds out of Chaldon take concrete farm track on L. Parking in farmyard beyond house.* Home-made teas. **Adm £3.50, chd free.** Sun 7 June (11-5).
Old-fashioned country garden, created from derelict site over 26yrs by present owners. Well-stocked herbaceous borders with old-fashioned roses, peonies, delphiniums. Wildlife pond and duck pond with ducks. Lovely views over surrounding farmland. Shetland pony. Some uneven paths.

68 6 UPPER ROSE HILL
Dorking RH4 2EB. **Peter & Julia Williams,** 01306 881315. *Town centre. From roundabout at A24/A25 junction follow signs through town centre towards Horsham. Turn L (under cedar tree) after Cricketers PH by flint wall. Parking available in rd & behind Sainsbury's (5 mins walk).* Home-made teas. **Adm £3, chd free.** Suns 31 May; 6 Sept (1.30-5.30).
Visitors also welcome by appt.
$1/_2$-acre plantsman's informal terraced garden on dry sand. Surprising secluded setting with striking outlook onto St Paul's Church. Planted for yr-round interest of foliage and form; fruit and vegetables, gravel bed and alpine troughs, borders and rockeries. Range of drought-tolerant plants. Autumn colour, grasses attractive into Oct.

69 VALE END
Chilworth Road, Albury GU5 9BE. **Mr & Mrs John Foulsham,** 01483 202594, daphne@dfoulsham.freeserve.co.uk. *4m SE of Guildford. From Albury take A248 W for $1/_4$ m.* Home-made teas. **Adm £3, chd free.** Sun 19, Wed 22 Apr (2-5). **Evening Opening** £5, wine, Sat 13 June (6-8.30). Wed 17 June (2-5). Visitors also welcome by appt.
1-acre walled garden on many levels in beautiful setting overlooking mill pond. Richly diverse planting of roses, shrubs, annuals and perennials on light sandy soil. Formal clipped yew walk with festooned rope swag, tiny courtyard, potager with fruit, vegetable and herb garden. Pantiled water cascade and newly-created gravel gardens. River and woodland walks from the garden gate.

70 VANN

Hambledon GU8 4EF. Mrs M Caroe, 01428 683413, www.vanngarden.co.uk. *6m S of Godalming. A283 to Wormley. Turn L at Hambledon. Follow yellow Vann signs for 2m. Please do not park in rd, park in field.* Home-made teas Mon 4 May only. **Adm £4.50, chd free (share to Hambledon Village Hall). Sun 29 Mar to Sat 4 Apr incl (10-6); Mon 4 May (2-6). Tue 5 May to Sun 10 May incl (10-6); Sun 7 June to Sat 13 June incl (10-6).**

English Heritage registered 4½ -acre garden surrounding Tudor and William and Mary house (not open) with later changes by W D Carôe. Old cottage garden, pergola, ¼ -acre pond, Gertrude Jekyll water garden, azaleas, new 'Centenary' garden, spring bulbs, woodland, mixed borders. Fritillaria *meleagris* in Mar/Apr. Island beds, crinkle crankle wall. Maintained by owner with 3 days' help per week. Deep water. Water garden paths not suitable for wheelchairs, but many others are. Please ring prior to visit to request disabled parking.

  🚶 ♿ 🐕 ☕ ☎

71 NEW VICARAGE COTTAGE

Brockham Green, nr Betchworth RH3 7JS. Mr & Mrs R Harman. *2m E of Dorking. Take signed rd from A25 between Dorking and Reigate, then ½ m to Brockham Green. No parking on Green, considerate parking on rd please.* Ploughman's lunches at garden (Sun only), home-made teas (Sat & Sun) in village hall from 2.30. **Adm £3, chd free. Sat 27, Sun 28 June (11-5).**

½ -acre cottage garden situated on the Green, next to church and in one of Surrey's most beautiful villages. Designed to complement the 400yr-old cottage. Gently curving borders surround and flow from a central ancient yew tree, with a mix of flowers, shrubs and roses. Pond, stumpery, small wild flower meadow, young orchard and kitchen garden. Lovely river walk to Betchworth Village.

  ♿ 🐕 🐾 ☕

WALBURY

See Hampshire.

72 WALNUT HOUSE

Gatton Close, Reigate RH2 0HG. Inger & Dirk Laan. *1m N of Reigate. M25 J8, then S on A217. After Esso garage, L into Raglan Rd, at Xrds L into Gatton Rd. After 500yds Gatton Close on L. Please park in Gatton Rd.* Home-made teas. **Adm £3, chd free. Sun 2 Aug (11-5). Evening Opening £5, wine & canapés, Wed 5 Aug (5.30-8.30).**

⅓ -acre garden of contrasting moods, leading the visitor through a shady intimate fernery into large water garden reflecting light from open skies. Romantic flower garden with unusual plants and old favourites. Pergola, greenhouse and small potager. Created by owners. Steep access slope.

  ♿ 🐕 ☕

Gently curving borders surround and flow from a central ancient yew tree . . .

73 WALTON POOR HOUSE

Ranmore RH5 6SX. Nicholas & Prue Calvert. *6m NW of Dorking. From Dorking take rd to Ranmore, continue for approx 4m, after Xrds in dip 1m on L. From A246 at East Horsley go S into Greendene, 1st L Crocknorth Rd, 1m on R.* Home-made teas. **Adm £3, chd free. Mon 4 May; Suns 7 June; 26 July (12-5.30).**

Tranquil, almost secretive, 4-acre mostly wooded garden in N Downs AONB, planted to show contrast between colourful shrubs and mature trees. Paths wind through garden to pond, hideaway dell and herb garden leading to herb nursery. Herb talk 3pm.

  ♿ 🐕 🐾 ☕

74 WESTWAYS FARM

Gracious Pond Road, Chobham GU24 8HJ. Paul & Nicky Biddle, 01276 856163. *4m N of Woking. From Chobham Church proceed over roundabout towards Sunningdale, 1st Xrds R into Red Lion Rd to junction with Mincing Lane.* Home-made teas.

Adm £3, chd free. Sun 10 May (10-5). Evening Opening £5, wine & canapés, Wed 13 May (6-8). Visitors also welcome by appt.

Open 8-acre garden surrounded by woodlands planted in 1930s with mature and some rare rhododendrons, azaleas, camellias and magnolias, underplanted with bluebells, erythroniums, lilies and dogwood; extensive lawns and sunken pond garden. Working stables and sandschool. Lovely Queen Anne House (not open) covered with listed *Magnolia grandiflora*. Victorian design glasshouse. Limited wheelchair access to woodland.

  ♿ 🐕 🐾 ☎

WHEATLEY HOUSE

See Hampshire.

WHISPERS

See Hampshire.

75 ♦ WINKWORTH ARBORETUM

Hascombe Road, nr Godalming GU8 4AD. The National Trust, 01483 208477, www.nationaltrust.org.uk. *2m S of Godalming on B2130. Coaches by written arrangement. Stn: Godalming 3m.* **Adm £5.60, chd £2.80, family ticket £12.50. Daily all yr, dawn to dusk. For NGS: Suns 19 Apr; 4 Oct (11-5).**

110 acres of rolling Surrey hillside set in a valley leading down to a reservoir and wetland area. Planted with rare trees and shrubs leading to impressive displays in spring with magnolias, azaleas and bluebells matched by the dramatic reds, golds and browns of maples, cherries etc during autumn. National Collection of Sorbus aria.

  NCCPG ☕

76 WINTERSHALL MANOR

Bramley GU5 0LR. Mr & Mrs Peter Hutley. *3m S of Bramley Village. On A281 turn R, then next R. Wintershall Drive next on L. Bus: AV33 Guildford-Horsham, alight Palmers Cross, 1m.* Cream teas. **Adm £3, chd 50p (share to Wintershall Charitable Trust). Sats 28 Mar; 25 Apr (2-5).**

2-acre garden and 200 acres of park and woodland. Bluebell walks in spring, wild daffodils, rhododendrons, specimen trees. Lakes and flight ponds; superb views. Chapel of St Mary, stations of Cross, Rosary Walk and St Francis Chapel. Some gravel paths and steep slopes.

  ♿ 🐕 ☕

77 WOODBURY COTTAGE
Colley Lane, Reigate RH2 9JJ.
Shirley & Bob Stoneley, 01737
244235. *1m W of Reigate. M25 J8,
A217 (direction Reigate). Immed before
level Xing turn R into Somers Rd, cont
as Manor Rd. At very end turn R into
Coppice Lane & follow signs to car
park. Garden is 300yds walk from car
park. Approach from A25 not
recommended.* Home-made teas.
Adm £3, chd free. Sats, Suns 4, 5
July; 5, 6 Sept (Sats 2-5, Suns 11-5);
Wed 9 Sept (2-5). **Evening
Opening**, £4, wine, Fri 10 July (5-8).
Visitors also welcome by appt for
groups of 10+.
Cottage garden of just under ¼ acre,
made and maintained by owners.
Garden is stepped on slope with mixed
planting, enhanced by its setting under
Colley Hill. A rich diversity of plants,
colour-themed, still vibrant in Sept.

78 WOODHILL MANOR
Woodhill Lane, Shamley Green
GU5 0SP, 01483 891004,
stephanie@smithkingdom.com,
www.woodhillmanor.com. *5m S of
Guildford. Directions on application
when booking visit.* Home-made teas.
Adm £4.50, regret no children owing
to deep ponds and steep steps.
Pre-booked visitors welcome
Fri 17, Wed 22, Thur 23 Apr; Weds,
Thurs, Fri 1, 9, 17, 23, 29 July; Fri 7
Aug (all 10.30-4.30). **Christmas
Celebration with mulled wine
and mince pies** Thur 17 Dec
(10.30-4). **Pre-booking for all
dates essential.** Groups of 5+, no
coaches.
Georgian manor house with glorious
mix of traditional and formal gardens
with views towards the S Downs.
Dramatic spring display of over 3000
tulips. Box parterres, extensively
planted colourful herbaceous beds,

courtyards with scented lavender and
rose displays in July. Wild flower
meadow walks and 20 acres of
parkland with mature trees incl
mulberry, tulip tree, monkey puzzles.
Newly-planted pond gardens.

79 WOTTON HOUSE
Guildford Road, Dorking RH5 6HS.
Principal Hayley. *3m W of Dorking.
On A25 towards Guildford. Gravel
driveway (signed), adjacent to Wotton
Hatch PH.* Light refreshments & home-
made teas (not NGS). Adm £2.50, chd
free. Suns 19, 26 July (11-4).
Now under new management, the
gardens are being restored to their
former glory. Widely held to be the first
example of an Italian-style garden in
England. The 20 acres of parkland
were created in 1640 by George
Evelyn and his brother John, the
eminent designer and diarist. Features
incl a terraced mount, classical garden
temple, statuary, tortoise house
(uninhabited), and grottoes.

Glorious mix of
traditional and
formal gardens
with views
towards the
South Downs . . .

Surrey County Volunteers

County Organiser
Mrs Gayle Leader, Stuart Cottage, East Clandon, Surrey GU4 7SF, 01483 222689

County Treasurer
Mr Roger Nickolds, Old Post House, East Clandon, Surrey GU4 7SE, 01483 224027, rogernickolds@hotmail.com

Publicity
Mrs Mary Farmery, Fairlawn, Camilla Drive, Westhumble, Surrey RH5 6BU 01306 640225, maryfarmery@hotmail.com

Assistant County Organisers
Mrs Anne Barnes, Spurfold, Radnor Road, Peaslake, Guildford, Surrey GU5 9SZ, 01306 730196
Mrs Maggie Boyd, Bardsey, 11 Derby Road, Haslemere, Surrey GU27 1BS, 01428 652283
Mr Keith Lewis, 41 Shelvers Way, Tadworth, Surrey KT20 5QJ, 01737 210707
Mrs Shirley Stoneley, Woodbury Cottage, Colley Lane, Reigate, Surrey RH2 9JJ, 01737 244235
Mrs Averil Trott, Odstock, Castle Square, Bletchingley, Surrey RH1 4LB, 01883 743100

Mark your diary with these special events in 2009

EXPLORE SECRET GARDENS DURING CHELSEA & HAMPTON COURT FLOWER SHOW WEEKS

Tue 19 May, Wed 20 May, Thur 21 May, Fri 22 May, Wed 8 July, Thur 9 July
Full day tours from £82 per person, 10% discount for groups
Advance booking required, telephone +44 (0)20 8693 1015 or email j.wookey@btinternet.com
Specially selected gardens in London, Essex, Kent, Hampshire and South Oxfordshire. The tour price includes transport and lunch with wine at a popular restaurant or pub.

HAMPTON COURT PALACE

Thur 2 Apr, Tue 23 June, Thur 25 June, Wed 15 July, Tue 4 Aug, Thur 10 Sept
Evening tours in the company of one of the Palace's specialist tour guides from 6.30 – 8pm
Tickets £6 per person. Advance booking required, telephone +44 (0)1483 211535 or
visit www.ngs.org.uk for more information
Gossip, scandal, murder, healing – you'll find it all within the Formal Gardens at Hampton Court Palace. Each tour will have its own unique feature whether it's the story of the Great Vine or the magic and mystery of the Maze.

FROGMORE – A ROYAL GARDEN (BERKSHIRE)

Tue 26 May 10am – 5.30pm (last admission 4pm)
Garden adm £4.50, chd free. Tickets available in advance or on the day.
Advance booking for groups and coaches, telephone
+44 (0) 1483 211535 or email orders@ngs.org.uk
A rare opportunity to explore 30 acres of landscaped garden, rich in history and beauty.

FLAXBOURNE FARM – FUN & SURPRISES (BEDFORDSHIRE)

Sun 7 June 10am – 5pm. Adm £5, chd free
No booking required, come along on the day!
Bring the whole family and have fun in this surprising and entertaining garden of 2 acres. Enjoy the large plant fair, live music, pets corner, birds of prey, dog agility show and much more.

WISLEY RHS GARDEN – MUSIC IN THE GARDEN (SURREY)

Fri 11 Sept 6 – 9pm
Adm (incl RHS members) £7, chd under 15 free
Save money on advance bookings for groups of 4 or more, telephone +44 (0)1483 211535 or
visit www.ngs.org.uk for more information
A special evening opening of this famous garden, exclusively for the NGS. Enjoy music and entertainment as you explore the gardens and the floral marquee on the first day of the Wisley Flower Show.

For further information visit www.ngs.org.uk or telephone 01483 211535

SUSSEX

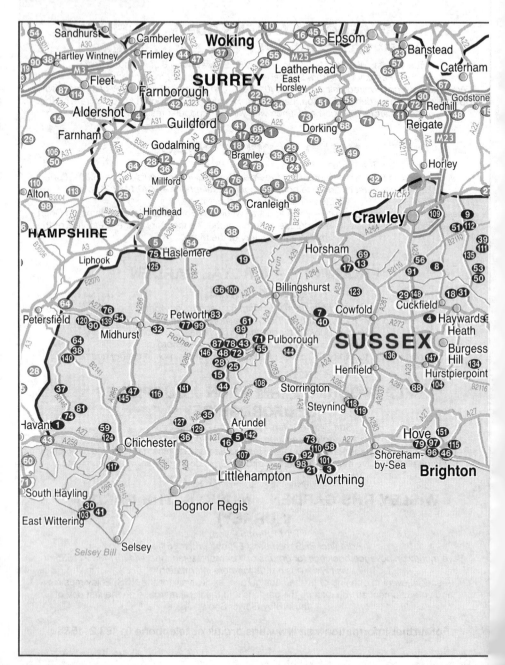

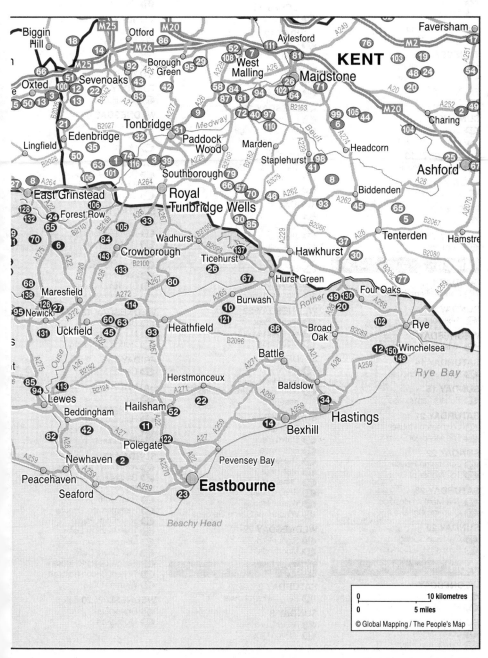

Opening Dates

February

SUNDAY 8
77 The Manor of Dean
81 Mitchmere Farm

WEDNESDAY 11
104 Pembury House

THURSDAY 12
81 Mitchmere Farm
104 Pembury House

FRIDAY 13
104 Pembury House

SUNDAY 15
37 Dormers
81 Mitchmere Farm

WEDNESDAY 18
104 Pembury House

THURSDAY 19
104 Pembury House

FRIDAY 20
104 Pembury House

SUNDAY 22
37 Dormers

March

SUNDAY 1
120 Sandhill Farm House

SUNDAY 8
1 Aldsworth House

WEDNESDAY 11
1 Aldsworth House

SATURDAY 14
22 Butlers Farmhouse

SUNDAY 15
22 Butlers Farmhouse

SATURDAY 21
74 Lordington House
77 The Manor of Dean

SUNDAY 22
74 Lordington House
77 The Manor of Dean

SATURDAY 28
79 The Martlets Hospice
93 Oakleigh Cottage

SUNDAY 29
93 Oakleigh Cottage
105 Penns in the Rocks

April

WEDNESDAY 1
15 Bignor Park
84 Moorlands

SUNDAY 5
11 Bates Green
88 Newtimber Place

WEDNESDAY 8
15 Bignor Park
84 Moorlands

SATURDAY 11
67 King John's Lodge

SUNDAY 12
19 Bradstow Lodge
67 King John's Lodge

MONDAY 13
61 Horsebridge House
67 King John's Lodge

WEDNESDAY 15
15 Bignor Park
19 Bradstow Lodge
84 Moorlands

SATURDAY 18
77 The Manor of Dean
117 Rymans
120 Sandhill Farm House

SUNDAY 19
1 Aldsworth House
66 Kiln Copse Farm
77 The Manor of Dean
101 18 Pavilion Road
117 Rymans
120 Sandhill Farm House

TUESDAY 21
1 Aldsworth House

WEDNESDAY 22
15 Bignor Park
66 Kiln Copse Farm
84 Moorlands

SATURDAY 25
38 Down Place
42 Firle Place
83 Moor Farm - **Pre booking essential**

SUNDAY 26
37 Dormers
38 Down Place
42 Firle Place
46 The Garden House
76 Malt House
94 Offham House
114 Rose Cottage
143 Warren House
149 Winchelsea Spring Gardens

WEDNESDAY 29
15 Bignor Park
84 Moorlands

May

SATURDAY 2
106 Perryhill Farmhouse

SUNDAY 3
4 Ansty Gardens
16 4 Birch Close

101 18 Pavilion Road
102 Peasmarsh Place
106 Perryhill Farmhouse
141 Upwaltham Barns

MONDAY 4
16 4 Birch Close
76 Malt House
134 Stonehealed Farm
141 Upwaltham Barns
143 Warren House

TUESDAY 5
76 Malt House

WEDNESDAY 6
10 Bateman's
15 Bignor Park
84 Moorlands

SATURDAY 9
8 Balcombe Gardens
67 King John's Lodge
133 Stone Cross House

SUNDAY 10
27 Clinton Lodge
45 Framfield Grange
54 Hammerwood House
67 King John's Lodge
86 Mountfield Court
124 Sennicotts
125 Shalford House
133 Stone Cross House

WEDNESDAY 13
15 Bignor Park
84 Moorlands
139 Trotton Old Rectory

FRIDAY 15
24 Caxton Manor

SATURDAY 16
24 Caxton Manor
30 Cookscroft
53 Ham Cottage
77 The Manor of Dean
135 Stonehurst

SUNDAY 17
6 Ashdown Park Hotel
7 Bakers House
30 Cookscroft
53 Ham Cottage
54 Hammerwood House
70 Legsheath Farm
77 The Manor of Dean
78 Manvilles Field
92 Oak Grove College
123 Sedgwick Park House
137 Tinkers Bridge Cottage
143 Warren House

WEDNESDAY 20
15 Bignor Park
84 Moorlands

SATURDAY 23
- **20** Brickwall
- **39** Duckyls Holt
- **53** Ham Cottage
- **83** Moor Farm - **Pre booking essential**
- **111** The Priest House

SUNDAY 24
- **12** Beauchamps
- **14** Bexhill Gardens
- **17** Blue Jays
- **32** Cowdray Park Gardens
- **39** Duckyls Holt
- **47** Gardeners Cottage
- **53** Ham Cottage
- **56** High Beeches
- **57** Highdown
- **67** King John's Lodge
- **101** 18 Pavilion Road
- **114** Rose Cottage
- **116** Roundhill Cottage

MONDAY 25
- **39** Duckyls Holt
- **67** King John's Lodge
- **116** Roundhill Cottage
- **143** Warren House

WEDNESDAY 27
- **15** Bignor Park
- **84** Moorlands
- **131** Sparrow Hatch

THURSDAY 28
- **31** Copyhold Hollow
- **131** Sparrow Hatch

FRIDAY 29
- **68** Latchetts

SATURDAY 30
- **23** 51 Carlisle Road
- **68** Latchetts
- **75** Lowder Mill

SUNDAY 31
- **1** Aldsworth House
- **23** 51 Carlisle Road
- **41** Earnley Grange
- **73** Longlands
- **75** Lowder Mill
- **99** 6 Park Terrace

June

MONDAY 1
- **36** Denmans Garden

TUESDAY 2
- **145** West Dean Gardens

WEDNESDAY 3
- **1** Aldsworth House
- **57** Highdown
- **84** Moorlands

THURSDAY 4
- **140** Uppark

FRIDAY 5
- **22** Butlers Farmhouse (Evening)
- **50** Great Lywood Farmhouse

SATURDAY 6
- **60** Hobbs Barton
- **72** Little Poynes
- **85** Mount Harry House & Mount Harry Lodge
- **120** Sandhill Farm House

SUNDAY 7
- **27** Clinton Lodge
- **35** Dale Park House
- **50** Great Lywood Farmhouse
- **52** Hailsham Grange
- **57** Highdown
- **60** Hobbs Barton
- **69** Leechpool Cottage
- **72** Little Poynes
- **80** Mayfield Gardens
- **94** Offham House
- **99** 6 Park Terrace
- **120** Sandhill Farm House

MONDAY 8
- **27** Clinton Lodge
- **60** Hobbs Barton

WEDNESDAY 10
- **84** Moorlands
- **110** 6 Plantation Rise

THURSDAY 11
- **71** Little Hill (Evening)
- **142** Warningcamp House

SATURDAY 13
- **23** 51 Carlisle Road
- **26** Church Settle Cottage
- **65** Kidbrooke Park (Day & Evening)
- **90** Nyewood House
- **96** 64 Old Shoreham Road
- **117** Rymans
- **150** Winchelsea's Secret Gardens

SUNDAY 14
- **3** Ambrose Place Back Gardens
- **7** Bakers House
- **71** Little Hill
- **89** North Springs
- **90** Nyewood House
- **101** 18 Pavilion Road
- **103** 33 Peerley Road
- **110** 6 Plantation Rise
- **113** Ringmer Park
- **117** Rymans
- **122** Sayerland House
- **138** Town Place

MONDAY 15
- **27** Clinton Lodge

WEDNESDAY 17
- **2** Alfriston Clergy House
- **8** Balcombe Gardens
- **84** Moorlands
- **139** Trotton Old Rectory

THURSDAY 18
- **82** Monks House
- **129** Slindon Gardens
- **138** Town Place

FRIDAY 19
- **9** Bankton Cottage (Evening)
- **46** The Garden House (Evening)
- **68** Latchetts
- **93** Oakleigh Cottage (Evening)

SATURDAY 20
- **21** 52 Brook Barn Way
- **38** Down Place
- **39** Duckyls Holt
- **67** King John's Lodge
- **68** Latchetts
- **95** Old Scaynes Hill House
- **111** The Priest House

SUNDAY 21
- **4** Ansty Gardens
- **21** 52 Brook Barn Way
- **38** Down Place
- **39** Duckyls Holt
- **67** King John's Lodge
- **73** Longlands
- **77** The Manor of Dean
- **78** Manvilles Field
- **95** Old Scaynes Hill House
- **97** Overstrand
- **113** Ringmer Park
- **114** Rose Cottage
- **129** Slindon Gardens

MONDAY 22
- **27** Clinton Lodge

WEDNESDAY 24
- **84** Moorlands
- **131** Sparrow Hatch

THURSDAY 25
- **131** Sparrow Hatch
- **138** Town Place

FRIDAY 26
- **100** Parsonage Farm (Day & Evening)

SATURDAY 27
- **13** 4 Ben's Acre
- **128** Sienna Wood
- **151** 22 Woodland Way

SUNDAY 28
- **19** Bradstow Lodge
- **27** Clinton Lodge
- **128** Sienna Wood
- **138** Town Place

July

WEDNESDAY 1
- **19** Bradstow Lodge
- **84** Moorlands

THURSDAY 2
- **140** Uppark

SATURDAY 4
- **9** Bankton Cottage

SUNDAY 5
- **52** Hailsham Grange
- **107** Pindars
- **138** Town Place
- **142** Warningcamp House
- **144** West Chiltington Village Gardens

MONDAY 6
27 Clinton Lodge
107 Pindars

WEDNESDAY 8
84 Moorlands

THURSDAY 9
18 Borde Hill Garden, Park & Woodland

FRIDAY 10
119 St Mary's House Gardens

SATURDAY 11
112 Ridge House
115 Round Hill Gardens
119 St Mary's House Gardens

SUNDAY 12
92 Oak Grove College
98 Palatine School Gardens
112 Ridge House
113 Ringmer Park
125 Shalford House
136 Sussex Prairies
138 Town Place
144 West Chiltington Village Gardens

WEDNESDAY 15
84 Moorlands

FRIDAY 17
68 Latchetts
109 Pine Tree Cottage (Evening)

SATURDAY 18
48 The Grange
68 Latchetts
91 Nymans
109 Pine Tree Cottage
126 Sheffield Park Garden
132 Standen

SUNDAY 19
11 Bates Green
48 The Grange
77 The Manor of Dean
118 Saffrons

WEDNESDAY 22
84 Moorlands
118 Saffrons

SUNDAY 26
58 Hill Barn Gardens
59 4 Hillside Cottages
63 The Hundred House

MONDAY 27
27 Clinton Lodge

WEDNESDAY 29
84 Moorlands

August

SATURDAY 1
15 Bignor Park
105 Penns in the Rocks

SUNDAY 2
15 Bignor Park

MONDAY 3
27 Clinton Lodge

WEDNESDAY 5
84 Moorlands

FRIDAY 7
68 Latchetts

SATURDAY 8
22 Butlers Farmhouse
68 Latchetts

SUNDAY 9
22 Butlers Farmhouse
147 Westfield

MONDAY 10
27 Clinton Lodge

WEDNESDAY 12
84 Moorlands

SATURDAY 15
9 Bankton Cottage
55 Heatherbank
106 Perryhill Farmhouse
130 South Grange

SUNDAY 16
55 Heatherbank
77 The Manor of Dean
106 Perryhill Farmhouse
130 South Grange

WEDNESDAY 19
29 Colwood House
84 Moorlands

SUNDAY 23
29 Colwood House

WEDNESDAY 26
84 Moorlands

FRIDAY 28
40 Durrance Manor (Evening)

SATURDAY 29
13 4 Ben's Acre

SUNDAY 30
40 Durrance Manor
51 Grove Farm House
67 King John's Lodge

MONDAY 31
67 King John's Lodge
136 Sussex Prairies

September

WEDNESDAY 2
10 Bateman's
84 Moorlands

SATURDAY 5
117 Rymans

SUNDAY 6
6 Ashdown Park Hotel
41 Earnley Grange
88 Newtimber Place
100 Parsonage Farm
107 Pindars
117 Rymans
125 Shalford House
134 Stonehealed Farm

WEDNESDAY 9
84 Moorlands

SUNDAY 13
11 Bates Green
77 The Manor of Dean
103 33 Peerley Road
142 Warningcamp House

WEDNESDAY 16
84 Moorlands

SATURDAY 19
120 Sandhill Farm House
121 Sarah Raven's Cutting Garden

SUNDAY 20
113 Ringmer Park
120 Sandhill Farm House

WEDNESDAY 23
84 Moorlands

SUNDAY 27
42 Firle Place
56 High Beeches

WEDNESDAY 30
84 Moorlands

October

WEDNESDAY 7
15 Bignor Park
84 Moorlands

TUESDAY 13
126 Sheffield Park Garden

WEDNESDAY 14
15 Bignor Park
84 Moorlands

WEDNESDAY 21
15 Bignor Park
84 Moorlands

SUNDAY 25
102 Peasmarsh Place

WEDNESDAY 28
15 Bignor Park
84 Moorlands

February 2010

SUNDAY 7
77 The Manor of Dean
81 Mitchmere Farm

TUESDAY 9
104 Pembury House

WEDNESDAY 10
104 Pembury House

THURSDAY 11
81 Mitchmere Farm
104 Pembury House

SUNDAY 14
81 Mitchmere Farm

TUESDAY 16
104 Pembury House

WEDNESDAY 17
104 Pembury House

THURSDAY 18
104 Pembury House

Gardens open to the public

- **2** Alfriston Clergy House
- **5** Arundel Castle & Gardens
- **10** Bateman's
- **18** Borde Hill Garden, Park & Woodland
- **27** Clinton Lodge
- **36** Denmans Garden
- **42** Firle Place
- **49** Great Dixter House & Gardens
- **52** Hailsham Grange
- **56** High Beeches
- **57** Highdown
- **67** King John's Lodge
- **82** Monks House
- **91** Nymans
- **111** The Priest House
- **119** St Mary's House Gardens
- **121** Sarah Raven's Cutting Garden
- **126** Sheffield Park Garden
- **132** Standen
- **140** Uppark
- **145** West Dean Gardens

By appointment only

- **25** Champs Hill
- **28** Coates Manor
- **33** Crown House
- **34** Dachs Halt
- **43** Fittleworth House
- **44** Five Oaks Cottage
- **64** Kent House
- **83** Moor Farm
- **87** New Barn
- **108** Pine Cottage
- **127** Sherburne House
- **146** Westacre

Also open by appointment ☎

- **7** Bakers House
- **8** 46 Westup Farm Cottages, Balcombe Gardens
- **8** 8 Winterfield, Balcombe Gardens
- **9** Bankton Cottage
- **11** Bates Green
- **13** 4 Ben's Acre
- **14** 41a Barnhorn Road, Bexhill Gardens
- **16** 4 Birch Close
- **19** Bradstow Lodge
- **21** 52 Brook Barn Way
- **23** 51 Carlisle Road
- **26** Church Settle Cottage
- **30** Cookscroft
- **35** Dale Park House

- **37** Dormers
- **38** Down Place
- **39** Duckyls Holt
- **40** Durrance Manor
- **41** Earnley Grange
- **46** The Garden House
- **48** The Grange
- **54** Hammerwood House
- **59** 4 Hillside Cottages
- **60** Hobbs Barton
- **68** Latchetts
- **70** Legsheath Farm
- **75** Lowder Mill
- **76** Malt House
- **77** The Manor of Dean
- **78** Manvilles Field
- **81** Mitchmere Farm
- **83** Moor Farm
- **84** Moorlands
- **90** Nyewood House
- **92** Oak Grove College
- **95** Old Scaynes Hill House
- **96** 64 Old Shoreham Road
- **98** Palatine School Gardens
- **99** 6 Park Terrace
- **100** Parsonage Farm
- **102** Peasmarsh Place
- **103** 33 Peerley Road
- **104** Pembury House
- **105** Penns in the Rocks
- **107** Pindars
- **110** 6 Plantation Rise
- **112** Ridge House
- **114** Rose Cottage
- **116** Roundhill Cottage
- **117** Rymans
- **120** Sandhill Farm House
- **122** Sayerland House
- **123** Sedgwick Park House
- **128** Sienna Wood
- **130** South Grange
- **134** Stonehealed Farm
- **136** Sussex Prairies
- **137** Tinkers Bridge Cottage
- **138** Town Place
- **141** Upwaltham Barns
- **142** Warningcamp House
- **144** Palmer's Lodge, West Chiltington Village Gardens
- **144** The Stone House, West Chiltington Village Gardens
- **151** 22 Woodland Way

The Gardens

ABBOTSMERRY BARN
See Kent.

1 ALDSWORTH HOUSE
Emsworth Common Road, Aldsworth PO10 8QT. Tom & Sarah Williams. *6m W of Chichester. From Havant follow signs to Stansted House until Emsworth Common Rd. Stay on this rd to reach Aldsworth. From Chichester take B2178; go straight on at Funtington, house 1st on R in Aldsworth (not in Emsworth).* Homemade teas. **Adm £3.50, chd free. Sun 8, Wed 11 Mar; Sun 19, Tue 21 Apr; (11-4); Sun 31 May (2-7); Wed 3 June (2-7).**
6-acre Victorian family garden being adapted to modern needs by plantaholic owners, with enthusiastic help from a terrier and spaniel. Unusual trees, shrubs and perennials incl hellebores, old apple trees, magnolias, roses and 120 clematis. Great views. Carpets of spring bulbs, particularly crocus, daffodils and bluebells. Gravel and walled gardens. Small arboretum. Showing of short DVD of garden in 1920s and 1930s.
  ♿ ✖ ⊗ ☕

2 ♦ ALFRISTON CLERGY HOUSE
Alfriston BN26 5TL. The National Trust, 01323 870001, www.nationaltrust.org.uk. *4m NE of Seaford. Just E of B2108, in Alfriston village, adjoining The Tye & St Andrew's Church. Bus: RDH 125 from Lewes, Autopoint 126 from Eastbourne & Seaford.* **Adm £4.30, chd £2.15. Mon, Wed, Thur, Sat, Sun: 28 Feb to 12 Mar & 2 Nov to 20 Dec (11-4); 14 Mar to 1 Nov (10-5). For NGS: Wed 17 June (10-5).**
Enjoy the scent of roses and pinks in a tranquil setting with views across the meandering R Cuckmere. Visit this C14 thatched Wealden hall house, the first building to be acquired by the National Trust in 1896. Our gardener will be available to talk to you and welcome you to this peaceful cottage garden.
✖

Victorian family garden being adapted to modern needs by plantaholic owners, with enthusiastic help from a terrier and spaniel . . .

Group opening

❸ AMBROSE PLACE BACK GARDENS
Richmond Road, Worthing BN11 1PZ. *'...a horticultural phenomenon'* The Telegraph 2005, '...ordinary people - extraordinary back gardens' The Times 2008, '...rivals Chelsea' GMTV 2008. Afternoon teas/cakes at 'Way-In Café', Worthing Tabernacle Church by £2 prepaid ticket only from 10 Ambrose Place or entry points. **Gardens combined adm £4, chd under 14 free. Sun 14 June (11-1 & 2-5).**
Take Broadwater Rd into town centre, turn R at Town Hall T-lights into Richmond Rd. Garden entrances on L opp Library. Parking in rds. Start Tour at Ambrose Villa in Portland Rd or 1 Ambrose Place next to St Paul's Community Centre. Featured widely in press and on radio. Limited access to most gardens.
✄ ⊛ ☕ 🌿

1 AMBROSE PLACE
Mrs M M Rosenberg
Traditional walled garden; shrubs, pond, climbing plants.

3 AMBROSE PLACE
Tim & Fiona Reynoldson
Delightful English cottage garden.

4 AMBROSE PLACE
Mark & Caroline Robson
Paved garden, raised herbaceous borders, lawn and flowering summer plants.

5 AMBROSE PLACE
Pat & Sue Owen
Paved town garden with raised borders, variety of flowering shrubs and herbaceous plants.

6 AMBROSE PLACE
Catherine Reeve
Lawned garden with charming colourful borders and summerhouse.

8 AMBROSE PLACE
Claire & Steve Hughes
Children's wonderland garden with colourful borders.

9 AMBROSE PLACE
Anna & Derek Irvine
Small courtyard with trough fountain leads through greenhouse to paved town garden with three further fountains and a brick rill.

10 AMBROSE PLACE
Alan & Marie Pringle
Mediterranean garden with Alhambra-inspired pond, cypress trees and lush borders.

11 AMBROSE PLACE
Mrs M Stewart
Mature garden with roses, summerhouse, flowering plants.

12 AMBROSE PLACE
Peter & Nina May
Rediscovered designer garden brought back to life.

13 AMBROSE PLACE
Linda Gamble
Charming courtyard garden with colourful seasonal flowers.

14 AMBROSE PLACE
Andy & Lucy Marks
Paved town garden, roses, flowering shrubs, summer perennials and fig tree.

AMBROSE VILLA
Mark & Christine Potter
Victorian-style secret garden with pond, mature trees and shrubs. Flower and vegetable borders and long-established fruit-bearing vine and fig. Delightful shady areas and summerhouse.

Group opening

❹ ANSTY GARDENS
Haywards Heath RH17 5AW. *3m W of Haywards Heath on A272. 1m E of A23.* Start in car park signed in Ansty village. Home-made teas at Barn House & Netherby (May) and at Whydown Cottage (June). **Combined adm £4, chd free. Suns 3 May; 21 June (1.30-6).**
All five gardens are very different. You will be assured of a very warm welcome from the owners and our helpers for the day. We will be happy to answer any questions, we are all 'hands-on gardeners'.
✄ ⊛ ☕

APPLE TREE COTTAGE
Deaks Lane. Mr & Mrs G J Longfield
2-acre garden surrounds C16 cottage (not open) with mature trees, herbaceous and raised beds, rockery, fernery and vegetable garden with fruit cage. Usual and unusual plants in cottage style. Views over farmland and woodland.

THE BARN HOUSE
Cuckfield Road. Mr & Mrs M Dykes
Pretty walled garden of formal design with box hedging and informal cottage planting. Pond surrounded by azaleas. Delightful views.

LEAFIELD
Bolney Road. Mr & Mrs Paul Dupée
2½ acres. Rockery and herbaceous borders, incl many hardy geraniums, acers, eucalyptus and other unusual shrubs. Meadow and woodland areas. Exhibition of owner's contemporary watercolours of flowers. Garden game for children.

NETHERBY
Bolney Road. Mr & Mrs R Gilbert
½-acre cottage garden, with 3 ponds and 2 Japanese bridges. Laburnum arch. Raised beds and vegetable garden. Statues, rhododendrons, camellias, acers and lawns. Home-made jams and chutneys for sale on 3 May.

WHYDOWN COTTAGE
Bolney Road. Mrs M Gibson & Lance Gibson
1-acre woodland garden, with water features. Many unusual trees, incl an embothrium. Fresh planting annually. Ideas for the smaller garden.
✄ ⊛

Ordinary people - extraordinary back gardens . . .

❺ ◆ ARUNDEL CASTLE & GARDENS
Arundel BN18 9AB. Arundel Castle Trustees Ltd, 01903 882173, www.arundelcastle.org. *In the centre of Arundel, N of A27.* **For admissions information, please phone or visit website. 4 Apr to 1 Nov Tues to Suns, + Mons in Aug & Bank Hol Mons.**
Home of the Duke and Duchess of Norfolk. 40 acres of grounds and garden. The Collector Earl's Garden based on early C17 classical designs.

2 restored Victorian glasshouses with exotic fruit and vegetables. Walled flower and kitchen gardens. Specialising in unusual tender perennials and plants for mild climates. C14 Fitzalan Chapel white garden.

6 ASHDOWN PARK HOTEL

Wych Cross RH18 5JR. Mr Kevin Sweet. *6m S of E Grinstead. Take A22, 3m S of Forest Row turn L at Wych Cross by garage, 1m on R. From M25 take M23 S, exit J10 on A264 to E Grinstead. Approach from S on A22, turn R at Wych Cross.* Teas (not NGS). **Adm £3.50, chd free. Suns 17 May; 6 Sept (2-5).** 186 acres of parkland, grounds and gardens surrounding Ashdown Park Hotel. Restoration work continues on the walled garden with the planting of herbaceous perennials, roses, lime trees, box hedging and wall-trained fruit trees. A peaceful oasis in the heart of Ashdown Forest. Woodland walks.

7 BAKERS HOUSE

Bakers Lane, Shipley RH13 8GJ. Mr & Mrs Mark Burrell. *5m S of Horsham. Take A24 to Worthing, then A272 W, 2nd turn to Dragon's Green. L at George & Dragon PH, Bakers Lane then 300yds on L.* Home-made teas. **Adm £4, chd free (share to St Mary the Virgin, Shipley). Suns 17 May; 14 June (2-6).** Visitors also welcome by appt, please apply in writing. Large Wealden garden, lake, laburnum tunnel, shrubs, trees, rose walks of old-fashioned roses; scented knot garden, bog gardens, lemon and olive walk. Gravel paths, partial wheelchair access.

Group opening

8 NEW BALCOMBE GARDENS

RH17 6JJ. *3m N of Cuckfield on B2036. From J10A on M23, follow B2036 S for 2½ m.* **Adm £4, chd free. Sat 9 May; Wed 17 June (12-5).**
Balcombe is an ancient village with 55 listed buildings incl the C15 parish church of St Mary. The village hall contains interesting murals on the theme of War and Peace, while slightly further afield is the famous Balcombe Viaduct and beautiful woods, lakes, millpond and reservoir. Generations of Culpepers lived locally in the C15

and C16. The 2 gardens opening for the NGS, several 100 yds apart, will especially appeal to plant lovers. Teas will be served in the Tea Rooms in the centre of the village.

46 WESTUP FARM COTTAGES

Balcombe. Chris & Sarah Cornwell, 01444 811891. *¼ m N of stn, turn L off B2036 immed before Balcombe Primary School (signed) ¾ m.* **Visitors also welcome by appt, groups of 4+, coaches welcome.**
Hidden in the countryside of the High Weald, this cottage garden contains unique and traditional features, linked by intimate paths through lush and subtle planting.

☎

NEW WINTERFIELD

Oldlands Ave. Sue & Sarah Howe, 01444 811380. *Just N of stn, R into Newlands, ¼ m signed.* **Visitors also welcome by appt to end June.**
Plantsman's garden incl herbaceous and shrub borders, pond, wild flowers, gravelled areas, alpine troughs, 'secret' garden and as many trees and shrubs as can be crammed into ⅓ acre.

A pair of scandalous swans hold sway . . .

---

9 BANKTON COTTAGE

Turners Hill Road, Crawley Down RH10 4EY. Robin & Rosie Lloyd, 01342 718907, rosie.lloyd@dsl.pipex.com. *4m W of East Grinstead. 2½ m E of M23 J10. On B2028 1m N of Turners Hill Xrds. Parking only on rd.* Home-made teas. **Adm £3.50, chd free. Sats 4 July; 15 Aug (2-5.30). Evening Opening £5, wine, Fri 19 June (6-8.30). Visitors also welcome by appt late May to mid Aug, for groups of 20+, coaches welcome.**

3½ acres of surprises: the walled garden, cottage garden in flavour and filled with an exuberance of flowers, sits alongside a formal lavender parterre and serpentine yew hedges. Nearby informal pond leads towards raised bed vegetable plot. Beyond the walls, shrubs, old fashioned roses and orchard lead to woodland and lake, where ducks, moorhens, terrapin and a pair of scandalous swans hold sway. Fernery, bog, gravel gardens. Well-stocked plant stall.

10 ◆ BATEMAN'S

Burwash TN19 7DS. The National Trust, 01435 882302, www.nationaltrust.org.uk. *6m E of Heathfield. ½ m S of A265 on rd leading S at W end of Burwash, or N from Woods Corner (B2096).* **Adm £7.10, chd £3.55. Sats to Weds 14 Mar to 1 Nov (11-4.30). For NGS: Weds 6 May; 2 Sept (11-4.30).** Home of Rudyard Kipling from 1902-1936. Kipling planted yew hedges and rose garden, as well as constructing the pear alley and pond. The mill, within the grounds, grinds local wheat into flour. Tour of garden by garden staff.

11 BATES GREEN

Arlington, nr Hailsham BN26 6SH. Carolyn & John McCutchan, 01323 485152, batesgreen@dsl.pipex.com, www.batesgreen.co.uk. *3½ m SW of Hailsham and of A22. 2m S of Michelham Priory. 2½ m N from Wilmington on A27. Bates Green on small back rd (Tyehill Road) running from Yew Tree Inn in the centre of Arlington village to Caneheath nr Old Oak Inn.* Light refreshments. **Adm £4, chd free. Suns 5 Apr; 19 July; 13 Sept (11-5). Visitors also welcome by appt.**
Plantsman's 2-acre tranquil garden with different areas of interest and colour through the seasons. Springtime incl narcissi, primroses, violets, wood anemones, early tulips and coloured stems of cornus. Summer progresses with alliums, hardy geraniums, kniphofias, hemerocallis, grasses, salvias and organic vegetables. Autumn peaks with asters, cyclamen, colchicum, dahlias, heleniums, miscanthus, verbenas and butterflies. New dry garden being created. Featured in 'BBC Homes & Antiques'.

12 BEAUCHAMPS
Float Lane, Udimore, Rye TN31 6BY. Matty & Richard Holmes. *3m W of Rye. 3m E of Broad Oak Xrds. Turn S off B2089 down Float Lane ½ m.* Home-made teas. **Adm £4, chd free (share to Friends of St Mary's Church, Udimore). Sun 24 May (2-6).** Nestling in the beautiful Brede Valley, this lovely informal garden, maintained by its owners, displays a wide range of unusual herbaceous plants, shrubs and trees incl fine specimens of *Cornus controversa* 'Variegata' and *Crinodendron hookerianum*. Small orchard, kitchen garden and copse. Many home-propagated plants for sale, incl some fine irises. Wheelchair access not recommended after wet weather.

An attractive
Edwardian
residential
seaside town . . .
noted for the
many enthusiastic
gardeners who
open to the
public . . .

13 4 BEN'S ACRE
Horsham RH13 6LW. Pauline Clark, 01403 266912. *From A281 via Cowfold, R into St Leonards Rd by PH & restaurant, after Hilliers Garden Centre into Comptons Lane. 5th R into Heron Way, 2nd L Grebe Crescent, 1st L Ben's Acre.* Home-made teas. **Adm £3, chd free. Sats 27 June; 29 Aug** (12.30-5). **Visitors also welcome by appt for groups of 10+.** Described as a little piece of heaven, set on the edge of St Leonards Forest and Horsham riverside walk. Plant lover's garden, 100ft x 45ft, using different levels and interesting design for shape, colour and texture. Relaxed planting of verbena, grasses and many flowers, ornamental trees and shrubs for colour and foliage, box hedging and topiary for formality. Water features, ornaments and pots. Summerhouse and arbour, with other seating for relaxing and viewing.

Group opening

14 BEXHILL GARDENS
TN39 3RJ. *½ m W of centre of Bexhill. Proceed to Little Common roundabout on A259, then see directions for each garden.* Home-made teas at 57 Barnhorn Road. **Combined adm £4, chd free. Sun 24 May (11-5).** An attractive Edwardian residential seaside town famous for its De La Warr Pavilion arts centre. Also noted for the many enthusiastic gardeners who open to the public.

1 ASHCOMBE DRIVE
Richard & Liz Chown. *Exit roundabout S into Cooden Sea Rd, 3rd L into Kewhurst Ave, 1st L into Ashcombe Dr, 400yds on R* Be surprised at what can be achieved in a modest space. Cleverly landscaped, this secret garden delights its visitors. Curvaceous beds and extravagant planting combine to make this a truly romantic garden.

41A BARNHORN ROAD
Pat Crouch, 01424 843415, patc6041@yahoo.co.uk. *At roundabout continue on A259 (Barnhorn Rd) approx 400 yds. Garden on L, park in adjacent rds.* **Visitors also welcome by appt June only, for groups of 10 or less.** Plantaholic's garden incl many geraniums, grasses, cornus, penstemons and over 60 varieties of clematis. Stile and folly are two quirky features to be seen. Featured on BBC TV Open Gardens.

NEW 57 BARNHORN ROAD
Trevor Oldham & John Vickers. Pleasant, spacious garden with lots of lawn and beds with mostly English summer flowers.

THE CLINCHES
Collington Lane East. Val & Ian Kemm. *Exit roundabout E through pelican lights. 1m over hill turn R into Sutherland Ave (signed town centre) & R into Collington Lane East* A pleasing informal garden, developed rather than planned, surrounds the house. It has different rooms and hidey holes

and well-stocked borders, water features and Gaudi-inspired steps.

66 CRANSTON AVENUE
Karen Hewgill. *From roundabout, take A259 E (towards Hastings), after approx 1m turn R into Sutherland Ave, 3rd turning on R into Cranston Ave* Potter round this surprising large town garden with themed areas full of interest incl a newly-enlarged vegetable garden.

15 BIGNOR PARK
Pulborough RH20 1HG. The Mersey Family, www.bignorpark.co.uk. *5m S of Petworth and Pulborough. Well signed from B2138. Nearest village Sutton.* Home-made teas 1, 2 Aug only. **Adm £3, chd free. Every Wed 1 Apr to 27 May (2-5); Sat 1, Sun 2 Aug (2-6); Every Wed 7 to 28 Oct (2-5).** 11 acres of garden to explore, with magnificent views of S Downs. Interesting trees, shrubs, wild flower areas with swathes of daffodils in spring. Walled flower and vegetable gardens. Plenty of seats for contemplation, and shelter if it rains. Temple, Greek pavilion, Zen pond and unusual sculptures. A peaceful garden with no traffic noise. Partial wheelchair access.

16 4 BIRCH CLOSE
Arundel BN18 9HN. Elizabeth & Mike Gammon, 01903 882722. *1m S of Arundel. From A27/A284 roundabout at W end of Arundel take Ford Rd. After ½ m turn R into Maxwell Rd. Follow signs for ½ m.* Home-made teas. **Adm £2.50, chd free. Sun 3, Mon 4 May (2-5). Visitors also welcome by appt in May only.** ⅓ acre of woodland garden on edge of Arundel with woods on three sides. Wide range of mature trees and shrubs (incl silver birch, chestnut, stewartia, acer, rhododendron, viburnum and cornus alternifolia) and many hardy perennials. Particular emphasis on spring flowers (bluebells, narcissi, tulips, alliums, camassia and forget-me-nots) and clematis (over 100 incl 11 different montana). All set in a tranquil setting with secluded corners, meandering paths and plenty of seating.

⑰ BLUE JAYS

Chesworth Close, Horsham RH13 5AL. Stella & Mike Schofield. *5mins walk SE of St Mary's Church. From A281 (East St) L down Denne Rd, L to Chesworth Lane, R to Chesworth Close. Garden at end of close with 4 disabled parking spaces. Other parking in Denne Rd car park; some spaces in Denne Rd, Normandy and Queensway, free on Suns.* Home-made teas. **Adm £2.50, chd free (share to North London Hospice). Sun 24 May (1.30-5.30).**
One-acre garden with rhododendrons, camellias and azaleas. Spring bulbs, mixed borders with cordylines and tree ferns are set in open lawns with gunnera and a water feature. Woodland path along stream and R Arun. Large WW2 pill box in corner of garden. Small orchard and vegetable plot.

  ♿ 🐕 ⊛ ☕

⑱ ♦ BORDE HILL GARDEN, PARK & WOODLAND

Balcombe Road, Haywards Heath RH16 1XP. Borde Hill Garden Ltd, 01444 450326, www.bordehill.co.uk. *1¹/₂ m N of Haywards Heath.* **Adm £7.50, chd £4, concessions £6.50. 20 Mar to 13 Sept & 24 Oct to 1 Nov (10-6 or dusk if earlier). For NGS: Thur 9 July (9-5).**
Botanically rich Grade II* garden with distinctive living rooms each with unique style, incl the Rose and Italian Gardens. Early spring-flowering magnolias, camellias, rhododendrons and azaleas give way to exuberant borders of roses and herbaceous plants. Woodland and lakeside walks with magnificent views. Children's adventure playground. Wheelchair access to formal garden (17 acres).

  ♿ ⊛ ☕

⑲ BRADSTOW LODGE

The Drive, Ifold RH14 0TE. Ian & Elizabeth Gregory, 01403 753248, bradstow-lodge@tiscali.co.uk. *1m S of Loxwood. From A272/A281 take B2133 (Loxwood). ¹/₂ m S of Loxwood take the Plaistow rd, after 800yds turn R into The Drive (by village shop). Follow signs. Parking in The Drive only, please park considerately.* Home-made teas. **Adm £3, chd free. Suns, Weds 12, 15 Apr; 28 June; 1 July (2-5). Visitors also welcome by appt, groups and societies welcome.**
Plantsman's garden of about ³/₄ acre created over the last 7yrs on a triangular plot to give rooms with a

---

wide range of plants, many unusual. Two ponds, bog garden, wild area, formal garden with box and yew topiary and knot garden, raised beds, greenhouses. Many pots and containers. Featured on BBC Southern Counties Radio.

  ♿ 🐕 ⊛ ☕ ☎

⑳ BRICKWALL

Rye Road, Northiam TN31 6NL. The Frewen Educational Trust Ltd. *8m NW of Rye. S end of Northiam High St at A28/B2088 junction. Rail and bus: Rye, Northiam to Hastings service.* Home-made teas. **House & garden £5. Garden only £3, chd free. Sat 23 May (2-5).**
Listed garden surrounding a Grade I listed Jacobean Mansion (also open) and currently housing school for dyslexic children. Gardens incl chess garden with topiary yew pieces and number of Stuart characteristics: brick walls, clipped yew and beech are particular features, also small arboretum. Some shallow steps.

  ♿ ☕

㉑ NEW 52 BROOK BARN WAY

Goring-by-Sea BN12 4DW. Jennie & Trevor Rollings, 01903 242431, tjrollings@gmail.com. *1m W of Worthing. Turn S off A259 into Parklands Ave, L at T-junction into Alinora Cres. Brook Barn Way immed on L.* Light refreshments & home-made teas. **Adm £3, chd free. Sat 20, Sun 21 June (1-5). Visitors also welcome by appt.**
Mature owner-designed garden by the sea, imaginatively blending traditional Tudor cottage garden with subtropical, Mediterranean and antipodean planting. Unusually designed structures, paths, arches and pond combine dense planting with shady viewpoints and sunny patios. Worthing in Bloom, Best Containers.

  ⊛ ☕ ☎ 🐕

Chess garden with topiary yew pieces . . .

㉒ BUTLERS FARMHOUSE

Butlers Lane, Herstmonceux BN27 1QH. Irene Eltringham-Willson, www.irenethegardener. zoomshare.com. *3m E of Hailsham. Take A271 from Hailsham, go through the village of Herstmonceux, turn R signed Church Rd then approx 1m turn R.* Home-made teas Sat & Sun only. **Adm Mar £3, Aug £4, chd free. Sat 14, Sun 15 Mar (2-5). Sat 8, Sun 9 Aug (2-5 with live jazz). Evening Opening £5, wine, Fri 5 June (5.30-8.30).**
Lovely rural setting for ³/₄ -acre garden surrounding C16 farmhouse (not open) with views of S Downs. Pretty in spring with primroses and hellebores. Mainly herbaceous with rainbow border, small pond with dribbling frogs and Cornish-inspired beach corners. Restored to former glory, as shown in old photographs, but with a few quirky twists. Recent projects incl a grass corner, poison garden and, still being developed, a secret jungle garden. Relax and listen to live jazz in the garden in August. Featured in 'Sussex Life' & 'Amateur Gardening'.

  ♿ 🐕 ⊛ 🛏 ☕

㉓ 51 CARLISLE ROAD

Eastbourne BN21 4JR. Mr & Mrs N Fraser-Gausden, 01323 722545, fgausden@ic24.net. *200yds inland from seafront (Wish Tower), close to Congress Theatre.* Home-made teas in May. **Adm £3, chd free. Sat 30, Sun 31 May (2-5); Sat 13 June, wine, £4 (12-2). Visitors also welcome by appt.**
Walled, S-facing garden (82ft sq) with mixed beds intersected by stone paths and incl small pool. Profuse and diverse planting. Wide selection of shrubs, old roses, herbaceous plants and perennials mingle with specimen trees and climbers. Constantly revised planting.

  🐕 ⊛ ☕ ☎

㉔ CAXTON MANOR

Wall Hill, Forest Row RH18 5EG. Adele & Jules Speelman. *1m N of Forest Row, 2m S of E Grinstead. From A22 take turning to Ashurstwood, entrance on L after ¹/₃ m, or 1m on R from N.* Home-made teas. **Adm £3.50, chd free. Fri 15, Sat 16 May (2-5).**
Delightful Japanese-inspired gardens planted with mature rhododendrons, azaleas and acers, surrounding large pond with massive rockery and

---

waterfall, beneath the home of the late Sir Archibald McIndoe (house not open). Elizabethan-style parterre at rear of house. Featured on BBC TV Open Gardens.

25 CHAMPS HILL
Waltham Park Road, Coldwaltham RH20 1LY. Mr & Mrs David Bowerman, 01798 831868, m.bowerman@btconnect.com. 3m S of Pulborough. On A29, turn R to Fittleworth into Waltham Park Rd; garden 400yds. Home-made teas by arrangement. **Adm £4, chd free. Visitors welcome by appt, preferably for groups of 10+. Mar, May and Aug best for viewing.**
27 acres of acid-loving plants around sand pits and woodland. Superb views. Sculptures.

26 NEW CHURCH SETTLE COTTAGE
Church Settle Lane, Wadhurst TN5 6NH. Sue & Pete Bridges, 01892 783857. 9m S of Tunbridge Wells. From B2099 Wadhurst to Ticehurst Rd take turning to Stonegate. R fork into Church Settle Lane, 1/2 m on L, parking in field. Home-made teas. **Adm £3, chd free. Sat 13 June (2-6). Visitors also welcome by appt.**
In a lovely rural setting, this is a true cottage garden packed with many old roses and perennials. Created over 15yrs from a rough field, with paths, pergolas and a large carp pond. Though only 3/4 acre, the garden offers an amazing display in variety and colour.

27 ◆ CLINTON LODGE
Fletching TN22 3ST. Lady Collum, 01825 722952, www.clintonlodgegardens.co.uk. 4m NW of Uckfield. From A272 turn N at Piltdown for Fletching, 11/2 m. Car park available (weather permitting) on Suns and Mons in June. **Adm £4, chd free.**
For NGS: Suns 10 May; 7 June, Mons 8, 15, 22, Sun 28 June; Mons 6, 27 July; 3, 10 Aug (2-5.30).
6-acre formal and romantic garden, overlooking parkland, with old roses, double herbaceous borders, yew hedges, pleached lime walks, copy of C17 scented herb garden, medieval-style potager, vine and rose allée, wild

flower garden. Canal garden, small knot garden and shady glade. Caroline and Georgian house, not open. Group visits by arrangement. Featured in 'Sussex Life', 'Wealden Times' & 'Country Life'.

28 COATES MANOR
Fittleworth RH20 1ES. Mrs G H Thorp, 01798 865356. 31/2 m SW of Pulborough. Turn off B2138 signed Coates. **Adm £3.50, chd free. £5 with light refreshments, by arrangement. Visitors welcome by appt, all year.**
1 acre, mainly shrubs and foliage of special interest, surrounding Elizabethan house (not open). Flowing design punctuated by clipped shrubs and specimen trees. Paved walled garden with interesting perennials, clematis, scented climbers and smaller treasures. Cyclamen, nerines, amaryllis, berries and coloured foliage give late season interest.

Though only 3/4 acre, the garden offers an amazing display in variety and colour . . .

29 COLWOOD HOUSE
Cuckfield Lane, Warninglid RH17 5SP. Mr & Mrs Patrick Brenan. 6m W of Haywards Heath, 6m SE of Horsham. Entrance on B2115 (Cuckfield Lane). From E, N & S, turn off A23, turn W towards Warninglid for 3/4 m. From W come through Warninglid village. Home-made teas. **Adm £4, chd free (share to Warninglid Village Hall). Wed 19, Sun 23 Aug (2-6).**
10 acres of garden, with mature and specimen trees from the late 1800s, lawns and woodland edge. Formal parterre, rose and herb gardens. 100ft terrace and herbaceous border overlooking flower-rimmed croquet lawn. Cut turf labyrinth and forsythia tunnel. Water features and fountains, ornaments, gazebos and pavilions. Pets' cemetery. Gravel paths.

30 COOKSCROFT
Bookers Lane, Earnley, nr Chichester PO20 7JG. Mr & Mrs J Williams, 01243 513671, williams.cookscroft@virgin.net, www.cookscroft.co.uk. 6m S of Chichester. At end of Birdham Straight A286 from Chichester, take L fork to E Wittering B2198. 1m on, before sharp bend, turn L into Bookers Lane. 2nd house on L. Home-made teas. **Adm £3, chd free. Sat 16, Sun 17 May (2-6). Visitors also welcome by appt, coaches easily accommodated.**
5-acre garden started from fields in 1988. Many trees grown from provenance seeds or liners. Collections of eucalyptus, birch, snake bark maples and unusual shrubs. 3 ponds with waterfalls. Cottage garden and Japanese garden. Interesting and developing garden, incl woodland area: what two fully-employed couples have achieved at the weekends!

31 COPYHOLD HOLLOW
Copyhold Lane, Borde Hill, Haywards Heath RH16 1XU. Frances Druce, www.copyholdhollow.co.uk. 2m N of Haywards Heath. Follow signs for Borde Hill Gardens. With BHG on L, over brow of hill and take 1st R signed Ardingly. Garden 1/2 m. Home-made teas. **Adm £3, chd free. Thur 28 May (2-4.30).**
Enchanting N-facing 2-acre cottage and woodland garden, in a steep-sided hollow surrounding C16 listed house (not open) behind 1000yr-old box hedge. Mixed borders, pond and bog garden. Mature woodland enhanced with camellias, rhododendrons, shrubs, non-native trees and bulbs. Wildlife encouraged. Rough hewn oak steps up 'Himalayan Glade'. Featured in 'Sussex Life'.

32 COWDRAY PARK GARDENS
Midhurst GU29 0AY. The Viscount & Viscountess Cowdray. 1m E of Midhurst on A272. Follow A272 towards Petworth and Haywards Heath, entrance on R 200yds past Cowdray Park Golf Club. From Petworth follow A272 towards Midhurst, entrance on L after entering park through wrought iron gates. Light refreshments & cream teas. **Adm £4, chd free. Sun 24 May (2-5).**
Avenue of wellingtonias, woodland walk; grass garden, rhododendrons, azaleas; lakes; large variety of trees

and shrubs, herb parterre. Lebanon cedar 300yrs old; pleasure garden surrounded by ha-ha, themed herbaceous border; laburnum tunnel, cherry avenue and valley garden. Deep unfenced water.

33 CROWN HOUSE

Sham Farm Road, Eridge TN3 9JU. Major L Cave (Retd), 01892 864389. *3m SW of Tunbridge Wells. Signed from A26 Tunbridge Wells to Crowborough rd, approx 400yds. Buses: 29 (¹/₂ hourly service), also 225, 228 & 229. In Eridge take Rotherfield turn S (Sham Farm Rd), 1st R, house 1st on L, short walk from bus stop.* Light refreshments. **Adm £4, chd free** (share to MS Society). **Visitors welcome by appt. Open most afternoons May to Oct for groups of up to 50. Please phone to confirm availability of proposed date.** Situated in an AONB, 1¹/₂ acres with pools and fountain, rose garden and rose walk, herbaceous borders and heather border, herb garden. Full size croquet lawn. Laid out as a series of garden rooms in the style of Gertrude Jekyll. Panoramic views of the High Weald and Eridge Park. Rose walk not suitable for wheelchairs.

This small garden shows what can be achieved if you're determined enough . . .

34 DACHS HALT

94 St Helens Road, Hastings TN34 2EA. Max & Lee Colton, 01424 420443. *1¹/₂ m N of town centre. From A21 take A2101 (Hastings town centre), L at roundabout, approx ¹/₂ m down St Helens Rd.* Teas by prior arrangement. **Adm £3, chd free** (share to RNLI). **Visitors welcome by appt spring to autumn for groups of 4+. Written confirmation will be requested for large groups.** Designed and maintained by owners with mobility problems. Full of ideas to help the disabled, this small garden

shows what can be achieved if you're determined enough. Divided into rooms by steps, paths, slopes and archways. Packed with plants and shrubs, ponds, pots and plenty of seats. Featured on BBC TV Open Gardens & in 'Amateur Gardening'.

35 DALE PARK HOUSE

Madehurst BN18 0NP. Robert & Jane Green, 01243 814260, robertgreen@farming.co.uk. *4m W of Arundel. Take A27 E from Chichester or W from Arundel, then A29 (London) for 2m, turn L to Madehurst & follow red arrows.* Home-made teas. **Adm £3.50, chd free. Sun 7 June (2-5). Visitors also welcome by appt.** Set in parkland on S Downs with magnificent views to sea. Large walled garden with 200ft herbaceous border, mixed borders and rose garden. Rose and clematis arches, interesting collection of hostas, foliage plants and shrubs, orchard and kitchen garden.

36 ◆ DENMANS GARDEN

Denmans Lane, Fontwell BN18 0SU. Michael Neve & John Brookes, 01243 542808, www.denmans-garden.co.uk. *5m from Chichester & Arundel. Off A27, ¹/₂ m W of Fontwell roundabout.* **Adm £4.95, chd (4-14) £3.95, seniors £4.75. Open daily (9-5, or dusk if earlier), not 25, 26 Dec & 1 Jan. For NGS: Mon 1 June (10.30-5).** Nearly 4-acre garden designed for yr-round interest through use of form, colour and texture. Home of John Brookes MBE, renowned garden designer and writer, it is a garden full of ideas to be interpreted within smaller home spaces.

37 DORMERS

West Marden PO18 9ES. Mr & Mrs John Cairns, 02392 631543. *10m NW of Chichester. On B2146. In centre of village turn up hill towards Rowlands Castle.* **Adm £3, chd free. Suns 15, 22 Feb (12-4); Sun 26 Apr (2-5). Visitors also welcome by appt in May & June.** Village garden on chalk, started from scratch in 1997. Cottage-style planting, mainly herbaceous and bulbs, hellebores in early spring. Each area with a different colour scheme, small but productive vegetable patch. Gravel paths.

38 DOWN PLACE

South Harting, Petersfield GU31 5PN. Mr & Mrs D M Thistleton-Smith, 01730 825374. *1m SE of South Harting. B2141 to Chichester, turn L down unmarked lane below top of hill.* Cream teas. **Adm £3, chd free** (share to Friends of Harting Church). **Sats, Suns 25, 26 Apr; 20, 21 June (2-6). Visitors also welcome by appt Apr to July.** 7-acre hillside, chalk garden on the N side of S Downs with fine views of surrounding countryside. Extensive herbaceous, shrubs and rose borders on different levels merge into natural wild flower meadow renowned for its collection of native orchids. Fully stocked vegetable garden and greenhouses. Spring flowers and blossom. Limited wheelchair access.

39 DUCKYLS HOLT

Selsfield Road, West Hoathly RH19 4QN. Mrs Diana Hill & Miss Sophie Hill, 01342 810282. *4m SW of East Grinstead, 6m E of Crawley. At Turners Hill take B2028. After 1m S fork L to West Hoathly. Garden on R immed beyond 30mph sign.* Home-made teas. **Adm £3.50, chd free. Sat, Sun, Mon 23, 24, 25 May; Sat 20, Sun 21 June (11-6). Opening with The Priest House 23 May, 20 June, combined adm £4. Visitors also welcome by appt late May & June.** Delightful cottage garden of approx 2 acres on many different levels. Small herb garden, colourful formal and informal plantings, herbaceous borders, rose border and formal rose garden, chickens and runner ducks (mink and fox permitting). Mature azaleas and rhododendrons in season. Limited parking.

40 DURRANCE MANOR

Smithers Hill Lane, Shipley RH13 8PE. Gordon & Joan Lindsay, 01403 741577, galindsay@dsl.pipex.com. *7m SW of Horsham. Take A24 to A272 (S from Horsham, N from Worthing), then turn W towards Billingshurst. Go 1.7m to 2nd turning on L Smithers Hill Lane signed to Countryman PH. Durrance Manor 2nd on L.* Home-made teas. **Adm £3.50, chd free. Evening Opening, wine, Fri 28 Aug (5.30-8.30). Sun 30 Aug (2-6). Visitors also welcome by appt.** 2-acre garden surrounding medieval hall house (not open) with Horsham stone roof. Uninterrupted views to S

Downs and Chanctonbury Ring over ha-ha. Colourful long borders, grass garden with complementary plants, walled gravelled garden with exotic planting, large pond, wild flowering meadow and orchard, greenhouse and vegetable garden. Gravel paths.

 ♿ ☕ ☎

④① EARNLEY GRANGE
Almodington Lane, Earnley PO20 7JS. Mr & Mrs I J Parker, 01243 512362, ij.parker@btconnect.com. *6m S of Chichester. A286 take L turn to Almodington Lane. End of lane, sharp R-hand bend, garden on L.* Home-made teas. **Adm £3.50, chd free. Suns 31 May; 6 Sept (2-5). Visitors also welcome by appt.**
Opportunity to see a newly-planted (2008) 4-acre garden designed by Chelsea and Hampton Court gold medallist Chris Beardshaw (The Flying Gardener). Features an English rose garden, lime walk, long borders, Italian garden, herb terrace and grass walks. Also an existing Victorian walled garden with greenhouse. Long herbaceous borders for all-yr interest, fruit trees and soft fruits.

 ♿ 🐾 ☕ ☎

EDENBRIDGE HOUSE
See Kent.

FELBRIDGE COPSE
See Surrey.

④② ◆ FIRLE PLACE
Lewes BN8 6LP. 8th Viscount Gage, 01273 858567, www.firleplace.co.uk. *3m E of Lewes. On A27 turn R from Lewes & L from Eastbourne. Follow tourist signs.* **House & garden £8, chd £5. Garden only £4, chd £2.50. Open Easter Sun & Mon, May Bank Hol Suns & Mons; then Weds, Thurs & Suns June to Sept (2-4.30). For NGS: Sat 25, Sun 26 Apr (10-5); Sun 27 Sept (12-5).**
'The Pleasure Grounds'. Wild woodland garden dating back to C16 currently undergoing renovation, situated above Firle Place (also open) giving far-reaching views over Firle Park towards the Sussex Weald. Woodland paths and avenues leading to hidden glades, each with themed plantings. Garden only open NGS days. April openings combine with Garden Show. Show entry ticket incl entry to garden £5, chd/conc £3, with conducted tours of Pleasure Grounds with head gardener.

 ⊕ ☕

④③ FITTLEWORTH HOUSE
Bedham Lane, Fittleworth RH20 1JH. Edward & Isabel Braham, 01798 865074. *3m SE of Petworth. Just off A283, midway between Petworth and Pulborough, 200yds along lane signed Bedham.* **Adm £3, chd free. Visitors welcome by appt May to July for groups of 4+, clubs and societies welcome. Also open by appt Manvilles Field.**
Mature 3-acre garden encompassing wisteria-covered Georgian House (not open). Magnificent cedar, rose garden, rhododendrons. Lawns and mixed borders, fountain. Working walled kitchen garden, wide range of vegetables grown using new and traditional methods. Apple tunnel and 150ft-long colour borders. Large 'Victorian' glasshouse and old potting shed.

 ♿ ☎

Working walled kitchen garden, wide range of vegetables grown using new and traditional methods . . .

④④ FIVE OAKS COTTAGE
West Burton RH20 1HD. Jean & Steve Jackman, 01798 831286/07939 272443, jestjsck@tiscali.co.uk. *5m S of Pulborough. Please ring or email for directions.* **Adm £2.50. Visitors welcome by appt. Regret not suitable for children.**
A botanical watercolourists' garden. Maintained in an ecologically-informal way, allowing plant populations to fluctuate naturally with an ever-critical artist's eye. We love to show our garden so please ring or email to agree a date to visit. We are happy to open

for just 1 or 2 people at a time, or for small groups. Tea and cake on request. Plants, plant supports and botanical cards for sale.

 🐾 ⊕ ☕ ☎

④⑤ FRAMFIELD GRANGE
Framfield TN22 5PN. Mr & Mrs Jack Gore. *3m E of Uckfield. From Uckfield take B2102 to Framfield 2¹/₂ m. Continue through Framfield on B2102. The Grange is approx ¹/₄ m E on R.* Home-made teas. **Adm £5, chd free. Sun 10 May (2-5).**
10 acres of garden with shrub borders, wild flower meadow with orchids and lakes. Woodland walks, bluebell glades. Many hybrids and species of rhododendrons and azaleas. Beautifully kept walled kitchen garden.

 ♿ ⊕ ☕

④⑥ THE GARDEN HOUSE
5 Warleigh Road, Brighton BN1 4NT. Bridgette Saunders & Graham Lee, 01273 702840, contact@gardenhousebrighton.co. uk. *1¹/₂ m N of sea front. 1st turning L off Ditchling Rd, heading N from sea front.* Home-made teas. **Adm £3, chd free. Sun 26 Apr (2-5). Evening Opening £4.50, wine, Fri 19 June (6-8.30). Visitors also welcome by appt.**
Tucked away in the heart of the city, this 'secret' walled garden is full of trees, shrubs, organic vegetables and herbaceous perennials, with a pond and many quirky and fun features. In Victorian times it was a market garden supplying cut flowers to Brighton's shops...now it's a delightful surprise. This is a garden in progress, using recycled materials. Most of the plants have been propagated by the garden owner. Featured on BBC TV Open Gardens.

 🐾 ⊕ ☕ ☎

④⑦ GARDENERS COTTAGE
West Dean PO18 0RX. Jim Buckland & Sarah Wain. *6m N of Chichester. Follow signs to West Dean Gardens and park in Gardens car park. Follow signs to cottage.* Home-made teas. **Adm £3, chd free. Sun 24 May (11-5).**
Small serene and secluded theatrical retreat with strong emphasis on texture, foliage and good structure created by trees. Topiary, labyrinthine paths, interesting spaces. Separate courtyard garden with pond.

 🐾 ☕

48 THE GRANGE

Fittleworth RH20 1EW. Mr & Mrs W Caldwell, 01798 865384, billcaldwell@btinternet.com. *3m W of Pulborough. A283 midway Petworth-Pulborough; in Fittleworth turn S onto B2138 then turn W at Swan PH.* Home-made teas. **Adm £3, chd free.** Sat 18, Sun 19 July (2-5.30). Visitors also welcome by appt, groups of 4+.

3-acre garden gently sloping to R Rother. Walled formal area divided by yew hedges nr pretty, late C17 house (not open), with old roses, thyme lawn, small potager and orchard. Shade areas contain an increasing collection of hellebores; masses of naturalised spring bulbs. Colour-themed herbaceous and mixed borders; hot garden. Gravel paths.

A real oasis in a most unexpected location . . .

49 ♦ GREAT DIXTER HOUSE & GARDENS

Northiam TN31 6PH. Olivia Eller/Great Dixter Charitable Trust, 01797 252878, www.greatdixter.co.uk. *8m N of Rye. 1/2 m NW of Northiam off A28.* **House & garden £8, chd £3.50. Garden only £6.50, chd £3.** Tues to Suns & Bank Hol Mons, 1 Apr to 25 Oct (House 2-5, Garden 11-5).

Designed by Lutyens and Nathaniel Lloyd whose son, Christopher, officiated over these gardens for 55yrs, creating one of the most experimental and constantly changing gardens of our time. Wide variety of interest from clipped topiary, wild meadow flowers, natural ponds, formal pool and the famous long border and exotic garden. A long and varied season is aimed for.

50 GREAT LYWOOD FARMHOUSE

Lindfield Road, Ardingly RH17 6SW. Richard & Susan Laing. *2 1/2 m N of Haywards Heath. Take B2028 for Ardingly. 2m from centre of Lindfield, turn L down single track.* Home-made teas. **Adm £3.50, chd free.** Fri 5, Sun 7 June (2-6).

Approx 1 1/2 -acre terraced garden surrounding C17 Sussex farmhouse (not open). Landscaped and planted since 1997, with views to S Downs. Featuring lawns and grass walks, mixed borders, rose garden, kitchen garden and orchard, walled garden with dovecote.

51 NEW GROVE FARM HOUSE

Paddockhurst Road, Turners Hill RH10 4SF. Mrs & Mrs Piers Gibson. *1/4 m W of Turners Hill on B2110.* Home-made teas. **Adm £4, chd free.** Sun 30 Aug (2.30-5.30).

4-acre classic terraced garden with views of S Downs. The garden incl a maze, ha-ha, lime walk, herb and vegetable gardens and a brilliant hot bed. Steep drops to different levels. Partial wheelchair access.

52 ♦ HAILSHAM GRANGE

Vicarage Road, Hailsham BN27 1BL. Noel Thompson Esq, 01323 844248, noel@hgrange.co.uk. *Adjacent to church in centre of Hailsham. Turn L off Hailsham High St into Vicarage Rd, park in public car park.* **Adm £3.50, chd free.** For NGS: Suns 7 June; 5 July (2-5.30).

Formal garden designed and planted in grounds of former early C18 Vicarage (not open). Series of garden areas representing modern interpretation of C18 formality; Gothic summerhouse; pleached hedges; herbaceous borders, colour-themed romantic planting in separate garden compartments. Group visits by arrangement. Some gravel paths.

53 HAM COTTAGE

Hammingden Lane, Highbrook, Ardingly RH17 6SR. Peter & Andrea Browne. *5m N of Haywards Heath. On B2028 1m S of Ardingly turn into Burstow Hill Lane. Signed to Highbrook, then follow NGS signs.* Home-made teas. **Adm £4, chd free.** Sats, Suns 16, 17, 23, 24 May (2-5.30).

8 acres of undulating garden mostly created from agricultural land. Interesting variety of trees and shrubs, rhododendrons, azaleas and camellias round the pond. 2 areas of woodland, one with a drift of bluebells, the other

with a sandstone outcrop, part of which forms a small amphitheatre. Stream-fed bog garden, formal garden with theme planting and vegetable garden, all created by present owners. Energy-saving devices on display: solar powered system for night-time greenhouse & house water heating; photovoltaic modules and wind turbine for lighting.

54 HAMMERWOOD HOUSE

Iping GU29 0PF. Mr & Mrs M Lakin, 01730 815627, amandalakin@btconnect.com. *3m W of Midhurst. 1m N of A272 Midhurst to Petersfield rd. Well signed.* Home-made teas. **Adm £3, chd free (share to Iping Church).** Suns 10, 17 May (1.30-5). Visitors also welcome by appt.

Large garden with some herbaceous planting although much admired for its rhododendrons, azaleas, acers, cornus and arboretum. 1/4 m walk to wild water garden.

55 NEW HEATHERBANK

20 London Road, Pulborough RH20 1AS. Colin & Dee Morley. *On A29 opp Esso garage in Pulborough, large eucalyptus tree in front garden.* Light refreshments & home-made teas. **Adm £3, chd free.** Sat 15, Sun 16 Aug (11-5).

A real oasis in a most unexpected location. A Mediterranean-style suburban garden (200ft x 40ft), with interesting features and well-stocked with many unusual plants, incl several tropical species.

56 ♦ HIGH BEECHES

Handcross RH17 6HQ. High Beeches Gardens Conservation Trust, 01444 400589, www.highbeeches.com. *5m NW of Cuckfield. On B2110, 1m E of A23 at Handcross.* **Adm £6, chd under 14 free.** Daily (not Weds) 21 Mar to 31 Oct 1-5. For NGS: Suns 24 May; 27 Sept (1-5).

25 acres of enchanting landscaped woodland and water gardens with spring daffodils, bluebells and azalea walks, many rare and beautiful plants, wild flower meadows and glorious autumn colours. Picnic area. National Collection of Stewartia.

57 ♦ **HIGHDOWN**
Littlehampton Road, Goring-by-Sea
BN12 6PF. Worthing Borough
Council, 01903 501054,
www.highdowngardens.co.uk/Highd
own/. *3m W of Worthing. Off A259.
Stn: Goring-by-Sea, 1m.* **Collection
box. Open daily Apr to Sept (10-6),
Mons to Fris Oct to Mar (10-4.30),
not Christmas period. For NGS: Sun
24 May; Wed 3, Sun 7 June (10-6).**
Famous garden created by Sir
Frederick Stern situated in chalk pit
and downland area containing a wide
collection of plants. Many plants were
raised from seed brought from China
by great collectors like Wilson, Farrer
and Kingdon-Ward. Green Flag Award.
Woodchip and grass paths and
slopes, may cause problems for
wheelchair users.
&. ✗ **NCCPG**

Group opening

58 **HILL BARN GARDENS**
Worthing BN14 9QG. *1 1/2 m N of
Worthing town centre. At junction of
A27/A24 (Grove Lodge roundabout),
take lane N towards Hill Barn Golf
Course. 1/4 m further on, park in public
car park on R.* Home-made teas.
**Combined adm £4, chd free (share
to Worthing & District Animal
Rescue Service). Sun 26 July (11-4).**
Six very different cottage gardens (incl
Worthing in Bloom winner 2007/2008)
in a peaceful semi-rural location
adjacent to S Downs. Children must
be supervised. Limited wheelchair
access to some gardens.
✗ ⊕ ☕

NEW **BRAEMAR**
51 First Avenue. Kevin &
Maggie McCormac
Entering through a yew arch, a
herbaceous border leads you past
this architecturally interesting
house (not open). A variety of
trees, plants and vegetables grow
in this mature garden which
surrounds the house.

1 GOLF COURSE COTTAGES
Tony & Ruth Patching
This plantsman's garden is formal
without being regimented.
Herbaceous border, shingle
garden and other interesting
features. Winner of Worthing in
Bloom Small Front Garden 2007
and 2008.

25 WARREN COTTAGES
Elaine Sinclair
Medium-sized wildly informal
chalk garden with many
interesting features. 3 small
ponds, cactus and courtyard
gardens and topiary within the
main garden. Resident cats,
rabbits and hens.

NEW **1 WATERWORKS
COTTAGES**
Teresa Gasson
Two small courtyard gardens with
shingle and brick-paved areas
surrounded by traditional flint
walls. Well-established grapevine
and a variety of pots and hanging
baskets.

NEW **2 WATERWORKS
COTTAGES**
Ann Maggs
Small cottage garden surrounded
by traditional flint walls with a
variety of pots and hanging
baskets.

NEW **3 WATERWORKS
COTTAGES**
Peter Vernon
Secluded small cottage garden
partly laid to lawn with small pond
and patio and an interesting
variety of plants and features.

59 **4 HILLSIDE COTTAGES**
Downs Road, West Stoke
PO18 9BL. Heather & Chris Lock,
01243 574802. *3m NW of Chichester.
From A286 at Lavant, head W for 1 1/2
m, nr Kingley Vale.* **Adm £3, chd free.
Sun 26 July (2-5). Visitors also
welcome by appt June, July & Aug.**
Garden 120ft x 27ft in established rural
setting, created from scratch in 1996.
Densely planted with mixed borders
and shrubs, large collection of roses,
clematis and fuchsias. Profusion of
colour and scent in an immaculately
maintained small garden.
✗ ☕ ☎

60 **HOBBS BARTON**
Streele Lane, Framfield, nr Uckfield
TN22 5RY. Mr & Mrs Jeremy Clark,
01825 732259,
hobbsbarton@btinternet.com. *3m E
of Uckfield. From Uckfield take B2102
E to Framfield, or approaching from S
leave A22 at Pear Tree junction S end
of Uckfield bypass. Garden signed
from centres of Framfield & Buxted.*
Home-made teas. **Adm £5 (Sat &
Sun), £4 (Mon), chd free. Sat 6, Sun
7, Mon 8 June (2-5.30). Visitors also
welcome by appt June & July only.**
In a peaceful pastoral setting, typical of
rural Sussex and well removed from
the noise of traffic, this is a mature
garden of 2 3/4 acres developed by the
present owners over the past 36yrs.
Wide sweeping lawns lead to areas
planted with many types of rose,
shrubberies and herbaceous borders;
numerous specimen trees incl
Metasequoia glyptostroboides,
liriodendron, giant prostrate junipers;
pretty water features; part-walled
vegetable and fruit garden. Developing
woodland garden. Lakeside walk.
&. ✗ ⊕ ☕ ☎

61 **HORSEBRIDGE HOUSE**
Fittleworth Road, Wisborough
Green RH14 0HD. J R & K D
Watson. *2 1/2 m SW of Wisborough
Green. From Wisborough Green take
A272 towards Petworth. Turn L into
Fittleworth Rd, signed Coldharbour,
proceed 2m. At sign 'Beware low flying
owls' turn R into Horsebridge House.
From Fittleworth take Bedham Lane,
2 1/2 m NE.* Home-made teas. **Adm
£3.50, chd free. Mon 13 Apr (10-4).**
Large formal garden divided into rooms
centred on 1920s croquet lawn.
Unusual hedging and shrub planting,
spring cherry, apple and pear blossom
with underplanted daffodils. Formal
vegetable garden with box hedging;
asparagus bed. Large play area for
children under 5 with parental
supervision. Woods and parkland.
&. ✗ ☕

Unusual hedging and shrub
planting, spring cherry, apple and
pear blossom with underplanted
daffodils . . .

Pond area
with some
subtropical
plants, secret
woodland copse
and orchard.
Bear Hunt for
under 5s . . .

63 NEW **THE HUNDRED HOUSE**
Pound Lane, Framfield
TN22 5RU. Dr & Mrs Michael
Gurney. *4m E of Uckfield. From
Uckfield take B2102 through
Framfield. 1m from centre of village
turn L into Pound Lane, then 3/4 m
on R.* Home-made teas. **Adm
£3.50, chd free.** Sun 26 July
(2-5).
Delightful garden with panoramic
views set in the grounds of the
historic The Hundred House. Fine
C17 stone ha-ha. 1 1/2 -acre garden
with mixed herbaceous borders,
productive vegetable garden,
greenhouse, ancient yew tree,
pond area with some subtropical
plants, secret woodland copse and
orchard. Beech hedge and field
walks. Bear Hunt for under 5s.

64 **KENT HOUSE**
ast Harting GU31 5LS. Mr & Mrs
avid Gault, 01730 825206. *4m SE
f Petersfield. On B2146 at South
arting take Elstead to Midhurst rd E
r 1/2 m. Just W of Turkey Island, turn
 up no through road for 400yds.*
dm £3, chd free. **Visitors welcome
y appt May to Aug. Refreshments
ossible by arrangement.**
1/2 -acre garden with fine trees, ha-ha,
ade-loving plants for Apr and May,
alled garden, panoramic views of the
owns from pretty Georgian house
ot open). Mixed borders of unusual
hrubs and herbaceous plants.

65 NEW **KIDBROOKE PARK**
Priory Road, Forest Row
RH18 5JA. Michael Hall School.
*1/4 m from village centre, fork down
Priory Rd at War Memorial.* Light
refreshments, home-made teas &
wine. **Adm £5, chd free (share to
Michael Hall School). Day &
Evening Opening with string
quartet, wine & nibbles** Sat
13 June (2-8).
Kidbrook Mansion (1734) is now
home to Michael Hall Steiner
Waldorf School. Grounds
landscaped by Humphry Repton
still retain many of his original
vistas, incl lakes, cascades,
ornamental bridges and C19
greenhouses. Original kitchen
garden in full use as a prolific
biodynamic plot. Weedy, but
wonderful. Much to explore in 60
acres. Organic produce for sale,
Mansion Market. Young people's
art and gardening workshop.

66 **KILN COPSE FARM**
Kirdford RH14 0JJ. Bill & Pat Shere.
*4m NE of Petworth. Take A283 from
Petworth then fork R signed Kirdford
& Balls Cross. Through Balls Cross,
over narrow bridge then 400yds on L.*
Home-made teas. **Adm £3.50, chd
free.** Sun 19, Wed 22 Apr (1-5.30).
2-acre garden on clay that has
gradually evolved to blend with the
natural woodland setting. Many
informal mixed shrub and herbaceous
borders, low-maintenance conifer
border, spacious lawns, vegetable
garden and ponds. Experience, too,
the joy of wild flowers and walking
through bluebell woods and fields to
be rewarded with lovely views. Partial
wheelchair access.

KIMPTON HOUSE
See Hampshire.

67 ◆ **KING JOHN'S LODGE**
Sheepstreet Lane, Etchingham
TN19 7AZ. Jill Cunningham, 01580
819232, www.kingjohnslodge.com.
*2m W of Hurst Green. A265 Burwash
to Etchingham. Turn L before
Etchingham Church into Church Lane
which leads into Sheepstreet Lane
after 1/2 m. L after 1m.* **Adm £3, chd
free. Open daily 10-4 £3.50.** For
NGS: Sat 11, Sun 12, Mon 13 Apr;
Sat 9, Suns 10, 24, Mon 25 May; Sat
20, Sun 21 June; Sun 30, Mon 31
Aug (2-5).
4-acre romantic garden for all seasons
surrounding an historic listed house
(not open). Formal garden with water
features, rose walk and wild garden
and pond. Rustic bridge to shaded ivy
garden, large herbaceous borders, old
shrub roses and secret garden. Further
4 acres of meadows, fine trees and
grazing sheep. Nursery. Featured in
'The English Garden' and 'Sussex
Life'.

68 **LATCHETTS**
Freshfield Lane, Danehill RH17 7HQ.
Laurence & Rebeka Hardy, 01825
790237, laurence@flb.uk.com. *5m
NE of Haywards Heath. SW off A275.
In Danehill turn into Freshfield Lane at
War Memorial. 1m on R (not Latchetts
Farmhouse).* Home-made teas. **Adm
£4, chd free (share to Danehill PCC).**
Fris, Sats: 29, 30 May; 19, 20 June;
17,18 July; 7, 8 Aug (1.30-5.30).
**Visitors also welcome by appt,
coaches welcome.**
Amazing 8-acre garden, stunning
setting, remarkable diversity of trees,
interest for all ages. Many new
areas. Immaculate lawns, colourful
borders, roses, dahlias, unusual
plants. Ponds, water features,
Christian walled garden, raised bed
vegetables. Mound, Sunken Garden,
woodland Fern Stumpery, 'Scary
Path', children's Safari Hunt.
Renowned home-made teas.
Featured in 'GGG', 'Daily Express'
and 'Sussex Life'.

69 **LEECHPOOL COTTAGE**
Leechpool Lane, Horsham
RH13 6AG. Margaret Penny. *1m N of
town centre. From Horsham stn N to
Harwood Rd B2195. After 2nd
roundabout 2nd L Woodland Way, to
Leechpool Lane. From N take by-pass
A264 Roffey after T-lights. Ist R
Woodland Way.* Home-made teas.
**Adm £2.50, chd free (regret not
suitable for small children).** Sun
7 June (12-5).
Artistic and quirky cottage garden,
made and maintained by owners.
Many interesting features incl topiary,
Italian-style courtyard, conservatory,
fountains, old-fashioned climbing
roses, small Japanese garden and
woodland stream. Featured in local
press.

70 LEGSHEATH FARM
nr Forest Row RH19 4JN. Mr & Mrs
M Neal, 01342 810230,
legsheath@btinternet.com. 4m S of
E Grinstead. 2m W of Forest Row, 1m
S of Weirwood Reservoir. Home-made
teas. Adm £5, chd free. Sun 17 May
(2-5.30). Visitors also welcome by
appt.
Panoramic views over Weirwood
reservoir. Exciting 10-acre garden with
woodland walks, water gardens and
formal borders. Of particular interest,
clumps of wild orchids, fine davidia,
acers, eucryphia and rhododendrons.
Mass planting of different species of
meconopsis on the way to ponds.
Some steep slopes.
♿ ❂ ☕ ☎

LEYDENS
See Kent.

Rose and grape arbour in the middle of box-hedged beds, hidden rhododendron dell . . .

71 LITTLE HILL
Hill Farm Lane, Codmore Hill,
Pulborough RH20 1BW. Barbara &
Derek James. 1m N of Pulborough.
Hill Farm Lane off A29 by The Rose
PH, garden 10th on L. Overflow
parking in field before garden entrance,
follow signs. Teas & wine. Adm £3,
chd free. Evening Opening, wine,
Thur 11 June (5-7). Sun 14 June
(2-5).
4 acres of formal gardens with sunken
rose garden and pond, tiered rock
garden with waterfall and pond, rose
and grape arbour in middle of box-
hedged beds, hidden rhododendron
dell. Some annuals, perennials, shrubs,
trees and small orchard, vegetable plot
and fruit cage. Wild flowers. Some
gravel and stone paths.
♿ ✖ ☕

72 LITTLE POYNES
Lower Street, Fittleworth RH20 1JE.
Wade & Beth Houlden. 3m W of
Pulborough. Off A283, between
Pulborough and Petworth. Lower St
B2138. Parking on School Lane, village
hall car park and in lane by St Mary's
Church. Home-made teas. Adm £3,
chd free. Sat 6, Sun 7 June (1-6).
Informal village garden of approx
1/2 acre. Sunny and shady areas
providing the opportunity for varied
planting and places to sit. Vegetable
area and cut flower beds.
✖ ☕

73 NEW LONGLANDS
74 Hayling Rise, High
Salvington, Worthing BN13 3AQ.
Chris & Bernice Young. 2m NW
of Worthing. From
Brighton/Worthing take A27
towards Arundel, up Crockhurst
Hill into Arundel Rd. Hayling Rise
on R by bus shelter. From A24 join
A27 and turn W to Crockhurst Hill,
as above. Home-made teas. Adm
£3, chd free (share to Clic
Sargent). Suns 31 May; 21 June
(2-5.30).
5yr-old suburban garden, 50ft
deep, 110ft wide, with a
magnificent oak tree. Informal beds
with diverse planting and emphasis
on perennials and shrubs. Over 30
varieties of hardy geraniums and
growing number of roses. Trellises
and relaxed seating in dappled
shade, even a 'bug hotel'.
✖ ❂ ☕

74 LORDINGTON HOUSE
Lordington, Chichester PO18 9DX.
Mr & Mrs John Hamilton. 7m W of
Chichester. On W side of B2146,
11/2 m S of Walderton, 6m S of South
Harting. Home-made teas. Adm
£3.50, chd free. Sat 21, Sun 22 Mar
(1.30-4.30).
Vestigial C17 garden layout, fine house
(not open). Large walled gardens,
elegant topiary and commanding
views. Kitchen garden and poultry.
Carpet of daffodils in spring. Owner-
gardeners negotiating steep learning
curve. Gravel paths, uneven paving,
slope to kitchen garden.
♿ ✖ ❂ 🛌 ☕

75 LOWDER MILL
Bell Vale Lane, Fernhurst, nr
Haslemere GU27 3DJ. Anne & John
Denning, 01428 644822. 11/2 m S of
Haslemere. 6m N of Midhurst. Follow
A286 out of Midhurst towards

Haslemere, through Fernhurst and take
2nd R after Kingsley Green into Bell
Vale Lane. Lowder Mill approx 1/2 m on
R. Home-made teas. Adm £3.50, chd
£1.50. Sat 30, Sun 31 May (11-5).
Visitors also welcome by appt for
groups of 20+ close to opening
dates.
C17 mill house and former mill set in
3-acre garden in beautiful valley below
Blackdown on the
Sussex/Surrey/Hampshire border. The
garden had been neglected before the
present owners began restoration in
2002. Work is still ongoing, incl the
lakeside walk. Stunning courtyard
between house and mill, streams,
waterfalls, unusual container planting
and restored greenhouse and cold
frames. Interesting raised vegetable
garden. Rare breed chicken and
ducks, as well as resident kingfishers.
Renowned for superb home-made
teas, served overlooking the mill lake.
Featured in 'Country Living'.
✖ ❂ ☕ ☎

76 MALT HOUSE
Chithurst Lane, Rogate GU31 5EZ.
Mr & Mrs G Ferguson, 01730
821433. 3m W of Midhurst. From
A272, 31/2 m W of Midhurst turn N
signed Chithurst then 11/2 m, very
narrow lane; or at Liphook turn off A3
onto old A3 (B2070) for 2m before
turning L to Milland, then follow signs
to Chithurst for 11/2 m. Adm £3, chd
free. Sun 26 Apr; Mon 4, Tue 5 May
(2-6). Visitors also welcome by appt.
6 acres; flowering shrubs incl
exceptional rhododendrons and
azaleas, leading to 50 acres of
arboretum and lovely woodland walks
plus many rare plants and trees. Some
steep slopes.
♿ ☕ ☎

77 THE MANOR OF DEAN
Pitshill, Tillington GU28 9AP. Mr &
Mrs James Mitford, 01798 860781,
emma@mitford.uk.com. 3m W of
Petworth. On A272 from Petworth to
Midhurst. Pass through Tillington
village. A272 then opens up to short
section of dual carriageway. Turn R at
end of this section and proceed N,
entrance to garden approx 1/2 m.
Home-made teas. Adm £3, chd free.
Sats, Suns: 8 Feb; 21, 22 Mar; 18,
19 Apr; 16, 17 May; Suns 21 June;
19 July; 16 Aug; 13 Sept (2-5); Sun
7 Feb 2010. Visitors also welcome
by appt, no parking for coaches.
Approx 3 acres. Traditional English
garden, herbaceous borders, a variety
of early-flowering bulbs and

snowdrops, spring bulbs, grass walks, walled kitchen garden with vegetables and fruit, some available for purchase. Asparagus bed. Lawns, rose garden and informal areas. Some building progress, areas clearly fenced off.

78 MANVILLES FIELD
Bedham Lane, Fittleworth RH20 1JH. Mrs P Aschan, 01798 865424. *3m SE of Petworth. Just off A283 between Petworth and Pulborough, 400yds along lane signed Bedham.* Adm £3, chd free. Suns 17 May; 21 June (2-5). Visitors also welcome by appt in May & June for groups of 5+. Also open by appt **Fittleworth House.**
2-acre established garden featuring a wonderful mix of shrubs, clematis, roses and herbaceous perennials. Established trees, orchard, lawns and lovely views.

Delightful country retreat of novelist Virginia Woolf with a tardis-like garden that grows and grows . . .

79 THE MARTLETS HOSPICE
Wayfield Avenue, Hove BN3 7LW, www.themartlets.org. *From Old Shoreham Rd (A270), 600yds W of A2023 junction, turn N into Holmes Ave. 1/4 m L into Wayfield Ave. From A27T Hove exit, take King George VI Ave. Turn L at 1st T-lights immed R into Holmes Ave, 1/2 m turn R into Wayfield Ave.* Light refreshments & teas. Adm £3, chd free (share to The Martlets Hospice). Sat 28 Mar (2-5).
1-acre garden with courtyard. Mainly informal plantings. Rose bower, water feature and wild flower bank. Peaceful garden with private secluded areas which are enjoyed by patients and their families. Maintained by volunteer gardeners who will greet visitors. Hospice Shop will be open.

Group opening

80 MAYFIELD GARDENS
TN20 6TE. *10m S of Tunbridge Wells. Exit A267 into Mayfield. At N end of village turn R at Budgens, signed car park. Follow yellow signs to first garden, detailed map available.* Homemade teas at Warren House. Combined adm £4, chd free. Sun 7 June (2-5.30).
Picturesque old Wealden village in conservation area dating back to Saxon times.

LAUREL COTTAGE
South Street. Barrie Martin
Cottage garden with variety of plants and shrubs and attractive view.

NEW ST ANTHONY'S
Sir John Nicholas
Medium sized garden with pretty borders, roses and raised vegetable beds.
&

SUNNYBANK COTTAGE
Fletching Street. Eve & Paul Amans
S-facing informal garden with views and well-stocked feature bank with numerous specimen shrubs.

UPPERCROSS HOUSE
South Street. Mrs Rosemary Owen. *Next to car park in South St*
Cottage garden with good views. Plenty of shrubs and plants and water feature.

WARREN HOUSE
The Warren. C Lyle
2-acre family garden with good range of shrubs, meadow and stream. Sculptures.
&

81 MITCHMERE FARM
Stoughton PO18 9JW. Neil & Sue Edden, 02392 631456, sue@mitchmere.ndo.co.uk. *5 1/2 m NW of Chichester. Turn off the B2146 at Walderton towards Stoughton. Farm is 3/4 m on L, 1/4 m beyond the turning to Upmarden.* Adm £3, chd free. Suns, Thurs, 8, 12, 15 Feb (11-4); 7, 11, 14 Feb 2010. Visitors also welcome by appt Jan & Feb only.
1 1/2 -acre garden in lovely downland position. Unusual trees and shrubs growing in dry gravel, briefly wet most

years when the Winterbourne rises and flows through the garden. Coloured stems, catkins, drifts of snowdrops and crocuses. Small collection of special snowdrops. Small formal kitchen garden, free-range bantams. Wellies advisable. Local artists' work exhibited and for sale. Local crafts for the garden for sale. Gravel and shallow steps but alternative grass paths.

82 NEW ◆ MONKS HOUSE
Rodmell, Lewes BN7 3HF, www.nationaltrust.org.uk. *From A27 SW of Lewes follow signs for Kingston and Rodmell village. Turn L at Abergavenny Arms, then 1/4 m.* Adm £3.80, chd £1.90. 1 Apr to 31 Oct, Wed & Sat only (2-5.30). For NGS: Thur 18 June (2-5.30). House **not** open.
Delightful country retreat of novelist Virginia Woolf with a tardis-like garden that grows and grows, full of cottage garden plants and sculpture. Summerhouse where she wrote and entertained the Bloomsbury Set. Cream teas available at the Abergavenny Arms.

83 MOOR FARM
Horsham Road, Petworth GU28 0HD. Richard Chandler, 01798 342161, richardandflo1@btinternet.com. *1m E of Petworth. Off A272, signed by cottage.* Adm £4, chd £2.50. Sat 25 Apr (4.30pm start), 23 May (2pm start). **Limited numbers, prebooking essential.** Visitors also welcome by appt April to July, for coaches and groups of 10+.
Enjoy the many pleasures of the countryside on this arable farm with Countryside Stewardship featuring wildlfe and wild flowers, lakes and birds. Take a farm trailer ride past bluebell woods and wildlife (and hope to hear the nightingales which are abundant in April and early summer). Learn what goes on in arable farming today and ask the questions you've always wanted answered! Do bring a picnic.

84 MOORLANDS
Friar's Gate, nr Crowborough TN6 1XF. Dr & Mrs Steven Smith & Dr Lucy & Mr Mark Love, 01892 652474. *2m N of Crowborough. St Johns Rd to Friar's Gate. Or turn L off B2188 at Friar's Gate signed Horder*

Hospital. Home-made teas. **Adm £4, chd free. Every Wed 1 Apr to 28 Oct (11-5). Visitors also welcome by appt.**
4 acres set in lush valley deep in Ashdown Forest; water garden with ponds, streams and river; primulas, rhododendrons, azaleas. River walk with grasses and bamboos. Rockery restored to original 1929 design. The many special trees planted 29yrs ago make this garden an arboretum.

85 MOUNT HARRY HOUSE & MOUNT HARRY LODGE
Ditchling Road, Offham BN7 3QW. Lord & Lady Renton, Mr & Mrs Stewart-Roberts. *2m N of Lewes. On S side of Ditchling Rd B2116, 1/2 m W of A275.* Home-made teas. **Adm £4, chd free (share to Sussex Ouse Conservation Society). Sat 6 June (2-5).**
2 adjoining 7-acre and 1-acre terraced gardens on chalk. Herbaceous and shrubbery borders, wild flower walk, specimen trees, laburnum walks, walled garden, dell garden, conservatory, ornamental tree nursery. In beautiful downland setting.

86 MOUNTFIELD COURT
nr Robertsbridge TN32 5JP. Mr & Mrs Simon Fraser. *3m N of Battle. On A21 London-Hastings; 1/2 m from Johns Cross.* Home-made teas. **Adm £3.50, chd free. Sun 10 May (2-5).**
3-acre wild woodland garden; walkways through exceptional rhododendrons, azaleas, camellias and other flowering shrubs; fine trees and outstanding views. Small paved herb garden.

87 NEW BARN
Egdean, nr Petworth RH20 1JX. Mr & Mrs Adrian Tuck, 01798 865502. *2m SE of Petworth. 1/2 m S of Petworth turn off A285 to Pulborough, at 2nd Xrds turn R into lane. Or 1m W of Fittleworth take L fork to Midhurst off A283.* 150yds turn L. **Adm £3, chd free. Visitors welcome by appt end May to end Sept.**
Converted C18 barn (not open) with 2-acre garden in beautiful peaceful farmland setting. Large natural pond and stream. Owner-maintained and planned for yr-round interest from snowdrops, camellias, spring flowers, masses of bluebells, azaleas, water-irises, roses, shrubs and herbaceous

through to autumn colour. Trees planted for flower, bark and leaf. Seats and a swing.

Gardens and woods full of bulbs and wild flowers in spring. In summer, roses . . .

88 NEWTIMBER PLACE
Newtimber BN6 9BU. Mr & Mrs Andrew Clay, www.newtimber.co.uk. *7m N of Brighton. From A23, take A281 towards Henfield. Turn R at small Xrds signed Newtimber in approx 1/2 m.* Home-made teas. **Adm £3.50, chd free. Suns 5 Apr; 6 Sept (2-5.30).**
Beautiful C17 moated house (not open). Gardens and woods full of bulbs and wild flowers in spring. In summer, roses, herbaceous border and lawns. Moat flanked by water plants. Mature trees. Wild garden, ducks, chickens and fish. Gravel drive, humped bridges. Unfenced moat; children must be supervised.

89 NORTH SPRINGS
Bedham, nr Fittleworth RH20 1JP. Mr & Mrs R Haythornthwaite. *Between Fittleworth and Wisborough Green. From Wisborough Green take A272 towards Petworth. Turn L into Fittleworth Rd signed Coldharbour. Proceed 1 1/2 m. From Fittleworth take Bedham Lane off A283 and proceed for approx 3m NE. Limited parking.* Home-made teas. **Adm £3, chd free. Sun 14 June (12-5).**
Hillside garden with beautiful views surrounded by mixed woodland. Focus on structure with a wide range of mature trees and shrubs. Stream, pond and bog area. Abundance of roses, clematis, hostas, rhododendrons and azaleas.

90 NYEWOOD HOUSE
Nyewood, nr Rogate GU31 5JL. Mr & Mrs C J Wright, 01730 821563, sue.j.warren@mac.com. *4m E of Petersfield. From A272 at Rogate take South Harting rd for 1 1/2 m. Turn L at pylon towards South Downs Hotel. Nyewood House 2nd on R over cattle grid.* Cream teas. **Adm £3, chd free. Sat 13, Sun 14 June (2-6). Visitors also welcome by appt April to July. Minibuses and groups of 10+.**
Victorian country house garden with stunning views of S Downs. 3 acres comprising formal gardens with rose walk and arbours, pleached hornbeam, colour-themed herbaceous borders, shrub borders, lily pond and kitchen garden with greenhouse. Wooded area featuring spring flowers followed by wild orchids. Featured in 'Chichester Observer'. Gravel driveway.

91 ♦ NYMANS
Handcross RH17 6EB. The National Trust, 01444 405250, www.nationaltrust.org.uk. *4m S of Crawley. On B2114 at Handcross signed off M23/A23 London-Brighton rd. Bus: 73 from Hove or Crawley & 271 from Haywards Heath.* **Adm £8.50, chd £4.30. All yr (not 25 Dec to 1 Jan) Wed to Sun & Bank Hols (10-5pm, 4pm Nov to Jan). For NGS: Sat 18 July (10-5).**
One of the greatest C20 gardens in the country with an important collection of rare plants, set around a romantic house and ruins in a beautiful wooded estate. Internationally renowned for its garden design, rare plant collection and intimacy. You can also enjoy wonderful views across the Sussex countryside and explore the ancient woodland, with lakes and wild flowers. Gravel paths.

92 OAK GROVE COLLEGE
The Boulevard, Worthing BN13 1JX. Jennie Rollings, 01903 708870, jrollings@wsgfl.org.uk. *1m W of Worthing. Turn S off A2032 at roundabout onto The Boulevard, signed Goring. School entrance 1st on L (shared entrance with Durrington High School).* Light refreshments & home-made teas. **Adm £3, chd free. Suns 17 May; 12 July (11-5). Also open 12 July Palatine School Garden, combined adm £3.50, chd free. Visitors also welcome by appt.**
An inspiring example of how special

needs children are transforming their new school grounds into a green oasis, comprising water wise gardens, memorial gardens, herb garden, large sensory courtyard with water feature, sculptures and mosaics. Extensive and unusual planting. Large food growing area with vegetable boxes and polytunnels. Living willow, reclaimed woodland, outdoor textiles and chicken run. Gold Award SE in Bloom Schools Competition. Best School Garden & Highly Commended Waterwise Garden for Worthing in Bloom. Wheelchair access may be restricted owing to ongoing projects.

& ❀ ☕ ☎

93 NEW OAKLEIGH COTTAGE
Back Lane, Cross in Hand TN21 0ND. Beth & Barry Simons. *2m from Heathfield. At Esso garage in Cross in Hand, A267, turn behind oak showroom into Back Lane. Garden 1m, turn R for parking at show sign.* Home-made teas. **Adm £3.50, chd free. Sat 28, Sun 29 Mar (10-4). Evening Opening £5.50, wine, Fri 19 June (6-8).**
Pretty cottage garden with a variety of habitats in 1 acre. Orchard with daffodils, secret garden of camellias, spring shrubbery, woodland garden and large herbaceous borders. Hellebores in spring and roses in summer are especially beautiful.

🚶 ❀ ☕

Orchard with
daffodils, secret
garden of
camellias, spring
shrubbery,
woodland garden
and large
herbaceous
borders . . .

94 OFFHAM HOUSE
Offham BN7 3QE. Mr S Goodman & Mr & Mrs P Carminger. *2m N of Lewes on A275. Cooksbridge stn ½ m.* Home-made teas. **Adm £4, chd free. Suns 26 Apr; 7 June (1-5).**
Fountains, flowering trees, double herbaceous border, long peony bed. 1676 Queen Anne house (not open) with well-knapped flint facade. Herb garden. Walled kitchen garden with glasshouses.

& ❀ ☕

OLD BUCKHURST
See Kent.

95 OLD SCAYNES HILL HOUSE
Clearwater Lane, Scaynes Hill RH17 7NF. Sue & Andy Spooner, 01444 831602. *2m E of Haywards Heath. On A272, 50yds down Sussex border path beside BP Garage shop, & opp Farmers Inn. No parking at garden (drop off only), please park considerately in village.* Home-made teas. **Adm £3, chd free (share to Court Meadow Assoc). Sat 20, Sun 21 June (2-5.30).** Visitors also welcome by appt June & July only for groups of 10+.
In memory of Sarah Robinson. Entrance archway with steps leading to 1-acre natural garden on S-facing slope of predominantly heavy clay. Mature trees and shrubs with some unusual specimens. Several colourful herbaceous borders and island beds with ornamental grasses. Many roses, small wild flower meadow with orchids, woodland walk, small orchard, fruit and vegetable area, bog garden and natural-looking pond. Entirely maintained by owners.

🚶 ❀ ☕ ☎

96 64 OLD SHOREHAM ROAD
Hove BN3 6GF. Brian & Muriel Bailey, 01273 889247, baileybm@ntlworld.com. *A270. On S side between Shirley Drive & Upper Drive.* Home-made teas. **Adm £2.50, chd free. Sat 13 June (2-5.30). Visitors also welcome by appt, groups of 4+.**
12.6m by 33.6m, designed, built and maintained by owners. S-facing on chalk with secluded terrace, conservatory, pergola, rose arbour, bog garden, arches, trellises, vegetable garden, alpine bed, parterre, ponds, waterfall, many clematis and hostas. Automatic watering.

& 🚶 ❀ ☕ ☎

97 NEW OVERSTRAND
20 Shirley Road, Hove BN3 6NN. Ivor & Anne O'Mahony. *A270, turn N into Shirley Drive, 1st R.* Home-made teas. **Adm £3, chd free (share to MS Treatment Centre). Sun 21 June (2-5.30).**
Large S-facing town garden with formal lawn, raised seaside planting, tropical area and many interesting, well-stocked perennial borders. Established trees, shrubs, rose-clad pergolas and bubbling water features. Lower garden with medicinal plants, fernery, tall grasses, fruit cage and vegetable area with charming vine-clad greenhouse.

🚶 ❀ ☕

98 PALATINE SCHOOL GARDENS
Palatine Road, Worthing BN12 6JP. William Bauress, 01903 242835. *Turn S off A2032 at roundabout onto The Boulevard, signed Goring. Take R turn at next roundabout into Palatine Rd. School approx 100yds on R.* Light refreshments & teas. **Combined adm with Oak Grove College £3.50, chd free. Sun 12 July (11-5).** Visitors also welcome by appt.
This many-roomed mature garden, with its varied planting never ceases to surprise visitors. Constructed by teachers, volunteers and children with special needs. Conservation and wildlife area, large and small ponds, bog garden, sea garden, oriental garden, dry gardens, thinking garden, rockeries, labyrinth, mosaics. Picnic areas, echiums and interesting tree collection.

& ☕ ☎

99 6 PARK TERRACE
Tillington, Petworth GU28 9AE. Mr & Mrs H Bowden, 01798 343588, isabellebowden@aol.com. *On A272, between Midhurst & Petworth. 1m W of Petworth, turn uphill at sign to Tillington Village, past Horseguards PH and church, no 6 is past village hall. Please do not park in residents' spaces but further up the lane.* Home-made teas. **Adm £3, chd free. Sun 31 May; Sun 7 June (11-6).** Visitors also welcome by appt. Coaches & groups up to 40 welcome. Lunches & teas on request.
Terraces under ivy, wisteria and roses. Small ponds, aviary, archways, topiaries, leafy tunnels and a large dome covered in fruit trees, clematis,

jasmine and roses. Sunset terrace with S Downs views. Raised dry beds, herbaceous beds, lots of shrubs, pigsty and greenhouse. Garden designed for entertaining. It provides lots of quiet retreats in complete privacy, basking to the sound of water from fountains made by Humphrey.

❀ ☕ ☎

100 PARSONAGE FARM
Kirdford RH14 0NH. David & Victoria Thomas, 01403 820295. *5m NE of Petworth. Take A283 from Petworth, fork R signed Kirdford and Balls Cross. After approx 5m and after Kirdford village sign on L, turn R just before L turn to Plaistow.* Home-made teas & wine. Adm £4, chd free (share to Kings World Trust for Children). Day & Evening Opening wine, Fri 26 June (2-9). Sun 6 Sept (2-6). Visitors also welcome by appt throughout the year.
Major garden under development, now growing to maturity with fruit theme and many unusual plants. 5 acres of formal gardens on a grand scale, C18 walled garden with borders in apricot, orange, scarlet and crimson, topiary walk, pleached lime allée, tulip tree avenue, rose borders, vegetable garden with trained fruit, lake, turf amphitheatre, recently planted autumn shrubbery and jungle walk. Owners and Head Gardener available to give advice.

& ✕ ☕ ☎

101 18 PAVILION ROAD
Worthing BN14 7EF. Andrew Muggeridge & Ya-Hui Lee. *Nr Worthing main stn.* Adm £2.50. Suns 19 Apr; 3, 24 May; 14 June (1-4). Town garden. This is a plantsman's garden: many unusual perennials, lots of grasses, many infill plants throughout the season. Sunflowers, leonotis and seasonal pots. The design is always changing, described as 'organised chaos', plenty to see. Regret not suitable for children or wheelchairs.

✕ ❀

102 PEASMARSH PLACE
Church Lane, Peasmarsh TN31 6XE. Viscount Devonport, 01797 223398, jmcarree@hotmail.com. *3½ m NW of Rye. From A268 in Peasmarsh take Church Lane (signed Norman Church), garden 1m on R after church.* Home-made teas. Adm £3.50, chd free. Suns 3 May (2-5); 25 Oct (11-4). Visitors also welcome by appt with conducted tours for small groups.

7-acre garden surrounding Peasmarsh Place (not open). Yew-enclosed rose garden and various features with an Alice in Wonderland connection. Fine display of spring flowers and autumn colour. Contains National Collections of limes and sweet chestnuts. Large and varied arboretum mostly planted since 1976 with fine walks and outdoor sculpture.

& ✕ ❀ ❀ NCCPG ☕ ☎

Walled garden with borders in apricot, orange, scarlet and crimson . . .

103 33 PEERLEY ROAD
East Wittering PO20 8PD. Paul & Trudi Harrison, 01243 673215, stixandme@aol.com. *7m S of Chichester. From A286 take B2198 to Bracklesham. Turn R into Stocks Lane then L at Royal British Legion into Legion Way & follow rd round to Peerley Rd halfway along.* Adm £2.50, chd free. Suns 14 June; 13 Sept (12-4). Visitors also welcome by appt.
Small garden 65ft x 32ft, 110yds from sea. Packed full of ideas and interesting plants using every inch of space to create rooms and places for adults and children to play. Specialising in unusual plants that grow well in seaside conditions. A must for any suburban gardener. Great winter interest. Advice on coastal gardening. Featured in 'Amateur Gardening'.

✕ ❀ ☎

104 PEMBURY HOUSE
Ditchling Road (New Road), Clayton, nr Hassocks BN6 9PH. Nick & Jane Baker, 01273 842805, www.pemburyhouse.co.uk. *6m N of Brighton. On B2112, 110 metres from A273. Some parking at the house, otherwise parking at village green.* Light refreshments & teas. Adm £3.50, chd free. Weds, Thurs, Fris 11 Feb to 20 Feb (11-4). Tues, Weds, Thurs 9 Feb to 18 Feb 2010. Visitors also

welcome by appt in February 2009/10 only, for groups of 15+, small coaches permitted.
Ours is a garden where the Christmas Day flower count often exceeds 50 different types. The success of our informal country garden depends not only on its flowers but on the shape, form and foliage of the carefully chosen planting. Depending on the vagaries of the season, winter-flowering shrubs, hellebores and drifts of snowdrops are usually at their best Feb. Over a long period, the hellebores are a great source of joy, with each individual flower asking to be turned up and admired. Winding paths give a choice of garden walks, with views to the S Downs and countryside. Lots of seats and secret places, and much development work since last yr. Wellies and winter woollies advised. Featured on BBC Gardeners' World and in 'Sussex Life'. Wheelchair access may be limited by soft ground.

& ❀ ☕ ☎

105 PENNS IN THE ROCKS
Groombridge TN3 9PA. Lady Gibson, 01892 864244. *7m SW of Tunbridge Wells. On B2188 Groombridge to Crowborough rd just S of Plumeyfeather corner.* Home-made teas. Adm £4, chd £1. Suns 29 Mar; 1 Aug (2.30-5.30). Visitors also welcome by appt.
Large wild garden with rocks, lake, C18 temple and old walled garden with herbaceous, roses and shrubs. House (not open) part C18. Dogs under control in park only (no shade in car park).

✕ ❀ ☕ ☎

106 PERRYHILL FARMHOUSE
Hartfield TN7 4JP. Mr & Mrs John Whitmore. *7m E of East Grinstead. Midway between E Grinstead & Tunbridge Wells. 1m N of Hartfield on B2026. Turn into unmade lane adjacent to Perryhill Nurseries.* Home-made teas. Adm £4, chd free. Sats, Suns 2, 3 May; 15, 16 Aug (2-5). 1½ acres, set below beautiful C15 hall house (not open), with stunning views of Ashdown Forest. Herbaceous and mixed borders, formal rose garden and climbing rose species, water garden, parterre, pergola. Many varieties of unusual shrubs and trees. Croquet lawn (open for play). Top and soft fruit. Productive Victorian greenhouse. Dahlia mania corner. Featured in 'GGG'.

& ✕ ❀ ☕

107 PINDARS

Lyminster, nr Arundel BN17 7QF. Mr & Mrs Clive Newman, 01903 882628, pindars@tiscali.co.uk. *2m S of Arundel. Lyminster on A284 between A27 & A259. 1m S of A27 Pindars on L. Park beyond house in designated field.* Home-made teas. **Adm £3, chd free. Sun 5, Mon 6 July; Sun 6 Sept (2-5). Visitors also welcome by appt.**
Long herbaceous borders surround lawns dotted with big tubs, and even bigger trees (eucalyptus, acer, birch and oak) form a background. Gravel gardens and a vegetable patch with unusual beans, squashes, salads. All this created from a field 40yrs ago. 2 Friendly Burmese cats and nice owners too! Some gravel paths.

108 PINE COTTAGE

Rackham, Pulborough RH20 2EU. Rob & Glenys Rowe, 01903 744115, glenysrowepc@aol.com. *4m S of Pulborough. From Pulborough take A283 to Storrington, after 4m turn into Greatham Rd. Follow Rackham signs. From Arundel take A284 then B2139 to Storrington. After Amberley turn L into Rackham St. Please park as indicated, no roadside parking please. Garden entrance via public footpath adjacent to Rackham Old School and Rackham Woods.* **Adm £3, chd free. Visitors welcome by appt from 18 May to 14 June, for groups of 10+, coaches permitted.**
4-acre garden developed in quiet harmony with the surrounding landscape of the Amberley wildbrooks and the S Downs. 3 large ponds, one with a well-established reed bed, a bog garden, wild flower areas, an organic kitchen garden and orchard. Relaxed planting with native species encourages a wide range of wildlife. Deep water, children must be strictly supervised.

A formal garden with soft edges . . . . with bold and dramatic blocks of colour . . .

109 NEW PINE TREE COTTAGE

32 Mount Close, Pound Hill, Crawley RH10 7EF. Zena & Barry Everest. *3m S of Gatwick. M23, J10A, 2nd exit N B2036. Straight over 2 roundabouts, at 3rd roundabout 1st L, 2nd R, straight over staggered Xrds.* Home-made teas. **Adm £3, chd free. Evening Opening,** wine, Fri 17 July (6.30-8). Sat 18 July (11-4).
1/4 -acre plot divided into 4 distinct areas. Front and back gardens planted with many colourful and unusual shrubs and perennials to complement this charming Sussex cottage. Front garden enhanced by fine-leaved lawn. Planting of the pond area is exuberant and colourful and a 25ft stepped pergola clothed with wisteria and clematis sits between this area and the terraced top garden. Well worth a visit! Partial wheelchair access.

110 6 PLANTATION RISE

Worthing BN13 2AH. Mr & Mrs N Hall, 01903 262206, trixiehall@btinternet.com. *2m from sea front on outskirts of Worthing. A24 meets A27 at Offington roundabout. Proceed into Offington Lane. Take 1st R into The Plantation, 1st R again to Plantation Rise. Please park in The Plantation, short walk to Plantation Rise.* Light refreshments & home-made teas. **Adm £3, chd (under 10) free. Wed 10, Sun 14 June (2-5). Visitors also welcome by appt all year for groups of 4-16, Wed & Thur pm.**
Previous winner 'Daily Mail' Garden of the Year and runner-up 'Times' Back Garden of the Year 2008, featuring pond, summerhouse, pergolas, shrubs, and perennials for all-yr colour. Garden 70ft x 80ft has been spectacularly landscaped by Nigel to give the impression of a much larger garden. Spring flowers and heathers in April. WC available on request. Steps, gravel paths.

111 ◆ THE PRIEST HOUSE

North Lane, West Hoathly RH19 4PP. Sussex Archaeological Society, 01342 810479, www.sussexpast.co.uk. *4m SW of East Grinstead. Turn E to West Hoathly 1m S of Turners Hill at the Selsfield Common junction on B2028. 2m S turn R into North Lane. Garden 1/4 m further on.* **House & garden adm £2, chd £1. Garden only £1, chd free. Mar to Oct, Tues to Sats & BH Mons (10.30-5.30), Suns (12-5.30). For NGS: Sats 23 May; 20 June (10.30-5.30). Also open within walking distance and with home-made teas, Duckyls Holt. Combined adm £4, chd free.**
C15 timber-framed house with cottage garden. Large selection of culinary and medicinal herbs in small formal garden with mixed herbaceous borders, plus long-established yew topiary, box hedges and espalier apple trees. Small woodland garden with fernery. Adm to Priest House Museum £1 for NGS visitors.

112 RIDGE HOUSE

East Street, Turners Hill RH10 4PU. Mr & Mrs Nicholas Daniels, 01342 715344. *4m SW of East Grinstead. 3m E of Crawley. On B2110, 5m SE of J10 M23. Via A264 & B2028. 30yds E of Crown PH on Turners Hill Xrds. Parking at recreation ground E of Ridge House.* Home-made teas. **Adm £3, chd free. Sat 11, Sun 12 July (2-6). Visitors also welcome by appt in June & July only, coaches permitted.**
A magical view of the High Weald greets the visitor. All-yr interest is offered by Nigel's Garden in its quiet corner together with the mixed borders, dell with its pond and the productive vegetable garden. Paths lead to unexpected vistas, and the large compost heaps and Victorian greenhouse with its reservoir should not be missed. Art groups welcome.

113 RINGMER PARK

Ringmer, Lewes BN8 5RW. Deborah & Michael Bedford. *On A26 Lewes to Uckfield rd. 1 1/2 m NE of Lewes, 5m S of Uckfield.* Home-made teas. **Adm £4, chd free. Suns 14, 21 June; 12 July; 20 Sept (2-5).**
Densely-planted 6-acre garden created by the owners over the last 20yrs. A formal garden with soft edges, the emphasis is on continuous flowering from spring bulb displays through to Oct, with bold and dramatic blocks of colour. Features incl a striking hot garden, rose garden, pergola covered with roses and clematis and bordered by peonies, double herbaceous borders and much more. Outstanding views of the S Downs. Featured in 'Country Life'.

114 ROSE COTTAGE
Hadlow Down TN22 4HJ. Ken & Heather Mines, 01825 830314, kenmines@hotmail.com. *6m NE of Uckfield. After entering village on A272, turn L (100yds) by phone box just after New Inn, follow signs.* Home-made teas. **Adm £3, chd free. Suns 26 Apr; 24 May; 21 June (2-5.30). Visitors also welcome by appt April to July, coaches permitted.**
Plantsman's 2/3 -acre garden. Old-fashioned roses, exuberant planting and luxuriance within a strong design results in a garden that visitors refer to as harmonious and tranquil and which evokes memories of childhood. Self-seeding is encouraged, so a constantly-changing garden. Collection of David Newman sculptures are integral to the design, further enhanced by Victorian church stonework. Bug hunt and fact sheets for children and adults. Featured in 'Amateur Gardening'.
🐾 ⊛ ☕ 🐌 ☎

Group opening

115 NEW ROUND HILL GARDENS
Brighton BN2 3RY. *1½ m N of Brighton pier. On A23 pass Preston Park, cinema and fire stn. At next T-lights turn L up hill (Ditchling Rd). Princes Cres 2nd R, Belton Rd then 1st L off Princes Cres.* Home-made teas. **Combined adm £3, chd free. Sat 11 July (12-5).**
Two city centre gardens opening for the first time this yr. Although only approx 200m apart, these hill-top gardens are very different - one L-shaped, the other terraced into steep slope. Both have a focus on plants, texture and colour. Map and full directions at www.roundhillgardens.co.uk.
🐾 ☕

NEW 1 BELTON CLOSE
Steve Bustin & John Williams.
Belton Close lies between 7 & 9 Belton Rd, off Princes Cres. No parking in Close
Only 4yrs old but packing a lot into an enclosed space. 15m mixed border, hot border, kitchen garden, greenhouse and many pots. Key plants incl bananas, ferns, sweet peas and dahlias.
♿

NEW 85 PRINCES CRESCENT
George Coleby
The owners of this small garden have used creative landscaping and plant selection to overcome the challenges of a steeply-sloping site surrounded by terraced houses, creating a surprisingly intimate and secluded urban oasis.

---

116 ROUNDHILL COTTAGE
East Dean PO18 0JF. Mr Jeremy Adams, 01243 811447. *7m NE of Chichester. Take A286 towards Midhurst. At Singleton follow signs to Charlton/East Dean. In East Dean turn R at Star & Garter Inn, Roundhill is approx 100yds.* Home-made teas. **Adm £3, chd free. Sun 24, Mon 25 May (12-4). Visitors also welcome by appt.**
1-acre country garden set in tranquil fold of the S Downs, designed in 1980 by Judith Adams whose inspiration came from French impressionists and continued by her daughter Louise, whose love of secret gardens, wild flower meadows and crumbly gothic ruins all show to delightful effect in a garden full of surprises. Come and enjoy.
🐾 ☕ ☎

These hill-top gardens are very different . . .

117 RYMANS
Apuldram PO20 7EG. Mrs Michael Gayford, 01243 783147, suzanna.gayford@talktalk.net. *1m S of Chichester. Take Witterings rd, at 1½ m SW turn R signed Dell Quay. Turn 1st R, garden ½ m on L.* Home-made teas. **Adm £4, chd free. Sats, Suns 18, 19 Apr; 13, 14 June; 5, 6 Sept (2-5). Visitors also welcome by appt.**
Walled and other gardens surrounding lovely C15 stone house (not open); bulbs, flowering shrubs, roses, ponds, potager. Many unusual and rare trees and shrubs. In late spring the wisterias are spectacular. The heady scent of hybrid musk roses fills the walled garden in June. In late summer the garden is ablaze with dahlias, sedums, late roses, sages and Japanese anemones.
⊛ ☕ ☎

118 NEW SAFFRONS
Holland Road, Steyning BN44 3GJ. Tim Melton & Bernardean Carey. *6m NE of Worthing. Exit roundabout on A283 at S end of Steyning bypass into Clays Hill Rd. 1st R into Goring Rd, 4th L into Holland Rd. Parking in Goring Rd and Holland Rd.* Home-made teas. **Adm £3, chd free. Sun 19, Wed 22 July (2-5.30).**
3/4 -acre garden with large lawns set around Edwardian house. Redesigned and replanted by owners since 2001 with emphasis on colour and texture. It features formal herbaceous beds, a long border of shrubs, trees, grasses and bamboos, a mixture of mature and younger specimen trees and a kitchen garden with large fruit cage and asparagus bed.
☕

119 ◆ ST MARY'S HOUSE GARDENS
Bramber BN44 3WE. Peter Thorogood & Roger Linton, 01903 816205, www.stmarysbramber.co.uk. *1m E of Steyning. 10m NW of Brighton in Bramber Village off A283.* **Adm £4, chd free. House open May to Sept, Suns, Thurs & BH Mons (2-6). Please phone or see website for details.** For NGS: **Fri 10, Sat 11 July (2-5.30). Gardens only open.**
Five acres of gardens, incl charming formal topiary, ancient ivy-clad 'Monk's Walk', large example of the prehistoric Ginkgo biloba, and magnificent Magnolia grandiflora around Grade I listed C15 timber-framed medieval house, once a pilgrim inn. The Victorian 'Secret' gardens also incl splendid 140ft fruit wall, rural museum, terracotta garden, the delightful Jubilee rose garden, pineapple pits and English poetry garden.
♿ 🐾 ⊛ ☕

120 SANDHILL FARM HOUSE
Nyewood Road, Rogate GU31 5HU. Rosemary Alexander, 01730 818373, www.rosemaryalexander.co.uk, r.a.alexander@talk21.com. *4m SE of Petersfield. From A272 Xrds in Rogate, take rd S signed Nyewood/Harting. Follow rd for approx 1m over small bridge. Sandhill Farm House on R, over cattle grid.* **Adm £3.50 (Mar £2.50), chd free. Sun 1 Mar (1-4); Sats, Suns 18, 19 Apr; 6, 7 June; 19, 20 Sept (2-5). Visitors also welcome by appt, groups of 10+.**

Front and rear gardens are broken up into garden rooms. Front garden incl small woodland area planted with early spring flowering shrubs and bulbs, white garden and hot dry terraced area. Rear garden has mirror borders, small decorative vegetable garden and 'red' border. Grit and grasses garden. Organic and environmentally friendly. Home of author and Principal of The English Gardening School. Featured in 'House & Garden'.

🐾 ✿ ☎

121 ◆ SARAH RAVEN'S CUTTING GARDEN
Perch Hill Farm, Willingford Lane, Brightling TN32 5HP. Sarah Raven, 0845 050 4849, www.perchhill.co.uk. *7m SW of Hurst Green. From A21 Hurst Green take A265 Heathfield Rd for 6m. In Burwash turn L by church, go 3m to Xrds at top of hill. At large green triangle, R down Willingford Lane, garden 1/2 m on R. Field parking, uneven ground.* **Adm £5, chd under 14 free. 25 Apr; 13 June; 22, 23 Aug (9.30-4). For NGS: Sat 19 June (10-4).** Sarah's inspirational, productive 2-acre working garden. Large cutting garden, vegetable, salad and herb garden, fruit garden and willow bed. Oast garden has an extravagant mix of colour and structure: salvias, cardoons, artichokes, dahlias, zinnias, gladioli, cannas, jungly corn and banana foliage. Group visits by arrangement. Featured in many publications and on BBC Gardeners' World.

&. 🐾 ✿ ☕

122 SAYERLAND HOUSE
Sayerland Lane, Polegate BN26 6QP. Penny & Kevin Jenden, 01323 485228, penny@jenden.net. *2m S of Hailsham, 1m N of Polegate. At Cophall roundabout on A27 take A22, turn L at 1st turning (100yds). Follow through Bay Tree Lane, turn sharp L into Sayerland Lane. From N on A22 turn L into Bay Tree Lane before roundabout.* Home-made teas. **Adm £4, chd free. Sun 14 June (2-6) with music. Visitors also welcome by appt.** 5-acre garden surrounding listed C15 house (not open). Several distinct garden areas. Walled garden with colour-themed herbaceous borders, enclosed rose garden, ponds, kitchen garden, wild flower areas and tropical beds. Many mature shrubs and specimen trees. Live music, plant sales, tombola, book stall.

&. 🐾 ✿ ☕ ☎

123 SEDGWICK PARK HOUSE
Horsham RH13 6QQ. John & Clare Davison, 01403 734930, clare@sedgwickpark.com, www.sedgwickpark.co.uk. *1m S of Horsham off A281. Take A281 towards Cowfold/Brighton. Hillier Garden Centre on R, then 1st R into Sedgwick Lane. After Sedgwick sign post, enter N gates of Sedgwick Park. Enter also by W gates via Broadwater Lane, from Copsale or Southwater A24.* Light refreshments & home-made teas. **Adm £4, chd free (share to Cancer Wise). Sun 17 May (11.30-5). Visitors also welcome by appt.** Extensive parkland, meadows and woodland. Formal gardens landscaped by Harold Peto featuring 20 interlinking pools, cascades and impressive water garden known as 'The White Sea'. Large Horsham stone terraces and lawns look out onto clipped yew hedging and mature trees incl rare, 'Champion' oak. Beautiful secluded rose walk and colourful borders. Azaleas, rhododendrons and colourful walkways form superb setting for the house. Beyond finest views to S Downs, Chanctonbury Ring and Lancing College Chapel. New labyrinth and organic vegetable garden. Uneven paving, slippery when wet; unfenced ponds and swimming pool.

&. ✿ ☕ ☎

On 18 July come and meet our NGS/NT Careership gardener and hear about his first year on the scheme . . .

124 SENNICOTTS
West Broyle, Chichester PO18 9AJ. Mr & Mrs James Rank. *2m NW of Chichester. From Chichester take B2178 signed Funtington for 2m. Entrance on R. Long drive, ample parking nr house. From Fishbourne turn N marked Roman Palace then straight on until T-junction. Entrance opp Salt Hill Rd.* Light refreshments &

home-made teas. **Adm £3.50, chd free. Sun 10 May (2-6).** Historic gardens set around a Regency villa (not open). Extensive rhododendron and azalea borders. Working walled kitchen and cutting garden. Avenues and walks. New fountain for 2009. Views across mature Sussex parkland to S Downs. Excellent home-made teas. Lots of space for children. A warm welcome. Gravel paths.

&. ✿ ☕

125 SHALFORD HOUSE
Square Drive, Kingsley Green GU27 3LW. Vernon & Hazel Ellis. *2m S of Haslemere. Just S of border with Surrey on A286. Square Drive is at brow of hill, to the E. Turn L after 0.2m and follow rd to R at bottom of hill.* Home-made teas. **Adm £3.50, chd free. Suns 10 May; 12 July; 6 Sept (2-6).** Highly regarded 10-acre garden designed and created from scratch over last 16yrs. Wonderful hilly setting with terraces, streams, ponds, waterfall, sunken garden, herbaceous borders, azaleas, walled kitchen garden, wild flower meadows with orchids. Prairie-style plantation and stumpery merging into 7-acre woodland. Further 30-acre wood with beech, rhododendrons, bluebells, ponds, Japanese-themed area and woodland walks.

🐾 ✿ ☕

126 ◆ SHEFFIELD PARK GARDEN
Sheffield Park TN22 3QX. The National Trust, 01825 790231, www.nationaltrust.org.uk. *10m S of E Grinstead. 5m NW of Uckfield; E of A275.* **Adm £7, chd £3.50, family £17.50. Open all yr; please phone or visit website for details. For NGS: Sat 18 July; Tue 13 Oct (10.30-5.30, last adm 4.30).** Magnificent 120 acres (40 hectares) landscaped garden laid out in C18 by Capability Brown and Humphry Repton. Further development in early yrs of this century by its owner Arthur G Soames. Centrepiece is original lakes, with many rare trees and shrubs. Beautiful at all times of the year, but noted for its spring and autumn colours. National Collection of Ghent azaleas. Dogs allowed on South Park, but not in garden. On 18 July come and meet our NGS/NT Careership gardener and hear about his first yr on the scheme. Please call for times.

&. 🐾 ✿ NCCPG

127 SHERBURNE HOUSE
Eartham, nr Chichester PO18 0LP.
Mr & Mrs Angus Hewat, 01243
814261, anne.hewat@virgin.net. *6m
NE of Chichester. Approach from A27
Chichester-Arundel rd or A285
Chichester-Petworth rd, nr centre of
village, 200yds S of church.* Adm
£3.50, chd free. Visitors welcome by
appt, groups and individuals,
refreshments by arrangement.
Chalk garden of approx 2 acres. Shrub
and climbing roses, lime-tolerant
shrubs, herbaceous, grey-leaved and
foliage plants, pots, water feature,
small herb garden, kitchen garden
potager with octagonal pergola, fruit
cage, wild flower meadow and
conservatory.

128 SIENNA WOOD
Coombe Hill Road, East Grinstead
RH19 4LY. Alison & Michael Brown,
01342 300653, a.brown@zoo.co.uk.
*1m W of E Grinstead, off B2110 E
Grinstead to Turners Hill. Garden is
1/2 m down Coombe Hill Rd on L.*
Cream teas. Adm £4, chd free. Sat
27 (2-6), Sun 28 June (11-5). Visitors
also welcome by appt.
Meander our peaceful 2 1/2 -acre
garden and lovely lakeside walk and
woodland behind. Start at the formal
borders surrounding the croquet lawn,
and via the rose garden to the old
apple orchard and summer borders;
then down past the wild garden to the
lake and back through the vegetable
garden. Many unusual trees and
shrubs. Child and wheelchair friendly.
Great teas! Prize quiz!

Large sunny
patio and small,
shady area
surrounded
by scented
plants . . .

Group opening

129 NEW SLINDON GARDENS
nr Arundel BN18 0RE. *4m E of
Arundel. From Slindon Xrds on A29
turn R into village if coming from N,
L if coming from S. Follow rd up
village for approx 1/2 m. The Well
House is on L just past Church Hill,
park in farm opp.* Teas at The Well
House. Combined adm £4, chd
free. Thur 18, Sun 21 June (2-5).
Two secluded gardens in the heart
of the old National Trust village of
Slindon, situated on the S side of
the Downs, based on chalk and
flint.

NEW COURT COTTAGE
Mark & Clare Bacchus
The mainly S-facing garden
occupies 1/3 acre with an
outstanding village view. It
features specimen shrubs, 2
good-sized 'hot' and 'cool' island
borders, a developing orchard, a
small kitchen garden and
greenhouse. It is bordered on one
side by a mature beech hedge.
Large sunny patio and small,
shady area surrounded by
scented plants. Visitors always
comment on the fine lawns. The
garden is tended with enthusiasm
by its amateur owners!

NEW THE WELL HOUSE
Sue & Patrick Foley,
www.wellhousegarden.com
Pretty village garden incl a walled
garden with traditional herbaceous
beds stocked with mixed
perennials, shrubs and roses.
Newly-designed side garden
around a pool, with roses,
shrubs, fruit trees and climbers
planted against a flint wall. Small
vegetable and cutting garden.

130 NEW SOUTH GRANGE
Quickbourne Lane, Northiam,
Rye TN31 6QY. Linda & Michael
Belton, 01797 252984,
belton.northiam@virgin.net.
*Between A268 & A28, 1km E of
Northiam. From Northiam centre
follow Beales Lane into
Quickbourne Lane, or Quickbourne
Lane leaves A286 approx 2/3 km S
of A28/A286 junction.* Light
refreshments & home-made teas.
Adm £3.50, chd free (share to
Friends of Barnetts).

Sat 15, Sun 16 Aug (11-5).
Visitors also welcome by appt
June to Sept, for min 10 max 20
visitors.
1/2 acre with annuals, a large variety
of herbaceous perennials, grasses,
shrubs and trees plus raised bed
and wildlife pond for yr-round
colour and interest. Vegetable
beds. 1/2 acre of orchard with rough
grass, 1/2 -acre wild wood. The
whole is managed to sustain a
wide range of wildlife.

131 SPARROW HATCH
Cornwell's Bank, nr Newick
BN8 4RD. Tony & Jane Welfare. *5m
E of Haywards Heath. From A272 turn
R into Oxbottom Lane (signed
Barcombe), 1/2 m fork L into Narrow
Rd, continue to T-junction & park in
Chailey Lane (no parking at house).*
Adm £2.50, chd free. Weds, Thurs
27, 28 May; 24, 25 June (2-5).
Delightful 1/3 -acre plantsman's cottage
garden, wholly designed, made and
maintained by owners. Many features
incl 2 ponds, formal and wildlife,
herbaceous borders, shady dell,
vegetables, herbs, alpines. Planned for
owners' enjoyment and love of growing
plants, both usual and unusual. Home
propagated and grown plants for sale.

132 ◆ STANDEN
West Hoathly Road, East Grinstead
RH19 4NE. The National Trust,
01342 323029,
www.nationaltrust.org.uk. *1 1/2 m S of
E Grinstead. Signed from B2110 &
A22 at Felbridge.* House & Garden
£8.20, chd £4.10. Garden only £4.90,
chd £2.45. Weds to Suns 14 Mar to
1 Nov, also Mons 27 July to 31 Aug
(11-5.30). Last entry to house 4pm.
For NGS: Sat 18 July (11-5.30).
Approx 12 acres of hillside garden,
divided into small compartments:
notably a quarry garden, kitchen
garden and bamboo garden with pool
and cascades. Woodland walks and
stunning views over the Medway and
Ashdown Forest. Ongoing restoration.

133 STONE CROSS HOUSE
Alice Bright Lane, Crowborough
TN6 3SH. Mr & Mrs D A Tate. *1/2 m
S of Crowborough. At Crowborough
T-lights (A26) turn S into High St, &
shortly R into Croft Rd. Straight over
2 mini roundabouts into Alice Bright
Lane. Garden on L at next Xrds about*

1½ m from T-lights. Home-made teas. **Adm £3, chd free. Sat 9, Sun 10 May (2-5.30).**
Beautiful 9-acre country property with gardens containing a delightful array of azaleas, rhododendrons and camellias, interplanted with an abundance of spring bulbs. The very pretty cottage garden has interesting examples of topiary and unusual plants. Jacob sheep graze the surrounding pastures. Gravel drive.

134 STONEHEALED FARM
Streat Lane, Streat BN6 8SA. Lance & Fiona Smith, 01273 891145, afionasmith@hotmail.com. *2m SE of Burgess Hill. From Ditchling B2116, 1m E of Westmeston, turn L (N) signed Streat, 2m on R immed after railway bridge.* Home-made teas. **Adm £3.50, chd free (share to St Peter & St James Hospice). Mon 4 May; Sun 6 Sept (2-6). Visitors also welcome by appt in May & Sept only for groups of 10+.**
1½ acres surrounded by fields with views to the S Downs. Terrace with seasonal pots, hidden front garden, shaded pond with serpentine bridge, kitchen garden, new lime walk, oak tree deck. Early-flowering shrubs, bulbs and emerging perennial foliage in May. Dramatic late summer colour and grasses in Sept. Featured in RHS 'The Garden'.

30,000 plants and 550 different varieties . . .

135 STONEHURST
Selsfield Road, Ardingly RH17 6TN. Mr & Mrs M Holman. *1¼ m N of Ardingly. On B2028 opp Wakehurst Place.* Home-made teas. **Adm £4, chd free. Sat 16 May (12-5).**
Gardens of approx 12 acres designed and laid out early in the last century by Thomas Mawson with a wealth of architectural brick and stone work. Fine views across the Cob Valley and to S Downs. Amongst established planting is large collection incl camellias, acers, rhododendrons and azaleas.

136 NEW SUSSEX PRAIRIES
Morlands Farm, Wheatsheaf Road, Henfield BN5 9AT. Paul & Pauline McBride, 01273 492608, morlandsfarm@btinternet.com, www.sussexprairies.co.uk. *2m E of Henfield on B2116 Wheatsheaf Rd (also known as Albourne Rd).* Home-made teas. **Adm £4, chd free (share to Canine Partners). Sun 12 July; Mon 31 Aug (11-5). Visitors also welcome by appt for groups of 10+.**
Prairie garden of approx 6 acres planted in the naturalistic style. This exciting new garden was planted in May 2008, using 30,000 plants and 550 different varieties. A colourful garden which also features a huge variety of unusual ornamental grasses, a cutting garden and a series of enclosed circular gardens with different themes. Surrounded by mature oak trees with views of Chanctonbury Ring and Devil's Dyke on the S Downs. Collection of sculptures within the garden.

137 TINKERS BRIDGE COTTAGE
Tinkers Lane, Ticehurst TN5 7LU. Mrs M A Landsberg, 01580 200272. *11m SE of Tunbridge Wells. From B2099 ½ m W Ticehurst, turn N to Three Leg Cross for 1m, R after Bull Inn. House at bottom of hill.* **Adm £5, incl tea, chd free. Sun 17 May (2.30-5.30). Visitors also welcome by appt.**
12 acres landscaped; stream garden nr house (not open) leading to herbaceous borders, wildlife meadow with ponds and woodland walks. Access over grass.

138 TOWN PLACE
Ketches Lane, Freshfield, nr Sheffield Park RH17 7NR. Mr & Mrs A C O McGrath, 01825 790221, mcgrathsussex@hotmail.com, www.townplacegarden.org.uk. *3m E of Haywards Heath. From A275 turn W at Sheffield Green into Ketches Lane for Lindfield. 1¾ m on L.* Cream teas. **Adm £5, chd free. Sun 14, Thurs 18, 25, Sun 28 June; Suns 5, 12 July (2-6). Visitors also welcome by appt 13 June to 11 July only, for groups of 20+, £7 per person.**
3 acres with over 600 roses, 150ft herbaceous border, walled herb garden, ornamental grasses, ancient

hollow oak, orchard and potager. 'Green' Priory Church and Cloisters. C17 Sussex farmhouse (not open).

139 TROTTON OLD RECTORY
Trotton GU31 5EN. Mr & Mrs John Pilley. *3m W of Midhurst. On S side of A272 at Trotton, opp church.* **Adm £4, chd free. Weds 13 May; 17 June (2-6).**
Yew hedges frame old-fashioned roses, perennials, shrubs and trees underplanted with spring bulbs in this typical English country garden of about 3 acres. Pleached limes, a laburnum tunnel, a small lake and bog garden all add to the interest as well as a productive vegetable garden with Victorian glasshouses.

140 ◆ UPPARK
South Harting GU31 5QR. The National Trust, 01730 825415, www.nationaltrust.org.uk. *1½ m S of S Harting. 5m SE of Petersfield on B2146.* House & garden £8.20, chd £4.10. Garden only £4, chd £2. Suns to Thurs 29 Mar to 29 Oct 11.30-5, House 12.30-4.30. For NGS: Thurs 4 June; 2 July (11.30-5).
Intimate restored picturesque garden nestles behind Uppark House, in contrast to the sweeping panoramic views to the S. Gardener leads tours at 12 and 2.30 to tell the history and development of the site. Fine restored mansion.

141 UPWALTHAM BARNS
Upwaltham GU28 0LX. Roger & Sue Kearsey, 01798 343145. *6m S of Petworth. 6m N of Chichester on A285.* Light refreshments, home-made teas & wine. **Adm £3.50, chd free (share to St Mary's Church). Sun 3, Mon 4 May (11-5). Visitors also welcome by appt for groups of 10+ in June, July, Sept & Oct, coaches permitted.**
Unique farm setting has been transformed into a garden of many rooms. Entrance is a tapestry of perennial planting to set off C17 flint barns. At the rear, walled terraced garden redeveloped and planted in an abundance of unusual plants. Extensive vegetable garden. New ideas for 2009. Roam at leisure, relax and enjoy at every season, with lovely views of S Downs and C12 Shepherds Church (open to visitors). Some gravel paths.

142 WARNINGCAMP HOUSE
Warningcamp, Arundel BN18 9QY. David & Sarah Houghton King, 01903 884254. *2m NE of Arundel off A27. Leaving Arundel towards Worthing cross railway bridge, take 1st L signed Burpham. Follow rd for approx 1m, take 1st L turn at junction and gate faces you.* Home-made teas. **Adm £3.50, chd free. Thur 11 June (10-5); Suns 5 July; 13 Sept (2-5). Visitors also welcome by appt June to Sept.**
Formal garden laid out in 1920s to reflect the Victorian house first built in 1820. Set in 11 acres of garden and fields, incl walled kitchen garden with cutting flowers and working glasshouse. Formal garden to front of house features scented 'peony and pinks' walk, roses, long borders, parterre and gravel garden. Old Victorian water pumps renovated this yr. Wonderful views of Arundel Castle and many places to sit. Gravel paths, some uneven surfaces.

143 WARREN HOUSE
Warren Road, Crowborough TN6 1TX. Mr & Mrs M J Hands. *1½ m SW of Crowborough Cross. From Crowborough Cross towards Uckfield A26, 4th turning on R. 1m down Warren Rd. From South 2nd L after Blue Anchor.* Home-made teas. **Adm £3, chd free. Sun 26 Apr; Mon 4, Sun 17, Mon 25 May (2-5).**
Beautiful house (not open) steeped in history with 9-acre garden and views over Ashdown Forest. Series of gardens old and new, displaying wealth of azaleas, rhododendrons, impressive variety of trees and shrubs. Sweeping lawns framed by delightful walls and terraces, woodlands, ponds, ducks.

Group opening

144 WEST CHILTINGTON VILLAGE GARDENS
RH20 2LA. *2m E of Pulborough. 3m N of Storrington. Palmers Lodge at Xrds in centre of village opp Queen's Head, The Stone House 400yds S of Palmer's Lodge, next to church.* Home-made teas at Palmer's Lodge. **Combined adm £4, chd free. Suns 5, 12 July (1.30-5.30).**
Two contrasting gardens in the heart of this delightful village.

PALMER'S LODGE
Broadford Bridge Road. Richard Hodgson, 01798 812751. Visitors also welcome by appt in July only, teas provided.
Charming ½ -acre plantsman's garden with colourful herbaceous border. Also shrubs, fruit and vegetable garden and small greenhouse.

NEW THE STONE HOUSE
Mark & Liz Lamport, 01798 817209, liz.lamport@btopenworld.com. Visitors also welcome by appt.
A small cottage garden in the village centre. The owners are enthusiastic plant lovers who have been developing the garden over 8yrs. Mixed flowers, fruit and vegetable borders and a collection of chillies and tomatoes.

145 ◆ WEST DEAN GARDENS
West Dean PO18 0QZ. Edward James Foundation, 01243 818210, www.westdean.org.uk. *5m N of Chichester. On A286.* **Adm £6.75, chd £3.25, concessions £6.25. Gardens open daily, Mar to Oct (10.30-5), Nov to Feb (11-4). For NGS: Tue 2 June (10.30-5).**
35-acre historic garden in tranquil downland setting. 300ft long Harold Peto pergola, mixed and herbaceous borders, rustic summerhouses, redeveloped water and spring garden, specimen trees. Restored 2½ -acre walled garden contains fruit collection, 13 Victorian glasshouses, apple store, large working kitchen garden, extensive plant collection. Circuit walk (2¼ m) climbs through parkland to 45-acre St Roche's Arboretum. National Collections of *Aesculus* and *liriodendron*.

146 WESTACRE
Burton Park Road, Petworth GU28 0JS. Mrs R Charles, 01798 344467. *2m S of Petworth, off A285 (Chichester rd). Turn L past garage onto Burton Rark Rd, garden ¼ m on L.* Light refreshments & home-made teas. **Adm £3.50, chd free. Visitors welcome by appt, groups of 15+.**
Old gardener (Gaywood Farm, Pulborough) learns new tricks! Started from scratch but framed by old forest trees and with glimpses of the Downs, this 4yr-old garden now has a pond

and bog gardens, a pergola leading to a potager, wall planting, terrace beds and raised shrub banks. Unusual plants are maturing well in much enriched poor sandy soil. Intriguing from spring to autumn.

147 WESTFIELD
Malthouse Lane, Hurstpierpoint BN6 9JX. Phil & Cherry Radford. *Next to Hurstpierpoint College. With College cricket pitch on your L, after 200m white rocks on grass verge. Parking opposite on playing field.* Home-made teas. **Adm £3.50, chd free. Sun 9 Aug (2-5).**
For garden lovers, this 'colonial-style' 1-acre garden is packed with tropical plants such as cannas, bananas, phormiums, palms and grasses and is surrounded by mature trees. For parents, Westfield is a great place to bring the children as there is a Treasure Hunt in the large woodland garden for them to enjoy.

Mixed
flowers, fruit
and vegetable
borders and a
collection of
chillies and
tomatoes . . .

148 WHITEHOUSE COTTAGE
Staplefield Lane, Staplefield RH17 6AU. Mr Barry Gray. *5m NW of Haywards Heath. E of A23 & 2m S of Handcross. In Staplefield at Xrds by cricket pavilion take turning marked Staplefield Lane for 1m.* **Adm £3, chd free. Open daily throughout the year during daylight hours, no appointment required.**
4 acres of woodland with mixed shrubs, paths beside stream linked by ponds.

149 NEW WINCHELSEA'S SPRING GARDENS
TN36 4EE. Home-made teas in Court Hall, High Street. **Combined adm £3, chd free. Sun 26 Apr (1-5).**
Winchelsea's Secret Gardens have been open in June for many years. This year, for the first time, there is the opportunity to view a selection of the gardens in spring. **Cleveland House, Rye View and South Mariteau** will be open on 26 Apr for bulbs and blossom. Please see Winchelsea's Secret Gardens for details.

A plantswoman's organised chaos! . . .

150 WINCHELSEA'S SECRET GARDENS
TN36 4EJ. *2m W of Rye. Parking in streets.* Light refreshments & home-made teas in The New Hall. **Combined adm £5, chd free. Sat 13 June (12-5).**
Winchelsea is a beautiful medieval town, founded in 1288 by Edward I. Notable buildings incl the splendid C14 church and Court Hall. It is one of the few surviving C13 English towns where the streets are laid out in a grid system. Because of this, the gardens are hidden behind old walls. Many of the gardens open this year have lovely water features and wonderful views of the sea or across the beautiful Brede Valley. Town maps given to all visitors.

AMERIQUE
Castle Street. Mr & Mrs D O'Brien
Mature garden, partly walled, extending to a wild area with herb garden to attract bees and butterflies. Old-fashioned roses - ramblers, scramblers and bush varieties abound.

THE ARMOURY
Castle Street. Mr & Mrs Jasper
Approx 1 acre of land divided into 10 garden rooms with different themes. Various water features, plenty of seating. Uneven paths.

CLEVELAND HOUSE
Rookery Lane. Mr & Mrs J Jempson
This beautiful 1⅓-acre walled garden has recently undergone a huge transformation due to box blight. New semi-wild area, borders, summerhouse and trees. Lovely views. Gravel paths.

FIVE CHIMNEYS
Mill Road. Tony & Sue Davis
Garden of approx ⅓ acre incl kitchen garden, separated from the main lawned area by a pleached hornbeam hedge, rose garden.

NEW KING'S LEAP
Castle Street. Philip Kent
Large cottage-style garden comprising mixed beds, woodland border and rockery, all packed with plants for colour and interest.

PERITEAU HOUSE
High Street. Dr & Mrs Lawrence Youlten
Old walled garden with herbaceous borders, fountain and 300yr-old yew tree.

RYE VIEW
The Strand. Howard Norton & David Page. *On A259, below the town entrance rd*
Garden created since 2006 with riverside views over Rye Marsh. A blend of formal and informal planting with a collection of silver plants and unusual shrubs.

SOUTH MARITEAU
German Street. Mr & Mrs Robert Holland
Part-walled garden of about ⅓ acre divided into 3 areas: seaside, romantic and orchard with C19 rockery.

THE WELL HOUSE
Castle Street. Alice Kenyon
Recently renovated partially walled garden using gravel as well as lawn. Existing trees to aim at all-yr interest.

NEW WINCHELSEA COTTAGE
High Street. Mr Nigel Ashton
Small courtyard garden.

151 NEW 22 WOODLAND WAY
Patcham BN1 8BA. Jean & Barry Hewland, 01273 508979. *N Brighton. From A23 (London Rd) at Patcham turn L into Peacock Lane, almost at top L into Woodland Way.* **Adm £3, chd free. Sat 27 June (2-5). Visitors also welcome by appt.**
Facing the S Downs, this 5yr old sloping garden on shallow chalk has no grass. Gravel paths, pond, vegetable and fruit patch and hundreds of plants. A plantswoman's organised chaos!

Sussex County Volunteers

East & Mid Sussex
County Organisers
Rosie & Robin Lloyd, Bankton Cottage, Turners Hill Road, Crawley Down RH10 4EY, 01342 718907, rosie.lloyd@dsl.pipex.com
Treasurer
Robin Lloyd, robin.lloyd@dsl.pipex.com

West Sussex
County Organiser
Jane Allen, Dyers House, Pickhurst Road, Chiddingfold, Surrey GU8 4TG, 01428 683130, nicholasallen@btinternet.com
Treasurer
Peter Edwards, Quince Cottage, The Street, Bury, Pulborough RH20 1PA, 01798 831900, peteredwards425@btinternet.com

WARWICKSHIRE
with Birmingham & part of West Midlands

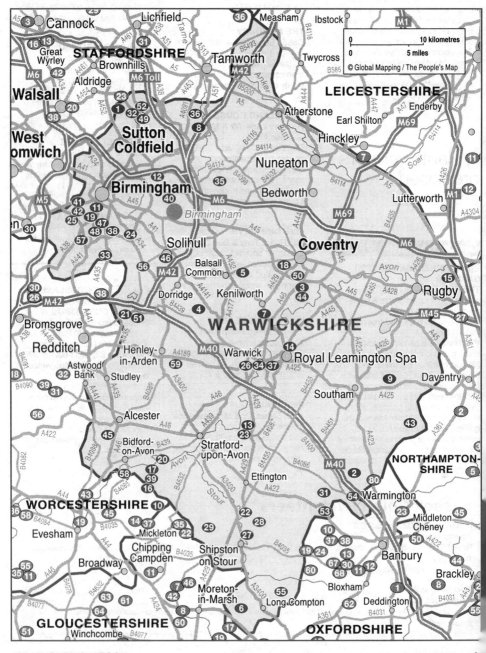

Opening Dates

February

SUNDAY 8
45 Ragley Hall Gardens

March

SUNDAY 8
20 Elm Close
59 Wootton Grange

April

SUNDAY 19
14 19 Church Lane
31 Ivy Lodge

WEDNESDAY 22
25 89 Harts Green Road

SUNDAY 26
41 50 Pereira Road

May

SUNDAY 3
3 Avondale Nursery
24 Hall Green Gardens
44 The Quarry Garden

MONDAY 4
3 Avondale Nursery
18 Earlsdon Gardens
44 The Quarry Garden

SUNDAY 10
20 Elm Close

TUESDAY 12
22 The Folly Lodge

WEDNESDAY 13
25 89 Harts Green Road

SATURDAY 16
51 Tanworth-in-Arden Gardens

SUNDAY 17
1 Ashover
51 Tanworth-in-Arden Gardens

SUNDAY 24
3 Avondale Nursery
6 Barton House
10 Broad Marston & Pebworth Gardens
44 The Quarry Garden

MONDAY 25
3 Avondale Nursery
8 Bridge House
10 Broad Marston & Pebworth Gardens
44 The Quarry Garden

SUNDAY 31
14 19 Church Lane

June

SUNDAY 7
16 Dorsington Gardens
30 Inglenook

32 18 Ladywood Road
36 Middleton Hall

SUNDAY 14
29 Ilmington Gardens
35 Maxstoke Castle
49 Stoneleigh House
50 Styvechale Garden Trail
54 Warmington Village Gardens

TUESDAY 16
22 The Folly Lodge

WEDNESDAY 17
25 89 Harts Green Road

SUNDAY 21
17 Dorsington House
27 Honington Village Gardens
39 The Old Rectory
52 91 Tower Road
55 Whichford & Ascott Gardens
57 Woodbrooke Quaker Study Centre

SUNDAY 28
5 Balsall Common Gardens
7 Bertie Road Gardens
12 Castle Bromwich Hall Gardens
21 Elmhurst
38 Moseley Gardens South

July

SUNDAY 5
23 Greenlands
28 Idlicote Gardens
48 The Stables Selly Park

SUNDAY 12
2 Avon Dassett Gardens
11 5 Carpenter Road
30 Inglenook
42 Pereira Road Gardens
47 Sir Johns Gardens

TUESDAY 14
22 The Folly Lodge

SATURDAY 18
4 Baddesley Clinton Hall
53 Upton House & Gardens

SUNDAY 19
15 Clifton Hall Farm
24 Hall Green Gardens
40 Park View Gardens
46 8 Rectory Road

WEDNESDAY 22
25 89 Harts Green Road

SUNDAY 26
33 Little Indonesia

August

SUNDAY 2
1 Ashover

SUNDAY 9
3 Avondale Nursery
56 Wits End

TUESDAY 18
22 The Folly Lodge

FRIDAY 21
13 Charlecote Park (Evening)

MONDAY 31
8 Bridge House

September

WEDNESDAY 9
25 89 Harts Green Road

SUNDAY 13
3 Avondale Nursery

TUESDAY 15
22 The Folly Lodge

SATURDAY 19
26 Hill Close Gardens

October

SATURDAY 3
45 Ragley Hall Gardens

February 2010

SUNDAY 7
45 Ragley Hall Gardens

Gardens open to the public

3 Avondale Nursery
4 Baddesley Clinton Hall
9 Bridge Nursery
12 Castle Bromwich Hall Gardens
13 Charlecote Park
25 89 Harts Green Road
26 Hill Close Gardens
34 The Master's Garden
36 Middleton Hall
37 The Mill Garden
44 The Quarry Garden
45 Ragley Hall Gardens
53 Upton House & Gardens

By appointment only

19 Edgbaston Garden Sculpture Trail
43 Priors Marston Manor Garden
58 Woodpeckers

Also open by appointment ☎

1 Ashover
2 Avon Dassett Gardens
6 Barton House
14 19 Church Lane
20 Elm Close
21 Elmhurst
22 The Folly Lodge
24 16, 28 & 37 Burnaston Road, Hall Green Gardens
24 36 Ferndale Road, Hall Green Gardens

㉝ Little Indonesia
㊶ 50 Pereira Road
㉜ 91 Tower Road
㉟ Springfield House, Warmington Village Gardens
㊺ Wits End
㊾ Wootton Grange

The Gardens

ARTHINGWORTH GARDENS
See Leicestershire & Rutland.

① ASHOVER
25 Burnett Road, Streetly B74 3EL.
Jackie & Martin Harvey, 0121 353
0547. *8m N of Birmingham. Off
B4138.* Cream teas. **Adm £3, chd
free.** Suns 17 May; 2 Aug (1.30-
5.30). Visitors also welcome by appt
from May-Aug, incl coaches.
Secluded 1/3 -acre, romantic country-
style garden, profusion of mixed
planting. Vibrant in May with tapestry
of azaleas, tulips and complementary
plants. In summer packed, colour-
themed herbaceous borders,
artistically planted with flowers and
foliage to give maximum effect of
colour, form and texture. Extended
hot border a special feature.
Established pond and waterfalls,
grasses and ferns.
✖ ✿ ☕ ☎

Group opening

② AVON DASSETT GARDENS
CV47 2AE. *7m N of Banbury. From
M40 J12 turn L & L again B4100. 2nd
L into village. Park in village & at top of
hill.* Home-made teas at Old Mill
Cottage. **Combined adm £5, chd free**
(share to Myton Hamlet Hospice).
Sun 12 July (2-6).
Small pretty Hornton stone village on
the side of the Avon Dassett hills,
popular for picnics and walking and
with views to the N and W. 2 churches
open for visitors.
✿ ☕

AVON COTTAGE
Mrs M J Edginton
Interesting contrasts between
cottage garden, courtyard and
vegetable garden.
♿

AVON HOUSE
Mrs L Dunkley
Mature garden, principally shrubs,
featuring hostas.
♿

THE COACH HOUSE
Bitham Hall. Mr & Mrs G J Rice,
01295 690255. Visitors also
welcome by appt all yr, groups &
coaches.
Sloping 2 acres, part of former
Victorian garden overlooking Edge
Hill. Walls give shelter and support
to many climbers and more tender
perennials and shrubs. Planted to
give yr-round interest. Woodland,
alpines, fruit and vegetables.
☎

HILL TOP FARM
Mrs N & Mr D Hicks
1 acre. Display of bedding plants,
perennials, shrubs, conifers and
heathers. Extensive kitchen
garden. Greenhouses.
✖ ✿

THE LIMES
Mr & Mrs B Anderson
Large ecological garden. Wide
variety of roses, shrubs and trees.
♿

OLD MILL COTTAGE
Mr & Mrs M J Lewis
Conservation garden of 3/4 acre
with shrubs, perennial borders
and rockeries. Collection of alpines
and herbs. Pond and tropical
garden. Mediterranean gravel
garden.
♿

THE OLD NEW HOUSE
Mr & Mrs W Allan
1-acre, formal rose garden,
herbaceous borders and specimen
trees.
♿

THE OLD RECTORY
Lily Hope-Frost
2-acre mature garden with
colourful terrace and wide stone
steps leading to fountain and
small wood, surrounding listed
house (not open) mentioned in
Domesday Book. Many places to
sit. Entrance to church through
walled garden.

ORCHARD END
Jill Burgess
1-acre garden with fruit trees, old
yew and box hedging, large pond
and herbaceous borders.
♿

POPPY COTTAGE
Mr & Mrs R Butler
Pretty cottage garden. Water
feature and kitchen garden.
♿

③ ◆ **AVONDALE NURSERY**
at Russell's Nursery, Mill Hill,
Baginton CV8 3AG. Mr Brian Ellis,
024 7667 3662,
www.avondalenursery.co.uk. *3m S
Coventry. At junction of A45/A46 take
rd to Baginton, 1st L to Mill Hill. Park in
Russell's Nursery.* **Adm £3.50, chd
free.** Mon to Fri, 10-12.30, 2-5, Sat
10-5, Sun 10.30-4.30. For NGS:
Suns, Mons 3, 4, 24, 25 May; Suns
9 Aug; 13 Sept (11-4). Also open
with **Styvechale Gardens** 14 June.
A plantsman's garden with a vast array
of ornamental grasses, impressive
collections of geums, geraniums,
sanguisorbas, asters, crocosmias and
much more. All plants are well labelled
and most for sale at the nursery.
4 additional themed show gardens,
prairie cottage, shade and gravel.
Unusual sculptures an added delight.
♿ ✿ ☕

Part of former
Victorian garden
overlooking
Edge Hill.
Walls give
shelter and
support to many
climbers . . .

④ ◆ **BADDESLEY CLINTON
HALL**
Knowle B93 0DQ. The National
Trust, 01564 783294,
www.nationaltrust.org.uk. *7 1/2 m NW
of Warwick. 3/4 m W of A4141 Warwick
to Birmingham rd nr Chadwick End.*
House & Garden £8.80, chd £4.40.
Garden only £4.40, chd £2.20.
Weds to Suns & BH Mons, 11 Feb to
1 Nov (11-5); 4 Nov to 20 Dec (11-4).
For NGS: Sat 18 July (11-5).
Medieval moated manor house little
changed since1634. Walled garden
and herbaceous borders, natural
areas, lakeside walk, nature trail. Partial
wheelchair access.
♿ ✖ ✿ ☕

Group opening

⑤ BALSALL COMMON GARDENS
CV7 7DG. *5m W of Coventry, 10m N of Warwick. 5m S of M42/M6 intersection. From T-lights at junction of A452/B4101, go E on B4101 towards Coventry for 1m. L into Hodgetts Lane.* **Combined adm £4, chd free (share to Balsall Village Hall). Sun 28 June (11-6).**
A variety of gardens to suit most interests. Map available at each garden. Please note that a car or cycle is necessary in order to get round to all these gardens.

ALDER HOUSE
Mr & Mrs M Hawley
Mixed borders of perennials, shrubs and trees, raised pond and wildlife pond.

THE BUNGALOW
Mr & Mrs G Johnson
2 acres with mixed borders, pond and lawns, a flower arranger's garden.

THE COTTAGE
Table Oak Lane. Enid & John Hinton
Purely perennials! From field to garden in 9 yrs. 1 acre; mixed beds, mature trees, wildlife waterlily pond, organic vegetable plot, pergola.

ELMCROFT
Hodgetts Lane. Mr & Mrs E Owen
Cottage garden with mixed shrub and herbaceous borders and containers. Small wildlife pond, ornamental raised koi tank and pagoda.

FIRS FARM
Mr & Mrs C Ellis
1-acre garden, courtyard with tubs, walled garden, formal garden with mixed borders and pergola supporting varieties of honeysuckle. Open grassed area with fruit and ornamental trees.

MERIGLEN
Mr & Mrs J Webb
Mixed borders of shrubs and perennials designed to save labour. Garden room and greenhouse.

THE PINES
Mr & Mrs C Davis
1½ -acre garden of interlinked areas incl herbaceous borders, pond, roses, vegetables, fruit, small herb garden, woodland area and apiary. All framed by hedges and shrubberies.

---

⑥ BARTON HOUSE
Barton-on-the-Heath GL56 0PJ. Mr & Mrs I H B Cathie, 01608 674303.
2m W of Long Compton. 2m off A3400 Stratford-upon-Avon to Oxford rd. 1¼ m off A44 Chipping Norton to Moreton-in-Marsh rd. Cream teas. **Adm £5, chd £2.50. Sun 24 May (2-6). Visitors also welcome by appt for groups of 25+.**
6½ acres with mature trees, azaleas, species and hybrid rhododendrons, magnolias, moutan tree peonies. National collection of arbutus. Japanese garden, catalpa walk, rose garden, secret garden and many rare and exotic plants. Victorian kitchen garden. Exotic garden with palms, cypresses and olive trees established 2002. Vineyard planted 2000 - free wine tasting. Manor house by Inigo Jones (not open). 12, 2metre high Pawlonia Fargesii seedlings, 5 new species of Arbutus.

Eight town gardens demonstrating a variety of ways, from traditional to modern, of using small spaces to make and enjoy a garden . . .

Group opening

⑦ NEW BERTIE ROAD GARDENS
Kenilworth CV8 1JP. *5m N of Warwick/Leamington. 5m S of Coventry. From A46, take A452 into Kenilworth. Follow signs for town centre. After r'about take 3rd R into Waverley Rd, Bertie Rd is 1st L. Parking in town centre car parks, adj Waitrose.* Light refreshments & teas at Bertie Court. **Combined adm £3.50, chd free (share to Life Path Trust). Sun 28 June (2-5).**
Eight town gardens accessed from a single street demonstrating a variety of ways, from traditional to modern, of using small spaces to make and enjoy a garden.

NEW 1 BERTIE COURT
Jacqueline and Peter Merry
Small picturesque garden with a central greenery isle surrounded by compact colourful borders and accessed by a willow-canopied gazebo.

NEW 3 BERTIE COURT
Hazel Gibbs
A garden for seniors - made for easy living with paving, decking and lots and lots of pots.

NEW 4 BERTIE COURT
Keith Deane
Very small garden reshaped since early 2007 to create a space both attractive to wildlife and containing as many native plants as space permits.

NEW 2(B) BERTIE ROAD
Dilys & Andrew Skinner
Small walled garden set on a number of levels with vegetables, herbs and flowers in raised beds with space to enjoy.

NEW 3 BERTIE ROAD
Stella & John Parkinson
Small informal cottage-style garden with crowded beds of mainly perennials and shrubs surrounding a lawn.

NEW 17 BERTIE ROAD
Mrs L Donald
A garden filled with shrubs and plants for peace and colour.

NEW 40 WAVERLEY ROAD
Catherine & Richard Sturt
Small family garden where a keen gardener takes on the foes of a bouncing brood, balls and a bunny but still manages to hang on to flowers, foliage and assorted wildlife.

NEW 42 WAVERLEY ROAD
Lee Thomas
Modern and traditional garden linked by curves with textured materials and plants offering yr-round colour. An ideal space for entertaining or for peace and tranquillity, surrounded by mature trees.

The foes of a bouncing brood, balls and a bunny . . .

⑧ BRIDGE HOUSE
Dog Lane, Bodymoor Heath B76 9JF. Mr & Mrs J Cerone. *5m S of Tamworth. From A446 head N on A4091, R at sign into Bodymoor Heath Lane. 3/4 m into village, R into Dog Lane. Immed after hump back bridge.* Home-made teas. **Adm £3, chd free.**

Mons 25 May; 31 Aug (2-5.30).
1-acre garden surrounding converted public house divided into smaller areas with a mix of shrub borders, azalea and fuchsia, herbaceous and bedding, orchard, kitchen garden and wild flower meadow. Pergola walk, wisteria, pond and lawns.
  ♿ ✿ ☕

⑨ ◆ BRIDGE NURSERY
Tomlow Road, Napton CV47 8HX. Christine Dakin, 01926 812737, www.bridge-nursery.co.uk. *3m E of Southam. Brown tourist sign at Napton Xrds on the A425 Southam to Daventry rd.* **Adm £2, chd free.** Apr-Oct (10-4).
Be inspired by the range of rare and unusual plants thriving in heavy clay soil. Our 1-acre garden is a fine example of mind over matter! Large pond and bamboo grove. New 2009: hedgerow walk, butterfly border, cutting garden. Wildlife abounds. As featured in *Gardens News* December 2008.
  ♿ ✿

Group opening

⑩ BROAD MARSTON & PEBWORTH GARDENS
Stratford-upon-Avon CV37 8XZ. *9m SW of Stratford-upon-Avon. On B439 at Bidford turn L towards Honeybourne, after 3m turn L at Xrds signed Pebworth.* Home-made teas. **Combined adm £4, chd free.** Sun 24, Mon 25 May (2-6).
The hamlet of Broad Marston, with priory and manor, and the village of Pebworth have properties from the time of Shakespeare to the C21. The simple country church is always open for quiet contemplation. WC at village hall.

NEW BANK FARM HOUSE
Front Street. Craig & Erica Chapman
Laid out in 2008 and still under development, this walled cottage style sloping garden includes chickens and a feature pond. Steep steps, deep water.

NEW BANK HOUSE
Front Street. CV37 8XQ. Clive Warren
1/2 -acre garden sloping SW with fruit trees, shrubs and pretty stone retaining walls.

1 ELM CLOSE
Mr & Mrs G Keyte
Small cottage garden, very well stocked and with many features of interest.
  ♿ ✿ ✿

NEW FELLY LODGE
Front Street. Mr & Mrs B Clatworthy
Re-built 4yrs ago this garden reflects the owner's changing preferences for different planting schemes. The emphasis is on perennials, shrubs and textures with pathways and pergola to create interest.

ICKNIELD BARN
Friday Street. Sheila Davies
Very small walled cottage garden which almost becomes a part of the living room! Designed for relaxation and pottering, yet still full of interest.

IVYBANK
Mr & Mrs R Davis
1/3 -acre garden with ferns, ivies, roses and shrubs. Nursery holds National Collection of Pelargoniums and Hederas.
  ♿ ✿ ✿

THE KNOLL
Mr K Wood
Cottage-style walled garden.

THE MOUNT
Mr & Mrs J Allott
Traditional garden with heavy clay soil overlying blue lias. Large lawn with perennial borders and rose arbour at rear. Front cottage garden.

NOLAN COTTAGE
Priory Lane. Mr & Mrs R Thomas
3/4 -acre cottage garden with ponds, mixed borders, vegetables, fruit and more. Wild area with a natural pond. Sit and enjoy on one of the many seats.
  ♿ ✿

NEW ORCHARD HOUSE
David & Susan Lees
S-facing garden which has been updated with new borders in the last 3 yrs, mature trees and an abundance of clematis.

PRIMROSE HILL
Richard & Margaret Holland
Split-level garden completely redesigned in 2007 and still settling in. Raised rose beds, upper and lower lawns, terrace, shrubbery, pergola, lavender borders and fish pond.
  ♿

BURBAGE GARDENS
See Leicestershire & Rutland.

⑪ NEW 5 CARPENTER ROAD
B15 2JT. Professor & Mrs Robert Allen. *2m SW Birmingham. From M6 J6 take A38 S to Priory Rd junction, signed Botanical Gardens. R turn to Carpenter Rd opp Hallfield School.* Cream teas. **Adm £3, chd free.** Sun 12 July (2-5).
1/2 -acre mature walled garden with mixed planting incl stunning herbaceous border. Productive kitchen garden with vegetables, soft fruit and Victorian style glasshouse.
  ✿ ✿ ☕

---

12 ◆ CASTLE BROMWICH HALL GARDENS

Chester Road. B36 9BT. Castle Bromwich Hall Gardens Trust, 0121 749 4100, www.cbhgt.org.uk. *4m E of Birmingham. 1m J5 M6 (exit N only).* Adm £3.50, chd 50p, concessions £3. Phone or check web for details of opening days & times. For NGS: Sun 28 June (1.30-5.30).

Restored C18 formal walled gardens provide visitors with the opportunity to see a unique collection of historic plants, shrubs, medicinal and culinary herbs and fascinating vegetable collection. Intriguing holly maze. Several fruits within the orchards and along the paths incl apple, pear, apricot, quince, medlar, fig and cherry. Guided tours, gift shop.

13 NEW ◆ CHARLECOTE PARK

Warwick CV35 9ER. The National Trust, 01789 470277, www.nationaltrust.org.uk. *5m E of Stratford-upon-Avon, 6m S of Warwick. From J15, Longbridge r'about take A429, follow signs.* Adm £4.40, chd £2.20, family £11. For NGS: Evening Opening Fri 21 Aug (6-8).

At this time of year you can see a wonderful colourful display in our parterre. As you walk round you will see borders full of interesting herbaceous plants and a special garden called the sensory garden where you can touch the plants and spend some time reflecting on what you have seen.

14 19 CHURCH LANE

Lillington CV32 7RG. David & Judy Hirst, 01926 422591. *1½ m NE Leamington Spa. Take A445 towards Rugby. Church Lane on R just beyond r'about junction with B4453. Garden on corner of Hill Close. Enter via driveway in Church Lane.* Adm £2, chd free. Suns 19 Apr; 31 May (2-5.30). Visitors also welcome by appt on Tues in Mar (for hellebores), Mons in June.

Enjoy a plantsperson's cottage-style garden with a country atmosphere. Visitors have been intrigued by the wide range of unusual plants and their combinations, different aspects and areas. Narrow paths, may not be suitable for very young or infirm.

15 CLIFTON HALL FARM

Lilbourne Road, Clifton-upon-Dunsmore CV23 0BB. Bob & Jenny Spencer. *2m E of Rugby. From Clifton Church take Lilbourne rd out of village. Ist farm on R, just past village sign.* Home-made teas. Adm £3, chd free. Sun 19 July (2-6).

A feast of flowers down on the farm. A garden blossoming with emerald lawns and billowing borders. Silvery foliage, waving grasses and 'pop' plants from hostas to alstromerias, bananas, tree ferns - it is all here! Farmer Bob's tractor display and a cuppa with Jenny will round off your visit. Vintage tractors and farm walk. Some gravel.

COLDOR

See Leicestershire & Rutland.

A feast of flowers down on the farm. A garden blossoming with billowing borders . . .

Group opening

16 DORSINGTON GARDENS

CV37 8AR. *6m SW of Stratford-upon-Avon. On B439 from Stratford turn L to Welford-on-Avon, then R to Dorsington.* Light refreshments & teas in the marquee at Dorsington Arboretum. Combined adm £5, chd free. Sun 7 June (12-5).

Pretty conservation area village. Maps given to all visitors. For information please phone 01789 721730. Children's entertainment, carriage rides, plant stall, open farm, garden of life-sized sculptures, rare tree arboretum, car display incl vintage Rolls Royces.

THE BARN

Mr & Mrs P Reeve
2 tier country garden with shrubs, herbaceous borders and vegetable patch.

COLLETTS FARM

Mr & Mrs D Bliss
Trees and shrubs, container flowers. Highly productive kitchen garden with fan-trained fruit.

DORSINGTON ARBORETUM

Mr F Dennis
12 acres with collection of several hundred trees from around the world leading to Udde Well Pond (ancient well) and willow walk.

DORSINGTON HOUSE

Mr & Mrs I Kolodotschko
(See separate entry).

MANOR HOUSE FARM

Mr & Mrs Coffey
Old farmhouse garden under restoration.

THE OLD MANOR

Mr F Dennis
3 acres with fairy walk, herb garden, ornamental fish pond, sunken water garden leading to Highfield, (Mr F Dennis) with its Mediterranean garden, container plants and bonsai collection.

SAPPHIRE HOUSE

Mrs D Sawyer
Orchard, vegetable garden, shrub beds, lawns and large walnut trees.

THE WELSHMAN'S BARN

Mr F Dennis
5 acres with Japanese garden, Oz maze, bronze sculpture garden of heroes, wild flower garden and stream.

17 DORSINGTON HOUSE

Barton Road. CV37 8AT. Mr & Mrs I Kolodotschko. *On B439 from Stratford. L to Welford-on-Avon, R to Dorsington.* Combined adm with The Old Rectory £3, chd free. Sun 21 June (2-5). Also open with Dorsington Gardens Sun 7 June.

Laid out in 2006, the garden was designed in conjunction with its contemporary house for yr-round interest through use of form, colour and texture. Nearly 5 acres, it forms various areas which are extensions of the internal spaces.

Our group of enthusiasts demonstrate how the varied use of design and planting can achieve 5 unique gardens . . . .

Group opening

18 EARLSDON GARDENS
CV5 6FS. *Coventry. Turn towards
Coventry at A45/A429 T-lights. Take
3rd L turn into Beechwood Ave,
Earlsdon Gardens.* Home-made teas.
**Combined adm £3, chd free. Mon 4
May (11-4).**
Selection of varied urban gardens,
maps provided.

59 THE CHESILS
John Marron & Richard Bantock
Herbaceous plants jostle for
attention in a richly planted garden
on several levels.

NEW 1 DORNEY CLOSE
CV5 6AN. Josie & Bill Howie
Well structured compact town
garden on different levels.Lots of
spring interest with bulbs,
hellebores and grasses.

40 HARTINGTON CRESCENT
Viv & George Buss
Surprisingly large garden with
interest for all ages, water feature
and fern garden.

114 HARTINGTON CRESCENT
Liz Campbell & Denis Crowley
Large, mature, pretty garden on
several levels with hidden aspects.

36 PROVIDENCE STREET
Rachel Culley & Steve Shiner
Large peaceful cottage garden.
Water features, packed
herbaceous borders, vegetable
plot, yr-round interest and colour.

87 ROCHESTER ROAD
Edith Lewin
Peaceful, mature cottage garden.

54 SALISBURY AVENUE
Peter & Pam Moffit
Plantaholic's garden with a large
variety of plants, clematis and small
trees, some unusual.

**19 EDGBASTON GARDEN
SCULPTURE TRAIL**
5 Farquhar Road East. B15 3RD.
John Alexander-Williams, 01214
541279, johnaw@blueyonder.co.uk.
*4m SW of Birmingham. Under 1m
from Birmingham Botanical Gardens.
Farquhar Rd East is a triangle off
Farquhar Rd, between Somerset &
Richmond Hill Rds in Edgbaston.*
Visitors welcome by appt·
Town garden of ¹/₃ acre. Evolved over
more than 23 yrs to provide interlinking
areas of interest with hidden walks and
arches designed to create sculpture
trail. Some 80 sculptures by owner
provide surprise and amusement and
set off very personal collection of
shrubs, trees and plants.

20 ELM CLOSE
Binton Road, Welford-on-Avon
CV37 8PT. Eric & Glenis Dyer, 01789
750793. *5m SW of Stratford. Off
B4390. Elm Close is between Welford
Garage & The Bell Inn.* Home-made
teas. **Adm £3, chd free. Suns 8 Mar;
10 May (2-5). Visitors also welcome
by appt in groups, 10+.**
Do come and see our hundreds of
hellebores, georgeous species and
herbaceous peonies, sumptuous tree
peonies, masses of late flowering
clematis, bulbs in profusion, numerous
japanese maples, hostas, daphnes
and many rare and unusual plants
providing colour at every season.
Featured in 'Cotswold Life'.

21 ELMHURST
Vicarage Hill, Tanworth-in-Arden
B94 5EA. Mr & Mrs R Lockwood,
01564 742641. *Off B4101, ³/₄ m from
village.* Home-made teas. **Adm £2.50,
chd free (share to St Mary
Magdalene Church). Sun 28 June
(2-6). Also open with Tanworth-in-
Arden Gardens 16, 17 May. Visitors
also welcome by appt for groups in
June & July.**
¹/₂ -acre with wide range of plants,
some unusual, for yr-round interest.
Herbaceous borders, woodland area,
rockery, small pond and interesting
features. Bark path to gravel area.

FARMWAY
See Leicestershire & Rutland.

22 THE FOLLY LODGE
Halford CV36 5DG. Mike & Susan
Solomon, 01789 740183,
SS@follylodge.eclipse.co.uk. *3m NE
Shipston-on-Stour. On A429 (Fosse
Way). In Halford take turning to Idlicote.
Garden on R past Feldon Edge.*
Home-made teas. **Adm £3, chd free.**
**Tues 12 May;16 June; 14 July;
18 Aug; 15 Sept (2-5). Visitors also
welcome by appt for groups 8+.**
A garden that displays imagination and
is crammed with surprising features
and striking plant combinations. A
relaxed and welcoming garden to sit in
and enjoy the atmosphere. Featured in
'Gardeners' World Magazine'. Gravel
paths.

23 GREENLANDS
Stratford Road, Wellesbourne
CV35 9ES. Elizabeth Street. *4m E of
Stratford-upon-Avon. Situated at the
Loxley/Charlecote crossroads on the
B4086, next to airfield.* **Adm £3, chd
free. Sun 5 July (11-5).**
1-acre with mature trees, shrubs,
herbaceous borders and semi-wild
areas. Winding paths and secluded
garden rooms. 2 gravel gardens and
tree lined vistas. A collection of old
farm implements. Flower paintings
from plants in the garden. Some gravel
and bark chip paths.

Group opening

24 HALL GREEN GARDENS
Birmingham B28 8DG. *Off A34, 3m
city centre, 6m from M42 J4. Take A34
to Hall Green, turn into Colebank Rd
where S Birmingham College is
situated.* Home-made teas at 16
Burnaston & 36 Ferndale Rd.
**Combined adm £3.50, chd free
(share to St Mary's Hospice). Suns
3 May; 19 July (2-5.30).**
Our group of enthusiasts demonstrate
how the varied use of design and
planting can achieve 5 unique gardens.

16 BURNASTON ROAD
Howard Hemmings & Sandra
Hateley, 0121 624 1488,
howard.hemmings@blueyonder.
co.uk. Visitors also welcome by
appt from mid-May to mid-Aug.
S-facing formal lawn and border
garden with interesting features inc
an unusual log display, multi-

coloured gravel, and bark covered shrub border, manicured conifers, water feature and archway leading to tranquil seating area.

28 BURNASTON ROAD
B28 8DJ. Mrs L A Mole, 0121 624 6159. Visitors also welcome by appt from May to Aug.
Small suburban garden with well-stocked borders. Minature stream edged by moisture loving plants which runs into wildlife ponds. Shade area, containers and small kitchen garden.

37 BURNASTON ROAD
Mrs C M Wynne-Jones, 0121 608 2397. Visitors also welcome by appt from mid-May to mid-Aug.
Tranquil garden with curving borders containing many different perennials, shade areas, soft fruit and vegetables, a surprise around the corner.

36 FERNDALE ROAD
Mrs A A Appelbe & Mrs E A Nicholson, 0121 777 4921. Visitors also welcome by appt all year.
Large suburban florist's garden with many unusual plants giving yr-round interest. Garden divided into distinct areas, large ornamental garden with pool and waterfalls, tree and soft fruit garden and side patio.

120 RUSSELL ROAD
Mr D Worthington
Plantsman's sub-divided garden designed by owner. Features formal raised pool, shrubs, climbers, old roses, herbaceous and container planting. Comprehensive overhaul of planting and some features in the last 3 yrs. Uneven paving.

Herbs and edible flowers border a path through the rockery . . .

HAMMOND ARBORETUM
See Leicestershire & Rutland.

25 ◆ 89 HARTS GREEN ROAD
Harborne B17 9TZ. Mrs Barbara Richardson, 0121 427 5200. *3m SE of Birmingham. Off Fellows Lane-War Lane.* Adm £2.50, chd free. For NGS: Weds 22 Apr; 13 May; 17 June; 22 July; 9 Sept (2-5).
Wildlife-friendly split-level garden protected by mature trees. Extensively planted with unusual herbaceous perennials, shrubs and climbers. Herbs and edible flowers border a path through the rockery and 50 varieties of hemerocallis in July. Large display of plants in containers featuring vegetables, half hardy perennials and shade plants. Pond.

26 ◆ HILL CLOSE GARDENS
Warwick CV34 6HF. Hill Close Gardens Trust, 01926 493339, www.hillclosegardens.com. *Town centre. Entry from Friars St by Bread & Meat Close. Car park by entrance next to racecourse.* Adm £3, chd free. Fri & Sun (2-5), Sat & BH Mons (11-5), 10 Apr-24 Oct. For NGS: Sat 19 Sept (11-5).
Restored GII* Victorian leisure gardens comprising 16 individual hedged gardens, 7 with brick summerhouses. Herbaceous borders, heritage apple and pear trees, C19 daffodils, many varieties of asters and chrysanthemums. Heritage vegetables. NCCPG plant exchange border, Victorian style glasshouse. Head Gardener's walk 2nd Fri in month. Designated wheelchair route. Manual and electric wheelchairs available.

Group opening

27 HONINGTON VILLAGE GARDENS
Shipston CV36 5AA. *1½ m N of Shipston-on-Stour. Take A3400 towards Stratford then turn R signed Honington.* Home-made teas. Combined adm £4, chd free. Sun 21 June (2.15-5.30).
C17 village, recorded in Domesday, entered by old toll gate. Ornamental stone bridge over the R Stour and interesting church with C13 tower and late C17 nave after Wren.

HOLTS COTTAGE
Mr & Mrs R G Bentley
Cottage garden being restored to original layout and opening onto parkland. Interesting trees incl fruit trees and shrubs with herbaceous borders and ponds.

HONINGTON GLEBE
Mr & Mrs J C Orchard
2-acre plantsman's garden consisting of rooms planted informally with yr-round interest in contrasting foliage and texture. Old walled garden laid out with large raised lily pool and parterre filled with violas and perennials.

HONINGTON HALL
B H E Wiggin
Extensive lawns and fine mature trees with river and garden monuments. Carolean house (not open). Parish church adjoins house.

MALT HOUSE RISE
Mr & Mrs M Underhill
Small garden, well stocked with interesting established shrubs and many container plants.

THE OLD HOUSE
Mr & Mrs I F Beaumont
Small structured cottage garden formally laid out with box hedging and small fountain. Informally planted, giving an almost billowing, frothy appearance.

ORCHARD HOUSE
Mr & Mrs Monnington
Small developing garden created by owners with informal mixed beds and borders.

Group opening

28 IDLICOTE GARDENS
CV36 5DT. *3m NE of Shipston-on-Stour.* Home-made teas at Badgers Farm. Combined adm £4, chd free (share to Idlicote Church). Sun 5 July (2-6).
Delightful hamlet with stunning views, large village pond and Norman church.

BADGERS FARM
Sir Derek & Lady Hornby
Lawns with panoramic views and herbaceous borders lead to encl rose garden, vegetable garden, pond and orchard walk.

2 BICKERSTAFF COTTAGES
Mr D Amos
Delightful small enclosed cottage garden with ornamental pond.

BICKERSTAFF FARM
Sir John & Lady Owen
Recently planted garden, mainly shrub borders and roses.

IDLICOTE HOUSE
Mrs R P G Dill
Extensive gardens with mature trees and shrubs, formal area and spectacular views. Enclosed vegetable garden with flower borders. Norman Church and C18 dovecote in grounds. Grade II listed C18 house (not open).

THE OLD FORGE
Mr & Mrs J Terry
Planted in 2003 for easy maintenance.

WOODLANDS
Captain & Mrs P R Doyne
Shrubs and herbaceous plants. Spectacular views beyond walled garden.

Group opening

29 ILMINGTON GARDENS
Ilmington CV36 4LA. *8m S of Stratford-upon-Avon. 4m NW of Shipston-on-Stour off A3400. 3m NE of Chipping Campden.* Light refreshments & teas in village hall. **Combined adm £5, chd free (share to Shipton Home Nursing). Sun 14 June (2-6).**
One of the most attractive ancient Cotswold villages with 2 greens, 2 inns, a Norman church and many interesting walled walkways and country footpaths. Glorious views and scenery. St Mary's Church open all day for Flower and Organ Festival. Ilmington traditional Morris dancers at Manor House.

THE BEVINGTONS
Mr & Mrs N Tustain
Hedges divide different garden areas surrounding long thatched cottage, once a row of three. Views over ponds in Bury Orchard in centre of village.

FOXCOTE HILL
Mr & Mrs M Dingley
Garden developed on sloping site on edge of village retaining most of old orchard with naturalised bulbs. Paths through orchard give views over countryside towards Edge Hill. Paved courtyard with fountain.

FOXCOTE HILL COTTAGE
Miss A Terry
Hillside garden with dry stone walls enclosing banks planted with alpines and bulbs.

NEW THE GRANGE
Mr & Mrs Iain Barker
A garden for an explorer. Perched high in Ilmington with spectacular views over the village and surroundings, the gardens lead from one secret to another. Orchard, pool garden, kitchen garden, vegetable garden, rose garden, woods, incl Tuines oak and 400yr old Turkey oak. Garden is a 200yd walk up steep driveway - no cars.

THE GREY HOUSE
Mr & Mrs B Blackie
Formal lawns and beds with orchard on elevated site surrounding Georgian farmhouse, overlooking village and distant views.

ILMINGTON MANOR
Mr & Mrs M Taylor
4-acre garden surrounding Elizabethan cotswold stone manor house. Hundreds of roses, extensive yew topiary, ornamental trees, shrub and herbaceous borders, gold fish pond. House not open.

30 INGLENOOK
20 Waxland Road, Halesowen B63 3DW. Ron & Anne Kerr. *1/4 m from Halesowen town centre. M5 J3 take A456 to Kidderminster, R at 1st island, 1st L into Dogkennel Lane. Waxland Rd 2nd L. 2 car parks in town centre, limited roadside parking.* Home-made teas. **Adm £2.50, chd free. Sun 7 June; 12 July (1-5).**
Charming garden featuring waterfalls which cascade over rocks down to ponds set within a woodland area. A path meandering through the trees brings you back to the lawn and patio. Hidden area hosts greenhouses, vegetable plots, asparagus beds and mixed borders. Enjoy panoramic views from the raised decked area with its semi-tropical planting overlooking terraces which display a wide variety of low-growing conifers.

A garden for an explorer. Perched high in Ilmington with spectacular views over the village . . .

31 IVY LODGE
Radway CV35 0UE. Mr Martin Dunne. *12m S of Warwick. From J12 M40 take B4451 to Kineton, B4086 S for 3m to signed turning, Radway.* **Adm £3.50, chd free. Sun 19 Apr (2-5).**
The garden planted in 1956 by the late Jim Russell and the current owner's mother Mrs Willis. They incorporated a 3-acre field to make a 4-acre garden. Large areas of bulbs and blossoming fruit trees. Grass paths wind through the wilder areas of the garden amongst the flower beds, shrubs and ornamental trees.

KILSBY GARDENS
See Northamptonshire.

32 18 LADYWOOD ROAD
Four Oaks, Sutton Coldfield B74 2SW. Ann & Ron Forrest. *2m N of Sutton Coldfield. Off A454, Four Oaks Road, nr stn.* Home-made teas. **Adm £3, chd free. Sun 7 June (1-5).**
Spacious informal garden on Four Oaks Estate. Approx 1 1/4 acres, secluded and densely planted with roses, peonies, irises and lupins in herbaceous beds. Pond with fountain. Feature cedar tree, azaleas and rhododendrons.

33 LITTLE INDONESIA
20 Poston Croft, Kings Heath B14 5AB. Dave & Pat McKenna, 0121 628 1397, patanddave76@yahoo.co.uk, www.littleindonesia.wordpress.com. *1 1/2 m from Kings Heath High St. Poston Croft is 6th L off Broad Lane, which is off A435 Alcester Rd.* Cream teas. **Adm £3, chd free. Sun 26 July (11-4). Visitors also welcome by appt, June - Aug, groups 10+.**
A garden that is the realisation of my dreams. An amazing plant paradise

with the feel of entering a jungle, even though we are in the heart of Birmingham. Planted so that it seems to go on for ever. Plants of unusual leaf shapes and textures. Bananas, cannas and grasses jostle with one another for space. A plantaholic's paradise. Featured on 'BBC Gardeners World', 'Midlands Today' and 'Central TV Weather' broadcast from garden. Steps down to garden, gravel paths.

🍴 🍲 ☎

㉞ ◆ THE MASTER'S GARDEN
Lord Leycester Hospital, Warwick CV34 4BH. The Governors. *W end of Warwick High St, behind hospital.* **Adm £2, chd free. Apr to Sept (10-4.30).**
Restored historic walled garden hidden behind the medieval buildings of this home for retired ex-servicemen, also open to the public. Mixed shrub and herbaceous planting with climbing roses and clematis, Norman arch, ancient Egyptian Nilometer, thatched summerhouse, gazebo, knot garden and C18 pineapple pit.

🍴

㉟ MAXSTOKE CASTLE
Coleshill B46 2RD. Mr & Mrs M C Fetherston-Dilke. *2¹/₂ m E of Coleshill. E of Birmingham, on B4114. Take R turn down Castle Lane, Castle drive 1¹/₄ m on R.* Home-made teas. **Adm £6.50, chd £4. Sun 14 June (11-4).**
Approx 5 acres of garden and grounds with herbaceous, shrubs and trees in the immed surroundings of this C14 moated castle. No wheelchair access to house.

♿ 🍴 ⊛ 🍲

㊱ ◆ MIDDLETON HALL
Tamworth B78 2AE. Middleton Hall Trust, 01827 283 095, middletonhalltrust.co.uk. *4m S of Tamworth, 2m N J9 M42. On A4091 between The Belfry & Drayton Manor.* **Adm £3, chd £1. Suns & Bank Hol Mons, Apr-Sept. For NGS: Sun 7 June (1-5).**
Two walled gardens set in 40 acres of grounds surrounding GII Middleton Hall, the C17 home of naturalists Sir Francis Willughby and John Ray. Large colour themed herbaceous borders radiating from a central pond, restored gazebo, pergola planted with roses and wisteria. Courtyard garden with raised beds. SSSI Nature Trail, craft centre, music in Hall. Gravel paths.

♿ ⊛ 🍲

㊲ ◆ THE MILL GARDEN
55 Mill Street, Warwick CV34 4HB. Julia (née Measures) and David Russell, 01926 492877. *Off A425 beside castle gate at the bottom of Mill St. Use St Nicholas car park.* **Adm £1.50, chd free with adult. 1 Apr to 31 Oct (9-6).**
This garden lies in a magical setting on the banks of the R Avon beneath the walls of Warwick Castle. Winding paths lead round every corner to dramatic views of the castle and ruined medieval bridge. This informal cottage garden is a profusion of plants, shrubs and trees. Beautiful all-yr, full of contrasting shapes and colours.

🍴 ⊛

Group opening

㊳ MOSELEY GARDENS SOUTH
Birmingham B13 9TF. *3m city centre. Halfway between Kings Heath and Moseley village. From A435 turn at the main Moseley T-lights on to St Mary's Row/Wake Green Rd. 1st R, Oxford Rd, then 1st R, School Rd. Prospect Rd is 3rd on L, Ashfield Rd is 4th on R.* Cream teas at 10 Grove Avenue. **Combined adm £3.50, chd free. Sun 28 June (2-6).**
Urban gardens to front and rear of inter-war and Victorian houses set in a quiet leafy suburb. Wildlife ponds, water features, easy maintenance design and planting, outdoor artwork, sculpture and vegetable plots. Limited wheelchair access.

🍴 ⊛ 🍲

7 ASHFIELD ROAD
Hilary Bartlett
Small garden with secluded woodland feel. Attractive pond with rockery, waterfall and shingle bank. Plant sale.

10 GROVE AVENUE
Anita & Steve Harding
Suburban garden with herbaceous borders, pond area and summer house.

19 PROSPECT ROAD
Mr A J White
Well planted suburban garden with plenty of colour.

NEW 46 SCHOOL ROAD
Jenny Hudson
Extensive garden with walled courtyard with arched entrance to garden, sculptures, herbaceous borders, 2 small ponds, unusual containers, mature trees and well maintained vegetable plot.

65 SCHOOL ROAD
Wendy Weston
Small shady garden with patio, pergola and pond. Designed for easy maintenance. Tricky gravel paths.

♿

㊴ THE OLD RECTORY
Dorsington CV37 8AX. Mr & Mrs N Phillips. Combined adm with **Dorsington House £3, chd free. Sun 21 June (2-5).**
2-acre Victorian garden with mature trees incl old espalier fruit trees. Box hedges, herbaceous borders, many old roses, large pool, small wood.

♿ 🍴

㊵ NEW PARK VIEW GARDEN
227 Gressel Lane. B33 9UL. Shirley & Jim Beveridge. *From Castle Bromwich take B4114 Chester Rd, turn into Hurst Lane which runs into Leaford Rd and Gressel Lane.* Cream teas. **Adm £2.50, chd free. Sun 19 July (1-5).**
Small garden evolving over 3 yrs. Growing and showing fuchsias our speciality. Shrubs, perennials, vegetable patch, many hanging baskets and containers. Koi pond with gazebo and small wildlife pond. An ideal example of a big garden approach to a small garden. Parking opposite.

🍴 ⊛ 🍲

A big garden approach to a small garden . . .

㊶ 50 PEREIRA ROAD
Harborne B17 9JN. Peg Peil, 0121 427 7573. *Between Gillhurst Rd & Margaret Grove, ¹/₄ m from Hagley Rd or ¹/₂ m from Harborne High St.* **Adm £2, chd free. Sun 26 Apr (2-5). Also open with Pereira Road Gardens.** Visitors also welcome by appt.
Plantaholic's garden with over 1000 varieties, many unusual. Large bed of plants with African connections. Many fruits, vegetables, herbs, grasses. Plant sales in aid of CAFOD.

🍴 ⊛ ☎

Unusual decking area surrounded by English country plants, steps to exotic area with summerhouse, on to the vegetables and a quiet pond . . .

Group opening

42 PEREIRA ROAD GARDENS
Harborne B17 9JN. *Between Gillhurst Rd & Margaret Grove, ¼ m from Hagley Rd or ½ m from Harborne High St.* Teas. **Combined adm £3.50, chd free. Sun 12 July (2-5).**
Bird Sanctuary also open.

10 PEREIRA ROAD
Muriel May
S aspect sloping garden with steps, shaded, mature silver birch and acid-loving shrubs, some landscaping.

14 PEREIRA ROAD
Mike Foster
Well established suburban garden with mixed herbaceous and shrub borders, small fruit and vegetable area. Wildlife friendly with 2 ponds and natural area.

NEW 48 PEREIRA ROAD
Rosemary Klem
Sloping S-facing site tiered with mature shrubs and koi pond.

50 PEREIRA ROAD
Peg Peil
(See separate entry).

55 PEREIRA ROAD
Emma Davies & Martin Commander
Sloping gravelled garden with mixed planting, grasses and small pond.

43 PRIORS MARSTON MANOR GARDEN
The Green, Priors Marston CV47 7RH. **Dr & Mrs Mark Cecil, 07758 360839,** clare.will@btopenworld.com. *8m SW of Daventry. Off A361 between Daventry and Banbury at Charwelton.* **Visitors welcome by appt during Aug, weekdays only, groups and individuals.**
Greatly enhanced by present owners to relate back to a Georgian manor garden. Wonderful walled kitchen garden provides seasonal produce and cut flowers for the house. Herbaceous flower beds and a sunken terrace with water feature by William Pye. Lawns lead down to the lake around which you can walk amongst the trees and wildlife with stunning views up to the house and the new garden aviary.

44 ◆ THE QUARRY GARDEN
Mill Hill, Baginton CV8 3AG. Russells Nurseries, www.russellsgardencentre.co.uk. *2m S Coventry centre. ¼ m from Lunt Roman Fort, opp Old Mill PH.* **Adm £3, chd free. 1 Feb-24 Dec. For NGS: Suns & Mons 3, 4, 24, 25 May (10.30-4.30).**
Stunning 6-acre quarry garden with a 35ft rock face. Ponds and rock features amongst a beautiful collection of magnolias and camellias followed by a blaze of colour with azaleas and rhododendrons amongst oaks, crategus, birches, conifers, heathers. Come and seek the centre of a mixed hedge maze adjacent to the quarry. Fun for all ages. Limited wheelchair access.

45 ◆ RAGLEY HALL GARDENS
Alcester B49 5NJ. **Marquess & Marchioness of Hertford, 07917 425664,** rossbarbour@ragleyhall.com. *2m SW of Alcester. Off A435/A46 8m from Stratford-upon-Avon.* **For opening times & prices see website or phone. For NGS: Sun 8 Feb (11-3) £3, chd free; Sat 3 Oct (10-6) £5, chd £5; Sun 7 Feb 2010 (11-3) £4, chd free.**
24 acres of gardens, predominantly mature broadleaved trees, within which a variety of cultivated and non-cultivated areas have been blended to achieve a garden rich in both horticulture and bio-diversity. The winter garden, spring meadows and

bulbs make way for summer meadows, herbaceous borders, annual bedding and new rose garden development providing a rich tapestry of colour and contrast all yr. 3 Oct children's playpark & café.

46 NEW 8 RECTORY ROAD
Solihull B91 3RP. **Nigel & Daphne Carter.** *Town centre. From M42 J5 follow town centre. 1st L after St Alphage Church.* Cream teas & wine. **Adm £2.50, chd free. Sun 19 July (12-5).**
Stunning town garden divided into areas. Unusual decking area surrounded by English country plants, steps to exotic area with summerhouse, on to the vegetables and a quiet pond. Places to sit. Unusual plants throughout the garden.

Group opening

47 SIR JOHNS GARDENS
B29 7EP. *S Birmingham. Off A441 nr Selly Park Tavern.* Home-made teas. **Combined adm £3.50, chd free. Sun 12 July (12-5).**
3 gardens with interesting features, created by 3 plantaholics.

SECRET GARDEN
73 Sir Johns Road. Mrs Carol Dockery
Tropical cordylines, banana, washitonia palms, rare yucca - on different levels leading to sun house with a Moroccan feel. To be featured in 'Amateur Gardening'.

47 SIR JOHNS ROAD
Julie & Steve Cray, sprca.org.uk
150x22ft. Side has seating and shade loving plants, patio with pot plants through to lawned area with cottage garden feel, pergola over agaves and succulents, arch through to area with exotic plants.

61 SIR JOHNS ROAD
Graham Allen
English natural organic garden with interesting plants, scree bed, pond, patios, range of pots and shrubs.

SOUTH KILWORTH GARDENS
See Leicestershire & Rutland.

Group opening

48 THE STABLES SELLY PARK
B29 7JW. *2m SW Birmingham. From A38 take Eastern Rd, R into Selly Wick Rd - which is also off A441. Park in rd.* Home-made teas at no 9. **Combined adm £3, chd free (share to St Marys Hospice). Sun 5 July (2-6).**
3 small interesting and different S and W facing gardens leading off a secluded private driveway in a peaceful mature woodland setting (designated Nature Conservation area) all landscaped and planted from 'building sites' since 1994.

3 THE STABLES
Mark Kenchington
Open plan front and secluded walled rear garden with over 150 different ornamental and flowering shrubs, trees, perennials and alpines. Lawn and patio with colourful pots and baskets, small kitchen garden with raised beds.

5 THE STABLES
Francis & Kate Peart
With woodland on its SE border, this compact and partially shaded garden was designed for low maintenance, featuring terracotta fountain, pots and a small pond for wildlife.

9 THE STABLES
Jeff & Heather Bissenden
Front garden recently landscaped with rockery, heathers, sunny and shady areas. Walled rear contains vegetables, ornamental shrubs and woodland, patio pots and hanging baskets containing a variety of pelargoniums.

Winner of Coventry Evening Telegraph Garden of the Year 2008 . . .

49 STONELEIGH HOUSE
17a Wentworth Road, Four Oaks Park B74 2SD. Richard & Gillian Mason. *1½ m N Sutton Coldfield on A5127. L at Four Oaks Station, 500yds on L.* Home-made teas. **Adm £3, chd free. Sun 14 June (1-5).**
½ -acre, mixed beds and borders with mature trees and rhododendrons. Ornamental and wildlife pond, raised beds vegetable plot, various pots and planters. Front garden wild flower meadow.

Group opening

50 STYVECHALE GARDEN TRAIL
Stivichall CV3 5BE. *From A45 take B4113, Leamington Road, towards Coventry. 2nd R into Baginton Road. The Chesils is 1st L.* Cream teas. **Combined adm £3, chd free (share to Myton Hospice). Sun 14 June (11-6).**
Maps at all gardens & St Thomas More's Church.

AVONDALE NURSERY
Mr Brian Ellis
(See separate entry).

59 THE CHESILS
John Marron & Richard Bantock
A modern take on a cottage garden where plants jostle and bustle for attention.

91 THE CHESILS
Graham & Pat White
A plantsman's garden designed as a series of rooms incl water, gravel and wildlife. The garden is bursting and brimming with unusual plants.

16 DELAWARE ROAD
Val & Roy Howells
Structural plants such as phormiums, bamboos and palms are imaginatively planted with herbaceous plants, acers and ferns in a garden that has the 'wow' factor.

2 THE HIRON
Sue & Graham Pountney
A series of ponds and stream run through this garden and are complemented with rich and fascinating planting. A serene garden for contemplation.

SMITHY COTTAGE
Jane & Peter Woodward
Winner of Coventry Evening Telegraph Garden of the Year 2008. This chocolate box garden with perennial borders, kitchen garden, pond and summerhouse terrace provides the perfect setting for a C17 cottage and blacksmith's forge.

21 STAMFORD AVENUE
Jan Cooper
A growing and impressive collection of heucheras is just one of the delights of this mature suburban garden.

6 TOWNSEND CROFT
Jean & John Garrison
Deep richly planted herbaceous borders that take your breath away. Mature trees, water features and a secret hidden garden. Heavenly.

Group opening

51 TANWORTH-IN-ARDEN GARDENS
B94 5EA. *9m S of Birmingham, between A435 & A3400. Just off B4101.* Home-made teas. **Combined adm £5, chd free (share to St Mary Magdalene Church). Sat 16, Sun 17 May (2-6).**
Lovely village with an interesting church.

ELMHURST
Vicarage Hill. Mr & Mrs Richard Lockwood
(See separate entry).

FAIRLAWNS
Mr & Mrs Ward
A garden of two halves; conifers, shrubs, ferns, hostas; gravel, slate, pebbles, water features with rock plants and other planting.

NEW KEWSTOKE
Mr & Mrs Mike Colyer
Approx 1 acre with extensive lawns, mature pines, sunken garden, shrubbery, rhododendrons, herbaceous border, courtyard, water feature.

THE SPINNEY
Mr & Mrs John Palmer
1/2 -acre garden on 3 sides, many mature trees, wide variety of shrubs incl rhododendrons, azaleas, camellias and magnolias in spring. 2 water features, sculptures and many plants in pots.

 ♿ ✖

Try the new human sundial . . .

THORPE LUBENHAM HALL
See Leicestershire & Rutland.

52 91 TOWER ROAD
B75 5EQ. Heather & Gary Hawkins, 0121 323 2561, heatherhawkins@talktalk.net. 3m N Sutton Coldfield. From A5127 at Mere Green Island, turn into Mere Green Rd, L at St James, L again. Cream teas. Adm £2.50, chd free. Sun 21 June (1.30-5.30). Visitors also welcome by appt, small groups, June & July.
163ft mature garden with curved borders and island beds, mixed shrubs and perennials thrive in this S-facing garden. Fish pond, rockery, vegetable plot and unusual cast iron water feature all provide additional interest and an ideal garden for both restful contemplation and hide and seek.

✖ ♿ ☕ ☏

53 ◆ UPTON HOUSE & GARDENS
Banbury OX15 6HT. The National Trust, 01295 670266, www.nationaltrust.org.uk. 7m NW of Banbury. On A422, 1m S of Edgehill. House & Garden Adm £8.90, chd £4.40. Garden only £5.25, chd £2.60. Mar-Oct, Sat-Wed (11-5). For NGS: Sat 18 July (11-5).
Extensive valley gardens with elements from medieval through to 1930s. Cascading terraces of colourful borders descend to a rare kitchen garden, with pools and a bog garden in the valley below. National Collection of Asters splendid in the autumn. Wide lawns surround house famous for an internationally important collection of fine art and porcelain. Garden tours.

✖ ♿ NCCPG ☕

WALTON GARDENS
See Leicestershire & Rutland.

Group opening

54 WARMINGTON VILLAGE GARDENS
OX17 1BY. 5m NW of Banbury. Off B4100. Home-made teas. Combined adm £4, chd free (share to Air Ambulance & Warmington Church). Sun 14 June (1-6).
A heritage and direction map given to all visitors to take you around this small charming village situated on the edge of the Cotswolds only a few miles from where the famous Battle of Edge Hill took place. The warm Hornton Stone Manor and houses are enhanced by the very varied and interesting gardens both large and small.

✖ ♿ ☕

3 COURT CLOSE
Mr & Mrs C J Crocker
Terraced garden with pockets of interest and lots of seating. Mixed planting for through the year colour with many aromatic plants. Water features incl spring fed well, mixed surfaces, patios with container planting, alpine bed. Sculptures by owner throughout the garden.

♿

THE MANOR HOUSE
Mr & Mrs G Lewis
Large garden, fruit and vegetable plot, flower beds, knot garden, topiary and box hedging.

♿

OLD MANOR COTTAGE
Mrs R Andrea
Cottage garden with wisteria archway. Water feature, mixed borders, quiet seating areas and terraced herb garden.

OLD RECTORY FARMHOUSE
Mr & Mrs J Deakin
1/3 -acre, still under re-development. Walled garden with mixed borders, small woodland walk, grassed area with ornamental trees. New for 2009, small greenhouse, extended paving, patio with tubs. No wheelchair access to woodland, some gravel.

♿

1 RECTORY CLOSE
Mrs J Adams
A garden that wraps around the house with beech hedge, stone wall, mature trees and shrubs, vegetable patch, 3 fruit trees, fruit cage and enclosed garden. Floral border and fully stocked fish pond.

SPRINGFIELD HOUSE
Jenny & Roger Handscombe, jenny.handscombe@virgin.net. Visitors also welcome by appt for small groups.
Interesting house (1539) set in 1/2 acre, very informal country garden.

♿ ♻ ☏

WESTERING
Mr & Mrs R Neale
Attractive 1/2 -acre garden with herbaceous borders stocked with many interesting and unusual plants, vegetable plot, pond and chickens.

♿ ♿

1 THE WHEELWRIGHTS
Ms E Bunn
Very small terraced walled garden with mixed surfaces, Hornton stone retaining walls and steps. Mostly shrubs, grasses and ferns with specimen fastigiate yews and ornamental vine. No gnomes! Steps, uneven surfaces.

2 THE WHEELWRIGHTS
Mrs C Hunter
Very small walled garden laid to grass, paving, flower beds and containers. Traditional planting of perennials. Steps, uneven surfaces.

Group opening

55 WHICHFORD & ASCOTT GARDENS
CV36 5PQ. 6m SE of Shipston on Stour. Turn E off A3400 at Long Compton for Whichford. Home-made teas served adjacent to Church. Combined adm £4, chd free. Sun 21 June (2-6).
Enjoy a stroll around two peaceful stone villages on the edge of the Cotswolds with C13 church, pottery and inn. Featured in 'Open Gardens of Hokkaido, Japan'.

♿ ☕

ASCOTT LODGE
Charlotte Copley
Beautiful views, lawns sloping down to pond, well stocked shrub borders, courtyard garden. Many interesting plants. Gravel paths.

✖

BROOK HOLLOW
John & Shirley Round
Terraced hillside garden with large variety of trees, shrubs and plants, stream and water features. Try the new human sundial and

competition for children. Wheelchair access to lower garden only.

THE OLD HOUSE
Terry & Barbara Maher
Undulating, softly planted gardens spilling down through mature trees and shrubs to wildlife ponds. Gravel paths.

THE OLD RECTORY
Peter & Caroline O'Kane
Informal garden structured around ponds and streams with interesting borders.

✗

SEPTEMBER HOUSE
Joan Clayton
Secluded peaceful garden, in full colour in June, with roses and other interesting plants.

NEW WHICHFORD HOUSE
Bridget & Simon Herrtage
Established garden recently replanted with new borders amidst mature trees and with glorious views of Brailes Hill. Finalist of 'Country Life' Best Parsonage Competition. Steep steps, gravel paths.

THE WHICHFORD POTTERY
Jim & Dominique Keeling,
www.whichfordpottery.com
Secret walled garden, unusual plants, large vegetable garden and rambling cottage garden. Adjoins the pottery and shop. Chelsea 2008 display award. Some narrow paths and steps.

56 WITS END
59 Tanworth Lane, Shirley B90 4DQ. Sue Mansell, 0121 744 4337, suemansell@talktsalk.net. *2m SW of Solihull. Take B4102 from Solihull, 2m. R at island onto A34. After next island (Sainsbury's) Tanworth Lane is 1st L off A34.* Home-made teas. **Adm £2, chd free.** Sun 9 Aug (2-5). Visitors also welcome by appt from June to Aug for groups of 10+.
Interesting all-yr-round plantaholic's cottage-style garden. Hundreds of perennials, alpines and shrubs, many rare and unusual in various shaped beds (some colour co-ordinated) and a spectacular late summer border. Gravel area, alpine sinks, rockery, extensive shade and small waterfall, river and bog. Millennium Wheel of sleepers and crazy paving in woodland setting.

❀ ☕ ☎

57 WOODBROOKE QUAKER STUDY CENTRE
1046 Bristol Road, Selly Oak B29 6LJ, www.woodbrooke.org.uk. *4m SW of Birmingham. On A38 Bristol Rd, S of Selly Oak, opp Witherford Way.* Light refreshments & teas. **Adm £3, chd £1.50.** Sun 21 June (2.30-5.30). 10 acres of organically-managed garden and grounds. Grade II listed former home of George Cadbury (not open). Herbaceous and shrub borders, walled garden with herb garden, potager and cutting beds, Chinese garden, orchard, arboretum, Victorian boat house, lake and extensive woodland walks. Very fine variety of trees. Craft stalls, boating on lake, bouncy castle.

& ✗ 🛏 ☕

58 WOODPECKERS
The Bank, Marlcliff, nr Bidford-on-Avon B50 4NT. Drs Andy & Lallie Cox, 01789 773416, andrewcox@doctors.org.uk. *7m SW of Stratford-upon-Avon. Off B4085 between Bidford-on-Avon & Cleeve Prior.* Visitors welcome by appt all year.
Peaceful 2½-acre plantsman's country garden designed and maintained by garden-mad owners since 1965. A garden for all seasons. Unusual plants, hidden surprises, interesting trees, colour-themed borders, potager and knot garden. Wooden sculptures of St Fiacre and The Green Man carved by the owner. Lovely garden buildings of framed green oak. Featured in 'Country Life'.

& ✗ ☎

59 WOOTTON GRANGE
Pettiford Lane, Henley-in-Arden B95 6AH. Mrs Jean Tarmey, 01564 792592. *1m E of Henley-in-Arden. Take 1st R off A4189 Warwick Rd on to Pettiford Lane, garden is 300yds on R. From A3400 in Wootton Wawen turn by craft centre on to Pettiford Lane, garden 1m on L.* Light refreshments & teas. **Adm £2.50, chd free (share to Air Ambulance).** Sun 8 Mar (10.30-3.30). Visitors also welcome by appt all year.
Early Victorian farmhouse (not open) surrounded by 1-acre country garden noted for snowdrops and hellebores in the spring. Wide variety of unusual plants for yr-round interest incl clematis, roses and alpines, ornamental grasses, vegetables and bog garden.

& ❀ ☕ ☎

Undulating, softly planted gardens spilling down . . .

Warwickshire and part of the West Midlands Volunteers

County Organiser, Warwickshire
Julia Sewell, Dinsdale House, Baldwins Lane, Upper Tysoe, Warwick CV35 0TX, 01295 680234, sewelljulia@btinternet.com

County Organiser, West Midlands
Jackie Harvey, Ashover, 25 Burnett Road, Streetly, Sutton Coldfield B74 3EL, 0121 353 0547

County Treasurer, Warwickshire
John Wilson, Victoria House, Farm Street, Harbury, Leamington Spa CV33 9LR, 01926 612572

County Treasurer, West Midlands
Martin Harvey, Ashover, 25 Burnett Road, Streetly, Sutton Coldfield B74 3EL, 0121 353 0547

Assistant County Organisers
Mary Lesinski, The Master's House, Lord Leycester Hospital, High Street, Warwick CV34 4BH, 01926 499918, lordleycester@btinternet.com
Janet Neale, Westering, The Green, Warmington, Banbury OX17 1BU, 01295 690515
Peter Pashley, Millstones, Mayfield Avenue, Stratford-upon-Avon CV37 6XB, 01789 294932, peter@peterpash.mail.co.uk

WILTSHIRE

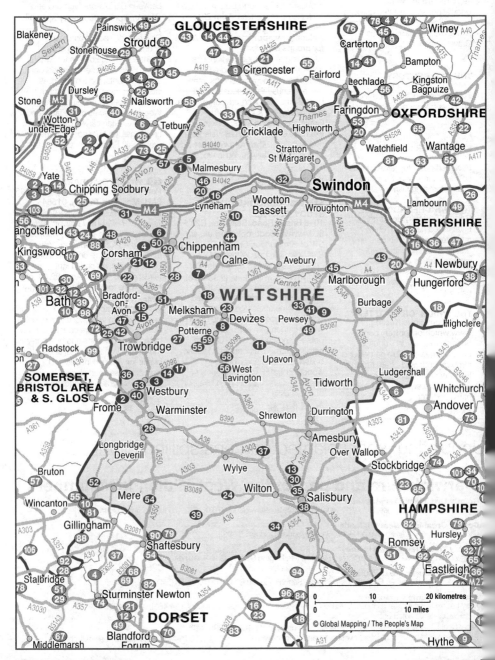

Opening Dates

February

SUNDAY 1
19 Great Chalfield Manor

SATURDAY 7
28 Lacock Abbey Gardens

SUNDAY 8
28 Lacock Abbey Gardens

SATURDAY 14
28 Lacock Abbey Gardens

SUNDAY 15
28 Lacock Abbey Gardens

March

SUNDAY 15
1 Abbey House Gardens

SUNDAY 29
37 The Mill House

April

WEDNESDAY 1
49 Sharcott Manor

SUNDAY 5
12 Corsham Court
47 Priory House
48 Ridleys Cheer
49 Sharcott Manor

SUNDAY 12
31 Littleton Drew Gardens

MONDAY 13
31 Littleton Drew Gardens

SUNDAY 19
8 Broadleas Gardens Charitable Trust
9 Broomsgrove Lodge
41 Oare House

FRIDAY 24
38 Mompesson House

SUNDAY 26
25 Iford Manor
30 Little Durnford Manor
40 Oak Tree Cottage
53 30 Tower Hill
55 Wellaway

May

SUNDAY 3
54 Waterdale House

WEDNESDAY 6
49 Sharcott Manor

SUNDAY 10
7 Bowood Rhododendron Walks

WEDNESDAY 13
18 Enfield

THURSDAY 14
18 Enfield

SATURDAY 16
15 The Courts
56 West Lavington Manor

SUNDAY 17
4 Biddestone Manor
11 Conock Manor
33 Manor Farm
48 Ridleys Cheer

WEDNESDAY 20
18 Enfield

THURSDAY 21
18 Enfield

SUNDAY 24
24 Hyde's House

WEDNESDAY 27
18 Enfield

THURSDAY 28
18 Enfield

FRIDAY 29
58 Windmill Cottage

June

WEDNESDAY 3
18 Enfield
49 Sharcott Manor

THURSDAY 4
18 Enfield

SATURDAY 6
14 Court Lane Farm

SUNDAY 7
10 33 Calne Road
12 Corsham Court
14 Court Lane Farm
17 Edington Gardens
50 Sheldon Manor

MONDAY 8
35 Mawarden Court

WEDNESDAY 10
10 33 Calne Road
18 Enfield

THURSDAY 11
18 Enfield

FRIDAY 12
58 Windmill Cottage

SATURDAY 13
34 Manor House
45 Poulton House

SUNDAY 14
6 Bolehyde Manor
13 The Court House
16 Dauntsey Gardens
22 Hazelbury Manor Gardens
27 Keevil Gardens

33 Manor Farm
42 The Old Malthouse
44 The Old Vicarage
46 The Pound House
47 Priory House
48 Ridleys Cheer
51 32 Shurnhold

WEDNESDAY 17
18 Enfield

THURSDAY 18
18 Enfield

SATURDAY 20
20 Great Somerford Gardens

SUNDAY 21
20 Great Somerford Gardens
21 Guyers House
26 Job's Mill
30 Little Durnford Manor

WEDNESDAY 24
18 Enfield

THURSDAY 25
18 Enfield
43 The Old Mill

FRIDAY 26
58 Windmill Cottage

SATURDAY 27
3 Beggars Knoll
37 The Mill House

SUNDAY 28
3 Beggars Knoll
37 The Mill House
39 North Cottage & Woodview Cottage (Day & Evening)
59 Worton Gardens

July

WEDNESDAY 1
49 Sharcott Manor

SATURDAY 4
39 North Cottage & Woodview Cottage

SUNDAY 5
5 Blicks Hill House

FRIDAY 10
58 Windmill Cottage

SATURDAY 11
2 Barters Nurseries

SUNDAY 12
47 Priory House
57 Whatley Manor

SATURDAY 18
52 Stourhead Garden

FRIDAY 24
51 32 Shurnhold (Evening)
58 Windmill Cottage

SUNDAY 26

(29) 130 Ladyfield Road and Hungerdown Allotments

August

SUNDAY 2

(32) Lydiard Park Walled Garden
(41) Oare House

WEDNESDAY 5

(49) Sharcott Manor

SUNDAY 16

(36) The Mead Nursery

FRIDAY 21

(44) The Old Vicarage

September

WEDNESDAY 2

(49) Sharcott Manor

SUNDAY 6

(49) Sharcott Manor

WEDNESDAY 9

(34) Manor House

SUNDAY 13

(55) Wellaway

FRIDAY 18

(51) 32 Shurnhold (Evening)

SATURDAY 19

(15) The Courts

January 2010

SUNDAY 31

(19) Great Chalfield Manor

February

SATURDAY 13

(28) Lacock Abbey Gardens

SUNDAY 14

(28) Lacock Abbey Gardens

SATURDAY 20

(28) Lacock Abbey Gardens

SUNDAY 21

(28) Lacock Abbey Gardens

Gardens open to the public

(1) Abbey House Gardens
(2) Barters Nurseries
(7) Bowood Rhododendron Walks
(8) Broadleas Gardens Charitable Trust
(12) Corsham Court
(15) The Courts
(19) Great Chalfield Manor
(25) Iford Manor
(28) Lacock Abbey Gardens
(32) Lydiard Park Walled Garden
(36) The Mead Nursery
(37) The Mill House
(38) Mompesson House
(50) Sheldon Manor
(52) Stourhead Garden
(54) Waterdale House

By appointment only

(23) Home Covert Gardens & Arboretum

Also open by appointment ☎

(3) Beggars Knoll
(4) Biddestone Manor
(5) Blicks Hill House
(6) Bolehyde Manor
(14) Court Lane Farm
(18) Enfield
(34) Manor House
(39) North Cottage & Woodview Cottage
(40) Oak Tree Cottage
(42) The Old Malthouse
(45) Poulton House
(46) The Pound House
(48) Ridleys Cheer
(49) Sharcott Manor
(51) 32 Shurnhold
(53) 30 Tower Hill
(58) Windmill Cottage

The Gardens

(1) ◆ ABBEY HOUSE GARDENS

Malmesbury Town Centre SN16 9AS. Barbara & Ian Pollard, 01666 827650, www.abbeyhousegardens.co.uk. *5m N of J17 M4. Beside C12 Abbey. Parking in town centre (short stay) or follow brown signs to long stay (via steps to gardens).* **Adm £6.50, chd £2.50, concessions £5.75. 21 Mar to 31 Oct incl. For NGS: Sun 15 Mar (11-5.30).**

5 beautiful acres planted by present owner. Over 130,000 spring bulbs especially tulips, 'medieval' herb garden, topiary, knot garden, herbaceous borders, laburnum walk. UK's largest private collection of roses (over 2000), unique auricula theatre, ornamental trees, rare plants, wooded walk to river, 'monastic' fish ponds, waterfall and fernery. Colour, peace and contrast.

♿ 🐕 ❀ ☕

See the spring in our peaceful 8 acres . . .

(2) NEW ◆ BARTERS NURSERIES

Chapmanslade BA13 4AL. Mr & Mrs Legh Walker, 01373 832512, www.barters.co.uk. *3m N of Warminster. On A3098, 1m from A36. From Frome take A3098 to Chapmanslade.* **Adm £3, chd free. Plant Centre open all year, phone or visit website for details. For NGS: Sat 11 July (12-5.30).**

A rare opportunity to look round this 10-acre shrub and perennial nursery. Guided tours at 12, 2 and 4pm lasting 1 hr. Meet the growers and find out more about commercial horticulture.

🐕 ❀ ☕

BATH PRIORY HOTEL

See Somerset & Bristol.

(3) BEGGARS KNOLL

Newtown. BA13 3ED. Colin Little & Penny Stirling, 01373 823383. *1m SE of Westbury. Turn off B3098 at White Horse Pottery, up hill towards the White Horse for 1km. Limited parking at end of drive.* Home-made teas. **Adm £3, chd free.** Sat 27, Sun 28 June (2-6). **Visitors also welcome by appt.**

A Chinese garden on the edge of Salisbury Plain? Unlikely but true ... remind yourselves of Beijing with a visit to 3 pavilions, a moon gate, zig-zag pathways, 3 ponds and a series of garden rooms filled with Chinese plants. Extensive potager with chickens, collections of podocarps and viburnums. Spectacular views to the Mendips.

🐕 ❀ ☕ ☎

(4) BIDDESTONE MANOR

Chippenham Lane, Biddestone SN14 7DJ. Rosie Harris, Head Gardener, 01249 713211. *5m W of Chippenham. On A4 between Chippenham & Corsham turn N. From A420, 5m W of Chippenham, turn S. Use car park.* Home-made teas. **Adm £3.50, chd free.** Sun 17 May (2-5). **Visitors also welcome by appt, groups of 10+ incl coaches.**

See the spring in our peaceful 8 acres with small lake and streams, more new seedings of wild flowers, arboretum with grasses and bulbs, walled kitchen garden, orchard, cutting garden, beautiful shrub borders. C17 Manor House (not open) with ancient dovecote.

♿ 🐕 ❀ ☕ ☎

5 BLICKS HILL HOUSE

Blicks Hill, Malmesbury SN16 9HZ.
Alan & Valerie Trotman, 01666
829669. $^{1}/_{2}$ m E of Malmesbury. W of
(A429) bypass, between r'abouts.
Home-made teas. **Adm £3.50, chd
free. Sun 5 July (11.30-5).** Visitors
also welcome by appt, groups 10+
incl coaches.
Stunning, and having the 'wow' factor
is how visitors describe this garden
situated on a 1-acre stepped and
sloping site. Mature trees give a
backdrop to the colourful beds and
borders which have all been created
since 2004. Unique pergola leading to
a woodland glade, new water feature
and stream constructed in green slate,
hanging baskets, tubs and bedding
plants add extra impact. Very much a
plantsman's garden. Gradual slope.

6 BOLEHYDE MANOR

Allington SN14 6LW. The Earl &
Countess Cairns. $1^{1}/_{2}$ m W of
Chippenham. On Bristol Rd (A420).
Turn N at Allington Xrds. $^{1}/_{2}$ m on R.
Parking in field. Home-made teas.
**Adm £3.50, chd 50p (share to
Kington St Michael Church). Sun 14
June (2.30-5.30).** Visitors also
welcome by appt. Please apply in
writing, giving an email address for
confirmation.
Series of gardens around C16 manor
house (not open), enclosed by walls
and topiary, densely planted with many
interesting shrubs and climbers, mixed
rose and herbaceous beds. Inner
courtyard with troughs full of tender
plants, wild flower orchard, vegetable,
fruit garden and greenhouse yard.
Collection of tender pelargoniums,
adventure tree house for children.
Some steps.

7 ◆ BOWOOD RHODODENDRON WALKS

Chippenham SN11 9PG. The
Marquis of Lansdowne, 01249
812102, www.bowood.org. $3^{1}/_{2}$ m SE
of Chippenham. Entrance off A342
between Sandy Lane & Derry Hill
villages. **Adm £5.60, chd free,
concessions £5.10. Late Apr to early
June. For NGS: Sun 10 May (11-6).**
This 60-acre woodland garden of
azaleas and rhododendrons is one of
the most exciting of its type in the
country. From the individual flowers to
the breathtaking sweep of colour
formed by hundreds of shrubs,
surrounded by carpets of bluebells,

this is a garden not to be missed.
Planting began in 1850 and some of
the earliest known hybrids feature
among the collection. Bowood House
and Gardens a separate attraction, 2m
from Rhododendron Walks.

8 ◆ BROADLEAS GARDENS CHARITABLE TRUST

Devizes SN10 5JQ. Lady Anne
Cowdray, 01380 722035,
broadleasgardens@btinternet.com.
1m S of Devizes. On A360 or follow
tourist signs from Long Street. **Adm
£5.50, chd £2.50, groups of 10+ £5.
Mar to Oct, Suns, Weds & Thurs.
For NGS: Sun 19 Apr (2-6).**
9-acre garden, a sheltered dell planted
with many unusual trees and shrubs.
Azaleas, rhododendrons and
magnolias with underplantings of
trilliums, erythroniums and many
others. Herbaceous borders and
perennial garden full of interesting
plants.

9 BROOMSGROVE LODGE

New Mill, Pewsey SN9 5LE. Diana
Robertson. 2m E of Pewsey. From
A345 take B3087 Burbage Rd, after
$1^{1}/_{2}$ m L to New Mill, through village
and past canal. Park in field. Light
refreshments & teas. **Adm £3, chd
free. Sun 19 Apr (2-6). Also open
Oare House.**
Alongside stunning views of Martinsell
Hill discover the imaginatively planted
herbaceous borders, large vegetable
garden, greenhouse and tunnel.
Sunken terrace full of vibrantly planted
pots and a 4-acre field to wander
around to admire the views.

10 33 CALNE ROAD

Lyneham SN15 4PT. Sue & Sam
Wright. 7m N of Calne. Next to RAF
Lyneham entrance. Home-made
teas. **Adm £2, chd 50p. Sun 7,
Wed 10 June (1-5).**
Approx $^{3}/_{4}$ -acre informal garden
comprising modest collection of
hostas, clematis and roses. Small
kitchen garden, pond and mature
orchard with bantams, chickens,
geese, doves and dovecote. Green
oasis surrounded by activity.

CHIFFCHAFFS
See Dorset.

CONHOLT PARK
See Hampshire.

Mature trees give a backdrop to the colourful beds and borders . . .

11 CONOCK MANOR

Chirton SN10 3QQ. Mrs Bonar
Sykes. 5m SE of Devizes. Off A342.
Cream teas. **Adm £3, chd free (share
to Chirton Church). Sun 17 May
(2-6).**
Mixed borders, flowering shrubs,
extensive replanting incl new
arboretum, interesting decorative
brickwork with tiled water runnels to
replace old borders. C18 house in
Bath stone (not open). Trees of interest
incl Liriodendron tulipifera, Zelkova,
Catalpa and many different magnolias.
Some gravel paths.

12 ◆ CORSHAM COURT

Corsham SN13 0BZ. Mr James
Methuen-Campbell, 01249 701610,
www.corsham-court.co.uk. 4m W of
Chippenham. S of A4. **House &
Garden £7, chd £3, concessions £6.
Garden only £2.50, chd £2,
concessions £1.50. Phone or visit
website for details. For NGS: Suns
5 Apr; 7 June (2-5.30).**
Park and gardens laid out by Capability
Brown and Repton. Large lawns with
fine specimens of ornamental trees
surround the Elizabethan mansion.
C18 bath house hidden in the grounds.
Spring bulbs, beautiful lily pond with
Indian bean trees, young arboretum
and stunning collection of magnolias.

13 THE COURT HOUSE

Lower Woodford SP4 6NQ. Mr &
Mrs J G Studholme. 3m N of
Salisbury. On Woodford Valley rd,
parallel to A360 & A345. Home-made
teas. **Adm £3, chd free. Sun 14 June
(2-6).**
$3^{1}/_{2}$ -acre garden on the banks of the
Avon. Herbaceous borders, waterside
planting, yew hedges, rambler roses
and wild flowers. Ancient site of
Bishop's Palace in the time of Old
Sarum.

14 COURT LANE FARM
Bratton BA13 4RE. Lt Col & Mrs
Anthony Hyde, 01380 830364. *2m E
of Westbury*. Off B3098. Home-made
teas. **Adm £3, chd free. Sat 6, Sun 7
June (12-6). Visitors also welcome
by appt.**
Cottage garden of 1 acre, informal,
mature and full of interest with
numerous rooms. Garden objects, incl
rural items, shepherd's hut,
contemporary sculpture and pottery.
Rambling and climbing roses tumble
over arches and banks. 80 varieties of
hardy geraniums, topiary and wildlife
pond.

15 ♦ THE COURTS
Holt BA14 6RR. The National Trust,
01225 782875,
courtsgarden@nationaltrust.org.uk.
*2m E of Bradford-on-Avon. S of B3107
to Melksham. In Holt follow NT signs,
park at village hall.* **Adm £6, chd £3.
14 Mar-1 Nov daily (excl Wed). For
NGS: Sats 16 May; 19 Sept (11-
5.30).**
Beautifully kept but eclectic garden.
Yew hedges divide garden
compartments with colour themed
borders and organically shaped
topiary. Water garden with 2 recently
restored pools, temple, conservatory
and small kitchen garden split by an
apple allée, all surrounded by 3½ acres
of arboretum with specimen trees.
Wheelchair access map at reception.

CROWE HALL
See Somerset & Bristol.

Group opening

16 DAUNTSEY GARDENS
SN15 4HW. *5m SE of Malmesbury.
Approach via Dauntsey Rd from Gt
Somerford, 1¼ m from Volunteer Inn.*
Home-made teas. **Combined adm
£5, chd free. Sun 14 June (1.30-5).**
Group of gardens centred around
historic Dauntsey Park Estate.

THE COACH HOUSE
Col & Mrs J Seddon-Brown
Small walled garden with thyme
terrace and gazebos, climbing
roses and clematis on walls. Mixed
borders of herbaceous plants and
shrubs. Mop-headed pruned
crataegus prunifolia line the drive. A
quiet and secluded spot.

NEW DAUNTSEY PARK
Mr & Mrs Giovanni Amati
Classical C18 country house
setting with views over the R Avon.
Spacious lawns with wonderful
mature trees in the shadow of St
James The Great Church.

THE GARDEN COTTAGE
Miss Ann Sturgis
Traditional walled kitchen garden
with organically grown vegetables,
yew topiary, apple orchard and
woodland walk.

IDOVER HOUSE
Mr & Mrs Christopher Jerram
Large mature country house
garden with glorious lawns and
mature trees and hedges incl 2
lofty wellingtonias. Formal
symmetrical rose garden in pink
and white, old fashioned borders,
duck ponds and kitchen garden.

THE OLD POND HOUSE
Mr & Mrs Stephen Love
2 acres clipped and unclipped!
Large pond with lilies and fat carp,
giraffe and turtle. Views across
Dauntsey Park.

DYRHAM PARK
See Somerset & Bristol.

Woodland
plants, bulbs
and lilies . . .
National
Collection of
evening
primroses,
with over
20 species . . .

Group opening

17 EDINGTON GARDENS
BA13 4QF. *4m NE of Westbury. On
B3098 between Westbury & West
Lavington. Park off B3098 in church
car park, in Monastery Rd opp
Monastery Garden House, or in car
park nr junction of B3098 and
Monastery Rd.* Home-made teas in
Parish Hall. **Combined adm £5, chd
free. Sun 7 June (2-6).**
Village map given to all visitors.

BECKETTS HOUSE
Mr & Mrs David Bromhead
An old 2½ -acre garden with varied
established hedges
compartmentalising the garden.
Borders, lawns, rockery, rose
garden, vegetable and fruit garden,
lake and lovely views. Gravel drive.

BONSHOMMES COTTAGE
Mr Michael Jones. *Through Old
Vicarage garden to avoid steep
steps*
¼ -acre hillside garden with mixed
herbaceous, roses, shrubs. Some
long-established Japanese
knotweed has been retained as a
practical feature.

THE MONASTERY GARDEN
Mr & Mrs Allanson-Bailey
2½ -acre garden with many
varieties of spring bulbs and shrub
roses, 3-acre additional walled
garden, medieval walls of national
importance.

THE OLD VICARAGE
Mr J N d'Arcy
2-acre garden on greensand on
hillside with fine views. Intensively
planted with herbaceous borders,
wall borders, gravel garden and
shrubs. Arboretum with growing
range of unusual trees. Woodland
plants, bulbs and lilies, with
recently introduced species from
abroad. National Collection of
evening primroses, with over
20 species.

NEW THE PLOUGH
Mr & Mrs N J Buckman
A well-stocked garden on 4 levels
with emphasis on shrubs
interspersed with perennials incl a
dwarf conifer bed and camomile
lawn the size of a handkerchief.

Rose hoops, climbing and shrub roses . . .

18 ENFIELD
62 Yard Lane, Netherstreet, Bromham SN15 2DT. Graham & Elizabeth Veals, 01380 859303, enfieldgarden@talktalk.net. *4m NW of Devizes. E off A342 into Yard Lane, garden 1/4 m on R. Limited parking.* Light refreshments & teas. **Adm £2.50, chd free. Every Weds & Thurs, 13 May to 25 June; (11-4.30).** Visitors also welcome by appt.
The cottage garden style of planting combines old favourites with many plants not commonly seen in gardens today. The 1/2 acre incl 4 separate areas and over 550 species and cultivars of herbaceous plants incl a significant collection of foxgloves planted in the last 3 yrs.

GANTS MILL & GARDEN
See Somerset & Bristol.

GILBERTS NURSERY
See Hampshire.

19 ◆ GREAT CHALFIELD MANOR
Melksham SN12 8NH. Mr & Mrs R Floyd & The National Trust, 01225 782239, patsy@greatchalfield.co.uk. *3m SW of Melksham. Take B3107 from Melksham then 1st R to Broughton Gifford. Follow sign for Atworth, turn L for 1m to Manor. Park on grass outside.* **Adm £3.50, chd free. Tues, Weds, Thurs & Suns Apr to end Oct, Suns 2-5, weekdays 11-5. House tours available, please phone or email for details. For NGS: Sun 1 Feb (2-4.30); Sun 31 Jan 2010. Adm charge also applies for NT Members on NGS days.**
Garden and grounds of 7 acres laid out 1905-12 by Robert Fuller and his wife to Arts and Crafts designs by Alfred Parsons, Capt Partridge and Sir Harold Brakspear. Incl roses, daffodils, spring flowers, topiary houses, borders, terraces, gazebo, orchard, autumn border. C15 moated manor (not open) and adjoining Parish Church. Snowdrops and aconites enhance the moat walk.

Group opening

20 GREAT SOMERFORD GARDENS
SN15 5JB. *4m SE of Malmesbury. 4m N of M4 between J16 & J17; 2m S of B4042 Malmesbury to Wootton Bassett rd; 3m E of A429 Cirencester to Chippenham rd.* Teas at The Mount House. **Combined adm £4, chd free. Sat 20, Sun 21 June (1.30-5.30).**
Medium-sized village, bordered by R Avon, with thriving community, school, pub, post office and general stores. Also has possibly the oldest allotments in the country which are well used. River walk.

CLEMATIS
Dauntsey Road. Mr & Mrs Arthur Scott
Small but active, charming village garden created about 20yrs ago. Very well stocked herbaceous borders, shrubs, fruit trees and a pond, with small collection of approx 20 clematis.

1 HOLLOW STREET
Bridget Smith
1/4 acre, next door to Old Maltings. Lilies, penstemons and other assorted perennials.

THE MOUNT HOUSE
Park Lane. Mr & Mrs McGrath
3 acres of lawns, herbaceous beds, shrubs, large trees, fruit and vegetables. Ancient motte area has been sympathetically replanted and meanders to the R Avon. Historic barn open.

SOMERFORD HOUSE
West Street. Mr & Mrs Martin Jones
3-acre garden developed over the last 29yrs which incorporates the original orchard and features roses, shrubs, old wisteria, perennials, rockery and pool, vegetables and soft fruit.

21 GUYERS HOUSE
Pickwick, Corsham SN13 0PS. Mr & Mrs Guy Hungerford. *4m SW of Chippenham. Guyers Lane signed directly off A4 opp B3109 Bradford-on-Avon turning.* **Adm £3, chd free. Sun 21 June (2-5.30).**
6-acre garden. Herbaceous borders,

yew walks, pleached hornbeam walk. Extensive lawns, ponds, walled garden, rose hoops, climbing and shrub roses, walled kitchen garden, orchard, herb garden. Gravel paths, garden can be viewed from grass paths.

22 HAZELBURY MANOR GARDENS
Wadswick, Box SN13 8HX. *5m SW of Chippenham, 5m NE of Bath. From A4 at Box, A365 to Melksham, at Five Ways junction L onto B3109, 1st L, drive immed on R.* Light refreshments & teas. **Adm £5, chd free. Sun 14 June (2-6).**
8 acres Grade II landscaped organic gardens around C15 fortified manor (not open). Impressive yew topiary and clipped beeches around large lawn, herbaceous and mixed borders ablaze in summer, laburnum and lime walkways, rose garden, stone circle and rockery. Walled kitchen garden.

HILL LODGE
See Somerset & Bristol.

HILLTOP
See Dorset.

HODGES BARN
See Gloucestershire North & Central.

23 HOME COVERT GARDENS & ARBORETUM
Roundway SN10 2JA. Mr & Mrs John Phillips, 01380 723407. *1m N of Devizes. On minor rd signed Roundway linking A361 to A342, 1m from each main rd.* Visitors welcome by appt.
Extensive garden on greensand created out of ancient woodland since 1960. Situated below the Downs with distant views. Formal borders around the house contrast with water gardens in the valley below. Wide range of trees, shrubs and plants grown for yr-round interest. Mar/Apr camellias, magnolias, erythroniums. May/June rhododendrons, malus, davidia, many flowering trees. July/Aug hydrangeas, eucryphias. Water gardens path very steep.

HOMEWOOD PARK HOTEL
See Somerset & Bristol.

HOOKSHOUSE POTTERY
See Gloucestershire North & Central.

24 HYDE'S HOUSE
Dinton SP3 5HH. Mr George Cruddas. *9m W of Salisbury. Off B3089 nr Dinton Church.* Teas. **Adm £4, chd free.** Sun 24 May (2-5).
3 acres of wild and formal garden in beautiful situation with series of hedged garden rooms. Numerous roses and borders. Large walled kitchen garden, herb garden and C13 dovecote. Charming C16/18 Grade I listed house (not open), with lovely courtyard. NT walks around park and lake. Some gravel, some steps, some modest slopes.

> Very pretty small garden with more than 25 clematis, climbing roses and a small fish pond . . .

25 ◆ IFORD MANOR
Lower Westwood, Bradford-on-Avon BA15 2BA. Mrs Elizabeth Cartwright-Hignett, 01225 863146, www.ifordmanor.co.uk. *7m S of Bath. Off A36, brown tourist sign to Iford 1m. Or from Bradford-on-Avon or Trowbridge via Lower Westwood village (brown signs).* **Adm £4.50, chd under 10 free, concessions £4.** For NGS: Sun 26 Apr (2-5).
Very romantic award-winning, Grade I listed Italianate garden famous for its tranquil beauty. Home to the Edwardian architect and designer Harold Peto 1899-1933. The garden is characterised by steps, terraces, sculpture and magnificent rural views. House not open.

26 JOB'S MILL
Crockerton BA12 8BB. Lady Silvy McQuiston. *1½ m S of Warminster. Down lane E of A350, S of A36 roundabout.* Home-made teas. **Adm £3, chd free (share to The Woodland Trust).** Sun 21 June (2-6).
Delightful medium-sized terraced garden through which R Wylye flows. Herbaceous border and water garden.

Group opening

27 KEEVIL GARDENS
BA14 6NA. *6m E of Trowbridge, S of A361. Gardens all within walking distance, nr E end of Main St. Park in Main St or Martins Rd.* **Combined adm £3.50, chd free.** Sun 14 June (2-6).
Quiet village with unspoiled largely C14-C18 main street lined with Grade I and Grade II listed houses and Grade I listed C13/C14 church of St Leonard.

FIELDHEAD HOUSE
Peter & Janie Dixon
Garden of former vicarage set in approx 2 acres. Contains roses, clematis etc with kitchen garden, pond, small orchard, fine hedging and Italianate swimming pool area (viewable but not open). Gravel paths.

LONGLEAZE HOUSE
John & Olga Gower Isaac
C18 village farmhouse (not open). 1-acre garden developed over last 10yrs with shrubs, climbers, species roses, herbaceous perennials, bulbs etc. Children's pirate ship. Gravel paths.

KEMPSFORD MANOR
See Gloucestershire North & Central.

28 ◆ LACOCK ABBEY GARDENS
Chippenham SN15 2LG. The National Trust, 01249 730459, www.nationaltrust.org.uk. *3m S of Chippenham. Off A350. Follow NT signs. Use public car park just outside Abbey.* **Adm £3, chd free.** Grounds Mar to Oct (11-5.30), winter weekends (11-4). For further details please phone or see website. For NGS: Sats, Suns 7, 8, 14, 15 Feb (11-4); 13, 14, 20, 21 Feb 2010. Adm charge also applies for NT Members on NGS days.
Victorian woodland garden with pond, botanic garden and exotic tree specimens. Display of early spring flowers with carpets of aconites, snowdrops, crocuses and daffodils. C13 Abbey with C18 Gothick additions.

29 NEW 130 LADYFIELD ROAD AND HUNGERDOWN ALLOTMENTS
SN14 0AP. Philip & Pat Canter and Chippenham Town Council. *1m SW of Chippenham. Between A4 Bath and A420 Bristol Rds. Signed off B4528 Hungerdown Lane which runs between the A4 & A420.* Home-made teas. **Adm £2.50, chd free.** Sun 26 July (1-5.30).
Very pretty small garden with more than 25 clematis, climbing roses and a small fish pond. Curved neat edges packed with colourful herbaceous plants and small trees. 2 patio areas with lush lawn, pagoda and garden arbour. Small allotment with 14 gardens next door. Wheelchair access to main allotment path only.

30 LITTLE DURNFORD MANOR
Salisbury SP4 6AH. The Earl & Countess of Chichester. *3m N of Salisbury. Just beyond Stratford-sub-Castle.* **Adm £3, chd £1.** Suns 26 Apr; 21 June (2-6).
Extensive lawns with cedars, walled gardens, fruit trees, large vegetable garden, small knot and herb gardens. Terraces, borders, sunken garden, water garden, lake with islands, river walks, labyrinth walk. Some steep slopes & gravel but mostly accessible.

Group opening

31 LITTLETON DREW GARDENS
SN14 7LL. *6m W of Chippenham. Nr The Gibb PH on B4039. Car parking on rd to Littleton Drew and walk down to Goulters Mill, or drive/walk up to Barton Cottage.* Cream teas. **Combined adm £3.50, chd free.** Sun 12, Mon 13 Apr (2.30-5).
Contrasting pair of gardens; one in valley beside Bybrook and the other a cottage garden in the village.

BARTON COTTAGE
Littleton Drew. Beryl Willis. *Turn N off B3095, 2nd cottage on L. Park opp*
Small garden surrounding Elizabethan Cotswold cottage. Densely planted with many unusual perennials, topiary, pond with ferns

and small potager incl espalier apples, standard redcurrant and gooseberries. Over 70 different clematis.

GOULTERS MILL FARM
The Gibb. Mr & Mrs Michael Harvey. *Parking at top of 300yd drive, elderly/disabled at the Mill* 3/4 -acre garden in a steep sided valley bordered by the beginnings of the Bybrook, threaded through with gravel paths, punctuated with topiary and mounds of shrubs and underplanted with an eclectic mix of perennials and self-sown annuals, dahlias and salvias. Hellebores, tulips, anemones, daphne bholua, sarcocca, and lonicera fragrantissima and later a heady mix of delphiniums, eremurus, aconites and asters. Bluebell wood a must in May, in June and July the N side of the valley is alive with harebells, rock roses, vipers bugloss and blue butterflies if you are lucky.

   🐕 ⊗ 🛏️

32 NEW ◆ LYDIARD PARK WALLED GARDEN
Lydiard Tregoze SN5 3PA. Swindon Borough Council, 01793 770401, www.lydiardpark.org.uk. *3m W Swindon, 1m from J16 M4. Follow brown signs from W Swindon.* House & Garden £4.50, chd £2.25, concessions £4. Garden only £2.50, chd £1, concessions £2. Tues to Suns, Mar to Oct (11-5), Nov to Feb (11-4). For NGS: Sun 2 Aug (11-5). Beautiful ornamental and flower C18 walled garden. Trimmed shrubs alternating with individually planted flowers and bulbs incl rare daffodils and tulips, sweet peas, annuals and wall-trained fruit trees. Park and children's playground.

   🐕 ☕

33 MANOR FARM
Huish SN8 4JN. Mr & Mrs J Roberts. *3m NW of Pewsey. Huish is signed from A345 by White Hart PH in Oare. Follow lane for 1m into Huish, turn R by dead-end sign.* Home-made teas. Adm £3, chd free. Sun 17 May; 14 June (2-5.30). Fine downland views surround this intriguing garden which has a surprise around every corner. Ongoing design

and planting schemes create new interest each year. Wide variety of clematis and roses, pleached lime walk, woodland pond and grotto. Landscaped farmyard featuring duckpond and thatched granary. No wheelchair access around pond, some narrow paths.

   🐕 ☕

34 MANOR HOUSE
Stratford Tony SP5 4AT. Mr & Mrs H Cookson, 01722 718496, lucindacookson@care4free.net. *4m SW of Salisbury. Take minor rd W off A354 at Coombe Bissett. Garden on S after 1m.* Home-made teas. Adm £3, chd free. Sat 13 June (11-5); Wed 9 Sept (2-5). Visitors also welcome by appt. Varied 4-acre garden. Formal and informal areas, small lake fed from R Ebble, herbaceous beds with colour through to late autumn incl many salvias. Pergola-covered vegetable garden, parterre garden, orchards, shrubberies, interesting mature and newly planted trees, many original contemporary features. Sitting areas to enjoy both internal and external views.

   🐕 ⊗ ☕ 📞

MARSHFIELD GARDENS
See Somerset & Bristol.

35 MAWARDEN COURT
Stratford Road, Stratford sub Castle SP1 3LL. Mr & Mrs Colin Harris. *2m WNW Salisbury. A345 from Salisbury, L at traffic lights, opp St Lawrence Church.* Adm £3, chd free (share to Friends of St Lawrence). Mon 8 June (2.30-5.30). Recently recreated garden, rose garden approached through a pergola flanked by a herbaceous border. Path through line of white beam leading towards R Avon and a woodland path through a plantation of poplars. Redesigned small ornamental lake by Thomas Hoblin (Chelsea Gold Medallist 2008).

   🐕

MAYO FARM
See Dorset.

36 ◆ THE MEAD NURSERY
Brokerswood BA13 4EG. Mr & Mrs S Lewis-Dale, 01373 859990, www.themeadnursery.co.uk. *3m W of Westbury. E of Rudge. Follow signs for Country Park at Brokerswood. Halfway between Rudge & Country Park.* Weds to Sats (9-5), Sun (12-5)

Feb to mid Oct. For NGS: Sun 16 Aug (12-5), £3 incl tea & home-made cake. 1 1/4 -acre nursery and garden giving ideas on colour and design with herbaceous borders, raised alpine beds, sink garden and bog bed. Well-drained Mediterranean-style raised bed and small wildlife pond. Nursery with extensive range of herbaceous perennials, alpines, pot-grown bulbs and grasses in peat free compost. Variety of stalls. Featured in 'Country Garden'.

   🐕 ⊗ ☕

Rare daffodils and tulips . . .

37 ◆ THE MILL HOUSE
Berwick St James SP3 4TS. Diana Gifford Mead, 01722 790331. *8m NW of Salisbury. S of A303, N of A36, on B3083, S end of village.* Adm £3, chd free. Apr-Oct. Please phone for details. For NGS: Sun 29 Mar; Sat 27, Sun 28 June (2-6). Surrounded by the R Till, millstream and a 10-acre traditional wet water meadow, this garden of wildness supports over 200 species of old fashioned roses rambling from the many trees. It is filled with butterflies, moths and insects. Birdsong is phenomenal in spring and summer. Herbaceous borders crammed with plants of yesteryear, unforgettable scents. Glorious spring bulbs. SSSI.

   🛏️ ☕

38 ◆ MOMPESSON HOUSE
The Close, Salisbury SP1 2EL. The National Trust, 01722 335659, www.nationaltrust.org.uk. *Enter Cathedral Close via High St Gate, Mompesson House on R.* Garden adm £1.50, chd free. Sat to Wed, Mar to Nov, 11-5. For NGS: Fri 24 Apr (11-4). Adm charge also applies for NT Members on NGS days. The appeal of this comparatively small but attractive garden is the lovely setting in Salisbury Cathedral Close, with a well-known Queen Anne house. Planting as for an old English garden with raised rose and herbaceous beds around the lawn. Climbers on pergola and walls, shrubs and small lavender walk. Cake stall.

   🐕 ⊗ ☕

39 NORTH COTTAGE & WOODVIEW COTTAGE
Tisbury Row, Tisbury SP3 6RZ.
Jacqueline & Robert Baker, Diane McBride,
robert.baker@pearceseeds.co.uk.
12m W of Salisbury. From A30 turn N through Ansty, L at T-junction, towards Tisbury. From Tisbury take Ansty rd. Entrance nr junction signed Tisbury Row. Home-made teas. **Adm £2.50, chd free. Day & Evening Opening** wine, Sun 28 June (2-8); Sat 4 July (2-6). Visitors also welcome by appt.
Two cottage gardens in lovely country setting continuously changing and developing. Fruit and vegetables, greenhouses and an allotment. 4-acre small holding containing orchard, ponds and coppice wood. Perennial and annual planting provides colour and variety. Coppicing and hedgelaying practised. Water features and unique sculptures around every corner. Pottery, jewellery crafts. Lace-making demonstration 28 June, charity dog show 4 July.
✿ ☕ ☎

40 OAK TREE COTTAGE
Hisomley, Dilton Marsh BA13 4DB.
Chris & Pam Good, 01373 822433,
christopher.good@tesco.net. *2m SW of Westbury. Signs from A36, A350 & A3098. Single track roads, park on grass inside property.* **Adm £2.50, chd free.** Sun 26 Apr (2-5). **Also open 30 Tower Hill.** Visitors also welcome by appt.
8 yrs ago our garden, vegetable garden and orchard did not exist. Imagination, hard work and good soil have provided what you see today. The garden around the house leads to over 50 old apple varieties in the orchard - then enjoy the view as you walk to the fledgling vineyard.
♿ ✖ ✿ ☕ ☎

OAKDENE
See Hampshire.

41 OARE HOUSE
Rudge Lane, Pewsey SN8 4JQ. Mr Henry Keswick. *2m N of Pewsey. On Marlborough Rd (A345).* Home-made teas. **Adm £3, chd free.** Suns 19 Apr; 2 Aug (2-6). **Also open 19 Apr Broomsgrove Lodge.**
Fine house (not open) in large garden with fine trees, hedges, spring flowers, woodlands, extensive lawns and kitchen garden. Partial wheelchair access, some steps and gravel paths.
♿ ☕

42 THE OLD MALTHOUSE
Lower Westwood BA15 2AG. Simon & Amanda Relph, 01225 864905. *2m SW of Bradford-on-Avon. Take B3109 S, R to Westwood at 1st Xrds after leaving Bradford-on-Avon, 300yds past The New Inn on R.* Home-made teas. **Adm £3, chd free (share to Tulsi Trust).** Sun 14 June (2-5). Visitors also welcome by appt.
1 acre. At front, small garden with unusual water feature. To the side, long border against N-facing wall with mainly white flowering shrubs and herbaceous plants. Through the wall to 3 garden rooms: lawn surrounded by shrubs, another small lawn with semi-circular flame border facing splendid magnolia across pond, gravel courtyard with 6 island beds, 2 lily ponds and sculptured water feature enclosed by rose-covered pergola on two sides. Some gravel paths.
♿ ✿ ☕ ☎

A whimsical garden of pollarded limes, stone sculpture, overflowing pots and herbaceous borders bursting with colour . . .

43 THE OLD MILL
Ramsbury SN8 2PN. Annabel Dallas. *8m NE of Marlborough. From A4 or B1492 head to Ramsbury. At The Bell PH follow sign to Hungerford. Garden behind yew hedge on R 100yds beyond The Bell.* Home-made teas. **Adm £3.50, chd free.** Thur 25 June (2-6).
Water running through a multitude of channels no longer drives the mill but provides the backdrop for a whimsical garden of pollarded limes, stone sculpture, overflowing pots and herbaceous borders bursting with colour. Paths meander by streams and over small bridges. Vistas are cut through trees to give dramatic views of the downs beyond.
✖ ☕

44 NEW THE OLD VICARAGE
Swindon Road, Hilmarton SN11 8SB. Lesley & George Hudson. *4m S of Wootton Bassett on A3102 between Lynham & Calne.* Home-made teas. **Adm £3, chd free.** Sun 14 June (11.30-5); Fri 21 Aug (2-5).
7-acre garden and paddock is the quintessential English garden incl a Victorian walled garden with an ornamental pond, wisteria-covered pergola and beautiful wide herbaceous borders, secret garden, woodland garden, large lawns. Formal garden circled by paddocks and wildflower meadow (best in June), orchard and kitchen garden. Restored over the last 5 yrs.
✖ ✿ ☕

45 POULTON HOUSE
Marlborough SN8 2LN. Mr & Mrs Martin Ephson, 01672 511705, eugenia@poultonhouse.com. *1/2 m E of Marlborough centre. Take Ramsbury rd from The Green in Marlborough 1/3 m, large white gates on L.* Light refreshments & teas. **Adm £3, chd free.** Sat 13 June (2-6). Visitors also welcome by appt.
7-acre garden round fine Queen Anne manor house (not open) with mature trees set in sweeping lawns. Many different aspects, incl walled garden with topiary, sunken rose and herb garden, orchard with mown geometric patterns. Long herbaceous borders, millennium rill, scented philadelphus walk and fine roses. Woodland path, riverside pool and wildlife area interplanted with native trees. Vegetable garden and wild flower meadow. Very limited wheelchair access.
✖ ✿ ☕ ☎

46 THE POUND HOUSE
Little Somerford SN15 5JW. Mr & Mrs Michael Baines, 01666 823212. *2m E of Malmesbury on B4024. In village turn S, leave church on R. Car park on R before railway bridge.* Home-made teas & wine. **Adm £3, chd free.** Sun 14 June (2-6). Visitors also welcome by appt.
Large well planted garden surrounding former rectory. Mature trees, hedges and spacious lawns. Well-stocked herbaceous borders, roses, shrubs, pergola, parterre, swimming pool garden, water, ducks, chickens, alpaca and horses. New raised vegetable garden and lots of places to sit!
♿ ✖ ✿ 🛏 ☕ ☎

PRIOR PARK LANDSCAPE GARDEN
See Somerset & Bristol

47 PRIORY HOUSE
Market Street, Bradford-on-Avon
BA15 1LH. Mr & Mrs Tim Woodall.
Town centre. Park in town centre. Take A363 signed Bath up Market St. House 500yds. Home-made teas.
Adm £2.50, chd free. Suns 5 Apr; 14 June; 12 July (2-5.30).
³/₄ -acre town garden, mostly formal. Spring garden, irises, roses and colour coordinated herbaceous borders. Knot garden in front of part Georgian House is an interpretation of the sash windows. Some steep parts.

48 RIDLEYS CHEER
Mountain Bower SN14 7AJ. Mr & Mrs A J Young,
antonyoung@ridleyscheer.co.uk. *9m WNW of Chippenham. At The Shoe, on A420 8m W of Chippenham, turn N then take 2nd L & 1st R.* Cream teas.
Adm £3.50, chd free. Suns 5 Apr; 17 May; 14 June (2-6). **Visitors** also welcome by appt.
1¹/₂ -acre informal garden with unusual trees and shrubs, incl acers, liriodendrons, magnolias, daphnes, hellebores, hostas and euphorbias. Over 125 different rose varieties incl hybrid musks, albas, tree ramblers and species roses, planted progressively over past 37yrs. Potager, miniature box garden, 2-acre arboretum planted 1989, and 3-acre wild flower meadow.

ST CHRISTOPHER'S
See Hampshire.

SANDLE COTTAGE
See Hampshire.

49 SHARCOTT MANOR
Pewsey SN9 5PA. Captain & Mrs D Armytage, 01672 563485. *1m SW of Pewsey. Via A345 from Pewsey towards Salisbury. Turn R signed Sharcott at grass triangle. 400yds up lane, garden on L over cattle-grid.* Home-made teas. **Adm £3, chd free.** Wed 1 Apr (11-5), Sun 5 Apr; (2-6); Weds 6 May; 3 June; 1 July; 5 Aug; Sept (11-5), Sun 6 Sept (2-6). **Visitors** also welcome by appt, groups & coaches.
-acre plantsman's garden on greensand, planted for yr-round interest. Mature trees with many tree rambler roses and densely planted borders with unusual plants and

climbers. Woodland walk carpeted with spring bulbs around ¹/₂ -acre lake, ornamental water fowl. Vegetable garden in raised beds. Hydrangeas and good autumn colour later. Gravel paths, grass slopes, wet areas.

Gardening on partial greensand gives us healthy borders of numerous herbaceous plants . . .

50 ◆ SHELDON MANOR
Chippenham SN14 0RG. Kenneth & Caroline Hawkins, 01249 653120, www.sheldonmanor.co.uk. *1¹/₂ m W of Chippenham. Take A420 W. 1st L signed Chippenham RFC, entrance approx ¹/₂ m on R.* **House & Garden £8. Garden only £4.50, chd under 12 free. Thurs, May, June & Sept (2-4).** For NGS: Sun 7 June (2-4).
Wiltshire's oldest inhabited manor house with C13 porch and C15 chapel. Gardens with ancient yews, mulberry tree and profusion of old-fashioned roses blooming in May and June. BBC TV location for Bone Kickers.

51 32 SHURNHOLD
Melksham SN12 8DG. Alvin & Judith Howard, 01225 704839, bolingbroke.design@tinyworld.co.uk. *¹/₄ m W of Melksham. On A365 nr George Ward School.* **Adm £2.50, chd free.** Sun 14 June (2-5). **Evening Openings** Fri 24 July; Fri 18 Sept (6-9.30). **Visitors** also welcome by appt.
A small eccentric garden with Chinese, Japanese, French and Roman styles with buildings, fountains and ponds. Floodlit on evening openings. Featured in 'Historic Gardens of Wiltshire'. Short steep drive, gravel paths.

SHUTE FARM
See Dorset.

SNAPE COTTAGE PLANTSMAN'S GARDEN
See Dorset.

52 ◆ STOURHEAD GARDEN
Stourton BA12 6QD. The National Trust, 01747 841152, www.nationaltrust.org.uk. *3m NW of Mere on B3092. Follow NT signs.* **House & Garden £11.10, chd £5.50. Garden only £6.60, chd £3.60. Opening times vary according to season; please see website or phone for details.** For NGS: Sat 18 July (11-5).
One of the earliest and greatest landscape gardens in the world, creation of banker Henry Hoare in 1740s on his return from the Grand Tour, inspired by paintings of Claude and Poussin. Planted with rare trees, rhododendrons and azaleas over last 250yrs.

53 NEW 30 TOWER HILL
Westbury BA13 3SP. Norman & Dot Eddolls, 01373 864938. *2m SW of Westbury. A3098 from Westbury to Frome.* Home-made teas. **Adm £2.50, chd free (share to Warminster & Westbury Visually Handicapped Club).** Sun 26 Apr (2-5). Also open **Oak Tree Cottage. Visitors** also welcome by appt.
¹/₂ -acre surrounds a 1930s bungalow with views to the Warminster Downs. Gardening on partial greensand gives us healthy borders of numerous herbaceous plants. 2 small fishponds and a rockery. Some gravel, slopes & steps.

54 ◆ WATERDALE HOUSE
East Knoyle SP3 6BL. Mr & Mrs Julian Seymour, 01747 830262. *8m S of Warminster. N of East Knoyle, garden signed from A350.* **Adm £4, chd free, concessions £3.** For NGS: Sun 3 May (12-6).
4-acre mature woodland garden with rhododendrons, azaleas, camellias, maples, magnolias, ornamental water, bog garden, herbaceous borders. Bluebell walk. New shrub border created by storm damage mixed with agapanthus and half hardy salvias.

12 acres of English country garden with 26 distinct rooms . . .

55 WELLAWAY

Close Lane, Marston SN10 5SN. Mr & Mrs P Lewis. *5m SW of Devizes. From A360, Devizes to Salisbury, R into Potterne through Worton, signed L to Marston, lane ½ m on L.* Home-made teas. **Adm £4, chd free. Suns 26 Apr; 13 Sept (2-6).**
2-acre flower arranger's garden comprising herbaceous borders, orchard, vegetable garden, ornamental and wildlife ponds, lawns and naturalised areas. Planted since 1979 for yr-round interest. Shrubberies and rose garden, other areas underplanted with bulbs or ground cover. Springtime particularly colourful with daffodils, tulips and hellebores.

56 NEW WEST LAVINGTON MANOR

1 Church Street, West Lavington SN10 4LA. Mr & Mrs Andrew Doman. *6m S of Devizes, on A360. House opposite White Street, where parking available.* **Adm £5, chd free (share to Church of All Saints). Sat 16 May (10-7).**
A 5-acre walled garden first established in C17 by John Danvers who brought Italianate gardens to the UK. Variety of formal and informal areas incl herbaceous border, Japanese garden, rose garden, orchard and arboretum with some outstanding specimen trees all centred around a trout stream and duck pond.

WESTON HOUSE
See Dorset.

57 NEW WHATLEY MANOR

Easton Grey SN16 0RB. Christian & Alix Landolt. *4m W of Malmesbury. From A429 at Malmesbury take B4040 signed Sherston. Manor 2m on L.* Teas (not NGS). **Adm £3.50, chd free. Sun 12 July (2-5.30).**
12 acres of English country garden with 26 distinct rooms each with a strong theme based on colour, scent or style. Original 1920s plan inspired the design and combines classic style with more contemporary touches. Specially commissioned sculptures.

WINCOMBE PARK
See Dorset.

58 WINDMILL COTTAGE

Kings Road, Market Lavington SN10 4QB. Rupert & Gill Wade, 01380 813527. *5m S of Devizes. Turn E off A360 1m N of West Lavington, 2m S of Potterne. At top of hill turn L into Kings Rd, L into Windmill Lane after 200yds. Limited parking.* **Adm £2.50, chd free. Fris 29 May; 12, 26 June; 10, 24 July (2-5.30). Visitors also welcome by appt late May to end July, for groups of 4+.**
1-acre cottage-style garden on greensand. Mixed beds and borders with long season of interest. Roses on pagoda, large vegetable patch for kitchen and exhibition at local shows, polytunnel and greenhouse. Whole garden virtually pesticide free for last 13yrs. New for 2009, a bog garden by a revamped pond, shade walk and prairie garden.

Group opening

59 WORTON GARDENS

SN10 5SE. *3m SW of Devizes. A360 Devizes to Salisbury, turn W in Potterne or just N of West Lavington. From Seend turn S at Bell Inn, follow signs to Worton.* Home-made teas at The Grange. **Combined adm £4, chd free. Sun 28 June (2-6).**

ASHTON HOUSE
Mrs Colin Shand
½ -acre garden in 3 sections, with herbaceous borders, many shrubs and birch grove, walled courtyard, small gravel garden and raised vegetable garden. House burnt down shortly before 2006 opening but garden being maintained while house rebuilt.

BROOKFIELD HOUSE
Mr & Mrs Graham Cannon
1-acre part-walled garden with mixed borders and separate fruit and vegetable garden, rose garden and fine views.

THE GRANGE
Mr & Mrs Simon Jacobs
Formal box hedging incl knot garden, pond garden, herbaceous borders, unusual trees, newly planted walled kitchen garden, rose garden and extensive lawns giving fine views all set around C17 timber framed house (not open). Some gravel paths.

NEW THE LITTLE HOUSE
Wendy & Steve Ellis
Small cottage garden on 3 levels. Structured beds with slate paths, terraced shrubbery bank and a dry gravel garden surrounded by climber-clad trellis.

Wiltshire County Volunteers

County Organisers
Sean & Kena Magee, Byams House, Willesley, Tetbury GL8 8QU, 01666 880009, sean@magees.demon.co.uk

Assistant County Organisers
Cosima Armytage, Sharcott Manor, Pewsey SN9 5PA, 01672 563485
Sarah Coate, Colts Corner, Upper Woodford, Salisbury SP4 6PA, 01722 782365
Jo Hankey, Mill Cottage, Burcombe, Wilton SP2 0EJ, 01722 742472, richard.hankey@virgin.net
Shirley Heywood, Monkton House, Monkton Deverill BA12 7EX, 01985 844486
Diana Robertson, Broomsgrove Lodge, New Mill, nr Pewsey SN9 5LE, 01672 810515, diana@broomsgrovelodge.co.uk
Anne Shand, Brow Cottage, Seend Hill, Seend, Melksham SN12 6RU, 01380 828866

Mark your diary with these special events in 2009

EXPLORE SECRET GARDENS DURING CHELSEA & HAMPTON COURT FLOWER SHOW WEEKS

Tue 19 May, Wed 20 May, Thur 21 May, Fri 22 May, Wed 8 July, Thur 9 July
Full day tours from £82 per person, 10% discount for groups
Advance booking required, telephone +44 (0)20 8693 1015 or email j.wookey@btinternet.com
Specially selected gardens in London, Essex, Kent, Hampshire and South Oxfordshire. The tour price includes transport and lunch with wine at a popular restaurant or pub.

HAMPTON COURT PALACE

Thur 2 Apr, Tue 23 June, Thur 25 June, Wed 15 July, Tue 4 Aug, Thur 10 Sept
Evening tours in the company of one of the Palace's specialist tour guides from 6.30 – 8pm
Tickets £6 per person. Advance booking required, telephone +44 (0)1483 211535 or
visit www.ngs.org.uk for more information
Gossip, scandal, murder, healing – you'll find it all within the Formal Gardens at Hampton Court Palace. Each tour will have its own unique feature whether it's the story of the Great Vine or the magic and mystery of the Maze.

FROGMORE – A ROYAL GARDEN (BERKSHIRE)

Tue 26 May 10am – 5.30pm (last admission 4pm)
Garden adm £4.50, chd free. Tickets available in advance or on the day.
Advance booking for groups and coaches, telephone
+44 (0) 1483 211535 or email orders@ngs.org.uk
A rare opportunity to explore 30 acres of landscaped garden, rich in history and beauty.

FLAXBOURNE FARM – FUN & SURPRISES (BEDFORDSHIRE)

Sun 7 June 10am – 5pm. Adm £5, chd free
No booking required, come along on the day!
Bring the whole family and have fun in this surprising and entertaining garden of 2 acres. Enjoy the large plant fair, live music, pets corner, birds of prey, dog agility show and much more.

WISLEY RHS GARDEN – MUSIC IN THE GARDEN (SURREY)

Fri 11 Sept 6 – 9pm
Adm (incl RHS members) £7, chd under 15 free
Save money on advance bookings for groups of 4 or more, telephone +44 (0)1483 211535 or
visit www.ngs.org.uk for more information
A special evening opening of this famous garden, exclusively for the NGS. Enjoy music and entertainment as you explore the gardens and the floral marquee on the first day of the Wisley Flower Show.

For further information visit www.ngs.org.uk or telephone 01483 211535

WORCESTERSHIRE

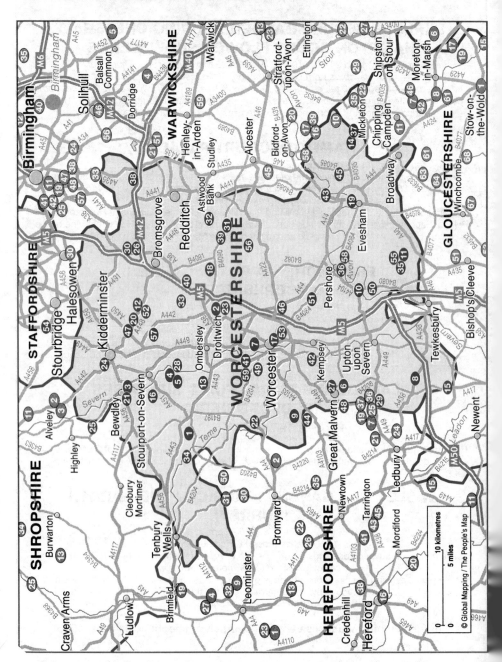

Opening Dates

February

SATURDAY 7
- (17) The Greyfriars

WEDNESDAY 18
- (12) Dial Park

THURSDAY 19
- (12) Dial Park

THURSDAY 26
- (39) Red House Farm

March

THURSDAY 5
- (39) Red House Farm

THURSDAY 12
- (39) Red House Farm

WEDNESDAY 18
- (47) Stone House Cottage Gardens

THURSDAY 19
- (39) Red House Farm

SUNDAY 22
- (29) Little Malvern Court

THURSDAY 26
- (39) Red House Farm

SATURDAY 28
- (47) Stone House Cottage Gardens

SUNDAY 29
- (12) Dial Park

April

THURSDAY 2
- (39) Red House Farm

SUNDAY 5
- (56) White Cottage

THURSDAY 9
- (39) Red House Farm

FRIDAY 10
- (46) Spetchley Park Gardens
- (47) Stone House Cottage Gardens

SUNDAY 12
- (2) 24 Alexander Avenue
- (14) Frogs Nest
- (37) 4 Poden Cottages
- (57) Whitlenge Gardens

MONDAY 13
- (14) Frogs Nest
- (15) Gadfield Elm House
- (37) 4 Poden Cottages
- (57) Whitlenge Gardens

THURSDAY 16
- (39) Red House Farm

SUNDAY 19
- (28) Little Larford
- (48) Tannachie

TUESDAY 21
- (32) The Mill House

THURSDAY 23
- (39) Red House Farm
- (47) Stone House Cottage Gardens

SATURDAY 25
- (10) Church Cottages
- (44) Shuttifield Cottage
- (53) The Walled Garden

SUNDAY 26
- (10) Church Cottages
- (28) Little Larford

TUESDAY 28
- (32) The Mill House

THURSDAY 30
- (39) Red House Farm

May

SATURDAY 2
- (44) Shuttifield Cottage

SUNDAY 3
- (16) Gladderbrook Farm
- (57) Whitlenge Gardens

MONDAY 4
- (29) Little Malvern Court
- (57) Whitlenge Gardens

TUESDAY 5
- (32) The Mill House

THURSDAY 7
- (39) Red House Farm

SUNDAY 10
- (55) Whitcombe House

THURSDAY 14
- (39) Red House Farm

SATURDAY 16
- (44) Shuttifield Cottage
- (47) Stone House Cottage Gardens

SUNDAY 17
- (25) Hunters End

THURSDAY 21
- (39) Red House Farm

SUNDAY 24
- (14) Frogs Nest
- (57) Whitlenge Gardens

MONDAY 25
- (14) Frogs Nest
- (15) Gadfield Elm House
- (57) Whitlenge Gardens

THURSDAY 28
- (39) Red House Farm

SATURDAY 30
- (10) Church Cottages
- (34) Orleton House
- (50) Two Gardens in Eckington
- (53) The Walled Garden
- (56) White Cottage

SUNDAY 31
- (5) Astley Towne House
- (10) Church Cottages
- (16) Gladderbrook Farm
- (30) Marlbrook Gardens
- (34) Orleton House
- (50) Two Gardens in Eckington
- (56) White Cottage

June

THURSDAY 4
- (39) Red House Farm

SATURDAY 6
- (1) Abberley Churches Open Gardens Weekend
- (36) Pershore Gardens
- (44) Shuttifield Cottage

SUNDAY 7
- (1) Abberley Churches Open Gardens Weekend
- (3) The Antiquary
- (23) Hiraeth
- (36) Pershore Gardens
- (41) Rose Cottage
- (59) Worlds End Nurseries

THURSDAY 11
- (39) Red House Farm

SATURDAY 13
- (27) Layton Avenue Gardens
- (45) South Littleton Gardens

SUNDAY 14
- (8) Birtsmorton Court
- (13) Eastgrove Cottage Garden Nursery
- (27) Layton Avenue Gardens
- (45) South Littleton Gardens
- (48) Tannachie
- (52) Tythe Barn House
- (55) Whitcombe House

WEDNESDAY 17
- (47) Stone House Cottage Gardens

THURSDAY 18
- (39) Red House Farm

FRIDAY 19
- (38) Pump Cottage
- (49) Treetops

SATURDAY 20
- (38) Pump Cottage
- (49) Treetops
- (53) The Walled Garden

SUNDAY 21
- (4) Astley Country Gardens
- (14) Frogs Nest
- (19) Harrells Hardy Plants Nursery Garden
- (25) Hunters End

MONDAY 22
- (38) Pump Cottage

WEDNESDAY 24
23 Hiraeth

THURSDAY 25
39 Red House Farm

SUNDAY 28
7 Beckett Drive Gardens
14 Frogs Nest
15 Gadfield Elm House
16 Gladderbrook Farm
21 High Bank

July

THURSDAY 2
37 4 Poden Cottages
39 Red House Farm

SATURDAY 4
44 Shuttifield Cottage

SUNDAY 5
3 The Antiquary
30 Marlbrook Gardens
46 Spetchley Park Gardens

THURSDAY 9
37 4 Poden Cottages
39 Red House Farm

SATURDAY 11
20 Harvington Hall

SUNDAY 12
19 Harrells Hardy Plants Nursery Garden
20 Harvington Hall
24 Honeybrook House Cottage
55 Whitcombe House
58 Wick Village
59 Worlds End Nurseries

THURSDAY 16
37 4 Poden Cottages
39 Red House Farm

SATURDAY 18
18 Hanbury Hall

SUNDAY 19
9 Bridges Stone Mill
23 Hiraeth
25 Hunters End
28 Little Larford
51 The Tynings

THURSDAY 23
37 4 Poden Cottages
39 Red House Farm

FRIDAY 24
47 Stone House Cottage Gardens

SATURDAY 25
34 Orleton House
53 The Walled Garden

SUNDAY 26
2 24 Alexander Avenue
5 Astley Towne House
16 Gladderbrook Farm
34 Orleton House

THURSDAY 30
37 4 Poden Cottages

39 Red House Farm

August

SATURDAY 1
51 The Tynings (Evening)

SUNDAY 2
21 High Bank
30 Marlbrook Gardens

THURSDAY 6
39 Red House Farm

SATURDAY 8
44 Shuttifield Cottage

SUNDAY 9
22 High View
26 Kokopelli

THURSDAY 13
39 Red House Farm

SATURDAY 15
54 Westacres

SUNDAY 16
7 Beckett Drive Gardens
54 Westacres

WEDNESDAY 19
23 Hiraeth

THURSDAY 20
39 Red House Farm

SATURDAY 22
47 Stone House Cottage Gardens

SUNDAY 23
24 Honeybrook House Cottage

THURSDAY 27
39 Red House Farm

SUNDAY 30
5 Astley Towne House
16 Gladderbrook Farm
57 Whitlenge Gardens

MONDAY 31
14 Frogs Nest
15 Gadfield Elm House
57 Whitlenge Gardens

September

THURSDAY 3
39 Red House Farm
47 Stone House Cottage Gardens

SATURDAY 5
30 Marlbrook Gardens (Evening)

SUNDAY 6
2 24 Alexander Avenue

THURSDAY 10
39 Red House Farm

SATURDAY 12
47 Stone House Cottage Gardens

SUNDAY 13
19 Harrells Hardy Plants Nursery Garden

42 Round Lodge

THURSDAY 17
39 Red House Farm

SATURDAY 19
44 Shuttifield Cottage

THURSDAY 24
39 Red House Farm

SATURDAY 26
44 Shuttifield Cottage

SUNDAY 27
5 Astley Towne House
44 Shuttifield Cottage

October

THURSDAY 1
39 Red House Farm

THURSDAY 8
39 Red House Farm

THURSDAY 15
39 Red House Farm

THURSDAY 22
39 Red House Farm

THURSDAY 29
39 Red House Farm

February 2010

SATURDAY 6
17 The Greyfriars

Gardens open to the public

13 Eastgrove Cottage Garden Nursery
17 The Greyfriars
18 Hanbury Hall
19 Harrells Hardy Plants Nursery Garden
20 Harvington Hall
29 Little Malvern Court
39 Red House Farm
40 Riverside Gardens at Webbs of Wychbold
46 Spetchley Park Gardens
47 Stone House Cottage Gardens
57 Whitlenge Gardens

By appointment only

6 Barnard's Green House
11 Conderton Manor
31 Meadow Farm
33 New House Farm
35 Overbury Court
43 St Egwins Cottage

Also open by appointment ☎

2 24 Alexander Avenue
3 The Antiquary
5 Astley Towne House

39 Red House Farm

⑫ Dial Park
⑮ Gadfield Elm House
⑯ Gladderbrook Farm
㉑ High Bank
㉒ High View
㉓ Hiraeth
㉔ Honeybrook House Cottage
㉕ Hunters End
㉖ Kokopelli
㉘ Little Larford
㉚ 24 Braces Road, Marlbrook Gardens
㉚ Oak Tree House, Marlbrook Gardens
㉚ Saranacris, Marlbrook Gardens
㉞ Orleton House
㊲ 4 Poden Cottages
㊳ Pump Cottage
㊹ Shuttifield Cottage
㊿ The Croft, Eckington
(51) The Tynings
(52) Tythe Barn House
�54 Westacres
�55 Whitcombe House
�56 White Cottage

The Gardens

Group opening

① ABBERLEY CHURCHES OPEN GARDENS WEEKEND
Abberley WR6 6UZ, 01299 896429. *12m NW of Worcester. On A443.* Light refreshments & teas. **Adm £6 (valid both days), chd free (share to Abberley Church). Sat 6, Sun 7 June (11.30-5).**
Varied collection of approx 12 gardens set against the beautiful Abberley Hills. Visitors will find the highest garden in Abberley with magnificent views; cottage gardens, farmhouse scented garden and gardens with views over Teme Valley. Individual garden details and map provided at village hall and gardens. Coffee, lunches and teas served from 10.30 at Abberley Village Hall.

⊗ ☕

② 24 ALEXANDER AVENUE
Droitwich Spa WR9 8NH. Malley & David Terry, 01905 774907. *1m S of Droitwich. Droitwich Spa towards Worcester A38. Or from M5 J6 to Droitwich Town centre.* **Adm £3, chd free. Suns 12 Apr; 26 July; 6 Sept (2-6). Visitors also welcome by appt.**
40 x 10metres garden is a lesson in what can be done in a small space. Turning a barren patch of grass into a paradise. High hedges, clad with clematis from the 100+ varieties

grown, obscure views of neighbouring houses. Borders filled with dazzling array of interesting plants, many rare. Fine collection of ferns. Alpines grow in stone troughs and gravel garden. 'A garden of immaculate artistry'. Featured in 'GGG' & 'Garden News'.

& ✕ ⊗ ☎

③ THE ANTIQUARY
48 High Street, Bewdley DY12 2DJ. Karen Raine, 01299 402430. *3m W of Kidderminster. (B4194) Bewdly Centre. Follow signs to garden parking in Gardener's Meadow car park by the river.* **Adm £2.50, chd free. Suns 7 June; 5 July (12-5). Visitors also welcome by appt.**
Hidden away behind unassuming High St, frontage 200ft SW facing walled town house garden with 4 distinct rooms separated by wisteria pergola and jasmine arch. Herbaceous garden, pond, herb garden, developing meadow, orchard area and vegetable plot. Free-range rare breed hens add charm to this tranquil oasis. Featured on Radio Hereford & Worcester - gardening slot.

✕ ☕ ⊗

Visitors will find the highest garden in Abberley with magnificent views . . .

Group opening

④ ASTLEY COUNTRY GARDENS
Astley, nr Stourport-on-Severn DY13 0SG. *3m SW of Stourport-on-Severn. Take A451 out of Stourport, turn L onto B4196 for Worcester. Start at Astley Village Hall where map and descriptions of gardens are available.* Home-made teas at Astley Towne House & Sandstone Barn. **Combined adm £5, chd free. Sun 21 June (11-5.30).**
A wonderful range of 8 gardens of great variety within country settings and owners' enccentricities in peaceful and colourful surroundings. Full days enjoyment with refreshments available at 2 locations. Cars advisable, parking available at each location.

⊗ ☕

ASTLEY TOWNE HOUSE
Tim & Lesley Smith. Also open Suns 31 May; 26 July; 30 Aug; 27 Sept.
2½ acres incl sub-tropical planting. Stumpery garden with tree ferns and woodland temple. Many features incl Mediterranean garden, tree house, revolving summerhouse and underground grotto with shell mosaics and water features. Featured on Hereford & Worcs radio, Finalist in 'Best Private Garden in Worcestershire'.

6 ELM GROVE
Michael & Audrey Ecob
Good example of what can be achieved in a small area on very sandy soil. The garden is a blaze of colour and contains some most unusual plants skilfully chosen to complement each other. Complete with vegetables, greenhouse and fishpool.

✕

NEW HALL BARN
Susan & Richard Chandler
Beautiful walled garden and peripheral areas, with small vegetable plot within the grounds of a grade II listed C18 barn conversion (not open). Access from rear of White House.

LONGMORE HILL FARMHOUSE
Larford Lane. Roger & Christine Russell
½ acre garden of C16 farmhouse (not open). Small feature courtyard leading to part-walled terrace and lily pond. Mixed borders, mature shrubs, climbing roses and clematis. Vegetable garden and small orchard area.

POOL HOUSE
Philip Siegert & Oonagh O'Sullivan
Lawns, with flowering tulip and handkerchief trees, lead down from one of the few Strawberry Hill Gothic houses in the Midlands, to a lovely lake with large tame carp which is fed by other lakes. Walled garden with tree peonies and old-fashioned roses. Garden cultivated organically and also home to the Pool House herds of British White Cattle and Black Welsh Mountain sheep.

SANDSTONE BARN
Julien & Helen Tanser. *Adjacent to Longmore Hill Farmhouse* Good plant stall from Little Larford, tea and cakes/cream teas and refreshments served in pretty walled courtyard, with mature and decorative planting. In combination with Longmore Hill Farmhouse.

NEW SWEVENINGS
John & Sam Glayzebrook
Picturesque country cottage garden with enclosed lawned areas, water feature, herbaceous and climbing plants and vegetable plot. Accessible from the White House garden.

THE SYTCH
Stan & Hilary Kilby. *Parking on main rd (100yd up bridleway)* Beautiful terrace with lawns leading to picturesque water feature and lake with views beyond. Mixed borders with productive vegetable garden, poultry and orchard. Pedigree flock of Bleu de Maine sheep.

THE WHITE HOUSE
Dunley. Tony & Linda Tidmarsh
Classical style garden divided by yew hedges, shrub borders and brick walls into separate 'rooms' around a central lawn. Variety features celebratory events in the owners family. Italian garden contains cascade made of copper, 4 pools, one incorporating the girls entrance to Tipton Boarding School. Superb climbing roses.

5 ASTLEY TOWNE HOUSE
Astley DY13 0RH. Tim & Lesley Smith, 01299 822299. *3m W of Stourport-on-Severn. On B4196 Worcester to Bewdley Road.* Home-made teas. **Adm £4, chd free.** Suns 31 May; 26 July; 30 Aug; 27 Sept (1-5). Open with **Astley Country Gardens** 21 June. Visitors also welcome by appt.
2½ acres incl sub-tropical planting. Winding paths of jungle garden incorporating bananas, palms and other rare and exotic plants. Features incl stumpery garden, woodland temple, tree top high safari lodge, revolving neo-classical summerhouse, 'mns with statuary and grotto

based on Greek mythology with water features and shell mosaics. Featured in 'Historic Gardens of Worcestershire' by Timothy Mowl.

6 BARNARD'S GREEN HOUSE
Hastings Pool, Poolbrook Road, Malvern WR14 3NQ. Mr & Mrs Philip Nicholls, 01684 574446. *1m E of Malvern. At junction of B4211 & B4208.* **Adm £3, chd free (share to Save the Children Fund).** Visitors welcome by appt.
Newly developed 2 acre garden with mature trees and 7 new shrub and herbaceous borders. The woodland has been replanted and incorporates a gravel garden, and stumpery. The rose garden is best in June and red garden superb in July/Aug. Vegetable garden, surrounded by roses, mixed borders. The millennium dome in the centre. 1635 half-timbered house (not open). Featured in 'Limited Edition'.

Group opening

7 BECKETT DRIVE GARDENS
Northwick WR3 7BZ. *1½ m N of Worcester city centre. Cul-de-sac off A449 Ombersley Rd directly opp Granthams garage, 1m S of Claines r'about on A449.* Home-made teas at 6 Beckett Drive. **Combined adm £3, chd free.** Suns 28 June; 16 Aug (10-5).
Two individual but contrasting gardens both with an abundance of plants and interesting design ideas. Compost advisors in attendance at no.5.

5 BECKETT DRIVE
Jacki & Pete Ager
Intriguing design ideas and something of interest around every corner. Flowerbeds are stocked with shrubs, perennials and alpines in a landscaped setting. The garden incls some unexpected and surprising features. New bed for sun-loving planting in 2009.

6 BECKETT DRIVE
Guy Lymer
Eclectic mix of planting, modern sculpture and water features with lighting for each. Established shrubs for yr-round interest are complemented by exotic plants, ornamental grasses and a natural arbour.

Tea and cakes, cream teas and refreshments served in pretty walled courtyard . . .

8 BIRTSMORTON COURT
nr Malvern WR13 6JS. Mr & Mrs N G K Dawes. *7m E of Ledbury. On A438.* Home-made teas. **Adm £4, chd free.** Sun 14 June (2-5.30).
Fortified manor house (not open) dating from C12; moat; Westminster pool, laid down in Henry VII's reign at time of consecration of Westminster Abbey; large tree under which Cardinal Wolsey reputedly slept in shadow of ragged stone; white garden. Potager; topiary.

9 BRIDGES STONE MILL
Alfrick Pound WR6 5HR. Sir Michael & Lady Perry. *6m NW of Malvern. From Worcester, take the A4103 Hereford rd to Bransford, at Bank House Hotel r'about take minor rd towards Leigh & Suckley. After 200yds, fork L towards Suckley. After 3m sign announces arrival at Alfrick Pound. 300yds beyond that, entrance gate to Bridges Stone Mill on L.* Home-made teas. **Adm £3.50, chd free.** Sun 19 July (2-5.30).
Formerly a cherry orchard adjoining the mainly C19 water mill, this is now a 2½ -acre garden laid out with trees, shrubs and mixed beds and borders; small lake, stream and brook. The garden is bounded by 200yd stretch of Leigh Brook (an SSSI), and a mill stream from the mill's own weir. Extensive all-yr round planting. Ornamental vegetable parterre completes the picture.

BROAD MARSTON & PEBWORTH GARDENS
See Warwickshire & part of West Midlands.

10 NEW CHURCH COTTAGES

Church Road, Defford WR8 9BJ. *3m SW of Pershore. A4104 Pershore to Upton Rd, turn into Defford, black & white cottages at side of church. Parking in village hall car park.* Home-made teas at no.1 (Apr), no.2 (May). **Combined adm £3, chd free (share to Air Ambulance). Sats, Suns 25, 26 Apr; 30, 31 May (11-5).**
2 countrymen's gardens containing specimen trees, water features, herbaceous borders, walled garden. Fruit and vegetables, poultry and new Japanese- style feature.

1 CHURCH COTTAGES
John Taylor
True countryman's ¹/₃ garden. Interesting layout, with new Japanese -style feature.Specimen trees; water features; vegetable garden; aviary, poultry and cider making.

NEW 2 CHURCH COTTAGES
Mark & Debra Fox
80 metres long cottage garden divided into rooms of varied styles. Herbaceous borders with bulbs, mature trees and shrubs, walled garden, water features and fruit trees.

11 CONDERTON MANOR

nr Tewkesbury GL20 7PR. Mr & Mrs W Carr, 01386 725389, carrs@conderton.wanadoo.co.uk. *5¹/₂ m NE of Tewkesbury. On Bredon - Beckford rd or from A46 take Overbury sign at Beckford turn.* **Adm £4. Visitors welcome by appt.**
7-acre garden with magnificent views of Cotswolds. Flowering cherries and bulbs in spring. Formal terrace with clipped box parterre; huge rose and clematis arches mixed borders of roses and herbaceous plants, bog bank and quarry garden. Many unusual trees and shrubs make this a garden to visit at all seasons. Contact owners to discuss wheelchair access.

12 DIAL PARK

Chaddesley Corbett DY10 4QB. David & Olive Mason, 01562 777451, olivemason@btinternet.com. *4¹/₂ m from Kidderminster, 4¹/₂ m from Bromsgrove. On A448 midway between Kidderminster & Bromsgrove.*

Limited parking at garden, or park in village or at village hall. Teas (Feb), Home-made teas (March). **Adm £2.50, chd free. Wed 18, Thur 19 Feb (11-4); Sun 29 Mar (2-5). Visitors also welcome by appt, all yr-round for groups & individuals, coaches permitted.**
A garden for all seasons with a wide variety of plants, many rare. Approx ³/₄ -acre in rural setting. Specialities incl large collection of snowdrops, old varieties of daffodils, primroses and hardy ferns. Small collection of country tools and bygones. Featured in 'Worcestershire Life'.

13 ◆ EASTGROVE COTTAGE GARDEN NURSERY

Sankyns Green, Shrawley WR6 6LQ. Malcolm & Carol Skinner, 01299 896389, www.eastgrove.co.uk. *8m NW of Worcester. On rd between Shrawley (B4196) & Great Witley (A443). Follow brown tourist signs to Sankyns Green.* Teas. **Adm £4, chd free. For regular opening details, please tel or see website. For NGS: Sun 14 June (2-5).**
Unpretentious garden surrounded by ancient cloud hedge and comprising many intimate areas, winding brick paths, great (alpine) wall of china, red hot Lloydian area, long blue, white and yellow border. Inspired planting invites quiet sitting. 2 acre arboretum with wide ride, and labyrinth. Excellent nursery. Wild flowers in glade. Old fashioned home-made teas in orchard with tablecloths and posies, plenty of space for chidren to run - home-made ice cream. Featured in 'Daily Telegraph' & 'Period Living'.

14 FROGS NEST

8 Stratford Road, Honeybourne, Evesham WR11 7PP. Nina & Steve Bullen. *6m E of Evesham. 5m N of Broadway, 5m S of Bidford. Parking at the Gate Inn.* Home-made teas. **Adm £3, chd free. Suns, Mons 12, 13 Apr; 24, 25 May; Suns 21, 28 June; Mon 31 Aug (11-6).**
A small garden but worth the journey! 2 quite different gardens make it a special visit. S-facing front garden is quite formal with herbaceous borders and tongue-in-cheek woodland walk complete with boathouse. N-facing back garden has ponds and all-yr colour interest. Garden to relax in. Featured in 'Amateur Gardening'.

15 GADFIELD ELM HOUSE

Malvern Road, Staunton GL19 3PA. Canon & Mrs John Evans, 01452 840302. *7m W of Tewkesbury. 12m S of Malvern. 1m from Staunton Cross on the Malvern Rd (B4208). 2m SE J2 M50.* Home-made teas. **Adm £2, chd free. Mons 13 Apr; 25 May; Sun 28 June; Mon 31 Aug (2-6). Visitors also welcome by appt.**
Garden created over 25yrs from scratch. Vistas, temples, statues, herbaceous borders. Field walk with view of Malverns, Bredon Hill and the Cotswolds. Rare breed poultry. Some gravel paths.

> # Field walk with view of Malverns, Bredon Hill and the Cotswolds . . .

16 GLADDERBROOK FARM

High Oak, Heightington, Bewdley DY12 2YR. Mike & Sue Butler, 01299 879923, sue.butler4@btinternet.com. *3m W of Stourport-on-Severn. Take A451 from Stourport. At Dunley turn R signed Heightington. After 2m turn R signed High Oak follow rd for ³/₄ m. Park at High Oak Farm by kind permission of Mr & Mrs T Sprague. Garden 100yds down lane.* Home-made teas. **Adm £3, chd free. Suns 3, 31 May; 28 June; 26 July; 30 Aug (12-5). Visitors also welcome by appt groups 10 - 25.**
Plantsman's 1-acre garden on heavy clay with stunning views, developed from a field since 2001. Unusual trees, shrubs, perennials and grasses. 2-acre spring wild flower meadow, developing arboretum, small orchard, vegetable plot, water feature and nursery with unusual plants for sale. Stout shoes advisable. Winner of Large Garden - Bewdley in Bloom.

17 ◆ THE GREYFRIARS
Friar Street, Worcester WR1 2LZ.
The National Trust, 01905 23571,
greyfriars@nationaltrust.org.uk. *In
Friar Street within the centre of
Worcester. Please use city car parks.*
**Adm £2 (incl NT members), chd free.
For NGS: Sat 7 Feb (12-4). Sat 6 Feb
2010.**
Delightful city garden created from the
clearance of back to back housing. An
archway leads through to the walled
garden containing a beautiful display of
spring bulbs incl snowdrops and
daffodils.

Paths lead from a garden of delight through the woodland to the sloping prairie garden . . .

18 ◆ HANBURY HALL
School Road, Droitwich WR9 7EA.
The National Trust, 01527 821214,
hanburyhall@nationaltrust.org.uk.
*3m NE of Droitwich. 6m S of
Bromsgrove. Signed off B4090 and
B4091.* **House & garden £7.60, chd
£3.80, garden only £5, chd £2.50.
For NGS: Sat 18 July (11-5.30).**
Re-creation of C18 formal garden by
George London. Parterre, fruit garden
and wilderness. Mushroom house,
Orangery and Ice house, William and
Mary style house dating from 1701.
Opportunity to meet the gardeners and
to see behind the scenes in the Walled
Garden.

**19 ◆ HARRELLS HARDY
PLANTS NURSERY GARDEN**
Rudge Road, Evesham WR11 4JR.
Liz Nicklin & Kate Phillips, 07799
577120/07733 446606,
www.harrellshardyplants.co.uk. *¼ m
from centre of Evesham. From High St
turn into Queens Rd opp Catholic
church. Turn R at end of Queens Rd,
then L into Rudge Rd. Approx 150yds
on R is a small lane to nursery
gardens.* **Adm £2.50, chd free. Open
Suns 10-12noon, & private visits.
For NGS: Suns 21 June; 12 July; 13
Sept (2-5).**
[..] garden on w-facing slope,
[..] and intensively planted with a

wide range of hardy perennials and
grasses, many unusual. Featuring large
collection of hemerocallis and jewel
bed, bog garden, the prairie, sunshine
bed (yellow flowers), mini cottage
garden, pink bed and many others.
Featured in 'Gloucester Echo'
magazine.

20 ◆ HARVINGTON HALL
Harvington DY10 4LR. The Roman
Catholic Archdiocese of
Birmingham, 01562 777846,
www.harvingtonhall.com. *3m SE of
Kidderminster. ½ m E of A450
Birmingham to Worcester Rd & about
½ m N of A448 from Kidderminster to
Bromsgrove.* **House & garden £7,
chd £4.50, concessions £6, garden
only £2.50, chd 50p. Wed to Sun Apr
to Sept, weekends Mar & Oct. For
NGS: Sat 11, Sun 12 July (11.30-4).**
Romantic Elizabethan moated manor
house with island gardens. Small
Elizabethan-style herb garden, tended
by volunteers from the Hereford and
Worcs Gardens Trust. The main Hall
gardens are also looked after by
volunteers. Tours of the Hall, which
contains secret hiding places and rare
wall paintings, are also available.

21 HIGH BANK
Cleobury Road, Bewdley DY12 2PG.
Stuart & Ann McKie, 01299 401342,
stuartmckie135@hotmail.com. *3½ m
W of Kidderminster. A456. ½ m W of
Bewdley town centre on B4190
(signed Tenbury). Parking available opp
garden entrance.* Home-made teas.
**Adm £2.50, chd free. Suns 28 June;
2 Aug (11-5). Visitors also welcome
by appt May - Aug.**
Beautiful garden approx 1/3-acre with
many old and protected trees.
Restored in keeping with Edwardian
house (not open). Featuring original
summerhouse, rhododendrons and
azaleas. Large collection of roses,
herbaceous borders, courtyard garden,
pergola walk and water features.
Garden is still being developed. 2nd
prize Large Garden - Bewdley in
Bloom.

22 HIGH VIEW
Martley WR6 6PW. Mike & Carole
Dunnett, 01886 821559,
mike.dunnett@virgin.net. *1m S of
Martley. On B4197 between Martley &
A44 at Knightwick.* Home-made teas.
Adm £3.50, chd free. Sun 9 Aug

(11-5). Visitors also welcome by
appt June to Sept for groups of 10+.
Intriguing 2½ acre garden developed
over the last 30yrs. Magnificent views
over the Teme valley. The garden has
many features incl patio container
planting, ponds and imaginatively
designed borders containing many
unusual trees, shrubs and herbaceous
plants selected for summer colour.
Access to garden via steep slopes and
steps - but the walk is well worth it.
Featured in 'Worcester News', Winner
- Private Garden - 'Herefordshire &
Worcestershre Life' Garden Awards.

23 HIRAETH
30 Showell Road, Droitwich
WR9 8UY. Sue & John Fletcher,
07752 717243 / 01905 778390,
jfletcher@inductotherm.co.uk. *1m S
of Droitwich. On The Ridings estate.
Turn off A38 r'about into Addyes Way,
2nd R into Showell Rd, 500yds on R.*
Home-made teas. **Adm £2.50, chd
free. Suns 7 June, 19 July (2-6);
Weds 24 June; 19 Aug (12-5).
Visitors also welcome by appt.**
Traditional cottage garden at rear
incorporating pool, waterfall feature,
200yr-old wooden stile and oak
sculptures. Time is needed to inspect
the collection of herbaceous plants,
hostas, ferns and other new and
unusual varieties. Front garden
contains numerous trees, shrubs and
ornamental barrels, rose arch, wood
and metal sculptures.

**24 HONEYBROOK HOUSE
COTTAGE**
Honeybrook Lane, Kidderminster
DY11 5QS. Gerald Majumdar, 01562
67930, www.cottagegarden.org.uk.
*1½ m N of Kidderminster. On A442
leaving Kidderminster towards
Bridgnorth, 300yds from the island at
the Three Crowns & Sugar Loaf PH
turn R into Honeybrook Lane.* Home-
made teas. **Adm £3.50, chd free.
Suns 12 July; 23 Aug (11-5). Visitors
also welcome by appt July & Aug
only, groups 10+.**
2 acre country garden with magnificent
views. Steep paths lead from the
cottage garden into a garden of delight
through the woodland to the sloping
prairie garden, down past shade
borders to the brook, wildlife pond,
herbaceous borders and long tree lined
walk. Developed since 2003. Featured
in 'Garden News'.

A walk with wildlife . . .

25 HUNTERS END
Button Bridge Lane, Button Bridge.
Kinlet DY12 3DW. Norma & Colin
Page, 01299 841055,
norma@normapage.wanadoo.co.uk.
*6m NW of Bewdley. A4194 from
Bewdley at Button Bridge, turn R
down Button Bridge Lane, garden
³/₄ m on L (look for horses heads).*
Cream teas. **Adm £3, chd free. Suns
17 May; 21 June; 19 July (2-5.30).
Visitors also welcome by appt
groups of 10+, no coaches, minibus
possible.**
This ³/₄ acre garden with plants and
decorative features which will create a
smile and a laugh from the beginning
to end of your tour. Quirky displays
scattered around enhance the humour.
To soak up the atmosphere and
tranquillity of the garden, just relax in
one of the many seating areas and
enjoy your tea and cake. Good
selection of quality plants for sale.
Featured in 'Amateur Gardening',
'Shropshire Star' & on BBC Radio
Worcs & Hereford.

26 KOKOPELLI
185 Old Birmingham Road,
Marlbrook, Bromsgrove B60 1DQ.
Bruce Heideman & Sue James, 0121
445 2741,
private@kokopelligardens.me.uk,
www.kokopelligardens.me.uk. *2m N
of Bromsgrove. 1m N of M42 J1,
follow B4096 signed Rednal. 1m S of
M5 J4, follow A38 signed Bromsgrove,
turn L at T-lights into Braces Lane, turn
R at Old Birmingham Rd.* Home-made
teas. **Adm £2.50, chd free (share to
Motor Neurone Disease). Sun 9 Aug
(1.30-6). Visitors also welcome by
appt, for goups of 10+.**
Developing organic garden with
winding path leading through 3
distinctly different areas finishing in
large fruit and vegetable garden
showcasing heritage varieties. Mix of
traditional cottage planting and exotics.
Vegetable garden features unusual
varieties. Extensive use of rainwater
harvesting, greenhouse features
passive solar heating and solar electric.
Featured in 'Garden News', 'Amateur
Gardening' & on BBC Radio Hereford
& Worcester.

Group opening

27 LAYTON AVENUE GARDENS
Malvern WR14 2ND. *7m S of
Worcester, 5m NW of Upton on
Severn. From Worcester approach
Malvern on A449. Turn L at r'about into
Townsend Way (signed A4208
Welland). After 3 r'abouts take 2nd R
(Charles Way), then 2nd L into Layton
Ave. From Upton approach Malvern on
A4211. Take 3rd exit at Barnards
Green r'about (Pickersleigh Rd). After
1m turn R at T-lights (signed A4208)
Worcester) take 2nd L, then 2nd L
again.* Home-made teas. **Combined
adm £3.50, chd free (share to
Acorns Hospice, Worcester). Sat 13,
Sun 14 June (11-4).**
This year a 3 garden group. The
addition of an extra neighbouring
garden brings yet more variety and
interest to your visit. Water features in
all gardens, interesting designs and
colourful planting plus a productive
vegetable garden. Exhibition of wood
carvings & paintings by Jenny Bradford
at no.22. Featured on BBC Hereford &
Worcester - Saturday am gardening
programe.

10 LAYTON AVENUE
David Ranford
Secluded and inviting this mature
garden wraps its self round the
house (not open). Seating areas
and courtyard fispond.

22 LAYTON AVENUE
Brian & Jenny Bradford
Plenty of places to sit and enjoy
this pleasant garden with its
feature gazebo, streamside areas
and pond. Still maturing, there are
extended and additional borders
incl new plants and interesting
foliage amongst the flowers.
Exhibition of woodcarving and
paintings.

NEW 159 PICKERSLEIGH ROAD
Phil & Karen Hopkinson. *Round
the corner from 10 Layton Ave*
Developing garden of 2 distinct
areas. Mixed borders,
incorporating pond, stream and
waterfalls, incl arbour and
pergolas. Good sized traditional
fruit and vegetable plot.

28 LITTLE LARFORD
Scots Lane, Astley Burf DY13 0SB.
Lin & Derek Walker, 01299 823270,
walker363@btinternet.com,
www.littlelarfordcottage.org.uk. *3m
W of Stourport-on-Severn. Take A451
from Stourport, turn L onto B4196 for
Worcester. After 1m turn L signed
Larford Lakes. Garden approx 1¹/₂ m
further on. Access via Larford Lane or
Seedgreen Lane.* Home-made teas.
**Adm £3, chd free. Suns 19, 26 Apr;
19 July (11-5).** Visitors also welcome
by appt April, early May & July,
groups of 10+.
Hillside ¹/₂ -acre garden surrounding
picturesque thatched cottage (not
open) in woodland setting. 'Tulip
Time' - many thousands of tulips in
ambitious bedding displays amongst
shrub and herbaceous borders.
Colourful containers and hanging
baskets, cut flower and vegetable
garden, glasshouse and frames. July is
'lily time'. Woodland walk with
numerous bird boxes and viewpoint
overlooking cottage towards Severn
valley. 'Nature Centre' A walk with
wildlife. Featured in 'English Garden'
(America), 'Garden Answers' &
'Garden News'.

29 ◆ LITTLE MALVERN COURT
Little Malvern WR14 4JN. Mrs T M
Berington, 01684 892988,
littlemalverncourt@hotmail.com,
www.marlbrookgardens.com. *3m
S of Malvern. On A4104 S of junction
with A449.* Teas & cakes. **Adm £4.50,
chd 50p. Weds & Thurs 22 Apr to 23
July. For NGS: Sun 22 Mar; Mon 4
May (2-5).**
10 acres attached to former
Benedictine Priory, magnificent views
over Severn valley. Intriguing layout of
garden rooms and terrace round
house designed and planted in early
1980s; water garden below feeding
into chain of lakes; wide variety of
spring bulbs, flowering trees and
shrubs. Notable collection of old-
fashioned roses. Topiary hedge and
fine trees. Featured in 'Worcestershire
Life'.

THE LONG BARN
See Herefordshire.

LONGACRE
See Herefordshire.

Group opening

30 MARLBROOK GARDENS
Bromsgrove B60 1DY. *2m N of Bromsgrove. 1m N of M42 J1, follow B4096 signed Rednal, turn L at Xrds into Braces Lane. 1m S of M5 J4, follow A38 signed Bromsgove, turn L at T-lights into Braces Lane. Parking available.* Home-made teas at St Lukes Church (Suns). **Combined adm £5, chd free. Suns 31 May; 5 July; 2 Aug (1.30-5.30). Evening Opening £6, wine & light refreshment, Sat 5 Sept (6.30-10).**
Experience the difference! Three stunning gardens of contrasting style, from gently sloping to challenging terraces. Why not join us for a glass of wine in September for our spectacular evening opening when all three gardens are illuminated with hundreds of lights. For more details visit www.marlbrookgardens.com. Featured in 'Daily Mail' weekend magazine.

24 BRACES LANE
Lynn & Alan Nokes, 0121 445 5520, alyn.nokes@virgin.net. Visitors also welcome by appt, groups of 20+.
Gentle sloping garden (175ft x 38ft) landscaped into 4 rooms. Mediterranean area with exotics some rare and unusual. Pond, stream and patio area planting for sunny and shady aspects and mature lawn and borders incl monochrome bed. Large vegetable garden with raised beds and greenhouses, seating in all areas.

OAK TREE HOUSE
504 Birmingham Road. Di & Dave Morgan, 0121 445 3595, meandi@btinternet.com. Visitors also welcome by appt, groups of 20+.
Plantsman's cottage garden overflowing with plants, pots and interesting artifacts. Wildlife pond, waterfall, alpine area, plenty of seating, secluded patio and rear open vista. Special interests incl scented plants and hostas. Hidden front garden. Featured in 'Garden News'.

SARANACRIS
28A Braces Lane. John & Janet Morgan, 0121 445 5823, saranacris@btinternet.com. Visitors also welcome by appt,

groups of 20+.
Riot of colour in an unusual terraced garden designed and built by owners in former sand quarry. 'Jungle style' planting with rare and exotic plants set amongst mature trees, ponds, stream and waterfalls. Roof garden, conservatory and glasshouse planted with gingers. Featured on Central TV News.

This is not a plantsman's garden - more a growing awareness of the dietary preferences of rabbits . . .

31 NEW MEADOW FARM
33 Droitwich Road, Feckenham B96 6RU. Robert & Diane Cole, 01527 821156, meadowfarm33@aol.com. *1/2 m W of Feckenham, on B4090. Droitwich Rd.* **Adm £5 tea incl, chd free. Visitors welcome by appt for groups min 15, coaches permitted.**
1 acre garden created since 1999 by enthusiastic husband and wife team, and intensively planted with herbaceous perennials. Particularly colourful between June and Sept, but planted for all season interest. 1¼ acre wild flower meadow, and ¾ acre nursery not normally open to the public. Worcestershire's best kept secret.

32 NEW THE MILL HOUSE
Ham Green Lane, Redditch B97 5UB. Jackie & Richard Raby. *8m W of Redditch, 8m S of Bromsgrove. Off B4090 Ham Green situated between Hanbury, Collow Hill & Feckenham.* Home-made teas. **Adm £4, chd free. Tues 21, 28 Apr; 5 May (10.30-4.30).**
The Mill House stands on the site of a corn mill recorded on the Blaygrave map of 1591. Set in a charming secluded location in the midst of ever encroaching countryside drifts of wild garlic mingled with bluebells flourish along the Swansbrook stream, sheltering abundant wildlife. This is not a plantsman's garden - more a growing awareness of the dietary preferences of rabbits.

33 NEW HOUSE FARM
Elmbridge Lane, Elmbridge WR9 0DA. Charles & Carlo Caddick, 01299 851249. *2½ m N of Droitwich Spa. From Droitwich take A442 to Cutnall Green. Take lane opp The Chequers PH and proceed 1m to T-junction, turning L towards Elmbridge Green & Elmbridge. Continue along lane passing church and church hall. At T-junction turn into Elmbridge Lane, garden on L.* Home-made teas. **Adm £3, chd free. Visitors welcome by appt April to Sept.**
This charming garden surrounding an early C19 red brick house, has a wealth of rare trees and shrubs under planted with unusual bulbs and herbaceous plants. Special features are the 'perry wheel', ornamental vegetable gardens. Water garden, dry garden and rose garden, mews, retreat, potager and greenhouse. Topiary and tropical plants complete the effect. Willow pottery. Haws watering cans.

THE ORCHARDS
See Herefordshire.

34 ORLETON HOUSE
Orleton, Stanford Bridge WR6 6SU. Jenny & John Hughes, 01584 881253, jenny@orleton.co.uk, www.orletonhouse.co.uk. *6m E of Tenbury Wells. 15m NW of Worcester. A443 from Worcester for 10m then B4203 towards Bromyard. Cross R Teme at Stanford Bridge then next R turn. 1m down this lane.* Wine, light refreshments & teas. **Adm £4, chd**

free. Sats, Suns 30, 31 May; 25, 26 July (11-5). Visitors also welcome by appt for groups of 15+, May to July. 4 acres of garden, adjoining paddocks and wooded areas surrounding a Jacobean grade 11 listed house (not open) amid breathtaking beauty of the Teme Valley. Colourful herbaceous borders with abundance of unusual plants sit alongside a stream with boardwalk and tree house. New lych gate leads to a white garden. Jenny's pottery workshop will be open. Jenny's pottery demonstrations will take place during the open days. Featured in the 'English Garden'.

  ⅄ ✖ ✪ ⊨ ☕ ☎

35 **OVERBURY COURT**
nr Tewkesbury GL20 7NP. Mr & Mrs Bruce Bossom, 01386 725111, garden@overburyestate.co.uk. *5m NE of Tewkesbury. Village signed off A46.* **Adm £3.50.** Visitors welcome by appt.
Georgian house 1740 (not open); landscape garden of same date with stream and pools; daffodil bank and grotto. Plane trees; yew hedges; shrubs; cut flowers; coloured foliage; gold and silver, shrub rose borders. Norman church adjoins garden. Some slopes, while all the garden can be viewed, parts are not accessible to wheelchairs.

  ⅄ ✖ ☎

Cottage garden with delightful country views . . .

Group opening

36 **PERSHORE GARDENS**
8 High Street, Pershore WR10 1BG. Janet Stott, 01386 555349, www.visitpershore.co.uk. *On the B4084 between Worcester and Evesham.* Tickets and maps can be obtained from Number 8 High St opp Angel Hotel. Teas at various locations. **Combined adm £5, chd free. Sat 6 (1-6), Sun 7 June (1-5).**
A variety of gardens tucked away behind the elegant facades of Pershore's town houses - tiny courtyards, walled gardens, formal gardens, some river frontages, plus the allotments and children's garden. Gardens in the centre of town and on outskirts start at Number 8. Featured in local press.

  ♿ ☕

THE PICTON GARDEN
See Herefordshire.

37 **4 PODEN COTTAGES**
Honeybourne WR11 7PS. Patrick & Dorothy Bellew, 01386 438996, pots@poden.freeserve.co.uk. *6m E of Evesham. At the Gate Inn take the Pebworth, Long Marston rd, turn R at end of the Village for Mickleton. 1m on Mickleton Rd.* Home-made teas. **Adm £3, chd free. Sun 12, Mon 13 Apr; every Thurs 2 July to 30 July; (2-6).** Visitors also welcome by appt anytime.
⅓ -acre cottage and rose garden which has been planted by the owners. Paths wind through mixed herbaceous borders. 100 different roses old and modern, shrubs, small terrace and pond. Fine views over the Cotswold Hills. All-yr colour. Small vegetable garden. Featured in NGS Teas - Promoted by 'Plus One Living' in Japan.

  ⅄ ✖ ✪ ☕ ☎

38 **PUMP COTTAGE**
Hill Lane, Weatheroak B48 7EQ. Barry Knee & Sue Hunstone, 01564 826250, barryknee.1947@btinternet.com. *3m E of Alvechurch. 1½ m from J3 M42 off N-bound c'way of A435 (signed Alvechurch). Parking in adjacent field.* Home-made teas. **Adm £3, chd free. Fri 19, Sat 20, Mon 22 June (11-5).** Visitors also welcome by appt Mar to Oct inclusive.
C19 cottage, charming 1 acre plantsman's garden, in rural setting. Extensively planted, cottage garden, paths meandering through rockery and water features, romantic area with trees, shrubs and roses. Large natural pool, water lilies, boardwalk, wildlife area. Continually developing with new planting and features, incl folly and bridge. Increased spring interest for spring 2009. Featured in 'Garden News'. Restricted wheelchair access, some slopes, steps and narrow paths.

  ♿ ✖ ☕ ☎

RAGLEY HALL GARDENS
See Warwickshire & part of West Midlands.

39 ◆ **RED HOUSE FARM**
Flying Horse Lane, Bradley Green B96 6QT. Mrs M M Weaver, 01527 821269, www.redhousefarmgardenandnursery.co.uk. *7m W of Redditch. On B4090 Alcester to Droitwich Spa. Ignore sign to Bradley Green. Turn opp The Red*

Lion PH. **Adm £2, chd free. Daily 26 Feb to 29 Oct. For NGS: Every Thurs 26 Feb to 29 Oct (11-5).**
Created as a peaceful haven from its working farm environment, this mature country garden offers yr-round interest. In densely planted borders a wide range of traditional favourites rub shoulders with the newest of introductions and make each visit a pleasurable and rewarding experience. Adjacent nursery open daily 10-5. Featured in 'Worcester Evening News', GGG & on Radio Hereford & Worcester.

  ✖ ✪

40 ◆ **RIVERSIDE GARDENS AT WEBBS OF WYCHBOLD**
Wychbold, nr Droitwich WR9 0DG. Webbs of Wychbold, 01527 860000, www.webbsdirect.co.uk. *2m N of Droitwich Spa. 1m N of M5 J5 on A38. Follow tourism signs from motorway.* **Adm free for NGS all yr. Open daily all yr except Easter Sun, Christmas & Boxing Day & Easter Sun.** For opening times please tel or see website.
Riverside gardens occupy 2½ -acres of themed gardens incl National Collection of *Potentilla fruticosa*, colour spectrum garden, white garden, dry garden, David Austin roses, grass garden and many others under continual development. The New Wave section opened in 2004; designed by Noel Kingsbury, this area features a series of plantings of naturalised perennials for differing situations. These are both eye catching and wildlife friendly. Once established they will require minimum maintenance.

  ♿ ✖ ✪ NCCPG ☕

41 **NEW** **ROSE COTTAGE**
Moseley Road, Hallow WR2 6NJ. Hazel Kemshall & Chris Neville. *3m NW of Worcester off A443. Turn at Hallow PO into Moseley Rd, garden ¼ m on R.* **Adm £2, chd free. Sun 7 June (11-5).** Also open **Worlds End Nursery.**
Cottage garden with delightful country views. Interesting layout complementing a mild slope, well-stocked herbaceous borders, gravel garden, variety of beds created for all-yr round interest. Peak summer flowering incls hardy geraniums, roses, traditional cottage garden plants against a background of mature trees, hedges and shrubs.

  ✖

42 **NEW** **ROUND LODGE**
5 Court Mews, Jennett Tree
Lane, Callow End WR2 4UA.
Cathy Snelgar. *5m S of
Worcester. From Worcester take
A449 Malvern Rd to Powick, L
onto B4429 signed Upton, to
Callow End, turn R in Jennett Tree
Lane, Stanbrook Abbey on corner.
Court Mews is approx ³/₄ m on L.
Disabled parking only next to
house, park in lane.* Home-made
teas. **Adm £3, chd free.** Sun 13
Sept (11-4).
¼ acre country garden within part
of early Victorian walled garden.
2 distinct areas divided by original
kitchen garden wall. Colour
themed borders, original pond,
island bed, lawns and terrace.
Through wall to small shade
garden, orchard and kitchen
garden. Delightful evocative garden
with many old features. Some
gravel paths.

43 **ST EGWINS COTTAGE**
1 Church Lane, Norton, Evesham
WR11 4TL. Anne & Brian Dudley,
01386 870486. *2m N of Evesham. On
B4088. Park in St Egwins Church car
park only (not in Church Lane).* **Adm
£2.50, chd free.** Visitors welcome by
appt 16 May to 16 Aug, individuals &
groups also welcome.
Plant lovers cottage garden, unusual
and traditional plants, ferns, hardy
geraniums, phlox, clematis, lobelia,
roses and shrubs. Apple tree border
with shade loving plants to give
colourful textured display. Paved/gravel
area with pots of ferns, hostas and
perennials. Strategically placed seats,
ensure that different aspects are
discovered as the garden is explored.

44 **SHUTTIFIELD COTTAGE**
Birchwood, Storridge WR13 5HA.
Mr & Mrs David Judge, 01886
884243. *8m W of Worcester. Turn R
off A4103 opp Storridge Church to
Birchwood. After 1¹/₄ m L down steep
tarmac drive. Please park on roadside
but drive down if walking is difficult.*
Adm £3.50, chd free. Sats 25 Apr; 2,
16 May; 6 June; 4 July; 8 Aug; 19
Sept (130-5.30); Sat 26, Sun 27 Sept
(2-5). Visitors also welcome by appt,
coaches by prior arrangement only.
Superb position and views.
Unexpected 3 acre plantsman's
garden with extensive herbaceous

borders, primula and stump bed, many
unusual trees, shrubs and perennials,
colour-themed for interest throughout
the year. Walks in the 20-acre wood
with ponds and natural wild areas
where anemones, bluebells,
rhododendrons and azaleas are a
particular feature in spring. Large old
rose garden with many spectacular
mature climbers. Good garden colour.
Small deer park, vegetable garden and
teas under thatch. Featurd in GGG.

Delightful evocative garden with many old features . . .

Group opening

45 **SOUTH LITTLETON
GARDENS**
nr Evesham WR11 8TH. Mr & Mrs
Barnsley. *4m NE of Evesham. On
B4085. Car parking and toilets on
recreation ground. Transport provided
to outlying gardens.* Home-made teas
at Friends Meeting House (Shinehill
Lane). **Combined adm £5, chd free.**
Sat 13, Sun 14 June (12-6).
Group of gardens around South
Littleton. in the heart of the beautiful
Vale of Evesham. Incl allotments and
new cottage created by one man for
the Senior Citizens Bungalows.
Gardens vary in size and character
from the traditional to the unusual.

46 ◆ **SPETCHLEY PARK
GARDENS**
Spetchley WR5 1RS. Mr John
Berkeley, 01453 810303,
www.spetchleygardens.co.uk. *2m E
of Worcester. On A44, follow brown*

signs. **Adm £6, chd free,**
concessions £5.50. Wed to Sun &
Bank Hols 21 Mar to 30 Sept 11-6;
Oct weekends 11-4. For NGS: Fri
10 Apr; Sun 5 July (11-5.30).
30-acre garden containing large
collection of trees; shrubs and plants,
many rare and unusual. Red and fallow
deer in nearby park. A wonderful
display of spring bulbs, but masses of
colour throughout spring and summer.
Every corner of this beautiful garden
reveals some new vista, some new
treasure of the plant world. Gravel
paths.

STANTON GARDENS
See Gloucestershire North &
Central.

47 ◆ **STONE HOUSE COTTAGE
GARDENS**
Stone DY10 4BG. James & Louisa
Arbuthnott, 01562 69902,
www.shcn.co.uk. *2m SE of
Kidderminster. Via A448 towards
Bromsgrove, next to church, turn up
drive.* **Adm £3, chd free.** Weds to
Sats 18 March to 12 Sept. For
NGS: Weds, Thurs, Fris, Sats 18,
28 Mar; 10, 23 Apr; 16 May; 17 June;
24 July; 22 Aug; 3, 12 Sept (10-5).
A beautiful and romantic walled garden
adorned with unusual brick follies. This
acclaimed garden is exuberantly
planted and holds one of the largest
collections of rare plants in the country.
It acts as a shop window for the
adjoining nursery. Partial wheelchair
access.

48 **TANNACHIE**
Harcourt Road, Malvern WR14 4DN.
Mr & Mrs R Morgan. *On western
slopes of Malvern hills. Off B4232,
1.2m N of Wyche Cutting. From Great
Malvern take A449 then B4218 to The
Wyche. Parking at Horseshoe bend on
B4232 or on Harcourt Rd.* Home-
made teas. **Adm £3, chd free.** Suns
19 Apr; 14 June (2-5).
Victorian garden, approx 1¹/₂ acres
currently undergoing restoration.
35 metre herbaceous border, terrace
with views to Hay Bluff, rock garden,
rhododendron area, sunken garden,
children's garden with fedge and
roundhouse, woodland, vegetable and
fruit garden. Magnolias, azaleas, giant
redwood, deodara cedar, crinodendro
hookerianum, gunnera, fig and vine.
Featured in 'NGS Newsletter'.

49 NEW TREETOPS

28 Hallow Lane, Lower Broadheath WR2 6QL. Ian & Ruth Edynbry. *3m N W of Worcester. B4204 (signed Martley) to Lower Broadheath, after PO 2nd R into Hallow Lane, for 300yds.* **Adm £3, chd free. Fri 19, Sat 20 June (1-5).**
The design is based on different 'rooms' a formal patio area with pergola, water garden, bordered by roses and shrubs. Glade with silver birch and acers. Feature of the garden 100 vines, herbaceous border, small soft fruit, vegetable area and orchard. NB No wine for sale.

Group opening

50 NEW TWO GARDENS IN ECKINGTON

WR10 3BH. *A4104 (from B4084 through Pershore) to Upton & Defford, L turn B4080 to Tewkesbury/Eckington, R Drakes Bridge Rd, L Manor Rd round s bend - 2nd entrance on R,* stonewall entrance. Home-made teas. **Combined adm £3.50, chd free (share to Cats Protection League). Sat 30, Sun 31 May (11-5).**
2 diverse garden, cottage and formal gardens with topiary, both incl ponds and wildlife set in lovely village of Eckington with riverside parking, picnic site. Gravel paths.

NEW BROOK HOUSE

Manor Road. Lynn Glaze
1acre cottage garden, perennial planting, large pond with koi carp, surrounded by alpine rockery.

NEW THE CROFT

Upper End. Mr & Mrs M J Tupper, 01386 750819. *Garden has electric gates, admission requires pressing a button on a VDU screen to obtain entrance.* **Visitors also welcome by appt.**
Formal garden with fish pond, topiary and dew pond with ducks and geese. Hedges and stone paths, gazebo overlooking the whole garden.

51 THE TYNINGS

Church Lane, Stoulton, nr Worcester WR7 4RE. John & Leslie Bryant, 01905 840189, john.bryant@onetel.com. *5m S of Worcester; 3m N of Pershore. On the B4084 (formerly A44) between M5 J7 & Pershore. The Tynings lies beyond the church at the extreme end of Church Lane. Ample parking.* Home-made teas. **Adm £3, chd free. Sun 19 July (2-5). Evening Opening £4, wine, Sat 1 Aug (6-8). Visitors also welcome by appt, mid May to mid Aug, coaches permitted.**
Plantsman's 1/2 -acre garden, in a rural setting with views of Stoulton Church, generously planted with unusual shrubs and trees. Island beds, herbaceous borders and water features contain an extensive (and growing) selection of lilies, euphorbias, berberis, euonymus and ferns. Wide variety of dahlias add colour throughout summer and autumn. Tree ferns, bamboos and bog garden add to the surprises round every corner. Plants labelled. Planting list available.

52 TYTHE BARN HOUSE

Chaddesley Corbett DY10 4QB. Judy & John Berrow, 01562 777014, j.berrow@virgin.net. *41/2 m from Bromsgrove; 41/2 m from Kidderminster. On A448. 150yds towards Kidderminster from the turn into Chaddesley Corbett village. Limited parking at garden. Parking in village (The Talbot) or at village hall (200 yds). Walking difficulties park in private lane.* Home-made teas. **Adm £2.50, chd free. Sun 14 June (2-5.30). Visitors also welcome by appt June & July, groups of 10+, coaches permitted.**
Approx 3/4 -acre romantic garden created in old farm rickyard, within old farm building complex in conservation area surrounded by sheep. Incl old and modern roses; herbs and herbaceous borders. Small terrace garden. Shrubs and trees together with vegetable plot and greenhouse. Lovely view of the church and surrounding countryside. Featured in 'Limited Edition', 'Garden News'.

53 THE WALLED GARDEN

6 Rose Terrace, off Fort Royal Hill, Worcester WR5 1BU. Julia & William Scott. *1/2 m from cathedral. Via Fort Royal Hill, off London Rd (A44). Park on first section of Rose Terrace & walk the last 20yds down track.* **Adm £2.50, chd free. Sats 25 Apr; 30 May; 20 June; 25 July (1-5).**
Peaceful oasis of organically grown aromatic, decorative culinary and medicinal herbs, vegetables, flowers and fruit trees in a C19 walled kitchen garden. Whilst preserving its history the garden is continuing to change and flourish. Featured in 'Kitchen Garden' magazine & on BBC Radio Hereford & Worcester.

54 WESTACRES

Wolverhampton Road, Prestwood DY7 5AN. Mrs Joyce Williams, 01384 877496. *3m W of Stourbridge. A449 in between Wall Heath (2m) & Kidderminster (6m). Parking Beechwood Bonsai (next door).* Home-made teas. **Adm £2.50, chd free (share to DEBRA). Sat 15, Sun 16 Aug (11-5). Visitors also welcome by appt.**
3/4 -acre plant collector's garden, many unusual varieties, formal area with large koi pool. Path to woodland with many acers, tree ferns and 80 varieties of hostas. Conifers Japanese style garden with bamboos and grasses. Covered tea area, small plant nursery.

55 WHITCOMBE HOUSE

Overbury, nr Tewkesbury GL20 7NZ. Faith & Anthony Hallett, 01386 725206, tonyhallett@nsl.eclipse.co.uk. *9m S of Evesham. 9m N of Cheltenham, 5m E of Tewkesbury. Signed Overbury take A46 at Beckford Inn or at r'about junction of A46, A435 & B4077 take small lane signed Overbury or take Bredon rd out of Tewkesbury. In village turn up hill, garden 1st on L before village hall.* Home-made teas. **Adm £3.50, chd free. Suns 10 May; 14 June; 12 July (2-5). Visitors also welcome by appt Apr to Sept, groups 10+, coaches welcome.**
Cotswold stone-walled 1 acre garden planted for every season with cool spring borders of blue, yellow and white merging into summer magnificence, pastel coloured herbaceous borders, flowering shrubs, self seeded primula, poppy, foxglove and arum lily. Completed by a

Gardens set in lovely village of Eckington with riverside parking . . .

magnificent burst of late summer gold, orange and red. 12 colour packed herbaceous borders framed by mature trees, shrubs, approx 100 roses provides a warm relaxing ambience in an ever changing spectacle. A stream runs over mini waterfalls and under the Captains Bridge. Its cool babble soothes and provides for easy reflection and peace. Kitchen garden, fig tree and collection of home produced plants complete the pure indulgence.

Becomes confetti capital when acres of farmland are in colourful bloom . . .

56 WHITE COTTAGE
Earls Common Road, Stock Green, nr Inkberrow B96 6SZ. Mr & Mrs S M Bates, 01386 792414, cranesbilluk@aol.com. *2m W of Inkberrow, 2m E of Upton Snodsbury. A422 Worcester to Alcester, turn at sign for Stock Green by Red Hart PH, 1¹/₂ m to T- junction, turn L.* **Adm £2.50, chd free, concessions £2. Sun 5 Apr (2-5); Sat 30, Sun 31 May (10-5). Visitors also welcome by appt groups welcome 10+.** 2 acres, herbaceous and shrub beds, stream and spring wild flower area, rose garden, raised woodland bed, large specialist collection of hardy geraniums and echinacea. Adjacent nursery. Featured in 'Cotswold Life' & on TV Gardeners World (talking about geraniums).

57 ◆ WHITLENGE GARDENS
Whitlenge Lane, Hartlebury DY10 4HD. Mr & Mrs K J Southall, 01299 250720, www.whit-lenge.co.uk. *5m S of Kidderminster, on A442. Take A449 from Kidderminster towards Worcester,* then A442 (signed Droitwich) over small island, ¹/₄ m, 1st R into Whitlenge Lane. Follow signs. **Adm £2.50, chd free. Open all yr except Christmas, Mon to Sat (9-5), Sun (10-5). For NGS: Suns, Mons 12, 13 Apr; 3, 4, 24, 25 May; 30, 31 Aug (10-5).** 3 acre show garden of professional designer with over 800 varieties of trees, shrubs etc. Twisted pillar pergola, camomile lawn, waterfalls and pools. Mystic features of the Green Man, 'Sword in the Stone' and cave fernery. Walk the labyrinth and take refreshments in The Garden 'Design Studio' tearoom. Featured in 'Limited Edition'.

Group opening

58 NEW WICK VILLAGE
WR10 3NU. *1m E of Pershore on B4084, signed Post to Wick, almost opp Pershore Horticultural College.* **Combined adm £5, chd free. Sun 12 July (2-5).** Wick becomes confetti capital when acres of farmland are in colourful bloom. Approx 10 gardens incl a romantic manor, cottage gardens with a twist, gardener's gardens with fruit and vegetables, gardens for wildlife and new gardens continuing their transformation to maturity.

NEW AALSMEER
Main Street. Peter Edmunds
Spring/early summer garden with a selection of shrubs and herbaceous.

NEW CONFETTI FIELD
School Lane.
10 acres of delphiniums ajacis and cornflowers. Known as 'confetti fields'. Cut flowers for sale. Featured in 'Saga' magazine.

NEW GLENMORE COTTAGE
Main Street. Susan Allard
Cottage garden for C21. Herbaceous beds with cottage garden favourites, pond and raised bed with Mediterranean theme. Wheelchair access via gate next to garage off Cook's Hill.

NEW THE OLD FORGE
Main Street. Sean & Elaine Young
Our garden is relatively young. We have introduced structures, and a pond to allow for a variety of perennials, grasses and shrubs. We plan to continue this development over next few years.

NEW TUDOR HALL
Main Street. Mr & Mrs A Smart
Garden inspired by Lawrence Johnson's 'Hidcote'. 0.3 acre site has been divided into interconnected hedge 'rooms'. Perennial and herbaceous borders, fun topiary and summer colour.

NEW VENEDIGER
Wick House Close. Alan & Barbara de Ville
0.2 acre sloping garden with lawns, herbaceous and small tree borders plus fruit trees and vegetable area.

NEW WAVENEY
Owletts Lane. Mr & Mrs G Burton
Small garden on sloping site. Herbaceous borders, pond, fruit and vegetables and overflowing pots.

NEW 5 WICK HOUSE CLOSE
Jill & Martin Willams
Lawned 60ft x 45ft garden bordered on 3 sides with shrubs and herbaceous plants featuring 2 giant Sequoia Wellingtonia. Garden is currently undergoing renovation to a designer by local designer Kate Smart.

NEW WICK MANOR
Main Street. Charles Hudson
Romantic manor garden, surrounded by an intresting garden that has evolved over several hundred years.

NEW WILLOW CORNER
Wick House Close. Marjorie Donaldson
Garden rises from the rear of the house with retaining wall and steps. Gravel area, rose and clematis arches, trees and borders stocked with mature shrubs.

NEW WOODWARDS HOUSE

Cooks Hill. **Garth & Lynne Raymer**
Large garden with 3 distinct zones. Redesigned house garden, incl walled area, raised pond and extensive rockeries. 2nd zone is a mature fruit and vegetable garden while at the top is a wilderness area. Sloped path to main area and up hill, on grass hereafter.

WOODPECKERS

See Warwickshire & part of West Midlands.

Fun topiary and summer colour . . .

59 WORLDS END NURSERIES

Moseley Road, Hallow WR2 6NJ. **Kristina & Robin Pearce,** 01905 640977, www.worldsendgarden.co.uk. *4m NW of Worcester. At Hallow PO follow lane to Sinton Green. Ignore L turn to Wichenford, garden next on R.* Teas. **Adm £3, chd free. Suns 7 June; 12 July (11-5).** Also open **Rose Cottage 7 June.**
³/₄ -acre garden laid out to a mixture of island beds and formal planting. Garden contains many unusual herbaceous plants, grasses, ferns and over 200 varieties of hostas all clearly labelled. Newly developed rill and alpine garden with stone troughs and raised beds was completed in 2008.

Worcestershire County Volunteers

County Organiser
Judy Berrow, Tythe Barn House, Chaddesley Corbett DY10 4QB, 01562 777014, j.berrow@virgin.net

County Treasurer
Cliff Woodward, 11 Trehernes Drive, Pedmore, Stourbridge DY9 0YX, 01562 886349

Publicity
David Morgan, Oak Tree House, 504 Birmingham Road, Marlbrook B61 0HS, 0121 445 3595, meandi@btinternet.com

Leaflet Coordinator
Alan Nokes, 24 Braces Lane, Marlbrook, Bromsgrove B60 1DY, 0121 445 5520, alyn.nokes@virgin.net

Assistant County Organisers
Richard Armitage, 11 Myatts Field, Harvington, Evesham WR11 8NG, 01386 871211
Valerie Austin, Primrose Cottage, 6 Wyre Hill, Bewdley DY12 2UE, Tel 01299 409441
Mike George, 55 Hawkwood Crescent, Worcester WR2 6BP, 01905 427567

YORKSHIRE

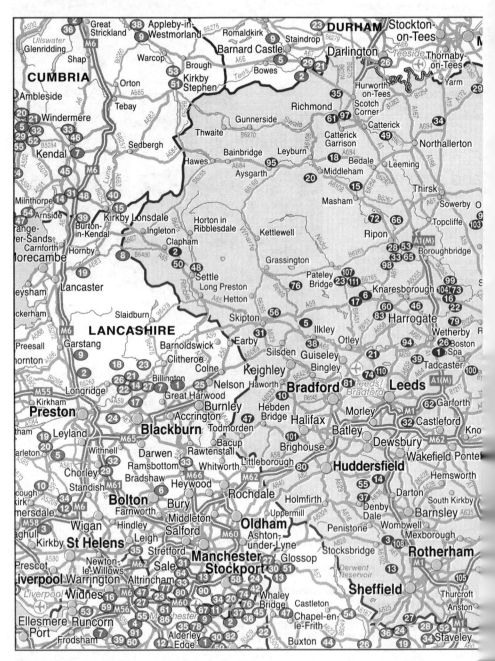

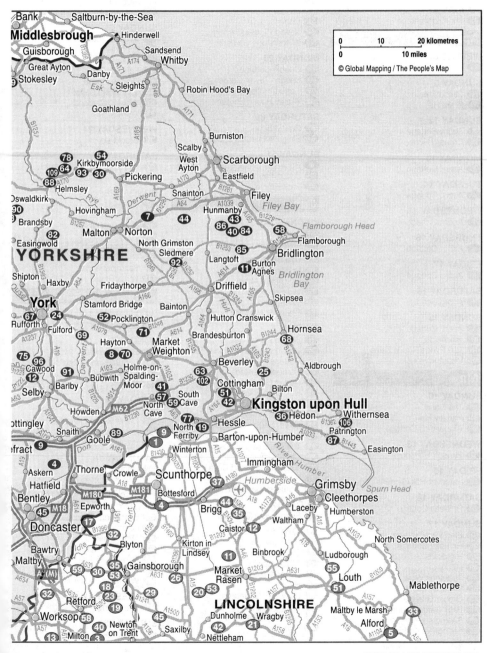

0   10   20 kilometres
0   10 miles
© Global Mapping / The People's Map

THE YELLOW BOOK | **601**

Opening Dates

March

SUNDAY 1
9 Bridge Farm House

SUNDAY 22
73 The Old Vicarage

April

WEDNESDAY 1
65 Newby Hall & Gardens

SUNDAY 5
15 Clifton Castle
30 Friars Hill

SUNDAY 12
1 Acorn Cottage
75 Orchard House

MONDAY 13
1 Acorn Cottage

TUESDAY 14
1 Acorn Cottage

WEDNESDAY 15
1 Acorn Cottage

THURSDAY 16
1 Acorn Cottage

FRIDAY 17
1 Acorn Cottage

SATURDAY 18
1 Acorn Cottage

SUNDAY 19
1 Acorn Cottage
37 Highfields
79 130 Prince Rupert Drive
100 Vicarage House

May

SUNDAY 10
19 The Court
34 Harlsey Hall
107 Woodlands Cottage

WEDNESDAY 13
5 Beacon Hill House

FRIDAY 15
76 Parcevall Hall Gardens

SATURDAY 16
29 Fir Trees Cottage

SUNDAY 17
7 Blackbird Cottage
29 Fir Trees Cottage
37 Highfields
39 Hillbark
44 Jacksons Wold
62 Millrace Nursery
75 Orchard House
83 RHS Garden Harlow Carr
89 Saltmarshe Hall
96 Stillingfleet Lodge

SATURDAY 23
64 Nawton Tower Garden

SUNDAY 24
21 Creskeld Hall
42 56 Hull Road
51 Linden House
64 Nawton Tower Garden
109 Wytherstone Gardens

MONDAY 25
16 Cobble Cottage
64 Nawton Tower Garden
99 Tinkers Hollow
101 Warley House Garden

SATURDAY 30
78 Pennyholme
93 Sleightholmedale Lodge

SUNDAY 31
8 Boundary Cottage
9 Bridge Farm House
77 Park House

June

WEDNESDAY 3
38 5 Hill Top
54 Low Askew

SATURDAY 6
11 Burton Agnes Hall
20 Coverham Abbey
72 Old Sleningford Hall
78 Pennyholme
93 Sleightholmedale Lodge

SUNDAY 7
11 Burton Agnes Hall
25 Dowthorpe Hall & Horse Pasture Cottage
35 Hartforth Gardens
36 Hedon Gardens
43 Hunmanby Grange
44 Jacksons Wold
45 Jasmine House
56 Lower Heugh Cottage Garden
61 Millgate House (Day & Evening)
69 The Old Coach House
72 Old Sleningford Hall
79 130 Prince Rupert Drive
97 Swale Cottage
109 Wytherstone Gardens

FRIDAY 12
90 Shandy Hall (Evening)

SUNDAY 14
4 B J Nurseries
6 Birstwith Hall
15 Clifton Castle
24 Derwent House
39 Hillbark
40 Holly Tree Cottage
63 Molecroft Cottage
66 Norton Conyers
68 Nutkins

84 The Ridings
91 Skipwith Hall
102 26 West End

FRIDAY 19
90 Shandy Hall (Evening)

SUNDAY 21
3 Avenue Cottage
10 Brookfield
22 Croft Cottage
49 Langton Farm
87 Ruston House
96 Stillingfleet Lodge
104 Whixley Gardens
108 Wortley Hall

WEDNESDAY 24
10 Brookfield

SATURDAY 27
27 Fernleigh
29 Fir Trees Cottage

SUNDAY 28
27 Fernleigh
29 Fir Trees Cottage
44 Jacksons Wold
48 Langcliffe Hall
50 Lawkland Hall
74 The Orchard
89 Saltmarshe Hall
111 Yorke House

July

WEDNESDAY 1
12 Cawood Gardens

SUNDAY 5
4 B J Nurseries
9 Bridge Farm House
34 Harlsey Hall
39 Hillbark

SUNDAY 12
12 Cawood Gardens
23 Dacre Banks Gardens
80 2 Prospect Place
86 Rustic Cottage

SATURDAY 18
52 Linden Lodge
82 Rewela Cottage
93 Sleightholmedale Lodge

SUNDAY 19
26 East Wing, Thorp Arch Hall
52 Linden Lodge
67 The Nursery
82 Rewela Cottage
85 Rudston House
93 Sleightholmedale Lodge
109 Wytherstone Gardens

WEDNESDAY 22
31 The Grange

SUNDAY 26
40 Holly Tree Cottage

59 39 Market Place
84 The Ridings
95 Stainsacre
106 Withernsea Gardens

August

SATURDAY 1
105 Winthrop Park Nature Therapy
and Sensory Garden

SUNDAY 2
32 Grasmere
49 Langton Farm
98 Thorpe Lodge

WEDNESDAY 5
31 The Grange

SATURDAY 8
58 Mansion Cottage

SUNDAY 9
58 Mansion Cottage

WEDNESDAY 12
31 The Grange

SATURDAY 15
83 RHS Garden Harlow Carr

SUNDAY 16
2 Austwick Hall
62 Millrace Nursery

SUNDAY 23
9 Bridge Farm House
14 The Circles Garden

SUNDAY 30
17 Cold Cotes

MONDAY 31
13 72 Church Street

September

SUNDAY 6
8 Boundary Cottage
55 Lower Crawshaw
96 Stillingfleet Lodge

SUNDAY 13
79 130 Prince Rupert Drive

SUNDAY 27
65 Newby Hall & Gardens

Gardens open to the public

11 Burton Agnes Hall
18 Constable Burton Hall Gardens
44 Jacksons Wold
47 Land Farm
65 Newby Hall & Gardens
66 Norton Conyers
76 Parcevall Hall Gardens
83 RHS Garden Harlow Carr
90 Shandy Hall
92 Sledmere House
96 Stillingfleet Lodge
110 York Gate

By appointment only

28 Field Cottage
33 Greencroft
41 Hotham Hall
46 Kelberdale
53 Littlethorpe Manor
57 Manor House
60 The Mews Cottage
70 The Old Priory
71 The Old Rectory
81 The Ranch House
88 Rye Hill
94 Spring Close Farm
103 The White House

Also open by appointment ☎

1 Acorn Cottage
2 Austwick Hall
4 B J Nurseries
6 Birstwith Hall
8 Boundary Cottage
9 Bridge Farm House
10 Brookfield
12 9 Anson Grove, Cawood Gardens
12 21 Great Close, Cawood Gardens
13 72 Church Street
16 Cobble Cottage
17 Cold Cotes
19 The Court
23 Low Hill, Dacre Banks Gardens
24 Derwent House
25 Dowthorpe Hall & Horse Pasture Cottage
26 East Wing, Thorp Arch Hall
29 Fir Trees Cottage
30 Friars Hill
31 The Grange
34 Harlsey Hall
37 Highfields
40 Holly Tree Cottage
43 Hunmanby Grange
45 Jasmine House
49 Langton Farm
55 Lower Crawshaw
56 Lower Heugh Cottage Garden
58 Mansion Cottage
59 39 Market Place
61 Millgate House
62 Millrace Nursery
64 Nawton Tower Garden
68 Nutkins
75 Orchard House
79 130 Prince Rupert Drive
80 2 Prospect Place
82 Rewela Cottage
85 Rudston House
86 Rustic Cottage
87 Ruston House
89 Saltmarshe Hall
93 Sleightholmedale Lodge
95 Stainsacre
98 Thorpe Lodge

100 Vicarage House
102 26 West End
105 Winthrop Park Nature Therapy and Sensory Garden
107 Woodlands Cottage
108 Wortley Hall
109 Wytherstone Gardens
111 Yorke House

The Gardens

1 ACORN COTTAGE
50 Church Street, Boston Spa
LS23 6DN. Mrs C M Froggatt, 01937
842519. *1m SE of Wetherby. Off A1
on A659 Church St opp Central
Garage.* Home-made teas. **Adm £3.50
incl teas, chd free. 12 Apr to 19 Apr
(11-5). Visitors also welcome by
appt Mid Mar to mid April only.**
You are invited to come and spend
peaceful time in this small well
established alpine garden full of spring
delights. Three generations of the
family have collected the plants and
bulbs, and these have recently been
rearranged and the garden significantly
altered for ease of maintenance and
access without losing the character
and uniqueness of this fine collection.
Featured in 'Garden News'. Some
small steps.

**ALKBOROUGH AND BURTON
STATHER GARDENS**
See Lincolnshire.

ASKHAM GARDENS
See Nottinghamshire.

You are
invited to come
and spend
peaceful time
in this small
garden full
of spring
delights . . .

2 AUSTWICK HALL
Town Head Lane, Austwick, nr Settle LA2 8BS. Eric Culley & Michael Pearson, 015242 51794, austwickhall@austwick.org, www.austwickhall.co.uk. *5m W of Settle. From A65 to Austwick Village. Pass Game Cock Inn on L. After Primary School turn L Town Head Lane.* Home-made teas. **Adm £2.50, chd free. Sun 16 Aug (12-5).** Visitors also welcome by appt.
Historic manor house and gardens set in the dramatic limestone scenery of the Yorkshire Dales. Formal terraces with herbaceous borders are divided by lawns, gravel paths and dry stone walls. Specimen trees, and juniper lined walk leads to jungle garden. Featured in 'Yorkshire Life'.
✕ ❀ ⌂ ☕ ☎

Fringed by ancient hedgerow which incl wild hops, honeysuckles and roses . . .

3 AVENUE COTTAGE
Wortley Village S35 7DB. Vega Shepley & Roger England. *9m NW of Sheffield, 5m SW of Barnsley. On A629 Huddersfield - Sheffield rd in Wortley village, signed Wortley Hall & Gardens.* Teas at Wortley Hall. **Sun 21 June (12-4)** combined with **Wortley Hall** adm £5.
Within the walled kitchen garden of Wortley Hall and attached to original gardener's cottage the garden overlooks the tree line of Wortley Hall Gardens. Gravelled island beds with Mediterranean style plantings are set in lawn. Areas for wildlife, large mixed shrubbery, and vegetable garden on raised beds. Garden is totally organic.
✕ ❀ ☕

4 NEW B J NURSERIES
Broad Lane, Sykehouse, Goole DN14 9AX. Jim & Linda Bennett, 01405 785277. *7m NE of Doncaster. M18 J6, A614 towards Goole. 1st L, follow rd to junction, approx 3m. Turn L, garden behind arena. From A19 towards Doncaster, L at Askern, 4m to Sykehouse.* Home-made teas. **Adm £3, chd free. Suns 14 June; 5 July (10-5).** Visitors also welcome by appt Apr to Sept, coaches or groups of 10+.
Ex-nursery now converted to 5-acre garden fringed by ancient hedgerow which incl wild hops, honeysuckles and roses. Very many unusually large mixed beds containing extensive range of herbaceous perennials, shrubs and grasses. Small lake and woodland walk encouraging wildlife. Adjacent nursery. Gravel paths.
♿ ✕ ❀ ☕ ⌂ ☎

5 BEACON HILL HOUSE
Langbar, nr Ilkley LS29 0EU. Mr & Mrs D H Boyle. *4m NW of Ilkley. 1¼ m SE of A59 at Bolton Bridge.* Home-made teas. **Adm £3, chd free** (share to Riding for the Disabled). **Wed 13 May (1.30-5).**
900ft up the southern slope of Beamsley Beacon, the garden is sheltered by woodland on the north and a Victorian windbreak to the west. Rhododendrons, magnolias and other early flowering shrubs and trees benefit from this. Later, large scrambling roses and borders with unusual plants provide interest.
✕ ❀ ☕

6 BIRSTWITH HALL
High Birstwith, nr Harrogate HG3 2JW. Sir James & Lady Aykroyd. *5m NW of Harrogate. Between Hampsthwaite & Birstwith villages, close to A59 Harrogate/Skipton rd.* Home-made teas. **Adm £3.50, chd free. Sun 14 June (2-5).** Visitors also welcome by appt, coaches permitted. Please write.
Large 8-acre garden nestling in secluded Yorkshire dale with formal garden and ornamental orchard, extensive lawns, picturesque stream, large pond and Victorian greenhouse.
♿ ❀ ☕ ☎

7 BLACKBIRD COTTAGE
Scampston YO17 8NG. Mrs Hazel Hoad. *5m E of Malton. Off A64 to Scarborough through Rillington, turn L signed Scampston only. Follow signs.* Home-made teas. **Adm £2.50, chd free. Sun 17 May (10-5).**
⅓ -acre plantswoman's garden made from scratch since 1986. Great wealth of interesting plants, with shrub and herbaceous border and a new themed gravel garden. Alpines a speciality. Please visit throughout the day to ease pressure on small but inspirational garden. Plants for sale by Rona Ashworth.
✕ ❀ ☕

BOTTESFORD GARDENS
See Lincolnshire.

8 BOUNDARY COTTAGE
Seaton Ross, York YO42 4NF. Roger Brook, 01759 319156, twinponds@talktalk.net. *5m SW of Pocklington. From A64 York, take Hull exit & immed B1228, approx 9m, then follow signs Seaton Ross. From M62 Howden N on B1228 approx 11m, R turn to Seaton Ross. Garden 1m before Seaton Ross. From Hull turn R 100yds before Seaton Ross.* Home-made teas. **Adm £3, chd free. Suns 31 May; 6 Sept (12-5).** Visitors also welcome by appt for guided tour and refreshments, May to October.
Third opening of horticulturist Roger Brook's ¾ -acre plantsman's garden. New features incl third pond, unlined 'streams' in the bog garden and 100 hardy cacti in the gravel garden. Garden includes 'roof garden without roof', extensive mixed and herbaceous borders, maturing specimen trees, unorthodox fruit and vegetables, alpine troughs and seasonal container displays. National Collection of Dicentra. Artist working in garden (Sept). Featured in 'Amateur Gardening' & 'The English Garden'.
♿ ✕ ❀ NCCPG ⌂ ☕ ☎

9 BRIDGE FARM HOUSE
Long Lane, Great Heck, Nr Selby DN14 0BE. Barbara & Richard Ferrari, 01977 661277. *6m S of Selby. 3m E of M62 (J34) A19 turn E at r'about to Snaith onto A645, straight on at T-lights then 1st R to Great Heck. House 1st on L, park in adjacent field.* Teas in church opposite. **Adm £2.50, chd free. Suns 1 May; 31 May; 5 July; 23 Aug (12-4).** Visitors also welcome by appt, groups of 10+, coaches permitted.
Large all-yr round organic garden designed and created by owners since 2002. Creatively planted with many unusual and interesting plants incl: long double borders, ponds, bog, gravel, pots, poultry, wildlife areas, working compost heaps, trees, woodland, spring interest borders and named varieties of snowdrops and hellebores.
♿ ✕ ❀ ☕ ☎

⑩ BROOKFIELD
Jew Lane, Oxenhope BD22 9HS.
Mrs R L Belsey, 01535 643070. *5m SW of Keighley. Take A629 towards Halifax. Fork R onto A6033 towards Haworth. Follow signs to Oxenhope. Turn L at Xrds in village. 200yds after PO fork R, Jew Lane.* Home-made teas. **Adm £3, chd free. Sun 21, Wed 24 June (1.30-5.30). Visitors also welcome by appt in May, June & July.**
1-acre, intimate garden, incl large pond with island, mallards, new apricot call ducks, and European pochard. Many varieties of candelabra primulas and florindaes, azaleas, rhododendrons. Unusual trees and shrubs, screes, greenhouse and conservatory. New series of island beds. Quiz for children.

🐕 ❀ ☕ ☎

⑪ ◆ BURTON AGNES HALL
Driffield YO25 4ND. Mrs S Cunliffe-Lister, 01262 490324, www.burtonagnes.com. *Between Driffield & Bridlington. Burton Agnes is on A614.* **Adm £4, chd £2.50, concessions £4 (donation to NGS) Gardener's Fair £4.50, chd £2.50, concessions £4. 1 April to Fri 31 Oct. For NGS: Gardener's Fair Sat 6, Sun 7 June (11-5).**
8 acres. Lawns with clipped yew and fountains; woodland gardens and walled garden containing potager; herbaceous and mixed borders; maze with thyme garden; jungle garden; campanula collection garden and coloured gardens containing giant games boards. Collections of hardy geraniums, clematis, penstemons and many unusual perennials.

♿ ❀ ☕

Group opening

⑫ CAWOOD GARDENS
YO8 3UG. *5m N of Selby. On B1223 5m NW of Selby & 7m SE of Tadcaster. Between York & A1 on B1222.* Light refreshments (Anson Grove) & home made teas (Ash Lea). **Combined adm £5, chd free. Wed 1, Sun 12 July (12-5).**
An attractive, historic, riverside village. C11 church also open. Village maps given at all gardens.

☕

9 ANSON GROVE
Tony & Brenda Finnigan, 01757 268888. Visitors also welcome by appt.

Small garden with tranquil pools and secluded sitting places. Narrow winding paths and raised areas give views over oriental styled pagoda, bridge and Zen garden.

🐕 ❀ ☎

ASH LEA
Michael & Josephine Welbourn
Shrubs and fernery lead to colourful formal borders, in contrast to a relaxed atmosphere by a clear pool, leading to dining area and traditional vegetable garden edged in clipped box.

21 GREAT CLOSE
David & Judy Jones, 01757 268571. **Visitors also welcome by appt, groups of 10+.**
All-yr interest, with mixed planting in ever-changing borders, incl vegetables, herbs, grasses and many unusual and some exotic perennials. Ponds, stream and rose walk make a colourful garden with small summerhouse and plenty of places to sit and enjoy the views.

🐕 ❀ ☎

Varieties of South African bulbs, half-hardy and tender plants . . .

⑬ 72 CHURCH STREET
Oughtibridge S35 0FW. Linda & Peter Stewart, 0114 286 3847, lindastewart@talktalk.net. *6m N of Sheffield. M1 (J36) A61 (Sheffield). Turn R at Norfolk Arms PH. In Oughtibridge follow one-way system turning L immed after zebra crossing.* Home-made teas. **Adm £2.50, chd free. Mon 31 Aug (11-4). Visitors also welcome by appt groups of 10+.**
Wildlife-friendly 1/3-acre garden on N-facing slope. Informal beds providing yr-long interest have mixed plantings of trees, shrubs, phormiums, bamboos, grasses, ferns, bulbs and perennials which lead to a natural stream with a backdrop of native woodland. Garden railway open nearby.

🐕 ❀ ☕ ☎

⑭ NEW THE CIRCLES GARDEN
8 Stocksmoor Road, Midgeley, nr Wakefield WF4 4JQ. Joan Gaunt. *Equidistant between Huddersfield, Wakefield & Barnsley, W of M1. Turn off A637 in Midgeley at the Black Bull PH (sharp bend) onto B6117 (Stocksmoor Rd). Please park on L adjacent to houses.* Home-made teas. **Adm £3, chd free. Sun 23 Aug (1.30-5).**
1/2-acre plantswoman's garden on gently sloping site overlooking fields and woods. Designed and maintained by owner. Interesting herbaceous and shrub plantings linked by grass and gravel paths, incl varieties of S African bulbs, half-hardy and tender plants, perennials, holly, fruit trees and ferns. Terrace with pots, greenhouse, circular gravel garden and woodland beds.

❀ ☕

CLIFF HOUSE
See Lincolnshire.

⑮ CLIFTON CASTLE
Ripon HG4 4AB. Lord & Lady Downshire. *2m N of Masham. On road to Newton-le-Willows & Richmond. Gates on L next to red telephone box.* Home-made teas. **Adm £3.50, chd free (share to Talking Space). Suns 5 Apr; 14 June (2-5).**
Fine views, river walks, wooded pleasure grounds with bridges and follies. Cascades, wild flower meadow and 19C walled kitchen garden.

♿ ☕

⑯ COBBLE COTTAGE
Rudgate, Whixley, Nr York YO26 8AL. John Hawkridge & Barry Atkinson, 01423 331419. *6m E of Knaresborough. 8m W of York. 3m E of A1 off A59 York - Harrogate.* **Combined Mon 25 May (11-5) with Tinkers Hollow adm £3, chd free. Combined Sun 21 Jun (11.30-5) with Whixley Gardens adm £5, chd free. Visitors also welcome by appt.**
Imaginatively designed, constantly changing, small cottage garden full of decorative architectural plants and old family favourites. Interesting water garden, containers and use of natural materials. Black and white courtyard garden and Japanese style garden with growing willow screen.

🐕 ❀ ☎

COBWEBS
See Lincolnshire.

17 COLD COTES
Cold Cotes Road, nr Kettlesing, Harrogate HG3 2LW. Penny Jones, Ed Loft, Doreen & Joanna Russell, 01423 770937, info@coldcotes.com, www.coldcotes.com. *7m W of Harrogate. Off A59. After Black Bull PH turn R to Menwith Hill/Darley.* Home-made teas. **Adm £3.50, chd free.** Sun 30 Aug (11-5). Visitors also welcome by appt, May-Sept.
Large peaceful garden with expansive views is at ease in its rural setting. Series of discreet gardens incl formal areas around house, streamside walk and sweeping herbaceous borders inspired by the designer Piet Oudolf which are at their height in late summer, lead to a newly developed woodland garden with wonderful autumn colour. Art & Craft activities.

🐾 ✿ 🏠 ☕ ☎

Large peaceful garden with expansive views is at ease in its rural setting . . .

18 ◆ CONSTABLE BURTON HALL GARDENS
nr Leyburn DL8 5LJ. Mr Charles Wyvill, 01677 450428, www.constableburtongardens.co.uk. *3m E of Leyburn. Constable Burton Village. On A684, 6m W of A1.* **Adm £3, chd 50p, concessions £2.50.** Daily 14 Mar to 27 Sept (9-6).
Large romantic garden with terraced woodland walks. Garden trails, shrubs, roses and water garden. Display of daffodils and over 5000 tulips planted annually amongst extensive borders. Fine John Carr house (not open) set in splendour of Wensleydale countryside.

♿ ✿

19 THE COURT
Humber Road, North Ferriby HU14 3DW. Guy & Liz Slater, 01482 633609, guy@guyslater.karoo.co.uk. *7m W of Hull. Travelling E on A63 towards Hull, follow sign for N Ferriby. Through village to Xrds with war memorial, turn R & follow rd to*

T-junction with Humber Rd. Turn L & immed R into unmarked cul-de-sac, last house on LH-side. Home-made teas. **Adm £2.50, chd free.** Sun 10 May (1-5). Visitors also welcome by appt.
Romantic, restful and secluded, informal garden with yr-round interest. Hidden seating areas and summerhouses, small pond and waterfall. $2/3$ -acre garden surrounded by trees contains laburnum and wisteria tunnel which leads to well-planted shady woodland area, around tennis court. Many interesting features, courtyards and a 'pretty potty patio'.

♿ ✿ ☕ ☎

20 COVERHAM ABBEY
Leyburn DL8 4RL. Mr & Mrs Nigel Corner. *A6108 to Middleham then Coverdale Road out of Middleham following signs to 'The Forbidden Corner', past pond on R. Drive at bottom of steep bank on L before Church.* Home-made teas. **Adm £3.50, chd free.** Sat 6 June (2-5).
Varied garden set within grounds of C13 Premonstratensian Abbey ruins. Knot garden and herbaceous borders.

♿ 🐾 ✿ ☕

21 CRESKELD HALL
Arthington, nr Leeds LS21 1NT. J & C Stoddart-Scott. *5m E of Otley. On A659 between Pool & Harewood.* Home-made teas. **Adm £3.50, chd free.** Sun 24 May (12-5).
Historic picturesque $3^{1/2}$ -acre Wharfedale garden with beech avenue, mature rhododendrons and azaleas. Gravel path from terrace leads to attractive water garden with canals set amongst woodland plantings. Walled kitchen garden and flower garden. Specialist nurseries.

♿ 🐾 ✿ ☕

22 CROFT COTTAGE
Green Hammerton, Nr York YO26 8AE. Alistair & Angela Taylor. *6m E of Knaresborough. 3m E of A1M adjacent to A59. Entrance through orchard off old Harrogate rd.* Home-made teas. **Adm £2.50, chd free.** Sun 21 June (11.30-5). Combined with **Whixley Gardens** adm £5.
Secluded $1/2$ -acre cottage garden divided into a number of garden rooms. Conservatory, clipped yew, old brick, cobbles and pavers used for formal areas leading to water feature, mixed borders and orchard with wild flowers.

🐾 ✿ ☕

23 DACRE BANKS GARDENS
nr Summerbridge, Nidderdale HG3 4EW. *4m SE of Pateley Bridge, 10m NW of Harrogate. On B6451. Limited wheelchair access. Parking at each garden.* Home-made teas. **Combined adm £5, chd free.** Sun 12 July (11-5).
Lovely walk between gardens along valley. Picnic area at Yorke House.

♿ ✿ ☕

LOW HALL
Mrs P A Holliday, 01423 780230, pamelaholliday@btinternet.com. Visitors also welcome by appt May, June, July & Sept.
Romantic walled garden on different levels around a C17 family home (not open) with shrubs, climbing roses, tender plants, herbaceous borders and pond garden. Mature yews and beech hedges. Limited access, 2 steps.

☎

YORKE HOUSE
Anthony & Pat Hutchinson
(See separate entry).

24 DERWENT HOUSE
59 Osbaldwick Village, Osbaldwick YO10 3NP. Dr & Mrs D G Lethem, 01904 410847, davidlethem@tiscali.co.uk. *2m E of York. On village green at Osbaldwick off A1079. Parking in old school yard opp church 14 June.* Home-made teas. **Adm £2.50, chd free.** Sun 14 June (1.30-5). Visitors also welcome by appt in June.
$3/4$ -acre, attractive village garden extended in 1984 to provide new walled garden, summer house, conservatories and terraces. Rose garden, box parterres, pelargoniums, hardy geraniums and ornamental allée of apple and pears. Double herbaceous border leads to meadow with species roses and eucalyptus.

🐾 ✿ ☕ ☎

25 DOWTHORPE HALL & HORSE PASTURE COTTAGE
Skirlaugh HU11 5AE. Mr & Mrs J Holtby, 01964 562235, john.holtby@farming.co.uk. *6m N of Hull, 8m E of Beverley. On the A165 Hull to Bridlington Rd halfway between Coniston & Skirlaugh on the RH-side travelling N. Signed at the bottom of*

drive which has white railings. **Adm £5, chd free. Sun 7 June (11-5). Visitors also welcome by appt.**
3½ acres owned by professional garden designer. Kitchen garden potager, orchards, shady area, herbaceous borders, beautiful pond with island and bridge with bog planting. Wild areas for the plentiful wildlife and birds. Horse Pasture Cottage has a cottage garden with woodland water feature.

Holmesfield. *1st R Greenhill Ave, then 2nd R Meadowhead Ave.* Light refreshments. **Adm £2.50, chd free. Sat 27, Sun 28 June (1-5).**
Plantswoman's ⅓ -acre cottage style garden with large variety of unusual plants set in differently planted sections to provide all-yr interest. Auricula theatre and paved area for drought resistant plants in pots. Seating areas to view different aspects of garden. Patio with gazebo and greenhouse.

Visitors also welcome by appt between 12 to 24 May and 16 to 28 June only.
1 acre mixed shrubaceous borders, large rockeries, spring bulbs, species tulips, mature conifers, fritillaries, erythroniums and secluded ornamental pond. Hosta collection and garden sculpture. Tranquil garden surrounded by farmland with views to Cleveland Hills and Roseberry Topping. Designed and maintained by owners since 1992 with low maintenance in mind. Large private cacti collection. Pelargonium Exhibition at weekend openings. Access via gravel drive.

Inspiring, imaginatively developed contemporary garden in parkland setting. Striking views, dramatic combinations of plants framed by yew hedges and trained trees . . .

30 FRIARS HILL
Sinnington YO62 6SL. Mr & Mrs C J Baldwin, 01751 432179, friars.hill@abelgratis.co.uk. *4m W of Pickering.* On A170. **Adm £3, chd free. Sun 5 Apr (1-5). Visitors also welcome by appt mid March - end July.**
1¾ -acre plantswoman's garden containing over 2500 varieties of perennials and bulbs, with yr-round colour. Early interest with hellebores, bulbs and woodland plants. Herbaceous beds. Hostas, delphiniums, old roses and stone troughs. Featured in local press.

26 EAST WING, THORP ARCH HALL
Thorp Arch LS23 7AW. Fiona & Chris Royffe, 01937 843513, plantsbydesign@btinternet.com, www.eastwinggardens.info. *1m S of Wetherby.* Take A659 into Boston Spa centre. Turn L opp Cost-Cutters over bridge to Thorp Arch, at end of Main St turn L into Thorp Arch Park & R over cattle grid. Home-made teas. **Adm £3.50, chd free. Sun 19 July (12-5). Visitors also welcome by appt May to Aug, groups of 15+.**
¾ -acre surrounding East Wing of C18 John Carr house (not open). Inspiring, imaginatively developed contemporary garden in parkland setting. Striking views, dramatic combinations of plants framed by yew hedges and trained trees. Courtyards, ponds, potager, earth sculpture and dry garden, newly designed features. Photographic exhibition.

FANSHAWE GATE HALL
See Derbyshire.

27 FERNLEIGH
9 Meadowhead Avenue, Sheffield S8 7RT. Mr & Mrs K Littlewood. *4m S of Sheffield city centre. A61, A6102, B6054 r'about, exit B6054 towards*

28 FIELD COTTAGE
Littlethorpe Road, Ripon HG4 3LG. Richard & Liz Tite, 01765 690996, liztite@btinternet.com. *1m SE of Ripon.* Off A61 Ripon bypass follow signs to Littlethorpe, continue straight on at church, (Littlethorpe Rd) round sharp LH-bend 250yds on LH-side by derestriction sign. **Visitors welcome by appt, groups of 20+, coaches permitted.**
1-acre plantsman's garden for all seasons. Walled garden, small pond, raised sleeper beds and gravel garden, vegetable/cut flower plot, Victorian-style greenhouse, extensive range of unusual and tender plants in containers. Varied range of planting material makes use of challenging areas.

FIELD HOUSE FARM
See Lincolnshire.

29 FIR TREES COTTAGE
Stokesley TS9 5LD. Helen & Mark Bainbridge, 01642 713066, mark@firtreespelargoniums.co.uk, www.firtreespelargoniums.co.uk. *1m S of Stokesley.* On A172 garden will be signed Pelargonium Exhibition. Home-made teas. **Adm £3, chd free. Sats Suns 16, 17 May; 27, 28 June (10-4).**

THE GARDEN HOUSE
See Lincolnshire.

THE GARDENS AT DOBHOLME FISHERY
See Derbyshire.

31 THE GRANGE
Carla Beck Lane, Carleton BD23 3BU. Mr & Mrs R N Wooler, 01756 709342. *1½ m SW of Skipton.* Turn off A56 (Skipton-Clitheroe) into Carleton. Keep L at Swan PH, continue through to end of village & turn R into Carla Beck Lane. From Skipton town centre follow A6131. Turn R to Carleton. Cream teas. **Adm £3.50, chd free (share to Sue Ryder Care Manorlands Hospice). Weds 22 July; 5, 12 Aug (1-5). Visitors also welcome by appt in groups 10+ during August.**
Now reaching maturity, a plantsman's garden of over 4 acres of different features restored by the owners during the last 12 years. Large herbaceous border with ha-ha, walled garden, rose and clematis walk, ornamental grass beds, water features and vegetable beds, some unusual mature tree

specimens. Formal parterre garden. Gravel paths, gentle slopes, a few steps & cobbled area.

  ♿ ✕ ⊗ ☕ ☎

32 NEW GRASMERE
48 Royds Lane, Rothwell LS26 0BH. Terry & Tina Cook. *5m S of Leeds, 6½ m N of Wakefield. M62 J30 follow A642 towards Leeds. Turn L after 200yds (Royds School) Pennington Lane follow rd for 1m. Car parking at school opp or in rd nr squash club.* Home-made teas. **Adm £2.50, chd free. Sun 2 Aug (12-5).**
Amongst old orchard trees is hidden a restful family suburban garden of ⅓ -acre. Wildlife encouraged by many nesting boxes, pond, wild flower area, log piles for hedgehogs and flowers to attract butterflies. Secluded summerhouse enclosed by colourful tapestry hedge and architectural planting. Developing vegetable garden.

⊗ ☕

33 GREENCROFT
Pottery Lane, Littlethorpe, nr Ripon HG4 3LS. Mr & Mrs David Walden, 01765 602487. *1m SE of Ripon. Off A61 Ripon bypass, follow signs to Littlethorpe. Turn R at church (Pottery Lane) to Bishop Monkton for 1½ m. On RH-side after Littlethorpe Pottery (open). Car parking in field opp and at Pottery.* **Visitors welcome by appt.**
½ -acre informal garden made and built by owners. Special ornamental features incl gazebo, temple, pavilion, stone wall with mullions, pergola and formal pool. Long herbaceous borders lead to circular enclosed garden planted with late flowering perennials, annuals and exotics. Log cabin with shingle roof built alongside large pond.

✕ ☎

GRINGLEY GARDENS
See Nottinghamshire.

34 HARLSEY HALL
Northallerton DL6 2BL. Sir Joseph & Lady Barnard, 01609 882203. *14m S of Teeside. 7m E of Northallerton. From Northallerton A684 N towards A19. 5m L to East Harlsey. R at Cat & Bagpipes. From N 14m S Teeside on A19. R ¼ m N of Tontine Inn. From S 12m N of A19. L ¼ m N of Tontine Inn.* Home-made teas. **Adm £3, chd free. Suns 10 May; 5 July (2-5). Visitors also welcome by appt.**
5 acres of grounds incl shrubs, herbaceous plants, climbing roses, lonicera and clematis. Terraced lawns down to a series of lakes planted with cedars, acers, gean cherries, oaks and rhododendrons. Visit early spring for daffodils followed by bluebells. Many wild flowers, primroses and violets. St Oswald's Church containing effigy of Geoffrey de Hotham.

⊗ ☕ ☎

Group opening

35 NEW HARTFORTH GARDENS
Richmond DL10 5JR. *4m N of Richmond. From Gilling follow signs for Hartforth, then Hartforth Village.* **Combined adm £5, chd free. Sun 7 June (11-5).**
♿

NEW EASINGTOWN
John & Kate Stephenson
The garden was designed and first planted 10yrs ago, in a linked series of walled enclosures. The exact origins are unknown, but during the C20 enclosures were used for agriculture. Gordon Long and Malcolm Hockham from Eggleston Hall and Louise Bainbridge from Richmond create 5 separate gardens.

NEW NO 1 HARTFORTH
Mark & Sandra Stephenson
½ acre of typical English country house - parts established 30yrs ago and extended over the past 10yrs. A very peaceful setting.

Group opening

36 HEDON GARDENS
HU12 8JN. *Follow A1033 from Hull, towards Hedon.* Teas at 32 Baxtergate. **Combined adm £4, chd free (share to St Augustine's Church Restoration Fund). Sun 7 June (1.30).**
Historic market town, with royal charters dating back to C12. Present mayor is its 661st. Town Hall open, which contains ancient and civic silver, incl England's oldest civic mace. St Augustine's Church 'The King of Holderness' open. Tickets (with map) on sale at each garden.

✕ ⊗ ☕

32 BAXTERGATE
John & Barbara Oldham
Well designed garden made in 7yrs by former owners of The White Cottage, Halsham. Gravel and raised beds with many unusual plants, minute vegetable garden and fish pond.

56 ROSLYN CRESCENT
Ernie & Monica Kendall
Small town garden for plant enthusiasts, with yr-round interest, featuring hostas, mini hostas, ferns and other shade loving plants.

> Amongst old orchard trees is hidden a restful family suburban garden of ⅓ -acre . . . log piles for hedgehogs and flowers to attract butterflies . . .

37 HIGHFIELDS
Manorstead, Skelmanthorpe HD8 9DW. Julie & Tony Peckham, 01484 864336, julie-tony@tiscali.co.uk. *8m SE of Huddersfield. M1 (J39) A636 towards Denby Dale. Turn R in Scissett village (B6116) to Skelmanthorpe. After 2nd Police Speed Check sign turn L (Barrowstead), continue to top of hill.* **Adm £2, chd free. Suns 19 Apr; 17 May (2-5). Visitors also welcome by appt 20 April to 30 June.**
Small garden which shows creativity within metres rather than acres! 2 ponds, gravel bed, box parterre with obelisk water feature, arbours, arches and vertical structures. Incl collection of 30+ hebes in raised beds, and growing collection of muscari and alpines.

⊗ ☕ ☎

38 NEW 5 HILL TOP
Westwood Drive, Ilkley
LS29 9RS. Lyn & Phil Short.
*1/2 m S of Ilkley town centre. Turn
S at town centre T-lights up Brook
St, cross The Grove taking Wells
Rd up to the Moors.* Home-made
teas. Adm £2.50, chd free. Wed
3 June (11-4.30).
Delightful 2/3 -acre steep N facing
garden on edge of Ilkley Moor.
Sheltered woodland of Victorian
origin underplanted with
naturalistic, flowing tapestry of
foliage, shade loving flowers,
shrubs and ferns amongst large
moss covered boulders. Natural
stream, bridges, meandering gravel
paths and steep steps give
'Dingley Dell' a touch of magic.
Summerhouse with stunning views
over Wharfedale and moors.

✕ ❀ ☕

39 HILLBARK
Church Lane, Bardsey, Nr Leeds
LS17 9DH. Tim Gittins & Malcolm
Simm, www.hillbark.co.uk. *4m SW of
Wetherby. Turn W off A58 into Church
Lane, garden on L before church.*
Home-made teas. Adm £3, chd free.
Suns 17 May; 14 June; 5 July (11-5).
Established, award winning 1-acre
country garden. 3 S-facing levels,
distinct intimate areas; hidden corners;
surprise views. Evergreen structure
blends with formal topiary and
perennial flowers. Dramatic specimen
yew. Small ornamental ponds,
summerhouse overlooking gravel, rock
and stream gardens, large natural
pond with ducks. Marginal planting incl
bamboo, gunnera and royal fern.
Woodland approached by bridge
across stream. Large rambling roses.
Unusual ceramics.

✕ ❀ ☕

40 HOLLY TREE COTTAGE
Back Street, Burton Fleming
YO25 3PD. Susan Cross, 01262
470347, skcross@hotmail.co.uk.
*1m NE of Driffield. 11m SW of
Scarborough, 7m NW of Bridlington.
From Driffield B1249 before Foxholes
turn R to Burton Fleming. From
Scarborough A165 R to Burton
Fleming.* Home-made teas. Combined
adm with The Ridings £4, chd free.
Suns 14 June; 26 July (1-5). Visitors
also welcome by appt.
The owners' 3rd NGS garden, but
different in size and shape. Superbly
designed small garden planted with

over 100 clematis and 50 roses, hardy
geraniums, unusual plants and shrubs
in colour-themed mixed borders.
Attractive seating areas, pergolas,
water features and wildlife areas.

❀ ☕ ☎

41 HOTHAM HALL
Hotham YO43 4UA. Stephen &
Carolyn Martin, 01430 422054. *15m
W of Hull. Nr North Cave, J38 of M62
turn towards North Cave, follow signs
for Hotham.* Visitors welcome by
appt.
C18 Grade II house (not open), stable
block and clock tower in mature
parkland setting with established
gardens. Lake with bridge over to
newly planted island (arboretum).
Garden with Victorian pond and mixed
borders. Selection of spring flowering
bulbs. Gravel paths.

&. ☎

42 56 HULL ROAD
Cottingham HU16 4PU. Keith &
Mary Gregersen. *NW edge of Hull.
From Hull, Cottingham Rd & Hull Rd
(continuation), L after West Bulls PH.
From Cottingham 1/4 m from r'about.*
Light refreshments & teas. Adm £3,
chd free. Sun 24 May (1-5). Also
open Linden House.
Immaculate well designed 1/3 -acre
suburban garden broken into several
distinct areas featuring mature trees,
mixed border, pond, fernery, gravel
garden and several seating areas.

&. ✕ ❀ ☕

Natural stream,
bridges,
meandering
gravel paths
and steep
steps give
'Dingley Dell'
a touch of
magic . . .

43 HUNMANBY GRANGE
Wold Newton YO25 3HS. Tom & Gill
Mellor, 01723 891636,
gill.mellor@btconnect.com,
www.hunmanbygrange.co.uk.
*121/2 m SE of Scarborough. Hunmanby
Grange is a farm between Wold
Newton & Hunmanby on the rd from
Burton Fleming to Fordon.* Home-
made teas. Adm £3, chd free. Sun
7 June (11-5). Visitors also welcome
by appt May to July.
3-acre garden created from exposed
open field, on top of Yorkshire Wolds
nr coast. Hedges and fences now
provide shelter from wind, making
series of gardens with yr-round interest
and seasonal highlights. The Wold Top
Brewery open. Featured in 'Hull Daily
Mail'.

&. ✕ ❀ ☕ ☎

44 ◆ JACKSONS WOLD
Sherburn. Mr & Mrs Richard
Cundall, 01944 710335,
www.jacksonswoldgarden.com.
*11m E of Malton, 10m SW of
Scarborough. A64 in Sherburn. T-lights
take Weaverthorpe Rd. R fork to
Helperthorpe. E + W Lutton.* Adm £3,
chd free. Tues, Weds May to July,
adm £2.50. For NGS: Suns 17 May;
7, 28 June (1-5).
2-acre garden with stunning views of
the Vale of Pickering. Walled garden
with mixed borders, numerous old
shrub roses underplanted with unusual
perennials. Woodland paths lead to
further shrub and perennial borders.
Lime avenue with wild flower meadow.
Traditional vegetable garden with
roses, flowers and box edging framed
by Victorian greenhouse. Adjoining
nursery.

&. ✕ ❀ ☕

45 JASMINE HOUSE
145 The Grove, Wheatley Hills,
Doncaster DN2 5SN. Ray & Anne
Breame, 01302 361470. *2m E of
Doncaster. 1m E of Doncaster Royal
Infirmary off A18. Turn R into Chestnut
Ave (Motor Save on corner).* Home-
made teas. Adm £2, chd free (share
to Aurora Trust Fund). Sun 7 June
(1-5). Visitors also welcome by appt.
Colourful tropical to traditional, plant
packed haven. A real surprise awaits
you on entering this town 'garden for
all seasons'. Climbers festoon
archways that lead to enclosed
gardens displaying the gardener's love
of rare and unusual plants, from ferns
and alpines to bonsai and tender
perennials. Featured on Sky TV.

✕ ❀ ☕ ☎

46 KELBERDALE
Wetherby Road, Knaresborough HG5 8LN. Stan & Chris Abbott, 01423 862140, chrisatkelberdale@btinternet.com. *1m S of Knaresborough. On B6164 Wetherby rd. House on L immed after new ring rd (A658) r'about.* Visitors welcome by appt May to July, groups of 15+, coaches welcome. Winner of 3 national awards, this owner-made and maintained plantsman's garden overlooking the R Nidd has a bit of everything. Full of yr round interest with large traditional herbaceous border, colour themed beds, pond and bog garden, alpine house and troughs and vegetable garden. The wild garden with large pond and meadow is a haven for wildlife.

  ⅋ ✕ ⊛ ☕ ☎

KEXBY HOUSE
See Lincolnshire.

47 ◆ LAND FARM
Colden, Hebden Bridge HX7 7PJ. Mr J Williams, 01422 842260, www.landfarmgardens.co.uk. *8m W of Halifax. From Halifax at Hebden Bridge go through 2 sets T-lights. Take turning circle to Heptonstall. Follow signs to Colden. After 2¾ m turn R at 'no through' rd, follow signs to garden.* Adm £4, chd free. Weekends & Bank Hols from begining of May to end Aug. 6 acres incl alpine, herbaceous, formal and newly developing woodland garden, meconopsis varieties in June, cardiocrinum giganteum in July. Elevation 1000ft N-facing. C17 house (not open). Art Gallery. Some steps.

  ⅋ ☕

48 NEW LANGCLIFFE HALL
nr Settle BD24 9LY. Mr & Mrs Robert Bell. *1m N of Settle. From Settle B6479 signed Stainforth & Horton-in-Ribblesdale. Car parking in courtyard or village.* Adm £3, chd free. Sun 28 June (1-5). The dramatic limestone peak of Blua is the backdrop to 9-acres of parkland and gardens at Langcliffe Hall (Grade II Jacobean Manor House - not open). Formal parterre and herbaceous borders drift into wild flower meadows. Stone pergola, sunken rose garden, pond, orchard, ponies and a donkey. Vegetable garden with fruit cage, greenhouse and potting shed.

✕ ⊛ ☕

49 LANGTON FARM
Great Langton, Northallerton DL7 0TA. Richard & Annabel Fife, 01609 748446. *5m W of Northallerton. B6271 in Great Langton between Northallerton and Scotch Corner.* Cream teas. Adm £3, chd free. Suns 21 June; 2 Aug (2-6). Visitors also welcome by appt. Riverside garden comprising formal and informal gravel areas, nuttery, romantic flower garden with mixed borders and pebble pool. Organic.

  ⅋ ✕ ⊛ ☕ ☎

50 LAWKLAND HALL
Austwick LA2 8AT. Mr & Mrs G Bowring. *3m N of Settle. Turn S off A65 at Austwick/Lawkland Xrds or Giggleswick/Lawkland Xrds signed Lawkland/Eldroth. Follow signs to Lawkland.* Home-made teas. Adm £3, chd free. Sun 28 June (11-5.30). Old stone walls and established hedges surround and divide garden of Grade I Elizabethan hall (not open) into smaller enclosures. Potting shed, heather-thatched gazebo in rose garden, summer house in kitchen garden. Relaxed, mixed planting styles rub shoulders with formality. Small lake attracts wildlife incl kingfishers and dragonflies. Plentiful seating and level underfoot with few steps.

✕ ⊛ ⊨ ☕

Formal parterre and herbaceous borders drift into wild flower meadows. Stone pergola, sunken rose garden, pond, orchard, ponies and a donkey . . .

51 NEW LINDEN HOUSE
16 Northgate, Cottingham HU16 4HH. Eric Nicklas. *4m NW of Hull. From A164 turn onto B1233 signed Cottingham, garden on L 50yds before railway Xing. From A1079, turn onto B1233, straight on at bowling club, over Xing then 50yds on R.* Light refreshments & teas. Adm £2.50, chd free (share to Dove House, Hull). Sun 24 May (10-5). Also open 56 Hull Road. This interesting small garden in which its thoughtfully curved lawn, numerous shrubs, pond and aviary blend well together. Special features also make this a garden well worth seeing.

  ⅋ ✕ ⊛ ☕

52 NEW LINDEN LODGE
Newbridge Lane, nr Wilberfoss YO41 5RB. Robert Scott & Jarrod Marsden. *10m E of York. A1079 Hull/York rd, E of Wilberfoss and NW of Barmby Moor. Take turn signed Bolton, onto Bolton Lane. At Xrds turn L, garden after wood on R.* Cream teas. Adm £3.50, chd free. Sat 18, Sun 19 July (11-5). 1-acre garden, owner-designed and constructed since 2000, with many choice and unusual plants and trees. Gravel paths edges with box and lavender lead to herbaceous/mixed borders, wildlife pond and summerhouse. Also to kitchen garden, glasshouse, orchard and woodland area and formal garden with pond and water feature. Craft stalls.

  ⅋ ✕ ⊛ ☕

53 LITTLETHORPE MANOR
HG4 3LG. Mr & Mrs J P Thackray, john_p_thackray@compuserve.com *Outskirts of Ripon by racecourse. Ripon bypass A61. Follow Littlethorpe Rd from Dallamires Lane r'about to stable block with clock tower. Map supplied on application.* (share to Environment & Arts Projects at Yorkshire Cancer Centre). Visitors welcome by appt May to Aug, groups of 20+, coaches permitted. 11 acres. Walled garden based on cycle of seasons with box, herbaceous, roses, gazebo. Sunken garden with white rose parterre, herb, brick pergola with blue and yellow borders. Terraces, formal lawns with

fountain pool, hornbeam towers, box headed hornbeam drive. Parkland with lake, classical pavilion, cut flower garden. Spring bulbs. Gravel paths. Small lake, unfenced.

⑤④ LOW ASKEW
Cropton YO18 8ER. Mr & Mrs Martin Dawson-Brown. *5m W of Pickering. Signed to Cropton from A170. Between the villages of Cropton & Lastingham.* Cream teas. **Adm £3, chd free.** Wed 3 June (2-5). Designed by present owners to harmonise with the ancient and beautiful valley of the R Seven in which garden is situated. Now in its 3rd decade new plantings and ideas underway. Plants stall incl rare pelargoniums. Enchanting riverside walk.

38 LOW STREET
See Lincolnshire.

Parterre for late-summer exotics; herbaceous border, glasshouse with productive garden . . .

⑤⑤ LOWER CRAWSHAW
Off Stringer House Lane, Emley, nr Huddersfield HD8 9SU. Mr & Mrs Neil Hudson, 01924 840980, nhudson42@btinternet.com. *8m of Huddersfield. From Huddersfield turn R to Emley off A642 (Paul Lane). M1 J39 (A636) direction Denby Dale, 5m after Bretton r'about turn R to Emley, 1/2 m beyond Emley village turn (Stringer House Lane) continue for 1 m. Car park in adjacent field.* Home-made teas. **Adm £3.50, chd free.** Sun Sept (12-5). Visitors also welcome by appt in June & July, groups of 20+.
3 acre garden in open country on

eastern slopes of the Pennines, surrounding 1690s farmhouse (not open) with extensive range of old farm buildings. Garden created by owners since 1996. Natural stream runs through the garden, dammed on several levels and opening into 2 large ponds. Walled vegetable garden created from old barn, enclosed rose garden, orchard, and courtyard. Naturalistic planting of shrubs, trees and perennials. Partial wheelchair access.

⑤⑥ LOWER HEUGH COTTAGE GARDEN
Kirk Lane, Eastby BD23 6SH. Trevor and Marian Nash, 01756 793702. *2 1/2 m NE of Skipton. Follow the A59/65 N ring rd around Skipton, turn at signs for Embsay (railway) and Eastby. In Embsay follow signs for Eastby & Barden onto Kirk Lane. 6th house on R.* Home-made teas. **Adm £3, chd free.** Sun 7 June (1-6). Visitors also welcome by appt for groups (2 to 30) any time of year.
Visit unique Japanese 'stroll through garden' extending over almost 1 acre. Main emphasis is on conifers, acers, bamboos, grasses, heathers set within landscaped beds amid manicured lawns and beech hedges. For 2009, the kaiyushiki gardens will feature additional streams and pools, extended woodland and karesansui beds while maintaining the existing rojiniwai, tea house, pavilion and rock gardens. Partial wheelchair access.

⑤⑦ NEW MANOR HOUSE
Church Street, North Cave, Brough HU15 2LW. Mrs Jacky Carver, 01430 422203, jacky@northcave.plus.com. *1 1/2 m from M62, J38. B1230 E of North Cave, leaving village next to church.* **Adm £5, incl tea.** Visitors welcome by appt for groups of 10+.
2-acre garden surrounding C18 farmhouse with octagonal dovecote, stream and lake. Parterre for late-summer exotics; herbaceous border, glasshouse with productive garden and small orchard. Naturalistic planting at rear running into 20yr-old arboretum with spring bulbs and wild flowers and woodland walk by lakeside.

⑤⑧ MANSION COTTAGE
8 Gillus Lane, Bempton YO15 1HW. Polly & Chris Myers, 01262 851404, chrismyers@tinyworld.co.uk. *2m NE of Bridlington. From Bridlington take B1255 to Flamborough. 1st L at T-lights, go up Bempton Lane, turn 1st R into Short Lane then L at T-junction. Cross railway into Bempton, Gillus Lane is L fork at church.* Delicious fresh lunches & home-made teas. **Adm £2.50, chd free.** Sat 8, Sun 9 Aug (10-4). Visitors also welcome by appt, incl groups, throughout Aug.
Peaceful hidden garden with many different views. New for 2009, white border, ornamental ironworks and globe garden. In the 100ft mixed border, scented border, bog garden and patio, cuttery and late flowering hot bed has a wide variety of exuberant perennial planting and grasses. Water features, pots, vegetables, summerhouse and conservatory complete the picture. Exhibition of Art by local artist.

⑤⑨ 39 MARKET PLACE
South Cave HU15 2BS. Lin & Paul Holland, 01430 421874, paulandlin@btinternet.com. *12m W of Hull. From A63 turn N to South Cave on A1034. House on LH-side opp PO, before Xrds.* Home-made teas. **Adm £2.50, chd free.** Sun 26 July (2-5). Visitors also welcome by appt.
Small walled garden with eclectic planting. Established trees, cottage garden plants and evergreen shrubs. Rockeries, gravel fernery with grasses and water feature. Interesting stonework and lots of nooks and crannies. A few shallow steps and gravel paths.

⑥⓪ THE MEWS COTTAGE
1 Brunswick Drive, Harrogate HG1 2PZ. Mrs Pat Clarke, 01423 566292, patriciamclarke@hotmail.com. *W of Harrogate town centre. From Cornwall Rd, N side of Valley Gardens, 1st R (Clarence Dr), 1st L (York Rd), 1st L (Brunswick Dr).* Home-made teas. **Adm £3.** Visitors welcome by appt.
Small tranquil garden on sloping site featuring a terracotta tiled courtyard with trompe-l'oeil. A garden of special interest to hardy planters over a long season; recommended for an August visit when a large collection of phlox paniculata is in flower.

MILL FARM
See Lincolnshire.

61 MILLGATE HOUSE
Millgate, Richmond DL10 4JN. Tim
Culkin & Austin Lynch, 01748
823571,
oztim@millgatehouse.demon.co.uk,
www.millgatehouse.com. *Centre of
Richmond. House is located at bottom
of Market Place opp Barclays Bank.
Next to Halifax Building Soc.* **Adm
£2.50, chd £1.50. Day & Evening
Opening Sun 7 June (8am-8pm).**
Visitors also welcome by appt.
SE walled town garden overlooking
R Swale. Although small, the garden is
full of character, enchantingly secluded
with plants and shrubs. Foliage plants
incl ferns and hostas. Old roses,
interesting selection of clematis, small
trees and shrubs. RHS associate
garden. Immensely stylish, national
award-winning garden. Featured in
'The Sunday Times' & 'Pink Paper'.

62 MILLRACE NURSERY
84 Selby Road, Garforth LS25 1LP.
Mr & Mrs Carthy, 0113 2869233,
carol@millrace-plants.co.uk. *5m E of
Leeds. On A63 in Garforth. 1m from
M1 J46, 3m from A1.* Home-made
teas. **Adm £2.50, chd free. Suns 17
May; 16 Aug (1-5).** Visitors also
welcome by appt.
Overlooking a secluded valley. Garden
developed over last 9yrs to incl large
herbaceous borders containing many
unusual perennials, shrubs and trees.
The immediate garden also incl an
ornamental pond, vegetable garden
and small woodland. The outer garden
leads through a wild flower meadow to
large bog garden and wildlife ponds.
Specialist nursery.

63 MOLECROFT COTTAGE
Northgate, Walkington HU17 8ST.
Keith & Beverley Reader. *2m SW of
Beverley. On B1230 in Walkington,
turn R by the Dog & Duck PH.* **Adm
£3, chd free. Sun 14 June (1.30-5).
Also open 26 West End.**
The quintessential English garden. This
1-acre plot incl Yorkshire terrace with
pots and pond. Traditional maintained
lawn and herbaceous border area with
trees, 78ft rose walk with many
clematis underplanted with hostas. Hot
gravel garden, vegetable plot, wild
garden and orchard.

64 NAWTON TOWER GARDEN
Nawton YO62 7TU. Douglas Ward
Trust, 01439 771218. *5m NE of
Helmsley. From A170, between
Helmsley & Nawton village, at Beadlam
turn N 2½ m to Nawton Tower.* **Adm
£1.50, chd 50p. Sat 23, Sun 24, Mon
25 May (2-5).** Visitors also welcome
by appt during late April & May,
coaches permitted.
Large garden; heathers,
rhododendrons, azaleas, shrubs,
bluebells, bulbs and trees. Limited
wheelchair access, some steps and
slopes.

The garden is full of character, enchantingly secluded . . .

65 ◆ NEWBY HALL & GARDENS
Ripon HG4 5AE. Mr R C Compton,
01423 322583, www.newbyhall.com.
*2m E of Ripon. Signed from A1 &
Ripon town centre.* **For opening
details please tel or see website.
For NGS: Wed 1 Apr; Sun 27 Sept
(11-5).**
40 acres extensive gardens laid out in
1920s. Full of rare and beautiful plants.
Formal seasonal gardens, stunning
double herbaceous borders to R Ure
and National Collection holder *Cornus*.
Miniature railway and adventure
gardens for children. Contemporary
sculpture park set in a peaceful
woodland (June - Sept).

66 ◆ NORTON CONYERS
Wath, nr Ripon HG4 5EQ. Sir James
& Lady Graham, 01765 640333,
norton.conyers@bronco.co.uk. *4 m
N of Ripon. Take Melmerby & Wath
sign off A61 Ripon-Thirsk. Go through
villages to boundary wall. Signed entry
300metres on R.* **Adm £4, chd under
14 free. Please phone for details.
For NGS: Sun 14 June (2-5).**
Large C18 walled garden of interest to
garden historians. Interesting iron
entrance gate; herbaceous borders,
yew hedges and Orangery (open to the
public) with an attractive little pond in
front. Small sales area specialising in
unusual hardy plants, fruit in season.
House, which was visited by Charlotte

Brontë and is an original of Thornfield
Hall in 'Jane Eyre' is closed for major
repairs. Gravel paths, slight slope to
orangery.

67 THE NURSERY
15 Knapton Lane, Acomb
YO26 5PX. Tony Chalcraft & Jane
Thurlow. *2½ m W of York. Follow
B1224 towards Acomb & York city
centre, from A1237 York ringroad. Turn
L at first mini r'about into Beckfield
Lane. Knapton Lane 2nd L after 150
metres.* Home-made teas. **Adm £2,
chd free. Sun 19 July (1-5).**
Attractive 1-acre organic fruit and
vegetable garden behind suburban
house created from previous nursery.
Bush and trained fruit trees (incl 40+
varieties apples and pears), large and
small greenhouses, productive
vegetables grown in bed and row
systems interspersed with informal
ornamental plantings providing colour
and habitat for wildlife.

68 NUTKINS
72 Rolston Road, Hornsea
HU18 1UR. Alan & Janet Stirling,
01964 533721, ashornsea@aol.com.
*12m NE of Beverley. On B1242 S-side
of Hornsea between Freeport & golf
course.* Home-made teas. **Adm £2.50,
chd free. Sun 14 June (11-4).**
Visitors also welcome by appt.
³/₄ -acre garden with good backbone
of mature plants and trees,
herbaceous borders, bog garden and
recently developed woodland garden
and stream-side area. Seating areas to
linger and enjoy different views of the
garden. Partial wheelchair access,
gravel paths and steps.

69 THE OLD COACH HOUSE
Church Lane, Elvington YO41 4AD.
Simon & Toni Richardson. *8m SE of
York. From A1079 immediately after
York outer ring road, turn on B1228 fo.
Elvington. Disabled parking only on
Church Lane. Please park in village.*
Light refreshments & teas at village ha
Adm £3, chd free. Sun 7 June (12-5
Delightful atmospheric owner-made
2-acre garden. Extensive mixed long
borders, hosta garden and large
natural wildlife pond leading to
summerhouse, vegetable garden and
long rose pergola. Enclosed flower
garden with ornamental pool adjacen*
to house. Village fête.

70 THE OLD PRIORY
Everingham YO42 4JD. Dr J D & Mrs
H J Marsden, 01430 860222,
marsd13@aol.com. *15m SE of York,
5¹/₂ m from Pocklington. 2m S of the
A1079 York-Hull Rd. Everingham has
3 access rds, the Old Priory is to the
east of the Village.* Visitors welcome
by appt. Garden at its best late May
& Jun, coaches permitted.
Country garden of 2 acres on dry
sandy loam and wet peat land.
Conservatory, polytunnels, walled
vegetable garden. Mixed herbaceous
borders drop down to bog garden
where paths bridge the stream into
less formal garden which leads to lake.
Short woodland walk. Children enjoy
the animals. Gravel around house.

OLD QUARRY LODGE
See Lincolnshire.

71 THE OLD RECTORY
Nunburnholme YO42 1QU. Mr & Mrs
M Stringer, 01759 302295. *13m SE of
York. Turn off Hull-York A1079 at
Hayton (between Beverley & York).
Follow signs to Nunburnholme.*
Visitors welcome by appt.
Secluded large garden informally
planted with shrubs, perfumed roses
and generous herbaceous borders
blending into attractive countryside.
Unspoilt peaceful streamside. Orchard
and vegetable areas.

72 OLD SLENINGFORD HALL
Mickley, nr Ripon HG4 3JD. Jane &
Tom Ramsden. *5m NW of Ripon. Off
A6108. After N Stainley turn L, follow
signposts to Mickley. Gates on R after
1¹/₂ m opp cottage.* Home-made teas.
Adm £3.50, chd free (share to
Holyrood House Centre For Health &
Pastoral Care). Sat 6, Sun 7 June
(1-5).
Early C19 house (not open) and
garden with original layout of interest to
garden historians. Many acres with
mature trees, woodland walk and
Victorian fernery. Romantic lake with
islands, watermill, walled kitchen
garden, long herbaceous border, yew
and huge beech hedges. Several plant
and other garden stalls. The garden
has been closed for the new
herbaceous border to be planted in the
walled garden, which is in the process
of being re-developed.

73 THE OLD VICARAGE
Church Street, Whixley, Nr York
YO26 8AR. Mr & Mrs Roger
Marshall. *6m E of Knaresborough, 8m
W of York. 3m E of A1 (M) off A59 York
to Harrogate.* Light refreshments &
teas. Adm £3, chd free. Sun 22 Mar
(11-4); Combined with Whixley
Gardens adm £5 Sun 21 June
(11.30-5).
Delightful ³/₄ -acre walled flower garden
with gravel and old brick paths leading
to hidden seating areas and garden
structures festooned with climbers.
Mixed borders, old roses, wall shrubs,
hardy and half hardy perennials, bulbs
and hellebores. Featured in 'Bises'
magazine.

74 NEW THE ORCHARD
4a Blackwood Rise, Cookridge
LS16 7BG. Carol & Michael
Abbott. *5m N of Leeds centre. Off
A660 (Leeds-Otley) N of A6120
Ring Rd bear L onto Otley Old Rd.
Before radio mast turn L (Tinshill
Lane). Please park in Tinshill Lane
after passing council flats.* Home-
made teas. Adm £2, chd free
(share to NeST Nephrotic
Syndrome Trust). Sun 28 June
(1-6).
¹/₄ -acre hidden suburban oasis of
peace and tranquillity. Differing
levels made by owners using old
stone, found on site, planted for yr
round interest. Long rockery, fruit
tree arbour and sheltered oriental
styled seated area linked by narrow
grass lawns and steps. Mixed
perennials, bulbs and pots
amongst paved and pebbled
areas. Children's quiz.

75 ORCHARD HOUSE
Appleton Roebuck, York YO23 7DD.
David & Sylvia Watson, 01904
744460. *8m SW of York. 3m from A64
Bilborough Top flyover on Main St in
Appleton Roebuck.* Home-made teas.
Adm £3, chd free. Suns 12 Apr;
17 May (11-5). Visitors also welcome
by appt, groups of 10+, coaches
permitted.
Fascinating 1-acre garden created and
maintained by owners in harmony with
surrounding countryside. Brimming
with unusual features and ideas. Paths
of brick, cobble and grass wind
through extensive colourful plants to
old oak revolving summerhouse,

exposed tree roots with sunken garden
and grotto. Parasol bed, 'torr' with
chapel of rest, lily pond, rill, stream,
wildlife pond.

76 ◆ PARCEVALL HALL GARDENS
Skyreholme BD23 6DE. Walsingham
College, 01756 720311,
www.parcevallhallgardens.co.uk.
*9m N of Skipton. Signs from B6160
Bolton Abbey-Burnsall rd or off B6265
Grassington-Pateley Bridge.* Adm
£5.50, chd £2.50, concessions
£4.50. Daily 1 April to 31 Oct. For
NGS: Fri 15 May (10-6).
The only garden open daily in the
Yorkshire Dales National Park. 24 acres
in Wharfedale sheltered by mixed
woodland; terrace garden, nose
garden, rock garden, fish ponds. Mixed
borders, tender shrubs (desfontainea,
crinodendron, camellias); autumn
colour. Birdwatching, old apple orchard
for picnics.

77 NEW PARK HOUSE
Creyke Lane, Welton HU15 1NQ.
Noel & Jane Thompson. *9m W of
Hull. From A63 E towards Hull,
follow signs for Welton. Park in
village. Creyke Lane is unmade rd
to side of Green Dragon PH, rough
for approx 50yds.* Adm £3, chd
free. Sun 31 May (11-4).
Informal 1-acre plot with mature
beech trees, the garden is planted
for yr-round interest. Featuring
naturalistic mixed planting,
woodland walk, copper rill,
pergolas, ornamental herb garden
and raised vegetable beds.

Naturalistic
mixed planting,
woodland walk,
copper rill,
pergolas,
ornamental herb
garden . . .

78 PENNYHOLME

Fadmoor YO62 7JG. Mr & Mrs P R Wilkinson. *7m NE of Helmsley. From A170 between Kirkbymoorside & Nawton, turn N. 1/2 m before Fadmoor turn L, signed 'Sleightholmedale only' continue N up dale, across 3 cattle grids, to garden. No buses.* Home-made teas. **Adm £3.50, chd free. Sats 30 May; 6 June (1-5).** Also open **Sleightholmedale Lodge.**
Enchanting 10-acre country garden. Unique river and dale setting. Extensive collection of magnificent rhododendrons and azaleas in mature oak wood circular walk. Currently developing traditional rose/mixed borders, water features, wildlife garden and tree garden.

PINEFIELDS

See Lincolnshire.

79 130 PRINCE RUPERT DRIVE

Tockwith, York YO26 7PU. Mr & Mrs B Wright, 01423 358791, www.dryad-home.co.uk. *7m E of Wetherby. From B1224 Wetherby/York rd turn N to Cattal, after 1m turn R at Xrds to Tockwith. 1st turning on R in village. Please do not park in the cul-de-sac.* Home-made teas. **Adm £2.50, chd free. Suns 19 Apr (1-4); 7 June; 13 Sept (1-5).** Visitors also welcome by appt groups of 10+.
1/2 -acre enthusiast's garden planted for yr-round interest from early hellebores, cyclamen and bulbs to late perennials and grasses mixed with our large fern collection, in beds connected by gravel paths. Many plants grown from seed, incl wild-collected seed. Rock and bog gardens, pond and pergola, glasshouses, shade house, kitchen garden with vegetables and trained fruit, small nursery.

80 2 PROSPECT PLACE

Outlane, Huddersfield HD3 3FL. Carol & Andy Puszkiewicz, 01422 376408, carol-puszkiewicz@talktalk.net. *5m N of Huddersfield. 1m N of M62. J24 (W) take A643 to J23 (E) follow A640 to Rochdale. Turn R immed before 40mph sign (Gosport Lane). Parking in adjacent field.* Home-made teas. **Adm £2.50, chd free. Sun 12 July (12-5).** Visitors also welcome by appt June & July, groups of 6+.
1-acre long, intimate garden high in the Pennines (900ft). Narrow paths lead from cottage herbaceous borders and pond to shade areas and secret garden with camomile lawn, chocolate and silver borders surrounding circular bed and productive kitchen garden with trained fruit and flowers. Evolving wild area with native trees, large pond with indigenous planting, narrow stream and meadow. Children's garden trail.

81 THE RANCH HOUSE

60 Clara Drive, Calverley, nr Leeds LS28 5QP. Preston Harrison, 0113 257 0114. *8m NW of Leeds. From A6120 ring rd, take A657 through Calverley. Turn R just before petrol stn. House 1/2 m on R.* Home-made teas. **Visitors welcome by appt May to Aug, groups of 10+, coaches permitted.**
2-acre garden created in 1998 by owner. Series of interconnecting areas separated by yew hedges are linked by grass paths. Rose and clematis arches provide a succession of harmonious plantings to the numerous herbaceous and mixed borders. Ponds; woodland garden has evolving underplanting beneath mature trees with shrubs and woodlanders creating a naturalistic atmosphere. Efficient composting system.

RENISHAW HALL GARDENS

See Derbyshire.

82 NEW REWELA COTTAGE

Skewsby, York YO61 4SG. John Plant & Daphne Ellis, 01347 888125, plantjohnsgarden@btinternet.com. *4m N of Sheriff Hutton. After Sheriff Hutton, towards Terrington, turn L towards Whenby & Brandsby. Turn R just past Whenby to Skewsby. Turn L into village. 400yds on R.* Light refreshments & teas. **Adm £2.50, chd free. Sat 18, Sun 19 July (10-6).** Visitors also welcome by appt.
3/4 -acre ornamental garden, designed by current owner, featuring a great number of unusual trees and shrubs, many architectural plants, softening features like the pond, pergola, natural stone sunken garden, breeze house, paths, decking, fruit cage and raised vegetable garden. Featured in 'The Evening Press'. Gravel paths with some fairly steep slopes. Wheelchairs may need assistance.

Brick pergola and arches covered with climbers lead to secret garden with lavender edged beds . . .

83 ♦ RHS GARDEN HARLOW CARR

Crag Lane, Harrogate HG3 1QB. Royal Horticultural Society, 01423 565418, www.rhs.org.uk/harlowcarr. *11/2 m W of Harrogate town centre. On B6162 (Harrogate - Otley).* **Adm £7, chd £2.50 6-16. Open all yr except Christmas Day,** for times see website or tel. For NGS: **Sun 17 May; Sat 15 Aug (9.30-5).**
One of Yorkshire's most relaxing yet inspiring locations! Highlights incl spectacular herbaceous borders, streamside garden, alpines, scented and kitchen gardens. 'Gardens Through Time', woodland and wild flower meadow. Events all yr. Gravel paths, gentle slopes.

84 THE RIDINGS

Bridlington Road, Burton Fleming YO25 3PE. Roy & Ruth Allerston. *11m NE of Driffield. 11m SW of Scarborough, 7m NW of Bridlington. From Driffield B1249 before Foxholes turn R to Burton Fleming. From Scarborough A165 R to Burton Fleming.* Home-made teas. **Adm £4, chd free. Suns 14 June; 26 July (1-5).** Combined with **Holly Tree Cottage.**
Tranquil cottage garden designed by owners in 2001 on reclaimed site. Brick pergola and arches covered with climbers lead to secret garden with lavender edged beds. Colour-themed mixed borders with old English roses. Paved terrace with water feature and farming bygones. New gravel garden Featured in 'The Journal'.

85 RUDSTON HOUSE

Long Street, Rudston, nr Driffield YO25 4UH. Mr & Mrs Simon Dawson, 01262 420400. *5m W of Bridlington. On B1253. S at Bosville Arms for approx 300yds*. Cream teas. **Adm £3.50, chd free. Sun 19 July (11-5).** Visitors also welcome by appt Jun-Aug, groups any size, coaches permitted.

Birthplace of authoress Winifred Holtby. Victorian farmhouse (not open) and 3 acres of exuberant garden with fine old trees, lawns, paths with clipped box hedges, conifers, shrubs, greenhouses, roses, interesting potager with named vegetable varieties, hosta beds with lilies, and short woodland walk, with pond. Plenty of seats and interesting corners and features; children love to explore. Partial wheelchair access, ramp access, gravel paths.

86 RUSTIC COTTAGE

Front Street, Wold Newton, nr Driffield YO25 3YQ. Jan Joyce, 01262 470710. *13m N of Driffield. From Driffield take B1249 to Foxholes (12m), take L turning signed Wold Newton. Turn L onto Front St, opp village pond, continue up hill garden on L*. Light refreshments in village hall. **Adm £2.50, chd free. Sun 12 July (11-4).** Visitors also welcome by appt.

Plantswoman's cottage garden of much interest with many choice and unusual plants, incl old-fashioned roses, fragrant perennials and herbs grown together with wild flowers to provide habitat for birds, bees, butterflies and small mammals. It has been described as 'organised chaos'! The owner's 2nd NGS garden.

Plenty of
seats and
interesting
corners and
features;
children love
to explore . . .

87 NEW RUSTON HOUSE

Kiln Lane, Patrington HU12 0RP. Chris & Peter Robinson, 01964 630336, cripetrob@btinternet.com. *15m E of Hull on A1033. Fork R in village, signed Easington. 1st R after passing church into Kiln Lane*. Home-made teas. **Adm £4, chd free. Sun 21 June (11-5).** Visitors also welcome by appt.

2½ acres, mixture of mature and younger trees, sunken garden with water feature, kitchen garden, fruit and vegetables, small woodland walk, wild area, rainwater collection and storage system. Pergola and other interesting features. Walled garden, greenhouse and conservatory.

88 RYE HILL

15 Station Road, Helmsley YO62 5BZ. Dr & Mrs C Briske, 01439 770669. *Centre of Helmsley. Signed at Helmsley bridge on A170 (Thirsk-Scarborough)*. Light refreshments. **Adm £2.50, chd free (share to St Catherine's Hospice).** Visitors welcome by appt, June & July only. Coaches permitted.

Plantswoman's garden designed, constructed and maintained by owners. Divided into interlinking compartments, each planted in different style: formal, woodland and cottage. Intense planting using unusual plants for yr-round colour and interest. Conservatory, well stocked with tender species, ponds and many architectural features. New projects each yr.

89 SALTMARSHE HALL

Saltmarshe DN14 7RX. Mr & Mrs Philip Bean, 01430 430199, pmegabean@aol.com. *6m E of Goole. From Howden (M62, J37) follow signs to Howdendyke & Saltmarshe. House in park W of Saltmarshe village*. Home-made teas. **Adm £3.50, chd free. Suns 17 May; 28 June (12-5).** Visitors also welcome by appt.

Large lawns, fine old trees, R Ouse and a Regency house (not open) with courtyards provide setting for shrubs, climbers, herbaceous plants and roses. Of special interest to plantsmen and garden designers are pond garden, walled garden and large herbaceous border. Approx 10 acres.

90 ◆ SHANDY HALL

Coxwold YO61 4AD. The Laurence Sterne Trust, 01347 868465. *N of York. From A19, 7m from both Easingwold & Thirsk, turn E signed Coxwold*. **Adm £2.50, chd £1. Garden Suns to Fris May to Sept 11-4.30. For NGS: Evening Openings Fris 12, 19 June (5-9).**

Home of C18 author Laurence Sterne. 2 walled gardens, 1 acre of unusual perennials interplanted with tulips and old roses in low walled beds. In old quarry, another acre of trees, shrubs, bulbs, climbers and wild flowers encouraging wildlife, incl over 140 recorded species of moths. Moth trap and release with Dr Dave Chesmorre. Featured in 'Country Life'. Partial wheelchair access.

91 SKIPWITH HALL

Skipwith, Selby YO8 5SQ. Mr & Mrs C D Forbes Adam. *9m S of York, 6m N of Selby. From York A19 Selby, L in Escrick, 4m to Skipwith. From Selby A19-York, R onto A163 to Market Weighton, then L after 2m to Skipwith*. Home-made teas. **Adm £4, chd free. Sun 14 June (1-5).**

4-acre walled garden, recreated over past 6yrs. Formal mixed borders, decorative kitchen garden with pool and maze, Italian garden, pleached trees, orchard with espaliers and fans, attractive woodland.

92 ◆ SLEDMERE HOUSE

Driffield YO25 3XG. Sir Tatton Sykes, 01377 236637, www.sledmerehouse.com. *7m W of Driffield. 17m from city of York, 10m from Beverley. Sledmere House is 35min drive from M62*. **House and Garden Adm £7.50, chd £3, concessions £7, Garden only Adm £5, chd £2, (RHS) concessions £4.50. For details of openings & times see website or tel.**

Award winning garden incl octagonal walled garden, herbaceous borders, roses, perennials, bulbs and parterre. Capability Brown landscaped park with mature beech trees and 'eyecatchers'. Sledmere Garden Show Sun 17 May. Yorkshire in Bloom - Gold.

93 SLEIGHTHOLMEDALE LODGE

Fadmoor YO62 6JG. Dr & Mrs O James, 01751 431942. *6m NE of Helmsley. Parking can be limited in wet weather.* Teas at Pennyholme May, June. **Adm £3.50, chd free. Sats 30 May; 6 June (1-5); Sat 18, Sun 19 July (2-6). Also open Pennyholme 30 May; 6 June. Visitors also welcome by appt.** Hillside garden, walled rose garden and herbaceous borders.

🛏 ☕ ☎

The most distant part of the garden is left to nature with wild pond and folly to add intrigue . . .

94 SPRING CLOSE FARM

Gill Lane, Kearby LS22 4BS. John & Rosemary Proctor, 0113 2886310. *3m W of Wetherby. A661 from Wetherby town centre, turn L at bottom of Spofforth Hill to Sicklinghall. 1m after village turn L at Clap Gate towards Kearby.* **Adm £5 incl light refreshments. Visitors welcome by appt May to Aug inclusive, groups of 10-40, coaches permitted.** Large mature yet evolving quiet country garden, originally an exposed site, now divided into garden rooms sheltered by clipped yew and beech hedging, with allées and tranquil water garden leading to new orchard with ha-ha and stunning views over Wharfe Valley. Underplanted roses, mulberry trees and herbaceous borders with archways to walled garden with small greenhouse, and enclosed cottage garden.

♿ 🐕 ☕ ☎

95 STAINSACRE

Carperby DL8 4DD. Colin & Pat Jackson, 01969 663740, stainsacrepat@hotmail.com. *7m W of Leyburn. From A684 1m N of Aysgarth Falls.* Home-made teas at village hall. **Adm £3.50, chd free. Sun 26 July (12-5). Visitors also welcome by appt, Jun - Aug.**

1-acre site on S-sloping hillside created by owners since 1996. Deep mixed borders and island beds with wide variety of hardy and unusual perennials. 2 small wildlife ponds and artificial stream. Open grassed area with native trees and gravel area with specimen hostas. Gravel and grass paths.

♿ 🐕 ⊛ ☕ ☎

96 ◆ STILLINGFLEET LODGE

Stewart Lane, Stillingfleet, Nr York YO19 6HP. Mr & Mrs J Cook, 01904 728506, www.stillingfleetlodgenurseries.co.uk. *6m S of York. From A19 York-Selby take B1222 towards Sherburn in Elmet.* Light refreshments & teas. **Adm £4, chd 5-16yrs 50p. Weds, Fris 15 Apr to 30 Sept; 1st & 3rd Sats each month 1-5. For NGS: Suns 17 May; 21 June; 6 Sept (1.30-5).** Plantsman's garden subdivided into smaller gardens, each based on colour theme with emphasis on use of foliage plants. Wild flower meadow and natural pond. 55yds double herbaceous borders. New modern rill garden. Adjacent nursery.

♿ 🐕 ⊛ ☕

97 SWALE COTTAGE

Station Road, Richmond DL10 4LU. Julie Martin & Dave Dalton. *Richmond town centre. On foot, facing bottom of Market Place, turn L onto Frenchgate, then R onto Station Rd. House 1st on R.* Home-made teas. **Adm £2.50, chd free. Sun 7 June (1-5).** ½-acre urban oasis on steep site, with sweeping views and hidden corners. Several enclosed garden rooms on different levels. Mature herbaceous, rose and shrub garden with some areas of recent improvement. Magnificent yew and cedar. Organic vegetables and soft fruit, pond, orchard, adjacent paddock with sheep and hens. Some steep slopes and rough paths.

♿ 🐕 ⊛ ☕

98 THORPE LODGE

Knaresborough Road, Ripon HG4 3LU. Mr & Mrs T Jowitt, 01765 602088, jowitt@btinternet.com, www.thorpelodge.co.uk. *1m S of Ripon. On Ripon-Bishop Monkton-Knaresborough rd ¾ m from Ripon bypass.* Home-made teas. **Adm £5, chd under 12 free. Sun 2 Aug (1-6). Visitors also welcome by appt.** Beautiful, large country garden of 12 acres with extensive colour-themed

flower borders, walled rose garden, canals and fruit trees. Pleached hornbeam walk and allées leads to walks through mature woodland with vistas and ponds. Courtyard with exotic shrubs and tender plants in pots. Area for picnics.

♿ ⊛ 🛏 ☕ ☎

99 TINKERS HOLLOW

Church Field Lane, Great Ouseburn, nr York YO26 9SG. Heather & Eric Sugden. *Between York & Harrogate off B6265. 4m E of A1 (M) J47, (A59) towards York. Before Green Hammerton take B6265 towards Boroughbridge. Follow signs to Great Ouseburn. Car parking at Tinkers Hollow.* **Combined with Cobble Cottage adm £3, chd free, Mon 25 May (11-5).** Just over 1 acre, with wide range of features. Ponds connected by waterfall and small stream help extend the diverse range of plants grown. Several pergola walk-ways provide interesting and varied routes linking bog, perennial and shrub borders. By complete contrast the most distant part of the garden is left to nature with wild pond and folly to add intrigue. All of the garden is accessible by wheelchair over the lawns.

♿ ⊛

100 VICARAGE HOUSE

Kirkby Wharfe LS24 9DE. Mr & Mrs R S A Hall, 01937 835458. *1m S of Tadcaster. (A162) turn L (B1223) after 1m turn L to Kirkby Wharfe. Parking on rd.* Home-made teas. **Adm £2.50, chd free. Sun 19 Apr (1-5). Visitors also welcome by appt May & June, groups of 10+.** Secluded 1-acre country garden surrounded by mature trees, colour-themed border, extensive herbaceous borders, raised beds. Species primula and aquilegias. Gravel pathways. Plant stall with Elizabethan primulas.

🐕 ⊛ ☕ ☎

101 WARLEY HOUSE GARDEN

Stock Lane, Warley, Halifax HX2 7RU. Dr & Mrs P J Hinton. *2m W of Halifax. From Halifax take A646 (Burnley). Turn R up Windleroyd Lane approx 1m after A58, A646 junction (King Cross). Turn L at T-junction into Stock Lane. Park on rd before Warley Village.* Home-made teas. **Adm £3, chd free. Mon 25 May (1-5).** Following the demolition of original early C18 house and years of neglect the partly walled 2½ -acre garden is being renovated by the present owners. Rocky path and Japanese style planting leads to lawns and lovely S-facing views over open countryside. The alpine ravine is now planted with ferns, and fine trees give structure to the developing woodland area. Drifts of groundcover, shrub and herbaceous plantings, wild flowers and heathers maintain constant seasonal interest. Japanese garden not accessible by wheelchair.

WEST BARN
See Lincolnshire.

102 26 WEST END
Walkington HU17 8SX. Miss Jennifer Hall, 01482 861705. *2m SW of Beverley. On the B1230, 100yds beyond Xrds in centre of village on the R. Teas at 18 West End (nearly next door).* **Adm £3.50, chd free. Sun 14 June (1.30-5). Also open Molecroft Cottage. Visitors also welcome by appt June & early July, for groups 6+.** Exceptionally charming and interesting 1-acre cottage garden opening into old wooded gravel pit still being developed by owner. Many rare plants collected over 22yrs.

Thousands of colourful and scented plants, to delight and stimulate the senses . . .

103 THE WHITE HOUSE
Husthwaite YO61 4QA. Mrs A Raper, 01347 868688. *5m S of Thirsk. Turn R off A19 signed Husthwaite. 1½ m to centre of village opp parish church.* **Visitors welcome by appt.** Come and meet the gardener, an enthusiastic plantswoman. Exchange ideas and visit a 1-acre country garden with walled garden, conservatory and gardens within the garden. Herbaceous - of special interest a fresh lavender and purple palette in late spring and a hot summer border. Many unusual plants and shrubs and a strong collection of clematis,

landscaping, planting and a recently extended and restructured bed of English and shrub roses in the old orchard. A garden for all seasons.

Group opening

104 WHIXLEY GARDENS
nr York YO26 8AR. *8m W of York, 8m E of Harrogate, 6m N of Wetherby. 3m E of A1(M) off A59 York-Harrogate. Signed Whixley.* Light refreshments & teas at The Old Vicarage. **Combined with Croft Cottage adm £5, chd free. Sun 21 June (11.30-5).**

ASH TREE HOUSE
High Street. Mr & Mrs E P Moffitt
Well designed unusual garden of approx ¼ -acre with extensive rockeries making full use of sloping site. Established herbaceous plants, shrubs and climbers achieve a cottage garden effect. Access only by steps.

THE BAY HOUSE
Stonegate. Mr & Mrs Jon Beckett
Densely planted courtyard garden on differing levels.

COBBLE COTTAGE
John Hawkridge & Barry Atkinson
(See separate entry).

THE OLD VICARAGE
Mr & Mrs Roger Marshall
(See separate entry).

105 NEW WINTHROP PARK NATURE THERAPY AND SENSORY GARDEN
Wickersley S66 1EE. David & Carol Bowser, www.winthroppark.co.uk. *4m E of Rotherham. M18 J1, follow A631 to Rotherham. In Wickersley turn L at r'about B6060 to Thurcroft, after 6 speed humps turn L (Newhall Ave).* Light refreshments & teas. **Adm £2, chd free. Sat 1 Aug (10-5). Visitors also welcome by appt groups and coaches.**
Derelict sewage treatment works, transformed by volunteers into a beautiful small nature therapy park. Paths lead to themed areas planted with thousands of colourful and scented plants, shrubs and young trees to delight and stimulate the senses as well as creating an oasis of rest, tranquillity

and peace. Unusual design features, garden art, sculpture, large working greenhouse and café.

Group opening

106 NEW WITHERNSEA GARDENS
HU19 2PL. *23m E of Hull, 16m S of Hornsea. Enter Withernsea from A1033 onto Hollym Rd. From Hornsea, B1242, through town onto Hollym Rd.* Home-made teas. **Combined adm £5, chd free. Sun 26 July (1-5).**
Two interesting, contrasting gardens opp each other in Withernsea.

NEW CRANFORD
Linda & Maurice Beever
Colourful herbaceous borders planted with annuals, perennials, grasses, evergreens, shrubs and trees. Pond feature, vegetable garden and chicken runs. Gold award & overall winner, Withernsea in Bloom.

NEW 54 HOLLYM ROAD
Mr Matthew Pottage
Plantsman's garden of approx ⅓ acre, consisting of a range of unusual herbaceous and woody subjects (some of which are only borderline hardy), a pond and topiary hedge. Well-presented and labelled collection of cacti and succulents on display in greenhouse and on patio.

107 WOODLANDS COTTAGE
Summerbridge, nr Harrogate HG3 4BT. Mr & Mrs Stark, 01423 780765, annstark@btinternet.com, www.woodlandscottagegarden.co.uk. *4m E of Pateley Bridge, 10m NW of Harrogate. On the B6165 (Ripley-Pateley Bridge) ½ m W of Summerbridge.* Home-made teas. **Adm £2.50, chd free. Sun 10 May (1.30-5). Visitors also welcome by appt.**
1-acre plantswoman's garden in Nidderdale. Garden is designed to harmonise with the surrounding countryside and has several differing areas of planting with many unusual plants, natural rock outcrops, wild flower meadow, productive fruit and vegetable garden. Some gravel paths.

108 WORTLEY HALL
Wortley Village S35 7DB, 0114
2882100, info@wortleyhall.com,
www.wortleyhall.com. *9m NW of
Sheffield & 5m SW of Barnsley. On
A629 Huddersfield - Sheffield rd in
Wortley village, signed Wortley Hall &
Gardens.* Light refreshments & teas.
Adm £5, chd free. Sun 21 June
(12-4). Combined with **Avenue
Cottage.** Visitors also welcome by
appt March to Oct, groups 15+.
26 acres of elegant Italianate gardens
set within landscaped parkland. Formal
gardens with sunken garden, arbour
and clipped yew balls all framed with
seasonal bedding and mixed borders
leading to walled organic kitchen
garden. Informal walks through
pleasure grounds reveal C18/19
plantings incl 500yr old hollow oak,
lake and ice house. Guided tours at
1pm and 3pm. Meet outside reception
door. No wheelchair access to kitchen
garden.

  ♿ ✂ ❀ ☕ ☎

109 WYTHERSTONE GARDENS
Pockley YO62 7TE. Lady Clarissa
Collin, 01439 770012,
newtontowerestate@tiscali.co.uk,
www.wytherstonegardens.co.uk. *2m
NE of Helmsley. Signed from A170.*
Light refreshments & home-made teas.
Adm £5, chd free. Suns 24 May;
7 June; 19 July (10-5). Visitors also
welcome by appt.
A true plantsman's garden set in 8
acres of rolling countryside on edge of
the N York Moors. The garden is
divided by beech hedges, creating
interlinked specialised 'feature'
gardens, incl Mediterranean, spring
(with large unusual collection of
clematis) ericaceous, terraced, fern,
paeonia, foliage and bamboo garden,
good small arboretum (incl the most
northerly Wollemia nobilis planted
outside). Plants not thought hardy in
the N of England grow happily on
Wytherstone's free draining soil.
Delightful on-site nursery where all the
plants are propagated from the garden.
Selling rare and unusual perennials.

  ♿ ✂ ❀ ☕ ☎

Many unusual
plants, natural
rock outcrops,
wild flower
meadow,
productive fruit
and vegetable
garden . . .

110 ◆ YORK GATE
Back Church Lane, Adel LS16 8DW.
Perennial, 0113 267 8240,
www.perennial.org.uk/yorkgate. *5m
N of Leeds centre. 2¼ m SE of
Bramhope, signed from A660. Park in
Church Lane nr church and take public
footpath through churchyard & straight
on to garden.* Adm £3.50, chd free.
Thurs, Suns & BH Mons, 5 Apr to
27 Sept (2-5), for evening opening
times please see website or tel.
1-acre masterpiece and outstanding
example of C20 English garden design,
noted for its striking architectural
features and exquisite vistas. Divided
into a series of smaller gardens with
different themes and contrasting styles,
it incl ponds, a dell with stream, white
garden, newer garden with grasses
and summer flowering perennials,
kitchen garden and famous herb
garden with topiary.

  ✂ ❀

111 YORKE HOUSE
Dacre Banks, nr Summerbridge,
Nidderdale HG3 4EW. Anthony &
Pat Hutchinson, 01423 780456,
pat@yorkehouse.co.uk,
www.yorkehouse.co.uk. *4m SE of
Pateley Bridge, 10m NW of Harrogate.
On B6451. Car park.* Cream teas.
Adm £3, chd free. Sun 28 June
(11-5). Combined with **Dacre Banks
Gardens** adm £5, 12 July. Visitors
also welcome by appt June/July,
groups of 10+, coaches permitted.
Flower arranger's 2-acre garden with
colour-themed borders full of flowering
and foliage plants and shrubs.
Extensive water feature incl large
ornamental ponds and stream. Other
features incl nut walk, rose walk,
patios, gazebo, Millennium garden and
wildlife area. The garden enjoys
beautiful views across Nidderdale.
Picnic area.

  ♿ ❀ ☕ ☎

Yorkshire County Volunteers

County Organisers
N Yorks - Districts of Hambleton, Richmond, Ryedale, Scarborough & Cleveland Jane Baldwin, Riverside Farm, Sinnington, York
  YO62 6RY, 01751 431764, wnbaldwin@yahoo.co.uk
E Yorks Sally Bean, Saltmarshe Hall, Saltmarshe, Goole DN14 7RX, 01430 430199, pmegabean@aol.com
West & South Yorks & North Yorks District of Craven, Harrogate, Selby & York Bridget Marshall, The Old Vicarage, Whixley, York
  YO26 8AR, 01423 330474, biddymarshall@btopenworld.com

County Treasurer
Angela Pugh, Savage Garth, Nun Monkton, York YO26 8ER, 01423 330456, angie.pugh@btinternet.com

Publicity
Felicity Bowring, Lawkland Hall, Austwick, Lancaster LA2 8AT, 01729 823551, diss@austwick.org

County Booklet & Advertising
Tim Gittins, Hillbark, Church Lane, Bardsey, Leeds LS17 9DH, 01937 574968, timgittins@aol.com

Assistant County Organisers
Deborah Bigley, The Old Rectory, Great Langton, Northallerton DL7 0TA, 01609 748915, debsandbobbigley@aol.com
Annabel Fife, Langton Farm, Great Langton, Northallerton DL7 0TA, 01609 748446, annabelfife@fsmail.net
Josephine Marks, Carlton Hall, Carlton Husthwaite, Thirsk YO7 2BR, 01845 501626, carlton331@btinternet.com
Louise Martin, Fawley House, 7 Nordham, North Cave HU15 2LT, 01430 422266, louisem200@hotmail.co.uk
West & South Yorks Jane Hudson, Lower Crawshaw, Emley, Huddersfield HD8 9SU, 01924 840980,
  janehudson42@btinternet.com

Mark your diary with these special events in 2009

EXPLORE SECRET GARDENS DURING CHELSEA & HAMPTON COURT FLOWER SHOW WEEKS

Tue 19 May, Wed 20 May, Thur 21 May, Fri 22 May, Wed 8 July, Thur 9 July
Full day tours from £82 per person, 10% discount for groups
Advance booking required, telephone +44 (0)20 8693 1015 or email j.wookey@btinternet.com
Specially selected gardens in London, Essex, Kent, Hampshire and South Oxfordshire. The tour price includes transport and lunch with wine at a popular restaurant or pub.

HAMPTON COURT PALACE

Thur 2 Apr, Tue 23 June, Thur 25 June, Wed 15 July, Tue 4 Aug, Thur 10 Sept
Evening tours in the company of one of the Palace's specialist tour guides from 6.30 – 8pm
Tickets £6 per person. Advance booking required, telephone +44 (0)1483 211535 or visit www.ngs.org.uk for more information
Gossip, scandal, murder, healing – you'll find it all within the Formal Gardens at Hampton Court Palace. Each tour will have its own unique feature whether it's the story of the Great Vine or the magic and mystery of the Maze.

FROGMORE – A ROYAL GARDEN (BERKSHIRE)

Tue 26 May 10am – 5.30pm (last admission 4pm)
Garden adm £4.50, chd free. Tickets available in advance or on the day.
Advance booking for groups and coaches, telephone
+44 (0) 1483 211535 or email orders@ngs.org.uk
A rare opportunity to explore 30 acres of landscaped garden, rich in history and beauty.

FLAXBOURNE FARM – FUN & SURPRISES (BEDFORDSHIRE)

Sun 7 June 10am – 5pm. Adm £5, chd free
No booking required, come along on the day!
Bring the whole family and have fun in this surprising and entertaining garden of 2 acres. Enjoy the large plant fair, live music, pets corner, birds of prey, dog agility show and much more.

WISLEY RHS GARDEN – MUSIC IN THE GARDEN (SURREY)

Fri 11 Sept 6 – 9pm
Adm (incl RHS members) £7, chd under 15 free
Save money on advance bookings for groups of 4 or more, telephone +44 (0)1483 211535 or visit www.ngs.org.uk for more information
A special evening opening of this famous garden, exclusively for the NGS. Enjoy music and entertainment as you explore the gardens and the floral marquee on the first day of the Wisley Flower Show.

For further information visit www.ngs.org.uk or telephone 01483 211535

Mark your diary with these special events in 2009

EXPLORE SECRET GARDENS DURING CHELSEA & HAMPTON COURT FLOWER SHOW WEEKS

Tue 19 May, Wed 20 May, Thur 21 May, Fri 22 May, Wed 8 July, Thur 9 July
Full day tours from £82 per person, 10% discount for groups
Advance booking required, telephone +44 (0)20 8693 1015 or email j.wookey@btinternet.com
Specially selected gardens in London, Essex, Kent, Hampshire and South Oxfordshire. The tour price includes transport and lunch with wine at a popular restaurant or pub.

HAMPTON COURT PALACE

Thur 2 Apr, Tue 23 June, Thur 25 June, Wed 15 July, Tue 4 Aug, Thur 10 Sept
Evening tours in the company of one of the Palace's specialist tour guides from 6.30 – 8pm
Tickets £6 per person. Advance booking required, telephone +44 (0)1483 211535 or visit www.ngs.org.uk for more information
Gossip, scandal, murder, healing – you'll find it all within the Formal Gardens at Hampton Court Palace. Each tour will have its own unique feature whether it's the story of the Great Vine or the magic and mystery of the Maze.

FROGMORE – A ROYAL GARDEN (BERKSHIRE)

Tue 26 May 10am – 5.30pm (last admission 4pm)
Garden adm £4.50, chd free. Tickets available in advance or on the day.
Advance booking for groups and coaches, telephone
+44 (0) 1483 211535 or email orders@ngs.org.uk
A rare opportunity to explore 30 acres of landscaped garden, rich in history and beauty.

FLAXBOURNE FARM – FUN & SURPRISES (BEDFORDSHIRE)

Sun 7 June 10am – 5pm. Adm £5, chd free
No booking required, come along on the day!
Bring the whole family and have fun in this surprising and entertaining garden of 2 acres. Enjoy the large plant fair, live music, pets corner, birds of prey, dog agility show and much more.

WISLEY RHS GARDEN – MUSIC IN THE GARDEN (SURREY)

Fri 11 Sept 6 – 9pm
Adm (incl RHS members) £7, chd under 15 free
Save money on advance bookings for groups of 4 or more, telephone +44 (0)1483 211535 or visit www.ngs.org.uk for more information
A special evening opening of this famous garden, exclusively for the NGS. Enjoy music and entertainment as you explore the gardens and the floral marquee on the first day of the Wisley Flower Show.

For further information visit www.ngs.org.uk or telephone 01483 211535

WALES

Cheshire & Wirral

Flintshire & Wrexham

Denbighshire & Colwyn

Gwynedd & Anglesey

WALES

Shropshire

Ceredigion

Powys

Herefordshire

Carmarthenshire & Pembrokeshire

Gwent

Glamorgan

The areas shown on this map are specific to the organisation of The National Gardens Scheme. The Gardens of England, listed by area, precede the Gardens of Wales.

Somerset, Bristol Area & S. Glos

CARMARTHENSHIRE & PEMBROKESHIRE

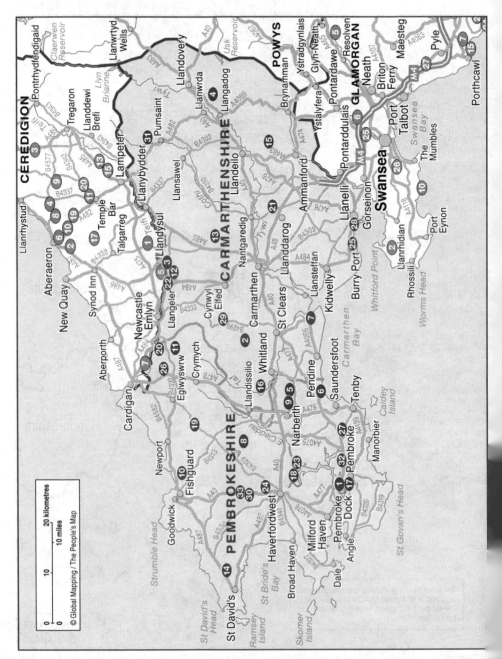

Opening Dates

February

SATURDAY 21
14 Golwg Yr Ynys

SUNDAY 22
14 Golwg Yr Ynys

SATURDAY 28
14 Golwg Yr Ynys

March

Every Sat & Sun
14 Golwg Yr Ynys

SUNDAY 8
20 Nant-yr-Eryd

April

Every Sat & Sun
14 Golwg Yr Ynys

SUNDAY 26
32 Upton Castle Gardens

May

SATURDAY 2
14 Golwg Yr Ynys

SUNDAY 3
14 Golwg Yr Ynys
27 Rosewood
30 Treffgarne Hall

SATURDAY 9
14 Golwg Yr Ynys

SUNDAY 10
11 Ffynone
14 Golwg Yr Ynys

SATURDAY 16
14 Golwg Yr Ynys
24 Poyston Hall
28 Stradey Castle Gardens

SUNDAY 17
6 Colby Woodland Garden
14 Golwg Yr Ynys
16 Llwyngarreg
24 Poyston Hall

SUNDAY 24
14 Golwg Yr Ynys

SATURDAY 30
14 Golwg Yr Ynys

SUNDAY 31
14 Golwg Yr Ynys
23 Picton Castle & Woodland Gardens

June

SATURDAY 6
14 Golwg Yr Ynys

SUNDAY 7
7 The Cors

14 Golwg Yr Ynys

FRIDAY 12
15 Llwyn Cyll

SATURDAY 13
14 Golwg Yr Ynys

SUNDAY 14
2 Blaendwr
5 Coed-y-Ffynnon
9 Dyffryn Farm
14 Golwg Yr Ynys

SATURDAY 20
3 Cilgwyn Bach Farm
5 Coed-y-Ffynnon
12 Glandwr
14 Golwg Yr Ynys
21 The National Botanic Garden of Wales (Evening)
29 Tradewinds
33 Weir Castle

SUNDAY 21
3 Cilgwyn Bach Farm
12 Glandwr
14 Golwg Yr Ynys
29 Tradewinds
33 Weir Castle

SATURDAY 27
14 Golwg Yr Ynys

SUNDAY 28
14 Golwg Yr Ynys
23 Picton Castle & Woodland Gardens

July

SATURDAY 4
14 Golwg Yr Ynys
22 The Old Vicarage

SUNDAY 5
2 Blaendwr
13 Glangwili Lodges
14 Golwg Yr Ynys
22 The Old Vicarage

SATURDAY 11
14 Golwg Yr Ynys

SUNDAY 12
13 Glangwili Lodges
14 Golwg Yr Ynys
27 Rosewood

SATURDAY 18
14 Golwg Yr Ynys
33 Weir Castle

SUNDAY 19
4 Cilgwyn Lodge
14 Golwg Yr Ynys
16 Llwyngarreg
25 Red Roofs
26 Rhosygilwen Mansion
33 Weir Castle

WEDNESDAY 22
25 Red Roofs

FRIDAY 24
1 Aderyn y Môr
17 Mead Lodge

SATURDAY 25
1 Aderyn y Môr
14 Golwg Yr Ynys
17 Mead Lodge

SUNDAY 26
1 Aderyn y Môr
14 Golwg Yr Ynys
17 Mead Lodge

MONDAY 27
1 Aderyn y Môr
17 Mead Lodge

August

SATURDAY 1
14 Golwg Yr Ynys

SUNDAY 2
10 Dyffryn Fernant
14 Golwg Yr Ynys

SATURDAY 8
14 Golwg Yr Ynys

SUNDAY 9
7 The Cors (Evening)
14 Golwg Yr Ynys

SATURDAY 15
14 Golwg Yr Ynys

SUNDAY 16
14 Golwg Yr Ynys
31 Ty'r Maes

WEDNESDAY 19
31 Ty'r Maes

SATURDAY 22
14 Golwg Yr Ynys

SUNDAY 23
14 Golwg Yr Ynys

SATURDAY 29
14 Golwg Yr Ynys

SUNDAY 30
14 Golwg Yr Ynys
29 Tradewinds

September

SUNDAY 6
14 Golwg Yr Ynys
30 Treffgarne Hall

SATURDAY 12
14 Golwg Yr Ynys

SUNDAY 13
14 Golwg Yr Ynys

SATURDAY 19
14 Golwg Yr Ynys

SUNDAY 20
14 Golwg Yr Ynys

SATURDAY 26
14 Golwg Yr Ynys

SUNDAY 27
14 Golwg Yr Ynys

October

Every Sat & Sun
14 Golwg Yr Ynys

November

Sats & Suns 1st-15th
14 Golwg Yr Ynys

Gardens open to the public

6 Colby Woodland Garden
10 Dyffryn Fernant
21 The National Botanic Garden of Wales
23 Picton Castle & Woodland Gardens
32 Upton Castle Gardens

By appointment only

8 Cwm Pibau
18 Millinford

Also open by appointment ☎

2 Blaendwr
4 Cilgwyn Lodge
5 Coed-y-Ffynnon
7 The Cors
9 Dyffryn Farm
11 Ffynone
12 Glandwr
14 Golwg Yr Ynys
15 Llwyn Cyll
16 Llwyngarreg
19 Moorland Cottage Plants
20 Nant-yr-Eryd
22 The Old Vicarage
24 Poyston Hall
25 Red Roofs
26 Rhosygilwen Mansion
29 Tradewinds
30 Treffgarne Hall
31 Ty'r Maes
33 Weir Castle

Colourful garden on a steep cliffside with a wide marine backdrop . . .

The Gardens

1 **NEW** **ADERYN Y MÔR**
4 Connacht Way, Llanion, Pembrokeshire SA72 6FB. Philip & Monica Geobey. *Pembroke Dock side, Cleddau Bridge roundabout, exit into Essex Road. Past traffic-calming. R into Connacht Way, L at T-junction.* Home-made teas. **Adm £2, chd free. Fri to Sun 24 to 27 July (11-5). Also open Mead Lodge.** An imaginative and colourful garden on a steep cliffside with a wide marine backdrop. Access by attractive, extensive stairway. Variety of plants, some exotic. 2 ponds. Seating areas at top and bottom of garden.
🐕 ☕

2 **BLAENDWR**
Cwmbach, Whitland, Carmarthenshire SA34 0DN. Arthur & Barbara Howells, 01994 448256, bahowells@hotmail.co.uk. *7m N of Whitland and St Clears. From St Clears town centre take Llanboidy rd through Llangynin, then keep R towards Blaenwawn; Blaendwr is approx 3m on R before Xrds. From Haverfordwest take Whitland bypass, turn L for Llanboidy. Turn R at 3rd Xrds and R again at next Xrds.* **Adm £2.50, chd free. Suns 14 June; 5 July (2-6). Visitors also welcome by appt.** 1/2 -acre carefully casual cottage garden. Borders of healthy perennials and clematis-covered pergolas on exposed hilltop location, with charming water features, children's garden and plentiful plant interest. Beautiful copper beech hedge, small organic vegetable garden, stunning views of surrounding country. Garden designed for wheelchair access, easy walking.
♿ 🐕 ☎

3 **CILGWYN BACH FARM**
Heol-y-Dderwen, Pont-Tyweli, Llandysul SA44 4RP. Jean & Ian Wilson. *15m N of Carmarthen. Turn off A486 Llandysul to Newcastle Emlyn rd at Half Moon PH (300yds from Llandysul bridge). Pass Jewson's building supplies on L, garden 2nd house on L.* Home-made teas. **Adm £2.50, chd free. Sat, Sun 20, 21 June (11-5). Also open Glandwr.** 1-acre garden with informally-planted raised beds, gravel walks, lawns and

old stone buildings. Small wildlife pond. Views of surrounding hills. Short walk in wild area. Best in Village, Llangeler Parish in Bloom.
🐕 ☕

4 **CILGWYN LODGE**
Llangadog, Carmarthenshire SA19 9LH. Keith Brown & Moira Thomas, 01550 777452, keith@cilgwynlodge.co.uk. *3m NE of Llangadog village. 4m SW of Llandovery. Turn off A40 into centre of Llangadog. Bear L in front of village shop then 1st R towards Myddfai. After 21/2 m pass Cilgwyn Manor on L then 1st L. Garden 1/4 m on L.* Home-made teas. **Adm £3, chd free. Sun 19 July (1-5). Visitors also welcome by appt, coaches and parties welcome.** Fascinating and much-admired 1-acre garden with something for everyone. Wide variety of herbaceous plants displayed in extensive colour-themed borders, over 250 varieties of hostas, a growing collection of clematis and many borderline hardy rare or unusual plants. Traditional vegetable and fruit garden and large waterlily pond. 10th anniversary of opening for the NGS. One part is wheelchair accessible the other has slopes and gravel paths.
♿ 🐕 ✿ ☕ ☎

5 **COED-Y-FFYNNON**
Lampeter Velfrey, Pembrokeshire SA67 8UJ. Col R H Gilbertson, 01834 831396. *21/2 m SE of Narberth. From Penblewin roundabout on A40 follow signs to Narberth & then to crematorium. Straight on through Llanmill & Lampeter Velfrey. Garden 1/2 m on L.* **Adm £2.50, chd free. Sun 14, Sat 20 June (2-6). Also open Dyffryn Farm. Visitors also welcome by appt June & July, groups welcome. Parking for one coach.** Enthusiast's 1-acre garden with over 140 varieties of old fashioned roses. Informal planting and very naturalistic garden style with ample provision for wildlife. Roses at their best early June to early July. Relaxed rural setting, lots of rough grass; don't expect manicured lawns.
♿ 🐕 ✿ ☕ ☎

6 ◆ **COLBY WOODLAND GARDEN**
Amroth, Pembrokeshire SA67 8PP. The National Trust, 01834 811885. *6m N of Tenby. 5m SE of Narberth. Signed by brown tourist signs on coast rd & A477.* **Adm £4.20, chd £2.10,**

family £10.50. Open daily Feb to Oct, Mon to Sun. For NGS: Sun 17 May (10-5).
8-acre woodland garden in a secluded and tranquil valley with fine collection of rhododendrons and azaleas. Walled garden open by kind permission of Mr and Mrs A Scourfield Lewis, with charming gazebo and rill. Steep areas. Some areas of woodland garden are not suitable for wheelchairs.

&. ✕ ❀ ☕

⑦ THE CORS
Newbridge Road, Laugharne, Carmarthenshire SA33 4SH. Nick Priestland, 01994 427219, www.the-cors.co.uk. *12m SW of Carmarthen. From Carmarthen, turn R in centre of Laugharne at The Mariners PH. At bottom of Newbridge Rd on R. Use public car parks, 5 mins walk.* Home-made teas. **Adm £3.50, chd free.** Suns 7 June (2-6). **Evening Opening** wine, 9 Aug (6-9). Visitors also welcome by appt.
Approx 2¹/₂ acres set in beautiful wooded valley bordering river. Large bog garden with ponds, gunnera, bamboos and tree ferns. Exceptional, elegant plantsman's garden with unusual architectural and exotic planting incl Tetrapanax papyrifer, Blechnum chilense, *chusan* palms and sculptures. Shortlisted 'Times Garden of the Year'.

&. ✕ ❀ ☕ ☎

⑧ CWM PIBAU
New Moat, Pembrokeshire SA63 4RE. Mrs Duncan Drew, 01437 532454. *10m NE of Haverfordwest. 3m SW of Maenclochog. Off A40, take B4313 to Maenclochog, follow signs to New Moat, pass church, then 2nd concealed drive on L, ¹/₂ m rural drive.* **Adm £3, chd free.** Visitors welcome by appt.
5-acre woodland garden surrounded by old deciduous woodland and streams. Created in 1978, contains many mature, unusual shrubs and trees from Chile, New Zealand and Europe, set on S-facing sloping hill. More conventional planting nearer house.

☎

⑨ DYFFRYN FARM
Lampeter Velfrey, Narberth, Pembrokeshire SA67 8UN. Dr & Mrs M J R Polson, Mr & Mrs D Bradley, 01834 861684, www.pembrokeshireplants.co.uk. *3m E of Narberth. From junction of A40 & A478 follow signs for*

crematorium, continue down into Llanmill. Then uphill, at brow turn L at Bryn Sion Chapel Xrds (before Lampeter Velfrey). After ¹/₂ m rd turns R under railway bridge. Dyffryn Farm straight ahead, parking under bridge and immed on R (14 June only). Home-made teas. **Adm £2.50, chd free (share to Paul Sartori Foundation).** Sun 14 June (1-5). **Also open Coed y Ffynnon.** Visitors also welcome by appt May to Sept £3 per person.
Large garden, in several areas on different levels, in 'naturalised' manner (not landscaped or contrived) using secluded valley backcloth. Highlights incl 70+ bamboos; grasses, herbaceous plants, unusual shrubs; stream, pond with island and small woodland; all in relaxed style with 'hidden' havens. Supervised children very welcome. Bamboo craft workshop.

❀ ☕ ☎

Large garden in 'naturalised' manner (not landscaped or contrived) using secluded valley backcloth . . .

⑩ ♦ DYFFRYN FERNANT
Llanychaer, Fishguard, Pembrokeshire SA65 9SP. Christina Shand & David Allum, 01348 811282, www.genuslocus.net. *3m E of Fishguard, then ¹/₂ m inland. A487 Fishguard to Cardigan. After approx 3m, at end of long straight hill, turn R signed Llanychaer with road signs 'unsuitable for long vehicles'. After exactly ¹/₂ m is Dyffryn track, on L behind LH bend, with wooden sign.* **Adm £4, chd free.** Wed - Sun and BH Mons 10-6 Easter to end Sept. For NGS: Sun 2 Aug (10-6).
The just-tamed meets the decidedly wild with a touch of the tropics in this adventurous 6-acre garden, making the most of dramatic landscape. Choice plants designed to be appreciated in contrasted areas. Lush bog garden, intriguing sculptures, obelisk, jungly courtyard, fernery, large pond, new grasses garden. Featured in 'Beautiful Britain' and GGG.

✕ ❀ 🛏

⑪ FFYNONE
Boncath, Pembrokeshire SA37 0HQ. Earl & Countess Lloyd George of Dwyfor, 01239 841610. *9m SE of Cardigan. 7m W of Newcastle Emlyn. From Newcastle Emlyn take A484 to Cenarth, turn L on B4332, turn L again at Xrds just before Newchapel.* Home-made teas. **Adm £3, chd free.** Sun 10 May (1-5). Visitors also welcome by appt.
Large woodland garden designated Grade I on Cadw register of historic gardens in Wales. Lovely views, fine mature specimen trees; formal garden nr house with massive yew topiary; rhododendrons, azaleas, woodland walks. House (also Grade I) by John Nash (1793), not open. Later additions and garden terraces by F Inigo Thomas c1904. Limited wheelchair access. Some steep paths.

&. ❀ ☕ ☎

⑫ GLANDWR
Pentrecwrt, Llandysul, Carmarthenshire SA44 5DA. Mrs Jo Hicks, 01559 363729. *15m N of Carmarthen, 2m S of Llandysul, 7m E of Newcastle Emlyn. On A486. At Pentrecwrt village, take minor rd opp Black Horse PH. After bridge keep L for ¹/₄ m. Glandwr is on R.* Cream teas. **Adm £2.50, chd free.** Sat, Sun 20, 21 June (11-5). **Also open Cilgwyn Bach Farm.** Visitors also welcome by appt.
Delightful 1-acre cottage garden, bordered by a natural stream with country views. Some single coloured beds and borders, a rockery and many shrubs and climbers. Walk in the mature woodland transformed into an adventurous intriguing place, with shade loving shrubs and plants, ground covers and many surprises. Best in village, Llangeler Parish in Bloom.

✕ ☕ ☎

⑬ GLANGWILI LODGES
Llanllawddog, Carmarthenshire SA32 7JE. Chris & Christine Blower. *7m NE of Carmarthen. Take A485 from Carmarthen. ¹/₄ m after Stag & Pheasant PH in Pontarsais turn R for Llanllawddog and Brechfa. ¹/₂ m after Llanllawddog Chapel, rd bears sharply R, Glangwili Lodges 100yds on R.* Light refreshments & teas. **Adm £3, chd free.** Sun 5, 12 July (11-5).
Ongoing development of 1-acre walled garden. Borders with unusual perennials and colourful cottage styling. Rockery, alpines, water

features, Koi pond, arbour, collection of maples and unusual trees. Walks by woodland stream with developing parkland area. Valley setting with superb views of the Gwili valley and Brechfa forest.

🏃 ♿ ☕

14 NEW GOLWG YR YNYS

Carnhedryn, St Davids, Pembrokeshire SA62 6XT. Paul & Sue Clark, 01437 721082, www.golwygyrynys.com. *4m E of St Davids, 11m SW of Fishguard, 2m N of Solva. Village of Carnhedryn, off A487 between Fishguard and St Davids.* Adm £2.50, chd free. Open Sats, Suns 21 Feb to 15 Nov. Feb, March, Oct, Nov (1-4). April, Sept (12-5). May, June, July, Aug (12-6). Excl Sats 23 May, 5 September. Visitors also welcome by appt.

A garden for plantaholics with yr-round floral colour and foliage interest. Intriguing layout of sheltered rooms full of surprises. Unfolds to reveal 1/4 acre of borders, colour themed beds packed with unusual shrubs and garden favourites. Particular specialities are Hebes (25 varieties) and Hydrangeas (13 varieties).

🏃 ♿ ☎

15 LLWYN CYLL

Trap, Carmarthenshire SA19 6TR. Liz & John Smith, 01558 822398, liz-johntrap@amserve.com. *3m SE of Llandeilo. In Trap turn towards Glanaman & Llandybie (at The Cennen Arms). Llwyn Cyll is 1/2 m on L adjoining Llwyn Onn. Parking limited.* Evening opening £3, wine Fri 12 June (4.30-8). Visitors also welcome by appt almost daily mid Apr to mid Sept. Please ring first to avoid disappointment.

31/2 -acre country garden of yr-round interest. Abundant, colourful terraced and walled borders, orchard, vegetable garden. Sun and shade areas with sympathetic planting. A plantsman's garden with many rarities and specimen trees. Up to 40 different magnolias in the arboretum, many in flower late Apr to early June. Scenic view of Castle Carreg Cennen. Featured in 'Carmarthenshire Life'.

🏃 ☎

Intriguing layout of sheltered rooms full of surprises . . .

16 LLWYNGARREG

Llanfallteg, Carmarthenshire SA34 0XH. Paul & Liz O'Neill, 01994 240717, lizpaulfarm@yahoo.co.uk. *19m W of Carmarthen. A40 W from Carmarthen, turn R at Llandewi Velfrey to Llanfallteg. Go through village, garden 1/2 m further on, 2nd farm on R.* Home-made teas. Adm £3.50, chd free. Suns 17 May; 19 July (2-6). Visitors also welcome by appt.

3-acre plantsman's garden with many rare trees. Bog garden, woodland gardens, deep borders, peat beds, gravel gardens, vegetable plot, several ponds. Rhododendrons, bamboos, magnolias, meconopsis, acers. Primulas and massed grasses among many unusual plantings. Beautiful even in the rain! Several deep water features. Young children must be closely supervised. Featured in 'Carmarthenshire Life' magazine and S4C's Wedi Tri programme.

♿ ♿ ☕ ☎

17 MEAD LODGE

Imble Lane, Pembroke Dock, Pembrokeshire SA72 6PN. John & Eileen Seal. *From A4139 between Pembroke and Pembroke Dock take B4322 signed Pennar and Leisure Centre. After 1/2 m turn L into Imble Lane. Mead Lodge at end.* Home-made teas. Adm £2.50, chd free (share to Paul Sartori Foundation). Fri 24 to Mon 27 July incl (11-5). Also open Aderyn-y-Môr.

Unexpected, secluded country garden, a relaxing oasis on S-facing slope overlooking the Pembroke River estuary. Varied 3/4 -acre garden reflects the owners' keen interest in ferns, grasses and herbs. Incl terraces with Chinese and Mediterranean influences, colour-themed beds, small arboretum, fernery and vegetable garden. Pond, bog garden and stream in development. Readings of garden-related poetry and prose on most days.

♿ ☕

18 MILLINFORD

Millin Cross, Pembrokeshire SA62 4AL. Drs B & A Barton, 01437 762394. *3m E of Haverfordwest. From Haverfordwest on A40 to Carmarthen, turn R signed The Rhos, take turning to Millin. Turn R at Millin Chapel then immed L over river bridge.* Adm £3 chd free. Visitors welcome by appt.

Spacious, undulating and peaceful garden of 4 acres on bank of Millin Creek. Varied collection of over 125 different trees, many unusual, plus shrubs, herbaceous plants and bulbs in beautiful riverside setting. Impressive terracing and water features. Visit in spring, summer and early autumn.

🏃 ☕ ☎

19 MOORLAND COTTAGE PLANTS

Rhyd-y-Groes, Brynberian, Pembrokeshire SA41 3TT. Jennifer & Kevin Matthews, 01239 891363, www.moorlandcottageplants.co.uk. *12m SW of Cardigan. 16m NE of Haverfordwest, on B4329, 3/4 m downhill from cattlegrid (from Haverfordwest) and 1m uphill from signpost to Brynberian (from Cardigan).* Adm £2.50, chd 50p (share to Paul Sartori Foundation). Daily (not Weds) 16 May to 6 Sept (10.30-5.30). Visitors also welcome by appt.

1-acre garden at 720ft on wild north-eastern slopes of the Preselis. Informal, enclosed abundantly planted area where carpets of spring flowers give way to jungly perennials, grasses and bamboos. This contrasts with new area of lawn and deep parallel borders providing spaciousness and stunning mountian views. Gardening without pesticides/fungicides encourages abundant wildlife. Diverse mollusc-proof plantings demonstrate what can be achieved without using any slug and snail controls. Adjoining nursery (open daily 10.30 to 5.30 (not Weds) 1 Mar to 30 Sept) specialising in hardy perennials, ornamental grasses & ferns.

🏃 ♿ ☎

20 NANT-YR-ERYD

Abercych, Boncath, Pembrokeshire SA37 0EU. Alan & Diana Hall, 01239 682489. *5m SE of Cardigan, 5m W of Newcastle Emlyn. Off B4332 Cenarth to Abercych, Boncath Rd. Turn N to Abercych, through village and take L fork.* Home-made teas. Adm £2, chd free (share to Paul Sartori Foundation). Sun 8 Mar (11-4).

Visitors also welcome by appt May, June, July.
Charming well-maintained cottage garden of 1-acre. 60 varieties of daffodils in spring. Mature and new topiary gardens. Exotic fernery and other displays in original outbuildings. Well worth visitng in summer, for beautiful roses including 'Rosa mundi', and 'William Lobb', 'Abraham Darby', 'Dortmund', and 'Abbotswood'. Also wild flower meadow.

✗ ♨ ☎

㉑ ◆ THE NATIONAL BOTANIC GARDEN OF WALES
Llanarthne, Carmarthenshire
SA32 8HG, 01558 668768,
www.gardenofwales.org.uk. *10 mins from M4. M4 W to Pont Abraham, then A48 to Cross Hands, half way between Cross Hands and Carmarthen, follow brown signs to NBGW.* NGS Adm £3, chd free. Open daily, not Christmas Day. Phone or see website for details.
For NGS: **Evening Opening Longest Day.** A Midsummer Night's Concert in the Great Glasshouse with Symphonica Tywi (6-10), wine, Sat 20 June.
The acclaimed Great Glasshouse, with Mediterranean plantings is the centre of this stunning young garden, set within 570-acres of Regency parkland. Double Walled Garden, containing the new Tropical House adjacent to Japanese and Bee gardens. Extensive herbaceous borders complement the scientific plantings. Informal wildlife areas (N. N. R. Designation 2008) and lakeside walks. Featured in 'The Garden'.

& ✗ ❀ ♨

㉒ THE OLD VICARAGE
Llangeler, Carmarthenshire
SA44 5EU. Mr & Mrs J C Harcourt,
01559 371168. *4m E of Newcastle Emlyn. 15m N of Carmarthen on A484. From N Emlyn turn down lane on L in Llangeler before church.* Cream teas.
Adm £2.50, chd free. Sat 4, Sun 5 July (11-6). Visitors also welcome by appt June, July, access for 29-seater coaches.
A garden gem created since 1993. Less than 1 acre divided into 3 areas of roses, shrubs and a semi-formal pool with an interesting collection of unusual herbaceous plants. Plant sale in aid of National Osteoporosis Society. Access is gravelled.

& ✗ ❀ ♨ ☎

㉓ ◆ PICTON CASTLE & WOODLAND GARDENS
The Rhos, Pembrokeshire
SA62 4AS. Picton Castle Trust,
01437 751326,
www.pictoncastle.co.uk. *3m E of Haverfordwest. On A40 to Carmarthen, signed off main rd.* Garden £4.95, chd £2.50, concessions £4.75. Daily 1 Apr to 30 Sept, not Mons (except BH Mons).
For NGS: Suns 31 May; 28 June (10.30-5.0).
Mature 40-acre woodland garden with unique collection of rhododendrons and azaleas, many bred over 41yrs, producing hybrids of great merit and beauty; rare and tender shrubs and trees incl magnolia, myrtle, embothrium and eucryphia. Wild flowers abound. Walled garden with roses; fernery; herbaceous and climbing plants and large clearly-labelled collection of herbs.

& ❀ ♨

㉔ NEW POYSTON HALL
Rudbaxton, Haverfordwest,
Pembrokeshire SA62 4DD. Mr & Mrs David Ellis, 01437 760887. *2m N of Haverfordwest. A40 Haverfordwest to Fishguard. R after Withybush Airfield, signed Clarbeston Road. Follow road, ignoring sign for Rudbaxton. Gates on L.* Adm £2.50, chd free (share to Paul Sartori Foundation). Sat, Sun 16, 17 May (1-5). Visitors also welcome by appt.
Spacious, tranquil grounds of historic mansion (childhood home of General Picton). Sloping lawns, imposing trees, small lake. Key elements of C18 design, spaces rather than flower beds. Formal garden with young yew walks. Children must be supervised.

♨ ☎

A town garden of approx ⅓ -acre in a coastal location . . .

㉕ NEW RED ROOFS
129 Elkington Road, Burry Port,
Carmarthenshire SA16 0AB.
Elaine Morgan, 01554 832418,
eddiemorgan44@hotmail.com.
4m W of Llanelli. A484. L at pelican crossing. Bear R. Garden 100 yds on R. Home-made teas. Adm £2, chd free. Sun 19, Wed 22 July (2-6). Visitors also welcome by appt late June to late July. Groups of 30 max.
A town garden of approx ⅓ -acre in a coastal location. Colourful perennial borders with a mix of unusual plants such as *Hedychium,* Oleander, Acacia dealbata and Roscoea. Small water feature with Koi pond, container grown plants incl bonsai and fuchsias. Seating in shaded areas.

& ❀ ♨ ☎

㉖ RHOSYGILWEN MANSION
Cilgerran, Cardigan, Pembrokeshire SA43 2TW. Glen Peters & Brenda Squires, 01239 841387, enquiries@retreat.co.uk. *5m S of Cardigan. From Cardigan follow A478 signed Tenby. After 6m turn L at Rhoshill towards Cilgerran. After ¼ m turn R signed Rhosygilwen. Mansion gates ½ m.* Light refreshments & teas (not NGS). Adm £3, chd free. Sun 19 July (11-5). Visitors also welcome by appt Mon to Fri (9-3). Coaches permitted.
20 acres of garden in 55 acre estate. Pretty ½ m drive through woodland planting. Spacious lightly wooded grounds for leisurely rambling, 1-acre walled garden fully productive of fruit, vegetables and flowers; authentically restored Edwardian greenhouses, many old and new trees, small formal garden. Gravel paths & slopes in some areas.

& ✗ ♨ ☎

㉗ ROSEWOOD
Redberth, nr Tenby, Pembrokeshire SA70 8SA. Jan & Keith Treadaway. *3m SW of Kilgetty. Coming from W, turn for Sageston and almost immed R towards Redberth. First cottage after village boundary sign. From E, turn for Redberth and continue along old A447, second cottage after village turn. Ample parking on roadside.* Adm £2.50, chd free (share to Paul Sartori Foundation). Suns 3 May; 12 July (1-5).
Intimate and well-maintained ¼ -acre garden, cleverly designed in different areas, with abundant, colourful mixed

plantings incl scattered exotic species and a National Collection of clematis (*subgenus viorna*) plus many other clematis in bloom all yr, but especially in summer.

28 STRADEY CASTLE GARDENS

Llanelli, Carmarthenshire SA15 4PL. Sir David Mansel Lewis. *1m NW of Llanelli town centre. Entrance approx ¾ m from Furnace off B4308 Furnace to Kidwelly rd.* Home-made teas. **Adm £4, chd free. Sat 16 May (2-5.30).** Enjoy a rural oasis and stroll in the extensive grounds of the mid-C19 mansion. Formal parterre, pond and herbaceous borders enhance the immediate house surrounds. The 'Wilderness' garden, with many fine shrubs and trees, has been restored and developed within the curtilage of the former C17 house. Some deep gravel.

29 TRADEWINDS

Ffynnonwen, Penybont, Carmarthenshire SA33 6PX. Stuart Kemp-Gee & Eve Etheridge, 01994 484744, ffynnonwen@hotmail.com. *10m NW of Carmarthen. A40 W from Carmarthen approx 4m, then turn R onto B4298 to Meidrim. In Meidrim R onto B4299 to Trelech. After approx 5½ m turn R at Tradewinds sign, then approx ½ m, next to 2nd farm.* **Adm £3, chd free. Sat Sun 20, 21 June; Sun 30 Aug (11-5).** Visitors also welcome by appt. 2½ -acre plantsman's garden with abundance of herbaceous perennials, shrubs and trees giving yr-round interest. Mixed borders, natural streams and natural pond. Picturesque garden in tranquil setting. 100ft grass, 100ft herbaceous and 80ft conifer borders - all new. Many new trees in arboretum. Art studio open.

30 TREFFGARNE HALL

Treffgarne, Haverfordwest, Pembrokeshire SA62 5PJ. Mr & Mrs Batty, 01437 741115. *7m N of Haverfordwest, signed off A40. Proceed up through village and follow rd round sharply to L, Hall ¼ m further on L.* Home-made teas. **Adm £3, chd free. Suns 3 May; 6 Sept (1-5).** Visitors also welcome by appt. 4-acre garden under development since 2003. Thriving in splendid hilltop location, substantial collection of exotics incl echiums, proteas, michelias, acacias, salvias and palms in superbly landscaped ½ -acre walled garden with double rill, pergola and statuary. Broadwalk with long border, rockery and gravel garden. Several smaller planting schemes. Rare & exotic plants for sale.

31 NEW TY'R MAES

Ffarmers, Llanwrda, Carmarthenshire SA19 8JP. John & Helen Brooks, 01558 650541, johnhelen@greystones140.freeserve.co.uk. *7m SE of Lampeter. 1½ m N of Pumsaint on A482, opposite turn to Ffarmers.* Home-made teas. **Adm £3, chd free (share to Pumsaint Women's Institute). Sun 16, Wed 19 Aug (1-5).** Visitors also welcome by appt. Recently developed 2½ -acre garden. Herbaceous and shrub beds, fruit, vegetables, new arboretum (200 types of tree), woodland dell, ponds, pergola, gazebos, post rope arcade covered in climbers, bulbs, annuals and perennials (many rare and unusual). Abundant colour March to October. Craft Stalls. Partial wheelchair access. Some gravel paths.

32 ◆ UPTON CASTLE GARDENS

Cosheston, Pembroke Dock, Pembrokeshire SA72 4SE. Prue & Stephen Barlow, 01646 689996, info@uptoncastle.com. *4m E of Pembroke Dock. 2m N of A477 between Carew and Pembroke Dock. Follow brown signs through Cosheston.* Cream teas on the lawn. **Adm £3, chd £1.50. Tues to Suns, Apr to Oct (10-5), also Mons in Aug and Bank Hols. For NGS: Sun 26 Apr (10-5).** 35 acres of mature gardens and arboretum with many unusual camellias, magnolias, rhododendrons and other rare trees and shrubs incl a 50yr-old Davidia (handkerchief tree). *Fagus sylvatica var. heterophylla, Drimys winteri,* formal rose gardens, herbaceous borders, Victorian kitchen garden (now being restored), woodland walk to the estuary and C13 chapel. Limited wheelchair access, disabled may be dropped at house.

33 WEIR CASTLE

Treffgarne, Wolfscastle, Pembrokeshire SA62 5LR. D J & D C Morris, 01437 741252. *On A40 between Haverfordwest and Fishguard. Approx 5m from Haverfordwest (before Wolfscastle). Just past signs for Treffgarne and Angling Centre, turn L up drive.* **Adm £2.50, chd free (share to Paul Sartori Foundation). Sats, Suns 20, 21 June; 18, 19 July (11-5).** Visitors also welcome by appt,coaches welcome. (The grounds of a farmhouse, not actually a castle.) Fairly steep hillside, richly planted with well-chosen shrubs and perennials, with attractive features and lovely views. The result of flair and imagination and brilliant use of a difficult site.

Mark your diary with these special events in 2009

EXPLORE SECRET GARDENS DURING CHELSEA & HAMPTON COURT FLOWER SHOW WEEKS

Tue 19 May, Wed 20 May, Thur 21 May, Fri 22 May, Wed 8 July, Thur 9 July
Full day tours from £82 per person, 10% discount for groups
Advance booking required, telephone +44 (0)20 8693 1015 or email j.wookey@btinternet.com
Specially selected gardens in London, Essex, Kent, Hampshire and South Oxfordshire. The tour price includes transport and lunch with wine at a popular restaurant or pub.

HAMPTON COURT PALACE

Thur 2 Apr, Tue 23 June, Thur 25 June, Wed 15 July, Tue 4 Aug, Thur 10 Sept
Evening tours in the company of one of the Palace's specialist tour guides from 6.30 – 8pm
Tickets £6 per person. Advance booking required, telephone +44 (0)1483 211535 or
visit www.ngs.org.uk for more information
Gossip, scandal, murder, healing – you'll find it all within the Formal Gardens at Hampton Court Palace. Each tour will have its own unique feature whether it's the story of the Great Vine or the magic and mystery of the Maze.

FROGMORE – A ROYAL GARDEN (BERKSHIRE)

Tue 26 May 10am – 5.30pm (last admission 4pm)
Garden adm £4.50, chd free. Tickets available in advance or on the day.
Advance booking for groups and coaches, telephone
+44 (0) 1483 211535 or email orders@ngs.org.uk
A rare opportunity to explore 30 acres of landscaped garden, rich in history and beauty.

FLAXBOURNE FARM – FUN & SURPRISES (BEDFORDSHIRE)

Sun 7 June 10am – 5pm. Adm £5, chd free
No booking required, come along on the day!
Bring the whole family and have fun in this surprising and entertaining garden of 2 acres. Enjoy the large plant fair, live music, pets corner, birds of prey, dog agility show and much more.

WISLEY RHS GARDEN – MUSIC IN THE GARDEN (SURREY)

Fri 11 Sept 6 – 9pm
Adm (incl RHS members) £7, chd under 15 free
Save money on advance bookings for groups of 4 or more, telephone +44 (0)1483 211535 or
visit www.ngs.org.uk for more information
A special evening opening of this famous garden, exclusively for the NGS. Enjoy music and entertainment as you explore the gardens and the floral marquee on the first day of the Wisley Flower Show.

For further information visit www.ngs.org.uk or telephone 01483 211535

CEREDIGION

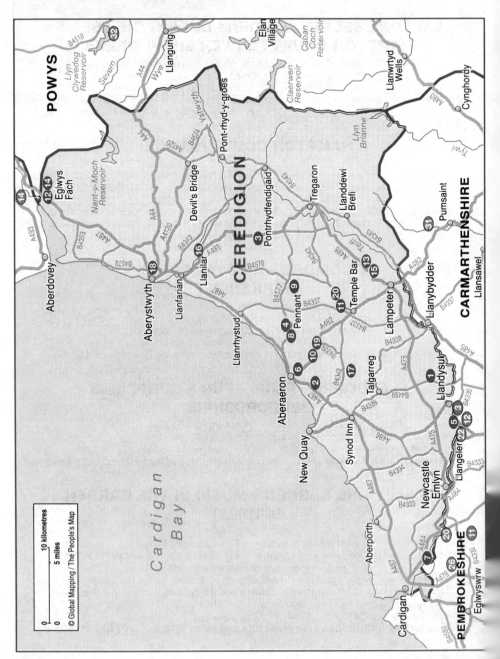

Opening Dates

February

SATURDAY 28
17 Perth Yr Eglwys

March

SUNDAY 1
17 Perth Yr Eglwys

May

SUNDAY 3
12 Llwyncelyn
14 The Mill House

SUNDAY 10
17 Perth Yr Eglwys
18 Plas Penglais

SUNDAY 17
2 Arnant House

SATURDAY 23
4 Dyffryn

SUNDAY 24
1 Alltyrodyn Mansion
4 Dyffryn

June

SUNDAY 7
3 Bwlch y Geuffordd

SUNDAY 14
16 Penbanc
20 Winllan Wildlife Garden

MONDAY 15
20 Winllan Wildlife Garden

TUESDAY 16
20 Winllan Wildlife Garden

WEDNESDAY 17
20 Winllan Wildlife Garden

THURSDAY 18
10 Llanerchaeron (Evening)
20 Winllan Wildlife Garden

FRIDAY 19
20 Winllan Wildlife Garden

SATURDAY 20
20 Winllan Wildlife Garden

SUNDAY 21
11 Llanllyr
20 Winllan Wildlife Garden

MONDAY 22
20 Winllan Wildlife Garden

TUESDAY 23
20 Winllan Wildlife Garden

WEDNESDAY 24
20 Winllan Wildlife Garden

THURSDAY 25
20 Winllan Wildlife Garden

FRIDAY 26
20 Winllan Wildlife Garden

SATURDAY 27
20 Winllan Wildlife Garden

SUNDAY 28
13 Maesyderi Farm
15 New Hall
20 Winllan Wildlife Garden

July

SUNDAY 5
6 Gerallt

SATURDAY 18
9 Isfryn

SUNDAY 19
9 Isfryn

SATURDAY 25
8 Gwynfryn Hall Garden

SUNDAY 26
5 Garregwen

August

SUNDAY 2
19 Ty Glyn Walled Garden

SUNDAY 16
7 Glanhelyg

September

SATURDAY 12
8 Gwynfryn Hall Garden

Gardens open to the public

10 Llanerchaeron
19 Ty Glyn Walled Garden

Also open by appointment ☎

1 Alltyrodyn Mansion
2 Arnant House
3 Bwlch y Geuffordd
11 Llanllyr
12 Llwyncelyn
13 Maesyderi Farm
14 The Mill House
15 New Hall
20 Winllan Wildlife Garden

1000ft high, 2-acre wildlife garden featuring lake with water lilies . . .

The Gardens

1 ALLTYRODYN MANSION
Capel Dewi SA44 4PS. Mr & Mrs Donald Usher, 01545 590206. *8m W of Lampeter, off A475. Take B4459 at Rhydowen to Capel Dewi. Entrance on R by South Lodge*. Home-made teas. **Adm £3, chd free (share to Capel Dewi Church). Sun 24 May (11-5). Visitors also welcome by appt.**
Early C19 garden. Approx 8 acres, mostly mature woodland with many fine trees. Old walled garden. Rare stone-built gothic cold bathhouse. Early C20 lake, Dutch garden and rhododendron plantings. Garden is best in spring when rhododendrons and azaleas are in bloom. Walled garden now being used for production of organic produce.
♿ ✖ ✿ ☕ ☎

2 ARNANT HOUSE
Llwyncelyn, Aberaeron SA46 0HF. Pam & Ron Maddox, 01545 580083. *On A487, 2m S of Aberaeron. Next to Llwyncelyn Village Hall. Parking in lay-by opp house*. Teas. **Adm £2.50, chd free. Sun 17 May (12-5). Visitors also welcome by appt.**
Garden created in 7yrs from derelict ground. 1-acre, in Victorian style and divided into rooms and themes. Laburnum arch, wildlife ponds, rotunda and tea house. Wide, long borders full of perennial planting with a good variety of species, numerous statues and oddities to be discovered. Several different magnolias, rhododendrons in May, 50 different types of Clematis.
♿ ✿ ☕ ☎

3 BWLCH Y GEUFFORDD
Bronant, Aberystwyth SY23 4JD. Mr & Mrs J Acres, 01974 251559, gayacres@aol.com. *6m NW of Tregaron. 12m SE of Aberystwyth off A485. Take turning opp Bronant school for 1½ m then turn L up a ½ m track*. Home-made teas. **Adm £3, chd 50p. Sun 7 June (11-6). Visitors also welcome by appt.**
1000ft high, 2-acre wildlife garden featuring lake with water lilies and a series of pools linked by waterfalls, a number of theme gardens, from Mediterranean to woodland and from oriental to exotic jungle with hut. Plenty of sympathetic seating and

large sculptures. Gravel paths but specialised wheelchair available for visitors weighing less than 10st.

 ♿ ✿ ☕ ☎

4 DYFFRYN
Pennant, Llanon, Ceredigion SY23 5PB. Mrs Jo Richards. *15m S of Aberystwyth on A487. From N through Llanon, L at Old Bakery, then 2nd L. From S through Aberarth, R uphill to Pennant, A4577. Follow signs.* Light refreshments & teas. **Adm £2.50, chd free. Sat, Sun 23, 24 May (11-5).**
²/₃ -acre garden now 28yrs old has matured into a W Wales rainforest with many mature trees and shrubs. Rooms with paving, water features and oriental touches - bamboos and grasses. Abundant birdlife and plenty of seats in different areas. Floral art exhibits, BBQ (weather permitting). Guide dogs permitted.

 ♿ 🐕 ✿ ☕

5 NEW GARREGWEN
Bangor Teifi, Llandysul SA44 5BS. Yvonne & Brian Smith, 01559 363586. *2m W of Llandysul. A486 centre of Llandysul main street. L up Sion Hill towards leisure centre. Garden on L after 2m.* Home-made teas. **Adm £3, chd free. Sun 26 July (11-6).**
Within 2 acres, an interesting mix of flowers, shrubs, vegetables and young unusual trees together with a wild life pond, lily and fish pond. Meandering stream in a woodland setting. Local artist Sally Pearce's studio will be open next door.

🐕 ✿ ☕

6 GERALLT
Bro Allt y Graig, Aberaeron SA46 0DU. Huw & Dilys Lewis. *Off A482 Aberaeron - Lampeter rd. Turn at D & L Davies Garage. Entry at first bend where road divides. Please park at Memorial Hall on A482 in Aberaeron.* Home-made teas. **Adm £3, chd free. Sun 5 July (11-5).**
Mature 1920s bungalow garden containing a large variety of shrubs, lavenders and roses such as 'Chapeau de Napoleon'. Sections include a pond-side area with gunnera and bamboo, a slate bed, woodland glade and a herb plot with a wide variety of herbs both culinary and medicinal.

🐕 ✿ ☕

7 GLANHELYG
Lon Helyg, Llechryd, Cardigan SA43 2NJ. Mike & Ann Williamson, www.glanhelyg.co.uk. *3m SE of Cardigan. From A484 Cardigan-Newcastle Emlyn, L into Lon Helyg 50yds after Llechryd sign, house at end.* Home-made teas. **Adm £2.50, chd free. Sun 16 Aug (1-6).**
3¹/₂ -acre woodland, meadow and walled garden. Recent imaginatively re-designed Victorian walled garden contains a large variety of plants, many semi-tender in prairie style planting. Art gallery. Gravel paths.

 ♿ ✿ ☕

8 NEW GWYNFRYN HALL GARDEN
Cilcennin Road, Pennant, Llanon SY23 5JW. Guy & Joanny Sansom. *3m S of Llanon. Situated on the edge of Pennant on Ciliau-Aeron to Pennant Road. Opposite entrance to Pennant car boot sale.* Home-made teas. **Adm £3, chd free. Sats 25 July; 12 Sept (11-6).**
Established ²/₃ -acre, owned by retired professional gardeners. Beautifully presented in a series of 'garden rooms'. Large pond, board walk, garden statuary. Many unusual semi-tropical plants, ferns, fuchsia and herbaceous perennials.

 ♿ 🐕 ✿ ☕

Beautifully presented in a series of 'garden rooms'. Large pond, board walk, garden statuary . . .

9 NEW ISFRYN
Bethania, nr Llanon SY23 5NP. Mrs Julie Langford. *15m SW Aberystwyth. B4337 from Llanrhystud or B4577 from Aberarth to Cross Inn. Turn R or continue along B4577 for 2m. At Xrds turn R. 3rd house on L.* Home-made teas. **Adm £3, chd free. Sat, Sun 18, 19 July (11-5).**
5-acre garden, ever evolving with shrub and herbaceous borders, kitchen garden incl poultry, fruit areas, vegetable beds and a polytunnel. A woodland with paths. A field with lawned paths, ducks, lake and natural areas. Children must be supervised. Eggs and produce available. Gentle slopes. WC facilities not wheelchair accessible.

 ♿ 🐕 ✿ ☕

10 ♦ LLANERCHAERON
Ciliau Aeron, Lampeter SA48 8DG. The National Trust, 01545 570200, www.nationaltrust.org.uk. *2¹/₂ m E of Aberaeron. On the A482 Lampeter to Aberaeron.* **Adm £3, chd free. House and Garden adm £6.90, Farm & Garden only adm £5.90. Mar to Jul, Weds to Suns, July to Aug, Tue to Suns, Sept to Nov, Weds to Suns (11-5).** Check website for details. For NGS: **Evening Opening,** wine, music & refreshments, **Thur 18 June (6-9).**
Llanerchaeron is a small C18 Welsh gentry estate set in the beautiful Dyffryn Aeron. The estate survived virtually unaltered into the C20. 2 extensive restored walled gardens produce home-grown vegetables, fruit and herbs for sale. The kitchen garden sits at the core of the estate with a John Nash villa built in 1795 and home farm, all virtually unaltered since its construction.

 ♿ 🐕 ☕

11 LLANLLYR
Talsarn, Lampeter SA48 8QB. Mr & Mrs Robert Gee, 01570 470900. *6m NW of Lampeter. On B4337 to Llanrhystud.* Home-made teas. **Adm £3.50, chd under 12 free. Sun 21 June (2-6).** Visitors also welcome by appt.
Large early C19 garden on site of medieval nunnery, renovated & replanted since 1989. Large pool, bog garden, formal water garden, rose & shrub borders, gravel gardens, laburnum arbour, allegorical labyrinth

and mount, all exhibiting fine plantsmanship. Yr-round appeal, interesting & unusual plants. Specialist plant fair by Ceredigion Growers Association.

 ⌖ ✕ ❀ ☕ ☎

12 LLWYNCELYN
Glandyfi, Machynlleth SY20 8SS. Mr & Mrs Stewart Neal, 01654 781203, joyneal@btinternet.com. *12m N of Aberystwyth. On A487 Machynlleth (5½ m). From Aberystwyth, turn R just before Glandyfi sign*. Home-made teas. **Adm £3.50, chd free combined with Mill House. Sun 3 May (11-6). Visitors also welcome by appt.**
13-acre woodland hillside garden/arboretum alongside Dyfi tributary. Collections of hybrid/species rhododendrons flowering Christmas-Aug. Mollis azaleas in many shades, bluebells in ancient oak wood. Rare species and hybrid hydrangeas. Large fernery, many overseas taxa added to natives. Formal garden contains terrace, parterre and potager. Large plant sale. Specialist plant fair by Ceredigion Growers Association. Gravel path.

 ⌖ ✕ ❀ ☕ ☎

13 MAESYDERI FARM
Llangybi, Lampeter SA48 8LY. Glenda Johnson, 01570 493221, www.oakmeadows-cockers.co.uk. *3m N of Lampeter, 6m S of Tregaron. On A485 midway betweeen Llangybi and Bettws Bledrws, opp layby*. Home-made teas. **Adm £3.50, chd free combined with New Hall. Sun 28 June (11-5). Visitors also welcome by appt.**
Created over the last 6yrs from rough pasture and maturing well. Designed and maintained by an enthusiastic plantswoman, containing many interesting trees, an eclectic mix of shrubs, cottage garden perennials, water & bog garden. Gravel areas with raised beds, a small woodland with shade-loving plants.

 ✕ ❀ ☕ ☎

14 THE MILL HOUSE
Glandyfi, Machynlleth SY20 8LY. Professor & Mrs J M Pollock, 01654 781342, jpol@waitrose.com. *Entrance at Llwyncelyn*. **Adm £3.50, chd free combined with Llwyncelyn. Sun 3 May (11-5). Visitors also welcome by appt May only. Limited access and parking.**
Picturesque garden of a former water mill with millstream, millpond, and

several waterfalls in woodland setting, about 1½ acres. Azaleas, rhododendrons and spring colour enhance waterside vistas, which have a Japanese theme.

 ✕ ☎

15 NEW HALL
Bettws Bledrws, Lampeter SA48 8NX. Maureen & Dave Allen, 01570 493188. *3m N Lampeter, 6m S Tregaron. On A485, 100yds from church*. Teas at Maesyderi Farm. **Adm £3.50, chd free combined with Maesyderi Farm. Sun 28 June (11-5). Visitors also welcome by appt.**
Cottage garden established in 2000 from derelict ground by keen plantswoman and her husband. Well stocked herbaceous borders incl interesting trees and shrubs, water garden and koi ponds with large gunneras and bog plants. Collection of Japanese acers.

 ✕ ☎

Large tropical glasshouse filled with beautiful and interesting exotic species . . .

16 PENBANC
Llanilar, Aberystwyth SY23 4NY. Enfys & David Rennie. *Off A487, 6m SE of Aberystwyth. From Llanfarian take A485 signed Tregaron for 2½ m. Turn L into lane immed after Cwmaur Estate. Penbanc in ½ m, overlooking river bridge. Park in field next to river*. Home-made teas. **Adm £3, chd free. Sun 14 June (2-6).**
½ -acre, S-facing sloping cottage garden alongside R Ystwyth with views over valley. Established orchards, large vegetable garden and densely planted herbaceous borders created in 2005, with masses of roses, clematis, campanula lactiflora, hardy geraniums, grasses and shrubs. Riverside wildlife walk.

 ✕ ❀ ☕

17 PERTH YR EGLWYS
Mydroilyn, Lampeter SA48 7QX. Elizabeth Gould & Christopher May. *Off A 487, 4m S of Aberaeron. Turn L at Llanarth, signed Mydroilyn. Through village to chapel, R to school, R again at school, 300yds*. Home-made teas 10 May only. **Adm £2.50 (Feb, Mar) £3, May, chd free. Sat 28 Feb; Suns 1 Mar (11-4); 10 May (11-5).**
3-acre established woodland garden. Drifts of snowdrops and cyclamen in early spring along with hellebores, camellias and early rhododendrons. In May, streamside walks and extensive bog gardens, large areas of azaleas, perennial borders and a vegetable garden. Plant sale 10 May only.

 ✕ ❀ ☕

18 PLAS PENGLAIS
Penglais Road, Aberystwyth SY23 3DF. Aberystwyth University. *NE of Aberystwyth on A487. Entrance alongside Penglais Lodge, opp side of rd to University Campus. Park on campus*. Home-made teas. **Adm £3, chd free. Sun 10 May (2-5).**
Sheltered garden of Georgian Mansion surrounded by native trees and carpeted with bluebells. Rockery, walled terrace, pond, extensive lawns, rhododendrons and many unusual specimen shrubs and trees. Remains of old Botany Dept 'order beds'. Large tropical glasshouse filled with beautiful and interesting exotic species. Some uneven paths, slippery ground. Soft ground in wet weather.

 ⌖ ✕ ❀ ☕

19 ◆ TY GLYN WALLED GARDEN
Ciliau Aeron, Lampeter, Cerdigion SA48 8DE. Ty Glyn Davis Trust, 01970 832268, www.tyglyndavistrust.co.uk. *3m SW of Aberaeron. Turn off A482 Aberaeron to Lampeter at Ciliau Aeron signed to Pennant. Entrance 700metres on L*. Refreshments. **Adm £2.50, chd free. For NGS: Sun 2 Aug (11-5).**
Secluded L-shaped walled garden in beautiful woodland setting alongside R Aeron, developed specifically for special needs children. S-facing productive terraced kitchen garden overlooks herbaceous borders, orchard and ponds with child orientated features and surprises amidst unusual shrubs and perennials. Newly planted fruit trees selected from former gardener's notebook of C19.

 ⌖ ✕ ❀

Garden includes a large pond, small woodland, 600 yards of riverbank walk and a 4-acre hay meadow with over 10,000 wild orchids including the rare Greater Butterfly Orchid . . .

20 WINLLAN WILDLIFE GARDEN
Talsarn SA48 8QE. Mr & Mrs Ian Callan, 01570 470612. *8m NNW of Lampeter. On B4342, Talsarn-Llangeitho rd.* **Adm £3, chd free. Daily Sun 14 June to Sun 28 June; (2-5). Visitors also welcome by appt daily 1 to 30 June.**
6-acre wildlife garden owned by botanists happy to share their knowledge with visitors. Garden includes a large pond, small woodland, 600yds of riverbank walk and a 4-acre hay meadow with over 10,000 wild orchids incl the rare Greater Butterfly Orchid.

Ceredigion County Volunteers

County Organiser
Jennifer Dyer, Robin Hill, Coed y Garth, Furnace, Machynlleth SY20 8PG, 01654 781223, jandrdyer@btinternet.com

County Treasurer
Rodney J Dyer, Robin Hill, Coed y Garth, Furnace, Machynlleth SY20 8PG, 01654 781223, jandrdyer@btinternet.com

Assistant County Organiser
Joy Neal, Llwyncelyn, Glandyfi, Machynlleth SY20 8SS, 01654 781203, joyneal@btinternet.com
Lisa Raw-Rees, The Old Mill, Water Street, Aberaeron SA46 0DG, 01545 570107, hywelrawrees@hotmail.com

Mark your diary with these special events in 2009

EXPLORE SECRET GARDENS DURING CHELSEA & HAMPTON COURT FLOWER SHOW WEEKS

Tue 19 May, Wed 20 May, Thur 21 May, Fri 22 May, Wed 8 July, Thur 9 July
Full day tours from £82 per person, 10% discount for groups
Advance booking required, telephone +44 (0)20 8693 1015 or email j.wookey@btinternet.com
Specially selected gardens in London, Essex, Kent, Hampshire and South Oxfordshire. The tour price includes transport and lunch with wine at a popular restaurant or pub.

HAMPTON COURT PALACE

Thur 2 Apr, Tue 23 June, Thur 25 June, Wed 15 July, Tue 4 Aug, Thur 10 Sept
Evening tours in the company of one of the Palace's specialist tour guides from 6.30 – 8pm
Tickets £6 per person. Advance booking required, telephone +44 (0)1483 211535 or
visit www.ngs.org.uk for more information
Gossip, scandal, murder, healing – you'll find it all within the Formal Gardens at Hampton Court Palace. Each tour will have its own unique feature whether it's the story of the Great Vine or the magic and mystery of the Maze.

FROGMORE – A ROYAL GARDEN (BERKSHIRE)

Tue 26 May 10am – 5.30pm (last admission 4pm)
Garden adm £4.50, chd free. Tickets available in advance or on the day.
Advance booking for groups and coaches, telephone
+44 (0) 1483 211535 or email orders@ngs.org.uk
A rare opportunity to explore 30 acres of landscaped garden, rich in history and beauty.

FLAXBOURNE FARM – FUN & SURPRISES (BEDFORDSHIRE)

Sun 7 June 10am – 5pm. Adm £5, chd free
No booking required, come along on the day!
Bring the whole family and have fun in this surprising and entertaining garden of 2 acres. Enjoy the large plant fair, live music, pets corner, birds of prey, dog agility show and much more.

WISLEY RHS GARDEN – MUSIC IN THE GARDEN (SURREY)

Fri 11 Sept 6 – 9pm
Adm (incl RHS members) £7, chd under 15 free
Save money on advance bookings for groups of 4 or more, telephone +44 (0)1483 211535 or
visit www.ngs.org.uk for more information
A special evening opening of this famous garden, exclusively for the NGS. Enjoy music and entertainment as you explore the gardens and the floral marquee on the first day of the Wisley Flower Show.

For further information visit www.ngs.org.uk or telephone 01483 211535

DENBIGHSHIRE & COLWYN

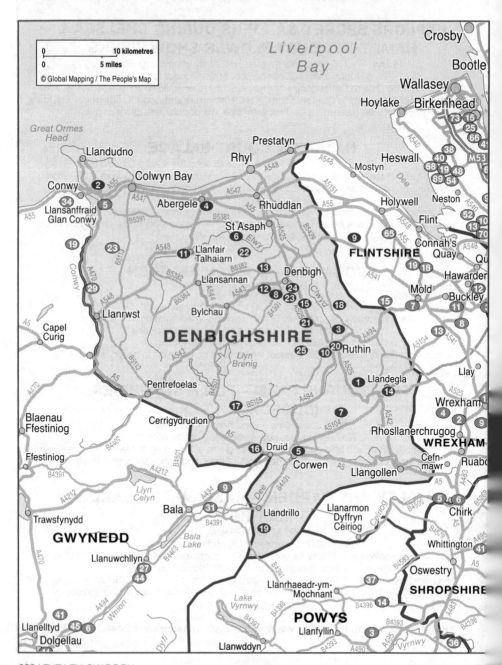

0 — 10 kilometres
0 — 5 miles
© Global Mapping / The People's Map

Liverpool Bay

Crosby
Bootle
Wallasey
Hoylake Birkenhead
73 15
25
66

Great Ormes Head
Llandudno
Prestatyn
Rhyl
Heswall
Mostyn
38
40
68 19 48
89 54
M53

Conwy 2
Colwyn Bay
Abergele 4
Rhuddlan
Holywell Neston
34
Llansanffraid 5
Glan Conwy
St Asaph 6
65
Flint
Connah's Quay
52
13
70
10

19
23
Llanfair Talhaiarn 11
22
9
FLINTSHIRE
19 18
Hawarden
12

29
Llansannan
13
Denbigh
15
Mold
Buckley
11
8

Llanrwst
Bylchau
12 24
8 23
15
18
15
7
13

Capel Curig
DENBIGHSHIRE
21
3
20
25 10 Ruthin
Llay

Pentrefoelas
Llyn Brenig
1 Llandegla
14
Wrexham
4 2 9

Blaenau Ffestiniog
Cerrigydrudion
17
7
Rhosllanerchrugog
WREXHAM
Cefn-mawr Ruabon

Ffestiniog
16 Druid
Corwen 5
Llangollen
5 6 Chirk

Llyn Celyn
9
Bala 31
Llandrillo
Llanarmon Dyffryn Ceiriog
Whittington 41

Trawsfynydd
19
Oswestry
A5

GWYNEDD
Bala Lake
Llanuwchllyn 27
44
Llanrhaeadr-ym-Mochnant
37
14
SHROPSHIRE

41
45 6
Llanelltyd
Dolgellau
Lake Vyrnwy
POWYS
Llanfyllin 3
36

Llanwddyn

Opening Dates

March

SUNDAY 8
8 Dolhyfryd

April

SUNDAY 26
20 Ruthin Castle

May

SATURDAY 2
7 Dibleys Nurseries

SUNDAY 3
5 Caereuni
7 Dibleys Nurseries

MONDAY 4
5 Caereuni
7 Dibleys Nurseries

SUNDAY 10
17 The Old Rectory, Llanfihangel Glyn Myfyr
24 Tros-y-Parc

WEDNESDAY 13
6 The Cottage Garden Melin-y-Ddol

SUNDAY 24
5 Caereuni
16 Maesmor Hall

MONDAY 25
5 Caereuni

WEDNESDAY 27
6 The Cottage Garden Melin-y-Ddol

June

FRIDAY 5
3 Bryn Celyn (Evening)

SUNDAY 7
3 Bryn Celyn
5 Caereuni

WEDNESDAY 10
6 The Cottage Garden Melin-y-Ddol

SUNDAY 14
13 Henllan Village Gardens

SUNDAY 21
6 The Cottage Garden Melin-y-Ddol
12 Gwaenynog

WEDNESDAY 24
6 The Cottage Garden Melin-y-Ddol

SUNDAY 5
5 Caereuni
17 The Old Rectory, Llanfihangel Glyn Myfyr

WEDNESDAY 8
6 The Cottage Garden Melin-y-Ddol

SUNDAY 12
15 Llanrhaeadr y.c. Gardens

WEDNESDAY 22
6 The Cottage Garden Melin-y-Ddol

SUNDAY 26
14 Llandegla Village Gardens

August

SUNDAY 2
5 Caereuni

WEDNESDAY 12
6 The Cottage Garden Melin-y-Ddol

TUESDAY 18
2 Bodysgallen Hall & Spa

WEDNESDAY 26
6 The Cottage Garden Melin-y-Ddol

SUNDAY 30
5 Caereuni
21 Stella Maris

MONDAY 31
5 Caereuni
21 Stella Maris

September

SUNDAY 6
5 Caereuni

SUNDAY 20
5 Caereuni

October

SUNDAY 4
5 Caereuni

SUNDAY 25
5 Caereuni

By appointment only

1 Arfryn
4 33 Bryn Twr & Lynton
9 Donadea Lodge
10 Firgrove
11 Garthewin
18 The Old Rectory, Llangynhafal
19 Rhyd Gethin
22 Tal-y-Bryn Farm
23 Trosyffordd
25 Tyddyn Bach

Also open by Appointment ☎

3 Bryn Celyn
8 Dolhyfryd
14 Glan-yr-Afon, Llandegla Village Gardens
14 Swn y Gwynt, Llandegla Village Gardens
15 Tan-y-Parc, Llanrhaeadr y.c. Gardens
18 The Old Rectory, Llangynhafal
20 Ruthin Castle
21 Stella Maris

The Gardens

1 ARFRYN
Pentrecelyn, nr Ruthin LL15 2HR. Mr & Mrs A O Davies, 01978 790475, arfrynpentrecelyn@btinternet.com. *4m S of Ruthin. On A525 Wrexham rd. At Llanfair Dyffryn Clwyd take B5429 to Graigfechan. Mold-Ruthin A494 to Llanbedr Dyffryn Clwyd turn L after village B5429 to Graigfechan.* **Adm £2.50, chd free. Visitors welcome by appt June, July only, groups 10+.** Situated on hillside 800ft above sea level. 2-acre garden designed for yr-round interest, overlooking wonderful views. Divided into separate rooms - secret garden filled with old roses and hardy geraniums, cottage garden, wild flower bank and lawned gardens with herbaceous and shrub beds. New polytunnel garden featuring half hardy plants, trachycarpus, musa, cannas, etc.

BANK HOUSE
See Cheshire & Wirral.

Secret garden filled with old roses and hardy geraniums . . .

2 BODYSGALLEN HALL & SPA

nr Llandudno LL30 1RS. Historic House Hotels Ltd. *2m from Llandudno. Take A55 to its intersection with A470 towards Llandudno. Proceed 1m, hotel is 1m on R.* Home-made teas. **Adm £3, chd 50p. Tue 18 Aug (1-5).**
Garden is well known for C17 box-hedged parterre. Stone walls surround lower gardens with rose gardens and herbaceous borders. Outside walled garden is a cascade over rocks. Enclosed working fruit and vegetable garden with espalier-trained fruit trees, hedging area for cut flowers with walls covered in wineberry and Chinese gooseberry. Restored Victorian woodland, walks with stunning views of Conwy and Snowdonia. Featured in House & Garden Magazine. Gravel paths and steep slopes.

& ✖ ❀ ⊫ ☕

3 BRYN CELYN

Llanbedr LL15 1TT. Mrs S Rathbone, 01824 702077, skrathbone@toucansurf.com. *2m N of Ruthin. From Ruthin take A494 towards Mold. After 1½ m, turn L at Griffin PH onto B5429. Proceed 1½ m; garden on R.* Home-made teas. **Adm £3, chd free (share to Llanychyn Church). Sun 7 June (2.30-6). Evening Opening** , light refreshments & wine Fri 5 June (6-8.30). Visitors also welcome by appt.
2-acre garden with lawns surrounded by mixed borders. Walled garden with old-fashioned roses, cistus, lavender, honeysuckle, box balls and fruit trees. Gazebo and pergola leading to Mediterranean garden and woodland. Cherry trees and spring bulbs, autumn colour.

& ✖ ❀ ☕ ☎

4 33 BRYN TWR & LYNTON

Abergele LL22 8DD. Mr & Mrs Colin Knowlson, 01745 828201, crk@slaters.com. *From A55 heading W, take slip rd to Abergele. Turn L at r'about then over T-lights; 1st L signed Llanfair T H. 3rd rd on L, No 33 is on L.* **Adm £3, chd free. Visitors welcome by appt anytime, with prior notice.**
2 connected gardens of totally differing styles, one cottage style of planting, the other quite formal. Approx ¾ acre in total, containing patio and pond areas; mixed herbaceous and shrub borders, many unusual plants. Large changes for 2009. Steps & steep paths in places.

✖ ❀ ☎

CAERAU UCHAF
See Gwynedd.

5 CAEREUNI

Ffordd Ty Cerrig, Godreír Gaer, nr Corwen LL21 9YA. Mr & Mrs Williams. *1m N of Corwen. Take A5 to Bala. Turn R at T-lights onto A494 to Chester. 1st R after lay-by; house ¼ m on L.* **Adm £2.50, chd free. Sun, Mons 3, 4, 24, 25 May; 7 June; 5 July; 2, 30, 31 Aug; 6, 20 Sept; 4, 25 Oct.**
Third of an acre international quirky themed fantasy garden with unique features incl; Japanese smoke water garden, old ruin, Spanish courtyard, Welsh gold mine, Chinese peace garden, woodman's lodge and jungle, Mexican chapel, 1950s petrol garage.

✖

International quirky themed fantasy garden with unique features . . .

6 THE COTTAGE GARDEN MELIN-Y-DDOL

Marli, Abergele LL22 9EB. Tom & Jenny Pritchard. *1½ m N of Llannefydd. 3m S of Bodelwyddan. 3m S of A55 between Llannefydd & Glascoed. On R Elwy adj to Pont-y-Ddol. Entrance on S side of bridge.* Home-made teas. **Adm £2.50, chd free (share to St Mary's Church, Cefn, 21 June only). Weds 13, 27 May; 10, 24 June; 8, 22 July; 12, 26 Aug (2-5). Sun 21 June (2-5.30).**
Many cottage garden plants in informal borders. Small bog areas, grass garden, laburnum arch, small wild flower meadow, fruit and vegetables, cut flower border. Elemental 'white witches' garden. Dyers and aromatherapy plant areas. Old mill stones from the mill are used throughout garden. Living willow structure. Hens. Riverside walk. Working cottage garden, sometimes repeat flowering sacrificed for seed production. All in magical setting. Adj nursery featuring plants propagated from garden.

✖ ❀ ☕

CYFIE FARM
See Powys.

---

7 DIBLEYS NURSERIES

Cefn Rhydd, Llanelidan LL15 2LG. Mr & Mrs R Dibley. *7m S of Ruthin. Take A525 to Xrds by Llysfasi Agricultural College. Turn onto B5429 towards Llanelidan. After 1½ m turn L, 1m up lane on L. Brown tourist signs from A525.* Home-made teas. **Adm £3, chd 50p (share to ActionAid). Sat, Sun, Mon 2, 3,4 May (10-5).**
Large arboretum with wide selection of rare and unusual trees.There will be a lovely display of rhododendrons, magnolias, cherries and camellias. Ride through the garden on a miniature railway. ¾ -acre glasshouses are open to show streptocarpus and other pot plants. National Collection of *Streptocarpus.*

✖ ❀ NCCPG ☕

8 DOLHYFRYD

yn Lawnt, Denbigh LL16 4SU. Captain & Mrs Michael Cunningham, 01745 814805, virginia@dolhyfryd.com. *1m SW of Denbigh. On B4501 to Nantglyn, from Denbigh - 1m from town centre.* Light refreshments & home-made teas; wine. **Adm £3, chd free. Sun 8 Mar (10-4). Visitors also welcome by appt.**
Established garden set in small valley of R Ystrad. Acres of crocuses in late Feb/early Mar. Paths through wild flower meadows and woodland of magnificent trees, shade-loving plants and azaleas; mixed borders; walled kitchen garden - recently re-designed. Many woodland and riverside birds, incl dippers, kingfishers, grey wagtails. Many species of butterfly encouraged by new planting. Much winter interest, exceptional display of crocuses. If wet, phone to visit on a sunny day. Mentioned on Radio Wales. Gravel paths, some steep slopes.

& ❀ ☕ ☎

9 DONADEA LODGE

Babell CH8 8QD. Mr P Beaumont, 01352 720204. *7m NE of Denbigh. Turn off A541 Mold to Denbigh at Afonwen, signed Babell; T-junction turn L. A55 Chester to Conwy take B5122 to Caerwys, 3rd turn on L.* **Adm £2.50 chd free. Visitors welcome by appt May to July.**
1-acre shady garden showing 25yrs of imaginative planting to enhance the magic of dappled shade, moving through different colour schemes, with each plant complementing its neighbour.

& ✖ ☎

Small established garden planted on incline with waterfall and ponds . . .

⑩ NEW FIRGROVE
Ruthin LL15 2LL. Philip & Anna Meadway, 01824 702677, panda.meadway@btinternet.com. 1½ m SW of Ruthin. Exit Ruthin on B5105 towards Cerrig Y Drudion. After church & inn, garden is ½ m on the R. Light refreshments & teas. Adm £3, chd free. Visitors welcome by appt May to Sept daily incl weekends (12-3.30). Groups max of 20 due to limited parking.
1½ -acre mature plantsman's garden that is still developing. A garden for all seasons whose microclimate allows tender and unusual shrubs to thrive. Some underplanted with Streptocarpus for the summer. A collection of large exotics for summer containers. Many varieties of Pittosporum, camellias, magnolias, buddleia colvii and alternifolia. Clematis up the trees.

🛏 ☕ ☎

⑪ GARTHEWIN
Llanfair T.H. LL22 8YR. Mr Michael Grime, 01745 720288. 6m S of Abergele & A55. From Abergele take A548 to Llanfair TH & Llanrwst. Entrance to Garthewin 250yds W of Llanfair TH on A548 to Llanrwst. Adm £3, chd free. Visitors welcome by appt in April, May & June.
Valley garden with ponds and woodland areas. Much of the 8 acres have been reclaimed and redesigned providing a younger garden with a great variety of azaleas, rhododendrons and young trees, all within a framework of mature shrubs and trees. Small chapel open. Rural Wales Award for Restoration and Enhancement of Historic Park and Garden.

☎

GRAFTON LODGE
See Cheshire & Wirral.

⑫ GWAENYNOG
Denbigh LL16 5NU. Major & Mrs Tom Smith. 1m W of Denbigh. On A543, Lodge on L, ¼ m drive. Home-made teas. Adm £3, chd free (share to St James' Church, Nantglyn). Sun 21 June (2-5.30).
2 acres incl the restored kitchen garden where Beatrix Potter wrote and illustrated the 'Tale of the Flopsy Bunnies'. Small exhibition of some of her work. C16 house (not open) visited by Dr Samuel Johnson during his Tour of Wales. 2009 is the 100th Birthday of 'The Tale of the Flopsy Bunnies'. Music.

♿ 🐕 ⊕ ☕

Group opening

⑬ NEW HENLLAN VILLAGE GARDENS
Henllan LL16 5AH. 2m NW of Denbigh. On B5382 Denbigh to Henllan Road. Teas in Church Institute. Combined adm £5, chd free (share to Henllan Church & Chapel). Sun 14 June (2-5).
Small village surrounded by farmland with Medieval church and thatched village pub.

☕

NEW BELVEDERE
Mr Gerraint Wyn Pritchard
Small garden with selection of plants and shrubs. Slate corner feature. Unusual display of hand crafted walking sticks made by the owner.

♿ 🐕

NEW 5 FFORDD BRYN Y GARN
Sue & Alec Rumbold
Plantswoman's garden making the most of a small space. Raised beds, pond, rockery and archways. Plant stall.

🐕 ⊕

NEW 51 GLASFRYN
Iris Baugh
Lawned garden sheltered by hedges and trees. Raised beds, wide variety of plants and roses. Different seating areas, decking and a variety of pot plants.

♿ 🐕

NEW MAES-Y-FFYNNON
Jane & Duncan Stewart
Medium sized garden with mixed range of shrubs and perennials. Wheelchair access to front garden only.

♿ 🐕

TAN Y GRAIG
Barbara & Jim Buchanan. Adm £2.50, chd free
Elevated ½ -acre garden with panoramic views, dissected by terraced walks and backed by a 50ft limestone cliff. Large rockery, shrub and perennial beds containing over 500 varieties of plants. Small nursery. All plants propogated from the garden.

♿ ⊕

NEW TY CRWN
John & Gaynor Kumria
Small established garden planted on incline with waterfall and ponds. Incls rockery, herb garden and bog garden.

🐕

Group opening

⑭ LLANDEGLA VILLAGE GARDENS
LL11 3AP. 10m W of Wrexham. Off A525 at Llandegla Memorial Hall. Parking & mini bus from hall. Cream teas at & in aid of Llandegla Memorial Hall. Combined adm £5, chd free. Sun 26 July (2-6).
Small picturesque village surrounded by moorland. Church with interesting features. Communal garden area by river.

⊕ ☕

ERRW LLAN
3 Maes Teg. Mr & Mrs Keith Jackson
¼ -acre garden made to attract wildlife. Plants grown for birds and butterflies. Trees for a variety of nesting sites. Pond to encourage frogs, toads, newts and damsel flies.

GLAN-YR-AFON
Mr & Mrs D C Ion, 01978 790286, val@dunvalion.co.uk. Visitors also welcome by appt.
1-acre informal country garden surrounding this 200yr old farmhouse on 3 sides with a wide variety of features incl stream, 2 ponds, herbaceous borders, rockery and several ancient trees.

🐕 ☎

NEW ISIS
Janet & David Rose
Small garden with perennials, raised vegetable beds and open outlook. Designed for pleasure with practicality.

OLD TY HIR FARM
Chester Road. Mr & Mrs D M Holder
1-acre open plan garden with wide variety of trees, shrubs and many secret areas to explore.

SWN Y GWYNT
Phil Clark, 01978 790344. Visitors also welcome by appt. 1/4 -acre plantsman's garden, shrubs and associated plants for shade. Some areas difficult.

Group opening

15 NEW LLANRHAEADR Y.C. GARDENS
Llanrhaeadc Y.C LL16 4NL. *3m S of Denbigh, 5m N of Ruthin. Take A525 from Denbigh or Ruthin. Follow signs at Llanrhaeadr.* Home-made teas at Tan-y-Parc. **Combined adm £5, chd free (share to Llanrhaeadr Church, St Dyfnog's Church). Sun 12 July (2-5).**
3 village gardens all different with superb views over farmland countryside in the beautiful Vale of Clwyd. Near St Dyfnog's Church with wonderful Jesse Window. Anvil Pottery.

NEW BRONDYFFRYN
LL16 4NH. Mrs D Roberts
Situated across two fields, 1/2 -acre garden with a wonderful view. Lawned areas with two pools, one with created waterfall. Small enclosed vegetable plot.

PARC BACH
Mrs Ivor Watkins
1/3 -acre garden making max use of all available space. Beds crammed full of unusual plants making a beautiful picture framed by wonderful views across the Vale of Clwyd. Productive and varied fruit garden, mostly on cordons and espalier. Garden slopes away.

NEW TAN-Y-PARC
LL16 4NL. Mrs Sandra Edwards, 01745 890807, dottycom3_@hotmail.com. **Visitors also welcome by appt July & Aug groups of 10 or more. Coaches permitted.** Small cottage garden, new planted borders in paddock area, greenhouse and raised vegetable plots, fruit bushes. Rear garden enclosed with beech hedges, 2 large raised beds. Pergola with grape vine.

16 MAESMOR HALL
Maerdy, Corwen LL21 0NS. Mr & Mrs G M Jackson. *5m W of Corwen. Take A5 from Corwen, through 2 sets of T-lights. In Maerdy take 1st L after church and opp The Goat PH.* Home-made teas. **Adm £3, chd free. Sun 24 May (1-5).**
Well-established garden with riverside and estate walks featuring a water garden and white plant garden. The rhododendrons are extensive and provide a fitting backdrop to the parkland. Large azalea beds are a mixture of colour. Wooded walks around the hall together with an arboretum are also an attraction. Latest addition is the largest rose carousel in Wales featuring over 80 roses from David Austin. Patios and front of hall displays. Enormous stone table has been brought down from the surrounding mountain - could have been King Arthur's. Gravel paths.

Look at the mountains and trees, listen to the river and birds, smell the roses . . .

17 THE OLD RECTORY, LLANFIHANGEL GLYN MYFYR
LL21 9UN. Mr & Mrs E T Hughes, 01490 420568, elwynthomashughes@hotmail.com. *2 1/2 m E of Cerrigydrudion. From Ruthin take B5105 SW for 12m to Llanfihangel Glyn Myfyr. Turn R just after Crown PH (follow signs). Proceed for 1/3 m, garden on L.* Home-made teas. **Adm £3, chd free (share to Cancer Research UK). Suns 10 May (2-5); 5 July (2-6). Visitors also welcome by appt Groups of 10+.**
Garden of approx 1 acre set in beautiful, tranquil, sheltered valley. A garden for all seasons; hellebores; abundance of spring flowers; mixed borders; water, bog, and gravel gardens; walled garden with old roses, pergola, bower and garden of meditation. Also incls hardy orchids and gentians. Some areas inaccessible for wheelchairs with slopes & steps.

18 THE OLD RECTORY, LLANGYNHAFAL
Denbieh, Nr Ruthin LL16 4LN. Mr & Mrs Henry Dixon, 01824 790254, sue@allthedixons.com. *3 1/2 m N of Ruthin. From Ruthin take A494; Llanbedr take B5429. After 1/2 m turn R signed 2 1/2 m Llangynhafal. Entrance on R at Xrds.* **Adm £3, chd free. Visitors welcome by appt April, May, June only.**
Extensive grounds centred on traditional walled gardens, with bulbs, unusual plants, orchards, blossom and vegetables. Installations, sculptures and water features link the C18 and C21.

19 NEW RHYD GETHIN
Pennant Road, Llandrillo, Corwen LL21 0TE. Tony & Jenny Leeson, 01490 440213, anthony.leeson@tesco.net. *Between Corwen & Bala. Take B4401 signed Llandrillo. In village turn at shop /PO. 50yds fork L onto Pennant Rd. 2m down single track. Fork R at telephone box.* Home-made teas. **Adm £3, chd free. Visitors welcome by appt May to Sept. Gardening clubs welcome. Sorry, access not suitable for coaches.**
Look at the mountains and trees, listen to the river and birds, smell the roses and let our garden touch your senses. Oh! to taste the teas and feel the peace of this garden

filled with old roses, shrubs and herbaceous plants. Mature woodland area with pond, rock garden.

✗ ⊨ ☕ ☎

20 RUTHIN CASTLE
Castle Street, Ruthin LL15 2NU. Ruthin Castle Ltd, 07834 211989, gardens_ruthincastle@hotmail. co.uk. *Turn L at Natwest Bank, on r'about in centre of Ruthin.* **Adm £3, chd free. Sun 26 Apr (11-5). Visitors also welcome by appt.**
Wonderfully exciting restoration project, progressing fast, of Victorian and formal gardens. Walkways, courtyards, rose garden, dry moats and dungeons in C13 castle ruins. Lawns with rare and beautiful trees. The hotel was frequented by Edward, Prince of Wales.

✗ ✿ ⊨ ☎

21 STELLA MARIS
Llanrhaeadr LL16 4PW. Mrs J E Moore, 01745 890475, mumjem@aol.com. *3m SE of Denbigh. Take A525 Denbigh to Ruthin rd. After 3m from Denbigh or 4m from Ruthin turn W to Mynydd Llech. Garden 1/2 m on L.* Home-made teas. **Adm £3, chd free. Sun, Mon 30, 31 Aug (2-6). Visitors also welcome by appt.**
1-acre garden created to enjoy the wonderful, ever changing views over the Vale of Clwyd. Good collection of specimen trees, interesting shrubs, herbaceous borders with all-yr round interest, gravel garden and ponds. All complement the outstanding scenery.

✗ ✿ ⊨ ☕ ☎

22 TAL-Y-BRYN FARM
Llannefydd LL16 5DR. Mr & Mrs Gareth Roberts, 01745 540256, laeth@villagedairy.co.uk. *3m W of Henllan. From Henllan take rd signed Llannefydd. After 21/2 m turn R signed Bont Newydd. Garden 1/2 m on L.* Light

refreshments & teas. **Adm by donation. Visitors welcome by appt 1 April to 1 Oct. Please book first.**
Medium-sized working farmhouse cottage garden. Ancient farm machinery. Incorporating ancient privy festooned with honeysuckle, clematis and roses. Terraced arches, sunken garden pool and bog garden, fountains and old water pumps. Herb wheels, shrubs and other interesting features. Lovely views of the Clwydian range. New water feature.

♿ ✗ ✿ ⊨ ☕ ☎

23 TROSYFFORDD
Ystrad LL16 4RL. Miss Marion MacNicoll, 01745 812247, marionphysio@btinternet.com. *11/2 m W of Denbigh. From A525 Denbigh to Ruthin rd, turn R in outskirts of Denbigh by swimming pool, on Ystrad rd signed Prion & Saron. Follow for 11/2 m, Trosyffordd is 2nd drive on R after 1st hill.* **Adm £2.50, chd free. Visitors welcome by appt May, June, July only. Coaches permitted.**
1-acre plantswoman's old fashioned cottage garden. Large collection of shrubs, trees, herbaceous and grasses. Teas for groups by arrangement.

♿ ✿ ☎

24 TROS-Y-PARC
Ystrad, Denbigh LL16 4RH. Stephen & Camilla Cheshire. *A525 Ruthin to Denbigh. At r'about follow sign to town centre. 2nd L after r'about into Ystrad rd signed to Prion & Saron. Entrance on L after 1/2 m.* Home-made teas. **Adm £3, chd free (share to St Kentigern Hospice, St Asaph). Sun 10 May (2-5.30).**
2 acres; established shrubs; lawns; wisteria clad pergola, hornbeam/beech cloister, mature trees, partly walled ha ha, woodland walk. Beautiful views across valley to Clwydian Hills. Gravel drive.

♿ ✗ ✿ ☕

25 TYDDYN BACH
Bontuchel, Ruthin LL15 2DG. Mr & Mrs L G Starling, 01824 710248, les.starling@boyns.net. *4m W of Ruthin. B5105 from Ruthin, turn R at Cross Keys towards Bontuchel/Cyffylliog. Through Bontuchel, river is now on R. Turn L up narrow rd, steep hill just before bridge. House 1st on L.* **Adm £2.50, chd free. Visitors welcome by appt July & August. Road not suitable for coaches.**
Mainly organic, very pretty cottage garden with prolific vegetable garden. Wildlife friendly with hedges and wood pile. Greenhouse packed with plants for both pots and the garden. Featured in 'Amateur Gardening'. Winner Rural Garden, Ruthin Show Society.

✗ ☎

Ancient
privy
festooned
with
honeysuckle,
clematis and
roses . . .

Denbighshire & Colwyn Volunteers

County Organiser
Sue Rathbone, Bryn Celyn, Llanbedr, Ruthin LL15 1TT, 01824 702077, skrathbone@toucansurf.com

County Treasurer
Elizabeth Sasse, Hendy, Trefechan Road, Afonwen, Mold CH7 5UP, 01352 720220

Publicity
Jessica Craft, Bryn Glas, Prion, Denbigh LL16 4RY, 01745 890251, jessiecraft8@aol.com

Assistant County Organiser
Fran Michels, Tyddyn Ucha, Graigfechan, Ruthin LL15 2HB, 01824 705750, jon.plants@btinternet.com

FLINTSHIRE & WREXHAM

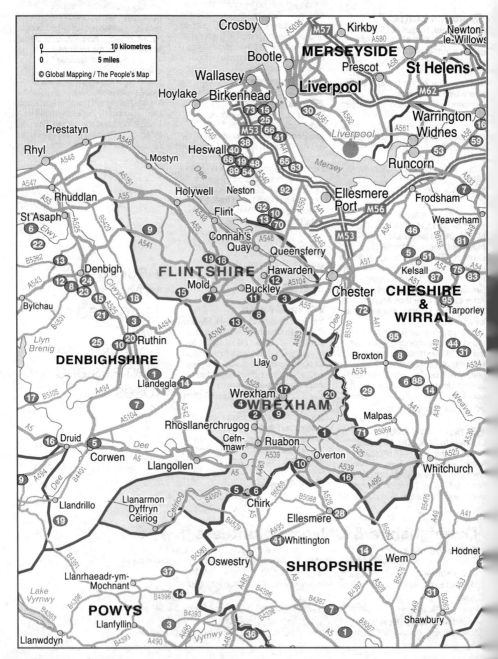

Opening Dates

March

SATURDAY 21
⑨ Erddig Hall

April

SATURDAY 4
⑱ 90 St Peters Park

SUNDAY 5
⑫ Hawarden Castle

SUNDAY 26
⑬ Leeswood Green Farm

May

SATURDAY 9
⑨ Erddig Hall

SUNDAY 17
⑲ Welsh College of Horticulture

SUNDAY 24
⑬ Leeswood Green Farm

June

SUNDAY 7
④ Bryn Amma Cottage

SUNDAY 14
⑩ The Garden House
⑭ Llangedwyn Hall

SUNDAY 28
⑥ Chirk Town Gardens
⑮ Pantymwyn Village Gardens

July

SATURDAY 11
⑰ Prices Lane Allotments

SUNDAY 12
⑦ The Cottage Nursing Home
⑩ The Garden House

SATURDAY 18
⑤ Chirk Castle
⑨ Erddig Hall

SUNDAY 19
③ Broughton & Bretton Allotments
⑪ Glan-y-Ffordd

August

SUNDAY 2
② Bramley House

SUNDAY 9
① Bangor-on-Dee Village Gardens

SUNDAY 16
⑧ Dove Cottage

SUNDAY 23
⑯ Penley Village Gardens

September

SUNDAY 6
⑩ The Garden House

⑲ Welsh College of Horticulture

SUNDAY 20
⑳ Yew Tree Villa

Gardens open to the public

⑤ Chirk Castle
⑨ Erddig Hall
⑩ The Garden House

Also open by appointment ☎

② Bramley House
⑬ Leeswood Green Farm
⑱ 90 St Peters Park

The Gardens

Group opening

① BANGOR-ON-DEE VILLAGE GARDENS
LL13 0JA. *6m S of Wrexham. On A525 Wrexham to Whitchurch rd. Turn L signed Bangor-on-Dee. Follow signs to gardens.* Home-made teas at Sunbank. **Combined adm £3, chd free (share to Retired Greyhound Trust & MS Society).** Sun 9 Aug (2-5.30).
Picturesque village on the R Dee, beautiful church, well known basket shop and race course.
♿ ✕ ❀ ☕

4 SANDOWN ROAD
Gill & Dave Williams
A garden for wildlife which incls, small pond, log-pile and planting to encourage bees, butterflies and birds. Small collection of hostas, exotics and alpines.
♿ ✕ ❀

SUNBANK
Laurels Avenue. Norman & Sylvia Jones
Approx 3/4 -acre well cared for garden set on 3 lawned levels with wide variety of shrubs and perennials. Surrounded by mature trees and farmland with interesting water features and magnificent views over village and surrounding countryside.
♿ ✕

BANK HOUSE
See Cheshire & Wirral.

② NEW BRAMLEY HOUSE
Bronwylfa Road, Legacy, Wrexham LL14 4HY. Susan & John Droog, 01978 846935, john_sue.droog@btinternet.com. *2m W of Wrexham. Leave A483 & take B5605 signed Johnstown. 1st R, after roundabout. L at T-junction on to B5097. After 1m follow signs for field parking.* Home-made teas. **Adm £2.50, chd free (share to Hope House Children's Hospice).** Sun 2 Aug (1.30-5.30). Visitors also welcome by appt, July & Aug, groups 10+, coaches permitted.
Set in 1/2 acre with open views across farmland to nearby woods. South facing, formal and gravel gardens to the front moving to mixed borders, shrubs, trees and large lawned area. Water features further complemented by a stream running through the main body of the garden. Raffle & tombola. Partial wheelchair access. Some gentle slopes. Garden visible from top path.
✕ ❀ ☕ ☎

Allotments

③ BROUGHTON & BRETTON ALLOTMENTS
Main Road, Broughton CH4 0NT. Broughton & Bretton Area Allotments Association. *5m W of Chester. On A5104 (signed Penyffordd) in village of Broughton.* Home-made teas at War Memorial Institute. **Adm £3, chd free (share to Nightingale House Hospice, Wrexham).** Sun 19 July (2-6).
Small collection of full and half sized allotment plots used by the local community to grow a mix of vegetables, flowers and soft fruit.
♿ ✕ ☕

a stream running through the garden . . .

④ BRYN AMMA COTTAGE

Frondeg, Wrexham LL14 4NB.
Gillian & Roger Nock. *3m W of
Wrexham. From A483 turn onto A525
towards Ruthin, after Coedpoeth
Village turn L in Minera on B5426
(Minera Hall Rd), 2m turn R into
unnamed lane with passing places,
follow signs to field parking.* Home-
made teas. **Adm £3, chd free. Sun
7 June (1-5).**
Approx 1/2 -acre constantly evolving
garden on hillside at over 900ft, nr
moorland with views over Wrexham.
Planted for yr-round interest, woodland
slopes to stream with cataracts, flag
iris, naturalised ferns and moisture-
loving plants. Lawned areas with
informal borders, bluebells, perennials,
rhododendrons, azaleas, ornamental
trees and shrubs. Gravel paths, steep
slopes.

Wildlife pond, places to sit and ponder . . .

⑤ ◆ CHIRK CASTLE

nr Wrexham LL14 5AF. The National
Trust, 01691 777701,
www.nationaltrust.org.uk. *7m S of
Wrexham, 2m W of Chirk Village.
Follow brown signs from A483 to Chirk
Village. 2m W on minor rds. Follow
brown signs.* **Garden & tower Adm
£6.50, chd £3.25. See website for
opening days & times. For NGS: Sat
18 July (10-5).**
5½ -acre hilltop garden with good
views over Shropshire and Cheshire.
Formal garden with outstanding yew
topiary. Rose garden, herbaceous
borders, more informal further from the
building with rare trees and shrubs,
pond, thatched hawk house, ha-ha
with terrace and pavilion. Lime tree
avenue with daffodils and statue.
Garden tours, plant identification quiz,
seed sowing for children. Information
on the NGS Gardeners' Careership.

Group opening

⑥ NEW CHIRK TOWN GARDENS

LL14 5PN. *10m SW of Wrexham.
See garden entries for directions.*
Home-made teas. **Combined
adm £3.50, chd free. Sun 28
June (2-5.30).**
Chirk is an attractive small town on
the Welsh border with great
historical interest including a
medieval castle now run by the NT.

NEW 81 MAES-Y-WAUN

Anne Davies. *Follow signs from
Whitehurst r'about passing
Kronospan factory on R. Take
next L. Third house on L*
Plantswoman's small garden
packed with interesting
perennials and shrubs. Wildlife
pond, places to sit and ponder.

9 THE PARKLANDS

Sarah Wilkie. *Through Chirk
Village, turn L at St Mary's Church
into Trevor Rd. Park here please.
Bear L then R into Shepherd's
Lane, then R into The Parklands*
Pleasantly situated in newly built
development on the edge of the
village. Front garden laid to lawn,
trees and shrubs. Smaller rear
garden of mixed planting, trees,
shrubs, perennials and climbers.
Small vegetable garden. Several
places to sit and enjoy the superb
views over surrounding
countryside.

NEW QUEEN ANNE COTTAGE

Whitehurst Gardens. Michael
Kemp. *A5 from Chirk to
Llangollen. 50m off Whitehurst
r'about, turning on R*
Small woodland cottage garden
on two levels set around C17
summerhoouse. Selection of trees,
shrubs, herbaceous and old roses.

⑦ ◆ THE COTTAGE NURSING HOME

54 Hendy Road, Mold CH7 1QS. Mr
& Mrs A G & L I Lanini. *10m W of
Chester. From Mold town centre take
A494 towards Ruthin. 2nd R into
Hafod Park. Straight on to T-junction.
Turn R onto Hendy Rd. Garden at
junction of Hendy Rd & Clayton Rd.*
Home-made teas. **Adm £2, chd £1**
(share to British Heart Foundation,
Mold). **Sun 12 July (2-5).**
Beautiful garden set in approx 1 acre.
Well-established shrubs, herbaceous
plants and abundance of colourful
window boxes and tubs. Heart-shaped
patio, incl water feature and pergola,
with natural reclaimed stone walling.

⑧ DOVE COTTAGE

Rhos Road, Penyffordd, Nr Chester
CH4 0JR. Chris & Denise Wallis. *6m
SW of Chester. From Chester A55 S
exit A550 follow signs for Corwen. Turn
L immed opp Penyffordd railway stn.
From Wrexham A541 for Mold, R at
Pontblyddyn for Chester, turn R immed
opp Penyffordd railway stn.* Home-
made teas. **Adm £3, chd free. Sun
16 Aug (2-5).**
Approx 1½ -acre garden, many shrubs
and herbaceous plants set informally
around lawns. Newly established
vegetable area, 2 ponds (1 wildlife),
summerhouse, pergola and woodland
planted area. Gravel paths, slight
incline.

⑨ ◆ ERDDIG HALL

nr Wrexham LL13 0YT. The National
Trust, 01978 355314,
www.nationaltrust.org.uk. *2m S of
Wrexham. Signed from A483/A5125
Oswestry rd; also from A525
Whitchurch rd.* **£3 donation to NGS
from Garden Tours. (Guided tours
12 and 3pm £3. Only tour proceeds
for NGS). For other opening details
& prices please tel or see website.
For NGS: Sats 21 Mar; 9 May; 18
July (11-5).**
Important, listed Grade 1, historic
garden. Formal C18 and later Victorian
design elements incl pleached lime tree
avenues, trained fruit trees, wall plants
and climbers, herbaceous borders,
roses, herb border, annual bedding,
restored glasshouse and vine house.
National Collection of Ivy. Guided tours
at 1 and 3pm by Head Gardener or
garden staff. Gravel paths & slopes.
Access leaflet available at the ticket
office.

⑩ ◆ THE GARDEN HOUSE

Erbistock LL13 0DL. Mr & Mrs S
Wingett, 01978 781149,
gardens@simonwingett.com. *5m
S of Wrexham. On A528 Wrexham to
Shrewsbury rd. Follow signs at
Overton Bridge to Erbistock Church.*
**Adm £3, chd free. Easter to Sept,
Wed to Fri (10-5).**

For NGS: Suns 14 June; 12 July; 6 Sept (2-5).
Shrub and herbaceous plantings in monochromatic, analogous and complementary colour schemes. Rose pergolas, National Collection of hydrangea (over 300 species and cultivars). Sculpture Garden. Large lily pond, Victorian dovecote.

⑪ GLAN-Y-FFORDD
Bannel Lane, Buckley CH7 3AP. Ken & Ann Darlington. *1m SE of Buckley. From Wrexham A550, at Penymynydd roundabout, L onto A5118 Mold. 250yds R for Buckley over railway bridge (T-lights). Fieldgate entrance on L 200yds after The Winding House. From Mold take A5118 off Wylla roundabout through Llong, pass cement works, take 2nd L to Buckley over railway bridge. Fieldgate entrance on L 200yds after Winding House. Parking in field with access to garden. We do not recommend parking on the busy rd.* Home-made teas. **Adm £2.50, chd free. Sun 19 July (2-5).**
Established garden on S-facing slope. Mixed borders of shrubs and herbaceous plants. Vegetable garden and greenhouse.

GRAFTON LODGE
See Cheshire & Wirral.

⑫ HAWARDEN CASTLE
Hawarden CH5 3PB. Sir William & Lady Gladstone. *6m W of Chester. On B5125 just E of Hawarden village. Entrance via farm shop.* Adm £3, chd £2. Sun 5 Apr (2-5).
Large garden and picturesque ruined castle. Take care and supervise children. Dogs on short leads only. Limited wheelchair access by grass paths.

18 HOLMWOOD DRIVE
See Cheshire & Wirral.

NGLEWOOD
See Cheshire & Wirral.

⑬ LEESWOOD GREEN FARM
Leeswood CH7 4SQ. Anne Saxon, 1352 771222, annemsaxon@yahoo.co.uk. *3m SE of Mold. 9m NW of Wrexham. Off A541 W. At Pontblyddyn, from Wrexham, turn L after garage into Mingle Rd. After 1/2 m at T-junction turn R. Garden after 50ys on R approached by 1/4 m lane. Park in village. Limited*

disabled or elderly parking at house. Home-made teas. **Adm £3, chd free. Suns 26 Apr; 24 May (2-5). Visitors also welcome by appt.**
Plantswoman's garden surrounding C15 farmhouse in lovely rural location. Many unusual trees, shrubs and perennials set around lawns, ornamental vegetable garden, orchard and paved areas with some unusual features. Small meadow, wildflowers and seating to enjoy the vistas. Gravel entrance.

⑭ LLANGEDWYN HALL
Llangedwyn SY10 9JW. Mr & Mrs T M Bell. *8m W of Oswestry. On B4396 to Llanrhaeadr-ym-Mochnant about 5m W of Llynclys Xrds.* Home-made teas. **Adm £3, chd free. Sun 14 June (12-5).**
Approx 4-acre formal terraced garden on 3 levels, designed and laid out in late C17 and early C18. Unusual herbaceous plants, sunken rose garden, small water garden, walled kitchen garden and woodland walk.

MAYLANDS
See Cheshire & Wirral.

THE OLD FARM
See Cheshire & Wirral.

Group opening

⑮ PANTYMWYN VILLAGE GARDENS
Mold CH7 5EN. *3m W of Mold. From Mold A541 to Denbigh turn L at first mini r'about, signed Pantymwyn approx 3m. From Ruthin A494 to Mold turn L after Flintshire Boundary signed Pantymwyn 1 1/2 m.* Home-made teas & plant sales at Wych Elm (not open). **Combined adm £4, chd free. Sun 28 June (2-6).**
Small scenic village with wonderful views of the Clwydian Range and Moel Famau. Close to Loggerheads Country Park - AONB. Live music at Bryn Mor. Displays by Welsh College of Horticulture Floristry Students.

THE BIRCHLINGS
Cilcain Road CH7 5EH. Mike & Ros Thomas
Gentle sloping garden with views of the hills. A garden for all seasons. Mixed borders, natural rock outcrops, pots, ponds and patios.

BRYN MOR
Cefn Bychan Road. Pam & Andy Worthington
Garden is compact and colourful incl an organic ornamental kitchen garden, shrubs and herbaceous borders.

COEDLE
Pant y Buarth. Richard & Shirley Hughes
Limestone hillside, developing garden, cottage style of approx 1/2 acre containing rockery, mixed shrub and herbaceous borders, small pond and woodland area.

GREENHEYS
Cefn Bychan Road. Roy & Carol Hambleton
Relaxed style planting of shrubs, perennials and climbers especially clematis. Occasional formal touches.

INCHCAPE
Cefn Bychan Rd. Matthew & Kay Roberts
Front garden designed around large limestone outcrops incl herbaceous borders. Back garden with unusual trees, shrubs and conifers.

LONG SHADOWS
Cefn Bychan Road. Dave & Agnes Christmas
Rocky garden filled with a mixture of flowering plants, mature trees, shrubs and hedges. Spectacular views of Moel Famau.

ROWANOKE
Pant y Buarth. Ron & Clare Exley
Limestone hillside garden with different levels. Variety of shrubs, trees, plants, and wildlife pond.

SOUTHERNWOOD
Cefn Bychan Road. Bill & Joan Chadwick
Small garden. Variety of colourful shrubs, flowers and pots.

Unique garden
cruck house . . .

As many herbaceous perennials and annuals as can be squeezed in . . .

Group opening

16 PENLEY VILLAGE GARDENS
LL13 0LS. *12m SE of Wrexham. On A539. Turn R when approaching Penley from Overton for Shilling Barn Cottage. L in village for Park Cottage.* Home-made teas at Park Cottage. **Combined adm £4, chd £1.** Sun 23 Aug (2-5).
Penley is noted for the only thatched primary school in Wales. It has war time connections with Polish freedom fighters and is the site of a Polish veterans' hospital.

PARK COTTAGE
Penley LL13 0LS. Dr S J Sime. *No parking at house please. Roadside parking in village, 250yd walk.* Home-made teas. **Adm £2.50, chd £1**
4-acres incl shade and grass gardens. Ponds, maze, orchard and vegetables. Large collection of unusual trees and shrubs. In August hydrangeas, hoherias, eucryphias and clethras are complemented by late flowering perennials and grasses.

NEW SHILLING BARN COTTAGE
Trevor & Jean Thomas
1/3 acre garden. Interest incl salvas, sempervivums, scented pelargoniums and as many herbaceous perennials and annuals as can be squeezed in. Vegetable garden. Collection of hardy and half-hardy fuchsias. Pebble drive and grass. Gentle slope.

Allotments

17 PRICES LANE ALLOTMENTS
Prices Lane, Wrexham LL11 2NB. Wrexham Allotment & Leisure Gardeners Association. *1m from town centre. From A483, take exit for Wrexham Ind Estate and follow A5152 towards the town centre. Allotments signed from there.* Home-made teas. **Adm £3, chd free.** Sat 11 July (12-6). 120 plus plots, growing a good variety of flowers, fruit and vegetables. Plots for the disabled and school children. Association shop, selling a wide range of garden requisites and seeds.

18 NEW 90 ST PETERS PARK
Northop CH7 6YU. Mr P Hunt, 01352 840758, philipbhunt@hotmail.co.uk. *3m N of Mold, 3m S of Flint. Leave A55 at Northop exit. Opp cricket ground, turn R. Fifth turning on R. Garden on R.* Home-made teas. **Adm £3, chd free.** Sat 4 Apr (2-5.30). **Visitors also welcome by appt.**
Garden designed and planted in last 30yrs by professional botanist and horticulturalist. It comprises mature trees and shrubs incl rare species: EMLA cloned malus and prunus cultivars, embothrium underplanted with spring flowering bulbs. Unique garden cruck house with sedum roof, beamed ceilings and inglenook fireplace and other interesting timber framed structures.

19 WELSH COLLEGE OF HORTICULTURE
Holywell Road, Northop CH7 6AA. M B Simkin (Principle), info@wcoh.ac.uk, www.wcoh.ac.uk. *10m W of Chester. Leave A55 at exit to Northop. From E carry on through T-lights in village. College on R after 1/2 m. From W, R at T-lights.* Home-made teas (not for NGS). **Adm £3, chd free. Suns 17 May; 6 Sept (1-4).**
Over 91 hectares of land. Developed over the past 50 yrs the picturesque surroundings provide a number of different landscaped areas. Favourites incl ornamental gardens, grass gardens, pinetum, courtyard, gold garden, winter stem bed, shrubbery, heather garden, rock gardens, and village beds. NCCPG fuchsia. Demonstrations every hour on horticultural practices.

WOODHILL
See Powys.

20 NEW YEW TREE VILLA
Bowling Bank, Is-y-Coed, Wrexham LL13 9RN. Marian & Jeff Hughes. *6m E of Wrexham. From Wrexham take A534 to Nantwich rd. R onto B5130 Holt - Cross Lanes rd for 2 1/2 m. Garden on R. Please park at Isycoed village hall.* Home-made teas. **Adm £3, chd free.** Sun 20 Sept (2-5). 1/4 -acre garden situated in small rural village. Densely planted with various shrubs, grasses and perennials providing late summer colour. Moon gate leads to open courtyard with water feature and many colourful pots. Gravel driveway & paths.

Flintshire & Wrexham Volunteers

County Organiser & Leaflet Coordinator
Angela Wilson, Penley Hall Stables, Penley, Wrexham LL13 0LU, 01948 830439, wilsons.penley@tiscali.co.uk

Assistant County Organiser
Anne Saxon, Leeswood Green Farm, Leeswood, Mold CH7 4SQ, 01352 771222, annemsaxon@yahoo.co.uk

County Treasurer
Mrs Wendy Sime, Park Cottage, Penley, Wrexham LL13 0LS, 01948 830126

Press & Publicity Officer
Ann Rathbone, Woodfield House, Station Road, Hawarden CH5 3EG, 01244 532948

Mark your diary with these special events in 2009

EXPLORE SECRET GARDENS DURING CHELSEA & HAMPTON COURT FLOWER SHOW WEEKS

Tue 19 May, Wed 20 May, Thur 21 May, Fri 22 May, Wed 8 July, Thur 9 July
Full day tours from £82 per person, 10% discount for groups
Advance booking required, telephone +44 (0)20 8693 1015 or email j.wookey@btinternet.com
Specially selected gardens in London, Essex, Kent, Hampshire and South Oxfordshire. The tour price includes transport and lunch with wine at a popular restaurant or pub.

HAMPTON COURT PALACE

Thur 2 Apr, Tue 23 June, Thur 25 June, Wed 15 July, Tue 4 Aug, Thur 10 Sept
Evening tours in the company of one of the Palace's specialist tour guides from 6.30 – 8pm
Tickets £6 per person. Advance booking required, telephone +44 (0)1483 211535 or
visit www.ngs.org.uk for more information
Gossip, scandal, murder, healing – you'll find it all within the Formal Gardens at Hampton Court Palace. Each tour will have its own unique feature whether it's the story of the Great Vine or the magic and mystery of the Maze.

FROGMORE – A ROYAL GARDEN (BERKSHIRE)

Tue 26 May 10am – 5.30pm (last admission 4pm)
Garden adm £4.50, chd free. Tickets available in advance or on the day.
Advance booking for groups and coaches, telephone
+44 (0) 1483 211535 or email orders@ngs.org.uk
A rare opportunity to explore 30 acres of landscaped garden, rich in history and beauty.

FLAXBOURNE FARM – FUN & SURPRISES (BEDFORDSHIRE)

Sun 7 June 10am – 5pm. Adm £5, chd free
No booking required, come along on the day!
Bring the whole family and have fun in this surprising and entertaining garden of 2 acres. Enjoy the large plant fair, live music, pets corner, birds of prey, dog agility show and much more.

WISLEY RHS GARDEN – MUSIC IN THE GARDEN (SURREY)

Fri 11 Sept 6 – 9pm
Adm (incl RHS members) £7, chd under 15 free
Save money on advance bookings for groups of 4 or more, telephone +44 (0)1483 211535 or
visit www.ngs.org.uk for more information
A special evening opening of this famous garden, exclusively for the NGS. Enjoy music and entertainment as you explore the gardens and the floral marquee on the first day of the Wisley Flower Show.

For further information visit www.ngs.org.uk or telephone 01483 211535

GLAMORGAN

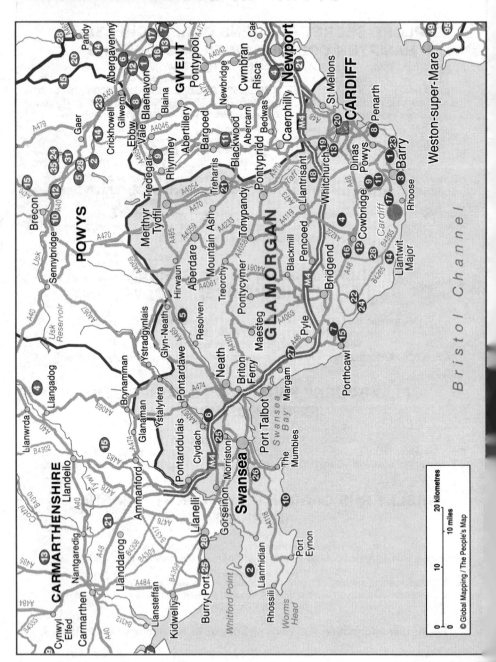

Opening Dates

April

SUNDAY 5
㉔ Slade

MONDAY 13
❼ Coedargraig Gardens

SATURDAY 25
⑬ Llandaff Gardens

May

SUNDAY 3
⑯ Penllyn Court
⑳ Penylan Gardens

MONDAY 4
❼ Coedargraig Gardens

FRIDAY 15
㉖ Touchwood
㉖ Touchwood

TUESDAY 19
㉖ Touchwood
㉖ Touchwood

SATURDAY 23
❸ The Birches

SUNDAY 24
❸ The Birches
㉑ Pontygwaith Farm

SUNDAY 31
❶ Barry Gardens
❹ Bordervale Plants

June

SUNDAY 7
⑫ Llanblethian Gardens
⑭ Llantwit Major & Llanmaes Gardens
⑮ Newton Village Gardens

SUNDAY 14
❻ Brynyrenfys
⑱ Pentyrch Gardens in June
㉕ Springfield

THURSDAY 18
❽ 77 Coleridge Avenue

SATURDAY 20
⑰ Penmark Village Gardens

SUNDAY 21
❷ Big House Farm
㉗ Twyn-yr-Hydd
㉘ Wilton Road Gardens

SUNDAY 28
⑪ Hen Felin & Swallow Barns
㉑ Pontygwaith Farm
㉒ St Brides C/W Primary School

July

SATURDAY 4
㉓ Sea Breeze

SUNDAY 5
㉓ Sea Breeze

SUNDAY 12
❶ Barry Gardens
❺ Brynheulog

SATURDAY 25
⑲ 89 Pen-y-Dre

SUNDAY 26
⑲ 89 Pen-y-Dre
⑳ Penylan Gardens

TUESDAY 28
⑳ Penylan Gardens (Evening)

August

SATURDAY 29
⑬ Llandaff Gardens

SUNDAY 30
❹ Bordervale Plants

September

SATURDAY 26
❽ 77 Coleridge Avenue

Gardens open to the public

❹ Bordervale Plants
❾ Dyffryn Gardens
㉖ Touchwood
㉗ Twyn-yr-Hydd

By appointment only

⑩ 11 Eastcliff

Also open by appointment

❶ 47 Aneurin Road, Barry Gardens,
❶ 11 Arno Road, Barry Gardens,
❺ Brynheulog
❻ Brynyrenfys
❽ 77 Coleridge Avenue
⑫ Glyndwr House, Llanblethian Gardens
⑫ Stallcourt Mews, Llanblethian Gardens
⑬ Gaynors Garden, Llandaff Gardens
⑭ Swinebridge Farm, Llantwit Major & Llanmaes Gardens
⑰ Gileston House, Penmark Village Gardens
⑳ 6 Alma Road, Penylan Gardens
㉑ Pontygwaith Farm
㉓ Sea Breeze
㉔ Slade
㉕ Springfield
㉖ Touchwood

The Gardens

Group opening

❶ BARRY GARDENS
Barry CF63 2AS. *6m SW of Cardiff. See garden entries for directions.* Home-made teas. **Combined adm £5, regret not suitable for young children. Suns 31 May, 12 July (2-6).** Barry enjoys panoramic views of the Bristol Channel and is close to the rural vale. It is close enough to Cardiff to enjoy the city.
☕

47 ANEURIN ROAD
Dave Bryant, 07894 339821, davebryant@uk2.net. *A4050 Cardiff to Barry, take roundabout L marked Barry Docks & Sully. At 2nd roundabout turn R towards Barry town centre, under railway bridge and up hill towards centre. Opp YMCA turn L, then 1st R.* **Visitors also welcome by appt.** Small ever changing front garden containing a wide range and variety of annuals, perennials and shrubs, displayed in over 600 various containers that change with both the seasons and flowering cycle of the plants. 2nd place Best Front Garden, Vale in Bloom. 2nd place Best Hanging Basket Display, Vale of Glamorgan.
✗ ✿ ☎

11 ARNO ROAD
Little Coldbrook. Debbie Palmer, 01446 743642, deb.palmer@ntlworld.com. *On A4050 Cardiff to Barry, take roundabout marked Barry Docks & Sully. 2nd R into Coldbrook Rd, 2nd L into Langlands Rd, then 6th R into Norwood Cres, 1st L into Arno Rd.* **Visitors also welcome by appt February.** A small plant lovers garden packed with alpines, climbers and perennials, many unusual. Fernery, ponds & rock garden. Snowdrops, hellebores and shurbs for early interest.
✗ ✿ ☎

1 NORTH WALK
Sue Hyett. *From A4050 at roundabout marked Barry & Barry College, turn L. Continue past Barry Hospital, garden by road sign for Barry College, before*

pedestrian crossing Plantsman's garden of many different parts: cottage garden overflowing with unusual plants, courtyard foliage garden, hot gravel garden, interesting succulent house and wildlife pond.

✈ ✿

---

2 BIG HOUSE FARM
Llanmadoc SA3 1DE. **Mr & Mrs M Mead.** *15m W of Swansea. M4 J47. Take A483 signed Swansea. Next roundabout R A484 signed Llanelli. 2nd roundabout L B4296 signed Gowerton. R at 1st T-lights onto B4295. 10m after Bury Green, R to Llanmadoc. Pass Britannia Inn, L at T-junction uphill past red tel box. 100 yds turn R. Honesty car park on R.* Home-made teas. **Adm £2.50, chd free.** Sun 21 June (2-6).
Mainly walled coastal garden, just under 1 acre, with stunning views. A variety of interesting plants and shrubs in mixed borders. Small Mediterranean garden and walled kitchen garden.
♿ ☕

3 THE BIRCHES
Dingle Close, Barry CF62 6QR. **Paul & Peta Goodwin.** *6m W of Cardiff. Into Barry from Cardiff on A4050. At 1st roundabout straight on (signed to airport), next roundabout L to Pontypridd Rd, next roundabout 2nd exit to Park Cres, next roundabout 4th exit to Park Rd. After approx 1/2 m bear L onto Porth Y Castell; 2nd L to Min Y Mor, 1st L Marine Drive and park. Walk 70yds down field, garden entrance through stone archway.* **Adm £3.50, chd free.** Sat, Sun 23, 24 May (2-6).
Large coastal garden with terraces and different rooms combining hard and soft landscaping. Mediterranean retreat, palm tree area, pergola, water features. Good design, beautiful plants and easy maintenance are equally important. Described as 'stunning' by many visitors. Still developing. Adjacent nature reserve with wood and wildflower meadow. Featured on BBC2's Open Gardens.
✈

4 ◆ BORDERVALE PLANTS
Ystradowen, Cowbridge CF71 7SX. **Mrs Claire Jenkins,** 01446 774036, www.bordervale.co.uk. *8m W of Cardiff. 10 mins from M4. Take A4222 from Cowbridge. Turn R at Ystradowen postbox, then 3rd L & proceed 1/2 m, following brown signs. Garden on R.*

Parking in rd past corner. Teas on 31 May only. **Adm £2.50, chd free. Fris, Sats, Suns & Bank Hols Mar to Sept.** For NGS: Suns 31 May; 30 Aug (10-5).
Within mature woodland valley (semi-tamed), with stream and bog garden, extensive mixed borders; wild flower meadow, providing diverse wildlife habitats. Children must be supervised. The nursery specialises in unusual perennials and cottage garden plants. Featured in 'South Wales Echo'. Steep slopes in garden.
♿ ✈ ✿ ☕

Croeso i bawb!

5 BRYNHEULOG
45 Heol y Graig, Cwmgwrach, Neath SA11 5TW. **Lorraine Rudd,** 01639 722593. *8m W of Neath. From M4 J43 take A465 to Glyneath, then rd signed Cwmgwrach. Entering village pass Dunraven PH, turn L at school sign, approx 100yds fork L into Glannant Place. Up hill, bear sharp R, approx 200yds turn L up steep track. 2nd house on L.* Home-made teas. **Adm £3, chd free.** Sun 12 July (10.30-5). Visitors also welcome by appt.
As seen on BBC TV Open Gardens! This keen plantswoman's hillside garden perfectly reflects the dramatic setting and surrounding natural beauty. Garden incl potager, tropical greenhouse, orchids and rose garden. 30ft polytunnel growing fruit and vegetables in raised beds. Wildflower area & wildlife garden.
✈ ✿ ☕ ☎

6 BRYNYRENFYS
30 Cefn Road, Glais, Swansea SA7 9EZ. **Edith & Roy Morgan,** 01792 842777. *8m N of Swansea. M4 J45, take A4067 R at 1st roundabout, then 1st R and follow yellow signs.* Home-made teas. **Adm £3, chd free (share to Swansea Alzheimers Society).** Sun 14 June (12-6). Visitors also welcome by appt April - July, coaches welcome.

If you love plants you'll be at home here. A small surprising garden full of interest. Unusual trees, shrubs and perennials vie for attention with the panoramic view. Wildlife and weed friendly with no bedding! Seating on different levels, so stay a while, unwind and be welcome. Croeso i bawb!
✿ ☕ ☎

7 COEDARGRAIG GARDENS
Newton, Porthcawl CF36 5SS. **Philip & Caroline Vaughan.** *2m from centre of Porthcawl. Take hill out of Porthcawl (A4106 Bridgend). House on L opposite White Lodge.* Light refreshments & teas. **Adm £3, chd free.** Mons 13 Apr; 4 May (10.30-4.30).
9 acres in the process of renovation. Masses of spring flowers - daffodils, tulips, crocus, grape hyacinth. Primrose banks, sweeping bluebell woods; azaleas, rhododendrons; formal terraced gardens; wildlife garden; orchard with hens; duck pond.
✈ ✿ ☕

8 77 COLERIDGE AVENUE
Penarth CF64 2SR. **Diana Mead,** 02920 703523, diana@dianamead.net. *3m SW of Cardiff. M4 J33 to Cardiff Bay. B4160 (B4055) for Penarth and Barry. At T-lights, straight across to next lights. Keep L, take 1st exit to Lower Penarth into Redlands Rd, then 4th L into Cornerswell Rd, 1st L into Coleridge Ave.* **Adm £2, chd free.** Thur 18 June; Sat 26 Sept (11-4). Visitors also welcome by appt all yr, not more than 10 people. Demonstration of watercolour flower painting can be included if requested.
Artist-gardener's small awkwardly shaped plot designed and planted to give seasonal colour and interest. Three linked areas; cottage style front with shaded fern bed, serpentine gravel path, shrubs, perennials. Side garden with apples, vegetables and herbs. Sheltered tiny rear garden with vine, tender plants, pear trees and frog pond. September opening for Autumn colour and fruit harvest. Art exhibition inspired by the garden.
✈ ✿ ☎

9 ◆ DYFFRYN GARDENS
nr Cardiff CF5 6SU. **Vale of Glamorgan Council,** 02920 593328, www.dyffryngardens.org.uk. *5m N o. Cardiff. Exit J33 from the M4, on the A4232 signed Barry; 1st interchange 4th exit A48 signed Cowbridge. In St*

Nicholas village turn L, Dyffryn is signed. **Mar-Oct (£6.50, chd £2.50, conc £4.50), Nov - Feb (£3.50, chd £1.50, conc £2.50). Mar to Oct (10-6), Nov to Feb (11-4), closed Tues & Weds.**
Outstanding Grade I listed Edwardian garden. Formal lawns; fountains and pools; seasonal beds; trees and shrubs. Garden rooms, incl Pompeian, Paved Court and Theatre garden. Arboretum contains trees from all over the world incl 13 champion trees - one the original *Acer griseum* collected by 'Chinese' Wilson. The gardens have recently been restored to Thomas Mawson's original 1904 design with help from Heritage Lottery Fund. Some gravel paths with slopes.
& ✿ ☎

⑩ 11 EASTCLIFF
Southgate SA3 2AS. Mrs Gill James, 01792 233310. *7m SW of Swansea. Take the Swansea to Gower rd & travel 6m to Pennard. Through village of Southgate & take 2nd exit off roundabout. Garden 200yds on L.*
Adm £3, chd free. Visitors welcome by appt.
Seaside garden, approx 1/3 acre, and developed in a series of island and bordered beds for all-yr interest. Large number of white, blue-green and unusual plants such as artemesia, melianthus, euphorbia, allium and Mediterranean plants. Woodland area and gravel bed.
& ✖ ☎

Group opening

⑪ HEN FELIN & SWALLOW BARNS
Dyffryn CF5 6SU. *3m from Culverhouse Cross roundabout. M4 J33, A4232 to Penarth, 1st exit to Culverhouse Cross roundabout. A48, follow signs to Cowbridge. At St Nicholas turn L at T-lights down Dyffryn Lane, past Dyffryn House. R at T-junction, both houses on L. Follow signs. Parking in paddock at rear of Hen Felin.* Hotdogs & hamburgers, cheese and wine. **Combined adm £4, chd free. Sun 28 June (12-7).**
Small hamlet in the middle of rich agricultural land. Fantastic community spirit but no pub, no church, no shop, no school. Garden opening in memory of Piers Frampton, much-missed neighbour. Local artists stall, face painting, music. Wheelchair access possible to most of the two gardens.
& ✿ ☕

THE BARNS
Mrs Janet Evans
10yr-old garden with packed herbaceous borders, formal and informal. Orchard, hens, riverside meadow, herb garden and lavender patio.
&

HEN FELIN
Rozanne Lord. *House at end of village on R before humpback bridge*
Beautiful cottage garden with stunning borders, wishing well, 200yr-old pig sty, secret garden, lovingly-tended vegetable patch and chickens. Mill stream running through garden with wildflower section and 200yr old oak tree surrounded by octagonal bench. Featured in 'South Wales Echo'.
& ✿

Group opening

⑫ LLANBLETHIAN GARDENS
Llanblethian CF71 7JU. *7m E of Bridgend. From Cardiff A48 W through Cowbridge, L up hill towards Llantwit Major. L at Cross Inn PH.* Home-made teas at Glyndwr and at the picturesque Vineyard Barn. **Combined adm £3.50, chd free (share to Diabetes UK). Sun 7 June (2-6).**
Picturesque hillside country village, quiet and unspoilt. Adjacent to popular market town of Cowbridge. Vine plants & sampling of Glyndwr's range of wines.
& ✿ ☕

GLYNDWR HOUSE
Richard & Susan Norris, 01446 774564, glyndwrvineyard@talktalk.net. Visitors also welcome by appt May and June. Groups of 10+.
Large informal gardens and 6-acre vineyard, producing award winning vines. Herbaceous borders, roses and climbers. Wildlife ponds, orchards, woodland walks and wildflowers. Chickens, ducks and pheasants roam freely. Featured in The Sunday Times. Some slopes.
& ✿ ⊨ ☎

STALLCOURT MEWS
Stallcourt Close. Dick & Beverly Tonkin, 01446 772704, beverlytonkin@btinternet.com. *Rear of Llanblethian Church.* **Visitors also welcome by appt.**
Front terraced courtyard garden.

Side and rear sloping garden with 60m stream (unfenced) and ponds. Largely impulse planting so quite varied; vegetable garden and short woodland walk. Featured in South Wales Echo. Steps to the courtyard garden. Rest of garden is sloping but accessible.
& ✿ ☎

Set in beautiful location along the River Taff . . .

Group opening

⑬ NEW LLANDAFF GARDENS
Llandaff, Cardiff CF5 2QH. *1m N of Cardiff. From Llandaff city and Cathedral along Cardiff Road, A4119. Take 2nd exit onto A4054, Bridge Road. Turn L at bus stop into Radyr Court Road. Park next to railings.* Light refreshments & teas. **Combined adm £3, chd free (share to Headway, Cardiff & Pursue Appeal). Sats 25 Apr; 29 Aug (11-4).**
Set in beautiful location along the River Taff and a short distance from the picturesque Llandaff Cathedral. These gardens offer interesting planting schemes that can be achieved in a small city space. The owners are enthusiastic gardeners who have many years of experience in horticulture and are more than happy to share their knowledge.
✖ ✿ ☕

NEW GAYNORS GARDEN
Gaynor Witchard, 02920 410359, gaynor.witchard@ntlworld.com. Visitors also welcome by appt September. Max of 12 people.
Sheltered sloping garden full of exotic species from the S & E hemispheres. Includes Dicksonia antarctica, Fatsia japonica, various palms and canna. Under a pergola covered in a mature grapevine and clematis, a deck path leads to a quiet area behind an octagonal greenhouse. Not suitable for those with walking difficulties.
✖ ✿ ☎

ROSEMARY'S GARDEN
Rosemary Edwards
Walk through a small woodland garden with specimen hydrangea and rhododendron, spring bulbs, stunningly white silver birch. Raised herb bed beside a decked path leading to seasonal containers and a pergola covered in 'Wedding Day' climbing rose.

Group opening

⑭ LLANTWIT MAJOR & LLANMAES GARDENS
Llantwit Major CF61 1SD. *5m S of Cowbridge. Off A48. Take B4270 from Cowbridge or B4265 from Barry. Follow signs to town centre and NGS arrows.* Home-made teas at Mehefin. Cream teas at Mintfield. BBQ at Flanders Barn. **Combined adm £5, chd free. Sun 7 June (11-5).**
Only a 30 minutue drive from Cardiff in the beautiful Vale of Glamorgan, Llantwit Major was home to Britains first monastic university. St Illtud's Church is dedicated to the Saint who gave his name to the town. This delightful town with ancient inns, town hall and houses of old stone is a short distance from the Heritage Coast with its walks and beaches. Llanmaes, a mile or so from Llantwit Major, is a pretty village which won the 'Best Kept Village' award in 2008, has an attractive village green and stream running through it. St Catwg, an early C13 Norman church, has a 15th rood screen carved from oak, reputedly the oldest and rarest in the Vale of Glamorgan, and a medieval wall painting of St George and the Dragon.

COLHUGH CHINE
Mrs K & Mr R Harris
1/2 -acre garden with mature trees set in valley overlooking farmland. Front garden features lawns, winter gardens and flower borders. Rear garden has terraces with rockeries and a stream.

FLANDERS BARN
Ann John
1-acre gardens of converted barn. Front garden based on drought tolerant perennials. Back garden is a work in progress; container garden, rockery, fruit trees, vegetable garden run on organic no-dig system. Wild areas, some managed.

GADLYS FARM HOUSE
Dot & Des Williams
1-acre of informal family garden surrounding a C17 farmhouse. Various sitting areas to relax amongst mature trees, herbaceous borders, summerhouse water feature and courtyard with planters.

MEHEFIN
Mrs Alison Morgan
1/3 acre south facing garden. Modern and old fashioned shrub roses in relaxed plantings. Scented plants, interesting colours and varieties. Sit in garden or conservatory and enjoy trees, flowers and ponds.

MINTFIELD
Susan & John Clarke
Pretty terraced garden with steps, formal lawns with perennial cottage borders, gravel garden with Mediterranian planting and grasses, step garden with hot planting.

OLD ROSEDEW HOUSE
Tina & Graham Benfield
Atmospheric 1/2 -acre walled garden attached to Grade 2 Listed C17 farmhouse. On various levels with lawns, stream, wildlife pond and bog plants, hidden corners, seats, cottage garden planting. Vegetable patch and chickens.

SWINEBRIDGE FARM
Anton Jones, 07973 963683. Visitors also welcome by appt.
Charming C16/17 farmhouse with walled garden, incl clipped box and yew trees. Terrace to sit, relax and ponder.

Wonderful views across the channel to Devon give an ever changing outlook . . .

Group opening

⑮ NEWTON VILLAGE GARDENS
Porthcawl CF36 5NT. *M4 J37, then A4229 to Porthcawl. Approx 3m A4106 to Bridgend. L at 1st roundabout, 2nd L to Newton.* Home-made teas at Newton Cottage & Tyn-y-Caeau Farm. **Combined adm £5, chd free. Sun 7 June (1-6).**
Charming seaside village with 800yr-old Norman church, village green and friendly pubs. Gardens range from small cottage to larger gardens with wonderful herbaceous borders.

LLWYNRHOS
Clevis Hill. Andrew & Liz Singer
Small cottage-style garden with large mixture of plants. Paths, steps and limestone walls renovated and considerable new planting over last 4 yrs. Patio garden with herbs and summer vegetables.

THE MOUNT
Mr & Mrs C J Russell
12ft limestone walls form a perfect backdrop for a variety of architectural plants in the side garden. Raised and walled beds at the front contain a variety of herbaceous planting and shrubs. Wonderful views across the channel to Devon give an ever changing outlook, what ever the gardening weather. Entry via steep hill.

NEWTON COTTAGE
Mr & Mrs J David
Large informal cottage garden. Mixed borders, good variety of shrubs, climbers and herbaceous plants. Newly-planted box garden. Kitchen garden.

THE OLD ORCHARD
Richard & Caroline Howe
Cottage garden with steps up to the rear gardens, populated with fruit trees, June-flowering roses, small herb garden and vegetable patch.

TYN-Y-CAEAU FARM
Tyn-y-Caeau Lane. Ian & Margaret John. *From Newton village return to A4106 Bridgend*

Rd, straight over roundabout into Tyn-y-Caeau Lane, approx 1m along lane.

Young garden with herbaceous borders, vegetable garden, ponds, wild flower meadow, orchard with fruit trees and hens. Wonderful panoramic view of Bristol Channel.

16 PENLLYN COURT

nr Cowbridge CF71 7RQ. Mr & Mrs John Homfray. *17m W of Cardiff. A48 W of Cardiff towards Bridgend. Bypass Cowbridge, turn R at Pentre Meyrick, then 2nd R, Penllyn Court on L.* Home-made teas. **Adm £3, chd free. Sun 3 May (2-6).**

Large family garden with semi-formal walled garden, orchard with fruit trees and bulbs, stumpery, mixed plantings of shrubs and spring flowers. Vegetable garden.

Group opening

17 PENMARK VILLAGE GARDENS

CF62 3BP. *4m W of Barry. Take B4265 from Barry to Penmark.* Home-made teas. **Combined adm £5, chd free. Sat 20 June (11-5).**

Quaint rural village with 800 yr old Norman church, excellent pub and fantastic community spirit. The 6 gardens are within a mile circular walk and feature an exciting and eclectic range of garden styles and planting. Live music, flower festival, scarecrow trail competition. Transport around gardens.

GILESTON HOUSE

Kath Linton, 01446 710666, gilestone@supanet.com. Visitors also welcome by appt May to July.

Original medieval 'strip' garden designed by current owners. 1-acre garden laid out with a series of curved lawns, abundantly stocked flower beds and shrubberies presenting an ever-changing vista round each corner. Plenty of seating areas to rest and enjoy the beautiful rural views.

GWAL EIRTH

Gwyn Grisley
Beautiful terraced garden created by keen gardener. Plantaholic's paradise filled with many varieties

of perennials, grasses, ferns and hostas. Samples of owner's pottery displayed throughout garden.

PENMARK PLACE

Mr & Mrs Andrew Radcliffe
C13 manor house with enclosed walled garden, large vegetable plot and orchard. Rose hedges, perennial beds, 100yr-old varieties of apple and pear.

SEFTON BUNGALOW

Cynthia John
Meandering stream with specimen trees situated on the lea of a field, with panoramic views. Garden with many plants of note.

NEW ST JUDE

Brian & Sarah Morris
Mature terraced garden with interesting mix of trees, shrubs, bulbs and perennials to give yr round interest. Includes small pond, pots and small vegetable garden.

NEW TOLZEY COTTAGE

Mr & Mrs A Matthews
Beautiful cottage garden with herbaceous borders, established shrubs and roses. Spectacular views over a valley. Known as 'best view in the village'.

Six small to medium sized gardens in easy walking distance . . . a warm welcome awaits you . . .

Group opening

18 NEW PENTYRCH GARDENS IN JUNE

CF15 9QD. Pentyrch. *2m N of Cardiff. M4 J32 - A470 to Merthyr. After 1/2 m exit signed Taffs Well & Radyr. 1st exit at r'about onto B4262 signed Radyr, Gwaelod & Pentyrch. Next r'about R. L at T-junc. 1st house on L.* Home-made teas. **Combined adm £5, chd free. Sun 14 June (11-6).**

Six small to medium sized gardens in easy walking distance, each with its own distinct style. See wildlife, recycling, prize winning vegetables, cottage and modern gardens incl three 'Cardiff in Bloom' prize winners. A warm welcome awaits you. Pentyrch Gardens host of Radio 4 Gardeners Question Time.

NEW 5 HEOL DAN Y RODYN

Stephen Evans
Haven for wildbirds with nest boxes and feeders plus large bog area for frogs and newts. Recycling is important with many of its features salvaged from other peoples waste. Packed with interest and beautifully kept.

NEW 9 HEOL Y PENTRE

Chris & Ken Rogers
Corner plot with perennial borders and acers. Climbers with small gravel garden. Winner of Cardiff in Bloom. Featured on 'Britains Best Gardens'.

NEW 14 MAES Y SARN

Yvonne & Anthony Krip
Front and rear garden designed to provide all year interest. Mature oak trees shelter packed borders containing a variety of shrubs and perennials, roses, clematis, hosta and acers. A 'lush peaceful haven' in the middle of Pentyrch.

NEW MAES-Y-GOF

Jeanette & Chris Troughton
Cottage garden with terracing, reclaimed from jungle 6 years ago. Redesigned and planted with bulbs, herbaceous roses, clematis, shrubs, palms and ferns. Patio, small pond and seating areas. Prize winner Cardiff in Bloom.

NEW 2 PENMAES

Chris & Helen Edwards
Small packed garden with 47 roses, clematis and fuchsia. Full colour and scent. Peaceful to sit in.

NEW TY DERI
Hanni & Lyn Davies
Award winning garden with specimen trees, water feature surrounded by seasonal herbaceous borders. Rear garden incl unusual plants, raised vegetable beds, large fruit cage and greenhouse. Winner Cardiff in Bloom for front garden. Slightly steep drive, small slope to front garden, partial access to rear garden.

19 NEW 89 PEN-Y-DRE
Rhiwbina, Cardiff CF14 6EL. Emil Nelz. *From M4 J32, take the A470 towards Cardiff. At t-lights turn L, continue to mini r'about turn R through village to t-lights. R at t-lights into Pen-y-Dre.* Light refreshments & teas. **Adm £2.50, chd free (share to Ty-Hafan Childrens Hospice). Sat, Sun 25, 26 July (11-5).**
Small garden with several different types of unusual plants. Palms, fern, oleander, magnolia etc. Fish pond with Koi carp. Conservatory with several cacti and succulents plus hibiscus and bougainvillea. Both front and back gardens have large selection of hollyhocks. Winner Cardiff in Bloom.

Group opening

20 PENYLAN GARDENS
Penylan, Cardiff CF23 5BD. *1½ m NE of Cardiff city centre. M4 J29, Cardiff E A48, then Llanedeyrn/Dock exit, towards Cyncoed and L down Penylan Hill. Marlborough Rd is L at T-lights at bottom of hill. Look out for NGS signs.* Light refreshments & teas. **Combined adm £4, chd free (share to Alzheimers Society, Cardiff & The Vale Branch). Suns 3 May; 26 July (2-6). Evening Opening** wine, **Tue 28 July (5-9pm).**
Victorian suburb of mostly terraced houses with small gardens and many parks.

6 ALMA ROAD
Melvyn Rees, 07903 456385, mel@tymel.demon.co.uk.
Visitors also welcome by appt.
S-facing terraced house garden 30ft x 15ft with many species from the S and E hemispheres, incl *Dicksonia antarctica, D. squarosa* and *Sophora* in a riot of exotic foliage. Slate used as paving material with gravel infill. Decking provides a raised seating area.

7 CRESSY ROAD
Victoria Thornton
Bijou terraced house garden. A secluded haven with an exotic mix of tropical planting, agaves, grasses, arisemea, woodland planting. Fern collection, wildlife pond, small conservatory housing forest cacti. Area winner Cardiff in Bloom.

102 MARLBOROUGH ROAD
Mrs Judith Griffiths
Come and discover a secret stone-walled garden behind a busy street. A garden of contrasts: Mediterranean-style sunny patio/shady areas. Wander through an informal mix of cottage garden plants, established shrubs and fruit trees.

NEW 128 PENYLAN ROAD
John & Judi Wilkins
A stone walled SE facing cottage style garden offering colour and tranquillity away from a busy main road.

21 PONTYGWAITH FARM
Edwardsville, nr Treharris CF46 5PD. Mr & Mrs R J G Pearce, 01443 411137. *2m NW of Treharris. N from Cardiff on A470. At r'about take A4054 (old Ponytpridd to Merthyr rd), travel N towards Aberfan for approx 3m through Quakers Yard and Edwardsville. 1m after Edwardsville turn very sharp L by old black bus shelter, garden at bottom of hill.* Light refreshments & teas. **Adm £3, chd free. Suns 24 May; 28 June (10-6). Visitors also welcome by appt May to Aug, large groups welcome.**
Large garden surrounding C17 farmhouse adjacent to Trevithick's Tramway. Situated in picturesque wooded valley. Fish pond, lawns, perennial borders, lakeside walk and rose garden. Grade II listed humpback packhorse bridge in garden, spanning R Taff, featured in film *Caught in the Act*; A lovely day out for all the family. Steep slope to river.

22 ST BRIDES C/W PRIMARY SCHOOL
Heol Yr Ysgol, St Brides Major CF32 0TB. *4m SW of Bridgend. From M4 J35 1st exit to A473. At 3rd r'about take 2nd exit to A48, over mini r'about. Next r'about 1st L to Ewenny Rd, signed Llantwit Major B4265. Continue to St Brides Major, R at Fox & Hounds, 1st L to Heol Yr Ysgol.* Home-made teas. **Adm £3, chd free. Sun 28 June (11-4).**
This school garden has been developed and maintained by the school's Gardening Club which meets weekly after school and has approx 40 members. Individual gardens within the school grounds incl: Warm Welcome Garden, Woodland, Organic Fruit and Vegetable Garden, Easter Garden, Jewish Garden, Sensory Garden, Patchwork Garden, Butterfly Garden, Flower Diary Garden, Woven Willow Playground, Maze, Nature Reserve and Wild flower Meadow, craft willow bed and Faith Garden.

Small Japanese garden holds 40 maples . . .

23 NEW SEA BREEZE
Oyster Bend, Sully CF64 5LW. Chris & Derek Richards, 02920 531214, orchid1552@hotmail.co.uk. *5m W of Penarth. From A4232 take A4055 to Dinas Powys. L at B4267 after Merry Harrier PH to Redlands Road. Cont on for approx 4m. In Sully L onto Clevedon Ave then R Smithies Ave. 1st L into Oyster Bend.* Light refreshments & teas. **Adm £2.50, chd free. Sat, Sun 4, 5 July (11-5). Visitors also welcome by appt Jul to Sept, small groups only.**
A plant person's garden near the sea, exciting around every corner. Coastal haven overflowing with unusual tropical plants. Colourful decking surrounds pond and tree seat. Braheas, iochromas and hedychiums. Small Japanese garden holds 40 maples in slate borders complementing granite pathways and Japanese sculptures.

24 SLADE

Southerndown CF32 0RP.
Rosamund & Peter Davies, 01656 880048,
ros@sladewoodgarden.plus.com.
5m S of Bridgend. M4 J35. Follow A473 to Bridgend. Take B4265 to St Brides Major. Turn R in St Brides Major for Southerndown. At Southerndown turn L opp 3 Golden Cups PH onto Beach Rd. Follow rd into Dunraven Park. Turn 1st L over cattle grid on to Slade drive. Home-made teas. **Adm £3, chd free. Sun 5 Apr (1-6). Visitors also welcome by appt.**
Woodland garden and walk. Display of early spring flowers: snowdrops, daffodils, crocus, cyclamen, bluebells. Mature specimen trees. Herbaceous borders, rose and clematis pergola terraced lawns, orchard, hens. Path to beach. Extensive views over Bristol Channel. Heritage Coast wardens will give guided tours of adjacent Dunraven Gardens with slide shows every 1/2 hr from 3pm.

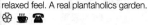

25 SPRINGFIELD

176 Clasemont Road, Morriston SA6 6AJ. Carole & Stuart Jones, 01792 773827. *4m N of Swansea. From M4 J46 follow A48 E for 1m. From Morriston Cross take A48 W for 1m, garden on A48 50yds from entrance to Morriston Golf Club.* Home-made teas & wine. **Adm £2.50, chd free. Sun 14 June (12-6). Visitors also welcome by appt.**
Small informal suburban garden with interesting mix of trees, shrubs, bulbs and perennials to give yr-round interest. Incl small pond and pebble pond and many containerised plants. Several seating areas give the garden a relaxed feel. A real plantaholics garden.

26 ◆ TOUCHWOOD

4 Clyne Valley Cottages, Killay, Swansea SA2 7DU. Carrie Thomas, 01792 522443, www.touchwoodplants.co.uk. *4m W of Swansea centre. Take A4118 (Gower rd) past Killay shops and over mini-r'about towards Gower. 2nd L (halfway down hill) into Clyne Valley Road, which leads to Clyne Valley Cottages.* **Adm £2, chd free. Open most days, phone or see website for details. For NGS: Fri 15, Tue 19 May (2-4.30). Also Evening Opening Fri 15, Tue 19 May (6-8). Visitors also welcome by appt for NGS during the Aquilegia season.**
Plantsman's intimate cottage garden, most items grown from seed. Annuals, biennials, perennials, bulbs, shrubs, grasses, climbers, herbs, vegetables and alpines. National Collection of *Aquilegia vulgaris*, hybrids and cultivars flowering May and beginning of June. Set in historical country park, nr Clyne and Singleton gardens. Featured in 'The Hardy Plant' & 'Swansea Life' magazines.

Pretty courtyard surrounded by barn conversions covered by climbers . . .

TREDEGAR HOUSE & PARK
See Gwent.

27 ◆ TWYN-YR-HYDD

Margam Country Park, Margam SA13 2TJ. Neath Port Talbot College, 01639 648261, robert.priddle@nptc.ac.uk. *2m W of Pyle. M4 J38, take A48 signed Margam Park. Pass entrance to Park, after 1/2 m turn L into garden.* **Adm £3.50, chd free. For NGS: Sun 21 June (11-3.30).**
Spread out over 11-acre site and containing gardens designed and constructed by horticulture students. Incl herb, prairie, woodland and a vegetable garden. Grounds also contain walled garden designed by Arts and Crafts designer Ralph Hancock. New for 2009 a collection of over 50 different varieties of Hebe.

Group opening

28 NEW WILTON ROAD GARDENS

CF71 7LP. Siginstone, Cowbridge. *3m SW of Cowbridge. W along A48 passing Cowbridge. L at Pentre Meyrick on B4268 (signed Llysworney/Llantwit Major). 1m after Llysworney turn L (signed Siginstone/Victoria Inn).* Light refreshments & teas at Hafod-y-Fro. **Combined adm £3, chd free. Sun 21 June (2-6).**
Siginstone is a rural village between the market town of Cowbridge and the historic town of Llantwit Major, near to the the heritage coast.

NEW HAFOD-Y-FRO
Rhodri & Kathy Williams
Pretty courtyard surrounded by barn conversions covered by climbers, pond and bog areas. Lawn leading to raised terrace. Summerhouse and waterfall. Annual, herbaceous, rose and shrub border sheltered by evergreens. Developing woodland and orchard.

NEW LANGLANDS
Eliz & Colin Davies
Evolving over 40 years, the garden is a series of spaces incl mature pleasure and Mediterranean courtyard areas, established pond and produce garden. Planted for year round interest with many features and resting places.

Glamorgan County Volunteers

County Organiser
Rosamund Davies, Slade, Southerndown, Glamorgan CF32 0RP, 01656 880048, ros@sladewoodgarden.plus.com

County Treasurer
Mr Gerry Long, Gwdi-Hw Cottage, Trerhyngyll, Cowbridge, Vale of Glamorga, 01446 774772, gerry.long@virgin.net

Assistant County Organiser
Melanie Hurst, Wolf House, Llysworney, Cowbridge, Vale of Glamorgan CF71 7NQ, 01446 773659, melanie@hurstcreative.co.uk

GWENT

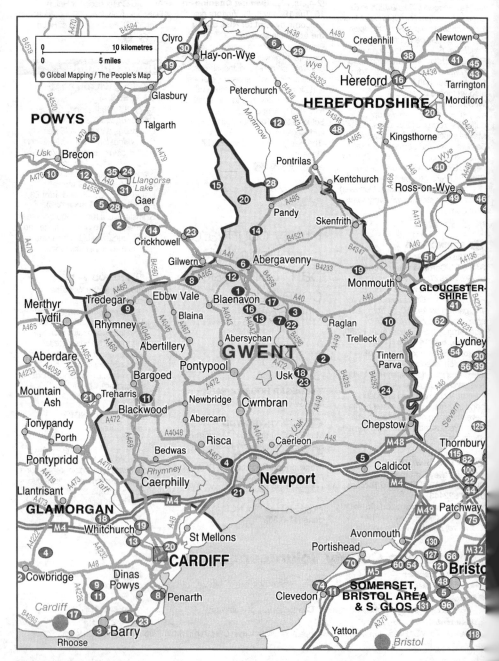

0 ___ 10 kilometres
0 ___ 5 miles
© Global Mapping / The People's Map

Opening Dates

March
SUNDAY 22
⑬ Llanover

April
SUNDAY 5
⑤ Dewstow Gardens & Grottoes

May
SUNDAY 10
⑩ High Glanau Manor

SATURDAY 16
⑮ Nant-y-Bedd
⑱ Plas Newydd Cottage

SUNDAY 17
⑥ Gardd-y-Bryn
⑮ Nant-y-Bedd

SATURDAY 23
⑪ Hillcrest Bungalow

SUNDAY 24
⑪ Hillcrest Bungalow

MONDAY 25
⑪ Hillcrest Bungalow

June
SATURDAY 6
㉒ Trostrey Lodge

SUNDAY 7
㉒ Trostrey Lodge

SUNDAY 14
⑫ Llanfoist Village Gardens
⑯ Ochran Mill

SUNDAY 21
⑭ Llanthony and District Gardens
㉑ Tredegar House & Park

FRIDAY 26
⑯ Ochran Mill (Evening)

SATURDAY 27
㉓ Usk Gardens

SUNDAY 28
① Castell Cwrt
㉓ Usk Gardens

July
SATURDAY 4
⑦ Glebe House

SUNDAY 5
⑦ Glebe House

SUNDAY 12
⑧ Graig Cottage
⑯ Ochran Mill

SATURDAY 18
⑨ 80 Gwent Way

SUNDAY 19
③ Clytha Park
⑨ 80 Gwent Way

WEDNESDAY 22
㉔ Veddw House (Evening)

August
SUNDAY 2
⑳ Three Wells

SATURDAY 8
⑪ Hillcrest Bungalow

SUNDAY 9
⑪ Hillcrest Bungalow
⑯ Ochran Mill

SUNDAY 23
④ Croesllanfro Farm

SUNDAY 30
② Cefntilla

MONDAY 31
② Cefntilla

September
SUNDAY 13
⑯ Ochran Mill

SUNDAY 27
⑤ Dewstow Gardens & Grottoes
⑲ Sunnyside

October
SUNDAY 4
⑯ Ochran Mill

Gardens open to the public
⑤ Dewstow Gardens & Grottoes
⑰ Penpergwm Lodge
㉑ Tredegar House & Park
㉔ Veddw House

Also open by appointment ☎
④ Croesllanfro Farm
⑦ Glebe House
⑨ 80 Gwent Way
⑩ High Glanau Manor
⑪ Hillcrest Bungalow
⑬ Llanover
⑭ 14 Grove Farm, Llanthony and District Gardens
⑯ Ochran Mill
⑲ Sunnyside
㉒ Trostrey Lodge

A restful mix
of formal and
informal in about
6 acres . . .

The Gardens

❶ CASTELL CWRT
Llanelen NP7 9LE. Lorna & John McGlynn. *1m S of Abergavenny. From Abergavenny/Llanfoist take B4269 signed Llanelen. After passing Grove Farm turn R up single track rd. Rd climbs up steeply over canal. Approx 500yds entrance to Castell Cwrt on L. Separate disabled parking available.* **Adm £2.50, chd free.** Sun 28 June (12-5).
Large informal family garden in 10-acre smallholding with fine views overlooking Abergavenny. Lawns with established trees and shrubs borders. Organic soft fruit and vegetable gardens. Hay meadow walk, livestock in fields and family pets. Children very welcome, animals to see and space to let off steam. Some gravel and grass paths.
♿ ✖ ⊛ 🍵

❷ CEFNTILLA
Usk NP15 1DG. Lord Raglan. *3m NE of Usk. From S, take B4235 Usk to Chepstow rd to Gwernesney & follow signs N to Cefntilla, about 1m. From N, take Chepstow rd S from Raglan & follow signs through Llandenny.* Homemade teas. **Adm £3.50, chd free (share to Young Carers - Monmouthshire Crossroads).** Sun, BH Mon 30, 31 Aug (12-5).
Rectangular former Jacobean garden area greatly extended in 1850s with woodland circumambulatory. Lawns set about with good trees, shrubs, colourful herbaceous borders, fine rosebeds, topiary walk with golden and Irish yews, handsome large lily pond. A varied yet restful mix of formal and informal in about 6 acres. Dogs on leads only.
♿ ⊛ 🍵

❸ CLYTHA PARK
Abergavenny NP7 9BW. Sir Richard Hanbury-Tenison. *Half-way between Abergavenny (4m) and Raglan (4m). On old road signed Clytha at either end. 100yds from garden through wood.* **Adm £3, chd free.** Sun 19 July (2-5).
Large C18 garden around 1½-acre lake with wide lawns and good trees. Visit the 1790 walled garden or walk around the lake on a serpentine path laid out over 250 yrs ago. Ravens always around and possibly the largest tulip tree in Wales.
♿ 🍵

4 CROESLLANFRO FARM

Rogerstone NP10 9GP. Barry & Liz Davies, 01633 894057, lizplants@gmail.com. *3m W of Newport. From M4 J27 take B4591 to Risca. Take 3rd R, Cefn Walk (also signed 14 Locks Canal Centre). Proceed over canal bridge, continue approx 1/2 m to island in middle of lane. White farm gate opp. Limited parking.* Home-made teas. **Adm £3.50, chd free. Sun 23 Aug (2-5.30). Visitors also welcome by appt Jun to end of Aug.**

An unexpected, ever evolving 1 1/2 -acre garden. Steps, terracing, folly, grotto and large sweeping borders of mass planted, late flowering perennials help to create a garden for all moods. From the primordial to the colonial garden there's a place here for everyone incl a treasure hunt for children. Some gravel paths and steps.

5 ◆ DEWSTOW GARDENS & GROTTOES

Caerwent, Caldicot NP26 5AH. John Harris, 01291 430444, www.dewstow.co.uk. *5m W of Chepstow. From A48 Newport to Chepstow rd, L to Caerwent & Dewstow golf club. Garden next to golf club. Coaches permitted.* **Adm £5, chd free. Daily 20 Mar to 18 Oct. See website for opening times. For NGS: Suns 5 Apr; 27 Sept (10.30-4).**

5-acre Grade 1 listed unique garden which was buried and forgotten after World War 11 and rediscovered in 2000. Created around 1895 by James Pulham & Sons, the garden contains underground grottoes, tunnels and ferneries and above ground stunning water features. You will not be disappointed. Wheelchair access very limited.

6 GARDD-Y-BRYN

The Hill Education & Conference Centre, Abergavenny NP7 7RP. Coleg Gwent. *1/4 m N of town centre. From A40 in Abergavenny, follow signs to Hill College.* Home-made teas. **Adm £3, chd free. Sun 17 May (2-6).**

Recently-restored Victorian walled garden on S-facing slope overlooking Abergavenny and surrounded by mature woodland. Divided into various themed gardens incl fruit, vegetables, flowers for cutting, wild garden. Unusual, interesting, trees and shrubs. Atmospheric Mediterranean garden with intriguing human sundial. New

Stumpery/fernery. Wonderful outdoor mural of Usk Valley and Sugar Loaf Mountain.

7 GLEBE HOUSE

Llanvair Kilgeddin NP7 9BE. Mr & Mrs Murray Kerr, 01873 840422, joanna@amknet.com. *Midway between Abergavenny (5m) and Usk (5m). On B4598.* Home-made teas. **Adm £3.50, chd free. Sat, Sun 4, 5 July (2-6). Visitors also welcome by appt 1 April to 6 May for tulips.**

1 1/2 acres with colourful herbaceous borders, S-facing terrace and climbers. Small ornamental vegetable garden with summerhouse. New green oak pergola. Old Rectory of St Mary's Llanvair Kilgeddin with its famous Victorian scraffito murals and set in picturesque Usk Valley with stunning all-round views.

Beautiful cottage garden on precipitious hillside with superb views . . .

8 NEW GRAIG COTTAGE

Rhonas Road, Clydach, Abergavenny NP7 0LB. Graham & Elizabeth Mills. *4 1/2 m NW of Abergavenny. A465 towards Merthyr Tydfil from Abergavenny. Approx 4m turn R to Clydach North over cattle grid, bear L up hill 1/2 m and follow signs for parking or park in village.* Home-made teas. **Adm £3, chd free. Sun 12 July (11-6).**

Beautiful cottage garden on precipitious hillside with superb views of Clydach Gorge, Llanwenarth Brest and Sugar Loaf Mountain. Garden set on four levels with steep steps. Luscious cottage style planting, pergolas, seating areas, pond, ornamental and fruit trees, shrubs, vegetable garden, small woodland bank, well stocked greenhouse, composting area.

THE GRIGGS

See Herefordshire.

9 NEW 80 GWENT WAY

Tredegar NP22 3HT. Mr Robert Edward, 01495 711413, robert-je@hotmail.com. *2m W of Ebbw Vale. From A465 take the A4048 to Tredegar and follow signs to Ashvale Industrial Park. Park on the service road to the industrial estate at the bottom of Gwent Way.* Home-made teas. **Adm £2.50, chd free. Sat, Sun 18, 19 July (2-5). Visitors also welcome by appt July to Aug, groups of 30 max.**

Small town garden crammed with interest front and back. Terraced front with small shrubbery, alpines, hanging baskets and pots. Sculpted metal pergola across width of back garden, two ponds and a rill, climbers on all walls and fences with numerous pots and hanging baskets. 1st prize winner Gwent in Bloom.

10 HIGH GLANAU MANOR

Lydart, Monmouth NP25 4AD. Mr & Mrs Hilary Gerrish, 01600 860005, helenagerrish@hotmail.co.uk. *4m SW of Monmouth. Situated on B4293 between Monmouth & Chepstow. Turn into 'Private Road' opp Five Trees Carp Fishery.* Home-made teas. **Adm £3.50, chd free. Sun 10 May (2-6). Visitors also welcome by appt through Cadw.**

Listed Arts and Crafts garden laid out by H Avray Tipping in 1922. Original features incl impressive stone terraces with far-reaching views over the vale of Usk, pergola, herbaceous borders, Edwardian glasshouse, rhododendrons, azaleas and tulips. Runner up NGS Gold Medal 'I own Britains Best Garden'.

11 HILLCREST BUNGALOW

Waunborfa Road, Cefn Fforest, Blackwood NP12 3LB. Mr M O'Leary and Mr B Price, 01443 837029, www.hillcrestgarden.co.uk. *3m W of Newbridge. Follow A4048 to Blackwood town centre or A469 to Pengam T-lights, then NGS signs.* Light refreshments. **Adm £3, chd free. Sat, Sun, Mon 23, 24, 25 May; Sat, Sun 8, 9 Aug; (12-6). Visitors also welcome by appt Apr-Sept, groups of any size welcome.**

Visit our 'Secret' Garden and experience a haven of treasures and tranquillity. Discover secluded gardens each cascading into the next, revealing a new delight around every corner. Find out where the garden ends and the distant valley view begins. Relax while enjoying a sublime cream tea. Then go round again!

Gallery created from the old cattle yard and parlour . . .

Group opening

12 LLANFOIST VILLAGE GARDENS
NP7 9PE. www.llanfoist-open-gardens.co.uk. *1m SW of Abergavenny on B4246. Map provided with ticket. Most gardens within easy walking distance of the village centre. Free minibus to others. Limited wheelchair access to some gardens.* Light refreshments & teas lunch at village hall. **Adm £5, chd free, unaccompanied 50p (share to Llanfoist Villagers Association).** Sun 14 June (10.30-5.30).
Make this a great day out. Visit around 15 exciting and contrasting village gardens, both large and small, set just below the Blorenge Mountain on the edge of the Black Mountains. This is our 7th annual event. A number of new gardens opening along with many regulars. Canal trips between gardens subject to water supply. Featured in local press.

13 LLANOVER
nr Abergavenny NP7 9EF. Mr & Mrs M R Murray, 07753 423635. *4m S of Abergavenny, 15m N of Newport. On A4042 Abergavenny - Pontypool.* Home-made teas. **Adm £4, chd free.** Sun 22 Mar (2-5). **Visitors also welcome by appt Jan to Mar, Oct to Dec for 10+ people.**
15-acre listed garden and arboretum with lakes, streams, cascades and a dovecote. Champion trees present incl *Quercus alba, Aesculus californica,*

Sorbus wardii, Betula costata and *Abies concolor.* The numerous magnolias, camellias and the avenue of spring bulbs should be in full bloom. Traditional Welsh dancing and harpist. Gravel and grass paths.

Group opening

14 LLANTHONY AND DISTRICT GARDENS
NP7 7LB. *5m N of Abergavenny. From Abergavenny roundabout take A465 N towards Hereford. 4.8m turn L onto Old Hereford Rd signed Pantygelli 2m. Myndd Ardrem 1/2 m on R, Mione on L. Directions to other gardens provided.* Light refreshments & teas. **Combined adm £5, chd free (share to Llanthony and District Garden Club).** Sun 21 June (10.30-4.30).
Located in an area of outstanding beauty within the Black Mountains rural communities of Fforest Coal Pit, Cwmyoy and the village of Llanvihangel Crucorney. The garden settings reflect the diversity of the local landscape with views across valleys, mountains and forests. Steep slopes but vehicular access to disabled parking (see Perthi Crwn).

NEW GROVE FARM
Walterstone. David & Christine Hunt, 01873 890293, davidbhunt@tiscali.co.uk. **Visitors also welcome by appt July & Aug. Max 15 people.**
Large tranquil courtyard with ponds, shrubs, specimen trees, greenhouse and gallery created from the old cattle yard and parlour. Banks of herbaceous borders, shrubberies and rose covered pergolas leading to vegetable and herb garden, wild pond and orchard. Please note there are a number of steep steps.

☎

MIONE
Llanvihangel Crucorney. Yvonne & John O'Neil
Established garden with wide variety of plants, many unusual. Pergola with climbing roses and clematis, wildlife pond, containers with diverse range of planting. Several seating areas, each with a different atmosphere. Summerhouse.

MYNYDD ARDREM
Llanvihangel Crucorney. Linda & Geoff Walsh
This lovely garden was re-started 7 yrs ago within established mature boundaries, in order to create a romantic setting for the Victorian house. Beautiful roses, clematis, herbaceous borders, shrubs, trees and a wisteria-clad pergola.

PERTHI CRWN
Cwmyoy. Jim Keates
Restored farmhouse garden with stunning views, SW aspect facing valley and mountainside beyond. Sunny, walled garden with fruit, vegetables and flowers, formal rose garden and newly-created wild flower bank.

❀

15 NANT-Y-BEDD
Grwyne Fawr, Fforest Coal Pit NP7 7LY. Sue & Ian Mabberley. *10m NW of Abergavenny. Turn into Llanvihangel Crucorney from A465 Abergavenny/Hereford rd. L at Skirrid Inn and L at bottom. After 1m L to Fforest Coal Pit. After 2m at the junction of five roads, straight ahead to Grwyne Fawr Reservoir and Forestry Commission 'Mynydd Du'. Nant y Bedd 5m.* **Adm £3, chd free (share to Llanthony & District Garden Club).** Sat, Sun, 16, 17 May (1-5).
A late spring 2-acre garden nestled high in the Black Mountains. An oasis in the forest managed organically. Vegetables, flowers, mature trees, water and rope suspension bridge over tumbling stream. Comments incl 'exceptionally creative and restful', 'a special atmosphere' and 'an inspirational experience'. Come and see this cherished garden in a magnificent National Park setting. 'Environmental Art' Stone Wall. Featured on BBC2 Open Gardens.

🐕 ❀

THE NEUADD
See Powys.

16 OCHRAN MILL
Llanover NP7 9HU. Elaine & David Rolfe, 01873 737809, elaine@ochranmill.co.uk. *3m S of Abergavenny. On A4042 midway between Llanover & Llanelen.* Home-made teas. **Adm £3, chd free.** Suns 14 June; 12 July; 9 Aug; 13 Sept; 4 Oct (1-5). **Evening Opening,** wine, Fri 26 June (6-9). **Visitors also**

welcome by appt for gardening groups/individuals. Coaches permitted.

Grade II listed water mill (not working) in approx 2-acres. An abundance of colour and lush growth packed with many varieties of herbaceous perennials and colourful shrubs. Interest from early spring to late autumn, hellebores, roses, asters and many more. 'Horticultural heaven' Andy Sturgeon. 'Inspiring' Elspeth Thompson. 'A garden rich in flowers' Stephen Anderton. Field for picnics & stream. Pinball and arcade collection (very popular with non-gardeners and children). New tea room. Gravel paths, gentle slopes.

🚶 🐕 ✿ ☕ ☎

17 ◆ **PENPERGWM LODGE**
nr Abergavenny NP7 9AS. Mr & Mrs Simon Boyle, 01873 840208, boyle@penpergwm.co.uk. *3m SE of Abergavenny, 5m W of Raglan. On B4598. Turn opp King of Prussia Inn. Entrance 150 yds on L.* **Adm £3.50, chd free. Daily Thur 2 Apr to Sun 20 Sept; (2-6).**
3-acre garden with Jubilee tower overlooking terraced ornamental garden containing canal, cascading water and new loggia at head of canal. S-facing terraces planted with rich profusion and vibrant colours all surrounded by spacious lawns and mature trees. Special plant nursery.

🚶 ✿ 🛏

Colourful, scented walled garden within the small orchard of a listed Regency house approached across a ha-ha past a spectacularly tall tulip tree in flower . . .

18 **PLAS NEWYDD COTTAGE**
Porthycarne Street, Usk NP15 1SA. Dr Pauline Ruth. *A449 to Usk. R at Three Salmons PH, R up Porthycarne Close opp Veterinary Hospital. Old coach house on L at top. Parking in town car parks.* Home-made teas. **Adm £3, chd free (share to Alzheimer's Society Befriending Scheme Monmouthshire). Sat 16 May (10-6).**
Old courtyard at front originally for coaches and horses for Georgian house next door. Now flagged and cobbled with sunny flower beds. Steeply terraced back garden to castle woods. Espalier trees, roses, shrubs and vegetables. Wide views to SW over Usk. Woodland at top.

☕

19 **SUNNYSIDE**
The Hendre NP25 5HQ. Helen & Ralph Fergusson-Kelly, 01600 714928, helen-fk@hotmail.com. *4m W of Monmouth. On B4233 Monmouth to Abergavenny rd. Parking in field 50m from garden.* Home-made teas. **Adm £3, chd free. Sun 27 Sept (12-5). Visitors also welcome by appt May to end Sept, eves & w/e for small groups.**
Listed house (not open) on old Rolls estate. Mature, sloping garden of 1/3 acre with lawns, trees, shrubs and herbaceous borders planted with interesting perennials and grasses for late season colour. Designed and planted by owner. Some gravel paths. Water feature. Seating areas to enjoy views over surrounding countryside.

🐕 ✿ ☕ ☎

20 **THREE WELLS**
Nr Llanvihangel Crucorney, Abergavenny NP7 7NR. Antony & Verity Woodward, www.thegardenintheclouds.com. *8m N of Abergavenny. Off A465 Abergavenny-Hereford rd. At Llanvihangel Crucorney turn downhill at Skirrid PH and 1st R over hump-back bridge. After 2/3 m, L by grass triangle and follow yellow signs. Challenging, very steep and narrow single track lanes. Reversing may be necessary for last 1 1/2 m. If wet, car park will be 15 minute walk.* Light refreshments & home-made teas. **Adm £3.50 (incl cup of tea), chd free (share to Longtown Mountain Rescue). Sun 2 Aug (12-6).**
Highest property opening in Britain? 6-acre smallholding in mountain setting (reaching nearly 1600ft) on Offa's Dyke

footpath in Brecon Beacons National Park. For anyone fit and intrepid who sees beauty in wild places - in upland wild-flower meadows, dry-stone walls and mountain springs, forgotten farm machinery in field corners and gateways framing 70-mile views.

☕

21 ◆ **TREDEGAR HOUSE & PARK**
Newport NP10 8YW. Newport City Council, 01633 815880, stephen.sully@newport.gov.uk. *2m SW of Newport town centre. Signed from A48 (Cardiff rd) & M4 J28.* **Adm £2.50, chd free. Wed to Sun (11-5). For NGS: Sun 21 June (11-5).**
Series of C18 walled formal gardens surrounding magnificent late C17 house (also open). Early C18 orangery garden with coloured mineral parterres. Open on NGS day Growing Space gardens maintained to a high standard by staff and clients with mental illnesses. Six separate areas incl bog garden, ornamental pond and secret cottage garden. Group visits by arrangement tel 01633 810718.

🚶 🐕 ✿

22 **TROSTREY LODGE**
Bettws Newydd, Usk NP15 1JT. Roger & Frances Pemberton, 01873 840352. *4m W of Raglan. 7m E of Abergavenny. Off the old A40 (unnumbered) Abergavenny - Raglan. 1m S of Clytha Gates and 1 1/2 m N of Bettws Newydd.* Home-made teas, Sun only. **Adm £3.50, chd free. Sat, Sun 6, 7 June (12-6). Visitors also welcome by appt June and July only.**
'This other Eden'...well, it is a colourful, scented walled garden within the small orchard of a listed Regency house (not open) which is approached across a ha-ha past a spectacularly tall tulip tree in flower. The garden is surrounded by green fields (ideal for picnics), very old oak trees and the R Usk.

✿ ☕ ☎

Group opening

23 **USK GARDENS**
Usk Town NP15 1AF, www.usktc.f9.co.uk. *From M4 J24 take A449, proceed 8m to Usk exit. Good free parking in town. Map of gardens provided with ticket.* **Adm £6, chd free (share to Usk Gardens Open Days Charities). Sat, Sun 27, 28 June (10-5).**

Proud winner of Wales in Bloom for many years with its colourful hanging baskets and boxes are a sight not to be missed! The town is a wonderful backdrop to the 25+ gardens from small cottages packed with colourful and unusual plants to large gardens with brimming herbaceous borders. Wonderful romantic garden around the ramparts of Usk Castle. Gardeners' market with wide selection of interesting plants. Featured in local press, BBC Gardeners' World & Gardeners' Question Time. Limited wheelchair access to some gardens.

&. ✖ ✿ ☕

My favorite NGS gardens include the Charles Jenks 'Garden of Cosmic Speculation' and the 'yew wave' garden at Veddw House' . . .

24 ◆ **VEDDW HOUSE**
Devauden NP16 6PH. Anne Wareham & Charles Hawes, 01291 650836, www.veddw.co.uk. *5m NW of Chepstow. Off B4293. Signed from PH on the green at Devauden.* **Adm £5.50, chd £1.50. Suns & Bank Hol Mons, 7 Jun to 31 Aug (2-5). For NGS: Evening Opening** wine, **Wed 22 July (5-7.30).**
My favorite NGS gardens include the Charles Jenks 'Garden of Cosmic Speculation' and the 'yew wave' garden at Veddw House' *Jane Owen. Financial Times.* A modern romantic garden.
&.

Gwent County Volunteers

County Organiser
Joanna Kerr, Glebe House, Llanvair Kilgeddin, Abergavenny NP7 9BE, 01873 840422, joanna@amknet.com

Assistant County Organiser
Sue Carter, St Pega's, 47 Hereford Road, Monmouth NP25 3HQ, 01600 772074, stpegas47@hotmail.co.uk

GWYNEDD, ANGLESEY & CONWY

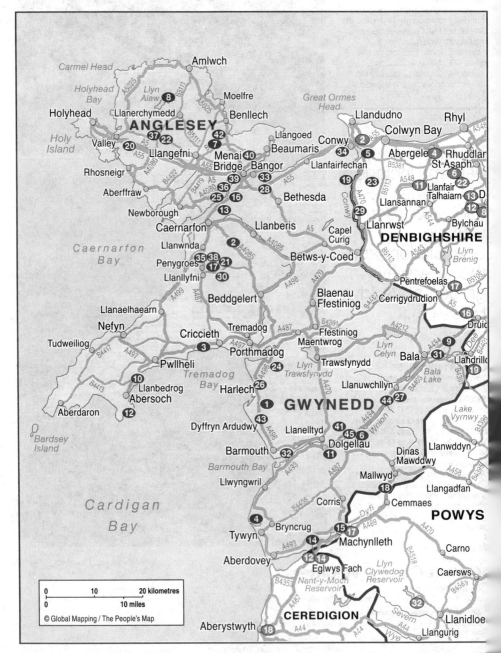

Opening Dates

February

SUNDAY 8
③③ Penrhyn Castle

April

SATURDAY 11
㉖ Llyn Rhaeadr

SUNDAY 12
③ Bont Fechan Farm
㉖ Llyn Rhaeadr

MONDAY 13
③ Bont Fechan Farm
㉖ Llyn Rhaeadr

TUESDAY 14
㉖ Llyn Rhaeadr

WEDNESDAY 15
㉖ Llyn Rhaeadr

SUNDAY 26
㉙ Maenan Hall

May

SATURDAY 2
㉚ Megans Wood Gwernoer Farm

SUNDAY 3
㉖ Llyn Rhaeadr
㉚ Megans Wood Gwernoer Farm
㉜ Pen y Bryn

MONDAY 4
㉓ Gyffylog

SUNDAY 10
⑲ Gilfach

WEDNESDAY 13
⑯ Foxbrush

SUNDAY 17
③ Bont Fechan Farm
⑥ Bryn Gwern
⑩ Coron
㉘ Llys-y-Gwynt

SUNDAY 24
⑬ Crug Farm
⑮ Felin y Ffridd
⑳ Gwaelod Mawr
㉟ Plas Mawr
㊲ Rhyd

SUNDAY 31
⑤ Bryn Eisteddfod
㊶ Ty Capel Ffrwd

June

SUNDAY 7
⑨ Caerau Uchaf
㊷ Ty Gwyn

SATURDAY 13
② Antur Waunfawr
⑧ Cae Newydd

③① Melin Meloch

SUNDAY 14
⑧ Cae Newydd
⑪ Craig y Ffynnon
⑫ Crowrach Isaf
⑲ Gilfach
③① Melin Meloch
③④ Pensychnant

TUESDAY 16
㉔ Hotel Maes-y-Neuadd

WEDNESDAY 17
⑯ Foxbrush

SATURDAY 20
㉕ Llanidan Hall

SUNDAY 21
⑭ Esgairweddan
㊵ Treffos School

SUNDAY 28
㉘ Llys-y-Gwynt

July

SATURDAY 4
㉕ Llanidan Hall

SUNDAY 5
⑦ Bryn Seiri
㉟ Plas Mawr
㊶ Ty Capel Ffrwd

SUNDAY 12
⑳ Gwaelod Mawr
③④ Pensychnant

SATURDAY 18
㊱ Plas Newydd Country House &
Gardens

SUNDAY 19
⑰ Gardd y Coleg

SATURDAY 25
① Aber Artro Hall
㊳ St John the Baptist & St George

SUNDAY 26
㊺ Tyn-Twll

August

SUNDAY 2
⑥ Bryn Gwern
㉑ Gwyndy
㊲ Rhyd
㊹ Tyn y Cefn

SUNDAY 9
㉖ Llyn Rhaeadr
③① Melin Meloch

MONDAY 10
㉖ Llyn Rhaeadr

TUESDAY 11
㉖ Llyn Rhaeadr

WEDNESDAY 12

㉖ Llyn Rhaeadr

THURSDAY 13
㉖ Llyn Rhaeadr

FRIDAY 14
㉖ Llyn Rhaeadr

SUNDAY 16
⑲ Gilfach

THURSDAY 20
㉔ Hotel Maes-y-Neuadd

MONDAY 31
㉓ Gyffylog

February 2010

SATURDAY 13
③③ Penrhyn Castle

Gardens open to the public

② Antur Waunfawr
⑬ Crug Farm
⑰ Gardd y Coleg
㉔ Hotel Maes-y-Neuadd
③③ Penrhyn Castle
③④ Pensychnant
㊱ Plas Newydd Country House &
Gardens

By appointment only

④ Bronclydwr
㉒ Gwyndy Bach
㉗ Llys Arthur
㊴ Tan Dinas
㊸ Ty Newydd

Also open by appointment ☎

③ Bont Fechan Farm
⑤ Bryn Eisteddfod
⑥ Bryn Gwern
⑦ Bryn Seiri
⑧ Cae Newydd
⑨ Caerau Uchaf
⑩ Coron
⑮ Felin y Ffridd
⑯ Foxbrush
⑲ Gilfach
⑳ Gwaelod Mawr
㉕ Llanidan Hall
㉖ Llyn Rhaeadr
㉘ Llys-y-Gwynt
㉚ Megans Wood Gwernoer Farm
㉟ Plas Mawr
㊲ Rhyd
㊹ Tyn y Cefn

The Gardens

❶ ABER ARTRO HALL

LL45 2PA. Paul & Carolyn Morgan. *Turn R off A496 in front of Victoria Inn in Llanbedr (L if coming from Harlech). After 1m turn R at sign Cwm Nantcol & follow arrows.* Light refreshments & teas. **Adm £4, chd free. Sat 25 July (11-5).**

Arts and Crafts 1910, 5-acre garden by architect Charles Edward Bateman. Terraced borders; riverside walk; fine trees, ponds. Hillside rock and wild garden leads to ancient woodland. Kitchen garden incl fruit pergola; secret Tuscan garden; William Morris 'wallpaper' garden. Tree house. playground. Partial wheelchair access, one steep slope - ask for reserved parking.

&. ❀ ☕

Views to Red Wharf Bay, the hills and Snowdonia . . .

❷ ◆ ANTUR WAUNFAWR

Bryn Pistyll, Waunfawr, Caernarfon LL55 4BJ. Menna Jones, 01286 650721, www.anturwaunfawr.org. *4¹/₂ m SE of Caernarfon. On A4085. Waunfawr village, turn L following signs, bear L for approx ¹/₂ m.* **Adm £2, chd free. Open all yr, see website for details. For NGS: Sat 13 June (11-3).**

Gardens and 7-acre Nature Park developed by Antur Waunfawr, a community venture providing employment opportunities for people with learning disabilities. Meadows, woodland walks, wildlife and ornamental ponds, soft fruit garden, herbaceous perennial beds. Well stocked wildlife plant nursery, greenhouses. Limited wheelchair access to garden.

&. ❀ ☕

ARFRYN
See Denbighshire & Colwyn.

BODYSGALLEN HALL & SPA
See Denbighshire & Colwyn.

---

❸ BONT FECHAN FARM

Llanystumdwy LL52 0LS. Mr & Mrs J D Bean, 01766 522604. *2m W of Criccieth. On the A497 to Pwllheli on L of main rd.* Home-made teas. **Adm £2, chd free. Sun 12, Mon 13 Apr; Sun 17 May (11-5). Visitors also welcome by appt.**

Cottage garden with rockery, fish pond, herbaceous border, steps to river. Large variety of plants. Nicely planted tubs; good vegetable garden and poultry. Rhododendron and azaleas. Shetland ponies.

&. ❀ ☕ ☎

❹ BRONCLYDWR

Rhoslefain, Tywyn LL36 9LT. Mr & Mrs Michael Bishton, 01654 710882, michael@bronclydwr.co.uk. *5m N of Tywyn. Take A493 Dolgellau to Tywyn rd. At Rhoslefain take Tonfanau rd for about ¹/₂ m. Fork L along private rd to end of tarmac rd then take unmade rd to large house on edge of wood.* **Adm £4, chd free. Visitors welcome by appt 23 May to 31 July.**

1-acre unique plantsman's garden of peaceful historic farmhouse overlooking Cardigan Bay. Many unusual and tender plants are grown incl protea, puya, amicia, echiums, watsonias, arums, euryops, restios etc. Interesting trees, shrubs, bamboos; bog garden and wild wooded area. Borders also contain many interesting hardy plants.

🐾 ❀ ☎

❺ BRYN EISTEDDFOD

Glan Conwy LL28 5LF. Dr Michael Senior, 01492 581175. *3¹/₂ m SE of Llandudno. 3m W Colwyn Bay. Up hill (Bryn-y-Maen direction) from Glan Conwy Corner where A470 joins A55.* Home-made teas. **Adm £2.50, chd 50p. Sun 31 May (2-5). Visitors also welcome by appt.**

8 acres of landscaped grounds incl mature shrubbery, arboretum, old walled 'Dutch' garden, large lawn with ha-ha. Extensive views over Conwy Valley, Snowdonia National Park, Conwy Castle, town and estuary.

&. ❀ ☕ ☎

❻ BRYN GWERN

Llanfachreth LL40 2DH. H O & P D Nurse, 01341 450255. *3m NE of Dolgellau. Do not go to village of Llanfachreth, stay on A494 Bala-Dolgellau rd: 13m from Bala. Take 1st Llanfachreth turn R. From Dolgellau 4th Llanfachreth turn L, follow signs. No coach parking.* Cream teas. **Adm £3,**

chd free. **Sun 17 May; Sun 2 Aug (10-5). Visitors also welcome by appt.**

Wander through 2 acres of trees and shrubs, incl acers, azaleas, pieris, rhododendrons, gunnera (watch it grow!) and bulbs in spring; hydrangeas, eucryphia, magnolias, embothriums, fuchsias and primulas during summer. Semi-wild cultivated garden, home to cats, dogs, chickens, ducks and wild birds. Eat your cream teas or just sit and become intoxicated with the smells and breathtaking views of Cader Idris. Wheelchair access to main area only.

&. 🐾 ❀ ☕ ☎

❼ NEW BRYN SEIRI

Talwrn, Llangefni LL77 8JD. Mr & Mrs Phillip Tolman, 01248 722911, bhive@btinternet.com. *3m N of Llangefni. From Llangefni take B5110 signed Benllech. 2m R to Talwrn. 1st L. (F)3/4(/F)m very sharp L hand bend. Do not go round bend. Bryn Seiri drive on R. Limited parking. May need to park in lane.* Home-made teas. **Adm £3, chd free. Sun 5 July (11-5). Visitors also welcome by appt May to Sept. June/July for roses. Everyone / small groups welcome. Sorry no coaches. Please phone first.**

A relaxed, colourful 2-acre cottage garden. Incl's generous herbaceous borders, developing sloped woodland garden, pergola, pond (unfenced), gravel garden, sloping lawns, dry stone walls and paths. Many roses and unusual shrubs. Views to Red Wharf Bay, the hills and Snowdonia. Some areas still under development. Mostly grass - not suitable for wheelchairs when wet. Some slopes & steps. Steep in parts.

&. 🐾 ☕

❽ CAE NEWYDD

Rhosgoch, Anglesey LL66 0BG. Hazel & Nigel Bond, 01407 831354, nigel@cae-newydd.co.uk. *3m SW of Amlwch. L immed after Amlwch Town sign on A5025 from Benllech, follow signs for leisure centre & Lastra Farm. After L turn for Lastra Farm, follow rd for approx 3m, pass through Rhosgoch, keep to main rd, follow signs for Llyn Alaw, ¹/₄ m. Garden/car park on L.* Light refreshments & teas. **Adm £3, chd free. Sat, Sun 13, 14 June (11-4). Visitors also welcome by appt Apr to Sept, incl small groups.**

Started 2002 from exposed 2½ -acre S-facing field, overlooking Llyn Alaw with panoramic views of Snowdonia. Come in April to see the spring borders and May onwards for the mixed beds of interesting shrubs, grasses and perennials; large wildlife pond, meadow area with cut paths and buddleias, vegetable garden with polytunnel and chicken run. Paved area near house with raised beds and formal pond. Sheltered mature paddock garden with pond/bog area, formal herb bed and walled former pigsty providing additional shelter. 2½-acre hay meadow best seen in early June.

9 CAERAU UCHAF
Sarnau, Bala LL23 7LG. Mr & Mrs Toby Hickish, 01678 530493, info@summersgardens.co.uk. *3m NE of Bala. From A5 N of Corwen turn L A494 to Bala. Approx 5m turn R into Sarnau, keep R up hill approx 1m. From Bala take A494 NE. After approx 3m turn L into Sarnau, keep R up hill approx 1m. Coaches strictly by appt.* Home-made teas. **Adm £3, chd free. Sun 7 June (2-5). Visitors also welcome by appt Coaches strictly by appointment.**
3-acres of gardens incl herbaceous borders, traditional vegetable garden, wildlife garden, woodland walks (some paths rather steep), fabulous views. Described by one visitor as 'An astounding feat at 1,000 feet above sea level'. Regular exhibitors and medal winners at RHS Flower Show, Tatton Park. Gravel paths, steep slopes but main gardens accessible.

10 CORON
Llanbedrog LL53 7NN. Mr & Mrs B M Jones, 01758 740296. *3m SW of Pwllheli. Turn R off A499 opp Llanbedrog Village sign, before garage, up private drive.* Cream teas. **Adm £3, chd free. Sun 17 May (11-5.30). Visitors also welcome by appt.**
5-acre mature garden featuring Davidia involucrata, overlooking Cardigan Bay. Pathways leading through extensively planted areas with rhododendrons, embothriom, azaleas, camellias, bluebell walks, wooded slopes and rock outcrops providing shelter for tender plants, lakes and bog gardens; orchards, walled vegetable and formal garden. Craft demonstration - weaving with willow & rushes.

11 CRAIG Y FFYNNON
Ffordd y Gader, Dolgellau LL40 1RU. Jon & Sh,n Lea. *Take Tywyn rd from Dolgellau main sq. Park on rd by Penbryn Garage. Walk up rd signed Cader Idris. Garden entrance on L 50yds from junction.* Home-made teas. **Adm £3, chd free (share to Eisteddfod Genedlaethol Cymru). Sun 14 June (11-5).**
N-facing 2-acre Victorian garden set out in 1870s. Majority of garden planted with mature specimen trees, rhododendrons and azaleas predominate. More formal herbaceous borders and greenhouse enclosed by box hedges. Wildlife pond; unusual shade-loving plants and ferns. Book reading, by local authors, of their new books.

12 CROWRACH ISAF
Bwlchtocyn LL53 7BY. Margaret & Graham Cook. *1½ m SW of Abersoch. Follow rd through Abersoch & Sarn Bach, L at sign for Bwlchtocyn for ½ m until junction and no-through rd - Cim Farm. Turn R, parking 50metres on R.* Cream teas. **Adm £2.50, chd free. Sun 14 June (11-4).**
2-acre plot incl 1 acre fenced against rabbits, developed from 2000. incl island beds, windbreak hedges and wide range of geraniums, shrubs and herbaceous perennials. Views over Cardigan Bay and Snowdonia. Grass and gravel paths, some gentle slopes.

Craft demonstration - weaving with willow & rushes . . .

13 ◆ CRUG FARM
Caernarfon LL55 1TU. Mr & Mrs B Wynn-Jones, 01248 670232, info@crug-farm.co.uk, www.crug-farm.co.uk. *2m NE of Caernarfon. ¼ m off main A487 Caernarfon to Bangor rd. Follow signs from roundabout.* **Adm £3, chd free. Tel or see website for regular opening times. For NGS: Sun 24 May (10-5).**
3 acres; grounds to old country house (not open). Gardens filled with choice,

unusual collections of plants. Collected by the Wynn Jones, winners of the Sir Bryner Jones Memorial Award for their contribution to horticulture.

CYFIE FARM
See Powys.

14 ESGAIRWEDDAN
Pennal SY20 9JZ. Mr & Mrs John & Annie Parry. *4m W of Machynlleth. From Machynlleth take A493 towards Aberdovey. Esgairweddan is on R between Pennal & Cwrt.* Home-made teas. **Adm £2.50, chd free. Sun 21 June (2-5).**
Small garden with 400yr-old farmhouse (not open), ¾ m drive from rd entrance leading through oak woodland with wonderful view of Dovey estuary.

15 FELIN Y FFRIDD
Ffriddgate SY20 8QG. Mr & Mrs J W Osselton, 01654 702548. *1m N of Machynlleth. From S, take A487 from Machynlleth to Dolgellau. After approx 1m turn R at B4404 to Llanwrin. Garden short distance on L before bridge. From N, take A487, turn L on B4404.* Cream teas. **Adm £3, chd free. Sun 24 May (2-5.30). Visitors also welcome by appt.**
Approx 1 acre, bordered by R Dulas. Lower garden has pond, gravel paths and old mill where woodland edge is being developed. Upper garden has grass paths, mixed borders and island beds, where conifers and viburnums contrast with colourful, scented azaleas and rhododendrons. Wide choice of home-grown plants for sale.

16 FOXBRUSH
Felinheli LL56 4JZ. Mr & Mrs B S Osborne, 01248 670463. *3m SW of Bangor. On Bangor to Caernarfon rd, entering village opp Felinheli signpost.* Cream teas. **Adm £2.50, chd free. Weds 13 May, 17 June (2-7). Visitors also welcome by appt March and end of June. Coaches welcome.**
Fascinating country garden created over 40 years around winding river. Rare and interesting plant collections incl rhododendrons, ferns, Hydrangea, clematis and roses cover a 45ft long pergola. Fan-shaped knot garden, 3 bridges and new plantings have replaced those lost in the horrendous devastation caused by floods of 2004.

A hidden gem in the middle of the Dyfi Forest . . .

17 ♦ **GARDD Y COLEG**
Carmel LL54 7RL. Pwyllgor Pentref
Carmel Village Committee, 01286
881843. *Garden at Carmel village
centre. Parking on site.* **Adm £2, chd
free.** For NGS: Sun 19 July (2-5).
Approx 1/2 acre featuring raised beds
planted with ornamental and native
plants mulched with local slate.
Benches and picnic area, wide
pathways suitable for wheelchairs.
Spectacular views. Garden created by
volunteers.
&. ✕

18 **NEW** **GARTHEINIOG**
Aberangell SY20 9QG. Revd
Michael & Mrs Angela Balchin.
*12m N of Machynlleth. Off the
A470. Turn for Aberangell where
the route will be signed.* Cream
teas. **Adm £3, chd free.** Sun
28 June (1-5pm).
A hidden gem in the middle of the
Dyfi Forest. 2-acre garden around
an old farmhouse, incl unusual
varieties of shrubs, flowers and
trees - giving yr round interest. Two
valleys with streams, ponds and
hillside plantings with wandering
grassy paths. Terraced cottage
garden with perennials and old
roses. Wildlife lake and riverside
walk in adjacent farmland.
❀ ✿ ☕

19 **GILFACH**
Rowen LL32 8TS. James & Isoline
Greenhalgh, 01492 650216. *4m S of
Conwy. At Xrds 100yds E of Rowen S
towards Llanrwst, past Rowen School
on L; turn up 2nd drive on L.* Teas.
Adm £2, chd free. Suns 10 May;
14 June; 16 Aug (2-5.30). **Visitors
also welcome by appt.**
1-acre country garden on S-facing
slope with magnificent views of the R

Conwy and mountains; set in 35 acres
of farm and woodland. Collection of
mature shrubs is added to yearly;
woodland garden, herbaceous border,
small scree bed and pool.
&. ✕ ✿ ☕ ☎

GRANDMA'S GARDEN
See Powys.

20 **NEW** **GWAELOD MAWR**
Caergeiliog, Anglesey LL65 3YL.
John & Tricia Coates, 01407
740080. *6m W of Holyhead.
1/2 m W of Caergeiliog. From A55
J4. R'about 2nd exit signed
Caergeiliog. 300yds, Gwaelod
Mawr is first house on L.* Home-
made teas. **Adm £3, chd free.**
Suns 24 May; 12 July (11-5).
**Visitors also welcome by appt
May, June, July only.**
2 1/2 -acre county garden. Lake
with island and random planting.
Laburnam arch leading to sunken
Monet-style garden with lily pond.
Large rock outcrop with palm
trees. Spanish style patio.
Japanese Koi carp pond and
Chinese themed garden. Large
variety of plants, shrubs and trees
throughout with individual seating
areas. Gravel paths.
&. ❀

21 **GWYNDY**
Y Fron LL54 7RE. David & Mary
Lloyd-Evans. *6m S of Caernarfon. At
Groeslon roundabout, approx 6m S of
Caernarfon on A487. Follow signs for
Groeslon, Carmel & Fron. After 2m at
30mph sign in Fron, turn L then immed
R up track for 1/4 m. Parking at
beginning of track or next to garden at
top of track.* Light refreshments. **Adm
£2.50, chd free.** Sun 2 Aug (11-5).
Exposed 1 1/2 -acre hillside garden
(altitude 1000ft). Mainly shrubs, small
trees, perennials, lawns and small
vegetable garden. Totally organic with
wildlife in mind. Glorious panoramic
views of the Nantlle Ridge and
surrounding area. Wheelchair access
dependent on several previous days of
dry weather as main access to garden
via grass. Gently sloping.
&. ✕ ❀ ☕

22 **GWYNDY BACH**
Llandrygarn LL65 3AJ. Keith & Rosa
Andrew, 01407 720651,
info@keithandrew-art.com. *5m W of
Llangefni. From Llangefni take B5109
towards Bodedern, cottage exactly 5m

out on the L.* **Adm £2.50, chd free.**
Visitors welcome by appt Apr to
Sept, coaches permitted.
3/4 -acre artist's garden, set amidst
rugged Anglesey landscape.
Romantically planted in intimate rooms
with interesting rare plants and shrubs,
box and yew topiary, old roses and
Japanese garden with large koi pond.
National Collection of Rhapis miniature
Japanese palms. Studio attached.
✕ **NCCPG** ☎

23 **NEW** **GYFFYLOG**
Ffordd Gyffylog, Eglwysbach,
Colwyn Bay LL28 5SD. Chris &
Carol Potten. *2m from Bodnant
Gardens. 1 1/2 m from Eglwysbach.
From A55 take A470 signed
Bodnant Gardens, passing
Bodnant Gardens on R towards
Eglwysbach. Before village pass
cream chapel on L. L at Ffordd
Gyffylog for 1m. At green railings
turn R, park in field at end of lane.*
Home-made teas. **Adm £3.50,
chd free.** Mons 4 May; 31 Aug
(11-5).
Set in 2-acres of woodland with
stunning views of the Snowdonia
foothills. Entrance is a Welsh slate
patio with water feature and knot
garden. Mature herbaceous flower
beds extend around the house.
Orchard, vegetable garden and
chickens. Footpath to waterfall.
Wildlife, photographic
opportunities, nature walks.
Eglwysbach Show Winner.
&. ❀ ☕

24 ♦ **HOTEL MAES-Y-NEUADD**
Talsarnau, nr Harlech LL47 6YA. Mr
& Mrs P Jackson & Mr & Mrs P
Payne, 01766 780200,
lynn@neuadd.com. *3m NE of
Harlech. Take B4573 old Harlech rd at
T-junction with A496. Hotel signed
1/4 m on L. Take small lane on L immed
after sign, just before small bridge on
bend. Hotel entrance & car park
1/2 m up hill, through small hamlet (tel
box on L). Follow brown signs.* **Adm
£3, chd under 12 free, concessions
£2.50.** Open daily except Christmas
and New Year (10-5). For NGS: Tue
16 June; Thur 20 Aug (10-5).
Gardens and grounds of country
house hotel, parts of which C14. Views
towards Snowdon, Cardigan Bay and
Lleyn Peninsula. 80 acres, meadows,
woodland walks, 2 working walled
gardens, unusual cultivars, cut flower
borders; innovative, intensive, organic

gardening methods with aesthetic appeal. Fruit and vegetables for sale. Suitable for assisted wheelchair users only. Slate & gravel paths to all vegetable gardens, gravel drive.

 ♿ 🐾 ◎ 🛌 ☕

25 LLANIDAN HALL

Brynsiencyn LL61 6HJ. Mr J W Beverley, 07759 305085, beverley.family@btinternet.com. *5m E of Llanfair Pwll. From Llanfair PG (Anglesey) follow A4080 towards Brynsiencyn for 4m. Turn at/opp Groeslon PH. Continue for 1m, garden entrance on R.* Teas. **Adm £2.50, chd free (share to CAFOD). Sats 20 June; 4 July (10-4). Visitors also welcome by appt.**
Walled garden of 1¾ acres. Physic and herb gardens, ornamental vegetable garden, herbaceous borders, water features and many varieties of old roses. Sheep, ponies, rabbits and hens to see. Children must be kept under supervision. Llanidan Church will be open for viewing. Gravel paths.

♿ 🐾 ◎ ☕ ☎

26 LLYN RHAEADR

Parc Bron-y-Graig, Centre of Harlech LL46 2SR. Mr D R Hewitt & Miss J Sharp, 01766 780224. *From A496 take B4573 into Harlech, take turning to main car parks S of town, L past overspill car park, garden 75yds on R.* **Adm £2.50, chd free (share to WWF). Sat 11 to Wed 15 Apr; Sun 3 May; Sun 9 to Fri 14 Aug; (2-5). Visitors also welcome by appt all year. Apr to June only, maximum 15 people per group.**
Small lake with 20 species of waterfowl with ducklings in spring and summer. Fish pond, waterfalls, woodland, rockeries, lawns, borders, snowdrops, daffodils, heathers, bluebells, ferns, camellias, azaleas, rhododendrons, wild flowers, views of Tremadog Bay, Lleyn Peninsula. Car park, toilets and refreshments all within 200yds in Harlech.

🐾 ☎

27 LLYS ARTHUR

Llanuwchllyn, nr Bala LL23 7UG. Mr & Mrs E Morgan, 01678 540233, tedanded@hotmail.co.uk. *On A494, on Dolgellau side of Llanuwchllyn, opp Penial Chapel, over bridge, 1st house on L.* **Visitors welcome by appt June to Sept, coaches and groups welcome.**
Nestled in foothills of Aran range, approx 1 acre of garden with

herbaceous borders, grassy paths, ponds, hidden statues, secret corners and vegetable garden. Lots of seating areas and many different plants making an interesting place for visitors morning, afternoon or evening. Chicken pen with 10 chickens incl 4 battery rescue.

🐾 ◎ ☎

An old mill with mill race intact - an oasis . . .

28 LLYS-Y-GWYNT

Pentir Road, Llandygai LL57 4BG. Jennifer Rickards & John Evans, 01248 353863. *3m S of Bangor. 300yds from Llandygai roundabout at J11 of A5 & A55, just off A4244. From A5 & A55 follow signs for services (Gwasanaethau) and find 'No Through Road' sign 50yds beyond. Turn R then L. (Sat Nav does not find us).* Home-made teas. **Adm £2.50, chd free. Suns 17 May; 28 June (11-4). Visitors also welcome by appt, coaches welcome.**
Rambling 2-acre garden in harmony with and incl magnificent views of Snowdonia. Incorporating large Bronze Age cairn. Designed to wander, with paths to provide shelter and interest. The exposed site planted for wind tolerance, yr-round colour and wildlife. Pond, waterfall and N-facing rockery. Good family garden.

♿ 🐾 ◎ ☕ ☎

29 MAENAN HALL

Maenan, Llanrwst LL26 0UL. The Hon Mr & Mrs Christopher Mclaren. *2m N of Llanrwst. On E side of A470, ¼ m S of Maenan Abbey Hotel.* Home-made teas. **Adm £3, chd £2. Sun 26 Apr (10.30-5.30).**
About 4 hectares of ground, some steeply sloping, with mature hardwoods; upper part has many ornamental trees, shrubs and roses, walled garden, borders and lawns, all with lovely views over Conwy valley and Snowdonia foothills. Rhododendrons, camellias, magnolias, pieris, hydrangeas and bluebells predominate in woodland dell. Many of the original plants are from Bodnant. Gravel paths and many slopes.

♿ ◎ ☕

30 MEGANS WOOD GWERNOER FARM

Nantlle LL54 6BB. Mrs Black, 01286 880913. *2m E of Penygroes. Halfway between Talysarn & Nantlle. On B4418 Penygroes to Rhyd-Ddu rd, past big house on L, 1st house on R up towards waterfall and park in field immed on L.* Light refreshments & teas. **Adm £3, chd free. Sat, Sun 2, 3 May (11-4). Visitors also welcome by appt in May.**
3-acre woodland garden set on steep hillside. Panoramic views of the Nantlle valley and Snowdon. Woodland underplanted with over 1000 rhododendrons, azaleas and camellias. Ornamental pond and waterfall on site of mines. 2 new gardens created in 2007. The first a memorial to Megan's husband, Reg, who had the vision to see the potential for turning a waste copper mine site into the garden we see today. The second a kitchen garden with greenhouse, fruit trees and shrubs.

🐾 ◎ ☕ ☎

31 NEW MELIN MELOCH

Llanderfel, Bala LL23 7DP. Richard & Beryl Fullard. *2m N of Bala. Main Bala Road A494. Turn to Llanderfel B4401. 1st house on L.* Cream teas. **Adm £3, chd free. Sat 13, Suns 14 June; 9 Aug (10-5).**
An old mill with mill race intact - an oasis. You will be amazed at the riot of colour and interesting planting arrangements around 3 ponds. Sit and become intoxicated with the smells and sights. River walk through field where bird watching is a must.

♿ 🐾 ◎ 🛌 ☕

14 THE MILL HOUSE

See Ceredigion/Cardiganshire.

32 PEN Y BRYN

Glandwr LL42 1TG. Phil & Jenny Martin. *2m E of Barmouth. On A496 7m W of Dolgellau, situated on N side of Mawddach Estuary. Park in or nr layby and walk L up narrow lane.* Cream teas. **Adm £3, chd £1.50 (share to Gwynedd Hospice at Home). Sun 3 May (11-5).**
A glorious hillside garden with panoramic views of The Mawddoch Estuary. Woodland walks awash with Bluebells in the spring. Lawns on different levels with vibrant

rhododendrons and azaleas, arches of clematis, honeysuckle and roses. Heather filled natural rocks, unusual conifer feature, a rock cannon and a pond for wildlife.

✈ ⊛ ☕

33 ◆ PENRHYN CASTLE
Bangor LL57 4HN. The National Trust, 01248 353084, www.nationaltrust.org.uk. *3m E of Bangor. On A5122. Buses from Llandudno, Caernarfon, Betws-y-Coed; alight: Grand Lodge Gate. J11 A55, signed from thereon.* Adm £1.50, chd free. Open daily (not Tues). Check website for times. For NGS: Sun 8 Feb (11-4); Sat 13 Feb 2010.
Large grounds incl Victorian walled garden; fine trees, shrubs, wild garden, good views. Snowdrop days. Partial wheelchair access, some uneven gravel/grass paths, some steps, bark chippings.

♿ ✈ ⊛ ☕

34 ◆ PENSYCHNANT
Sychnant Pass, nr Conwy LL32 8BJ. Pensychnant Foundation Wardens Julian Thompson & Anne Mynott, 01492 592595, julian.pensychnant@btinternet.com. *2¹/₂ m W of Conwy. At top of Sychnant Pass between Conwy & Penmaenmawr. From Conwy turn L into Upper Gate St by Heddlu/Police; after 2¹/₂ m Pensychnant's drive signed on R. From Penmaenmawr, fork R by Mountain View PH; summit of Sychnant Pass after walls, Pensychnant's drive on L.* Adm £2, chd 50p. House, exhibition and nature reserve open Wed to Sun, 1 Apr to 30 Sept (11-5). For NGS: Suns 14 June; 12 July (11-5).
Diverse herbaceous borders surrounded by mature shrubs, banks of rhododendrons, ancient and Victorian woodlands. 12 acre woodland walks with views of Conwy Mountain and Sychnant. Woodland birds. Picnic tables, archaeological trail on mountain. A peaceful little gem. Large Victorian gothic house (open) with art exhibition. Partial wheelchair access, please phone for advice.

♿ ✈ ⊛ ☕

2-acre wildlife garden with streams . . .

35 NEW PLAS MAWR
Groeslon, Caernarfon LL54 7UF. Mrs Pam Marchant & Mrs Tracey Jones, 01286 830628. *Off A487 Cearnarfon - Porthmadog road. From Cearnarfon take 3rd exit at Groeslon r'about. Property is approached accross cattle grid immed to the R.* Home-made teas. Adm £2.50, chd free (share to Wales Air Ambulance). Suns 24 May; 5 July (1-5). Visitors also welcome by appt May to Aug. Groups of 4+.
2-acre wildlife garden with streams, ponds and woodland walks. Cultivated areas incl herbaceous borders, rockeries, vegetable garden, polytunnel and greenhouse. Plenty to delight children with dens and places to explore. Wellies advisable and adult supervision essential.

✈ ⊛ ☕ ☎

36 ◆ PLAS NEWYDD COUNTRY HOUSE & GARDENS
Anglesey LL61 6DQ. The National Trust, 01248 714795, www.nationaltrust.org.uk. *2m S of Llanfairpwll. A55 junctions 7 & 8 on A4080.* House and Garden Adm £7.50, chd £3.75, Garden only adm £5.50, chd £2.75. Sats to Weds, 28 Mar to 4 Nov (11-5.30, house 12-5). For NGS: Sat 18 July (11-5).
Plas Newydd is a beautiful C18 country house with spectacular panoramic views across the Menai Strait to Snowdonia. Set in beautiful gardens, there are tranquil walks, an Australasian arboretum and a pretty Italianate Terrance Garden. The house is also famous for its association with the 1st Marquess of Anglesey. A new exhibition room features changing displays of work by local artists. Some slopes & gravel paths.

♿ ✈ ☕

37 ◆ RHYD
Trefor, Anglesey LL65 4TA. Ann & Jeff Hubble, 01407 720320, jeffh43@btinternet.com. *7m W of Llangefni. Nr Holyhead. From Bodedern 2¹/₄ m along B5109 towards Llangefni, turn L.* Home-made teas. Adm £2.50, chd free. Suns 24 May; 2 Aug (11-5). Visitors also welcome by appt coaches permitted.
5 acres of gardens, arboretum, meadows and nature reserve. Herbaceous beds, pergolas, ponds, stream, rockery, garden room, decking and fernery. Many species of roses,

climbing and standard. Clematis and rhododendron. Wide variety of herbaceous plants especially hosta and primula. Many places to sit and ponder or watch the wildlife.

♿ ✈ ⊛ ☕ ☎

38 ◆ ST JOHN THE BAPTIST & ST GEORGE
Lon Batus, Carmel LL54 7AR. Bishop Abbot Demetrius. *7m SE of Caernarfon. On A487 Porthmadog Rd, at Dinas roundabout exit 1st L to Groeslon, turn L at PO for 1¹/₂ m. At village centre turn L & L again at Xrds.* Home-made teas. Adm £1, chd free. Sat 25 July (2-5).
Holy community in the making under the authority of The Orthodox Catholic and Holy Synod of Malan. This is not a garden in the traditional sense but a spiritual retreat from the stresses and strains of modern life, surrounded on all sides by space and rural tranquillity. We are privileged to share a glimpse of a more contemplative life.

✈ ☕

39 ◆ TAN DINAS
Llanfairpwll, Anglesey LL61 5YL. Charles Ellis, 01248 714373, charles.ellis@tesco.net. *2m W of Menai Bridge. On main rd between Llanfairpwll & Britannia Bridge, 250yds from the Marquess of Anglesey's column. Parking in Column car park, access via path through Column woods. Visitors cars can unload but not park at garden.* Adm £2, chd free. Visitors welcome by appt.
An interesting 1¹/₂ -acre cottage garden. Overlooked by the Marquess of Anglesey's Column, 200yds from the Menai Straits. Carefully designed and planted on 3 levels; shrubbery, large pond garden and heather garden. Careful planting ensures all-yr colour. Many interesting trees and shrubs are now reaching maturity.

✈ ⊛ ☎

40 ◆ TREFFOS SCHOOL
Llansadwrn, Anglesey LL59 5SL. Dr & Mrs Humphreys. *2¹/₂ m N of Menai Bridge. A5025 Amlwch/Benllech exit from the Britannia Bridge onto Anglesey. Approx 3m turn R towards Llansadwrn. Entrance to Treffos School is 200yds on LH-side.* Cream teas. Adm £2.50, chd free. Sun 21 June (1-4).
7 acres, child-friendly garden, in rural location, surrounding C17 house now run as school. Garden consists of mature woodland, underplanted with

spring flowering bulbs and rhododendrons, ancient beech avenue leading down to rockery, herbaceous borders and courtyards. Garden trails & art /craft activities for children.

♿ 🐕 ✿ ☕

TY CAPEL DEILDRE
See Powys.

41 TY CAPEL FFRWD
Llanfachreth LL40 2NR. Revs Mary & George Bolt, 01341 422006. *4m NE of Dolgellau, 18m SW of Bala. From A470 nr Dolgellau take A497 towards Bala. Turn L after 200yds signed Dolgellau. 1st R signed Llanfachreth, 4m. Uphill to village, L at T-junction, past war memorial on L, 1/2 m. Park nr chapel, walk 30yds downhill to garden. No parking beside cottage. From S via Trawsfynydd, go through Ganllwyd, 1st L signpost Llanfachreth. Follow NGS signs.* Cream teas. **Adm £3, chd free.**
Suns 31 May; 5 July (1-5).
1-acre cottage garden, started from nothing, still being created. A stream, the ffrwd, runs through garden, flowers and azaleas fill the bank with colour in spring. Wide collection of plants, many unusual. Trees blend into surrounding countryside. Mature roses incl climbers. Hostas, lilies and meconopsis blend together in small bluebell wood. Fuchsias and lilies fill large pots on patio where home-made teas can be enjoyed beside stream. A wild primrose, blue bell 'way marked' walk from garden. Some steep paths.

✿ ☕

Sculpture of a 40ft sleeping giant . . .

42 NEW TY GWYN
Llanbedrgoch LL76 8NX. Keith & Anna Griffiths. *2m inland W of Red Wharfe Bay. A5025 from Menai Bridge through Pentraeth. Turn L to Llanbedrgoch. L at staggered Xrds in village on road to Talwrn. After 1m turn R up unmade road of concrete strips. Garden 1m on L at bottom of small dip.* Home-made teas. **Adm £3, chd free.**
Sun 7 June (11-5).
Wildish 9-acres incl wild flower meadow, limestone pavement and hazel copses together with landscaped formal lawns and gardens separated into a number of 'green rooms' of different interest incl gazebo and fish pond, small walled garden, topiary yews and box hedging. Adjacent to several SSSI's, incl Cors Goch, an International Wetlands Nature Reserve.

🐕 ☕

43 TY NEWYDD
Dyffryn Ardudwy LL44 2DB. Guy & Margaret Lloyd, 01341 247357, guylloyd@btinternet.com. *51/2 m N of Barmouth, 41/2 m S of Harlech. A496 Barmouth to Harlech rd, 1/2 m N of Dyffryn Ardudwy, area sometimes referred to as Coed Ystumgwern. At bus shelter and phone box turn down lane towards sea, driveway 30yds on L.* Home-made teas. **Adm £2.50, chd free. Visitors welcome by appt** April to Sept inclusive. Individuals or groups.
31/2 acres of maritime garden and pasture, diversely planted with trees and shrubs for yr-round interest. Some areas still being developed. Extensive vegetable and fruit areas. Greenhouse and polytunnel for overwintering tender subjects, propagation, spring/summer bedding and summer salads. Interesting plant sales area.

🐕 ✿ ☕ ☎

44 TYN Y CEFN
Llanuwchllyn LL23 7UH. Trevor and Diane Beech, 01678 540551. *6m W of Bala. From Bala take A494 towards Dolgellau. Small lane on L approx 21/2 m after Llanuwchllyn. From Dolgellau take A494 towards Bala. Small lane on R approx 4m after turn to Drws y Nant. Light refreshments & teas.* **Adm £2.50, chd free. Sun 2 Aug (12-5). Visitors also welcome by appt July & Aug, no coaches.**
1-acre very exposed sloping meadow garden at foot of the Aran with panoramic views. Features sheltered, enclosed garden for tender plants and trees. Wildlife area incl 2 ponds and developing woodland area to attract birds. Mature shrub beds and feature trees incl majestic eucalyptus. Display of garden sculptures created by the owners. Featured in 'Amateur Gardening' magazine. Steep slopes and unfenced ponds.

✿ ☕ ☎

45 TYN-TWLL
LL40 2DP. Sue & Pete Nicholls, 01341 450673, sue-nicholls@hotmail.com. *11/2 m NE of Llanfachreth. From Dolgellau on Bala rd (A494), 1st L to Llanfachreth opp Brithdir sign. Continue up hill, 1st R then 1st L and follow signs to Tyn Twll.* Cream teas and light refreshments. **Adm £2.50, chd free.**
Sun 26 July (10-5).
Created by 2 artists, Tyn Twll is set in 21/2 acres of ancient woodland with imaginative architectural features using local materials. Traditional planting, rockeries, walled fruit and vegetable garden, short woodland walk and pond area in sheltered setting, providing a haven for wildlife. Recent addition sculpture of a 40ft sleeping giant - inspired by Welsh legends. Some uneven ground and sloping slate paths.

♿ ✿ ☕ ☎

POWYS

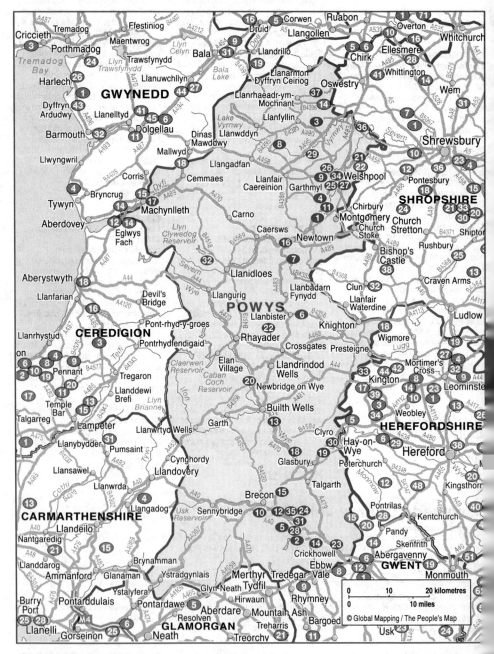

Opening Dates

April

SUNDAY 5
21 Maesfron Hall and Gardens

SUNDAY 12
27 Rowan

MONDAY 13
33 The Walled Garden

SUNDAY 26
1 Abernant

May

SATURDAY 2
29 Tan-y-Llyn

SUNDAY 3
29 Tan-y-Llyn

MONDAY 4
20 Llysdinam

SUNDAY 10
13 Glanwye
14 Gliffaes Country House Hotel

SATURDAY 16
9 Dingle Nurseries & Garden
11 Glansevern Hall Gardens

SUNDAY 17
3 Bodynfoel Hall
9 Dingle Nurseries & Garden
18 Llanstephan House

SUNDAY 24
27 Rowan

MONDAY 25
8 Cyfie Farm

WEDNESDAY 27
17 Grandma's Garden

June

SATURDAY 6
29 Tan-y-Llyn
34 Welshpools Secret Gardens

SUNDAY 7
10 Ffrwdgrech House
11 Glansevern Hall Gardens
29 Tan-y-Llyn
33 The Walled Garden
34 Welshpools Secret Gardens

SUNDAY 14
23 The Neuadd

SUNDAY 21
6 Cwmllechwedd Fawr
1 Treberfydd
32 Ty Capel Deildre

SUNDAY 28
1 Abernant
2 Glanusk

July

SATURDAY 4
7 Cwm-Weeg
29 Tan-y-Llyn

SUNDAY 5
15 Glyn Celyn House
29 Tan-y-Llyn

SUNDAY 12
19 Llowes Gardens
28 Talybont Gardens

SATURDAY 18
25 Powis Castle Garden

August

SATURDAY 8
34 Welshpools Secret Gardens

SUNDAY 9
20 Llysdinam
34 Welshpools Secret Gardens

September

SUNDAY 13
21 Maesfron Hall and Gardens

SATURDAY 19
11 Glansevern Hall Gardens

October

SATURDAY 17
9 Dingle Nurseries & Garden

SUNDAY 18
9 Dingle Nurseries & Garden

Gardens open to the public

2 Ashford House
7 Cwm-Weeg
9 Dingle Nurseries & Garden
11 Glansevern Hall Gardens
17 Grandma's Garden
25 Powis Castle Garden

By appointment only

4 Cil y Wennol
5 Coity Mawr
16 Glynderyn
22 Mill Cottage
24 The Old Vicarage
26 Rose Cottage
30 Tawryn
35 The Wern
36 Westlake Fisheries & Camping
37 Woodhill

Also open by appointment ☎

1 Abernant
3 Bodynfoel Hall

8 Cyfie Farm
20 Llysdinam
21 Maesfron Hall and Gardens
27 Rowan
29 Tan-y-Llyn
32 Ty Capel Deildre
33 The Walled Garden
34 Welshpools Secret Gardens

The Gardens

1 ABERNANT
Garthmyl SY15 6RZ. J A & B M
Gleave, 01686 640494,
johngleave@virgin.com. *Mid-way
between Welshpool (9m) & Newtown
(9m) on A483. 1½ m S of Garthmyl.
Approached over steep humpback
bridge, then straight ahead through
gate. No parking for coaches.* Home-
made teas. **Adm £3, chd free. Suns
26 Apr; 28 June (12-5.30). Visitors
also welcome by appt Apr to July.
Groups welcome.**
Approx 3 acres incl cherry orchard,
roses, knot garden, lavender, box
hedging, rockery, pond, shrubs,
ornamental trees, potager, raised
specimen fern beds in natural setting.
Examples of archaic sundials, fossilised
wood and stone heads. Additional
woodland of 9-acres, pond and stream
with borrowed views of the Severn
Valley.
✗ ☙ ⊛ ☕ ☎

Archaic
sundials,
fossilised
wood and
stone heads . . .

2 ◆ **ASHFORD HOUSE**
Talybont-on-Usk LD3 7YR. Mrs E
Anderson, 01874 676271. $6^1/_2$ m SE
of Brecon. Off A40 on B4558. 1m SE
of Talybont-on-Usk. Adm £2.50, chd
free. Every Tues, Apr to Sept (2-6).
1-acre walled garden surrounded by
woodland and wild garden approx
4 acres altogether. Mixed shrub and
herbaceous borders; meadow garden
and pond; alpine house and beds;
vegetables. A relaxed plantsman's
garden. Weekly openings mean visitors
may enjoy a peaceful garden in its
everyday state.
&. ⊛

3 **BODYNFOEL HALL**
Llanfechain SY22 6XD. Trustees of
Bodynfoel Estate, 01691 648486,
bonn@talktalk.net. 10m N of
Welshpool via A490 towards Llanfyllin.
Take B4393, follow signs. Home-made
teas. Adm £3.50, chd free,
concessions £2. Sun 17 May (2-6).
Visitors also welcome by appt
June/July only.
Approx 5 acres of garden, woodland
and ponds. Wide variety of trees,
shrubs, rhododendrons and azaleas
with woodland walks. Pondside
planting links the 3 ponds. Mixed
borders and paths surround the house,
with lawns and ha-ha offering far-
reaching views into Shropshire. North
Powys Youth Music Trust will be
playing during the afternoon. One
steep area unsuitable for wheelchairs.
&. ⊛ ☕ ☎

4 **CIL Y WENNOL**
Berriew, Welshpool SY21 8AZ. Willie
& Sue Jack, 01686 640757,
williejack@btinternet.com. 5m SW of
Welshpool. Berriew is off the A483
Welshpool to Newtown rd. By Berriew
School take B4385 towards Castle
Caereinion. Cil y Wennol is $^3/_4$ m along
the B4385. Cream teas. Adm £5 (incl
tea & cake), chd free (share to
Rekindle Home). Visitors welcome
by appt June to Aug. Groups of
10-20 only.
$3^1/_2$ -acre established garden set
around Tudor cottage (not open). Long
curving drive, through terraced
landforms leads to front garden of
traditional formal cottage design with
more recent influences. Rear gardens:
sweeping array of new-style prairie
planting, spectacular views, enclosed
vegetable garden, croquet lawn.
Crescent-shaped hedges, slate walls,
amphitheatre steps and congruent
sculptures. Some steep steps.
🐕 ⊛ ☕ ☎

5 **COITY MAWR**
Talybont-on-Usk LD3 7YN. Mr & Mrs
William Forwood, 01874 676664. 6m
SE of Brecon. Leave Talybont village
on B4558 towards Brecon. Approx
$^1/_2$ m at pink cottages take L signed
Talybont reservoir, then 1st R up to rd
junction; turn L to Coity Mawr at top on
R. Adm £3, chd free. Visitors
welcome by appt Spring to Autumn,
please telephone first.
$4^1/_2$ acres at 850ft created over 15yrs;
work still in progress incl Cornus
Wood. Terraced with spectacular view
of Black Mountains across Usk valley.
Mature trees, unusual plants and
shrubs; rose and water gardens;
parterre; willow arbour.
&. 🐕 ⊛ ☎

Sweeping
array of new-
style prairie
planting . . .

6 **CWMLLECHWEDD FAWR**
Llanbister LD1 6UH. John
Underwood. 12m N of Llandrindod
Wells. Leave A483 at Llanbister on
B4356 to Knighton. After 2m bottom
of hill at bridge immed turn sharp L,
following hedge on R for $^1/_3$ m. Or leave
A488 at Monaughty on B4356 to
Llanbister. After 7m take R fork before
bridge. Home-made teas. Adm £3,
chd free. Sun 21 June (2-5).
2-acre garden at 1100ft in 4 distinct
parts. At front of house layout is a
horseshoe with interesting mixed
planting, leading to orchard and highly
productive vegetable garden.
Woodland garden planted around
steep dingle which runs to large oval
pool.
🐕 ⊨ ☕

7 ◆ **CWM-WEEG**
Dolfor, Newtown SY16 4AT.
Dr W Schaefer & Mr K D George,
01686 628992,
wolfgang.schaefer@virgin.net. $4^1/_2$ m
SE of Newtown. Take A489 E from

Newtown for $1^1/_2$ m, turn R towards
Dolfor. After 2m turn L down farm
track. Light refreshments & teas. Adm
£3, chd free. Suns 17 May - 13 Sept
(11-5). For NGS: Evening Opening
Sat 4 July (7-10). Visitors also
welcome by appt.
$2^1/_2$ -acre garden set within 22 acres of
wild flower meadows and bluebell
woodland with stream centred around
C15 farmhouse (open by prior
arrangement). Formal garden in English
landscape tradition with vistas, grottos,
lawns and extensive borders terraced
with stone walls, translates older
garden vocabulary into an innovative
C21 concept. Featured on 'I Own
Britains Best Home & Garden'.
🐕 ☕

8 **CYFIE FARM**
Llanfihangel, Llanfyllin SY22 5JE.
Group Captain Neil & Mrs Claire
Bale, 01691 648451,
info@cyfiefarm.co.uk. 6m SE of Lake
Vyrnwy. B4393 from Llanfyllin. After
approx 4m, L signed
Llanfihangel/Dolanog B4382. After
leaving Llanfihangel towards Dolanog,
1st L. 3rd farm on L. Home-made
teas. Adm £3.50, chd free. Mon
25 May (2-5). Visitors also welcome
by appt.
1-acre hillside country garden with
spectacular views of Vyrnwy Valley and
Welsh Hills. Terraced formal areas with
roses, mature shrubs, herbaceous
borders. Walks through garden on
different levels, leading to informal
areas with mature trees,
rhododendrons, azaleas, heathers.
Stepped path to lower summerhouse
where wild garden, bluebell bank views
and peaceful location enjoyed.
🐕 ⊛ ⊨ ☕ ☎

9 ◆ **DINGLE NURSERIES &
GARDEN**
Welshpool SY21 9JD. Mr & Mrs D
Hamer, 01938 555145,
info@dinglenurseryandgarden.co.uk.
2m NW of Welshpool. Take A490
towards Llanfyllin and Guilsfield. After
1m turn L at sign for Dingle Nurseries
Garden. Adm £3, chd free. Open all
yr (9-5). For NGS: Sats, Suns 16,
17 May; 17,18 Oct (9-5).
4-acre garden on S-facing site, sloping
down to lake. Beds mostly colour
themed with a huge variety of rare and
unusual trees and shrubs. Set in hills of
mid Wales this beautiful and well
known garden attracts visitors from
Britain and abroad.
⊛ ☕

⑩ FFRWDGRECH HOUSE

Brecon LD3 8LB. Mr & Mrs Michael Evans. ½ m W of Brecon. Enter Brecon from A40 bypass. Take 3rd turning on R, Ffrwdgrech Road. In ¾ m at oak gate, Lodge on L. Home-made teas. **Adm £3, chd free. Sun 7 June to (2-5).**
7-acre Victorian pleasure garden, lake, specimen trees incl fine examples of ginko, swamp cyprus, davidia involucrata, sub tropical shrubs, rhododhendrons and azaleas. Beautiful stream and waterfall, woodland walks. Views of Brecon Beacons.

Formal garden with box balls, borders, rose pergola and beech hedge . . . the garden is harmonised by the R Usk . . .

⑪ ◆ GLANSEVERN HALL GARDENS

Berriew SY21 8AH. G & M Thomas, 01686 640644, glansevern@yahoo.co.uk. 5m SW of Welshpool. On A483 at Berriew. Signposted. **Adm £5, chd free, concess £4. Fris, Sats & Bank Hol Mons 7 May to 26 Sept (12-5). For NGS: Sats 16 May, 19 Sept (12-5); Sun 7 June NGS Plant Fair (11-5).**
20-acre mature garden situated nr banks of R Severn. Centred on Glansevern Hall, a Greek Revival house dated 1801 (not open). Noted for variety of unusual tree species; much new planting; lake with island; woodland walk; large rock garden and grotto. Roses and herbaceous beds. Water garden and large walled garden, with fruit, vegetable and ornamental planting. Interesting shelters and follies. Walk down to R Severn through Folly garden. Majority accessible to wheelchair users.

⑫ GLANUSK

Llanfrynach, Brecon LD3 7UY. Mike & Lorraine Lewis. 1½ m SE of Brecon. Leave A40 signed Llanfrynach, Pencelli. Cross narrow bridge (R Usk), 40 metres on R. Home-made teas. **Adm £3, chd free. Sun 28 June (2-6).**
2-acre garden ranging from an orchard surrounded by specimen trees and roses to a bank with waves of prairie grasses, perennials and a formal garden with box balls, borders, rose pergola and beech hedge. The garden is harmonised by the R Usk, the criss-crossing of numerous paths and an ancient yew.

⑬ GLANWYE

Builth Wells LD2 3YP. Mr & Mrs H Kidston. 2m SE Builth Wells. From Builth Wells on A470, after 2m R at Lodge Gate. From Llyswen on A470, after 6m L at Lodge Gate. Home-made teas. **Adm £3, chd free. Sun 10 May (2-5).**
Large Edwardian garden, spectacular rhododendrons, azaleas. Herbaceous borders, extensive yew hedges, lawns, long woodland walk with bluebells and other woodland flowers. Magnificent views of upper Wye Valley.

⑭ GLIFFAES COUNTRY HOUSE HOTEL

Crickhowell NP8 1RH. Mr & Mrs N Brabner & Mr & Mrs J C Suter. 2½ m NW of Crickhowell. 1m off A40. Home-made teas. **Adm £3, chd free. Sun 10 May (2-5).**
Large garden; spring bulbs, azaleas and rhododendrons; ornamental pond; heathers, shrubs and ornamental trees; fine maples; superb position high above R Usk.

⑮ GLYN CELYN HOUSE

Felinfach, nr Brecon LD3 0TY. Mr & Mrs N Paravicini. 4m NE of Brecon. On A470 east of Brecon on hill above Felinfach. Home-made teas. **Adm £3, chd free. Sun 5 July (2-5).**
7-acre sloping garden still in the making after 14yrs. 2 streams supply water to fountains and lake. Mixed planting within yew and hornbeam hedges. Woodland walks lead to lake and unusual grotto. Well-established and newly planted trees. Pretty kitchen garden with raised beds and rose and sweet pea covered arches. Glorious views over the Black Mountains.

⑯ NEW GLYNDERYN

Milford Road, Newtown SY16 3HD. Janet & Frank Podmore, 01686 626745. ½ m W of Newtown. B4568 Newtown - Aberhafesp Rd. 1st gate passed Dolerw Park Drive on L. Home-made teas. **Adm £4 (incls homemade tea), chd free. Visitors welcome by appt all yr. Coach drop off only.**
Much loved secluded garden in decline, being lovingly restored by plant enthusiast. ¼ -acre garden with long curved pergola for wisteria and clematis, raised alpine, herbaceous and rose beds. Small pond, trees, shrubs, camellias, azaleas, rhododendrons and bulbs begin colourful yr-round interest garden. Small fruit and vegetable area.

⑰ ◆ GRANDMA'S GARDEN

Plas Dolguog Estates, Machynlleth SY20 8UJ. Diana & Richard Rhodes, 01654 702244, diana@sol-star.fsnet.co.uk. 1½ m E of Machynlleth. Turn L off A489 Machynlleth to Newtown rd. Follow brown tourist signs to Plas Dolguog Hotel. **Adm £3.50, chd £1.50. Weds & Suns all yr (10-5). For NGS: Wed 27 May (10-5).**
Inspiration for the senses. Old and new areas, 7 sensory gardens, riverside boardwalk, stone circle, wildlife pond, willow arbour, strategic seating. Continuous new attractions. Wildlife abundant. 9 acres in which to find peace. Sculptures, poetry, arboretum. Great for children and access. Braille information available. David Bellamy Gold Award for Conservation. Access statement available.

THE GRIGGS
See Herefordshire.

HERGEST CROFT GARDENS
See Herefordshire.

HILL HOUSE FARM
See Herefordshire.

LITTLE HELDRE
See Shropshire.

⑱ LLANSTEPHAN HOUSE

nr Brecon LD3 0YR. Lord & Lady Milford. 10m SW of Builth Wells. Leave A470 at Llyswen onto B4350. 1st L after crossing river in Boughrood. Follow yellow signs. From Builth Wells leave A470 at Erwood Bridge. 1st L *then follow signs*. Home-made teas. **Adm £3, chd free. Sun 17 May (2-5).** Large garden with rhododendrons, azaleas, shrubs, water garden, shrub roses, walled kitchen garden, greenhouses and very fine specimen trees. Beautiful views of Wye Valley and Black Mountains.

LLANTHONY AND DISTRICT GARDENS
See Gwent.

Group opening

19 LLOWES GARDENS
nr Hay-on-Wye HR3 5JA. *3¹/₂ m W of Hay-on-Wye. On A438 between Clyro and Glasbury-on-Wye at Llowes. Follow yellow signs in village.* Home-made teas. **Combined adm £5, chd free. Sun 12 July (2-6).**
2 very interesting, very different gardens full of exciting structural and colour ideas. Flower festival in the church with Celtic Cross and Kilvert associations.

2 MILL COTTAGES
Lyn & Chris Williams. *In village*
Fascinating long narrow garden with a series of individual areas imaginatively planted. Features a variety of unusual stonework, interesting collection of grasses and many hidden surprises.

PLAS WYE
Geoff & Helen Hardy
Mature 1-acre densely planted colourful garden in a series of interconnecting areas cleverly linked over different levels. Water features, roses, laburnum arch and views of the Black Mountains.

LLWYNCELYN
See Ceredigion/Cardiganshire.

20 LLYSDINAM
Newbridge-on-Wye LD1 6NB. Sir John & Lady Venables-Llewelyn & Llysdinam Charitable Trust, 01597 860190, elster@f25.com. *5m SW of Llandrindod Wells. Turn W off A470 at Newbridge-on-Wye; turn R immed after crossing R Wye; entrance up hill.* Home-made teas. **Adm £3 chd free** (share to NSPCC). **Mon 4 May; Sun 9 Aug (2-6). Visitors also welcome by appt.**

Large garden. Azaleas, rhododendrons, water garden and herbaceous borders, shrubs, woodland garden, Victorian kitchen garden and greenhouses. Fine view of Wye Valley. Some gravel paths and slopes.

unusual stonework . . . collection of grasses and many hidden surprises . . .

21 MAESFRON HALL AND GARDENS
Trewern, Welshpool SY21 8EA. Dr & Mrs T Owen, 01938 570600, www.maesfron.co.uk. *4m E of Welshpool. On A458 Shrewsbury to Welshpool road.* Home-made teas. **Adm £3, chd £1. Suns 5 Apr; 13 Sept (2-5). Visitors also welcome by appt.**
Georgian house (not open) built in Italian villa style set in 4 acres of S-facing gardens on lower slopes of Moel-y-Golfa with panoramic views of The Long Mountain. Terraces, walled kitchen garden, tropical garden, restored Victorian conservatories, tower and shell grotto. Woodland and parkland walks with wide variety of trees. Buttington Church open for visitors.

22 MILL COTTAGE
Abbeycwmhir LD1 6PH. Mr & Mrs B D Parfitt, 01597 851935. *8m N of Llandrindod Wells. Turn L off A483 1m N of Crossgates roundabout, then 3¹/₂ m on L, signed Abbeycwmhir. Limited parking.* **Adm £3, chd free. Visitors welcome by appt May only (10-6).**
¹/₃ -acre streamside garden in spectacular valley setting, consisting mainly of mature, rare and unusual trees and shrubs, particularly interesting to the plantsman. Rockery with numerous ericaceous plants and interesting water feature.

THE MILL HOUSE
See Ceredigion/Cardiganshire.

NANT-Y-BEDD
See Gwent.

---

23 THE NEUADD
nr Crickhowell NP8 1SP. Robin & Philippa Herbert. *1m NE of Crickhowell. Leave Crickhowell by Llanbedr rd. At junction with Great Oak Rd bear L and continue up hill for 0.9m, garden on L. Ample parking.* Home-made teas. **Adm £3, chd free. Sun 14 June (2-6).**
Garden under continuing restoration and development. At 750ft in Brecon Beacons National Park. Decorative walled garden, sunken garden, winter garden, rock garden with pool and springs. Woodland walk and paths. Unusual plants and trees. Owner is wheelchair user but some paths are steep.

24 THE OLD VICARAGE
Llangorse LD3 7UB. Major & Mrs J B Anderson, 01874 658639. *6¹/₂ m E of Brecon on B4560, 4m off A40 at Bwlch. Park in Llangorse village and approach through churchyard.* **Adm £2.50, chd free. Visitors welcome by appt April to Sept, plants always available.**
Small family garden maintained by owners; interesting herbaceous and shrub borders; lawns, trees and vegetables.

25 ◆ POWIS CASTLE GARDEN
Welshpool SY21 8RF. The National Trust, 01938 551929, www.nationaltrust.org.uk. *1m S of Welshpool. Turn off A483 ³/₄ m out of Welshpool, up Red Lane for ¹/₄ m.* **House and Garden Adm £11; chd £5.50, Garden only Adm £8, chd £4, under 5s free. Check website for opening dates & times. For NGS: Sat 18 July (11-5.30).**
Laid out in early C18 with finest remaining examples of Italian terraces in Britain. Richly planted herbaceous borders; enormous yew hedges; lead statuary, large wild flower areas. One of the National Trust's finest gardens. National Collection of *Laburnum*. Talks with Careership Student 11.30 & 3. Step-free route map around garden. Some gravel paths.

26 ROSE COTTAGE
Welshpool SY21 9JE. Peter & Frances Grassi, 01938 553723, frances@anngardening.fsnet.co.uk *3m N of Welshpool. 1m from Dingle Nursery, please telephone for directions.* Home-made teas. **Adm £ chd free. Visitors welcome by appt**

June to Aug for groups & individuals.
S-facing 1-acre garden set in wooded valley and bordered by farmland. Small stream meanders through site, dammed to form pools teeming with wildlife. Stylish summerhouse at pool edge, elegant fruit cage, rustic archways, bespoke chicken hut all add extra interest to informal ribbon borders, raised beds, vegetable garden and small orchard.

27 ROWAN
Leighton, Welshpool SY21 8HJ. Tinty Griffith, 01938 552197. *2m E of Welshpool. From Welshpool take B4388 (Buttington to Montgomery). At Leighton turn L after school then at church straight ahead between stone pillars. 1st on R, parking in churchyard.* Home-made teas. **Adm £3, chd free. Suns 12 Apr; 24 May (2-5). Visitors also welcome by appt April 12th to end July.**
1 acre of traditional plantsman's country garden with village church as backdrop. Discrete paths meander around island beds and mixed borders with irises, roses, unusual and rare plants, trees dripping with climbers and a series of planted pools and marshy areas. Views over Montgomeryshire countryside. Leighton Church open. Slopes slippery if wet, gravel paths.

Group opening

28 TALYBONT GARDENS
Talybont-on-Usk LD3 7JE. *6m SE of Brecon. Off A40 signed Talybont-on-Usk. Follow yellow signs to gardens.* Home-made teas at the Malt House. **Combined adm £6, chd free (share to Arthritis Research Campaign). Sun 12 July (2-6).**
Three garden gems beautifully structured. Great use of space, colour and planting, specimen trees.

LONICERA
Station Road. Gareth & Eirona Davies
1/2-acre garden of varied interest incorporating several small feature gardens. Rose garden; heather garden with conifers; herbaceous and woody perennials; colourful summer bedding displays; window boxes, hanging baskets and patio tubs forming extensive frontage display; greenhouses.

NEW THE MALT HOUSE
Mike & Lyn Bugler. *From Station Road, R into village. First house on R*
2 1/2-acre mixed garden incorporating a cottage garden, rockery and hosta collection. Many choice specimen trees and featuring a journey through the 'millennium forest'. Ornamental and wildlife ponds and riverside walk.

TY CAM
Harry Chapman. *Next to White Hart PH*
Small garden of secret surprises on 3 levels with steps built on a railway embankment. Attractive features incl patios, decks, pergolas, ponds and waterfalls. Many choice herbaceous plants, trees and shrubs.

29 TAN-Y-LLYN
Meifod SY22 6YB. Callum Johnston & Brenda Moor, 01938 500370, info@tanyllyn-nursery.co.uk. *1m SE of Meifod. From Oswestry on A495 turn L in village, cross R Vyrnwy & climb hill for 1/2 m bearing R at Y-junction.* Home-made teas. **Adm £3, chd free (share to Alzheimer's Society Montgomeryshire). Sats, Suns 2, 3 May; 6, 7 June; 4, 5 July; (2-5). Visitors also welcome by appt.**
S-facing sheltered 3-acre garden, surrounded by small hills, fields and forest. Steeply sloping, the paths, beds and hedges have been laid out to complement the contours of the hill. Extensive collection of plants in containers, herb garden, thorn grove, pond, orchard and wilderness. Exhibitions, events and entertainments.

30 TAWRYN
6 Baskerville Court, Clyro HR3 5SS. Chris & Clive Young, 01497 821939. *1m NW of Hay-on-Wye. Leave A438 Hereford to Brecon rd at Clyro. Baskerville Court is behind church and Baskerville Arms Hotel. Please park in village.* Home-made teas. **Adm £2.50, chd free. Visitors welcome by appt Spring to Autumn, please telephone first (10-6).**
1-acre steeply-terraced garden on an oriental theme. Come and see the Ghost Dragon and the River of Slate. Lots of new crooked paths and

planting. Stunning views of the Black Mountains and Kilvert's Church. Colour all yr. Talks on NGS history and fundraising by Chris.

31 TREBERFYDD
Bwlch, nr Brecon LD3 7PX. David Raikes, www.treberfydd.com. *6 1/2 m E of Brecon. From Crickhowell leave A40 at Bwlch and take B4560 then L for Penorth. From Brecon leave A40 at Llanhamlach. 2 1/2 m sign for Llangasty Church, entrance over cattle grid.* Tel 01874 730205/07796 897540 or email david.raikes@btinternet.com for further directions. Home-made teas. **House and garden adm £5, garden only adm £3, chd free. Sun 21 June (1-5).**
10 acres of lawns, peaceful woodland walks, rose beds and herbaceous borders designed in 1852 by W A Nesfield for imposing Victorian Gothic house. Cedar of Lebanon 155 yrs old. Yews, holly oaks, copper beech, orchards and rockery. Wonderful position nr Llangorse Lake. Beacons nursery within walled garden. Tours of the house.

A journey through the 'millennium forest' . . .

32 TY CAPEL DEILDRE
Llanidloes SY18 6NX. Dr Beverley Evans-Britt, 01686 412602. *4 1/2 m N of Llanidloes. Go N from Llanidloes on B4518. 2m turn L on Clywedog rd, signed scenic route, 2 1/2 m on R by nature walk lay-by.* Light refreshments & teas. **Adm £3.50, chd £1 (share to Chernobyl Children's Project). Sun 21 June (2-5.30). Visitors also welcome by appt May to Aug. Coaches welcome.**
2-acre garden of almost 100% organic plants has been personally created on a former waste site over 30 years. A 1350ft windy location with stunning views of Llyn Clywedog. It consists of ponds surrounded by walks and marginal gardens, herbaceous borders containing many rare perennials, rose and begonia gardens and lawns. Demonstration by local beekeepers with virtual hives.

UPPER TAN HOUSE
See Herefordshire.

33 THE WALLED GARDEN
Knill, nr Presteigne LD8 2PR. Dame
Margaret Anstee, 01544 267411. *3m
SW of Presteigne. On B4362 Walton-
Presteigne rd. In Knill village turn R
over cattle grid, keep R down drive.*
Adm £3, chd free. Mon 13 Apr; Sun
7 June (2-6). Visitors also welcome
by appt, please ring first.
4 acres: walled garden; river, bog
garden and small grotto; primulas; over
100 varieties of roses, shrub, modern
and climbing; peonies; mixed and
herbaceous borders; many varieties of
shrubs and mature trees; lovely spring
garden. Nr C13 church in beautiful
valley. Some narrow paths and uneven
ground.

Happily
released
house plants . . .

Group opening

**34 NEW WELSHPOOLS
SECRET GARDENS**
High Street, Welshpool
SY21 7JP. *Off A458 in Welshpool.
Follow signs.* Combined adm
£3.50, chd free. Sats, Suns 6,
7 June; 8, 9 Aug (2-5).
2 very different hidden gems.
Weave through jungle growth
above you, rare planting at your
feet, be amazed at paths secreted
away and stumble across hidden
pools. Every surface covered,
containers dripping with happily
released house plants, statues and
Mediterranean arbour.

NEW OAK COTTAGE
Tony & Margaret Harvey, 01938
559087,
tony@montgomeryshire.eu.
Visitors also welcome by appt
May only, individuals and small
groups.
A plantsman's small and hidden
garden providing an oasis of green
in the town centre. Gravel paths
and stepping stones meander
through a wide variety of plants,
incl unusual species. Alpines are a
favorite (more enthusiasm than
knowledge!). Runner Up
'Welshpool in Flowers'.

NEW VICTORIA HOUSE
Rita Wyatt
Established secret walled garden in
town centre. Packed with wide
variety of plants and Wild Dingle
area. Lavender bags and herbs for
sale.

35 THE WERN
Llanfihangel Talyllyn LD3 7TE. Neil &
Lucienne Bennett, 01874 658401.
*4m E of Brecon. From Brecon, leave
A40 (S) at 1st exit onto B4558 to
Groesffordd. Follow rd to Llanfihangel
Talyllyn. Take 2nd R (no through rd) in
front of converted barns to end. From
Crickhowell leave A40 (N) at Bwlch. R
onto B4560. At Llangorse turn L to
Llanfihangel Talyllyn. Take 'no through
rd' (2nd L), follow to end.* Home-made
teas. Adm £3, chd free. Visitors
welcome by appt 1 May - 15 Sept.
Garden groups especially welcome.
Mini buses but no coaches (narrow
road).
1-acre garden of unusual trees, shrubs
and plants. Many young acers,
rhododendrons and azaleas. Hot
border with banana, cannas and
tender plants. Secluded herb garden.
Ornamental grass and bamboo garden
leading to woodland walk crossing

stream. Charming, productive fruit
and vegetable garden and polytunnel
surrounded by damsons and plums.
No disabled access to woodland
walk.

**36 WESTLAKE FISHERIES &
CAMPING**
Domgay Road, Four Crosses
SY22 6SJ. Lynn Mainwaring, 01691
831475. *9m N of Welshpool.* Turn off
A483 in Four Crosses, signed
Pysgodfa Fishery. Follow brown tourist
signs. Domgay Rd approx 1m. Home-
made teas. Adm £3, chd free.
Visitors welcome by appt all yr.
A quiet scenic environment of 38
acres, managed organically on the R
Vyrnwy with lakes and pools. 2-acre
garden containing mixed borders, fish
lawn, orchard, potager, herb and
cutting garden, large vegetable garden
(many unusual varieties grown),
greenhouses and fruit cage. Birch walk
and purple hazel walk lead to lake
walks and wildlife area.

37 WOODHILL
Moelfre, Oswestry SY10 7QX. Janet
Randell, 01691 791486,
www.pco.powys.org.uk/woodhill.
9m W of Oswestry. Adm £3, chd 50p,
disabled free (share to Woods, Hills
& Tracks). Visitors welcome by appt,
open all yr, short notice OK.
6 acres. Informal garden designed with
wheelchair users in mind set amidst
wonderful views of the surrounding hills
and mountains on the foothills of The
Berwyns nr Snowdonia. Footpaths for
disabled access totalling 3/4 m, young
arboretum, picnic spot overlooking
stream, ponds and wetlands.
Sheltered arbour in more formal
setting. All-yr interest: bluebell wood in
spring; roses in summer; trees, shrubs
and berries in autumn; scented winter
shrubs. 1000 trees and shrubs planted
informally. Abundant wildlife sightings.

Powys County Volunteers

County Organisers
South Shân Egerton, Pen-y-Maes, Hay-on-Wye HR3 5PP, 01497 820423, sre@waitrose.com
North Angela Hughes, Castell y Gwynt, Montgomery SY15 6HR, 01686 668317, r.dhughes@btinternet.com

County Treasurer
Penny Davies, Plas Derwen, Llansantffraid, Powys SY22 6SX, 01691 828373, digbydavies@aol.com

Publicity
North Carol Parry, Plas Robin, Llandyssil, Powys SY15 6LQ, 01686 668963, carolsummers@btinternet.com

Assistant County Organisers
North Penny Davies, Plas Derwen, Llansantffraid, Powys SY22 6SX, 01691 828373, digbydavies@aol.com

Mark your diary with these special events in 2009

EXPLORE SECRET GARDENS DURING CHELSEA & HAMPTON COURT FLOWER SHOW WEEKS

Tue 19 May, Wed 20 May, Thur 21 May, Fri 22 May, Wed 8 July, Thur 9 July
Full day tours from £82 per person, 10% discount for groups
Advance booking required, telephone +44 (0)20 8693 1015 or email j.wookey@btinternet.com
Specially selected gardens in London, Essex, Kent, Hampshire and South Oxfordshire. The tour price includes transport and lunch with wine at a popular restaurant or pub.

HAMPTON COURT PALACE

Thur 2 Apr, Tue 23 June, Thur 25 June, Wed 15 July, Tue 4 Aug, Thur 10 Sept
Evening tours in the company of one of the Palace's specialist tour guides from 6.30 – 8pm
Tickets £6 per person. Advance booking required, telephone +44 (0)1483 211535 or visit www.ngs.org.uk for more information
Gossip, scandal, murder, healing – you'll find it all within the Formal Gardens at Hampton Court Palace. Each tour will have its own unique feature whether it's the story of the Great Vine or the magic and mystery of the Maze.

FROGMORE – A ROYAL GARDEN (BERKSHIRE)

Tue 26 May 10am – 5.30pm (last admission 4pm)
Garden adm £4.50, chd free. Tickets available in advance or on the day.
Advance booking for groups and coaches, telephone
+44 (0) 1483 211535 or email orders@ngs.org.uk
A rare opportunity to explore 30 acres of landscaped garden, rich in history and beauty.

FLAXBOURNE FARM – FUN & SURPRISES (BEDFORDSHIRE)

Sun 7 June 10am – 5pm. Adm £5, chd free
No booking required, come along on the day!
Bring the whole family and have fun in this surprising and entertaining garden of 2 acres. Enjoy the large plant fair, live music, pets corner, birds of prey, dog agility show and much more.

WISLEY RHS GARDEN – MUSIC IN THE GARDEN (SURREY)

Fri 11 Sept 6 – 9pm
Adm (incl RHS members) £7, chd under 15 free
Save money on advance bookings for groups of 4 or more, telephone +44 (0)1483 211535 or visit www.ngs.org.uk for more information
A special evening opening of this famous garden, exclusively for the NGS. Enjoy music and entertainment as you explore the gardens and the floral marquee on the first day of the Wisley Flower Show.

For further information visit www.ngs.org.uk or telephone 01483 211535

Early Openings 2010

Don't forget early planning for 2010

Gardens across the country open from early January onwards – before the new Yellow Book is published – with glorious displays of colour including hellebores, aconites, snowdrops and carpets of spring bulbs.

Bedfordshire

31 JANUARY
King's Arms Garden

Buckinghamshire

21 FEBRUARY
Magnolia House, Grange Drive
Woodburn
28 FEBRUARY
Quainton Gardens

Cheshire & Wirral

16 JANUARY
Ness Botanic Gardens
7 FEBRUARY
Dunham Massey

Cornwall

6 & 14 FEBRUARY
Coombegate Cottage

Cumbria

28 FEBRUARY
Summerdale House

Devon

3, 10, 17, 24 JANUARY
Sherwood
31 JANUARY
Cherubeer Gardens
Little Cumbre
Sherwood
7 FEBRUARY
Cherubeer Gardens
Little Cumbre
Pikes Cottage
Sherwood
14 FEBRUARY
Little Cumbre
Pikes Cottage
Sherwood
21 FEBRUARY
Little Cumbre
21 FEBRUARY
Pikes Cottage
Sherwood
28 FEBRUARY
Pikes Cottage
Sherwood

Essex

21 FEBRUARY
Green Island

Gloucestershire

31 JANUARY
Home Farm
7 FEBRUARY
Trench Hill
14 FEBRUARY
Home Farm
Trench Hill

Gwynedd

13 FEBRUARY
Penrhyn Castle

Hampshire

7 FEBRUARY
The Down House
14 FEBRUARY
Bramdean House
21 FEBRUARY
Little Court
22 FEBRUARY
Little Court
23 FEBRUARY
Little Court

Herefordshire

4, 11, 18 & 25 FEBRUARY
Ivy Croft

Kent

14 FEBRUARY
Mere House
18 FEBRUARY
Broadview Gardens

Lancashire Merseyside & Greater Manchester

14 & 21 FEBRUARY
Weeping Ash

Lincolnshire

27 & 28 FEBRUARY
21 Chapel Street

Nottinghamshire

7 & 28 FEBRUARY
The Beeches

Somerset & Bristol Area

31 JANUARY
Rock House

Surrey

14 & 17 FEBRUARY
Gatton Park

Sussex

7 FEBRUARY
The Manor of Dean
Mitchmere Farm
9 FEBRUARY
Pembury House
10 FEBRUARY
Pembury House
11 FEBRUARY
Mitchmere Farm
Pembury House
14 FEBRUARY
Mitchmere Farm
16 FEBRUARY
Pembury House
17 FEBRUARY
Pembury House
18 FEBRUARY
Pembury House

Warwickshire & part of West Midlands

7 FEBRUARY
Ragley Hall Gardens

Wiltshire

31 JANUARY
Great Chalfield Manor
13, 14, 20 & 21 FEBRUARY
Lacock Abbey Gardens

Worcestershire

6 FEBRUARY
The Greyfriars

Garden Visiting Around the World

Heading off on holiday? Whether you're planning a short trip north of the border or across the channel or a longer visit down under or to our see our North American cousins, why not visit a few of the wonderful gardens open for charity elsewhere in the world?

America

GARDEN CONSERVANCY
Publication Open Days Directory
W www.gardenconservancy.org
Visit America's very best rarely seen private gardens. The Open Days Program is a project of The Garden Conservancy, a non-profit organisation dedicated to preserving America's gardening heritage.

VIRGINIA'S HISTORIC GARDEN WEEK
18 – 25 April 2009
W www.MyCapitalGardensUSA.co.uk
W www.vagardenweek.org
Every year Virginia plays host to Historic Garden Week and 2009 represents the 76th anniversary. Visitors will be able to step through the gates of more than 250 of Virginia's most beautiful gardens, homes and historic landmarks during 'America's Largest Open House'.

Australia

AUSTRALIA'S OPEN GARDEN SCHEME
Contact Neil Robertson
E national@opengarden.org.au
W www.opengarden.org.au
More than 700 inspiring gardens drawn from every Australian state and territory including tropical gardens, arid-zone gardens as well as featuring Australia's unique flora.

Belgium

JARDINS OUVERTS DE BELGIQUE – OPEN TUINEN VAN BELGIË
Publication Catalogue of private Belgian Open Gardens, published annually in March
Contact Dominique Petit-Heymans
E info@jardinsouverts.be
W www.jardinsouverts.be
A non-profit organisation founded in 1994. Most of the proceeds from entry fees support charities chosen by garden owners.

Monticello, home of Thomas Jefferson

France

E jardinsetsante@wanadoo.fr
W www.jardins-sante.org
Founded in 2004, Jardins et Santé is an association with humanitarian aims. It was created and is run by a team of volunteers. The funds raised through garden openings are used to finance scientific research in the field of neurology. Contributions are also made to the development of the therapeutic role of the garden, particularly in hospitals and retirement homes. In January 2007 a research grant was presented to Mme Seegmuller, of the University Hospital of Strasbourg, to contribute to clinical studies in focal epilepsy in children and adolescents.

Donations have also been allocated to assist in the creation of several projects including:

- a garden in a residential centre for elderly patients with dementia at the teaching hospital in Rouen.
- a garden activity centre for autistic young adults in the Vaucluse area.
- a vegetable plot at a centre for autistic adolescents and young adults in Saint-Florent-sur-Cher.
- an ornamental garden and a potager at a home in the Isère region for adults with severe epilepsy.

The 2008 grant will be attributed at the end of the year to a project on clinical research into autism.

Japan

THE N.G.S. JAPAN
Contact Tamie Taniguchi
E tamieta@syd.odn.ne.jp
W www.ngs-jp.org
The N.G.S. Japan was founded in 2001. Most of the proceeds from the entry fees support children's and welfare charities as nominated by owners and Japanese garden conservation.

Netherlands

NETHERLANDSE TUINENSTICHTING (DUTCH GARDEN SOCIETY, NTS)
Publication Open Tuinengids, published annually in March.
E info@tuinenstichting.nl
W www.tuinenstichting.nl
The Dutch Garden Society was founded in 1980 to protect and restore gardens public parks and cemeteries.

New Zealand

PRIVATE GARDENS OF NEW ZEALAND/ GARDENS TO VISIT
W www.gardenstovisit.co.nz
The New Zealand website showcases private gardens of New Zealand which also operate B&Bs and farm stays. In addition some properties can also provide venues for private and corporate hospitality and weddings. Properties may also feature plant, art and sculpture sales, picnics, fishing and garden tours.

Scotland

GARDENS OF SCOTLAND
Contact Paddy Scott
T 0131 226 3714
E info@sgsgardens.co.uk
W www.gardensofscotland.org
Founded in 1931, Scotland's Gardens Scheme facilitates the opening of Scotland's finest gardens to the public. 40% of funds raised goes to charities nominated by each garden owner whilst 60% net goes to the SGS beneficiaries - The Queen's Nursing Institute Scotland, Maggie's Cancer Caring Centres, The Gardens Fund for the National Trust for Scotland, Perennial and The Royal Fund for Gardeners' Children.

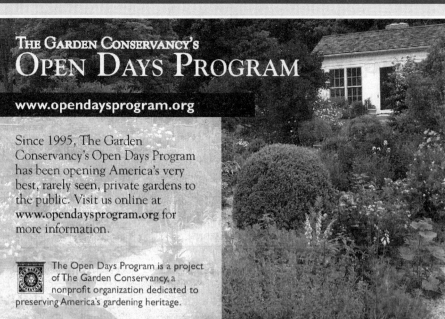
A catalogue record of this book is available from the British Library.

Typeset in Helvetica Neue font family by Chat Noir Design, France.

The papers used by The National Gardens Scheme are natural recyclable products made from wood grown in sustainable forests.

ISBN 978-1-905942-12-1
ISSN 1365-0572
EAN 9 781905 942008

© The National Gardens Scheme 2009

First published February 2009

National Plant Collections in the NGS

Almost 100 of the gardens that open for The National Gardens Scheme are custodians of National Plant Collections®, the National Council for the Conservation of Plants and Gardens (NCCPG), although this may not always be noted in the garden descriptions.

The NCCPG can be contacted at 12 Home Farm, Loseley Park, Guildford, Surrey GU3 1HS Tel: 01483 447544 Fax: 01483 458933. Website: www.nccpg.com

NCCPG

A

ACER (EXCL JAPONICUM, PALMATUM CVS.) BETULA, ZELKOVA
Hergest Croft Gardens
Herefordshire

AESCULUS, LIRIODENDRON
West Dean Gardens
Sussex

ANEMONE (JAPANESE) AND HELLEBORUS
Broadview Gardens
Kent

ANEMONE NEMOROSA CVS.
Kingston Lacy
Dorset

AQUILEGIA VULGARIS (CVS. & HYBRIDS)
Touchwood
Glamorgan

ARALIACEAE, PODOCARPACEAE, EUCALYPTUS
Meon Orchard
Hampshire

ARBUTUS
Barton House
Warwickshire
Dunster Castle Gardens
Somerset & Bristol Area

ARUNCUS, FILIPENDULA
Windy Hall
Cumbria

ASTER (AUTUMN FLOWERING)
The Picton Garden
Herefordshire

ASTER AMELLUS, CORDIFOLIUS, ERICOIDES
Upton House & Gardens
Warwickshire

ASTILBE, HYDRANGEA AND POLYSTICHUM (FERNS)
Holehird Gardens
Cumbria

ASTILBE, IRIS ENSATA, TULBAGHIA
Marwood Hill
Devon

B

BERBERIS, MAGNOLIA, RHODODENDRON (KNAPHILL AZALEAS)
Sherwood
Devon

BRUGMANSIA
Valducci Flower & Vegetable Gardens
Shropshire

BRUNNERA, OMPHALODES
Hearns House
Oxfordshire

BUDDLEJA, CLEMATIS VITICELLA
Longstock Park Water Garden
Hampshire

C

CAMELLIA & RHODODENDRON INTRODUCED TO HELIGAN PRE-1920
The Lost Gardens of Heligan
Cornwall

CARPINUS BETULUS CVS.
West Lodge Park
Hertfordshire

CEANOTHUS
Eccleston Square, SW1
London

CENTAUREA
Bide-a-Wee Cottage
Durham & Northumberland

CLEMATIS (SUBGENUS VIORNA)
Rosewood
Carmarthenshire & Pembrokeshire

CLEMATIS VITICELLA
Hawthornes Nursery Garden
Lancashire, Merseyside & Greater Manchester

CLEMATIS VITICELLA CVS. LAPAGERIA ROSEA & CVS.
Roseland House
Cornwall

COLCHICUM
Felbrigg Hall
Norfolk

CORNUS (EXCL. C FLORIDA CVS.)
Newby Hall & Gardens
Yorkshire

CORYDALIS
164 Point Clear Road
Essex

CROCOSMIA
The Crocosmia Gardens
Lincolnshire

CYCLAMEN (EXCL PERSICUM CVS.)
Higher Cherubeer
Devon

CYDONIA OBLONGA
Norton Priory Museum & Gardens
Cheshire & Wirral

D

DAPHNE, GALANTHUS
Brandy Mount House
Hampshire

DICENTRA
Boundary Cottage
Yorkshire

E

EUONYMOUS (DECIDUOUS)
East Bergholt Place
Suffolk

EUPHORBIA
University of Oxford Botanic Garden
Oxfordshire

F

FUCHSIA (HARDY)
Welsh College of Horticulture
Flintshire & Wrexham

G

GENTIANA (AUTUMN FLOWERING)
Newton Farm
Devon

GEUM
1 Brickwall Cottages
Kent

GREVILLEA
Pine Lodge Gardens & Nursery
Cornwall

GUNNERA
The Mowle
Norfolk

H

HAMAMELIS
Swallow Hayes
Shropshire

HEDERA
Erddig Hall
Flintshire & Wrexham

HELENIUM
Holbrook Garden
Devon

HELENIUM CVS
Yew Tree House
Cheshire & Wirral

HELIOTROPIUM
Hampton Court Palace
London

HELIOTROPIUM ARBORESCENS CVS.
The Homestead
Leicestershire & Rutland

HEUCHERA AND SCHIZOSTYLIS
Cliffe
Devon

HOSTA (MINIATURE)
Upper Merton House
Gloucestershire North & Central

HOSTA (MODERN HYBRIDS)
Cleave House
Devon

HYDRANGEA
The Garden House
Flintshire & Wrexham

I

IRIS (DYKES MEDAL WINNERS)
Myddelton House Gardens
London

J

JUGLANS
Wimpole Hall
Cambridgeshire

L

LABURNUM
Powis Castle Garden
Powys

LAMIUM
12 Darges Lane
Staffordshire

LATHYRUS (EXCL ODORATUS CVS.)
Weaver's Cottage
Cambridgeshire

LEUCANTHEMUM SUPERBUM (CHRYSANTHEMUM MAXIMUM)
Shapcott Barton Estate
Devon

LIGULARIA
Fell Yeat
Cumbria

M

MALUS (ORNAMENTAL)
Barnards Farm
Essex

MENTHA, NEPETA, ORIGANUM
Iden Croft Herb Gardens
Kent

N

NYSSA, OXYDENDRUM
Exbury Gardens & Steam Railway
Hampshire

O

OENOTHERA SPP.
The Old Vicarage
Wiltshire

ORIGANUM, SANGUISORBA, THYMUS
Chesters Walled Garden
Durham & Northumberland

P

PAEONIA (PRE-1900 AND EARLY POST 1900 CVS.)
Green Cottage
Gloucestershire North & Central

PELARGONIUM, HEDERA
Ivybank
Warwickshire

PENNISETUM, CEANOTHUS (DECIDUOUS CVS.) AND PHYGELIUS
Knoll Gardens
Dorset

PENSTEMON
Mews Cottage
Dorset

PENSTEMON CVS. AND SALVIA (TENDER)
Kingston Maurward Gardens
Dorset

PHOTINIA, AZARA
Trelissick
Cornwall

PLANTS SELECTED BY SIR FREDERICK STERN
Highdown
Sussex

POTENTILLA FRUTICOSA
Riverside Gardens at Webbs of Wychbold
Worcestershire

Q

QUERCUS
Chevithorne Barton
Devon

R

RHAPIS CVS. & SPP.
Gwyndy Bach
Gwynedd

RHODODENDRON (GHENT AZALEAS)
Sheffield Park Garden
Sussex

RHODOHYPOXIS
Newton Farm
Devon

RODGERSIA
The Gate House
Devon

ROSA (PRE-1900 SHRUB ROSES)
Mottisfont Abbey & Garden
Hampshire

ROSA (PRE-1900)
Broomfield Hall
Derbyshire

ROSA (RAMBLING)
Moor Wood
Gloucestershire North & Central

S

SALVIA SPP.
2 Hillside Cottages
Hampshire

SARCOCOCCA
Capel Manor Gardens
Hertfordshire

SAXIFRAGA (SUBSECTS. KABSCHIA & ENGLERIA)
Waterperry Gardens
Oxfordshire

Accommodation available at NGS Gardens

We feature here a list of NGS garden owners or county volunteers who offer accommodation. We have listed them by Yellow Book county and indicated whether they offer Bed & Breakfast (**B&B**), Self-Catering (**SC**), or Hotel (**H**) accommodation. You will also find a reference to accommodation in the main directory with their garden entry, unless the property owner is a member of the county team and does not open their garden.

Bedfordshire

LUTON HOO HOTEL, GOLF AND SPA
The Mansion House, Luton Hoo
LU1 3TQ
Elite Hotels (Rotherwick) Limited
T 01582 734437
E enquiries@lutonhoo.co.uk
W www.lutonhoo.com
Accommodation A luxury 5* hotel with 144 rooms, 18 hole golf course, magnificent spa with swimming pool and 1,065 acres of parkland and gardens created by the famous landscape designer Capability Brown.
H

Berkshire

LITTLECOTE HOUSE HOTEL
Littlecote, Hungerford RG17 0SU
Warner Leisure Hotel Group
T 01488 682509
E functions.littlecote@bourne-leisure.co.uk
W www.warnerleisurehotels.co.uk
Accommodation Commanding an excellent location in the heart of the Berkshire countryside, the hotel has 198 bedrooms including beautifully refurbished 'Historic' rooms and suites in the Old House, luxurious contemporary 'Signature' rooms and comfortable 'Ambassador' rooms in the new wing.
H

Buckinghamshire

THE OLD VICARAGE
Padbury, Buckinghamshire
MK18 2AH
Mr & Mrs. H. Morley-Fletcher
T 01280 813045
E belindamf@freenet.co.uk
Accommodation Twin or double bedroom with private bathroom in a Victorian house, surrounded by 2½ acres of garden. Breakfast comes from our organic garden, or from local sources wherever possible. Convenient for Silverstone, Stowe and Addington Manor Equestrian Centre.
B&B

Cambridgeshire

CHURCHILL COLLEGE
Storey's Way, Cambridge CB3 0DS
T 01223 336164
E accommodation@chu.cam.ac.uk
W www.churchillconferences.co.uk
Accommodation Comfortable student accommodation available on a bed and breakfast basis during College vacation periods only.
B&B

KENILWORTH SMALLHOLDING
West Drove North, Walton Highway, Wisbech PE14 7DP
Marilyn Clarke
T 01945 881332
E j.f-m_clarke@tiscali.co.uk
W www.kenilworthhouse.co.uk

Accommodation Self contained double room with ensuite shower and large verandah overlooking garden. Entrance lobby adjacent to bedroom provides exclusive access for residents and contains fridge stocked for self catering breakfast, kettle and microwave.
SC

SOUTH FARM
South Farm, Shingay-cum-Wendy SG8 0HR
Philip Paxman
T 01223 207581
E philip@south-farm.co.uk
W www.south-farm.co.uk
Accommodation 2 self-contained apartments for 2 or 4 each. They can be self catering. Also 3 double ensuite rooms. Dinner and lunch available. Prices from £80 per night or £70 single. Not usually available Saturdays.
B&B SC

Carmarthenshire & Pembrokeshire

DYFFRYN FERNANT
Llanychaer, Fishguard SA65 9SP
Christina Shand
T 01348 811282
E christina.shand@virgin.net
W www.genuslocus.net
Accommodation Cosy one roomed converted barn in the heart of the garden with wood burning stove. Sleeps 4. Secluded, romantic and peaceful. Self catering.
SC

Cornwall

BONYTHON MANOR
Cury Cross Lanes, nr Helston TR12 7BA
Richard & Sue Nathan
T 01326 240234
E sue@bonythonmanor.co.uk
W www.bonythonmanor.co.uk
Accommodation 4 properties sleeping 10, 6, 4 and 2. All 5* accommodation with ensuite facilities and private gardens. Bookings

through 'Rural Retreats' - 01386 701177. www.ruralretreats.co.uk. Cottage refs: Bonython Farmhouse – CW042, Mews Cottage – CW047, St Corantyn Cottage - CW048, Spring Water Barn - CW058.
SC

CARWINION
Mawnan Smith, Falmouth TR11 5JA
A & J Rogers
T 01326 250258
E jane@carwinion.freeserve.co.uk
W www.carwinion.co.uk
Accommodation 1 double, 2 twin/double ensuite rooms in quiet country house set in 14 acres of valley garden. Children & dogs welcome. Rooms from £80 per night. Single occ. £50. SC flat sleeps 2. Cottage sleeps 6.
B&B SC

CREED HOUSE
Creed, Grampound, Truro TR2 4SL
Mr & Mrs Jonathan Croggon
T 01872 530372
E jrcroggon@btinternet.com
Accommodation Georgian Rectory - guest wing with one twin, one double - both with ensuite, sitting room, continental breakfast. Prices £90 per night.
B&B

EDNOVEAN FARM
Perranuthnoe, Penzance TR20 9LZ
Christine & Charles Taylor
T 01736 711883
E info@ednoveanfarm.co.uk
W www.ednoveanfarm.co.uk/gardens
Accommodation Granite barn above Mount's Bay, stunning views; formal parterre giving way to open terraces; Italian & gravel gardens. Four poster beds, roll top baths, and patchwork quilts. 3 ensuite rooms with private terrace. 5 diamonds.
B&B

HALLOWARREN
Carne, Manaccan, Helston TR12 6HD
Amanda Osman
T 01326 231224
W www.stanthony.co.uk
Accommodation Victorian cottage - sleeps 2, part of period Cornish farmhouse. All seasons. Traditional barn - sleeps 5. Full central heating. Both equipped to very high standard with all linen supplied. Atmospheric setting in woodland garden bordering stream.
SC

HIDDEN VALLEY GARDENS
Treesmill, nr Par PL24 2TU
Patricia Howard
T 01208 873225
E hiddenvalleygardens@yahoo.co.uk
W www.hiddenvalleygardens.co.uk
Accommodation New, fully equipped, SC accommodation for 2 or 4 in Garden Studio & West Wing stone barn conversions set in 'hidden' valley with a delightful 4 acre display garden. Inside and outside dining. £230 - £380 pw for 2 persons.
SC

TREGOOSE
Grampound, Truro TR2 4DB
Anthony & Alison O'Connor
T 01726 882460
W www.tregoose.co.uk
Accommodation 1 double room (four poster), ensuite. 1 twin, ensuite bath with shower over. 1 double with private bath/shower. Prices from £49 pppn.
Member of County Team
B&B

TREWOOFE ORCHARD
Lamorna, Penzance TR19 6BW
Barbara & Dick Waterson
T 01736 810214
E trewoofe@waterson.org.uk
W www.lamorna-valley.co.uk
Accommodation 1 double ensuite, 1 twin with private bathroom (both with baths). From £80 per night per room. Reduced single rate from Oct - April incl. Three night minimum July - Sept incl. Secluded and tranquil. Non smoking. Special diets catered for.
B&B

Cumbria

BRACKENRIGG LODGE
Windy Hall Road, Bowness-on-Windermere LA23 3HY
Lynne Bush
T 015394 47770
E lynne@brackenriggs.co.uk
W www.brackenriggs.co.uk
Accommodation Ideally located, tranquil, rural 3 acre setting, home of roe deer & red squirrels. Close to the village and lake. Resident owner guarantees comfortable, clean accommodation. A real home from home. (SC - 1 apartment & 1 cottage).
SC

CASTLE GREEN HOTEL
Castle Green Lane, Kendal LA9 6RG
T 01539 73400
E reception@castlegreen.co.uk
W www.castlegreen.co.uk
Accommodation Set in 14 acres of natural woodland, yet only 5 miles from the M6 and 8 miles from Windermere. The Hotel boasts 100 bedrooms, AA rosette, restaurant, pub in the grounds and Health & Fitness Club.
H

LANGHOLME MILL
Woodgate, Lowick Green, Ulverston LA12 8ES
Mr & Mrs G Sanderson
T 01229 885215
E info@langholmemill.co.uk
Accommodation Ten minutes from Lake Coniston with stunning views, this C17 corn mill comprises 4 double bedrooms & large garden designed around the mill race featuring rhododendrons, hostas & acers. Ideal for walkers & families.
SC

LINDETH FELL COUNTRY HOUSE HOTEL
Lyth Valley Road, Bowness-on-Windermere LA23 3JP
Air Cdr & Mrs P A Kennedy
T 01539 443286
E kennedy@lindethfell.co.uk
w www.lindethfell.co.uk
Accommodation On a tree lined drive above Lake Windermere, standing in magnificent private gardens. 14 bedrooms, singles, doubles and family rooms. Price from £50 B&B. Five course dinner available. Many awards including AA Top 200 hotel and Gold Award. A 3* Country House Hotel.
H

RYDAL HALL
Rydal, Ambleside LA22 9LX
Diocese of Carlisle
T 015394 32050
E mail@rydalhall.org
W www.rydalhall.org
Accommodation Rydal Hall is a Grade 2 listed house situated in the heart of the English Lake District with recently restored Thomas Mawson Gardens. A number of rooms have a wonderful view down the Rothay Valley.
B&B SC

SWINSIDE END FARM
Scales, High Lorton, Cockermouth CA13 9UA
Karen Nicholson
T 01900 85410
E swinside@supanet.com
Accommodation Farmhouse: 3 double bedrooms and 1 twin room, all ensuite. Guest sitting room. Prices from: £32 pppn for one night, £25 pppn for two nights and £23.50 pppn for three or more nights.
B&B

Denbighshire & Colwyn

BODYSGALLEN HALL
Bodysgallen Hall & Spa, Llandudno
L30 1RS
Historic House Hotels Ltd.
T 01492 584466
E info@bodysgallen.com
W www.bodysgallen.com
Accommodation Standing in 200
acres of gardens and parkland,
Bodysgallen Hall provides all that is
best in country house hospitality. 31
rooms and suites, an award winning
restaurant and a health and fitness
spa are here to indulge in.
H

FIRGROVE
Llanfwrog, Ruthin LL15 2LL
Anna & Philip Meadway
T 01824 702677
E panda.meadway@btinternet.com
W www.firgrovecountryhouse.co.uk
Accommodation A small Georgian
country house offering 5* B&B
accommodation in a peaceful, rural
setting. Three double bedrooms
equipped with every need of the
modern day visitor. Evening meals are
available with prior notice.
B&B

THE OLD RECTORY
Llanfihangel Glyn Myfyr,
Cerrigydrudion LL21 9UN
Mr & Mrs E T Hughes
T 01490 420568
E elwynthomashughes@hotmail.com
Accommodation Luxury rural
retreat set in idyllic garden and
countryside. 1 family room, ensuite, 1
family room with private bathroom.
Guest lounge. Price from £30 pppn.
B&B

RHYD GETHIN
Pennant Road, Llandrillo, Corwen
LL21 0TE
Tony & Jenny Leeson
T 01490 440213
E anthony.leeson@tesco.net
Accommodation Former C16
stone farmhouse in a riverside setting
in a secluded wooded valley. One
bedroom with kingsize four poster
bed and ensuite shower room. One
bedroom with kingsize bed and
private bathroom. Outstanding rural
views. £35pppn.
B&B

RUTHIN CASTLE
Castle Street, Ruthin LL15 2NU
Ruthin Castle Ltd
T 01824 702664
E reservations@ruthincastle.co.uk
W www.ruthincastle.co.uk
Accommodation A magical 62
bedroom hotel in a parkland setting,
rich in history and character, 23 miles

from Chester. The medieval castle,
built by Edward 1, & owned by the
monarchy for extended periods, was
re-built in 1826. B&B from £60 pppn.
H

STELLA MARIS
Llanrhaeadr, Denbigh LL16 4PW
Mrs Jane Moore
T 01745 890475
E mumjem@aol.com
Accommodation Suite of bright
comfy rooms. Lounge with
kitchenette, spacious bedroom with
kingsize bed, sofa bed & ensuite
shower room. Peaceful location with
wonderful views. Good gardens,
restaurants, health spa and country
walks nearby. Dogs welcome.
B&B SC

TAL-Y-BRYN FARM GUEST HOUSE
Tal-y-Bryn Farm, Llannefydd,
Denbigh LL16 5DR
Gareth & Falmai Roberts
T 01745 540208
E llaeth@villagedairy.co.uk
W www.villagedairy.com
Accommodation C16 farmhouse,
lovely views and garden with lovely
historical walks. 3 double guest
rooms with ensuite facilities. TV and
internet connections. Tea & coffee
facilities. No dogs please.
B&B

Derbyshire

BRICK KILN FARM
Hulland Ward, Ashbourne DE6 3EJ
Mrs Jan Hutchinson
T 01335 370440
Accommodation The property is a
small holding in a rural setting. Dogs,
horses and hens are kept. Available
are two bedrooms, one twin and one
double, bathroom with bath, shower.
B&B

THE CASCADES
Clatterway, Bonsall DE4 2AH
Mr & Mrs A Clements
T 01629 822464
E info@cascadesgardens.com
W www.derbyshiregarden.com
Accommodation Set in a beautiful
4 acre garden within The Peak District
National Park and close to
Chatsworth. Cascades offers a range
of luxury 5* accommodation. Ideal for
a relaxing short break or holiday.
B&B

THE RIDDINGS FARM
Kirk Ireton, Ashbourne DE6 3LB
Mr & Mrs P R Spencer
T 01335 370331
W http.members.lycos.co.uk/
ivycottage
Accommodation Delightful,
peacefully situated barn conversion
looking over Carsington Water.

Spacious 2 bedroomed,
accommodation, sleeps 3. Sorry no
pets, no smoking. Towels, linen
(duvets) and electricity included.
£250- £350 per week.
Member of County Team
SC

SHATTON HALL FARM COTTAGES
Shatton Hall Farm, Bamford, Hope
Valley S33 0BG
Angela Kellie
T 01433 620635
E ahk@peakfarmholidays.co.uk
W www.peakfarmholidays.co.uk
Accommodation Three
comfortable stone cottages, each
with two double bedrooms, open plan
living area. 4* accommodation,
around listed Elizabethan farmhouse.
Secluded location with good access
and within easy reach of Chatsworth
House and Haddon Hall.
SC

Devon

ASHWELL
East Street, Bovey Tracey, Newton
Abbot TQ13 9EJ
Diane Riddell
T 01626 830031
W www.ashwell-bb.com
Accommodation Ashwell is an
elegant William IV house with 2 large
bright and comfortable bedrooms with
ensuite facilities. Enjoy home-baked
bread, fresh eggs from our free range
hens and home made preserves.
See Bovey Tracey Gardens for details
of garden
B&B

BROOK
East Cornworthy, Totnes TQ9 7HQ
Mr & Mrs P Smyth
T 01803 722424
Accommodation One twin room
with ensuite shower room. Cottage
set in lovely tranquil valley within
walking distance of the River Dart and
Dittisham. The garden extends to
3 acres.
See East Cornworthy Gardens for
details of garden
B&B

THE CIDER HOUSE
Buckland Abbey, Yelverton PL20 6EZ
Mrs Sarah Stone
T 01822 853285
E sarah.stone@cider-house.co.uk
W www.cider-house.co.uk
Accommodation House formerly
part of Cistercian monastery of
Buckland; 1 double & 1 twin room
each with private bathroom, plus extra
twin room if required. Minimum stay 2
nights. £80 per room per night. Cottage
sleeps 5 in 3 bedrooms; sitting room
with log fire, dining room, kitchen.
Walled garden, use of tennis court.
Member of County Team
B&B SC

DARTINGTON HALL
Dartington Hall Gardens, Totnes
TQ9 6JE
Dartington Hall Trust
T 01803 847147
E bookings@dartingtonhall.com
W www.dartingtonhall.com
Accommodation There are 51
bedrooms within the C14 medieval
courtyard, most retaining their original
character. From beamed ceilings to
an etching of a C15 Spanish galleon
carved onto a wall, history can be
discovered all over the courtyard and
gardens.
H

KINGSTON HOUSE
Staverton, Totnes TQ9 6AR
Michael & Elizabeth Corfield
T 01803 762235
E info@kingston-estate.co.uk
W www.kingston-estate.co.uk
Accommodation Kingston House,
5 Diamonds - Gold award, has 3
beautiful suites and 9, 5* cottages.
The house is set in the gardens,
offering delicious food using garden
produce whenever possible, excellent
wine list. Price on application.
B&B SC

LITTLE ASH FARM
Fenny Bridges EX14 3BL
Sadie & Robert Reid
T 01404 850271
Accommodation Ensuite family
room sleeps 4. Family suite, twin and
double with bathroom. Single,
ensuite. All rooms have TV and tea
tray. Full breakfast in large
conservatory overlooking garden.
From £24. Non smoking.
B&B

NORTH BORESTON FARM
Halwell, Totnes TQ9 7LD
Rob & Jan Wagstaff
T 01548 821320
E borestongarden@btinternet.com
Accommodation Converted old
granary. Comfortably furnished living
room and well equipped kitchen
upstairs; bedroom (sleeps 2) with
ensuite shower room downstairs.
French windows onto own terrace.
Covered parking. Ideally located for
best of coast, Dartmoor and great
gardens.
SC

THE OLD RECTORY
Ashford, Barnstaple EX31 4BY
Ann Burnham
T 01271 377408
E annburnham@btinternet.com
Accommodation You will enjoy
your stay at the recently renovated
Old Rectory. Attractive bedrooms
with full ensuite. Delicious breakfasts;
dinner or supper on request. The
view is superb. Log fires in winter.
B&B

RECTORY GARDEN COTTAGE
The Old Rectory, Littleham, Bideford
EX39 5HW
Mrs C Smith
T 01638 674756 (Agent)
E admin@shhl.co.uk
W www.rectory-garden-
cottage.co.uk
Accommodation Spacious
cottage with own pretty and very
private garden. Lovely views over
gardens of The Old Rectory and
wooded countryside. Well equipped,
modern kitchen. Sleeps 3: one
kingsize bed , ensuite shower room,
one single with bathroom.
SC

REGENCY HOUSE
Hemyock, Cullompton EX15 3RQ
Mrs Jenny Parsons
T 01823 680238
E jenny.parsons@btinternet.com
Accommodation Regency House
is the most beautiful, spacious,
Georgian rectory. Accommodation:
double room, ensuite, 1 twin with
private bathroom. Price £45 pppn.
Dexter cattle, Jacob sheep and
horses live here too. Excellent pub in
Culmstock.
B&B

SOUTH HEATHERCOMBE
Heathercombe North, Manaton,
Newton Abbot TQ13 9XE
**Mrs Julia Holden & C & M Pike
Woodlands Trust**
T 01647 221350
E bandb@heathercombe.com
W www.heathercombe.com
Accommodation Comfortable, well
equipped accommodation in C15
Dartmoor longhouse. Twin/double
ensuite bedroom & twin/double family
room; whirlpool bath, TV/DVD, tea &
coffee making, guest's lounge with
log fire, conservatory. Delicious
breakfasts. Dogs welcome (kennels).
From £30 pn. See Heathercombe for
details of garden.
B&B

ST MERRYN
Higher Park Road, Braunton
EX33 2LG
Ros Bradford
T 01271 813805
E ros@st-merryn.co.uk
W www.st-merryn.co.uk
Accommodation Lovely house set
in peaceful garden. 1 single/twin with
private bathroom. 1 double (kingsize
bed) with private bathroom. 1 double
(kingsize bed), ensuite shower room.
Minimum stay 2 nights. Strictly no
smoking. Prices from £30pp.
B&B

WESTCOTT BARTON
Middle Marwood, Barnstaple
EX31 4EF
Howard Frank
T 01271 812842
E westcott_barton@yahoo.co.uk
W www.westcottbarton.co.uk
Accommodation Pretty bedrooms
(4 double, 1 twin), all ensuite, all with
colour TV and tea/coffee making
facilities. Breakfast is a movable feast
and evening meals are available on
request. No smoking or pets. Not
suitable for children under 12 yrs.
£45 per person.
B&B

WHITSTONE FARM
Whitstone Lane, Newton Abbot
TQ13 9NA
Katie & Alan Bunn
T 01626 832258
E katie@whitstonefarm.co.uk
W www.whitstonefarm.co.uk
Country house with stunning views
over Dartmoor. 1 super kingsized (or
twin) room, 1 kingsized room, 1
double sized room - all ensuite.
Prices from £70 per night. Single
occ. from £49. Come and be
pampered.
B&B

WINSFORD WALLED GARDEN
Halwill Junction EX21 5XT
Aileen Birks & Michael Gilmore
T 01409 221477
E muddywellies@
winsfordwalledgarden.com
W www.winsfordwalledgarden.com
Accommodation Top quality
double ensuite accommodation,
located within Victorian walled
summer flower garden containing
1000's of varieties. Wander inside the
most ornate and innovative Victorian
greenhouses anywhere in the South
West filled with bougainvillea and
tropical hibiscus. £35 pppn & £45
single occupancy.
B&B

Dorset

DOMINEYS COTTAGES
Domineys Yard, Buckland Newton
nr Dorchester DT2 7BS
Mr & Mrs W Gueterbock
T 01300 345295
E cottages@domineys.com
W www.domineys.com
Accommodation 3 delightful highly
commended 2 bdrm self-catering
cottages. Maintained to exceptional
standards - TB4*. Enchanting
gardens peacefully located in
Dorset's beautiful heartland. Flower
decked patios and heated summer
pool. Babies & children over 5 years
welcome. Regret no pets.
SC

HIGHER MELCOMBE MANOR
Higher Melcombe, Melcombe
Bingham, Dorchester DT2 7PB
**Michael Woodhouse & Lorel
Morton**
T 01258 880251
E lorel@lorelmorton.com
Accommodation 3 double
bedrooms, 2 with ensuite bathrooms
and 1 with bathroom along the
corridor. All recently refurbished.
Historic C16 manor house with two
acres of garden in a glorious setting.
Near to the Dorset Gap with its
wonderful walks and breathtaking
views.
B&B

KNOWLE FARM
Uploders, Bridport DT6 4NS
Alison & John Halliday
T 01308 485492
W www.knowlefarmbandb.com
Accommodation Welcoming,
relaxing village base for the delights
of West Dorset and beyond. Top
quality accommodation in C18
longhouse. Every attention to detail.
Super breakfasts. Double, ensuite;
twin with private bathroom. Sorry no
pets, smoking or children under 12.
From £37.50 pppn.
B&B

Durham & Northumberland

CHESWICK HOUSE
Cheswick, Berwick-upon-Tweed
TD15 2RL
Jean & Peter Bennett
T 01289 387387
E info@cheswickhouse.co.uk
W www.cheswickhouse.co.uk
Accommodation Detached
picturesque lodge. Cosy lounge with
wood burner. Four-poster bedroom.
Garden Wing – 3 bedroom apartment
sleeps 5. Large lounge, master
ensuite with four poster. Both one
mile from heritage coast within
secluded private estate. Tennis court.
SC

THORNLEY HOUSE
Thornley Gate, Hexham NE47 9NH
Eileen Finn
T 01434 683255
E e.finn@ukonline.co.uk
W web.ukonline.co.uk/e.finn
Accommodation Beautiful country
house, 1 mile west of Allendale, near
Hadrian's Wall. 3 bedrooms with
facilities, TV & tea makers. 2 lounges
with Steinway grand piano and
plasma TV. Resident Maine Coon
cats. B&B from £28 pppn - £175pw.
B&B

Flintshire & Wrexham

DOVE COTTAGE
Rhos Road, nr Chester CH4 0JR
Mr & Mrs C Wallis
T 01244 547539
E dovecottage@supanet.com
W www.visitwales.com
Accommodation Delightful C17
farmhouse. Luxurious
accommodation. 2 double rooms,
ensuite. Single occ. £35-£40, double
£60 per night. Convenient for
Chester & N Wales.
B&B

THE GARDEN HOUSE
Erbistock, LL13 0DL
Mr & Mrs S Wingett
T 01978 781149
E art@simonwingett.com
W www.simonwingett.com
Accommodation Luxurious 2
bedroomed cottage, sleeps 4/5,
situated by the Welsh River Dee in 5
acres of garden. Log burner, open
plan.
SC

WYCH ELM
Cefn Bychan Rd, Mold CH7 6EL
Martin & Gillian Fraser
T 01352 740241
E gandmfraser@btinternet.com
W www.wychelmbandb.co.uk
Accommodation Cedar shingle
house in woodland setting with fine
views of the Clwydian Hills. Mold 4
miles, Chester 17 miles. An excellent
base to explore this undiscovered
corner of Wales. Twin/king with
private bathroom, double with en
suite shower. From £27.50pppn.
See Pantymwyn Village Gardens for
details of Garden

Glamorgan

FLANDERS BARN
Flanders Road, Llantwit Major
CF61 1RL
Ann John
T 01446 794711
E davidp.john@hotmail.co.uk
W www.flandersbarn.co.uk
Accommodation Cottage annexe
of grade 2 listed barn. Lounge with
log fire, fridge and TV. Double
bedroom, ensuite shower room.
Sleeps 2-4. Price from £70pn, incl
breakfast.
See Llantwit Major & Llanmaes
Gardens for details of garden
B&B

GLYNDWR HOUSE & VINEYARD
Llanblethian, Cowbridge CF71 7JF
Richard & Susan Norris
T 01446 774564
E glyndwrvineyard@talktalk.net
W www.glyndwrvineyard.com

Accommodation An oasis of
peace and calm, set amidst
orchards, vineyard, herbaceous
borders, wildflowers and ponds. The
twin bedded room has its own
verandah and kitchen. Beautifully
situated for walks, a nearby pub and
the historic market town of
Cowbridge.
See Llanblethian Gardens for details
of garden
B&B SC

MEHEFIN
Sigginston Lane, Llanmaes, Llantwit
Major CF61 2XR
Bryn & Alison Morgan
T 01446 793427
E bb@mehefin.com
W www.mehefin.com
Accommodation Privately owned
B&B in attractive, award winning
village. Two double ensuite
bedrooms. 18 miles from Cardiff.
Close to Dyffryn Gardens and approx
1 hrs drive to National Botanic
Garden of Wales.
See Llantwit Major & Llanmaes
Gardens for details of garden
B&B

Gloucestershire

BERRYS PLACE FARM
Bulley Lane, Churcham GL2 8AS
Mr G & Mrs A Thomas
E 01452 750298 / 07950 808022
W g.j.thomas@btconnect.com
Accommodation Traditional
farmhouse B&B with fishing lake. 6
miles west of historic Gloucester,
approx 9 miles to Cheltenham Spa
and race course and within easy
reach of the Cotswolds, Forest of
Dean and Wye Valley. £35 pppn.
B&B

BYAMS HOUSE
Willesley, Tetbury GL8 8QU
Kena & Sean Magee
T 01666 880009
E sean@magees.demon.co.uk
Accommodation Two bedroomed
cottage which sleeps 4 in a peaceful,
rural setting near Westonbirt
Arboretum. Convenient for Bath and
Cheltenham. £40 single, £75 double
occupancy. Full English breakfast.
Member of County Team
B&B

COOPERS COTTAGE
Wells Cottage, Wells Road, Bisley
Stroud GL6 7AG
Mr & Mrs Michael Flint
T 01452 770289
E flint_bisley@talktalk.net
Accommodation Attractive old
beamed cottage, non-smoking,
sleeps 2-4. Stands apart in owners'
large, beautiful garden with lovely
views. Furnished & equipped to high
standard. Very quiet, good walking.

Village shop & 2 pubs nearby. See Wells Cottage for details of garden.
SC

KEMPSFORD MANOR
High Street, Kempsford, Fairford GL7 4EQ
Mrs Z Williamson
T 01285 810131
E ipek.williamson@tiscali.co.uk
W www.kempsfordmanor.co.uk
Accommodation C17-18 manor house set in peaceful gardens. Fine reception rooms. 3-4 double bedrooms. Price from £40 single occ. Ideal retreat. Home grown organic vegetables. Suitable for small conferences and marquee receptions. 1 mile from Wiltshire border.
B&B

KINGSCOTE PARK HOUSE
Kingscote Park, Kingscote, Tetbury GL8 8YA
Geoffrey Higgins
T 01453 861050
E rebecca@matara.co.uk
W www.kingscotepark.co.uk
Accommodation Kingscote Park House: Relax in our beautiful Regency family home, with close family and friends – sleeps up to 16 people. Zen rooms: 3 new Zen inspired attic rooms, with queen-size futon beds within the Matara centre. See The Matara Garden for details of garden
B&B SC

OWLPEN MANOR
Owlpen, Uley, Dursley GL11 5BZ
Lady Karin Mander
T 01453 860261
E sales@owlpen .com
W www.owlpen.com
Accommodation Nine SC cottages on 215 acre estate. Cosy retreats for just two or up to nine. Most have log burners or open fires. Home made take-away food and breakfast hampers available. Pets welcome.
SC

Gwent

THE HILL
Pen Y Pound Road, Abergavenny NP7 7RP
Coleg Gwent
T 01495 333777
E sam.brooks@coleggwent.ac.uk
W www.thehillabergavenny.co.uk
Accommodation The Hill offers 48 ensuite bedrooms, an executive suite and a self-contained lodge that sleeps 5. Please phone for more information and special offers. See Gardd-y-Bryn for details of garden.
B&B SC H

PENPERGWM LODGE
Abergavenny NP7 9AS
Mr & Mrs S Boyle
T 01873 840208
E boyle@penpergwm.co.uk
W www.penplants.com
Accommodation A large rambling Edwardian house in the lovely Usk valley. Pretty bedrooms have garden views, bathrooms share a corridor, breakfast and relax in the spacious and comfortable sitting room. Great walking in nearby Brecon Beacons National Park.
B&B

Gwynedd

HOTEL MAES-Y-NEUADD
Talsarnau, nr Harlech LL47 6YA
Peter & Lynn Jackson & Peter Payne
T 01766 780200
E maes@neuadd.com
W www.neuadd.com
Accommodation 15 individually designed ensuite double/twin rooms. C14 manor house with bar, terrace, lounge, conservatory and highly acclaimed restaurant serving fresh, local produce and home grown fruit & vegetables. B&B from £49.50.
H

MELIN MELOCH
Llanderfel, Bala-Gwynedd LL23 7DP
Richard Fullard
T 01678 520101
Accommodation A self contained pretty granary with one double and one twin room. Bed and breakfast is £30 pppn.
B&B

Hampshire

APPLE COURT
Hordle Lane, Hordle, Lymington SO41 0HU
Charles & Angela Meads
T 01590 642130
E applecourt@btinternet.com
W www.applecourt.com
Accommodation Cottage annexe next to Apple Court. 2 bedrooms, sleeps 4. Kitchen, dining room, conservatory/lounge. Non-smoking. Regret no dogs. Beautiful location near New Forest, Lymington. From £400 per week.
B&B

12 CHRISTCHURCH ROAD
Winchester SO23 9SR
Mrs P Patton
T 01962 854272
E pjspatton@yahoo.co.uk
W www.visitwinchester.co.uk/ site/where-to-stay
Accommodation An elegant Victorian house on the south side of city. Easy walk to city centre and close to long distance footpaths.

Home made bread, preserves and local produce. Well behaved dogs welcome. Luggage can be transported for walkers. From £40 per room.
B&B

Herefordshire

BROBURY HOUSE
Brobury, Hereford HR3 6BS
Prof & Mrs Cartwright
T 01981 500229
E enquiries@broburyhouse.co.uk
W www.broburyhouse.co.uk
Accommodation House - B&B: Large double room, ensuite. 1 double & 1 twin large rooms each with private shower room, all with beautiful garden views. Prices from £35 pppn. Cottages - 2 spacious, recently refurbished, self catering cottages. Peak period price £440.
B&B SC

CAVES FOLLY NURSERY
Evendine Lane, Colwall WR13 6DY
Bridget Evans
T 01684 540631
E bridget@cavesfolly.com
W www.cavesfolly.co.uk
Accommodation SC cottage on organic nursery. Idylic setting in Malvern Hills AONB. Available to let nightly or weekly. Sleeps 6. Also self-catering B&B - choose your organic breakfast from our shop. £35 per person.
B&B SC

THE GREAT HOUSE
Dilwyn, Hereford HR4 8HX
Tom & Jane Hawksley
T 01544 318007
W www.thegreathousedilwyn.co.uk
Accommodation 3 double/twin, ensuite bathrooms. Private sunny sitting room with door to garden. Beams, panelling, flag stone floors and enormous log fires. Price from £45pppn, single suppl. £10. Dinner by arrangement from £20. Licensed. Wolsey Lodge.
B&B

HOLME LACY HOUSE HOTEL
Holme Lacy, nr Hereford HR2 6LP
Warner Leisure Hotel Group
T 01432 870870
E events.holmelacy@bourne-leisure.co.uk
W www.warnerleisurehotels.co.uk
Accommodation Set in the idyllic Wye Valley, this is a magical Grade I listed mansion with 179 bedrooms. The Historic Rooms and Suites are in the Old House, whilst the contemporary 'Signature' rooms and comfortable 'Ambassador' rooms are in the new wing.
H

HOPE END HOUSE
Hope End, Ledbury HR8 1JQ
Mr & Mrs PJ Maiden
T 01531 635890
E sharonmaiden@btinternet.com
W www.hopeendhouse.com
Accommodation Hope End House, surrounded by 100 acres of historic parkland, where once Elizabeth Barrett roamed. This romantic house has peace at its heart. Our accommodation has been awarded 5*. Our gardens tranquil and peaceful.
B&B

SHIELDBROOK
Kings Caple, Hereford HR1 4UB
Susan & Oliver Sharp
T 01432 840670
E susansharp95@btinternet.com
Accommodation Comfortable double room with double bed and wash basin in room in a traditional 300 year old house. Well situated for garden visits. £40 pppn.
B&B

Hertfordshire

WEST LODGE PARK
Cockfosters Road, Hadley Wood Barnet EN4 0PY
Beales Hotels
T 0208 216 3900
E westlodgepark@bealeshotels.co.uk
W www.bealeshotels.co.uk
Accommodation 59 bedrooms including Superior, Executive rooms with views over our arboretum. If you are looking for something more modern, try our Chestnut Lodge rooms which can be found in a separate lodge in our gardens.
H

Isle of Wight

NORTHCOURT
Northcourt Gardens, Main Road Shorwell PO30 3JG
Mr & Mrs J Harrison
T 01983 740415
E christine@northcourt.info
W www.northcourt.info
Accommodation B&B in large C17 manor house in 15 acres of exotic gardens, on edge of the downs. 6 double/twin rooms, all ensuite. Price from £60 per room. Also wing of house for up to 14 self-catering.
B&B SC

Kent

BOYTON COURT
Sutton Valence ME17 3BY
Richard & Patricia Stileman
T 01622 844065
E richstileman@aol.com
Accommodation Country house in quiet location with lovely garden. 2 double rooms (1 kingsize, 1 twin) with

ensuite bathrooms. Both with spectacular views. £105 pn. Single occ. £65. Detached SC stable suite. £105 B&B, £85 pn or £450 per week (SC).
B&B SC

CANTERBURY CATHEDRAL LODGE
Cathedral House, 11 The Precincts Canterbury CT1 2EH
Dean & Chapter of Canterbury
T 01227 865350
E stay@canterbury-cathedral.org
W www.canterburycathedrallodge.org
Accommodation 30 ensuite rooms situated within the Precincts, all with stunning views of The Cathedral. 2 minutes from city centre, shops, restaurants and cafes. 10% off the normal tarriff when mentioning this on reservation.
B&B

3 CHAINHURST COTTAGES
Dairy Lane, Chainhurst TN12 9SU
Heather Scott
T 01622 820483 / 07729 378489
E heatherscott@waitrose.com
W www.chainhurstcottages.co.uk
Accommodation Comfortable, modern accommodation with private entrance and ensuite bathroom in quiet rural location with good local pubs. Ideal touring base for historic properties and gardens including Leeds Castle & Sissinghurst Garden. Visit Britain - 4* Silver award. £80 pn, £50 single occ.
See Chainhurst Cottage Gardens for details of garden
B&B

COTTAGE FARM
Cacketts Lane, Cudham TN14 7QG
Phil & Karen Baxter
T 01959 534048/532506
E karen@cottagefarmturkeys.co.uk
Accommodation Delightful country cottage: 1 double and 1 twin room, living room, kitchen and bathroom. Full central heating. From £350 per week self catering. B&B £35 pppn based on 2 sharing double/twin room. £45 single occ.
B&B SC

HOATH HOUSE
Chiddingstone Hoath, Edenbridge TN8 7DB
Mervyn & Jane Streatfeild
T 01342 850362
E janestreatfeild@hoath-house.freeserve.co.uk
W www.hoathhouse.co.uk
Accommodation Rambling medieval and Tudor house in extensive gardens with fine views. Convenient for Penshurst, Chartwell and Hever and recommendations for NGS openings across Kent. 2 twin rooms sharing 'Art deco' bathroom,

1 double, ensuite. Good access to London and Gatwick
Member of County Team
B&B

MISTRAL
Oxenturn Road, Wye TN25
G P Chapman & S M Chapman
T 01233 813011
E geoff@chapman.invictanet.co.uk
W www.chapman.invictanet.co.uk
Accommodation Mistral B&B is a 4* modern establishment located in Wye, with easy access to the village and North Downs. Wye has a rail link to London, Ashford International (Eurostar) and Canterbury. Garden enthusiasts welcome.
See Wye Gardens for details of garden
B&B

ROCK FARM HOUSE
Gibbs Hill, Nettlestead, Maidstone ME18 5HT
Mrs S E Corfe
T 01622 812244
W www.rockfarmhousebandb.co.uk
Accommodation Delightful C18 Kentish farmhouse in quiet, idyllic position on a farm with extensive views. 4 diamond B&B with 1 double and 1 twin room, both ensuite. Price £75, single occ £50.
B&B

THE SALUTATION
Knightrider Street, Sandwich CT13 9EW
Mr & Mrs D Parker
T 01304 619919
E dominic@the-salutation.com
W www.the-salutation.com
Accommodation 10 bedrooms available within 3 cottages within the estate, offering exclusive and private bed and breakfast.
B&B

WICKHAM LODGE
The Quay, High Street, Aylesford ME20 7AY
Cherith & Richard Bourne
T 01622 717267
E wickhamlodge@aol.com
W www.wickhamlodge.co.uk
Accommodation Beautifully restored house offering every modern comfort situated on the river bank in Aylesford, one of the oldest and most picturesque villages in Kent. Cherith & Richard provide a warm and hospitable welcome for their guests.
B&B SC

Lancashire Merseyside & Greater Manchester

MILL BARN
Goose Foot Close, Samlesbury Bottoms, Preston PR5 0SS
Chris Mortimer
T 01245 853300
E chris@millbarn.net
Accommodation Mill Barn is a converted barn. 1 double & 1 twin room, neither ensuite. Guests are accommodated as house guests & have full access to all shared rooms - lounge, conservatory, studio etc. as well as the garden.
Member of County Team
B&B

THE RIDGES
Weavers Brow, Cont. Cowling Road Limbrick Heath Charnock, Chorley PR6 9EB
John & Barbara Barlow
T 01257 279981
E barlow.ridges@virgin.net
W www.bedbreakfast-gardenvisits.com
Accommodation 3 bedrooms, 1 double ensuite, 1 twin & 1 single sharing a private bathroom. Dining room. Prices from £70 double & £40 single.
B&B

SEFTON VILLA
14 Sefton Drive, Sefton Park Liverpool L8 3SD
Mrs Patricia Williams
T 0151 281 3687
E seftonvilla@live.co.uk
W www.seftonvilla.co.uk
Accommodation Victorian house. Decorated in period style with kingsize bed and ensuite with shower. Tea & coffee facilities, TV, hairdryer.
See Sefton Park Gardens for details of garden
B&B

Lincolnshire

BRUNESWOLD COACH HOUSE
The Coach House, 1A Hereward Street, Lincoln LN1 3EW
Jo & Ken Slone
T 01522 568484
E kenjo@bruneswoldcoachhouse.co.uk
W www.bruneswoldcoachhouse.co.uk
Accommodation Ground level self catering B&B accommodation within the garden of a Victorian town house in uphill Lincoln, brimming with plants and sculpture. 5 minutes walk away from the historic quarter of Lincoln. Off-road parking. See The Coach House for details of garden.
SC

GOLTHO HOUSE
Lincoln Road, Goltho, Market Rasen LN8 5NF
Mrs D Hollingworth
T 01673 857768
E s.hollingworth@homecall.co.uk
W www.golthogardens.com
Accommodation 1 double room with four poster bed, 1 double room with half tester bed, 1 double room - all share a private bathroom.
B&B

London

38 KILLIESER AVENUE
SW2 4NT
Winkle Haworth
T 020 8671 4196
E winklehaworth@hotmail.com
W www.specialplacestostay.com
Accommodation Luxurious and stylish accommodation, 1 twin bedded room, 1 single - both with private bathroom. Price from £90. Single occ. £60. English breakfast incl.
Member of County Team
B&B

28 OLD DEVONSHIRE ROAD
SW12 9RB
Georgina Ivor
T 020 8673 7179
E georgina@balhambandb.co.uk
W www.balhambandb.co.uk
Accommodation 1 spacious double room with private bathroom in elegant mid Victorian house. 5 minutes from Balham tube and mainline stations; great variety of local restaurants. Price from £90. Single occ £60. English breakfast included.
B&B

Norfolk

BAGTHORPE HALL
Bagthorpe, King's Lynn PE31 6QR
Mrs Gina Morton
T 01485 578528
E enquiries@bagthorpehall.co.uk
W www.bagthorpehall.co.uk
Accommodation 2-3 large double bedrooms ensuite, big comfortable beds, organic and homemade breakfast. From £70 for double incl breakfast. £40 single.
B&B

BAY COTTAGE
The Old Cottage, Colby Corner Nr Aylsham NR11 7EB
Stuart Clarke
T 01263 734574
E enchanting@btinternet.com
W www.enchantingcottages.co.uk
Accommodation 4* ETB graded country cottage with large garden. Sleeps 7 in 3 bedrooms, plus a self contained garden, oak framed annexe with wheelchair access, which sleeps 2. See The Old Cottage for details of garden.
SC

CONIFER HILL
Starston, Harleston IP20 9NT
Richard & Tish Lombe Taylor
T 01379 852393
E richard.taylor55@virgin.net
Accommodation Victorian house on a hill – unusual for Norfolk! Comfy sitting room, TV and log fire. Swimming pool. Children over 6 years welcome. Dogs by arrangement. 1 twin, ensuite. 1 twin & 1 double let to same party only. £35 pppn.
B&B

MANOR HOUSE FARM
Wellingham, King's Lynn PE32 2TH
Robin & Elisabeth Ellis
T 01328 838227
W www.manor-house-farm.co.uk
Accommodation Award winning conversion in garden. 2 large airy double bedrooms, ensuite. Comfortable, sitting room with wood burning stove, TV and books etc plus small kitchen. Breakfast in dining room of main house. Also beautiful barn with SC for 2.
B&B SC

THE OLD RECTORY
Ridlington, North Walsham NR28 9NZ
Peter & Fiona Black
T 01692 650247
E blacks7@email.com
W www.oldrectory.northnorfolk.co.uk
Accommodation House: 1 double bedroom, ensuite; 1 double with wash basin and private bathroom. Garden room: large studio, double/twin beds, plus sofa bed, ktichen and bathroom. Prices from £50 per night. 1½ miles from East Ruston Old Vicarage Gardens
Member of County Team
B&B SC

SALLOWFIELD COTTAGE
Wattlefield, Wymondham NR18 9NX
Caroline Musker
T 01952 605086
E caroline.musker@tesco.net
W www.sallowfieldcottage.co.uk
Accommodation One double ensuite, one double with private bathroom and one single with private shower. The cottage is in a quiet location well away from the road surrounded by its own garden with a large pond.
B&B

STABLE COTTAGE
Bolwick Hall, Marsham Norwich NR10 5PU
Mr & Mrs G Fisher
T 01263 732131
E gandcfisher@supanet.com
W www.bolwick.com

Accommodation Grade 2 listed cottage with private garden surrounded by Hall gardens with lake and tennis court. Sleeps 7 with 4 bedrooms. See Bolwick Hall for details of garden.
SC

Northamptonshire

DALE HOUSE
Yew Tree Lane, Spratton NN6 8HL
Fiona Cox
T 01604 846458
E cjcatdalehouse@aol.com
Accommodation Double room with kingsize bed and own bathroom in annexe. SC or B&B. Parking in private drive. Quiet views overlooking garden and open countryside.
See Spratton Gardens for details of garden
B&B SC

HUNT HOUSE QUARTERS
Hunt House, Main Road, Kilsby, Rugby CV23 8XR
Linda Harris
T 01788 823282 / 0775 3679308
E luluharris@hunthouse.fsbusiness.co.uk
W www.hunthousekilsby.com
Accommodation The Hunt House Quarters is set in a beautiful thatched hunting lodge and covered stables. 4 courtyard rooms are finished to luxury standard. Tranquil setting. AA 4* Highly Commended award.
See Kilsby Gardens for details of garden
B&B

THE OLD VICARAGE
Broad Lane
Evenley, Brackley, NN13 5SF
Philippa Heumann
T 07774 415 332
E philippaheumann@andreas-heumann.com
Accommodation Elegant Regency vicarage set in large attractive garden in the picturesque village of Evenley. Two twin bedrooms, two bathrooms. Ideally situated for visiting gardens in Central England –approx 5 miles J10 M40. B&B – single £35, double £70 pn.
Member of County Team
B&B

Nottinghamshire

GRINGLEY HALL
Gringley on the Hill, Doncaster DN10 4QT
Dulce & Ian Threlfall
T 01777 817262
E dulce@gringleyhall.fsnet.co.uk
W www.gringleyhall.co.uk
Accommodation Regency house located on the borders of Nottinghamshire, Lincolnshire and South Yorkshire. The setting for the true story 'Lemon Curd and

Grandfather's Whiskers'. Spacious, comfortable, ensuite rooms and seriously delicious breakfasts using homemade produce. SC cottages on request.
See Gringley Gardens for details of garden
B&B SC

THORESBY HALL HOTEL & SPA
Thoresby Park, nr Ollerton, Newark NG22 9WH
Warner Leisure Hotel Group
T 01623 821000
E thoresbyhall.reception@bourne-leisure.co.uk
W www.warnerleisurehotels.co.uk
Accommodation A majestic Victorian mansion set on the edge of the ancient Sherwood Forest with 221 bedrooms. The magnificent Historic Rooms in the Old House, the contemporary 'Signature' rooms with every modern facility to the comfortable 'Ambassador' rooms in the new wing.
H

Oxfordshire

BROUGHTON GROUNDS FARM
North Newington, Banbury OX15 6AW
Andrew and Margaret Taylor
T 01295 730315
E info@broughtongrounds.co.uk
W www.broughtongrounds.co.uk
Accommodation One double, one twin and one single room in C17 farmhouse, on working mixed farm, located on the Broughton Castle Estate. Beautiful views and peaceful location. Prices: £30 pppn.
B&B

BUTTSLADE HOUSE
Temple Mill Road, Sibford Gower Banbury OX15 5RX
Mrs Diana Thompson
T 01295 788818
E janthompson50@hotmail.com
W www.buttsladehouse.co.uk
Accommodation Sympathetically restored stables of C17 farmhouse in tranquil English country garden. 1 double and 1 twin bedded room with private sitting rooms and own bathrooms. Own bread & cakes baked daily, seasonal fruit from garden. SC available, please enquire.
See Sibford Gower Gardens for details of garden
B&B SC

CHAPMANS BARN
Chapmans, Nottingham Fee, Blewbury OX11 9PG
Jenny Craig
T 01235 851055
E bnb@chapmansbarn.com
W www.chapmansbarn.com
Accommodation A private annexe to a C17 thatched cottage with 1 bedroom (single, double, twin)

ensuite bathroom, sitting room, nestled at the foot of the Berkshire downs. Sun - Thurs £60, Fri/Sat £80. See Blewbury Gardens for details of garden
B&B

GOWERS CLOSE
Sibford Gower, Banbury OX15 5RW
Judith Hitching and John Marshall
T 01295 780348
E j.hitching@virgin.net
Accommodation C17 thatched cottage has 1 double and 1 twin, both ensuite, with low beams and log fires, enchanting garden for pampered guests to enjoy. Close to Hidcote, Kiftsgate and many Cotswold gardens. Price from £35 pppn.
See Sibford Gower Gardens for details of garden
B&B

SOUTH NEWINGTON HOUSE
South Newington, Banbury OX15 4JW
Roberta & John Ainley
T 01295 721207
E rojoainley@btinternet.com
W www.southnewingtonhouse.co.uk
Accommodation Cottage annexe: Bedroom (kingsize), sitting room, shower room & kitchen. House: 2 doubles (kingsize) & 1 twin all with private bathrooms. Prices £80 - £100 per room per night. Single occ. £50 - £60.
Member of County Team
B&B SC

Powys

CWMLLECHWEDD FAWR
Llanbister, Llandrindod Wells LD1 6UH
John Underwood
T 01597 840267
E postmaster@cwmllechwedd.u-net.com
W www.cwmllechwedd.u-net.com
Accommodation One double, one twin room both with ensuite bathrooms. Evening meals available. Early C19 brick farmhouse in rural mid Wales.
B&B

CYFIE FARM
Llanfihangel, Llanfyllin SY22 5JE
Neil & Claire Bale
T 01691 648451
E info@cyfiefarm.co.uk
W www.cyfiefarm.co.uk
Accommodation This beautiful, remote, 5* (Gold), C17 Welsh Longhouse, boasts a magnificent peaceful setting with stunning views. Relax all day in your own luxurious suite of rooms. Cordon Bleu cuisine. Hot tub & sauna spa.
B&B SC

MILL COTTAGE
Abbeycwmhir, Llandrindod Wells
LD1 6PH
Mr & Mrs B D Parfitt
T 01597 851935
E nkmillcottage@yahoo.co.uk
W www.Abbeycwmhir.co.uk
Accommodation C18 cottage in a
peaceful village in the beautiful
Cambrian mountains. 1 double/twin
with private bathroom. 2 singles (one
with dressing room and basin).
Private bathroom. Evening meals by
arrangement. Ideal for walkers and
cyclists.
B&B

PLAS DOLGUOG HOTEL
Solstar, Dolguog Estates Felingerrig,
Machynlleth SY20 8UJ
Mr Anthony & Mrs Tina Rhodes
T 01654 702244
E res@plasdolguog.co.uk
W www.plasdolguog.co.uk
Accommodation Family run hotel,
David Bellamy Conservation Award, 9
acres including Grandma's Garden.
Family & ground floor rooms - all
individual with ensuite facilities. Cu
Og's restaurant offers panoramic
views over the Dyfi Valley &
Snowdonia National Park. See
Grandma's Garden for details of
garden.
B&B

THE WERN
Llanfihangel Talyllyn, Brecon LD3 7TE
Lucienne and Neil Bennett
T 01874 658401
E lucienne_bennett@hotmail.com
W www.bennettthewern.vispa.com
Accommodation The Wern B&B
for Horse and Rider is situated in the
Brecon Beacons National Park. The
Evening meals available. The food
provided is from produce from our
gardens. Our guests have full use of
our gardens and terraces.
B&B

Shropshire

BROWNHILL HOUSE
Ruyton XI Towns, Shrewsbury
SY4 1LR
Yoland & Roger Brown
T 01939 261121
E brownhill@eleventowns.co.uk
W www.eleventowns.co.uk
Accommodation Old world
standards, modern facilities & relaxed
atmosphere. Unique 2 acre garden -
must be seen to be believed. Easy
access - Chester to Ludlow,
Snowdonia to Ironbridge and loads of
wonderful gardens. Find out all about
us on our website.
B&B

MAREHAY FARM
Gatten, Pontesbury, Shrewsbury
SY5 0SJ
Carol & Stuart Buxton
T 01588 650289
Accommodation 2 ensuite rooms,
one twin, one double in one of the
last idyllic areas of England. Far from
the madding crowd and noble strife!
B&B from £27.50 per person.
B&B

Somerset, Bristol Area & S Glos

THE BEANACRE BARN
Church Farm House, Turners Court
Lane, Binegar, Radstock BA3 4UA
Susan & Tony Griffin
T 01749 841628
E smgriffin@beanacrebarn.co.uk
W www.beanacrebarn.co.uk
Accommodation In the Mendip
Hills 4m north of Wells. Imaginatively
converted, beautifully furnished and
particularly spacious, beamed barn.
All modern facilities and comfort in a
traditional setting. Sleeps 2+2. Own
south-facing garden and patio.
Peaceful country retreat. See Church
Farm House for details of garden.
SC

BEECH HOUSE
Yate Road, Iron Acton BS37 9XX
John & Hazel Williams
T 01454 313679
E bandb@beech-house.biz
W www.beech-house.biz
Accommodation Farmhouse
accommodation serving farmhouse
breakfast. Accredited by tourist
board. All rooms ensuite, hospitality
tray, TV and internet. Some with far
reaching rural views. Gardens open
to residents all year round. Sorry no
pets or children.
B&B

BINHAM GRANGE
Old Cleeve, Minehead TA24 6HX
Marie Thomas
T 01984 640056
E mariethomas@btconnect.com
W www.binhamgrange.co.uk
Accommodation A warm welcome
awaits you at Binham Grange,
mentioned in the 13th century in
association with Cleeve Abbey.
Rooms are individually decorated
with antiques, books and flowers.
Local produce, herbs and vegetables
from own garden simply prepared.
B&B

CHERRY BOLBERRY FARM
Furge Lane, Henstridge,
Templecombe BA8 0RN
Mrs Jennifer Raymond
T 01963 362177
Accommodation Farmhouse B&B
on working organic dairy farm with
Jersey cattle & Oxford sheep. 1

double and 1 twin, £25pppn. Very
peaceful setting in no through lane
with far reaching views.TV, tea &
coffee facilities. Full English breakfast
- mainly home produced produce -
served in conservatory overlooking
garden. Use of swimming pool.
B&B

CRICKET ST. THOMAS HOTEL
nr Chard, Somerset TA20 4DD
Warner Leisure Hotel Group
T 01460 30111
E hazel.malcolm@bourne-
leisure.co.uk
W www.warnerleisurehotels.co.uk
Accommodation Cricket St
Thomas is an elegant mansion C1820,
set in the heart of Somerset. The 217
bedrooms including the beautiful
'Royale' rooms in the Old House, with
contemporary 'Signature' rooms and
the comfortable 'Ambassador' rooms
in the new building.
H

EMMAUS HOUSE RETREAT & CONFERENCE CENTRE
Emmaus House, Clifton Hill, Clifton
BS8 1BN
Sisters of La Retraite
T 0117 907 9950
T administration@emmaushouse.
org.uk
W www.emmaushouse.org.uk
Accommodation C18 listed
building in the heart of Clifton. 23
single rooms, 7 ensuite. Prices pppn
from £40 standard to £45 ensuite.
Continental breakfast. Award winning
gardens with extensive views. Nightly
'curfew' 10.30 pm. Latest check-in
9.00 pm.
B&B

FARNDON THATCH
Puckington, Ilminster TA19 9JA
Bob & Jane St John Wright
T 01460 259845
E janesjw@yahoo.com
1 double room, ensuite. 1
double/twin with private bathroom.
C16 thatched cottage in idyllic
setting. 1 acre garden with fine views.
Occasional evening meal. No
smoking.
B&B

GANTS MILL & GARDEN
Gants Mill Lane, Bruton BA10 0DB
Alison & Brian Shingler
T 01749 812393
E shingler@gantsmill.co.uk
W www.gantsmill.co.uk
Accommodation C18 farmhouse
in rural valley, by historic watermill
now generating electricity. Spacious,
comfortable, pretty, bedrooms with
lacy four-poster stargazer beds. Wide
choice of healthy and wicked
breakfasts with best local ingredients.
£35 pppn. Vacancies on website.
B&B

HANGERIDGE FARMHOUSE
Hangeridge Farm, Wrangway,
Wellington TA21 9QT
Mrs J M Chave
T 01823 662339
E hangeridge@hotmail.co.uk
W www.hangeridge.co.uk
Accommodation A family run B&B.
Located in Wrangway near Wellington
on the Somerset/Devon border. Very
peaceful setting down a country lane,
on the edge of the Blackdown Hills.
One double room with private
bathroom and a twin bedded room.
£25 pppn.
B&B

HARPTREE COURT
East Harptree, Bristol BS40 6AA
Mr & Mrs Charles Hill
T 01761 221729
E location.harptree@tiscali.co.uk
W www.harptreecourt.co.uk
Accommodation 2 double rooms
ensuite and 1 twin room in elegant
period house surrounded by beautiful
landscaped grounds. £100 B&B with
afternoon tea per room pn. £65 single
occ. Evening meal by arrangement.
5* Highly Commended.
B&B

HOMEWOOD PARK HOTEL
Abbey Lane, Hinton Charterhouse,
Bath BA2 7TB
von Essen Hotels
T 01225 723731
E info@homewoodpark.co.uk
W www.homewoodpark.co.uk
Accommodation Beautifully
refurbished, this country house hotel
near Bath is one of the loveliest in the
West Country. 19 Contemporary
bedrooms, individually furnished to a
high standard. B&B prices from
£125.00 per room. See website for
special offers.
H

KNOLL COTTAGE
Stogumber, Taunton TA4 3TN
Elaine & John Leech
T 01984 656689
E mail@knoll-cottage.co.uk
W www.knoll-cottage.co.uk
Accommodation Visit Britain 4*.
Secluded rural location between the
Quantocks and Exmoor. Beautiful 2
acre garden. Two ensuite bedrooms
with kingsize beds in recently
converted stables. Double from £60.
Single from £35. Dogs welcome.
B&B

**SELF REALIZATION MEDITATION
HEALING CENTRE**
Self Realization Meditation Healing
Centre Charitable Trust, Laurel Lane
Queen Camel, Yeovil BA22 7NU
Charitable Trust - SRMHC
T 01935 850266
E info@selfrealizationcentres.org
W www.selfrealizationcentres.org

Accommodation The
accommodation is comfortable,
simple, home style and non-smoking
with beautiful vegetarian meals
available. The spacious grounds
include meditation rooms, a heated
indoor therapy pool and a lovely
sitting room with a log fire.
B&B SC

STOBERRY HOUSE
Stoberry Park, Wells BA5 3LD
Mr and Mrs Tim Young
T 01749 672906
E stay@stoberry-park.co.uk
W www.stoberry-park.co.uk
Accommodation Uniquely situated
in 26 acres of parkland within walking
distance of City of Wells. Breathtaking
views over cathedral and Vale of
Avalon. Luxurious B&B with
individually decorated ensuite
bedrooms, very comfortable reception
rooms, warm welcome into the family
home.
B&B SC

WOODLAND COTTAGE
Oldbury-on-Severn BS35 1PL
Jane Perkins
T 01454 414570
E jane.perkins@simtec.ltd.uk
Accommodation 1 twin room with
shared bathroom. Price £20 pppn
Member of County Team
B&B

Suffolk

ROSEMARY
Rectory Hill, East Bergholt, Colchester
CO7 6TH
Mrs Natalie Finch
T 01206 298241
Accommodation Situated in the
heart of Constable country within easy
reach of Harwich and Flatford. Garden
featured on Gardener's World. 3 twin
rooms - with hand basins, 1 single
room. Shared bathroom. Price £29
single, £58 twin.
B&B

Surrey

GREAT FOSTERS
Stroude Road, Egham TW20 9UR
The Sutcliffe Family
T 01784 433822
E reservations@greatfosters.co.uk
W www.greatfosters.co.uk
Accommodation More than 4
centuries of celebrated history have
enriched Great Fosters with
remarkable heritage. Countless
original features remain, with
bedrooms varying from historic
grandeur to more contemporary in
style. Double/twin rooms start from
£165 per night.
H

SPRING COTTAGE
Smithwood Common Road, Cranleigh
GU6 8QN
Mr & Mrs David Norman
T 01483 272620
E norman.springcott@btinternet.com
Accommodation 1st floor
accommodation in newly built barn. 1
double bedroom, bathroom, large
sitting room with TV. Lovely views
towards N and S downs. Good
walking and cycling. Enjoy garden in
all seasons. Prices from £70 pn.
Single occ. £45.
B&B SC

WOTTON HOUSE
Principal Hayley Hotels & Conference
Venues, Guildford Road, Dorking
RH5 6HS
Hayley Conference Centres
T 01306 730000
E wotton@hayleycc.co.uk.
W www.hayley-conf.co.uk
Accommodation Wotton House
has 111 ensuite facilities. 91 double
rooms, 20 twins and 5 adapted for
disabled use. Each room has: Wi-Fi,
TV, Safe, tea & coffee making facilities,
hairdryers, trouser press & iron. Dry
cleaning service.
H

Sussex

BUTLERS FARMHOUSE
Butlers Lane, Flowers Green,
Herstmonceux BN27 1QH
Irene Eltringham-Willson
T 01323 833770
E irene.willson@btinternet.com
W www.irenethegardener.zoomshare.
com
A charming C16 farmhouse in 5 acres
of idyllic, quiet countryside. Enjoy
breakfast overlooking fantastic views
of the South Downs. 2 double rooms.
Laze around outdoor swimming pool.
Herstmonceux and Pevensey Castles
nearby. From £75.
B&B

COPYHOLD HOLLOW
Copyhold Lane, Lindfield, Haywards
Heath RH16 1XU
Frances B G Druce
T 01444 413265
E yb@copyholdhollow.co.uk
W www.copyholdhollow.co.uk
Accommodation Guests' sitting
room with inglenook fireplace, oak
beams, cotton sheets, ensuite
bedrooms, C16 home surrounded by
countryside. Double/twin £45/£50
pppn, single £50/£55 pn. 4*(Gold
Award).
B&B

HAILSHAM GRANGE
Hailsham BN27 1BL
Noel Thompson
T 01323 844248
E noel-hgrange@amserve.com
W www.hailshamgrange.co.uk
Accommodation is available in the main house (a former vicarage circa 1700) & adjoining Coach House. Hailsham Grange exemplifies the classic English style which is synonymous with relaxed comfortable living & old fashioned hospitality. Rates range from £75 - £110 per room pn.
B&B

HAM COTTAGE
Highbrook, Ardingly RH17 6SR
Mr & Mrs P Browne
T 01444 892746
E aegbrowne@btinternet.com
Accommodation C18 cottage set in 8 acres of landscaped gardens within the heart of Sussex, providing 2 double & 1 twin room each with its own bathroom.
B&B

LORDINGTON HOUSE
Lordington, Chichester PO18 9DX
Mr & Mrs John Hamilton
T 01243 375862
E audreyhamilton@onetel.com
Accommodation Comfortable accommodation offered in double, twin and single rooms with own bath/shower. All rooms have fine views over AONB. Breakfast times flexible. Packed lunches and supper by arrangement.
B&B

MOOR FARM
Horsham Road, Petworth GU28 0HD
Richard Chandler
T 01798 342161
E richardandflo1@btinternet.com
Accommodation B&B accommodation on large working arable farm, well off the road, lakeside setting, within sight of Petworth Park. Bring your own horse and explore the local bridleways. Coarse fishing on site. Good parking.
B&B

MORLANDS FARM
Wheatsheaf Road, Henfield BN5 9AT
Pauline McBride
T 01273 492 608
E morlandsfarm@btinternet.com
W www.sussexprairies.co.uk
Accommodation Set within the beautiful Sussex Prairie landscape, our farmhouse offers the highest standard of comfort. Three double bedrooms all with ensuite facilities. Unlimited access to the Prairie Garden. Breakfast sourced from our farm and garden and quality local suppliers. From £45pppn. See Sussex Prairie for details of garden.
B&B

NETHERBY
Bolney Road, Ansty, Haywards Heath RH17 5AW
Mr & Mrs Russell Gilbert
T 01444 455888
E susan@gilbert58.freeserve.co.uk
Accommodation A warm welcome awaits you in this cosy Victorian cottage set in ½ acre garden. Firm beds (2 doubles, 1 twin), excellent breakfasts and sinks in all rooms. Rates £35 pppn. Pets by arrangement.
See Ansty Gardens for details of garden
B&B

PINDARS
Lyminster Road, Lyminster, Arundel BN17 7QF
Jocelyne & Clive Newman
T 01903 882628
E pindars@tiscali.co.uk
W www.pindars.co.uk
Accommodation Comfortable, friendly country house with special emphasis on hospitality and good food. Delicious and varied breakfasts, imaginatively cooked. Evening meals on request, with vegetables from the prolific garden! Prices from £65 pn.
B&B

73 SHEEPDOWN DRIVE
Petworth, West Sussex, GU28 0BX
Mrs Angela Azis
T 01798 342269
Accommodation 2 twin with shared bathroom. Prices from £60 per room. Single from £35. A short walk from the historic town, no. 73 lies in a quiet 70s cul-de-sac and has glorious views.
NGS Vice-President
B&B

SOUTH GRANGE
Quickbourne Lane, Northiam, Rye TN31 6QY
Mr & Mrs Belton
T 01797 252984
E belton.northiam@virgin.net
W www.southgrange-northiam.co.uk
Accommodation consists of one double, one twin-bedded and one single room with use of a large private bathroom in a modern detached house situated on a quiet country lane on the edge of the village.
B&B

Warwickshire & part of West Midlands

SPRINGFIELD HOUSE
School Lane, Warmington, Banbury OX17 1DD
Roger & Jenny Handscombe
T 01295 690286
E jenny.handscombe@virgin.net
W www.stayatspringfield.co.uk
Accommodation C16 house with log fires and flagstone floors. 2 well appointed rooms with king or super-king beds and private bathroom. Handy for Cotswolds, Compton Verney and Shakespeare. No Smoking. From £25pppn.
See Warmington Village Gardens for details of garden
B&B

WOODBROOKE QUAKER STUDY CENTRE
1046 Bristol Road, Selly Oak, Birmingham B29 6LJ
T 0121 472 5171
E enquiries@woodbrooke.org.uk
W www.woodbrooke.org.uk
Accommodation Enjoy our beautiful grounds, award-winning hospitality, peaceful environment and Grade 2 Listed building. Set in the former home of George Cadbury, the famous Quaker and chocolate maker, why not take a short break to unwind? B&B (ensuite) from only £45.
B&B

Wiltshire

BECKETTS HOUSE
Tinhead Road, Edington, Westbury BA13 4PJ
Mrs Susan Bromhead
T 01380 830100
E sue@bromhead.org
Accommodation Attractive C16/17/18 listed house, in lovely village, set in 2¼ acres, tennis court, lake, summer house & superb views. 3 large twin beds, ensuite/private bathrooms. Guests' drawing room. Walks on doorstep. Longleat, Bath, Salisbury nearby.
See Edington Gardens for details of garden
B&B

BROOMSGROVE LODGE
New Mill, nr Pewsey SN9 5LE
Peter & Diana Robertson
T 01672 810515
E diana@broomsgrovelodge.co.uk
W www.sawdays.co.uk
Accommodation Thatched house with very comfortable twin and single accommodation. Own chickens and large vegetable garden. Close to Marlborough and the canal, with wonderful views over Pewsey Vale and Martinsell Hill.
B&B

GOULTERS MILL FARM
The Gibb, Burton, Chippenham SN14 7LL
Alison Harvey
T 01249 782555
E alison@harvey3512.freeserve.co.uk
Accommodation Delightful rooms in old mill house, all ensuite and equipped with kingsized beds. Convenient for Bristol, Bath or Cotswolds. The house is set in cottage gardens in a steep sided valley.

See Littleton Drew Gardens for details of garden
B&B

IDOVER HOUSE
Dauntsey, Chippenham SN15 4HW
Caroline & Christopher Jerram
T 01249 720340
E christopher.jerram@humberts.co.uk
Accommodation 2 twin bedded rooms each with ensuite bathrooms. A family house full of history and a delightful garden, including formal rose garden and herbaceous and shrub borders edging the lawns. Swimming pool, tennis court and croquet lawn available for guests. See Dauntsey Gardens for details of garden
B&B

THE MILL HOUSE
Berwick St James, Salisbury SP3 4TS
Diana Gifford Mead/ Michael Mertens
T 01722 790331
W www.millhouse.org.uk
Accommodation 4 ensuite, 2 single rooms from £60 pp single, £85, double. High quality accommodation. Very quiet, beautiful garden. Highly sourced and organic food. Part of old farm.
B&B

THE POUND HOUSE
Little Somerford, Chippenham SN15 5JW
Mrs Michael Baines
T 01666 823212
E squeezebaines@yahoo.com
Accommodation 2 twins, shared bathroom. 2 doubles, own bathrooms. Aga breakfast, home-laid eggs. Old rectory, large well planted garden, beautiful trees, lots of animals! Pets by arrangement. 4 miles from J17 M4. Ideal for Cotswolds and Bath. £35 pppn.
B&B

RIDLEYS CHEER
Mountain Bower, Chippenham SN14 7AJ
Sue & Antony Young
T 01225 891204
E sueyoung@ridleyscheer.co.uk
Accommodation 1 double with private bathroom. 1 double and 1 twin bedded room with shared bathroom. Prices from £90 per night. Single occ from £55. Dinner £40 per head.
B&B

Worcestershire

MILL HOUSE COTTAGE
The Mill House, Ham Green Lane. Ham Green, Redditch B97 5UB
Mr and Mrs R H Raby
T 01527 545598
E hot2trott@btinternet.com
Accommodation SC cottage. Secluded rural situation, next to main house. Large comfortable sitting room with inglenook fireplace, kitchen breakfast room. Downstairs toilet and shower room. Open-tread staircase to spacious double bedroom. Tariff – single £40 pn. Double £60 pn.
B&B SC

ORLETON HOUSE
Orleton, Stanford Bridge WR6 6SU
Jenny and John Hughes
T 01584 881253
E jenny@orleton.co.uk
W www.orletonhouse.co.uk
Accommodation Luxury SC accommodation for two people. Bedroom with sitting area, bathroom and dining kitchen. £75 pn. Breakfast and/or dinner extra by arrangement.
SC

Yorkshire

AUSTWICK HALL
Town Head Lane, Austwick, Lancaster LA2 8BS
Eric Culley and Michael Pearson
T 015242 51794
E austwickhall@austwick.org
W www.austwickhall.co.uk
Accommodation 5*, Silver Award Luxury Guest Accommodation. An Historic Manor House set in 13 acres. The four ensuite bedrooms provide spacious accommodation individually decorated and furnished with antiques. Dinner available.
B&B

BOUNDARY COTTAGE
Seaton Ross, York YO42 4NF
Roger Brook
T 01759 319156
E twinponds@talktalk.net
Accommodation Homely accommodation for visitors to my gardens (Boundary Cottage and/or Bolton Percy Churchyard). B&B £30 pppn.
B&B

COLD COTES
Cold Cotes Road, Felliscliffe, Harrogate HG3 2LW
Ed Loft
T 01423 770937
E info@coldcotes.com
W www.coldcotes.com
Accommodation Cold Cotes' guests say this is a special place to stay, tranquil setting, beautiful and comfortable rooms, excellent breakfast, an inspiring garden, with service second to none. We have 5 ensuite guest rooms and facilities for small events. Prices from: double £80.
B&B

DOWTHORPE HALL
Skirlaugh, Hull HU11 5AE
Caroline Holtby
T 01964 562235
E john.holtby@farming.co.uk
Accommodation Dowthorpe Hall provides a twin room, ensuite, a double room with own bathroom & a single room, all offering the ultimate in luxury. Caroline, a cordon bleu cook, is happy to offer evening meals with home grown ingredients.
B&B

LAWKLAND HALL
Austwick, via Lancaster LA2 8AT
Mr & Mrs Giles Bowring
T 01729 823551
E diss@austwick.org
Accommodation Relaxed, spacious Elizabethan country house. Choose from 1 double and 3 twin bedrooms. Large, comfortable drawing room overlooking the garden. £40 pp bed & breakfast served in oak panelled dining room. Member of County Team
B&B

MILLGATE HOUSE
Millgate, Richmond DL10 4JN
Tim Culkin & Austin Lynch
T 01748 823571
E oztim@millgatehouse.demon.co.uk
W www.millgatehouse.com
Accommodation Prepare to be amazed – something very special – exceptional taste, furnishings from all over the world, stunning position, celebrated garden –. breakfasts are superb. National Award winning garden.
B&B SC

RIVERSIDE FARM
Sinnington, York, Yorkshire YO62 6RY
William and Jane Baldwin
T 01751 431764
E wnbaldwin@yahoo.co.uk
Accommodation Situated in stunning, quiet village, Georgian farmhouse offers high class accommodation, private sitting room, wonderful atmosphere. 1 kingsize double ensuite. 1 twin with private bathroom. 1 single room. Price £32.50 pppn. £40 for single occ. Member of County Team
B&B

SLEIGHTHOLMEDALE LODGE
Kirbymoorside, York YO62 6JG
Mrs R James
T 01751 431942
E info@shdcottages.co.uk
W www.shdcottages.co.uk
Accommodation Peaceful, warm cottages round a stone courtyard, adjoining a working farm and garden. Max price – high season - £480 per cottage per week.
SC

THORPE LODGE
Knaresborough Road, Ripon
HG4 3LU
Tommy & Juliet Jowitt
T 01765 602088
E jowitt@btinternet.com
W www.thorpelodge.co.uk
Accommodation Listed Georgian
house with 2 large double/twin rooms,
both ensuite bath & shower, television
and tea/coffee making facilities. Own
sitting room and entrance. Dogs kept
and welcome. From £80 pn including
full English breakfast, £55 single occ.
Excellent pubs nearby.
B&B

WORTLEY HALL
Wortley, Sheffield S35 7DB
Jonathan da Rosa
T 0114 2882100
E info@wortleyhall.org.uk
W www.wortleyhall.org.uk
Accommodation The hall has 49
ensuite bedrooms. There is also a lift
to the first floor. All bedrooms have a
direct telephone line and internet
connection, colour television, tea
making facilities and shower. Some
rooms have a bath.
B&B

Bring your
own horse
and explore
the
bridleways . . .

Garden Index

This index lists gardens alphabetically and gives the Yellow Book county section in which they are to be found.

www.ngs.org.uk

W